STRENGTH TO STRENGTH

Program in Judaic Studies
Brown University
Box 1826
Providence, RI 02912

Number 363
STRENGTH TO STRENGTH

edited by
Michael L. Satlow

STRENGTH TO STRENGTH

ESSAYS IN APPRECIATION OF SHAYE J. D. COHEN

Edited by

Michael L. Satlow

Brown Judaic Studies
Providence, Rhode Island

Library of Congress Cataloging-in-Publication Data
is available from the Library of Congress.

ISBN 9781946527110 (pbk.)
ISBN 9781946527127 (hbk.)
ISBN 9781946527134 (ebk.)

Printed on acid-free paper.

Contents

Abbreviations

AB	Anchor Bible
ABD	*Anchor Bible Dictionary*. Edited by David Noel Freedman. 6 vols. New York: Doubleday, 1992
ABRL	Anchor Bible Reference Library
AbrN	*Abr-Nahrain*
AbrNSup	Abr-Nahrain Supplements
AcBib	Academia Biblica
AcOr	*Acta Orientalia*
AGJU	Arbeiten zur Geschichte des antiken Judentums und des Urchristentums
AIL	Ancient Israel and Its Literature
AIPHOS	*Annuaire de l'Institut de philologie et d'histoire orientales et slaves*
AJA	*American Journal of Archaeology*
AJEC	Ancient Judaism and Early Christianity
AJP	*American Journal of Philology*
ANRW	*Aufstieg und Niedergang der römischen Welt: Geschichte und Kultur Roms im Spiegel der neueren Forschung*. Part 2, *Principat*. Edited by Hildegard Temporini and Wolfgang Haase. Berlin: de Gruyter, 1972–
AOAT	Alter Orient und Altes Testament
APF	*Archiv für Papyrusforschung*
ASH	Ancient Society and History
ASOR	American Schools of Oriental Research
AuOr	*Aula Orientalis*
AYB	Anchor Yale Bible
BAI	*Bulletin of the Asia Institute*
BASOR	*Bulletin of the American Schools of Oriental Research*
BBR	*Bulletin for Biblical Research*
BCH	*Bulletin de correspondance hellénique*
BEATAJ	Beiträge zur Erforschung des Alten Testaments und des antiken Judentums
BHT	Beiträge zur historischen Theologie
Bib	*Biblica*
BibInt	Biblical Interpretation Series
BibInt	*Biblical Interpretation*

BibOr	Biblica et Orientalia
BIES	*Bulletin of the Israel Exploration Society*
BJS	Brown Judaic Studies
BJSUCSD	Biblical and Judaic Studies from the University of California, San Diego
BMI	Bible and Its Modern Interpreters
BN	*Biblische Notizen*
BZAW	Beihefte zur Zeitschrift für die alttestamentliche Wissenschaft
CBET	Contributions to Biblical Exegesis and Theology
CBQ	*Catholic Biblical Quarterly*
CBQMS	Catholic Biblical Quarterly Monograph Series
CCSL	Corpus Christianorum: Series Latina. Turnhout: Brepols, 1953–
CEJL	Commentaries on Early Jewish Literature
CHANE	Culture and History of the Ancient Near East
CIIP	*Corpus Inscriptionum Iudaeae/Palaestinae: A Multi-lingual Corpus of the Inscriptions from Alexander to Muhammad.* Berlin: de Gruyter, 2010
CIJ	*Corpus Inscriptionum Judaicarum.* Edited by Jean-Baptiste Frey. 2 vols. Rome: Pontifical Biblical Institute, 1936–1952
CIL	*Corpus Inscriptionum Latinarum.* Berlin: Reimer, 1862–
CJAn	Christianity and Judaism in Antiquity
CRINT	Compendia Rerum Iudaicarum ad Novum Testamentum
CSHJ	Chicago Studies in the History of Judaism
CTU	*The Cuneiform Alphabetic Texts from Ugarit, Ras Ibn Hani, and Other Places.* Edited by Manfred Dietrich, Oswald Loretz, and Joaquín Sanmartín. Münster: Ugarit-Verlag, 1995
DCLS	Deuterocanonical and Cognate Literature Studies
DJD	Discoveries in the Judaean Desert
DNP	*Der neue Pauly: Enzyklopädie der Antike.* Edited by Hubert Cancik and Helmuth Schneider. Stuttgart: Metzler, 1996–
DSD	*Dead Sea Discoveries*
ECL	Early Christianity and Its Literature
EDSS	*Encyclopedia of the Dead Sea Scrolls.* Edited by Lawrence H. Schiffman and James C. VanderKam. 2 vols. New York: Oxford University Press, 2000
ErIsr	*Eretz Israel*
EncJud (1971)	*Encyclopaedia Judaica.* Edited by Cecil Roth. 16 vols. Jerusalem: Encyclopedia Judaica, 1971
EncJud (2007)	*Encyclopaedia Judaica.* Edited by Fred Skolnik and Michael Berenbaum. 2nd ed. Detroit: Macmillan Reference, 2007
EPRO	Etudes préliminaires aux religions orientales dans l'empire romain

FAT	Forschungen zum Alten Testament
FC	Fathers of the Church
FJTC	Flavius Josephus: Translation and Commentary
FRLANT	Forschungen zur Religion und Literatur des Alten und Neuen Testaments
GLAJJ	*Greek and Latin Authors on Jews and Judaism.* Edited by Menahem Stern. 3 vols. Fontes ad res Judaicas spectantes
HAT	Handbuch zum Alten Testament
HBM	Hebrew Bible Monographs
HCS	Hellenistic Culture and Society
HR	*History of Religions*
HS	*Hebrew Studies*
HSM	Harvard Semitic Monographs
HSS	Harvard Semitic Studies
HUCA	*Hebrew Union College Annual*
ICC	International Critical Commentary
IEJ	*Israel Exploration Journal*
IG	*Inscriptiones Graecae. Editio Minor.* Berlin: de Gruyter, 1924–
IJO	*Inscriptiones Judaicae Orientis.* Edited by David Noy and H. Bloedhorn. 3 vols. TSAJ 99, 101–102. Tübingen: Mohr Siebeck 2004
Int	*Interpretation*
ISBL	Indiana Studies in Biblical Literature
JAAR	*Journal of the American Academy of Religion*
JAJ	*Journal of Ancient Judaism*
JANER	*Journal of Ancient Near Eastern Religions*
JANES	*Journal of the Ancient Near Eastern Society*
JAOS	*Journal of the American Oriental Society*
JBL	*Journal of Biblical Literature*
JCS	*Journal of Cuneiform Studies*
JCP	Jewish and Christian Perspectives
JE	*The Jewish Encyclopedia.* Edited by I. Singer. 12 vols. New York: Funk & Wagnalls, 1926
JECS	*Journal of Early Christian Studies*
JEH	*Journal of Ecclesiastical History*
JIGRE	*Jewish Inscriptions of Graeco-Roman Egypt.* Edited by William Horbury and David Noy. Cambridge: Cambridge University Press, 1992
JIWE	David Noy. *Jewish Inscriptions of Western Europe.* 2 vols. Cambridge: Cambridge University Press, 1993–1995
JJMJS	*Journal of the Jesus Movement in Its Jewish Setting*
JJS	*Journal of Jewish Studies*
JNES	*Journal of Near Eastern Studies*
JNSL	*Journal of Northwest Semitic Languages*

JPSTC	JPS Torah Commentary
JQR	*Jewish Quarterly Review*
JRA	*Journal of Roman Archaeology*
JRASup	Journal of Roman Archaeology Supplements
JRS	*Journal of Roman Studies*
JSJ	*Journal for the Study of Judaism in the Persian, Hellenistic, and Roman Period*
JSJSup	Supplements to the Journal for the Study of Judaism
JSNT	*Journal for the Study of the New Testament*
JSNTSup	Journal for the Study of the New Testament: Supplement Series
JSOT	*Journal for the Study of the Old Testament*
JSOTSup	Journal for the Study of the Old Testament: Supplement Series
JSP	*Journal for the Study of the Pseudepigrapha*
JSPSup	Journal for the Study of the Pseudepigrapha Supplements
JSQ	*Jewish Studies Quarterly*
JTS	*Journal of Theological Studies*
LAI	Library of Ancient Israel
LEC	Library of Early Christianity
LHBOTS	Library of Hebrew Bible/Old Testament Studies
LSAWS	Linguistic Studies in Ancient West Semitic
MGWJ	*Monatschrift für Geschichte und Wissenschaft des Judentums*
MIFAO	Mémoires publiés par les membres de l'Institut français d'Archéologie Orientale
MTSR	*Method and Theory in the Study of Religion*
NEAEHL	*The New Encyclopedia of Archaeological Excavations in the Holy Land.* Edited by Ephraim Stern. 4 vols. Jerusalem: Israel Exploration Society & Carta; New York: Simon & Schuster, 1993
NIGTC	New International Greek Testament Commentary
NIV	New International Version
NJPS	New Jewish Publication Society Version
NRSV	New Revised Standard Version
NRT	*La nouvelle revue théologique*
NTOA	Novum Testamentum et Orbis Antiquus
OBO	Orbis Biblicus et Orientalis
OeO	Oriens et Occidens
OGIS	*Orientis Graeci Inscriptiones Selectae.* Edited by Wilhelm Dittenberger. 2 vols. Leipzig: Hirzel, 1903–1905
OLA	Orientalia Lovaniensia Periodica
Or	*Orientalia*
OTL	Old Testament Library

OTP	*The Old Testament Pseudepigrapha.* Edited by James H. Charlesworth. 2 vols. New York: Doubleday, 1983–1985
PAAJR	*Proceedings of the American Academy for Jewish Research*
PACS	Philo of Alexandria Commentary Series
PG	*Patrologia Cursus Completus: Series Graeca.* Edited by Jacques-Paul Migne. 162 vols. Paris, 1857–1886
PHSC	Perspectives on Hebrew Scriptures and Its Contexts
PL	*Patrologia Cursus Completus: Series Latina.* Edited by Jacques-Paul Migne. 217 vols. Paris, 1844–1864
PMLA	*Proceedings of the Modern Language Association*
Proof	*Prooftexts*
PTSDSSP	Princeton Theological Seminary Dead Sea Scrolls Project
PW	*Paulys Real-Encyclopädie der classischen Altertumswissenschaft.* New edition by Georg Wissowa and Wilhelm Kroll. 50 vols. in 84 parts. Stuttgart: Metzler and Druckenmüller, 1894–1980
PWSup	Supplement to PW
RAC	*Reallexikon für Antike und Christentum.* Edited by Theodor Klauser et al. Stuttgart: Hiersemann, 1950–
RB	*Revue biblique*
RevQ	*Revue de Qumran*
RGRW	Religions in the Graeco-Roman World
RHR	*Revue de l'histoire des religions*
RIMA	The Royal Inscriptions of Mesopotamia, Assyrian Periods
SAOC	Studies in Ancient Oriental Civilization
SBLDS	Society of Biblical Literature Dissertation Series
SBT	Studies in Biblical Theology
ScrHier	Scripta Hierosolymitana
SC	Sources chrétiennes
SCS	Septuagint and Cognate Studies
SDSSRL	Studies in the Dead Sea Scrolls and Related Literature
SemeiaSt	Semeia Studies
SFSHJ	South Florida Studies in the History of Judaism
SHR	Studies in the History of Religions
SIr	Studia Iranica
SJ	Studia Judaica
SJC	Studies in Jewish Civilization
SJLA	Studies in Judaism in Late Antiquity
SJMT	Studies in Judaism in Modern Times
SNTSMS	Society for New Testament Studies Monograph Series
SPhiloA	*Studia Philonica Annual*
SR	*Studies in Religion*
SStLL	Studies in Semitic Languages and Linguistics
STDJ	Studies on the Texts of the Desert of Judah

StPatr	Studia Patristica
StPB	Studia Post-biblica
TSAJ	Texte und Studien zum antiken Judentum
TUGAL	Texte und Untersuchungen zur Geschichte der altchristlichen Literatur
TynBul	*Tyndale Bulletin*
UF	*Ugarit-Forschungen*
USQR	*Union Seminary Quarterly Review*
VC	*Vigiliae Christianae*
WAW	Writings from the Ancient World
WGRWSup	Writings from the Greco-Roman World Supplements
ZAC	*Zeitschrift für Antikes Christentum*
ZAW	*Zeitschrift für die alttestamentliche Wissenschaft*
ZPE	*Zeitschrift für Papyrologie und Epigraphik*

Shaye J. D. Cohen
An Appreciation

Nearly everything about assembling this volume was easy. The first group of stealthily invited contributors—mostly students and present and former colleagues of Shaye—almost all enthusiastically accepted and recommended others whose life Shaye has touched, who almost all enthusiastically accepted and so on. In fact, I am sure that had I not wanted to keep this volume secret (for fear of embarrassing Shaye) that many others too would have joined, swelling the volume to at least twice its present size. This speaks to the impact that Shaye has had over his long, distinguished, and continuing career and the gratitude that so many of us have for him as both a scholar and a teacher.

Even in the best of circumstances, writing for Shaye is not an easy thing. Shaye is notoriously sharp and critical (more on which below), and it is hard to escape the feeling that he is looking over your shoulder as you write. As an editor, this was a bit of a boon. The quality of the essays was high and the authors were eager for suggestions for further improvements. Even the deadlines were, by and large, observed. My colleagues at Brown Judaic Studies, many of whom were Shaye's as well when he was at Brown for a decade, were delighted to publish this collection in his honor.

In fact, the only difficult thing about this volume was finding a suitable title. When I reflected on Shaye's accomplishments and asked the contributors for their thoughts as well, I could not stop thinking of the many areas of Shaye's strengths and the ways in which his scholarship has made such a deep impact on the field. Ultimately, what came to mind was the phrase traditionally recited at the completion of the public reading of a book of the Torah in the synagogue, *ḥazaq, ḥazaq, venitḥazzeq,* which translates something along the lines of "Be strong, be strong, and we will be strengthened." There is something elusive about the meaning and history of this phrase that I think would appeal to Shaye, but what appealed to me was its dimension of reciprocity. With its clear, sharp conclusions, Shaye's scholarship invites—almost challenges—its readers to engage. Shaye doesn't simply move from one area of his many strengths to another, he creates ongoing conversations from which he, and we, continue to learn. His academic lectures are, similarly, peppered with questions and requests for further dialogue. The title of this volume, *Strength to Strength,* is meant, however imperfectly, to evoke this reciprocal dimension of Shaye's work and character.

While the essays in this volume are arranged in a rough chronological sequence, many engage directly with Shaye's scholarship and might alternatively have been organized thematically. In this field, engagement with Shaye's scholarship is by no means difficult. From the publication of his dissertation on Josephus, Shaye's scholarly works have been landmarks in a remarkable variety of subjects. While a full scholarly retrospective is beyond the scope of this introduction, it is worth singling out a few areas in which Shaye's scholarship has been transformative and continues to reverberate:

Josephus and historiography. Shaye's dissertation put Josephus squarely in the context of ancient historiography and reignited an older scholarly debate that has still not been settled on how we are to understand Josephus and his motives.

Pharisees and rabbis. In a string of studies, Shaye discussed how little we know about the Pharisees and the tenuous connection that they may have had to the rise of the classical rabbis. His article "Yavneh Revisited" posited that the rabbis actually sought to distance themselves from the Pharisees in an attempt to develop a nonsectarian outlook—a narrative that is woven into the structure of his popular textbook *From the Maccabees to the Mishnah*. At the same time, though, his articles "Epigraphical Rabbis" and "The Place of the Rabbis in the Jewish Society of the Second Century" set the foundations for the now widely popular view that the rabbis who produced what would become Jewish classics were relatively marginal and uninfluential in their time.

Identity and intermarriage. What seemed to engage Shaye most, however, was the issue of Jewish identity, in all of its many dimensions. Perhaps not coincidentally, this interest corresponded to increased anxiety in the American Jewish community about intermarriage and Jewish identity. In a series of studies, Shaye argued that the Jewish prohibition on intermarriage was relatively late; that Jewish identity was often fluid, subjective, and perspectival into late antiquity; and that the ideas that Jewish identity devolved through the matrilineal line and that there was an objective ceremony to mark "conversion" to Judaism were rabbinic innovations.

Gender. Shaye was among the earliest scholars to step, gingerly, into scholarly awareness of gender in the study of the Jews of late antiquity. In one set of essays he argued that rabbinic attitudes toward menstruants changed sharply, and more negatively, over time. He brought together this interest with that of identity in his provocatively titled book *Why Aren't Jewish Women Circumcised? Gender and Covenant in Judaism.*

Jews and gentiles. The question of "us" cannot be studied apart from "them"; it is the "them" that helps to define the "us." Shaye's work on Jewish–Christian relations, mainly in antiquity but also sometimes through the present day, continues to explore how these boundaries were and continue to be constructed and what is at stake in such constructions.

Shaye's impact extends beyond his scholarship. He has, of course, developed a cohort of PhD students and currently teaches one of the largest undergraduate classes at Harvard University. More significantly, though, he has brought ancient Judaism to a much larger audience. With his book *From the Maccabees to the Mishnah* (now in its third edition, and translated into multiple languages) and many survey articles—not to mention his teaching for the wider community—he has reached far and wide and helps to bring responsible scholarly narratives into the public square. He has appeared in several mainstream documentaries and has a MOOC. In each of these venues his natural verve and wit are in full display. He is now editing a new annotated translation of the Mishnah that brings together both his deep scholarship and his desire to make it accessible to a wider public.

Like all of us, Shaye is complex. In a necrology of his teacher, Morton Smith, Shaye wrote, "Smith was blessed with extraordinary integrity and honesty. If he felt that something was worthless drivel, he said so, and, when reviewing a book, he said so in print. His criticisms were always sharp and sharply expressed, but everyone will admit that his criticisms were directed *ad rem,* not *ad hominem.*"[1] Much the same could be said about Shaye. His critiques, whether in print, at conference presentations, or on student papers, are direct, unsparing, and impersonal. At the same time, he is receptive to critique of his own work and seeks to find something to learn from all scholarship. More than once, after quickly dismantling a conference presentation, he would later and informally talk of what he had learned from the paper, only moving to the negative if prodded. At Harvard, he is also known for his whimsical ties, which landed him in an article in the campus paper in an article entitled, "Harvard's Next Top Model: Teacher Edition."

Shaye often jokingly describes himself as a "failed *yeshivah bocher.*" A graduate of Yeshiva College, he studied for his PhD at Columbia University while getting his rabbinical ordination at the Jewish Theological Seminary of America. I was never exactly sure what the "failed" part of this phrase meant, aside from his obvious move away from, or at least to the

1. Shaye J. D. Cohen, "Morton Smith (1915—1991)," *PAAJR* 58 (1992): 37–40, here 39–40.

edge of, Orthodoxy (as illustrated by the way he plays with and tosses his *kippah* around while teaching) and into academic Jewish studies (although these are not mutually exclusive). The "*yeshiva bocher*" is clearer. Although trained traditionally, Shaye draws a bright line between the academic study of Jewish history and its confessional practice. Whether or not Jewish descent was always traced through the matrilineal line, for example, is for him a purely historical question; how that research is put to use and what it means for modern Jews are not his concerns. But at the same time he remains visibly and unapologetically Jewish and Zionist. When the Presbyterian Church voted to divest from Israel, he thought long and hard about publishing the third edition of his book with their press and, in a compromise, was permitted to include a new preface with a scathing indictment of that vote.

The preparation of this volume was immeasurably aided by the advice of Shaye's wife, Miriam May. In addition to blunting a bit of Shaye's edge, Miriam has warmly welcomed scores of his students and colleagues into their lives. I am also delighted that their son Jonathan Cohen, currently pursuing a PhD in American history, agreed to go outside of his comfort zone to engage some of his father's work from a very different angle.

Finally, on behalf of all of the contributors, let me extend our thanks to Shaye. Our engagement with you and your work has made us all better, and this volume is but a small token of appreciation.

Michael L. Satlow
31 July 2018

Signs of Poetry Past

Literariness in Pre-Biblical Hebrew Literature

EDWARD L. GREENSTEIN
Bar-Ilan University

In the present essay I will briefly explore the extent to which we can reconstruct the earliest literature of Israel and consider the ways in which it is literary. I will then compare the literariness of the pre-biblical Hebrew works with that of the Bible. Is the Hebrew Bible literary in the same ways that some of its components are? In what ways can we say that the incorporation of earlier literary material into the narrative framework of the Bible alters its literary character? Since I am attempting to cover a lot of ground, I will necessarily be sparing in my examples and in the number of arguments I might marshal in making my points.

The earliest surviving Hebrew literature comprises relatively short texts such as the torso of a poem in an extrabiblical inscription and several brief compositions that seem to have had an independent career prior to their incorporation into the framework of biblical narrative.[1] Let us look first at the inscription, written on the doorway of a ninth-century BCE building in the area between the Negev and the Sinai Peninsula. Writing on the doorways of buildings was a common practice in the ancient

1. For a survey of poems and snatches of poems incorporated into the Torah, see, e.g., Robert H. Pfeiffer, *Introduction to the Old Testament* (New York: Harper & Row, 1948), 271–81; cf. Julius A. Bewer, *The Literature of the Old Testament*, 3rd ed. rev. Emil G. Kraeling, Records of Civilization, Sources and Studies 5 (New York: Columbia University Press, 1962), 1–31. For some pertinent studies, see, e.g., James W. Watts, *Psalm and Story: Inset Hymns in Hebrew Narrative*, JSOTSup 139 (Sheffield: JSOT Press, 1992); Steven Weitzman, *Song and Story in Biblical Narrative: The History of a Literary Convention in Ancient Israel* (Bloomington: Indiana University Press, 1997); Walter J. Houston, "Misunderstanding or Midrash? The Prose Appropriation of Poetic Material in the Hebrew Bible (Part 1)," *ZAW* 109 (1997): 342–55. The present article is derived from a lecture I have given, first in June 2010 at a conference in honor of Prof. Lawrence Besserman, at the Hebrew University of Jerusalem, and again in November 2012 at Brandeis University. My continued research on ancient Hebrew poetry and on pre-biblical Israelite epic in particular is supported by a grant from the Israel Science Foundation (673/16). I appreciate the research assistance I have received from my former student Dr. Adi Marili. It is a pleasure to publish this article in honor of my longtime colleague and friend Prof. Shaye J. D. Cohen.

Near East (cf., e.g., Deut 6:9; 11:20).[2] In the entrance to a long storeroom at Kuntillet ʿAjrud, the site of a way station established by Israelite traders,[3] a text was inscribed on plaster.[4] The very beginning of the inscription is lacking, and one cannot be sure how far it extends; but parts of six lines are preserved.[5] These lines describe a theophany of the high god El or just *'ēl*—God—and it is likely that Israel's God, YHWH, is named (line 2 with some restoration). Telltale signs of parallelism, along with the hymnic content, suggest that the text belongs to a poem. In it the deity shines forth (ובזרח אל) as the earth quakes (ברעש), "the mountains melt and the hills are crushed" (וימסנ הרמ וידכנ גבנ<נ>מ). The people are bidden to "ready themselves to bless Baal (or the Lord) on the day of battle" (הכנ [ל]ברכ בעל בימ מלח[מה]) and to praise (?) "the name of El (or God) on the day of battle" ([...] לשמ אל בימ מלח[מה]).[6]

The images and phrases of this fragment are virtually all familiar from the Bible, a fact that bespeaks an ancient Hebrew literary tradition. The shining forth of God is attested in the Blessings of Moses (Deut 33:2); the melting of the mountains is found in Mic 1:4 and in Ps 97:5, the terms for "the hills" and for "crushing" occur in relatively early biblical psalms (68:16-17 and 93:3), the phrase "on the day of battle" is found in Hos 10:14 and Amos 1:14, and the command to ready oneself and to bless God has its biblical parallels as well (e.g., Amos 4:12; Judg 5:2, 9). The inscription recalls one biblical passage in particular, the archaic hymn that constitutes Hab 3.[7] There God comes forth from the south together

---

2. See, e.g., Karel van der Toorn, *Scribal Culture and the Making of the Hebrew Bible* (Cambridge: Harvard University Press, 2007), 12–13.

3. See, e.g., Nadav Na'aman, "The Inscriptions of Kuntillet 'Ajrud through the Lens of Historical Research," *UF* 43 (2011): 299–324; Na'aman, "A New Outlook at Kuntillet 'Ajrud and Its Inscriptions," *Maarav* 20 (2013): 39–51; André Lemaire, "The Kuntillet 'Ajrud Inscriptions Forty Years after Their Discovery," in *Alphabets, Texts and Artifacts in the Ancient Near East: Studies Presented to Benjamin Sass*, ed. Israel Finkelstein, Christian Robin, and Thomas Römer (Paris: Van Dieren, 2016), 196–208.

4. Shmuel Aḥituv, Esther Eshel, and Ze'ev Meshel, "The Inscriptions," in Ze'ev Meshel, *Kuntillet 'Ajrud (Ḥorvat Teman): An Iron Age II Religious Site on the Judah-Sinai Border* (Jerusalem: Israel Exploration Society, 2012), 110–14; cf. F. W. Dobbs-Allsopp, J. J. M. Roberts, C. L. Seow, and R. E. Whitaker, eds., *Hebrew Inscriptions: Texts from the Biblical Period of the Monarchy with Concordance* (New Haven: Yale University Press, 2005), 286–89. The text is written in Hebrew but in Phoenician script; see Aḥituv, Eshel, and Meshel, "Inscriptions," 133; Dobbs-Allsopp et al., *Hebrew Inscriptions*, 287; Alice Mandell, "'I Bless You to YHWH and His Asherah'—Writing and Performativity at Kuntillet 'Ajrud," *Maarav* 19 (2012): 132–33 n. 4, with extensive bibliography.

5. Reading according to Shmuel Aḥituv, *Echoes from the Past: Hebrew and Cognate Inscriptions from the Biblical Period*, trans. Anson F. Rainey (Jerusalem: Carta, 2008), 324–29.

6. Given the preposition ל preceding the noun phrase שמ אל, "name of El/God," one should restore a verb of praising that ordinarily takes that preposition before the object, such as הודה, הלל, שיר, זמר; see Aḥituv, *Echoes from the Past*, 327.

7. See David A. Robertson, *Linguistic Evidence in Dating Early Hebrew Poetry*, SBLDS

with an entourage of minor deities and demons. His majestic aura covers the heavens and the earth. And as he glows (ונגה כאור תהיה; v. 4), "the everlasting mountains break apart, the primeval hills sink low" (v. 6). Both here and in the inscription the mountains shiver at the appearance of the deity. Habakkuk's poem goes on to delineate the roar of the ocean and the halting of the sun and moon at the apex of the sky as every part of creation reacts to the advance of the deity (vv. 10–11). It is possible that in the missing lines of the inscription as well, responses from the sky, the sea, and other parts of nature are enumerated.

The dramatic nexus between theophany and the cataclysmic response of nature is well known from the second-millennium BCE epic of the Canaanite storm god Baal from Ugarit,[8] from such biblical poems as Pss 29 and 114—where the mountains skip like young rams (vv. 6 and 4, respectively)—in Ps 18 (= 2 Sam 22),[9] and in the prose account of the Sinai revelation in the Torah, where the mountain trembles as God descends upon it (Exod 19:18).[10] In Ps 18 the theophany is incorporated into a prayer of thanksgiving, but in Pss 29 and 114, the divine epiphany comprises nearly all the composition.[11] One event and the response to it are virtually

---

3 (Missoula, MT: Society of Biblical Literature, 1972), 155 (conclusion based on preceding analyses); cf. Frank Moore Cross, *From Epic to Canon: History and Literature in Ancient Israel* (Baltimore: Johns Hopkins University Press, 1998), 45–46; Theodore Hiebert, *God of My Victory: The Ancient Hymn in Habakkuk 3*, HSM 38 (Atlanta: Scholars Press, 1986). The suggestion is that the poem, or parts thereof, were incorporated from older sources; see, e.g., Patrick D. Miller Jr., *The Divine Warrior in Early Israel*, HSM 5 (Cambridge: Harvard University Press, 1973), 118. Robertson's study has been critiqued especially in Robyn C. Vern, *Dating Archaic Biblical Hebrew Poetry: A Critique of the Linguistic Arguments*, PHSC 10 (Piscataway, NJ: Gorgias, 2011). However, see the thorough linguistic critique of Vern's work by Na'ama Pat-El and Aren Wilson-Wright in *HS* 54 (2013): 387–410. Biblical translations are my own.

8. See esp. *KTU* 1.4 vi 25–37; for a convenient presentation of the text and a translation, see Mark S. Smith, "The Baal Cycle," in *Ugaritic Narrative Poetry*, ed. Simon B. Parker, WAW 9 (Atlanta: Scholars Press, 1997), 136–37.

9. For a comparison of Ps 29 to Ps 18, see Edward L. Greenstein, "YHWH's Lightning in Psalm 29:7," in *Let Your Colleagues Praise You: Studies in Memory of Stanley Gevirtz*, vol. 2, ed. Robert J. Ratner, Lewis M. Barth, Marianne Luijken Gevirtz, and Bruce Zuckerman, *Maarav* 8 [1992]: 49–57, esp. 57.

10. See, e.g., Samuel E. Loewenstamm, "The Trembling of Nature during the Theophany," in *Comparative Studies in Biblical and Ancient Oriental Literatures*, AOAT 204 (Neukirchen-Vluyn: Neukirchener Verlag; Kevelaer: Butzon & Bercker, 1980), 173–89. In the LXX and several modern readings based on it, the trembling of Mount Sinai (ויחרד כל־ההר מאד) is harmonized to accord with the trembling of the congregated people below (v 16: ויחרד כל־העם). In the Ugaritic passage (n. 8 above) and elsewhere (e.g., Ps 97), however, the response to the storm god's appearance occurs both in nature and among people; see already Edward L. Greenstein, review of *The Torah: A Modern Commentary*, by W. Gunther Plaut, *Journal of Reform Judaism* 29 (1982): 80–86, here 82–83.

11. Cf. Claus Westermann, *Praise and Lament in the Psalms*,trans. Keith R. Crim and Richard N. Soulen (Atlanta: John Knox, 1981), 96. Westermann maintains that theophanies, even in nonliturgical contexts like the Song of Deborah (Judg 5) and the Blessings of Moses

all that are described in the inscription from Kuntillet 'Ajrud, and that is about all that is ever described in any of the many Hebrew poems that are embedded within the Bible.

Biblical scholars have devoted a good deal of study to the apparently autonomous poems that are embedded within biblical narrative. The longer ones include, for example, the Blessings of Jacob (Gen 49), the Song at the Sea (Exod 15), the Oracles of Balaam (Num 22–24), the Song of Moses (Deut 32), the Blessings of Moses (Deut 33), the Song of Deborah (Judg 5), the Prayer of Hannah (1 Sam 2), David's Lament over Saul and Jonathan (2 Sam 1), David's Song of Thanksgiving for having been rescued from Saul (2 Sam 22 = Ps 18), and many additional shorter poems, to some of which I shall soon turn. Most of these poems are widely regarded as among the earliest texts in the Bible.[12] In addition to these songs embedded in narrative, there are several archaic psalms and the prayer of Habakkuk, to which I have made reference above.

In biblical narrative we also encounter, as mentioned, short songs. Some of them, like the Song of Lamech (Gen 4:23–24),[13] David's elegy over Abner (2 Sam 3:33–34),[14] the taunting of Samson by the Philistines (Judg 16:23–24),[15] and the jingle that the women of Israel sing about Saul and David—"Saul has smitten thousands, and David tens of thousands" (1 Sam 18:7 = 1 Sam 21:12 = 29:5)[16]—may well be complete.[17] The last-cited instance is particularly compelling because it is quoted three times, all in exactly the same form.[18] It seems like a fixed and complete jingle, like

---

(Deut 33), belonged originally to the genre of psalms; however, the evidence of the poem found at Kuntillet 'Ajrud may undermine that claim.

12. See recently Augustinus Gianto, "Archaic Biblical Hebrew," in *Periods, Corpora, and Reading Traditions*, vol. 1 of *A Handbook of Biblical Hebrew*, ed. W. Randall Garr and Steven E. Fassberg (Winona Lake, IN: Eisenbrauns, 2016), 19–29, here 20–21; Paul Korchin, "Glimpsing Archaic Biblical Hebrew through Thetic Grammar," *HS* 58 (2017): 49–79, here 57.

13. See, e.g., Stanley Gevirtz, *Patterns in the Early Poetry of Israel*, 2nd ed., SAOC 32 (Chicago: University of Chicago Press, 1973), 25–34.

14. For a reconstructed reading of this lament, see Elisha Qimron, "The Lament of David over Abner," in *Birkat Shalom: Studies in the Bible, Ancient Near Eastern Literature, and Postbiblical Judaism Presented to Shalom M. Paul on the Occasion of His Seventieth Birthday*, 2 vols. (Winona Lake, IN: Eisenbrauns, 2008), 1:143–47.

15. See, e.g., Westermann, *Praise and Lament*, 90.

16. See, e.g., Gevirtz, *Patterns in the Early Poetry*, 15–24; but note the critical remarks of M. O'Connor, "War and Rebel Chants in the Former Prophets," in *Fortunate the Eyes That See: Essays in Honor of David Noel Freedman in Celebration of His Seventieth Birthday*, ed. Astrid B. Beck et al.; Grand Rapids: Eerdmans, 1995), 322–37, here 329–30.

17. See F. W. Dobbs-Allsopp, *On Biblical Poetry* (Oxford: Oxford University Press, 2015), 75.

18. There is a slight difference between the so-called rebel chant, a couplet to which a single line is attached in 2 Sam 20:1 and to which an additional couplet is attached in 1 Kgs 12:16; see O'Connor, "War and Rebel Chants," 330–33. For the present purposes, it should be observed that, either way, the song is short and apparently complete.

a riddle that is found embedded but has an autonomous existence.[19] We cannot know for sure without having independent texts to compare, but we can sometimes bring comparative evidence to bear. In Num 21, having mentioned a particular well in the region of Moab from which the Lord gave water to Israel, the narrator introduces a song:

> Then Israel sang this song:
> "Arise, O well! / Sing to it!
> The well the princes have dug, / the people's-leaders have excavated,
> With their staffs, / with their walking-sticks" (vv. 17–18).[20]

Contrary to the claim that this short piece is no more than a fragment of a larger work,[21] this song may well constitute the entire poem. The poem bears a strong resemblance to a Bedouin song recorded over a century ago:

> Spring up, O well, / flow copiously.
> Drink and disdain not, / with a staff we have dug it.[22]

This song and others like it are meant to induce the water to rise in the well, perhaps even magically.[23] Songs like this belong to popular lore.[24]

Another example of a short song that may seem like no more than a snatch of something larger is the boastful song of Lamech in praise of ven-

---

19. Compare, of course, Samson's riddle, which is in verse form, and the corresponding solution to it, which is formulated similarly (Judg 14:14, 18). On the form, double entendre, and contextual function of Samson's riddle, see, e.g., James L. Crenshaw, *Samson: A Secret Betrayed, A Vow Ignored* (Atlanta: John Knox, 1978), 99–120; Claudia V. Camp and Carole R. Fontaine, "The Words of the Wise and Their Riddles," in *Text and Tradition: The Hebrew Bible and Folklore*, ed. Susan Niditch, SemeiaSt (Atlanta: Scholars Press, 1990), 127–51.

20. For a brief analysis of the poetics, see Edward L. Greenstein, "Hebrew Poetry: Biblical Poetry," in *The Princeton Encyclopedia of Poetry and Poetics*, ed. Roland Greene, 4th ed. (Princeton: Princeton University Press, 2012), 602–3.

21. So, e.g., William Foxwell Albright, *Yahweh and the Gods of Canaan: A Historical Analysis of Two Contrasting Faiths*, The Jordan Lectures (Garden City, NY: Doubleday, 1968), 44.

22. Alois Musil, *Arabia Petraea*, 3 vols. (Vienna: A. Hölder, 1907–1908), 3:259]; translation from Bewer, *Literature of the Old Testament*, 4.

23. See, e.g., George B. Gray, *A Critical and Exegetical Commentary on Numbers*, ICC (1903; repr., New York: Scribner's Sons, 1920), 288–89; cf. Alexander Rofé, *Introduction to the Literature of the Hebrew Bible*, Jerusalem Biblical Studies (Jerusalem: Simor, 2009), 414–15. Compare t. Sukkah 3:3. For a different view, see, e.g., Jacob Milgrom, במדבר *Numbers: The Traditional Hebrew Text with the New JPS Translation*, JPSTC (Philadelphia: Jewish Publication Society, 1990), 460–61.

24. See, e.g., Terry Giles and William J. Doan, *Twice-Used Songs: Performance Criticism of the Songs of Ancient Israel* (Peabody, MA: Hendrickson, 2009), 124.

geance—a favorite theme of the Arab poets[25]—embedded in the narrative of Cain and his descendants in Gen 4:23:

> Lamech said to his (two) wives:
> "Adah and Zillah, / listen to my voice!
> O wives of Lamech, / give ear to my utterance!
> I would kill a man for only wounding me,
> A youth for merely bruising me.
> Though Cain may be avenged seven-fold,
> Lamech (will be avenged) seventy-seven-fold!"

This song recalls the boast of a mercenary warrior in the Ugaritic epic of Aqhat, from the mid-second millennium BCE. The boast is formulated in no more than a couplet: "May the hand that slew Valiant Aqhat, / Slay enemies by the thousand!"[26] It also recalls a three-line declaration from elsewhere in the same epic, where the goddess Anath takes pride in her ultimate responsibility for the murder of the Valiant Aqhat: "For his staff I slew him! / I truly slew him for his bow! / For his darts I ended his life!"[27]

Brief songs like these are both occasional—there are specific circumstances that occasion them—and instrumental (in the sense suggested by literary critic Derek Attridge)—they serve a practical purpose and are not intended for enjoyment alone.[28] Yet they may be used either in or out of their characteristic life settings.[29] They can exist as autonomous poems; but they can also be adapted for use in larger contexts. Classical Arabic

25. See, e.g., Morris S. Seale, *The Desert Bible: Nomadic Tribal Culture and Old Testament Interpretation* (London: Weidenfeld & Nicolson, 1974), 131–34; cf., e.g., Johannes Pedersen, *Israel: Its Life and Culture*, 4 vols. in 2 (London: Oxford University Press; Copenhagen: Pio-Branner, 1926), 1:380; John Skinner, *A Critical and Exegetical Commentary on Genesis*, 2nd ed., ICC (Edinburgh: T&T Clark, 1930), 120. For early Arabic literature, compare the following excerpt: "Out of vengeance I wounded 'Abdalqais with a spear and made a wound so great that it would have been filled with light had not blood poured out from it on all sides"; quoted in Felix Klein-Franke, *The Ḥamāsa of Abū Tammām* (Leiden: Brill, 1972), 158.

26. *KTU* 1.19 iv 58–59; trans. in Edward L. Greenstein, "The Role of the Reader in Ugaritic Narrative," in *"A Wise and Discerning Mind": Essays in Honor of Burke O. Long*, ed. Saul M. Olyan and Robert C. Culley, BJS 325 (Providence, RI: Brown Judaic Studies, 2000), 148. For the text and a comparable translation, see Simon B. Parker, "Aqhat," in Parker, *Ugaritic Narrative Poetry*, 78.

27. *KTU* 1.19 i 13–16; my translation. For the text and a comparable translation, see Parker, "Aqhat," 67.

28. Derek Attridge, *The Singularity of Literature* (London: Routledge, 2004), 6–10 and passim.

29. On the functionality of (some, perhaps even most) ancient Near Eastern literature, see Edward L. Greenstein, "Verbal Art and Literary Sensibilities in Ancient Near Eastern Context," in *The Wiley-Blackwell Companion to Ancient Israel*, ed. Susan Niditch, Wiley Blackwell Companions to Religion (West Sussex, UK: Wiley Blackwell, 2016), 457–75, here 459–61.

poetry can be presented either in whole form—the "ode" (*qaṣīda*)—or in fragmentary form—the "snatch" (*qiṭ'a*).[30]

In the early Middle Ages, Muslim poets began collecting long and short poems of the pre-Islamic Arab poets and arranging them in anthologies by theme. The most famous of these works is the *Ḥamāsa* of Abū Tammām from the ninth century.[31] It includes eleven sections on a variety of subjects, beginning with *ḥamāsa* ("bravery, courage"), which gives its name to the entire compilation.[32] It would seem that sometime in the early monarchic period, ancient Israelite poets or scribes did something similar: they collected diverse Hebrew poems and wrote them on the same scroll, in *səpārîm*.[33] Of the two poetic collections that are mentioned in the primary biblical narrative, "The Book of the Wars of YHWH" and "The Book of Yashar," the latter can be more completely reconstructed.

The Book of Yashar contained a number of poems that are included in the Bible.[34] One is the Lament of David over Saul and Jonathan, to which I shall return below. The Book of Yashar also included the poem, possibly an epic,[35] from which the following verse of Joshua was excerpted:

> O sun at Gibeon, be still (or dark)![36]
> And moon in the Valley of Ayalon!
> . . . .
> Until a nation avenges its enemies! (Josh 10:12)

---

30. Charles James Lyall, *Translations of Ancient Arabian Poetry: Chiefly Pre-Islamic* (London: Williams & Norgate, 1930), xix.

31. See D. M. Dunlop, *Arab Civilization to A.D. 1500*, Arab Background Series (New York: Praeger, 1971), 41.

32. See, e.g., Klein-Franke, *Ḥamāsa of Abū Tammām*, esp. 42, 149.

33. So, e.g., Gray, *Numbers*, 284–85. For an important comparative perspective, see Geo Widengren, "Oral Tradition and Written Literature among the Hebrews in the Light of Arabic Evidence, with Special Regard to Prose Narratives," *AcOr* 23 (1959): 201–62. For ספר as any written work, see, e.g., Eduard Nielsen, *Oral Tradition: A Modern Problem in Old Testament Introduction*, SBT 11 (London: SCM, 1954), 45–46 and cf. 40–41; Aḥituv, *Echoes from the Past*, 439; Katherine M. Stott, *Why Did They Write This Way? Reflections on References to Written Documents in the Hebrew Bible and Ancient Literature*, LHBOTS 492 (New York: T&T Clark, 2008), 2–4.

34. Much of the following section is drawn from my article "What Was the Book of Yashar?" *Maarav* 21 (2014 [appeared 2017]: 25–35.

35. See, e.g., Sigmund Mowinckel, "Hat es ein israelitische Nationalepos gegeben?" *ZAW* 53 (1935): 133–34. I am using the term *epic* to denote a relatively long narrative poem about a hero or heroes, human, divine, or both.

36. It is clear from the following verse (13) that the scribe who incorporated this verse (12) into the narrative interpreted דום to be from דמם ("to stand/be still"). However, it is possible that in its original context דום was derived from דום ("to grow dark"). Akkadian *da'āmu* is used of the moon in eclipse; see, e.g., Francesca Rochberg-Halton, "Canonicity in Cuneiform Texts," *JCS* 36 (1984): 140. Cf. Hezi Yitzhaqi, Daniel Vainstub, and Uzi Avner, "'Sun, Stand Still over Gibeon; and Moon, in the Valley of Aijalon'—Annular Solar Eclipse on October 30, 1207 BCE?" [Hebrew], *Beit Mikra* 61 (2016): 196–238.

It is unclear who is speaking—the deity, in which case, "the divine command indicates the power of God over cosmic forces in waging war," or a person, in which case "the poem is an incantation or an omen directed to the sun as a cosmic power."[37] Either way, it is a verse extract embedded in a prose narrative.[38]

Based on a possible misreading of the Septuagint, there is probably another reference to the Book of Yashar in 1 Kgs 8:12–13, where we find a poetic prayer of Solomon upon the dedication of the temple. The Greek translator seems to have read שיר ("song"; Greek ᾠδῄ), which is apparently a metathesis of ישר.[39] I have argued that we can find within the Bible yet another poem from the Book of Yashar—the poem that gave its name to the book.[40] In order to establish my case, I return to the text introducing the Lament of David.

David is said to have given an order to teach the Judeans קשת, "The Bow," which is then said to be "written in the Book of Yashar." "The Bow" is the name of the song. As Morris Seale explains in his book *The Desert Bible,* an anthropological study seeking to provide some background to the Bible with the aid of ethnographic information concerning nomadic Arabs, songs can be named for a prominent word in the lyrics.[41] The chapter titles in the Qur'an are also taken from catchwords in the *sūrah* that follows. The word *qešet* ("bow") appears in the verse: "Jonathan's bow never retreated, / Saul's sword never returned empty." Since the lament focuses on Jonathan and Saul and expresses a special affection for Jonathan, it makes sense that a word from this verse would give the title to the poem.

Another poem that was meant to be written down and taught to the Israelites is the Song of Moses (Deut 32),[42] known by Jews as *Ha'ăzînû,*

---

37. Thomas B. Dozeman, *Joshua 1–12: A New Translation with Introduction and Commentary,* AYB 6B (New Haven: Yale University Press, 2015), 432, 441–42.

38. For the embedding and its possible meaning in its new context, see, e.g., Giles and Doan, *Twice-Used Songs,* 35–36.

39. See, e.g., Otto Eissfeldt, *The Old Testament: An Introduction,* trans. Peter R. Ackroyd (New York: Harper & Row, 1965), 133; Mordechai Cogan, *1 Kings: A New Translation with Introduction and Commentary,* AB 10 (New York: Doubleday, 2000), 281. For an extremely skeptical view, see Kristin De Troyer, "'Is This Not Written in the Book of Jashar?' (Joshua 10:13c): References to Extra-Biblical Books in the Bible," in *The Land of Israel in Bible, History, and Theology: Studies in Honor of Ed Noort,* ed. Jacques van Ruiten and J. Cornelis de Vos, VTSup 124 (Leiden: Brill, 2009), 45–50.

40. Greenstein, "What Was the Book of Yashar?"

41. Seale, *Desert Bible,* 19–20. See also Nielsen, *Oral Tradition,* 49; A. A. Anderson, *2 Samuel,* WBC 11 (Dallas: Word, 1989), 15; Kevin L. Spawn, *"As It Is Written" and Other Citation Formulae in the Old Testament: Their Use, Development, Syntax, and Significance,* BZAW 311 (Berlin: de Gruyter, 2002), 61–62; Giles and Doan, *Twice-Used Songs,* 27-28. For a brief history of research on the meaning (and reading) of קשת here, see Spawn, *"As It Is Written,"* 59–62.

42. See Deut 31:19; cf. v. 30. On the incorporation of this song within the book of Deu-

"O give ear!," the word that opens the poem. Using the same principle of naming a poem in antiquity by means of a key word that evokes the main subject of the poem, let us look for the poem's original name. The Song of Moses has as its main theme Israel's God YHWH and his on-again off-again relationship with Israel. In the poem, unreliable Israel is nicknamed somewhat ironically *Yəšūrûn*, "The Upright One" (Deut 32:15; see also Deut 33:5, 26; Isa 44:2), a name that plays on one of the epithets of the Lord in the opening verses of the song, ישר, "Upright." The Lord is praised as "A faithful God, without corruption; / Just and upright [ישר] is he." To me it seems apparent that the ancient name of the poem was *Yāšār* and that the scroll in which this poem held a prominent place was "The Book of Yashar."[43]

Ancient Hebrew authors, such as those who composed the biblical narrative, would find in texts like the Book of Yashar sources for the poems they would incorporate into their compositions. It is often impossible to tell whether a short poem is an excerpt from a larger piece or a self-contained song already removed from its original context. In Num 21:14, "The Book of the Battles of YHWH" (ספר מלחמות ה') is cited as the source for part of a boundary description. A brief snatch (for the term, see above) is quoted in order to confirm that the Arnon River, which extends eastward from the middle of the Dead Sea, is the historical border between Moab and the Amorites (see v. 13). This passage is notoriously difficult, but if the *nota accusativi* את, which is out of place in a presumably early poem,[44] is parsed as an imperative of the verb אתה,[45] the passage makes good sense:

אֶת-וָהֵב בְּסוּפָה / וְאֶת-הַנְּחָלִים אַרְנוֹן;
וְאֶשֶׁד הַנְּחָלִים / אֲשֶׁר נָטָה לְשֶׁבֶת עָר / וְנִשְׁעַן לִגְבוּל מוֹאָב.

teronomy, see Mark Leuchter, "Why Is the Song of Moses in Deuteronomy?," *VT* 57 (2007): 295–317.

43. See Anderson, *2 Samuel*, 14.

44. See, e.g., David N. Freedman, "Prose Particles in the Poetry of the Primary History," *Divine Commitment and Human Obligation: Selected Writings of David Noel Freedman*, 2 vols., ed. John R. Huddlestun (Grand Rapids: Eerdmans, 1997), 171–82; cf. Gianto, "Archaic Biblical Hebrew," 22; Chaim Cohen, "Diachrony in Biblical Hebrew Lexicography and Its Ramifications for Textual Analysis," in *Diachrony in Biblical Hebrew*, ed. Cynthia L. Miller-Naudé and Ziony Zevit, LSAWS 8 (Winona Lake, IN: Eisenbrauns, 2012), 364–66.

45. I am indebted for this insight to Prof. Richard C. Steiner, who finds precedents to this suggestion in Midrash Leqaḥ Ṭov to our passage; and Duane L. Christensen, "Num 21:14-15 and the Book of the Wars of Yahweh," *CBQ* 36 (1974): 359–60. For a broader discussion of this passage and the "Book of the Battles of YHWH" in general, see my "What Was the Book of the Wars of the Lord?" *TheTorah.com*, https://thetorah.com/what-was-the-book-of-the-wars-of-the-lord/.

Come[46] to Waheb in a storm[47] / and come to the streams of the
 Arnon,
The watershed of the streams, / bending[48] toward the settled plain
 (or Ar);
And leaning on the border of Moab.

The structure and content of this reading can be supported by comparing the so-called Heshbon song, probably a fragment, that is embedded nearby (Num 21:27-30):

עַל-כֵּן יֹאמְרוּ הַמֹּשְׁלִים:
בֹּאוּ חֶשְׁבּוֹן—תִּבָּנֶה / וְתִכּוֹנֵן עִיר סִיחוֹן.
כִּי־אֵשׁ יָצְאָה מֵחֶשְׁבּוֹן, / לֶהָבָה מִקִּרְיַת סִיחֹן; / אָכְלָה עָר מוֹאָב, / בַּעֲלֵי בָּמוֹת אַרְנֹן.
אוֹי־לְךָ מוֹאָב, / אָבַדְתָּ עַם־כְּמוֹשׁ;
נָתַן בָּנָיו פְּלֵיטִם / וּבְנֹתָיו בַּשְּׁבִית / לְמֶלֶךְ אֱמֹרִי סִיחוֹן;
וַנִּירָם אָבַד חֶשְׁבּוֹן עַד־דִּיבֹן; / וַנַּשִּׁים עַד־נֹפַח אֲשֶׁר עַד־מֵידְבָא.

Thus say the poets:
Come to Heshbon—let it be rebuilt! / And let the City of Sihon be
 reestablished!
For a fire went out from Heshbon, / a flame from the Town of
 Sihon;
It consumed the Steppe of Moab, / the dwellers of the Arnon's
 plateau.
Woe to you, O Moab! / You are destroyed, People of Chemosh![49]
Your sons have been made into fugitives, / and your daughters into
 captives
To the King of the Amorites, Sihon.
We have cast them down to destruction, from Heshbon to Dibon;[50]
We have devastated up to Nophah, from Asher (?) to Medeba.

In the Heshbon Song, as in the extract from the Arnon boundary passage, there is a summons to the addressee to "come" and witness the substance of the bard's claim—using the poetic (old Northwest Semitic) verb אתה

46. If the imperative is singular, it is apocopated. If it is plural, which seems preferable to me (see immediately below), the *vav* of the plural has been lost by haplography.

47. Perhaps to the site of a theophany; see Nah 1:3-4, where YHWH appears in a "storm" (סופה) and exerts control over the waters.

48. The relative pronoun אשר is, like את (see above with n. 44) unexpected in an archaic poem, but it is occasionally found; see Freedman, "Prose Particles."

49. Chemosh was, of course, the national god of Moab, known not only from the Bible but also from the mid-ninth century BCE inscription of King Mesha of Moab.

50. The verse is problematic; see Jacob Milgrom, במדבר *Numbers*, 182.

in the Arnon verse and the regular Hebrew בא in the Heshbon Song. But whereas the Heshbon Song continues to be quoted, the Arnon verse has no continuation.

Here we can be certain that the enigmatic line (who is being addressed? what are they meant to witness?) has been excerpted from a larger work.[51] In the case of the Song of the Well, which is quoted in the same chapter, however, we cannot be sure that the poem has been reproduced in full or whether, as has been suggested, it has been taken from a larger epic poem.[52] Similarly, it is unclear whether the couplet from Josh 10 cited above—"O sun at Gibeon, be still (or dark)! /And moon in the Valley of Ayalon!"—has been excerpted from an epic account of an Israelite battle and/or whether it has been taken out of context and adapted to a new setting.[53]

The question of whether there had once been epic poems in ancient Israel, as there were in pre-Israelite Canaan, has been controversial, with scholars like Sigmund Mowinckel, Umberto Cassuto, W. F. Albright, Frank Moore Cross, Frank H. Polak, Yair Zakovitch, and myself on the pro side, and scholars like Shemaryahu Talmon, Charles Conroy, and Robert S. Kawashima, on the other.[54] I want to address this question head-on in

---

51. The questions of who is/are being addressed and to what purpose pertain to the Heshbon Song as well. It seems to be an Israelite taunt song, making a mockery of a defeated Moabite enemy, but it could be an import from a Transjordanian work; see the discussion in Philip J. Budd, *Numbers*, WBC 5 (Waco, TX: Word, 1984), 243-46.

52. See, e.g., Baruch A. Levine, *Numbers 21–36: A New Translation with Introduction and Commentary*, AB 4A (New York: Doubleday, 2000), 91.

53. See above with n. 35; cf., e.g., Mowinckel, "Israelitische Nationalepos," 133; Trent C. Butler, *Joshua 1–12*, 2nd ed., WBC 7A (Grand Rapids: Zondervan, 2014), 483–84.

54. Mowinckel, "Israelitische Nationalepos"; Umberto Cassuto, "Israelite Epic" [1943], in *Biblical and Oriental Studies*, trans. Israel Abrahams, 2 vols. (Jerusalem: Magnes, 1975), 2:69-109; Albright, *Yahweh and the Gods of Canaan*; Frank Moore Cross, *Canaanite Myth and Hebrew Epic: Essays in the History of the Religion of Israel* (Cambridge: Harvard University Press, 1973); Frank H. Polak, "Epic Formulas in Biblical Narratives and the Roots of Early Hebrew Prose" [Hebrew], *Te'uda* 7 (1991): 9–53; Yair Zakovitch, "Yes, There Was an Israelite Epic in the Biblical Period," *International Folklore Review* 8 (1991): 18–25; Edward L. Greenstein,"From Oral Epic to Writerly Verse and Some of the States in Between" (presentation at the Society of Biblical Literature Annual Meeting, 2006); Shemaryahu Talmon, "Did There Exist a Biblical National Epic?" *Literary Studies in the Hebrew Bible* (Jerusalem: Magnes, 1993), 91–111; Charles Conroy, "Hebrew Epic: Historical Notes and Critical Reflections," *Bib* 61 (1980): 1–30; Robert S. Kawashima, *Biblical Narrative and the Death of the Rhapsode*, ISBL (Bloomington: Indiana University Press, 2004). Niditch observes that many features of biblical narrative resemble those of ancient Near Eastern epic, but she remains ambivalent concerning the question of an early Israelite epic ("The Challenge of Israelite Epic," in *A Companion to Ancient Epic*, ed. John Miles Foley, Blackwell Companions to the Ancient World: Literature and Culture (Malden, MA: Blackwell, 2005), 277–87. For the affinity of biblical narrative to earlier Canaanite (Ugaritic) narrative, see Edward L. Greenstein, "Biblical Prose Narrative and Early Canaanite Narrative," in *Essays on Hebrew Literature in Honor of Avraham Holtz* [Hebrew], ed. Zvia Ginor (New York: Jewish Theological Seminary), 9–29 [Hebrew].

what follows, but we ought first to take stock of some of those features that characterize the pre-biblical poetry of ancient Israel.

The somewhat haphazard corpus of early Hebrew poems represents an array of genres. The larger poems break down into victory songs, hymns of praise, blessings and curses, psalms of thanksgiving, and laments. All these genres are lyric in some way—none is narrative. There may be narrative sections within some of the poems, but there is no consecutive and chronologically ordered story, which is overall characteristic of both pre-biblical Canaanite epic and of biblical narrative.[55] Even the Heshbon Song cited in the name of the ballad singers (*hammōšəlîm*) in Num 21:27-29 (see above),[56] which has a narrative cast to it, is set within a different genre—the taunt song—in which the speakers mock the defeated Moabites.

Early Hebrew poetry is also distinguished by special language.[57] The definite article *ha-*, the marker of the direct object *'et*, and the relative pronoun *'ăšer* are for the most part absent; and when they are occasionally found we may suspect that later scribes have introduced them under the influence of later usage.[58] The fact that these linguistic features were a trait or convention of early Hebrew poetry can be shown by inspecting the poetry of Job. Although Job was written in the Persian period, it adopts the practices of archaic Hebrew poetry and very deliberately archaizes, using the definite article, the object marker, and relative pronoun very sparingly.[59]

---

55. See Meir Sternberg, "Time and Space in Biblical (Hi)story Telling: The Grand Chronology," in *The Book and the Text: The Bible and Literary Theory*, ed. Regina M. Schwartz (Oxford: Blackwell, 1990), 81–145; Greenstein, "Biblical Prose Narrative"; Samuel E. Balentine, "The Prose and Poetry of Exile," in *Interpreting Exile: Displacement and Deportation in Biblical and Modern Contexts*, ed. Brad E. Kelle, Frank Ritchel Ames, and Jacob L. Wright, AIL 10 (Atlanta: Society of Biblical Literature, 2011), 345–46; notwithstanding Robert S. Kawashima, "From Song to Story: The Genesis of Narrative in Judges 4 and 5," *Proof* 21 (2001): 151–78; David H. Richter, "Genre, Repetition, Temporal Order: Some Aspects of Biblical Narratology," in *A Companion to Narrative Theory*, ed. James Phelan and Peter J. Rabinowitz, Blackwell Companions to Literature and Culture 33 (Oxford: Blackwell, 2005), 285–98, here 291–92.

56. Some find the last lines of the song in verse 30, but they can discern in it poetry only after they have emended it; see, e.g., Levine, *Numbers 21–36*, 82, 108–9.

57. See, e.g., Gianto, "Archaic Biblical Hebrew"; Korchin, "Glimpsing Archaic Biblical Hebrew"; Gregory Mobley, *The Empty Men: The Heroic Tradition of Ancient Israel*, ABRL (New York: Doubleday, 2005), 20.

58. See David Noel Freedman, "Pottery, Poetry, and Prophecy: An Essay on Biblical Poetry," *JBL* 96 (1977): 5–26, here 6–8; Freedman, "Prose Particles"; Cohen, "Diachrony in Biblical Hebrew Lexicography," 364–65.

59. See, e.g., Nahum M. Sarna, "Notes on the Use of the Definite Article in the Poetry of Job," in *Texts, Temples, and Traditions: A Tribute to Menahem Haran* (ed. Michael V. Fox et al.; Winona Lake, IN: Eisenbrauns, 1996), 279–84. C. L. Seow's assertion that there are "numerous examples of prose particles" in the poetry of Job is an exaggeration (*Job 1–21: Interpretation and Commentary*, Illuminations (Grand Rapids: Eerdmans, 2013), 24. Deliberate

Early Hebrew poetry also employs special grammar.[60] Most salient is the use of the prefixed and suffixed verb forms without the so-called *vav*-consecutive that characterizes biblical prose.[61] A special vocabulary defines early Hebrew poetry as well. Certain terms such as *təhôm* ("the sea"), *māḥaṣ* ("to strike, to slay"), and *'imrâ* ("utterance") occur only in poetic passages, and some terms, for example, *mišpətayim* ("animal pens"), occur only within the corpus of archaic poems.[62]

Two additional rhetorical features of early Hebrew poetry may be mentioned. One is a high degree of verbal repetition and assonance.[63] An extreme instance is the Song of Deborah (Judg 5).[64] The phenomenon embraces the length of the poem. Here is simply one brief illustration (vv.4–5):

ה' בְּצֵאתְךָ מִשֵּׂעִיר / בְּצַעְדְּךָ מִשְּׂדֵה אֱדוֹם / אֶרֶץ רָעָשָׁה /
גַּם-שָׁמַיִם נָטָפוּ / גַּם-עָבִים נָטְפוּ מָיִם:
הָרִים נָזְלוּ / מִפְּנֵי ה' זֶה סִינַי / מִפְּנֵי ה' אֱלֹהֵי יִשְׂרָאֵל:

---

archaizing is evident also in the conservative orthography of the MT of Job; see C. L. Seow, "Orthography, Textual Criticism, and the Poetry of Job," *JBL* 130 (2011): 63–85.

60. See, e.g., Patrick D. Miller, "The Theological Significance of Biblical Poetry," in *Israelite Religion and Biblical Theology: Collected Essays*, JSOTSup 267 (Sheffield: Sheffield Academic, 2000), 233–49, esp. 235–45, where the flexibility of form and syntax characteristic of biblical verse are underscored.

61. See esp. Tania Notarius, *The Verb in Archaic Biblical Poetry: A Discursive, Typological, and Historical Investigation of the Tense System*, SStLL 68 (Leiden: Brill, 2013).

62. See, e.g., Frank M. Cross Jr. and David Noel Freedman, *Studies in Ancient Yahwistic Poetry*, SBLDS 21 (Missoula, MT: Scholars Press, 1975), 29; Gianto, "Archaic Biblical Hebrew," 27. The verb רצד ("skip"; cognate to רקד) and the noun גבנן ("hill"), which appears in the poem from Kuntillet 'Ajrud as well (see above), occur only in Ps 68:16–17. They are early equivalents of רקד and הר־גבעה; see Ps 29:6; 114:4; cf. Joel 2:5. The phrase תועפת ראם ("ram's horns") occurs only in the Oracles of Balaam (Num 23:22, 24:8); its equivalent קרני ראם occurs in the Blessings of Moses (Deut 33:17). For recent studies of archaic Hebrew vocabulary, see Cohen, "Diachrony in Biblical Hebrew Lexicography"; Tania Notarius, "Lexical Isoglosses of Archaic Hebrew: פלילים (Deut 32:31) and כן (Judg 5:15) as Case Studies," *HS* 58 (2017): 81–97. For a detailed discussion of תועפת, see Chaim Cohen, "The Well-Attested BH-Akk. Simile כראם (Ps 92:11) / כמו בן־ראמים (Ps 29:6) = Akk. *kīma rīmi / rīmāniš* and Its Semantic Equivalent כאביר (Isa 10:13 [*Kethiv*] in the Speech of the Assyrian King," in *Marbeh Ḥokmah: Studies in the Bible and the Ancient Near East in Loving Memory of Victor Avigdor Hurowitz*, ed. Shamir Yona et al. (Winona Lake, IN: Eisenbrauns, 2015), 84–85 n. 5.

63. This feature characterizes much ancient Near Eastern verse; see, e.g., Greenstein, "Verbal Art and Literary Sensibilities," 457–75. For repetition as an epic feature in ancient Hebrew poetry, see, e.g., Albright, *Yahweh and the Gods of Canaan*, 4–28. For an exemplary study of punning in archaic Hebrew poetry, see Stanley Gevirtz, "Of Patriarchs and Puns: Joseph at the Fountain, Jacob at the Ford," *HUCA* 46 (1975): 33–54.

64. See, e.g., Michael D. Coogan, "A Structural and Literary Study of the Song of Deborah," *CBQ* 40 (1978): 143–66; Susan Niditch, *Judges: A Commentary*, OTL (Louisville: Westminster John Knox, 2008), 77.

O YHWH, when you go forth [בצאתך] from Seir,
When you march forth [בצעדך] from the region of Edom,
The earth quakes.
The heavens precipitate, / The clouds precipitate water.
The mountains melt down, / In the presence of YHWH of Sinai,
In the presence of YHWH, God of Israel.

The combined phenomena of repetition and assonance (sibilants in the first triplet, labials in the next couplet, liquids in the last triplet) is reminiscent of Ugaritic epic,[65] a topic to which I will return.

The last feature of archaic Hebrew poetry I will address here is, on the one hand, the paucity of figurative language and, on the other, that the most prevalent use of the imagery is that from the domain of animals. This is not surprising, for animal imagery is a noted feature of the Ugaritic poetry that lies in the background of Hebrew literature and of Arabic poetry, which, we have seen, exhibits many similarities to the biblical corpus.[66] In the Oracles of Balaam, for example, most of the images involve animals, especially the lion. Take, for example, the following passage (23:24; cf. 24:9):

Here is a people that stands up like a lion, / stands erect like a lion.
It will not lie down till it's eaten its prey,
And has drunk the blood of its victims.

Animal imagery is salient in the blessings of Jacob and of Moses,[67] as well as in Ps 29 and many other early Hebrew poems.

In fact, certain of the lines concerning animals that we find in the Blessings of Jacob and in the Oracles of Balaam are virtually identical to lines we find in the Blessings of Moses as well.[68] There are actually quite

65. See, e.g, Baruch Margalit, "Alliteration in Ugaritic Poetry: It Role in Composition and Analysis," *UF* 11 (1979): 537–57 (part 1); and *JNSL* 8 (1980): 57–80 (part 2).

66. Let these two examples stand for the lot. From the Ugaritic epic of Kirta (*KTU* 1.14 iv 29–31): "Like a locust swarm, they inhabit the steppe; / Like crickets, the desert's edge" (text and translation in Edward L. Greenstein, "Kirta," in Parker, *Ugaritic Narrative Poetry*, 19). Compare the proximate image of the locusts, which proceed in formation (lines 17–18), to Prov 30:27. From the "Al-Find of the Banū Zimmān": "We strode as stalks a lion forth / at dawn, a lion wrathful-eyed" (trans. in Lyall, *Translations of Ancient Arabian Poetry*, 5; cf. Jer 4:7 etc. For animal imagery in Proverbs, see Tova L. Forti, *Animal Imagery in the Book of Proverbs* (VTSup 118; Leiden: Brill, 2007). For lion imagery, see Brent A. Strawn, *What Is Stronger than a Lion? Leonine Image and Metaphor in the Hebrew Bible and the Ancient Near East*, OBO 212 (Fribourg: Academic Press; Göttingen: Vandenhoeck & Ruprecht, 2005). For animal imagery in Akkadian epic, see Michael P. Streck, *Die Bildersprache der akkadischen Epik*, AOAT 264 (Münster: Ugarit-Verlag), 172–76.

67. See Gen 49:9, 11, 14, 17, 21, 22, 27; Deut 33:17, 19, 20, 22.

68. Compare, e.g., Gen 49:9 with Num 23:24 and Deut 33:20; Num 23:9 with Deut 33:28; Num 23:22 with Deut 33:17; see Budd, *Numbers*, 263.

a number of nearly identical lines shared by several of the early Hebrew poems, leading one to wonder whether they are all influenced by the same now-lost classic or whether the stock of available material was severely limited.[69]

Be that as it may, the corpus of early Hebrew poetry clearly served as a resource for later Hebrew poets. The influence of these classic poems was great, and they can be shown to have been widely used throughout biblical literature. No one, to my knowledge, has ever assembled all the pertinent evidence for this phenomenon, but most of the examples have been noted here and there in the literature. One striking example is the line "Yah is my power and my might, and he has become my savior" (עזי וזמרת יה ויהי לי לישועה; Exod 15:2a), which recurs word for word in Isa 12:2 and Ps 118:14. The Song of Moses (Deut 32)—which I identify as the Song of Yashar (see above)—has a particularly extensive impact.[70] There are dozens of echoes in the Prophets, in Psalms, and in Job.[71]

One example of this phenomenon is found in Prov 3:20, a passage recounting God's creation of the earth and the sky: "In his wisdom the watery deeps were split open, / and the skies dripped dew." The verb for "dripped," רעף, is simply a metathesized form of the verb ערף, which is used in Deut 32:2. This can be demonstrated by comparing Job 36:28, where we find the verb רעף in a similar context and in parallelism with the verb נזל ("to drip)," which is found together with ערף in Deuteronomy. Here is the verse Deut 32:2 in Everett Fox's translation:

> Let my teaching drip like rain, / let my words flow like dew,
> Like droplets on new-growth, / like showers on grass.[72]

The second line of the couplet from Prov 3, with its combination of "dew" and "drip," is clearly influenced by the verse in the classic song.

---

69. Thanks to these similarities, some textual difficulties may be cleared up. For example, Gen 49:10b can be restored by comparison with Ps 68:30. See, e.g., Cross and Freedman, *Ancient Yahwistic Poetry*, 83; Chaim Cohen, "Jewish Medieval Commentary on the Book of Genesis and Modern Biblical Philology, Part 3: Genesis 37–49," in *Zaphenath-Paneah: Linguistics Studies Presented to Elisha Qimron on the Occasion of His Sixty-Fifth Birthday*, ed. Daniel Sivan, David Talshir, and Chaim Cohen [Hebrew] (Beer-sheva: Ben-Gurion University Press, 2009), 271–73—but neither bases the reading on Ps 68.

70. See, e.g., Dov Rappel, *The Ha'azinu Song with Introduction and Commentary* [Hebrew] (Tel Aviv: Yediot Ahronot, 1996).

71. For Jeremiah, see Leuchter, "Why Is the Song of Moses in Deuteronomy?," 304. For Job, see my "Parody as a Challenge to Tradition: The Use of Deuteronomy 32 in the Book of Job," in *Reading Job Intertextually*, ed. Katharine Dell and Will Kynes, LHBOTS 574 (New York: Bloomsbury T&T Clark, 2013), 66–78.

72. Everett Fox, *The Five Books of Moses: Genesis, Exodus, Leviticus, Numbers, Deuteronomy; A New Translation with Introductions, Commentary, and Notes*, Schocken Bible 1 (New York: Schocken, 1995), 1002.

The first line of the couplet in Prov 3:20 is drawn from yet another source. The phrase "the watery deeps were split open" (תהומות נבקעו) is a paraphrase of a snatch of poetry embedded in the midst of the flood narrative in Gen 7:11.[73] The full couplet reads:

נִבְקְעוּ כָּל־מַעְיְנֹת תְּהוֹם רַבָּה / וַאֲרֻבֹּת הַשָּׁמַיִם נִפְתָּחוּ׃

All the springs of the great watery deep split open,
And the windows of the sky opened up.

The form and language of this couplet leave no doubt that it was incorporated into the prose narrative from elsewhere—biblical prose will sometimes wax poetic in dialogue,[74] but almost never in the discourse of the narrator. Whenever one encounters such a burst of verse, one must suspect a quotation from a source. So our verse in Prov 3 is a combination of classical quotations—one from Deut 32 and the other from the source of Gen 7.

The other half of the couplet found in Gen 7:11 is borrowed, in a manner reminiscent of Prov 3:20, in Isa 24:18:

כִּי-אֲרֻבּוֹת מִמָּרוֹם נִפְתָּחוּ / וַיִּרְעֲשׁוּ מוֹסְדֵי אָרֶץ׃

For the windows from on high opened up,
And the earth's foundations quaked.

The second line of the Isaian couplet is an echo of another archaic Hebrew poem, the one found in Ps 18:8, which is also embedded in 2 Sam 22:

וַתִּגְעַשׁ וַתִּרְעַשׁ הָאָרֶץ / וּמוֹסְדֵי הָרִים יִרְגָּזוּ

The earth rumbled and quaked, / and the earth's foundations
trembled.

To me it seems very unlikely that the poets in Isaiah and Proverbs would both find inspiration in an isolated couplet embedded in the dry prose of Gen 7. Rather, they were drawing on a poem, probably an epic poem, about the great flood, from which the author of Gen 7 also drew. Behind the prose narrative of the Bible lie early Hebrew epic poems.[75]

---

73. See recently Jason M. H. Gaines, *The Poetic Priestly Source* (Minneapolis: Fortress, 2015), 158, 200–201.

74. See my "Direct Discourse and Parallelism," in *Discourse, Dialogue and Debate in the Bible: Essays in Honour of Frank H. Polak*, ed. Athalya Brenner-Idan, HBM 63 (Sheffield: Sheffield Phoenix, 2014), 79–91.

75. See the references in n. 55 above. The likelihood of a pre-biblical epic of the flood can be supported by invoking not only the Mesopotamian tradition of a flood epic (see Y. S. Chen, *The Primeval Flood Catastrophe: Origins and Early Development in Mesopotamian Tradi-*

As was said above, there is no full epic poem among the archaic songs and snatches that can be found in embedded form in biblical narrative.[76] Yet there are several sorts of evidence that can be adduced to establish the existence of pre-biblical Hebrew epics.[77] I will illustrate three of them here. First, in the midst of narrative prose we occasionally find a burst of classical poetry. The couplet cited above from the flood story, in Gen 7:11, is as obvious an example as one can find. There are others.[78] Second, archaic terms that occur almost exclusively in biblical verse occasionally turn up in narrative prose. An example is the word *təhôm*, a poetic synonym of the term for "sea" in Ugaritic and in biblical poetry. Its only attestation outside of poetry is in the creation story, just once, in Gen 1:2—in a chapter that exhibits additional telltale signs of an epic background.[79] Third, and most important: pre-biblical Canaanite epic from Ugarit is characterized by the use of formulas such as "He/she raised his/her eyes and saw" and

tions, Oxford Oriental Monographs [Oxford: Oxford University Press, 2013], esp. 197–252) but also the Ras Shamra (ancient Ugarit) version of the Babylonian flood epic in which the episode of the birds has recently been identified; see Guy Darshan, "The Calendrical Framework of the Priestly Flood Story in Light of a New Akkadian Text from Ugarit (RS 94.2953)," *JAOS* 136 (2016): 507–14.

76. The Song at the Sea (Exod 15) and the Song of Deborah (Judg 5), which are sometimes cited as narrative poems (e.g., Gaines, *Poetic Priestly Source*,13), are not essentially narrative; they are rather victory hymns embedding narrative passages, and not necessarily in chronological order (see above with n. 56). For the nature of such poems, see, e.g., Murray H. Lichtenstein, "Biblical Poetry," in *Back to the Sources: Reading the Classic Jewish Texts*, ed. Barry W. Holtz (New York: Summit, 1984), esp. 107–14, on the Song at the Sea. The same approach may be applied to the Song of Deborah; contrast the misguided analyses of Kawashima ("From Song to Story") and of Walter J. Houston ("Misunderstanding or Midrash? The Prose Appropriation of Poetical Material in the Hebrew Bible [Parts 1 and 2]," *ZAW* 109 [1997]: 342–55, 534–48), who assume that the prose narratives in Exod 14 and Judg 4 were created on the basis of the earlier songs. The hypothesis of early epic versions of both narratives can account for the resemblances and differences between the juxtaposed verse texts.

The suggestion of Cross and others that there was a full-length pre-biblical Israelite epic is very unlikely in view of the evidence of the relatively short biblical poems and the modest length of the Ugaritic epics (possibly no longer than one thousand lines each); see Dobbs-Allsopp, *On Biblical Poetry*, 249–52; and see further below.

77. See esp. Cassuto, "Israelite Epic."

78. For example, Gen 2:5 with its basically balanced parallelism seems to be excerpted from a creation epic; see Mowinckel, "Israelitische Nationalepos," 146. Numbers 22:3–6 comprises mainly couplets that appear to derive from an epic poem concerning Balaam. The Deir 'Alla inscription from ca. 800 BCE, together with the reference in Mic 6:5, supports this conclusion; see, e.g., Budd, *Numbers*, 263.

79. Polak indicates the poetic features but goes too far in maintaining that the prose narrative of Gen 1:1–2:4a is essentially a poem. It does not comprise a continuous sequence of couplets (and triplets). A comparison with any passage from Ugaritic epic will immediately reveal the generic distinction. See Frank H. Polak, "Poetic Style and Parallelism in the Creation Account (Genesis 1.1–2.3)," in *Creation in Jewish and Christian Tradition*, ed. Henning Graf Reventlow and Yair Hoffman, JSOTSup 319 (Sheffield: Sheffield Academic, 2002), 2–31.

"He/she raised his/her voice and cried."[80] These formulas have precise parallels in the Bible, where the verb for "raising up," the noun for "eyes," and sometimes the verb for "crying out," are identical to the terms in the Canaanite formulas.[81] There can be no doubt of a historical connection between the Canaanite formulas and their biblical doubles.

The formula for raising the eyes and seeing occurs about twenty times in biblical narrative prose.[82] The formula for raising the voice and crying out occurs a dozen times in biblical narrative prose.[83] And yet these formulas never occur in any archaic biblical poem. In some late biblical prophetic texts, in poetry, they are attested only in the imperative—"O lift up your eyes and see!"[84] The third- and first-person use of epic formulas is found in the Bible only in narrative prose.

So how can narrative formulas known from second-millennium Canaanite epic get absorbed into biblical prose narrative? Not directly from Canaanite epic, which antecedes the development of biblical prose narrative. Not from the archaic poetry that is found in the Bible, which, as we have seen, is never essentially narrative and in any event contains no such formulas. Not from biblical poetry at all, where it is employed only relatively late and only in the imperative. The only realistic explanation is that the formulas were known from early Hebrew epic, which is not preserved in full form anywhere in the Bible. In the same way that the authors of biblical prose narrative occasionally drew on the corpus of archaic Hebrew poetry, they drew on pre-biblical Hebrew epic, which also belonged to that corpus.[85]

Scholars have suggested that among the epics that predate biblical

---

80. See the comprehensive extension of Cassuto's observations ("Israelite Epic," 74–76) in Polak, "Epic Formulas."

81. See my "Trans-Semitic Idiomatic Equivalency and the Derivation of Hebrew *ml'kh*," *UF* 11 (1979): 329–36; cf. Polak, "Epic Formulas"; and Polak, "Linguistic and Stylistic Aspects of Epic Formulae in Ancient Semitic Poetry and Biblical Narrative," in *Biblical Hebrew in Its Northwest Semitic Setting: Typological and Historical Perspectives*, ed. Steven E. Fassberg and Avi Hurvitz, Publication of the Institute for Advanced Studies, the Hebrew University of Jerusalem 1 (Jerusalem: Magnes; Winona Lake, IN: Eisenbrauns, 2006), 285–304.

82. E.g., Gen 13:10, 14; 18:2; 22:4, 13; 24:63, 64; 31:1; 33:5; 37:25; 43:29; Num 24:2; Josh 5:13; Judg 19:17; 1 Sam 6:13; 2 Sam 18:24; Zech 2:1, 5; 5:9, 6:1; Dan 8:3; 10:5; 1 Chr 21:16; and cf. Job 2:12. In the imperative, it occurs in Gen 31:14.

83. E.g., Gen 21:16; 27:38; 29:11; Judg 2:4; 9:7; 21:2; 1 Sam 11:4; 24:17; 2 Sam 3:32; 13:36; Job 2:12; Ruth 1:9, 14. The formulaic "he lifted up his legs and went" occurs only in Gen 29:1 and would appear to be a later imitation of an epic formula.

84. See Isa 40:26, 49:18, 60:4, Jer 3:2, 13:20, Zech 5:5. Cf. Michael P. Maier, "'Lift Up Your Eyes and Look Around!' Point of View in Isaiah 60," *BN* 169 (2016): 54; Frank H. Polak, "Oral Platform and Language Usage in the Abraham Narrative," in *The Formation of the Pentateuch: Bridging the Academic Cultures of Europe, Israel, and North America*, ed. Jan C. Gertz et al.; FAT 111 (Tübingen: Mohr Siebeck, 2016), 424–26.

85. See Frank H. Polak, "Epic Formulas in Biblical Narrative: Frequency and Distribution," in *Actes du seconde colloque international "Bible et informatique: Méthodes, outils, résultats,*

narrative prose are verse poems about the combat between YHWH God of Israel and a personified Sea and about the exodus from Egypt and the crossing of the sea.[86] If such epics existed and if their language was borrowed by later narrators and poets, it would explain the fact that certain phrases and motifs are disseminated fairly widely in biblical literature. To assemble a complete catalogue of such phrases would entail a full-blown research project,[87] but a few examples are the following: YHWH's growling at the Sea (using the verb גער) and blasting it with the wind of his nostrils (רוח אפו);[88] the Lord's splitting of the water (using the verb בקע) and allowing the people to cross on dry land (using the terms חרבה or יבשה);[89] and the sea water covering over the enemy or victim (using the verb כסה).[90]

Some scholars have suggested that in early Israel there was not only epic verse but also an epic poem, originally oral, relating in succession the major episodes of Israel's national story—from Jacob and the sojourn in Egypt through the exodus and on to the conquest of the Transjordan and Canaan.[91] I cannot accept such a far-reaching theory.[92] For one thing, the archaic poems, even at their lengthiest, are fairly short. Even the Ugaritic epics extended for no more than about twelve hundred lines each. Moreover, the styles of the archaic Hebrew poems vary widely. For example, whereas the deletion or gapping of the main verb in the second of a two-line couplet is very common in most early Hebrew verse, as it is in Ugaritic,[93] the Song at the Sea in Exod 15 shows not a single example of gapping.[94]

---

ed. R. F. Poswick et al. (Geneva: Slatkine, 1989), 435–88, here 474–75; Dobbs-Allsopp, *On Biblical Poetry*, 242–43.

86. See, e.g., Cassuto, "Israelite Epic," 71–73. On the combat myth, see now Noga Ayali Darshan, *Treading on the Back of the Sea: The Combat between the Storm-God and the Sea in Ancient Near Eastern Literature [Hebrew]* (Jerusalem: Bialik Institute, 2016). See above concerning the pre-biblical flood epic reflected in Gen 7:11.

87. I am engaged in such a project, with support of the Israel Science Foundation (see n. 1 above).

88. E.g., Exod 15:8, 10; Isa 50:2; Nah 1:4; Ps 18:17 (= 2 Sam 22:16); 104:6-7; 106:9.

89. E.g., Exod 14:16, 21, 22, 29; Josh 3:17; 2 Kgs 2:8; Ps 78:13. The verse Neh 9:11 appears to be a direct borrowing from Exod 14.

90. E.g., Exod 14:28; 15:5, 10; Ezek 26:19; Ps 78:53; 106:11; Job 22:11; 38:34; cf. Hab 2:14; Ps 104:6; Job 36:30.

91. See, e.g., Cross, *From Epic to Canon*, 43–46.

92. See Dobbs-Allsopp, *On Biblical Poetry*, 250–52; see also Freedman, "Pottery, Poetry, and Prophecy," 18–20.

93. See my "Two Variations of Grammatical Parallelism in Canaanite Poetry and Their Psycholinguistic Background," *JANES* 6 (1974): 87–105; and Cynthia L. Miller, "Patterns of Verbal Ellipsis in Ugaritic," *UF* 31 (1999): 333–72; cf. her "A Linguistic Approach to Ellipsis in Biblical Poetry (or, What to Do When Exegesis of What Is There Depends on What Isn't)," *BBR* 13 (2003): 251–70.

94. See M. O'Connor, *Hebrew Verse Structure* (Winona Lake, IN: Eisenbrauns, 1980), 471–72.

In comparing the relatively few epics from the ancient Near East that have survived in writing, one does not find such stylistic diversity.

On the other hand, a comparison of the ancient Near East's most famous epic poem, the Epic of Gilgamesh, can be instructive.[95] Epic poems about episodes in Gilgamesh's career circulated independently for centuries before a poet decided to draw on some of them and compose an extensive epic in writing. The standard version of the epic was written by a poet-scribe in the latter part of the second millennium BCE, and in its fullest form reached fewer than three thousand lines. There is no evidence to support the theory that an entire Epic of Gilgamesh ever existed in oral form.[96]

It would seem that the archaic pre-biblical poetry of Israel has been preserved for the most part as it was incorporated into a prose narrative of Israel's traditional history, extending from the creation of the world through the middle of the Babylonian exile in the middle of the sixth century BCE. This narrative is highly rhetorical—rich in literary tropes and allusions. And yet it is also instrumental: it manifests the clear purpose of tracing the history of the people from its first inhabitation of its homeland to its exile from that land and of its dependence on the good graces of its God if it ever wants to return to its land.[97]

The incorporation of archaic Hebrew verse within the framework of biblical prose narrative is also instrumental. A poem such as Deut 32—"the Song of Yashar" or *Ha'azinu*—has the express purpose of serving as testimony to the fact that the people had been warned of the consequences of breaking the covenant with God.[98] Explicit citations from the Book of Yashar or the Book of the Battles of YHWH are apparently adduced in order to authenticate a particular tradition or attest to its antiquity.[99] The embedding of excerpts from ancient poems or entire poems may have served a similar purpose.

But from an aesthetic or literary point of view, these poems serve additional functions. They stop the action and lend drama, emotion,

---

95. For the background and development of the epic, see Jeffrey H. Tigay, *The Evolution of the Gilgamesh Epic* (Philadelphia: University of Pennsylvania Press, 1982); A. R. George, *The Babylonian Gilgamesh Epic: Introduction, Critical Edition and Cuneiform Texts*, 2 vols. (Oxford: Oxford University Press, 2003); David Damrosch, *The Buried Book: The Loss and Rediscovery of the Great Epic of Gilgamesh* (New York: Henry Holt, 2006).

96. See Benjamin R. Foster, *The Epic of Gilgamesh: A New Translation, Analogues, Criticism* (New York: Norton, 2001), xiv.

97. See my "The Torah as She Is Read," in *Essays on Biblical Method and Translation*, BJS 92 (Atlanta: Scholars Press, 1989), 29–51.

98. See Isaac Rabinowitz, *A Witness Forever: Ancient Israel's Perception of Literature and the Resultant Hebrew Bible*, ed. Ross Brann and David I. Owen, Occasional Publications of the Department of Near Eastern Studies and the Program of Jewish Studies, Cornell University 1 (Bethesda, MD: CDL Press, 1993).

99. See, e.g., Stott, *Why Did They Write This Way?*, 55–58.

and subjectivity to a narrative.[100] In their new contexts, the old songs are reperformed,[101] and, as they are, the old songs are—to the extent they are already known—defamiliarized—placed in new settings where their literary features remain salient but their function and perhaps even their reference have significantly changed. As they are embedded in and subordinated to biblical narrative, the archaic songs are redefined as dialogue within narrative.[102] They are highly expressive still, but they seem to lose something of the lyrical quality they seem once to have possessed back when they were autonomous poems.

100. See Lichtenstein, "Biblical Poetry."

101. See, in general, Giles and Doan, *Twice-Used Songs*; and, for Deut 32, Leuchter, "Why Is the Song of Moses in Deuteronomy?"; Keith A. Stone, *Singing Moses's Song: A Performance-Critical Analysis of Deuteronomy's Song of Moses*, Ilex Foundation Series 17 (Boston: Ilex Foundation / Washington DC: Center for Hellenic Studies, Trustees of Harvard University, 2016).

102. All biblical poetry is direct discourse of some kind; see my "Direct Discourse and Parallelism." Cf. Rolf A. Jacobson, *"Many are Saying": The Function of Direct Discourse in the Hebrew Psalter*, JSOTSup 397 (London–New York: T & T Clark International, 2004).

Prohibited Bodies in Leviticus 18

WILLIAM K. GILDERS
Emory University

There is no law that is not inscribed on bodies. Every law has a hold on the body.

—Michel de Certeau[1]

Leviticus 18, the second chapter in the portion of the book of Leviticus that has been conventionally referred to as the Holiness Code,[2] specifies sexual behavior that YHWH prohibits the Israelites to engage in, identifies such behavior as characteristic of the Egyptians and Canaanites, and warns of the dire national consequence for failing to abide by the prohibitions. The sexual prohibitions are set out in two main units, one concerned with behavior commonly characterized as "incest" (18:6–18) and the other dealing with other proscribed sexual acts (18:19–23).[3] This

---

When I was a doctoral student in the Judaism in Antiquity program at Brown University, I studied rabbinic texts on sexuality and marriage with Shaye J. D. Cohen, in the course of which I discovered an interest in ancient Israelite laws about sexuality and kinship and in exploring those texts through concepts and models drawn from the social sciences. Now, as I prepare a commentary on Leviticus for the Old Testament Library series published by Westminster John Knox Press, I have returned to that old interest. Thus, it seems appropriate to offer some material related to that work-in-progress as my contribution to this volume. My thanks to Michael Satlow for helpful feedback on a draft of this study and to my research assistant, Richard A. Purcell, for his attention to detail and thoughtful suggestions. All weaknesses in this work, of course, are my sole responsibility.

1. Michel de Certeau, *The Practice of Everyday Life*, trans. Steven Rendall (Berkeley: University of California Press, 1984), 139.

2. Leviticus 17–26 (excluding Lev 27 as a late addition to the book).

3. Interpreters differ over whether to assign Lev 18:18, which prohibits a man from taking his wife's sister as an additional wife during his wife's lifetime, to the first unit or the second. Erhard S. Gerstenberger places it with 18:19–23 as one of the "forbidden vices" (*Leviticus: A Commentary*, trans. Douglas W. Stott, OTL [Louisville: Westminster John Knox, 1996], 251–54). Jacob Milgrom places 18:18 in the category of incest prohibitions with 18:6–17 (*Leviticus 17–22: A New Translation with Introduction and Commentary*, AB 3A [New York: Doubleday, 2000], 1523–24); see also Susan Rattray, "Marriage Rules, Kinship Terms and Family Structure in the Bible," in *Society of Biblical Literature 1987 Seminar Papers*, ed. Kent Harold Richards (Atlanta: Scholars Press, 1987), 537–44, here 537. Adrian Schenker also places 18:18 with the incest prohibitions but marks it as belonging to a subcategory along with the prohibitions of 18:17 ("What Connects the Incest Prohibitions with the Other Prohibitions Listed

two-part sexual code clearly regulates bodies, those of Israelites as well as of non-Israelites resident in the land of Israel (18:26). The incest prohibitions, in particular, focus on the body in two ways: referring to *flesh* (using two Hebrew words with largely overlapping semantic ranges, שאר and בשר) and to the treatment of *nakedness* (ערוה). The terms for *flesh* indicate what conventional Western kinship norms conceptualize as consanguinity (shared blood),[4] while the term for *nakedness* is a euphemism for the genitals, and the repeated idiom of *uncovering nakedness* indicates sexual activity.[5] My goal in this paper is to deepen and extend understanding of this body terminology by clarifying the cultural conceptions of the dressed and undressed body reflected in the text and how those conceptions are related to the text's language of embodied kinship. In brief, I will elucidate the ways Lev 18 prohibits the sexual uncovering of specific human bodies. I will attend mainly to the incest prohibitions, although some brief attention will be given to the additional rules (18:19–23) in order to develop an understanding of how the whole of Lev 18 deals with the sexual body.

This study works from a basic proposition of much of the scholarly work on the body that has been carried out over the past forty years within a variety of disciplinary fields, including biblical studies. While the body is a concrete physical reality, that reality is always experienced through a variety of sociocultural practices, especially discourse. It is in this sense that the body can be spoken of as *constructed*.[6] Of particular relevance to my treatment of the sexual laws of Lev 18 is Michel de Certeau's eloquent statement about the relationship between law and the body, which follows immediately after the words quoted as the epigraph to this essay:

> From birth to mourning after death, law "takes hold of" bodies in order to make them its text. Through all sorts of initiations (in rituals, at school, etc.), it transforms them into tables of the law, into living tableaux of rules and customs, into actors in the drama organized by social order.... the law constantly writes itself on bodies. It engraves itself on parchments made from the skin of its subjects. It articulates them in a juridical corpus. It makes its book out of them.[7]

---

in Leviticus 18 and 20?," in *The Book of Leviticus: Composition and Reception*, ed. Rolf Rendtorff and Robert A. Kugler, VTSup 93 [Leiden: Brill, 2003], 162–85, here 163–65).

4. Milgrom, *Leviticus 17–22*, 1533; Eve Levavi Feinstein, *Sexual Pollution in the Hebrew Bible* (New York: Oxford University Press, 2014), 109, 239 n. 41.

5. See, e.g., Gerstenberger, *Leviticus*, 244 n. 1: the idiom לגלות ערוה "refers to the forbidden act of 'uncovering the pubic region,' but here implies sexual activity"; see also Milgrom, *Leviticus 17–22*, 1534.

6. Elizabeth A. Castelli, "The Body," in *The Cambridge Companion to Ancient Mediterranean Religions*, ed. Barbette Stanley Spaeth, Cambridge Companions to Religion (Cambridge: Cambridge University Press, 2013), 252–80, here 252–53.

7. De Certeau, *Practice of Everyday Life*, 139–40.

In this study, I will explore how a particular collection of laws that deals with sexual relationships "writes itself" upon the bodies its authors assumed and pictured, constructing them as subject to its regulations.

Preliminary Observations on Leviticus 18:6–18 as a Kinship Code Written on Bodies

In the anthropological study of kinship, any particular system is presented and interpreted from the perspective of a single participant within that system, conventionally designated "ego."[8] Analysis of the incest prohibitions in Lev 18:6–18 according to this approach is facilitated by the fact that they are explicitly directed to ego, who is addressed in the second masculine singular. Ego is an adult Israelite male in relation to whom Israelite women are designated as kin with whom he may or may not enter into sexual relations (with marriage being the assumed normative context for such relations). Most of the prohibited unions are clear, although a couple of them have produced conflict among interpreters.[9] These are the relatively unambiguous rules: ego may not engage in sexual relations with his mother (18:7); with any other wife of his father (18:8); with a half-sister who is the daughter of his father or of his mother (18:9); with the daughters of his own sons and daughters (18:10); with his father's sister (18:12); with his mother's sister (18:13); with his father's brother's wife, who is specified as belonging to the category of paternal aunt (דודה) (18:14); with his daughter-in-law (כלה), further specified as his son's wife (18:15); with his brother's wife (18:16); with a woman and her daughter or with a woman and her son's daughter or daughter's daughter (18:17); and with a woman and her sister during the woman's lifetime (18:18).

Leviticus 18:6 introduces the incest prohibitions, deploying the body terminology that will function throughout the code: איש איש אל־כל־שאר בשרו לא תקרבו לגלות ערוה אני ה׳ ("Not one of you may approach his close bodily kin[10] to uncover nakedness! I am YHWH!"). In my view, this prohibitive commandment sets out a general principle and prohibition, which could stand on its own insofar as the identity of women included under the des-

8. Ernest L. Schusky, *Manual for Kinship Analysis*, 2nd ed., Studies in Anthropological Method (New York: Holt, Rinehart & Winston, 1972), 9–10.

9. The one rule that presents real exegetical difficulty is the prohibition of ego having a sexual relationship with his father's wife's daughter, who is specified as מולדת אביך (18:11). I will address its interpretation below in my systematic examination of the incest rules.

10. As Milgrom observes (*Leviticus 17–22*, 1533), שאר בשרו (literally, "flesh of his flesh") is a superlative, "implying that the subject is the close relatives"; this interpretation is reflected in my translation.

ignation שאר בשרו were known.[11] The collection of prohibitive laws that follows (18:7–18) functions, therefore, to clarify and supplement the general principle, not to exhaustively "unpack" it.

The idiom שאר בשרו occurs only one other time in Leviticus (and nowhere else in the Hebrew Bible), in Lev 25:49b. There, it refers to male kin (in addition to the already specified brother [אח], paternal uncle [דוד], and paternal uncle's son [בן־דוד]; 25:48–49a) who are qualified to redeem an Israelite from indenture to a resident alien: משאר בשרו ממשפחתו ("one of his close bodily kin from his kin group"[12]). This usage helps to clarify that the idiom refers to a smaller subgroup within the larger kin network (משפחה).

According to Susan Rattray, the one source that serves to identify the female kin included under שאר בשרו is Lev 21:2, which identifies family members for whom a priest may contract death uncleanness.[13] Those relatives are referred to as שארו הקרב אליו ("his bodily kin who are close to him"), which requires us to ask whether שארו הקרב אליו and שאר בשרו are indeed synonymous idioms. Rattray, followed by Milgrom, maintains that they are, noting that Num 27:11 appears to use the formula שארו הקרב אליו ממשפחתו ("his bodily kin who are close to him from his kin group") synonymously to the usage of שאר בשרו ממשפחתו ("his close bodily kin from his kin group") in Lev 25:49. Thus, Lev 21:2 serves as the key for understanding the meaning and function of Lev 18:6 in relation to 18:7–18, as well as addressing the issue of the apparent absence of ego's full sister and his daughter from the set of prohibitions in Lev 18:7–18. On this interpretation of שאר בשרו in Lev 18:6 as synonymous with שארו הקרב אליו in Lev 21:2, ego's full sister and daughter are included implicitly in Lev 18:6 just as they appear explicitly in Lev 21:2.

Rattray's and Milgrom's understanding of Lev 18:6 can be challenged by noting that the very first explicit prohibition after that verse refers to ego's mother, who would clearly already be included under שאר בשרו and should not need to be referred to explicitly any more than ego's full sister or daughter.[14] This critique, however, misses the point that the specific rules that follow Lev 18:6 should be understood not simply as supplemental to but as elaborating on and clarifying the basic rule in various

---

11. In basic agreement with Milgrom, *Leviticus 17–22*, 1527–30, 1533, who follows Rattray, "Marriage Rules," 542, who explains that the purpose of the laws in 18:7–18 is "to indicate *who else* is forbidden by extension from the basic relationships" covered by 18:6 (Rattray's emphasis).

12. For the translation "kin group" for משפחה, see Jacob Milgrom, *Leviticus 23–27: A New Translation with Introduction and Commentary*, AB 3B (New York: Doubleday, 2001), 2148, 2238.

13. Rattray, "Marriage Rules," 542.

14. Feinstein, *Sexual Pollution*, 172; Milgrom, *Leviticus 17–22*, 1529.

ways. The first elaboration and clarification concern the status of ego's father's wife, who is not ego's own mother (18:8), to present which the text must first clarify specifically why ego's mother is prohibited (18:7). This specification also functions as a concrete example of the application of the general rule, analogous to the listing of the relatives in Lev 21:2 to make clear who is included as שארו הקרב אליו. Therefore, Lev 18:6 should be understood as a general prohibition against sexual relations with the close bodily kin specified in Lev 21:2, which is elaborated and clarified in the rules that follow.

Leviticus 18:7 begins the elaboration and clarification of the general prohibition, deploying the idiom of *uncovering nakedness* in an arresting manner to make its point about the prohibition of mother–son incest. Ego is addressed directly (as in all of the prohibitive commandments through to 18:23): ערות אביך וערות אמך לא תגלה אמך[15] הוא לא תגלה ערותה ("Your father's nakedness, that is, your mother's nakedness,[16] you must not uncover. She is your mother. You must not uncover her nakedness."). The simple declaration, "she is your mother," reflects the taken-for-granted nature of this incest prohibition, but it is placed after a motive that appears to explain precisely why such a union is problematic. Ego's having sexual relations with his mother would not simply confuse the categories of mother and son, but would constitute a violation of his father.

Interpreters disagree about the precise sense of "your father's nakedness" and the offense indicated by warning ego not to uncover it. Does the term "nakedness" in construct with the designation of a male figure indicate *his* genitals or female genitals under his control?[17] From Lev 18:7 through 18:17, every prohibitive commandment begins with the word ערוה as a euphemism for genitals within a context focused on sexual behavior. In addition, the word ערוה occurs in Lev 18:18 (and in 18:19, the first law of the second unit of prohibitions). Leviticus 18:6–19 clearly connects the cultural category of nakedness with sexuality. In the discussion to follow, I will explore that cultural connection, to clarify how a term that refers to the uncovered body can specify the genitals and how an idiom that literally means "uncover nakedness" can refer to sexual activity. On the basis of this exercise, I will return to the question of whose "nakedness" (that is, genitals) is referred to in constructions such as "your father's nakedness" (ערות אביך).

---

15. Throughout this study, I will quote the consonantal MT. As is common, the *written* (*ketiv*) form הוא (3ms) is *read* (*qere*) as the 3fs (היא), correcting an apparently widespread scribal error.

16. The *vav*-conjunction before "your mother" is best understood as explicative. See Milgrom, *Leviticus 17–22*, 1537.

17. For these distinct options, see Milgrom, *Leviticus 17–22*, 1536–37.

Nakedness as an Israelite Cultural Category

The best-known biblical text relevant to the question of ancient Israelite conceptions of bodily undress is Gen 2–3 (specifically 2:25; 3:7, 10–11), although Genesis uses the adjective ערום rather than the noun ערוה.[18] According to Gen 2:25, the first human couple were left unclothed after their creation by YHWH and were unconcerned about their condition: ויהי שניהם ערומים האדם ואשתו ולא יתבששו ("Now the two of them were naked, the human being and his wife, but they were unabashed"[19]). While the narrator tells the reader about the couple's nakedness, they themselves were unconscious of it, as the continuation of the narrative makes clear. Only after both of them had eaten from the fruit of the forbidden tree of the knowledge of good and evil did they know that they were naked (3:7). This knowledge followed from their eyes being opened (ותפקחנה עיני שניהם), which suggests a conception of nakedness being in the eye of the beholder. Before eating of the forbidden fruit, the couple presumably would have seen their own genitals, but would not have evaluated them as any different from others parts of their bodies (such as their hands).[20] Seeing, in this context, indicates a particular evaluation of what was seen. When they became aware of their condition, the couple responded in line with ancient Israelite cultural modesty norms, making "aprons" or "loincloths" (חגרת), that is, coverings for their genitals (and perhaps also their buttocks). Notably, there is no indication that the woman covered her breasts.

The story of the first humans becoming aware of their nakedness resonates remarkably with present-day body theory, which distinguishes the "pre-cultural nude body" from the culturally constituted body, the object of "the gaze": "The cultural component must exist for the nude body to exist, meaning in effect that the *culturally constituted gaze* defines the nude body it sees."[21] In the narrative of Gen 3, the bodies of the first man and woman become culturally nude when parts of them can been seen as needing to be covered.

---

18. H. Niehr ("עָרוֹם," *TDOT* 11:354) asserts that ערום has "no discernable sexual connotations," in clear distinction from ערוה. The two terms, however, do have significantly overlapping semantic ranges, and the narrative in Gen 2–3 draws attention to how the couple covered their *genitals* once they became aware of their nakedness. Thus, it is incorrect to draw a sharp lexical distinction.

19. For the translation "unabashed," see Gordon J. Wenham, *Genesis 1–15*, WBC 1 (Waco, TX: Word, 1987), 71.

20. Umberto Cassuto, *A Commentary on the Book of Genesis*, trans. Israel Abrahams, 2 vols. (Jerusalem: Magnes, 1961–1964), 1:137 (referencing Obadiah Sforno).

21. Florence Dee Boodakian, *Resisting Nudities: A Study in the Aesthetics of Eroticism* (New York: Peter Lang, 2008), 10–11 (emphasis in the original).

The next relevant text in the narrative sequence of Genesis, the account of Noah's drunken undress and the responses of his three sons (Gen 9:20–27), is an Aaronide composition, from the same larger tradition as Lev 18 and sharing key terminology with it, making it particularly significant. According to this narrative, when Noah became intoxicated with wine, he uncovered himself (ויתגל) inside his tent (9:21), that is, in private, not as a public display.[22] His son Ham saw his father's nakedness (ערות אביו), which he reported to his brothers, who were outside the tent (9:22). Shem and Japeth responded to this information by draping a mantle across their shoulders and walking backwards into the tent to cover their father's nakedness (ויכסו את ערות אביהם), keeping themselves from seeing Noah's condition, in explicit contrast to Ham (9:23).[23]

Some interpreters, ancient and modern, have understood the statement that Ham saw Noah's nakedness as a euphemism for a more serious offense, indicating that Ham raped or castrated his father.[24] The rape interpretation of the text draws on the fact that the other occurrence of the expression "father's nakedness" (ערות אב) is in Lev 18 with clear reference to sexual activity. As I will demonstrate below, however, the genitive combination of nakedness with a designation for a male individual in Leviticus need not refer to sexual activity with that person. Moreover, the description of the response by Shem and Japeth to Ham's report indicates that the issue of concern was the seeing of Noah's exposed body; the two took careful measures to avoid this.[25]

On its own, the text is unclear about what constituted Noah's nakedness. However, in view of the data in Gen 2–3 and other biblical texts, it is reasonable to conclude that the exposure of Noah's genitals was at issue. The behavior of Shem and Japeth in contrast to that of Ham suggests a cultural norm that a son should avoid seeing his father's genitals whenever possible. Ham's offense presumably lay not in having (accidently) encountered his father in a state of nakedness but, first, in failing to cover him immediately and, second, in reporting his vulnerable condition to his brothers so that they might also see his exposure.[26] Again, the *gaze* is at issue.

---

22. Nahum M. Sarna, *Genesis* בראשית: *The Traditional Hebrew Text with the New JPS Translation*, JPSTC (Philadelphia: Jewish Publication Society, 1989), 65.

23. See Sarna, *Genesis*, 66: "The Hebrew word order is the reverse of that which tells of Ham's behavior in verse 22. The chiasm points up the contrast between their conduct and his."

24. Ibid., 63–64, 66, 357 n. 7.

25. This straightforward interpretation of the story is reflected in the LXX translation, Jub 7:1–2, Philo, *QG* 2.70, and Josephus, *Ant.* 1.6.3. As Sarna notes, this is the interpretation in *all* of the "earliest postbiblical traditions" (*Genesis*, 66).

26. Josef Scharbet emphasizes Ham's filial obligation to cover his father in order to

Another text from the same large body of Aaronide composition as Gen 9:20–27 and Lev 18 is of particular significance for this investigation: the instruction in Exod 28:42 concerning the attire of the Aaronide priesthood, specifying that priests must wear מכנסי־בד לכסות בשר ערוה ממתנים ועד־ירכים ("linen undergarments to cover naked flesh; they must be from the hips to the thighs.").[27] It is not clear what form this undergarment is to take, whether a loincloth or pants or breeches.[28] Nevertheless, the specification of the coverage area of the garment indicates that preventing exposure of the genitals (and perhaps also the buttocks) is at issue.[29]

Outside of the Pentateuch, but closely related to the Holiness tradition, Ezekiel refers to nakedness in unambiguously sexual terms. In Ezek 16, Jerusalem is personified as a woman involved in a relationship with YHWH. At the beginning of the narrative, YHWH describes coming upon Jerusalem as an abandoned newborn infant given no after-birth care (16:4–6). It is only when the female child arrives at sexual maturity that her nakedness becomes a fact of note (16:7): שדים נכנו ושערך צמח ואת ערם ועריה ("your breasts stood firm and your hair sprouted, but you remained unclothed and naked").[30] The combination of the two adjectival forms in this context seems to emphasize the *complete* nakedness of personified Jerusalem, ערם, as in a number of other contexts, referring to the physical lack of clothing (e.g., Gen 2:25, Isa 58:7), while עריה emphasizes the exposure of the genitals. YHWH declares that, when he saw the mature but still naked female and judged her to be at the "age for love" (עת דדים), he spread part of his garment over her, "and I covered your nakedness" (16:8) (ואכסה ערותך). The deity's action here is the precise opposite of the behavior referred to in Lev 18, covering rather than uncovering, and the use of the term ערוה indicates the genitals, as becomes abundantly clear from its usage further on in the text.

When personified Jerusalem betrays her relationship with YHWH, she is crudely described as promiscuously spreading her legs (16:25).[31] This promiscuous behavior meant that her nakedness was uncovered (16:36):

---

spare him disgrace, an obligation he failed to discharge (*Genesis 1–11*, NEchtB [Würzburg: Echter, 1983], 100).

27. The garment is referred to also in Exod 39:28; Lev 6:3; 16:4; Ezek 44:18.

28. See Cornelis Houtman, *Exodus*, 4 vols., HCOT (Leuven: Peeters, 2000), 3:482–83. The noun is based on the root כנס ("gather"), which may suggest a loincloth, perhaps similar to the traditional Hindu dhoti made famous by Mohandas Gandhi. Houtman, however, identifies the garment as an "apron" or "skirt," worn "around the waist covering the abdomen, the behind and the thighs, extending down to the knees" (483).

29. The same anxiety about exposure of genitals (and buttocks) is reflected in a non-Aaronide text (Exod 20:26), which prohibits using steps to ascend an altar, אשר לא־תגלה ערותך עליו ("whereupon your nakedness must not be uncovered").

30. See also 16:22, which states that personified Jerusalem was ערם ועריה during her "youth" (נעוריך).

31. Ezek 16:25: ותפשקי את־רגליך לכל־עובר ("and you spread your legs for every passer-by");

ותגלה ערותך. YHWH declares that his violent punitive response will be to uncover the woman's nakedness to the sight of all with whom she had fornicated: וגליתי ערותך אלהם וראו את־כל־ערותך ("I will uncover your nakedness to them and they will see all your nakedness") (16:37). Yhwh will turn her over to the control of her former lovers, who will completely strip her, returning her to her original state of being "unclothed and naked" (עירם ועריה) (16:39).[32]

Public exposure of the genitals and buttocks is explicitly identified in two other notable texts as a humiliation for those subjected to it.[33] In 2 Sam 10:4, Hanun, the king of Ammon, mistreats envoys sent by David by having their beards half-shaved and their robes cut in half to their buttocks. Due to this treatment, the men were greatly humiliated or shamed (נכלמים מאד) (10:5). Isaiah 20 reports that YHWH commanded Isaiah to go about in public "naked" (ערום) and barefoot for a period of three years (20:2–3) as a "sign and portent" of what the Egyptians and Ethiopians would suffer at the hands of the Assyrians, who would take captives away ערום ויחף וחשופי שת ערות מצרים ("naked and barefoot, buttocks uncovered—Egypt's nakedness") (v. 4). Given the meaning attached to Isaiah's public nakedness, it seems appropriate to imagine that it would have been humiliating to the prophet himself and scandalous to those who encountered it. Indeed, it would have lacked social impact had such public nakedness not been a violation of established norms. It was appropriate only because it was a performance in response to divine command.[34]

The data I have surveyed here[35] point to an Israelite conception of modesty that defines nakedness as the exposure of the genitals and buttocks—especially the genitals—and identifies a feeling of shame as the normative response to such a condition of exposure. There is little evidence of any distinction between exposure in a same-sex context and that in a different-sex context. Nakedness, as the exposure of genitals, is closely linked to sexuality, especially illicit conduct. The use of "nakedness" as a euphemism for the genitals indicates the cultural norm that genitals are properly to be kept covered and that an attitude of shame always attends their exposure. It is important to note that the idiom "uncover nakedness"

---

the NJPS translates the Hebrew literally, while the NRSV renders it euphemistically as "offering yourself to every passer-by."

32. See also Ezek 23:18.

33. Saul M. Olyan, "Honor, Shame, and Covenant Relations in Ancient Israel and Its Environment," *JBL* 115 (1996): 201–18, here 212–13.

34. *Pace* William H. C. Propp, *Exodus 19–40: A New Translation with Introduction and Commentary*, AB 2A (New York: Doubleday, 2006), 185, who refers to Isaiah's prophetic sign act as evidence that "nudity per se was not too indecent for Israelites."

35. See also 1 Sam 20:30; 2 Sam 6:14, 20; Isa 47:3; Amos 2:16; Mic 1:11; Nah 3:5; Hab 2:15; Lam 4:21.

is never used to refer to licit sexual activity, which suggests cultural anxiety about all sexual activity, even what was deemed licit.

Incest and Uncovering Naked Flesh (Lev 18:6–18)

I return now to the incest prohibitions in Lev 18:6–18 to read them in light of the evidence I have adduced for Israelite norms about exposure of the genitals. Each of the specific prohibitions in Lev 18:7–17 begins with the Leitwort ערוה, which highlights the importance of this cultural body category. The activity that ego is forbidden to engage in with designated women is literally the uncovering of nakedness. While the idiom clearly refers to sexual activity, its literal sense is not lost in the context but serves an important role in defining the motivation for incest avoidance. This is made clear in the very first of the specific prohibitions—against ego having a sexual relationship with his mother (18:7). As I noted above, this prohibitive commandment begins with a reference to ego's father's nakedness before referring to his mother's nakedness and proceeding to make clear that it is the focus of the rule. The explicit motive given for the prohibition is a simple appeal to the fact that the woman in question is ego's mother, as if it is self-evident that a son would not have a sexual relationship with his mother.[36] This motive is supported implicitly by the initial reference to the father's nakedness, which indicates that a sexual relationship between ego and his mother would necessarily implicate ego's father. Milgrom suggests that ego is being warned that a sexual relationship with his mother would amount to a sexual relationship with his father.[37] However, this is an unnecessary interpretive move. Rather, the reference to the father's nakedness should be understood in relation to the straightforward sense of the narrative about Noah's nakedness in Gen 9. It was inappropriate for a son to voluntarily look upon his father's uncovered genitals. According to Lev 18:7, ego's sexual involvement with the mother would amount to the uncovering of his father's genitals to him, violating the normative boundary.

An alternative approach is to understand "your father's nakedness" as meaning the female sexuality that belongs exclusively to ego's father.[38] This interpretation is undermined by the declaration in Lev 18:10 that ego's granddaughters' nakedness is his nakedness.[39] Clearly, that verse cannot

36. Feinstein, *Sexual Pollution*, 109–10.

37. Milgrom, *Leviticus 17–22*, 1537.

38. Jonathan R. Ziskind, "The Missing Daughter in Leviticus XVII," *VT* 46 (1996): 125–30, here 129.

39. Biblical Hebrew lacks a term that is equivalent to English "granddaughter." Thus, the offspring are designated as "your son's daughter" and "your daughter's daughter."

be referring to ego's sexual access to his granddaughters, because that is what the text in fact prohibits. Thus, some interpreters have extended the concept to refer to control over a woman's sexuality.[40] Yet a man would not, in fact, be the one responsible for guarding his granddaughters' sexuality; that responsibility would belong to their fathers, especially in the case of daughters of ego's daughters, who would be married into other men's patriarchal households. I conclude, therefore, that Lev 18:10 refers to ego's own nakedness (his own genitals), just as Lev 18:7 refers to ego's father's nakedness (his genitals). The motive offered to ego in Lev 18:10 is that a sexual relationship with a granddaughter would amount to a degrading self-exposure—like Noah's. The reference to "nakedness" highlighs ego's physical kinship with his granddaughters while not explicitly deploying the idiom of שאר בשר.

Leviticus 18:8 follows and depends integrally on the prohibition in Lev 18:7. Since a sexual relationship between ego and his mother would implicate ego's father, it follows quite logically that the same would be true of a sexual relationship between ego and any other woman with whom his father is involved. Thus, the rule against a relationship between ego and a wife of his father who is not ego's mother is supported by the motive statement, ערות אביך הוא ("she is your father's nakedness").

Leviticus 18:9 explicitly prohibits ego to have a sexual relationship with a half-sister, either paternal or maternal, and thereby implicitly prohibits a relationship with a full sister[41] but offers no clear motive for the prohibition. The text does not identify the nakedness of ego's half-sister as the nakedness of ego's father or as the nakedness of ego's mother's husband, which might be expected if the idiom referred to sexual proprietorship or control. The absence of the idiom here is evidence that it does not have the meaning of sexual proprietorship or control.

The prohibition of a sexual relationship with a daughter of ego's father's wife (Lev 18:11) lacks the motivation of identifying the woman's nakedness with nakedness of any other male. Instead, the rule is motivated by a simple declaration that the woman is ego's sister. This identity appears to be justified by the woman's specification as מולדת אביך, which must mean something other than that she is a biological daughter of ego's father—a category of sister already treated in Lev 18:9.[42] Milgrom may be correct that the idiom means "of your father's clan," identifying

40. Milgrom, *Leviticus 17–22*, 1541, citing Sarah J. Melcher, "The Holiness Code and Human Sexuality," in *Biblical Ethics and Homosexuality*, ed. Robert L. Brawley (Louisville: Westminster John Knox, 1996), 87–102, here 94.

41. If ego may not have a sexual relationship with either a sister who is the daughter of his father or who is the daughter of his mother, it follows necessarily that he cannot have a relationship with a full sister, who is the daughter of both of his parents. Thus, the full sister is not absent from the code.

42. John E. Hartley, *Leviticus*, WBC 4 (Dallas, TX: Word, 1992), 295.

the woman as a member of ego's father's larger kin group.[43] However, I would suggest an alternative understanding that is consistent with the usage of מולדת in Lev 18:9, where the word seems to have the sense of "originating by birth." In Lev 18:9, ego is told that any daughter of his father or mother is his sister, whether she belongs to the household ("originating by birth in the household"; מולדת בית) or whether she belongs to another household ("originating by birth outside [the household]"; מולדת חוץ). In Lev 18:11 we can understand מולדת אביך as meaning "originating by birth to your father," that is, born into the father's household, while not being ego's father's biological daughter; presumably, this scenario would result when ego's father took a woman as his wife who was already pregnant with another man's child. Whatever the case may be, it is clear that Lev 18:11 identifies a woman as ego's sister who is not his father's biological ("flesh") daughter.

Leviticus 18:12 prohibits ego from having sexual relations with his father's sister using the established idiom about uncovering nakedness. But in this case, the prohibition is motivated by noting that the woman is the "flesh" (שאר) of ego's father (that is, his bodily kin), harking back for the first time to the language of the general rule in Lev 18:6. This specification that ego's father's sister is ego's father's "flesh" further supports the understanding that a prohibition of a sexual relationship between a man and his full sister is included under the prohibition set out in Lev 18:6 against a man having a sexual relationship with any of "his close bodily kin" (שאר בשרו). However, Lev 18:12 fails to explain why ego may not have a relationship with a woman who is "flesh" of his father. It is probable that the woman's identity as ego's father's sister is precisely the key point of concern. As his father's direct offspring, an extension of his father, so to speak, ego is bound by the same restriction as his father. He may not have a sexual relationship with this close bodily relative who is forbidden to his father.

Leviticus 18:13 prohibits ego from having a sexual relationship with his mother's sister, motivating the rule by identifying the woman as ego's mother's flesh (כי־שאר אמך הוא). The language of this rule follows that of the previous one. Here, however, it seems to warn ego that a sexual relationship with his mother's sister, who shares "flesh" with his mother, would implicate him in a relationship with his own mother (which, of course, is prohibited by Lev 18:6–7). Thus, reference to close bodily kinship is inscribed differently when it motivates a prohibition against intercourse with a close female relative of ego's father than when a relationship with a female relative of ego's mother is prohibited.

Leviticus 18:14 prohibits ego from having a sexual relationship with

43. Milgrom, *Leviticus 17–22*, 1515, 1539–40, 1541–42. See also Feinstein, *Sexual Pollution*, 105, 236 n. 22.

his father's brother's wife, a woman with whom he has no bodily kinship. The wording of this rule follows that of Lev 18:7. The prohibited act is first identified as ego uncovering the nakedness of his father's brother, which is then explained as being the act of drawing near to his wife. To this is added a simple motive statement that she is ego's paternal aunt (דודה),[44] which seems to make the prohibition in Lev 18:12, against ego having a relationship with his father's sister, apply to his father's brother's wife. The reference to the paternal uncle's nakedness makes perfect sense in a cultural context in which a father's brother had a status comparable to ego's father. Just as ego would not uncover his father's nakedness, so he would not uncover his father's brother's nakedness. As in Lev 18:7–8, the idiom here does not indicate sexual involvement between ego and his father's brother, but a violation of the norms of modesty and propriety.

Leviticus 18:15 prohibits ego from having a sexual relationship with his daughter-in-law (כלה), specified as his son's wife in the motive statement for the rule. In this rule, the daughter-in-law's nakedness is not identified as ego's son's nakedness, which might be expected if the idiom referred to the man's proprietorship over his wife's sexuality or if the language of a father's nakedness in relation to his son were a warning against the equivalent of same-sex, father–son, incest. The absence of the language here makes sense, however, if a son's obligation to avoid seeing his father's nakedness were not mirrored by an obligation for his father to avoid seeing his son's nakedness. As cross-cultural studies of modesty norms demonstrate, such rules are frequently hierarchical in their mobilization, with lower-status individuals prohibited from seeing their superiors naked while superiors may see their inferiors naked.[45] The tradents could not have warned ego against a relationship with his daughter-in-law on the basis of the offense of uncovering his son's nakedness, since there was no cultural norm against a father seeing his son's genitals. Nor could they have appealed to "flesh," since the woman is an affine, bodily kin of neither man. Thus, they were left to prohibit ego from uncovering his daughter-in-law's nakedness simply by referring to the fact that she is his son's wife, appealing to an implicit concern not to confuse social roles.[46]

Leviticus 18:16 prohibits a sexual relationship between ego and his

---

44. According to most interpreters, the term דודה means "paternal aunt" as the term דוד means "paternal uncle," there being no specific Hebrew terms for maternal aunts or uncles. See Milgrom, *Leviticus 17–22*, 1543–44.

45. On this normative pattern as it presented itself in rabbinic culture, see Michael Satlow, "Jewish Constructions of Nakedness in Late Antiquity," *JBL* 116 (1997): 429–54, here 438–40.

46. In this case, therefore, I agree with Schenker's explanation of the incest laws as based on a concern with maintaining clear social roles ("Incest Prohibitions," 166–67, 170, 181). I do not believe, however, that this is a sufficient explanation for every prohibition in the collection.

brother's wife, motivating this prohibition with the declaration that the woman's nakedness is ego's brother's nakedness (ערות אחיך הוא). In view of the absence of a comparable motive in the previous prohibition about a father's relationship with his son, it appears that norms of modesty and propriety do apply between adult brothers, meaning that sexually mature and, therefore, married or marriageable brothers are expected to avoid seeing one another's genitals.

Leviticus 18:17 is the final prohibition to begin with the word ערוה, marking the end of a block of prohibitive commandments that are conceptually united around norms for the proper treatment of the genitals, marked for their sexual function. This verse prohibits ego from having sexual relations with a woman and her daughter; it also prohibits ego from having sexual relations with the woman's son's daughter or her daughter's daughter (the woman's granddaughters). The motive for these prohibitions is that they are "her flesh."[47] To this motive is added the designation of the act of violating the prohibition as "depravity" (זמה).[48] The appeal to the category of "flesh" here appears designed to mark the prohibited women as equivalent to ego's prohibited "flesh" on the basis of his relationship with the woman. While the text does not specify it, it appears that the woman's daughter is equated with ego's daughter (prohibited to him by Lev 18:6, and also a fortiori by Lev 18:10) and the woman's granddaughters are equated with ego's granddaughters, prohibited by Lev 18:10.

This legislative move by which women who are not actually ego's physical ("flesh") kin are made such through the mechanism of ego's physical union with his wife exemplifies the ways in which law defines and constructs (or, to use de Certeau's language, "writes") the body within particular cultural contexts. In the order envisaged by the tradent(s) behind Lev 18:6–17, a woman's daughters and granddaughters, who are not actually "flesh" kin of her husband, can be constituted as "flesh" by a text that is presented as a divine decree. Likewise, a woman who is the daughter of ego's father's wife, but not ego's "flesh" sister, can be constituted as a sister by a decree that highlights the woman's relationship with ego's father, a relationship itself constituted by the woman's membership in the father's household (Lev 18:11).

Leviticus 18:18 does not open with the word ערוה, although it does contain a reference to uncovering nakedness and is linked with the prior block of laws by its concern with prohibiting a sexual union involving closely related individuals. In this case, ego is prohibited from taking a woman as a wife in addition to her sister, which is characterized as causing

47. Reading with the LXX and revocalizing the Hebrew consonants as שְׁאֵרָהּ against the MT's vocalization of שַׁאֲרָה.

48. Milgrom, *Leviticus 17–22*, 1548.

rivalry or strife. The act also necessarily involves uncovering nakedness. The usage of the idiom here highlights its negative connotation. While every sexual act presumably involves the uncovering of genitals, it is only in the case of illicit unions that this fact is highlighted. I would suggest, therefore, that the idiom גלה ערוה can always be appropriately rendered as "illicitly uncover genitals," referring either to the sexual acts that attend such uncovering or to violations of codes of propriety and modesty, which are equated in their severity with illicit sexual behavior.

The Additional Prohibitions (Lev 18:19–23) and the Exhortation (Lev 18:24–30)

The rest of the prohibitions in Lev 18 (vv. 19–23) are directed against behaviors that fall outside the framework of unions that violate kinship norms. I will treat them here only very briefly to highlight the ways in which they add to the chapter's construction of the body. Leviticus 18:19 prohibits intercourse with a menstruating woman, making further use of the idiom גלה ערוה in the sense of "illicitly uncover genitals." Leviticus 18:20 prohibits adultery by telling a man not to place his penis (שכבת)[49] "for seed" (לזרע) into a fellow Israelite's wife, which would result in his becoming unclean by her. A bodily act will produce a negative bodily consequence. Leviticus 18:21 prohibits offering children (literally, "seed," זרע) in sacrifice. The designation of children as "seed" appears to be the means by which the tradent(s) included this prohibition within the context of a set of laws governing sexual behavior, marking children as the products of the body of the man addressed by the code. Leviticus 18:22 prohibits a man from dealing sexually with a male body as he would with a female body. Leviticus 18:23 prohibits a male from engaging in bestiality by bluntly commanding him not to place his penis into an animal's body, which would result in his becoming unclean by it (just as he would become unclean by committing adultery). It also tells the male addressee that a woman is forbidden to offer herself to an animal.

The chapter ends with a general exhortation (18:24–30), resuming the plural address of the introductory verses, in which YHWH warns the Israelites not to make themselves unclean by the proscribed acts by which the nations YHWH is expelling from the land made themselves unclean. YHWH also indicates that the code applies equally to Israelites and to resident aliens and designates all of the prohibited actions as "repulsive" (תועבת), whereas the code of prohibitions had applied the label only to male–male intercourse (18:22). YHWH emphasizes that the behavior of

49. For this translation, see Milgrom, *Leviticus 17–22*, 1550.

the previous residents of the land made the land unclean, which resulted in it "vomiting" them out (18:25), whereas the Israelites will not suffer expulsion if they abide by the prohibitive commandments and so avoid making the land unclean.

Conclusions

What counts as "nakedness" is culturally specific.[50] In some societies, the buttocks may be exposed while the genitals must be covered; in others, both areas of the body must be "properly" covered. In some societies, a woman with uncovered breasts is not judged to be "naked," while in others the breasts must be kept covered in public in most circumstances. There are cultures in which an individual is not "naked" so long as their body is painted. In the case of ancient Israel, as indicated by the evidence I have examined, the cultural norm seems to have been to define nakedness primarily as the exposure of the genitals, with the buttocks also an area of concern. This norm applied equally to men and women and appears to have applied to many same-sex contexts and relationship patterns as well as to relationships between the sexes. I could find no evidence that a woman with uncovered breasts was considered naked.

In Lev 18, the idiom of "uncovering nakedness" is employed as a euphemism for the sexual act without losing its literal sense as referring to the exposure of the genitals. This fact explains why it can be used to refer to both the sexual act with a woman and the offense against the man to whom she licitly belongs. In the former usage, "uncovering nakedness" indicates the sexual act; in the latter, it refers to a violation of cultural norms of modesty and propriety. Modern readers who approach the text from a cultural context in which there are appropriate settings in which males can expose their genitals and buttocks to one another without violating norms of modesty[51] may find it difficult to grasp that the offense

50. On this principle, see Adeline Masquelier, "Dirt, Undress, and Difference: An Introduction," in *Dirt, Undress, and Difference: Critical Perspectives on the Body's Surface*, ed. Adeline Masquelier (Bloomington: Indiana University Press, 2005), 1–33, esp. 9. Masquelier draws particular attention to T. O. Beidelman, "Some Nuer Notions of Nakedness, Nudity, and Sexuality," *Africa: Journal of the International African Institute* 38 (1968): 113–32. As Masquelier notes, this article demonstrates that the Nuer, often characterized by ethnographers as going about "naked," "held to complex notions relating to matters of dress, ornamentation, and undress."

51. The most common North American setting is the athletic locker room and its communal shower facility, although there has been a notable shift in expectations about modesty over the last thirty years as popular media reports have noted. See, e.g., Choire Sicha, "Men's Locker Room Designers Take Pity on Naked Millennials," *New York Times*, December 3, 2015, https://www.nytimes.com/2015/12/04/fashion/mens-style/mens-locker-room-designers-take-pity-on-naked-millennials.html.

against males articulated by Lev 18 is simply the transgression of modesty standards. Nevertheless, this is the best way to understand the text in its own cultural context. For the tradents behind the incest laws of Lev 18, there were adult males who were required to avoid seeing other specified males naked (that is, with their genitals exposed). Violation of this norm was a serious offense, as the narrative about Noah and Ham demonstrates. The bodies "written" by the laws of Lev 18 must keep genitals covered except for licit sexual relationships, and even such approved relationships are fraught with the norms of modesty, which are deployed to dissuade illicit sexual relationships.

Leviticus 18 as a whole inscribes, writes, and engraves itself (to use de Certeau's words) upon a male body that is restricted in various ways in its sexual expression. The adult male Israelite addressed by the commandments may not have sexual relationships with women who are identified as his "flesh," whose bodies are physically close to his within the kinship system. Moreover, the laws inscribe some women who are not actually "flesh" kin as being constituted as such by divine decree. Ego may not uncover the nakedness of any of these proscribed women. In some cases, the act of uncovering a woman's nakedness is equated with uncovering the nakedness of the man with whom she is licitly united (for example, ego's father's brother, in the case of that man's wife). The fact that the woman's husband has uncovered her nakedness, that is, her genitals, implicates his own genitals, so that ego would also uncover them through intercourse with the woman—and would violate the strong norms of propriety and modesty.

The laws are also inscribed upon the bodies of all Israelites and of non-Israelites resident in their land. Violation of the sexual prohibitions set out in the code at the core of Lev 18, according to the concluding exhortation of the chapter, generates a form of uncleanness that affects the bodies engaged in the violation and is passed on to the land. Contamination of the land with bodily generated uncleanness will result in the expulsion of those bodies from the land. This severe warning constructs the bodies of all residents of the land of Israel (both Israelite citizens and non-Israelite resident aliens) as potent actors, whose cultural performance determines the ultimate survival of their society.

The Territoriality of YHWH in Biblical Texts

SAUL M. OLYAN
Brown University

The original ethnic-territorial meaning of *Ioudaios*, *yehudi*, and related terms was brought into relief by Shaye J. D. Cohen in pioneering studies such as "*Ioudaios*, *Iudaeus*, Judaean, Jew." Cohen argued that, before the middle of the second century BCE, *ioudaios* "should be translated not as 'Jew,' a religious term, but as 'Judaean,' an ethnic-geographic term."[1] Cohen's ideas have contributed significantly to an ongoing debate that has yet to subside. Scholars continue to dispute when in antiquity we ought to translate these terms as "Judean" and when—if at all—to render them as "Jew."[2] Thus, scholars have paid significant attention in recent times to the ethnic-territorial dimension of being a Judean. Less attention, however, has been devoted to evidence that suggests that not only Judeans, but YHWH himself, had a significant territorial character. Most scholars of Israelite religion have neglected materials that emphasize the territoriality of YHWH; instead, they have focused on texts that speak of YHWH's universal reach and catholic concerns, often in order to reconstruct a supposed move among Judeans toward monotheism.[3] It is my purpose here

---

1. Shaye J. D. Cohen, "*Ioudaios, Iudaeus,* Judaean, Jew," in *The Beginnings of Jewishness: Boundaries, Varieties, Uncertainties*, HCS 31 (Berkeley: University of California Press, 1999), 69–106; quotation from 70.

2. See, among others, Steve Mason, "Jews, Judaeans, Judaizing, Judaism: Problems of Categorization in Ancient History," *JSJ* 38 (2007): 457–512; Daniel Boyarin, "Rethinking Jewish Christianity: An Argument for Dismantling a Dubious Category (to which is Appended a Correction of my *Border Lines*)," *JQR* 99 (2009): 7–36; Seth Schwartz, "How Many Judaisms Were There? A Critique of Neusner and Smith on Definition and Mason and Boyarin on Categorization," *JAJ* 2 (2011): 208–38, esp. 221–38; Cynthia Baker, "A 'Jew' by Any Other Name?," *JAJ* 2 (2011): 153–80; Michael L. Satlow, "Jew or Judaean?," in *"The One Who Sows Bountifully": Essays in Honor of Stanley K. Stowers*, ed. Caroline Johnson Hodge et al., BJS 356 (Providence, RI: Brown Judaic Studies, 2013), 165–75; John J. Collins, *The Invention of Judaism: Torah and Jewish Identity from Deuteronomy to Paul*, The Taubman Lectures in Jewish Studies 7 (Oakland: University of California Press, 2017), 2–19, 189–95.

3. Among the reconstructions that say little or nothing about texts that assume or assert YHWH's territoriality are Patrick D. Miller, *The Religion of Ancient Israel*, LAI (Louisville:

to address this imbalance in biblical scholarship by considering a number of texts that suggest that YHWH had significant ties to his land. These links are so substantial that, according to some of these texts, YHWH's interests did not extend beyond his territory and the people living there, and he could only be worshiped in his land. These texts are monarchic, exilic, and postexilic in origin and stand in tension with other pre-587 and post-587 passages that assume or assert YHWH's concern for other lands and peoples and his exercise of power in international contexts on behalf of his own people or others. These very different, coexisting perspectives on YHWH's interests and activity bring into relief the diversity of ideological viewpoints that may be discerned in the biblical anthology.[4] I offer this study as a tribute to Shaye J. D. Cohen, my former colleague at Brown, from whom I have learned much over many years and whose uncompromising intellectual honesty is an example to colleagues and students alike.

Readers are no doubt familiar with texts that speak of YHWH's universal reach and his concern for his people—whether as a whole or individually—when they reside in other lands. Like other ancient West Asian deities, YHWH is not infrequently portrayed exercising power in lands other than Judah/Israel to the detriment of enemies and the benefit of his people or individual worshipers.[5] Examples include the ark narrative, in

---

Westminster John Knox, 2000); John Day, *Yahweh and the Gods and Goddesses of Canaan*, JSOTSup 265 (Sheffield: Sheffield Academic, 2000); and Ziony Zevit, *The Religions of Ancient Israel: A Synthesis of Parallactic Approaches* (New York: Continuum, 2001). Rainer Albertz mentions the ideology of YHWH's territoriality in passing—as a characteristic allegedly of the prestate period, with 1 Sam 26:19 as an example of its supposed survival—but does not seem to view it as vibrant during the sixth century (*A History of Israelite Religion in the Old Testament Period*, 2 vols., OTL [Louisville: Westminster John Knox, 1994], 228, 377, 413). A recent contribution that addresses issues of territoriality in Israelite religion directly is David Frankel, *The Land of Canaan and the Destiny of Israel: Theologies of Territory in the Hebrew Bible*, Siphrut 4 (Winona Lake, IN: Eisenbrauns, 2011), although, like so many scholars, he adheres to the monotheistic developmental paradigm (e.g., 199: "With the development of the monotheistic outlook, the exclusion of other lands as legitimate places for the worship of the Lord became problematic"). On monotheism itself as a problematic concept in texts such as Isaiah 40–55, which clearly recognizes the existence, volition, and agency of nonobvious beings other than YHWH, see my article "Is Isaiah 40–55 Really Monotheistic?," *JANER* 12 (2012): 190–201.

4. Such ideological diversity is evident also when one considers texts that address the status of YHWH's covenants with Israel, Levi, and David after 587 or when one considers the distribution of holiness among persons (e.g., priests, Levites, Israel). On the former, see Saul M. Olyan, "The Status of Covenant during the Exile," in *Berührungspunkte: Studien zur Sozial- und Religionsgeschichte Israels und seiner Umwelt; Festschrift für Rainer Albertz zu seinem 65. Geburtstag*, ed. Ingo Kottsieper, Rüdiger Schmitt, and Jakob Wöhrle, AOAT 350 (Münster: Ugarit-Verlag, 2008), 333–44. For the latter, see Saul M. Olyan, *Rites and Rank: Hierarchy in Biblical Representations of Cult* (Princeton: Princeton University Press, 2000), 27–35, 121–22.

5. Other deities are also often portrayed as active on the international scene, for example, Assur, who leads Assyrian armies to victory, as in Shalmaneser III's Monolith Inscription (see A. Kirk Grayson, *Assyrian Rulers of the Early First Millennium BC, II: [858–745 BC]*, RIMA 3 [Toronto: University of Toronto, 1996], 14, lines 22–23; 15, lines 30, 32–33), or Shamash, who

which YHWH wreaks havoc on the Philistines and their god Dagon in Philistia (1 Sam 5–6) or the exodus account, in which he demonstrates his power over Pharaoh and promises to "render judgments against all the gods of Egypt" in Egypt (Exod 12:12).[6] A number of other texts portray YHWH as a "redeemer" (*gōʾēl*) of his people in Babylon, acting decisively to defeat the Babylonians and return the exiles to their land by means of a new exodus (Isa 43:14–15, 16–21).[7] Such decisive action includes YHWH's raising up of his "messiah," Cyrus of Persia, in order to vanquish Babylon for Israel's sake (Isa 45:1–7). Daniel 3 describes YHWH's demonstration of his might in Babylon through his protection of Shadrach, Meshach, and Abednego from the effects of Nebuchadnezzar's fiery furnace. In addition, there are passages such as 1 Kgs 8:46–50, which speaks of YHWH hearing the prayers of exiled, penitent Israelites and acting in their favor while they are in far-off lands. Perhaps most striking are texts that assert that YHWH's power to act is without any territorial limitation, extending even to Sheol and/or the heavens: "YHWH kills and makes to live, / he brings [people] down to Sheol and raises [them] up" (1 Sam 2:6). Amos 9:2 is similar: "Were they to dig down to Sheol, / from there my hand would take them. / Were they to ascend to the heavens, / from there I would bring them down." These are but a few of the passages that suggest that YHWH's might and his concerns extend well beyond the land of Israel and its denizens. Wherever YHWH has interests, he acts decisively to further them according to these texts.[8]

In addition to texts that portray YHWH's universal reach and his active concern for Israelites, whether they are in the land or abroad, there are a number of biblical passages that suggest that YHWH's interests extend beyond his people. According to Amos 9:7, YHWH not only brought the Israelites up from the land of Egypt but also was responsible for the mass migrations of other peoples such as the Philistines and Arameans. Thus, not only is YHWH active on the international scene; according to this passage, his motivations go well beyond a concern for Israel or Israelites alone. A number of prophetic utopian texts envision Jerusalem as a magnet for the nations, who will come there to worship Israel's God in

---

accompanies Iahdun-Lim of Mari to the sea, where the king wins victories (Douglas Frayne, *Old Babylonian Period [2003–1595 BC]*, RIMA: Early Periods 4 [Toronto: University of Toronto Press, 1990], 605, lines 31–33). Such activity is obviously not unique to YHWH.

6. See, similarly, Jer 43:12. All translations in this essay are my own.

7. On the theme of a new exodus in Isa 40–55, see, e.g., 43:16–21, 51:9–11, 52:11–12.

8. Both the ark narrative and the Song of Hannah (1 Sam 2:1–10) are very likely preexilic in origin. On the ark narrative, its extent, and its date, see, e.g., Nathaniel B. Levtow, *Images of Others: Iconic Politics in Ancient Israel*, BJSUCSD 11 (Winona Lake, IN: Eisenbrauns, 2008), 132–43; on the Song of Hannah and its date, see P. Kyle McCarter Jr., *I Samuel: A New Translation with Introduction, Notes, and Commentary*, AB 8 (Garden City, NY: Doubleday, 1980), 74–76.

his temple. Among these is Isa 2:2–4: "At a future time, / the mountain of the temple of YHWH will be established, / As the highest of mountains, / lifted up above the hills, / and all the nations will flow to it." Another such passage is Isa 66:18–21, which describes YHWH gathering all nations to come to see his glory in Jerusalem, and 66:23, which speaks of "all flesh" coming "to bow down before" YHWH. Not only is YHWH Israel's God and Jerusalem his place of worship according to these texts; YHWH is also a god who takes an interest in other peoples and acts decisively in their favor, including them in his cult and his future redemption.[9]

In contrast to these well-known texts, a number of other biblical passages bear witness to the idea that YHWH's interests, his activity, and even his worship are limited to his land and the people residing in it. Exiled Judeans are beyond YHWH's orbit according to a number of texts. To leave the land of Israel is effectively to be removed from YHWH's presence—to be "far from YHWH"—and to lack an inheritance stake in the land (*môrāšâ*), as exiles are told by denizens of Jerusalem according to Ezek 11:15.[10] The last part of the allegedly popular saying of the exiles quoted in Ezek 37:11—"we are utterly cut off"—is likely a statement about the relationship of the exiles to YHWH specifically. Just as the dead are forgotten by YHWH and "cut off from" YHWH's "hand"—that is, his active intervention or power—according to Ps 88:6, so, too, according to the saying of Ezek 37:11, are the exiles entirely separated from YHWH.[11] Other sixth-century texts claim that the exiles exist outside of YHWH's sphere of interest, YHWH having rejected, abandoned, or forgotten them.

---

9. Frankel discusses some of the prophetic and psalmic texts that express these sentiments (*Land of Canaan*, 155–56).

10. As Moshe Greenberg puts it, "Here expulsion from YHWH's land is equated with a severance of ties with YHWH and hence of title to his land. By this reasoning, the homelanders claimed all the property left by the exiles" (*Ezekiel 1–20. A New Translation with Introduction and Commentary*, AB 22 [Garden City, NY: Doubleday, 1983], 189). As Greenberg and others note, Ezekiel's response reflects a different viewpoint: YHWH is with the exiles, even if only in a diminished way—as a *miqdāš mĕʿaṭ*—and although he removed them (*rḥq hiphil*) from the land and scattered them, he will eventually gather them and return them to their land (ibid., 190). Frank Moore Cross has argued that *rḥqw* in Ezek 11:15 has a dual meaning. Reading a perfect like most scholars rather than the MT's imperative, Cross renders *rḥqw mʿl yhwh* both as "they are far from" YHWH and as "they have forfeited (all) claim upon" YHWH and YHWH's land, basing the latter rendering on comparative legal evidence ("A Papyrus Recording a Divine Legal Decision and the Root *rḥq* in Biblical and Near Eastern Usage," in *Texts, Temples, and Traditions: A Tribute to Menahem Haran*, ed. Michael V. Fox et al. [Winona Lake, IN: Eisenbrauns, 1996], 311–20, here 320). In this, his understanding is close to that of Greenberg. On *môrāšâ* as a landed inheritance, see, e.g., Exod 6:8, Ezek 25:10, 33:24.

11. Ezekiel 37:1–10 and 12–14 are both intended to refute the negative perspective of the saying. On this, see Saul M. Olyan, "'We Are Utterly Cut Off': Some Possible Nuances of *nigzarnû lānû* in Ezek 37:11," *CBQ* 65 (2003): 43–51; and "Unnoticed Resonances of Tomb Opening and Transportation of the Remains of the Dead in Ezekiel 37:12–14," *JBL* 128 (2009): 491–501. I develop the argument regarding Ps 88:6 and Ezek 37:11 in detail in these articles.

These include the saying of Isa 40:27, attributed to the people: "My way is hidden from YHWH, / My claim is ignored by my god" as well as the nickname "Banished One" (*niddāḥâ*), used of the exiles in the figure of personified Zion according to Jer 30:17.[12] The idea that the exiles are separated from YHWH might also be expressed through metaphors of divorce or the sale of children into slavery, both of which would involve physical removal from the locus of the home: "It was on account of your sins that you were sold, / It was because of your transgressions that your mother was sent away" (Isa 50:1).[13] The abandonment theme, along with the motifs of YHWH forgetting, ignoring, or banishing the exiles, each central to the articulation of the idea of the exile as a profound punishment for Judeans, is very likely related to established notions of YHWH's territoriality expressed explicitly by texts such as Ezek 11:15.[14]

YHWH's territory and YHWH's worship are inextricably bound according to a number of biblical texts. To be outside the borders of YHWH's land excludes one from YHWH's worship and having "a portion in YHWH" (*ḥēleq bayhwh*), according to one viewpoint entertained in Josh 22:24-27. The rhetorical question of the exiles in Ps 137:4—"How can we sing a song of YHWH in an alien land?"—is similar in its assumption that YHWH's worship is restricted to his own territory. When David complains to Saul that he has been exiled from the land on account of Saul's hostility—literally, "driven out from being attached to the patrimony (*naḥălâ*) of YHWH"—he emphasizes the cultic effects of his banishment, suggesting that he must now "serve" "other gods" (1 Sam 26:19).[15] The story of the Aramean commander Naaman's attempt to practice devotion to YHWH from the foreign city of Damascus includes the rather unusual request that he be given a load of Israelite soil to import to Syria in order to make it possible for him to worship YHWH there (2 Kgs 5:17–18). Appar-

---

12. Derivatives of *niphal ndḥ* ("to be banished," "cast out") are used of exiles in a variety of biblical texts (e.g., Deut 30:4, Isa 11:12, 27:13, 56:8, Jer 40:12, 43:5, 49:5, Ps 147:2).

13. Although scholars continue to debate the precise meaning of YHWH's questions in the first part of Isa 50:1, it is clear that the metaphors of divorce and the sale of children into slavery are employed in this passage to speak of the separation of the exiles from YHWH.

14. The abandonment theme is extended also to the land itself, the city of Jerusalem, and those remaining in the land in a number of texts concerned with the unprecedented catastrophe of 587 BCE. The land is said to be abandoned by YHWH in the saying quoted in Ezek 8:12: "YHWH does not see us; YHWH has abandoned the land"; the statement of YHWH in Jer 12:7 is similar: "I have forsaken my house, / I have abandoned my heritage." In Isa 49:14, personified Zion claims that "YHWH has forsaken me, / My lord has forgotten me." Famously, Lam 5:20 suggests both abandonment and forgetting on YHWH's part: "Why have you forgotten us perpetually, / Forsaken us for so long?" Finally, according to Isa 62:4, Zion will no longer be called "Abandoned One" or the land of Judah, "Desolate One," when YHWH restores their fortunes.

15. For the land as Israel's patrimony (*naḥălâ*) rather than YHWH's, see Ps 105:11; for the people as YHWH's patrimony, see Deut 32:9.

ently, the assumption behind Naaman's request is that such devotion to YHWH would otherwise be impossible in an alien land.[16] Finally, just as Israelites must serve the gods of the nations where they reside according to a text such as 1 Sam 26:19, foreigners in YHWH's land are obligated to offer him the reverence he is due in the manner he expects it according to some texts.[17] They must follow "the custom of the god of the land" (*mišpaṭ ʾĕlōhê hāʾāreṣ*) or suffer dire consequences if they do not (2 Kgs 17:26).[18]

The notion of YHWH's territoriality is manifest also in a series of texts that cast Sheol as a place apart from YHWH's activity and interests.[19] As I have mentioned, Ps 88:6 speaks of the dead as forgotten by YHWH and "cut off from" his "hand." A series of rhetorical questions in verses 11–13 illustrates exactly what this means: "Do you do wonders for the dead? / Do the shades rise and praise you? / Is your covenant loyalty [*ḥesed*] spoken of in the grave? / Your faithfulness in the place of perishing [*ʾăbaddôn*]? / Are your wonders known in the darkness? / Your righteousness in the land of forgetfulness?" These verses make clear that YHWH forgets about

16. It is an error to assume, as some do, that the primary or sole reason YHWH may not be worshiped in an alien land according to the texts I have discussed is because all foreign lands are polluted and polluting (see, e.g., Albertz, *History of Israelite Religion*, 377, who cites some of these texts and speaks of alien lands as "cultically unclean"). Although there are a few biblical texts that seem to suggest that alien lands are "ritually" unclean (Hos 9:3, Amos 7:17, Ezek 4:13), nothing like this is hinted at in texts such as 1 Sam 26:19, 2 Kgs 5:17–18, or Ps 137:4, as others have observed (e.g., Andrea Allgood, "Foreign Lands—Multiple Perspectives: Foreign Land Impurity in the Hebrew Bible, Its Context, and Its Ideological Underpinnings" [PhD diss., Brown University, 2014], 308–9). And although Josh 22:19 raises the possibility that Transjordanian territory might be polluted, Frankel has made a good case that that verse should be understood as a secondary addition to the text (*Land of Canaan*, 189–91). Frankel raises doubts even about Hos 9:3, Amos 7:17, and Ezek 4:13 as evidence that alien lands defile, though here I think his skepticism goes too far (ibid., 197–99).

17. See, similarly, Frankel, *Land of Canaan*, 150–51, 200.

18. In contrast, other biblical texts require only some aliens in the land or none at all to embrace cultic obligations. When aliens are so obligated, often it is resident aliens (*gērîm*) specifically, e.g., Exod 12:19; Lev 17:10, 12, 13, 15, all from the Holiness source. Contrast Exod 12:43–49, also a Holiness text, which obliges "all of the congregation of Israel" to "make" the Passover and allows resident aliens (*gērîm*) to do so only if they are circumcised, which suggests that they are not obligated. Yet another position is reflected in Deut 14:21, in which Israelites are forbidden to eat any carcass; instead, they should give carcasses to the resident alien or sell them to other foreigners. Here, resident aliens are clearly excluded from this cultic obligation. Yet, according to Deut 16:11, 14, *gērîm* are obligated to observe pilgrimage festivals. On the complex biblical representations of aliens and their cultic obligations, see further my discussion in *Rites and Rank*, 68–81. Frankel understands the obligations of the resident alien in H texts (his P) to "reflect" the idea that all denizens of a god's territory must "comply with the demands of the God of the land" (*Land of Canaan*, 153). He likely has a point, although the obligations of the resident alien, even according to H, are not always the same as those of the native, as I note above with respect to Exod 12:43–49.

19. Contrast other texts that I have mentioned, such as 1 Sam 2:6 and Amos 9:2, which speak of YHWH's interests and agency extending even to Sheol.

the dead and does nothing for them. The dead, in turn, cannot worship YHWH or even remember his acts of covenant loyalty.[20] According to Ps 6:6, the dead do not even remember YHWH; according to Ps 28:1, were YHWH to be unresponsive to a living petitioner, he would be counted with the dead. Other texts also bear witness to this ideology of utter separation from YHWH in Sheol (e.g., Isa 38:18–19 and Ps 115:17–18, which contrast the lot of the dead and that of the living).

It is striking how similar the ideas expressed in these texts regarding YHWH's relationship with the dead are to notions about YHWH's relationship to exiles and fugitives who have left the land. Just as the dead cannot worship YHWH, so exiles are separated from his cult according to texts such as Ps 137:4 and 1 Sam 26:19. And just as YHWH is said to have abandoned or forgotten the dead, so he ignores the exiles and does not act on their behalf, according to the sayings quoted in Isa 40:27 and Ezek 37:11. Even derivatives of the verb *ʾbd* (primarily "to perish"), part of the distinct vocabulary of descriptions of Sheol (e.g.,*ʾăbaddôn*, Ps 88:12), are used of exiles, as in Isa 27:13: "Those who are perishing [*hāʾōbĕdîm*] in the land of Assyria will come, / the banished ones [*hanniddāḥîm*] in the land of Egypt, / They will bow down to YHWH, / on the holy mountain in Jerusalem."[21] The notion that the dead are entirely cut off from YHWH may well have been an elaboration of the idea that a god's interests, activity, and worship do not extend beyond the borders of his territory.

20. On the ideas of this psalm, see the articles cited in n. 11 as well as the treatment of Martin Leuenberger, "Das Problem des vorzeitigen Todes in der israelitischen Religions- und Theologiegeschichte," in *Tod und Jenseits im alten Israel und in seiner Umwelt: Theologische, religionsgeschichtliche, archäologische und ikonographische Aspekte*, ed. Angelika Berlejung and Bernd Janowski, FAT 64 (Tübingen: Mohr Siebeck, 2009), 163–67. On *ḥesed* as loyalty to a covenant, see, e.g., Exod 20:6, Deut 5:10, 2 Sam 10:2, Jer 2:2, and Frank Moore Cross, "Kinship and Covenant," in *From Epic to Canon: History and Literature in Ancient Israel* (Baltimore: Johns Hopkins University Press, 1998), 5–7, 9, and n. 12, who traces the term back to familial settings.

21. See also the saying of Ezek 37:11, which employs the same verb to describe the hopelessness of the exiles—"Our hope has perished" (*wĕʾābĕdâ tiqwātēnû*)—as well as various passages that speak of exiles perishing, e.g., Lev 26:38: "You shall perish [*waʾăbadtem*] among the nations; the land of your foes shall consume [*wĕʾākĕlâ*] you. And as for those who remain among you, they shall rot because of their iniquity in the land of your enemies"; and Jer 27:10, "I shall drive you out and you shall perish" (*wĕhiddaḥtî ʾetkem waʾăbadtem*). Deuteronomy 26:5, an obscure passage that has elicited much debate, also associates the verb *ʾbd* with residence in an alien land, in this case as a refugee, though its precise meaning there is unclear. Some have argued that *ʾbd* in Lev 26:38 cannot mean "perish" and must mean "be lost" or something similar, given that the text mentions survivors (e.g., Jacob Milgrom, *Leviticus 23–27: A New Translation with Introduction and Commentary*, AB 3B [New York: Doubleday, 2000], 2326; see also *HALOT* s.v. *ʾbd* for this interpretation). This argument, however, is unconvincing, since the text also states that "the land of your foes shall consume you," suggesting death for at least some if not many exiles. In short, the fact that some exiles are said to survive does not exclude "perish" as the most appropriate rendering of *ʾbd* in Lev 26:38.

Although only a few texts survive that bring into relief beliefs about what we might call YHWH's territorial character, the ideas expressed by these texts were likely popular in many circles and should certainly be considered by anyone seeking to reconstruct Israelite religion in all its diversity.[22] In addition to the important evidence of material culture, which has received much attention from specialists in recent years, texts that do not reflect dominant biblical ideologies also have the potential to significantly enrich our understanding of Israelite religion and help us to reconstruct the contours of debates about YHWH, his interests, his activity, and his worship.[23] Among these are passages that emphasize YHWH's territoriality.

22. Frankel describes the idea that YHWH is to be worshiped only in his land as "axiomatic" before the exiles of north and south (*Land of Canaan*, 137; see also 141).

23. The material evidence of Israelite religious practice suggests profound diversity and complexity through many centuries. On this material, see, e.g., Zevit, *Religions of Ancient Israel*; and Othmar Keel and Christoph Uehlinger, *Gods, Goddesses, and Images of God in Ancient Israel*, trans. Thomas H. Trapp (Minneapolis: Fortress, 1998).

Jerusalem in Greek and Latin Literature

ISAIAH M. GAFNI
The Hebrew University of Jerusalem
and Shalem College

In a brief article supporting Ed Sanders' concept of a "common Judaism" that existed in the late Second Temple period,[1] Shaye Cohen noted that, among the five areas of Jewish life cited by Sanders, was broad Jewish support for the Jerusalem temple. As evidence for the existence of a common Judaism, Sanders cited a wide array of Second Temple texts but, for whatever reason, chose not to include among those sources the writings of Greek and Latin authors. In a sweeping survey of classical literature as it related precisely to the features of common Judaism, Cohen convincingly proved that Greek and Latin literature dovetails quite well with the testimony of the other sources, and he proceeded to quote, albeit in a very few lines, how this is the case regarding what Greek and Latin authors had to say about Jerusalem.[2] In tribute to a dear friend and brilliant scholar, I have chosen to expand on Cohen's assertion, by presenting in greater detail the references to Jerusalem in classical literature.

The city of Jerusalem is mentioned nowhere in Greek literature prior to the conquests of Alexander the Great. Beginning with the late fourth century, however, and until the destruction of the Second Temple and beyond, the city assumed a constantly growing place in the works of Greek and Latin authors.[3] Pliny's famous reference to Jerusalem, "by far

---

1. Shaye J. D. Cohen, "Common Judaism in Greek and Latin Authors," in *Redefining First-Century Jewish and Christian Identities: Essays in Honor of Ed Parish Sanders*, ed. Fabian E. Udoh, with Susannah Heschel, Mark Chancey, and Gregory Tatum, CJAn 16 (Notre Dame, IN: University of Notre Dame Press, 2008), 69–87. For Sanders' thesis on "common Judaism," see E. P. Sanders, *Judaism: Practice and Belief, 63 B.C. – 66 C.E.* (Philadelphia: Trinity Press International, 1992), 47; Sanders, "The Dead Sea Sect and Other Jews: Commonalities, Overlaps and Differences," in *The Dead Sea Scrolls in Their Historical Context*, ed. Timothy H. Lim et al. (Edinburgh: T&T Clark, 2000), 7–43.

2. Cohen, "Common Judaism," 77.

3. For brief surveys on Jerusalem in classical literature, see Menahem Stern, "'Jerusalem, the Most Famous of the Cities of the East' (Pliny, Natural History 5.60)" [Hebrew], in *Studies in Jewish History: The Second Temple Period*, ed. Moshe Amit, Isaiah Gafni, and Moshe

the most famous city of the East and not of Judaea only" (*Nat.* 5.70), might be considered the apex of the growing spread of allusions to Jerusalem. These references include foundation stories of the city, its topography and geography, the nature of Jewish worship in its temple, and the numerous military confrontations between the rulers and residents of the city and various Greek and Roman generals. The common denominator in almost all of these allusions is the link they draw between the history and status of the city and the overall history of the Jewish people. As we proceed, it will become apparent that Greek and Latin authors ultimately came to recognize that Jerusalem held a very special place in the hearts and minds of Jews throughout the diaspora. The city would ultimately be perceived as a Jewish capital, rather than merely a Judean one. This survey does not set out to shed light on the *history* of Jerusalem in the classical era, but rather to describe what a specific intellectual and ruling society knew, or thought it knew, about Jerusalem. This knowledge may advance our understanding of practical actions, at times violent, taken not only toward the city and its inhabitants but also toward Jews residing far from the city itself. Nevertheless, I will attempt to separate references to Jerusalem in classical literature from the more general descriptions of Jews and Judaism,[4] notwithstanding the fact that the attitude of certain authors toward the Jewish people frequently played a role in their descriptions of the city.

As is the case with numerous references to Jews in classical literature, the statements we possess did not necessarily reach us in their original formulation but frequently were refashioned in the process of transmission. The transmitters or copyists frequently added to or omitted from the text they received, either in line with their personal attitude toward Jews or as a consequence of their role or status within their unique gentile environment. Thus, for example, one of the earliest descriptions of the topography and water supply of Jerusalem was written by Timochares,[5]

David Herr (Jerusalem: Yad Izhak Ben-Zvi, 1991), 518–30; Rivka Fishman-Duker, "Jerusalem: Capital of the Jews. The Jewish Identity of Jerusalem in Greek and Roman Sources," *Jewish Political Studies Review* 20.3–4 (Fall 2008): 119–40.

4. For general surveys on Jews and Judaism in classical literature, see Louis H. Feldman, "The Jews in Greek and Roman Literature" [Hebrew], in *The History of the Jewish People: The Diaspora in the Hellenistic-Roman World*, ed. Menahem Stern (Tel-Aviv: Am Oved, 1983) 265–85; M. Stern, "The Jews in Greek and Latin Literature," in *The Jewish People in the First Century: Historical Geography, Political History, Social, Cultural and Religious Life and Institutions*, ed. Shmuel Safrai and Menahem Stern, 2 vols., CRINT 1 (Assen: Van Gorcum, 1976), 2:1101–59; Peter Schäfer, *Judeophobia: Attitudes toward the Jews in the Ancient World* (Cambridge: Harvard University Press, 1997). Unless otherwise cited, all the translations of Greek and Latin authors are based on the translations provided in Menahem Stern, *Greek and Latin Authors on Jews and Judaism*, 3 vols., Fontes ad res Judaicas spectantes (Jerusalem: Israel Academy of Arts and Sciences, 1976–1984; henceforth *GLAJJ*). The translations of Josephus and Philo are from the LCL editions, which served as the source for Stern's translations as well.

5. On Timochares, see *GLAJJ* 1:134–37; Bezalel Bar-Kochva, "Jerusalem and Its Sur-

a second-century BCE historian who recorded the annals of King Antiochus VII Sidetes and possibly served as court historian in the king's entourage.[6] His description did not reach us directly, but as a quotation in the works of the church father Eusebius, who also did not have access to the original description but relied on the text found in Alexander Polyhistor's collection on the Jews.[7] Timochares relates how difficult it was to conquer Jerusalem, because it is surrounded by valleys and enjoys a bountiful supply of water (in contrast to the dry area surrounding the city). His presentation here clearly set out to praise Antiochus Sidetes, who overcame these obstacles and nevertheless subdued the city, although he refrained from taking total control. Interestingly, Timochares' description reached the hands of the noted geographer Strabo (first century BCE–first century CE), possibly also through an intermediary. Strabo, however, employed the description for a totally different purpose, namely, to explain why Moses chose this site for the establishment of Jerusalem (in line with foundation stories to be taken up below). Because the area is rocky and the surroundings dry, no one would be jealous of the city and wish to go to war over it (Strabo, *Geogr.* 16.2.36).[8] This explanation dovetailed nicely with Strabo's positive image of Moses. Thus, we find that Greek and Latin authors, when writing about Jerusalem, frequently were influenced by their personal beliefs or agenda, and therefore we must constantly be on guard and resist automatically "accepting what these texts describe as an ultimate truth."[9]

Not only do we frequently possess second- or third-hand versions of an original statement regarding Jerusalem, at times we cannot even be certain that the words were actually issued by the purported author and not by others—perhaps even Jews—for propagandist purposes. The famous example for these doubts is the descriptions of Jerusalem attributed to Hecataeus of Abdera and transmitted by Josephus in his *Against Apion* (1.183–204). In a lengthy section on Jerusalem we encounter statements about the antiquity of the city and its size and beauty; it is presented as the only fortified city of the Jews in the land of Israel. Hecataeus goes on to describe the temple compound with its altar, and the service of the priests within its confines. Many have cast doubts about the authenticity of this passage in *Against Apion*; some consider it to be a propagandistic Jewish composition, projected as the writing of a noted Hellenistic historian,

---

roundings in a Seleucid Work from the Beginnings of the Hasmonean State" [Hebrew], *Cathedra* 128 (2008): 5–18; Bar-Kochva, *The Image of the Jews in Greek Literature: The Hellenistic Period*, HCS 51 (Berkeley: University of California Press, 2010), 458–68.

6. Bar-Kochva, "Jerusalem and its Surroundings," 14–16.

7. On Alexander Polyhistor, see Stern, *GLAJJ* 1:157–64.

8. Menahem Stern, "Strabo on the Jews" [Hebrew], in Stern, *Studies in Jewish History: The Second Temple Period*, 518–30.

9. Bar-Kochva, "Jerusalem and its Surroundings," 16.

whereas others maintain that, even if originally written by Hecataeus, the passage underwent a significant revision under a Jewish hand.[10]

Similar questions accompany the entire corpus of Greek and Latin references to Jews and Judaism, and statements about Jerusalem are no exception. We can never be entirely certain which statements emerged from Jewish circles and were absorbed into classical literature, and which had their genesis within non-Jewish circles. What can be done is to examine the picture of Jerusalem in Greek and Latin literature by specific topics. These include foundation stories, the names applied to Jerusalem, the appearance and character of the city, military confrontations and conquests, and the variegated—and sometimes bizarre—reports about the cult practiced in the city.

Foundation Stories of Jerusalem in Greek and Latin Literature

Beginning with the section by Hecataeus of Abdera located in his *History of Egypt* and considered the more authentic of the sections on Jerusalem attributed to him,[11] the founding of Jerusalem was linked by numerous Greco-Roman writers to the various "exodus" narratives that became a staple among Greek and Latin authors. Much research has been devoted to the origins of these reports, which clearly were not based on the biblical account.[12] These stories were intended either to augment or to cast

10. Stern, *GLAJJ* 1:22–24; Bezalel Bar-Kochva, *Pseudo-Hecataeus, On the Jews: Legitimizing the Jewish Diaspora*, Hellenistic Culture and Society 21 (Berkeley: University of Califorinia Press, 1996), 249–52 (and Bar-Kochva's conclusion that the words attributed to Hecataeus in *Against Apion* reflect the views of a Jew from the Egyptian Hellenistic diaspora).

11. Quoted by Diodorus Siculus, *Bib. hist.* 40.3 (Stern, *GLAJJ* 1:26–27).

12. Greco-Roman authors were rarely familiar with any of the biblical accounts of Jewish history. There were, to be sure, some Greek writers who were able to link Jerusalem with King Solomon; Menander of Ephesus (second century BCE) reports that the temple of Jerusalem was built in the twelfth year of King Hiram of Tyre, in whose day there lived a young man named Abdemun, who succeeded in solving riddles posed by King Solomon (Josephus, *Ag. Ap.* 1:120, 126). Another Greek author of the second century BCE, Dius, describes a similar connection, whereby Solomon sent riddles to Hiram and asked for others from him "on the understanding that the one who failed to solve them should pay a sum of money to him who succeeded. Hiram agreed and, being unable to guess the riddles, spent a large sum of his wealth on the fine." Afterwards, however, the riddles were solved by one Abdemun of Tyre, who succeeded in confounding Solomon with his own riddles, and thus the Israelite king "paid back to Hiram more than he had received" (*Ag. Ap.* 1.114–115). A third Greek author, Laetus (also second century BCE), who translated the works of Phoenician writers into Greek, claims that King Solomon married Hiram's daughter and that the Tyrian king supplied trees for the building of the temple, a detail that agrees with the biblical account (for this source, see Stern, *GLAJJ* 1:128–30).

aspersions on the historical image of the Jewish nation. Frequently they followed the dictates of the ethnography that was common throughout the Hellenistic world (as in the case of Hecataeus), but at times they were incorporated into mythic frameworks that developed in Egypt without any prior connection to Jews.[13] The common thread in most of these stories is their narrative about a specific group that under dire conditions left the land of Egypt, suffered as a result of this emigration or expulsion, finally reached a safe haven, and there founded the city of Jerusalem. This nucleus, however, quickly became fragmented into numerous and very different versions, and it is apparent that the various storytellers were not only influenced by different sources but fashioned their reports in accordance with their personal disposition toward the Jewish people.

Hecataeus' version came down to us through Diodorus the Sicilian's *Bibliotheca historica* (40.3).[14] In it he describes the need felt by the Egyptians to banish from their midst alien settlers, who apparently were the cause for the local gods' wrath and ensuing calamities. Those that were expelled headed in various directions, among them to Greece, an indication that the fugitives were not necessarily from the lowest and negative elements of society. Rather, the masses that followed Moses to Judea had prominent partners that followed noted Greek leaders such as Danaus and Cadmus to other renowned locations. The masses, however, "were driven into what is now called Judea, which is not far distant from Egypt, and was at that time utterly uninhabited." This is a significant point, as it emphasizes Hecataeus' sympathetic position, although it clearly contradicts not only the biblical account but also those later versions that became a staple among less friendly authors. The latter went out of their way to stress that the fugitives arrived at populated territory and cruelly took control of the land. Hecataeus evinces a distinct admiration for Moses and projects him as a model leader totally in line with Greek ethnography: he captures the land, establishes a constitution for its citizens, and is the founder of its polis. Thus, Moses "on taking possession of the land ... founded, besides other cities, one that is now the most renowned of all, called Jerusalem."

13. For a summary of the different versions of the exodus story in classical literature, see Feldman, "Jews in Greek and Roman Literature," 270–73; John G. Gager, *Moses in Greco-Roman Paganism*, SBLMS 16 (Nashville: Abingdon, 1972), 113–33 ("Moses and the Exodus"); Schäfer, *Judeophobia*, 15–33; E. Gruen, "The Use and Abuse of the Exodus Story," in his *Heritage and Hellenism: The Reinvention of Jewish Tradition*, HCS 30 (Berkeley: University of California Press, 1998), 41–72; John J. Collins, "Reinventing Exodus: Exegesis and Legend in Hellenistic Egypt," in his, *Jewish Cult and Hellenistic Culture: Essays on the Jewish Encounter with Hellenism and Roman Rule*, JSJSup 100 (Leiden: Brill, 2005), 44–57; Bar-Kochva, *Image of the Jews* (see the index under Exodus story; expulsion from Egypt).

14. This passage, based on Hecataeus' work on ancient Egypt, is in truth a third-hand version, given that Diodorus' words were preserved in the *Bibliotheca* of Photius, the patriarch of Constantinople in the ninth century CE; see Stern, *GLAJJ* 1:26–27.

Hecataeus continues to describe Moses' legislative achievement as well as the establishment of the temple, all in terms of total adoration. Similar praise for Moses is found in the writings of Strabo the geographer. According to Strabo, Moses departed from Egypt willfully, as he could not accept the cultic behavior of the land, and he "persuaded not a few thoughtful men and led them away to this place where the settlement of Jerusalem now is; and he easily took possession of the place, since it was not a place that would be looked on with envy, nor yet one for which anyone would make a serious fight. For it is rocky, and, although it itself is well supplied with water, its surrounding territory is barren and waterless" (*Geogr.* 16.2.36).[15]

In contradistinction to the accounts supplied by Hecataeus and Strabo, other Greek authors provide far less sympathetic versions. One of these is the account provided by the third-century BCE Egyptian priest Manetho, recorded by Josephus (*Ag. Ap.* 1.73–91, 93–105). The story there recounts the ancient Egyptian tradition about the Hyksos, shepherds who invaded Egypt and took control of the land but were ultimately banished and traversed the desert to Syria. But fearing the Assyrians, who had taken control over much of Asia, "they built in the land now called Judaea a city large enough to hold all those thousands of people, and gave it the name of Jerusalem" (*Ag. Ap.* 1.90). It is apparent that, in attaching the founding of Jerusalem to the memory of the Hyksos, the Jews assumed a negative image in Egyptian eyes, and this tendency increased in the writings of other Greek authors. Diodorus Siculus quotes the companions of King Antiochus VII Sidetes telling the king, as he laid siege to Jerusalem, that the Jews were misanthropes who consider all men to be their enemies, were banished from Egypt as lepers, and ultimately "occupied the territory round about Jerusalem and ... made their hatred of mankind into a tradition" (*Bib. hist.* 39–40.1.2).[16] Describing the banished as lepers became a staple of the foundation story and is repeated by Lysimachus, a Greek-Egyptian of the second or first century BCE, and one of the quintessential anti-Jewish Greek authors.[17] Lysimachus also supplies

15. Stern, *GLAJJ* 1:295.

16. A bit further on Diodorus recounts that Antiochus IV Epiphanes, upon entering the temple, found a marble statue of a heavily bearded man seated on an ass with a book in his hands and assumed this was an image of "Moses the founder of Jerusalem"; on this see below.

17. Stern, *GLAJJ* 1:382–386; according to Stern, Lysimachus' narrative is based on a source different from that of Manetho. Not only is the king's name different, but he also makes no mention of the Egyptian tradition regarding the Hyksos and the crimes of the banished while still in Egypt. Instead he stresses their cruelty, pillage, and destruction of temples upon arriving in Judaa. Lysimachus also does not claim that Moses was an Egyptian priest, as stated by Manetho. It is also noteworthy that Lysimachus claims that the banished

an interesting detail regarding the original name of Jerusalem. At first the city was called "Hierosyla," meaning the despoiling of sanctuaries, in line with their violent activity upon reaching their ultimate destination. Only after some time and upon attaining power did they change the name to "Hierosolyma" and called themselves "Hierosolymites."[18]

The conquest of Jerusalem by Pompey in 63 BCE, and its later destruction by Titus during the Great Revolt, enhanced the interest of Latin authors in the history of the city and in the history of the Jewish nation in general.[19] One outstanding example of this interest is in the detailed account of Tacitus in the fifth book of his *History* (5.2–13).[20] Of the six versions of the origins of the Jewish people cited by Tacitus, three refer in one way or another to the city of Jerusalem. One version reports that "in the reign of Isis the superfluous population of Egypt, under the leadership of Hierosolymous and Iuda, discharged itself on the neighboring lands." A similar tradition is found in the works of Plutarch (*Is. Os.* 37),[21] who relates that the god Typhon fled the battlefield (in his war against the goddess Isis) on the back of an ass for seven days, "and that after he made his escape he became the father of sons, Hierosolymous and Judaeus." Plutarch notes that this is an attempt "to drag Jewish traditions into legend," and scholars have suggested that the allusion here might be to the slander that the Jews worship the ass (see below). Another version cited by Tacitus claims that the Jews have an illustrious pedigree "being the Solyma, a people celebrated in Homer's poems, who founded a city and gave it the name Hierosolyma." As we shall see presently, the term "Solyma" was connected with Jerusalem as far back as the Hellenistic period, and by Tacitus' days this connection had become well known, although both those who wished to glorify Jewish roots and those who disparaged them would equally cite this term.[22]

Tacitus ultimately reaches his sixth version of Jewish origins, with which he claims "most authors agree." Here he reverts to the tale of the expulsion of the lepers from Egypt to the desert, their leader Moses, and

---

people arrived at a land that was already settled, in direct contrast to Hecataeus' claim that the land at the time was "utterly uninhabited." Unlike Stern, Schäfer (*Judeophobia,* 28) suggests that Lysimachus had before him the writings of Hecataeus and Manetho but revised them in order to emphasize his anti-Jewish attitude.

18. On the names of Jerusalem in classical literature, see below.

19. Like Pliny, Tacitus refers to Jerusalem as "a famous city" (*Hist.* 5.2.1).

20. Stern, *GLAJJ* 2:17–63; and see the extensive bibliography there, 6. See also Johanan Hans Levy, "Tacitus on the Origin of the Jews" [Hebrew], in his *Studies in Jewish Hellenism* (Jerusalem: Mossad Bialik, 1960), 115–208.

21. See Levy, "Tacitus on the Origin," 119 n. 7; Stern, *GLAJJ* 1:563.

22. See Levy, "Tacitus on the Origin," 119 n. 10; Stern, *GLAJJ* 2:34–35.

the herd of asses that led them to a source of water. Finally, "they marched six days continuously, and on the seventh seized a country, expelling the former inhabitants; there they founded a city and dedicated a Temple." It appears that hundreds of years passed from the time the legend connecting the exodus from Egypt with the founding of Jerusalem first appeared, until Tacitus' day, when this "knowledge" became the accepted truth among most Greek and Latin authors.

Names of Jerusalem in Greek and Latin Literature

Clearchus of Soli (fourth–third century BCE), commonly considered a disciple of Aristotle and a near-contemporary of Hecateaeus of Abdera, also mentions Jerusalem. In a passage quoted by Josephus (*Ag. Ap.* 1.176–183), Clearchus describes a meeting between Aristotle and a Jew and quotes Aristotle's description of the event.[23] "The district which they inhabit is known as Judaea. Their city has a remarkably odd name: They call it Hierusaleme." As noted by Menahem Stern, "this form for Jerusalem is unique to Greek literature, whose authors consistently use the plural form Hierosolyma."[24] We already noted above that at least one Greek-Egyptian author, Lysimachus, set out to denigrate the Jews by claiming that their city was initially called Hierosyla, "because of their sacrilegious propensities." Only later, he says, did they change the name to its present one. These, however, are not the only attempts to explain the origin of the name Jerusalem. As noted above, Tacitus cited a connection between the name of the city and the figure of Hierosolymus, who, according to Plutarch, was one of the two sons of the god Typhon. Tacitus also recalled a tradition that the Jews were descendants of the Solymi, a celebrated tribe mentioned in Homer's poems, and they founded the city named after them. The first author to refer to the Jews as Solymites was Manetho, who in the same context also refers to the city of Jerusalem.[25] It appears, however, that this connection, or at least the term, was popular also among Hellenistic Jewry. Josephus also received this tradition and thus claims that Melchizedek was responsible for changing the name of the city from "Solyma" to Jerusalem (*J.W.* 6.438).[26]

---

23. For the entire passage see Johanan Hans Lewy, "Aristotle and the Jewish Sage according to Clearchus of Soli," *HTR* 31 (1938): 205–35.

24. Stern, *GLAJJ* 1:51.

25. Josephus, *Ag. Ap.* 1.248, following the reference to Jerusalem in 241.

26. See also Josephus, *Ant.* 1.180; 7.67; *Ag. Ap.* 1.172–174. Josephus also interprets the words of the poet Choerilus, who alludes to "the Solymian hills" as a reference to the Jewish nation, because these hills "are in our country and inhabited by us" (*Ag. Ap.*1.173–174). See: Louis H. Feldman, *Jew and Gentile in the Ancient World: Attitudes and Interactions from Alexander to Justinian* (Princeton: Princeton University Press, 1993), 191–92, 520–22 nn. 55–57.

While Tacitus considered the link between the Solymites and the Jewish people and Jerusalem to be laudatory, other Latin authors referred to this connection in far less flattering tones. Valerius Flaccus (second half of the first century CE) praised the Flavian dynasty for its military successes but refers to one of the family, probably Titus, as having become "foul with the dust of Solyma" (*Argon.* 1.13).[27] Martial refers to "Solyma now consumed by fire" (*Epigr.* 7.55.7)[28] and elsewhere derides a "circumcised poet ... born in the very midst of Solyma" (*Epigr.* 9.95.4).[29] Pausanius (second century CE) refers to the grave of Helen (probably the queen from Adiabene) located in the city of Solyma (*Descr.* 7.16.5),[30] and in a work by Philostratus (second–third century CE) Titus is quoted in a letter declaring that "I have captured Solyma" (*Vit. Apoll.* 6.29).[31] It is even possible that Jews residing outside the land of Israel established a settlement called Solyma, in memory of their city and (first) temple, which were destroyed. The Greco-Roman historian Asinius Quadratus (early third century CE), in his work on Parthia, refers to "Solyma, a city of the Assyrians ... founded after the capture of the Jerusalem Temple." Stern has noted that it was customary to refer to Babylonia as Assyria (thus, for example, Strabo), and so it is possible that the reference here is to an ancient Jewish settlement founded by those exiled to Babylonia following the destruction of Jerusalem (= Solyma) by the Babylonians. This bit of information conjures up the Jewish tradition in Babylonia regarding the synagogue in Nehardea built by Yekhoniah king of Judah, using in part stones taken from the destroyed temple, and possibly even a city built in Babylonia by the exiled king.[32] In any case, it appears that the name "Solyma," although in use from the Hellenistic period (at least beginning with Manetho), became increasingly popular among Latin authors following the destruction of the Second Temple.

Descriptions of Jerusalem in Classical Literature

Descriptions of Jerusalem frequently appear in classical literature in connection with military engagements between the city and various foreign armies, and therefore emphasis was often placed on the strength of the city, its fortifications, and the topographical conditions that rendered its

27. Stern, *GLAJJ* 1:504.
28. Ibid., 1:526.
29. Ibid., 1:528.
30. Ibid., 2:196.
31. Ibid., 2:342.
32. For the reference to Asinius Quadratus, see Stern, *GLAJJ* 2:345–46; Menahem Stern, "The Assyrian Jerusalem in a Fragment of the Work of Asinius Quadratus," [Hebrew], in Stern, *Studies in Jewish History: The Second Temple Period*, 549–51.

conquest a formidable task.[33] The fortification of Jerusalem was noted already by Agatharchides of Cnidus, a historian of the second century BCE, who reported how Ptolemy I Lagos was able to conquer the city primarily because the local population refused to take up arms on the Sabbath. Josephus quotes this source twice. In the more complete rendition (*Ag. Ap.* 1.209), Jerusalem is described as "the most strongly fortified of cities," whereas in the shorter version (*Ant.* 12.5) Agatharchides calls it "a strong and great city."[34] He does not explain what rendered the city "strong," and the earliest explanation for this appears in the words attributed to Timochares, cited above:

> Timochares says in the History of Antiochus that Jerusalem has a circumference of 40 stades.[35] It is hard to capture her, as she is enclosed on all sides by abrupt ravines. The whole city has a plenitude of running waters, so that the gardens are also irrigated by the waters streaming from the city. An area extending to a distance of 40 stades from the city is waterless; beyond the 40 stades the land becomes moist again.[36]

As noted by Bezalel Bar-Kochva, Timochares exaggerated regarding both the circumference of the city[37] as well as the plentiful source of water available to the besieged population, on the one hand, and the surrounding aridity that impeded its conquest by Antiochus Sidetes, on the other. This was done to enhance the Seleucid monarch's achievement. Stern also cites another passage quoted by Eusebius (*Praep. ev.* 9.36.1), entitled *Schoinometresis Syriae* ("The Land-Survey of Syria"), written approximately around 100 BCE, which describes Jerusalem as "situated on a high and rough terrain; some parts of the wall are built of hewn stone, but most of it consists of gravel. The city had a circumference of 27 stades, and in that place there is a fount from which water spouts in abundance."[38]

A description similar to that of Timochares appears in Strabo's *Geog-*

---

33. We already noted that one of the first descriptions of the city, its dimensions, and its geography was attributed to Hecataeus of Abdera (Josephus, *Ag. Ap.* 1.197–199), but most likely this was the work of a Jew from Hellenistic Egypt.

34. For both passages see Stern, *GLAJJ* 1:104–9.

35. One stadium = approximately 200 meters.

36. Timochares, *Antiochi,* quoted by Eusebius, *Praep. ev.* 9.35.1.

37. According to Bar-Kochva this circumference, approximately 8 km, is almost twice the true circumference of Jerusalem in the Hasmonean period and, according to Josephus (*J.W.* 5.159), that of the Great Revolt as well. By that time, the city had grown considerably in comparison to the earlier Hasmonean era yet was only about 35 stades in circumference. For Timochares' statement, see Bar-Kochva, "Jerusalem and Its Surroundings,"6.

38. For this text, see Stern, *GLAJJ* 1:137–38; Stern, "Jerusalem, the Most Famous of the Cities," 525; Stern suggests that the author may have been Xenophon of Lampsacus, who also served as a source for Pliny's *Historia naturalis*. If so, the text would have been written almost contemporaneous with Timochares.

raphy (16.2.36). Moses took possession of Jerusalem, a place "rocky, and although it itself is well supplied with water, its surrounding territory is barren and waterless, and the part of the territory within a radius of sixty stadia is also rocky beneath the surface."[39] Scholars have noted the similarity to Timochares' description, but there are also significant differences, such as the choice of Jerusalem by Moses because the area was rocky and thus would not be looked on with envy—with no mention of how difficult it would be to capture the city. Bar-Kochva has therefore suggested that Strabo's source was Poseidonius,[40] who reworked Timochares in an effort to render him closer to his own worldview, which strove to present the Jews in Moses' day as evincing the religious, social, and political ideals of the Stoic philosophy, a peace-loving community without any defensive fortifications.[41] Nevertheless it is noteworthy that further on in Strabo's *Geography*, as he describes Pompey's capture of Jerusalem, he reports that Jerusalem was "a rocky and well-walled fortress, and though well supplied with water inside, its outside territory was wholly without water; and it had a trench cut in rock ... and, from the stone that had been hewn out, the wall of the Temple was fenced with towers" (*Geogr.* 16.2.40).[42] Diodorus Siculus also describes the siege placed by Antiochus Sidetes on Jerusalem, but his description of the city's fortification is far more limited, noting only that upon subduing the city he dismantled its walls (*Bib. hist.* 34–40.1.5).[43]

As noted, Jerusalem was considered by numerous Greek and Latin authors to be a heavily fortified city, which enabled it to withstand more than one siege. When Pliny refers to Machaerus in the Transjordan, he calls it "next to Jerusalem the most important fortress in Judaea" (*Nat.* 5.72). Needless to say, the city's conquest by the Flavian emperors enhanced the image of Jerusalem as a heavily fortified city, and this knowledge served a major role in Flavian propaganda, which strove to project the new dynasty as having completed a major achievement. Prior to that, Livy underscored Pompey's achievement in conquering the city, and therefore wrote that the Roman general "conquered the Jews and captured their temple Jerusalem,[44] never invaded before" (*Per.* 102).[45] As for the Flavian achievement,

---

39. Stern, *GLAJJ* 1,300.

40. Strabo's dependence on Poseidonius for his knowledge of Moses and the Jewish religion has received extensive attention; see Stern, "Strabo and the Jews," 438–42, who cites additional sources for Poseidonius.

41. Bar-Kochva, "Jerusalem and Its Surroundings," 10–12.

42. On this passage, see Bar-Kochva, "Jerusalem and Its Surroundings," 10 n. 17.

43. Stern, *GLAJJ* 1:182–185. Scholars assume that Diodorus took this from Poseidonius, and, according to Bar-Kochva, the latter received the report from Timochares but reworked it to meet his own needs.

44. Livy was not the only author to identify the temple with Jerusalem, as will be noted below.

45. Stern, *GLAJJ* 1:329. Livy's statement is obviously an exaggeration, for the temple

words of a similar vein are found in a Latin inscription from the year 80 CE, inscribed on an arch erected in the Circus Maximus that commemorated Titus' victory over the Jews and Jerusalem, a city that generals, kings, and nations prior to him either unsuccessfully attempted to conquer, or did not even try to conquer.[46] As in the case of Livy, the inscription ignores a long list of generals and kings who successfully conquered the city, from the late first-temple period and throughout the Hellenistic and Roman periods.

The most detailed description of Jerusalem's fortifications was supplied by Tacitus, who included in his report on the fighting detailed descriptions of the city's walls and other fortifications:

> The city stands on an eminence, and the Jews had defended it with works and fortifications sufficient to protect even level ground; for the two hills that rise to a great height had been included within walls that had been skillfully built, projecting out or bending in so as to put the flanks of an assailing body under fire. The rocks terminated in sheer cliffs, and towers rose to a height of sixty feet where the hill assisted the fortifications, and in the valleys they reached one hundred and twenty.... An inner line of walls had been built around the palace, and on a conspicuous height stands Antony's tower.... The temple was built like a citadel, with walls of its own, which were constructed with more care and effort than any of the rest; the very colonnades about the temple made a splendid defense. Within the enclosure is an ever-flowing spring; in the hills are subterraneous excavations, with pools and cisterns for holding rain-water." (*Hist.* 5.11–12)

Tacitus proceeds to explain that the founders of the city prepared all these fortifications because they foresaw the many wars the city would be forced to endure "because the ways of their people differed so from those of the neighbors," and so they expected long sieges. In addition to the fortifications, Tacitus goes on to describe the different forces in the Jewish camp, claiming that the entire number of the besieged came to six hundred thousand: "there were arms for all who could use them ... both men and women showed the same determination.... Such was the city and people against which Titus Caesar proceeded; since the nature of the ground did not allow him to assault or employ any sudden operations, he decided to use earthworks and mantlets" (*Hist.* 5.13).

---

and the city had previously been conquered by Ptolemy I, Antiochus VII Epiphanes, and to a degree by Antiochus VII Sidetes as well. Livy's intention was to extoll Pompey's achievement, as did Josephus (*Ant.* 14.71). Quite possibly Livy and Josephus drew from the same source; see Stern, *GLAJJ* 1:329.

46. *CIL* 6, #944."gentem Iudeorum domuit et urbem Hierusolymam, omnibus ante se ducibus regibus gentibus aut frustra petitam aut omnino."

Jerusalem and the Temple: Contents and Worship in Classical Literature

The notoriety of Jerusalem among Greek and Latin authors was definitely enhanced by word of the temple in its midst. This connection was so entrenched that at times authors actually identified the temple and the city as one. The most famous example of this appears in Polybius' description of the fifth Syrian war in the late second century BCE. Polybius reports that the Jews of Judea transferred their allegiance to Antiochus III, noting that the Jews who came over to him resided in "the temple called Jerusalem, concerning which we have more to say, especially concerning the renown of the temple" (*Hist.* 16.39.4–5; Josephus, *Ant.* 12.136). As noted above, when Livy describes the city's conquest by Pompey, he also refers to the Jews' temple of Jerusalem. Elsewhere, however, Livy adds an important detail that reflects what various Greek and Latin authors attributed to the Jerusalem temple. In the *Scholia in Lucanum,* Livy is quoted as follows: "They [= the Jews] do not state to which deity pertains the temple at Jerusalem, nor is any image found there, since they do not think the God partakes of any figure" (2.593).[47]

The absence of any image in the Jewish temple was usually perceived by Roman authors as praiseworthy, and prior to the words of Livy we might note a statement by Varro, quoted by Augustine (*Civ.* 4.31).[48] He states that from ancient times the Romans worshiped gods without an image and suggests that if this had continued, "our worship of the gods would be more devout. And in the support of his opinion he adduces, among other things, the testimony of the Jewish race."[49] Noteworthy in this context are the contradictory statements of Tacitus. When he reports the conquest of the city by Pompey, the historian claims that, following the Roman general's entry into the temple, "it was a matter of common

---

47. Stern, *GLAJJ* 1:330; Schäfer (*Judeophobia*, 38) stresses the words *non niminant* ("do not state") and suggests the possibility that it was the secrecy surrounding the Jewish cult that aroused the Greek and Latin response. In a similar manner, Tacitus (*Hist.* 5.8.1) notes that only Jews were allowed to approach the doors of the temple, "and all, save the priests, were forbidden to cross the threshold." This suggestion of a degree of mystery and secrecy surrounding the temple may have contributed to the interest shown by Greeks and Romans concerning the temple.

48. For the source for Varro, see Stern, *GLAJJ* 1:207. The connection between a lack of any image applied to the deity and Jewish beliefs from the time of Moses was also noted by Strabo, *Geogr.* 16.2.35.

49. Josephus (*Ag. Ap.* 2.83–84) states that when Antiochus Epiphanes raided the temple "he found nothing there to deserve ridicule," and Josephus goes on to claim that "these facts are attested by many sober historians" naming specifically Polybius, Strabo, Nicolaus of Damascus, Timagenes, Castor the chronicler and Apollodorus. See Stern, *GLAJJ* 1:115.

knowledge that there were no representations of the gods within, but that the place was empty and the secret shrine contained nothing" (*Hist.* 5.9.1).[50] But just a few lines prior to that, in his summary of the various accounts about Jewish origins, Tacitus relates that, in their wanderings through the desert, the Israelites were led to a source of water by a herd of wild asses, and therefore "they dedicated in a shrine, a statue of that creature whose guidance enabled them to put an end to their wandering and thirst" (*Hist.* 5.4.2). Tacitus' lack of consistency has received considerable attention, and apparently he was the recipient of diverse sources, both positive and negative, regarding the contents of the Jewish temple and the Jews' manner of worship.[51] Tacitus' reference to the image of an ass in the temple appears in his sixth version of the origin of the Jews, which he designated as the one with which "most authors agree." It is quite possible that Tacitus copied this bit of information from a general narrative that he received, without necessarily identifying with this particular detail.[52]

In any case, the information about the image of an ass, or the head of an ass, placed in the Jerusalem temple resonated in numerous Greek and Latin works, and it is even possible to trace the development of the tradition. The first author to mention it is Mnaseas of Patara (ca. 200 BCE). His report came down to us third-hand, with Josephus quoting Apion, who attributes the story to Mnaseas. The latter, in describing a lengthy war between the Jews and the Idumeans, reports that a scoundrel by the name of Zabidus succeeded in stealthily entering the sanctuary, where he "snatched up the golden head of the pack-ass" and made off with it to the Idumean city of Dora (*Ag. Ap.* 2.112–114). The report does not state explicitly that the Jews worshiped the image that was snatched, but in another text quoted by Josephus we read that "within this sanctuary … the Jews kept an ass's head, worshipping that animal and deeming it worthy of the deepest reverence" (*Ag. Ap.* 2.80).. The charge about ass worship probably had its origins in Egypt and was most likely connected with attempts to identify the Jewish god with the evil Egyptian god Seth (referred to as Typhon by the Greeks), who was also known to have the image of an ass.[53] The charge seems to have split into a variety of versions, and thus

---

50. The connection between Pompey's conquest and the lack of an image in the temple is repeated by Cassius Dio, *Hist. rom.* 37.17.2: "They never had any statue of him even in Jerusalem itself."

51. See Stern, *GLAJJ* 2:37; Feldman, "Jew and Gentile," 499.

52. Further on in his survey (*Hist.* 5.5), Tacitus compares the beliefs of the Egyptians with those of the Jews: "The Jews conceive of one god only, and that with the mind only; they regard as impious those who make from perishable materials representations of gods in man's image … therefore they set up no statues in their cities, still less in their temples"; see D. Rokeaḥ, "Tacitus and the God of Israel" [Hebrew], *Zion* 55 (1990): 265–68.

53. We already noted Plutarch's tradition that connected Typhon's flight from battle on the back of an ass and the two sons he had later: Hierosolymus and Judaeus (see n. 21 above).

Diodorus Siculus reports that when Antiochus IV Epiphanes entered the innermost sanctuary, "where it was lawful for the priest alone to enter," he encountered a marble statue of a heavily bearded man seated on an ass with a book in his hand, and assumed it was Moses "the founder of Jerusalem (*Bib. hist.* 34–35.1.3).[54] The story here appears in the context of another "Jerusalem" episode, namely, the siege laid by Antiochus VII Sidetes on the city, at which time the king's friends reminded him of the ancient enmity between his ancestors and the Jews. That event, however, ended only with the dismantling of the walls of Jerusalem and the exacting of tribute, rather than the outright annihilation of the Jews as urged by his friends.

The charge of ass worship was not the sole defamation of Jews in Greco-Roman literature, and Josephus cites another "discovery" made by Antiochus IV Epiphanes upon entering the temple. According to Apion, the king encountered a Greek in the temple who was being fattened for slaughter as a sacrifice, for the Jews have a custom whereby they snatch a Greek every year, "fatten him up for a year, and then convey him to a wood, where they slew him, sacrificed his body with their customary ritual, partook of his flesh, and, while immolating the Greek, swore an oath of hostility to the Greeks." (*Ag. Ap.* 2.95).[55] It appears that in this instance as well the claims, which had their origins in Egypt, possibly as far back as the Persian period, subsequently reached circles close to the Seleucid court during Antiochus Epiphanes' reign and ultimately found their way to the works of Timochares, Posidonius, Diodorus, and Apion. Some of the charges were expunged in line with the aims and disposition of the authors,[56] while elsewhere they persisted, given the interest of authors such as Apion in perpetuating the Greek–Egyptian animosity toward Jews.

Beyond the traditions regarding ass worship and blood libel, on the one hand, and the lack of idols or images, on the other hand, Greek and Latin literature knows very little about the religious practices in the temple,

---

54. Bar-Kochva suggests that Diodorus received this story from Poseidonius, whose source was Timochares; this version is less extreme, as it does not claim that the ass was the object of veneration but merely a means of travel for Moses. The statue of Moses may have been employed to honor the founder of the cult, not to serve as an object of worship. For the stages in the development of the charge and its different versions, see Bar-Kochva, *Image of the Jews*, 206–49; Schäfer, *Judeophobia*, 55–65.

55. For the origins of this claim and its permutations, see B. Bar-Kochva, "The Hellenistic 'Blood Libel': Its Contents, Sources and Transmission " [Hebrew], *Tarbiz* 65 (1995–1996): 347–74; Bar-Kochva, *Image of the Jews*, 253–79.

56. The blood libel is explicitly mentioned by only one other Greek writer, the first-century CE (?) historian Damocritus. His report reached us through a tenth-century text, and there he, like Apion, mentions both charges: "They used to worship an asinine golden head, and that every seventh year they caught a foreigner and slaughtered him. They used to kill him by carding his flesh into small pieces." See Stern, *GLAJJ* 1:530–31; Schäfer, *Judeophobia*, 62–65.

on regular weekdays as well as during festivals. Hecataeus of Abdera, in the text quoted by Diodorus, makes the general observation that Moses "instituted their forms of worship and ritual" and that "the sacrifices he established differ from those of other nations." He claims that the priests were also the nation's judges and law keepers, in addition to their role in the temple. The priest outstanding for his wisdom is called the high priest, and he is considered God's messenger who announces the ordinances in public gatherings. As he does this the gathered Jews bow before him.[57]

Reference to a specific festival can be found in the writing of Plutarch, in a passage from the *Quaestiones convivales* that addresses the possible connection between the Jewish religion and the cult of Dionysus. Following an ambiguous reference to a fast day, Plutarch (as presented by Moiragenes the Athenian) draws a comparison between a number of Dionysiac ceremonies and temple practices during the festival of Sukkot. The author appears to have some knowledge about the "Procession of Branches," the musical activity of the Levites, and possibly even the extension of the holiday following Sukkot (*Quaest. conv.* 4.4.6.2).[58] The festival of Sukkot is mentioned in another text attributed (erroneously) to Plutarch. It relates that when Antiochus VII Sidetes laid siege to Jerusalem, the Jews asked for a cease-fire for seven days "for their most important festival." Antiochus not only granted this but also offered bulls and incense to the priests. The Jews were amazed and, immediately following the festival, placed themselves in his hands.[59]

References to the Conquest of Jerusalem by Pompey

Pompey's conquest of Jerusalem and Judea's entry into Rome's political sphere left a strong impression in classical literature, and in this context Jerusalem was frequently discussed.[60] Cicero, in his *Pro Flacco* (28.67), notes

57. Hecataeus, *Aegyptiaca*, in Diodorus, *Bib. hist.* 40.3.3–6. It is obvious that Hecataeus did not base his report on the biblical account but rather relied on oral tradition that he received, possibly from a Jewish source. Moreover, the image of the priests here agrees far more with the reality of the Hellenistic period than the biblical era, although he, too, is not aware of the hereditary element connected to the high priesthood. On Hecataeus' passage, see Gager, *Moses in Greco-Roman Paganism*, 26–37; Stern, *GLAJJ* 1:29–32. The other passage from Hecataeus, quoted by Josephus in *Against Apion*, provides additional information regarding temple activity (the existence of an eternal light, priestly abstinence from wine while in the temple), but, as noted above, this passage was likely the work of a Jewish author and not Hecataeus.

58. Stern, *GLAJJ* 1:553–54; Schäfer, *Judeophobia*, 53–54.

59. Plutarch, *Apothegmata*, quoted by Stern, *GLAJJ* 1:563–64; for a parallel version, see Josephus, *Ant.* 13.241–242; for the story's source, see Bar-Kochva, *Image of the Jews*, 413–17.

60. I will not take up those passages that connect Pompey with the internal confrontations within the Jewish leadership of Jerusalem, such as Diodorus' report concerning the two

that, when Pompey captured the city and entered as victor, he touched nothing in the shrine, and Cicero cites this as an example of Pompey's wisdom.[61] In his letter to Atticus from the year 59 BCE, Cicero refers to Pompey as "Hierosolymarius." (*Att.* 2.9.1). However, Cicero's references to Jerusalem are important for another reason, as he is the first author to testify explicitly that "every year it was customary to send gold to Jerusalem on the order of the Jews from Italy and from all our provinces" (*Flac.* 28.67).[62] The reference here is to the sending of *shekalim* from the Jewish diaspora to Jerusalem, a custom attested primarily in rabbinic literature.[63] Cicero, in defending Flaccus for attempting to stem the ongoing flow of funds to Jerusalem, makes it clear that to his mind "even while Jerusalem was standing and the Jews were at peace with us, the practice of their sacred rites was at variance with the glory of our empire, the dignity of our name, the customs of our ancestors" (*Flac.* 28.69).

Jerusalem's conquest by Pompey was recounted by some authors in an interesting context, reminiscent of the fall of the city to Ptolemy I as reported by Agatharchides of Cnidus. As noted above, that historian attributed the fall of the city to the Jews' refusal to take up arms on the Sabbath. Similarly, Josephus (following Strabo[64]) claims that the city was taken "in the third month, on the fast day" (*Ant.* 14.66).[65] Given that the "third month" refers here to that of the siege (and not the third month of

---

brothers, Hyrcanus II and Aristobulus II, who appeared before Pompey (*Bib. hist.* 40.2; Stern, *GLAJJ* 1:185), or the allusion to Aristobulus' surrender in an inscription set up by Pompey (Diodorus, *Bib. hist.* 40.2; compare Plutarch, *Pomp.* 45.5). Moreover, it is certain that major passages produced by Nicolaus of Damascus that described events in Jerusalem were incorporated into Josephus' writing; these were taken up in an important study by Menahem Stern, "Nicolaus of Damascus as a Source of Jewish History in the Herodian and Hasmonean Age," in Stern, *Studies in Jewish History: The Second Temple Period*, 445–64.

61. Cicero refutes the claim that Pompey did this out of religious feelings toward the Jews (see Josephus, *Ant.* 14.72; *J.W.* 1.153) but claims that Pompey was careful not to supply his critics with opportunity for gossip.

62. Strabo (quoted by Josephus, Ant. 14.111–113) relates that already during the reign of Mithridates VI Eupator, king of Pontus in 88 BCE, the Jews of Asia Minor dispatched funds to Jerusalem.

63. Tacitus also refers to this, as he relates that "the worst rascals among other peoples…kept sending tribute and contributing to Jerusalem" (Hist. 5.5.1); further on in that passage (5.8.1) we read that in Jerusalem "was a temple possessing enormous riches". For the entire issue see Stern's long note in GLAJJ,1, 198-199.

64. Josephus cites both Strabo and Nicolaus of Damascus as his sources, but the changing of "Sabbath" to "fast day" is likely the work of Strabo, as Nicolaus spent much time in Jerusalem and would have been cognizant of the nature of the Jewish Sabbath.

65. This date—the third month—was still cited by Byzantine authors; see: Eutropius, *Breviarium ab Urbe Condita* 6.14.2; the latter also refers to Jerusalem as "the nation's capital" (*caput gentis*), the very same title given to the city by Tacitus (*Hist.* 5.8.1: *Hierosolyma genti caput*). Elsewhere (*Hist.* 2.78.4) Tacitus claims that Caesarea was the capital of Judea, but there the reference is to the capital of the province, whereas here Tacitus refers to Jerusalem as the national capital of the Jews (see Stern, *GLAJJ* 2:46).

the Jewish calendar), with the siege beginning in the spring (*J.W.* 1.149), it is inconceivable that the "fast" here refers to the Day of Atonement. As noted by numerous scholars, the text here might be yet another example of classical writers believing that the Sabbath was a fast day.[66] It should be noted, however, that certain Jewish circles did, in fact, fast on the Sabbath, and thus there might even be some credibility to statements by Greek and Latin authors that project the Sabbath as a day of fasting.[67]

Cassius Dio also describes the conquest of Jerusalem by Pompey as taking place on a specific Jewish day when the besieged refrained from work. While most of the city was taken by the Roman general without any trouble, the temple itself was a far more serious undertaking: "It was on high ground and was fortified by a wall of its own, and if they had continued defending it on all days alike, he could not have got possession of it." But the Jews "made an exception on what are called the days of Saturn, and by doing no work at all on those days afforded the Romans an opportunity to batter down the wall ... thus the defenders were captured on the day of Saturn, and all the wealth (of the temple) was plundered" (*Hist. rom.* 37.1.17).[68] The refusal of Jews to fight on the Sabbath became so entrenched in the minds of classical writers that at least one first-century Latin author, Frontinus, claims that the fall of the city to Titus was also a result of Jewish abstaining from fighting on Sabbath, although by that time the rebels no longer strictly adhered to this practice (*Strategmata* 2.1.17).[69]

As already noted, Tacitus also describes Pompey's conquest of the city, noting that the Roman commander entered the sanctuary but found no representations of the gods therein. He also reports that, while the walls of the city were razed, the temple remained standing (*Hist.* 5.9.1). We should note that, when Tacitus wrote this report, the city of Jerusalem had been destroyed for a second time, and Tacitus claims that the residents of Jerusalem had drawn lessons from Pompey's conquest and subsequently fortified the city and its walls in preparation for a future confrontation (*Hist.* 5.12.2).[70] It appears that, with each successive fall of

---

66. See Stern, "Strabo on the Jews", 428–29; Stern, *GLAJJ* 1:276–77; the same interpretation may apply to Strabo (*Geogr.* 16.2.40), who relates that Pompey waited for the fast day, when Jews abstain from work (Stern, *GLAJJ* 1:307). For Sabbath as a fast day in classical literature, see also Schäfer, *Judeophobia*, 88–90.

67. See Yitzhak D. Gilat, "On Fasting on the Sabbath" [Hebrew], *Tarbiz* 52 (1982–1983): 1–16.

68. The plundering of the temple by Pompey as described by Cassius Dio contradicts the report by Cicero (and Josephus) quoted above, and it is possible that Cassius Dio referred to plundering by the soldiers, and not to Pompey specifically (see Stern, *GLAJJ* 2:353).

69. Stern, *GLAJJ* 1:510–11.

70. Tacitus claims that during Claudius' reign the Jews purchased the right to build the walls of Jerusalem. This would apparently refer to the rebuilding project of Agrippa I (Stern, *GLAJJ* 2:58).

the city to a Roman army, Greek and Latin authors recalled the chain of conquerors going back to Pompey. Thus, for example Appian, the Alexandrian historian of the second century CE, recounts the three routs of Jerusalem at the hands of Roman generals: Pompey, who "destroyed their greatest, and to them holiest city, as Ptolemy, the first king of Egypt had formerly done; it was afterward rebuilt and Vespasian destroyed it again, and Hadrian did the same in our time" (*Syriacus liber* 50.252).[71] There were some authors who even considered Pompey's conquest to have signaled the establishment of Judea as a Roman province,[72] although this probably took place only upon the banishment of Herod's son Archelaus from the country in 6 CE.

From the Destruction of Jerusalem and the Temple to the Bar-Kokhba Uprising

With the exception of Josephus, Tacitus provides the most detailed description of the events in Jerusalem on the eve of the destruction (*Hist.* 5.10-13). He informs us that the war began under the Judean procurator Florus. Tacitus considers that governor, as well as Felix, one of his predecessors, who "practiced every kind of cruelty and lust," responsible for the outbreak of hostilities, rather than explicitly blaming the Jewish rebels.[73] Tacitus describes the failure of Cestius Gallus, the governor of Syria, to quell the outbreak of the uprising at its earliest stages and goes on to describe briefly the dispatch of Vespasian to Judea, his success in subduing the territory save for Jerusalem, the Roman civil war that temporarily put the war on hold, and finally Titus' appearance before the walls of Jerusalem.[74] Tacitus was also aware of the divisions within the Jewish camp, and he describes the tripartite division of the city among the three leaders: Simon Bar Giora, John of Gischala, and the priest Eleazar ben Simon (*Hist.* 5.12.13).[75]

---

71. Stern, *GLAJJ* 2:179. Appian has routinely been cited by those who claim that Bar-Kokhba conquered Jerusalem and therefore the city was destroyed by Hadrian. But Appian's statement that the city was destroyed is unclear, for, as already noted, in Pompey's time only the walls were destroyed. In fact, elsewhere (*Mithridates liber*, 106.498) Appian reports only that Pompey "captured their holiest city, Jerusalem" (Stern, *GLAJJ* 2:560).

72. Thus Ammianus Marcellinus, *Res gestae* 14.8.12 (Stern, *GLAJJ* 2:604).

73. Stern, *GLAJJ* 2:53.

74. Tacitus claims that Vespasian almost succeeded in completing the war with the Jews, with the laying of the siege being the only obstacle, coupled with the blind "*superstitio*"' of the Jews (*Hist.* 2.4.3).

75. The division he describes is identical to that of Josephus (*J.W.* 5.248–254). On this, and some minor differences that nevertheless do appear, see Stern, *GLAJJ* 2:59.

An account of the fall of Jerusalem is missing in Tacitus' report,[76] but he does record the appearance of all sorts of celestial omens that foretold the imminent destruction. His statement about the ancient Jewish prophecies that "this was the very time when the east should grow strong and that men starting from Judaea should possess the world" appears to be a definite allusion to messianic beliefs that encouraged the rebels, and very similar expectations are described by Josephus as well (*J.W.* 6.312). Both historians interpreted the prophecies as pointing to Vespasian and Titus. It appears that prophecies about the transfer of rule in the world to different Eastern elements were widespread among various Roman circles, and Suetonius also relates that astrologers had promised Nero rule of the East, "expressly naming sovereignty of Jerusalem" (*Nero* 40).[77]

Roman historiography was keenly aware of the emotional ties that continued to exist between the Jews and the city of Jerusalem, and the most explicit testimony of this may be Cassius Dio's explanation of the causes of the Bar-Kokhba uprising:

> At Jerusalem he [= Hadrian] founded a city in place of the one which had been razed to the ground, naming it Aelia Capitolina, and on the site of the temple of the god he raised a new temple to Jupiter. This brought on a war of no slight importance nor of brief duration. For the Jews deemed it intolerable that foreign races should be settled in their city and foreign religious rites planted there. (*Hist. rom.* 69.12.1–2)

Many years and bloody confrontations would have to pass before Roman historians would realize how far-fetched was Strabo's claim that Jerusalem "was not a place that would be looked on with envy, nor yet one for which anyone would make a serious fight."

Conclusion

It appears that Greek and Roman authors were keenly aware of the bond between Jerusalem and the Jewish nation, throughout the Second Temple period and in the immediate aftermath of the destruction. Two authors, Tacitus and Eutropius, referred to it as the nation's "capital," and the

---

76. In addition to Josephus, the fullest description of the armed confrontation in Jerusalem led by Titus in the final days and up to the destruction is provided by Cassius Dio, *Hist. rom.* 67.4–7.

77. Suetonius mentions Jerusalem a number of times; in his words about Augustus (*Aug.* 93) he claims that the emperor praised his grandson Gaius for not praying in Jerusalem while passing through Judea. He also describes Titus' actions in the final stages of the war, claiming that in the final attack on Jerusalem "he slew twelve of the defenders with as many arrows," taking the city on his daughter's birthday (*Tit.* 5:2).

foundation of the city became a staple in the ethnographic accounts of the origins of the Jewish people. The story of the exodus, in all its variant versions known to Greek authors, almost always ends with the founding of Jerusalem. In addition, there was no lack of attempts to insert the founding of the city into Egyptian and Greek mythology. Side by side, Tacitus recounts the attempts to connect the founding of the city with the Solymites, mentioned favorably by Homer, and with Hierosolymus and Iuda, the sons of the Egyptian god Typhon. Attempts to label any given story as having a Jewish connection were frequently achieved by attaching to it the name Jerusalem, as did Manetho in his version of the Hyksos tradition. One could have read his entire account without being aware of any connection to Jewish history, but as soon as he concluded his narrative by stating that those banished from Egypt built a city named Jerusalem, he contextualized the story within a contemporary framework that could only arouse animosity toward the Jews within certain Egyptian circles. From a city with "a remarkably odd name" (Clearchus of Soli) Jerusalem had indeed become "the most famous city of the East".

No Ancient Judaism

DANIEL BOYARIN
University of California – Berkeley

In seeking to honor my friend and colleague of more than four decades, Professor Shaye Cohen, I have decided to abduct and conjoin several passages from my forthcoming book *Judaism: The Genealogy of a Modern Notion*[1] in the interest of bringing one of its central arguments into sharp focus in a forum for which it is supremely relevant.

In general, I would suggest, users of the language who utilize *Judaism* to refer to something that persists from Moses Our Rabbi to Moses Mendelssohn are indeed willy-nilly speaking normatively. They have an a priori idea of what Judaism *is* and believe that a certain essence can be traced in all forms of the alleged "religion" throughout this history; therefore, even if *Judaism* be a modern term, it picks out some unique and real thing in the world.[2] This is a perfectly legitimate sort of normative

---

1. Daniel Boyarin, *Judaism: The Genealogy of a Modern Notion*, Key Words for Jewish Studies (New Brunswick, NJ: Rutgers University Press, 2018).

2. I wish to add here that I have misconstrued the argument of Evan M. Zuesse, "Phenomenology of Judaism," in *The Encyclopaedia of Judaism*, ed. Jacob Neusner, Alan J. Avery-Peck, and William Scott Green (Leiden: Brill, 2005), vol. 3:1968–86 (consulted online on 5 July 2018, http://dx.doi.org/10.1163/1872-9029_EJ_COM_0141) in a previous publication of mine. He certainly does not exclude such entities as Karaism, Qumran, or the Sadducees from his phenomenology of Judaism. Indeed, he writes explicitly, "Applying these criteria, it will be seen that Ethiopian, Sadducean, and Karaite Judaism all conform to normative Judaism, as does, of course, Rabbinic Judaism." I regret my earlier sloppy reading of his essay. Nonetheless, I remain deeply skeptical of any attempts to construct a "Judaism" from the Bible to modernity that can be described phenomenologically as a singular and uniform phenomenon. Perhaps the blindness is mine, but I continue not to understand claims such as, "Judaism therefore is different from the folkist religions and even from its daughter religions. It is the only religion in antiquity (or even in the modern period) to have arisen de novo by creating its own people and explicitly structuring the entire society in terms of religious norms. The ideals are at the source of the society, not the other way around." Whence came this religion? Presumably, and on reading further in Zuesse, for sure, from G-d: "The source of scriptural norms was therefore not the people but God and the one-time revelation that created the people, preserved in Judaism's scriptures. This revelation is theological at root and is not merely to be determined by social-anthropological, historical, or other folkist criteria." This hardly sounds like phenomenology to me but the most traditional

statement, a theological claim if you will—and, as such, successful within a given language game, but hardly one that is justifiable within the language game of historiography.

The best example of such an approach outside of the pulpit would be George Foot Moore's works, especially as signified by his aptly titled, "The Rise of Normative Judaism." Moore (15 October 1851–16 May 1931) was one of the most respected scholars of his time (with good reason) and taught generations of students at Harvard. It is easy to get a sense of Moore's approach from the very opening of this extended essay:

> THE centuries which we designate politically by the names of the dominant powers of the age successively as the Persian, Greek, and Roman periods of Jewish history constitute as a whole an epoch in the religious history of Judaism. In these centuries, past the middle of which the Christian era falls, Judaism brought to complete development its characteristic institutions, the school and the synagogue, in which it possessed, not only a unique instrument for the education and edification of all classes of the people in religion and morality, but the centre of its religious life, and to no small extent also of its intellectual and social life. Through the study of the Scriptures and the discussions of generations of scholars it defined its religious conceptions, its moral principles, its forms of worship, and its distinctive type of piety, as well as the rules of law and observance which became authoritative for all succeeding time. In the light of subsequent history, the great achievement of these centuries was the creation of a normative type of Judaism and its establishment in undisputed supremacy throughout the wide Jewish world.[3]

It is clear already—and Moore goes on to state explicitly—that this stipulative "normative Judaism," which really for him means "Judaism" *tout court*, is the Judaism defined by the Mishnah. Startlingly, for Moore, "Judaism" is so reified that it can actually have agency: "Judaism saw in [Ezra] the restorer of the law."[4] This "Judaism" manifests, for Moore as "rabbinic texts," as becomes lucidly explicit in his further citations. Thus, with respect to the introduction of the Mishnah known as the Chapters of the Fathers, Moore writes:

> With the authenticity of these utterances we are not here concerned; what is beyond question is that they are set down at the beginning of the Sen-

form of transcendental theology. In any case, Zuesse explicitly describes his own account as normative, so we are essentially in agreement. See too Evan M. Zuesse, "Five Types of Judaism? Reflections on the Inner Logic of Judaism as Revealed by Niebuhr's Phenomenological Typology," *Review of Rabbinic Judaism* 5 (2005): 430–51.

3. George Foot Moore, *The Rise of Normative Judaism* (Cambridge, MA: Reprinted from *HTR* 17 [1924] 307–73 and 18 [1925] 1–38), 307.

4. Ibid., 308.

> tences of the Fathers as recognized fundamentals of Judaism, and if any one should choose to rename the collection "Maxims of the Pharisees," the significance of the sayings would not be diminished.[5]

Moore's work is admirable, and his scholarship is excellent in its studious effort to redeem "Judaism" from the prejudiced anti-Judaism of many of his peers and predecessors among Protestant Bible scholars, and in part that effort conditions his very exclusive identification of the ideologies and practices of the Rabbis (= the Pharisees, for him) with the very essence of "Judaism." His view of things on this score is entirely consonant with that of Orthodox Jewish tradition. Since it has been established by historians by now that it was not the case that even after Yavneh the Pharisees and then the Rabbis were the de facto leaders of Palestinian Jewry, let alone world Jewry, acceptance of this narrative must be counted a normative judgment, one that a historical scholarship cannot countenance. What is more to the point is that, as I would suggest, any assertion of there having been a "Judaism" as an essential object involves such normative judgments.

In another crucial paper, Moore shows that he understands well the issue itself, even if, of course, not as applicable to his own work, writing that "Christian investigation and discussion of the terms Memra and Shekinah have thus in all stages been inspired and directed by a theological motive, and the results come around in a circle to the theological prepossessions from which they set out."[6] Thus, in this very paper, for instance, Moore excludes a particular interpretation implying a divine intermediary owing alone to the alleged total absence of a comparable idea in any "exoteric teaching of Judaism."[7] By this he must indeed mean, as I have already shown, the putative "Judaism" of the Mishnah and its sequels, for had he had recourse to the texts known as Pseudepigrapha, he would have found ample evidence for the ideas of divine intermediaries.[8] As Annette Yoshiko Reed sums up Moore's intervention, she finds him "refracting Second Temple Judaism through yet another later lens and claiming Rabbinic sources as the crux of a timelessly normative Judaism from which 'pseudepigrapha' (and earliest Christianity) are categorically excluded" (Reed in an unpublished paper). It would hardly be inapposite to refer to Moore's linear history of the rise of "normative Judaism" and its eventual triumph over all, false, rivals as exactly what Walter Benjamin

---

5. Ibid., 327.
6. George Foot Moore, "Intermediaries in Jewish Theology: Memra, Shekinah, Metatron," *HTR* 15 (1922): 42.
7. Ibid., 55.
8. Daniel Boyarin, "Daniel 7, Intertextuality, and the History of Israel's Cult," *HTR* 105 (2012): 135–62.

has famously elegized: "The nature of this sadness stands out more clearly if one asks with whom the adherents of historicism actually empathize. The answer is inevitable: with the victor." Put more crudely, Churchill described this as writing the history of the winners. My contention here is that hypostases such as "Judaism," when they are not attested within the language of a given culture, nearly inevitably—try as we might to avoid this result—lead to consequences structurally like those of Moore. My first task in this paper, then, will be to show that there was no such signifier in ancient Jewish writing.

Was There Any Ancient Judaism Then?

Steve Mason famously argued against the meaningful usage of the term *Judaism* in antiquity.[9] I have strongly assented to his position, which I am developing further here. Seth Schwartz makes two arguments against the claim that there is no "Judaism" as the name of a "religion" in antiquity. The first is based on Shaye Cohen's argument from so-called conversion.[10] The argument runs as follows: if there was a "religious" ceremony by which others became Jews, then Judaism was necessarily a religion. To be sure, this argument begs the question by assuming the existence or relevance of a "religious" ceremony as opposed to some other kind of ceremony. Furthermore, Schwartz, in defending Cohen against Mason, somewhat misunderstands Mason's point, in my opinion. The point is not that peoplehood [*ethnos*, *genos*, or even *polis*] did not incorporate a strong cultic component in antiquity, but precisely that worship and peoplehood are so inextricably tied to each other in antiquity that moving from one people to another (or even from the province of one *polis* to another) necessarily involved adopting new gods and new practices associated with them. With her usual clarity and pithiness, Paula Fredriksen has argued, "Jews may be one of the few Western groups now for whom ethnicity and religion closely coincide, [but in antiquity] it was the least odd thing about them."[11] And as Elizabeth Castelli has well phrased this very point with respect to the Romans:

> From the vantage point of a post-Enlightenment society that understands the separation of the political and the religious as an ideal to be protected, the Roman imperial situation requires careful attention to the myriad

---

9. Steve Mason, "Jews, Judaeans, Judaizing, Judaism: Problems of Categorization in Ancient History," *JSJ* 38 (2007): 457–512.

10. Shaye J. D. Cohen, *The Beginnings of Jewishness: Boundaries, Varieties, Uncertainties*, HCS 31 (Berkeley: University of California Press, 1998).

11. Paula Fredriksen, "Mandatory Retirement: Ideas in the Study of Christian Origins Whose Time Has Come to Go," *SR* 35 (2006): 231–46.

> ways in which "Roman religion" might, it could be defensibly argued, not quite exist. That is, insofar as practices that could conventionally be called "religious" intersected so thoroughly with political institutions, social structures, familial commitments, and recognition of the self-in-society, there is very little in ancient Roman society that would not as a consequence qualify as "religious."[12]

For the most part, this inextricable tie holds with respect to Judeans in antiquity as well, with only one nonconclusive exception. On the one hand, the case of the so-called "conversion" (forced) of the Idumeans and similar cases fits this notion of an inextricable linkage well; they were annexed to the Judeans and thus required to behave accordingly. On the other hand, Cohen and Schwartz are undoubtedly correct to point to the conversion of Antiochus in 2 Macc 9:17 who "becomes a Jew" [Ιουδαῖον ἔσεσθαι][13] as a case in which he "becomes a Jew" without stopping to be a Seleucid, providing us with the single case from antiquity of one who becomes a *Ioudaios* while retaining a non-*Ioudaios* "ethnic" identity. The second case adduced by them, however, goes exactly in the opposite direction. Achior in Judith (14:10) does not become a Jew but "becomes added to the House of Israel": "When Achior saw all that the God of Israel had done, he believed firmly in God. So he was circumcised, and was added to the house of Israel, remaining so to this day."[14] If anything, this strongly supports Mason's point. Achior didn't convert to a religion but, having learned to trust its god, he joined an *ethnos*. Following Cohen's reasoning adopted by Schwartz, after all, one could conclude that the Book of Ruth is evidence for conversion to "Judaism" as well. Moreover, as has been recently shown, the rejection of any notion of the possibility of assimilation to the Jewish People was much more widespread than Schwartz recognized at the time of his writing.[15] Acknowledging, then, the significance of the single case in Maccabees as perhaps a harbinger of something yet to come, it remains the case that Mason was correct in seeing Judean identity as parallel, *grosso modo*, with such identities as Ephesian, Athenian, and Roman.

Schwartz, however, makes yet another point against Mason (and thus implicitly against me as well). Arguing that "the Jews' religion was

12. Elizabeth A. Castelli, *Martyrdom and Memory: Early Christian Culture Making*, Gender, Theory, and Religion (New York: Columbia University Press, 2004), chapter 2.

13. Seth Schwartz, "How Many Judaisms Were There? A Critique of Neusner and Smith on Definition and Mason and Boyarin on Categorization," *JAJ* 2:233.

14. ἰδὼν δὲ Αχιὼρ πάντα, ὅσα ἐποίησεν ὁ Θεὸς τοῦ Ισραήλ, ἐπίστευσε τῷ Θεῷ σφόδρα καὶ περιετέμετο τὴν σάρκα τῆς ἀκροβυστίας αὐτοῦ καὶ προσετέθη πρὸς τὸν οἶκον Ισραὴλ ἕως τῆς ἡμέρας ταύτης.

15. Matthew Thiessen, *Contesting Conversion: Genealogy, Circumcision, and Identity in Ancient Judaism and Christianity* (New York: Oxford University Press, 2011).

unusually tightly integrated and its administration was concentrated in the hands of an unusually unified clerisy," he wishes to derive from this point the conclusion that the Jews did, in fact, have a religion which we might as well name "Judaism." Formally, at least, this is a classic example of *petitio principii*, otherwise known as "begging the question," assuming the conclusion in the premises themselves. Beginning his sentence with the subject, "The Jews' religion" disqualifies it a priori as an argument for the existence of such an entity. What of the substance of the argument, however? Schwartz finds it very telling that the Jews around the world converge in certain practices and diverge in others. The question still remains whether the name for the practices in which they converge ought to be Judaism, a religion, or not. The actual evidence, therefore, for Schwartz's claim that "even before the rise of Christianity some people did think in terms of Judaism, in a sense much like the modern one"[16] is to all intents and purposes, nonexistent or, at any rate, so rare as to be inconsequential. Moreover, his sequel: "and others thought that allegiance to the Jewish God and acceptance of his laws made you not simply pious but Jewish," actually serves well the present argument.

Does *Ioudaismos* Mean Judaism? 2 Maccabees and Paul

Cognoscenti will immediately object: but there is a term in ancient Judean writing that means Judaism (and is, moreover, precisely cognate to it), to wit Judeo-Greek *Ioudaismos*. The burden of the present section is, then, to demonstrate that this is not the case.

In an article published in Hebrew some years ago, Yehoshua Amir gathered the material on the word *Ioudaismos* as it appears from the pens of Jews. Considering all of it together (a total of seven attestations, four of which are found in one context), Amir opines, "Following the first survey of the material, it is possible to sum up that the word Ιουδαϊσμός represents the complex of behavior that is obligated by the fact that someone is a Jew and that this behavior is considered a value for which it is worthy to fight and even to die."[17] As Amir shows, and the point is well known indeed, nouns in *-ismos* are the verbal nouns formed from verbs in *-izō* quite regularly in Greek (he claims over a thousand examples). The important question, then, is what does the verb from which the noun is derived

16. S. Schwartz, "How Many Judaisms?," 238.

17. Yehoshua Amir, "The Term Ιουδαϊσμός: On the Self Understanding of Hellenistic Judaism," in *Proceedings of the Fifth World Congress of Jewish Studies, the Hebrew University, Mount Scopus-Givat Ram, Jerusalem, Jerusalem [sic], 3–11 August, 1969* (Jerusalem: World Union of Jewish Studies, 1972–1973), 264.

mean. There are quite a number of *-izō* verbs derived from proper nouns in which the verb means acting like a member of a group, or identifying with a group, so *mēdizō* would mean acting like a Mede or taking the side of the Medes. Amir points out that this is usually assigned to someone who is not a Mede himself, and it is frequently a pejorative term.[18] *Hellēnismos*, on the other hand, is something to which Greeks aspire, namely, the proper usage of the Greek language in writing, while *barbarismos* is the opposite of that (a usage still current in English where an error can be called a "barbarism"). In the Jewish usage, however, in 2 Maccabees, the term *Hellēnismos* is used by Jews with reference to other Jews who act like Greeks and are loyal to the Greek cause, thus similar to *Medismos* in the mouths of Greeks.[19] Here, however, is where I part company with Amir. Amir regards the development of this usage of *Hellēnismos* as issuing from the need for the Jewish writer to have a word that means "all of the signs of Hellenistic culture as one entity," because he wants *Ioudaismos* to function as such for Judeans, and he requires a word that is opposite to *Ioudaismos*. *Ioudaismos* is, moreover, according to Amir, a unique term marking the fact that it was only the Judeans of all the peoples in the Mediterranean world who deemed it necessary to have a name for all the signs of their own culture as one entity. In other words, according to Amir, first came the desire for a word that means "Judaism," and thence *Hellēnismos* as its opposite.[20]

Disagreeing with Amir as to the uniqueness in sense of *Ioudaismos*, Mason insists that *Ioudaismos* is no different in sense from the other ethnic verbal nouns in *-ismos* and remarks that Amir's argument of a unique status for *Ioudaismos* as the only noun in the entire ancient world that represents an entire culture or religion,

> seems a lot to claim for a word that is absent from all Hellenistic-Judaean texts but 2 and 4 Maccabees, completely passed over by Graeco-Roman observers of the *Ioudaioi*, and unparalleled even in contemporaneous Hebrew or Aramaic. A better explanation of this rarity, in light of the usage of parallel forms (above), seems to be that the particular circumstances calling for the usage of this word, which always risked negative connotations, rarely occurred.[21]

---

18. Amir, "Term Ιουδαϊσμός," 265.

19. See, e.g., 2 Macc 4:13: ἦν δ' οὕτως ἀκμή τις Ἑλληνισμοῦ καὶ πρόσβασις ἀλλοφυλισμοῦ διὰ τὴν τοῦ ἀσεβοῦς καὶ οὐκ ἀρχιερέως Ἰάσωνος ὑπερβάλλουσαν ἀναγνείαν, which Schwartz translates: "And there was such an apogee of Hellenism and inroad of foreignism due to the extreme impurity of that impious and unhighpriestly Jason." In a context in which behaving ("improperly") like a Greek would be designed *Hellēnismos* and even *allophylismos*, acting like a foreigner, can be found, it is hardly surprising to find the antonym of these as *Ioudaismos*.

20. Amir, "Term Ιουδαϊσμός," 266.

21. Mason, "Jews, Judaeans, Judaizing, Judaism," 465.

So far so good. Mason sees *Ioudaismos* as back-formed from *Hellēnismos*, which I will presently suggest is more plausible than the opposite. In my opinion, however, Mason overstates the case, insisting that *Ioudaismos* consists of a countermovement against *Hellēnismos* engaged in bringing back, that is, Judaizing (in the transitive sense), the Judean defectors to *Hellēnismos*:

> Judas' antidote to this Hellenizing (Ἑλληνισμός) was a counter-movement, a bringing back of those who had gone over to foreign ways: a "Judaizing" or Judaization, which the author of 2 Maccabees programmatically labels Ἰουδαϊσμός. The noun appears only in such contexts as these, evidently, because of its inherent sense of (re)alignment. This programme of Judas Maccabeus and his Asidaeans in 2 Maccabees (cf. 14.6) is not then "Judaism" as a system of life, but a newly coined counter-measure against Ἑλληνισμός.[22]

Let us review the argument. In pre-Christian antiquity, the term *Ioudaismos* appears essentially in only one literary context, namely, the accounts of the resistance of the Maccabees to *Hellēnismos*. Expanding implicitly but significantly on an argument that had been made earlier,[23] Mason argues that the word *Ioudaismos* appears only in this particular literary and historical context because it precisely fits that context and perhaps no other in Jewish antiquity.[24] It fits, moreover, into a paradigm of other terms formed the same way in Greek as a verbal noun from a particular kind of verb, neither of which has the slightest bit to do with the naming of a religion.[25] *Ioudaizō* would mean, in the same way, to act like a Judean, and the verbal noun formed from it, *Ioudaismos* would simply be the nominal form of that verb, so "acting like a Judean." No more, no less, just like *Hellēnismos*, acting, talking, writing like a Greek.[26] To get a sense of how

22. Ibid., 467.

23. Inter alia in Daniel Boyarin, "Semantic Differences: Linguistics and 'the Parting of the Ways,'" in *The Ways That Never Parted: Jews and Christians in Late Antiquity and the Early Middle Ages*, ed. Adam H. Becker and Annette Yoshiko Reed, TSAJ 95 (Tübingen: Mohr Siebeck, 2003), 65–85. The point about *Ioudaismos* had, moreover, already been anticipated as far back as Jonathan A. Goldstein, *II Maccabees: A New Translation with Introduction and Commentary*, AB 41A (New York: Doubleday, 1983).

24. Mason, "Jews, Judaeans, Judaizing, Judaism." Let it, nonetheless, be said clearly that (as Seth Schwartz has already noted), I have accepted some of Mason's conclusions and not others (I see, however, no flaw in that; we are, after all, dealing here in scholarly "facts" and their interpretation, not authority).

25. Cf. Martha Himmelfarb, "Judaism and Hellenism in 2 Maccabees," *Poetics Today* 19 (1998): 196. I think that Himmelfarb gets this one (uncharacteristically) exactly upside down. Starting from *Ioudaismos* as the given and translating it as "Judaism," she assumes that *Hellēnismos* here must mean "Hellenism," not "hellenizing."

26. It does need to be conceded that, as attested in the literature, *Hellēnismos* generally is used positively and quite restricted to writing style. Nonetheless, given the productivity of

active this kind of formation was in Greek, it should be enough to cite the following humorous example: Kenneth Dover cites the appearance of the word *euripidaristophanizein* ("to act like Euripides and Aristophanes"), penned by a rival comic poet who considered Aristophanes entirely too intellectual by half.[27] The hypothetical verbal noun from the verb would be exactly *euripidaristophanismos*, hardly the name of an institution, an abstraction, a religion, or even an entire cultural pattern. Hence, Mason is on good comparative lexical grounds in denial of such an idiosyncratic interpretation to the one single form from this highly productive Greek paradigm, *Ioudaismos*.

To be sure, as Seth Schwartz has well remarked, Mason's reading will work fine perhaps for such contexts as 2 Macc 14:37. (Although I disagree with Daniel Schwartz's interpretation of this passage at a key point, I shall nonetheless cite here his excellent translation, only exchanging *Ioudaismos*—the term in question—for Schwartz's "Judaism"):

> Someone informed to Nicanor about Raziz, one of the elders of Jerusalem—a man who loved his fellow-citizens and had a very good reputation, who due to the goodwill toward him was called "Father of the Jews." In the foregoing times of strife he had brought in a decision for *Ioudaismos* and with complete intensity had risked body and soul for *Ioudaismos*.[28]

In this passage, it is indeed quite easy to see how having made a decision for *Ioudaismos* means deciding for loyalty to the Judean ways and polity and even for a revival movement meant to reinvigorate such feelings in the backsliders. However, regarding a passage such as 2 Macc 8:1, the case is much harder to make:

> Judas Maccabaeus and those with him, on the other hand, had been going in and out and around secretly to the villages, summoning their kinsmen and those who remained in *Ioudaismos*.[29]

---

this paradigm, and especially its utility for "othering," *hellēnizō* would seem to be a perfectly ordinary formation to indicate Judeans acting like Greeks and being loyal to the Hellenic cause.

27. Kenneth James Dover, *Aristophanic Comedy* (Berkeley: University of California Press, 1972), 214.

28. Ραζὶς δέ τις τῶν ἀπὸ Ιεροσολύμων πρεσβυτέρων ἐμηνύθη τῷ Νικάνορι, ἀνὴρ φιλοπολίτης καὶ σφόδρα καλῶς ἀκούων καὶ κατὰ τὴν εὔνοιαν πατὴρ τῶν Ιουδαίων προσαγορευόμενος. 38 ἦν γὰρ ἐν τοῖς ἔμπροσθεν χρόνοις τῆς ἀμειξίας κρίσιν εἰσενηνεγμένος Ιουδαϊσμοῦ, καὶ σῶμα καὶ ψυχὴν ὑπὲρ τοῦ Ιουδαϊσμοῦ παραβεβλημένος μετὰ πάσης ἐκτενίας. Translation of Daniel R. Schwartz, *2 Maccabees*, CEJL (Berlin: de Gruyter, 2008), 465.

29. Ιουδας δὲ ὁ καὶ Μακκαβαῖος καὶ οἱ σὺν αὐτῷ παρεισπορευόμενοι λεληθότως εἰς τὰς κώμας προσεκαλοῦντο τοὺς συγγενεῖς καὶ τοὺς μεμενηκότας ἐν τῷ Ιουδαϊσμῷ προσλαμβανόμενοι συνήγαγον εἰς ἑξακισχιλίους.

As Seth Schwartz has correctly observed, it is much more difficult to understand the term here as referring to this recovery operation.[30] We need not, however, go from there to taking *Ioudaismos* here as meaning "something very much like Judaism,"[31] as that would presuppose a lexically and grammatically sui generis development of the vocable and the paradigm to which it belongs in this and only this context out of all of Greek literature. If we translate in both cases simply as fealty to the ways and cause of the Jews, then I think there is no difficulty. In the first instance, we find Razis jeopardizing life and limb for the Jewish way of life, while in the second case, those who had remained "in *Ioudaismos*" means those who had remained loyal to the historical practices—the *nomoi* or the *ethē* of the *patrie*—of the Judeans. *Ioudaismos* means the practice of such loyalty. The correct translation would be "had remained in Judaizing," or perhaps better "Jewing!"

As Mason correctly notes, it is only in Christian usage that *ioudaizō* has religious moment, per se. See his note on the cognate grammatical form *romaizō* in Josephus, *War* 2:562 as well:

> This is the only occurrence of ῥωμαΐζω in Josephus, and the first attestation in Greek literature, though from now on the verb begins to be used heavily by others: Dio Chrysostom (Or. 37.4), Appian (Annib. 177-78; Lib. 304-5; Mac. 7.1; Illyr. 40; Mithr. 5, 107, 109, 182; Bell. civ. 1.5.41; 2.13.91), Philostratus (Vit. Apoll. 5.36), Cassius Dio (50.6.4; 51.1.5). Once again, Josephus stands at the beginning of a trend. In form the verb belongs to a class that had gained prominence during the Persian and then Peloponnesian wars, half a millennium earlier: μηδίζω, περσίζω, λακωνίζω, ἀττικίζω—indicating political alignment with another (normally greater) city or power, usually a forced choice for weaker states in times of crisis (e.g., "Atticize or Laconize?"); cf. Thucydides 3.61.2; Xenophon, Hell. 6.3.14. Even if it was unavoidable, the identification with foreign states implied by the verb carried less-than-noble connotations. In the 2nd century BCE the author of 2 Maccabees ironically adjusted ἑλληνίζω, which had meant simply "to express oneself in Greek" and its condition Ἑλληνισμός for the same purpose: to indicate the shameful adoption of a Greek cultural program by Judean élites, to which he contrasted (with another neologism) the noble counter-measure of Ἰουδαϊσμός—the ongoing condition of the verb ἰουδαΐζω.... The appearance of ῥωμαΐζω in Josephus and his later Greek contemporaries may result from their reappropriation of the older Greek style that marked this period. Judaizing (*Ioudaismos*) is no more a religion than Atticizing is and, once again I emphasize that we do not have here an abstract noun for an institution but a verbal noun for

30. S. Schwartz, "How Many Judaisms?," 225.
31. Ibid., 226.

> an activity or set of activities (such as driving out the "barbarians" for instance or remaining steadfast in the commandments).[32]

Since *Ioudaismos* is formed grammatically from the verb *ioudaizō*, observing how that verb appears in a crucial Greek source—Josephus—ought to help us sort its meaning as the verbal noun as well. There are two occurrences of this verb in Josephus's corpus, both close to each other in *War*. The first is at 2.454:

> And thus were all these men barbarously murdered, excepting Metilius; for when he entreated for mercy, and promised that he would *ioudaizō*, and be circumcised, they saved him alive, but none else.[33]

The second is found only a few sentences later at 2.463:

> So the day time was spent in shedding of blood, and the night in fear, which was of the two the more terrible; for when the Syrians thought they had ruined the Jews, they had the *ioudaizontas* in suspicion also; and as each side did not care to slay those whom they only suspected on the other, so did they greatly fear them when they were mingled with the other, as if they were certainly foreigners.[34]

As Mason has remarked in his commentary ad loc., the only earlier usage of *ioudaizō* is to be found in the Septuagint to Esther, where it translates *mityahedim*, acting like Jews, even pretending to be Jews, in order to save their skins. Josephus's usage seems consistent, if not modeled, on that instance and incident. Although Josephus, as pointed out already, never uses *Ioudaismos*, his (rare) usage of the verb from which this gerund is derived, suggests a similar meaning as that which I have argued for in 2 Maccabees (with almost the opposite moral evaluation, however).

I, therefore, like Mason, disagree with Amir and maintain that *Hellēnismos* comes first with *Ioudaismos* a back formation, but I disagree with Mason somewhat about the semantic effect of the coinage. If we think of *Hellēnismos* in the mouths of Judeans about other Judeans as exactly analogous to the use of *Medismos* by Greeks about other Greeks, we can see easily that it is the primary term in this binary opposition. *Hellēnismos*, on this account, means acting like a Greek and being loyal to the Greek

---

32. Steve Mason, *Flavius Josephus: Translation and Commentary* (Leiden: Brill, 2000).

33. οἱ μὲν οὖν οὕτως ὠμῶς ἀπεσφάγησαν ἅπαντες πλὴν Μετιλίου, τοῦτον γὰρ ἱκετεύσαντα καὶ μέχρι περιτομῆς ἰουδαΐσειν ὑποσχόμενον διέσωσαν μόνον, τὸ δὲ πάθος Ῥωμαίοις μὲν ἦν κοῦφον, ἐκ γὰρ ἀπλέτου δυνάμεως ἀπαναλώθησαν ὀλίγοι, Ἰουδαίων δὲ προοίμιον ἁλώσεως ἔδοξεν.

34. καὶ τὰς μὲν ἡμέρας ἐν αἵματι διῆγον, τὰς δὲ νύκτας δέει χαλεπωτέρας· καὶ γὰρ ἀπεσκευάσθαι τοὺς Ἰουδαίους δοκοῦντες ἕκαστοι τοὺς ἰουδαΐζοντας εἶχον ἐν ὑποψίᾳ, καὶ τὸ παρ᾽ ἑκάστοις ἀμφίβολον οὔτε ἀνελεῖν τις προχείρως ὑπέμενεν καὶ μεμιγμένον ὡς βεβαίως ἀλλόφυλον ἐφοβεῖτο.

cause. *Ioudaismos* would be then seen as a natural back-formed opposite to indicate acting loyally to the Judean way of life and polity. Goldstein has made substantially the same point, arguing that "Greeks never forgot the history of the Persian wars of the sixth and fifth centuries B.C.E., in which one who deserted the cause of the Greeks to collaborate with their enemies was said to 'Medize.'... The implied antonyms of 'Medize' and 'Medism' were 'Hellenize' and 'Hellenism,' which would mean 'be loyal to the Greek cause.'"[35] I am suggesting precisely the same origin and semantics for *Ioudaismos*. This usage is, to be sure, it would seem, initially unique to Judeans, but it is a natural development in the particular circumstances of the Maccabean conflicts. The positive sense of *Ioudaismos*, acting like a Judean, is analogous to the positive sense of *Hellēnismos*, writing like a Greek, even though the latter is more restricted in its scope.[36] In other words, rather than seeing *Hellēnismos* as coined by Jews in order to have an opposition to *Ioudaismos,* I argue for the opposite: *Ioudaismos* was formed as the opposite to hellenizing disloyalty to mean Judaizing loyalty. It certainly does not attest, *pace* Amir and from Amir to Schwartz and thence to Davies, to an alleged new consciousness on the part of the Jews that they have a thing, an institution, a "Judaism." I believe that this will fit all of the ancient (pre-Christian) contexts well, avoiding Seth Schwartz's strictures, in that it does not involve "fancy exegesis," and that loyalty and adherence to Jewish (or Judean) ways is not reducible to being a member of a religion that we (now) call Judaism. Since all of the members of the paradigm of nouns of this form, the aforesaid *Medismos*, siding with the Persians, *Attikismos*, siding with Athens, are gerunds and not abstract nouns, there is no justification to read *Ioudaismos* as other than such a gerund as well. To be sure, in Greek, as far as I know, only *Ioudaismos*, *Rōmaizo* ("speak Latin, hold with Rome, be of the Roman party [Appian]"), and *Hellēnismos* (in that sense of writing like a Greek) have positive valence, nonetheless it seems by far best to understand and translate it as "Judaizing," in the sense of acting like a Judean without going so far as Mason and asserting that it is a transitive verb always meaning returning other Jews to the fold.. (I speculate that had we Persian "loyalists" writing Greek, for them too *Hellēnismos* would be pejorative and *Medismos* a term of praise). Thus by somewhat softening up Mason's interpretation, I think that the major outlines of his argument can be strongly maintained.

If we examine, moreover, the last to be considered of the usages of the word in 2 Maccabees, we will see this suggestion borne out (or at the very least, uncontradicted). Thus, the very first time the word appears (in the world to the best of our knowledge), we find it in 2:21:

---

35. Goldstein, *II Maccabees*, 230 n. 13

36. Ibid., 230 n. 13.

> And the heavenly apparitions which occurred for those who nobly with manly valor strived for *Ioudaismos*.[37]

There were heavenly apparitions in honor of those who strived with one another for *Ioudaismos*.[38] There is no reason here not to imagine that *Ioudaismos* means exactly what it ought to, namely, dedication to the ways of the Judeans and partisanship for their cause against their oppressors, the "barbarians."[39] Only an a priori and anachronistic idea of *Ioudaismos* as an abstract name for a "religion" or the name of an institution would lead one to imagine "Judaism" here.

An important argument against the notion that *Ioudaismos* was conceived of as a "religion"—even *avant la lettre*—can be found in the text itself, in the letter of Antiochus V in 2 Maccabees 11:

> 22 The king's letter was as follows: "King Antiochus to his brother Lysias: greetings.
>
> 23 Now that our father has passed over to the gods, in our desire that the people of the kingdom be untroubled and take care of their own affairs, 24 and having heard that the Jews did not willingly concur in their change[40] to Greek ways by my father, but rather, preferring their own way of life, ask that their own regulations be allowed to them— 25 now then, in our policy that this people too should be untroubled, we have decided to restore the Temple to them and that they should conduct their civic behavior according to the customs of their ancestors. 26 So you will do well if you send to them and give them the right hand, so that in perceiving our policy they will be in good spirits and happily go about taking care of their own affairs"[41]

---

37. καὶ τὰς ἐξ οὐρανοῦ γενομένας ἐπιφανείας τοῖς ὑπὲρ τοῦ Ιουδαϊσμοῦ φιλοτίμως ἀνδραγαθήσασιν ὥστε τὴν ὅλην χώραν ὀλίγους ὄντας λεηλατεῖν καὶ τὰ βάρβαρα πλήθη διώκειν. Translation slightly modified from D. R. Schwartz, *2 Maccabees*, 170. See next note.

38. Goldstein writes "vied with one another," utilizing the more usual meaning of φιλοτίμως, while D. Schwartz translated "fought with manly vigor for *Ioudaismos*." My "strived for" is meant to capture this ambiguity.

39. Goldstein keenly observes, "Our verse contains the earliest known occurrence of the Greek word *Ioudaismos* ('Judaism'). The writer probably chose deliberately to use a word of this form in the same context as 'barbarian,' for he thus induced his literate Greek audience to remember the struggle of the loyal Hellenes against the 'barbarian' Persians and against the 'Medism' of Greek collaborators with the Persian empire" (*II Maccabees*, 192 n. 21).

40. I have converted Schwartz's "conversion" to "change," as Schwartz's translation rather sells the pass by using such a marked term as "conversion." The Greek is μεταθέσει, which might be translated as "displacement" also.

41. See also Cana Werman, "On Religious Persecution: A Study in Ancient and Modern Historiography," *Zion* 81 (2016): 18–19 (Hebrew with English summary). Werman cites the less clear second letter there vv. 27-37 rather than this one, but nonetheless reads that letter very similarly to my own interpretation of the significance of this one. See also next note.

Now what must be observed here is that nowhere in this text is there an indication that it was a religion, *Ioudaismos*, that had been under attack and was now being restored to freedom and legitimacy, but rather Judaic customs versus Greek customs, their "civic behavior"—indeed the "customs of the ancestors," just as we find in Josephus. To be sure, these are, at least ostensibly, the words of a Greek, not a Judean, but it is at least in part the *imaginaire* of those very Greeks that is in question here. We have here, in effect, an implicit interpretation of the terms *Ioudaismos* and *Hellēnismos*, the former being glossed as "preferring their own way of life" and "conducting their civic behavior according to the customs of their ancestors," while *Hellēnismos*, we may take it, is "changing to Greek ways." In that sense, it is perfectly intelligible that there would have been a party among the Judeans who rejected every possible accommodation to Greek culture, whether or not it involved a specific violation of the Torah.[42]

A very recent scholarly controversy will help us to understand the intervention being made here as well as to get a further glimpse at the stakes of the question. The controversy is around an interpretation of the Hasmonean revolt published by Sylvie Honigman in 2014.[43] I am not interested, nor competent, to judge the rights and wrongs of her historical reconstruction, which seems to my untutored eye to be both brilliant and flawed, but in how the failure to pursue certain theoretical moves to their logical conclusion undermines certain of the arguments of both Honigman and her opponents, especially Cana Werman.[44] The part of the question that concerns me here is, obviously, the interpretation of *Ioudaismos*. As I have argued in the first chapter of my forthcoming book, it is vain to even inquire whether something in the premodern world was "religious" or "political," as neither of these concepts had currency and any given discourse could be, *in our eyes*, one or the other, or both, while in antiquity the whole distinction is nugatory. Thus, although Honigman explicitly rejects the "instrumentalist" view whereby so-called religion is a smoke screen for so-called political objectives, she forgets the "so-called" too often and feels called upon to write sentences, "From this perspective, the contrasted pairing of *Ioudaismos* and *Hellēnismos* in 2 Maccabees can be seen to have a political connotation."[45] What Honigman seems to miss

42. Himmelfarb, "Judaism and Hellenism." Cf. Werman, "On Religious Persecution," 18–19. While I agree with Werman that this text all but refutes Honigman's thesis (see below immediately), it does little to support Werman's notion of a separate "religious" sphere either.

43. Sylvie Honigman, *Tales of High Priests and Taxes: The Books of the Maccabees and the Judean Rebellion Against Antiochos IV* (Berkeley: University of California Press, 2014).

44. Werman, "On Religious Persecution."

45. Honigman, *Tales of High Priests*, 145. Incidentally, I quite agree with her explanation of why *Ioudaismos* and *Hellēnismos* do not appear together in the same context in 2 Maccabees; namely, that they don't belong together within the narration, although I don't need to

is that by asserting that the persecution of the Judeans by the Seleucids was *not* a "religious persecution," she still accepts the existence and reality of the category "religion," to the same extent as her adversaries. Honigman makes an important step forward in realizing that the category of "religion" is anachronistic as applied to 2 Maccabees but undermines this insight by continuing to refer to politics, *as an alternative to "religion."*[46]

There certainly are elements of what *we would call* religious persecution related in 2 Maccabees, but there is nowhere the slightest indication that they considered it to be different from any other kind of persecution.[47] We need not—particularly I need not as I am not a positivist historian—dismiss them, explain them away, or account for them as "politics" incognito. The vital point to make is that, given that there is not the slightest shred of evidence for "religion" and "politics" as separate spheres in ancient Judea, it is impossible to engage in an argument of whether something is "religion" or "politics" within that cultural formation, within that form of life. No commentators, it seems, ever asked themselves whether

---

accept her construction of the text or her appeal to royal inscriptions to conclude thus. See also Erich Gruen, "Hellenism and Persecution: Antiochus IV and the Jews," in *Hellenistic History and Culture*, ed. Peter Green, HCS 9 (Berkeley: University of California Press, 1993), 238–64. The contrast is within the semantic system of the text as a whole not an immediate context. (Consequently, refuting her reconstruction of the royal narrative does not, *pace* Werman, force us to accept older interpretations). Finally, Honigman refers to *Ioudaismos* as an abstraction (e.g., Honigman, *Tales of High Priests*, 199) without once, to the best of my memory, attempting to demonstrate this anachronistic grammatical construal, while I argue, with Mason, that it is a verbal noun, a gerund, no more an abstraction than "walking" or "eating." Now, again, Honigman clearly gets the error of translating *Ioudaismos* and *Hellēnismos* as "Judaism" and "Hellenism" and then referring to their modern meanings, but she hasn't gone far enough.

46. So, for instance, Honigman writes, "Put simply, 'religion' ('Judaism') and 'culture' ('Hellenism') fail to match any recognizable semantic fields in the social and cultural environment of the author." So far, so excellent, but then "and therefore it is impossible that the author was restricting his own understanding of *Hellēnimos* to 'cultural' aspects" (Honigman, *Tales of High Priests*, 202). The problem here, of course, is that the notion that something refers to "culture," an anachronism as well to be sure, implies that it is out of the sphere of a putative "religion," rather than seeing that a culture, according to most modern construals, incorporated so-called religion (as well as the military, economic relations, etc.). Honigman's oddly restricted and restrictive sense of what "culture" means has led her quite widely astray (*Tales of High Priests*, 212), and moreover given power to her opponents.

47. I would like to clear up a bit of terminological unclarity that has entered our discourse, namely, the use of "second-order" to mean the application of *our* categories to cultures that demonstrably made no such distinctions. In truth, this is correctly designated "third-order reflection," the first order being the phenomena themselves, the second order the categories made by the people being studied, the third the application of anachronistic categories of our own. As I have made eminently clear by now, I have no interest in such third-order analysis, as it teaches us about ourselves primarily; it is the second order that captures my attention, with thanks to Anders Klostergaard Petersen for the terminological clarification, although he himself *does* seek the third order. What interests me is the categories that *they* made—and the categories that they didn't make.

a given persecution, building a *gymnasion*, or eating pig was a religious persecution or a political one.

Ioudaismos may be the name for a righteous social order as Honigman claims, and one of that sort may have been refounded by Judas, but it makes no sense to claim that *Ioudaismos*'s only extension is the order founded by Judas. Similarly, when the text says, "and the heavenly apparitions which occurred for those who nobly fought with manly valor for *Ioudaismos*, so that although they were few number they plundered the entire country and chased away the barbarian hordes and retook the temple which was spoken of throughout the entire civilized world and liberated the city, and firmly reestablished the laws that were about to be abolished, the Lord having become merciful toward them in total grace—" (2 Macc 2:21–22),[48] it indicates that *Ioudaismos* was an existing thing for which these soldiers fought. *Ioudaismos* is, in short, the social order that obtained in Judea in the time of Seleukos IV and Onias; it is being fought for and ultimately *re*-established by Judas and his followers. This does not constitute a semantic conflation of *Ioudaismos* with the activity of Judas and his men.[49] An analogy: there is a political party in the United States called the Democrats, which presumably fights for democracy, but certainly does not imply that the word/concept *democracy* is applicable only when speaking about the U.S. Democratic party! It, accordingly, strikes me as slightly preposterous to imagine that "the label (*Ioudaismos*) refers to the rules of a particular dynasty."[50] Rather say: *Ioudaismos* is an ideal that the author of 2 Maccabees considers realized in his time (or the time he writes about) only in and by the Hasmonean dynasty—quite a different kettle of fish.

By far, then, in my opinion, the most compelling interpretation of *Ioudaismos* is that it follows the semantic/grammatical pattern so well attested

48. 21 καὶ τὰς ἐξ οὐρανοῦ γενομένας ἐπιφανείας τοῖς ὑπὲρ τοῦ Ἰουδαϊσμοῦ φιλοτίμως ἀνδραγαθήσασιν ὥστε τὴν ὅλην χώραν ὀλίγους ὄντας λεηλατεῖν καὶ τὰ βάρβαρα πλήθη διώκειν 22 καὶ τὸ περιβόητον καθ' ὅλην τὴν οἰκουμένην ἱερὸν ἀνακομίσασθαι καὶ τὴν πόλιν ἐλευθερῶσαι καὶ τοὺς μέλλοντας καταλύεσθαι νόμους ἐπανορθῶσαι τοῦ κυρίου μετὰ πάσης ἐπιεικείας ἵλεω γενομένου αὐτοῖς

49. I, therefore, agree with Werman's rejection of Honigman's explanation of *Ioudaismos* but not for the same reasons (Werman, "On Religious Persecution," 16–18). Our differences emerge especially on p. 17, where Werman assumes that refutation of Honigman's interpretation necessitates a return to the notion that there is a religion ("a personal religion" no less) called "Judaism" in antiquity. In fine, my own reading of *Ioudaismos/Hellēnismos* is closer to Werman than to Honigman but does not support in any way the idea central to Werman's argument of a distinct "religious" persecution, still less of the existence of *yahadut* (a verbal anachronism by about a millennium and a conceptual one of about two millennia, as documented extensively in Boyarin, *Judaism*). Werman simply assumes that if Honigman can be dismissed then we are perforce left with the older historical doctrine of a "religion" called *yahadut*, quite thoroughly disregarding all other scholarship and all other published ideas and interpretations.

50. Honigman, *Tales of High Priests*, 145.

in Greek (Amir's one thousand examples) of acting in a certain way (generally "ethnic" but not by any means always). That is, that it means, to behave as a Judean, sincerely or not as the case may be. It is indeed, if not the opposite, a member of the paradigm that includes *Hellēnismos* and in contrast with it, as well. As such, 2 Maccabees [4:11–14a] states:

> Indeed, [Jason] abrogating the benevolent royal privileges which had been fixed for the Jews through the agency of Johanan and abolishing the regular civic usages, he innovated lawless practices. With relish he laid the foundations for a gymnasium directly beneath the acropolis, making the strongest of the ephebes submit to (wearing) sun-hats. There was such an apex of *Hellenismos* and inroad of foreignism [*allophylismos*] due to the extreme impurity of that impious and unhighpriestly Jason that the priests were no longer enthusiastic about the altar ministries. Rather, in their disdain for the Temple, and in their lack of concern for sacrifices, they hurried to participate in the lawless distributions in the palaestra which followed upon the call of the discus; Considering the ancestral values to be worthless, they considered the Greek honors to be the best.[51] (trans. D. Schwartz)

Once again, we have a fairly clear set of glosses on *Hellēnismos*, wearing funny Greek-style hats, exercising in a gymnasium, losing interest in the temple and sacrifices, and preferring sporting competitions. On the other hand, we may with a fair degree of confidence conclude that continuing "the regular civic usages" is what is known in this book as *Ioudaismos*. In neither this nor the above such catalogue discussed are specifically "religious" violations singled out as such, as a separate category and a separate semantic field. The argument is not, of course, that the issue is secular as opposed to religious or political as opposed to religious but that those very distinctions do not obtain for this text and for this form of life. From the above discussion I conclude that by far the best way of interpreting *Ioudaismos* is following the Judean way of life, sacrifices, temples, kings, taxes, everything, what Josephus refers to as the *nomoi* of the Fathers and the practices of the *politeuma*.

51. 11 καὶ τὰ κείμενα τοῖς Ιουδαίοις φιλάνθρωπα βασιλικὰ διὰ Ιωάννου τοῦ πατρὸς Εὐπολέμου τοῦ ποιησαμένου τὴν πρεσβείαν ὑπὲρ φιλίας καὶ συμμαχίας πρὸς τοὺς Ῥωμαίους παρώσας καὶ τὰς μὲν νομίμους καταλύων πολιτείας παρανόμους ἐθισμοὺς ἐκαίνιζεν 12 ἀσμένως γὰρ ὑπ' αὐτὴν τὴν ἀκρόπολιν γυμνάσιον καθίδρυσεν καὶ τοὺς κρατίστους τῶν ἐφήβων ὑποτάσσων ὑπὸ πέτασον ἤγαγεν 13 ἦν δ' οὕτως ἀκμή τις Ἑλληνισμοῦ καὶ πρόσβασις ἀλλοφυλισμοῦ διὰ τὴν τοῦ ἀσεβοῦς καὶ οὐκ ἀρχιερέως Ἰάσωνος ὑπερβάλλουσαν ἀναγνείαν 14 ὥστε μηκέτι περὶ τὰς τοῦ θυσιαστηρίου λειτουργίας προθύμους εἶναι τοὺς ἱερεῖς ἀλλὰ τοῦ μὲν νεὼ καταφρονοῦντες καὶ τῶν θυσιῶν ἀμελοῦντες ἔσπευδον μετέχειν τῆς ἐν παλαίστρῃ παρανόμου χορηγίας μετὰ τὴν τοῦ δίσκου πρόσκλησιν 15 καὶ τὰς μὲν πατρῴους τιμὰς ἐν οὐδενὶ τιθέμενοι τὰς δὲ Ἑλληνικὰς δόξας καλλίστας ἡγούμενοι.

The Pauline Moment

This interpretation explains well the usage of *Ioudaismos* in the Pauline epistles as well. Paul's usage of *Ioudaismos* seem also to bear out the interpretation of *Ioudaismos* as a verbal noun, a practice and not an abstraction. Paradoxically his usage in Galatians has typically been taken as evidencing the exact opposite. The most important passage is Gal 1:13–14, where we read [words to be discussed below are left untranslated]: "For you have heard of my *anastrophē* then in *Ioudaismos,* how I persecuted the congregation of God and tried to destroy it. And I had advanced in *Ioudaismos* beyond many of my own age among my people, so extravagantly zealous was I for the traditions of my ancestors." Let us begin with the word *anastrophē* usually translated as "life," as in "former life." Mason has argued, "The accompanying noun ἀναστροφή is stronger than '[my former] life,' as often translated (e.g., NRSV, ASV). It should indicate some sort of 'bent, inclination' or 'turning toward' something, 'a going back' to it, or a 'preoccupation' with it (cf. LSJ s.v.). The zeal mentioned in 1:14 confirms this sense."[52] Mason is right, in my opinion, that "former life" rather prejudices the case and does not correspond to the most frequent usages of this work in Greek. Once again, however, I think we need not go quite as far as he does, and I would prefer to translate "conduct," as we find it, for instance in Tob 4:14: *πρόσεχε σεαυτῷ, παιδίον, ἐν πᾶσι τοῖς ἔργοις σου καὶ ἴσθι πεπαιδευμένος ἐν πάσῃ ἀναστροφῇ σου,* where the last phrase translates well as "be well instructed in all of your conduct," paralleling the first clause, which would read "be careful in all of your works." Paul, then, would be referring to his former conduct in Judaizing, namely, his persecution of the Congregation of God. The use of *Ioudaismos* in the second verse makes this point even stronger. One does not advance in an institution, for instance, an alleged "religion" (except, perhaps, by being promoted within it, obviously inapplicable here), but in a practice, the practice of Judaizing in which Paul was more advanced because he was more learned and zealous than the others. Finally, Paul's usage of the verbal noun *Ioudaismos* must be interpreted with reference to his use of the verb as well. As remarked above, in Gal 2:14, Paul inveighs:

> But when I saw that they were not straightforward about the truth of the gospel, I said to Cephas before them all, "If you, though a *Ioudaios,* live like a gentile [*ethnikōs*] and not like a *Ioudaios* [*Ioudaikōs*], how do you force the gentiles to *Ioudaizein*?"[53]

52. Mason, "Jews, Judaeans, Judaizing, Judaism," 469.

53. ἀλλ' ὅτε εἶδον ὅτι οὐκ ὀρθοποδοῦσιν πρὸς τὴν ἀλήθειαν τοῦ εὐαγγελίου, εἶπον τῷ Κηφᾷ ἔμπροσθεν πάντων Εἰ σὺ Ἰουδαῖος ὑπάρχων ἐθνικῶς καὶ οὐκ Ἰουδαϊκῶς ζῇς, πῶς τὰ ἔθνη ἀναγκάζεις ἰουδαΐζειν;

which clearly means to live according to Judean ways as the opposite of living in the gentile manner. *Ioudaismos*, the noun derived from this verb, clearly means as well, then, Judaizing, living according to Judean ways and not being a member of an institution called "Judaism." That this is the case is shown by Mason's observation that "Paul denounces Peter because, though Peter allegedly lives as a foreigner [lit., ethnically DB] and not as a Judaean [Judaically, DB] (ἐθνικῶς καὶ οὐχὶ Ἰουδαϊκῶς), 'you compel the foreigners to Judaize' (τὰ ἔθνη ἀναγκάζεις ἰουδαΐζειν; Gal 2:14)—a cultural movement that Paul connects tightly with circumcision and observance of Judaean law (2:12, 21)."[54] Since ethnicizing is surely not observing a religion, neither is Judaizing here and hence certainly also not the noun derived quite regularly from this verb, *Ioudaismos*. Our honoree, I would argue, did well indeed to name his work, *The Beginnings of Jewishness* and not *The Beginnings of Judaism*.

When the apostle says that formerly he was very advanced in *Ioudaismos*, he is surely referring not to an abstract category or an institution but to the study of and learned practice of Judean ways of loyalty to the traditional practices of Judeans, described by his contemporary Josephus as "the ancestral [traditions] of the *Ioudaioi*" (τὰ πάτρια τῶν Ἰουδαίων; *Ant.* 20.41 and passim). Now again one might be tempted simply to gloss this as well as the Jewish religion were it not for the fact that this is exactly the usage that we find in Thucydides describing the Plataeans Medizing, namely, that they are accused of "forsaking *their* ancestral traditions" (παραβαίνοντες τὰ πάτρια; Thucydides 3.61.2), and I daresay no one has yet considered *Medismos* the name of a religion.[55] A final argument that *Ioudaismos*, in Paul, is not the name for the Jewish religion is the following: Paul never considered himself anything other than a Jew. Were *Ioudaismos* to mean the entirety of Judaic practice and belief, or the religion of the Jews, this verse would constitute a reading of himself out of it. It follows that *Ioudaismos*, if Paul is out of it, *simply cannot* be read as the alleged Jewish religion or even as a name for all that Jews do! It must mean, in his work, therefore, perhaps, study and keeping of the rejected Pharisaic paradosis (see Mark 7:3, where *Ioudaioi* seem to be identified with Pharisees). Once again, I arrive at results very similar—if not identical—to those of Mason but by slightly different routes of interpretation. *Ioudaismos*, "Judaizing," seems in all of these cases to mean hanging on (zealously) to the customs (traditions of the ancestors) of the Judeans. Any other interpretation (and there are some that seem possible within the context alone) involves importing the later sense of -ism words, as the names of institutions or, at least, movements, and applying them anachronistically to *Ioudaismos*.

---

54. Mason, "Jews, Judaeans, Judaizing, Judaism," 464.
55. Ibid., 463.

Is There Any Ancient Judaism Now?

Recognizing well the overweening normativity of the category "Judaism" when applied to antiquity, some major scholars of the twentieth century sought to disturb that normativity by introducing the term and concept of "Judaisms"—pluralized. In such fashion, they meant to disrupt both traditional and scholarly (such as Moore's) assignment of the term "Judaism" to the norms, leadership, and practices of the Rabbis. The initial moves in this direction came from Erwin Goodenough via his recognition that the "Judaism" of Philo and other Hellenistic Jews was significantly different from that of the Palestinians.[56] Pride of place in this movement certainly goes, however, to Jacob Neusner, who provided the first attempt at an actual definition of a "Judaism," one that would purportedly be neither essentialistic nor normative.[57] Here is, perhaps, Neusner's most succinct attempt at a definition:

> [A Judaism] is composed of three elements: a world view, a way of life, and a social group that, in the here and now, embodies the whole. The world view explains the life of the group, ordinarily referring to God's creation, the revelation of the Torah, the goal and end of the group's life in the end of time. The way of life defines what is special about the life of the group. The social group, in a single place and time, then forms the living witness and testimony to the system as a whole and finds in the system ample explanation for its very being. That is a *Judaism*.[58]

Oddly enough, it seems that the alleged "Judaism" of the Mishnah and the Talmuds, inherited by medieval Jewry and passed on to modernity, would not qualify as a "Judaism" on Neusner's account, since according to him, in the same site, "The first requirement is to find a group of Jews who see themselves as 'Israel.'... That same group must tell us that it uniquely constitutes 'Israel,' not *an* Israel."[59] The Rabbis, of course, contend that they have the true and correct interpretation of Torah but explic-

---

56. Erwin R. Goodenough, *By Light, Light: The Mystic Gospel of Hellenistic Judaism* (New Haven: Yale University Press; London: H. Milford, Oxford University Press, 1935).

57. Jacob Neusner, recently deceased, was a revolutionary figure in the study of ancient Jewry, one of the first to seek to put that study right in the middle of the humanities in the American academy. He succeeded perhaps at that project more fully than in his own scholarly constructions, which have tended more and more to seem wildly overdrawn and schematized, as in the instance being presented here. I have found Michael Satlow, "Defining Judaism: Accounting for 'Religions' in the Study of Religion," *JAAR* 74 (2006): 843–47 very helpful in laying out Neusner's views here and pointing to their weaknesses.

58. Jacob Neusner, *The Way of Torah: An Introduction to Judaism*, Religious Life of Man (Encino, CA: Dickenson, 1974), 8.

59. Ibid., 7.

itly deny that others—who may be sinners in their eyes—are not "Israel." This is particularly salient, because, as Michael Satlow makes clear, for all Neusner's talk of "Judaisms," it is essentially the history of the rabbinic tradition that he is setting out.[60] In any case, it is clear that Neusner's monothetic definition will not serve to include all of the entities that he himself (and certainly we) might be tempted to incorporate as Judaisms were we engaging in that very practice.

Satlow has attempted to improve on Neusner's view by tempering it with the proposal of Jonathan Z. Smith that we move toward a polythetic definition—virtually identical to Wittgenstein's "family resemblances"—that is a "map[ping] of characteristics that may or may not be shared by the members of a group. Two specific members of a group might share several of these characteristics, some overlapping set, or even none at all."[61] To put it in Smith's own language, "we need to map the variety of Judaisms, each of which appears as a shifting cluster of characteristics which vary over time."[62] Taking Smith's call as a program, Satlow proposes to carry it out.

Satlow begins by positing three maps: "A polythetic description of Judaism, I suggest, comprises of three maps that for heuristic purposes I would label, Israel, discursive tradition, and practice."[63] Attempting to finally get rid of the lingering (or actually clear and present) essentialisms of Neusner's approach, Satlow argues that "'Israel,' then, first and foremost indicates a mode of determining the scope of the data: for the academic student of religion, any Jewish community or individual that self-identifies as 'Jewish,' or part of Israel, 'counts' to the same degree as any other."[64] The other two maps are defined by Satlow as, "How do they [the given 'Israels'] accept or reject their received texts and their discourses, and how do they use (or not) this tradition to authorize and inform their beliefs and values?" and then, "What are their religious practices, and how do they justify and explain them?"[65] I shan't go into the details of Satlow's working out of his proposal, as I wish to query its very foundations, even while recognizing how much of an advance it is over Neusner's essentialism, or the grosser normative essentialisms of early scholarship such as Moore's. The most salient difficulties that I find with Satlow's proposal are that, beginning with any community that self-identifies with "Israel," it then proceeds to posit and investigate precisely the same set: beliefs

---

60. Satlow, "Defining Judaism," 845.

61. Ibid.

62. Jonathan Z. Smith, *Imagining Religion: From Babylon to Jonestown* (Chicago: University of Chicago Press, 1982), 18.

63. Satlow, "Defining Judaism," 846.

64. Ibid., 847.

65. Ibid., 846–47.

and "religious" practices that mark nearly any other praxis of the study of "religions." It has given, in fact, a monothetic definition of a "Judaism," to wit that it must identify itself as an Israel. In fine, we end up with "Israels"—monothetically, if expansively defined—and their "religions."[66] On my view, a genuinely polythetic analysis, starting from the data and not from any preconceived definition would lead, in a grossly cropped example, to something like the following results:

	Rabbis	Matthew	Sadducees	Marcion
Resurrection	+	+	-	-
God of Israel as Creator	+	+	+	+ (The Evil Creator)
Jesus as Savior	-	+	-	+
Call Themselves "Israel"	+	+	+	-

This is a synecdochical sample of a polythetic, or family resemblance, classification. Each of these entities shares at least one characteristic with at least one other, but none of them share all characteristics. Even the one characteristic that seems to be shared by all, Israel's God as creator, is so sharply different in Marcion, for whom Israel's God is not the true God but some evil underling, as to constitute a difference rather than a shared feature. There are ways in which the Rabbis and the Gospel of Matthew

66. Insofar as this would result in a kind of dialect map of features and characteristics joining and separating one group to and from the others, we might very well have a polythetic account of what joins and separates all groups that call themselves "Israel," but we have not advanced much beyond the dialect map model for describing the different proposed (or identified) "Israels" (Seth Schwartz, "How Many Judaisms," 219.) This model had explicitly recognized that groups that we call "Judaisms" frequently had overlapping characteristics shared with groups that we call "Christianities" but which divided them from other groups called "Judaisms" and "Christianities" respectively (Daniel Boyarin, *Dying for God: Martyrdom and the Making of Christianity and Judaism,* The Lancaster/Yarnton Lectures in Judaism and Other Religions for 1998 (Stanford, CA: Stanford University Press, 1999). Seth Schwartz is exactly right in claiming that such polythetic methods end up including much of what we (or even they) called Christianity within the same complex as rabbinic, Qumran, and other groups and texts. For me, and I imagine for Satlow, this is not a negative consequence. Schwartz's general critique of polytheticism (including, of course, mine but especially J. Z. Smith's) is well worth reading carefully ("How Many Judaisms," 219–21), although, naturally, I am much less concerned than Schwartz to find a way to place a boundary between "Judaism" and "Christianity" prior to the fourth century.

are closer to each other than the Rabbis and the Sadducees (as pointed out by Justin Martyr, lo these two millennia ago). Unless we decide to identify one characteristic as marking off something that we nominate Judaism and something that we nominate Christianity, an anachronistic and/or normative move, there is little reason to see the Gospel and Marcion as belonging to one group and the Rabbis and the Sadducees to another. Note please that there is no feature that joins the Rabbis and Marcion. Nevertheless, the Gospel shares distinctive features with the Rabbis that differentiate the Gospel from Marcion. The Gospel *does* share with Marcion the feature of Jesus as savior. Therefore, all of these entities belong in the same family (polythetic aggregate), a family that I would hesitate to call Judaisms (Marcion indeed!), still less, Judaism! Now of course this analysis would need to be much more extensive with many other known groups included and many other parameters as well, but this is sufficient, I think, to indicate what a polythetic (family resemblance) classification would look like and why it wouldn't produce "Judaisms" without some dogmatic border being advanced.

While Satlow makes real progress over earlier monothetic versions of defining "Judaism," either inchoate or explicit, he nevertheless leaves us with the question of why we should seek to define something that no one knows of at the time about which the research is being done. If it is "Israels" that are the object of study, then why not just say that? We end up with a polythetic definition of a word that didn't exist. What is gained by adding another layer of abstraction between us and the data by referring to them as "Judaisms"? It is considerations like these, *inter alia*,[67] that first led me to consider the possibility that it is not helpful to think in terms of "Judaisms."

Philological Investigations

How does one show that a beloved term such as "Judaism" is an anachronism? First, obviously, by simply showing that a word for it does not exist in several central Jewish languages. Notably, the argument that the very rare Second Temple Judeo-Greek word *Ioudaismos* does not mean anything like later "Judaism" has already been made.[68] Second, by arguing that without a word, there is no concept. For this we need a bit of theory.

---

67. See, e.g., Daniel Boyarin, "Beyond Judaisms: Meṭaṭron and the Divine Polymorphy of Ancient Judaism," *JSJ* 41 (2010): 323–65, although I am certainly not the only proponent of such views..

68. Mason, "Jews, Judaeans, Judaizing, Judaism," 457–512; and, for discussion, see Daniel Boyarin, "Rethinking Jewish Christianity: An Argument for Dismantling a Dubious Category (to Which Is Appended a Correction of My *Border Lines*)," *JQR* (2009): 9–12, which itself needs updating and correction now. See now Boyarin, *Judaism*, for extensive documen-

Ludwig Wittgenstein wrote, "Philosophy must not interfere in any way with the actual use of language, so it can in the end only describe it" (PI 124).[69] In contrast to some Wittgenstein scholars, I take him at his word here.[70] The project of the *Philosophical Investigations* is, I am convinced, to produce an actual description of language as a means of communication, nothing more, nothing less.

Wittgenstein famously remarked, "For a *large* class of cases—though not for all—in which we employ the word 'meaning' it can be defined thus: the meaning of a word is its use in the language" (PI 43). This basic statement is what underlies the significance of Wittgenstein's contribution: a change from a conception of meaning as representation to a view that looks to use as the crux of the matter. A commentator on Wittgenstein has helpfully phrased it: "Traditional theories of meaning in the history of philosophy were intent on pointing to something exterior to the proposition which endows it with sense. This 'something' could generally be located either in an objective space, or inside the mind as mental representation. Rather, when investigating meaning, the researcher must 'look and see' the variety of uses to which the word is put."[71] Without going into excessive detail here, it will be seen, nonetheless, that if the project of assessing meaning is the observation of the usage of a word, then, without a word, it is impossible to ascribe a meaning, a concept.[72]

If the meaning of the word is its use, then the interpretation of the word both for the speaker/writer and the hearer/reader is affected by all of the myriad ways that the word has been used before, setting up an endless oscillation of meaning effects.[73] Again, taking this very seriously as a plausible description of actual natural language, I suggest that Wittgenstein implies that we don't walk around with a lexicon in our heads, a list of words and definitions, but with a *Zettelkasten* (box of note slips) of thousands and thousands of half-remembered prior uses of words and

---

tation of this lack in Jewish languages from Judeo-Greek through Judeo-Arabic, pre-modern Hebrew, and Yiddish.

69. Ludwig Wittgenstein, *Philosophische Untersuchungen / Philosophical Investigations*, trans. G. E. M. Anscombe, P. M. S. Hacker, and Joachim Schulte (Malden, MA: Wiley-Blackwell, 2009),

70. Cf. Barry Stroud, "Wittgenstein on Meaning, Understanding, and Community," in *Wittgenstein—Eine Neubewertung / Towards a Re-Evaluation*, ed. R. Haller and J. Brandl (Vienna: Hölder-Pichler-Tempsky, 1990)

71. Lois Shawver, "Commentary on Wittgenstein's Philosophical Investigations," http://users.rcn.com/rathbone/lwtocc.htm.

72. See especially the now classic articulation of this point for the history of ideas: Quentin Skinner, "Meaning and Understanding in the History of Ideas," *History and Theory* 8 (1969): 37.

73. An unpublished lecture of Hans Sluga's, once heard, set me thinking this way. This is where a certain understanding of Wittgenstein meets Bakhtin's "alien word," Kristeva's "intertextuality," as well.

phrases that we pull out of our memories in appropriate (or seemingly appropriate) contexts. As one important Wittgenstein scholar has put it, "The point is that words are ultimately connected to the world by training, not by translation."[74] Or as Stanley Cavell has articulated essentially the same point: "Instead, then, of saying either that we *tell* beginners what words mean or that we *teach* them what objects are, I say: We initiate them, into the relevant forms of life held in language and gathered around the objects and persons of our world."[75]

Another of Wittgenstein's philosophical investigations sharpens our philological investigation:

> If "X exists" is meant simply to say: "X" has a meaning,—then it is not a proposition which treats of X, but a proposition about our use of language, that is, about the use of the word "X".

In other words, if the statement "Red exists" is true then this means that "Red" has a meaning in a given language, and the statement "red does not exist" means the opposite:

> But what we really *want* is simply to take "Red exists" as the statement: the word "red" has a meaning. Or perhaps better: "Red does not exist" as "'Red' has no meaning". (Wittgenstein 28–29)

Closet Platonists that we are, we are tempted to take "red exists" as a metaphysical statement, one that would necessitate something like, or at least analogous to, an Idea or Form. What Wittgenstein is claiming, in a non-Platonic thinking, however, is that the sentence "red exists" ought really to be understood as a statement about a given language, namely, that within that language, the word "red" has meaning. If, for example, the sentence "Judaism exists," then, only means that the term "Judaism" has meaning, the term "Judaism" cannot have meaning in a language that doesn't have a word for it. Since the sentence is only a statement about language (and not about the metaphysical being of "redness"), then where there is no word for "red," redness is not meaningful. Where there is no word for "Judaism," Judaism is not meaningful as a concept, ergo "Judaism" does not exist in that linguistic-cultural system.[76] This helps us to

---

74. David Bloor, *Wittgenstein, a Social Theory of Knowledge*, Contemporary Social Theory (London: Macmillan, 1983), 27.

75. Stanley Cavell, *The Claim of Reason: Wittgenstein, Skepticism, Morality, and Tragedy* (Oxford: Clarendon, 1979), 178.

76. See Jonathan Z. Smith, *Relating Religion: Essays in the Study of Religion* (Chicago: University of Chicago Press, 2004), 133–34, making a not dissimilar argument, but cf. ibid., 144 n. 51. Just to clarify at this point: this is not a claim that first-order phenomena do not exist that are not named in the language but only that the abstractions that organize phenomena into

begin to answer what difference it makes when a language has no word that is used as we use "religion," or more specifically for the current case, "Judaism." I fully subscribe to this Wittgensteinian position, here only barely sketched in, of course.

Since, following Wittgenstein, the statement "Judaism exists" makes no ontological sense and only has meaning in a language in which the word *Judaism* (or cognate) exists, it would follow that any talk of "Judaism" in antiquity, or in the Middle Ages for that matter, is *eo ipso* an ideological intervention, an assertion precisely of the timelessness of the abstract entity Judaism, a Form in the Platonic sense which can exist without anyone knowing that it does. As Theodor Adorno has written in a somewhat different context, "This kind of writing does not criticize abstract fundamental concepts, aconceptual data, or habituated clichés; instead, it presupposes them, implicitly but by the same token with all the more complicity."[77]

Language as "Form of Life"

When we divide the usage of a word into distinct and discrete meanings and submeanings as the practice of traditional lexicons, we are not actually describing the usage of the other language and its accompanying conceptual system but imposing the abstractions and categories of our language and conceptual system on them.[78] Thus, frequently enough, when we say that a given word has two meanings in some foreign language, all we are saying is that English has no word that matches the semantic range of that foreign tongue.[79] Only the usage of the other language will teach us what

second-order categories cannot be asserted except through their usage in language. I have argued against the use of third-order categories (drawn from *our* culture and languages) elsewhere (Daniel Boyarin, "The Concept of Translation in American Religious Studies," *Critical Inquiry* 44 [2017]: 17–39). See also n. 44 above.

77. Theodor W. Adorno, "The Essay as Form," in *Notes to Literature*, ed. Rolf Tiedemann, trans.Shierry Weber Nicholsen, 2 vols., European Perspectives (New York: Columbia University Press, 1991–1992),1:6.

78. For a version of this idea, see Anna Wierzbicka, *Understanding Cultures through Their Key Words: English, Russian, Polish, German, and Japanese*, Oxford Studies in Anthropological Linguistics (New York: Oxford University Press, 1997). See the extraordinarily sharp statement of John Locke quoted there on p. 4. Already then, and by him, it was clearly understood that abstractions are frequently (even usually) untranslatable. It is not inapposite to observe here, although the force of this observation will appear later, that the account that J. Z. Smith (*Relating Religion*, 127–31) gives of the philological dismantling of the concept of *mana* between Émile Durkheim and Claude Lévi-Straus matches the sorts of arguments that are being mounted against *religion* in, e.g., Carlin A. Barton and Daniel Boyarin, *Imagine No Religion: How Modern Categories Hide Ancient Realities* (Bronx, NY: Fordham University Press, 2016).

79. See C. P. Jones, "῎Εθνος and γένος in Herodotus," *CIQ* NS 46 (1996): 316, who, in an exemplary study, makes this point compellingly.

its living speakers consider to be within single categories and divided into separate ones. Asserting the existence of ancient religion or ancient Judaism is an imposition of our language on theirs, one valid for the pulpit perhaps but not for describing a form of life.[80]

Wittgenstein has brilliantly formulated what was for me, before reading him, a hunch: "And to imagine a language means to imagine a form of life [PI §19]."[81] Although the meaning of "forms of life" in Wittgenstein is much contested,[82] I have found most helpful the account given by P. M. S. Hacker.[83] Crucial to understanding Wittgenstein here is the recognition that already, "Wilhelm von Humboldt in his On Language (1836) linked the idea of forms of life with customs and habits of a language-using community."[84] As Hacker emphasizes, correctly in my view, this is *not* a philosophical term of art but common German usage. And Hacker explicitly remarks that Wittgenstein is using the term in this "humdrum" fashion. "Form of life" is, therefore, something quite close to our notion of culture while bypassing many of the theoretical problems that have arisen with that term.[85] (In fact, in my work henceforth, I intend to use "form of life" precisely where I once would have written "culture.")[86] The novelty

80. See too, "I've suggested elsewhere … that the attribution of implicit meanings to an alien practice regardless of whether they are acknowledged by its agents is a characteristic form of theological exercise, with an ancient history" (Talal Asad, "The Concept of Cultural Translation in British Social Anthropology," in *Writing Culture: The Poetics and Politics of Ethnography*, ed. James Clifford and George E. Marcus, [Berkeley: University of California Press, 1986], 161). Compare too Skinner's similar use of "mythology" (Skinner, "Meaning and Understanding," 7–10) or "metaphysical belief" (ibid., 19–20).

81. Wittgenstein, *Philosophische Untersuchungen / Philosophical Investigations*.

82. J. F. M. Hunter, "'Forms of Life' in Wittgenstein's 'Philosophical Investigations,'" *American Philosophical Quarterly* 5 (1968): 233–43.

83. P. M. S. Hacker, "Forms of Life," *Nordic Wittgenstein Review*, special issue (2015): 1–20.

84. Ibid., 2.

85. I would generally associate my view with the interpretation described by Anna Boncompagni: "If forms of life are to be found on an empirical level, and if we identify them with the social and cultural features of a human society, then we can affirm that each human aggregate constitutes a form of life, if it is characterized by the existence of shared practices and a shared background of knowledge, language, know-how, history, culture. Each form of life is then a possible subject for anthropological research. Empirical pluralism can be associated, for instance, with Max Black, Naomi Scheman, Norman Malcolm" (Boncompagni, "Elucidating Forms of Life: The Evolution of a Philosophical Tool," *Nordic Wittgenstein Review*, special issue [2015]: 165). For a good account of the problems attending "culture," see Benson Saler, *Conceptualizing Religion: Immanent Anthropologists, Transcendent Natives, and Unbounded Categories*, SHR 56 (Leiden: Brill, 1993), 232–33.

86. For "form of life" as "converging on the idea of culture," see G. P. Baker, *Wittgenstein: Understanding and Meaning*, vol. 1 of *An Analytical Commentary on the Philosophical Investigations*, part 2, *Exegesis 1–184* (Hoboken, NJ: Wiley, 2008), 74. In the Brown Book, Wittgenstein observes that to imagine a language is to imagine a culture. (Ludwig Wittgenstein, *Preliminary Studies for the 'Philosophical Investigations,' Generally Known as the Blue and*

of Wittgenstein's §19 is not, then, in the concept of "form of life" but only this: that to investigate a language means to investigate a form of life:

> To conclude: the expression "form of life" plays a very small role in Wittgenstein's later philosophy. No aura or mystique should be allowed to attach itself to his notion of a form of life. In itself it is of no great moment. What *is* of great moment is the larger body of thought of which the concept of a form of life is merely a surface ornament. That larger body of thought is the ethnological conception of language as a form of activity embedded in the ways of living of a language-using community. That activity is normative, i.e. rule-governed—but not in the manner of a calculus; rather in the manner of a game.[87]

In order to make sense of Hacker, I would insist that his statement that "form of life" is not of great moment, comes simply to claim that Wittgenstein himself is neither coining nor referring to a new philosophical concept with that usage (of no great *moment*) but deploying it to make an argument that is of great moment at that moment.[88] It would follow, therefore, what the language lacks, the form of life cannot comprise.[89]

As Hacker sums up, as lucidly as could be hoped for, "In short, human beings in different epochs, in different cultures, have different forms of life. Different educations, interests and concerns, languages, different human relations and relations to nature and the world constitute distinct forms of life. For different cultures form different conceptual structures, adopt distinctive forms and norms of representation, limited only by the vague boundaries of the concept of a form of representation or a language."[90] In investigating a language, we are investigating a form of life. A form of life that has no word that means "religion" cannot have religion in it, nor can there be a "Judaism" without a word that refers to it.

Brown Books [Oxford: Blackwell, 1969], 134). Since that book was written in English, it is clear that, for him, *Lebensform* is a virtual equivalent of English "culture," but, paradoxically for English, "form of life," seems less theoretically pitfall-ridden than "culture."

87. Hacker, "Forms of Life," 18.

88. I must confess that "merely a surface ornament" confounds me quite totally.

89. As Hacker so well sums up his compelling point: "Wittgenstein's aim was to undermine such conceptions of philosophy, philosophy of logic and language [as those of Frege, Russell, and his own *Tractatus*] and to replace them with an anthropological and ethnological conception. According to the latter (which incidentally harmonizes 'in the large' with von Humboldt's observations on thought and language), language is not the totality of sentences that can be generated from a set of primitive indefinables, definitions, formation- and transformation-rules. It is rather an uncircumscribable motley of human activities, of the playing of language-games, in the medley of human life" (Hacker, "Forms of Life," 4).

90. Hacker, "Forms of Life," 11.

Early Jewish Knowledge of Greek Medicine

PIETER W. VAN DER HORST
Utrecht University

Ever since the start of his academic career, Shaye Cohen has had a keen interest in the relations between early Judaism and Greco-Roman culture. It seemed fit, therefore, to dedicate to him a modest contribution in this area of research. It will deal with a fascinating aspect of these relations, namely, the influence of Greek medical knowledge on Jewish intellectuals in the Hellenistic and Roman periods.

The Hebrew Bible does not display much interest in medical knowledge, and physicians are rarely mentioned.[1] The prevailing opinion of the biblical authors is that God is the dispenser of life and death and that as such he is the source of both health and disease, the latter being regarded as punishment or trial inflicted by God, and the first as a sign of his favor. God is, therefore, the only healer.[2] In view of this, it is all the more striking that in the postbiblical Hellenistic and Roman era Jews soon developed a vivid interest in things medical and initiated a very long history of Jewish involvement in medical science. It is the modest aim of this paper to show, first, that there is evidence for involvement in Greek medicine of Jewish physicians in the Hellenistic and Roman world, and, second, that Jewish doctors and other intellectuals such as rabbis demonstrably adopted and adapted theories and insights developed by Greek physicians and other thinkers *in medicis*.

A first sign of a change in attitude toward medicine may perhaps be found already in the LXX version of Exod 21:19. The Hebrew text says that, when two men have been fighting and A has beaten up B to such a degree that he has to take to bed, if B arises again A has to pay him only for

1. If physicians are mentioned at all, it is sometimes in a negative way, e.g., 2 Chr 16:12.

2. E.g., Gen 20:17, Exod 15:26 ("I the Lord am your healer"), Num 12:13, Deut 32:39, Pss 6:3, 30:3, 41:5, 103:3, Job 5:17–18, Isa 19:22. See further Owsei Temkin, *Hippocrates in a World of Pagans and Christians* (Baltimore: Johns Hopkins University Press, 1991), 86–88; Howard Clark Kee, "Medicine and Healing," *ABD* 4:659–64. See also Fridolf Kudlien, "Gesundheit," *RAC* 10:935; Kudlien, "Heilkunde," *RAC* 14:236–39; and Gary B. Ferngren, "Krankheit," *RAC* 21:981.

the loss of time (employment) and "arrange for his full recovery" [*rappô' yərappē'*] (NRSV). The LXX is more explicit here and says that A has to compensate for the costs of B.'s medical treatment [*apoteisei ... ta iatreia*].[3] (And Josephus goes even further when in his rewording of this passage he says that A has "to pay the doctors' bill" [*Ant.* 4.277: *apotinetō ... hosa tois iatrois edōken*[4]). But this LXX verse is an uncertain case.

It is at the beginning of the second century BCE that Ben Sira provides us with the first certain indication of the existence of Jewish medical experts.[5] Differing from what we find in the Hebrew Bible, he exhorts his readers to honor physicians for their God-given skills. "Knowledge makes the doctor distinguished and gives him access to those in authority" (38:3).[6] That Ben Sira is speaking here about Jewish (not pagan) doctors can confidently be inferred from the following passage, where it is said that the doctors "will also beseech the Lord" (38:14). It is very improbable that Ben Sira would have said this about pagan physicians.[7] It should be admitted that in Ben Sira's opinion God remains the ultimate healer (see 38:9: "it is He who heals") and uses the physician only as his tool, but the fact that this "tool" is to be honored is an important first step toward a full-fledged Jewish medical profession. His plea for respect for physicians and his justification of medicine before pious Jews were certainly facilitated by "the expansion of medical practice following the increasing influence of Hellenistic culture and science in Palestine."[8] It is striking, though, that in approximately the same period as Ben Sira, the author of the book of Tobit tells us that doctors were unable to heal the disease of the story's protagonist, only the angel Raphael (= God heals!) could do so. Here the tension between advocates of medicine and their opponents becomes visible.

3. The Vulgate makes it even more explicit: *ut... inpensas in medicos restituat.* See also the remarks in John W. Wevers, *Notes on the Greek Text of Exodus*, SCS 30 (Atlanta: Scholars Press, 1990), 332.

4. In this context Samuel S. Kottek remarks that in general "Josephus not infrequently adds to his version of the Bible medical interventions that do not appear in the canonical texts" (*Medicine and Hygiene in the Works of Flavius Josephus*, Studies in Ancient Medicine 9 [Leiden: Brill, 1994] 25). The *iatrikē* (female doctor) that is found in the manuscripts of Josephus's *Vita* 185 may be a copyist's error; see Steve Mason, *Life of Josephus*, Flavius Josephus: Translation and Commentary 9 (Leiden: Brill, 2001), 94.

5. On this passage, see Sijbolt J. Noorda, "Illness and Sin, Forgiving and Healing: The Connection of Medical Treatment and Religious Beliefs in Ben Sira 38, 1–15," in *Studies in Hellenistic Religions*, ed. Maarten J. Vermaseren, ÉPRO 78 (Leiden: Brill, 1979), 215–24; Larry P. Hogan, *Healing in the Second Temple Period*, NTOA 21 (Freiburg: Universitätsverlag; Göttingen: Vandenhoeck & Ruprecht, 1992), 38–48.

6. Translation by Patrick W. Skehan and Alexander A. Di Lella, *The Wisdom of Ben Sira: A New Translation with Notes*, AB 39 (Garden City, NY: Doubleday, 1987).

7. See Temkin, *Hippocrates in a World of Pagans and Christians*, 90.

8. Noorda, "Illness and Sin," 224. See also Martin Hengel, *Judentum und Hellenismus: Studien zu ihrer Begegnung unter besonderer Berücksichtigung Palästinas bis zur Mitte des 2. Jh.s v. Chr.*, WUNT 10 (Tübingen: Mohr Siebeck, 1969), 440.

"[T]hough a *modus vivendi* was established between Judaic religious healing and secular medicine, the antagonism was not basically eliminated."[9]

These documents show that the existence of Jewish physicians in the Hellenistic period was a distinct possibility. In order to make the step from possibility to reality we have to turn our attention to another type of evidence, most of which is from the Roman and early Byzantine period, that is, Jewish inscriptions.[10]

Let me begin with an important warning by first presenting an inscription that in several older publications figures as an epitaph of a Jewish doctor (e.g., in Frey's *CIJ* 2, no. 1419). It is *IJO* 3, App. 21, from Antoninopolis Constantia in northern Syria: *Isaakēs iatros*. Its most recent editors, however, rightly stress that, by the time the inscription was carved (late fourth to early fifth century CE), this originally Jewish name was also in use among Christians.[11] So-called Jewish names can never be a safe criterion for determining the Jewishness of an inscription unless they are accompanied by corroborative indicators of Jewishness.[12] In what follows, therefore, I will deal only with inscriptions that can be regarded as Jewish with a reasonable or high degree of certainty.

The harvest is not rich. Jews much more often mention the functions or offices they had in their synagogues than their secular professions. Many Jewish physicians, therefore, may go unidentified as such. Hence we probably see only the tip of the iceberg.

I leave aside here *JIGRE* 30, an epitaph from late second-century BCE Leontopolis. There is no uncertainty in this case about the Jewishness of the deceased but there is about his profession. The deceased man, Demas, is said to have helped many people by his *sophia*, and some scholars have taken this to be a reference to his work as a physician, assuming that *sophia* here refers to his medical skills. But *sophia* can denote the skills of any profession, so this interpretation is unwarranted.[13]

The next item is unproblematic: *JIWE* 1:76 is a fifth-century CE epitaph

---

9. Temkin, *Hippocrates in a World of Pagans and Christians*, 93.

10. For what follows I am much indebted to Fridolf Kudlien, "Jüdische Ärzte im Römischen Reich," *Medizinhistorisches Journal* 20 (1985): 36–57. Kudlien lists (36–37) several older scholarly publications that are now outdated; his own survey needs to be updated as well (this will be done below in the main text). For a concise summary of Kudlien's findings, see his article "Heilkunde," *RAC* 14:223–49, esp. 236–42).

11. David Noy and Hanswulf Bloedhorn, eds., *Inscriptiones Judaicae Orientis*, vol. 3, TSAJ 102 (Tübingen: Mohr Siebeck, 2004), 242–43.

12. I hasten to add that, of course, it cannot be *excluded* that Isaac was a Jewish doctor. See the discussion of this tricky criteriological problem in my *Ancient Jewish Epitaphs: An Introductory Survey of a Millennium of Jewish Funerary Epigraphy (300 BCE–700 CE)*, CBET 2 (Kampen: Kok Pharos, 1991), 16–18; and in my *Saxa judaica loquuntur: Lessons from Early Jewish Inscriptions*, BibInt 134 (Leiden: Brill, 2015), 8–12.

13. *Pace* Kudlien, "Jüdische Ärzte," 55. An even weaker case is *JIGRE* 40, where the fact that the deceased boy's name, Machaon, has led some scholars to speculate that his family

from the Jewish burial place of Venosa (southern Italy) and it calls the deceased, Faustinus, *gerousiarchon* [read *gerousiarchōn*, with omega] *archiatros*, "head of the council of elders (and) chief doctor."[14] This second title "could refer to someone working in the imperial palace or to a municipal employee."[15] *Archiatroi* had a high status and they probably enjoyed immunity from various obligations, among which would have been the paying of certain taxes (*ateleia*).[16] Faustinus was probably employed by the town of Venosa, which would imply that he was working not only for the Jewish community. However, the word *gerousiarchōn*, which is usually interpreted as a variant form of *gerousiarchēs*, can also be taken as a genitive plural, so that Faustinus would then be the personal physician of the leaders of the council of elders of the synagogue. That would imply that he did work for the Jewish community. But it has been objected that "it is hard to imagine that Venosa had enough gerousiarchs to justify their own chief doctor."[17] That objection may be countered, however, by the observation that Faustinus may have worked for both the municipality and the Jewish council of elders, and that it was only the latter profession that he found prestigious enough to have it put on record.[18] We know yet another Jewish *archiatros*, from Rome. *JIWE* 2, no. 341, a third- to fourth-century epitaph from the Jewish catacomb of Vigna Randanini, reads: *Aulus Vedius collega archiatros*.[19] And, finally, we have the epitaph of a Jewish *archiatros* from second-century CE Ephesus. In it, Julius and his wife Julia say that the Jewish community of Ephesus takes care of their sarcophagus (*tautēs tēs sorou kēdontai hoi en Ephesōi Ioudaioi*).

Actually we have only three inscriptions that inform us about the existence of Jewish doctors. It is striking, however, that all three are *archiatroi*, that is, public doctors or private physicians of rulers, who belong to the higher strata of society and are proud to have this fact recorded on their tombstones.[20] Apparently, the less prestigious common doctors (the "gen-

---

was active in medicine since Machaon is the name of one of the two sons of the Greek healing god Asclepius.

14. That the inscription is Jewish is confirmed not only by the fact that the final line reads *shalom shalom* in Hebrew characters but also by the presence of pictures of a shofar and a lulav.

15. D. Noy in *JIWE* 1:102.

16. See Emil Schürer, *The History of the Jewish People in the Age of Jesus Christ (175 B.C.–A.D. 135)*, rev. ed. Geza Vermes, Fergus Millar, and Martin Goodman, 3 vols. (Edinburgh: T&T Clark, 1973–1987), 3:23.

17. Noy in *JIWE* 1:101.

18. I am inclined to follow here Kudlien, "Jüdische Ärzte," 44, *contra* van der Horst, *Ancient Jewish Epitaphs*, 29.

19. *Collega* probably means that he was a member of a *collegium* (of doctors?).

20. On *archiatroi*, see further Gregory H. R. Horsley, *New Documents Illustrating Early Christianity: A Review of the Greek Inscriptions and Papyri Published in 1977*, NewDocs 2 (North Ryde, NSW: Ancient History Documentary Research Centre, Macquarie University, 1982),

eral practitioners") did not find it worthwhile to mention their professions in their epitaphs (if they had an epitaph at all). Moreover we should take into account that we have epitaphs of fewer than 0.1 percent of the Jews who lived in the ancient world between Alexander the Great and Muhammad.[21] As we will now see, literary evidence makes clear that Jewish doctors were a far from negligible part of late antique society.

Let me begin with some anonymous Jewish doctors. Several non-Jewish authors refer to remedies that they know had been developed by Jewish medical experts. For instance, Celsus, an early first-century CE encyclopedist, writes in his *De medicina* 5.19.11 (*GLAJJ*, vol. 1, no. 150)[22] that some physicians attribute an effective medication for the treatment of skull fractures to an *auctor Iudaeus*. This expression may either refer to a Jewish medical writer whose name Celsus does not know or it may refer to an author called *Iudaeus/Ioudaios*. That *Iudaeus/Ioudaios* could be a proper name is proved by other inscriptions. For example, a manumission inscription from Delphi, *IJO* 1 Ach42, records the manumission of a male slave "Ioudaios by name, Ioudaios by nation" (*hōi onoma Ioudaios, to genos Ioudaion*). And in *IJO* 1 Ach44 it is Ioudaios son of Pindarus who gives a slave his freedom back. In *De medicina* 5.22.4 (*GLAJJ* no. 151), Celsus mentions the (same?) man again, this time calling him only Iudaeus (without auctor). Whichever interpretation of *Iudaeus* one adopts here is irrelevant for our purposes; in any case it refers to a Jewish doctor whose remedies are mentioned with approval.[23]

In the second half of the second century CE, the famous and prolific physician and philosopher Galen, who spent some time in Palestine, refers several times to a doctor he calls Rufus from Samaria but who is also explicitly called a Jew by him, not a Samaritan (but Galen may not have known the difference between Jews and Samaritans).[24]. He quotes from Rufus's writings, which seem to have been mainly commentaries on Hippocratic works. In this respect Rufus was a precursor of Asaph ha-Rophe, except for the fact that Rufus was more of a compiler than an original thinker. Galen says

---

10–25; Vivian Nutton, "Archiatroi," *DNP* 1:990–91. It is also to be noted that our three *archiatroi* are from both the eastern and the western parts of the Roman Empire and that they range chronologically from the second to the fifth centuries CE.

21. See my *Ancient Jewish Epitaphs*, 73–74.

22. Henceforth *GLAJJ* refers to the three-volume work by Menahem Stern, *Greek and Latin Authors on Jews and Judaism*, Fontes ad res Judaicas spectantes (Jerusalem: Israel Academy of Sciences and Humanities, 1974–1984).

23. On the various meanings of *Ioudaios/Iudaeus*, see Shaye J. D. Cohen, *The Beginnings of Jewishness: Boundaries, Varieties, Uncertainties*, HCS 31 (Berkeley: University of California Press, 1999), 69–106; see also his article "Ioudaios" in *The Eerdmans Dictionary of Early Judaism*, ed. John J. Collins and Daniel C. Harlow (Grand Rapids: Eerdmans, 2010), 769–70. This is not the place to enter the ongoing debate about the proper translation of the term *Ioudaios*. For the sake of convenience and clarity I stick to the traditional usage.

24. See *GLAJJ* nos. 382, 384, 385, 390.

that Rufus "lacked the ability to interpret books of antiquity independently; Rufus had collected interpretations from commentaries written by others, since they were all in his possession."[25] Galen also criticizes Rufus's insufficient knowledge of the Greek language. It is a less-than-flattering picture that Galen draws here of our Jewish doctor, but it does show a lively interest in the Hippocratic tradition on the part of a Jewish doctor.

The fifth-century church historian Socrates writes that, during the riots that broke out between Christians and Jews in Alexandria under Bishop Cyril (early fifth century), a Jewish physician named Adamantius fled to Constantinople, only to return later after the riots had subsided (*Hist. eccl.* 7.13). Some other cases of presumably Jewish physicians in Alexandria are very dubious. [26]

Also in the early fifth century, the Christian physician Marcellus Empiricus of Bordeaux writes that "for the spleen there is a special remedy which was recently demonstrated by the patriarch Gamaliel on the basis of approved experiments" (*De medicamentis* 23.77).[27] It is not improbable that the Gamaliel referred to is Gamliel VI, the last Jewish patriarch of Palestine, who is known for his good contacts with pagan Greek intellectuals, among them Libanius, the famous Antiochian professor of rhetoric, with whom he had a lively correspondence (from 388 to 394).[28] What is reported in ancient sources about this Gamaliel/Gamliel evokes an image

25. Stern in *GLAJJ* 2:309 n. 7. The relevant passages from Galen are not included in *GLAJJ* since they have been preserved only in a medieval Arabic translation of Galen's commentary on Hippocrates's *Epidemiae.* See the edition by Franz Pfaff in *Galeni in Hippocratis Epidemiarum libros commentarii,* Corpus medicorum graecorum 5.10.2.2 (Berlin: Akademie-Verlag, 1956).

26. In his otherwise excellent book, *Alexandria in Late Antiquity: Topography and Social Conflict* (Baltimore: Johns Hopkins University Press, 1997), Christopher Haas sees more evidence of Jewish doctors in Alexandria than is warranted (113 with notes). I also leave aside here the dubious case of the early fifth-century physician Agapius of Alexandria, whom Salo W. Baron surmises to have been Jewish (*Social and Religious History of the Jews,* 2nd rev. ed., 18 vols. (New York: Columbia University Press, 1952–1983), 8:241. The same applies perhaps to a fifth-centuryAlexandrian physician thought to be Jewish by Jean Juster, *Les Juifs dans l'Empire Romain: Leur condition juridique, économique et sociale,* 2 vols. (Paris: Geuthner, 1914), 2:255. Kudlien ("Jüdische Ärzte," 40) rightly raises objections to the fact that Stern sees references to Jewish physicians in Lucian of Samosata (*GLAJJ* nos. 372 and 374).

27. For a more detailed study of this passage, see my "The Last Jewish Patriarch(s) and Graeco-Roman Medicine," in *Jews and Gentiles in the Holy Land in the Days of the Second Temple, the Mishnah and the Talmud,* ed. Menahem Mor et al. (Jerusalem: Yad Ben-Zvi, 2003), 87–96. See also the brief treatment in Martin Jacobs, *Die Institution des jüdischen Patriarchen: Eine quellen- und traditionskritische Studie zur Geschichte der Juden in der Spätantike,* TSAJ 52 (Tübingen: Mohr Siebeck, 1995), 331–32. The passage from Marcellus's *De medicamentis* is not included in *GLAJJ* because Marcellus was a Christian author. On Marcellus, see Fritz E. Kind, "Marcellus (58)," PW 14.2 (1930) 1498–1503; and Alain Touwaide, "Marcellus (8)," *DNP* 7:851–52.

28. See *GLAJJ* nos. 495–504.

of a wealthy, learned, open-minded, and powerful patriarch who was well versed in Greek culture and also in its medical achievements. He was a welcome guest at the Theodosian court (as was Marcellus Empiricus!) until he fell out of favor and was deposed in 415. We do not know whether Gamaliel practiced medicine himself or whether he had only theoretical knowledge of the discipline.[29] The fact that some rabbis were also active as physicians[30] —for example, Mar Samuel (b. Ber. 58b)—shows that rabbinic scholarship could go hand in hand with a medical profession. The patriarchs were not necessarily always rabbis, but they did belong to the same cultural milieu. So a patriarch in the role of physician is well imaginable. But even if Gamaliel was not a medical practitioner, he certainly was a man with an interest in and knowledge of Greek medical matters, and he shared his ideas with a non-Jewish physician. He then may also have shared his knowledge with rabbis. It is striking that in the series of treatments discussed in b. Giṭ. 69b, much attention is paid to diseases of the spleen,[31] precisely the topic with which Gamaliel too had occupied himself. (The fact that this information is found in the Bavli and not in the Yerushalmi does not invalidate its relevance).[32]

Indeed, in rabbinic literature we find telling examples of this interest in Greek medicine. In this corpus, which was definitely not written by medical doctors, one is confronted with an impressive quantity of Greek medical knowledge.[33] A striking example of this is the considerable amount of scientific gynecological, sexological, and embryological lore and science in the treatise Niddah in both Talmudim. For instance, as I have demonstrated at length elsewhere, rabbinic discussions in this tractate (and elsewhere as well) clearly demonstrate that several rabbis

---

29. When Wilhelm Bacher writes, "Gamaliel VI appears to have been a physician" ("Gamaliel VI," *JE* 5:563), he too easily overlooks other possibilities.

30. For references, see Catharina Hezser, "Representation of the Physician in Jewish Literature from Hellenistic and Roman Times," in *Popular Medicine in Graeco-Roman Antiquity: Explorations*, ed. William V. Harris, Columbia Studies in the Classical Tradition 42 (Leiden: Brill, 2016), 173–97. Note that some rabbis detest doctors and say that "the best of the physicians is destined for Gehenna" (m. Qidd. 4:14).

31. The magical elements in the recipes in this Bavli passage are nicely paralleled by those in a recently published Greek magical papyrus; see Roelof van den Broek, "A Greek Iatromagical Papyrus (Utrecht Copt. Ms. B3.8),," *ZPE* 202 (2017): 208–13.

32. Chronologically the last mention of a Jewish doctor in the Roman Empire is a very brief remark in the *Philosophical History* (formerly *Life of Isidorus*) of Damascius from the early sixth century. Damascius states only that the renowned physician Gesius took over almost all of the students of his own teacher, the Jewish doctor Domnus (fr. 128 ed. Polymnia Athanassiadi = *GLAJJ* no. 551). There is no further information about Domnus.

33. See, in general, Fred Rosner, *Medicine in the Bible and the Talmud: Selections from Classical Jewish Sources*, Library of Jewish Law and Ethics 5 (New York: Ktav, 1977); Julius Preuss, *Biblisch-talmudische Medizin* (Wiesbaden: Fourier-Verlag, 1992 [orig. 1911]); Samuel Krauss, *Talmudische Archäologie*, 3 vols. (Leipzig: Fock, 1910–1912), 1:252–67.

had extensive knowledge of Greek theories about the viability of a seven-month fetus, about the way an embryo comes into being, and about the much-debated existence of female semen as a contribution to embryogenesis. The rabbis were even able to develop their own specific variants of these Greek theories.[34] Let me give an example of the latter.

The ancient Greeks were very inventive in developing theories about embryogenesis. Apart from the traditional view (i.e., that the father alone makes the child and provides the substance for its coming-into-being and development, the mother being no more than the hothouse), there were three main theories developed by the early Greek philosophers and physicians: the encephalo-myelogenous doctrine, the pangenesis doctrine, and the haematogenic doctrine.[35] These theories were developed because the traditional view could not explain why children not only resembled their father but often also their mother. As a consequence, the essence of all three theories is the identification of the mother's contribution to the coming-into-being of an embryo. For instance, in the encephalo-myelogenous doctrine it is stated that there is a continuum of "brains–spinal marrow–sperm"; hence "sperm is a drop of brain" (thus Pythagoras according to Diogenes Laertius 8.28). Plato speaks of the "generative marrow" (*Tim.* 77D), and he says that "marrow runs from the head down the neck and along the spine and is indeed ... called seed" (*Tim.* 91A; my translation). It is clear that this doctrine in principle leaves room for a female contribution in the process of conception since the brains–marrow–semen continuum is not restricted to males. Indeed, we find that several adherents of this doctrine adopt the *epikrateia* principle as far as embryogenesis is concerned. The principle of *epikrateia* (predominance) is best illustrated by the short statement in Cen-

34. On Greek embryological knowledge in early rabbinic Judaism and in Qumran, see P. W. van der Horst, "Seven Months' Children in Jewish and Christian Literature from Antiquity," in my *Essays on the Jewish World of Early Christianity*, NTOA 14 (Fribourg: Universitätsverlag; Göttingen: Vandenhoeck & Ruprecht, 1990), 233–48 (this study was republished in a slightly revised version in *Korot: The Israel Journal of the History of Medicine and Science* 23 (2015–2016) 73–98; see also van der Horst "Sarah's Seminal Emission: Hebrews 11:11 in the Light of Ancient Embryology," in my *Hellenism – Judaism – Christianity: Essays on Their Interaction* (Kampen: Kok Pharos, 1994, 2nd ed., 1998), 203–23; and van der Horst, "Bitenosh's Orgasm (1QapGen 2:9-15)," *JSJ* 43 (2012): 613–28. Much of what follows is based upon these earlier studies.

35. For details, see Erna Lesky, *Die Zeugungs- und Vererbungslehren der Antike und ihr Nachwirken*, Abhandlungen der Geistes- und Sozialwissenschaftlichen Klasse; Jahrg. 1950, 19 (Mainz: Akademie der Wissenschaften, 1951). Fridolf Kudlien, "Zur Erforschung archäisch-griechischer Zeugungslehren," *Medizinhistorisches Journal* 16 (1981): 323–39. Hans-Joachim von Schumann, *Sexualkunde und Sexualmedizin in der klassischen Antike* (Munich: UNI-Druck, 1975), 102–204. Marie-Hélène Congourdeau, *L'embryon et son âme dans les sources grecques (VIe siècle av. J.-C.-Ve siècle apr. J.-C.)* (Paris: Association des Amis du Centre d'Histoire et Civilisation de Byzance, 2007).

sorinus, *De die natali* 6.4: "Alcmaeon[36] said that the sex of that parent would be realized [in the embryo] whose semen was most abundant [in coition]" (frag. 24A14 Diels-Kranz). That is to say, if the woman's sperm prevails in quantity at ejaculation,[37] a girl will be born, and if the man's, a boy. This principle, that the seed of either parent can be "overruled" by the other's seed, is not limited to Pythagorean circles but occurs with various modifications in several ancient theories of sex differentiation.

Some—but not all—rabbis adhered to the view that a woman produced her own sperm. For example, in Gen. Rab. 17:8 we read: "Why does a man deposit his sperm within a woman while a woman does not deposit her sperm within a man? It is like a man who has an article in his hand and seeks a trustworthy person with whom he may deposit it."[38] And in a *baraita* in b. Nid. 31a we read:

> Our rabbis taught: There are three partners in (the conception of) a human being, the Holy One —blessed be He—, his father, and his mother. His father supplies the semen of the white substance out of which are formed the child's bones, sinews, nails, the brains in his head and the white in his eye. His mother supplies the semen of the red substance out of which are formed his skin, flesh, hair, blood, and the black of his eye. The Holy One—blessed be He—gives him the spirit and the breath, beauty of features, eyesight, the power of hearing, the ability to speak and to walk, understanding and discernment.[39]

Although the term *epikrateia* is of course not used by the rabbis, the principle was adopted by them. Within the framework of their double-seed theory, the rabbis developed their own version of the *epikrateia* principle. This version states that if a man emits his semen first, the child will be a girl, but if the woman emits her semen first, the child will be a boy (see, e.g., b. Ber. 54a, b. Nid. 70b–71a, etc.).[40] This theory of crosswise sex determination—strange at first sight—was supported by an intriguing exegesis of the unique verbal form *tazria'* in Lev 12:2 and of Gen 46:15. In b. Nid. 31a we read the following interesting discussion:

> Rabbi Isaac citing Rabbi Ammi [or: Assi] stated: If the woman emits her semen [*hiphil* of *zr'*, as in Lev 12:2] first, she bears a male child, if the man

---

36. An early Pythagorean physician.

37. It was assumed that during her orgasm a woman emits her seed into her own uterus.

38. Note that "deposit" is also the original meaning of the Greek *katabolē, sc. spermatos* (ejaculation). Translations of rabbinic literature are from the Soncino editions, sometimes with slight modifications.

39. Cf. also b. Qidd. 30b; Qoh. Rab. 5.10.2.

40. These and other passages are discussed by Rosner, *Medicine in the Bible and the Talmud*, 173–75.

> emits his semen first, she bears a female child; for it is said: "If a woman emits semen [*tazria'*] and bears a male child" [Lev 12:2]. Our Rabbis taught: At first it used to be said that, if the woman emits her semen first, she bears a male child, and if the man emits his semen first, she bears a female child, but the Sages did not explain the reason, until Rabbi Zadok came and explained it: "These are the sons of Leah whom she bore unto Jacob in Paddan-Aram, with his daughter Dinah" [Gen. 46:15]. Scripture thus ascribes the males to the females and the females to the males.

This last sentence makes clear how Gen 46:15 was understood: because this biblical text speaks of "sons of Leah" and of "his [Jacob's] daughter Dinah," Scripture evidently implies that the fact that sons were born was due to Leah and that a daughter was born was due to Jacob. This fact, combined with the conviction that the unique *hiphil* form of *zr'* in Lev 12:2 implies female seminal emission, seems to lead inevitably to this specifically rabbinic doctrine of sex differentiation. The obvious problem of a double pregnancy with both a male and a female embryo was elegantly solved as follows: "It may equally be assumed that both [man and woman] emitted their semen simultaneously, the one resulting in a male and the other in a female" (b. Nid. 25b and 28b).

It is obvious that these arguments were not the fruit of an indigenous development of Jewish ideas about semen, nor were they the result of exegesis of Lev 12:2 and Gen 46:15. The fact that these biblical texts are adduced only in a context of discussion of *epikrateia* as the dominant principle of sex determination makes it highly probable that these biblical passages were taken into service only a posteriori as a scriptural prop to this theory. The Greek theory had already been adopted by the rabbis before the exegetical justification was found. It seems very probable that in this respect, too, the rabbis were indebted to Greek medicine.

Another well-attested instance of the influence of Greek medical theories on early Judaism is the theory of the viability of seven-months' children and the non-viability of eight-months' children. Several ancient Greek physicians wrote about this topic.[41] Its influence on Jewish writers we see for the first time in the first-century CE author of the Liber Antiquitatum Biblicarum when he has God say about Isaac's birth:

> I gave him Isaac and formed him in the womb of her who bore him and commanded to restore him quickly and give him back to me in the seventh month. Therefore, every woman who gives birth in the seventh month, her child will live. (LAB 23:8)

41. See, e.g., Hermann Grensemann (ed.), *Hippokrates: Über Achtmonatskinder; Über das Siebenmonatskind* (Corpus medicorum graecorum 1.2.1; Berlin: Akademie-Verlag, 1968). For more references, see my "Seven Months' Children."

The idea of Isaac being a seven-months' child is found also in b. Roš Haš. 11a, where it is applied to Samuel as well, and in other midrashic sources the same motif is applied to Moses (see, e.g., Tg. Ps.-J. on Exod 2:2; Exod. Rab. 1:19–20; cf. b. Nid. 38b and b. Yebam. 42a).[42] That the rabbis were aware of the Greek origin of this idea is hinted at in Gen. Rab. 14.2:

> There is a viable birth at nine [months] and a viable birth at seven [months]. R. Huna said: When the foetus is so formed as to be born at seven months, and it is born either at seven or at nine months, it is viable; if born at eight months, it cannot live. When it is formed so as to be born at nine but yet it is born at seven months, it cannot live, and all the more so if it is born at eight months. R. Abbahu was asked: "How do we know that when the foetus is fully developed at seven months it is viable?" "From your own [language] I will prove it to you", replied he: "Live, seven; go [away], eight."[43]

The "Hebrew" of the final words is: *zyt' 'ypth 'yth 'ktw*. As Saul Lieberman has convincingly argued, "Since *zêta* equals 7 and *êta* 8, the cryptogram has to be deciphered as: *zê ta hepta <mallon> ê ta oktô*, i.e. 'infants of seven [months] are more likely to survive than those of eight [months]."[44] The unmistakable reference to the numerical value of Greek letters clearly indicates that the rabbis were aware of the Greek origin of these embryological theories.

Much more could be said about this fascinating topic. I hope that what little I have presented in this short paper suffices to show that, after the biblical period, Jews adopted and adapted Greek medical knowledge and accorded physicians a high status. It seems that interpreting the Bible in light of Greek medical theories enabled the rabbis and others to overcome the biblical rejection of medicine to such a degree that the Talmud even stipulates that rabbis should never settle in a city where there are no physicians (b. Sanh. 17b).[45]

---

42. The same motif was applied to New Testament figures (mainly Jesus and Mary) in post-New Testament Christian literature; for discussion see my "Seven Months' Children."

43. For more passages, see Preuss, *Biblisch-talmudische Medizin*, 456–57.

44. Saul Lieberman, *Hellenism in Jewish Palestine: Studies in the Literary Transmission, Beliefs and Manners of Palestine in the I Century B.C.E.–IV Century C.E.*, 2nd ed., Texts and Studies of the Jewish Theological Seminary of America 18 (New York: Jewish Theological Seminary of America, 1962), 77. A less likely explanation is offered by H. Freedman in a note to his translation in *Midrash Rabbah* (London: Soncino, 1939), 1:112 n. 1: "*Zeta*, the Greek letter *Zeta*, whose numerical value is seven, is phonetically like *Zetu* [= *zētō*], let it live!, while *eta* (the letter *ē*), whose numerical value is eight, sounds like *itu* [*itō*], let it go! (i.e. die)." Both scholars agree, however, in the derivation of the wordplay from the Greek.

45. See Krauss, *Talmudische Archäologie*, 1:264.

The Problem of the Hyphen and Jewish/ Judean Ethnic Identity

The Letter of Aristeas, the Septuagint, and Cultural Interactions

BENJAMIN G. WRIGHT
Lehigh University

The Hyphen and Ethnic Identity: Two Contemporary Views

In his study of contemporary American ethnic identity, Matthew Jacobson writes, "Ethnic hyphenation, if not neutral, has at least become a natural idiom of national belonging in this nation of immigrants."[1] Indeed, America has become a nation composed of hyphenated ethnic identities—Italian-American, African-American, Irish-American, and so forth—and these hyphens have done and continue to do important work in the construction of an American identity, so much so that Jacobson can note that in the early twentieth century to represent oneself via a hyphenated designator was seen in the larger culture as decidedly *un*-American. In the last fifty years, by contrast, those same identifiers have come to express a quintessential Americanism founded on the idea of the immigrant.[2] In each case, the hyphen does a lot of work in communicating ethnic identity. It can be constructive—that is, pulling the two identifiers on each side together—but it also can signify a tension between the two elements. The hyphenated identifier might be applied by an external, third-person authority as an ascription, or it can be expressed as a first-person affiliation, that is, one's internal sense of belonging to a group. In the early twentieth century, whatever the first-person affiliation might have been, external authorities understood particularization of a person as Irish-American, say, to suggest that the Irish part detracted from the idea of participating fully in Americanism, that it denoted a holding back from integration.

1. Matthew Frye Jacobson, *Roots Too: White Ethnic Revival in Post-Civil Rights America* (Cambridge, MA: Harvard University Press, 2006), 10.
2. Ibid., 9–10; see also 21–22.

More recently, for some groups, the hyphenated identifier acts as a positive affiliation and has come to convey "national belonging," signifying, for instance, "I am Irish, but at the same time I am fully American." It thus articulates the constructive aspects of the hyphen, while at the same time eliding the tension previously attached to such terms.

Yet, as Jacobson shows, these hyphenated ethnic identifiers have, since the 1960s especially, pushed in a quite different direction, working to create American identities that could be deployed to absolve those who use them from certain anxieties attached to being American, specifically being a white American. The appeal, through use of the hyphen to equate Americanism with *European* immigration, allowed many white Americans to retreat from the uncomfortable implications of white privilege in the civil rights era in which those privileges were identified and challenged.[3]

Moreover, the hyphen subtly roots ethnic identity in a notion of common descent (i.e., *Portuguese*-American) at the same time that it exposes ethnic identity as extending beyond genetic or lineal kinship and into matters of the social and cultural attachments that create ethnic bonds (Irish-*American*), especially through appeals to ethnic heritage.[4] Looked at in this way, ethnic identification is a social performance that is conditioned by cultural factors as much as, if not perhaps more than, dependence on the idea of common descent. These performances can change in different circumstances depending on how individuals want to present themselves, and they can be marshaled in the service of social and cultural ends.

The changing valence of hyphenated designators that look backwards to an immigrant past, especially in the critical social and cultural work they do for arguing about what is (or is not) quintessentially American, illustrates the role they play in the historiography of contemporary America. The history written in and by a hyphen-nation does not simply chronicle the past (no history ever does), but it plays a role in contemporary social and political discourse—as Jacobson puts it, historiography is a "presentist pursuit." The goal is to create a *usable* past, one that serves present needs.[5]

---

3. Ibid., 9: "[O]urs has become a hyphen nation. Like those who came before, this mode of American nationalism is founded in large part on white primacy.... If hyphen-nationalism has articulated and celebrated one myth of origins for the United States and its white population, then it has effaced an older one. Ellis Island remembrance, that is, has perhaps entailed an even more portentous *forgetting* [italics original] of the gradual and violent history of this settler democracy in the making long before the first immigrants of the Castle Garden–Ellis Island variety ever came ashore. Indeed, in order fully to understand how white primacy in American life survived the withering heat of the civil rights era and multiculturalism, we must understand the displacement of Plymouth Rock by Ellis Island in our national myth of origins."

4. See Jacobson, *Roots Too*, 59–60.

5. Ibid., 10.

Writing specifically about contemporary Judaism, Shaul Magid examines the complications of how Jewish ethnicity works in what he calls a postethnic America.[6] Following David Hollinger, Magid understands American Jews as participating in an American culture that is postethnic—that is, in which ethnic identity is neither fixed and stable nor a simple matter of common descent; rather identity is performed.[7] The traditional boundaries of ethnicity, like those of gender and sexual orientation, "are constructed rather than essential categories, hybridity serving as an alternative structure and not an occasion for the dissolution of essential communities."[8] Thus, one can speak of *ethnic identity* as distinguished from *ethnicity*, ethnic identity indicating someone's "self-perception of being a member of an ethnic group."[9] Ethnic identity differs from ethnicity in that the former is fluid and constructed, whereas the latter depends on notions of genealogical or lineal descent. Of course, in both communal and individual instances, ethnicity might constitute one facet, and often a critical one, of ethnic identity.

Within this postethnic America, the relationship between ethnic identity and religion has become increasingly fraught—for Jews between Jewishness and Judaism, although Magid observes, "The vexing relationship between religion/culture and ethnicity as markers of identity is not unique to the American Jewish experience; it has existed in various forms for most of Jewish history."[10] In a postethnic Jewish America, though,

> Jews can, and are, inventing and reinventing new forms of religion, "new" Judaisms through religious syncretism, by using Judaism as a template for world ecological concerns, and by creating new rituals to mark communal, national, and global events that have nothing whatsoever to do with Jews, Jewish history or the Jewish myth. These new practices are often not exclusive to "Jews" and have been increasingly integrated into other religions.[11]

Jewishness, as a matter often both of ascription (by some external authority) and of affiliation (one's internal sense of belonging), is often

6. Shaul Magid, *American Post-Judaism: Identity and Renewal in a Postethnic Society*, Religion in North America (Bloomington, IN: Indiana University Press, 2013).

7. Magid, *American Post-Judaism*, 19. David Hollinger's book, *Postethnic America: Beyond Multiculturalism* (New York: Basic Books, 1995) also is an important influence on Jacobson's study.

8. Ibid., 23.

9. Ibid., 21, citing Bethamie Horowitz, "Old Casks in New Times: The Reshaping of Jewish Identity in the 21st Century," in *Ethnicity and Beyond: Theories and Dilemmas of Jewish Group Demarcation*, ed. Eli Lederhendler, Studies in Contemporary Judaism 25 (New York: Oxford University Press, 2011), 79–90.

10. Magid, *American Post-Judaism*, 25.

11. Ibid., 34.

"invented," with respect to the religion "Judaism" or apart from it. Jewishness, then, might be described as a "performative act rather than an inherited state."[12] As a speech act meant to influence others' perceptions, the structure of the performance actualizes and displays this invented ethnic identity.

The work of Jacobson and Magid has potential benefits for thinking about Jews and Jewishness in the ancient world, both inside and outside of Judea, since Jews lived as a minority in a Mediterranean world dominated by Hellenistic culture. We often think of ancient Jews as the equivalent of a hyphen-nation; they are Hellenistic Jews or Jewish Hellenes, with an implicit hyphen joining the adjective and the noun. The major difference between ancient Jews and contemporary Americans, of course, is that in the contemporary American context both groups and individuals apply these labels to themselves; they are often a self-designation, a matter of affiliation. For ancient Jews, modern scholars apply the label; that is, they ascribe such an identity to ancient people. In an analogous way that the hyphen can imply a certain tension or contestation between the two elements in American hyphenated designators, especially when ascribed, when scholars of ancient Judaism ascribe the descriptor Hellenistic, implicitly Hellenistic-Jewish, to ancient Jews, an unarticulated tension between the Hellenistic and the Jewish lies beneath the surface. Even though many scholarly books and articles have argued for the integration (to varying degrees) of Jews in the Hellenistic world, the use of the hyphen, either implicitly or explicitly, carries with it a suggestion of contestation between the two elements. The older models of Hellenistic and Jewish cultural clashing might not be so operative any more, but to the extent that the hyphenated designator Hellenistic-Jewish or the identifier Hellenistic Jew continues to be used, tension remains nonetheless.[13]

Moreover, to situate and to identify ancient Jews in this way often assumes an essentializing view of culture. The contrast between "Hellenism" and "Judaism" articulated in 2 Maccabees portrays these "-isms" as static and essentially at odds with one another, and these essentialized "-isms" have fixed the parameters for much modern scholarly discussion. As Michael Satlow points out, even though 2 Maccabees employs the terms, they are "second-order" categories that might have heuristic value for modern scholars, but he concludes that even the term "Judaism" does

12. Ibid., 30.

13. See Michael L. Satlow, "Beyond Influence: Toward a New Historiographic Paradigm," in *Jewish Literatures and Cultures: Context and Intertext*, ed. Anita Norwich and Yaron Z. Eliav, BJS 349 (Providence, RI: Brown Judaic Studies, 2008), 37–53, here 37–38, where he cites the studies of Shaye Cohen, Erich Gruen, Seth Schwartz, Peter Schäfer, and Yaron Eliav as examples of this recent move to contest the language of "influence," "assimilation," "conflict," "acculturation," etc.

not work as an analytical category.[14] Rather, ancient Jews, in groups and as individuals, are the social actors on which scholars must focus. Beyond the obfuscatory character of categories such as "Judaism," or "Jewish culture," Satlow argues that Jewish identity in antiquity was more fluid than scholars often recognize, particularly in light of the complexities of identifying ancient texts and artifacts, such as inscriptions, as uncontestably Jewish.[15]

Given the potential fluidity of ethnic identity in antiquity, as in modern cultures, and the problematic implications that accompany hyphenated designators to describe some ancient Jews, I am taking my cue from Magid's and Jacobson's analyses, all the while recognizing that the Hellenistic Mediterranean was not like contemporary postethnic America. Even so, both Jacobson's analysis of the hyphenated ethnic designator and Magid's emphasis on how American Jews perform their Jewishness provide approaches to think with, as one way to move beyond the often unspoken conflict and tension in juxtaposing "Hellenism" and "Judaism," as well as circumventing some of the problems of how one might pin down notions of ethnic identity in ancient texts.

Of course, in the ancient world, an important facet of identity was one's ethnic identity, which itself was not necessarily static or fixed. The recent debates about the use of the term "Jew" or "Judean" reveal some of the issues at stake in thinking about ethnicity and ethnic identity in the ancient world.[16] As Satlow points out, the choice of translating the Greek word *ioudaios* as "Jew" or "Judean" seems to be between understanding the term as an ethno-geographical marker or as a religious

---

14. Satlow writes: "Yet I am becoming increasingly convinced that particularly for historians of the Jews of antiquity, 'Judaism' as an analytical category is more pernicious than useful. Terms such as 'Judaism' or 'Jewish culture' immediately imply a model of culture that separates 'Jewish' from 'non-Jewish' culture. Unless used with extensive qualifications, the terms obscure the ongoing messy negotiations that constitute culture. At the same time, they obscure agency. Jews exist not Judaism" ("Beyond Influence," 43). He largely reserves the category "Judaism" as a descriptive category that denotes "the worldview and rituals of a particular group of Jews" (44).

15. See ibid., 45, and the literature cited there. See, for example, the methodological discussions in Robert A. Kraft, "The Pseudepigrapha in Christianity" and "The Pseudepigrapha and Christianity Revisited: Setting the Stage and Framing Some Central Questions," in *Exploring the Scripturesque: Jewish Texts and Their Christian Contexts*, JSJSup 137 (Leiden: Brill, 2009), 3–33, 35–60, respectively.

16. See Steve Mason, "Jews, Judaeans, Judaizing, Judaism: Problems of Categorization in Ancient History, *JSJ* 38 (2007): 457–512; Adele Reinhartz, "The Vanishing Jews of Antiquity," *Marginalia Review of Books*, June 24, 2014, http://marginalia.lareviewofbooks.org/vanishing-jews-antiquity-adele-reinhartz/. Also Michael Satlow, "Jew or Judaean?" in *"The One Who Sows Bountifully": Essays in Honor of Stanley K. Stowers*, ed. Caroline Johnson Hodge et al., BJS 356 (Providence, RI: Brown Judaic Studies, 2013), 165–75.

identifier.[17] Yet, he demonstrates that *ioudaios*, as employed by the Greek ethnographers, was itself a flexible term. They "recognized the inherent, emic looseness of the category of *ethnos* and manipulated it for their own ends."[18] Notwithstanding the issue of whether we can talk about "religion" in antiquity apart from broader cultural attachments and practices in which religious behavior is embedded, ethnicity and ethnic identity in antiquity, as in the contemporary contexts that Jacobson and Magid have studied, was not always determined and delineated via fixed group boundaries. Rather, ethnic identity was constantly constructed in public performance and was recreated in each performance, and thus it was constructed contingently, both personally and socially. Moreover, performers and audience might well have had different perspectives on the meaning of any given performance.[19] Texts, as special kinds of speech acts, as a type of public performance whose aim was to influence, offer opportunities for understanding how ancient ethnic identities were deployed, but they also have significant limitations, since many texts exist as one-time performances (at least for modern scholars) and often we possess little information about their authors and/or their contexts—in some cases not having them in the original language or even lacking certainty about what it was.

A good case in point is the Letter of Aristeas, whose author tells the story of the translation of the Septuagint through the voice of a gentile courtier of King Ptolemy II Philadelphus. To describe this anonymous author as a hellenized Jew (or Jewish Hellene) does not really have much analytical utility in the end. In a way, all Jews in this period, particularly those in Egypt, were hellenized to some degree or another by the mere fact that they lived in a world dominated by the successors of Alexander the Great. In addition, if the term "Hellenistic Jew" carries with it some inherent tension between the adjective and the noun, especially in terms of ethnic identity, we have to ask if there is indeed evident any perceptible tension between these two constructs in the text itself, and, if there is, what that tension might be and how any tension might play into the performance of ethnic identity in the work. By asking how this author performs his Jewishness, we might be able to bring different perspectives to these questions.

---

17. Satlow, "Jew or Judean?," 166.

18. Ibid., 175. Josephus as well seems occasionally to view the term *ioudaios* in cultural terms (171). On some problems of the terms *ethnos* and *genos* in ancient texts as indicators of ethnicity, see also Erich Gruen, "Did Ancient Identity Depend on Ethnicity? A Preliminary Probe," *Phoenix* 67 (2013): 1–22.

19. Satlow, "Jew or Judaean?," 166–67.

Ethnicity and Ethnic Identity in Ptolemaic Egypt

Before moving to consider Aristeas, the context of ethnic identification in Ptolemaic Egypt deserves brief consideration. After all, Jews living in Egypt would have been subject to external ascription from Ptolemaic authorities as well as identifying ethnically in some way through affiliation. In a recent monograph, Stewart Moore examines ethnicity and ethnic boundaries in Ptolemaic Egypt, also working with notions of ethnic identity that are not founded on lineal descent but that rather are embedded in discourse.[20] He focuses primarily on ethnic boundary markers that distinguish one ethnic group from another in Hellenistic Egypt, and some of his analysis will overlap with mine. Sylvie Honigman also treats ethnic identity in Ptolemaic Egypt, and she emphasizes that legal and social uses of ethnic identities are interdependent; "in a state culture in which the administrative structures and the social groups are one and the same, we must accept that the legal and social uses of ethnicity are interdependent—the administrative uses of the ethnic labels documented in the papyri both reflected and affected the way ethnic and social identities were constructed in Ptolemaic society."[21]

Two examples will suffice for my purposes. The first is the use of double names in different linguistic and social contexts—the use of Greek names in Greek documents and Egyptian names in Demotic documents. Moore cites the case of one Menches of Kerkeosiris, also called Asklepiades, a village scribe/secretary (*kommogrammateus*) who used his Egyptian name in official documents but his Greek name in his private communications. As a result of this practice, the contemporary scholar might not be able in some cases to determine lineal descent based on the type of name that a person had. More significantly, however, a person could employ different ethnic signals or markers in order to have the desired impact in specific social and/or cultural contexts.[22] Ascriptions might also change in different linguistic environments. For example, someone identified in a Greek text as a "Persian of the *epigonē*" or "Persian by descent" might be identified in a Demotic text as a "Greek, born in Egypt." By the second century BCE, apparently, Egyptians recruited as soldiers were admitted into this class of "Persians," which seems to have been a secondary class of

20. Stewart Moore, *Jewish Ethnic Identity and Relations in Hellenistic Egypt: With Walls of Iron?* JSJSup 171 (Leiden: Brill, 2015).

21. Sylvie Honigman, "'Jews as the Best of All Greeks': Cultural Competition in the Literary Works of Alexandrian Judaeans of the Hellenistic Period," in *Shifting Social Imaginaries in the Hellenistic Period: Narrations, Practices, and Images*, ed. Eftychia Stavrianopoulou (Leiden: Brill, 2013), 208–32, here 210.

22. See Moore, *Jewish Ethnic Identity*, 58–59.

Greeks. Thus, a "Persian" in this sense was an occupational designation, as was "Greek" (*Wynn*) in Demotic.[23]

The second example comes from Willy Clarysse's and Dorothy Thompson's study of census lists in the third century BCE, which were compiled primarily for purposes of taxation.[24] Clarysse and Thompson found that the lists were organized into various *ethnē*, some of which had a privileged status when it came to being exempted from or liable for paying certain taxes. Some of these *ethnē* might be what we would more commonly think of as kinship groups based on lineal descent; others were based on occupation or status, such as teachers, actors, or victors in athletic contests.[25]

Of the groups earmarked for special tax consideration, the designation "Hellene" might be the most illustrative. In the papyri that Clarysse and Thompson published, Hellenes were generally exempt from the one-*obol* tax, and this category seems to have stood along with the occupational *ethnē* as a favored tax status. Yet the term does not simply indicate someone of Greek descent. In fact, as Thompson observes, the label denotes "a superior tax status. It differed from other occupational designations … in that it might be applied to those who held various jobs at the same time as enjoying that status."[26] Some of the people categorized as Hellenes for tax purposes (whom Clarysse and Thompson call "tax-Hellenes") were Jews and even some Egyptians. From the town of Trikomia, for instance, we find listed as not subject to the one-*obol* tax and thus Hellenes for tax purposes, Jews and Thracians.[27] Thompson sums up the situation nicely, and her remarks form an appropriate segue to the discussion of Aristeas:

> Perceptions of Greek ethnicity in terms of origin form only part of the picture. Greek ethnicity and Greek culture cannot stand apart. If culture was originally an expression of ethnicity—Greek culture belonged to Greeks as did Egyptian to Egyptians—then in the new world that followed Alexander this was no longer clear. As ethnic identity became more blurred—with mixed marriages and the status of tax Hellene—so culture itself

---

23. Ibid., 49, relying on the analysis of Katelijn Vandorpe, "Persian Soldiers and Persians of the Epigone: Social Mobility of Soldiers-Herdsmen in Upper Egypt," *APF* 54 (2008): 87–108.

24. Willy Clarysse and Dorothy J. Thompson, *Counting the People in Hellenistic Egypt*, 2 vols., Cambridge Classical Studies (Cambridge: Cambridge University Press, 2006). See also Moore, *Jewish Ethnic Identity*, 58–62, where he discusses Clarysse and Thompson.

25. See the comments on *ethnos* in Gruen, "Did Ancient Identity Depend on Ethnicity?," 1–2.

26. Dorothy J. Thompson, "Hellenistic Hellenes: The Case of Ptolemaic Egypt," in *Ancient Perceptions of Greek Ethnicity*, ed. Irad Malkin, Center for Hellenic Studies Colloquia 5 (Washington, DC: Center for Hellenic Studies, 2001), 301–21, here 311.

27. The papyrus is P.Count 26, published in Clarysse and Thompson, *Counting the People*, 1:357–77; see the discussion in 2:145.

(language, education, the gymnasium) increasingly became the defining feature of Greekness. At the same time a growing number of individuals moved easily between the two worlds. And whether it was the Greek or Egyptian face (or sometimes both together) that they presented depended simply on the particular moment of time and the context in which they happened to be. It is only when we realize the complexities and fluidity of personal identity in this world that the role of ethnicity, language, and culture in Ptolemaic Egypt may begin to be assessed.[28]

The Performance of Judeanness/Jewishness in the Letter of Aristeas

The Jew who produced the Letter of Aristeas clearly had a Greek education, and he produced a Hellenistic literary text in the form of a Greek book in which he employs Greek rhetorical style and Greek literary forms but also in which he performs rhetorically his (and that of his co-ethnics) Judeanness by a variety of means.[29] In his study of Aristeas, Moore detects strong ethnic boundaries, which are "well-placed and well-patrolled."[30] The author shows no anxiety that appropriating Greek culture will compromise this identity. Thus, Moore concludes, Aristeas does not focus on ethnic boundaries per se but on the "cultural stuff" that these boundaries encompass. Moreover, he argues that, by representing the Septuagint as the product of *Judean* translators, not Alexandrian ones, the author of Aristeas (hereafter Ps.-Aristeas) is encouraging his Alexandrian Jewish readers "to add to their understanding of their ethnic boundaries and markers a greater sense of devotion to Jerusalem itself."[31] While I agree with much of Moore's overall reading of Aristeas, I disagree with his claim that Ps.-Aristeas shows no anxiety about his and his readers' Judeanness being compromised by their appropriation of Greek culture. I do think that the book reveals some anxiety about Judean participation in the larger cultural and social world of Alexandria, as I shall argue below.

A modern reader is struck immediately by the fact that the narrator of this text is explicitly not a Jew. Thus, through the pseudepigraphic voice

---

28. Thompson, "Hellenistic Hellenes," 316.

29. For more detail, see Benjamin G. Wright III, *The Letter of Aristeas: 'Aristeas to Philocrates' or 'On the Translation of the Law of the Jews'*, CEJL (Berlin: Walter de Gruyter, 2015) and "Greek *Paideia* and the Jewish Community in the Letter of Aristeas," in *Second Temple Jewish Paideia in Context*, ed. Jason M. Zurawski and Gabriele Boccaccini, BZNW 228 (Berlin: de Gruyter, 2017), 93–112. I have taken the term *Judeanness,* despite its awkwardness, from Moore and use it in line with Honigman's position, with which I largely agree, that in Aristeas the term *ioudaioi* "retained its political/ethnic value both in real society and in the literary works produced by Alexandrian Judeans" ("Jews as the Best," 209).

30. Moore, *Jewish Ethnic Identity*, 210.

31. Both quotations come from Moore, *Jewish Ethnic Identity*, 210.

of "Aristeas," a gentile courtier of Ptolemy II Philadelphus, we hear about Jews and who they are. For the purposes of understanding the performance of Judeanness in this text, the choice of the gentile narrator stands out. John Barclay concludes from the use of a gentile narrator that the implied reader of the text was gentile.[32] I am more persuaded that the function of this narrator makes the best sense with a Jewish audience in mind. Ps.-Aristeas's gentile narrator communicates to Jews that elite Greeks "get" their behaviors and practices, even if some of them might seem strange to a Greek audience.[33] Moreover, if Ps.-Aristeas is concerned about revalorizing ethnic boundaries and identity, then a Jewish audience is practically required.

Within the narrative, we hear three other significant voices: two gentiles—Ptolemy II Philadelphus and his chief librarian Demetrius of Phalerum—and one Judean—Eleazar, the high priest in Jerusalem. All three are filtered through the Greek (but still Jewish) voice of "Aristeas," who quotes them—the king in letters and in the questions posed at the series of symposia held in honor of the translators, Demetrius in two short memoranda to Ptolemy, and Eleazar at length in an *apologia* for the Jewish law. In the way that he conducts this complex chorus of voices, we can derive important insight into how Ps.-Aristeas performs Judeanness in the text.

The place to begin, however, is not with any single voice but with what might be the most important single term, *ioudaios,* and its attendant adjective *ioudaikos*. Do the terms indicate lineal descent? Geographical origins? Religious/cultural affiliation? Some combination of these ascriptions? *Ioudaios* and *ioudaikos* appear eighteen times in Aristeas. Some of these connect a specific people, who have their own laws, language, and customs, to a place called Judea. Almost all of the early uses of the terms in §§1, 6, 10–12, 15, and 22–24 establish this overall meaning.[34] (The other occurrences come in §§28, 30, 35, 38, 121 [adjective], 176 [adjective], 305, 308; see below.)

Aristeas §1 refers to Eleazar, "the high priest of the Judeans." Since "Aristeas" is being sent in a delegation to Jerusalem to fetch translators, whose leader is Eleazar, geography takes precedence, although lan-

32. John M. G. Barclay, *Jews in the Mediterranean Diaspora: From Alexander to Trajan (323 BCE–113 CE)* (Edinburgh: T&T Clark, 1996), 148.

33. For a fuller argument, see Benjamin G. Wright, "Pseudonymous Authorship and Structures of Authority in the *Letter of Aristeas*," in *Scriptural Authority in Early Judaism and Ancient Christianity*, ed. Isaac Kalimi, Tobias Nicklas, and Géza Xeravits, DCLS 16 (Berlin: de Gruyter, 2013), 43–61, esp. 53–61; and Letter of Aristeas §§19–20, 62–64.

34. Shaye J. D. Cohen restricts the meaning more than I would for Aristeas, specifically to the connection between the people and the place. See *The Beginnings of Jewishness: Boundaries, Varieties, Uncertainties*, HCS 31 (Berkeley: University of California Press, 1999), 84.

guage and cultural connections certainly factor in as well, as we see later in the text.

Aristeas §6 has the phrase *tou genous tōn Ioudaiōn*, "the race of the Judeans." The use of *genos* here is the only place in Aristeas where *ioudaios* and lineage might converge, although as Erich Gruen has shown, the term can also connote "community" or "collectivity" without indicating descent or lineage.[35] Even if the phrase denotes lineage in this passage, this component of ethnic identity plays a very minor role in how ethnic identity is constructed in Aristeas.

In Aristeas §§10–11 (§30), we hear of the "laws of the Judeans" as well as the language these people speak—Aramaic, not Greek—which suggests a cultural interpretation of Judean ethnic identification. Demetrius's reference to the language of Judeans does not serve as a universal statement, however, since he specifically refers to Judea as the place where the inhabitants speak this language.[36]

Aristeas §§22–24 focuses on war captives taken by Ptolemy I. *Ioudaioi* come from the "country of the Judeans." See especially §23, where Judeans are said to be removed from Judea and taken into Egypt.

Five passages stand in need of special comment, however, which fall under and reinforce the general meaning I gave above. First, in §38, as part of a letter that Ptolemy sends to Eleazar asking for Judean translators, he says, "Now since we desire to show favor to them [i.e., Judeans in Egypt] and *to all Judeans throughout the world and to future generations* (πᾶσι τοῖς κατὰ οἰκουμένην Ἰουδαίοις καὶ τοῖς μετέπειτα), we have decided that your law shall be translated into Greek letters from the Hebrew letters spoken by you." This is a remarkable statement, since, although a gentile king ostensibly says it and thus it serves as an ascription of Judeanness, the idea that having the Judeans' law in Greek would benefit all Judeans currently living as well as all future Judeans comes from a Judean pen. With respect to the meaning of *ioudaios* here, Ps.-Aristeas seems to indicate that anyone living anywhere who might affiliate through attachment to the laws of the Judeans qualifies as a Judean. Thus, in the case of the law in Aristeas, ascription and affiliation fuse together as a central aspect, perhaps *the* critical indicator of Judean ethnic identity.

Second, the translation of the laws introduces one complication. In §11, Demetrius tells the king that the Judeans "are supposed to use Syrian (characters). This is not so, but they use another style." Demetrius attributes the use of special characters to Judeans living *in Judea*, however, as

35. Gruen, "Did Ancient Identity Depend on Ethnicity," 13–14.

36. The idea that there is a Judean language appears in other texts as well. So, for example, Neh 13:23–24 notes that, upon his arrival in Judea, Nehemiah discovered Jews who had intermarried and the children "could not speak the language of Judah but spoke the languages of various peoples" (NRSV).

I noted above. His statement is part of an answer to the king's question of why the laws of the Judeans are not in the library. Demetrius responds that they need to be translated, because "*in Judea* they use their own characters." Third, in §15, we read that the law "has been laid down for all Judeans." Here the law applies to Judeans everywhere (also in §38) even though it has not been translated into Greek as yet. "Aristeas" is not making a statement about language and ethnic identity, however, but he is urging the king to release the Judean slaves in his kingdom, whose captivity, "Aristeas" argues, compromises the mission of translation. Thus, whereas at first blush §11 and §15 might appear to privilege language as a central component of Judean ethnic identity, it does not function that way. Rather, it is a commitment to the law that takes precedence both for those living in Judea and elsewhere.

The fourth passage, §305, describes the translators' activities. After rising and greeting the king, they go to their designated place for working: "and as is the custom of *all* the Judeans (ἔθος ἐστὶ πᾶσι τοῖς Ἰουδαίοις), when they had washed their hands in the sea in order that they might offer prayer to God, they turned to reading and explication of each detail." One might ask who the *all* is in this sentence. Is it those who live in Judea? Or all Judeans *in the world*, as in §38? I take it to refer to all those throughout the world, since in §15 and §38, where all Judeans are mentioned explicitly, Judeans everywhere in the world are meant. In this passage, as elsewhere in Aristeas, a gentile observes/knows about a Judean practice, asks what it means, and the Judeans explain. In this case "they explained that it is a testimony that they have done no wrong" (§306). Washing one's hands before prayer is given a moral significance, a significant interpretive move, as we will see in Eleazar's speech as well. Judeanness, then, includes cultural practices to which all Judeans adhere, which set them apart from Greeks and which Ps.-Aristeas feels the need to explain.

The fifth passage comes from the scene of the acceptance of the translation. In §308, Demetrius brings together "the people of the Judeans" (τὸ πλῆθος τῶν Ἰουδαίων) for the reading of the translation, which the people then accept à la biblical scenes of acceptance of something as authoritative and binding.[37] From the enumeration of the representatives of the groups of Judeans in §310, it seems as if the "multitude/people" of the Judeans comprised the translators, the members of a Judean *politeuma* in Alexandria, and "the people." The inclusion of those who are clearly Alexandrian with the Judean translators suggests that the designation "Judeans" does not only refer primarily to those who come from Judea, whether that connection is present or ancestral. These people have gathered for a reading of the translation of the law, and thus, the laws and customs that these

37. See Harry M. Orlinsky, "The Septuagint as Holy Writ and the Philosophy of the Translators," *HUCA* 46 (1975): 89–114. See also Wright, *Letter of Aristeas*, 442–45.

people practice constitute the central feature of identity. Indeed, in §311, we find another reference to the *ethos* of the Judeans, who are wont to place a curse on anyone who might think to change any part of the text.

So, Ps.-Aristeas makes a significant aspect of Judeanness an affiliation with habits and customs of a particular people, who might or might not reside in or come from Judea. The term *ioudaios* in Aristeas, then, does not mean primarily to be part of a kinship group or particular lineage. Rather, it has several components. As expressed in the term *ioudaios,* Judeanness can mean: (1) belonging to a particular *genos* (lineage group or collectivity) and/or *ethnos*; (2) who are governed by and abide by their own laws; (3) who practice a set of habits and customs characteristic of these people; and (4) who have at least some connection with the country of Judea. The significance of this last component is perhaps the most difficult to determine, since Ps.-Aristeas refers at times to all Judeans throughout the world, on the one hand, and yet, on the other, throughout the text he assumes a relatively close connection between Judeans and the institution of the high priesthood and temple in Judea. Whether Ps.-Aristeas thinks that all of these characteristics *in toto* constitute Judean ethnic identity or whether any single component or combination of components would suffice is not immediately clear. For the most part, however, when Ps.-Aristeas refers to Judeans, we are warranted in thinking that for him Judean ethnic identity consists at least partially in some connection to and/or association with the land of Judea, whether any Judean lives in Judea or looks to Judea as an ancestral homeland.

Of the voices that our author creates to tell his story, Demetrius's makes the briefest appearance, informing the king of the special character of the law (§31) and the intricacies of which language Judeans use. "Aristeas's," Eleazar's, and Ptolemy's voices tell us much more. Each one contributes important aspects of Ps.-Aristeas's idea of what constitutes Judean identity. One voice, Eleazar's, explains how Judean cultural practices that might be perceived as separating Judeans from Greeks really do not do so. The other two voices establish that Judeans are in fact Greeks, in the sense that we saw above in the Ptolemaic-period Egyptian papyri.

As to the voice of "Aristeas," throughout the story, our author takes pains to have him certify that he witnessed every event that he narrates, and he thus functions as the primary conduit of information about Judeans. As a rule, the character of "Aristeas" helps to place Judeans firmly within the bounds of mainstream Hellenistic culture. He points out Judean difference only *after* Eleazar's speech in which *accounting for* difference is a major theme. Early in the work, in the famous §16, "Aristeas" informs the king that Judeans "revere God, the overseer and creator of all things, whom all, even we, also worship, O King, using different names, Zeus and Dis." This equation exemplifies the way that Ps.-Aristeas employs Greek philosophical ideas that would presumably resonate with an educated and elite

Jewish audience, and it fits into larger arguments in Aristeas that Judeans excel at Greek philosophy—likely trading on well-known tropes about the Jews as a philosophical people. Other voices, such as Demetrius's in §31, where he calls the law philosophical, echo this portrayal. Indeed, Honigman takes §31 as evidence of a strategy of cultural competition in which Ps.-Aristeas positions Judeans as the *best* of all Greeks.[38] Later on, our narrator, by giving a blow-by-blow description of the seventy-two questions and answers in the symposia, represents the translators, who have come from Jerusalem, as philosophers who surpass any that the king has in his retinue. Moreover, he notes specifically that they have been prepared in Greek literature as well as their own literary traditions (§121), which prepares the reader for the translators' answers in the symposia as well as their bona fides for making the translation. By exploiting philosophical ideas and categories extensively throughout the work and by representing the translators as philosophers, Ps.-Aristeas, at the very least, situates Judeans within the larger mainstream of educated Hellenistic culture.

The narrator "Aristeas" also offers a long description of Judea, Jerusalem, and the surrounding areas as evidence of his travel to the high priest Eleazar to fetch the men who will translate the Jewish laws into Greek. In an idealized description, Ps.-Aristeas constructs Judea as an ideal Greek *polis,* a city par excellence, which rivals, indeed outshines, even Alexandria.[39] In a *synkrisis* (§§107–111), comparing the cities of Jerusalem and Alexandria, he rewrites a section of the Pseudo-Aristotelian tractate *Athenian Constitution* in which Jerusalem surpasses Alexandria, since it possesses the optimal relationship between the city and the country.[40] Thus, Judeans, both those who come from Jerusalem and those in the diaspora whose origins can be traced there, qualify as Greeks, just as do others who come from such *poleis* as Athens, Thebes, Sparta, and so on.[41] This idea is further emphasized in §182, where "Aristeas" reports that the protocols undertaken for the Judean translators comported with those given representatives from other cities: "For however many cities [*poleis*] have their own customs for drink and food and bedding, that number [i.e., of officials] was also assigned to them, And so things were prepared according

38. Honigman, "Jews as the Best." See below for more consideration of her overall thesis.

39. See Cohen, *Beginnings of Jewishness,* 126, where he argues, "The Letter of Aristeas views Judaeans everywhere as 'citizens' of the polity governed by Eleazar, the high priest of Jerusalem."

40. See Wright, *Letter of Aristeas,* 223–25; and Hongiman, "Jews as the Best," 227–28. Honigman argues that this *synkrisis* intends to link Jerusalem with Athens and thus as the source of Alexandrian culture. I am not convinced that this is the case. Rather, the comparison with Alexandria is to show that Judeans come from a *polis,* and thus they qualify as Greeks in Ptolemaic Egypt.

41. See Honigman, "Jews as the Best," 209.

to these customs whenever someone might come before the king so that being disturbed by nothing, they would pass the time cheerfully."[42]

The voice of the king further underscores the status of Judeans as Greeks who come from a *polis*. When Ptolemy writes to Eleazar, greeting him by his title of high priest, he essentially recognizes the Judean as a head of state. In Ptolemaic letters of this period, the use of the title to an addressee can indicate the addressee's equal or independent status.[43] Thus, the king recognizes Eleazar as the leader of a people who are constituted as a Greek city, and, as we saw above, people who reside in Egypt from such places are recognized as Greeks/Hellenes for various legal purposes. When it comes to the symposia, outside of the individual questions and answers, which as a rule represent the Judean translators as philosophers, the king unfailingly and heartily approves of whatever answers he receives. Thus, the approbation of the king certifies these Judeans as Greeks who fit well into the mainstream of Greek life in Alexandria.

Through each of these two figures, Ps.-Aristeas portrays Judeans as hailing from a *polis* governed by an independent leader recognized as such by Ptolemy himself, who, as excellent philosophers, can compete with Greeks on their own ground. At every turn, these Gentile voices emphasize the compatibility, even the equality, of Judeans and Greeks.[44] Difference is for the most part ignored. Ps.-Aristeas's gentile characters extend an external ascription that Judeans can be classified as Greeks, and within the social world of Hellenistic Alexandria in the late second century BCE, Judeanness includes or can encompass Greekness as part of ethnic identity. In this ascription, a potentially hyphenated identity, Jew-Hellene, serves as a means for gentiles to incorporate and accept Jews into the majority Greek *ethnos* of Hellenistic Alexandria.

When we get to the figure of Eleazar, we encounter perhaps the most important voice in Aristeas. The high priest's long speech, covering §§128–171, serves as the primary vehicle by which Ps.-Aristeas admits to Jewish difference and at the same time explains why Judeans are not really as different from Greeks as they might seem, even though they observe cultural practices that set them apart and that might appear to align them with Egyptians. In addition, coming from the mouth of the leader of the Judeans, the aspects of Judeanness that appear in his speech count as matters of affiliation rather than of ascription. The speech, which is prompted

42. Ibid., 208.

43. On the letter, see Wright, *Letter of Aristeas*, 158–62.

44. Some scholars argue that Ps.-Aristeas is making an argument for the superiority of Jews over Greeks. See, e.g., Erich Gruen, *Heritage and Hellenism: The Reinvention of Jewish Tradition*, HCS 30 (Berkeley: University of California Press, 1998), 216; and Gruen, "Jewish Perspective on Greek Culture and Ethnicity," in *Hellenism in the Land of Israel*, ed. John J. Collins and Gregory E. Sterling, Christianity and Judaism in Antiquity 13 (Notre Dame, IN: University of Notre Dame Press, 2001), 62–93.

by a question from "Aristeas" about Judean legislation "concerning food and drink and those beasts considered unclean" (§128), encompasses two basic topics, worship of idols and kosher law, although a short section also treats *tefillin* and *mezuzot*. With respect to idol worship, Eleazar, via indirect speech reported by "Aristeas," makes the claim that the Judean god is the only or unique god, employing the term *monos*. Honigman suggests that this use deliberately differs from what might be the more usual term in philosophy, *heis*, and thus Ps.-Aristeas is arguing that, by maintaining that God is unique, Judean philosophy goes further than any other Greek philosophical school.[45] This assertion would cohere well with the performance of the translators in the symposia that come after Eleazar's speech.

In his attack on idol worship, Eleazar reserves his most vehement language for Egyptians and others like them who "rely upon wild beasts and most serpents and animals and worship these, and they sacrifice to them, both alive and dead" (§138). His rejection of theriolatry, a practice that fascinated some ancient writers but was subjected to scorn by others, repudiates any ethnic connection to Egyptians.[46] When treating Greek worship, Eleazar reduces polytheism to Euhemerism, which, as Honigman notes, "re-directs his attacks from the Greeks in general to a specific philosophical movement, but in doing so further redefines the philosophical (and social) boundaries between insiders and outsiders."[47] Ps.-Aristeas, through the voice of Eleazar, marginalizes a philosophical movement that other Hellenistic philosophical schools had already subjected to criticism.[48] Greek outsiders become Judean outsiders as well, and symbolically Judeans stand with Greeks in their philosophical critique of these ideas.

Eleazar's rejection of idol worship and polytheism concludes with perhaps the most famous passage in Aristeas: "Therefore, the lawgiver ... fenced us around with unbroken palisades and with iron walls that we might not intermingle at all with any other nations, being pure in both body and soul, having been set free from vain opinions, revering the only and powerful God above all of creation" (§139). In the context of Eleazar's speech, although this statement might seem to separate Judeans from all non-Judeans, it might not really. The tone and tenor of earlier paragraphs frame Gentiles who share monotheism with Judeans—particularly Ptolemy II (cf. §16) and "Aristeas" himself—and Judeans as being on the same side, standing apart from those who remain mired in idolatry and poly-

45. Honigman, "Jews as the Best," 216.

46. See Wright, *Letter of Aristeas*, 261–63.

47. Honigman, "Jews as the Best," 220. Moore does not read this section as essentially a critique of Euhemerism, but he writes, "As for the Greeks, the question remains, what sort of Greeks would its author have believed capable of assenting to Eleazar's public lambasting of the patrimonial gods and their image-venerating rites?" (*Jewish Ethnic Identity*, 224). If one accepts Honigman's reading, then the issue in the text is not so starkly set out.

48. Honigman, "Jews as the Best."

theism.[49] Thus, as in other passages in Aristeas, the author arrays Judeans and educated, elite Greek against folks who do not think the same way as they do. Yet, at the same time, Ps.-Aristeas affirms in his use of *monos* for God, that one important marker of Judeanness and something that sets Judeans apart is worship of a god who is considered unique from all others and the creator of the cosmos.

At the beginning of his treatment of the food laws, Eleazar confronts the matter of Judean difference with the statement, "Do not come to the exploded conclusion that Moses legislated these matters on account of a curiosity with mice and weasels or similar creatures" (§144). The language of the section presumes that Judeans in Alexandria practice avoidance of certain foods and that this custom might separate them from Greeks. In a nutshell, Eleazar gives symbolic meanings to the food laws that have moral implications.[50] Judean legislation commands abstention from certain foods and permits the eating of others—in this case certain birds—in order to inculcate moral values, primarily justice. Judeans also eat ruminants in order to remind them of the "ruling and preserving nature of God" (§157). They share these moral values with elite Greeks, who agree on the need for justice and recollection of divine preservation.[51] Moore makes the tentative suggestion that Ps.-Aristeas might want to distinguish Judeans from Egyptians, who also prohibited certain foods but within the structure of a system of animal worship.[52] In this reading, as they do elsewhere, Judeans stand with Greeks over against Egyptians. Thus, Judeanness, as expressed in adherence to Judean laws, includes keeping the food laws given in Mosaic legislation. Even if such practices potentially divide Judeans from Greeks, Ps.-Aristeas contends, the reason for these peculiar Judean practices coincides with Greek values of justice and proper moral behavior.

Throughout this section, Eleazar appeals to the Judeans' "legislation" (*nomothesia*), which was given by the "lawgiver" Moses. Somewhat surprisingly, Ps.-Aristeas does not attribute the giving of the law to God. Rather, God prepared Moses's mind "for knowledge of all things" (§139), and thus God equipped him to give the Judeans their legislation. The focus on Moses as the lawgiver, especially in light of Ps.-Aristeas's portrayal of Judeans as the citizens of a Greek *polis*, places him in the company of other famous Greek lawgivers, such as Solon and Lycurgus. Moreover, since Eleazar authorizes the translation and offers authoritative interpretations of Mosaic law in Greek, which depend in places on the

49. See Wright, *Letter of Aristeas*," 264. Also Honigman, "Jews as the Best," 219–20.

50. For the full argument, see the appropriate paragraphs in Wright, *Letter of Aristeas*.

51. This section also includes a condemnation of male prostitution and incest, which Honigman connects to critiques of Cynics and early Stoics ("Jews as the Best," 221).

52. Moore, *Jewish Ethnic Identity*, 227.

language of the Septuagint, he functions as a type of Moses for the giving of the law a second time, only this time in its Greek form and for a people who reside in Egypt with no need to escape.[53] Within the narrative world of the text, Greeks understand why Judeans follow their laws, and they accept them as the laws constitutive of a particular people. Moreover, the Greeks in Aristeas abide by these laws in their interactions with Judeans. Thus, Judeanness includes observing the stipulations of the law but also recognizing that these laws have symbolic meanings that accompany the practice. In the same breath, however, Ps.-Aristeas implicitly represents the laws of the Judeans as comparable to the laws of Greek cities that were laid down by famous lawgivers.

These different narrative voices, then, allow Ps.-Aristeas to construct a Judean identity through ascription and affiliation. In the voice of Eleazar, he can affirm a kind of hyphenated identity that allows Jews to invent or reinvent a "new" form of Judaism, to paraphrase Magid, that allows room for them to affiliate as Hellenes as well. Gentile voices ascribe Greekness to the Judeans, even minimizing some of the unique aspects of Judean identity while at the same time also providing space for Judeans to affiliate as Jews and as Hellenes. Moreover, the gentile narrator confirms the centrality of the "laws of the Judeans," in this case the Greek Pentateuch that has been translated from a Hebrew text authorized by the ruler of the Judeans, as the governing constitution of a Hellenistic people. This same narrator assures the Judean community of Alexandria that gentiles appreciate the Septuagint as its foundational legislation and that it constitutes a central feature of their identity.[54] Much like contemporary bearers of hyphenated identities, Judeans in Alexandria could continue to practice their ancestral laws and customs while at the same time identifying as Hellenes, both by external ascription and internal affiliation.

In terms of how Ps.-Aristeas performs Judeanness in his work, then, Judean ethnic identity includes abiding by Judean laws, observing specifically Judean practices along with a connection to Judea, whether that connection is through residing in or having an ancestral homeland in Judea. Worship of the Judean god, who is thought to be unique and the creator, forms a significant and central component of Judeanness. More than that, however, Judean ethnic identity in Alexandria has Greekness as a component, perhaps even subsuming aspects of Judeanness under Greekness.

---

53. Ps.-Aristeas rewrites the exodus narrative in order to authorize the giving of the law in Egypt through the beneficence of a kind pharaoh (Ptolemy II) and a second Moses (Eleazar). On this idea, see Wright, *Letter of Aristeas*; Sylvie Honigman, *The Septuagint and Homeric Scholarship in Alexandria: A Study in the Narrative of the* Letter of Aristeas (London: Routledge, 2003); and Arkady Kovelman, *Between Alexandria and Jerusalem: The Dynamic of Jewish and Hellenistic Culture*, Brill Reference Library of Judaism 21 (Leiden: Brill, 2005).

54. See Wright, "Pseudonymous Authorship."

Throughout Aristeas, our author takes pains to show that Judeans in Alexandria differ little from any other people whose origins can be traced to a Greek *polis* with their own laws and *ethos*. Furthermore, Aristeas offers tantalizing suggestions that Judeans, like other Greeks, saw themselves as separate from Egyptians. I agree fully with Moore, who maintains that ethnic identity and relations in Ptolemaic Egypt must take into consideration relations among Judeans, Greeks and Egyptians.[55] Ps.-Aristeas's performance of Judeanness also bears out Honigman's premise that

> insofar as the ethnic labels used in the Ptolemaic administrative papyri corresponded to genuine social categories and document a peculiar two-tiered construction of Greek ethnicity, there is no reason to doubt that the *Ioudaioi* settled in Alexandria, and in Egypt as a whole, in Ptolemaic times were defined by the royal administration as a sub-group within the immigrant community of the Greeks. Moreover, I take for granted that the Judaeans themselves endorsed this two-tiered construction of ethnicity and perceived themselves as a sub-category of the Greeks.[56]

Why was it important for Ps.-Aristeas to work so hard to present Judeans in this light to a Judean audience that must have had a high enough level of education to be able to see what he was up to? Honigman answers that, unlike other areas of the Hellenistic world, where a three-tiered classification system of Greek, hellenized Barbarians, and everybody else operated, the Alexandrian social reality was two-tiered, comprising the categories of Greeks and Egyptians, with no room for hellenized Barbarians. As a result, Ps.-Aristeas worked to construct a Judean identity that fit within this system and that presented Judeans not just as Greek but the best of all Greeks. Whether the point is that Judeans are the best of or equal to Greeks, this interpretation would appeal to an educated Judean audience, and it accounts for a Judean desire to fit into the Ptolemaic system. To be classified as and to present oneself publicly as a Hellene undoubtedly was perceived as having social advantages.

The fact that Ps.-Aristeas labors to include Judeans as a type of Greek could reveal some anxiety that Judeans might not be accepted as Greeks. Moore points to a complex of traditions that connect Judeans with Egyptians, from ethnographers who trace Judean origins back to Egyptians to traditions about Judeans being inhospitable and possessing ridiculous laws (such as food prohibitions).[57] If we take into account that these traditions circulated in Egypt, we might interpret Ps.-Aristeas's efforts to portray Judeans as Greeks as reflecting an anxiety on his or his audience's

55. Moore, *Jewish Ethnic Identity*, chap. 2.
56. Honigman, "Jews as the Best," 211–12.
57. Moore, *Jewish Ethnic Identity*, 137–46, and the literature cited there.

part that they might be confused with or identified as Egyptians. Not only does our author show the positive connections between Judeans and Greeks, but he works to explain away those practices that might connect them with Egyptians. Thus, constructing an ethnic identity of Judeanness that accommodates or encompasses Greekness accomplishes strategic social goals for Ps.-Aristeas. In addition, all of the Greeks in the book accept Judeans who practice Judean customs, and they acknowledge the Septuagint as legislation laid down by an early lawgiver, which legitimately serves to govern them. Consequently, Ptolemy goes further than having food prepared according to Judean requirements; he also abides by other Judean practices in the symposia, for example, by sending away the sacred heralds and those who usually offered prayers in favor of prayer by one of the Judean translators (§184). The clear implication of §186 is that the king and all those gathered at the symposium also ate the food prepared according to Judean dietary requirements. In Ps.-Aristeas's view, any anxiety about whether Judeans would be considered Greeks or Egyptians ought to be allayed by the way that elite Greeks in his story deal with Judeans. Judeans are Greeks, and the Greeks who matter treat them that way. Thus, he fashions Judeans' Greekness through literary strategies that invoke both ascription and affiliation.

Yet I do not think that this anxiety warrants the hyphenated adjective Hellenistic-Jewish or the implicitly hyphenated Hellenistic Jew, if that hyphenation implies a tension between being Jewish and/or being Greek. Although Ps.-Aristeas exhibits *anxiety* about Judeans being accepted as Greeks—that is, through ascription from external authorities and sources—I do not see this kind of *tension* in *Aristeas,* particularly in terms of affiliation. Although our author might have or be aware of some anxiety that Judeans might not be classified as Hellenes, he makes the clear case for Judeans being identified as Greek *in terms of ethnic identity rather than ethnicity* to use the distinction I made above. If we leave the world of the narrative for the moment and consider Ps.-Aristeas himself through his literary product, we encounter someone who had a Greek education, who employed Greek rhetorical and literary devices, who knew Hellenistic and Classical Greek sources. This is a person whose level of education and literary persona present him as a Greek. His Judeanness shines through in his use of the Septuagint, which, as part of the Judean literary heritage, would not have been taught in a Greek school. Yet he approaches the Septuagint as he does his Greek sources. Sometimes he quotes, often he paraphrases, and he subjects the exodus story to a dramatic reconfiguration, indeed an inversion, from a story about a people escaping Egypt and an oppressive pharaoh and receiving the law through divine agency from the hand of God's human messenger Moses to a story of a second Moses, through his appointed deputies, giving the law in Greek in Egypt where a benevolent pharaoh facilitates the entire enterprise. In this way, he creates a *usable* history that situates Judeans in Alexandria as maintaining those aspects of Judeanness that he considers central at the same time that he can efface the problematic aspects of that history and claim Greekness as well. In the end, the people accept this second law as authoritative and binding, and it stands alongside and independent of the Hebrew law as containing all that Moses ordained for the Judean people.

In the Letter of Aristeas, then, the construction of ethnic identity extends well beyond claims to ethnicity, to common descent. The author presents Judean ethnic identity as multifaceted, analogous in some ways to modern American and Jewish identities. The extent to which Judean identity might have been *fluid* cannot be as easily determined, since we have but one performance of that identity from this anonymous Jew. Some might call it a hybrid identity, but even that term suggests a kind of cultural compromise, and, in the way that Homi Bhaba uses the term, a subversion of the dominant culture that I do not find in Aristeas.[58] The various features that we see in Aristeas convince me that the *tension* of the hyphen and the implicit compromise of the term *hybrid* are not operative in this text. Our author presents himself and other elite Judeans as Greeks while at the same time claiming a Judean identity. In Ps.-Aristeas's eyes, educated, elite Judeans in Alexandria would affiliate with his self-representation, an identity that educated, elite Greeks both ascribe to them and affirm.

58. See Homi Bhaba, *The Location of Culture* (London: Routledge, 1994).

What Did They See When They Read the Genesis Apocryphon in the First Decade after Its Publication?

MOSHE J. BERNSTEIN
Yeshiva University

I. The Challenge of "Newness"

One of the first things that we do after deciphering and transcribing (and translating) a hitherto unknown text is to look for something like it, something that appears to be of a similar nature to it, and to which it can be compared. Well-worn categories and nomenclature make us comfortable, and, if we can satisfactorily show that a new text has some features that enable us to group it with earlier ones with which we are familiar, we often stop searching for even more appropriate and fine-tuned categories to apply to it. As a result, once we have "discovered" the correct classification for a new work, we often put any further thoughts on this matter aside and proceed to analyze it as if its generic assignment were complete. This procedure, needless to say, may be convenient, but it often leaves us well short of our goals.

I stress that this is not a question that pertains to the text under discussion in this essay, the Genesis Apocryphon, alone, but to all of the Qumran texts that were not copies or translations of works already known.[1] And

---

Dear Shaye, It's been nigh unto a half-century since Thucydides, Book VI, engaged us for a summer of light reading. I've always valued our friendship as our careers proceeded along usually parallel, but occasionally intersecting, lines, and it is a genuine pleasure to be able to contribute to this volume in your honor.

This essay, in suitably different form, will, D.v., be the opening chapter in a planned volume tentatively titled *Reading the Genesis Apocryphon: A Multigeneric Approach*. I thank Professor Shalom Holtz and Ms. Judith C. Bernstein for their critical reading of earlier versions.

1. Four others of the Cave 1 scrolls fall into that category: the War Scroll (1QM), the Community Rule (1QS), the Thanksgiving Hymns (1QH), and the pesher on Habakkuk (1QpHab).

the Apocryphon at least gives its reader running texts for many lines at a time; imagine what confronted the earliest modern readers of the Dead Sea fragments, of which there are many more than actual Dead Sea Scrolls! They saw bits and pieces of leather with writing on them, sometimes legible, sometimes illegible, and had to identify what sorts of texts they were, name them, and classify them. It was not an easy task. And then for those of us who actually produced the official editions of these texts in the 1990s, there ensued an added dilemma of choosing between following or deviating from the naming and classifying of those early scholars. Names, and the genres that they imply, set the agenda for future research, and it often takes a conscious effort to detach oneself from the nomenclature determined by one's predecessors and to view a newly discovered work through unprogrammed (untinted?) lenses.[2]

II. The Publication History of the Genesis Apocryphon

The first "discovery" of the Dead Sea Scrolls in 1947 included seven manuscripts, in various stages of preservation. Because of the nature of its physical condition and its deterioration over the centuries, the Genesis Apocryphon (1QapGen ar) was the last of them to be unrolled, deciphered, and published, and when it was first made public, in 1956, only five (II and XIX–XXII) of its twenty-two (now twenty-three) surviving columns could be transcribed to any substantial degree.[3] In the course of

---

2. This topic remains, to my mind, one of the most underacknowledged significant issues in Qumran scholarship. I have dealt with it in "The Contours of Genesis Interpretation at Qumran: Contents, Contexts and Nomenclature," in *Studies in Ancient Midrash*, ed. James L. Kugel (Cambridge, MA: Harvard Center for Jewish Studies, distributed by Harvard University Press, 2001), 57–85, and briefly from a somewhat broader perspective in "Biblical Interpretation in the Dead Sea Scrolls: Looking Back and Looking Ahead," *The Dead Sea Scrolls and Contemporary Culture: Proceedings of the International Conference Held at the Israel Museum, Jerusalem (July 6–8, 2008)*, ed. Adolfo D. Roitman, Lawrence H. Schiffman, and Shani L. [Berrin] Tzoref; STDJ 93 (Leiden: Brill, 2010), 141–59, here 154–55 [= my *Reading and Re-reading Scripture at Qumran*, 2 vols., STDJ 107 (Leiden: Brill, 2013) (hereafter *RRSQ*), 1:64–92 and 2:686–704, here 699–700, respectively].

3. *Editio princeps*: Nahman Avigad and Yigael Yadin, *A Genesis Apocryphon: A Scroll from the Wilderness of Judaea* (Jerusalem: Magnes Press and Heikhal Ha-Sefer, 1956). In addition to the publication of columns II and XIX–XXII, the editors present the reader on pp. 18–22 with a limited number of citations of legible material from other columns. Despite the undoubted wisdom of the initial editors in the employment of an indefinite article before the work's name since there was no reason to title it with a definite article as unique or special, it has since become conventional to refer to it as "the Genesis Apocryphon," and I maintain that convention throughout this essay. Daniel A. Machiela (*The Dead Sea Genesis Apocryphon: A New Text and Translation with Introduction and Special Treatment of Columns 13–17*, STDJ 79 [Leiden: Brill, 2009], 1) suggests that the definite article owes its origin to E.Y. Kutscher, "The

time, the condition of the manuscript worsened further, on the one hand, while the photographic and other reconstructive technologies that could enable the reading of more of the surviving text improved markedly, on the other. As a result, when these technologies were applied to the manuscript in the 1990s, the amount of readable material that was added to the initial publication was unfortunately not as great as it would have been had those techniques been available earlier.[4]

The contents of the Apocryphon comprise a retelling of the story of Gen 5 through 15, although we cannot tell how much earlier in Genesis the story may have begun or where its endpoint might have been.[5] The opening section (columns 0–V) deals with the period up to the birth of Noah, with column II, the best preserved of them and the only one published by Avigad and Yadin, containing an emotional dialogue between Lamech's parents at the birth of their *Wunderkind*. Columns VI–XVII have Noah as their central figure; the preflood and postflood parts of the narrative are represented in varying degrees of preservation, while the story of the flood itself is missing virtually completely. Column XVIII, which contained the transition between the story of Noah and the story of Abram, is completely unreadable, and columns XIX–XXII include the story of Abram from his descent to Egypt with Sarai through the beginning of his dialogue with God following the war with the kings found in Gen 14. The narrative of the Apocryphon, which is largely, although not completely, told in first-person narration by the major character on the scene in each section, varies in the degree of its adherence to the biblical version of the stories, with some parts such as XXI, 23–XXII, 26 staying fairly close to the Bible, and others, such as columns II–V, not being immediately recognizable as narrowly biblical in nature.

Language of the 'Genesis Apocryphon'," in *Aspects of the Dead Sea Scrolls*, ed. Chaim Rabin and Yigael Yadin, ScrHier 4 (Jerusalem: Magnes, 1958), 1–35. I note, however, that Franz Rosenthal also employs it consistently in his review of the *editio princeps* in *JNES* 18 (1959): 82–83.

4. The unpublished columns were published in Jonas C. Greenfield and Elisha Qimron, "The Genesis Apocryphon Col. XII," in *Studies in Qumran Aramaic*, ed. Takamitsu Muraoka, AbrNSup 3 (Leuven: Peeters, 1992), 70–77; and Matthew Morgenstern, Elisha Qimron, and Daniel Sivan, "The Hitherto Unpublished Columns of the Genesis Apocryphon," *AbrN* 33 (1995): 30–54. At the Society of Biblical Literature Annual Meeting in 1991, Bruce Zuckerman and Michael Wise presented a reconstruction of the fragments of the Apocryphon that had been published in DJD I as 1Q20 and demonstrated that we possess material to the right of "column 1." They designated that text as "column 0," and that designation has been employed by subsequent students of the Apocryphon.

5. The left edge of column XXII shows stitching followed by a fairly straight edge, indicating that the subsequent material was cut off in antiquity. Matthew Morgenstern's theory ("A New Clue to the Original Length of the Genesis Apocryphon," *JJS* 47 [1996]: 345–47), based on the numeration on the sheets of the manuscript, that there originally was a great deal of text preceding the surviving material, has not been widely accepted.

III. Why Should We Care?

I should like to reframe my title query somewhat unusually as follows: when the scholars of the first decade after its initial publication looked at the newly deciphered text of the already named Genesis Apocryphon, what did they see? How did their perception affect further names that they suggested for the text, classifications in which they categorized it, questions that they asked of it, descriptions that they applied to it, and interpretations that they imposed on it? I shall discuss the answers to these questions as they are presented, roughly chronologically, in a variety of works in Qumran scholarship in the first decade after the Apocryphon was published, both those focusing on the Apocryphon and those presenting a broader perspective on Qumran literature. I cannot emphasize too strongly that my focus in this essay will be on perceptions, and not on the very important, and still-debated, question of generic classification, although I shall refer throughout to the generic assignments made by scholars in that first decade. This essay can only lay the groundwork for a fuller discussion of the generic "history" of the Apocryphon, and my detailed treatment of that issue must await a future occasion.[6] The endpoints of the chronological framework for the discussion are, more or less, the years of publication of the *editio princeps* of the "newly discovered" manuscript by Avigad and Yadin and of the first edition of the magisterial, and still standard, commentary on it by the late Joseph A. Fitzmyer.[7]

More than one reader may very well ask at this point why should we care, more than six decades after the initial publication of the Genesis Apocryphon, how its early scholarly readers read and interpreted it? The answer, in my view, is that in the case of a text such as the Apocryphon, which has been classified and read in *so many* different ways since its initial publication, *and* whose textual remains were *not all published simultaneously,* the history of its interpretation becomes a virtual and vital part of its interpretation. As we trace the paths down which earlier scholars walked in attempting to understand the text, the processes and strategies which they employed in reading the Apocryphon, and the lenses through which they examined it, we actually begin to understand the work more fully. Even some of the "false starts" made by those first readers of the

6. In the planned volume referred to in the opening note above; its prospective title should make it clear that I do not believe that a single generic classification can suffice for the Genesis Apocryphon. For the present, see my "The Genre(s) of the Genesis Apocryphon," in *Aramaica Qumranica: The Aix-en-Provence Colloquium on the Aramaic Dead Sea Scrolls,* ed. Katell Berthelot and Daniel Stökl Ben Ezra, STDJ 94 (Leiden; Brill, 2010), 317–43 [=*RRSQ* 1:217–38].

7. Joseph A. Fitzmyer, *The Genesis Apocryphon of Qumran Cave I: A Commentary,* BibOr 18 (Rome: Pontifical Biblical Institute, 1966). The most recent edition of Fitzmyer is *The Genesis Apocryphon of Qumran Cave 1 (1Q20): A Commentary,* 3rd ed., BibOr 18B (Rome: Biblical Institute Press, 2004).

Apocryphon in the 1950s and 1960s can aid in our attempt to assign the Apocryphon to a literary genre and to read it more "correctly."

IV. What Did They See and Say?

We can actually begin our survey well before the initial publication of the scroll, with a number of observations that John C. Trever made about it when he was among those who initially examined the newly discovered scrolls in Jerusalem in 1948. He was the first to notice that the scroll was written in Aramaic, based on the words אנשא לארעא in a piece of the manuscript now known as the "Trever fragment."[8] Then, based on the occurrences of the names בתאנוש and למך in column II of the Apocryphon, he "concluded that this must be the Apocryphal Book of Lamech, mentioned once in a Greek list of apocryphal books."[9] Without anything more to go on beyond what he saw in that column, Trever simply assumed that what was before him had to be the same work as one whose title was already known. That was perhaps a "normal" reaction to the discovery of a hitherto unknown document, and his incorrect identification did no harm other than to create a temporary misnomer for the Apocryphon.

The first editors, Nahman Avigad and Yigael Yadin, rejected Trever's identification of the scroll as "the lost *Book of Lamech*," because they had available a fuller range of its contents than had been available to him. They chose the title *A Genesis Apocryphon* because they "realized that Lamech is dealt with in only part of the book, and that the rest of it retells stories from *Genesis* in the manner of a number of apocryphal books. The chapters which are extant are concerned with Lamech, Enoch, Noah, Abram."[10] They designated the manuscript by two of its prominent qualities: it is based on the (biblical) book of Genesis and it contains material that is not to be found in any form of that book of which we are aware.[11] I do not have any problem with the use of the term Genesis (or with referring to it as a

---

8. John C. Trever, "Preliminary Observations on the Jerusalem Scrolls: D. The Unidentified Fourth Scroll," *BASOR* 111 (1948): 14–16. The "Trever fragment" is a piece that was detached from column I of the Apocryphon. See the plate with IMneg 6x6 in Machiela, *Dead Sea Genesis Apocryphon*, 151.

9. John C. Trever, "Identification of the Aramaic Fourth Scroll from 'Ain Feshkha," *BASOR* 115 (1949): 8–10. See further W. F. Albright's editorial comments there (9–10 n. 4).

10. Avigad and Yadin, *Genesis Apocryphon*, 7–8.

11. My formulation, employing the word "biblical" (even parenthetically), is intended quite consciously to confront one of the issues that are uppermost in the minds of many contemporary scholars of those works of Second Temple literature that bear some relationship to the books that we refer to today as "the Hebrew Bible." The book of Genesis existed (in more than one text form), and it is clear to me and to most other scholars, based on the number of clear-cut verbatim citations from Genesis, that the narrative in the Apocryphon is based on it (as well as conjectured oral traditions and the creativity of the final composer)

"biblical" book), but I have never been comfortable with the term "apocryphon" for any of the Qumran texts to which it has been applied, because it does not furnish a really valuable descriptor of those documents in any useful way. More neutral terms, like "narrative," would have been less likely to have an impact on the way that later scholars think about a work than a loaded term like "apocryphon," with its implications of noncanonicity and spuriousness. Nevertheless, in the case of a text that has been studied as much and for as long as the Genesis Apocryphon has been, we are unlikely to be able to change its long-time designation, even if we had a theoretically better option available (and I am not sure that one is). We should note, however, that the naming or designation of the scroll in terms of its relationship to an already existing literary work will be shown to have had substantial impact on its interpretation.

In their detailed summary of the more and less readable columns of the scroll, Avigad and Yadin indicated that they immediately recognized its connections to the literature of Second Temple Judaism, especially Enoch and Jubilees.[12] Or, to put it differently, they saw the Apocryphon as a (literary) text from the Second Temple era. In the course of their summary of the contents of the scroll, they pointed to similarities and differences between the new text and the books of Enoch and Jubilees, even suggesting that, in a case where "the version in the scroll is fuller and more detailed than that in *Jubilees*, [it] gives the impression of having possibly been a source on which the writer of *Jubilees* drew."[13] There are relatively few references to targumic and midrashic literature in their summary, and even when the editors point out the very "targumic" nature of the last segment of the Apocryphon, the one dealing with the war of the four kings against the five, parallel to Gen 14, they refrain from locating it in the targumic genre.[14]

When coming to characterize the nature of the scroll, although without the somewhat more sophisticated "generic" analysis or terminology in which more recent scholarship engages, Avigad and Yadin concluded

---

and actually serves as a commentary on Genesis. It is therefore heuristically convenient to employ the term "biblical."

12. Avigad and Yadin, *Genesis Apocryphon*, 16–37.

13. Ibid., 21. In the concluding section of their introduction (38), Avigad and Yadin go even further, suggesting that "*the scroll may have served as a source for a number of stories told more concisely in those two books* [Enoch and Jubilees; italics in the original]." In light of what we now know of the date and composition of Enoch based on its Aramaic remains at Qumran, at least half of that suggestion now appears preposterous. The relationship of the Apocryphon to Jubilees, on the other hand, is still being debated in 2018.

14. It is in this section, with its wealth of place-names that demand identification in contemporary terms, that Avigad and Yadin (34–35) introduce data from the Aramaic versions of the Pentateuch to compare the way that the Apocryphon refers to the locations with the way that they are handled in the later targumim.

with two very important observations: first, that the scroll "is actually a sort of apocryphal version of stories from *Genesis*, faithful for the most part, to the order of the chapters in Scripture.... though the narrative of the scroll is in large part couched in the first person."[15] Second, "The work is evidently a literary unit in style and structure, though ... it may perhaps be divisible into books—a Book of Lamech, a Book of Enoch, a Book of Noah, a Book of Abraham."[16] What they saw, then, was a first-person narrative in Aramaic, parallel to the narratives in Genesis, that exhibited signs of unity within a divisible structure, which "may be described as the earliest Aramaic example of pseudoepigraphic [*sic*] literature that has come down to us."[17] Because they describe the text rather than classify it by any of the terms that many subsequent scholars would employ, their characterization of the Apocryphon is meaningful without being constrictive. They tell us how they see it, without putting it into a box.

One of the most unusual, and unfortunately overlooked, reactions to the Apocryphon came in a review of that first edition by Yehoshua Grintz in a somewhat obscure Israeli Hebrew-language journal.[18] What Grintz saw was a narrative similar to the late-medieval *Sefer ha-Yashar*, collecting traditional aggadic material and integrating it into a sequential narrative, following the order of the Pentateuch.[19] In contrast to the medieval work, the author of the Apocryphon employed first-person narration to accomplish his task, perhaps imitating the style found in "Ahiqar the Wise" and, to a limited degree, in Tobit.[20] Like Avigad and Yadin, Grintz saw the background of the Apocryphon as identical to that of Enoch and Jubilees, but he postulated further that the author of the Apocryphon "expands the story from wherever he is able—whether from other sources or from his imagination."[21] Note that Grintz, too, chooses not to use the words "targum"

15. Ibid., 38.

16. Ibid.

17. Ibid., 39. The term *pseudoepigraphic* may be less significant than it appears to be, since the modern Hebrew introduction (p. לב) from which the English was translated, has הספרים החיצונים, "outside books," at that point, a term traditionally associated in Hebrew with books of a noncanonical nature, regardless of purported authorship.

18. Y. M. Grintz, "אגדת־בראשית מימי בית שני" [Genesis-aggada from the Second Temple era], review of Avigad and Yadin, מגילה חיצונית לבראשית, *Molad* 15 (1957): 385–89.

19. What is remarkable about Grintz's use of the *Sefer ha-Yashar* as his theoretical later analogue for the Apocryphon is that only a few years later Geza Vermes employed that work as a paradigmatic late example of the literary form that he would designate "rewritten Bible." Yet no one seems to remember that Grintz, to a limited degree, got there first.

20. Grintz, "אגדת־בראשית," 386. For discussion of the relationship of Tobit and the Apocryphon, see further James E. Miller, "The Redaction of Tobit and the Genesis Apocryphon," *JSP* 8 (1991): 53–61.

21. Grintz, "אגדת־בראשית," 385. On 387 and 388, Grintz argues forcefully against the position of Avigad and Yadin that the Apocryphon is a source for Jubilees and Enoch but posits rather that it draws upon those earlier books.

or "midrash" to describe the Apocryphon, and, in fact, he stresses, quite correctly in my view, the difference between classical midrash, where the story or interpretation is attached to the biblical verses, and the Apocryphon, where the narrative is presented independently of any link to the biblical text. It is unfortunate that some of his perceptive remarks did not have greater impact on the subsequent study of the Apocryphon.

Like the initial editors and Grintz, J. T. Milik avoided the superficial analogies with targum and midrash when looking at the Apocryphon, and he emphasized his decision explicitly. Shortly after the initial publication, he wrote, "The *Genesis Apocryphon*, even if it contains sections translated verbatim from the Hebrew of Genesis, is no true Targum or Midrash. Rather it is an ambitious *compilation of traditional lore concerning the Patriarchs*, preserving the popular form of the pseudepigraph (the Patriarchs themselves being the narrators)."[22] Milik looked past the passages where the Apocryphon renders the Hebrew text of Genesis into Aramaic in the manner of a targum and discounted whatever seeming points of contact it might have with midrash and saw two essential features of the Apocryphon: its anthological or compilatory nature and its (largely) first-person narrative. Whether the Apocryphon should ultimately be described as a "compilation," or whether we can come up with a more appropriate and narrowly focused rubric, that term might serve more suitably as its description than "targum" or "midrash." The relationship between the first-person narrative and the pseudepigraphy may also not be obvious, but they are both among the genuinely distinguishing qualities of the Apocryphon.[23]

But Milik clearly did not see the Apocryphon quite the same way that Avigad and Yadin did. He refers to it as the "not too appropriate title 'A Genesis Apocryphon'," and cites approvingly the name suggested "more plausibly" by Israeli scholar David Flusser, "*Sefer 'abôt*, 'the Book of the

22. J. T. Milik, *Ten Years of Discovery in the Wilderness of Judaea*, trans. John Strugnell, SBT 26 (London: SCM, 1959), 31 [emphasis added]. On p. 35, Milik describes the Apocryphon as a "collection of pseudepigraphic material concerning the Patriarchs arranged in a chronological order." Note the similarity between Milik's remarks and Grintz's, despite their somewhat divergent approaches.

23. Milik's use of the term *pseudepigraphic* may be more meaningful than Avigad and Yadin's, but it raises the interesting question of how we define pseudepigraphy. Is any Second Temple work with first-person speeches by biblical characters to be considered "pseudepigraphic"? I have discussed this issue in "Pseudepigraphy in the Qumran Scrolls: Categories and Functions," in *Pseudepigraphic Perspectives: The Apocrypha and Pseudepigrapha in Light of the Dead Sea Scrolls; Proceedings of the Second International Symposium of the Orion Center for the Study of the Dead Sea Scrolls and Related Literature, 12–14 January, 1997*, ed. Michael E. Stone and Esther G. Chazon, STDJ 31 (Leiden: Brill, 1999), 1–26 [= *RRSQ*, 2:421–47].

Patriarchs'."[24] Milik's preference, however, was for "an Aramaic title, *Ketāb 'abāhān*," with similar meaning.[25] Note that both Flusser and Milik avoid the perhaps "loaded" term "Apocryphon" and, at the same time, also steer clear of any indication in its name that the work is based on or related in any way to the scriptural book of Genesis (although the reference to "patriarchs" is probably meaningful only with a connection to Genesis).

Sometimes, however, the perception of the scholar is apparently affected by his or her interests beyond the strictly academic, and it is particularly striking that two of the very distinguished Christian early scholars of Qumran virtually ignored the contents of the Apocryphon when taking note of its existence. Millar Burrows wrote, "The most significant aspect of the document, however, is its language. Here we have for the first time an extended text of a dialect of Aramaic used by Jews in Palestine in the time of Christ. For the study of the Gospels, and in particular the words of Jesus, this is very important."[26] Frank Cross observed, "The seventh of these scrolls recently has had preliminary publication under the title *A Genesis Apocryphon*. It is an elaboration of Genesis in Aramaic, and will prove most useful as a basis for linguistic analyses of the Aramaic of Palestine in a little-known era."[27] When Burrows and Cross looked at the Apocryphon relatively early in the history of modern Qumran and Second Temple scholarship, they saw only a text in Aramaic that could

24. Ibid., 14 and n. 1. Flusser himself, in his review of Avigad and Yadin (*Kiryat Sefer* [1956–57]: 379–83, here 379 n. 3) attributes the suggestion to Benjamin Mazar. In the review, Flusser refers to the Apocryphon as "this historical romance" (in quotation marks), pointing out, tongue-in-cheek or otherwise, yet another possible classification for the work (379).

25. Milik, *Ten Years*, 14 n. 1. Fitzmyer (*Commentary*, 16 n. 19) suggests gently that כתב אבהתא, "book of *the* patriarchs," with a definite article, would be superior to Milik's suggestion, "book of patriarchs."

26. Millar Burrows, *More Light on the Dead Sea Scrolls* (New York: Viking, 1958), 8.

27. Frank Moore Cross, *The Ancient Library of Qumran and Modern Biblical Studies*, 2nd ed. (Garden City, NY: Doubleday, 1961), 33. Similar remarks appear in the final paragraph of Roland de Vaux's review of Avigad and Yadin (*RB* 64 [1957]: 625): "ce nouveau texte est surtout intéressant par sa langue.... on devine déjà tout le profit qu'en tirera l'étude de l'araméen que Jésus parla et dans lequel l'Évangile fut d'abord annoncé." De Vaux, however, had already devoted a couple of pages to other significant contributions of the Apocryphon. My observation in this paragraph should not be taken to underestimate the contribution of the Apocryphon to the history of Aramaic, especially in Palestine, and we observe that the significance of this text for the history of Aramaic was noted by Avigad and Yadin as well (39), as "[filling] a distinct gap in the history of Aramaic during one of the most decisive periods of its development." André Dupont-Sommer, too, likewise indicated the value of the Apocryphon's Aramaic for evaluating the Aramaic of Jesus (*The Essene Writings from Qumran*, trans. Geza Vermes [Oxford: Blackwell, 1961], 281; translated from the second revised and enlarged edition of *Les Écrits esséniens découverts près de la mer Morte* [Paris: Payot, 1960]; 3rd ed., virtually unchanged from 2nd ed., 1968). What is striking about the remarks by Burrows and Cross is that they seemed to see nothing else of value or interest or importance in this text.

be of service in the interpretation of the Palestinian Aramaic of the era of Jesus. None of the other associations or identifications that engaged even early students of the Apocryphon appeared to pique their interests.

It is similarly unsurprising, on the other hand, that when a Jewish scholar like Manfred Lehmann looked at the Apocryphon, he could see it only as a work related in some way to the later rabbinic targumim and midrashim. Writing in the first volume of *Revue de Qumran,* he noted that all through the Apocryphon, "we find shorter or longer passages of literal translations of the Biblical text interwoven in the midrashic portions."[28] Lehmann moves quickly from this assertion about literal translations in the Apocryphon to a claim that the Genesis Apocryphon was somehow an ancestor of the later targumim, particularly the Palestinian ones. Those Aramaic versions are not as strictly limited to precise rendering of the biblical text as is Onqelos and intersperse their translations of the text with nonbiblical material of a midrashic nature. Lehmann claims, in effect, that if the Apocryphon's Aramaic conforms closely to the biblical text, it resembles a literal targum, while if it blends translation with "midrashic" additions, it can be compared to a more midrashic sort of targum. Once again, the familiar furnishes a comfortable framework for looking at the Apocryphon. But Lehmann's examples simply demonstrate that a text retelling the story of Genesis in Aramaic will frequently *resemble* a targum, not that it *is* a targum, and certainly cannot support the claim that "it can be safely said that 1 Q *Genesis Apocryphon* offers important evidence on the existence of early targumic versions of *Genesis* certainly much before the time modern scholars would have us believe till now."[29]

The second half of Lehmann's article then deals with what he sees as parallels between the Apocryphon and classical midrashic literature. What he has observed correctly is that both the Apocryphon and the later midrashim respond creatively to similar gaps and other stimuli in the biblical text, but his alleged parallels are not parallel. To cite but one example, Lehmann writes, "The question as to the identity of the refugee referred

28. Manfred R. Lehmann, "1Q Genesis Apocryphon in the Light of the Targumim and Midrashim," *RevQ* 1 (1958–1959): 249–63, here 252. The opening words of the article are telling as to his stance: "The publication of parts of the Dead Sea *Genesis Apocryphon* from 1 Qumran brings us to an example of Biblical text treatment much closer to traditional Jewish literature than was hitherto known from Qumran." Lehmann writes further that "this Scroll fits squarely into the main stream of Targumim and Midrashim, and probably represents the oldest prototype of both available to us" (251). I have discussed the views of Lehmann and Matthew Black (presented below) in greater detail in "The Genesis Apocryphon and the Aramaic Targumim Revisited: A View from Both Perspectives," in *The Dead Sea Scrolls in Context: Integrating the Dead Sea Scrolls in the Study of Ancient Texts, Languages, and Cultures,* ed. Armin Lange, Emanuel Tov, and Matthias Weigold, 2 vols., VTSup 140 (Leiden: Brill, 2011), 2:651–71, here 652–54) [= *RRSQ* 1:266–85, here 267-69].

29. Lehmann, "1Q Genesis Apocryphon," 263.

to in Genesis 14,13 has evidently occupied the author of 1 Q *Gen. Ap.* just as it has provoked different midrashic solutions."[30] But the Apocryphon's identification and the two midrashic ones to which he alludes are not the same and thus cannot be claimed to constitute a "parallel." The dual effort on Lehmann's part to link the Apocryphon simultaneously with targum and with midrash points to the fact that he was not interested in a careful and narrow generic classification of the Apocryphon per se but rather in the location of the Apocryphon loosely within the traditions of early Jewish biblical interpretation.

Matthew Black, a Christian scholar who certainly could not be said to share Lehmann's instinctive tendency to locate the Apocryphon within the traditions of classical Jewish literature, explicitly questioned Avigad and Yadin's characterization of the Apocryphon shortly after the appearance of Lehmann's article. He wondered "whether, in fact, this is an adequate or even correct description of the character of this old Aramaic text" and suggested that "too much stress on the apocryphal character of the scroll may have the effect of obscuring or even misrepresenting its essential nature."[31] Citing Paul Kahle as the originator of the idea, Black suggests that this Aramaic document might be "an early specimen of a written Aramaic Pentateuch Targum from Palestine, perhaps a prototype and forerunner of the old Palestinian Targum ... and of the so-called Fragment Targum." Because he was focused on the "targumic aspects of the Apocryphon," Black could assert that "the division of the text into a series of 'Books', a 'Book of Lamech', a 'Book of Enoch', a 'Book of Noah', a 'Book of Abraham', seems unnecessary," since "like any other Targum text, the Aramaic translation is simply following the sections of Scripture in their canonical order."[32] Black has moved from a tentative hypothesis ("perhaps") to a virtual assertion in a few pages. His surprising (to us) conclusion is "The new scroll is almost certainly our oldest written Palestinian Pentateuch Targum."[33]

---

30. Ibid., 261.

31. Matthew Black, *The Scrolls and Christian Origins: Studies in the Jewish Background of the New Testament* (New York: Charles Scribner's Sons, 1961), 193. "Appendix C" of the volume (192–98) is entitled "Aramaic Texts from Qumran," but, in point of fact, deals almost exclusively with the Apocryphon.

32. Ibid., 195. We should note that the evidence for the targumic nature of the scroll derives almost entirely from the Abram material, especially column XXII, which is much closer to the biblical text than the material in column II, the only other one published at that time. By the time that Black published this, Kahle himself had moved away from his initial identification of the Apocryphon as a targum and referred to it as a "Midrash Book" and "Midrash Scroll" (*The Cairo Geniza*, 2nd ed., Schweich Lectures 1941, Oxford: Blackwell, 1959], 198). He would seem to have been in favor of some sort of anthological classification of the Apocryphon, writing, "The impression is given that we have here extensive Midrashic material which it was desired to have at hand."

33. Black, *Scrolls and Christian Origins*, 198. Black himself, some years later, also changed

Gad B. Sarfatti begins his treatment of the Apocryphon with the following description: "*The Genesis Apocryphon from the Wilderness of Judea* is a composition that follows the tracks of the book of Genesis and describes the incidents related in it with expansions and noticeable additions."[34] Accepting the characterization by the editors that the scroll belongs to the category "apocryphal literature" (ספרות חיצונית), in particular Enoch and Jubilees, Sarfatti asserts that "several of the stories in the scroll ... are not the product of the free imagination of the composer, like many stories in apocryphal literature, but flow from the biblical verses according to the same methodological principles according to which rabbinic *aggada* developed."[35] He points to such features as "resolution of difficult verses," "interpretation of juxtapositions," "identification of unnamed characters," "moving details from one section to another," and "filling out of details" as common to the Apocryphon and to rabbinic midrash.[36]

But, while Sarfatti indicates that the Apocryphon and rabbinic midrash employ analogous methods in their reading of the biblical text and characterizes them both by Isaac Heinemann's term ביאור יוצר ("creative interpretation"), he makes the very important point that there is a significant *formal* distinction between them. The midrash "exposes its way of interpretation and the steps of its work, while the scroll hides them, and presents us with a complete and polished literary product." He proceeds to offer an example, presenting what he sees as an interpretation of the Apocryphon in the way that a midrash would have expressed it and concludes, "but the scroll presents us with a complete literary artefact, so that the reader does not know how the story is held in the biblical verses, or what are its exegetical motivations."[37] Without using the term "genre," Sarfatti makes a valuable statement about how formal generic distinctions should make us very hesitant to use terms like "midrash" to describe the Genesis Apocryphon.

The future editor of the Apocryphon, Joseph A. Fitzmyer, published the modestly titled, but characteristically thorough and rich, essay, "Some

---

his mind about the generic identification, writing of the Apocryphon, "The new Aramaic document is a kind of *midrash* on Gen. xii and xiv" (*An Aramaic Approach to the Gospels and Acts*, 3rd ed. [Oxford: Clarendon, 1966], 40).

34. Gad B. Sarfatti, "Notes on the Genesis Apocryphon" [Hebrew], *Tarbiz* 28 (1959): 254–59, here 254.

35. Ibid. In a postscript to the article (259), he notes that Lehmann, in the article discussed above, had alluded to several of the same rabbinic passages that he had in conjunction with the Apocryphon.

36. Sarfatti, "Notes on the Genesis Apocryphon," 254–57.

37. Ibid., 257. Sarfatti argues that Heinemann (דרכי האגדה [Jerusalem: Magnes, 1954], 176) had claimed that this mode of rabbinic reading was not carried out by the pseudepigraphical literature but that, in actuality, the Apocryphon does so, although presenting its results differently.

Observations on the *Genesis Apocryphon*," in 1960, and it is unfortunate that it does not seem to have had much impact on ensuing scholarship.[38] Showing broad familiarity with everything that had been written to date on the Apocryphon, and characterizing the text as "a narrative based on several episodes in the biblical Genesis, sometimes with considerable elaboration, especially in columns 19-22, where Gn 12-15 are translated, paraphrased or expanded," his goal was "to point out the significance of various aspects of this document for different areas of biblical study. In particular, we may single out the significance which the *Genesis Apocryphon* has for the study of the Aramaic language, for the study of the OT and for the study of the NT."[39] No less than Burrows or Cross, he is interested in the value of this new Aramaic document for the recovery of the language of Jesus, but he goes far beyond that narrow concern in the remainder of the article.

From the standpoint of our limited current interest, Fitzmyer approves of the choice of the title "A Genesis Apocryphon," by the editors, who

> [obviously chose] the latter word to avoid an explicit identification of the document with either a Targum or a Midrash.... For though there are sections where the Hebrew text of Genesis is reproduced in a literal, word-for-word Aramaic version (resembling a Targum), there are also sections which expand the biblical version (in the manner of a haggadic midrash). Some of the additional material which makes up the expansion is found in other midrashim, but some of it appears here for the first time. The interest which the OT scholar will have in the Targumic aspect of the scroll is derived from the interpretative translation which it offers of the Biblical text.[40]

Without saying a word about genre, he emphasizes the value of the neutral term chosen by the editors over the narrower (and to him, unsuitable) terms midrash and targum. If only subsequent scholars had paid attention to these remarks, they might have avoided the comfortable route of trying to identify the Apocryphon as something familiar rather than something new and different.

Dupont-Sommer saw four parts in the narrative: stories of Lamech (cols. I–V), Noah (VI–XV), and Abram (XVIII–XXII), interrupted by the "table of the peoples" (XVI–XVII); he observed that "it is the patriarchs themselves who recount the events of their lives."[41] He, too, opted for a long-known genre for his analogue, choosing "midrash" rather than "tar-

---

38. Joseph A. Fitzmyer, "Some Observations on the *Genesis Apocryphon*," *CBQ* 22 (1960): 272–91.

39. Ibid., 278.

40. Ibid., 280–81.

41. Dupont-Sommer, *Les Écrits esséniens*, 292–93; Eng. *Essene Writings*, 280. It is perhaps

gum": "the present scroll is a precious example of Essene *midrash,* and it is interesting to compare it with one or the other of the Rabbinic *midrashim*."[42] Dupont-Sommer's analogizing of the Apocryphon to rabbinic midrash, however, did not blind him to its obvious links to Second Temple literature. Of the Apocryphon and Jubilees he writes, "It is clear not only that they originate from the same environment, but also that one of them must have served as a source for the other."[43] He also furnishes the readers of his translation of the scroll with the parallel in 1 Enoch 106–107 to column II of the Apocryphon, noting that, while in Enoch the story is told by Enoch, in the Apocryphon it is told by Lamech, "[b]ut this is only a secondary variant; the story is exactly the same."[44]

The first systematic attempt to look at the Apocryphon in a really different fashion came in the now classic presentation by Geza Vermes in 1961 of the "new" category "rewritten Bible." He included in this classification "the Palestinian Targum and Jewish Antiquities, Ps-Philo and Jubilees, and the recently discovered 'Genesis Apocryphon'," and characterized the genre as "a substantial narrative where the midrashist inserts haggadic development into the biblical narrative—an exegetical process which is probably as ancient as scriptural interpretation itself."[45] Vermes looked at the Apocryphon not standing alone but in the context of a variety of other works from late antiquity and found a way to describe those works not in terms of what they look like but in terms of what they actually do.

Despite this conceptual breakthrough, however, which saw the Apocryphon as belonging to a hitherto unrecognized generic category, Vermes could not tear himself away completely from the classical categories that had attracted Lehmann, Black, and Dupont-Sommer, among others. After a thorough discussion of the Abram section of the Apocryphon, he writes, "Genesis Apocryphon occupies a privileged position in midrashic literature in that it is the most ancient midrash of all. With its discovery the lost link between the biblical and Rabbinic midrash has been found."[46] It

---

worthy of note that Dupont-Sommer did not see the "table of the peoples" section, which deals with Noah's division of the earth among his children, as belonging to the Noah story.

42. Dupont-Sommer, *Essene Writings*, 280, citing Lehmann's article in n. 2. It is interesting that Dupont-Sommer subsequently writes of the latter portion of the Apocryphon, the third-person narrative beginning at XXI, 23, "the additions and modifications are so relatively insignificant that it may almost be regarded as a simple paraphrase of the biblical text in the targumic manner" (Eng., 291 n. 2).

43. Ibid. (Eng.), 281.

44. Ibid. (Eng.), 284.

45. Geza Vermes, *Scripture and Tradition in Judaism: Haggadic Studies*, 2nd ed., StPB 4 (Leiden: Brill, 1973), 95. The following chapter of the book (96–126), is a study of midrashic interpretation of the portion of the Abram story covered by the Apocryphon.

46. Ibid., 124.

appears that he is employing the term "midrash" in the same way that we shall see that Hubert Lignée does, and rather more loosely than Lehmann, for example. "Midrash," in this usage, is not a form or genre of rabbinic literature but some sort of nebulously defined approach to reading and interpreting Scripture.

The most substantial introduction to the Apocryphon in those early years, apart from the one in the *editio princeps*, is probably the one by Hubert Lignée, prefaced to his French translation.[47] Approaching the issue of literary genre explicitly, he observed "points de contact avec d'autres ouvrages apocryphes ou pseudépigraphiques, déjà connus (en particulier le livre des *Jubilés*) et aussi avec des compositions plus classiques du judaïsme rabbinique: Midrashim et Targumim."[48] Despite his realizing that the Apocryphon is intimately connected with the literature of the Second Temple era, Lignée suggested that, if the classification "midrash" is applicable to a variety of works and not only the later rabbinic type, "c'est dans cette catégorie que le present *Apocryphe* se range tout naturellement."[49] He both ate his cake by leaving the Apocryphon in its Second Temple milieu and had it through the employment of the term "midrash." The category "midrash" must become very expansive in order to include works like the Apocryphon, but many scholars were, and still are, prepared to make that adjustment in order to find a landing place for the Apocryphon.

Targum, however, that other previously known genre, also exercised an attraction on Lignée, although he eventually did reject it as a location for the Apocryphon.[50] The fact that the story of the Apocryphon adhered so closely to the form of the Genesis narrative was not evidence enough for him to make the identification. Too much, he suggested, was lacking from the classic form of targum, as the term came to be used in later Judaism, for the Apocryphon to fit into it.[51] Apparently, in Lignée's view (and probably that of many other scholars as well), "midrash" as a category is a broader and more malleable term than "targum" is.[52]

---

47. Hubert Lignée,"L'Apocryphe de la Genèse," in *Les textes de Qumran traduits et annotés*, ed. Jean Carmignac et al., 2 vols., Autour de la Bible (Paris: Létouzey et Ané, 1961–1963), 2:207–19.

48. Ibid., 209.

49. Ibid., 210.

50. Here we must recall once again that columns XIX–XXII, which are the most "targum-like" in the Apocryphon, constituted the lion's share of the earliest published material from the Apocryphon. If the entire text had been published at one time, it is very unlikely that "targum" would have played as significant a role in the generic debate as it did.

51. Lignée, "L'Apocryphe de la Genèse," 214.

52. I have criticized the unconstrained use of the term "midrash," especially as applied to the Apocryphon, in "The Genre(s) of the Genesis Apocryphon" (see n. 7 above), 325–29 [= *RRSQ*, 1:224–29]. Suffice it for the present to quote, once again, the well-formulated remark made over five decades ago by A. G. Wright, "The Literary Genre Midrash," *CBQ* 28 (1966):

William H. Brownlee began his description of the Apocryphon with "an Aramaic version of Genesis,"[53] which he then modified with the observation that it

> resorts to another device in order to rewrite Genesis. Each major character is allowed to tell his own story in the first person. This allows for intimacies of detail omitted in the OT Genesis. Although it is written in Aramaic, it follows the Hebrew text so closely that at certain points it will be of value for textual criticism.[54]

Brownlee then asserts further, "A new form of the story appears in the Genesis Apocryphon."[55] Notice the tension in this description between the "versional" nature of the Apocryphon that is said to be close enough to the original to be useful for textual criticism and its novel first-person narrative style and the newness of its story.[56] Brownlee seems to have been grappling with the difficulty of trying to describe features or qualities that did not quite fit together in the picture that he was drawing in the mid-1960s.

Finally, writing about a decade after Avigad and Yadin's publication of the Apocryphon, and in the same year Fitzmyer's commentary appeared, Addison G. Wright set out the inconsistencies that already existed in characterizing the Apocryphon by pointing to its being described as targum or midrash, on the one hand, and a "compilation of traditional lore" and an "Apocryphon," on the other.[57] Wright leaned toward classifying the Apocryphon as "targum" because it "very much resembles a targum in that it sets out to give the full biblical text, rather literally for Gn 14, and elsewhere in much the same free and paraphrastic way that characterizes many sections of the Pentateuchal Palestinian targums." He refrained

---

108: "The word as currently used in biblical studies is approaching the point where it is no longer really meaningful and where some of the material designated as midrash resembles the later rabbinic midrash in a very superficial way. *And surprisingly very few voices have been raised in protest*" (emphasis added).

53. William Hugh Brownlee, *The Meaning of the Qumrân Scrolls for the Bible*, Richards Lectures 1958 (New York: Oxford University Press, 1964), 52.

54. Ibid., 73.

55. Ibid., 74.

56. On p. 81 n. 39, Brownlee makes the somewhat surprising statement, "The Genesis Apocryphon might be described as a sort of Targum except for the fact that each major character speaks in the first person" (referring to Black, *Scrolls and Christian Origins*, 192–98). It should have been obvious that even if all those first-person speeches were turned back into third-person, the text would not have been a targum. But the superficial attractiveness of the comfortable generic classification as targum blinded Brownlee to its inherent difficulties.

57. Addison G. Wright, "The Literary Genre Midrash (Part Two)," *CBQ* 28 (1966): 424-425. He presents the classifications of Black, Lehmann, Vermes, Lignée, and Milik, among others.

from accepting this analysis only because "the autobiographical form found in some sections of G[enesis] A[pocryphon] is not a normal targumic feature, and this may be an indication that the nature of the work is other than targumic."[58] His conclusion is almost certainly correct, but his reasoning would not be replicated by any contemporary scholar today.

Wright followed his somewhat unusual analysis with the conclusion that the Apocryphon may be "a collection ... of assorted material to elucidate the biblical text and expand on it in the spirit of L[iber] A[ntiquitatum] B[iblicarum], for certainly a large number of alterations and additions to the biblical text are for exegetical purposes."[59] Wright's "collection of assorted material" appears to echo Milik's "compilation of traditional lore," and his search for something to which the Apocryphon can be compared has led him, consciously or unconsciously, to one of the other works that Vermes employs as a paradigm of "rewritten Bible," although he did not explicitly link his classification to those of either of his predecessors. His stress on "exegetical purposes" may actually be seen to point in the direction of reading the Apocryphon as a commentary on the Hebrew Bible. Wright finally located the Apocryphon "somewhere between a targum and LAB," but concluded, "At present, it can be said that the expansions on Gn in GA are certainly midrash and that there is some degree of probability to the view that the whole work is."[60] His inability to make up his mind, and his moving back and forth between targum, midrash, and other generic classifications are generated in part by the genuine difficulty in categorizing the Apocryphon and in part by the lack of rigor that pervaded scholarship in this area in those early years.

V. Synthesis and Conclusions

As promised initially, the foregoing survey of how the Apocryphon was viewed concludes about a decade after its initial publication, and just before the publication of the first edition of Fitzmyer's commentary. I embarked upon it because I thought that it would be valuable for my study in 2018 to observe what scholars *saw*, or thought they saw, when they first looked at the Apocryphon in those early years, and I was not disappointed. Even without a formal tabulation of the results, we can see that many readers of the Apocryphon saw in it what was familiar to them, whether or not the analogy was fully appropriate. It was connected to its "contemporaries," 1 Enoch and Jubilees; it resembled rabbinic midrash; it looked something like an Aramaic targum. Even Vermes, who had the

---

58. Wright, "Literary Genre," 425–26.
59. Ibid., 426.
60. Ibid.

insight to compare the Apocryphon with several other works of antiquity that did not necessarily resemble it formally and to create for them a new generic classification, "rewritten Bible," could not get away from "midrash" when he actually discussed the Apocryphon. We observe that it was difficult to describe the outstanding features of the Apocryphon, apart from perhaps its first-person narration, without resorting to the few analogies that were available at that time.

There was, it is now obvious to us in hindsight, one feature of the Apocryphon that was not seen, or was overlooked, by virtually all of those first readers, and that is its lack of unity on several levels.[61] There are several very reasonable explanations for this seeming oversight by so many outstanding scholars. First, it is quite natural to take for granted that an apparently chronologically sequential composition on a single roll of leather is a single work. Second, the fact that only columns II and XIX–XXII were made available, in toto, prevented those early readers from seeing the variations and stylistic discontinuities that we now can perceive as running through the whole of the Apocryphon. Third, and this is a point which might be said to cut both ways, the above-cited initial description of the Apocryphon by Avigad and Yadin as a "literary unit in style and structure, though … it may perhaps be divisible into books" may have inadvertently established a parameter under which the Apocryphon was to be evaluated. Avigad and Yadin's "literary unity" carried more weight than their "perhaps divisible" did. The literary unity of the Apocryphon was rarely challenged.

The apparent inability to view the Apocryphon as other than a single integrated work acted as an additional constraint on what those first readers of the Apocryphon saw when they read it. It virtually forced those early scholars who were describing or classifying the Apocryphon into the unfortunate position of choosing between the Scylla of "targum" and the Charybdis of "midrash." Those who gravitated to the number of passages where there are Aramaic translations of biblical verses, of which there are many in columns XIX–XXII, saw targum, while those who focused on the nontranslation material, whether in column II or in XIX–XXII, which expanded the biblical narrative in a variety of ways, saw in it an antecedent, or collateral ancestor, of rabbinic midrash. The significance of first publication cannot be overstated when it comes to those scholars who chose targum since it is only in columns XIX–XXII that we can speak of the text of the Apocryphon resembling that of an Aramaic version in any way. If any other section had had priority, such identification would never

61. I have laid the groundwork for broader discussion of the unity of the Apocryphon in "Divine Titles and Epithets and the Sources of the Genesis Apocryphon," *JBL* 128 (2009): 291–310, and "Is the Genesis Apocryphon a Unity? What Sort of Unity Were You Looking For?," *Aramaic Studies* 8:1/2 (2010): 107–34 [= *RRSQ* 1:195–216 and 239–65, respectively].

have taken place. Lonely column II was apparently not sufficient to give an impression of what the whole of columns 0–XVIII would have looked like to overcome the effect of XIX–XXII.

I can perhaps point to three early observers of the Apocryphon who didn't "see" in the same way that most others did, and whose choice of descriptive terminology therefore pointed away from the generic choice between targum and midrash and toward obvious comparisons to other works to which the Apocryphon might be related, even if they do not move beyond that. Grintz's "narrative," Milik's "compilation," and Wright's "collection" are terms that indicate the absence of a clear generic decision, of some uncertainty about how we should classify the Apocryphon.[62] The latter two, who actually employ terminology that also could be claimed to deny the "unity" of the Apocryphon, are the only scholars who come close to reading the Apocryphon not as something *like* something else, but *as itself*, who were willing, to some degree, to allow the work to speak to them on its own terms. But each of them described the Apocryphon in the vaguest, most unspecific terms, as they bent over backward to avoid the generic trap into which almost all other scholars were falling.

I want to stress again in conclusion that it is very easy for us to look back and point to failings and shortcomings of the scholarship that was done a half-century ago; it is likely that the same may be done to us and our scholarship in another generation or less. What are valuable in a survey such as the one that we have just presented are the theoretical lessons that we can extrapolate from it about keeping our eyes and minds open when we confront material that is completely new to us. It is comfortable and reassuring to classify a new text or document together with something familiar and recognizable. But that comfort comes at the cost of overlooking what is not obvious and often leads us to the kinds of dead-ends that we have seen in this exercise, and sometimes it takes a decade or two before we can walk back from that dead-end, look at the work with fresh eyes, and proceed down the path that will lead us to a more appropriate name, classification, and interpretation of an ancient text.

---

62. I could actually claim that Grintz is making a "generic" choice (although I suspect that he was not overly concerned with genre in his review) that could ultimately lead to what I believe is a satisfactory overall approach to the Apocryphon. Wright's discussion, cited above, actually shows some of his thought processes and indicates why he was uncomfortable locating the Apocryphon in any specific available generic pigeonhole. Because of Milik's much briefer discussion, it is hard to be sure what was motivating him.

The Tetragrammaton in the Habakkuk Pesher

TIMOTHY H. LIM
New College, University of Edinburgh

A striking feature of the Habakkuk Pesher is its representation of the four letters of YHWH, or the Tetragrammaton, in paleo-Hebrew script while the rest of 1QpHab is written in square, Aramaic script. There is no doubt that this manner of presenting the scroll was intended by the scribe, and not the result of an error or secondary insertion.[1] The paleo-Hebrew script was used exclusively for the divine name YHWH; other divine names of El, Eloha, and Sebaot were written in the same square script as the rest of the scroll. Why did the scribes write the Tetragrammaton in the way that they did?[2]

It is commonly thought that the writing of YHWH in paleo-Hebrew script was intended to guard the divine name from improper use.[3] The specific nature of this guarding varies in scholarly explanations. Mathias Delcor attributed the Habakkuk Pesher's writing of the divine name in "caractères phéniciens" to the great respect that the Jews had for the ineffable name and the convention of making the four letters sacrosanct

---

It is a pleasure to dedicate this article to an esteemed colleague and good friend, Shaye J. D. Cohen.

1. Hartmut Stegemann believed that YHWH was written by a later hand and inserted into the copied scroll (ΚΥΡΙΟΣ Ο ΘΕΟΣ *und* ΚΥΡΙΟΣ ΙΗΣΟΥΣ: *Aufkommen und Ausbreitung des religiösen Gebrauchs von* ΚΥΡΙΟΣ *und seine Verwendung im Neuen Testament* [Bonn Habilitationsschrift, 1969], 91 n. 502). However, the Tetragrammaton was written in the same ink as the rest of the scroll and without any false spacing that would indicate that the name was inserted after the rest of the scroll had been written.

2. Two hands have been identified: scribe A copied col. I–XII, 13 and scribe B XII, 13–XIII, 4.

3. See recently, e.g., George J. Brooke, "Physicality, Paratextuality and Pesher Habakkuk," in *On the Fringe of Commentary: Metatextuality in the Ancient Near Eastern and Ancient Mediterranean Cultures*, ed. Sydney H. Aufrère, Philip S. Alexander, and Zlatko Pleše in association with Cyril Jacques Bouloux, OLA 232 (Leuven: Peeters, 2014), 175–93, here 190: "The standard opinion is that the use of the paleo-Hebrew for the tetragrammaton is done to protect the name from abuse."

with these "curieuses graphies."[4] Had the letters of the divine name been written in the Aramaic script, then Delcor believed that readers of the scroll may have been liable to read and pronounce the name of YHWH, a blasphemy punishable by death. He pointed to the contemporary evidence of LXX Lev 24:16 and its rendering of the Hebrew "one who will blaspheme" by the Greek "one who will pronounce."

Jonathan Siegel, on the other hand, argued that it was the sectarian belief in "the permanence of the Divine Name" that was behind the Qumran practice of writing the Tetragrammaton in paleo-Hebrew script.[5] Basing himself on the rabbinic discussion of the writing of the divine names, and the prefixes and suffixes attached to them, Siegel sought the explanation in the scribal practice of erasures and cancellations, arguing that the Qumran practice is to be explained by "the palaeographical reflection of a significant theological consideration."[6] For him, the writing of the Tetragrammaton in paleo-Hebrew script is a scribal convention used to guard the divine name from being erased.

Different Ways of Profaning the Divine Name

There is one passage in the Habakkuk Pesher that appears to say something about the profanation of the divine name. In 1QpHab II, 4, the line reads: [ויחללו] את שו[ם]קודשו "[and they defiled] his holy Na[me]." The clause is badly damaged by a tear down the middle of the column and a sizable hole that extends to line 6. On the online image of the Digital

4. Mathias Delcor, "Des diverses manières d'écrire le tétragramme sacré dans les anciens documents hébraïque," *RHR* 147 (1955): 145–73, here147.

5. Jonathan Siegel, "The Employment of Paleo-Hebrew Characters for the Divine Names at Qumran in the Light of Tannaitic Sources," *HUCA* 42 (1971): 159–72. Siegel saw particularly significance in (1) the representation of the two Tetragrammata in 11QPs[a] XVI, 7 and XXI, 2 that could not be erased but were canceled from reading by the addition of dots above and below them; and (2) examples of the writing of the prefixes and suffixes along with YHWH in paleo-Hebrew script in 4QIsa[c]. He cited Patrick Skehan's preliminary summary ("The Text of Isaias at Qumran" *CBQ* 15 [1955]: 40–43, here 42–43). An example can be found in 4Q53, frag. 12, col. II, line 30 (Isa 26:4) in E. Ulrich et al., eds., *Qumran Cave 4.X: The Prophets*, DJD XV (Oxford: Clarendon, 1997), 45–74, here 59. For Siegel, the scribe of this scroll indicated that neither the divine name nor the prefixes and suffixes could be erased.

6. Siegel, "Employment of Paleo-Hebrew Characters," 171. A third explanation that the paleo-Hebrew script was used to mark out 1QpHab as nonbiblical can be set aside, since biblical scrolls are also written in paleo-Hebrew script (e.g., 4QIsa[c] [4Q57]). For a summary of biblical texts written in paleo-Hebrew script, see K. Matthews, "The Background of Paleo-Hebrew Texts at Qumran," in *The Word of the Lord Shall Go Forth: Essays in Honor of David Noel Freedman in Celebration of His Sixtieth Birthday*, ed. Carol L. Meyers and M. O'Connor, ASOR Special Volume Series 1 (Winona Lake, IN: Eisenbrauns, 1983), 554–68.

Dead Sea Scrolls, the two fragments should be moved farther apart.[7] Preserved is a particle (את), followed by specks of varying sizes consistent with the letters *shin* and *qoph*. The above restoration is widely followed.[8] Elisha Qimron suggested a slightly longer beginning, [וביא חללו], which can be translated as "[and because they defiled]."[9] Bilha Nitzan justifies the restoration by a reference to CD XV, 3 and its biblical source text Lev 22:32.[10] Delcor, moreover, sees the abuse in CD XV as not only the pronunciation of the divine name YHWH but also the abbreviation of it. He interprets the CD passage with m. Shevu'ot 4:13, where the prohibition concerns the pronunciation of the divine name in an abbreviated form of the Tetragrammaton.[11]

The Damascus Document's statement about the profanation of the divine name occurs in a context very different from that of the Habakkuk Pesher. I translate CD XV, 1–3 as follows:

> [He sh]all (add: אל, not) swear, neither by aleph and lamed, nor by aleph and dalet, the exception (to this rule) are the oaths of the ones entering (reading: שבועת הבאים)[2] by the curses of the covenant. And the torah of Moses he shall not call to mind, for in it are all the declarations of the Name. [3] And if he swears, then he transgresses, and defiles the Name (וחלל את השם).

The final clause, "he defiles the Name," is clearly the supposed source of the reconstruction of 1QpHab II, 4. Before we examine it, let us note some commonly accepted emendations of the opening lines of CD XV. The particle אל is added to the beginning of the line to negate the verb [יש]בע. This restoration is required by the sense, and also the syntax, a negation usually precedes כי אם.[12] The scribe incorrectly wrote שבועת הבנים ("the oaths

7. See the images of the Digital Dead Sea Scrolls of the Shrine of the Book, Israel Museum (http://dss.collections.imj.org.il/habakkuk). The fragments are not placed so closely in *The Dead Sea Scrolls of St. Mark's Monastery*, ed. Millar Burrows with the assistance of John C. Trever and William H. Brownlee (New Haven, CT: The American Schools of Oriental Research, 1950), plate LV.

8. William H. Brownlee, *The Midrash Pesher of Habakkuk*, SBLMS 24 (Missoula, MT: Scholars Press, 1979), 53; Maurya P. Horgan, *Pesharim. Qumran Interpretations of Biblical Books*, CBQMS 8 (Washington, DC: Catholic Biblical Association of America, 1979), part I, p. 4; Horgan, "Pesharim," in *Pesharim, Other Commentaries, and Related Documents*, vol. 6B of *The Dead Sea Scrolls: Hebrew, Aramaic, and Greek Texts with English Translations*, ed. James H. Charlesworth et al., PTSDSSP 6B (Tübingen: Mohr Siebeck, 2002), 162 n. 28; and Bilha Nitzan, מגילת פשר חבקוק. ממגילות מדבר יהודה *(1QpHab)* (Jerusalem: Bialik, 1986), 152.

9. Elisha Qimron, מגילות מדבר יהודה החיבורים העבריים כרך ראשון (Jerusalem: Ben Zvi, 2010), 246.

10. Nitzan, מגילת פשר חבקוק, 153 n. 4.

11. Delcor, "Des diverses manières," 159.

12. Elisha Qimron, "שבועת הבאים in the Damascus Document 15:1-2," *JQR* 81.1–2 (1990): 115.

of the sons"), and it is widely accepted that it should be corrected to שבועת הבאים (cf. הבא בברית, line 5), referring to the oaths of those entering the covenant. There are supralinear dots above כי בה כל פרוש השם, implying that the final clause of line 2 should be removed from reading or in subsequent copying, since it imputes to the torah of Moses all the declarations of the divine name.

The context of CD XV, 1–3 concerns the swearing of oaths. It is generally agreed that the letters *aleph* and *lamed* are abbreviations of the first two letters of the divine name Elohim, and that *aleph* and *daleth* the first two letters of Adonai. Chaim Rabin pointed out that the law refers to the prohibition of swearing by any of the names of God, with the sole exception of swearing by "the curses of the covenant."[13]

CD XV, however, is not a general law referring to the prohibition against using all divine names; it refers to the use of the two divine names Elohim (or Eloha) and Adonai. Only two divine names can be represented by the initial letters *aleph-lamed* or *aleph-daleth*. The law specifies against oaths that use Elohim and Adonai. The subsequent exception clause (כי אם) is not exclusive ("only") but iterative ("except for"). The sectarian is not to swear by oaths using Elohim or Adonai. But the oaths of those entering the covenant are exempted from this prohibition. The Damascus Document's law is consistent with what Josephus says about the Essenes, who are obliged to take "tremendous oaths" (ὅρκοι φρικώδεις) before they are allowed to touch the common food (*War* 2.139–142).

The use of CD XV, 1–3 to explain 1QpHab II, 4 is questionable, ostensibly focusing on the similarity of the formulation of the clause "and he defiles the Name" (וחלל את השם). The texts are similar but not the same: 1QpHab II, 4 has the longer form of "my holy Name." To be sure, the substantive השם is a biblical circumlocution or synonym for Adonai and YHWH found in the biblical texts, CD XV, 1–3, and 1QpHab II, 4, but the divine name can be defiled in different ways. It is not necessarily about the use of the divine names in swearing oaths.

The biblical source text in CD XV has been traced by Nitzan to Lev 22:32. This supposed biblical source text, however, does not concern the swearing of oaths as such, but the general admonition of keeping and guarding the divine commandments. The call to holiness, exemplified by "I am YHWH," requires Israelites to refrain from profaning "my holy Name" (ולא תחללו את שם קדשי), so that the Lord's name will be sanctified (Lev 22:32).

---

13. Chaim Rabin, *The Zadokite Documents* (Oxford: Clarendon, 1954), 71–73, followed by Joseph M. Baumgarten and Daniel R. Schwartz, "Damascus Document (CD)," in *Damascus Document, War Scroll and Related Documents*, vol. 2 of *The Dead Sea Scrolls: Hebrew, Aramaic, and Greek Texts with English Translations*, ed. James H. Charlesworth et al., PTSDSSP 2 (Tübingen: Mohr Siebeck, 1995), 37 n. 126.

There is no reason to limit the reason for defiling the divine name to the swearing of oaths. The profanation of God's name is a concept found in many biblical texts, especially in the Priestly literature (e.g., Lev 18:21, 19:12, 21:6, 22:2, Jer 34:16). Different reasons are given for the defilement of the divine name: the holy name is profaned in the worship of Molech (Lev 20:3); in the greed, social injustice, and sexual misconduct of Israel (Amos 2:7); and in idolatrous worship (Ezek 20:39; cf. Ezek 36:20-23, 39:25, 43:7). The priests, the sons of Aaron, are holy to God and do not profane the name of God, because they carry out the offerings by fire. They remain so on the condition that they do not marry a prostitute, a defiled woman, or a divorcée (Lev 20:6–7).

Several points are borne out by examining the rationale for the reconstruction of 1QpHab II, 4 from CD XV, 3: (1) CD's use of the defilement formula in a context prohibiting the swearing of oaths is not dependent on Lev 22:32, which concerns the observance of the divine commandments generally. (2) In the biblical texts there are many ways by which an Israelite could defile the divine name. (3) The profanation formula in 1QpHab II, 4 and CD XV, 1–3 is similar but not the same. The Habakkuk Pesher, but not CD, qualifies "the Name" with "my holiness." And (4) the accepted restoration of 1QpHab II, 4 does not have to be explained by the rationale found in CD XV, 1–3.

Swearing Oaths in the Rule of the Community

Before we examine what defiling or profaning the divine name means in 1QpHab II, 4, it is salutary to examine one other passage that has been interpreted to mean a prohibition against the pronunciation of the divine name. "[T]he paleo-Hebrew script," stated George Brooke, "would have reduced the chance that a reader would inadvertently pronounce the divine name."[14] Brooke did not say where he found evidence for this explanation. Others have understood a passage in the Rule of Community as a sectarian statement against the pronunciation of the divine name. 1QS VI, 27 reads as follows: [וא]שר יזכיר דבר בשם הנכבד על כול ה [ ].[15] This has been translated by Michael Wise, Martin Abegg, and Edward Cook as "Anyone who speaks aloud the M[ost] Holy Name of God, [whether in …]."[16] The bottom of column VI is partly mutilated, but the translators have understood it as an infraction relating to the pronunciation of the divine name.

14. Brooke, "Physicality," 191.

15. See the images of the Digital Dead Sea Scrolls, http://dss.collections.imj.org.il/community.

16. Michael Wise, Martin Abegg Jr., and Edward Cook, *The Dead Sea Scrolls. A New Translation* (San Francisco: HarperCollins, 1996), 135.

The context is the multiyear initiation process of the volunteer who is joining the *yaḥad* (1QS VI, 24–27). The precepts by which he is to be judged, in an inquiry to determine his suitability, include this clause putatively prohibiting the pronunciation of the divine name.

But what does the clause mean? Literally, it means "and whoever will cause a matter/word to be remembered in the Name, which (ה) is honoured over/according to all *h*[ ]." The end of the line is not preserved, and Qimron has restored it to [הכ]תוב בתורה, "which is written in the torah."[17] But the source of this biblical passage is not found in the Torah. The source text is traced to Deutero-Isaiah, where the context concerns the swearing of oaths. In Isa 48:1, the prophet calls his hearers to account, invoking the triple designation of "the house of Jacob," "Israel," and "the loins of Judah" and charging them for falsely "swearing by the name of YHWH" and "invoking the God of Israel." Preben Wernberg-Møller points out that יזכיר in 1QS VI, 27 is to be understood by its sense in Isa 48:1, where the verb is used in parallel with נשבעים.[18] He translates the line as "[The one w]ho makes an oath in the honoured name."[19] 1QS VI, 27 is a prohibition against swearing oaths by invoking the divine and honoured name and is consistent with the law expressed in CD XV, 1–3. It is not a prohibition against pronouncing the holy name of God as such.

Treachery and Unfaithfulness in the Renewed Covenant

When we turn to the Habakkuk Pesher, it is evident that 1QpHab II, 4 has nothing to do with the swearing of oaths or pronouncing of the Tetragrammaton. The first four lines of 1QpHab, column II, read as follows:

> [1] foretold (Hab 1:5d). *vacat* [The interpretation of the passage concerns] the traitors with the man [2] of the lie, because [they did] n[ot believe in the words of] the Teacher of Righteousness, (which were) from the mouth of [3] God. And concerns the trai[tors to the] new [covenant], bec[au]se [4] they did not remain faithful in the covenant of God, [and defiled] His [ho]ly Na[me].[20]

17. Qimron, מגילות מדבר יהודה, 220.

18. Preben Wernberg Møller, *The Manual of Discipline. Translated and Annotated with an Introduction*, STDJ 1 (Leiden: Brill, 1957), 29, 112 n. 86.

19. Ibid., 29.

20. Translation from my commentary on Habakkuk Pesher (in preparation) to be published in the Oxford Commentary on the Dead Sea Scrolls series (http://www.ocdss.div.ed.ac.uk).

The reconstructed clause, "[and defiled] His [ho]ly Na[me]" occurs in line 4 and at the end of the second of three pesherite comments on Hab 1:5b. In the MT, this biblical verse refers to YHWH's command for the righteous to look at the amazing work that he is doing in their days: "Look at the nations and see! Be amazed! Be astounded! For I am doing a work in your days, and you will not believe when told" (NRSV).

The pesherist, however, read Hab 1:5b differently. He understood יסופר not as "told" but "foretold." This predictive interpretation of the verb is in keeping with the pesherist's hermeneutics of reading into the prophetic oracles of old a prediction of events that were taking place in his time, the middle of the first century BCE, concerning the traitors, the Liar, and the Teacher of Righteousness. He read a variant in בוגדים ("traitors"; LXX: οἱ καταφρονηταί) instead of the graphically similar בגוים ("the nations") of the MT. In the MT, the preposition *bet* is required by the verb "to see," but in the pesherite variant it serves as the first radical of *bgd*, "to act or deal treacherously."

For the pesherist, the biblical verse refers to those whom he calls "trai[tors to the] new [covenant]," and their treachery is explained as some form of abandonment of the faith in the covenant. William Brownlee is partly correct to say that "[o]ne is not to think of profanity in the use of God's name."[21] He interprets this passage as a reference to the defection of those who joined the sect and subsequently fell away (cf. CD XX, 10–15).

But the clause "they defiled his holy name," does concern profanity, except that the nature of the profanity is not in the taking the divine name in vain in oaths or pronouncing the ineffable Tetragrammaton. Given that the pesherist labels the perpetrators as "traitors of the new covenant" and describes them as being unfaithful to the covenant, it can be inferred that the profanity concerns the breaking of the "new" or better "renewed" covenant, as understood by the sect.

What the pesherist says about the nature of the defilement of the divine name in 1QpHab II, 4 is evocative of the themes of Ezek 36:16–38, where YHWH's wrath was poured out on Israel, who committed bloodshed and idolatry that defiled the land. In verse 20, YHWH commands the prophet to declare that he (YHWH) is about to act because the house of Israel "have profaned my holy Name" (ויחללו את שם קדשי). Moreover, the house of Israel committed these morally impure deeds "among the nations" (בגוים; v. 22). The defilement formula is identical to 1QpHab II, 4, with the minor adaptation of the first- to third-person suffix on "holiness."

---

21. Brownlee, *Midrash Pesher of Habakkuk*, 55.

Divine Names in the Habakkuk Pesher

No explanation is given in the Habakkuk Pesher for writing the Tetragrammaton in paleo-Hebrew script. An examination of passages in the Damascus Document and Rule of the Community yielded a different explanation for the defilement of the holy name, relating to the swearing of oaths. In this situation, we should turn to the evidence of the Habakkuk Pesher scroll itself to see how the divine names are used and presented.

We need to establish what evidence there is in the Habakkuk Pesher rather than impose explanations derived externally from other Dead Sea Scrolls, the LXX, rabbinic texts, and early Jewish literature in general, since scribes of antiquity followed different practices.[22] Even within the one genre of the continuous pesher, the scribal practice of representing the divine name varies.[23] Only one copy of the Habakkuk Pesher (1QpHab) is extant, copied by two hands, the first scribe penned the words of column I, 1 to column XII, 13, and the second, column XII, 13–XIII, 4.[24] Because of the mutilation of line 17 of column XII, where the pesher cites Hab 2:20 and references YHWH, it is unclear whether there was any difference in practice between scribes A and B.

Four divine names are attested in the Habakkuk Pesher scroll: Eloha (אלוה), Sebaot (צבאות), El (אל), and YHWH (יהוה). Adonai (אדוני) and Elohim (אלהים) are not used, but the latter would presumably have been attested in Hab 1:12 had the biblical verse been preserved at the end of column IV (MT: אלוהי). Elohim also occurs in MT Hab 3:18, but chapter 3 of the prophecy is absent in 1QpHab. The related divine name, Eloha, a back-form of the plural, is used in the citation of Hab 1:11b (1QpHab IV, 10, 13). In the prophecy of Habakkuk, it refers to the Chaldeans placing their strength as "their god" (לאלוהו). Sebaot is used once as a divine epithet, juxtaposed to the Tetragrammaton (יהוה צבאות), in a citation of Hab 2:13 in 1QpHab X, 7. The scribe wrote YHWH in paleo-Hebrew script and Sebaot in square script.

The two divine names, El and YHWH, are used distinctly in the pesher. The Tetragrammaton (יהוה) is always written in paleo-Hebrew script and occurs exclusively in biblical quotations of the prophecy of Habakkuk. This divine name appears four times in the scroll in VI, 14; X, 7, 14; and XI,

---

22. Emanuel Tov judiciously summed up the matter: "It is unclear why certain scribes used paleo-Hebrew characters for the Tetragrammaton, while others wrote the Tetragrammaton in square characters" (*Scribal Practices and Approaches Reflected in the Texts Found in the Judean Desert,* STDJ 54 [Leiden: Brill, 2004], 240).

23. E.g., $4QpPs^b$ (4Q173), frag. 5, line 4, writes לאל, including the preposition, in paleo-Hebrew script (MT: ליהוה).

24. Some of the corrections and changes may be attributed to scribe A or B, but in most cases there is insufficient writing available for comparison.

10. It may also have been used in other places where the biblical lemmata are not preserved and the corresponding MT has YHWH (I, 1; IV, 17 [2x]; and XII, 17).

By contrast, El (אל) is the divine name that the pesherist consistently used in his sectarian comments (I, 6, 11; II, 3, 4, 8, 9, 11, [15]; V, 2, 3, 4; VII, 1, 4, 8, 13; VIII, 2, 10, 11, [17]; IX, 10; X, 3, 13; XI, 3, [15]; XII, 5, 9; XIII, 3). He does not use the Tetragrammaton in his comment of I, 11, "they rejected the law of God" (מאשו בתורת אל). The *sin* (ש) of מאש is either a variant spelling of מאס or a scribal error (cf. V, 11–12: מאס את התורה). This clause is dependent on Isa 5:24 and in the MT and 4QpIsa^b (4Q162) II, 7 יהוה (in square script) is the divine name used. It is difficult to escape the impression that the use of El for YHWH in this clause is part of an intentional avoidance strategy.

There is a discernible pattern of scribal practice. In 1QpHab II, 4, the pesherist uses El in the biblical expression "the covenant of God" (ברית אל), whereas the MT and Qumran biblical texts consistently use the Tetragrammaton (ברית יהוה; e.g., Num 10:33; Deut 10:8). The pesherist's use of El rather than YHWH in the construct is consistent with the practice of other sectarian scrolls (e.g., CD III, 11; V, 12; VII, 5; XIII, 14; XIV, 2; XX, 17; 1QS [II, 26]; V, 8; X, 10; 4Q267 frag. 9, col. 5, line 4 [in paleo-Hebrew script; cf. frag. 3, line 7]; 4Q280 frag. 2, line 6; 4Q491 frag. 11, col. 2, line 18; 6Q15 frag. 5, line 5). It has been suggested that there is a tendency to use generic divine names for the Tetragrammaton in the sectarian scrolls.[25]

Substitutes for the Divine Name

The Habakkuk Pesher attests to other references to God beyond the divine names. The substantive צור ("rock") refers to God in the citation of Hab I, 12b–13b, and the pesherist replicates this usage in the quotation of the biblical passage (1QpHab V, 1–2). It is not a divine name as such but a stock, biblical and figurative use of a geological term to express the qualities of support and defense thought to be found among God's attributes.

Another substitute is the use of "truth" for the Tetragrammaton. When the pesherist states that the Wicked Priest "was reckoned to the name of truth" (1QpHab VIII, 9), he is using not biblical language but sectarian terminology.[26] The phrase שם האמת ("the name of truth") is not used in the biblical texts. In the different versions of the Rule of the Community, "truth" is used as a substitute for "YHWH." The citation of Isa 40:3 in one

---

25. So Martin Rösel, *Adonaj—warum Gott "Herr" genannt wird*, FAT 29 (Tübingen: Mohr Siebeck, 2000), 209.

26. The formulation נקרא על שם האמת should be translated as "reckoned to" rather than "called by" the name of truth (cf. Gen 48:6).

recension of the Rule of the Community (4Q259) reads "the way of truth" (דרך האמת; col. 3, line 4) for "the way of YHWH" (דרך יהוה; 1QS VIII, 3).

The Habakkuk Pesher, 1QpHab, and the Divine Names

It is generally agreed that 1QpHab is a copy of the Habakkuk Pesher, evidenced by the errors in the scroll that could only be interpreted as scribal mistakes of copying. The writing of YHWH in paleo-Hebrew script is a scribal feature of 1QpHab; it is not necessarily a feature of the supposed original composition of the Habakkuk Pesher. The pesherist may or may not have written the Tetragrammaton in paleo-Hebrew script.

Presumably what he did do was to use YHWH only when he was quoting the biblical texts.[27] He did not limit this practice to the Tetragrammaton, but he also wrote Eloha and Sebaot when he quoted the prophecy of Habakkuk. In his comments, he used El, and other circumlocutions and substitutes. There is an unmistakable tendency to use certain divine names in the biblical quotations, and other ones in his comments.

Scribal Attitudes to the Writing of the Divine Names

The scribes who copied 1QpHab committed errors in relation to the writing of the divine name El. In line 1 of column VII, scribe A confused the preposition and divine name, writing אל only once in the clause "and God spoke to Habakkuk." A correction written by the same, or a different, hand added another אל above the line and between the words אל and חבקוק. It is likely that the scribal correction was adding the preposition rather than the divine name, since the pesherist followed the verb–subject sentence construction (cf. col. VII, 8, דברו הנבאים), and had he been inserting "God" one would have expected him to place the supralinear correction between the אל and וידבר. This scribal error was not in the writing of the divine name as such, but the morphologically identical אל of the preposition and divine name was the cause of the scribal error of haplography.

In column I, line 10, the final letter of תורה, in the clause "therefore the law will grow numb," was incorrectly written as a *tav* before being reformed to a *heh*. The scribal error of writing the *tav* was influenced by

27. It is, of course, theoretically possible that the scribe systematically changed the pattern of use of divine names in his *Vorlage*, but this seems unlikely, if the other scribal interventions are anything to go by. Discernible scribal changes in 1QpHab are ad hoc or concern orthographical and morphological variants.

the phrase בתורת אל in the clause "who rejected the torah of God" written directly below it in line 11, and the mistake was corrected to *heh* once it was realized that the word תורה was not part of a construct.

In column II, line 2, the first word of the phrase מפיא אל ("from the mouth of God") is written with a final *aleph* that augments the word. The spelling could be explained as the use of a digraph (יא-), but five lines later the same word is spelled without the final *aleph* in the phrase מפי הכהן ("from the mouth of the priest," lines 7–8). The final *aleph* of מפיא is probably a dittography that wrongly anticipates the *aleph* of the following word אל.

By contrast, there is no scribal mistake associated with the writing of the divine names of Eloha, Sebaot, and Yhwh. The writing of the Tetragrammaton is further distinguished from the former two divine names by the fineness of its strokes and the use of the paleo-Hebrew script. For the scribes who copied 1QpHab, YHWH clearly had a significance that the other two divine names, Eloha and Sebaot, did not.

Conclusions

The common scholarly view that the writing of the Tetragrammaton in paleo-Hebrew script in the Habakkuk Pesher was used to protect the divine name from abuse has been examined in the foregoing discussion. I eschewed explanations that were drawn from external sources, and I sought a largely descriptive discussion of the use of the divine names, including the writing of the Tetragrammaton in paleo-Hebrew script. I conclude that no single reason can explain all the features of the writing of the divine names.

The first half of the paper interrogated the claims that the convention can be explained by the concern for the inadvertent pronunciation of YHWH. The reconstruction of 1QpHab II, 4 led me to suggest that the defilement or profanation of the divine name is not the consequence of swearing oaths with the divine name but rather of the breaking of the renewed covenant.

In the second half of the paper I scrutinized internal evidence for clues to explain the presentation of the divine names. Central to the approach adopted above is the distinction that I draw between the composition of the Habakkuk Pesher and the scribal copying of 1QpHab. I demonstrated that the pesherist used certain divine names (Eloha, Sebaot, and Yhwh) when he quoted from the prophecy of Habakkuk, but he opted for El and other circumlocutions in his comments. He may or may not have written YHWH in paleo-Hebrew script. If he did so, then the special orthography had no bearing on his understanding of the prophet's words. The writing of YHWH in paleo-Hebrew script would have simply reflected a particular convention that he was following.

The scribes who copied 1QpHab did write the Tetragrammaton in paleo-Hebrew script. But they did not do so for the other two divine names, Eloha and Sebaot, despite the fact that they were also found in the biblical quotations. They treated the writing of YHWH differently from the other two divine names by writing the Tetragrammaton in paleo-Hebrew script and Eloha and Sebaot in square script. The fact that they reserved the paleo-Hebrew script only for the name YHWH suggests that they held it in a special regard. The nature of that regard has sometimes been explained in terms of a greater degree of sanctity, but there is no evidence in the commentary to substantiate or otherwise deny that supposition. The explanation, however, remains plausible.

They did not write El and other substitutes for the divine name in a special script. Moreover, the scribes who copied 1QpHab made errors associated with the reading of the divine name El. They did not commit similar errors when copying Eloha, Sebaot, and YHWH. It is possible that they took greater care in the writing of all three divine names of Eloha, Sebaot, and Yhwh, in a way that they did not with El.

The pesherist who wrote the sectarian commentary known as the "Habakkuk Pesher" and the scribes who copied 1QpHab considered the Tetragrammaton a special case among the divine names used in the prophecy of Habakkuk and in the sectarian comments associated with it. In varying ways, they showed by their use and scribal practice that YHWH is more important than the other divine names Eloha, Sebaot, and El.

Laws Pertaining to Purification after Childbirth in the Dead Sea Scrolls

LAWRENCE H. SCHIFFMAN
New York University

The purpose of this paper is to investigate the laws pertaining to purification after childbirth found in the Damascus Document (Zadokite Fragments). In innumerable cases, the Jewish legal rulings of the Dead Sea Scrolls texts have been found to agree with the Sadducean/Zadokite trend in Jewish law. In the investigation of laws pertaining to purification after childbirth we will see that this approach and the Pharisaic-rabbinic tradition[1] seem to have reached essentially the same conclusions based on exegesis of the material in Leviticus. We will see, however, that the sectarians and the book of Jubilees gave a particular explanation for the length of the periods of impurity not paralleled in the Pharisaic-rabbinic trend. Study of this issue should remind us of the extent to which aspects of Judaism in general, and Jewish law in particular, were shared among the various groups of Jews that made up the complex landscape that we term Second Temple Judaism.

A word is in order about the literary character of the text that we will be discussing. The particular fragment reads almost like rewritten Bible[2]

This paper is offered in honor of our friend and colleague Shaye Cohen in recognition of years of friendship and collegiality, and with thanks for his important scholarly contributions.

1. By this term I mean to designate the Second Temple system of Jewish law that can be reconstructed based on anti-Pharisaic polemics in Dead Sea Scrolls texts, use of New Testament reports, and early rabbinic sources. This system of Jewish law competed with the Sadducean/Zadokite system documented in Dead Sea Scrolls, the book of Jubilees, and some other Second Temple texts.

2. Despite the complex history that led to the emergence of our corpus of Hebrew Scriptures, the term "rewritten Bible" refers to Second Temple texts that adapt and rewrite literary materials that were later included in that canon. That is a sense in which this term is used here. Note that the term *sefer* ("book") in the Qumran corpus is used only for books included in the later canon of the Hebrew Bible, although in one instance *sefer serekh* is used for sectarian text. Our view is that the Dead Sea sectarians held authoritative a set of texts including all those in our Hebrew Bible except Esther, as well as some additional books such

since its verbiage is derived from the Bible. Just as Tannaitic literature included legal discussion in both scriptural order and in abstract, apodictic form, the same is the case in the Dead Sea Scrolls. Whereas the *serakhim*, lists of laws in apodictic form, may be compared with mishnaic laws, the Temple Scroll—rewritten Bible—can be compared to the scriptural order of Tannaitic midrash.[3] Nevertheless, it is clear from examining some smaller halakhic fragments that some seemingly apodictic legal discussions, organized around common subject matter and even having titles, are, in fact, internally organized in scriptural order.[4] Certainly, the influence of the Bible on Qumran halakhic texts cannot be overestimated, both in terms of legal derivation and literary form. This feature will be observed in the text we are discussing here. As observed long ago, in Qumran texts we sometimes find substitution of postbiblical terminology for that used in the Hebrew Bible. However, the opposite tendency—use of archaic, biblically based language—is more common.[5]

4Q266, a manuscript of the Damascus Document (Zadokite Fragments), takes up the question of purification after childbirth (4Q266 [4QD[a]] 6 II, 5–10):[6]

(5) ואשה אשר֯ [תזרי]ע֯ וילדה זכר [וטמאה א]ת֯ שבעת [הימים]
(6) [כ]י֯[מי] נ֯ד֯ת֯ [דאותה וביום השמיני ימול בשר] ע֯ר֯ל֯ת֯[ו]
(7) [ושלושת ושלושים יום תשב בדם טוהרה ואם נקבה תלד]
(8) [וטמאה שבועים כנדת ד]אותה ו֯[ששה וששים יום תשב בדם]
(9) [טוהרה והיאה] לא תוכל [קודש ולא תבו אל המקדש]
(10) [כי מ]שפט מות הו[אה

---

as Jubilees. See Lawrence H. Schiffman, "Memory and Manuscript: Books, Scrolls, and the Tradition of the Dead Sea Scrolls," in *New Perspectives on Old Texts: Proceedings of the Tenth International Symposium of the Orion Center for the Study of the Dead Sea Scrolls and Associated Literature, 9–11 January 2005*, ed. Esther G. Chazon and Betsy Halpern-Amaru, in collaboration with Ruth Clements, STDJ 88 (Leiden: Brill, 2010), 133–50.

3. Lawrence H. Schiffman, "Legal Texts and Codification in the Dead Sea Scrolls," in *Discussing Cultural Influences: Text, Context, and Non-Text in Rabbinic Judaism*, ed. Rivka Ulmer, Studies in Judaism (Lanham, MD: University Press of America, 2007), 1–39.

4. Charlotte Hempel, *The Laws of the Damascus Document: Sources, Tradition and Redaction*, STDJ 29 (Leiden: Brill, 1998), 49; Erik Larson, Manfred Lehmann, and Lawrence H. Schiffman, in Joseph M. Baumgarten et al., *Qumran Cave 4.XXV: Halakhic Texts*, DJD XXXV (Oxford: Clarendon, 1999), 25–51; Aharon Shemesh, "4Q251: Midrash Mishpaṭim," *DSD* 12 (2005): 280–302.

5. Chaim Rabin, *Qumran Studies*, Scripta Judaica 2 (Oxford: Oxford University Press, 1957), 108–11.

6. Joseph M. Baumgarten, ed., *Qumran Cave 4.XIII: The Damascus Document (4Q266–273)*, DJD XVIII (Oxford: Clarendon, 1996), 55–56. The translation is Baumgarten's. For an earlier discussion, see Lawrence H. Schiffman, "Laws Pertaining to Women and Sexuality in the Early Stratum of the Damascus Document," in *The Dead Sea Scrolls and Contemporary Culture: Proceedings of the International Conference Held at the Israel Museum, Jerusalem (July 6–8, 2008)*, ed. Adolfo D. Roitman, Lawrence H. Schiffman, and Shani Tzoref, STDJ 93 (Leiden: Brill, 2011), 557–59.

(5) And a woman who [conceiv]es and bears a male child [shall be unclean] for the seven [days,]
(6) [as] in [the day]s of her menstru[al impurity. And on the eighth day the flesh of his] foreskin [shall be circumcised. For]
(7) [thirty-three days she shall remain in her blood purification. If she bears a female child]
(8) [she shall be unclean two weeks as in her menst]ruation. [For sixty-six days she shall remain in her blood]
(9) [purification. And she] shall not eat [any hallowed thing, nor come into the sanctuary,][7]
(10) [for] it is a capital [of]fense.

This passage is closely based on Lev 12:2–8. At the end, we are told that the parturient (like the menstrually impure woman and one who has had an irregular flow) may not eat of holy foods or enter the sanctuary, and that violation of either of these two regulations constitutes a capital crime (lines 9–10). Our text has rearranged the biblical order of these restrictions in order to make the points that they apply after the birth of both male and female offspring and that they apply both to the times of "impure blood" (the seven and fourteen days) and to those of "pure blood" (the additional thirty-three or sixty-six days). From the Bible, we would not have known that violation of this regulation would constitute a capital crime, but our text makes that claim. All in all, the reordering of biblical passages falls under the rubric of rewritten Bible, a fair description of the style of our passage from the Damascus Document.

Regarding the text's emphasis on the fact that the offerings occur after both periods have elapsed and that only then may the parturient eat of holy food or enter the temple, rabbinic tradition is in full agreement.[8] Clearly, the sectarians determined that eating holy foods or entering the sanctuary while menstrually impure was a capital crime. The rabbis understood Lev 15:31 (*ve-lo' yamutu be-ṭumatam*), referring to a woman who has a blood flow outside of the period of menstruation, to refer to *karet* (excision).[9] One may also compare Lev 7:20–21, which mentions the punishment of *karet* for anyone who eats *shelamim* sacrifices while impure.[10] The same punishment

---

7. For the omission of א from the spelling of תוכל and תבו, see Elisha Qimron, *The Hebrew of the Dead Sea Scrolls*, HSS 29 (Atlanta: Scholars Press, 1986), 23–26; Eric D. Reymond, *Qumran Hebrew: An Overview of Orthography, Phonology, and Morphology*, RBS 76 (Atlanta: Society of Biblical Literature, 2014), 43–47, 77–87.

8. Rashi and Ramban to Lev 12:4, b. Hul. 31a; Maimonides, *H. Bet ha-Beḥirah* 7:15.

9. Sifre Num. 125 (ed. Haim S. Horovitz [Jerusalem: Wahrmann, 1966], 161) as interpreted by Rashi to Lev 15:31; see Baumgarten, DJD XVIII:56.

10. Cecilia Wassen, *Women in the Damascus Document*, AcBib 21 (Atlanta: Society of Biblical Literature, 2005), 56 n. 35 for some reason contains numerous errors. Numbers 7:20–21 should be corrected to Lev 7:20–21. Numbers 22:23 is also incorrect, but Lev 22:23 is also irrelevant. It is most probably an error for Lev 22:2–3, which is also cited by her. The refer-

is prescribed in Lev 22:2–3 for priests who eat sacrifices in a state of impurity. All this evidence would seem to imply that we are talking about death at the hands of heaven or *karet*.[11] However, the term משפט מות appears only in Deut 21:22, where it refers to a crime punishable by execution. This also appears to be the case with the sectarian term דבר מות, "capital case."[12] Nonetheless, it does appear from all this evidence that in our passage this expression is a reference to the divinely administered punishment of excision, and not to death at the hands of a human court.[13]

This topic is also taken up in 4Q265 (Miscellaneous Rules), which gives an explanation for the number of days of impurity and purity that, as we will see below, is also paralleled in Jub. 3:8–14.[14] It should be remembered that Miscellaneous Rules includes material found in both the Rule of the Community and the Damascus Document.[15] It remains to be seen if Miscellaneous Rules should be viewed as a composite text based on those to which it is parallel or if it is an independent redaction including some of the very same building blocks (*serakhim*) of which the redactors compiled these larger texts. 4Q265 (4QMisc Rules) 7, 11–17 states:[16]

(11) *vacat* בשבוע הראיש֯[ון נברא האדם וקודש לא היה לו עד]
(12) אשר לא הובא אל גן עדן ועצם [מעצמיו לוקחה לאשה וקודש לא]
(13) [ה]יה לה עד אשר לא הובאה אצ[לו אל גן עדן אחר שמונים יום]
(14) [כי] קדוש גן עדן וכול ה֯אב אשר בתוכו קודש֯ [לכן אשה אשר ילדה זכר]
(15) וטמאה שבעת ימים כימי נדת דותה תטמא ושל[שים ושלשת ימים תשב בדם]
(16) טהרה *vac* ואם נקבה תלד וטמאה [שבעים כנדתה וששים יום וששת ימים]
(17) [תש]ב בדם טוהרה בכול קודש [לא תגע ואל המקדש לא תבוא עד מלאת]

(11) *vac* In the fir[st] week [Adam was created, but he had nothing sacred (?) until]
(12) he was brought to the Garden of Eden. And a bone[of his bones was taken for the woman, but nothing sacred (?)]
(13) did she [ha]ve until she was brought to h[im in the Garden of Eden after eighty days,]
(14) [for] the Garden of Eden is sacred and every young shoot which is in its midst is a consecrated thing. [Therefore a woman who bears a male]

---

ence to Lev 7:20 at the end of the note is a correct reference that had been incorrectly referred to at the beginning of the note as Num 7:20–21.

11. Ibid., 55.

12. For use of this expression, see ibid., 55 n. 33; Lawrence H. Schiffman, "Halakhic Terminology in the Dead Sea Scrolls," *RevQ* 93 (2009): 115–33.

13. Wassen, *Women in the Damascus Document*, 56.

14. Martha Himmelfarb, "Impurity and Sin in 4QD, 1QS, and 4Q512," *DSD* 8 (2001): 29; Wassen, *Women in the Damascus Document*, 55; W. R. G. Loader, *The Dead Sea Scrolls on Sexuality: Attitudes Towards Sexuality in Sectarian and Related Literature at Qumran* (Grand Rapids: Eerdmans, 2009), 151–52; Ian C. Werrett, *Ritual Purity and the Dead Sea Scrolls*, STDJ 72 (Leiden: Brill, 2007), 55–60.

15. Lawrence H. Schiffman, "Serekh-Damascus," *EDSS* 2:868–69.

16. Baumgarten in DJD XXXV:70–71.

(15) shall be impure seven days, as in the days of her menstruation shall she be impure, and th[irty three days shall she remain in the blood]
(16) of her purity. *vac* And if she bears a female she shall be impure [two weeks as in her menstruation, and sixty-six days]
(17) [shall she remai]n in the blood of her purity. [No]consecrated thing [shall she touch, nor shall she enter the sanctuary until the completion of][17]

Lines 11–14 represent a narrative regarding the chronology of the placing of man and woman in the garden of Eden. Lines 14–17 (after the transitional use of *la-khen*) are another rewritten version of Lev 12:1 through almost the end of verse 4, where the text breaks off at the bottom of the column. Note that this passage leaves out Lev 12:3, which discussed circumcision on the eighth day. This is not necessarily because of any disagreement with that passage but, rather, because our text is emphasizing the purity regulations—specifically the number of days: seven or fourteen impure days and thirty-three and sixty-six pure days.

Whereas the laws in Leviticus are intended to ensure the purification of the mother after childbirth, Miscellaneous Rules has understood these regulations as applying to the newborn.[18] The text essentially treats Adam and Eve as newborn children and transfers to them the purificatory rites required for the mother in Leviticus.[19] The garden of Eden is considered as if it were a divine temple in which only those who had been fully purified were permitted to enter. Therefore, each entered the garden only after purification, requiring forty days for Adam and eighty for Eve.

Otherwise, the text in Miscellaneous Rules requires the same purification rituals as does that of the Damascus Document. The only difference is the extensive etiology provided in Miscellaneous Rules that is not present in the Damascus Document. The only explanation for this etiology is that Miscellaneous Rules has drawn upon Jubilees or a very similar textual tradition.[20]

---

17. Trans. Baumgarten, DJD XXXV:70–71.The sentence would most probably have ended with ימי טהרה, "the days of her purification" (Lev 12:4), and then would have continued in parallel with the description of the offering in verses 6–8. Alternatively, the offering might have been omitted as not applicable because the sectarians abstained from temple worship since they disapproved of the way it was conducted.

18. This approach is rejected in Sifra Parashah 1:8 (*Sifra*, ed. Isaak H. Weiss [Vienna: J. Schlossberg, 1861–1862; repr., New York: Om, 1946], 58a).

19. Joseph M. Baumgarten, "Purification after Childbirth and the Sacred Garden in 4Q265 and Jubilees," in *New Qumran Texts and Studies: Proceedings of the First Meeting of the International Organization for Qumran Studies*, ed. George J. Brooke and Florentino García Martínez, STDJ 15 (Leiden: Brill, 1994), 5–6. For a shorter discussion, see idem, DJD XXXV:60–61.

20. Cf. Aharon Shemesh, "Megillah 4Q265 u-Ma`amado shel Sefer ha-Yovelim ba-'Adat ha-Yaḥad," *Zion* 73 (2007–2008): 20–25.

The parallel in Jub. 3:8–14 is as follows:[21]

8. In the first week was Adam created, and the rib—his wife: in the second week. He showed her unto him: and for this reason the commandment was given to keep in their defilement, for a male seven days, and for a female twice seven days.
9. And after Adam had completed forty days in the land where he had been created, we brought him into the garden of Eden to till and keep it, but his wife they brought in on the eightieth day, and after this she entered into the garden of Eden.
10. And for this reason the commandment is written on the heavenly tablets in regard to her that gives birth: if she bears a male, she shall remain in her uncleanness seven days according to the first week of days, and thirty and three days shall she remain in the blood of her purifying, and she shall not touch any hallowed thing, nor enter into the sanctuary, until she accomplishes these days which (are enjoined) in the case of a male child.
11. But in the case of a female child she shall remain in her uncleanness two weeks of days, according to the first two weeks, and sixty-six days in the blood of her purification, and they will be in all eighty days.
12. And when she had completed these eighty days we brought her into the garden of Eden, for it is holier than all the earth besides and every tree that is planted in it is holy.
13. Therefore, there was ordained regarding her who bears a male or a female child the statute of those days that she should touch no hallowed thing, nor enter into the sanctuary until these days for the male or female child are accomplished.
14. This is the law and testimony which was written down for Israel, in order that they should observe (it) all the days.[22]

The narrative is mixed with the legal rulings in this version of the story. 4Q265 has omitted all references to the heavenly tablets, assuming as we do that the author had the Jubilees version available to him. There can be no question that the law found in 4Q266 is itself derived from the conceptual framework of Jubilees, taken over in Miscellaneous Rules. It is

---

21. Trans. Robert H. Charles, *The Book of Jubilees or the Little Genesis* (1902; repr., Jerusalem: Makor, 1971–1972), 24–25.

22. See Charles, *Book of Jubilees*, 22–24; James L. Kugel, "Jubilees," in *Outside the Bible: Ancient Jewish Writings Related to Scripture*, ed. Louis H. Feldman, James L. Kugel, and Lawrence H. Schiffman (Philadelphia: Jewish Publication Society; Lincoln: University of Nebraska Press, 2013), 296–97; Kugel, *A Walk through Jubilees: Studies in the Book of Jubilees and the World of Its Creation*, JSJSup 156 (Leiden: Brill, 2012), 38–40; Michael Segal, *The Book of Jubilees: Rewritten Bible, Redaction, Ideology and Theology*, JSJSup 117 (Leiden: Brill, 2007), 47–58; Cana Werman, *Sefer ha-Yovelim: Mavo', Targum u-Ferush* [*The Book of Jubilees: Introduction, Translation, and Interpretation*], Ben Mikra' la-Mishnah [Between Bible and Mishnah] (Jerusalem: Yad Izhak Ben-Zvi, 2015), 185, 191–92.

apparent, therefore, that this law belongs to the pre-Maccabean stratum of sectarian halakhah.[23]

A number of ancient texts absorbed the tradition regarding the entry of Adam and Eve into the garden of Eden after forty and eighty days, respectively.[24] In the Jewish tradition it is found in the medieval Midrash Tadshe,[25] a text that is to some extent directly dependent on the book of Jubilees.[26] We should emphasize that these texts seek to explain the purity regulations of Lev 12 based on the garden of Eden story. Further, the garden of Eden narrative is being used here to explain the differing impurity and purity periods for infant boys and girls.

In the imagery of both Miscellaneous Rules and Jubilees we see the concept that the garden of Eden is to be considered a prototype for the Jerusalem temple area. For this reason, the rules of sanctity and holiness required for entry into the temple are required in the garden. Hence, Adam and Eve could not enter the garden until they had completed the purificatory rites that were transferred to them, as newborns, from the laws of Leviticus pertaining to the mother.[27]

From a somewhat later period, this law is found in Josephus's review of biblical law in *A.J.* 3.269:

> Women after childbirth are forbidden by him to enter the Temple or to touch the sacrifices until 40 days have elapsed, if it is a male infant; double that number is prescribed for the birth of a female. But they enter at the end of the aforesaid term to offer sacrifices, which the priests apportioned to God. (Thackeray, LCL)[28]

Curiously, this text deals with the laws pertaining to purification after childbirth only from the point of view of the final readmission of the parturient into the temple. It makes no distinction between the periods of impure and pure blood. For this reason it does not mention the seven- and fourteen-day periods of impurity. The only likely explanation for this phenomenon is that Josephus sought to summarize biblical legislation for his non-Jewish readers, for whom the minor details were unnecessary.

---

23. See Lawrence H. Schiffman, "Pre-Maccabean Halakhah in the Dead Sea Scrolls and the Biblical Tradition," *DSD* 13 (2006): 348–61; Armin Lange, "Pre-Maccabean Literature from the Qumran Library and the Hebrew Bible," *DSD* 13 (2006): 277–305.

24. Charles, *Book of Jubilees*, 22–23.

25. Adolph Jellinek, *Bet Ha-Midrash*, 6 parts in 2 vols. (Jerusalem: Wahrmann, 1967), pt. 3:164–93.

26. Charles, *Book of Jubilees*, 22–23 nn. 8–14. See the parallel to Jubilees in section 15 (p. 178).

27. Baumgarten, "Purification after Childbirth," 7–10.

28. Cf. the translation of Louis H. Feldman, *Judean Antiquities 1–4*, Flavius Josephus: Translation and Commentary 3 (Leiden: Brill, 2000), 311.

The most significant question regarding the relationship of Pharisaic-rabbinic views to the laws pertaining to purification after childbirth has to do with the understanding of the two periods of time that are designated in Lev 12. The passage speaks of the period of impurity, similar to that of menstrual impurity, of seven days after the birth of a boy and fourteen days after the birth of a girl. The text also speaks of longer periods, namely, of thirty-three more days for a boy and sixty-six more days for a girl during which the mother is in a state of "blood of purity." According to rabbinic exegesis,[29] the first stage is a period of absolute impurity in which the woman is enjoined from relations with her husband and is prohibited from eating holy foods or entering the sanctuary. For this purpose, the sanctuary is defined as the entire *temenos*—the Temple Mount.[30] Thereafter, during the second period, she is still forbidden from eating holy foods or entering into the temple precincts, but she is permitted relations with her husband since she is in a period of "pure blood," and this blood is clearly not menstrual and does not originate in the uterus. During tannaitic times, and one would assume beforehand, this meant that it was permitted to have relations after the initial period if immersion took place, even if there continued to be bleeding during the second period of time.[31] The lengths of these two periods were defined differently for women who had delivered male and female children, following the Torah. Eventually, apparently in the early Middle Ages, the custom spread to forbid relations until all bleeding had stopped and there had been a seven-day period of purification on analogy with the law of the *zavah*,[32] thus rendering this Torah law no longer operable.[33] In this case, it appears that Tannaitic practice regarding the two different kinds of blood and the two periods represented the dominant explanation of Lev 12 in antiquity. Hence, we can assume that sectarian and Pharisaic-rabbinic practices were uniform on this particular issue. There seems to be no reason to assume that the later rabbinic stringency has its origins in Second Temple sectarianism.

A variety of stringencies relating to impurity came into practice toward the end of the talmudic period and in the gaonic era, spreading

---

29. Summarized in Maimonides, *H. Meṭam'e Mishkav u-Moshav* 5:4 based on m. Nid. 10:6.

30. M. Kel. 1:8; Maimonides, *H. Bi'at ha-Miqdash* 3:3. Cf. Ibn Ezra to Lev 12:4.

31. Sifra Tazria' Pereq 2:4 (ed. Weiss, 59a) and Rashi, Ibn Ezra, and Nahmanides to Lev 12:4.

32. A woman who had experienced nonmenstrual bleeding.

33. Cf. Maimonides, *H. 'Issure Bi'ah* 11:5–7. Even longer periods of waiting before returning to sexual relations after childbirth became customary in some Jewish communities. See Shulhan 'Aruch, Yoreh De`ah 194:1 (in the gloss of Moses Isserles). On the controversy over the prohibition of relations during the entire period of post-partum bleeding, see Eric (Yitzhak) Zimmer, *'Olam ke-Minhago Noheg: Peraqim be-Toledot ha-Minhagim, Hilkhotehem, ve-Gilgulehem* (Jerusalem: Merkaz Shazar, 1996), 220–39.

throughout the Jewish communities in the early Middle Ages.[34] Attempts have been made to explain these stringencies as arising from Karaite influence or from ancient sectarian traditions.[35] Some of the stringencies are found in a posttalmudic work known as Baraita' de-Niddah.[36] It is a mistake to trace these stringencies to Second Temple times and to assume that they were Sadducean when they are not found in relevant Qumran texts that deal with the same issues. On the other hand, certain of the stringencies are indeed documented in Qumran texts such as the *bet ha-ṭema'ot*, "house of the impure" (the noun is feminine), the special house to which menstrually impure women were exiled, mentioned possibly in one vocalization of the Mishnah (m. Nid. 7:4)[37] and required by the Temple Scroll (XLVIII, 14–16).[38] There, places for menstrually impure women are listed with places for other impure persons and termed *meqomot ... le-nashim be-heyotam be-niddat ṭum'atam uvlidtam*, "places ... for women in their menstrual impurity and after birth." It is certain that a variety of historical causes contributed to the onset of such stringencies at the beginning of the Middle Ages, and ancient sectarianism was only one of those causes. In fact, tendencies toward greater stringency in these issues can be observed within the talmudic corpus and so seem to have been part of the general trajectory.

---

34. See Shaya J. D. Cohen, "Purity and Piety: The Separation of Menstruants from the Sancta," in *Daughters of the King: Women and the Synagogue; A Survey of History, Halakhah, and Contemporary Realities*, ed. Rivka Haut and Susan Grossman (Philadelphia: Jewish Publication Society, 1993), 103–15.

35. Yedidya Denari, "Ḥillul ha-Qodesh 'al yede Niddah ve-Taqqanat 'Ezra," *Te'udah* 3 (1983): 17–37.

36. Michael J. Goldman, "*Baraita de-Niddah*," *EncJud* (1971), 4:194. The text is discussed and published in Chaim M. Horowitz, *Tosfata' `Atiqata'* (Frankfurt: C. M. Horowitz, 1889), sections 4–5.

37. The vocalized MSS Antonin (Abraham I. Katsch, *Ginze Mishnah* [Jerusalem: Mossad Harav Kook, 1970], 189, pl. 144), Kaufmann (Jerusalem: Sifriyat Meqorot 1967–1968), and Parma "B" de Rossi 497 (Introduction by Moshe Bar-Asher [Jerusalem: Makor, 1971]) have *bet ha-ṭema'ot*, "the house of the impure women." MS Paris 328–29 (Introduction by Moshe Bar-Asher [Jerusalem: Makor, 1973]) vocalized *bet ha-ṭum'ot*, "places of impurity." From Maimonides, *Perush ha-Mishnayot* (trans. Joseph Kafah [Jerusalem: Mossad Harav Kook, 1963], 3:381) it seems that Maimonides read *bet ha-ṭum'ot*. The parallel in t. Nid. 6:15 has *merḥaṣa'ot shel nashim*, "women's bath houses." Cf. Chanokh Albeck, "Hashlamot ve-Tosafot" in *Shishah Sidre Mishnah* (Jerusalem: Bialik Institute; Tel Aviv: Dvir, 1952–1959), 6:588–89.

38. See Yigael Yadin, *The Temple Scroll*, rev. ed., 3 vols. (Jerusalem: Israel Exploration Society and Shrine of the Book, 1983), 1:305–7; Lawrence H. Schiffman, "Matthew 9:20–22: 'And Behold, a Woman Who Had Suffered from a Hemorrhage'—The Bleeding Woman in Mark, Matthew, and Luke: Perspectives from Qumran and Rabbinic Literature," in *The Gospels in First-Century Judaea: Proceedings of the Inaugural Conference of Nyack College's Graduate Program in Ancient Judaism and Christian Origins, August 29th, 2013*, ed. R. Steven Notley and Jeffrey P. Garcia, Jewish and Christian Perspectives 29 (Leiden: Brill, 2016), 9–15. Samaritan and Ethiopian Jews followed a similar practice. See also Josephus, *A.J.* 3.261 regarding the desert camp of Israel.

Conclusion

The investigation of this law has been most fruitful. We have examined a regulation that was part of the Sadducee/Zadokite legal system before the Qumran sect came into being, as can be seen from the Jubilees parallel. Yet it generally agreed with the views of the later Tannaim. The study of large numbers of such laws in comparison with later rabbinic texts has yielded evidence of a rich and complex situation. In some areas of Second Temple law, we deal with ancient controversies between the two systems, the Sadducee/Zadokite and the Pharisaic-rabbinic. In other situations, no doubt interpretations of the Torah part of the common Judaism of Second Temple times, Tannaitic rulings that we believe go back to temple times were in agreement with the prescriptions of the sectarians. Sometimes we find a mixture of matters of controversy and matters of agreement.

The comparison of these probably pre-Maccabean laws continues to confirm our view that many laws found in the Tannaitic corpus may be shown to go back into Pharisaic times. The Qumran sect, or those whose legal tradition they inherited and passed on, polemicized, either directly or indirectly, against Pharisaic views. All this testifies not only to the existence of many Pharisaic-rabbinic laws before the destruction of the temple but also to the fructifying debate over these legal rulings that was already going on by around the time of the Maccabean revolt. This conclusion is itself one of the major results of the study of the halakhic material in the Dead Sea Scrolls.

In the case of our particular law regarding women who had given birth, we find that the explicit laws of the Torah, stated in the Damascus Document, are virtually the same in both halakhic traditions. They were held to more or less literally by both the sectarians and the Pharisaic-rabbinic tradition. At the same time, the Dead Sea Scrolls legal tradition, as embodied in Miscellaneous Rules, itself a text dependent on the Damascus Document, included also a narrative and rearranged order of laws that appears to depend on Jubilees. It seems, therefore, that in regard to this particular law we find unanimous legal rulings already in the pre-Maccabean period and an etiology dependent on a chronology of weeks that explained the law to the readers of Jubilees and the followers of the Qumran sect.

Philo and Jewish Ethnicity

ERICH S. GRUEN
University of California–Berkeley

Philo of Alexandria would seem to stand on the margin of two cultures. A devout Jew steeped in the Bible and its traditions, he was also deeply learned in Greek philosophy, literature, and legend. Philo serves frequently as the quintessential example of the thinker who straddled both worlds, a blend of the biblical exegete and the Hellenic philosopher. If anyone in antiquity were to explore in depth the question of how to reconcile Jewish identity with absorption in the cultural universe of Hellas, it should certainly have been Philo. The issue of how he struck a balance between Judaism and Hellenism has frequently exercised scholarly speculation.[1]

Yet that issue seems to have left Philo largely unmoved. The two worlds did not collide in his work, nor did they stand side by side in some stately juxtaposition. Philo belonged to an elite Jewish family in Alexandria, fully integrated in the intellectual society of cultivated Jews fluent in Greek who commanded both the Greek Bible and the literature and

---

I am delighted to dedicate this piece to Shaye Cohen, an old friend with whom I have had numerous productive and entertaining conversations over the years, including an annual lunch at the SBL, a regular highlight of that convention (which is not always full of highlights). Shaye's work on Jewish ethnicity and the malleable boundaries between Jew and gentile has been an invaluable guide and prod for some of my own thinking on those subjects, even when, perhaps especially when, we reach different conclusions. I look forward to a trenchant critique of this paper.

1. Among numerous treatments of this topic, see, e.g., Erwin Ramsdell Goodenough, *An Introduction to Philo Judaeus*, 2nd ed. (Oxford: B. Blackwell, 1962); Samuel Sandmel, "Philo Judaeus: An Introduction to the Man, His Writings, and His Significance," in *ANRW* II.21.1 (1984): 31–36; Alan Mendelson, *Philo's Jewish Identity*, BJS 161 (Atlanta: Scholars Press, 1988), 115–38; Jutta Leonhardt-Balzer, "Jewish Worship and Universal Identity in Philo of Alexandria," in *Jewish Identity in the Greco-Roman World / Jüdische Identität in der griechisch-römischen Welt*, ed. Jörg Frey, Daniel R. Schwartz, and Stephanie Gripentrog, AJEC 71 (Leiden: Brill, 2007), 29–53, with valuable bibliography; Cynthia M. Baker, "'From Every Nation under Heaven': Jewish Ethnicities in the Greco-Roman World, in *Prejudice and Christian Beginnings: Investigating Race, Gender, and Ethnicity in Early Christian Studies*, ed. Laura Nasrallah and Elisabeth Schüssler-Fiorenza (Minneapolis: Fortress, 2009), 86–91.

learning of Hellas.[2] For Philo, no reconciliation was necessary. He conveys a seamless whole that did not require adjustment or accommodation—let alone agonizing.[3]

How then did Philo understand what it meant to be Jewish? Did he have a conception of Jewish ethnicity? Did he define or articulate it? Wherein lay the distinctiveness of his people in the broader Greco-Roman society? What stood at the core of Jewish identity in the philosopher's construct? Indeed, one might go further and ask whether he worried very much about the issue at all.

I

Philo regularly divided the world into Hellenes and *barbaroi*, with nothing in between.[4] That apportionment, of course, simply echoed standard Hellenic verbiage. Philo duplicated the demarcation that the Greeks conventionally provided. The prevailing distinction was that of language: *barbaroi* spoke in a variety of bewildering tongues, the sole common denominator being that none was Greek. Philo embraced the customary formula. Where then did the Jews fit? In a cultural divide that allowed for just two parts, they presumably stood with the *barbaroi*. For some that might seem quite surprising. Yet it is important to note that the term *barbaros* itself did not necessarily or even usually carry a negative connotation. The dichotomy in nearly all of its appearances in Philo reflected stock phraseology without the application of a pejorative judgment.

On occasion, indeed, the category of "barbarian" could engender a most positive assessment—especially if it included Jews. So, for instance,

---

2. For the circumstances of Philo's life (what little is known of it), see Peder Borgen, "Philo of Alexandria: A Critical and Synthetical Survey of Research since World War II," in *ANRW* II.21.2 (1984): 98–154, here 108–15; R. Barraclough, "Philo's Politics: Roman Rule and Hellenistic Politics," in *ANRW* II.21.2 (1984); 417–553, here 421–41; J. Morris, "The Jewish Philosopher Philo," in Emil Schürer, *The History of the Jewish People in the Age of Jesus Christ (175 B.C.–A.D. 135)*, rev. ed. by Geza Vermes, Fergus Millar, and Martin Goodman, 3 vols., (Edinburgh: T&T Clark, 1973–1987), III.2:813–19; Daniel R. Schwartz, "Philo, his Family, and his Times," in *The Cambridge Companion to Philo*, ed. Adam Kamesar, Cambridge Companions (Cambridge: Cambridge University Press, 2009), 9–31; Torrey Seland, "Philo of Alexandria: An Introduction," in *Reading Philo: A Handbook to Philo of Alexandria*, ed. Torrey Seland (Grand Rapids: Eerdmans, 2014), 3–9; Maren R. Niehoff, *Philo of Alexandria: An Intellectual Biography* (New Haven: Yale University Press, 2018), 1–22.

3. The smooth presentation does not, however, preclude some inner tension. See E. S. Gruen, "Jewish Literature," in *The Oxford Handbook of the Second Sophistic*, ed. Daniel S. Richter and William A. Johnson (New York: Oxford University Press, 2017), 640–42.

4. Examples abound in his texts. See, e.g. *Spec.* 1.211, 2.44; *Mos.* 2.27; *Prob.* 138; *Legat.* 8, 141; *Opif.* 128; *Conf.* 6. 190; *Ebr.* 193; *Decal.* 153; *Praem.* 165; *Prov.* 2.15; *Abr.* 136; *Ios.* 134. Cf. Ellen Birnbaum, "Philo on the Greeks: A Jewish Perspective on Culture and Society in First Century Alexandria," *SPhiloA*, 13 (2001): 37–58, here 42-48.

Philo adapts a famous tale that pairs Alexander the Great with the celebrated Indian wise man Calanus. In Philo's version, Alexander wished to exhibit to the Greek world the alien wisdom of the "barbarian" and thus put pressure on Calanus to accompany him and add to his own fame as he traveled east and west. The Indian sage declined, and his retort demonstrated the virtue of the wise man who could successfully speak truth to power (*Prob.* 94–96). Philo expanded the motif of Eastern acumen on a broader scale in his comparison of Hellene and barbarian, this time bringing the Jews into the picture. Whereas all lands contain numerous wealthy, renowned, and pleasure-loving persons, so he claims, the intelligent, just, and astute constitute only a small number. As illustration, he notes the Seven Sages of Greece, and in the "barbarian" world he identifies the magi of Persia, the gymnosophists of India (who included Calanus), and the Jews in Palestinian Syria, most particularly their men of eminent virtue, sagacity, and devoutness, the Essenes (*Prob.* 73–76).[5] The *barbaroi* are thus at least on a par with the Greeks and even eclipsed them, especially when the Jews form part of the barbarian ranks.

Yet Philo the Jew could hardly leave it at that. Jews did not simply fall into the bland classification of non-Greeks. In matters of importance Philo makes sure to single out Jews from both Greeks and "barbarians."[6] The Jewish people corrected the principal error into which both Greeks and barbarians fell, namely, the worship of objects created by men (*Spec.* 2.165–166).[7] He sets Moses apart as the best of all lawgivers anywhere, superior to those who stem from Greeks or barbarians (*Mos.* 2.12). He proceeds to place Jews in a special category by themselves. In Philo's formulation, almost no community among Greeks or *barbaroi* adopts the practices of any other one, indeed generally rejects them. He cites as examples Athenians and Spartans in the first category, Egyptians and Scythians in the second. Jews, on the other hand, stand as a beacon for all, as Greeks and barbarians alike are drawn to Jewish usages like observance of the Sabbath. His people, so he maintains, have earned the admiration of all

---

5. On Philo's attitude toward non-Jewish intellectuals generally, see the remarks of Ellen Birnbaum, "Portrayals of the Wise and Virtuous in Alexandrian Jewish Works: Jews' Perceptions of Themselves and Others," in, *Ancient Alexandria between Egypt and Greece*, ed. W. V. Harris and Giovanni Ruffini, Columbia Studies in the Classical Tradition 26 (Leiden: Brill, 2004), 147–57.

6. See the useful discussion of K. Berthelot, "Grecs, Barbares et Juifs dans l'oeuvre de Philon," in *Philon d'Alexandrie: Un penseur à l'intersection des cultures gréco-romaine orientale juive et chrétienne: Actes du colloque international organisé par le Centre interdisciplinaire d'étude des religions et de la laïcité de l'Université libre de Bruxelles (Bruxelles, 26–28 juin 2007)*, ed. Sabrina Inowlocki and Baudouin Decharneux, Monothéismes et philosophie (Turnhout: Brepols, 2011), 47–61.

7. Rightly noted by Berthelot, "Grecs, Barbares," 59. Cf. *Her.* 169.

nations. In this framework, Jews occupy a distinctive place, one that is neither Hellenic nor "barbarian" (*Mos.* 2.17–21).

Philo could turn to this same purpose the iconic tale of Abraham's willingness to sacrifice his son Isaac. The philosopher responded vigorously to those who made light of this deed, both Greeks and barbarians. Greeks pointed to legends like that of Agamemnon's sacrifice of his daughter for the sake of his nation, and "barbarians" cited those for whom child sacrifice is an ingrained practice of their society. The latter noted that even Indian gymnosophists immolate themselves to prevent succumbing to old age. Greeks and barbarians alike could thus claim that Abraham's act was nothing special. Philo took umbrage. He rejected the parallels and insisted that the righteousness of Abraham was not dictated by custom, compulsion, or national necessity but solely by obedience to God (*Abr.* 178–199). However much the philosopher may deplore the practice of human sacrifice itself, his point here transcends any stigmatizing of the "barbarians." In Philo's conception, Abraham stands apart from both Greek and barbarian.

Only rarely does Philo employ the term *barbaros* in its adverse significance.[8] In connection with the foul practice of revenue collectors who inflict harsh penalties not only on property but on the bodies of debtors and innocent families, he brands the perpetrators as "barbarians by nature," lacking civilized *paideia*.[9] That passage stands almost alone in the Philonic corpus as a purely negative characterization of *barbaroi* as a body. To be sure, Philo's denunciation of the emperor Gaius in the *Legatio ad Gaium* fiercely censures the practice of *proskynēsis* as a "barbarian" act of abject prostration which had been introduced into Italy, to the shame of the noble Roman tradition of freedom.[10] Even here, however, the reference to the "barbaric" custom need not imply that the label itself signifies degradation, simply that the practice derived from a non-Roman nation (namely, Persia).

In brief, Jews could be included among *barbaroi* or be distinguished from them (as from Greeks), depending on context. Philonic usage encompassed both. It is plain that the term *barbaros* lacked any consistent designation of ethnicity. Hence, it could hardly serve to delineate, whether as parallel or as contrast, a Jewish sense of ethnic identity. Nor did Philo intend it for that purpose.

---

8. The discussion of K. Goudriaan, "Ethnical Strategies in Graeco-Roman Egypt," in, *Ethnicity in Hellenistic Egypt*, ed. Per Bilde et al., Studies in Hellenistic Civilization 3 (Aarhus: Aarhus University Press, 1992), 82–85, puts too much emphasis on the negative. And it is somewhat misleading to claim that Philo was conducting an "ethnical strategy."

9. Philo, *Spec.* 3.163–164: βάρβαροι τὰς φύσεις, ἡμέρου παιδείας ἄγευστοι.

10. Philo, *Legat.* 116: βαρβαρικὸν ἔθος. Cf. also *Legat.* 215.

II

Where, then, might one find Philo's notion of Jewish ethnicity? It would seem useful to look for clues in Philo's use of ethnically loaded language. The philosopher refers frequently to the *Ioudaioi* as a *genos* or an *ethnos*. On the face of it, scrutiny of those passages might tease out a Philonic conceptualization of Jewish ethnicity. In fact, however, the inquiry produces only mixed and ambiguous results, very far from a clear-cut signification.

Genos in Philo's works cannot be pinned down to a consistent definition. It often means little more than a category or a species, lacking any ethnic resonance.[11] Further, it can designate a family rather than a large collective, or, by contrast, a much larger group, namely, mortal creatures generally or indeed all of humankind. Philo affixes the label *genos* generously.[12] The word *ethnos* is equally malleable. It appears in Philo regularly to denote what might be termed "nation" in a wide and unspecific sense, without ethnic implications.[13] The phraseology itself does not solve the problem.

Should Jews be defined as a descent group, stemming from Abraham, and linked thereafter by genealogy? Philo does on occasion employ language to suggest such a lineage. He depicts the union of Abraham and Sarah as one that will produce not just a family of sons and daughters but an entire *ethnos*, one that will be most beloved of God (*Abr.* 98). He also quotes Genesis in having God promise Abraham that he will turn into a great *ethnos* (*Migr.* 1; cf. 68; *Her.* 277). Abraham is described as the earliest of the *ethnos* of the Jews (*Virt.* 212).

The language is evocative. But how far does it provide precision?[14] Philo, to be sure, identifies Abraham, Isaac, and Jacob as founders of the *ethnos* (*Praem.* 57). Elsewhere, however, he presents the same three as originators of the *genos* (*Mut.* 88; cf. *Spec.* 2.217; *Virt.* 206–207). The terms, it appears, are interchangeable, hardly clear-cut delimitations. And the overlap proceeds. Philo can speak of Abraham as leader of the *ethnos* and the *genos*.[15] How to interpret that? Does Philo indicate two separate units? He evidently chose not to be explicit. That may frustrate the scholar, but it also suggests the indifference of Philo to exactitude on the matter. Nor do the Israelites have a monopoly on the patriarchs. The seed of Abraham

---

11. E.g., Philo, *Opif.* 16; *Leg.* 1.14; *Cher.* 106; *Agr.* 144; *Spec.* 2.35; *Aet.* 117.

12. Family: e.g., Philo, *Det.* 25, 99; *Post.* 109; *Flacc.* 13; mortal creatures: e.g., *Leg.* 1.4, 1.16; *Plant.* 14; *Migr.* 69; humankind: e.g., *Opif.* 79; *Gig.*1; *Praem.* 8; *Legat.* 68.

13. E.g., Philo, *Mos.* 1.88, 1.123; *Spec.* 1.7, 1.78–79; *Praem.* 7, 57; *Legat.* 10, 19; *Prob.* 137, etc.

14. Philo reproduces the passage in the Scriptures on which God forecasts that Isaac's seed will be a blessing to all the *ethne* of the earth; *Her.* 8. Transmission of that text implies that descent from the patriarchs did not limit itself to the *ethnos* of the Hebrews.

15. Philo, *Her.* 278: τὸν ἔθνους καὶ γένους ... ἡγεμόνα ... ἐθνάρχης γὰρ καὶ γενάρχης.

through Isaac engenders all the *ethnē* of the earth (*Her.* 8; cf. *QG* 3.42). Philo can even designate the three founders as *genarchai* of the *ethnos* (*Somn.* 1.167). And there are added complications. Philo names Shem, one of the sons of Noah, as the root, Abraham as the tree, and Isaac as the fruit of the *genos* from whom sprang the seed that produced Jacob and the twelve tribes. At first glance, this formulation appears to indicate a direct lineage that defines the nation. Yet it should be noted that the imagery forms part of a common Philonic allegory in which the patriarchs advance reason and virtue, thereby to overcome the passions (*Sobr.* 65–66; *Somn.* 1.159, 166–172). Further overlap occurs when Philo describes Moses as a Chaldean by *genos* and seventh in descent from Abraham who was founder of the *ethnos* of the Jews (*Mos.* 1.5, 7; cf. *Virt.* 212). The terminology is plainly malleable rather than fixed. Philo, for instance, refutes those who call Moses an Egyptian by insisting that he was not only a Hebrew but of the purest *genos* of the Hebrews.[16] That surprising statement would allow the inference that Hebrews consisted of more than one *genos*. Whether that was the philosopher's intent remains obscure. In any case, God's choice of Moses as leader of his people had nothing to do with his genealogy. It was a prize for his love of virtue and the nobility of his soul (*Mos.* 1.148–149). The ostensibly ethnic terminology has different and wider significance. Philo has Joseph boast of belonging to the *genos* of the Hebrews, but he characterizes the *genos* as advancement beyond the perception of the senses to the life of the mind (*Migr.* 20). Even Philo's reproduction of God's message to Rebekah in Genesis that she had two *ethnē* in her womb transformed the genealogical meaning into an allegorical one. The two *ethnē* represented conflict in the soul between reason and irrationality, between baseness and virtue, between liberty and enslavement. Indeed Rebekah carried in her womb the sources of good and evil.[17] Philo's language of ethnicity is supple and pliable. It does not easily serve to pinpoint Jewish lineage.

III

In Philo's treatises, Jewish identity eludes simple definition by ancestry and descent. His vision was broader. The philosopher indeed freed the concept from the limits of the bloodline. Kinship in his formulation takes on a transformative character.

The founder of the nation himself plays a pivotal and evocative role. Philo stresses that Abraham's roots lay elsewhere than in (what would become) the homeland of the clan. The forefather stemmed from Chaldea,

16. Philo, *Mut.* 117: τὸν οὐ μόνον Ἑβραῖον, ἀλλὰ καὶ τοῦ καθαρωτάτου γένους ὄντα Ἑβραίων.
17. Philo, *Sacr.* 4; *Leg.* 3.88–89. Cf. *Sacr.* 134–135; Mos. 1.237–242. The Genesis passage is 25:23.

that is, Babylonia, the land of astrology and numerology. His migration to the future territory of Israel constituted the determinative act. But in Philo's depiction, this went beyond mere geography. The journey was a spiritual and intellectual one. Abraham moved from the myopia of polytheism, star worship, and false science to an authentic grasp of the universe as created and governed by God. He was, in fact, the first proselyte, as the philosopher conceives him, the quintessential model for all who abandoned the fraudulent ways and vacuous beliefs of their own ancestors to embrace the truth of the sole divinity.[18] The scales fell from Abraham's eyes. He dismissed his long-held Chaldean creed that equated the created world with the creator and acknowledged instead the invisible force that determined the visible world (*Abr.* 67–80; *Somn.* 160–161; *Praem.* 58). And Philo goes further. Perhaps the most notable aspect of his formulation comes in the depiction of Abraham's journey as a reaching for "kinship" with God.[19] The metaphorical use of the term serves him well. Philo injects kinship as a critical ingredient in his characterization of spiritual relationship. But the "kinship" goes well beyond the idea of a bloodline.

Ethnic solidarity did not distinguish the Jews. They consisted of a motley group almost from the start. Philo notes that intermarriage between peoples and between classes occurred already in the patriarchal period (*Virt.* 223–225). And when Moses led his people out of Egypt, they were a "mixed and rough multitude," as the book of Exodus affirms (12:38) and Philo reiterates.[20]

In the *Special Laws*, Philo expands upon Moses's exhortation to the Israelites in Deut 17:15 to choose a leader after his death from among their "brothers" and not set a "foreigner" above them. That might seem to suggest that a kinship bond defined the Israelites, excluding the outsider on ethnic grounds. But Philo's elaboration on the passage moves it onto a different plane. For him the liabilities of the foreigner rested on moral grounds. He is undesirable because of greed and selfishness; he would strip the people of their own land and possessions and send them into impoverished exile (*Spec.* 4.157–158). The philosopher engages in this form of verbal manipulation more than once. He pits the terms ὁμοεθνεῖς and ἀλλοτρίοι against one another in a seemingly ethnic differentiation. Yet this opposition, far from definitive, can be dissolved by a superabundance of virtues. The differentiation then becomes metamorphosed into nothing less than a kinship connection. The ostensibly ethnic contrast turns

18. Philo, *Virt.* 212–219, at 219: οὗτος ἅπασιν ἐπηλύταις εὐγενείας ἐστι κανών ... καλὴν δ' ἀποικίαν στειλαμένοις πρὸς ἔμψυχον τῷ ὄντι καὶ ζῶσαν πολιτείαν, ἧς ἔφορος καὶ ἐπίσκοπος ἀληθεία. Cf. *Hyp.* 6.1. See the comment of Walter T. Wilson, *Philo of Alexandria, On Virtues*, PACS 3 (Leiden: Brill, 2011), 409–10, with references.

19. Philo, *Virt.* 218: τῆς πρὸς θεὸν συγγενείας ὀρεχθέντα. Cf. Wilson, *On Virtues*, 409.

20. Philo, *Migr.* 154–155: τὸν ἐπίμικτον καὶ δασὺν τοῦτον ὄχλον; *Mos.* 1.147.

into an ethnic blending.[21] And Philo can go further still. He asserts that, in truth, kinship is not measured by blood alone but by similarity of actions and pursuit of the same goals (*Virt.* 195–196). Indeed, the philosopher describes the highest form of kinship, συγγένεια, in remarkable and unexpected fashion. He sets it in political, institutional, and ideological terms. It is a single type of constitution, the same law, and one god by whom all members of the *ethnos* are chosen.[22] Philo's sense of kinship easily transcends family ties.

In an even more striking passage, from the *De Virtutibus*, Philo has Moses express the fact that the whole *ethnos* from the start had the most compelling kinship with God, far more genuine than that of a blood-tie, making it the heir of all good things that human nature allows.[23] The formulation signifies that kinship in its purest sense eclipses any relationship by blood, a metaphorical notion that removes it from the bounds of a descent group.

The notorious apostasy of those Israelites who turned to worship of the golden calf, gave rise to another notable pronouncement by Moses as framed in Philo's narrative. Here again kinship took on a quite unconventional shape. The lawgiver, furious at the backsliders, authorized his zealous followers, the Levites, to slaughter at will those who abandoned the precepts of the Lord. His exhortation urged them to slay kinsmen and friends alike. The notion of genuine kinship and friendship was framed solely as the piety of good men.[24] An even blunter statement appears elsewhere, as Philo deconstructs the idea of συγγένεια. What are termed συγγένειαι, he says, that is, relationships stemming from blood ancestors, marriage, or other similar origins, should be cast aside if they do not lead to the honor of God, the indissoluble bond of unifying good will (*Spec.* 1.317). In Philo's conceptualization of συγγένεια, the metaphorical trumps the physical.

IV

The philosopher's devotion to allegory also permits him to transfigure dramatically perhaps the most fabled story of ethnic contrast, that of

---

21. Philo, *Spec. Leg.* 2.73: ἡ δ' ἀλλοτριότης ἀκοινώνητον, εἰ μὴ καὶ ταύτην τις ὑπερβολαῖς ἀρετῶν μεθαρμόσαιτο πρὸς συγγενικὴν οἰκειότητα.

22. Philo, *Spec.* 4.159: ἡ δ' ἀνωτάτω συγγένειά ἐστι πολιτεία μία καὶ νόμος ὁ αὐτὸς καὶ εἷς θεός ᾧ πάντες οἱ ἀπὸ τοῦ ἔθνους προσκεκλήρωνται.

23. Philo, *Virt.* 79: ἐξ ἀρχῆς τὸ σύμπαν ἔθνος ὑπολαβὼν ἔχειν ἀναγκαιοτάτην συγγένειαν, πολὺ γνησιωτέραν τῆς ἀφ' αἵματος, πάντων ἀγαθῶν ὧν δὴ ἀνθρωπίνη φύσις χωρεῖ κληρονόμον ἀπέφηνεν. Cf. Wilson, *On Virtues*, 193–94.

24. Philo, *Mos.* 2.169–171: συγγενεῖς καὶ φίλους ἀποκτεινάτω φιλίαν καὶ συγγένειαν ὑπολαβὼν εἶναι μόνην ἀνδρῶν ἀγαθῶν ὁσιότητα.

Sarah and Hagar. The handmaiden of the Hebrew Sarah was herself an Egyptian by birth but was pressed into service to provide Abraham with an heir. The troubled tale needs no recounting here. Its implications for differentiation between the *ethnē* and its consequences for the history of the patriarchs loom large. Philo's introduction of allegory into the analysis of the narrative, however, substantially softens the ethnic edge. His principal treatment of the disparity between the women occurs in the *De Congressu.*[25] In that work, the inferiority of Hagar to Sarah becomes allegorized as a distinction between the preliminary studies, such as grammar, geometry, music, and rhetoric, on the one hand, and wisdom, philosophy, and virtue, on the other. Hagar emblematizes the first, Sarah the second. But Philo does not denigrate the προπαιδεύματα. They are the necessary preparatory instruction for the acquisition of virtue (*Congr.* 24).[26] Hagar as handmaiden to Sarah represents the "encyclical instruction" vital for the acquisition of wisdom (*Congr.* 9; cf. 154–156). As Philo states explicitly, he is talking not about the two women but about minds—the one engaged in propaedeutic learning, the other struggling to attain virtue.[27] This skirts the whole issue of ethnicity as a determinative distinction.[28] The same holds for the contrast that Philo draws between Ishmael and Isaac. The difference between the sons of Hagar and Sarah respectively is put in allegorical terms as well: Ishmael, although the older half-brother, is the inferior in intellectual advancement, as are the *encyclia* to the true learning of the virtues (*Sobr.* 8–9). Ethnicity does not come into play.

Another passage sets the matter in a dramatically different light. In the *De Abrahamo* Sarah remarks to Abraham that Hagar was an Egyptian by birth, but a Hebrew by choice.[29] That statement seems to reintroduce ethnic differentiation. But it does so in a most evocative fashion. Hagar's ethnicity plainly did not determine her identity. She had chosen to become a Hebrew. Embrace of a preferred way of life outstripped ancestry.[30]

---

25. See the discussions by Sarah Pearce, *The Land of the Body: Studies in Philo's Representation of Egypt*, WUNT 208 (Tübingen: Mohr Siebeck, 2007), 167–77; Beth A. Berkowitz, "Allegory and Ambiguity: Jewish Identity in Philo's 'De Congressu,'" *JJS* 61 (2010): 3–9.

26. Discussion of the *propaideumata*, or the *mesē paideia* occurs in *Congr.* 11–23; cf. *QG* 3.19. See the valuable treatment by Pearce, *Land of the Body*, 167–77, with further references and bibliography. See esp. 170 n. 284.

27. Philo, *Congr.* 180; cf. 139–141; *Mut.* 255; *Somn.* 1.240. A somewhat more negative version in *Cher.* 8–10.

28. One might note that Paul (Gal 4:21–31) also reconceives Hagar and Sarah in allegorical terms, though quite different from those of Philo.

29. Philo, *Abr.* 251: γένος μὲν Αἰγυπτίαν, τὴν δὲ προαίρεσιν Ἑβραίαν.

30. It is worth noting that Philo associates the name Hagar with the circumstances of a πάροικος (*Congr.* 20, 22). That is a term used elsewhere to designate a sojourner or indeed a proselyte. See below.

V

Egyptians, as is well known, are principal targets of abuse by Philo. For some scholars, Philo manipulated Egypt as a constructed "Other" in order to establish a Jewish identity.[31] Expressions of hostility are numerous. No need to collect them here.[32] Egyptian animal worship draws some of his fiercest denunciation.[33] Philo also makes more general reference to the Egyptians' impiety and atheism (*Post.* 2; *Fug.* 180; *Mos.* 2.193–94). And he can mold the nation to his own allegorical purposes: Egypt serves as the land of the senses, the source of the passions, by contrast with reason and mind, the origin of genuine understanding (*Congr.* 83–85; *Mut.* 118).[34]

Yet the idea of Egypt simply as a concocted "Other" to set off the Jews by contrast may go too far. Much of the tirade comes in Philo's *In Flaccum* and *Legatio ad Gaium*, treatises that dealt with the Jews' dreadful ordeal in Alexandria in 38 CE, when Philo himself was personally and passionately engaged (e.g., *Flacc.* 17, 29; *Legat.* 120, 205). They need not have general resonance.[35] And the criticism of Egyptian animal worship paralleled that of many Greek and Roman writers.[36] The practice engendered widespread scorn. It would not readily contribute to the building of a special Jewish identity.

The picture is more complicated. Other comments of Philo cast Egyptians in a different light. At the beginning of the *De specialibus legibus* (1.2),

---

31. This is the view urged by Sarah Pearce, "Belonging and Not Belonging: Local Perspectives in Philo of Alexandria," in *Jewish Local Patriotism and Self-Identification in the Graeco-Roman Period*, ed. Siân Jones and Sarah Pearce, JSPSup 31 (Sheffield: Sheffield Academic, 1998), 88–97, and Maren Niehoff, *Philo on Jewish Identity and Culture*, TSAJ 86 (Tübingen: Mohr Siebeck, 2001), 45–74.

32. See the instances cited and discussed by Mendelson, *Philo's Jewish Identity*, 115–22; Pearce, "Belonging and Not Belonging," 79–105; Niehoff, *Philo on Jewish Identity*, 45–74, P. W. van der Horst, *Philo's Flaccus: The First Pogrom; Introduction, Translation, and Commentary*, PACS 2 (Leiden: Brill, 2003), 105–6; and the splendid study by Pearce, *Land of the Body*, esp. 45–80. See also Dorothy I. Sly, *Philo's Alexandria* (London: Routledge,1996), 111–14; Katell Berthelot, "The Use of Greek and Roman Stereotypes of the Egyptians by Hellenistic Jewish Apologists, with Special Reference to Josephus' *Against Apion*," in *Internationales Josephus-Kolloquium: Aarhus 1999*, ed. Jürgen U. Kalms, Münsteraner judaistische Studien 6 (Münster: Lit, 2000), 205-–7, 213–14.

33. See, most notably, Philo, *Dec.* 76–80; *Cont.* 8–9; cf. *Mos.* 2.161–162, 270; *Spec.* 1.79; *Legat.* 163. See the thorough discussion with references by Pearce, *Land of the Body*, 280-308.

34. He indulges in this form of metaphor with other peoples as well: Amalekites (*Migr.* 143–144), Canaanites (*Sacr.* 90; *Congr*, 83–85), Chaldeans (*Mut.* 16), Moabites, Ammonites, and Amorites (*Leg.* 3.228–232; *Post.* 177).

35. Pearce, *Land of the* Body, 54–80.

36. K. A. D. Smelik and E. A. Hemelrijk, "Egyptian Animal Worship in Antiquity," in *ANRW* II.17.4 (1984): 1955–97; Holger Sonnabend, . *Fremdenbild und Politik: Vorstellungen der Römer von Ägypten und_dem Partherreich in der späten Republik und frühen Kaiserzeit*, Europäische Hochschulschriften 3.286_(Frankfurt am Main: P. Lang, 1986), 120–24.

he pays respect to the Egyptian people for their large population, their antiquity, and their devotion to philosophy. In recounting (or constructing) Moses's education, Philo has Egyptians teach him the fundamentals of mathematics, music, Chaldean astronomy, and the philosophical symbolism of hieroglyphics, before he went on to Greek *paideia* (*Mos.* 1.23–24). Such remarks problematize any stark picture of Egyptian baseness.

Did Philo brand Egyptians with a character and nature fundamentally antithetical to Jewish qualities? Contrasts in customs, conventions, and beliefs, even drastic ones like animal worship, do not amount to ethnic differences. Indications of basic character traits are few indeed. Philo does claim on one occasion that Egyptian character is excessively arrogant by nature.[37] But he does not here compare Egyptians with other nations; he points rather to the hauteur of the Egyptian elite toward the ambitions of the common people.[38] In a different context Philo speaks of a propensity to stir up seditions and of jealousy as a feature of Egyptian nature (*Flacc.* 17, 29).[39] The complaints, however, come in the *In Flaccum*, where the narrative of events, the circumstances, and Philo's own experiences inclined him to hyperbole. Vitriol regarding Egyptian character appears once in the *Legatio ad Gaium* as well (166), also, of course, affected by those events. Nothing quite comparable can be found elsewhere in his corpus. This does not render meaningless the numerous hostile aspersions cast by the philosopher. But the disparagement of Egyptians falls into a category rather different from a judgment about inherent inferiority. Jewish ethnicity is not at issue.[40]

VI

The subordination of ethnicity in Philo's framing of the nation's identity can be illustrated in a quite different way: the philosopher's attitude toward intermarriage. He embraces the biblical prohibitions expressed most firmly in Exod 34:11–16 and Deut 7:1–4. Those pronouncements forbade marriages between Israelites and a whole range of specified peoples including Amorites, Hittites, Canaanites, and others. Philo endorses and even extends the ban. Since those ancient peoples no longer existed in his

37. Philo, *Agr.* 62: Αἰγυπτιακὸν ἐκ φύσεως καὶ διαφερόντως ἐστὶν ὑπέραυχον.

38. Philo, *Agr.* 62: ὡς χλεύην καὶ πλατὺν γέλωτα ἡγεῖσθαι τὰς τῶν δημοτικωτέρον ἀνθρώπων περὶ βίον σπουδάς τε καὶ φιλοτιμίας.

39. Cf. also *Legat.* 162, referring to Alexandrians.

40. Philo also occasionally, though very rarely, contrasts Jews with other peoples; *Spec.* 1.312–313; *Virt.* 34. The criteria, however, are not ethnic. His sneers about the savagery of Germans, Parthians, Sarmatians, and Scythians are delivered from a Roman, not a Jewish, perspective (*Legat.* 10). He can also offer quite positive appraisals of other nations, notably the Indians (*Somn.* 2.56; *Prob.* 75, 93–97).

day, he gives a blanket injunction against marriage with any non-Israelite (ἀλλοεθνής). But it is noteworthy that this divine interdiction was not issued on the grounds of alien ethnicity. The Bible is explicit, and Philo follows suit. Marriage with foreigners must be avoided, lest those Israelites who indulge in it fall prey to the customs, practices, and gods of others, and thus stray from the path of true worship (*Spec.* 3.29; cf. *Mos.* 1.296–298).[41] This prohibition speaks not to the inherent character of the ἀλλοεθνής but to the mode and objects of worship. The ban targets idolatry rather than ethnicity.[42]

Philo, in fact, when he expresses the nature of Jewish commonality, does so almost always in terms of customs, practice, and adherence to tradition. Some selective instances can provide illustration. When Joseph rejects the advances of Potiphar's wife, he delivers a speech, according to Philo, worthy of his *genos*. The patriarch declared that the descendants of the Hebrews follow customs and laws chosen especially for them (*Ios.* 42). When Moses and Aaron made their case to Pharaoh, they boldly boasted that the customs of their people shunned the norm and set them apart from all other nations.[43] Philo maintains that the *ethnos* of the Jews possesses distinctive laws, necessarily rigorous for they serve as training for the highest standard of virtue. The very founders of the *ethnos* implemented the eminently desirable forms of righteousness and virtue that were passed on to their descendants (*Spec.* 4.179–181). Allusion to the descent group is bound up inextricably with proper behavior in accord with the laws.

The combination has special force for Philo. When Moses rebukes those of his followers who sought preference in the distribution of land, Philo supplies him with a notable speech. The leader exclaims that the whole of his people is greater than its parts, and that all are entitled to equal honor. He proceeds to outline the features that unite them: a single *genos*, the same fathers, one house, the same customs, a commonality of laws, and countless other matters, each of which links together the kinship and binds it fast for good will.[44] That declaration encompasses both genealogical bonds and the unity of customs, laws, and a host of shared

41. See Sarah Pearce, "Rethinking the Other in Antiquity: Philo of Alexandria on Intermarriage," *Antichthon* 47 (2013): 140–55.

42. One might note also Philo's reference to the mixed multitude that followed Moses out of Egypt, as Exodus reported. Philo sees them primarily as the children of mixed marriages between Hebrews and Egyptians, a fact that does not disturb him (*Mos.* 1.147). See further the policy of intermarriage with handmaidens from Mesopotamia and the generous treatment of their children, evidently approved by Philo (*Virt.* 223–225).

43. Philo, *Mos.* 1.87 (with regard to sacrifices): μὴ κατὰ τὰ αὐτὰ ταῖς τῶν ἄλλων ἀνθρώπων γινομένας, ἀλλὰ τρόπῳ καὶ νόμῳ διαφεύγοντι τὴν κοινότητα διὰ τὰς τῶν ἐθῶν ἐξαιρέτους ἰδιότητας.

44. Philo, *Mos,* 1.324: πάντες ἐστὲ ἰσότιμοι, γένος ἕν οἱ αὐτοὶ πατέρες, οἰκία μία, ἔθη τὰ αὐτά, κοινωνία νόμων, ἀλλὰ μυρία, ὧν ἕκαστον τὴν οἰκειότητα συνδεῖ καὶ πρὸς εὔνοιαν ἁρμόζεται.

practices. Genealogy alone is an inadequate measure of ethnicity. Even more noteworthy, the very power of common customs and adherence to tradition, in Philo's striking formulation, gives kinship itself its meaning. The text holds real significance. Although the notion of race or ethnicity as a marker of Jewishness appears from time to time in the Philonic corpus, it is decidedly ancillary to other features that expressed Jewish identity, that is, shared conventions, respect for traditions and laws, and relations to the divine that provided common purpose.

The Jews, of course, are distinctive. They are the "chosen people," as Philo observes more than once.[45] Wherein lies their distinction? Does the award of divine favor to the Hebrews accord them a privilege that adheres to their stock and is transmitted through genealogy? Philo recounts the biblical story of the Mesopotamian seer Balaam (without giving the name) who was summoned by the king of Moab to curse the Hebrews but ended by blessing them. The Philonic narrative, while omitting the more fanciful features of the tale (like the talking donkey), has Balaam stick to his resolve and affirm the special status of the Hebrews who dwell alone and apart from all other *ethnē*. As Philo insists, however, this separation has nothing to do with geography but only with the distinctiveness of their chosen customs and their resistance to mingling with others who do not share their traditional practices. As for their relationship with God, Philo applies an allegorical interpretation: although their bodies may have been fashioned from human seeds, their souls were engendered by divine ones, thereby giving them a near kinship to God.[46] The linkage recurs here between the Jewish way of life and a kinship relation, with the latter embedded in the former. At the same time, the philosopher distinguishes sharply between a physical engendering and the more meaningful association of the *psychē* with God as exemplified by the nation's commitment to its traditions.

Philo asks an explicit question drawn from Deuteronomy: what is this great nation that brings God so near to them and earns them his favor? (Deut 4:5–8). His answer is that they are lovers of wisdom and knowledge, people who seek after greatness, which consists first and foremost in proximity to God (*Migr.* 53–60; see also *QG* 2.65). Here again it is the character of the people, not anything inherited in the bloodline, which earns them the benefactions of the Lord. Philo reasserts more than once the point that the quality of the descent group is intricately intertwined with allegiance to its chosen code of laws and the highest standards of virtue. The founders of the nation passed that legacy to their descendants, but its endurance lay in the exercise of righteousness and virtue (*Spec.* 4.179–181). The

45. E.g., Philo, *Conf.* 56: γένος γάρ ἐσμεν τῶν ἐπιλέκτων; *Praem.* 123: λαὸς ἐξαίρετος; *Post.* 91–92: τὸ ἐπίλεκτον γένος Ἰσραήλ. Cf. *Legat.* 3–4.

46. Philo, *Mos.* 1.278–279: τὰ μὲν σώματ' αὐτοῖς ἐξ ἀνθρωπίνων διεπλάσθη σπερμάτων, ἐκ δὲ θείων ἔφυσαν αἱ ψυχαί; διὸ καὶ γεγόνασιν ἀγχίσποροι θεοῦ. Cf. Num 22–24.

code of laws by which they lived came straight from the mouth of God, a feature deliberately chosen for the *ethnos*.[47] Philo indeed boasts that the laws of his people are emulated everywhere and predicts that nations will overturn their own native traditions and embrace the laws of his nation alone (*Mos.* 2.43–44). The *ethnos* that Moses led, an *ethnos* more populous and more powerful than his own native land of Egypt, indeed an *ethnos* that would be held more sacred than all others, was appointed to offer up prayers for humankind itself in warding off evils and sharing what is good (*Mos.* 1.149; cf. *Spec.* 2.167; *QG* 2.58). The values of the *ethnos,* no mere genealogy, characterized, in Philo's representation, the "chosen people."

Does the philosopher employ phraseology that might have racial resonance and a pejorative tone? The words ἀλλόφυλος, ἀλλοεθνής, and ἀλλογενής do crop up—but only very rarely, a total of fourteen times in the whole of Philo's corpus. They designate persons or people distinct from Jews but do not necessarily convey a negative characterization.[48] Only a few instances occur in an unfavorable context.[49] The majority of them lack any pejorative overtone.[50] A particular example is worth noting. Philo affirms that one should not practice injustice toward those of a different *ethnos*. Indeed, if they are guilty of nothing other than being of another *genos*, they are blameless.[51] That generous statement delivers the clear message that, however one understands these ostensibly ethnic terms, they do not designate an alien race incompatible with coexistence.

VII

The dissolution of ethnic boundaries is no better illustrated than by the encouragement and welcome of proselytes.[52] The practice receives warm endorsement by Philo and forms a repeated motif in his writings. The

47. Philo, *Spec.* 2.189–190: τοῦτο μὲν τοῦ ἔθνους.

48. E.g., Philo, *Her.* 42; *Somn.* 1.161; *Spec.* 4.16; *Virt.* 160, 222; *Prob.* 93; *Legat.* 183, 211.

49. Philo, *Spec.* 1.56; *Legat.* 200. The reference to *allogeneis* in *Spec.* 1.124, who are not permitted to share in sacred matters, given the context, probably means non-priests, rather than foreigners.

50. This holds also for the term ἀλλότριος, in various forms, which Philo uses much more frequently. But a large proportion is adjectival, meaning only "belonging to another" or "different from"; e.g. Philo, *Leg.* 2.40, 3.22; *Cher.* 9; *Plant.* 143; *Sobr.* 3; *Conf.* 115; *Her.* 105; *Mut.* 197. The noun form regularly refers to "foreigner" or "alien" as distinct from indigenous or familial, or simply to something that belongs to another; e.g., Philo, *Post.* 109; *Agr.* 84; *Her.* 44; *Spec.* 1.340, 2.123, 3.9, 4.70; *Virt.* 89; *Praem.* 139; *Legat.* 72. Rarely does the term carry a negative connotation or convey disparagement with regard to ethnic differentiation.

51. Philo, *Virt.* 147: μηδένα τῶν ἑτεροεθνῶν ἀδικεῖν, οὐδὲν ἔχοντας αἰτιάσασθαι ὅτι μὴ τὸ ἀλλογενές, ὅπερ ἐστὶν ἀναίτιον. Wilson oddly puts a negative interpretation on this (*On Virtues*, 322–23).

52. On Philo's view of proselytes, see the important treatment by Ellen Birnbaum, *The*

philosopher pays due homage to the biblical pronouncements in Leviticus, Deuteronomy, and elsewhere, wherein the Lord enjoins Israelites to treat the aliens like the native born, to love them as you do yourself, for you were once aliens in the land of Egypt (Lev 19:33–34; Deut 10:18–19).[53] Philo offers an extended version of this doctrine in *De Virtutibus*, employing the terms ἔπηλυς ("incomer") and πάροικος ("sojourner") more or less interchangeably. And he reinforces the biblical command by asserting that Israelites treat immigrants as friends and kinsmen (συγγενεῖς), thus a notable lifting of barriers.[54] Those proselytes who have abandoned their native land, friends, and relatives to join the Israelite community for reasons of virtue and piety should have all the privileges of the indigenous.[55] Philo indeed concocts or transmits a radical revision of the Tamar story which has her as an *allophylos* from Palestinian Syria who discarded all her idols and became a convert by entering the life of piety (*Virt.* 220–222).[56] Philo finds the ultimate eradication of differences in Lev 25:23, where God declares that all the land is mine, and those who dwell on it are merely proselytes and sojourners before me.[57] For Philo this justifies a bold universalism in which God alone is a full citizen of the world, while all others are visitors and aliens.[58] The leveling is drastic. Israelites and non-Israelites stand on the same plane, and ethnic differences disappear. The proselyte is no inferior figure. Indeed Abraham himself, as Philo represents him, is the first proselyte, a Chaldean immigrant who set the pattern for future mingling of peoples (*Virt.* 219; *Somn.* 1.160).[59]

The welcoming of proselytes and their integration into the community form a central ingredient of Jewish identity.[60] Ethnicity becomes quite irrelevant. In Philo's presentation, those who have cast away false deities

---

Place of Judaism in Philo's Thought: Israel, Jews, and Proselytes, BJS 290 (Atlanta: Scholars Press, 1996), 195–209.

53. It is noteworthy that the Septuagint uses the term προσήλυτος to signify "stranger" or "alien." That made it easier for Philo to transfer the concept to proselyte or convert, although the biblical term in this context had a different connotation. Cf. Deut 23:7–8, where the LXX uses the term πάροικος.

54. Philo, *Virt.* 102–108, esp. 103: ἀγαπᾶν τοὺς ἐπηλύτας, μὴ μόνον ὡς φίλους καὶ συγγενεῖς ἀλλὰ καὶ ὡς ἑαυτούς; 106: οὐ βδελύξῃ, Αἰγύπτιον, ὅτι πάροικος ἐγένου κατ' Αἴγυπτον. See the valuable commentary by Wilson, *On Virtues*, 257–62.

55. Philo, *Spec.* 1.51–53; 1.308–309; 4.176–178; *Somn.* 2.273; *Virt.* 219; *Praem.* 152. See the discussion of Terence L. Donaldson, *Judaism and the Gentiles: Jewish Patterns of Universalism (to 135 CE)* (Waco, TX: Baylor University Press, 2007), 235–45; *Virt.* 220–221; cf. Donaldson, *Judaism*, 251–53; Wilson, *On Virtues*, 410.

56. See Donaldson, *Judaism and the Gentiles*, 251–53; Wilson, *On Virtues*, 410. Philo's version bears little resemblance to the tale in Gen 38.

57. Lev 25.23 LXX: ἐμὴ γάρ ἐστιν ἡ γῆ, διότι προσήλυτοι καὶ πάροικοι ὑμεῖς ἐστε ἐναντίον μου.

58. Philo, *Cher.* 119-121: μόνος κυρίως ὁ θεὸς πολίτης ἐστί, πάροικον δὲ καὶ ἐπήλυτον τὸ γενητὸν ἅπαν; cf. 108.

59. Cf. Wilson, *On Virtues*, 409–410.

60. Philo, *Virt.* 182; *Mos.* 2.44; *Spec.* 2.118–119; *Legat.* 211.

and embraced the true God must be reckoned as our dearest friends and closest kinsmen. Their actions, showing a God-loving disposition, supply the greatest expression of friendship and kinship relations.[61] By setting the blend of Jew and convert in terms of close family bonds, Philo effectively blunts the force of ethnic differentiation.

The other side of this coin warrants mention. The receipt of proselytes into Jewish communities had its counterpart in the spread of Jews into foreign communities stretching across the Mediterranean and beyond from Italy to Iran. Philo himself, of course, was a diaspora Jew. He took immense pride in the dispersal of his people over islands and continents, delineating in detail the numerous sites in Europe, Asia, and Africa where Jews had settled, representing them indeed even as *apoikiai*, as if the Jews had sent out colonies in familiar Hellenic fashion (*Praem.* 165; *Flacc.* 45–46; *Legat.* 281–283). The relationship between the diaspora communities and the Judean homeland is too large a topic for treatment here.[62] Philo's comments, however, are worth attending to. Attachment to the homeland was vital for Jewish identity. The philosopher underscores the fact that Jerusalem remains the "metropolis," the mother-city, for all Jews scattered far and wide around the world, no matter where they dwell. Yet each individual community that houses the settlers of the diaspora is reckoned by them now as their *patris*, the fatherland, the site where they were born and raised, and one which many of them had inherited from fathers, grandfathers and even distant ancestors who came as initial settlers of the *apoikia*.[63] The descent group, in short, is tied to the location of individual communities. Jewish identity retains an indissoluble connection to the temple and the Holy City, to the ancient lore of the nation, which all Jews share. But the direct link with ancestors is traced to the founders of each diaspora settlement. Ethnicity does not reduce itself to the legacy of Abraham.

VIII

Philo's conception of Jewish ethnic identity is slippery, ambiguous, and forever elusive. He felt no urgency in providing a definition. For the Jewish intellectual enmeshed in a Hellenic cultural environment, the question was immaterial. Jews could be numbered among the *barbaroi* when

61. Philo, *Virt.* 179: φιλτάτους καὶ συγγενεστάτους ὑποληπτέον, τὸ μέγιστον εἰς φιλίαν καὶ οἰκειότητα παρασχομένους θεοφιλὲς ἦθος.

62. See Erich S. Gruen, *Diaspora: Jews amidst Greeks and Romans* (Cambridge: Harvard University Press, 2002), 232–252.

63. Philo, *Flacc.* 46: μητρόπολιν μὲν τὴν ἱερόπολιν ἡγούμενοι, καθ' ἣν ἵδρυται ὁ τοῦ ὑψίστου θεοῦ νεὼς ἅγιος, ἃς δ' ἔλαχον ἐκ πατέρων καὶ πάππων καὶ τῶν ἔτι ἄνω προγόνων οἰκεῖν ἕκαστοι πατρίδας νομίζοντες, ἐν αἷς ἐγεννήθησαν καὶ ἐτράφησαν; εἰς ἐνίας δὲ καὶ κτιζομένας εὐθὺς ἦλθον ἀποικίαν στειλάμενοι, τοῖς κτίσταις χαριζόμενοι.

he divided the world between Greeks and non-Greeks but could also be separated from both categories when he wished to stress the superiority of his people's achievements. Philo frequently applied to Jews what appeared to be ethnic language like *genos* or *ethnos,* but the terms had such wide and varied significance that they could not deliver (and were not meant to deliver) any precise or consistent designation of identity. The philosopher's allegorical massaging of "kinship" terminology lifted it out of the realm of blood relationship to a higher order of meaning. The harsh strictures leveled at Egyptian practices and beliefs did not aim to mark out Jewish ethnic distinctiveness. Philo conveyed a complex bundle of traits that constituted Jewishness. Custom, laws, connections with the divinity, and biblical lore, scrutinized for its allegorical significance and philosophical meaning, took central place, indeed served to define "kinship" itself. Jews were "chosen" for the practice of virtue, rationality, and righteousness, not for their ancestry. The embrace of proselytes, the acceptance of intermarriage, and the adaptation to life in diaspora communities where Jews were a minority, all features stressed by Philo, cast any sense of ethnic distinctiveness in the shade. Racial differentiation was not on the philosopher's agenda.

Josephus's "Samaias-Source"

TAL ILAN
Freie Univeristät Berlin

In his *Jewish Antiquities* books 14–15, Josephus mentions three times a certain "Samaias the Pharisee." This person does not appear in Josephus's earlier version of the history of this period, presented in his *Jewish War* book 1. In their study of Josephus's sources, nineteenth-century scholars had surmised that, when writings *Antiquities*, Josephus employed sources that had not been available to him when he wrote his earlier work.[1] The Samaias episodes clearly belong among these. The questions, what sort of sources they were and how many, have been the subject of an extensive debate, and no definite conclusions have been put forward. It seems to me, however, that, if a certain person is mentioned three times, on three separate occasions only in *Antiquities*, and in two cases his mention includes a cross-reference to his earlier or later appearance, all three stories belong to one source. In the following lines I will argue that this source, Josephus's "Samaias-source," was also known to, and used by, the editors of the Babylonian Talmud (henceforth *Bavli*). In this article, a comparison of several elements that are common to Josephus and the *Bavli*, will outline the "Samaias-source" and flesh out its ideology and theology.

At an early stage in his career, the recipient of this volume, my dear friend Shaye Cohen, had declared his intention to someday produce a corpus of all the parallels between Josephus and rabbinic literature (Shaye J. D. Cohen, "Parallel Historical Traditions in Josephus and Rabbinic Literature," *Proceedings of the World Congress of Jewish Studies* B/1 [Jerusalem: World Council of Jewish Studies Press, 1987], 14–17). When in 2010, Vered Noam and I set out on a similar venture, we asked him what had become of these plans and he gave us a free hand to pursue our project. The project is now out (Tal Ilan and Vered Noam, in collaboration with Meir Ben Shahar, Daphne Baratz and Yael Fisch, *Josephus and the Rabbis* [Hebrew] [Jerusalem: Yad Ben-Zvi, 2017]). This article, devoted gratefully to Shaye, is an outcome of my intensive interaction with these sources. It engages in some methods that may be considered by many today as outdated but which as Daniel R. Schwartz has recently shown (in his *Reading the First Century: On Reading Josephus and Studying Jewish History of the First Century*, WUNT 300 [Tübingen: Mohr Siebeck, 2013]) can still produce interesting and useful results. I am grateful to Vered Noam for having read an earlier version of this article and for suggesting many useful corrections. The end result is, of course, completely my responsibility.

1. For a listing of such sources, see Gustav Hölscher, "Josephus," *PW* 18: 1973–74.

Samaias in the Writings of Josephus

Josephus mentions Samaias three times in *Antiquities*, twice in association with another sage, described as his teacher and a Pharisee—Pollion.[2] I analyze the information Josephus provides on these men in order to see the relationship between them and between their immediate and wider contexts

The first reference to Samaias appears in *Ant.* 14. It describes how this person was involved in Herod's trial at the time when he was not a king but the newly appointed governor of Galilee and the son of the Idumean convert Antipater, advisor to the Hasmonean ruler (Hyrcanus II), and a commoner (in Greek *idiotēs*). In this capacity, Herod had executed a certain Hezekiah, whom he considered to be a rebel, but certain Jews viewed this action as murder and demanded that Herod be brought to trial. Herod indeed appeared for his hearing but brought with him a small army. This of course made all the judges terrified and they let him go. At this point "someone named Samaias, an upright man, and for that reason superior to fear," reprimanded his colleagues, stating that although "this fine fellow, Herod, who is accused of murder ... stands here clothed in purple, with the hair of his head carefully arranged, and with his soldiers around him, in order to kill us if we condemn him ... it is not Herod whom I should blame ... but you and the king for giving him such great license." He ends by warning his colleagues: "Be assured, however, that God is great, and this man, whom you now wish to release for Hyrcanus's sake, will one day punish you and the king as well" (*Ant.* 14.173–174).[3]

In this text we learn that Samaias was "an upright man." This description is clearly favorable to Samaias and indicates that it was written by a friendly author. This author, however, does have an enemy—Herod—"this fine fellow ... who is accused of murder." The events described in this text are also clearly divided between the fearless bravery of Samaias, who stands in this duel armed only with justice and righteousness, and the cowardice of Herod, who has no justice or righteousness on his side—only an armed and dangerous unit of soldiers.

Contrary to what we would have expected, however, the confrontation between Herod and Samaias does not end with the strong (but wicked)

2. Earlier scholars of Jewish history were interested in identifying these two scholars with Shammai and Hillel (m. Avot 1:12): Joseph Klausner, *History of the Second Temple Period* [Hebrew] (Jerusalem: Ha-Ma'arav, 1950), 3:362–63 and earlier bibliography; Abraham Schalit, *König Herodes: Der Mann und seiner Werk*, SJ 4 (Berlin: de Gruyter 1969), 768–71; or Shemaiah and Abtalion (m. Avot 1:10), Zachariah Frankel, *Hodegetik zur Mischna, Tosefta, Mechilta, Sifra und Sifri* [Hebrew] (Warsaw: M. Y. L. Tsaylingold 1923), 39; Emil Schürer, *The History of the Jewish People in the Age of Jesus Christ (175 BC–AD 135)*, rev. and ed. Geza Vermes, Fergus Millar, Martin Goodman, and M. Black, 3 vols. (Edinburgh: T&T Clark, 1973–1987), 2:362–63.

3. All translations are from the Loeb Classical Library.

killing the weak (but righteous); nor does it end with a miraculous delivery of the latter. It ends with a bond of friendship sealed between the two: "when Herod assumed royal power he killed Hyrcanus and all the other members of the Synhedrion with the exception of Samaias. Him he held in the greatest honor." This conclusion is unexpected and indicates that, despite the existence of heroes and villains here, they do not always stand on two sides of a divide. Politics and history are complicated, and sometimes changing sides is required.

The text ends with a cross-reference: "And on these events we shall speak in the proper place." Although scholars have shown that Josephus's cross-references are erratic and not always fulfilled,[4] this one is, at the beginning of book 15. In this second Samaias-source insert, we learn that "[w]hen Herod had got the rule of all Judaea into his hands, he showed special favor to those of the city's populace who had been on his side, while he was still an *idiotēs*." Among these were "Pollion the Pharisee and his disciple Samaias, for during the siege of Jerusalem these men had advised the citizens to admit Herod." These words are followed by the cross-reference "This same Pollion had once, when Herod was on trial for his life, reproachfully foretold to Hyrcanus and the judges that if Herod's life was spared, he would (one day) persecute them all. And in time this turned to be so, for God fulfilled his words" (*Ant.* 15.2–3).

The story here is closely tied with the previous one—not only does it tell what Josephus had promised would be told in his previous mention of Samaias, but it also refers back to the previous episode. As there, here too Samaias (and Pollion) appear righteous, and Herod a murderer, but they are now allies—*realpolitik* requires that the righteous ally themselves with the wicked in order to survive and save what can be salvaged. In fact, the two snippets may be considered doublets, or mirror images one of the other, had not the Pharisee Pollion suddenly appeared out of nowhere. Indeed, Josephus not only relegates Samaias to the position of disciple of the greater Pollion, he even seems to make the mistake of assigning to Pollion the action he had assigned to Samaias in book 14.[5]

The third occurrence of the two Pharisees, also in book 15, does not include a cross-reference, but it clearly refers to the same two people and is thus also derived from the same source. This is not just because of the names but also because of their common agenda—the righteous Pharisees

4. Justus von Destinon, *Die Quellen Flavius Josephus in der Jüd. Arch. Buch XII-XVII = Jüd. Krieg Buch I* (Kiel: Lipsius & Tischer, 1882), 21–29; Hölscher, "Josephus," 1970–82; Hans Drüner, *Untersuchung über Josephus* (Marburg: Ioh. Hamel, 1896), 70–76, 82–94; H. Peterson, "Real and Alleged Literary Projects of Josephus," *AJP* 79 (1958): 247–59; D. R. Schwartz, "Κατὰ τοῦτον τὸν καιρόν: Josephus Source on Agrippa II," *JQR* 72 (1982): 245–46.

5. However, see Benediktus Niese, *Flavii Iosepphi Opera et Aparato Critico*, vol. 3, *Antiquitatum Iudaicarum, Libri XI–XV* (Berlin: Weidmann,1885), 333 n. to line 11, where both in Manuscript E and in the Latin version, the text here reads "Samaias."

resist the wicked Herod but are not punished, because they are his allies. The text talks of a time when Herod demanded of "the rest of the populace ... that they submit to taking an oath of loyalty (to him).... Most of the populace yielded to this demand out of compliance or fear, but those who ... objected he got rid of" (*Ant.* 15.369). The story continues with him exempting the Pharisees from this oath, because of Pollion and Samaias (*Ant.* 15.370).

In this event, Herod is described as asking something unreasonable and alien to, if not to say transgressive against Jewish law—the taking of an oath of loyalty to the king (which could be considered to be taking the name of God in vain [Exod 20:6]). The law-abiding Pharisees, Pollion and Samaias, resist this demand, and not only are they not punished, but their other disciples are also exempted from the oath. Again, being allies of Herod protects them from his wrath, even though they (and the author who writes about them) clearly view him as a wicked king.

The Samaias-source thus consistently displays the same story line: Herod the wicked is presented as the mirror image of Samaias (and Pollion) the righteous, even though they are not necessarily enemies. The Pharisees wisely ally themselves with the wicked king, while not compromising their principles, and thus persevere. Implicitly, this story line also gives Herod a positive trait: he knows he is wicked and recognizes and cherishes righteousness in others.

The Context of the Samaias Inserts: The Relationship between *Antiquitites* 14 and 15

In this section I place the "Samaias-source" inserts within the larger context of the Josephus's narrative, in order to see what were Josephus's other sources and concerns and how he used the "Samaias-source" to support or contradict them.

1. *Herod's Trial*

The context in which the first Samaias pericope is inserted is Herod's trial before Hyrcanus II. Josephus had written about this trial in *Jewish War* as well.[6] *Antiquities* 14 had been used by Richard Laqueur as the test case

6. For a synopsis of *Antiquities* and *War* here, see Richard Laqueur, *Der jüdische Historiker Flavius Josephus: Ein biographischer Versuch auf neuer quellenkritischer Grundlage* (Darmstadt: Münchow, 1920), 128–230; Joseph Sievers, *Synopsis of the Greek Sources for the Hasmonean Period: 1–2 Maccabees and Josephus, War 1 and Antiquities 12–14*, SubBi 20 (Rome: Pontificio Istituto Biblico, 2001), 280–85.

for proving the older and by now nearly universally accepted thesis that, in the earlier *War*, Josephus had used Nicolaus of Damascus's *Universal History*, and later, in *Antiquities* he used his old composition and made changes in it, based on new sources.[7] This indeed seems to be the case in Josephus's retelling of the trial of Herod. The text of *War* is almost verbally repeated in *Antiquities*. Nevertheless, the tone is critically different. *War* presents both Herod and Hyrcanus in a bad light: Hyrcanus is sluggish and therefore incompetent to rule (1.203, 212),[8] although Nicolaus emphasized that he loved Herod (1.211).[9] Herod is young and temperamental and thus quick to kill (1.203–204).[10] However, there is also a truly positive hero in *War* and it is Antipater, who remains loyal to Hyrcanus, even though he could replace him (1.207),[11] and he advises Herod not to depose Hyrcanus but to remember his kind acts in the past (1.213)[12].

Because his story had to be pro-Herodian, this seems to have been the story line Nicolaus chose. He was of course well aware that it is hard to portray a private person (*idiotēs* in Greek), who is not a king, appearing in court with a private army, positively. Yet he could apparently not brush away the entire event as though it had never happened. It was too well known, both in Jerusalem and in Rome. So he portrayed Antipater as the positive Herodian figure; Hyrcanus as incompetent; and Herod as young and impetuous. Nicolaus would like us to believe that Herod will not behave so in the future.

The trial itself is portrayed minimally in *War*, making it unclear whether it ever took place. In *War* 1.210 we hear that Herod was summoned to the trial and came armed. According to *War* 1.211, the governor of Syria demanded that Hyrcanus drop the charges, which he gladly did. In 1.212, we hear that Herod intended to return with an army and punish Hyrcanus, but if there was no trial, it is not clear why he should have done this.

This state of affairs changes dramatically in *Antiquities*. Herod is presented even more negatively than in the previous composition. In 14.165

---

7. Laqueur, *Der judische Historiker Flavius Josephus*, 128–34.

8. On this being the way Nicolaus portrayed Hyrcanus, see Daniel R. Schwartz, "Josephus on Hyrcanus II," in *Josephus and the History of the Greco-Roman Period: Essays in Memory of Morton Smith*, ed. Fausto Parente and Joseph Sievers, StPB 41(Leiden: Brill, 1994), 210–32.

9. Copied in *Ant.* 14.170.

10. Copied in *Ant.* 14.158–159. Although, as the story will progress, it will be clear that this was conceived as negative, when it happened, many inhabitants of Syria (of which Nicolaus was of course a native) sang Herod's praise for this action (*War* 1.205, copied in *Ant.* 14.160). This small snippet reminds one of the songs of praise that were sung to David when he excelled in his wars against the Philistines, which enraged the aging King Saul (1 Sam 18:7). I have shown in the past, that Nicolaus always portrays Herod as a new David; see Tal Ilan "King David, King Herod and Nicolaus of Damascus," *JSQ* 5 (1998): 195–240.

11. Copied in *Ant.* 14.162.

12. Copied in *Ant.* 14.181.

he is designated as "tyrant" by his detractors; his acquisition of the governorship of Coele-Syria and Samaria is described as resulting from a bribe (14.180); as in the Samaias episode, here too the verb used to describe Herod's action is not the neutral Greek *kteinō/apokteinō* ("kill") used elsewhere (*War* 1.204, 209[13]), but the very specific and negative verb *phoneuō* ("murder," *Ant.* 14.168).[14] Hyrcanus, on the contrary, is portrayed less negatively. Despite his sluggishness (which is unchanged), he is persuaded to put Herod on trial because he is touched by the lament of the mothers of the men Herod had executed (*Ant.* 14.168). Antipater is the figure that undergoes the most dramatic disfigurement. Not only has he now become responsible for advising Herod to come to his trial armed (*Ant.* 14.159), he is described, like his son, as giving bribes and as lying about it (14.164). Like father like son, Herodians in this story are wicked.

These changes in the *Antiquities* story are clearly of a piece with the Samaias insertion. The body that now judges Herod is the Synhedrion, replacing an impersonal report in *War*.[15] In *Ant.* 14.177 we read, out of the blue (and actually in contradiction to the Samaias-source) that "the Synhedrion was bent on putting Herod to death." In *Ant.* 14.212, instead of the neutral "second summons" of *War* 1.212, we read that Herod decided that "if he were again summoned before the Synhedrion" he would refuse to come.[16] Even the "knaves at court" of *War* 1.213 become "members of the Synhedrion" (*Ant.* 14.179).

I believe these changes in rhetoric and presentation are the result of the insertion of the Samaias-source, which now sets the tone. There is a new positive hero in this story—Samaias—and it is his story that makes Herod more wicked and makes some elements, like the Jewish Synhedrion[17] and the Jewish law, so much more important. Josephus's decision to use this

13. Copied in *Ant.* 14.159, 167, respectively.

14. Cf. in the Samaias text in *Ant.* 14.173.

15. *Ant.* 14.167: "of our Law, which forbids us to slay a man, even an evildoer, unless he was first condemned by the Synhedrion to suffer his fate"; *War* 1. 209: "his country's laws, which do not permit anyone to be put to death without a trial."

16. Cf. also *War* 1.214; *Ant.* 14.180.

17. The issue of this "foreign body" both here and in rabbinic literature has been thoroughly discussed in Adolf Buchler, *Das Synedrion in Jerusalem und das grosse Beth-Din in der Quaderkammer des jerusalemischen Tempels* (Vienna: Verlag der Israel-Theol. Lehranstalt, 1902); Solomon Zeitlin, "Political Synedrion and the Religious Sanhedrin," *JQR* 36 (1945–1946): 109–40; Hugo Mantel, *Studies in the History of the Sanhedrin*, HSS 17 (Cambridge: Harvard University Press, 1961), 54–101; Shmuel Safrai, "Jewish Self-Government," in *The Jewish People in the First Century: Historical Geography, Political History, Social, Cultural and Religious Life and Institutions*, ed. Shmuel Safrai and Menahem Stern, 2 vols., CRINT section 1 (Assen: Van Gorcum, 1974–1976), 1:379–400: Elias Rivkin, "Beth Din, Boule, Sanhedrin: A Tragedy of Errors," *HUCA* 46 (1975): 181–99; Joshua Efron, *Studies on the Hasmonean Period*, SJLA 39 (Leiden: Brill, 1987), 287–338; David M. Goodblatt, *The Monarchic Principle: Studies in Jewish Self-Government in Antiquity*, TSAJ 38 (Tübingen: Mohr Siebeck, 1994), 76–130; Lester L. Grabbe, "Sanhedrin, Sanhedriyyot or Mere Invention?," *JSJ* 39 (2008): 1–19.

story is part of his own revisionist approach to Nicolaus's worldview and to the change in emphasis and interpretation of the events that his second composition repeatedly stresses.[18]

2. *Herod's Conquest of Jerusalem*

The second Samaias episode is also embedded in a context that derives from Josephus's *War*, but not in such a direct way. In *Antiquities*, Josephus relates the conquest of Jerusalem by Herod twice: once at the very end of book 14, and again at the beginning of book 15. As we have seen, book 14 follows closely on the heels of Nicolaus's account, as retold by Josephus in *War*. However, the Samaias insertion on Herod's conquest of Jerusalem is recounted at the beginning of book 15, whose relation to *War* is more complex. The topic is the tragic demise of the Hasmonean dynasty and the enthronement of Herod. In *War* (based on Nicolaus), when describing Antigonus's execution, Josephus writes, "This prisoner to the last, clinging to forlorn hope to life, fell under the axe, a fitting end to his ignominious career" (1.457). This description mourns neither the last scion of a magnificent dynasty nor the tragic figure of a fallen king; the description has sympathy neither for Antigonus nor for the Hasmoneans. Yet this changes in *Antiquities*. Antigonus is executed because of a bribe made by Herod, who is afraid of competition from the Hasmoneans (14.490).[19] In other words, Herod's wickedness is emphasized rather than Antigonus's supposed false claim to kingship. Even more dramatic are the words of Strabo about Antigonus's execution, which Josephus cites at the end of his report on the fall of Jerusalem: "Not even under torture would [the Jews] submit to proclaiming [Herod] king, so highly did they regard their former king" (*Ant.* 15.9–10). Both reports emphasize the dramatic nature of this event, so strongly played down in *War*. These descriptions of the execution of the last Hasmonean monarch fit well with the encomium for the Hasmoneans that Josephus proclaims at the very end of *Ant.* 14: "The Asmonean line came to an end after a hundred-and-twenty-six years. Theirs was a splendid renowned house because of both their lineage and their priestly office, as well as the things which its founders achieved on behalf of the nation" (*Ant.* 16.187). Spoken like the true Hasmonean that Josephus was (*Vita* 2).

The other insertions in *Antiquities* are no less dramatic, pointing to the historical importance Josephus assigned to the hour; he compares the fall of Jerusalem to Herod to its earlier fall to Pompey (*Ant.* 14.487), both events marking the demise of the Hasmonean dynasty—the beginning of its

---

18. On this topic in general see Schwartz, *Reading the First Century* (for a specific example of *Ant.* 14 versus *War* 1, see 18–22, 96).

19. Cf. *Ant.* 14.180, discussed above.

downfall and the end. When Pompey came, the two Hasmonean siblings, Hyrcanus II and Aristobolus II, were squabbling over the monarchy. Josephus does not fail to mention this when he adds at the end of his encomium here: "But they lost their royal power through internal strife" (*Ant.* 14.490).

The Samaias-source is inserted in this overall report of Herod's conquest of Jerusalem as part of the description of Herod's persecution of his opponents. *War* (based on Nicolaus) had already described this shortly: "by the award of honors [Herod] attached more closely to himself those who espoused his cause, while he exterminated the partisans of Antigonus" (*War* 1.358); *Antiquities* expands on this by stating that "[h]e also killed forty-five of the leading men of Antigonus' party" (*Ant.* 15.6). The anti-Herodian nature of Josephus's source is further indicated by the new king being accused of overtaxing the Jews during the sabbatical year, in which they incurred no income. The story of Polion and Samaias (*Ant.* 15.3–4) is inserted right at the beginning of this chain of accusations. Again, as in the case of Herod's trial, we have the same positive and negative heroes. Herod kills people (the ones Samaias had prophesied that he would someday kill) and abrogates the Jewish law (this time the sabbatical year). Samaias and Polion survive because they are politically savvy. After learning in the previous story that Herod cannot be overcome by mere righteousness, they follow the wise saying that "if you can't beat 'em, join 'em." The source does not criticize them for this, though it continues to be anti-Herodian.

3. The Pharisees' Exemption from Pledging Allegiance to Herod

The third Samaias insertion in *Antiquities* has no direct context taken from *War*. This is because, as all Josephus scholars have observed,[20] whereas in the other books on Herod in *Antiquities* (14, 16, and 17) Josephus was highly indebted to his account in *War* (influenced, as stated, by Nicolaus of Damascus), when he wrote *Ant.* 15, he wrote differently. This is evident first by the information that, in book 15 is spread over 425 passages while in *War* it is told in only 85 passages (459–544).[21]

The two main themes of these passages in *War* are Herod's systematic annihilation of the Hasmoneans, on the one hand, and his magnifi-

20. E.g., H. St. J. Thackeray, *Josephus: The Man and the Historian,* The Hilda Stich Stroock Lectures (New York: Jewish Institute of Religion Press, 1929), 65; Shaye J. D. Cohen, *Josephus in Galilee and Rome: His Vita and Development as a Historian,* Columbia Studies in the Classical Tradition 8 (Leiden: Brill, 1979), 52–58.

21. Compare *Ant.* 14—491 passages, told in *War* in 239 passages (120–458); *Ant.* 16—404 passages, told in *War* in 107 passages (445–551); *Ant.* 17 until Herod's death—199 passages, told in *War* in 122 passages (552–673).

cent building projects, with the temple as its crowning glory, on the other. Josephus condenses these two themes together in two clusters: first the building projects (*War* 1.401–425); then the murder of Hasmoneans (*War* 1.431–444). The two parts are connected one to the other with the words "But in revenge for public prosperity, Fortune visited Herod with troubles at home" (*War* 1.431). In *Ant.* 15, on the other hand, Josephus intersperses these themes among others and the order is generally reversed—first the murder of the Hasmoneans and then the building projects. I explained elsewhere this phenomenon as arising from the fact that Josephus had not read Nicolaus's relevant account for this period when he wrote his earlier narrative but that the missing Nicolaus volumes had meanwhile come to his attention.[22] This, in my view, dictates the general conclusion that the source used by Josephus in *War* to describe Herod's relations with the Hasmoneans was not Nicolaus. The third Samaias insert is thus embedded in a Nicolean but non-*War* context.

The immediate context in which the Samaias-source is inserted, although it begins in a seemingly positive representation of Herod—he remitted the taxes of the people, in direct contradiction to what we saw above, about how he had over-taxed the people in the sabbatical year—the narrator explains this not as an act of benevolence but as a desperate move to win back the favor of the people (*Ant.* 15.365). This report is followed by a listing of all the reasons why he had no favor with them: He had turned his kingdom into a police state; people were not allowed to meet or express their opinion freely; Herod had spies everywhere, and even he himself spied on the people, dressing as a commoner and listening to their conversations; he executed people who spoke against him without trial (*Ant.* 15:366–367); finally, he required the people to take an oath of loyalty to him. This entire passage is the most negative representation of Herod in all of Josephus's writings.

The narrative now continues with two groups whom Herod exempted from this oath. One of them is related in the Samaias insert, according to which Samaias's prediction of Herod's future actions had vouched the Pharisees this privilege. A similar story is then told about a certain Menahem, who won for the Essenes the same privilege, by predicting to Herod the child his future kingship (*Ant.* 15.371–376). The similarity between the central motif in both stories is hard to miss. In both, a class of Jews (a sect if you will) is exempt from taking the oath because of a righteous individual who had supported Herod when he was an aspiring youngster. If these stories do not derive from the same source, there was a very tight editing here. Who was this editor? Was it already the editor of the

---

22. Tal Ilan, *Integrating Women into Second Temple History*, TSAJ 76 (Tübingen: Mohr Siebeck, 1999), 110.

Samaias-source or was it Josephus? Both answers are possible, but I tend toward the former.

That the information provided here on the oath of allegiance does not derive from Nicolaus can be shown from another angle. Apparently, we do have Nicolaus's version of the association between the oath Herod demanded of his people and the special case of the Pharisees' refusal to comply with it. It is not in *Antiquities* 15, either because here Josephus chose to use his Samaias-source to relate this episode, or because Nicolaus himself had only told the entire episode in flashback. In any case, in *Ant.* 17.42, when Josephus relates the exploits of one of Nicolaus's most maligned heroines—the nameless sister-in-law of Herod, his brother Pheroras's wife—he refers back to this episode and to what he perceives as her role in it. He claims that "when the whole Jewish people affirmed by an oath that it would be loyal to Caesar and to the king's government, [the Phrisees] ... refused to take this oath, and when the king punished them with a fine, Pheroras's wife paid the fine for them." Since this tradition portrays the Pharisees negatively, and the king as their victim, while the other one from the Samaias-source is pro-Pharisaic and Herod is described in it as a bloodthirsty tyrant, I would argue that this is the Nicolean version of this event.

If we sum up the information we can glean from the three Samaias insertions, we see that (1) the first pericope stands on its own within an extended Nicolaus account; (2) the second pericope is also surrounded by a recognizable Nicolean background, although it is supported in its immediate context by other visibly non-Nicolean additions; (3) the third pericope, in contrast, is surrounded by a very long, non-Nicolean account, the end of which (the story of Menahem's prediction and the exemption of the Essenes from taking the oath) is very similar to the narrative of the exemption of the Pharisees from the oath because of Samaias.

This probably leads to the conclusion that the Samaias-source comprised an extended account, which included much more information beyond the three notes on this sage and his colleague, Pollion. Yet to know anything further about this source, we need to look beyond Josephus. This is where rabbinic literature comes in.

The Samaias-Source in Rabbinic Literature

In a project on which Vered Noam and I have been working in the last decade, we investigated all the parallels between the writings of Josephus and those in the entire corpus of rabbinic literature of which we were aware. In our investigation we discovered that, of the thirty-five parallel traditions we identified, twenty-eight have parallels in the *Bavli*, but only five are unique to it, having arrived there through no earlier rabbinic composition from the land of Israel.[23] In a previous study, Noam and I identified the earliest two traditions (of these five), both telling of the Hasmoneans and the Pharisees, as deriving from a single source—a Pharisaic account that sought to downplay the conflict between the Pharisees and the Hasmoneans and to accuse their opponents (whoever they were) of misrepresenting them.[24] In this article I will argue that the other three traditions that we identified as having come down directly to Babylonia with no intervening rabbinic source from the land of Israel, also all derive from one source—the same Samaias-source on which Josephus also drew and which was probably also Pharisaic. I turn now to the three sources in question

1. *The Story of King Yannai's Trial (b. Sanh. 19b)*

This source tells how King Yannai was ordered by the sages (headed by Shimeon ben Shetah) to stand trial for a murder his slave had committed. He comes to trial, but all the judges, except Shimeon ben Shetah, are filled with fear and fail to judge him. Thereupon, Shimeon ben Shetah curses them and they are all struck by an angel and die. The story is told in the *Bavli* in Hebrew.

The source has been identified by scholars many years hence as a parallel to the first Josephan Samaias insertion, based on the many thematic similarities between them.[25] In both, a servant of the king/ruler is required to stand trial for murder; in both, the court convened fears to judge him; in both, a brave sage predicts that this cowardice will lead to the death of the judges; and in both, they are indeed killed as a direct result of their failure.[26]

---

23. See Ilan and Noam, *Josephus and the Rabbis*, 65–69.

24. Tal Ilan and Vered Noam, "Remnants of a Pharisaic Apologetic Source in Josephus and the Babylonian Talmud," in *Tradition, Transmission, and Transformation from Second Temple Literature through Judaism and Christianity in Late Antiquity: Proceedings of the Thirteenth International Symposium of the Orion Center for the Study of the Dead Sea Scrolls and Associated Literature, Jointly Sponsored by the Hebrew University Center for the Study of Christianity, 22–24 February, 2011*, ed. Menahem Kister et al., STDJ 113 (Leiden: Brill, 2015), 112–33.

25. E.g., Abraham Geiger, *Urschrift und Übersetzungen der Bibel in ihrer Abhängigkeit von der innern Entwickelung des Judenthums* (Breslau: Julius Hainauer, 1857), 144–45; Joseph Derenbourg, *Essai sur l'histoire et la géographie de la Palestine d'après les Thalmuds et les autres sources rabbiniques* (Paris: Imprimerie Imperiale 1867), 146–48; Laqueur, *Der jüdische Historiker Flavius Josephus*, 176; Hugo Mantel, "Herod's Trial" [Hebrew], *Bar Ilan* 1 (1963): 168; Schürer, *History of the Jewish People*, 1:252 n. 31; Efron, *Studies on the Hasmonean Period*, 190–97; Goodblatt, *Monarchic Principle*, 112; Schwartz, "Josephus on Hyrcanus II," 23.

26. I discuss these in detail both in Ilan and Noam, *Josephus and the Rabbis*, 1:349–72; and

There are, however, also major differences between the two sources, most striking of which is the names of the protagonists. In Josephus's account, they are Herod and Samaias. Here they are King Yannai and Shimeon ben Shetah, two classical adversaries of the *Bavli*.[27] The other differences between Josephus's narrative and this one are that it is not Yannai who is on trial but his slave; the king does not refuse to be judged but refuses to stand up during the proceedings; the judges are afraid to judge Yannai, not because he has a small army waiting outside but merely because he is a king.

There are also traces of two retellings of similar events in the literature of the land of Israel (which the *Bavli* may have known), and each displays some of the features that differentiate this *Bavli* story from Josephus's narrative, but both lack the one feature that makes Josephus and tractate Sanhedrin so similar, namely, that the king's slave was brought to trial for murder. My thesis is that these sources from the land of Israel told a story about Shimeon ben Shetah and a Hasmonean king (probably Yannai), onto which the *Bavli* mounted his evidence from the Samaias-source. I concentrate here on one of them, which is closer and more intriguing—the post-*Bavli*, Tanhuma (*shoftim* Warsaw 7; Buber 6).[28]

It is well known that occasionally the Tanhuma was influenced by the *Bavli*, but in other cases it preserves older traditions from the land of Israel, and in some cases the two are evident in the same pericope.[29] The story in which the king's slave is told looks very much like the story in the *Bavli* but includes one major and striking difference. The story ends not with the death by heaven of the cowardly judges, as in the *Bavli*, but with

---

in my forthcoming "The Tanhuma on a Hasmonean King: Between Tannaitic Sources and the Babylonian Talmud," in *Studies in Tanhuma*, ed. Ronit Nikolsky and Arnon Atzmon.

27. B. Ber. 48a; b. Soṭah 47a; b. Sanh. 107b; cf. y. Ber. 7:2, 11b; Scholion to Megillat Ta'anit 28th Tevet. On this see, on the one hand, Efron, *Studies on the Hasmonean Period*, 143–218; and Daniel R. Schwartz, "Herod in Ancient Jewish Literature," in *The World of the Herods*, ed. Nikos Kokkinos, vol. 1 of *The International Conference, The World of the Herods and the Nabataeans, Held at the British Museum, 17–19 April 2001*, OeO 14 (Stuttgart: Steiner, 2007) 49–50; but, on the other hand, see Ilan and Noam, *Joesphus and the Rabbis*, 1: 289–91.

28. The other, earlier retelling derives from the remains of a lost Tannaitic halakhic midrash on Deuteronomy, preserved in a commentary on Deuteronomy, composed by the Karaite Yeshu'a ben Yehudah in Judeo-Arabic, with citations from the midrash interspersed in it, in Hebrew. The reconstructed midrash was published by Menahem I. Kahana, *Sifre Zuta on Deuteronomy: Citations from a New Tannaitic Midrash* [Hebrew] (Jerusalem: Magnes, 2002), 282: "And they said concerning 'The two parties [to the dispute] shall stand [before the LORD]' (Deut 19:17), even concerning a king and a commoner (הדיוט, *idiotēs*) and they told a lengthy episode about Yannai the king in a court case he had with a poor person before Shimeon ben Shetah."

29. As shown for example by Ronit Nikolsky, "From Palestine to Babylonia and Back: The Place of the Bavli and the *Tanhuma* on the Rabbinic Cultural Continuum," in *Rabbinic Traditions between Palestine and Babylonia*, ed. Ronit Nikolsky and Tal Ilan, AJEC 89 (Leiden: Brill, 2013), 311–33.

the king being humbled when witnessing this event and accepting the authority of the court to judge him. This conclusion is the exact opposite of the one presented in the *Bavli*, where this episode ends with the enactment of the rule that a king cannot be put to trial (m. Sanh. 2:2).[30]

My conclusion from the rabbinic retelling(s) is that there had existed an early source in the land of Israel that told of a civic dispute between King Yannai and a commoner, and the difficulties the court headed by Shimeon ben Shetah faced in judging the case fairly. When this story came to the hands of the *Bavli* editors, they identified similarities between it and the story of Herod's trial in the Samaias-source, which, as I am arguing here, was at their disposal. Instead of discarding either, they harmonized the two narratives, maintaining the names of the protagonists from the land of Israel, and actually the frame and the language, but replacing the civil case with a murder trial and the commoner with the king's slave (both from the Samaias-source). This, in the *Bavli*'s opinion, as we will see in the next source I discuss, is a fitting description of Herod—he was the slave of the House of Hasmonai, and Yannai was of course the quintessential Hasmonean king. Working in this way is an editorial characteristic of the *Bavli*; it maintains the form of a story it receives from land-of-Israel sources it considers authoritative but changes its content completely.[31]

2. *The "Herod Narrative"*[32]

The *Bavli* tells the story of Herod's rise to power within a discussion of the halakhic permissibility to tear down an old synagogue in order to build a new one. The point of contact between this case and Herod's story is the temple. Herod had torn down the old temple in order to build a new one. How had he dared to do it? This is the opportunity the *Bavli* takes to tell the entire story. It is told in Aramaic and is interspersed with editorial remarks, as is typical of the work of the *Bavli* editors.[33] In the following I

30. Another striking difference is the Tanhuma's failure to name the king of the House of Hasmonai who is brought to trial, but I have no explanation for this.

31. See my detailed discussion in Ilan and Noam, *Josephus and the Rabbis*, 1:71–72, 361–67.

32. Much has been written about this story in the *Bavli*. Only recently, see Eli Yassif, *The Hebrew Folktale: History, Genre, Meaning*, Folklore Studies in Translation (Bloomington: Indiana University Press, 1999), 141–42; Richard Kalmin, *Jewish Babylonia between Persia and Roman Palestine* (Oxford: Oxford University Press, 2006), 50–53; Yonatan Feintuch, "External Appearance versus Internal Truth: The Aggadah of Herod in Bavli Bava Batra," *AJS Review* 35 (2011): 85–104; Jeffrey L. Rubenstein, "King Herod in Ardashir's Court: The Rabbinic Story of Herod (B. Bava Batra 3b–4a) in Light of Persian Sources," *AJS Review* 38 (2014): 249–74.

33. On such editorial work, see Jeffrey L. Rubenstein, *Talmudic Stories: Narrative Art, Composition and Culture* (Baltimore: John Hopkins University Press, 1999), 51.

reproduce the composition as I think the *Bavli* received from the Samaias-source, and in the notes I remark on what I have left out.

Part 1: (2) Herod was the slave of the House of Hasmonai.[34]

(4) One day he heard it being said:[35] Every slave who rebels at this time will succeed. He stood up and murdered all his masters.[36]

Part 2: (8) He left Baba ben Buta (alive) to advise him. He made a crown of thorns for (Baba) and picked out his eyes. One day (Herod) came and set in (Baba's) presence. He said to him: Has the master (i.e. you) seen what this bad slave (i.e. Herod) has done? He said to him: What can I do to him? (Herod said): The master can curse him. (Baba) said to him: It is written: "Even in private you shall not curse a king" (Eccl 10:20). He said to (Baba): These words apply to a king, but this one is an *idiotēs*.[37] He said to (Herod): Even if he was just rich, it is written; 'In your bedchamber do not curse a rich man" (ibid.). Even if he were just a leader (*nasi*) it is written: "a leader in your folk you shall not curse" (Exod 22:27). (Herod continued, though): This refers to one who does what your folk does. (Baba) said: I fear him, lest someone go to him and tell him. (Herod protested): But now, is there anyone with us? (Baba) said to him: "the birds

---

34. Unit (1) reads: "How did Baba ben Buta advise Herod to destroy the Temple?" followed by an Amoraic discussion.

35. I usually translate from the version of MS Paris 1337. This manuscript has here "he heard a heavenly voice." I have chosen here to follow MS Escorial G-I-3, because its avoidance of an involvement of the supernatural is closer to the Samaias-source.

36. Units (3) and (5) which enclose these words read: "(3) He saw that (female) child … (5) He left that child. When she saw that he intended to marry her, that child went up to the roof and fell from the roof and died. When she fell she said: Whoever says: I am from the house of Hasmonai is a slave. And she fell and died." Both are foreign elements, interlaced within units (2) and (4), which are genuine Samaias-source texts. This "foreign" unit told of Herod's marriage to a Hasmonean princess, and her death. In Josephus, Herod executes the princess (*War* 1.438–444; *Ant.* 15:218–237), while here she commits suicide. There are textual reasons for considering this story to be a late insertion, see Ilan and Noam, *Josephus and the Rabbis*, 1:398–400.

Following these two units, two additional foreign elements are mentioned: "(6) He interred her in honey for seven years. There are those who say, he had intercourse with her and those who say he did not have intercourse with her. Whoever says he had intercourse with her, it was to satisfy his sexual drive. Whoever says he did not have sexual intercourse with her, why did he do so? So that it will be said: he married a princess." This is a Babylonian expansion and interpretation of a tradition from the land of Israel. In the Tannaitic midrash Sifre Deuteronomy 241 we read of a sexual act that is considered a doubtful transgression and is designated "the act of Herodes" (מעשה הירודס).

"(7) He asked: Who expounds the verse: "You shall put a king from among your brothers on you" (Deut 17:15)? The Rabbis. He stood up and murdered all the rabbis." This unit is a Babylonian expansion and exegesis of m. Soṭah 7:8, in which the same verse is used in order to bring Agrippa, Herod's grandson, into the fold. The two references demonstrate the *Bavli*'s historical awareness of the family relationship between the two kings. It does not belong to the original story.

37. Based on MS Escorial G-I-3 (הדיוט) and also MS Vatican 115 (מלך הדיוט הוא), which I prefer here because it is verbally close to the Samaias-source.

> of the air will pass on the message" (Eccl 10:20). He said to (Baba): Had I known that you are so humble I would not have done so (i.e killed the sages). What is the repentance of this man (i.e. Herod)? He said to him: Since he put out the light of the world, let him go and busy himself with the light of the world. He put out the light of the world—the rabbis, as it is written: "for the lamp is commandment and the Torah is light" (Prov 6:23); let him go and busy himself with the light of the world, the Temple, as it is written: "And all the nations shall gather to it" (Isa 2:2).[38]
>
> Part 3: (10) (Herod) said to him: I fear the kingdom of Rome.[39] (Baba) said to him: Send a messenger who will go for a year and come back a year, and while this happens, destroy and build it. (Herod) did so. When (the messenger) came back, they (i.e. Rome) sent to him: If you have not destroyed, don't destroy; If you have destroyed, don't build. If you have destroyed and built, you are a bad slave. One seeks advice after the fact? Although your weapons are on you, your book is here. You are not a *rex*,[40] nor the son of a *rex*. Herod('s kingdom) will be made a *colonia*.[41]

The story consists of three parts. Part 1 relates how Herod the slave murdered the house of his masters and became king. Part 2 relates how Herod left one of his opponents (perhaps from the house of his masters) alive to consult with him, blinded him and (pretending to be someone else) attempted to persuade him to curse the king. However, he failed. In part 3, the person he had left alive advises Herod to build the temple anew as repentance for his sins. Herod follows his advice, even though he rightly fears the power of Rome, whose words end the entire unit, describing Herod as a wicked slave who will lose his kingdom as a result of this action, and it will become a Roman province (*colonia*). Just as Herod killed his masters, so too others will take over his royal power, and it will not remain in his family.

Both *rex* and *colonia* are loanwords from Latin, a language that is very rare in (though not completely absent from) the *Bavli*. Such words usually indicate that we are looking at a story that was not invented in Babylonia but rather imported to it via the land of Israel. This would certainly be true if this story were a retelling based on the Samaias-source. It is interesting that, except for these words in Latin, and the biblical quotations, which

---

38. Followed by unit (9), a typical editorial "there are those who say (איכא דאמרי), offering an alternative interpretation for the last clause just cited.

39. I follow MSS Munich 95 and Vatican 115.

40. The MSS read here רכא or ריכא, and this appears to be a very old version, since the explanation of this word by the Babylonian editor in the next unit uses the biblical words רך (2 Sam 3:39) and אברך (Gen 41:43) to explain it. The idea that the Latin *rex* is intended was suggested by Rubenstein, "King Herod in Ardashir's Court," 252.

41. Units (11) and (12) are clearly editorial units. Unit 11 interprets the difficult term *rekhah*, just mentioned and unit (12) is taken wholesale from a discussion of Herod's temple in b. Sukkah 51b.

are in Hebrew, the entire story is told in Aramaic. This may have been the original language in which the Samaias-source was transmitted, as two internal wordplays in this narrative imply. The first is the interpretation of one of the verses cited:

> Since he put out the light of the world, let him go and busy himself with the light of the world. He put out the light of the world—the rabbis, as it is written: "for the lamp is commandment and the Torah is light" (Prov 6:23); let him go and busy himself with the light of the world the Temple, as it is written: "And all the nations shall flow to it" (Isa 2:2).

Note that the prooftext for the temple being the "light of the world" does not have the word "light" in it. In Aramaic, though, the Hebrew word used for "shall flow" (נהרו) means "shall give light." Thus, the prooftext is only understandable in an Aramaic context.

The second clear Aramaic context of the story is the message Rome sends to Herod: "You are a bad slave. One seeks advise after acting?" In Aramaic, three words here have a double meaning. The word עבדא means both "slave" and "deed," and, deriving from it, עבדין means both "acting" and "slaves"; the word מתמלכין means both "seeking advice" and "becoming king." The Romans may thus also be telling Herod: "Bad deed, since slaves have become kings." If the original language of the Samaias-source was Aramaic, it would of course have been accessible both to Josephus and to the *Bavli*.

The similarity between this core story of the Babylonian Herod narrative and the Samaias-source is associated with the second and third Samaias insertions in Josephus. Here and in the second Samaias insertion, situated in the middle of the account of Herod's conquest of Jerusalem from the hands of the last Hasmonean king, Herod kills all remaining supporters of the Hasmonean house but leaves one person alive (in *Antiquities*, Samaias; here, Baba ben Buta). In both, Herod is described as a commoner (*idiotēs*, הדיוט) and a former servant/slave of the Hasmoneans. In common with the third Samaias insertion (about the Pharisees' exemption from the oath of loyalty to Herod) the *Bavli* story also describes Herod's going out among his subjects in disguise, so as to hear them curse him and then denounce them. In the *Bavli* he makes sure his interlocutor does not recognize him by making him blind. In both, Herod became king based on a prediction. In the *Bavli* this is merely something that was being said, or a heavenly voice, while in the Samaias-source it is made by Menahem the Essene [42]

---

42. Jeffrey Rubenstein ("King Herod in Ardashir's Court") had recently argued that the Herod story in the *Bavli* is based on a similar story told in the Sasanian court about its founder, Ardashir, who had been the servant of the previous ruling house, and, on hearing a

Up to now we have identified in the *Bavli's* Herod narrative elements in common with the Samaias-source. We can now go a step further and identify Samaias-source elements in Josephus, based on the *Bavli*'s Herod narrative.

My first suggestion touches on the name of the sage the *Bavli* chose to give to Herod's interlocutor—not Samaias but rather Baba ben Buta. This sage is known from the rabbinic mythological past. Twice he is mentioned in the Tosefta[43] and another three traditions about him are unique to the *Bavli*.[44] One of them is our text. Perhaps the *Bavli* chose Baba here because he is described as the student of Shammai the elder, that is, someone to be dated to the days of the Second Temple, the days of Herod.[45] It is my contention, however, that his name was chosen here because it reminded the Babylonian editor of another episode related in the Samaias-source about a group of people, Hasmonean supporters, mentioned in Josephus, *Ant.* 15.260–266 by the name of "the sons of Baba." I am not the first person to argue for the similarity in name between the two.[46]

The story of the sons of Baba is told in flashback about "When Antigonus was king and Herod's force was besieging the city of Jerusalem, [and] under the stress of the miseries that came upon the besieged, many of them called upon Herod for help and were already placing their hopes on him. But the sons of Baba, who had a high position and great influence with the masses, remained loyal to Antigonus and were always speaking ill of Herod and exhorting the people to preserve for the kings the

---

prediction that he would become king, had killed the entire royal family. He might be right in general but probably not about the prediction, which is likely derived from the Samaias-source.

43. Once as a student of Shammai the elder, whose actions take place in the temple court (t. Ḥag. 2:11), and once as bringing a unique sacrifice to the temple (t. Ker. 4:4).

44. In b. Giṭ. 57a he is again presented as a disciple of Shammai (obviously based on t. Ḥag. 2:11), close to the destruction of the temple. On this story, see now Judith Baskin, "Rabbinic Forensics: Distinguishing Egg White from Semen," in *Sources and Interpretations in Ancient Judaism: Studies for Tal Ilan at Sixty*, ed. Meron Piotrkowski, Geoffrey Herman, and Saskia Dönitz, AJEC 104 (Leiden: Brill, 2018), 252-67. In b. Ned. 66b he is involved in a comic story of a Babylonian husband who marries a woman from the land of Israel. On this story, see Reuven Kiperwasser, "Wives of Commoners and the Masculinity of the Rabbis: Jokes, Serious Matters and Migrating Traditions," *JSJ* 48 (2017): 418–45. Obviously, the Babylonians found Baba, as a name, amusing. And indeed the name is never recorded for Babylonians, see Tal Ilan, *Lexicon of Jewish Names in Late Antiquity*, vol. 4, *The Eastern Diaspora 330 BCE–650 CE*, TSAJ 148 (Tübingen: Mohr Siebeck 2011), 63–64, where variants of the name בבי from the Eastern Diaspora are recorded, but not the form Baba, as opposed to vol. 1, *Palestine 330 BCE–200 CE*, TSAJ 91 (Tübingen: Mohr Siebeck, 2002) 80, from the land of Israel, where this is almost the only form recorded; and see also vol. 2, *Palestine 200–650*, TSAJ 126 (Tübingen: Mohr Siebeck, 2012) 70–72, for the later period in the land of Israel.

45. And we can add that, if the *Bavli* identified Samaias with Shammai the Elder (see n. 3 above), then they thought Baba was his disciple.

46. See Schwartz, "Herod in Ancient Jewish Literature," 49.

power which was theirs by birth" (*Ant.* 15.262–63). The purpose of the flashback is to explain why Herod had executed his brother-in-law Costobarus "when Herod was in control of things after the capture of the city, Costobarus was appointed to block the exits and guard the city in order to prevent the escape of those citizens who were in debt or followed a policy of opposition to the king. Since Costobarus knew that the sons of Baba were held in esteem and honor by all the people, and believed that by saving them he would have an important part in any change of government, he removed them from danger and hid them on his estate" (*Ant.* 15.264). When Herod was informed of this by his sister some years later, when she wished herself rid of her husband, he executed his brother-in-law and the sons of Baba.

The connection of this story to the second Samaias snippet is explicit. The time both took place (even though in this case it is in flashback) is Herod's capture of Jerusalem from the hands of the Hasmonean Mattathias Antigonus, and the topic is his persecution of the followers of the Hasmoneans. The death of the sons of Baba is described as producing the result that "none was left alive of the family of Hyrcanus and the kingdom was wholly in Herod's power, there being no one of high rank to stand in the way of his unlawful acts" (*Ant.* 15.266). This is clearly the very same result described at the end of book 14 and the beginning of book 15, which the death of Antigonus himself at the hands of the Romans, and of his followers at the hands of Herod, had produced. Yet we would not have been able to identify this insert as belonging to the Samaias-source (because it is positioned chronologically so far from the events to which it refers), had the *Bavli* not designated Herod's interlocutor Baba.

My second suggestion for identifying a Samaias-source pericope, based on the *Bavli*'s Herod narrative, touches on the construction of the temple. In *Antiquities* 15, the account of this proceeding follows immediately after the third long Samaias-source insertion, directly after the story of Menahem's prediction to Herod and the exemption of the Essenes from taking an oath of allegiance. It begins with a typical Nicolean praise for Herod's noble intentions and continues with a long speech Herod delivered, in which he both praises himself and demonstrates his love for his people (*Ant.* 15.380–387). This speech may have been composed by Josephus himself, but even if it was, it was certainly influenced by an earlier one that Nicolaus had written for his master. It is, however, not followed by jubilations; rather, "most of the people were astonished by this speech.... And ... they were dismayed by the thought that he may tear down the whole edifice and not have sufficient means to bring his project to completion" (*Ant.* 15.388).

This text does not sound very pro-Herodian. The suspicion voiced in it comes from a people who mistrust and dislike their king. This is not Nicolean but fits well the ideology of the Samaias-source. A similarity between the Herod narrative in the *Bavli* and Josephus's retelling of the same event can be further detected as Josephus relates how Herod reacted to this fear by cooperation. He gathered all the necessary building material and equipment in advance and trained priests to construct the temple, thus winning the trust of the people (*Ant.* 15.389–390), just as Herod of the *Bavli*'s Herod narrative gains Baba ben Buta's approval and forgiveness for his previous sins by doing the same. The fear the people voice here, in Josephus's narrative, is the one voiced in the Herod narrative by Herod himself and echoes the command of Rome to Herod there not to rebuild the temple if he had already pulled it down.[47]

3. *The War between the Sons of the House of Hasmonai*

As stated above, there are five traditions in the *Bavli* that have parallels in Josephus but not in any earlier source from the land of Israel. Two of them Vered Noam and I identified as a deriving from a Pharisaic source.[48] Of the three remaining traditions, two have been discussed. I suggest that the third such pericope also derives from the Samaias-source. My argument for this is the tradition's historical setting and theological outlook. Historically, the story is located in the period in which the demise of the Hasmoneans begins. Theologically, it is the story about the impiety of the sibling rivalry between the two Hasmonean contenders, Hyrcanus and Aristobolus, the reason, according to the Samaias-source for the fall of the Hasmoneans.

The *Bavli* begins the story with the words, "When the kings of the House of Hasmonai laid siege one on the other, Hyrcanus was within and Aristobulus was without" (b. Men. 64b).[49] Then it continues by telling how an agreement between the two that those who laid siege would provide those besieged with sacrifices was broken when the besieging party sent the besieged a pig. This brought about a drought.

This story, like the story Yannai's trial before Shimeon ben Shetah (and unlike the Herod narrative), is told in Hebrew. This is not, I think, an indication that the Samaias-source was originally in Hebrew but rather that, as in the case of the trial of Herod, the *Bavli* used an old Hebrew tradition from the land of Israel claiming, "In the days of the Wicked Kingdom they would lower two boxes with gold and they would raise for them two sheep. In the end they lowered two boxes with gold and they raised

47. See Schwartz, "Herod in Ancient Jewish Literature," 48.
48. Ilan and Noam, "Remnants of a Pharisaic Apologetic Source."
49. With parallels in b. Soṭah 49b; b. B. Qam. 82b.

for them two pigs" (y. Ta'an. 4:6, 68c).[50] Following this event, Jerusalem is destroyed and the temple burnt.

The language of this tradition is strikingly similar to the one in the *Bavli* story on the two Hasmonean brothers. In both, Jerusalem is under siege and the enemies, who lay the siege, supply the besieged with sacrifices. In both, a catastrophe follows the replacement of legitimate sacrificial animals with a pig. However, the besieging enemy in the *Yerushalmi* is Rome (the Wicked Kingdom) and the catastrophe that follows is the destruction of the temple. I argue that the *Bavli* "corrected" this information based on the Samaias-source: The besieging party became Hyrcanus's army (which is besieging his brother Aristobolus's troops) and the catastrophe that follows is a drought, which the *Bavli* editors identify as the one described in m. Men. 10:2.

In *Ant.* 14 Josephus tells a strikingly similar story. The reason I think it is derived from the Samaias-source is that *Ant.* 14, in which it is embedded, usually follows Nicolaus's Herodian account in great detail and faithfully. This insertion,[51] next to the Samaias insertion on Herod's trial, is the largest intrusion of the narrative in the entire book (*Ant.* 14.25–28). The parallel between this insertion and the *Bavli* story is clear. In both, Jerusalem is under siege by Hyrcanus, and Aristobolus is inside the city. In both, Hyrcanus's camp promises to supply the besieged with sacrifices. In both, this promise is not kept (although only in the *Bavli*, based on its *Yerushalmi* parallel, is the legitimate sacrificial animal replaced by a pig). In both, following the breach of contract, a drought hits the country.

Conclusion

Let me try very briefly to reconstruct the outline and message of the Samaias-source. It related how the Hasmonean siblings, Hyrcanus and Aristobolus, had sinned by engaging in war with one another, instead of showing brotherly love, and although both brothers failed to gain the upper hand, their actions brought a desecration of the temple and a drought. In *Ant.* 14, immediately following this event, Rome arrived in Judea and the Roman general Pompey successfully captured Jerusalem. After describing the fall of the city, Josephus decries these events: "For this misfortune which befell Jerusalem Hyrcanus and Aristobolus were

50. The story is told in the *Yerushalmi* next to another one of a similar form that relates a similar episode in the time of the early Hasmoneans and the Antiochean decrees, on which see Vered Noam, *Shifting Images of the Hasmoneans: Second Temple Legends and Their Reception in Josephus and Rabbinic Literature* (Oxford: Oxford University Press 2017), chapter 6.

51. Tied together with another one of the same nature, about Honi the rainmaker (*Ant.* 14.22–24), well known from the Mishnah (m. Ta'an. 3:1); see Noam, *Shifting Images*, chapter 6.

responsible, because of their dissension" (*Ant.* 14.77). The *Bavli* tells the episode of the sibling war with a very similar tone and message.

The punishment that the Hasmoneans suffered for sibling war and the desecration of the temple was, according to the Samaias-source that a slave of the family—Herod—an *idiotēs* and an Idumean convert—took over their kingdom and murdered them and all their followers. This is demonstrated in *Antiquities* in the story of Herod's trial. In failing to convict him, Hyrcanus's cowardice and that of his fellows in the Synhedrion bring about their own death at the hand of the slave. The *Bavli* too knew this story.

With the fall of Jerusalem to Herod, Samaias, according to *Antiquities* went over to Herod's side. Josephus ends book 14 with the demise of the Hasmoneans and again decries their sibling rivalry, which had brought it on: "they lost their royal power through internal strife" (14:491). The Samaias-source, however, is never blind to Herod's misdeeds. When explaining how Samaias's sagacity in joining Herod bought privileges for his Pharisee sect, he relates Herod's reign of terror. In the end, the Samaias-source finds Herod's building of the temple his one redeeming feature. This is very similar to the story told by the *Bavli* in its Herod narrative, which, however, ends with another message, missing from the Josephus Samaias snippets I identified, that Herod himself was punished for his misdeeds, by Rome's taking his kingdom from him and making it into a Roman colony.

The Two Gentlemen of Trachonitis

A History of Violence in Galilee and Rome (Josephus, Vita *112–113 and 149–154)*

DUNCAN E. MACRAE
University of California, Berkeley

Two powerful men, fleeing loyalist territory, ride into a rebel town, bringing arms and money. The local people are suspicious: these new arrivals belong to another ethno-religious group and should demonstrate their loyalty. The rebel general, however, dismisses these demands as coercion and insists that the refugees be treated as guests. Resentment grows. The local people now accuse the outsiders of witchcraft, claiming that they have harmed their efforts against the Empire. Again, the rebel leader stands against the crowd and mocks the idea that witchcraft can do real harm. His stand has little effect: the people attempt to lynch the refugees and the leader engineers their "escape," back into the enemy lands whence they had fled.

Readers of Josephus's *Vita* will recognize the story, the episode of the gentile refugees from Trachonitis, which the historian tells during his long account of his time as "governor" of Galilee in 66–67 CE. The narrative is not found in parallel sections of his *Bellum judaicum*, or any other historical source, and it seems to have no impact on the larger story of the revolt or even the machinations around personal leadership in Galilee that loom so large in the *Vita*. Perhaps consequently, it has attracted little direct comment or extended study from scholars.[1] Nevertheless,

Shaye Cohen generously supervised a "Special Topic" on Hellenistic and early Roman Judea when I was a graduate student in the Harvard Classics Department. At a key moment in my academic career, Shaye broadened my horizons. One of our areas of study was the *Vita* of Josephus: in notes from a meeting with him on 17 September 2009, I find that I wrote and underlined that the work was "a v. interesting window into the local issues"; this chapter is a belated investigation of one of those "local issues" and is offered in thanks for the initiation into Josephus and his world.

1. The exception is study of the demand that the refugees be circumcised, which has figured in studies of conversion to Judaism: see Shaye J. D. Cohen, "Respect for Judaism by Gentiles according to Josephus," *HTR* 80 (1987): 409–30, here 421–23; Simon Claude Mimouni,

the episode represents well the challenge and value for historians of the Roman world-at-large of studying Josephus's account of his time in Galilee. In this particular case, Josephus provides us with a rare and relatively detailed account of an outburst of popular violence in which he personally participated and that has the potential to help us understand the dynamics of intracommunal violence in ancient communities.

The problem of violence in antiquity has attracted growing interest from ancient historians, in part due to contemporary experiences and the realization that forms of violence outside the conventional sphere of "war" were pervasive in ancient societies, despite the classical ideal of "order."[2] For students of the Roman Empire, this new historiography of ancient violence can also join with the well-established study of riots in the cities of the empire (though the latter scholarship has often approached the problem from the perspective of "order").[3] One of the central challenges of studying violence, however, is that the term is extremely hard to define and may well be, as Brent Shaw has recently lamented, "radically undertheorized": some social theorists see violence almost everywhere in human society and as integral to all institutions, while others narrowly define it as illegitimate or illegal force.[4] Fortunately, Shaw and Ari Bryen,

---

La circoncision dans le monde judéen aux époques grecque et romaine: Histoire d'un conflit interne au judaïsme, Collection de la Revue des études juives 42 (Paris: Peeters, 2007), 93–94.

2. See the representative essays in Jerzy Styka, ed., *Violence and Aggression in the Ancient World*, Classica Cradoviensia 10 (Kraków: Księgarnia Akademicka, 2006); Martin Zimmermann, ed., *Extreme Formen von Gewalt in Bild und Text des Altertums*, Münchner Studien zur Alten Welt 5 (Munich: Herbert Utz, 2009); Werner Riess and Garrett G. Fagan, eds., *The Topography of Violence in the Greco-Roman World* (Ann Arbor: University of Michigan Press, 2016); Ioannis K. Xydopoulos, Kostas Vlassopoulos, and Eleni Tounta (eds.), *Violence and Community: Law, Space and Identity in the Ancient Eastern Mediterranean World* (London: Taylor & Francis, 2017). See also the works of Brent Shaw and Ari Bryen, cited below. The centrality of war to ancient societies has long been recognized, for instance in the important essay by M. I. Finley, *Ancient History: Evidence and Models* (London: Penguin Books, 1985), 67–87.

3. On urban riots during the empire (Rome itself looms large in these studies, for evidentiary reasons), see Ramsay MacMullen, *Enemies of the Roman Order: Treason, Unrest, and Alienation in the Empire* (Cambridge: Harvard University Press, 1966), 163–91; Thomas W. Africa, "Urban Violence in Imperial Rome," *Journal of Interdisciplinary History* 2 (1971): 3–21; W. J. Slater, "Pantomime Riots," *ClAnt* 13 (1994): 120–44; Paul Erdkamp, "'A Starving Mob Has No Respect': Urban Markets and Food Riots in the Roman World, 100 BC–400 AD," in *The Transformation of Economic Life under the Roman Empire: Proceedings of the Second Workshop of the International Network Impact of Empire (Roman Empire, c. 200 B.C.–A.D. 476), Nottingham, July 4–7, 2001*, ed. Lukas de Blois and John Rich (Amsterdam: Gieben, 2002), 93–115; Benjamin Kelly, "Riot Control and Imperial Ideology in the Roman Empire," *Phoenix* 61 (2007): 150–76.

4. Brent D. Shaw, *Sacred Violence: African Christians and Sectarian Hatred in the Age of Augustine* (Cambridge: Cambridge University Press, 2011), 4. This is not the place for an extended discussion of the history of theories of violence: the influence of Hobbes's polemic view of society, Max Weber's identification of the state as a monopoly of legitimate violence, and the ambiguity of the German word *Gewalt* have cast long shadows. For introductions

in sophisticated studies of violence in the Roman Empire, have argued convincingly for an approach to understanding violence in our evidence for antiquity as inseparably composed of rough actions (punching, kicking, beating, stabbing, burning) and rhetorical claims (insults, threats, complaints, charges, memorializations).[5] Following this lead has utility for the ancient historian: it means that representations of violence were not independent from the perpetration of harm, but rendered it legible to participants. In this way we can interpret violence as part of the wider tangle of social interactions between individuals and groups, rather than view it as an ineluctable breakdown of society.

The story of the refugees from Trachonitis in the *Vita* is well suited to analysis on these terms, since Josephus presents us with an extended cycle of violent words and actions in a particular local context. I turn to this narrative, therefore, to examine how Josephus relates this violent episode in one of his texts and to ask what was behind this instance of communal violence. In this case, I argue, the violence that appears at first sight to be a matter of "horizontal" local relationships in Galilee is a product of the "vertical" interactions between provincial actors and the Roman imperial center. This is not to claim that the fate of the refugees was Rome's "fault" or simply a mechanical consequence of the revolt, but rather to explore how local interactions in the Roman world, even violent ones, could be shaped by imperial power.

This argument involves facing up to the problem, approached directly by Shaye Cohen's *Josephus in Galilee and Rome*, of how to read the *Vita*: how can we move from tendentious narrative to historical questions?[6] As the work of Shaye and other Josephan scholars has emphasized, we must not

---

to modern thinking about violence for students of premodern societies, see Ari Z. Bryen, *Violence in Roman Egypt: A Study in Legal Interpretation* (Philadelphia: University of Pennsylvania Press, 2013), 65–73; Roderick Campbell, "Introduction: Toward a Deep History of Violence and Civilization," in *Violence and Civilization: Studies of Social Violence in History and Prehistory*, ed. Roderick Campbell, Joukowsky Institute Publication 4 (Oxford: Oxbow Books, 2014), 1–22.

5. Shaw, *Sacred Violence*, 4: "The violent deeds were living extensions of the rhetoric in which their values and causes were formed. The acts of physical harm and material damage served specific tactical ends that must be understood.... The interpretations and representations of violence fed on themselves and were seedbeds for novel and innovative acts of physical harm." Bryen, *Violence in Roman Egypt*, 74: "Violence is not so much a thing to be defined as it is a label used in a process of defining the actions of another, and locating those actions (and sometimes also the motives and character) of others within a discourse of claim-making. In other words, using the label 'violent' to describe an action or a person is a way of declaring unacceptable something that another thought appropriate, natural, or necessary." My reading of the books by Shaw and Bryen has particularly informed my approach in this essay.

6. Shaye J. D. Cohen, *Josephus in Galilee and Rome: His Vita and Development as a Historian*, Columbia Studies in the Classical Tradition 8 (Leiden: Brill, 1979).

ignore the literary or rhetorical qualities of the text; however, neither do we need to abandon historical questions about the world that the author represents.[7] I start with the story as told by Josephus, before turning to the perspective of "the crowd" in Taricheae. In the conclusion, I consider the sources of this outbreak of local violence in the context of the Roman imperial system.

Josephus: Facing Down the Mob

It was Josephus who made the episode of the refugees into a violent story: decades later, as author of his autobiographical *Vita*, he chose to memorialize this story as an outbreak of xenophobic violence.[8] Understanding the violence in Taricheae, therefore, means following the way that Josephus told the story and used the language of violence to cast the crowd as a mob and their demands as coercive and irrational.

Josephus tells the story of the refugees in two parts. In the first section (112–113), the author relates how two men of significance (μεγιστᾶνες) came to him from Trachonitis, an area under the control of Agrippa II, bringing arms, horses, and money.[9] This was the start of the trouble:

> The Judaeans were insisting that they [the refugees] be circumcised if they wished to live among them, but I did not allow them to be forced to do this [οὐκ εἴασα βιασθῆναι], saying that every man should worship God according to his own choice and not from violence [μὴ μετὰ βίας], and that it was necessary that those who had fled to us for safety should not come to regret it. The mass was persuaded, and I provided generously to the new arrivals for all their usual sustenance.[10]

---

7. Writing history from Josephus has been at the center of much methodological debate since *Josephus in Galilee and Rome*: see James S. McLaren, *Turbulent Times? Josephus and Scholarship on Judaea in the First Century CE*, JSPSup 29 (Sheffield: Sheffield Academic, 1998); Steve Mason, "Contradiction or Counterpoint? Josephus and Historical Method," *Review of Rabbinic Judaism* 6 (2003): 145–88; Steve Mason, "What Is History? Using Josephus for the Judaean-Roman War," in *The Jewish Revolt against Rome: Interdisciplinary Perspectives*, ed. Mladen Popović, JSJSup 154 (Leiden: Brill, 2011), 155–240; Zuleika Rodgers, ed., *Making History: Josephus and Historical Method*, JSJSup 110 (Leiden: Brill, 2007); Daniel R. Schwartz, *Reading the First Century: On Reading Josephus and Studying Jewish History of the First Century*, WUNT 300 (Tübingen: Mohr Siebeck, 2013).

8. Numerical references in the text without qualification refer to the *Vita*.

9. Josephus does not specify where the refugees found him, but the logic of the story and the location of his regular headquarters strongly support Taricheae (Magdala) as the location of the story. Steve Mason provides learned and full commentary (*Life of Josephus* [Boston: Brill, 2003], 75–76 and 86–87).

10. *Vita* 113: τούτους περιτέμνεσθαι τῶν Ἰουδαίων ἀναγκαζόντων, εἰ θέλουσιν εἶναι παρ' αὐτοῖς, οὐκ εἴασα βιασθῆναι, φάσκων δεῖν ἕκαστον κατὰ τὴν ἑαυτοῦ προαίρεσιν τὸν θεὸν εὐσεβεῖν, ἀλλὰ μὴ μετὰ

The passage opens with a group that Josephus calls "Judeans" (Ἰουδαῖοι). Only here in the *Vita* does the writer refer to the ordinary people of Galilee in this way; elsewhere he uses the term Galileans (Γαλιλαῖοι) or the name of a particular community.[11] The effect is to suggest that the call for circumcision of the Trachonitans comes from a group whose Judean identity has become salient. In his response, Josephus makes clear that he sees this demand as violent, by twice employing forms of the morally loaded word βία (violence, force), and contrasting it with both the choice (προαίρεσις) belonging to all people in matters of worship and the safety (ἀσφάλεια) that the refugees had sought among the rebels.[12] The construction of the insistence on circumcision as violent is successful, according to its proponent: "the mass" is persuaded (πεισθέντος δὲ τοῦ πλήθους).

The author leaves off from this story to relate three other events: a successful military operation against the Romans, an attempt by John of Gischala to strip Galilean support from Josephus, and the notorious Dabaritta affair. In the latter story, Josephus was accused of misappropriating funds from a bandit raid and, under the threat of execution, was forced to appease the people of both Taricheae and Tiberias with promises to use the funds for the construction of fortifications. The placement of the story of the refugees allows the historian to comment ironically, as Steve Mason has argued, on his interactions with the people of Taricheae.[13] In his speech in self-defense on the use of the Dabaritta funds (142), Josephus flatters the townspeople by remarking on their exceptional hospitality (τὴν γὰρ πόλιν ταύτην φιλοξενωτάτην οὖσαν ἐπιστάμενος). Mason suggests that the ironic juxtaposition of this compliment with the treatment of the noble refugees that falsifies it is intended to signal to readers that Josephus was willing to control the masses through flattery, as any good statesman might be expected to do.[14] Even with such rhetorical maneuvers, the historian writes, he was able to avoid an attack by an armed gang on his lodgings only through a demonstrative act of discipline against the most aggressive member of the opposition.

At this moment in his narrative (149–154), Josephus claims that "certain men" (τινες) incite the people of Taricheae, now "a mob" (ὄχλος), to

---

βίας, χρῆναι δὲ τούτους δι' ἀσφάλειαν πρὸς ἡμᾶς καταφυγόντας μὴ μετανοεῖν. πεισθέντος δὲ τοῦ πλήθους τοῖς ἥκουσιν ἀνδράσιν τὰ πρὸς τὴν συνήθη δίαιταν ἅπαντα παρεῖχον δαψιλῶς.

11. Cohen, *Josephus in Galilee*, 206–7.

12. See W. E. Moore, "ΒΙΑΖΩ, ΑΡΠΑΖΩ and Cognates in Josephus," *NTS* 21 (1975): 519–43, for the clear negative moral semantics of βία (and consistent link with physical violence) in Josephus; and Mason, *Life of Josephus*, 75–76, on the philosophical and rational connotations of the latter two terms.

13. Steve Mason, "Figured Speech and Irony in T. Flavius Josephus," in *Flavius Josephus and Flavian Rome*, ed. Jonathan Edmondson, Steve Mason, and James Rives (Oxford: Oxford University Press, 2005), 243–88, here 279–80.

14. Mason, *Life of Josephus*, xlv, citing Plutarch, *Precepts of Statescraft* 818e–819b.

repeat the demand for circumcision as a condition of residence for the refugees. They also add a charge that the incomers were sorcerers and were helping the Romans, which the historian casts as irrational nonsense (φλύαρος).[15] I will discuss below this accusation as a claim of violence, but it is significant that Josephus refutes that proposition directly in a second speech:

> When I learned of these claims, I again taught the people that they should not persecute those who had fled to them; I mocked the nonsense of the accusation of witchcraft, pointing out that the Romans would not maintain so many soldiers, if they could defeat their enemies with sorcerers. When I had said this, they were persuaded for the moment, but, when they had withdrawn, they were whipped up again by wicked men against the notables. At a certain moment, they armed themselves and advanced upon the house of the refugees in Taricheae to kill them.[16]

Josephus presents this as an authoritative address—he "teaches the people" (τὸν δῆμον ἀνεδίδασκον), no longer a mob, apparently, but a *dēmos*, a less threatening collectivity—and makes a rhetorical contrast between the nonexistent sorcerers and actual, violent Roman soldiers. The attempt to de-escalate fails, real harm *is* now imminent, and Josephus scrambles to avert the killing, which he says would have been the completion of "a defilement" (μύσος). Finally, he reluctantly sends the two refugees back to royal lands, via the lake. They would be pardoned, but he has himself become the victim of the violence (βιασθείς). This, he writes, was the end of the story: *καὶ τὰ μὲν περὶ ἐκείνους τοῦτ᾽ ἔσχε τὸ τέλος*.

Josephus tells the story artfully: the division of the episode in the wider narrative of the *Vita* emphasizes the repetitive nature of the local hostility to the Trachonitans and works to increase the drama before the final outcome.[17] Initially, each part follows a parallel structure: ill feeling toward the notable arrivals leads to open hostility from the local people before Josephus intervenes successfully with speech to dampen their aggression. In the conclusion of the second section, however, Josephus does not try to calm a third outbreak of hostility with rhetoric but concedes that the refugees must leave. Repetition also highlights difference: the second part

---

15. The transmitted text for the accusation of sorcery (149) is clear in sense, but it is hard to determine the exact phrase Josephus used: see Mason, *Life of Josephus*, 86 n.704.

16. *Vita* 150–151: πυθόμενος δὲ περὶ τούτων ἐγὼ πάλιν τὸν δῆμον ἀνεδίδασκον μὴ δεῖν διώκεσθαι τοὺς καταφυγόντας πρὸς αὐτούς· τὸν δὲ φλύαρον τῆς περὶ τῶν φαρμάκων αἰτίας διέσυρον, οὐκ ἂν τοσαύτας μυριάδας στρατιωτῶν Ῥωμαίους λέγων τρέφειν, εἰ διὰ φαρμακέων (P: φαρμάκων) ἦν νικᾶν τοὺς πολεμίους. ταῦτα λέγοντος ἐμοῦ πρὸς ὀλίγον μὲν ἐπείθοντο, πάλιν δ᾽ἀναχωρήσαντες ὑπὸ τῶν πονηρῶν ἐξηρεθίζοντο κατὰ τῶν μεγιστάνων, καί ποτε μεθ᾽ ὅπλων ἐπὶ τὴν οἰκίαν αὐτῶν τὴν ἐν Ταριχέᾳ ἀπῆλθον ὡς ἀναιρήσοντες.

17. Mason points out the habit of Josephus to divide stories for the sake of suspense (*Life of Josephus*, xxiii).

of the story involves not just the crowd but the incitement of the mass by wicked leaders (πονηροί), which works as both explanation and a link to neighboring episodes.

In sum, the historian characterizes the crowd and its demands as violent and irrational. Rather than see this attitude as reflective of Josephus's actual sentiments, I suggest that we read this violent tale as strategic and as part of his elite social performance, at Rome and even decades after the event.[18] As Shaye argued in his *Josephus in Galilee and Rome*, the *Vita* is more than just a defensive reply to Justus of Tiberias, as it used to be read but also gives a broader account of the author's *ethos* in the context of Galilean politics of the mid-60s CE.[19] This episode fits one of the key arenas for that account of self: the interaction between elites—Josephus and his rivals—and the masses in Galilean towns.

The elite class in the Roman Empire, a culturally integrated group of rulers of both the empire and its subject communities, had a strong moral vision of the expected behavior of the masses and the appropriate responses of members of their own class. From their perspective, the crowd in the imperial cities could be expected to be fickle and prone to spasms of violence, the stereotypical mob.[20] Indeed, Cicero and Horace portray Judeans as particularly prone to coercive uproar.[21] On the other side, Benjamin Kelly has recently argued that the elite were expected to respond to the crowd with personal appeals and seek alternatives to the use of (Roman) force.[22] The ideal was propagated in the famous first simile of the *Aeneid*, which compares the end of a storm at sea to the resolution of an urban riot by the mere appearance of a distinguished noble (*Aen.* 1.148–156). The story type was familiar in the eastern regions of the empire too: an anecdote from Philostratus's *Life of Apollonius of Tyana* (1.15) tells of an extreme case, when the hero, who had undertaken a vow of silence, managed to quell a crowd brandishing torches in Pamphylian Aspendos

18. Cohen suspects a Roman audience for the story (*Josephus in Galilee*, 147 n. 159).

19. Ibid., 101–80. The work of Mason has broadened this reading of the *Vita* as a positive account of Josephus's *ethos* and emphasizes a Roman audience: see Mason, "Should Any Wish to Enquire Further (*Ant.* 1.25): The Aim and Audience of Josephus's *Judean Antiquities/Life*," in *Understanding Josephus: Seven Perspectives*, ed. Steve Mason, JSPSup 32 (Sheffield: Sheffield Academic, 1998), 64–103, here 103; *Life of Josephus*, xlvii–l. See also Jerome H. Neyrey, "Josephus' Vita and the Encomium: A Native Model of Personality," *JSJ* 25 (1994): 177–206.

20. Zvi Yavetz captures the moral view that underlies the stereotypical depiction of the urban crowd at Rome (*Plebs and Princeps* [Oxford: Oxford University Press, 1969], 141–55).

21. Cicero, *Flac.* 66–67: *ob hoc crimen hic locus abs te, Laeli, atque illa turba* [sc. the Judeans] *quaesita est; scis quanta sit manus, quanta concordia, quantum valeat in contionibus … multitudinem Iudaeorum flagrantem non numquam in contionibus pro re publica contemnere gravitatis summae fuit*; Horace, *Sat.* 1.4.142–143: *ac veluti te / Iudaei cogemus in hanc concedere turbam.*

22. Kelly, "Riot Control," 160–62. Cf. Wilfried Nippel, *Public Order in Ancient Rome*, Key Themes in Ancient History (Cambridge: Cambridge University Press, 1995), 106, assuming that the ideal was a practical reality.

by significant gestures and a strongly worded letter.[23] Two well-known speeches by Josephus's near contemporary Dio Chrysostom, to the peoples of Prusa and Alexandria, can similarly be read as bravura performances of elite persuasion in the face of a riotous populace (*De tumultu* and *Ad Alexandrinos*). Kelly suggests that such stories reflect an actual elite ambivalence about using force to repress urban protest; more probably (and more cynically) the story type justified the social prominence of local elites, the fact that they did at times have to make political and economic concessions to restless urban populations, and state violence as a response of last resort to a truly intractable crowd.

Although conditions in Galilee during the revolt were irregular—probably strikingly so to Roman readers—the crowd at Taricheae and Josephus played their roles perfectly: an unreasonable mob and a persuasive elite.[24] Even modern readers have assented to the narrative: Per Bilde, for instance, suggests that the crowd at Taricheae was made up of "religious fanatics."[25] The arguments that Josephus claims to have used in the moment play to his readership too. His refusal to accept the circumcision of the refugees is defended with philosophical ideals of freedom of choice and a hint of the widespread philosophical notion that one divine principle lurks behind all systems of worship.[26] His rationalizing mockery of witchcraft and appeal to Roman military logistics likewise speak to the values of an imperial readership.[27] Finally, the violence of the crowd may also have been an explanation for the specific outcome of this incident: Josephus's choice to extradite the refugees back to Roman territory rather than allow the (polluting) violation of Mediterranean norms of hospitality.

The violence in Taricheae, therefore, was extremely useful to the historian writing in Domitianic Rome. Rather than constituting a threat to his social performance, the violence was an integral part of Josephus's rhetorical display, because it permitted him to match the imperial expectation of local elites as keepers of order in the face of the irrational mob. Recent

---

23. See also Lucian, *Demon.* 64 for a similar story, set in Athens.

24. A. M. Eckstein argues that the narrative of the rational statesman restraining an irrational people is a distinctively Polybian theme in Josephus ("Josephus and Polybius: A Reconsideration," *ClAnt* 9 [1990]: 175–208, here 195–98); my argument here is that it is better understood as an adoption of Roman imperial discourse.

25. Per Bilde, *Flavius Josephus, between Jerusalem and Rome: His Life, His Works and Their Importance*, JSPSup 2 (Sheffield: JSOT Press, 1988), 44.

26. Peter Van Nuffelen has studied imperial philosophical (harmonizing) theories of traditional cults (*Rethinking the Gods: Philosophical Readings of Religion in the Post-Hellenistic Period*, Greek Culture in the Roman World [Cambridge: Cambridge University Press, 2011]). Cohen argues that the negative view of conversion here (found also in the *Antiquitates*) is part of an apology for Judaism in a Roman context ("Respect for Judaism," 428).

27. The Josephan interest in Roman military organization is well known (esp. *B.J.* 3.70–109) and is a "Polybian" touch (Shaye J. D. Cohen, "Josephus, Jeremiah, and Polybius," *History and Theory* 21 [1982]: 366–81, here 368).

studies have convincingly argued for Josephus's actual social marginality in Rome, but this episode fits with his concern, particularly visible in the *Vita*, to present a provincial elite "face" to his readers.[28]

The People: Fear and Loathing in Taricheae

We could leave the story there, with Josephus's retrospective account of violence in Galilee, but I contend we should also try to reconstruct the story on a different plan from the *Vita*, to understand the position of "the crowd" and their final turn to riot. I have already emphasized the extent to which that account is shaped by its author, but I see no reason to suspect that he was making up the basic claims of the people or the eventual denouement of the episode. If this is correct, we are able to take them at their word and to use contextual and comparative evidence to find a different pattern of violence at Taricheae from the one that Josephus presents.[29]

First, we should look briefly at the wider context of the episode in the late first-century southern Levant. By late 66 CE, Taricheae was a city at war, a participant community in the Great Revolt against Rome. The revolt had commenced earlier in the year in Jerusalem, with local conflict there and in Caesarea and an ensuing destructive march on Judea led by Cestius Gallus.[30] At this moment, Josephus claims, significant communal violence burst out in the hellenized cities and towns of southern Syria between Judeans and their Syrian neighbors (*B.J.* 2.457–265 and 559–561; *Vita* 25–27). He mentions clashes at Philadelphia, Heshbon, Gerasa, Pella, Scythopolis, Gadara, Hippos, Kedasa, Ptolemais, Gaba, Sebaste, Ascalon, Anthedon, Gaza, and Damascus. Over the previous decades, these urban

---

28. On the social position of Josephus at Rome, see Hannah Cotton and Werner Eck, "Josephus' Roman Audience: Josephus and the Roman Elites," in Edmondson, Mason, and Rives, *Flavius Josephus and Flavian Rome*, 37–52; Jonathan J. Price, "The Provincial Historian in Rome," in *Josephus and Jewish History in Flavian Rome and Beyond*, ed. Joseph Sievers and Gaia Lembi, JSJSup 104 (Leiden: Brill, 2005), 101–18. For a reminder, though, both that ancient publication was a local affair and that Josephus assumed an elite audience, see Steve Mason, "Of Audience and Meaning: Reading Josephus' *Bellum Judaicum* in the Context of a Flavian Audience," in *Josephus and Jewish History in Flavian Rome and Beyond*, 71–100.

29. A methodological point: since the following analysis consciously goes beyond the text, we are not able to "prove" it in the typical manner of significant quotation from ancient sources. Instead, this is an argument from contextual and comparative probability. In order to limit this argument, however, I assume that the reported demands of the crowd, even if not the manner in which they put them, are real and sincere; it might be possible make an argument that this whole dispute was, for example, "in the final analysis" about peasant resentment of the rich, but there could be no kind of check on this argument.

30. See now Steve Mason, *A History of the Jewish War, AD 66–74* (Cambridge: Cambridge University Press, 2016), 281–334, on the first phase of the uprising.

communities seem to have come to encompass side-by-side citizen bodies, ethnic Syrians, Arabs, and Itureans living in political communities understood in Greek terms (as *poleis*) and Judeans living according to their own ancestral norms.[31] It is impossible to know how harmonious or contentious these arrangements had been, but the outbreak of the revolt and the arrival of large Roman military formations generated murderous riots between the two groups in cities across the region.[32] In the lachrymose account of Josephus, the Judeans suffered more harm than they inflicted, though we should note that in the *Vita* he was intent on using these events to portray the "necessity" (ἀνάγκη) of the revolt (27).

None of the cities mentioned in the previous paragraph were in Galilee.[33] The region was not, however, free from violence: part of Cestius Gallus's strategy for containing the incipient uprising was a *razzia* into the lower Galilee under the command of Caesennius Gallus, which Josephus claims led to the deaths of two thousand rebels (*B.J.* 2.510–512). In the years before the revolt, Galilean society itself had been divided: outside of two larger settlements, at Sepphoris and Tiberias, there is good evidence that the population was polarized between people living according to the particular cultural patterns of Judea and those who had adopted the practices of the wider Hellenistic cultural koine. Recent archaeological analysis by Andrea Berlin has emphasized that the two groups were distinguished even in terms of quotidian material culture.[34] Communities like the town

---

31. Nathanael Andrade captures well the double nature of these urban communities in the first century ("Ambiguity, Violence, and Community in the Cities of Judaea and Syria," *Historia: Zeitschrift für Alte Geschichte* 59 [2010]: 342–70).

32. See Martin Goodman, *The Ruling Class of Judaea: The Origins of the Jewish Revolt against Rome, A.D. 66–70* (Cambridge: Cambridge University Press, 1987), 18, arguing that this violence was "the consequence not the cause of the revolt"; *pace* Uriel Rappaport, "Jewish–Pagan Relations and the Revolt against Rome in 66–70 C.E.," *Jerusalem Cathedra* 1 (1981): 81–95. Only in Caesarea in early 66 CE did the violence seem to anticipate conflict between the imperial state and Judeans. Note also, for the sake of comparison, the connection of war and (what he calls) massacre in Jacques Sémelin, *Purify and Destroy: The Political Uses of Massacre and Genocide*, Comparative Politics and International Studies (New York: Columbia University Press, 2007), 131–47.

33. The history of Galilee before and during the revolt has been the subject of extensive study (in part because the question overlaps with the quest for the historical Jesus): see, with varied positions on the Judean identity of the region, Seán Freyne, *Galilee, from Alexander the Great to Hadrian, 323 B.C.E. to 135 C.E: A Study of Second Temple Judaism*, University of Notre Dame Center for the Study of Judaism and Christianity in Antiquity 5 (Notre Dame, IN: University of Notre Dame Press, 1980); Freyne, "The Revolt from Regional Perspective," in *The First Jewish Revolt: Archaeology, History and Ideology*, ed. Andrea M. Berlin and J. Andrew Overman (London: Routledge, 2002), 43–56; Richard A. Horsley, *Galilee: History, Politics, People* (Valley Forge, PA: Trinity Press International, 1995); Mark A. Chancey, *The Myth of a Gentile Galilee: The Population of Galilee and New Testament Studies*, SNTSMS 118 (Cambridge: Cambridge University Press, 2002).

34. Andrea M. Berlin, "Romanization and Anti-Romanization in Pre-Revolt Galilee,"

of Taricheae (Magdala) avoided imported pottery from the Mediterranean coast and adopted the use of lamps manufactured in Jerusalem. Whether we choose to think about this population as primarily an ethnic or religious group, they were living according to the ancestral norms of the inhabitants of Judea and were sentimentally attached to the cult practiced in Jerusalem. In Taricheae itself, this attachment was apparently materialized: a recent excavation of a remarkable pre-70 CE synagogue in the settlement revealed a large stone block that was carved with a menorah, a symbol of the temple cult.[35] In the opening phase of the revolt, in 66–67, the town seems to have served as the headquarters for Josephus, who had been sent to Galilee from Jerusalem. The nature of his mission has been highly controversial, but he was accepted in Taricheae as a man of authority.[36] In the *Bellum judaicum* Josephus portrays the natives of Taricheae as opposed to the revolt and friendly to Agrippa, though this is hard to reconcile with their actual behavior (3.492); he also reveals that the town had filled with Judean refugees by the time of the arrival of the Flavians (*B.J.* 3.463, 542). The actual composition of "the crowd" in our story, therefore, could have been a mix of locals and other refugees; as mentioned above, the term *Judean* used by Josephus seems to indicate that it was this common identity rather than place of origin that was significant in the moment.

The gentile refugees at the center of the story in the *Vita* were from Trachonitis, an area of basalt uplands (the modern Leja in Syria) to the northeast of Galilee and south of Damascus. Josephus is otherwise laconic about the identity of these two men, though this place of origin can tell us something about who they were. In the 60s CE, Agrippa II was the nominal ruler of this territory, which was settled by a people that our sources call "Itureans." The area was notorious for banditry, which both Josephus (*A.J.* 15.344; 16.274) and Strabo (*Geogr.* 16.2.20) regard as the characteristic way of life in the region.[37] In a wide-ranging study of "banditry" in

in Berlin and Overman, *First Jewish Revolt*, 57–73; Berlin, "Jewish Life before the Revolt: The Archaeological Evidence," *JSJ* 36 (2005): 417–70; Berlin, "Identity Politics in Early Roman Galilee," in Popović, *Jewish Revolt against Rome*, 69–106. See, though, the caution in Mark A. Chancey, "Archaeology, Ethnicity, and First-Century C.E. Galilee: The Limits of the Evidence," in *The Wandering Galilean: Essays in Honour of Seán Freyne*, ed. Zuleika Rodgers, JSJSup 132 (Leiden: Brill, 2009), 205–18.

35. Mordechai Aviam, "The Decorated Stone from the Synagogue at Migdal: A Holistic Interpretation and a Glimpse into the Life of Galilean Jews at the Time of Jesus," *NovT* 55 (2013): 205–20; Richard Bauckham and Stefano De Luca place the stone in the context of the current state of archaeological work in Taricheae/Magdala ("Magdala as We Now Know It," *Early Christianity* 6 [2015]: 91–118).

36. Cohen, *Josephus in Galilee*, 209. For the controversy regarding Josephus's mission, see the opinionated summary by Bilde, *Flavius Josephus*, 43–46.

37. See also *OGIS* 424, a decree of a "King Agrippa" from Seeia, a sanctuary in Trachonitis, which asserts that people in the area live like wild beasts (θηριώδης κατάστασις) and are accustomed to "hide in holes" (ἐνφωλεύσ[αντες]), almost certainly anti-"bandit" polemic.

Syria, Shaw has persuasively argued that this label was applied to the pre-political mode of economy and governance (mafioso-like "big men") that was common in the mountainous borderlands of the late Hellenistic and Roman Near East.[38] Bandits of this kind could be persuaded to cooperate with more complex forms of polity, often as providers of military man-power, but were liable to exercise independent agency. The status term that Josephus applies to the two refugees, μεγιστᾶνες, may support the idea that they were men of this sort: elsewhere he uses the term for powerful feudal lords in the courts of Achaemenid Persia, Adiabene, and Parthia. Given the ecology of their origin and their decision to defect from the king, the likelihood is that the refugees were such "bandits" from Trachonitis; it is perhaps little wonder that they came to Josephus with weapons, horses, and money (112: ἐπαγόμενοι τοὺς ἑαυτῶν ἵππους καὶ ὅπλα, χρήματα δ' ὑποκομίζοντες). As we have seen, they were coming into a tense situation, in a region that was already polarized and now shaken by the start of a conflict.

As we read it in the *Vita*, the population's first response to these new arrivals was to make circumcision a condition of their sojourn. We have seen how Josephus casts this demand as coercive and religious (about how to worship god), but we should be open to the possibility that it may not have been understood that way by those people who were making it. In the previous months and across the region, a wave of communal violence had crashed over the mixed communities of the southern Levant. By contrast, the people of Taricheae offered a different possibility: since the Trachonitans had made the choice to join their revolt, they proposed an entrance into their Judean political community.[39] Circumcision was *the* way to cross over to becoming a Judean in the Second Temple period; as Josephus himself puts it in the second part of his story, the expectation of the crowd was for the refugees to adopt their customs (149: μεταβῆναι ... εἰς τὰ παρ' αὐτοῖς ἔθη).[40] There was precedent for understanding such a crossing in political terms: when the Hasmonean Aristobulus had made

38. Brent D. Shaw, "Lords of the Levant: The Borderlands of Syria and Phoenicia in the First Century," *Scripta Classica Israelica* 33 (2014): 225–42, esp. 234–36 on Zenodorus, an Augustan-period big man in Trachonitis, building on his "Bandits in the Roman Empire," *Past & Present* 105 (1984): 3–52, and "Josephus: Roman Power and Responses to It," *Athenaeum* 83 (1994): 357–90.

39. For the revolt as an attempted revolutionary foundation of a new community, see now James S. McLaren and Martin Goodman, "The Importance of Perspective: The Jewish–Roman Conflict of 66–70 CE as a Revolution," in *Revolt and Resistance in the Ancient Classical World and the Near East: In the Crucible of Empire*, ed. John J. Collins and J. G. Manning, CHANE 85 (Leiden: Brill, 2016), 205–18.

40. On circumcision and becoming a Judean or Jew in the Second Temple period, see John J. Collins, "A Symbol of Otherness: Circumcision and Salvation in the First Century," in *Seers, Sybils and Sages in Hellenistic-Roman Judaism*, JSJSup 54 (Leiden: Brill, 1997), 211–35; Shaye J. D. Cohen, *The Beginnings of Jewishness: Boundaries, Varieties, Uncertainties*, HCS 31

conquests in Iturean lands, the population had adopted the customs of the Judean conquerors, including circumcision, as a symbol of their bond with the polity.[41] It is clear, however, that the incomers were reluctant to become Judean on these terms.

The next phase of the dispute was much less pacific; the refusal of the refugees to become Judean seems to have stoked distrust and fear in the crowd. Now the locals claimed that *they* were the victims of violence, with a new charge that the Trachonitans were sorcerers and using unseen magic to hinder the war effort against the Romans (149). We should not forget that the origin and status of the Trachonitans may have encouraged a perception that they had previously been bandit leaders and dangerous men. It is easy to agree with Josephus that the idea that they were sorcerers must have been nonsense, but much evidence points to the intensity of the fear of witchcraft in the Roman Mediterranean.[42] Shaw has compared the attitude of the crowd in Taricheae with the story in the Synoptic Gospels of Jesus's exorcism of the demon called Legion as both constituting magical explanations of Roman military power.[43] Comparative evidence from further afield may also provide a parallel for the link between militarized violence and an accusation of witchcraft: the Americanist Mary Beth Norton has suggested that the famous witch-hunt that started in Salem Village in 1692 was grounded in settler anxieties regarding contemporary wars with the native populations of New England. Notably, accusers there claimed that the minister George Borroughs, the alleged ringleader of the witches, had bewitched the soldiers who had failed to protect Maine settlers from Wabanaki raids in the preceding decade.[44] In this light, the accusation that the refugees were sorcerers signified a perception that they had, in cooperation with the Romans, harmed the community.

Josephus makes it seem that he was able to cast doubt on this accusation, at least for a short while, but even he admits that this persuasion was short-lived. He writes that the crowd was incited again by "wicked men," but his choice, years later in a work that is often dedicated to the settling

---

(Berkeley: University of California Press, 1999), 123–25; Mimouni, *La circoncision dans le monde judéen aux époques grecque et romaine*.

41. Cohen, *Beginnings of Jewishness*, 109–39. In *A.J.* 13.318, Josephus casts this as coercive (he uses the same verb as for the crowd in Taricheae—ἀναγκάζω), but as Cohen points out, an alternative version found in the Greek historical tradition implies voluntary acculturation (*Beginnings of Jewishness*, 112–13, 136–37).

42. For this fear, see the illuminating study by R. Gordon, "Imagining Greek and Roman Magic," in *Witchcraft and Magic in Europe: Ancient Greece and Rome*, ed. Bengt Ankarloo and Stuart Clark (Philadelphia: University of Pennsylvania Press, 1999), 159–275. In Taricheae, the accusation could also have been supported by an appeal to biblical law, which forbids the presence of (foreign) sorcerers among the people (Deut 18:10).

43. Shaw, "Josephus," 365. Cf. Mark 5:1–20, Matt 8:28–34, and Luke 8:28–39.

44. Mary Beth Norton, *In the Devil's Snare: The Salem Witchcraft Crisis of 1692* (New York: Alfred A. Knopf, 2002), 120–32.

of scores, not to name names suggests either that he only supposed such agents or that he was making excuses. In addition, the authority of Josephus may well have been shaken by the Dabaritta affair. At any rate, the crowd's perception of violence on the other side provoked them to action; they seized arms and marched on the residence of the refugees. In doing so, they were not persecuting innocent men but responding to violence with violence. It is possible that even here we are faced with something closer to a threat than actual attempted murder: Josephus still has time to dig a canal (διώρυγα) for their escape.

This is a different story of violence from the one told directly by Josephus in the *Vita*. Violence was located not in an unreasonable and murderous crowd but in the harm perpetrated against the Judeans by the Romans and by the gentile inhabitants of southern Syria. In response to such violence, the crowd had responded first with an attempt to integrate the outsiders into their distinct Judean community and then, when the Trachonitans had been linked with the losses suffered at the hands of the Romans, with a final resort to self-defense.

Galilean Violence as Roman Imperial Violence

The riot at Taricheae was a contingent and local event. The violence there was the result of a unique chain of decisions by Josephus, the Trachonitan nobles, and the people of Taricheae. It is only legible to us because of the choices made by Josephus as author and various communities of copyists to preserve the story in the *Vita*. But these accidents of chance should not prevent us from asking about the social forces that fomented the intracommunal violence. Each of the two stories of the incident that I have (re)told in this chapter offers a different answer to this question: Josephus blames the attachment to identity and xenophobia of the crowd; the people of Taricheae, if we take their enunciated claims seriously, blame the men from Trachonitis and, beyond them, the Romans.

The impression given by Josephus is that the violence arose from an irrational mobilization of Judean identity. In this, he anticipates (for different reasons) a significant current of modern liberal and secular discourse that casts groups with strong ethnic and religious identities as susceptible to violence.[45] There is also an old school of thought, dating back at least to Hume and more recently associated with Jan Assmann, that sees monotheism as inherently intolerant.[46] Anthropological and historical studies

---

45. For a recent representative of this view, see Vasily Rudich, *Religious Dissent in the Roman Empire: Violence in Judaea at the Time of Nero*, Routledge Monographs in Classical Studies (New York: Routledge, 2015), 322–23 (on the violence of "irrational" religious dissent).

46. David Hume argued for monotheistic intolerance in his *Natural History of Religion*

of ethnic and "sacred" violence, however, have raised significant doubts about the necessity of such connections.[47] As was the case in Galilee before the revolt, mixed populations can coexist in single urban or regional spaces for long periods even when group boundaries are firmly drawn; it almost always takes more than simple difference to provoke groups to rampage.

Instead, I propose that we consider the answer of the crowd and understand the violence in Taricheae as a response to Roman power. We will, of course, have to leave behind their idea that the Romans and Trachonitans relied on witchcraft but look instead for a more realistic mechanism. Much work since the 1970s on the political structure of the early and high Roman Empire has converged on a model that is dominated by the limited capacity of the state.[48] The basic constraints and technological conditions of a premodern agrarian economy left the central government with relatively weak ability to impinge on social life. Instead, the Roman imperial régime was reliant on local elites, who were bound to the center largely by discursive means: a bundle of shared values, common narratives and language for the mutual recognition of status.[49] This rather pacific scholarly image of the empire, however, must be tempered by the fact that the Roman state maintained an army of significant size (as Josephus pointed out to the crowd at Taricheae) and did use this military power against internal populations, at least intermittently.[50] The response to the Great Revolt is a famous example of the application of state violence, but imperial history contains many others, often on a much smaller scale.[51]

It is these two modes of imperial rule—the poetics and the pragmatics of empire—that each produce the violence that we have encountered in

---

(1757); for his modern successor, see Jan Assmann, *The Price of Monotheism* (Stanford, CA: Stanford University Press, 2010).

47. For criticism of the analytical concept of "identity," see Rogers Brubaker and Frederick Cooper, "Beyond 'Identity,'" *Theory and Society* 29 (2000): 1–47. On the insufficiency of ethnic or religious identity as an explanation of intracommunal violence in particular historical cases, see David Nirenberg, *Communities of Violence: Persecution of Minorities in the Middle Ages* (Princeton: Princeton University Press, 1998), 18–124; Shaw, *Sacred Violence,* 771 and passim.

48. The model is presented accessibly in Peter Garnsey and Richard P. Saller, *The Roman Empire: Economy, Society and Culture,* 2nd ed. (Oakland: University of California Press, 2015). See also Fergus Millar, "The World of the Golden Ass," *JRS* 71 (1981): 63–75, for a brilliant illustration of the model from a single source.

49. Clifford Ando, *Imperial Ideology and Provincial Loyalty in the Roman Empire,* Classics and Contemporary Thought (Berkeley: University of California Press, 2000); Carlos F. Noreña, *Imperial Ideals in the Roman West: Representation, Circulation, Power* (Cambridge: Cambridge University Press, 2011).

50. See, recently, Christopher J. Fuhrmann, *Policing the Roman Empire: Soldiers, Administration, and Public Order* (Oxford: Oxford University Press, 2012); and Gil Gambash, *Rome and Provincial Resistance* (New York: Routledge, 2015).

51. Thomas Pekáry gives a list of known disturbances ("*Seditio*: Unruhen und Revolten im römischen Reich von Augustus bis Commodus," *Ancient Society* 18 [1987]: 133–50).

Taricheae. On the one hand, the shared discourse by which metropolitan and local elites, including Josephus, coordinated the governance of even small communities was behind the production of the story of violence in the *Vita*. As we have seen, the story corresponds to the imperial plot of good elite facing down irrational mob; by writing it into his autobiography the historian was engaged in a project of self-fashioning. The logic of this story type, particularly its production of images of unruly populations, also justified the application of the other form of Roman governmental power: military force. Thus, on the other hand, the march of Cestius Gallus with the Twelfth Legion to southern Syria, the raid by Caesonnius Gallus into the lower Galilee, and the fighting that followed seem to have been a key factor in the physical violence in Taricheae. The fear that was engendered by these destructive military maneuvers led to the salience of group identity, indicated also by the riots in southern Syrian cities in 66 CE, to the sense of victimhood and, finally, to the violence that manifested at Taricheae.[52] In this sense, the crowd was right: the violence at Taricheae was Roman imperial violence.

52. Cf. Shaw, *Sacred Violence*, 796–801, 805–6, for the application of state violence as provocative of waves of sectarian violence in both the Africa of Augustine and Northern Ireland in the wake of Bloody Sunday (30 January 1972).

Why "Common Judaism" Does Not Look like Mediterranean Religion

STANLEY STOWERS
Brown University

In a volume celebrating the scholarship of Ed Sanders, Shaye Cohen considered the evidence of Greek and Roman writings for Sanders's notion of "common Judaism."[1] Cohen's careful analysis and good judgment manifest in that article have characterized his career.[2] There he makes a point important for my effort here: These writers mention things distinctive of Jews but have almost nothing to say about what was common across the Mediterranean. Thus, for instance, they say nothing about Jewish hymns and prayers. The ancient writers evidence a practice notable in modern scholarship, but what exactly is the price to pay for characterizing Jewish religion by difference only?

Ed Sanders's idea of common Judaism has been a hit, albeit with a number of dissenters.[3] The idea beautifully expresses intuitions underlying conceptions of Jewish and Christian origins that have been and still are normative for many. In my estimation, there is clearly something right about "common Judaism." There were, for instance, social mechanisms that allowed for ethnic-religious self-identification and identification by others. But the idea contradicts much of the scholarship about social groups that has become dominant in the social sciences, parts of the humanities, and the mind sciences in the last several decades. The academy is in the midst of a major revolution in thinking about social groups.[4] I will briefly discuss why the common belief/practice model that "common Judaism"

1. Shaye J. D. Cohen, "Common Judaism in Greek and Latin Authors," in *Redefining First-Century Jewish and Christian Identities: Essays in Honor of Ed Parish Sanders*, ed. Fabian Udoh, with Susannah Heschel, Mark Chancey, and Gregory Tatum, Christianity and Judaism in Antiquity 16 (Notre Dame, IN: University of Notre Dame Press, 2008), 69–87.

2. It was my good fortune to have Shaye as a colleague for several years

3. E. P. Sanders, *Judaism: Practice and Belief 63 BCE–66 CE* (Philadelphia: Trinity Press International, 1992), 45–314.

4. Rogers Brubaker, *Ethnicity without Groups* (Cambridge: Harvard University Press, 2004).

assumes cannot adequately deal with the dynamics of ancient Mediterranean religion, although it may be a good place to begin inquiry, and then lay out some proposals for theorizing that religion, including Judaism.

Psychology and other fields have shown dramatically that we know far less than we think we know.[5] With unrealistic confidence individuals hold fragmentary outlines of knowledge, and what is known varies greatly across individuals in a population. This overconfidence has in many ways served the species well. The unfounded confidence has made us bold about acting and going forward even when we really do not know. The mentally efficient fragments and outlines often pay off because they allow us just enough information to discover where to go for types of expertise or to technologies of knowledge for answers. Brain/mind with intrinsic limits could not survive unless efficient and adapted to the resources of the social environment. The key resource of social environments comes in that many people in any culture are experts in some small corner of knowledge. They know a lot about a little. Humans have been successful not because all share deep funds of common knowledge, that is, cultures, but because of the networks that connect individuals to experts, and now especially to knowledge technologies (e.g., books, libraries, television, the internet, computers, smart phones). Even though the technologies of writing and literacy had already had a transformative effect on Mediterranean cultures in the relevant period of antiquity, few individuals were highly literate. These well-established findings about—to cite a recent book title—the knowledge illusion, are important both for the practices of historians and for the way that historians understand cultures and the knowledge/knowledge practices that characterize them.[6]

In a 2008 book, the anthropologist Scott Atran and the psychologist Douglas Medin write, "it is just a non-starter to treat or define cultures and groups in terms of shared properties."[7] What could be more counterintuitive to us traditional historians! The ways that humans, including us twenty-first century academics, think intuitively about social groups has also been the object of some intensive cross-cultural study. We intuitively attribute something like essential natures to both natural kinds and social groups.[8] Critically self-reflective biologists, for instance, frequently write about how difficult it is for them to think about species in Darwinian rather

5. The bibliography is enormous. A pioneer has been Nobel Prize laureate Daniel Kahneman, e.g., *Thinking Fast and Slow* (New York: Farrar, Straus & Giroux, 2011).

6. Steven Sloman and Philip Fernback, *The Knowledge Illusion: Why We Never Think Alone* (New York: Riverhead Books, 2017).

7. Scott Atran and Douglas Medin, *The Native Mind and the Cultural Construction of Nature*, Life and Mind (Cambridge, MA: MIT Press, 2008), 265.

8. Ibid., 20–23.

than essentializing ways.[9] Scholars in many areas of the academy have long understood aspects of this problem of essentializing and have tried to introduce variation into descriptions of social groups. So one begins with an integrated entity (e.g., a culture, a religion) and then talks about variation within the unity, but with no escape from the mode of thought. Social theory in the last two centuries was dominated by three ideas that surely had something to do with those centuries being the great age of the nation-state: societies or cultures as superorganisms, as machines with functional parts, and as integrated systems. These models have been largely abandoned in light of vast quantities of detailed data about some cultures and the increasingly powerful methods of analysis.

Traditional social analysis in the humanities and social sciences has proceeded by the principle of synthesis. Bronislaw Malinowski wrote, "We are not interested in what A or B may feel *qua* individuals.... we are interested only in what they feel and think *qua* members of a given community [where] their mental states receive a certain stamp, become stereotyped by the institutions in which they live."[10] This largely ahistorical consensual view of cultures, or of religions, based on intuitive ideas, treats individuals as passive recipients of the culture by causally opaque and rather uniform kinds of absorption such as influence, imitation, instruction, and rule following. This intuitive model simply assumes that habits, procedures, beliefs, and norms are transmitted intact. But empirical investigation of "cultural learning" has found just the opposite.[11] Cultural transmission involves constant and large amounts of "error," variation, and change. The implicit view of mind as a culture sponge that indiscriminately soaks up whatever the culture offers has been central to not only a now old-fashioned sociology and anthropology but also to poststructuralist thought.

Historians of antiquity have no way of doing large and representative studies of cultural matters, but we can learn from our colleagues who do have such data and use less-intuitive and more-realistic models of culture. Philo and Josephus, to take examples that have been central to dominant constructions of "Judaism," can speak with great confidence about what Judeans think and do. They often generalize about Jews with little hesitation. But even before the recent revolution regarding knowledge in cul-

---

9. Michael Ghiselin, "Categories, Life and Thinking," *Behavioral and Brain Sciences* 4 (1981): 269–313.

10. Bronislaw Malinowski, *Argonauts of the Western Pacific* (New York: Dutton, 1922), 23. See Atran and Medin, *Native Mind*, 220.

11. Jean Lave and Etienne Wenger, *Situated Learning: Legitimate Peripheral Participation*, Learning in Doing (New York: Cambridge University Press, 1991); Dan Sperber, *Explaining Culture: A Naturalistic Approach* (Oxford: Blackwell, 1996); Scott Atran, "The Trouble with Memes: Inference versus Imitation in Cultural Creation," *Human Nature* 12 (2001): 351–81.

tures, we knew on some level that they could not have known these things about the millions of Jews living across the Mediterranean and West Asia. They could not have had a representative basis for most of their claims. Their confident statements and descriptions combine characteristic overconfidence with the impulse of literate elites to institute the normative, that is, to say what they think Jews ought to think and do. I believe that the blending of the normative and the descriptive characterizes much scholarship on ancient Jews and Christians. It would be one way to explain statements such as the ones from a recent volume on Sanders's notion of common Judaism:

> Jews from Italy, Egypt, Mesopotamia, and Jerusalem believed that God had given the Torah to Israel, rescued Israel from Egyptian bondage, and would in some fashion free Israel in the future again. Included within common Judaism was a commitment to the sacrificial system, the temple, observance of Sabbath and festivals, circumcision, purity, dietary laws, and charity. True, profound differences existed. While Torah, synagogue and purity were important for all Jews, their language, function and significance differed.[12]

Similarly, Roman Catholics revere the authority of the Vatican, obey the church's teachings, do not practice artificial birth control and share a common religiosity around the world.

In sociology, history, and other areas, the new approach to similarity and difference, to stability and change, across groups and cultures has usually been some form of network theory and network analysis.[13] In anthropology and areas of cognitive studies, epidemiological methods that chart the acquisition, transmission, and distribution of knowledge (beliefs/cognitions/discursive artifacts) and practices have become important and are often used together with the network theory.[14] Scholars using the two different but related approaches typically find vastly varied distributions of knowledge across putative cultures with a central role for networks of experts and connections or lack of connections by degree to these networks by nonexpert populations.

Atran and Medin with their research teams, for instance, spent two decades studying the Itza' Maya, the Spanish-speaking Ladinos, and the immigrant Q'eqchi' Maya of the great Petén forest region, populations much less socially and culturally complex than the Jews of the ancient

---

12. Wayne O. McCready and Adele Reinhartz, "Introduction: Common Judaism and Diversity within Judaism," in *Common Judaism: Explorations in Second-Temple Judaism*, ed. Wayne O. McCready and Adele Reinhartz (Minneapolis: Fortress, 2008), 219–20.

13. An excellent introduction is Charles Kadushin, *Understanding Social Networks: Theories, Concepts and Findings* (New York: Oxford University Press, 2012).

14. Ibid., 136–61; Atran and Medin, *Native Mind*, 209–23.

Mediterranean.[15] Their focus was on folkbiological knowledge of these populations who have depended on agroforestry for livelihoods and culture. They consciously began with conceptions not too different from "common Judaism" in identifying the peoples above as cultures. But the researchers crafted various experiments with the goal of understanding the distribution of knowledge/practices, the relations of such distributions to social formations, and the causal processes involved.

One method was to use the Cultural Consensus Model, a means for understanding similarity and differences within and across groups.[16] The teams adapted this model, long tested and widely used in the social sciences, to the conditions of the Maya and Ladinos. Even when this tool discovers a high degree of concordance about a cultural item, the approach does not assume uniformity but measures degrees of competence relative to the overall consensus. The ability to competently "perform" the cultural item can vary greatly. But the CCM does not reveal how cultural transmission works, nor does it map transmission and variation. Toward the latter two goals, Atran and Medin began with the intuitive and folk idea of the three cultural groups to identify "representative" individuals to query from each. But then they employed a technique that did not assume the three groups in intuitive ways. For each group they chose six men and six women who were not related by marriage or kinship. Each person was asked to name the seven people outside their own households who were most important to their lives and to rank these according to degree of importance. The informants were also asked to describe the ways that the people in this social network were important to their lives. Some time later, the same people were asked to prioritize the seven people "to whom you would turn if there were something you did not understand and wanted to find out about the forest/fishing/hunting." And they were asked about kinds of information that they would seek from such experts. The investigators then used the snowball method. They asked the same questions of the first and last persons named by the informants and so on. The result was two networks, one of social relations and the other of experts with connections or lack thereof between the two at various points.

The resulting "maps" rendered visually as three-dimensional topologies showed the pathways along which knowledge was stored, lost, distributed, and assimilated. Sometimes subgroups appeared clearly as in the genders among the Ladinos. Itza' were the least interconnected socially, but had the most prestigious experts. The Ladinos and their expert networks depended on the Itza' experts for the flow of knowledge that clearly clustered in densities among both with certain individuals (experts) being

15. Atran and Medin, *Native Mind*, 161–223, and bibliography.

16. Ibid., 57–60.

hyperconncted in some network. One surprise came from finding that the Itza' and Ladinos, but not the Q'eqchi' networks, even cultures, were blending, especially due to the Ladino dependence on Itza experts. The authors write, "Analyses within the Itza' sample revealed little residual agreement and this agreement was inconsistent across different tasks. In no case could we discern relationships between residual agreement and social or expert network proximity."[17] The Ladinos showed the most convergence of social and expert networks. The Q'eqchi' are highly corporate and focused on local social relations with few native experts. The Itza' example shows that experts can form rather autonomous networks of experts who only indirectly affect the broader culture. In this case, there were two distinct networks of forest/farming/hunting/fishing experts.

A great deal more could be said about Atran and Medin's study and their work with similar methods in Wisconsin and the Middle East. The point here is only to illustrate how their and other network and epidemiological research shows that our intuitive ideas about the commonality and boundedness of cultures and groups ranges from misleading to radically distorted. Vital takeaways appear from this sort of analysis, lessons for how historians should envision the culture(s) of the ancient Judeans and their religion. For one, there can be broad agreement across a population of individuals who identify most strongly with X group (e.g., ethnicity) and the widely shared belief that the X group shares beliefs and practices, when in reality there are actually enormous differences and a lack of commonality in many areas. Asking a Josephus, a Philo, or a rabbi, self-identifying experts on Judeans, needs the caution that they often likely project themselves onto Jews in general. Indeed, the belief in the belief of essential commonality may be the most widely shared thing by many groups. Second and related to that belief is often the conviction or assumption that one ought to be subject to the norms of the group. But then there are wide differences in what individuals consider the norms to be and how to interpret and apply them. Additionally, differences between conviction and practice are always present. Of course, a unified, comprehensive, and centralized educational, legal, and court system with experts serving the entire population and efficient methods of enforcement would somewhat limit diversity regarding norms in some areas of social life. But ancient Jewish populations did not have such a system. Nor did any other ancient people.

In addition to the histories of the populations/cultures, the environments, the cultural materials and social organization, such network approaches consider the constraints of broadly human mental organization to be a key factor. An enormous amount of progress has been made in

---

17. Atran and Medin, *Native Mind*, 213.

cognitive studies that can only be ignored at the risk of making the humanities esoteric clubs.[18] Structuralists and poststructuralists widely believed that the only significant mental organization was that binary oppositions structured language/thought. In a 1974, interview, Claude Lévi Strauss, who largely invented this view, said when asked about these binary operators, "When I started there was still no science of mind. Saussure, Marx, Mauss, and music were my guides. Since then things have changed. Psychology now has something to say."[19] That this binary view of language still has great influence in parts of the humanities, but none in linguistics, witnesses to the former's sometimes extreme isolation from the rest of the academy. All ideas and theories about how cultural items are produced, transmitted, and acquired presuppose some view of mind, even if it is the modernist idea of mind as the blank slate and culture sponge.

Atran and Medin follow the consensus in cognitive studies. Their focus was the distribution and variation of folkbiological knowledge. Anthropologists have studied folk biology in numerous cultures and found a common cognitive structure. Independently, psychologists have found the basic categories upon which folk biology depends in young children. For example, "From an early age, it appears, humans cannot help but conceive of any object they see in the world as either being or not being an animal, and there is evidence for an early distinction between plants and nonliving things."[20] With such categories go certain inferential structures. They are not dogmatic about this evidence for an evolutionarily developed mind but follow consensus in thinking it strong enough to use it as a hypothesis, a part of possible explanations. It certainly has vastly more evidence than the blank-slate model. The nested taxonomy found in all cultures so far studied is kingdoms, life forms, and generic species. Where great culturally specific variation occurs is within species. There can also be intermediate taxa between life form and generic species. For the Maya and Ladinos, these categories are hugely important and shape their central practices, the way they relate to their environment and their everyday reasoning. Three elements come together to shape their reasoning and knowledge: mind, culture, and the causal relation to the natural environment. The latter, for example, actually perceiving and relating to trees, is required to activate mental structures and cultural knowledge. Atran and Medin write, "We suggest that much of the cultural transmission and stabilization of ideas ... involves the communication of poor, fragmentary, and elliptical bits of information that manage to trigger rich and prior

---

18. Edward Slingerland, *What Science Offers the Humanities: Integrating Body and Culture* (Cambridge: Cambridge University Press, 2008).

19. Atran and Medin, *Native Mind*, 283 n. 4.

20. Ibid., 29.

inferential structure."[21] My attempt to theorize aspects of Mediterranean religion also attempts to relate tendencies of mind, culture, and environment.

Those who work in ancient Judaism and other religion in the Roman Empire, cannot do the kind of work that Atran and Medin do, but historians can be sensitive both in the critical use of the evidence and in theory formation. I have argued that religion across the ancient Mediterranean shows common patterns so that it can with profit be analyzed into modes.[22] These modes partly follow from an understanding of the ancient cultures as distributed, even if we possess the evidence to see only fragments of social and cultural networks. My approach attempts to chart ways that religious practices clustered and interconnected or did not connect in the larger social landscape, partly based on propensities demonstrated by cognitive scientists.

I hold that ancient Judaism fits the pattern. On this view, all the cultures of the ancient Mediterranean were in many ways distinctive, but none was unique, incomparable. But the notion of common Judaism illustrates a wider approach in which Judaism is so different that it only marginally counts as Mediterranean religion, if at all. Sanders, I think, did not mean "common Judaism" in this way, but it has clearly come to be so used. I aim to outline briefly my analytical theory of Mediterranean religion and then notice the ways in which common Judaism does and does not fit. The first mode upon which the second and third depend is the religion of everyday social exchange. The second is civic religion and the third the religion of literate religious experts whose writing and literate practices exhibit an important degree of cultural autonomy.[23] The religion of the ancient Judeans drew on all three modes with variation across time and place. Charting those variations, including the relative dominance of particular modes, can be an aid to critical historiography.

Culturally, religion in Judea during the three centuries before the Roman destruction of the temple in Jerusalem was a combination of broader Mediterranean and West Asian religion with certain peculiarities. My three modes are analytically useful precisely because they fit broadly

---

21. Ibid., 158.

22. Stanley K. Stowers, "The Religion of Plant and Animal Offerings versus the Religion of Meanings, Essences and Textual Mysteries," in *Ancient Mediterranean Sacrifice: Images, Acts, Meanings*, ed. Jennifer Wright Knust and Zsuzsanna Várhelyi (New York: Oxford University Press, 2011), 35–56; Stowers, "Why Expert versus Non-Expert Is Not Elite versus Popular Religion: The Case of the Third Century," in *Religious Competition in the Greco-Roman World*, ed. Nathaniel P. DesRosiers and Lily C. Vuong, WGRWSup 10 (Atlanta, GA: SBL Press, 2016), 139–53.

23. I also argue for a fourth mode that seems to become clearly visible only in the third and fourth centries CE in my "Religion of Plant and Animal Offerings," 49-51; "Why Expert versus Non-Expert," 139-53.

across the cultures. This allows one to then study the interaction of the three modes that characterizes the religion of the various cultures. The method, I believe, encourages thinking about the religion of ancient Jews without constructing "Judaism" according to an always-essential exceptionalism.

For cognitive and social reasons that I cannot discuss here, the mode I call the religion of everyday social exchange (RESE) is most basic.[24] It can and frequently does exist even apart from the other two modes, but those modes base themselves partly on the RESE. The religion of everyday social exchange features approachable deities and similar nonevident beings (NEBS) such as "local" gods, the beloved dead, the familiar heavenly bodies, angels, demons, ghosts, divinized humans, and spirits. Participants imagine that these beings affect their lives in personally relevant and tangible ways such as giving humans the offspring of animals and plants, children, weather, health and illness, help and hindrance with the contingencies of life and so on. Humans in turn want to build and maintain positive long-term relationships with the beings most relevant to their lives. Some ancients thought of these beings as serving under a high ruling god, but that did not eliminate the everyday and local qualities. Any approach that treats the ancients as if they lived in our disenchanted world with a distant theoretical god rather than in a day-to-day environment filled with palpably present, but normally unseen, beings is, I would argue, a massive distortion.

People intuitively deemed it right and fair to give gifts and thanks for the benefits that the gods and NEBS gave to them. Practices of gift giving (e.g., food and drink, incense, votives, praising by prayer, recognitions at meals, blessings, lamp lightings, dedications, hymns, flowers, bathing and dressing up, various entertainments and aesthetic presentations) and reciprocity were central, but also healings, exorcism, divinatory practices, apotropaic objects, and so on. Some beings were imagined to have characters making them not so positively approachable and were placated or avoided. The religion characterized farms, neighborhoods, households, and their members. The optimal social and physical environment for the religion was agricultural, although extension of the practices to contexts of nonagricultural production was normal. At least 90 percent of Jews lived in agricultural contexts.[25]

The most important practices of the RESE were gift giving to gods/NEBS, divinatory practices in which gods/NEBS provide information in the form of signs and traces, and prayer. In this mode people were typically modest about their knowledge of gods/NEBS, their intentions and

24. Ibid.

25. A figure widely held for the whole empire; see, e.g., Catherine Hezser, *Jewish Literacy in Roman Palestine*, TSAJ 81 (Tübingen: Mohr Siebeck, 2001), 34–35, 476.

moods. This contrasts sharply with the claims to certain knowledge of the second mode of literate religious experts who often appealed to texts. Individuals, however, can participate in more than one mode, especially in different situations and contexts, without noticing contradictions. Psychologists find such compartmentalizing to be a central characteristic of the mind.[26]

What I call "civic religion," a mode closely related in many ways to the RESE, featured practices from the RESE (e.g., prayer, offerings, divination) but reshaped and organized them together with other practices according to civic interests and principles of civic power. I use "civic" as a catchall for the religion of cities, kingdoms, and similar social formations based on the prestige and power of hereditary classes. As a central underlying principle of this mode, some portion of the aristocracy claimed the authority to represent the whole ethnic/citizen population before the gods. So, for instance, a small number of Roman elite ran the "religion of Rome." Most of the population never directly participated in these "official" cultic activities. These elite conducted the rites on behalf of Rome and its entire population. The masses mostly carried on the practices of everyday social exchange, but the RESE especially came together with civic religion in offerings made by individuals and families in temples and in festivals. In rituals, festivals, and many other practices celebrating cities, kingdoms, and ethnicities, civic religion was the major producer of ideologies that justified and naturalized the rule of aristocracies and that aimed to crystallize the solidarity of the relevant populations.

One misunderstanding needs correction, namely, the notion that the RESE somehow originated from the elites and civic religion. The opposite is the case. Offerings, honoring, seeking signs, prayer, apotropaic practices, and many other things were historically ubiquitous before and apart from cities, and in remote rural populations, and the practices were continued even when cities were destroyed and populations displaced. One does not need a temple in order to pray or to have a dream from a god, or to offer a bit of bread to a NEB. This misunderstanding seems to arise partly from the fact that people did, even in the RESE, often shape prayers or images of gods and many other things after dominant civic models. Further, civic religion entered homes and lives by way of civic festivals and so on. But the fundamental practices of civic religion came to it from the RESE in the sense that it was more fundamental because highly intuitive.

Civic religion tended to make these practices splendid and big. Offerings were made in temples, not houses, streets, or fields, and were set apart by being purified from birth, death and other pollutions of the

---

26. Andrew Shtulman, *Scienceblind: Why Our Intuitive Theories about the World Are So Often Wrong* (New York: Basic Books, 2017).

house and family. Civic religion thus created a structural hierarchy over the religion of families and households. The impurity of the latter was a threat to the presence of the gods on behalf of the city. Altars, libation cups, and divine representations often became magnificent works of art. Prayers and hymns became literary pieces to glorify the city, the ethnicity, their histories, their futures, and the city's gods. Festivals, although often agricultural, also celebrated the same, drawing in the participation of the nonelite on a large scale. Civic religion shared long-term generalized reciprocity with the RESE. The gods of the city gave benefits to the city and its inhabitants. The city in turn gave back gifts to thank and honor the gods. Events and circumstances might be read as signs of stresses and fractures in the city's relationship with a god. Thus, rites to reestablish the relationship and thus reinstitute normal exchange might be carried out. Both modes related to the gods/NEBS within an environment that was largely agricultural with fruit, grain, and animal offerings from the land. By contrast, the religion of literate experts focused on intellectual practices using the technologies of books, writing, and the exchange of writings by way of specialized social networks usually flourished in an urban context.

The religions that we moderns know and often simply equate with religion and "religions" (e.g., Judaism, Christianity, Islam, Buddhism) are institutionalized social formations dominated by experts in texts. The number of truly literate people—enough to write or competently interpret complex texts—was very small in antiquity. Yet nearly all of our conceptions of Judean, Christian, and other religion in antiquity come from this tiny but powerful caste to whom we owe the literary sources. The distinctive outlook from the vantage of the world viewed through texts and textual traditions counts as a third mode of religiosity. By contrast, the person who offered a sacrificial animal did not need to be literate, and the practice did not depend on writings and their interpretation. Any illiterate farmer could offer cakes, light a lamp, beg a NEB for help or sacrifice. While the religion of the expert might include the practices of the RESE, might even be parasitic upon them, the religion of the specialist could not exist without writings, high literacy, and networks of literate production and exchange.

Any textual practice, including writing, reading, and interpretive practices, introduces modifications into, or over against, the RESE and civic religion.[27] To write about the rules for sacrificing in a temple is not the same thing as sacrificing in the temple. Scholars have constantly confused creating norms via writing or stipulating a meaning with the practices themselves. The kinds of novelty and degree of difference from the RESE and civic religion varied greatly among kinds of experts in the field.

---

27. Jack Goody, *The Logic of Writing and the Organization of Society* (Cambridge: Cambridge University Press, 1986).

The field had many subfields, for example, ethnic, social rank, educational opportunity. It also had two poles in dynamic and creative tension.[28] On one side, experts were not very entrepreneurial and depended on kings, aristocratic priesthoods, patrons, and the scribal needs of aristocrats. Experts on this pole tended to intellectualize and textualize religious practice, but they took a much less radical position than those on the other pole. By the second century CE, for instance, the dominant Greek and Latin rhetorical culture, the orators and writers of the "Second Sophistic," and certain kinds of philosophers represented the dominant pole. An opposing pole of certain sorts of philosophers, Christian teachers, and many sorts of independent operators defined themselves in opposition to the dominant pole. The traditionally legitimized experts, in their view, had been corrupted by the money, power, and prestige that belonged to the dominant pole. Truth, morals, and the legitimate interpretation of texts could only come from those who had not sold out, those who showed disinterest in money, wealth, and power and who possessed a greater devotion, more faithful to the texts and their truth. The Gospels use John the Baptist as this sort of ideal semi-autonomous pole figure to legitimate Jesus, and Josephus claims that he spent three years with a similar figure named Banus (*Vita* 2). Experts on this side had no position by inheritance or bestowal and could gain legitimacy only by outdoing other specialists in displaying disinterest and novelty. Unsurprisingly, these entrepreneurs often criticized reciprocity as the mode of relating to the gods. The gods could not be bribed, bargained with, or honored with petty offerings. The gods wanted obedience, true beliefs, and the right inner formation of individuals.

This breezy review of the modes—distinctive concentrations of linked practices partly shaped by cognitive constraints—of ancient Mediterranean religiosity has aimed to bring standard conceptions of Judaism, including common Judaism, into comparison. In addition to an exaggerated commonness across this "Judaism," other broad features stand out. These include the supposed highly literate and intellectualistc nature of the common religion and its relative lack of reciprocal exchange with the divine, especially apart from the temples. The religion of mundane social exchange is nearly invisible in those accounts of Judaism. More broadly, while localism—local variation and the importance of place/local context—was central for all other peoples, for Jews, on this view, common

28. My account is indebted to Pierre Bourdieu; see the following works by Bourdieu: "Genesis and Structure of the Religious Field," *Comparative Social Research* 13 (1991): 1–44; "Legitimation and Structured Interests in Weber's Sociology of Religion," in *Max Weber: Rationality and Modernity*, ed. Scott Lash and Sam Whimster (London: Allen & Unwin, 1987), 119–36; *The Rules of Art: Genesis and Structure of the Literary Field* (Cambridge: Polity Press, 1996); *The Field of Cultural Production* (New York: Columbia University Press, 1993).

translocal belief and practice greatly eclipsed localism. If this picture is true, ancient Judaism was radically different from the religion of everyone else in the Mediterranean and West Asia. It looked more like the religion that has emerged in Western modernity. Of course this exceptionalism is precisely what scholars often want and frequently explain as due to the unique "Bible-based" monotheism of Judaism. Jews, unlike everyone else, did not live in a world filled with all sorts of unseen beings in a grand hierarchy reaching up to the highest god. Unlike all other peoples, Jews lived in a disenchanted world.

Looking more closely at the three interacting modes of religion from the vantage of its theorization, the most important civic religion seems to have organized itself around the temples, especially the Jerusalem temple, of course, but also the temple at Leontopolis. The most important aristocracy for civic religion was the priesthood, which formed a hierarchy from the highly aristocratic down to common priests who were only marginally so based on certain inherited prerogatives. The nonpriestly aristocracies of Judea and surrounding areas were similar to others in West Asia and the Eastern Mediterranean. A key difference from most areas, except Egypt, appears in that the hereditary priesthood monopolized the claim to religiously represent the whole ethnic population. The hereditary priesthood and temple in Jerusalem, with its legally mandated economic support from Judean agriculture, largely but not totally preempted the typical kind of economic basis for civic religion in the benefactions of the aristocracies. *The nonpriestly aristocracy could not claim to represent the whole "citizen" body before God.*

Reciprocity with the Judean supreme god was also the central principle in Judean civic religion and its RESE. This claim runs counter to the way that scholarship has often represented the temple as either an occasion for "the life of Torah" or a system for dealing with human sinfulness.[29] The goal of generalized reciprocal exchange in both the RESE and civic religion is the maintenance of long-term relationships with the divine. Typically, a calendar of festivals was also central to the Jerusalem temple's civic religion.

This reciprocity has been demonstrated for the representations of "the temple" and offerings in the Hebrew Bible and Jewish writings in the extremely important scholarship of Aaron Glaim.[30] He shows how the language of the Hebrew Bible regarding offerings is steeped in conceptions of gift giving and reciprocity. The so-called critique of sacrifice in the prophets gets an analysis showing that the real concern is the issue of God not accepting gifts when the relationship has been violated, a classic

29. Sanders, *Judaism: Practice and Belief*, 92–118, and variously through 119–278.

30. Aaron Glaim, "Reciprocity, Sacrifice, and Salvation in Judean Religion at the Turn of the Era" (PhD diss., Brown University, 2013).

topic in ancient reciprocity.[31] Chapters demonstrate that Philo, the Dead Sea Scrolls, Paul, and early rabbinic texts also have the temple and offerings focused on reciprocity, even though each of these adds certain twists characteristic of literate experts and sometimes criticisms of reciprocity as a mode of relating to God.

The religion of literate experts, with its intensively interactive field of exchange, was clearly important during the so called Second Temple period. The tiny but sometimes influential schools of Sadducees, Pharisees, Essenes, and probably others formed associations of literate experts. Josephus for good reasons found these people to resemble Greek philosophers. At times, schools and individuals were part of the heteronomos pole of the field as they advised rulers, the high priesthood, and the aristocracy. At other times, individuals and groups were rather freelance actors working to create their own legitimacy among interested fellows and followers. The authors of the Dead Sea Scrolls worked, it seems, in semi-autonomy over against the pole legitimated by established institutions. Josephus and other sources mention many teachers and figures working out of Judean literate exchange. Heidi Wendt has shown that freelance Jewish religious experts in such things as divinatory practices, healing, purifications, and so on were so common across the eastern Roman Empire that "a Judean" like "a Persian (*magus, magos*)," "a Chaldean," and sometimes "an Egyptian" became the designation for a type of ethnically coded religious expert (e.g., "I sought out a Judean/Chaldean/Magus to discover what the god wanted me to do").[32] Many of these were literate experts. Roman authorities were anxious about such freelance operators. Wendt shows that the supposed expulsions of the Jewish population from Rome were actually expulsions of such Jewish experts (i.e., "x expelled the Jews.").

The role of the priesthood in literate exchange presents enormous questions with quite limited evidence, but at least the more well-to-do portions of the priesthood were moderately to highly literate and the temple itself probably a center of textual learning. The presence of the temple and the importance of the sacred writings created conditions for freelance

---

31. Glaim's important point about God or gods not accepting sacrifice needs to be stressed but has been misrepresented by Joshua Schwartz (review of *Sacrifice, Cult, and Atonement in Early Judaism and Christianity: Constituents and Critique*, ed. Henrietta L. Wiley and Christian A. Eberhart, *Review of Biblical Literature* [http://www.bookreviews.org] (2018). Contra Schwartz, Glaim does not argue that the Hebrew Bible represents anger as the cause of God's refusal. Rather, the refusal is basic to gift giving in relationships. Imagine a person whose best friend began an affair with his wife that ruined their relationship. If the offending former friend appeared unrepentant with a gift as if nothing were wrong, the offended friend would not accept it as if the relationship was just fine. This is the idea in the misnamed prophetic critique of sacrifice.

32. Heidi Wendt, *At the Temple Gates: The Religion of Freelance Experts in the Early Roman Empire* (New York: Oxford University Press, 2016).

teachers and schools to thrive and compete in Jerusalem. This temple culture participated in broader West Asian patterns. Of course, outside of Roman Palestine, we have much evidence for an extensive and vigorous Judean subfield of literate production and exchange in Greek that largely follows Hellenistic literary traditions and practices with expertise often focused on Greek translations of the Scriptures.

The extant sources for Judaism in this period focus overwhelmingly on the civic religion of the temple and the religion of literate experts. Likewise, the interests of the Mishnah and the Talmuds is in the civic religion of the temple and their own tradition of literate exchange focused on law. Even when they write about what happens in households, their interest is in legal interpretation and in extending the practices of civic religion with its focus on celebrating the people and on corporate ethnicizing social thought into the domestic sphere (e.g., marriage, purity, festivals, prayer, funerary practices). Interestingly, the RESE does show up here and there in all of these sources but usually when, as for example, Josephus narrates events from everyday life and in "historical" storytelling. In a well-known instance, he touts his own divinatory skills and their role in the war with Rome (*War* 4.629). It would be foolish to believe that he never practiced divinatory skills in order to make decisions about his own life. Literate experts with their central interest in determining what should be normative, also frequently mention current everyday practice when they criticize certain practices from the RESE.[33] They otherwise have little or no interest in it. Josephus and Philo occupy most of their pages with anachronistic writing about representations of the temple, laws, and narratives from Scripture as if they represented the way things were for Judeans in their contemporary world. Rabbis often write as if the system of the temple and its law were still in effect. Just as contemporary Greek and Latin writers looked back to the writings, culture, and language of classical Athens as if these were contemporary, Jewish writers lived out fantasies about the presence of the Judean past in a rarified world of literary and legal imagination. The religion of everyday social exchange was too basic, too contemporary, and too commonplace to even be noticed by our sources except incidentally.

But incidental mentions in writings and nonliterary sources provide much evidence. Briefly, I will discuss some of the practices. But to grasp the RESE, these practices must be understood as part of a local and everyday world full of gods and nonevident beings with whom people imagined living day to day and who were often treated with patterns of long-term exchange. That exchange most centrally concerns coping with life, family, farm, and shop.

---

33. A theme of Wendt (*At the Temple Gates*).

It has been standard in the past to describe Jews in this period as "strict monotheists." Scholars should now know better, and I will not reargue the matter.[34] I have no doubt that Jews generally revered their "one god" as the legitimate object of honor and as the high god. Psychologists who have studied cognition about gods have shown quite convincingly that, even though literate authorities tend to advocate nonintuitive ideas about God, as, for example, that God is transcendent, omniscient, omnipresent, three in one, and an incomparable cosmic emperor (the idea seen widely in ancient Jewish writings), people not highly educated into such conceptions use intuitive thinking that treats even God as local, limited by time and space and possessing humanlike desires, emotions, and moods.[35] Thus, God can be treated as fitting the conditions of the RESE. Further, scholars have, I believe, argued convincingly that most Jews in this period believed in the existence of the gods of the other peoples.[36] They also often thought that these gods should be respected, but perhaps not honored in any way comparable to the Judean god. Certainly there were exclusive conditions and rules for God's temple in Jerusalem. In reality there were probably a range of ways to react to and relate to these gods, frequently considered to have been appointed by God.

The instance of a certain Moschos, who identified himself as a Jew in an inscription, is probably not atypical. In a dream, two local gods had commanded him to free his slave. With the inscription in the god's temple, Moschos announces his obedience to the divine commands. As Paula Fredriksen writes, there is no reason to conclude that Moschos saw his acts as diminishing his dedication to the Judean god.[37] Other nonliterary evidence shows Jews practicing this local religiosity of negotiating everyday life lived in an environment filled with gods and other nonevident beings.

Karen Stern has shown how scholars have resorted to the most specious sorts of arguments in attempts to render those who wrote graffiti at a temple of Pan either subtle monotheists or bad Jews.[38] But two of

---

34. I have treated this issue in "Gods, Monotheism and Ancient Mediterranean Religion," Culture and Religion of the Ancient Mediterranean Seminar, Brown University, 11 September 2012.

35. Justin L. Barrett and Frank C. Keil, "Conceptualizing a Non-Natural Entity: Anthropomorphism in God Concepts," *Cognitive Psychology* 31 (1996): 219–47; Justin L. Barrett, "Theological Correctness: Cognitive Constraints and the Study of Religion," *MTSR* 11 (1999): 325–39.

36. Paula Fredriksen, *Paul: The Pagan's Apostle* (New Haven: Yale University Press, 2017), 32–60.

37. Ibid., 46.

38. Karen Stern, "Vandals or Pilgrims? Jews, Travel Culture, and Devotional Practice in the Pan Temple of Egyptian El-Kanais," in *"The One Who Sows Bountifully": Essays in Honor of Stanley K. Stowers*, ed. Caroline Johnson Hodge et al., BJS 356 (Providence, RI: Brown Judaic Studies, 2013), 177–88.

the inscriptions and perhaps a third witness to the intuitive localism and sense of gratitude that belongs to the RESE. She shows that, without thinking that they would be considered heretics, they proudly proclaimed themselves Jews/Judeans as they thanked and blessed this god of the desert for safe travel. What was their theology? We know little except that they presumably honored the Judean god and did not see thanking Pan for help in his territory as a conflict. In all likelihood the epistemological modesty of the RESE is at play here. Unlike the literate experts, they had little or no investment in beliefs that were not practical and palpable.

Even Second Isaiah, supposedly the pinnacle of an evolution to monotheism, has God with hosts in heaven and a sea god enemy.[39] Yahweh was not without other gods, even if literate authorities sometimes told people that God was in a class of his own, and the other "gods" should not be called gods. In addition to many texts in the Hebrew Bible, Philo speaks of gods and certain of the Dead Sea Scrolls describe the gods in God's heavenly court or temple.[40] In Josephus's story (*War* 6.300) about the withdrawal of divine presence from the temple, a voice "as of an assembled army, says 'we are leaving here.'" Josephus has no problem with the idea of an army of NEBS stationed in the temple of the one God. Through Christianity we have inherited a dualistic picture of God with his administering angels opposed to Satan with his demons. But the very numerous types of NEBS that work for God and those who were seen as ambiguous, unreliable, or even in rebellion were not divided into two neat camps during the Second Temple period.[41]

The experts whose imaginations thrived from texts with long interpretive traditions and the elite of civic religion who were entirely focused on the divine histories of specific sites tell stories and execute rites with definite claims about identified deities involved. But in everyday life it was not like that. In Greek religion one has the same contrast between the writers, official civic contexts, and everyday life. In the latter, one rarely called on or identified a particular god or NEB. Rather, one spoke of "whichever divine one" or "the one who hears" or "the divine one."[42] One might get a message in a dream or see a sign in the sky or role dice for a yes or no from a NEB, and yet not know—at least not for certain—which god or NEB sent the message; yet one could be confident that it was a divine message. A person might call on "all who watch over us" or "God

39. Saul M. Olyan, "Is Isaiah 40–55 Really Monotheistic?," *JANER* 12 (2012): 190–201.

40. See esp. the *Songs of the Sabbath Sacrifice* (4Q400–407); Philo, e.g., *Spec.* 1.13–15.

41. Emma J. Wasserman, *Apocalypse as Holy War: Divine Politics and Polemics in the Letters of Paul*, AYBRL (New Haven: Yale University Press, 2018). Wasserman's book is the definitive account of the way that Jewish writers depict God as emperor of a divine hierarchy with many low-level gods and NEBS.

42. Robert Parker, *Polytheism and Society at Athens* (Oxford: Oxford University Press, 2005), 140.

and all his holy ones" or to the "spirit who has helped us in the past." These ambiguous identifications are not the kinds of things that a Philo, a Josephus, or a rabbi would write in books, but they were probably typical of the RESE. The farmer who acted so modestly at home would likely feel not the slightest contradiction in reciting lines about the God of Abraham, Isaac, and Jacob in a civic context, but might hesitate at the presumption that the one God who ruled the universe had spoken directly to him about his crops.

Finally, one needs to mention the famous dead, the beloved dead, and the annoying dead. Across the Mediterranean, massive evidence exists, especially archeological, for exchange with the beloved dead in varied forms and with varieties of local practices that range from leaving clear evidence to activities that would barely leave traces.[43] This topic for Judaism usually gets confounded and bypassed in that scholars slide quickly into discussions of "Jewish beliefs about the afterlife." Evidence shows that, even when people officially held some view such as that the dead became stars or slept until the resurrection, they also thought the dead had an existence near their tombs. In such cases, the cognitively intuitive overpowers the cognitively difficult on a practical level. The husband felt the presence of his wife at the tomb.

If a Judean woman's recently deceased husband appeared to her in a dream and warned her about an impending business transaction and complained of his thirst, I suspect that many, especially among the 90-plus percent who lived in rural areas with little influence from literate experts, would have gone to the tomb and poured a libation. She probably would have considered the exchange a private matter between her and her husband. There would be no trace in the archaeological record. The reaction to the text where Tobit exhorts (4:17), "Pour your bread and your wine on the tomb of the righteous, and do not give to sinners," should not be reflection on some rabbinic prohibition with the conclusion that the text depicts a practice that good Jews did not countenance. Rather, such gift giving and exchange with the dead was probably so basic and common that the author of Tobit mentioned it without a thought. To interaction with the beloved dead one can add interaction with the famous dead such as the patriarchs, whose supposed tombs had vigorous histories. Scholars have detailed the evidence for such tomb practices and, as Pieter W. van der Horst emphasizes, it is likely that Jews went to these tombs for "intercessions and miracles."[44] Finally, similar arguments could be made about the unhappy dead and practices to keep them away.

---

43. For bibliography, see Hans-Josef Klauck, *The Religious Context of Early Christianity* (Minneapolis: Fortress, 2003), 68–69, 70.

44. Pieter W. van der Horst, *Japheth in the Tents of Shem: Studies on Jewish Hellenism in Antiquity*, CBET 32 (Leuven: Peeters, 2002), 119–37; Jack N. Lightstone, *The Commerce of*

Very quickly I will mention some practices important to the RESE for which we have evidence. One of the most important with much evidence in this period is votive offerings.[45] Here one requests some help or benefit from a god or NEB and promises to give a gift in return when the boon has been granted. We hear in the literary sources and inscriptions especially about votive gifts given to the temple in Jerusalem, sometimes to synagogues and in public settings, but surely more important to everyday religion were small and more private exchanges. A mother promises to light lamps in honor of the deity for a month if her son recovers from an illness. A farmer whose crop was bountiful pours wine at the base of a tree where he had heard words of encouragement in the wind. Afterwards he might repeat yearly.

Other practices include healing via a god or NEB, local funerary rites, hundreds of forms of divination, oaths calling on the divine as witness, exorcisms, apotropaic practices (e.g., against evil eye, spirits of illness, ghosts), numerous methods of honoring (or gift giving to) NEBS in homes and fields, prayers focused on local needs, some household purifications, incantations, spells, and various local (rather than civic) rites of life passage and life crisis.[46] Against common assumptions, some evidence also exists for domestic sacrifice of animals.[47] For Jews, it seems, keeping the Sabbath was both very widespread and a practice of the RESE that also linked to civic religion and the book religion of literate experts. The book of Tobit attempts to depict episodes from everyday life, albeit in a theologically correct way. Tobit exhibits numerous links to literature and literate traditions of religious experts. The angel Raphael receives one of Tobit's prayers and heals Tobit and Sarah. Disguised as a human, the angel also provides practical strategic information to Tobit (about Sarah). The narrative has a focus on issues regarding family and marriage. In one episode, a carefully prepared fried fish liver becomes an apotropaic device that

---

the Sacred: Mediation of the Divine among Jews of the Greco-Roman World, new ed. (New York: Columbia University Press, 2006), 41–62.

45. Michael L. Satlow, "Giving for a Return: Jewish Votive Offerings in Late Antiquity," in *Religion and the Self in Antiquity*, ed. David Brakke, Michael L. Satlow, and Steven Weitzman (Bloomington: Indiana University Press, 2005), 91–108; Anne Katrine de Hemmer Gudme, *Before the God in This Place for Good Remembrance: A Comparative Analysis of the Aramaic Votive Inscriptions from Mount Gerizim*, BZAW 441 (Berlin: de Gruyter, 2013).

46. Jennifer Eyl, "'By the Power of Signs and Wonders': Paul, Divinatory Practices, and Symbolic Capital" (PhD diss., Brown University, 2011); Veit Rosenberger, ed., *Divination in the ancient World: Religious Options and the Individual* (Stuttgart: Franz Steiner, 2013); Gideon Bohak, *Ancient Jewish Magic: A History* (Cambridge: Cambridge University Press, 2008); John H. Elliott, *Beware the Evil Eye: The Evil Eye in the Bible and the Ancient World* (Eugene, OR: Cascade, 2016).

47. Jordon Rosenblum, "Home Is Where the Hearth Is? A Consideration of Jewish Household Sacrifice in Antiquity," in Johnson Hodge et al, *"One Who Sows Bountifully,"* 153–63.

drives demons away. In spite of the highly intellectualized theological framework, one can see in Tobit practices of the RESE. Raphael's role is of special interest. We know from both literary and nonliterary sources that Raphael gained a reputation as a healing NEB, a kind of Judean Asclepius. He was also one who received prayers from individuals and carried them to God, at least in literary sources. Some texts from everyday religiosity address prayers to him.[48]

A more thorough discussion of the modes would emphasize their often dynamic and interactive character, including the ways that the RESE interacted with the festivals and offering practices of the temples. So-called voluntary associations would also play a major role in the picture of Jewish religion. Many pre-70 CE synagogues or houses of prayer would fall into this category. Such associations typically involved extensions of the RESE and were often organized on the basis of households or neighborhoods or trades with local religious practices relevant to these social sites.[49] But such extensions, especially away from Judea, through patronage by local elites and as community centers, connected the mode of everyday religion with civic religion. Literate experts also sometimes had roles as teachers, leaders, and advisors in connection with associations and in that way Judean associations had some interaction with the field of literate experts.

"Common Judaism" and most consensus models of "Second Temple Judaism," generalize the religion of literate experts. It seems that nothing is more central to the imagination of this supposed religiosity than the image of millions of Jews across the Mediterranean pouring into synagogues to study Torah and pray each Sabbath. I obviously cannot critique this model here, but at least I can point to its role in creating the idea of a religion in which the central practices of its individuals focused on deep knowledge of extensive writings and the idea that these writings minutely governed the lives of individuals. It seems to me that such a religion would require an enormous infrastructure for which we lack evidence. It would require nearly universal literacy, individual possession of the writings, and an educational system in which the probably millions of Jews spent large amounts of time on a regular basis hearing instruction from experts. Literate experts would have to have been in charge of the religion of Judeans, as they apparently were centuries later. Instead of the handful of remains of Jewish meeting places, we would be finding many thousands of buildings able to accommodate numbers very much larger

---

48. "Raphael," *Dictionary of Deities and Demons in the Bible*, ed. Karel van der Toorn, Bob Becking, and Pieter W. Van Der Horst, 2nd ed. (Leiden: Brill, 1999), 688.

49. I argue this case in an unpubished paper, "Locating the Religion of Associations."

than in most finds.[50] Again this sounds suspiciously like conditions that emerged only in Western modernity with the printing press, universal education, and so on. Of all the ethnicities in the Mediterranean, only the Jews would not possess a basic religiosity that focused on interaction and exchange with gods and NEBS who inhabited the local environments of their lives.

Studies of modern religious populations where universal literacy prevails, where the religious institutions have large comprehensive educational systems (e.g., catechism through university), and where building infrastructures that can accommodate a large proportion of their population at any one time do not lend credibility to the idea that even such conditions would succeed. A large-scale survey in 2010 by the Pew Research Center showed that Protestants and Roman Catholics had little knowledge of basic information about the Bible and their own traditions.[51] Other studies have consistently yielded similar results. It is not that these people have not heard the correct teachings. Rather, just as the cognitive scientists predict, some religious representations rely on intuitive mental tools and others use nonintuitive mechanisms supporting teachings only acquired and held with great difficulty and needing constant reinforcement. Perhaps the religiosity of the Jews of the centuries before 70 CE was unique and shared little with everyone else in their world, but the modes of religiosity based on clusters of practices and cognitive propensities should at least raise questions about models like common Judaism.

---

50. Chad Scott Spiegel, *Ancient Synagogue Seating Capacities: Methodology, Analysis and Limits*, TSAJ 149 (Tübingen: Mohr Siebeck, 2012).

51. See DesRosiers and Vuong, *Religious Competition*, 133–36, for references and discussion.

Paul's Scriptures

MICHAEL L. SATLOW
Brown University

Again and again throughout his long and distinguished scholarly career, Shaye has been drawn to the issue of identity. Was Herod a Jew? Was Timothy? Who exactly was a Jew—or should we say "Judean"?—and how would anyone know? How do you become a Jew? Can a woman be a Jew? If you were a Jew, whom could you marry? If you were a Jew, what kind of Jew were you? Would you have followed the teachings of the rabbis? If you were a "rabbi," would you have followed the teachings of the rabbis? I do not think that it would be an exaggeration to say that in the aggregate the answers that Shaye has offered in these explorations have fundamentally transformed the field, leading to a much more nuanced and fluid sense of religious, ethnic, and gender identity in antiquity.[1] This paper, offered as a token tribute to my teacher, draws on Shaye's insights as they might apply to the apostle Paul.[2]

There is now a broad scholarly consensus that Paul was a Jew and should be considered within a Jewish "matrix" or "context."[3] Recog-

1. See the bibliography of Shaye's works in this volume. Several of these contributions are collected in his books, *The Beginnings of Jewishness: Boundaries, Varieties, Uncertainties*, HCS 31 (Berkeley: University of California Press, 1999), and *Why Aren't Jewish Women Circumcised? Gender and Covenant in Judaism* (Berkeley: University of California Press, 2005). Earlier relevant bibliography can be found in those works as well.

2. Shaye has touched on Paul in several articles but has not dealt directly with Paul's identity. For a recent essay, see his "From Permission to Prohibition: Paul and the Early Church on Mixed Marriage," in *Paul's Jewish Matrix*, ed. Thomas G. Casey and Justin Taylor (Mahwah, NJ: Paulist, 2011), 259–91.

3. This reevaluation of Paul is seen to have begun with E. P. Sanders, *Paul and Palestinian Judaism: A Comparison of Patterns of Religion* (Philadelphia: Fortress, 1977), although the phrase "the new perspective" was coined by James D. G. Dunn. This approach has generally been focused on explicating Paul's theology rather than the social-historical concerns focused on here. For an assessment of the new perspective, see Dunn, *The New Perspective on Paul*, WUNT 185 (Tübingen: Mohr Siebeck, 2004), 1–110. See more recently Mark D. Nanos and Magnus Zetterholm, eds., *Paul within Judaism: Restoring the First-Century Context to the Apostle* (Minneapolis: Fortress, 2015); Gabriele Boccaccini and Carlos A. Segovia, eds., *Paul the Jew: Rereading the Apostle as a Figure of Second Temple Judaism* (Minneapolis: Fortress, 2016).

nizing, however, that one cannot speak of a single "Jewish" context in antiquity, scholars have readily understood Paul as a "Hellenistic Jew" and have attempted to situate his writings among those of other Hellenistic Jews, even while recognizing that the line between "hellenized" and "Judean" can be quite blurry, if it exists at all.[4] Often following the narrative of Acts, Paul is cast as a fundamentally hellenized diaspora Jew whose first language was Greek; who received an education typical of a Jewish middle-class boy; and who then honed some of his scriptural skills as a Pharisee in Jerusalem before his sudden acceptance of Christ. Even the ordinarily skeptical E. P. Sanders almost takes for granted the fact that Paul received a solid childhood education in the Greek Bible, primarily in the diaspora.[5]

In this essay I will develop an alternative hypothesis: that Paul was a Jerusalem Jew, most likely from a relatively affluent family, who in all likelihood spent few if any of his formative years outside of Judea; whose native language was Aramaic but who received a Greek education in Jerusalem, like many affluent Jerusalem Jews; and who developed an increasing understanding of and appreciation for the Septuagint during his travels to diaspora Jewish communities. The narrative in Acts, that is, is fundamentally incorrect. In the latter part of the essay I suggest that this narrative helps us to see Paul's practice of scriptural citation in a new light.

A Jew from Jerusalem

The argument that Paul was born in the diaspora rests primarily on two pieces of evidence. The first is Acts 22:3, which purportedly cites Paul as saying, "I am a Jew, born in Tarsus in Cilicia, but brought up in this city at the feet of Gamaliel, educated strictly according to our ancestral law...."[6] The second piece of evidence is Paul's unquestionable command of Greek

---

See also Alan Segal, *Paul the Convert: The Apostolate and Apostasy of Saul the Pharisee* (New Haven: Yale University Press, 1990); and Daniel Boyarin, *A Radical Jew: Paul and the Politics of Identity*, Contraversions 1 (Berkeley: University of California Press, 1994).

4. For a theoretical reflection on this point, see Anders Klostergaard Petersen, "Paul the Jew was also Paul the Hellenist," in Boccaccini and Segovia, *Paul the Jew*, 273–99.

5. E. P. Sanders, "Paul's Jewish Matrix: The Scope and Nature of the Contributions," in Casey and Taylor, *Paul's Jewish Matrix*, 51–73. For a more nuanced example of this narrative, see James Albert Harrill, *Paul the Apostle: His Life and Legacy in Their Roman Context* (Cambridge: Cambridge University Press, 2012), 23–45.

6. Translations of all New Testament texts are from the New Revised Standard Version. See also Acts 21:39, in which Paul also states that he is from Tarsus, and 9:11, in which Paul is identified as being from Tarsus. According to Acts 9:30 and 11:25 Paul's missionizing began in Tarsus.

and, especially, the broad correspondence between his scriptural citations and the extant text of the Septuagint. The problem, though, is that Paul himself never mentions that he was born outside of Judea and there is no reason to think that he could not have learned Greek in Jerusalem.

Previous scholars have noted these issues. W. C. van Unnik, for example, concludes that, "although Paul was born in Tarsus, it was in Jerusalem that he received his upbringing in the parental home just as it was in Jerusalem that he received his later schooling for the rabbinate."[7] Martin Hengel cautiously subscribes to van Unnik's reconstruction, although Paul's masterly command of Greek suggests that we should not "see him as the purest kind of Palestinian Jew."[8]

In his letters, Paul offers few autobiographical details confined to four short passages:

Romans 11:1: "I myself am an Israelite, a descendant of Abraham, a member of the tribe of Benjamin."

2 Corinthians 11:22: "Are they Hebrews? So am I. Are they Israelites? So am I. Are they descendants of Abraham? So am I."

Galatians 1:13–14: "You have heard, no doubt, of my earlier life in Judaism. I was violently persecuting the church of God and was trying to destroy it. [14]I advanced in Judaism beyond many among my people of the same age, for I was far more zealous for the traditions of my ancestors."

Philippians 3:4–6: "If anyone else has reason to be confident in the flesh, I have more: [5]circumcised on the eighth day, a member of the people of Israel, of the tribe of Benjamin, a Hebrew born of Hebrews; as to the law, a Pharisee; [6]as to zeal, a persecutor of the church; as to righteousness under the law, blameless."

In these passages, Paul consistently (although not explicitly in Galatians) identifies himself as an Israelite or "from the people [*genos*] Israel." That claim and that of being from the "seed" (*sperma*) of Abraham are relatively clear: his parents identified as Israelites or, as we might say, "Jews,"

---

7. W. C. van Unnik, *Tarsus or Jerusalem, the City of Paul's Youth* (London: Epworth, 1962), 52. See also his rejoinder to critique in van Unnik, "Once Again: Tarsus or Jerusalem," in *Sparsa Collecta: The Collected Essays of W. C. van Unnik*, 4 vols., NovTSup 29, 30, 31, 156 (Leiden: Brill, 1973–2014), 1:321–27.

8. Martin Hengel, "The Pre-Christian Paul," in *The Jews among Pagans and Christians*, ed. Judith Lieu, John North, and Tessa Rajak (London: Routledge, 1992), 29–52, here 38. See also Jörg Frey, "The Jewishness of Paul," in *Paul: Life, Setting, Work, Letters*, ed. Oda Wischmeyer (London: T&T Clark, 2012), 56–95. Frey (58–60) reviews the evidence and then somewhat arbitrarily decides that Paul was shaped to at least some degree in Tarsus.

although he never explicitly uses that word. Three other claims that he makes in these passages deserve more attention.

First is his claim to be a "Hebrew" (2 Cor 11:22; Phil 3:5). It is possible that this is a mere rhetorical flourish that simply reiterates Paul's claim to be an Israelite.[9] The problem, however, is that it seems repetitive: Why emphasize both that he is a Hebrew and an Israelite? It is possible that Paul here means to refer to his linguistic ability. If this is the case, then Paul would be claiming here that he was a native speaker of "Hebrew," that is, the Aramaic vernacular, and the child of native Aramaic speakers.[10]

Second, Paul claims to be, "according to the law, a Pharisee" (Phil 3:5). Much has been made of this claim (e.g., van Unnik's conclusion that it was "schooling for the rabbinate"), and a full discussion is beyond the scope of this paper. I wish only, then, to make the following observations:

1. There are no Pharisees attested outside of Judea and Galilee.[11] Paul must have affiliated with the Pharisees when he was actually there.
2. Paul never claims simply "to be" a Pharisee; only to be one who was a Pharisee "according to the law" (*kata nomon*). The phrase appears in the New Testament only in Hebrews, where it can mean "according to Scripture" (10:8) or "established custom" (7:16; 8:4). Josephus's use of the term is similarly ambiguous (*Ant.* 1.338; 3.264, 4.139, 19.293). Since in this context Paul cannot mean "according to Scripture" he must mean something like, "according to established customs, I follow the Pharisees."
3. If this is indeed Paul's meaning, then his affiliation with the Pharisees might be similar to that of Josephus. Josephus states that in his nineteenth year he ἠρξάμην τε πολιτεύεσθαι τῇ Φαρισαίων αἱρέσει κατακολουθῶν (*Life* 12). Steve Mason renders it, "I began to involve myself in public life, deferring to the philosophical school of the Pharisees."[12] That is, Josephus is claiming not to have any particularly deep knowledge of the Pharisees but that he acted in public according to their norms. The language is different, but Paul might be claiming something similar.

---

9. John Reumann, *Philippians: A New Translation with Introduction and Commentary*, AYB 33B (2008; repr., New Haven: Yale University Press, 2012), 483.

10. See the discussion in Richard I. Pervo, *Acts: A Commentary*, Hermeneia (Minneapolis: Fortress, 2009), 154, who nevertheless arbitrarily asserts that the passages in Paul denote "a proud self-designation" rather than a statement of language. On the use of "Hebrew" to mean "Aramaic," see Martin Hengel, *Between Jesus and Paul: Studies in the History of Earliest Christianity* (Philadelphia: Fortress, 1983), 9–11. Jerome reports a tradition that Paul's parents were from Giscala in Judea and had been driven into exile in Tarsus, thus making him a "Hebrew of Hebrews" (*Comm. Phlm* 23 [PL 26:633]).

11. The arguments to the contrary are weak and refuted by Hengel, "The Pre-Christian Paul," 36-7.

12. Steve Mason, *The Life of Josephus*, FJTC 9 (Leiden: Brill, 2001), 20–21.

4. The "Pharisaic curriculum," often mentioned by scholars, is far from certain. There is almost no evidence, in fact, that Pharisees were fluent in *written* Scripture; they are most known for their facility with ancestral traditions or laws.[13] Paul himself suggests this in Gal 1:14: he is devoted to τῶν πατρικῶν μου παραδόσεων. The term *paradosis* is often associated with the Pharisees but is not explicitly connected to Scripture.[14]

Paul's evocation of the Pharisees, then, may reveal little; it is certainly no proof of his deep learning in Scripture. Instead, it could well point to his attraction to the religious customs and norms distinctive to the Pharisees of Judea. Whether he studied with the Pharisees (as asserted in Acts) or in some sociological sense was a "member" (whatever that may have meant in this context) of a Pharisaic group is impossible to determine from his words alone.

Third, in Rom 11:1 and Phil 3:5 Paul provides the detail that he is from the tribe of Benjamin. These references have typically been taken in one of two ways. Either they reveal that he has a tradition in his family that he truly descends from the tribe of Benjamin, thus enhancing his prestige, or that the notice is meant to evoke a web of biblical texts that would similarly enhance his prestige. There is, however, a third possibility that scholars have previously overlooked. Paul might be using the term as a toponym, meant to indicate that he was from the area of the tribe of Benjamin, to wit, Jerusalem.

The evidence on all sides of this question is sparse, so before reviewing the literary references to tribal identity in contemporaneous Jewish literature it is worth noting the evidence that we do not have and the possible significance of its absence. To my knowledge, there is not a single extant Jewish inscription or documentary papyrus, from any time in antiquity, that notes tribal affiliation.[15] Priestly (and Levitical) status was noted, but no other tribes—including that of Benjamin—can be found in the very places that one might most expect relatively affluent Jews to note their prestigious lineages. Among the Dead Sea Scrolls, outside of scriptural and archaizing texts there is no mention of tribal identity aside from priests and Levites.[16] Josephus too never assigns a tribal identity (except

13. For examples, see Josephus, *War* 2.162; *Ant.* 13.297.

14. Albert I. Baumgarten, "The Pharisaic Paradosis," *HTR* 80 (1987): 63–77.

15. The one possible exception to this is on a single Aramaic ostracon from Maresha that mentions someone from what appears to read מטה דאין. This appears to be a non-Jewish clan identification. See Esther Eshel, "Inscriptions in Hebrew, Aramaic and Phoenician Script," in *Maresha Excavations Final Report*, ed. Amos Kloner et al., IAA Reports 45 (Jerusalem: Israel Antiquities Authority, 2010), 3:35–88, no. 63.

16. Mention of the tribes in biblical contexts can be found in, for example, 4Q365, 4Q377, and 11QTemple.

for priests) to any non-biblical personage. The tribe of Judah would be evoked by later writers to signal Davidic and messianic descent, but this is largely artificial.[17] This lack of evidence suggests that tribal identity had long ceased to be important to Jews in the Second Temple period.

Use of tribal identity as a toponym is uncommon but not unattested in ancient Jewish literature. Jeremiah 8:16 mentions "Dan" as a place rather than a lineage. Among the literary references to tribes in Jewish literature from the Second Temple period, one uses tribal language as a toponym. According to 2 Macc 3:4, Simon, a priest, is identified as "from the tribe of Benjamin" according to the LXX. Simon, however, is, as we know from the narrative of 2 Maccabees, a priest; he cannot be from the lineage of Benjamin.[18] It would make perfect sense, then, that here the reference to the tribe of Benjamin means only that he is from the area of Benjamin. The Latin and Armenian translations, however, state instead that Simon is from the clan of Bilgah. These appear to me to be ancient corrections of the *lectio difficilor* in the LXX, but it is hard to know for certain.

Although the general concept of "the twelve tribes" is mentioned throughout the New Testament and other Jewish texts, identifications of individuals as members of specific tribes are rare.[19] When they do appear, according to Carey Moore, they "represented the general area from which these people descended rather than their actual tribe or bloodlines."[20] The identification of Judith and her family with the tribe of Simon (Jdt 6:15; 8:2; 9:2) may have a geographical resonance, although the evocation of Simon (and his slaughter of his sister Dinah's rapists) is literarily powerful. In Tobit, for the story to work Tobit must be identified with a northern tribe (Tob 1:4), in this case Naphtali. In the New Testament, aside from Paul only Anna the prophet is associated with a tribe, Asher (Luke 2:36). The reason for this identification is not entirely clear. Anna is described as having lived much of her life as widow in the Jerusalem temple, so it is possible that the tribal identification is meant to convey that she originally came from some distance to take up residence.[21]

Paul's own brief words, then, are at least consistent with the following reconstruction. Paul was born in or around Jerusalem, or at least

17. Although he exaggerates the role of tribal lineage, still useful is the survey of Joachim Jeremias, *Jerusalem in the Time of Jesus: An Investigation into Economic and Social Conditions during the New Testament Period* (Philadelphia: Fortress, 1969), 275–77.

18. On the different witnesses and the argument for this reading (if not interpretation), see Daniel R. Schwartz, *2 Maccabees*, CEJL (Berlin: de Gruyter, 2008), 95–96, 189–90.

19. The "twelve tribes" are mentioned, for example, in Matt 19:28; Luke 22:30; Ecclus 44:23.

20. Carey A. Moore, *Judith: A New Translation with Introduction and Commentary*, AB 40B (Garden City, NY: Doubleday, 1964), 168.

21. Cf. Joseph A. Fitzmyer, *The Gospel according to Luke (I–IX): Introduction, Translation, and Notes*, AB 28 (Garden City, NY: Doubleday, 1981), 431.

lived there from a young enough age that he could consider himself a "Benjaminite." His native language was Aramaic. He did not necessarily receive any formal education in the reading of Scriptures (in any language) while in Jerusalem, although he was attracted to Pharisaic practices and perhaps even studied those practices (not necessarily in written form) with teachers.

We might also make two further inferences. Paul knew Greek, not only the language but also literary and rhetorical techniques. It is thus likely that he learned it as part of his upbringing. If so, then it is also likely that Paul's parents were affluent enough to hire good tutors for him. Despite being a speaker of Aramaic, Paul's formal education would then (at least partially) have been in Greek.

Just because this reconstruction is possible does not, of course, make it correct. It differs from the picture presented in Acts. It also faces the test of plausibility: Can we imagine Jerusalem producing a Jew like Paul? I will here briefly sketch the evidence that suggests that this reconstruction is plausible, and perhaps even likely.

Despite attempts to argue for the extensive use of Hebrew, even multilingualism, in Jerusalem in the first century CE, the linguistic environment of Jerusalem was dominated by Aramaic.[22] Those in the upper classes would also receive tutoring in Greek. Knowledge of Hebrew, though, appears to have been scarce and was perhaps largely confined to scribes.[23] This is why, outside of the products of the nationalistic uprising of 66–73 CE, there is very little evidence for the everyday use of Hebrew in the first century CE; almost all extant inscriptions are in Aramaic and Greek. Nor would we expect any deep knowledge of Scripture, even among the (non-

---

22. The issue of the "language environment" of first-century Jerusalem has been extensively discussed and is still unsettled. A recent volume pushes toward seeing Hebrew as far more commonly known than has often been thought; see Randall Buth and R.Steven Notley, eds., *The Language Environment of First Century Judaea: Jerusalem Studies in the Synoptic Gospels*, JCP 26 (Leiden: Brill, 2014).

23. A fuller defense of this position is beyond the scope of this paper, but see the inscriptions collected in *CIIP*, vol. 1. Nearly all of the nonfunerary inscriptions are in Greek and Aramaic. The funerary inscriptions tend to be very short (often just a name), and it is sometimes unclear if those that use Semitic scripts are more "Hebrew" or "Aramaic." See also Jonathan J. Price and Haggai Misgav, "Jewish Inscriptions and Their Use," in *The Literature of the Sages*, ed. Shmuel Safrai, 2 vols., CRINT 2.3 (Assen: Van Gorcum; Minneapolis: Fortress, 2006), 2:461–83. A linguistic analysis of these inscriptions can be found in Guido Baltes, "The Use of Hebrew and Aramaic in Epigraphic Sources of the New Testament Era," in Buth and Notley, *Language Environment*, 35–65. While Baltes arrives at the conclusion that Hebrew was widely used, his own data suggest the opposite: by his counting, only 67 of the 726 inscriptions contained in *CIIP* and that date between 100 BCE and 70 CE contain "primary" or "secondary" language markers in Hebrew (51). See the analysis in Hanan Eshel, "The Hebrew Language in Economic Documents," in *Jesus' Last Week*, ed. R. Steven Notley, Marc Turnage, and Brian Becker, JCP 11, Jerusalem Studies in the Synoptic Gospels 1 (Leiden: Brill, 2006), 245–58, who sees very little Hebrew in these documents.

scribal) upper classes. There were synagogues in first-century Jerusalem (although we cannot gauge how popular they were) that might have read Scripture in an ad hoc fashion, perhaps accompanied by oral (probably on the fly) Aramaic translations.[24]

To test this reconstruction of Paul as a plausible product of first-century Jerusalem one can compare him to Josephus. Josephus was just a little younger than Paul. His first language was Aramaic. He learned enough Greek to compose literary works in it, even if he had assistants and was embarrassed by his pronunciation (*C. Ap.* 1.50; *A.J.* 20.262–265). His knowledge of Hebrew appears to have been shaky.[25] He claims to have followed the customs of the Pharisees and to have been expert at ancestral practices, but if his earliest extant work, the *Bellum judaicum*, is representative, then he had little familiarity with written Scripture while in Jerusalem.[26] His first intensive engagement with written Scripture was in its Greek translation when he arrived in Rome.[27]

Paul's trajectory was similar to Josephus's. Paul demonstrates a deep command of Scripture. It was a command, though, picked up outside of Judea and in Greek translation. This reconstruction of Paul's education helps to solve some puzzles about his use of Scripture that have long troubled scholars.

The Evidence of Acts

The reconstruction that I have offered above is in conflict with Acts. Yet a careful, if brief, examination of Acts can explain how and why the author of Acts made the mistakes he (?) did.

Paul claims in Acts 22:3 to have been educated "at the feet of Gamaliel." There is, of course, no way to know if this was actually true. However, it suspiciously embellishes Paul's own claim in his letters to have

---

24. Lee I. Levine, *The Ancient Synagogue: The First Thousand Years* (New Haven: Yale University Press, 2000), 42–73. In the rabbinic period, there are already relatively well-established Aramaic translations of Scripture, Targum Onkelos and Targum Jonathan. The rabbis knew of or developed the ritual of translating regular scriptural readings into Aramaic. According to Levine, "*Targumim* were in use in the first century, first and foremost (although by no means exclusively) in a synagogue setting" (150). Much more than this is hard to know for certain.

25. Tessa Rajak neatly summarizes the issue but presses the evidence too hard when she concludes that Josephus was "totally at home in both" Aramaic and Hebrew (*Josephus, the Historian and His Society*, 2nd ed., Classical Life and Letters (London: Duckworth, 2002), 230–32, here 232). Josephus's demonstrated knowledge of Hebrew is far more limited.

26. Seth Schwartz, *Josephus and Judean Politics*, Columbia Studies in the Classical Tradition 18 (Leiden: Brill, 299), 25: "there is little evidence he knew the biblical texts at all."

27. Michael Tuval, *From Jerusalem Priest to Roman Jew: On Josephus and the Paradigms of Ancient Judaism*, WUNT 357 (Tübingen: Mohr Siebeck, 2013), 260–74.

followed the Pharisees; Acts turns him into a disciple of the very paragon of what was imagined to be a Pharisee, Gamaliel himself.[28] One would expect no less from Paul's most admiring biographer.

The second suspicious claim in Acts 22:3 is that Paul was born in Tarsus (found also in 21:39). Van Unnik reads the entire verse as factually correct but conventional, indicating that Paul may have been born in Tarsus but for all intents and purposes he was really from Jerusalem. While this may be correct (and would comport with my reconstruction), it may well be possible to go further. This claim might instead be invented by the author, a literary flourish that advances the plot. "Purely redactional," in the words of Hans Conzelmann.[29]

Why would the author of Acts make up a birthplace for Paul? It is clear from other places in Acts that the author does not hesitate to create details when it suits his purpose.[30] In the context of the narrative of Paul's capture in Acts 21–22, his assertion of birth outside of Egypt, and as a Greek speaker, is crucial. But I think that it is also possible that the author of Acts, or his source, genuinely and sincerely inferred that Paul was from the Greek world. If the author was familiar with Paul's letters, he would know that Paul had a good knowledge of Greek and Greek Scripture and traveled throughout the eastern Mediterranean basin. Many decades removed from a Jerusalem long since destroyed, the author of Acts would not have known about what was typical in first-century Jerusalem. So the author made a speculation that was reasonable enough to have shaped scholarly discourse to this day.

A couple of other details in Acts can be similarly explained. Acts gives Paul the name Saul (7:58; 13:9). Whether or not the author was working from a source (perhaps even an urban legend), it fits nicely with 13:21, where Paul evokes "Saul, son of Kish, from the tribe of Benjamin." Paul/Saul share a lineage, perhaps in parallel to Christ/David (13:22). The author of Acts might have extrapolated from Paul's own assertion that he is a Benjaminite, understanding the claim to be one of lineage rather than geography.

Also from Acts comes the idea that Paul was middle or lower class. In Acts 18:3 and 20:34, he claims to work with his own hands as a tent-maker.

---

28. See also Acts 23:6 and 26:5, in which Paul emphasizes his actual identity as a Pharisee.

29. Hans Conzelmann, *Acts of the Apostles: A Commentary on Acts of the Apostles*, Hermeneia (Philadelphia: Fortress, 1987), 183.

30. The highly improbably temple-visiting, Scripture-reading Ethiopian eunuch met by a disappearing apostle (Acts 8:26–40) comes to mind as an example. This raises the interconnected questions of the genre and accuracy of Acts. Pervo reviews these positions, particularly whether Acts is to be considered historiography or fiction (*Acts*, 14–18). Below I develop a limited argument that Acts can be understood as (flawed) historiography, but my larger argument would work just as well if it was a fiction.

This claim might have been derived from 1 Cor 9:6–7, 15, in which he claims to earn a living with his own hands. Such an upbringing, however, pointedly raises the question of how he would have acquired command of literary Greek.

Acts says nothing that directly contradicts Paul's own words in the letters about his upbringing, but instead, as we might expect in such a literary treatment, expands and embellishes them.[31] If this is right, then Acts offers us a lively and smart reconstruction based on evidence similar to our own but does not possess independent facts that throw any light on Paul's upbringing.

Paul and Scripture

Understanding Paul not as a native Greek-speaking "Hellenistic Jew" but as a native Aramaic-speaking Jerusalem Jew with a Greek education that would have been typical of upper classes has several potential consequences. Here I will look at just one example of how it might help us to better understand Paul, namely, his use of Scripture.

Paul cites Scripture frequently, if unevenly, in his extant letters. In what follows, I discuss three dimensions of Paul's use of Scripture: (1) the language and version that he uses; (2) the parts of Jewish Scripture that he favored; and (3) the purpose to which he puts these citations. It is important to note that my discussion is limited to Paul's direct citations, almost always introduced with a citation formula. "Echoes" and "resonances" of Scripture in Paul's writings might be useful for gauging Paul's general familiarity with the contents of Scripture, but they are not as useful in answering the specific questions that interest us here.[32]

Language. Modern scholars have reached a near-consensus that Paul predominantly referenced the Septuagint in his letters.[33] Yet this conclusion is not without the major problem that, while many of Paul's citations of earlier Scripture seem to come directly from the Septuagint, most of his citations do not.

---

31. This, however, is not an argument that Acts is correct. The conflation of historiography and accuracy is present in Stanley E. Porter, "The Portrait of Paul in Acts," in *The Blackwell Companion to Paul*, ed. Stephen Westerholm (Chichester: Wiley-Blackwell, 2011), 124–38.

32. See Richard B. Hays, *Echoes of Scripture in the Letters of Paul* (New Haven: Yale University Press, 1989). For a trenchant critique of this approach, see Paul Foster, "Echoes without Resonance: Critiquing Certain Aspects of Recent Scholarly Trends in the Study of the Jewish Scriptures in the New Testament," *JSNT* 38 (2015): 96–111.

33. The classic study, still relied on by modern scholars, is E. Kautzsch, *De Veteris Testamenti locis a Paulo Apostolo allegatis* (Leipzig: Metzger & Wittig, 1869).

Table 1 is a tabulation of the data provided by E. Earle Ellis. Ellis categorized each of Paul's citations according to one of five categories:

1. In agreement with the LXX and the Hebrew
2. In agreement with the LXX against the Hebrew
3. In agreement with the Hebrew against the LXX
4. At variance with the LXX and the Hebrew where they agree
5. At variance with the LXX and the Hebrew where they vary[34]

Some of the verses fall betwixt and between his schema, so he additionally notes that some verses within each of these categories show only a "slight variation" or a "difference in word order." For the purpose of these statistics I have amalgamated these into their respective categories. Note that 1 Thessalonians, Philemon, and Philippians do not contain any direct citations.[35]

Table 1
Number (Percent of Total Number in Epistle) of Scriptural Citations in Each of Ellis's Categories[36]

	1	2	3	4	5
Romans	12 (22%)	9 (15%)	1(2%)	11 (21%)	21 (39%)
1 Corinthians	2 (13%)	2 (13%)	1 (6%)	4 (25%)	7 (33%)
2 Corinthians	3 (38%)	0	1 (13%)	3 (38%)	1 (13%)
Galatians	2 (20%)	2 (20%)	0	3 (30%)	3 (30%)

As this table illustrates, on a simple quantitative level it is hard to make a compelling case that Paul was primarily reliant on the Septuagint. In no single letter does Paul use the Septuagint version for more than 40% (categories 1 and 2 combined) of his citations. Instead, the bulk of his citations fall into categories 4 and 5, unattested text forms.

Previous scholars have proposed, very roughly, three kinds of accounts that reconcile these data with the thesis that Paul relied pri-

34. E. Earle Ellis, *Paul's Use of the Old Testament* (Edinburgh: Oliver & Boyd, 1957), 150.

35. The lack of citations from these three letters might be due to their short length. I suspect, though, that the absence is better explained by their intended audiences. These three letters are all addressed to gentile congregations (rather than what I believe to be the "mixed" congregations in Rome, Corinth, and Galatia) who Paul (probably rightly) assumed would not understand scriptural citations. I do not deal with Paul's audience here, but it must be taken seriously. See Christopher D. Stanley, *Arguing with Scripture: The Rhetoric of Quotations in the Letters of Paul* (New York: T&T Clark, 2004), 38–61; Stanley, "Paul's Use of Scripture: Why Audience Matters," in *As It Is Written: Studying Paul's Use of Scripture*, ed. Stanley E. Porter and Christopher D. Stanley, SBLSymS 50 (Atlanta: Society of Biblical Literature, 2008), 125–55.

36. Due to amalgamations and some other anomalies in determining proper categories, the rows do not always add up to 100%.

marily on the Septuagint.[37] The first kind of account ascribes divergences from the Septuagint (or some related Greek translation) to Paul's "faulty" memory. This account assumes that Paul learned written Scripture carefully, in both Greek and Hebrew, but when he was writing he tended to quote from memory rather than look each citation up in multiple, bulky scrolls.[38] The second kind of account, focusing on the fact that some of Paul's citations are in verbatim agreement with extant written versions of Scripture (and more specifically the Septuagint), claims that Paul must have been using a written source. In this account, the written base text might be a version (or versions) of Scripture that is no longer extant, or a collection of relevant verses that perhaps were modified during the course of composition or transmission.[39] The third kind of account posits that Paul knew the "correct" version of Scripture but changed it when it suited his needs.

These explanations have many variations. For the purposes of this paper it is worth noting a few insights on which previous research largely agrees:

1. Paul had access to and consulted the Septuagint. We do not know whether, when writing his letters, he consulted a full version (which, given the difficulty of finding specific references in bulky scrolls seems unlikely) or a smaller, previously compiled collection of quotations (which he himself may have created), but at least at times he probably consulted written versions for his quotations.[40]
2. Paul did not know Hebrew, or at least did not know Hebrew Scripture well. There is no real evidence that Paul consulted or knew a

37. The problem and different proposed solutions are nicely summarized by Christopher D. Stanley, *Paul and the Language of Scripture: Citation Technique in the Pauline Epistles and Contemporary Literature*, SNTSMS 74 (Cambridge: Cambridge University Press, 1992), 3–30.

38. Ellis, *Paul's Use of the Old Testament*, 14–15; see Stanley, *Paul and the Language of Scripture*, 16–17, for a quick summary and rejection of the argument. In his argument against Paul's citation of Scripture by memory, Stanley raises the legitimate point that in some cases Paul almost surely does cite from a written text (17 n. 49). Below I propose a model that addresses this objection.

39. For a summary of this argument (even if he largely rejects it), see R. Timothy McLay, *The Use of the Septuagint in New Testament Research* (Grand Rapids: Eerdmans, 2003), 25–30. See also Stanley, *Paul and the Language of Scripture*, 67–79; Stanley E. Porter, "Paul and His Bible: His Education and Access to the Scriptures of Israel," in Porter and Stanley, *As It Is Written*, 97–124, here 122.

40. For a review of the arguments for Paul's primary use of the Septuagint, see Ellis, *Paul's Use of the Old Testament*, 11–13, and the literature cited there. For the idea that Paul compiled his own notebook of scriptural citations from which he later drew for his letters, see Dietrich-Alex Koch, *Die Schrift als Zeuge des Evangeliums: Untersuchungen zur Verwendung und zum Verständnis der Schrift bei Paulus*, BHT 69 (Tübingen: Mohr, 1986), 92–101; Stanley, *Paul and the Language of Scripture*, 69–74.

written version of Hebrew Scripture (as strikingly seen in the verses that fall into category 3 in table 1). This reinforces the hypothesis offered above that Paul did not know Hebrew, or at least was unacquainted with or unable to access Jewish Scriptures in Hebrew.

3. Paul might have known some Scripture in Aramaic translation. Crawford H. Toy proposed that Paul knew Scripture through its oral Aramaic recitation, perhaps in the synagogue.[41] This proposal has not gained wide acceptance, but it also has not been refuted.[42]
4. Paul cited versions of Scripture that were favorable for the points that he was trying to make with them.[43] This does not necessarily mean that Paul knew all of the different versions of a citation and deliberately chose the one that he could best use, even altering it when necessary. At the same time, Paul has a pattern of departing from the Septuagint's version when another version better serves his purposes.

Before showing how the reconstruction above helps to synthesize these data, we should consider the scriptural books with which Paul is acquainted.

Paul's Scriptural Books. Paul cites from fifteen of the books that comprise our Hebrew Bible. His citation sources, by letter, are found in table 2.

Table 2
Sources of Paul's Direct Citations[44]

	Gn	Ex	Lv	Dt	1 Kgs	2 Kgs	Isa	Jer	Hos	Joel	Hab	Mal	Ps	Prov	Job
Rom	5	3	2	6	2		16		2	1	1	1	13	1	
1 Cor	2	1		1			5	1	1				3		1
2 Cor		1	1	1		1	2	1					1		
Gal	4		2	2			1				1				
Totals	11	5	5	10	2	1	24	2	3	1	2	1	17	1	1

Paul cites most from Isaiah, Psalms, Genesis, Deuteronomy, Exodus, Leviticus, and Hosea, with only one or two citations from the remaining books.[45] To a large degree this mirrors the pattern found in the Dead Sea

41. Crawford Howell Toy, *Quotations in the New Testament* (New York: Scribner's Sons, 1884), xiv–xviii.

42. Stanley, *Paul and the Language of Scripture*, 13, 22–24.

43. Ibid., 348–50.

44. Data follow Ellis, *Paul's Use of the Old Testament*, 150–52.

45. This largely mirrors quotation patterns elsewhere in the New Testament (with the exception of Leviticus). See David McCalman Turpie, *New Testament View of the Old: A Contribution to Biblical Introduction and Exegesis* (London: Hodder & Stoughton, 1872), 7.

Scrolls. The most frequently found manuscripts of "biblical" texts among the Dead Sea Scrolls were, in order, Psalms, Deuteronomy, Genesis, Isaiah, Exodus, and Leviticus.[46] Paul's choice of books thus appears to align with those most popular in Palestine.

One explanation for this correspondence between the most popular biblical books at Qumran and the books that Paul most frequently cites is that these books were the most well-known books in Judea, where Paul was first exposed to Scripture. Paul gravitated to citing the texts that he did not only because they served his purpose but also because he knew them better than other biblical texts. It is worth noting that in more or less contemporaneous texts produced by diaspora Jews, far less use is made of books such as Isaiah and Psalms. Paul's older contemporary Philo, for example, was hardly interested in non-pentateuchal biblical texts.[47]

Before continuing this line of inquiry, it is worth considering the evidence in a more fine-grained way. There is very little evidence that Paul knew the Bible in Hebrew at all; the citations that Ellis assigns to category 3 (following the Hebrew against the Septuagint) come from Job (two) and Exodus (one), and don't tell us very much. There may not yet have been a Greek translation of Job, and the difference of wording of the citation of Exodus between the MT and the Septuagint makes no difference to Paul's argument (2 Cor 8:15, citing Exod 16:18). There is substantially more evidence, as noted above, that Paul knew Scripture in Greek. Below is the list of books, by letter, that Paul cites that Ellis assigns to category 2 (following the Septuagint against the Hebrew).

Table 3
Books Cited That Fall into Ellis's Category 2

Romans	Genesis, Psalms, Isaiah, Proverbs, Deuteronomy
1 Corinthians	Genesis, Isaiah
2 Corinthians	0
Galatians	Genesis, Isaiah

This could be seen as a challenge to the hypothesis that Paul's knowledge of biblical books popular in Judea derived from his upbringing there. That is, if this were the case, we would expect that citations from these books in particular would follow the Hebrew—why, instead, do they fol-

46. James VanderKam and Peter Flint, eds., *The Meaning of the Dead Sea Scrolls: Their Significance for Understanding the Bible, Judaism, Jesus, and Christianity* (San Francisco: HarperCollins, 2002), 150.

47. Gregory E. Sterling, "The Interpreter of Moses: Philo of Alexandria and the Biblical Text," in *A Companion to Biblical Interpretation in Early Judaism*, ed. Matthias Henze (Grand Rapids: Eerdmans, 2012), 415–35, here 424–27.

low the Septuagint? Here, though, the picture is actually more muddled. Paul never consistently and clearly follows one textual version for his citations of a given biblical book, even within the same letter. In Romans, for example, Paul's citations of Isaiah fall into Ellis's categories 4 and 5 (both unattested textual forms), with the bulk actually falling into category 5. In 1 Corinthians, Paul uses different textual versions in his two citations of *the very same chapter* of Genesis. In 6:16 he cites a version of Gen 2:24 that falls into category 2, but in 15:45 he cites a version of Gen 2:7 that falls into category 4. For the citation of Gen 2:24, it would not have made a difference to Paul's argument had he used the Septuagint or the Hebrew version. His citation of Gen 2:7, however, contains a divergence from all known versions that is critical for Paul's argument.[48] Did Paul here have two different versions of Genesis, on two different scrolls, open in front of him as he composed the letter? Did he have one scroll that diverged from the textual versions that are now extant? Did he simply insert a critical word into his citation in 1 Cor 15:45 in order to make a better argument, hoping that no one would notice?

The reconstruction offered above provides a way to answer these questions. Paul almost never cites the Hebrew version of Scripture because he did not know Hebrew. He does at times appear to be consulting written versions of the Septuagint, but primarily he worked from memory of verses that he knew in Aramaic. This is why in the overwhelming majority of cases Paul's citations match neither the extant Greek nor Hebrew versions; they were filtered through both a translation and the vagaries (and desires) of memory. When Paul "miscites" Gen 2:7, he did not deliberately change what he knew to be the correct text. Rather, he cited it as he remembered it, with perhaps his memory adjusting the wording to better fit what he understood to be the true meaning of the verse. This was not a "memory lapse" because Paul had less interest in citing the precise wording of Scripture than he did in conveying its true (in his mind) meaning.[49]

Usage. Finally, an analysis of the way in which Paul uses Scripture also can largely be explained by the model offered in this essay.

---

48. Paul's citation calls Adam "the *first* man." The word "first" is not found in any other version but is necessary for Paul in order to make the contrast with "the last man," Christ.

49. The theory that Paul cited from memory, as noted above, has a long and distinguished scholarly history. The claim that Paul "miscites" Scripture, though, which arises from a priori assumptions and value judgments about Paul's education and the primacy of written Scripture, has made scholars uneasy. I am suggesting a model meant to be value neutral that, in large measure, comports with Leonard Greenspoon, "By the Letter? Word for Word? Scriptural Citation in Paul," in *Paul and Scripture: Extending the Conversation*, ed. Christopher D. Stanley, ECL 9 (Atlanta: Society of Biblical Literature, 2012), 9–24 (although I disagree with him on several specific points).

Paul's introductions to direct scriptural citations—his so-called "introductory formulae"—and the purpose to which he uses these citations tend to resemble Palestinian Jewish literature to a far greater extent than they resemble Jewish literature written in Greek, presumably outside of Palestine. Due to the scant and selective nature of the evidence, this is not a particularly strong argument, but nevertheless it helps to buttress the conclusions reached above.

Paul's preferred introductory formulae are "as it is written" and "Scripture says."[50] Only a handful of times does he cite Scripture with a formula that begins with a character (David, Isaiah, Moses, and, in just a few cases, God) who "says" the scriptural verse.[51] As scholars have, again, long noted, the phrase "as it is written" is more common in Palestinian Jewish literature such as the Dead Sea Scrolls and later rabbinic literature than in Greek Jewish literature.[52] The authors of the latter texts prefer to quote Scripture in the name of a character, especially Moses. Moreover, the Greek phrase "as it is written" is rarely used in contemporaneous non-Jewish Greek or Latin literature to introduce a citation. Paul appears to be following a distinctly Palestinian pattern of introducing Scripture.

A comparative analysis of the reasons that Paul cites Scripture yields murkier results. Scholars have developed competing schema for classifying Paul's use of scriptural citations.[53] Nearly all of Paul's citations, however, really fall into one of two types. Most of his citations are deployed in order to make christological claims about how we are to understand the world and our relationship to it in light of Christ. Most of the remainder of his citations attempt to prescribe proper behavior. Both Palestinian and non-Palestinian Jewish literature cite Scripture for proof of proper or normative behavior. While neither branch of literature obviously uses Scripture to make christological arguments, they both use it to make larger claims about the nature of the world. This is especially clear in Philo, who often reads Scripture as encoding some deeper truth about the nature of the world.[54] Such a use of Scripture in Palestinian literature is far less common but not completely unattested; some of the Dead Sea Scrolls, for example, use Scripture to reveal the state of affairs under the "new covenant."[55] Nevertheless, Ellis concludes that "where distinguishable, with

50. Ellis, *Paul's Use of the Old Testament*, 22–25, 48–49; Turpie, *New Testament View of the Old*, 340–41.

51. The vast bulk of these exceptions are found in Romans: 4:7, 8; 7:7; 9:15; 10:16, 19, 20; 11:4, 9, 10; 15:12.

52. For a careful and nuanced statement on the introductory formulas in the New Testament and the Mishnah, see Bruce Manning Metzger, "The Formulas Introducing Quotations of Scripture in the NT and the Mishnah," *JBL* 70 (1951): 297–307.

53. See Steve Moyise, "Quotations," in Porter and Stanley, *As It Is Written*, 15–28.

54. Hindy Najman, "A Written Copy of the Law of Nature," *SPhiloA* 15 (2003): 54–63.

55. Joseph A. Fitzmyer, "The Use of Explicit Old Testament Quotations in Qumran Lit-

few exceptions [Paul's literary methods] point to a Palestinian rather than a Hellenistic Judaism."[56]

Conclusions

Over the past few decades there has been an increasing awareness of Paul's "Jewishness" and its importance for understanding his activities. Much of this research, however, has remained grounded in assumptions about Paul's "Hellenistic" upbringing followed by his "rabbinical" training. In this essay I have argued for another, more nuanced understanding of Paul's upbringing. Paul was a "Hellenistic Jew" from Jerusalem, whose childhood and education would not have been very different from many of his affluent neighbors like Josephus. His native tongue was Aramaic, the language in which he would have orally learned Scripture in an ad hoc fashion. During his sojourn outside of Judea and through his trips to synagogues there he became familiar with written Jewish Scripture, in Greek.

There are two primary ramifications of this argument. The first involves audience. It is by no means obvious that Paul's invocation of Scripture and its authority "worked" for his audience. After all, why would gentile readers of his letters have given authority to the cryptic citations of Jewish Scripture? How might they have regarded it? The argument here sensitizes us to the possibility that Paul and his audience had different assumptions about scriptural authority based at least in part on their social locations.

The second ramification is for the cluster of questions generally tied to the "new perspective." These questions generally place Paul in a "Jewish" context but sometimes do not adequately address the question of what that actually means. Just as Shaye's work has forced us to reconsider what it meant to be a "Jew" in antiquity, it is my hope that this study will help us to recognize how our preconceptions about the artificial boundaries of "Hellenistic Judaism" might be reconfigured in a productive manner.

---

erature and the New Testament," *NTS* 7 (1961): 297–333: "The conclusion drawn from these details is that the exegetical practices of the New Testament writers is quite similar to that of their Jewish contemporaries, which is best illustrated by the Qumran literature" (330). See also Sarianna Metso, "Biblical Quotations in the Community Rule," in *The Bible as Book: The Hebrew Bible and the Judaean Desert Discoveries*, ed. Edward D. Herbert and Emanuel Tov (London: British Library and Oak Knoll Press, 2002), 81–92.

56. Ellis, *Paul's Use of the Old Testament*, 83.

Galatians 6:12 on Circumcision and Persecution

MARTIN GOODMAN
University of Oxford

Among the many areas of Jewish Studies to have been profoundly affected by the insights of Shaye Cohen, none is of greater significance than his manifold contributions to understanding Jewish identity in antiquity, not least in relation to the history of conversion.[1] He has repeatedly demonstrated through meticulous scholarship how careful readings of specific texts in context can deepen understanding and complicate long-held assumptions about Jewish history. I hope that the following short note may be seen as an appropriate tribute.

Paul's letter to the Galatians is generally agreed to have been composed in the late forties or mid fifties CE. Commentators, including Shaye in the *Jewish Annotated New Testament*, accept that the epistle is genuine and explain its contents and tone as the product of the specific situation of the churches in Galatia to whom Paul wrote.[2]

The main text of the letter was presumably dictated to a scribe, since Paul added the following note at the end:

> [11]See what large letters I make when I am writing in my own hand! [12]It is those who want to make a good showing in the flesh that try to compel you to be circumcised—only that they may not be persecuted for the cross of Christ. [13]Even the circumcised [or, better, (see below) "those who are being circumcised"] do not themselves obey law, but they want you to be circumcised so that they may boast about your flesh. [14]May I never boast of anything except the cross of our Lord Jesus Christ, by which the world has been crucified to me, and I to the world. [15]For neither circumcision nor uncircumcision is anything; but a new creation is everything!

1. Shaye J. D. Cohen, *The Beginnings of Jewishness: Boundaries, Varieties, Uncertainties*, HCS 31 (Berkeley: University of California Press, 1999).

2. Shaye J. D. Cohen, "The Letter of Paul to the Galatians," in *The Jewish Annotated New Testament*, ed. Amy-Jill Levine and Marc Zvi Brettler, 2nd ed. (Oxford: Oxford University Press, 2017), 373.

> [16]As for those who will follow this rule—peace be upon them, and mercy, and upon the Israel of God. (Gal 6:11–16 RSV)

Paul's assertion in 6:12 raises difficult questions for modern interpreters. To what sort of persecution did Paul refer, and who would persecute whom for failing to circumcise gentile Christians in Galatia, and why?

Commentators generally recognize this as a puzzle and have made manifold suggestions. Perhaps the persecutors were non-Christian Jews upset that gentile Godfearers were being enticed away from synagogues into Paul's Christian communities, attracted by admission without circumcision.[3] Perhaps the persecutors were Jews from Judea, transferring into Galatia a Judean campaign for conversion of gentiles by the forcible circumcision of males.[4] Perhaps they were local Jews in Galatia who made gentiles who had become Christians and been circumcised feel uncomfortable within the Jewish community if they did not force other gentile Christians also to be circumcised.[5]

Shaye himself states, with characteristic caution, that "Jews who do not believe in Christ are persecuting (what exactly this means is unclear) Jews who do believe in Christ, presumably because the former suspect the latter of rejecting the Torah and effacing the boundary between Jews and gentiles."[6] But it remains puzzling why non-Christian Jews should persecute Christian Jews for failure to circumcise Christian gentiles, thereby leaving those gentiles in their status as gentiles.

The following suggestion starts from the observation that Gal 6:12 is part of a postscript (6:11–18) to the epistle written by Paul himself to add to the letter he had dictated. Since publication of the great commentary on Galatians by Hans-Dieter Betz, it has been standard to accept his assertion that this postscript is the "hermeneutical key to the intentions of the Apostle [in the letter as a whole]."[7] But what if the postscript, scribbled with distinctively large letters (6:11), was actually adding something new in relation to the predicament of Paul's correspondents in order to add even more force to his furious denunciations in the body of the epistle?

---

3. Anthony E. Harvey, "The Opposition to Paul" in *Studia Evangelica, Vol. IV–V: Papers Presented to the Third International Congress on New Testament Studies Held at Christ Church, Oxford, 1965*, ed. Frank Leslie Cross, 2 vols., TUGAL 102–103 (Berlin: Akademie-Verlag 1968), 4:319–32.

4. F. F. Bruce, *The Epistle to the Galatians: A Commentary on the Greek Text*, NIGTC (Exeter: Paternoster, 1982), 269.

5. Mark D. Nanos, "The Inter- and Intra-Jewish Context of Paul's Letter to the Galatians" in *The Galatians Debate: Contemporary Issues in Rhetorical and Historical Interpretation*, ed. Mark D. Nanos (Peabody, MA: Hendrickson, 2002).

6. Cohen, "Galatians," 386.

7. Hans-Dieter Betz, *Galatians: A Commentary on Paul's Letter to the Churches in Galatia*, Hermeneia (Philadelphia: Fortress, 1979), 312–13.

The postscript must have been intended to be intelligible to the recipients of the letter in Galatia, but that need not mean that it simply echoes what is said in the document to which it was appended. The main epistle and the postscript both encouraged Paul's gentile Christians to resist those who wished them to be circumcised, but neither Paul's arguments nor the identity or alleged motivation of those urging circumcision necessarily remained the same.

I can see no reason to differ from the consensus that those opposed by Paul in the main text of Galatians were ethnic Jews who had accepted Christ who wanted gentiles in Galatia who accepted Christ to become circumcised proselytes as the hallmark of the people of God, nor that these Jewish Christ-followers probably had some links with the Jerusalem church and bolstered their arguments theologically from biblical texts, especially the narratives about Abraham.[8] But by contrast, in the postscript in 6:13, I suggest that Paul appears to envisage those who "want you to be circumcised so that they may boast about your flesh" as gentile Christians who are undergoing circumcision. This seems to me much the most natural way to understand his use of the present participle to refer to "those who are being circumcised [*peritemnomenoi*]."[9]

If it is such gentile Christians who are urging circumcision on fellow gentiles to avoid persecution "for the cross of Christ" (6:12), and if we ask from what source gentile Christians in Galatia might have expected persecution for adopting Christianity without becoming Jews, it is not hard to find an answer. Paul's teaching to his gentile converts was not always consistent (as can be seen not least in his rhetoric about the significance of circumcision in Gal 5:2–12), but he does not seem to have wavered in his insistence that his flock must demonstrate their faith in Christ by abjuring the worship of other gods. It is true that this is not a theme emphasized in Paul's letter to the Galatians as it is elsewhere in his correspondence, but Gal 4:8 and 5:20 take it for granted that the recipients of the epistle have abandoned their previous life as pagans and "turned to God from idols" (so Paul in 1 Thess 1:9, the earliest of his letters to survive).

The people who will have objected to this rejection of pagan worship by Galatian gentiles will not have been local Jews but local pagans. It is not accidental that accounts of Christian martyrdoms at the hands of gentile authorities stress so consistently hostility to the refusal of Christians to recognize the gods of the community—hence the account of Christian trials by the younger Pliny over half a century later in Pontus, just north of

8. John M. G. Barclay, "Mirror-Reading a Polemical Letter," *JSNT* 31 (1987): 73–93.

9. Johannes Munck argued already in the 1950s that the opposition to Paul in Galatia comprised a group of law-observant gentiles (*Paul and the Salvation of Mankind* [London: SCM, 1959], 87–89), but he has persuaded few New Testament scholars because his hypothesis fails to distinguish the opponents in the letter from those attacked in the postscript.

Galatia, clearly implies that the main issue at stake was the neglect of the traditional cults (Pliny, *Ep.* 10.96).

It is not possible to demonstrate conclusively that pagan converts to Christianity could avoid such persecution by their gentile neighbors for their rejection of ancestral religion if they were thought by those gentiles to have become Jews. But it might at the very least have seemed a tactic worth trying by gentile Christians when they came under pressure from their erstwhile pagan co-religionists, since there seems no doubt that gentiles in the cities of the early Roman Empire recognized, however grudgingly, the validity of proselyte conversion, however distasteful they found it. Nor should it be doubted that gentiles were well aware that adoption of Judaism also involved withdrawal from the traditional religious practices of the polytheistic community which the proselyte left behind. As Tacitus remarked sourly in the early second century CE, proselytes "renounce their ancestral religions" and "those who are converted to their ways [i.e., of the Jews] follow the same practice [i.e., circumcision], and the earliest lesson they receive is to despise the gods" (*Hist.* 5.5.1–2).

I suggest, therefore, that Gal 6:12 refers to gentile Christians in Galatia trying to avoid persecution by their gentile neighbors for abandoning the religious practices of the community. Such abandonment simply "for the cross of Christ" ran the risk of intense hostility from puzzled neighbors, just as the *nomen Christianum* evoked distaste for Pliny half a century later (Pliny, *Ep.* 10.96). Jews, by contrast, practiced a permitted religion, with privileges long woven into the fabric of civic life.[10] Demonstrating Jewish identity was not altogether easy either for a born Jew or a proselyte, but non-Jews fastened on male circumcision as an identity marker, as shown most starkly in the awful account by Suetonius of the public stripping of an old man in a Roman court which he witnessed in Rome as a boy during the rule of Domitian: for the court the exposure of the defendant's circumcision was enough to make him liable to the Jewish tax levied on all Jews after 70 CE (*Dom.* 12.2).

If gentile Christians in Galatia could be accused by Paul of having undergone circumcision simply for such social and political reasons rather than out of theological conviction, this might explain his otherwise odd assertion in the postscript that "those who are being circumcised do not themselves obey the law" (6:13). Their pressure on other gentile Christians in their community to undergo circumcision along with them could be explained by their desire to avoid being stigmatized by association with "atheists" who (in the eyes of pagans) had rejected worship of the gods for no reason apart from the new-fangled notion of salvation through Christ alone.

---

10. Miriam Pucci Ben Zeev, *Jewish Rights in the Roman World: The Greek and Roman Documents Quoted by Josephus Flavius*, TSAJ 74 (Tübingen: Mohr Siebeck, 1998).

If this analysis is correct, the alignment of this sociological polemic with the theological arguments in the rest of the epistle will have been made by Paul as he came to pen his final urgent message in a postscript to his backsliding community. I do not think that such conflation by Paul of two different issues as a way to bolster his polemic should really be a surprise. Paul's rhetoric was frequently innovative and inventive—indeed, the emphasis on male circumcision so that it alone can become a metonym for Jewishness, which is at the heart of the epistle to the Galatians, seems to have been one such rhetorical innovation.[11]

I suggest, in sum, that Gal 6:12 should not be taken as evidence that Jewish followers of Jesus were in danger of persecution by fellow non-Christian Jews if they did not demand circumcision of the Galatian gentiles who believed in Christ. Rather it should be seen as a reflection of a crisis within the Galatian gentile Christian community, where the danger of persecution came not from Jews but from their gentile neighbors.

---

11. Judith M. Lieu, *Christian Identity in the Jewish and Graeco-Roman World* (Oxford: Oxford University Press, 2004), 128.

Early Rabbinic Midrash between Philo and Qumran

STEVEN D. FRAADE
Yale University

The subject of this essay was inadvertently suggested at the 2011 meeting of the Society of Biblical Literature. In a panel discussion of my then recently published volume of essays, titled *Legal Fictions*,[1] Moshe Bernstein commented that it was impossible to think that the early rabbis simply woke up one morning and began "doing *midrash halakhah*," that is, the *explicit* deriving or justifying of laws from Hebrew Scriptures in the form of running commentaries on scriptural books, or sections thereof, something for which we have no exact prerabbinic antecedents. Bernstein made this comment in support of the extensive and important work that he and others have done in seeking in the Dead Sea Scrolls the missing link, as it were, between the Hebrew Bible and early rabbinic law and legal interpretation.[2]

For a long time since the initial discovery of the Dead Sea Scrolls in 1947, but especially of late, this has been a burgeoning area of scholarship that has yielded very significant results, even if allowing for exaggerated claims of having discovered long-lost links in the chain of midrashic tradition, especially in its legal (or in rabbinic terms, halakhic) aspects. In addition to the groundbreaking work of American scholars such as Bernstein, Lawrence Schiffman, and Joseph Baumgarten, I would highlight the

---

It is my pleasure to contribute to this well-earned tribute to Shaye Cohen, who has so ably modeled how to traverse the seeming gap between Jews writing and thinking in Hebrew and Greek.

1. Steven D. Fraade, *Legal Fictions: Studies of Law and Narrative in the Discursive Worlds of Ancient Jewish Sectarians and Sages*, JSJSup 147 (Leiden: Brill, 2011).

2. Moshe J. Bernstein, "4Q252: From Re-Written Bible to Biblical Commentary," *JJS* 45 (1994): 1–27; Bernstein, "4Q252: Method and Context, Genre and Sources," *JQR* 85 (1994): 61–79; Moshe J. Bernstein and Shlomo A. Koyfman, "The Interpretation of Biblical Law in the Dead Sea Scrolls: Forms and Methods," in *Biblical Interpretation at Qumran*, ed. Matthias Henze, SDSSRL (Grand Rapids: Eerdmans, 2005), 61–87. Now, thankfully, Bernstein's collected articles have been published as *Reading and Re-Reading Scripture at Qumran*, 2 vols., STDJ 107 (Leiden: Brill, 2013).

recent books by Israeli scholars such as Vered Noam and Aharon Shemesh, for which I might be permitted to refer to my review of the latter.[3] It is fair to say that, today, any critical scholar working on early rabbinic law and legal hermeneutics cannot afford to ignore the comparative insights provided by the Dead Sea Scrolls, especially in light of their chronological, geographical, and, perhaps most importantly, linguistic proximity.

As I and others have argued, however, there are difficulties with a linear, developmental model that leads directly from the Hebrew Bible to the Dead Sea Scrolls to early rabbinic halakhah, and midrash halakhah in particular, whether in terms of form, content, or conception. To begin with, among the approximately thousand texts of the Dead Sea Scrolls, we have very few examples of explicit midrash halakhah, that is, the deriving or justifying of law from Scripture in such a way as to differentiate between the two, that is, to lead the reader/auditor from one to the other, as in the format of the continuous commentary. The same can be said for midrash aggadah, but that is not my focus here. I have argued elsewhere that in both cases the search has been largely (but not entirely) in vain.[4] Underlying my arguments is the assertion that the formal traits of commentary (lemma, linking language, comment) are central to its rhetorical function. As Heinrich von Staden says of an entirely different type of ancient commentary, "In the commentaries using full, complete lemmata, the formal arrangement of the two ancient texts—the original and the exegetical—has significant implications for the socio-scientific dynamics of the triangle author-commentator-reader."[5]

---

3. Vered Noam, מקומראן למהפכה התנאית: היבטים בתפיסת הטומאה (Jerusalem: Yad Itzhak Ben-Zvi, 2010) (English title: *From Qumran to the Rabbinic Revolution: Conceptions of Impurity*); Aharon Shemesh, *Halakhah in the Making: The Development of Jewish Law from Qumran to the Rabbis*, Taubman Lectures in Jewish Studies (Berkeley: University of California Press, 2009). Cf. Steven D. Fraade, review of *Halakhah in the Making: The Development of Jewish Law from Qumran to the Rabbis*, by Aharon Shemesh, *JSJ* 43 (2012): 131–35.

4. Steven D. Fraade, "Looking for Legal Midrash at Qumran," in *Biblical Perspectives: Early Use and Interpretation of the Bible in Light of the Dead Sea Scrolls; Proceedings of the First International Symposium of the Orion Center for the Study of the Dead Sea Scrolls and Associated Literature, 12–14 May, 1996*, ed. Michael E. Stone and Esther G. Chazon, STDJ 28 (Leiden: Brill, 1998), 59–79 (= Fraade, *Legal Fictions*, 145–67); Fraade, "Looking for Narrative Midrash at Qumran," in *Rabbinic Perspectives: Rabbinic Literature and the Dead Sea Scrolls; Proceedings of the Eighth International Symposium of the Orion Center for the Study of the Dead Sea Scrolls and Associated Literature, 7–9 January, 2003*, ed. Steven D. Fraade, Aharon Shemesh, and Ruth A. Clements, STDJ 62 (Leiden: Brill, 2006), 43–66 (= Fraade, *Legal Fictions*, 169–92).

5. Heinrich von Staden, "'A Woman Does Not Become Ambidextrous': Galen and the Culture of Scientific Commentary," in *The Classical Commentary: Histories, Practices, Theory*, ed. Roy K. Gibson and Christina Shuttleworth Kraus, Supplements to Mnemosyne 232 (Leiden: Brill, 2002), 109–39, here 127. For the "turn to commentary" in ancient Judaism, see Steven D. Fraade, *From Tradition to Commentary: Torah and Its Interpretation in the Midrash Sifre to Deuteronomy*, SUNY Series in Judaica (Albany: State University of New York Press, 1991), 1–23.

In an article that appeared in a themed issue of Dead Sea Discoveries devoted to "The Rise of Commentary Texts in Ancient Near Eastern, Greek, Roman, and Jewish Cultures," Maren Niehoff, in comparing what she calls the "commentary culture(s)" in the land of Israel, comes to much the same negative conclusion, albeit somewhat overstated to my mind, in reviewing previous scholarship:

> The image, which emerges from these scholarly investigations, is one of homogeneous, internal development. Jews created a commentary culture from within their own community, transmitting from generation to generation their insights into their canonical books. On this reconstruction, the outside world and its Hellenistic culture mattered little, as Jews were engaged in a rather unique hermeneutic enterprise in Hebrew or Aramaic.[6]

Some Oddities of Midrash When Viewed Comparatively

To be more specific, we search largely (but not entirely) in vain among the Dead Sea Scrolls for several characteristic and ubiquitous traits of Tannaitic midrash halakhah, which, I would argue cut across the Tannaitic midrashic corpora, irrespective of variations of hermeneutical terminology and posture, and irrespective of the assignment of the collections to the "schools" of either Rabbi Akiva or R. Ishmael. These traits I take to be (1) the *explicit* interpretation of one verse by means of another, commonly from different parts of Scripture, that is, the employment of secondary lemmata (*Ὅμηρον ἐξ Ὁμήρου σαφηνίζειν* ["explaining Homer from Homer"], attributed to Aristarchus); (2) the adducing of multiple legal opinions and/or scriptural interpretations, to be found on virtually every page of early rabbinic literature (whether Mishnah, midrash, or gemara),[7] and (3), perhaps most significantly and strikingly, the dialectical and dialogical rhetoric of "question and answer," whether between the midrashic text and Scripture, whether among its named or anonymous rabbinic tradents, or whether between the midrashic text and its readers/auditors, often beginning with an interrogative interrogation of a scriptural lemma in what might be thought of in literary terms (e.g., responding to inner-scriptural redundancies, gaps, or contradictions). It is not that specimens of these traits (especially the first two) cannot be found among the Dead Sea

6. Maren R. Niehoff, "Commentary Culture in the Land of Israel from an Alexandrian Perspective," *DSD* 19 (2012): 442–63, here 443.

7. See Steven D. Fraade, "Rabbinic Polysemy and Pluralism Revisited: Between Praxis and Thematization," *AJS Review* 31 (2007): 1–40 (= *Legal Fictions*, 427–75).

Scrolls, but that they are so few and far between, relative to their ubiquity in early rabbinic midrash, as to be exceptions that prove the overarching rule of their absence. These traits differentiate early rabbinic midrash from both the predominance of "rewritten Bible" and the limited purview of continuous Dead Sea Scroll pesharim, the two most common forms of scriptural interpretation at Qumran.

Notwithstanding the long-noted similarities between citation language in early rabbinic midrash and Qumran exegesis, most commonly employing a form of the verbs אמר, and כתב,[8] we find nothing in Qumranic antecedents to rabbinic legal midrash that is analogous to such anonymous exegetical interlocutors, as expressed by. . . אחרים אומרים ("others say ...") or . . . יש אומרים ("there are those who say ..."), or to such dialogical rhetorical expressions as . . . אתה אומר . . . או אינו אלא ("You say ... but it can only mean..." [school of R. Ishmael]), . . . יכול ("might it be possible [to say]?" ["school" of R. Akiva]), . . . שומע אני ("I might understand it [to mean] ..." ["school" of R. Ishmael]), מה תלמוד לומר ("What does this come to teach?" ["school" of R. Akiva, but also of R. Ishmael]); למה נאמר ("Why is this said?" ["school" of R. Ishmael]); and . . . מניין ("Whence [do we learn this]?" ["school" of R. Akiva]); מה אני צריך ("For what do I need [this verse]?" ["school of R. Akiva"]); etc. While these rhetorical expressions might appear more or less frequently depending on whether a midrashic collection is assigned to the "school" of R. Akiva or R. Ishmael, their dialogical rhetorical posture is common to all.

To focus on another trait of tannaitic midrash, there is only one clear example in all of the Dead Sea Scrolls of a continuous scriptural commentary (pesher) that adduces multiple interpretations of a scriptural lemma (1QpHab I, 16–II, 10), but in that case, as I have previously argued,[9] they are not three alternative interpretations but a single threefold interpretation in that the pesher decodes the prophetic lemma so as to apply to three sequential chronological periods (past, present, future) in the life of the interpretive community.[10]

---

8. See, most recently, Daniel A. Machiela, "The Qumran Pesharim as Biblical Commentaries: Historical Context and Lines of Development," *DSD* 19 (2012): 313–62, esp. 321–24.

9. Fraade, *From Tradition to Commentary*, 5–6.

10. Another example that is sometimes cited is 4Q169 (4QpNah) 3–4 I, 1–11, where the word for "lion" (ארי) is given several interpretations. However, that is not a multiple interpretation since each interpretation is to a different occurrence of the word in the lemma. On the topic more broadly, see Matthias Weigold, "Ancient Jewish Commentaries in Light of the Dead Sea Scrolls: Multiple Interpretations as a Distinctive Feature," in *The Hebrew Bible in Light of the Dead Sea Scrolls*, ed. Nóra Dávid et al., FRLANT 239 (Göttingen: Vandenhoeck & Ruprecht, 2012), 281–94.

From Alexandria Shall Come Forth Torah

Curiously, in order to find antecedents to these defining characteristics of the early rabbinic "culture of commentary," we have to turn to a very different geographic, cultural, and, I should stress, linguistic environment, to that of Alexandria Egypt, and in particular to the works of Philo of Alexandria, and his Alexandrian predecessors (especially Demetrius and Aristobulus, second century BCE, whose works of biblical interpretation and commentary have survived only in fragments). Here, too, there is a long scholarly lineage going back to the origins of the Wissenschaft des Judentums, but more recently to the classic works of Yitzhaq Baer, David Daube, Henry Fischel, Elimelech Epstein Hallewy, and Saul Lieberman. There has been, however, a recent renewal of scholarly interest in the Hellenistic antecedents and analogues to early rabbinic scriptural hermeneutics, most especially as embodied in Tannaitic midrash halakhah, as argued by Philip Alexander and Chaim Milikowsky.[11]

Similarly, there has been a renewed effort to explore the possible influence of Hellenistic forms of commentary on the Qumran pesher, especially in articles by Markus Bockmuehl and Reinhard Kratz, and a book by Pieter B. Hartog.[12] The essays in Maren Niehoff's edited volume, *Homer and the*

11. See Philip S. Alexander, "Quid Athenis et Hierosolymis? Rabbinic Midrash and Hermeneutics in the Greco-Roman World," in *A Tribute to Geza Vermes: Essays on Jewish and Christian Literature and History*, ed. Philip R. Davies and R. T. White, JSOTSup 100 (Sheffield: JSOT Press, 1990), 101–24; Chaim Milikowsky, "Rabbinic Interpretation of the Bible in the Light of Ancient Hermeneutical Practice: The Question of the Literal Meaning," in *"The Words of a Wise Man's Mouth Are Gracious" (Qoh 10,12): Festschrift for Günter Stemberger on the Occasion of His 65th Birthday*, ed. Mauro Perani, SJ 32 (Berlin: de Gruyter, 2005), 7–28.

12. See Markus Bockmuehl, "The Dead Sea Scrolls and the Origins of Biblical Commentary," in *Text, Thought, and Practice in Qumran and Early Christianity: Proceedings of the Ninth International Symposium of the Orion Center for the Study of the Dead Sea Scrolls and Associated Literature, Jointly Sponsored by the Hebrew University Center for the Study of Christianity, 11–13 January, 2004*, ed. Ruth A. Clements and Daniel R. Schwartz, STDJ 84 (Leiden: Brill, 2009), 3–29; Reinhard Gregor Kratz, "Text und Kommentar: Die Pescharim von Qumran im Kontext der hellenistischen Schultradition," in *Von Rom nach Bagdad: Bildung und Religion in der späteren Antike und im klassischen Islam*, ed. Peter Gemeinhardt and Sebastian Günther (Tübingen: Mohr Siebeck, 2013); Kratz, "Text and Commentary: The Pesharim of Qumran in the Context of Hellenistic Scholarship," in *The Bible and Hellenism: Greek Influence on Jewish and Early Christian Literature*, ed. Thomas L. Thompson and Philippe Wajdenbaum, Copenhagen International Seminar (London: Routledge, 2014), 212-29; and for a critical assessment, Machiela, "Qumran Pesharim as Biblical Commentaries," 344–56; Pieter B. Hartog, *Pesher and Hypomnema: A Comparison of Two Commentary Traditions from the Hellenistic-Roman World*, STDJ 121 (Leiden: Brill, 2017). See, as well, Armin Lange and Pleše Zlatko, "The Qumran Pesharim and the Derveni Papyrus: Transpositional Hermeneutics in Ancient Jewish and Ancient Greek Commentaries," in *The Dead Sea Scrolls in Context: Integrating the Dead Sea Scrolls in the Study of Ancient Texts, Languages, and Cultures*, ed. Armin Lange, Emanuel Tov, and Matthias Weigold, 2 vols., VTSup 140 (Leiden: Brill, 2011), 2:895–922; Lange and Zlatko, "Transpositional Hermeneutics: A Hermeneutical Comparison of the Derveni Papyrus, Aris-

Bible in the Eyes of Ancient Interpreters (2012), similarly explore the parallels of Jewish commentaries (from the Second Temple to rabbinic period) to Homeric scholarship.[13] This scholarship emphasizes the shared rabbinic-Hellenistic Jewish commentary trait (but with important differences) of both acknowledging and incorporating *multiple* human interpretations of divinely revealed Scriptures.[14] While the fit is at best imperfect, the points of similarity are highly suggestive of a shared "culture of commentary," mutatis mutandis.[15]

From Babylonia Shall Come Forth Torah

In addition to fruitful comparisons of Tannaitic midrash halakhah with the Dead Sea Scrolls and Philo, there has been a recent return to the question of whether and to what extent early rabbinic scriptural commentary, as others have argued for the Qumran pesharim,[16] draws, even if indirectly, upon the rich tradition of Mesopotamian divinatory commentary, as applied to dreams, visions, and omens, for both structural and hermeneutical antecedents and influences.[17] Although the scholarly lineage of this line of inquiry is less robust than that of possible Hellenistic interlocu-

---

tobulus of Alexandria, and the Qumran Pesharim," *JAJ* 3 (2012): 15–67. Most recently, see the special issue of *DSD* 24 (2017) on the theme "The Dead Sea Scrolls in Their Hellenistic Context," edited by Pieter B. Hartog and Jutta Jokiranta, who provide an excellent introduction (339–55) on the same theme. Of particular relevance to our topic in that special issue of *DSD*, is Benjamin G. Wright, "Were the Jews of Qumran Hellenistic Jews?," *DSD* 24 (2017): 356–77, with regard to "Commentary" (367–68), assessing Bockmuehl and Hartog in particular.

13. Maren R. Niehoff, ed., *Homer and the Bible in the Eyes of Ancient Interpreters*, Jerusalem Studies in Religion and Culture 16 (Leiden: Brill, 2012).

14. Niehoff, "Commentary Culture," 445–48.

15. For a much fuller treatment, see, most recently, Yakir Paz, "Rabbinic Biblical Exegesis in Light of the Homeric Commentaries" (PhD diss., Hebrew University of Jerusalem, 2014).

16. See Martti Nissinen, "Pesher as Divination: Qumran Exegesis, Omen Interpretation and Literary Prophecy," in *Prophecy after the Prophets? The Contribution of the Dead Sea Scrolls to the Understanding of Biblical and Extra-Biblical Prophecy*,ed. Kristin De Troyter and Armin Lange, CBET 52 (Leuven: Peeters, 2009), 43–60; Uri Gabbay, "Akkadian Commentaries from Ancient Mesopotamia and Their Relations to Early Hebrew Exegesis," *DSD* 19 (2012): 267–312; Machiela, "Qumran Pesharim as Biblical Commentaries, 327–34; Alex P. Jassen, "The Pesharim and the Rise of Commentary in Early Jewish Scriptural Interpretation," *DSD* 19 (2012): 363–98, esp. 385–98. Most recently, see Bronwon Brown-deVost, "The Compositional Development of Qumran Pesharim in Light of Mesopotamian Commentaries," *JBL* 135 (2016): 525-41; Brown-DeVost, *Commentary and Authority in Mesopotamia and Qumran*. Journal of Ancient Judaism Supplements 29 (Göttingen: Vandenhoeck & Ruprecht, 2018).

17. Machiela (see previous note) argues that the Mesopotamian influence was mediated by the Jewish Aramaic tradition of dream, vision, and omen interpretation, as found, most notably, in the book of Daniel and in the Aramaic Book of Giants. Jassen (see previous note) advances a similar line of argument.

tors, it too has important antecedents, especially in two important articles that appeared in the same year (1987): one by Stephen Lieberman, and another by Antoine Cavigneaux, both of which suggest an ancient Near Eastern backdrop to aspects of early rabbinic hermeneutics.[18] After all, even as some of the hermeneutical rules (*middot*) first attributed to Hillel may have their closest analogues in the methods of Alexandrian Homeric commentators (as per Daube and Lieberman[19]), rabbinic literature itself *imagines* them to have been imported by Hillel from *Babylonia*.[20] In this regard, recent consideration of this avenue of cultural transmission has been greatly in the debt of my Yale colleague Eckart Frahm, who recently published a volume titled *Babylonian and Assyrian Text Commentaries: Origins of Interpretation*,[21] and who, in a final chapter titled "The Legacy of Babylonian and Assyrian Hermeneutics,"[22] takes on with fresh energy and insight the question of possible connections between Abraham's (and Hillel's) homeland and early rabbinic midrash.

Once again, however, the similarities (e.g., multiple interpretations set alongside one another) are only as telling as the differences (e.g., no application of this commentary genre to legal, narrative, or historical texts). Nevertheless, the ancient Near Eastern scholastic legacy continued well into Greco-Roman times and the land of Israel. If I have emphasized the *dialogical* similarities between Tannaitic midrash and Hellenistic commentary ("how do you know that x means y?"), I would emphasize now that the *deictic* decoding manner of the same midrashic texts ("x means y") can be fruitfully compared to similar methods in Babylonian commentaries, notwithstanding their other differences. For example, note how lexical equivalencies that are midrashically denoted by the expression אין ... אלא ... ("x can only mean y"), or how the demonstrative pronouns (זה, אלה, הוא) are used to connect scriptural signifier with midrashic

18. Stephen Lieberman, "A Mesopotamian Background for the So-Called Aggadic 'Measures' of Biblical Hermeneutics," *HUCA* 58 (1987): 157–225; Antoine Cavigneaux, "Aux sources du midrash: L'herméneutique babylonienne," *AuOr* 5 (1987): 243–55. See also Jeffrey Tigay, "An Early Technique of Aggadic Exegesis," in *History, Historiography and Interpretation: Studies in Biblical and Cuneiform Literatures*, ed. H. Tadmor and M. Weinfeld (Jerusalem: Magnes, 1983), 169–89.

19. David Daube, "Rabbinic Methods of Interpretation and Hellenistic Rhetoric," *HUCA* 22 (1949): 239–65; Daube, "Alexandrian Methods of Interpretation and the Rabbis," *Festschrift Hans Lewald* (Basel: Helbing & Lichtenheim, 1953), 27–44 (reprinted in *Essays in Greco-Roman and Related Talmudic Literature*, ed. Henry A. Fischel [New York: Ktav, 1977], 165–82); Saul Lieberman, "Rabbinic Interpretation of Scripture," in *Hellenism in Jewish Palestine: Studies in the Literary Transmission, Beliefs and Manners of Palestine in the I Century B.C.E.–IV Century C.E.* (New York: Jewish Theological Seminary of America, 1962), 47–82.

20. See y. Pesaḥ. 6:1, 33a; b. Pesaḥ. 66a; but not in t. Pesaḥ. 4:13–14.

21. Eckart Frahm, *Babylonian and Assyrian Text Commentaries: Origins of Interpretation*, Guides to the Mesopotamian Textual Record 5 (Münster: Ugarit-Verlag, 2011).

22. Ibid., chapter 12, 368–83.

signified, a feature shared with apocalyptic manners of vision decoding.[23] These are similar to ancient Near Eastern analogues of mantic decoding, as they are, mutatis mutandis, to the sorts of decoding found in the Qumran pesharim. Needless to say, we often find the two manners of commentary, dialogical and deictic, occupying the very same page of Tannaitic midrashic commentary, neither of them being a pure type that is exclusive of the other. In this regard (and others) rabbinic midrash halakhah is considerably more heterogeneous in form than either the Qumran pesher or Philo's allegorical commentaries.

A Case Study: Neither Either/Or nor Neither/Nor

Let us now look at a short, specific sample of Tannaitic legal exegesis to get a closer look at the heterogeneity of forms and methods therein employed, some of which are more deictic, and therefore closer to the ancient Near Eastern and Qumranic models of textual decoding, and some of which are more dialogical, and therefore closer to the Hellenistic models of commentary, while not being reducible to either. The commentary is that of Sifre Deut. (§156) to Deut 17:14–20 on the "law of the king," treated by me elsewhere in greater length and depth (and in comparison with the Temple Scroll among other texts).[24] To begin with, it is important to note that some individual interpretations are attributed to individual named Tannaitic sages, while the commentary as a whole, and its editorial voice, is anonymous, a combination that contrasts with earlier forms of Jewish scriptural interpretation of all types. This is an unusual characteristic—of blended anonymity and attribution— that I have begun to treat elsewhere, but which requires much more attention in all branches of early rabbinic literature.[25]

In commenting on the scriptural phrase ואמרת אשימה עלי מלך ("[when]

23. See Martha Himmelfarb, *Tours of Hell: An Apocalyptic Form in Jewish and Christian Literature* (Philadelphia: University of Pennsylvania Press, 1984); Himmelfarb, *Ascent to Heaven in Jewish and Christian Apocalypses* (New York: Oxford University Press, 1993).

24. Steven D. Fraade, "'The Torah of the King' (Deut. 17:14–20) in the Temple Scroll and Early Rabbinic Law," in *The Dead Sea Scrolls as Background to Postbiblical Judaism and Early Christianity: Papers from an International Conference at St. Andrews in 2001* ed. James R. Davila, STDJ 46 (Leiden: Brill, 2003), 25–60, esp. 49–58 (= Fraade, *Legal Fictions*, 285–319). For the Palestinian Talmud on the same, see Steven D. Fraade, "Priests, Kings, and Patriarchs: Yerushalmi Sanhedrin in Its Exegetical and Cultural Settings," in *The Talmud Yerushalmi and Graeco-Roman Culture*, ed. Peter Schäfer, 3 vols., TSAJ 93 (Tübingen: Mohr Siebeck, 2002), 3:315–33 (= Fraade, *Legal Fictions*, 323–44).

25. Steven D. Fraade, "Anonymity and Redaction in Legal Midrash: A Preliminary Probe," in מלאכת מחשבת: מחקרים בהתהוות ועריכת הספרות התלמודית (*Malekhet Mahshevet: Studies in the Redaction and Development of Talmudic Literature*), ed. Aaron Amit and Aharon Shemesh (Ramat-Gan, Israel: Bar-Ilan University Press, 2011), 9*–29*.

you say, 'I will set a king over me, [as do all the nations about me]'") (Deut 17:14), the midrashic commentary (§156) juxtaposes two interpretations, attributed to two mid-second-century named sages, Rabbis Nehorai and Judah, that are diametrically opposed to each other in their valuation of Israel's expressed desire for a king. It is as if the commentary stages a dialogue between them. R. Nehorai understands the verse to express denigration of Israel, taking his cue presumably from the verse's attributing the people's desire for a king to their wish to be like the surrounding non-Israelite peoples, reinforced by citation of a verse from 1 Sam 8:7. The latter verse understands the people's desire for a king as a repudiation of direct theocratic rule, that is, by God himself.

In stark contrast, R. Judah relies on the succeeding verse in Deuteronomy (17:15) to argue by way of a rhetorical question, and scriptural prooftext, how could the people be faulted for wishing to fulfill an *emphatic, direct* מצוה מן התורה ("command from the Torah"; presumably with divine authority) to establish a monarchy, שום תשים עליך מלך ("Surely, set a king over you!")? This is followed immediately by another rhetorical question, it not being clear which sage, if either, is asking it: If the desire to establish a monarchy was in fulfillment of a scriptural command, why were the people later "punished" for following through on that desire (alluding here to Samuel's predictions of the terrible consequences of establishing a monarchy, in 1 Sam 8)? In response we are told (again, it's not being clear by whom) that their error was not in establishing a monarchy per se, but in doing so before the appointed time.[26]

Although the two views of R. Nehorai and R. Judah remain unresolved, the presumed rhetorical conclusion would seem to favor R. Judah's view: they sought to fulfill a positive commandment but got the timing wrong. As if to give R. Nehorai another shot, the next phrase of the lemma, ככל הגוים אשר סביבותי ("as do all the nations about me"), is next cited, but with R. Nehorai's comment alone, that if the people's motivation for desiring a king was to be like the nations, it must have been to follow the nations in idolatrous worship, reinforced with a citation of 1 Sam 8:20.[27] Thus, the Sifre's commentary on Deut 17:14 constructs several "dialogues," both explicit and implicit: between Rabbis Nehorai and Judah, between Deut 17:14 and 15, between the lemma and 1 Sam 8, between the commentary's voices, both attributed and anonymous, between the biblical text and the implied auditor of the midrashic text, and, of course, between two very different views (already inner-scriptural) of Israelite monarchy.

In turning next its direct attention to Deut 17:15 as lemma, the commentary (§157) shifts from its previous dialogical mode to a more deictic mode of commentary, in which each textual element of the lemma

26. For further discussion, see Fraade, "'Torah of the King,'" 49–50 n. 62.
27. Compare t. Sanh. 4:5, discussed in Fraade, "'Torah of the King,'" 50 n. 63.

in succession is provided with its succinct, declarative decoding, without recourse to attributions, dialogical rhetoric, or prooftexts. Scripture denotes the appointment not of a one-time king but of a monarchic dynasty; it excludes the appointment of a queen; it requires the prophetic selection of the king; and it requires that the king be from within the land of Israel, and from among the people of Israel.[28]

The commentary next shifts back to a dialogical mode in probing the meaning of the second occurrence of תשים עליך מלך ("Establish over you a king") in Deut 17:15. In encountering this phrase a second time within the same verse (the first being שום תשים עליך מלך), the anonymous voice of the commentary rhetorically asks, הלא כבר נאמר ("has it not already been said?"), and ומה תלמוד לומר ("so what is the meaning of this [seeming redundant scripture]?"). The answer to these rhetorical questions is that the repeated phrase comes to accentuate the awesomeness of the king (emphasizing the word עליך, "over you"). For added emphasis and specificity, the commentary now uses the phrase מכאן אמרו ("from here [= this verse] they said") to introduce the mishnaic tradition (from Sanh. 2:5) that, in keeping with the king's august status, no one is to use his regalia or to see him exposed. Thus, to the dialogical mix is added reference or allusion to another intertext, here that being the Mishnah, as we shall see again shortly. This practice, of explicitly drawing (and marking) mishnaic discourse into the structure of midrashic commentary (and vice versa), relatively common in Tannaitic midrash of both the R. Akiva and R. Ishmael schools, is remarkable for its lack of antecedent in the commentary modes of either Qumran or Philo. It should be noted, however, that, although parts of our midrashic commentary are to found in the Mishnah (Sanh. 2:4–5), there they do not proceed in scriptural order as they do here, since there they can be rearranged for rhetorical effect (leaving the king's awesomeness for last), whereas here the order of the scriptural text determines the order of midrashic comments.[29]

As an example of multiple interpretations of the same lemma, here marked by the phrase דבר אחר ("another matter"),[30] our commentary attends to another seeming redundancy in Deut 17:15, in that the verse states, [מקרב אחיך] תשים עליך מלך ("[from among your brothers] establish over yourselves a king"),[31] followed by לא תוכל לתת עליך איש נוכרי ("You shall not establish over yourselves any foreigner"). This seeming repetition of the same requirement is decoded in deictic fashion as denoting, first, a positive obligation and, second, a negative prohibition (failure at

28. For elaboration, see Fraade, "'Torah of the King,'" 50–51 nn. 65–67.

29. See ibid., 43–44, 51 n. 68.

30. On which see above, at nn. 7, 9, 14.

31. For this as the text-critically correct form of the lemma (*pace* Finkelstein's edition), see Fraade, "'Torah of the King,'" 51 n. 69.

each being punishable in its own right).[32] The expression מכאן אמרו ("from here [= this verse] they said") is employed again (but without reference to any rule recognizable from our Mishnah), to introduce a tradition that would provide an additional solution to the problem of the redundancy of לא תוכל לתת עליך איש נכרי ("you shall not establish over yourselves any foreigner"). Since that clause, viewed atomistically, does not refer specifically to a king, it can be freed from its scriptural context to refer to appointed communal leaders (פרנסים) more broadly, who must be men and not women.[33]

Finally (for present purposes), the last clause of Deut 17:15, אשר לא אחיך הוא ("who is not your kinsman"), is treated. Rather than interpreting the clause per se (perhaps its meaning was self-evident, but it too could have been understood as being redundant), the comment uses the lemma to recall a purportedly historical incident from late Second Temple times, more fully narrated in the Mishnah (Soṭah 7:8), in which King Agrippa publicly reads from sections of Deuteronomy as part of the septennial הַקְהֵל ceremony during the festival of Sukkot (Deut 31:9–13). Rabbinic tradition conflates the הקהל ceremony with the king's obligation to read from a Torah scroll (Deut 17:19), which larger passage (Deut 17:14–20) would be read by the king on the occasion of הקהל. On one such occasion, when King Agrippa came to our verse (17:15), with its prohibition of appointing a gentile as king, he began to weep, since, as the grandson of Herod he was partly Edomite, and possibly illegitimate as king. The assembled people allayed his fears by acclaiming him to be one of them, thereby confirming him as legitimate king and reader of Scripture on this occasion. In proclaiming, אחינו אתה אחינו אתה ("You are our brother, you are our brother"), they are speaking as much to the biblical lemma (אשר לא אחיך הוא) as to Agrippa: the scriptural exclusion does not apply to him/you.[34]

In linking the lemma to a "historical" figure and event, this brief comment might be compared to the practice of the Qumran pesharim, which systematically decode each successive word or clause of the prophetic scriptural lemmata so as to refer to "historical" figures and events in the present-day life of the community.[35] But that is about as far as the comparison goes. The Qumran pesharim, especially the continuous ones, apply only to what are, or are understood to be, prophetic Scriptures, pre-

---

32. Ibid., 51 n. 70.

33. On the term and function of the פרנס, see ibid., 51–53; Fraade, "Local Jewish Leadership in Roman Palestine: The Case of the *Parnas* in Early Rabbinic Sources in Light of Extra-Rabbinic Evidence," in *Halakhah in Light of Epigraphy*, ed. Albert I. Baumgarten, Hanan Eshel, Ranon Katzoff, and Shani Tzoref, JAJSup 3 (Göttingen: Vandenhoeck & Ruprecht, 2011), 155–73.

34. See Fraade, "'Torah of the King,'" 45–47.

35. For an excellent summary of current scholarship on the pesher, see Shani Berrin, "Qumran Pesharim," in Henze, *Biblical Interpretation at Qumran*, 110–33.

sumed to be predictive (ominous) of the eschatological future, and are never applied to a legal scriptural text such as ours.[36] By contrast, there is no sense in our midrash that Deut 17:15 is being understood as being predictive of a future event. Furthermore, the "historical" fulfillments of the *predictive* biblical lemmata in the pesharim are understood to take place in eschatological times (אחרית הימים), whereas the Agrippa incident is rabbinically understood as having taken place in prior "historical" time. The Agrippa story, in its truncated "citation" as a comment to Deut 17:15, is simply a "historical" anecdote in which the commented upon lemma plays an uninterpreted role on one occasion of its being publicly read.

I hope to have demonstrated, in this one, limited textual sample, the *heterogeneous* nature of early rabbinic scriptural commentary in combining deictic and dialogic modes of interpretive discourse. While primary attention is paid therein to the sequence of scriptural words, phrases, and clauses that make up the base scriptural text, a plethora of "voices"—whether named or anonymous, whether scriptural or mishnaic, whether declarative or rhetorical—occupy the midrashic commentary's discursive world. Those diverse "voices" are enabled to converse with one another (as with the presumed midrashic student or auditor), in forms and manners that can be presumed in some cases to be "borrowed"—from both ancient Near Eastern and Greco-Roman cultures of commentary—while in others to have been transformed, and yet in others to be rabbinically "original."

Conclusion

The land of Israel (including the environs of Qumran) is and was traversed by well-traveled economic and cultural crossroads over land and sea, extending in virtually every direction and connecting diverse multilingual and multicultural realms, many of which were homes to Jewish communities (including Alexandria and Babylonia). It should not be surprising, therefore, that ancient Jewish cultural productions, such as early rabbinic midrash, Philonic allegorical commentary, and Qumran pesher embody linguistic and rhetorical choices between a wide array of intersecting options, only some of which have survived, that developed and persisted over time. This makes the tracing of their separate lineages all the more difficult, if not impossible.

If the academic scholarly penchant for extrarabbinic comparison and contextualization would belie the origins of midrash halakhah as spontaneous combustion, we should beware, if I may switch metaphors, of

36. For the Temple Scroll's "rewriting" of our pericope, see Fraade, "'Torah of the King,'" 31–39.

putting all of our comparative eggs into any one basket (nor is any one such basket free of its own heterogeneity). Just as it is unlikely that the early rabbis woke up one morning and suddenly began doing midrash halakhah, it is also unlikely that we can understand its origins in terms of a simple *linear* development from any *one* comparative, cultural direction.

If I may even more widely generalize, long-lasting and wide-ranging cultural "revolutions" (as I would characterize the rabbinic culture of commentary) are rarely if ever the product of sudden, singular, homogeneous propellants. In short, we need to broaden our comparative gaze(s) in multiple directions. Even so, there will be distinctive features of Tannaitic midrash halakhah (as of the commentaries of Philo and Qumran) that lack clear antecedents or analogues. The broader comparative lens allows us to view both these distinctive and shared features in sharper relief, even if it does not permit us unilinearly to trace the "origins" of midrashic commentary to any one time, place, motivation, or interpretive culture, but to appreciate the rich multiplicity of intersecting and interacting possibilities and their incorporation into a variety of exegetical rhetorical forms and functions.

Charity as a Negative Obligation in Early Rabbinic Literature

GREGG E. GARDNER
The University of British Columbia

Mishnah Pe'ah is perhaps the foundational work on Jewish thought on philanthropy. This tractate, together with Tosefta Pe'ah, works out a legal system for allocating agricultural produce from the householder (i.e., landowner or his agent) to the underprivileged.[1] These texts are presented as elucidations and expansions of the poor offerings mentioned briefly in the Hebrew Bible:

> 9When you reap the harvest of your land, you shall not reap all the way to the edges of your field, or gather the gleanings of your harvest. 10You shall not pick your vineyard bare, or gather the fallen fruit of your vineyard; you shall leave them for the poor and the stranger: I the Lord am your God. (Lev 19:9–10 NJPS)

> 19When you reap the harvest in your field and overlook a sheaf in the field, do not turn back to get it; it shall go to the stranger, the fatherless, and the widow—in order that the Lord your God may bless you in all your undertakings. 20When you beat down the fruit of your olive trees, do not go over them again; that shall go to the stranger, the fatherless, and the widow. 21When you gather the grapes of your vineyard, do not pick it over again; that shall go to the stranger, the fatherless, and the widow. (Deut 24:19–21 NJPS)

Typical of early rabbinic approaches to law, as succinctly described by Shaye Cohen, Mishnah and Tosefta Pe'ah draw upon concepts in the

---

Earlier research on this topic was undertaken as a Starr Fellow in Judaica at Harvard University (2009–2010). I thank Shaye Cohen, director of Harvard's Center for Jewish Studies during my fellowship, for supporting my research. I thank Michael Satlow for his helpful comments on an earlier draft of this paper. All remaining errors are my own.

1. On Mishnah Pe'ah, see my translation and annotation of the tractate in *The Mishnah: An Annotated Translation*, ed. Shaye J. D. Cohen et al.; (Oxford: Oxford University Press, forthcoming).

Hebrew Bible, elevate them to legal categories, and flesh them out in encyclopedic detail.[2] These discussions would later become central to rabbinic and Jewish approaches to poverty relief; for example, they become fodder for Maimonides's classic discourses on care for the poor.[3] What is often obscured and overlooked is that the Tannaim themselves do not identify these agricultural allotments as *tsedaqah,* or charity. Indeed, it was once common for scholars—perhaps too heavily influenced by traditional, apologetic, and harmonizing interpretations—to discuss all forms of poverty relief as "charity."[4] "Charity" would have been the most well-known, easily practiced, and laudatory form of support for the poor among both Jews and non-Jews—especially as the agricultural context of the biblical writings became less applicable to increasingly urbanized Jewish communities over time. Moreover, the somewhat indiscriminate use of "charity" by scholars is a product of the broad connotations of "charity" in English, where it denotes an array of emotions and actions such love, kindness, affection, generosity, spontaneous goodness, a lenient disposition, and benevolence.[5] The recent increase in critical scholarship on wealth and poverty, however, has prompted scholars to be more precise in their terminology and in identifying types of care for the poor.[6] For the study of

2. Shaye J. D. Cohen, "The Judaean Legal Tradition and the *Halakhah* of the Mishnah," in *The Cambridge Companion to the Talmud and Rabbinic Literature,* ed. Charlotte Elisheva Fonrobert and Martin S. Jaffee (New York: Cambridge University Press, 2007), 134.

3. Maimonides, *Mishneh Torah, Laws on Gifts for the Poor.* Maimonides himself notes that his *Mishneh Torah* draws upon the Mishnah, Tosefta, Sifra, Sifre, Jerusalem Talmud, and Babylonian Talmud; see Abraham Cronbach, "The Maimonidean Code of Benevolence," *HUCA* 20 (1947): 471. Because the Babylonian Talmud lacks an Order of Seeds, Maimonides's "Book of Seeds" draws more heavily upon the Tosefta and Palestinian Talmud than other portions of the *Mishneh Torah;* see Mark R. Cohen, "Maimonides and Charity in Light of the Geniza Documents," in *The Trias of Maimonides: Jewish, Arabic, and Ancient Culture of Knowledge = Die Trias des Maimonides: jüdische, arabische und antike Wissenskultur,* ed. Georges Tamer, SJ 30 (Berlin: de Gruyter, 2005), 66.

4. E.g., Judah Bergmann, *Ha-Tsedakah be-Yisra'el* [Hebrew] (Jerusalem: R. Mas, 1944; repr. 1974); Ephraim Urbach, "Political and Social Tendencies in Talmudic Concepts of Charity" [Hebrew], *Zion* 16 (1951): 1–27.

5. *Oxford English Dictionary* (Oxford New York: Oxford University Press, 2000), s.v. "charity."

6. For recent scholarship on wealth and poverty in the Jewish tradition, see, among others, Gregg E. Gardner, "Who Is Rich? The Poor in Early Rabbinic Judaism," *JQR* 104 (2014): 515–36; Gardner, *The Origins of Organized Charity in Rabbinic Judaism* (New York: Cambridge University Press, 2015); Gardner, "Pursuing Justice: Support for the Poor in Early Rabbinic Judaism," *HUCA* 86 (2016): 37–62; Alyssa M. Gray, "The Formerly Wealthy Poor: From Empathy to Ambivalence in Rabbinic Literature of Late Antiquity," *AJS Review* 33 (2009): 101–33; Gray, "Redemptive Almsgiving and the Rabbis of Late Antiquity," *JSQ* 18 (2011): 144–84; Leonard J. Greenspoon, ed., *Wealth and Poverty in Jewish Tradition,* SJC 26 (West Lafayette, IN: Purdue University Press, 2015); Tzvi Novick, "Charity and Reciprocity: Structures of Benevolence in Rabbinic Literature," *HTR* 105 (2012): 33–52; Michael L. Satlow, "'Fruit and the Fruit of Fruit': Charity and Piety in Late Antique Judaism," *JQR* 100 (2010): 244–77;

classical rabbinic literature, I have argued elsewhere that the most precise usage of the English "charity" is to parallel the additional meaning that the early rabbis appended to *tsedaqah* (which meant only "righteousness" in the Hebrew Bible)—namely, as almsgiving or the provision of material support to the poor without an expectation that it would be returned or repaid.[7] This definition of charity also maps nicely onto that of ethical theorists, as I will discuss below.

The harvest gifts discussed above, however, are not identified in early rabbinic texts as *tsedaqah*, as they differ conceptually from "charity."[8] In the laws of harvest gifts, the landowner surrenders nothing of his (the rabbis envision the actors—landowners, benefactors, and the poor—as male in these texts) own to the poor. His obligation is simply to refrain from interfering with the allocation of provisions from God to the poor. There is no redistribution from one human to another but only a single distribution from God to the poor—they are a gift from God, not from human landowners.[9] The laws of harvest gifts leave little, if any, room for personal discretion by humans, thereby precluding the generosity and liberality that are hallmarks of charity.[10] The Tannaim present the laws of harvest gifts as determinate, defining in high detail the actors, goods, and methods of allocation. Harvest gifts also include a clear set of correlative rights, as the Tannaim identify which elements of the harvest belong to the landowner and which produce belongs to the poor. The poor have an actionable claim to the specific stalks that fell to the ground as gleanings, those growing at the edge of the field, and so on.[11] In general, the attributes

---

Michael L. Satlow, ed., *Judaism and the Economy: A Sourcebook* (Routledge, forthcoming); Yael Wilfand, *Poverty, Charity and the Image of the Poor in Rabbinic Texts from the Land of Israel*, SWBA 2.9 (Sheffield: Sheffield Phoenix, 2014).

7. On the terms *charity* and *tsedaqah*, see my discussion in *Origins of Organized Charity*, 26–32.

8. As George Lakoff and Mark Johnson show (*Metaphors We Live By* [Chicago: University of Chicago Press, 1980; repr. 2003]), terminology is inseparable from conceptualization.

9. I thank Joshua Weinstein for this phrasing. The rabbis abide by the biblical theology that all land and its produce belong to God. Thus, as a precondition for claiming produce for himself, the landowner must satisfy God's claims to the yield by allocating certain items to those under God's special care—the poor and the priests. See Roger Brooks, *Support for the Poor in the Mishnaic Law of Agriculture: Tractate Peah*, BJS 43 (Chico, CA: Scholars Press, 1983), 17–19; Gardner, "Pursuing Justice," 37–62.

10. See, e.g., t. Pe'ah 4:18, where King Munbaz gives his treasures away to those in need, and my discussion in Gregg E. Gardner, "Competitive Giving in the Third Century CE: Early Rabbinic Approaches to Greco-Roman Civic Benefaction," in *Religious Competition in the Third Century C.E.: Jews, Christians, and the Greco-Roman World*, ed. Jordan D. Rosenblum, Lily C. Vuong, and Nathaniel P. DesRosiers, JAJSup 15 (Göttingen: Vandenhoeck & Ruprecht, 2014), 81–92. Nevertheless, it is possible that some sources (e.g., m. Pe'ah 1:2) preserve a competing view that would allow the householder to exercise a degree of discretion.

11. Perhaps to protect the rights of the poor or to adhere as closely as possible to the biblical wording of these laws (or perhaps to limit the landowner's obligation), harvest gifts

of these laws are undergirded by and flow from their negative character: the performer fulfills the commandment by *refraining* from certain actions.

The laws of harvest gifts map nicely onto how modern scholars of philosophy and ethics view the concept of justice, which they often define by contrasting it with charity.[12] Charity is incompletely or "imperfectly" defined, as the identities of the actors (e.g., benefactor, recipient) are left indeterminate. Charity grants the giver a great deal of personal discretion in deciding when, what, and to whom one gives. Norms of charity do not specify the place or time for when it should be given. Nor do they indicate how much each individual should give to the poor. This model is largely consistent with early rabbinic conceptualizations of *tsedaqah* or charity. Tannaitic texts instruct that charity consists of monetary or material support for the poor—but nowhere do they specify how much each individual should give, what the individual should give, or precisely when or how often.[13] The early rabbinic conceptualization of charity does not grant a poor individual the right over any particular asset in the possession of a potential benefactor.

Models of charity and justice can help us illuminate with greater insight and precision rabbinic approaches to care for the poor, as well as tease out their implications. Whereas harvest laws are negative in character, aligning with justice, for the most part the Tannaim present charity as a positive obligation. At the same time, however, ancient rabbinic thought on the topic is complex and never as consistent as modern scholars would like it to be. In this vein, the Tannaim's texts on care for the poor include discussions and ideas that prompt us to challenge the way that we think of justice and charity, and suggest that their bifurcation can be problematized.

First, while many aspects of Tannaitic charity are left to the personal discretion of the giver, the act itself is deemed involuntary—it is a divine commandment to perform charity, even if the method of performance is not perfectly defined. Third, as I will elaborate upon below, Tannaitic texts

---

are not fungible. Unlike the Second Tithe, which can be converted to other forms of wealth, the poor have a claim over the specific produce of harvest gifts. While one might say that what happens to grow in a corner or fall to the ground is entirely accidental, Brooks suggests that others might see this as divine choice in selecting the specific produce that belongs to the poor (*Support for the Poor*, 18).

12. J. B. Schneewind, "Philosophical Ideas of Charity: Some Historical Reflections," in *Giving: Western Ideas of Philanthropy*, ed. J. B. Schneewind, Philanthropic Studies (Bloomington: Indiana University Press, 1996), 59, 67; and, in the same volume, Allen Buchanan, "Charity, Justice, and the Idea of Moral Progress," 99.

13. This is clearly the case for charity laws on individual giving. For the subcategory of communal charity, the Tosefta prescribes that the *tamhui* (soup kitchen) and *quppa* (charity fund) should provide certain things, such as enough bread for two meals per day, certain clothes, and so on. The texts, however, do not specify how much or what each non-poor individual is obligated to donate to the *tamhui* or *quppa*. On communal, institutional giving, see further Gardner, *Origins of Organized Charity*.

occasionally present charity as a negative obligation. Eventually, from the few seeds planted by the Tannaim, charity's sense as a negative obligation would grow alongside its positive one—challenging later rabbinic thinkers to reconcile the two. Perhaps most famously, in his effort to classify commandments as positive or negative, Maimonides would write that one who refuses a beggar misses an opportunity to fulfill a positive commandment and transgresses a negative commandment.[14]

Charity as a Negative Obligation

The Tannaim, perhaps drawing upon a handful of received traditions from the Second Temple era, take up the concept of charity and discuss it extensively. There are discussions of charity scattered throughout the Tannaitic corpus, including a large block of discourse at the end of Tosefta Pe'ah (4:8–21). For the most part, charity is conceptualized as a positive obligation, fittingly motivated by a carrot: the promise of personal recompense from God for giving to the poor. We see this, for example, in discussions of charity where the giver earns *sakhar* (payment), treasures, and *perot* (fruit, profits), which are often paid out in the afterlife (e.g., t. Pe'ah 4:17–18). On occasion, however, charity is also motivated by a stick: the threat of personal punishment by God if one refuses to give when asked by a poor person. We see this in t. Pe'ah 4:20:

> R. Yehoshua ben Qorkhah said:
> "From where do we know that anyone who lifts his eyes[15] from charity [*tsedaqah*] is an idol worshiper?
> As it is said: *Be careful that you do not entertain a wicked* [*bly'l*] *thought, thinking, ["The seventh year, the year of remission, is near," and therefore view your needy neighbor with hostility and give nothing; your neighbor might cry to the Lord against you, and you would incur guilt.]* (Deut 15:9)[16]
> And there it says: *that some scoundrels* [*bly'l*] *[from among you] have gone [and subverted the inhabitants of their town, saying, "Come let us worship other gods"].* (Deut 13:14 NJPS)
> Just as *bly'l* refers to idolatry there [in Deut 13:14],
> So too *bly'l* refers to idolatry here [in Deut 15:9]." (t. Pe'ah 4:20)[17]

The Tosefta makes its point on exegetical grounds, using a characteristically rabbinic form of argumentation, the verbal analogy (*gezerah shewa*).[18]

---

14. See Maimonides, *Mishneh Torah,* in the enumeration of the commandments (i.e., Sefer Ha-Mitzvot), positive commandment 195 and negative commandment 232.
15. That is, he is distracted from or otherwise fails to give charity.
16. Translation based on NRSV, with my modifications.
17. Translations of rabbinic texts are my own, unless otherwise noted.
18. Eduard Lohse and Günter Mayer, *Die Tosefta, Seder I: Zeraim, 1.1: Berakot – Pea,*

The sense of *bly'l* as indicating idolatry is fairly clear in Deut 13:14, which discusses scoundrels (*bly'l*) who worship idols—an association that the Tosefta reads into the use of *bly'l* in Deut 15:9, which warns against failing to extend loans to the poor in the years leading up to the seventh-year remittance of debt. Idolatry may be considered a form of "persuasive rhetoric" that the rabbis used to make or enforce legal points.[19] Idolatry was particularly potent as it came to be identified as a defining metaphor for non-Jewishness.[20] We see this, for example, in discussions of table commensality, which warns that certain eating habits are akin to worshiping idols.[21] Similarly, in t. Pe'ah 4:20, idolatry is deployed to warn against failing to give—it is used in the service of presenting charity as a negative commandment. By framing a failure to give as idolatry, the Tosefta casts this negative obligation as a potential offense against God. Instead of a social responsibility, t. Pe'ah 4:20 is part of a broader understanding that charity is primarily an obligation with respect to God.[22] This is brought out in the subsequent passage in the Tosefta, t. Pe'ah 4:21:

> R. Elazar son of R. Yose said:
> From where do we learn that charity [*tsedaqah*] and acts of reciprocal kindness [*gemilut ḥasadim*] are great peace[-makers] and great intercessors between Israel and their father in heaven?
> *For thus says the Lord: Do not enter the house of mourning, [or go to lament, or bemoan them; for I have taken away my peace from this people, says the Lord, my steadfast love* [*ḥesed*] *and mercy* [*raḥamim*]. (Jer 16:5 NRSV)
> *Steadfast love* [*ḥesed*] is acts of reciprocal kindness [*gemilut ḥasadim*].
> *Mercy* [*raḥamim*] is charity [*tsedaqah*].
> It teaches that charity [*tsedaqah*] and acts of reciprocal kindness [*gemilut ḥasadim*] are great peace[-makers] between Israel and their father in heaven.

This passage, which concludes the tractate and punctuates its extended discourse on charity, sees charity primarily as a means to connect humans and God; social ethics would be included under the umbrella category of

---

ed. G. Kittel et al. (Stuttgart: Kohlhammer, 1999), 158 n. 161; see generally H. L. Strack and Günter Stemberger, *Introduction to the Talmud and Midrash*, trans. M. N. A. Bockmuehl (Minneapolis: Fortress, 1996), 18–19.

19. Michael L. Satlow, *Tasting the Dish: Rabbinic Rhetorics of Sexuality*, BJS 303 (Atlanta: Scholars Press, 1995), 8.

20. Sacha Stern, *Jewish Identity in Early Rabbinic Writings*, AGJU 23 (Leiden: Brill, 1994), 196–97.

21. Jordan D. Rosenblum, *Food and Identity in Early Rabbinic Judaism* (New York: Cambridge University Press, 2010).

22. Similarly, see Benjamin Porat, "Charity and Distributive Justice," in *Windows onto Jewish Legal Culture: Fourteen Exploratory Essays*, ed. Hanina Ben-Menahem, Aryeh Edrei, and Neil S. Hecht, 2 vols., (London: Routledge, 2011), 2:60.

gemilut ḥasadim or "acts of reciprocal kindness."[23] It is certainly possible that charity can also create peace (and solidarity) between humans, but that aspect is not brought out in this passage. Notably, intercession with God is brought about by benefactors giving, as the poor are not intercessors in this passage. As is typical of early rabbinic discussions of charity, in t. Pe'ah 4:20–21 the poor are backgrounded if not nearly invisible.[24] The invisibility and backgrounding of the poor may be a product of the fact that the authors and redactors of these texts were themselves not poor but rather generally well-off.[25]

Returning to the discussion of charity as a negative commandment in t. Pe'ah 4:20, this approach may be profitably compared to a passage in the Second Temple-era book of Tobit:[26]

> 6 … To all those who practice righteousness 7 give alms from your possessions, and do not let your eye begrudge the gift when you make it. Do not turn your face away from anyone who is poor, and the face of God will not be turned away from you. (Tob 4:6b–7 NRSV)

Here, too, charity is cast as a negative commandment, as one who refuses to give will be punished by God. The punishment is "measure-for-measure," as turning one's face away from the poor will result in God turning away God's face from the would-be benefactor.[27] As in the Tosefta, the poor play a very small role, cast as mere background to the main action, which is between God and the would-be benefactor. The punishment is exacted by God without any kind of intervention or intercession by the beggar. By contrast, as we will see, the poor are more visible in two other Tannaitic texts that cast charity as a negative commandment.

A second text on charity as a negative commandment is Sifre Deut. 117, an interpretation and discussion of Deut 15:9:

> *He will cry out to the Lord against you, and you will incur guilt* (Deut 15:9 NJPS).

---

23. Gregg E. Gardner, "From the General to the Specific: A Genealogy of 'Acts of Reciprocal Kindness' (*Gemilut Hasadim*) in Rabbinic Literature," in *Religious Studies and Rabbinics: A Conversation*, ed. Elizabeth Shanks Alexander and Beth A. Berkowitz, Routledge Jewish Studies Series (London: Routledge, 2017), 209–25.

24. On the visibility of the poor in classical rabbinic texts on charity, see among others Gray, "Formerly Wealthy Poor," 101–33.

25. Gardner, "Who Is Rich?," 515–36.

26. On care for the poor in Tobit, see Gary A. Anderson, *Charity: The Place of the Poor in the Biblical Tradition* (New Haven: Yale University Press, 2013); David J. Downs, *Alms: Charity, Reward, and Atonement in Early Christianity* (Waco, TX: Baylor University Press, 2016), 58–70.

27. On the principle of measure-for-measure, or *talion*, in early rabbinic literature, see Ishay Rosen-Zvi, "Measure for Measure as a Hermeneutical Tool in Early Rabbinic Literature: The Case of Tosefta Sotah," *JJS* 57 (2006): 269–86.

> *He will cry out* (Deut 15:9). Or contrariwise, one might think that he is commanded to cry out; therefore Scripture says elsewhere, *else he will cry to the Lord against you* (Deut 24:14). Again, one might think that if he cries out against you, a sin is charged against you, but if he does not cry out against you, no sin is charged against you; therefore the verse goes on to say, *and you would incur guilt* (Deut 15:9)—in any event. If so, why does the verse end with *else he will cry to the Lord against you* (Deut 24:14)? Because I, (the Lord) will exact punishment more quickly in response to the one who cries out than to the one who does not cry out. (Sifre Deut. 117 on 15:9; trans. Hammer, with my emendations)[28]

To better identify and appreciate the contribution of the rabbis, it is worth taking a moment to discuss Deut 15:9 in its biblical context. The verse refers to extending loans in the years leading up to the septennial cancellation of debts (Deut 15:7–11). While this is certainly laudable behavior and an act of obedience with respect to God, it is not rendered by the Hebrew Bible as charity per se. As a loan, Deut 15:7–11 does not map onto what came to be understood as charity, which is the surrender of one's assets with the assumption that the recipient will not provide compensation in return. More broadly, it is highly unlikely that the concept of charity appears anywhere in the Hebrew Bible, whether in Deut 15 or elsewhere. The term *tsedaqah* does not denote "charity" in Biblical Hebrew.[29] Moreover, biblical texts on care for the poor do not include prescriptions that would necessarily lead to the development of the concept of charity in a form similar to its postbiblical conceptualization. As with many concepts, postbiblical writings (including rabbinic texts) may retroactively claim that charity has a basis in the Hebrew Bible, but we cannot demonstrate that the specific form of charity (as it would come to be understood in postbiblical texts) necessarily derives from any particular source in the Hebrew Bible.[30]

In any case, the Tannaim read Deut 15:9 as addressing their conceptualization of charity: the borrower in Deut 15:9 is not asking for a loan—but rather for charity.[31] And the text does not warn against failing to lend, but

---

28. Reuven Hammer, *Sifre: A Tannaitic Commentary on the Book of Deuteronomy*, Yale Judaica Series 24 (New Haven: Yale University Press, 1986), 162–63.

29. Ahuva Ho, *Ṣedeq and Ṣedaqah in the Hebrew Bible*, American University Studies 7.78 (New York: P. Lang, 1991); Gardner, *Origins of Organized Charity*, 26–33; A. Hurvitz, "The Biblical Roots of a Talmudic Term: The Early History of the Concept of *tsedaqah* [= charity, alms]" [Hebrew], *Language Studies II–III* (1987): 155–60; Franz Rosenthal, "Sedaka, Charity," *HUCA* 23 (1950–1951): 411–30. The closest to "charity" that we find in the Hebrew Bible is the Aramaic *tsidqah* in Dan 4:24.

30. Here I adapt and apply the general observations and wording of Cohen, "Judaean Legal Tradition," 125.

31. Elsewhere, however, the Tannaim's development of the *prosbul*, a legal arrangement that circumvents the cancellation of debts in the seventh year (m. Shevi'it 10:3–7), can be understood as reinforcing the sense that Deut 15 addresses a loan that needs to be repaid.

rather against failing to give charity. In the rabbinic reading, Deut 15:9 indicates that the spurned beggar cries out to God against the failed benefactor. Despite the poor individual's presence and activity, his agency is severely limited: the midrash indicates that his cry does not directly provoke a punishment. Rather, the poor's cry only determines the speed of God's reaction, as the failed benefactor will be punished even without the poor's intervention.

A third early rabbinic text that conceptualizes charity as a negative commandment is in the Mekilta of Rabbi Ishmael:

> If the poor man stretches out his hand towards the householder, and the householder gives willingly, then *the Lord giveth light to the eyes of both* (Prov 29:13). If, however, the poor man stretches out his hand towards the householder, and the latter is unwilling to give, then *the Lord is the maker of them all* (Prov 22:2) – He who had made the one poor will in the end make him rich, and He who had made the other rich will in the end make him poor. (Mekhilta of R. Ishmael, Amalek, Yitro, Parashah 2, on Exod 18:13–17; trans. Lauterbach, with my modifications)[32]

This text from the Mekilta indicates that one who fails to give upon solicitation will be subject to personal punishment. The punishment is measure-for-measure and has significant material consequences: the potential benefactor will become poor. The threat of a reversal of fortune is employed in other early rabbinic texts on care for the poor, though there it is used to warn against pretending to be poor or infirmed in order to receive rabbinically prescribed poverty relief.[33] The Mekilta's use of the principle of measure-for-measure is more similar to the passage from Tob 4:6b–7 discussed above, as it is meant to dictate the behavior of the benefactor, rather than the beggar.

As in Sifre Deut. 117, here too in the Mekilta the poor individual is highly visible and has a degree of agency, as he initiates the process by soliciting alms. The poor man reaches out his hand—imagery that is frequently used in religious texts on charity.[34] That is, the poor initiate the process and the obligation by soliciting a well-off individual for alms. By comparison, the laws of harvest gifts are initiated simply by time—when

---

32. Jacob Z. Lauterbach, *Mekhilta de-Rabbi Ishmael: A Critical Edition, Based on the Manuscripts and Early Editions* (Philadelphia: Jewish Publication Society, 2004), 288; see also H. S. Horovitz and I. A. Rabin, eds., *Mechilta d'Rabbi Ismael* [Hebrew] (2nd ed., 1931; repr., Jerusalem: Shalem Books, 1997), 201–2.

33. Mishnah Pe'ah 8:9; t. Pe'ah 4:12–14; and Gregg E. Gardner, "Charity Wounds: Gifts to the Poor in Early Rabbinic Judaism," in *The Gift in Antiquity*, ed. Michael L. Satlow, Ancient World: Comparative Histories (Chichester: Wiley-Blackwell, 2013), 173–88.

34. E.g., m. Shabbat 1:1; t. Pe'ah 4:18. Outside of the rabbinic tradition, see, e.g., 2 En. 51:1; Sir 7:32; Acts of Thomas 2.

the harvest begins, in compliance with the biblical instructions, "*when* you reap ..." (Lev 19:9 and Deut 24:19). By contrast, in the passages discussed here, the obligation is initiated by the poor man's request—wherever and whenever it is made. Indeed, this may be a product of the realities of the time, as the poor in the Roman world were known to approach well-off individuals for alms on an ad hoc basis—particularly in marketplaces and near religious institutions but also occasionally at the doorway of one's home.[35] Whereas negative obligations (such as harvest gifts) are usually perfectly defined, here the temporal ambiguity adds an element of imperfection—the timing is left to the discretion of one of the parties. In this way, the poor man in the Mekilta is given a degree of agency.

As in Sifre Deut. 117, however, likewise in the Mekilta the poor's agency is significantly dampened, as the recompense or punishment is dispensed by God and is not a direct result of active intercession by the poor individual (e.g., by crying out or praying). The limited agency of the poor in these texts becomes all the more conspicuous when compared to other, similar religious models of giving—especially those that cast charity as a negative obligation.

The Poor as Intercessors and the Triadic Model of Giving

Scholars have identified certain "systematic patterns" that are common to multiple religious traditions' conceptualizations of charity.[36] These patterns are composed of a web of norms, virtues, theological validations, exclusionary rules, individual responsibilities, and so on.[37] One such pattern is the "triadic model" of giving: upon receiving alms, a beggar offers prayers that prompt divine powers to reward the benefactor. Conversely, a spurned beggar would curse a failed benefactor, prompting a punishment from the divine. Reciprocity and exchange are triangulated between three parties—benefactor, beneficiary, and the divine.[38]

In writings from the biblical and postbiblical tradition, the triadic model is evident in Hellenistic Jewish, early Christian, and Amoraic texts, where rewards for charity are often triggered by the poor, who intercede

35. Gardner, *Origins of Organized Charity*, 5–6; m. Shabbat 1:1; t. Pe'ah 4:8.

36. Julia R. Lieberman and Michal Jan Rozbicki, "Introduction," in *Charity in Jewish, Christian, and Islamic Traditions* (ed. Julia R. Lieberman and Michal Jan Rozbicki; Lanham, MD: Lexington Books, 2017), viii.

37. Ibid.

38. For example, Thierry Kochuyt outlines a "triadic model" of religiously inspired charity in Islamic thought ("God, Gifts and Poor People: On Charity in Islam," *Social Compass* 56 [2009]: 98–116).

by offering prayers to God on behalf of the benefactor.[39] We see this, for example, in Clement of Alexandria's *Salvation of the Rich*, where the poor serve as advocates on behalf of the rich.[40] Similarly, in the Shepherd of Hermas, the poor are depicted as rich in prayer, as they provide essential intercession with God on behalf of a benefactor (Herm. Sim. 2.5–7).[41] The triadic model is often employed within the framework of redemptive almsgiving.[42]

Like Tannaitic texts, Amoraic writings include depictions of the poor with little agency. Salient examples are passages in which the poor ask for alms by inviting a potential benefactor to "gain merit through me." By taking possession of alms, the poor in these texts complete the transaction, thereby fulfilling the benefactor's religious obligation to give charity. The poor in these texts, however, do not actively effect recompense or punishment for a failure to give by crying out or some other method. Rather, the poor are depicted as weak and dependent upon the giver—their very survival requires immediate generosity as they can die if benefactors merely delay their gifts.[43]

In other Amoraic texts, however, the poor are much more active and have significantly more agency, as with typical models of triadic giving. We see a range of attitudes, from the poor and rich being symbiotic (they enable each other to gain benefit), to suggestions that the poor individual gives more to the benefactor than he receives.[44] We also see the rabbis

---

39. On the poor as intercessors in ancient Judaism and Christianity, see Gary A. Anderson, *Sin: A History* (New Haven: Yale University Press, 2009), 147, 151; Anderson, *Charity*, 25, 31, 67; Gray, "Redemptive Almsgiving," 145–69, 183; Richard Finn, *Almsgiving in the Later Roman Empire: Christian Promotion and Practice (313–450)* (Oxford: Oxford University Press, 2006), 30, 180, 205; Anneliese Parkin, "An Exploration of Pagan Almsgiving," in *Poverty in the Roman World*, ed. Margaret Atkins and Robin Osborne (Cambridge: Cambridge University Press, 2006), 78; Satlow, "Fruit and the Fruit of Fruit," 245, 274.

40. Downs, *Alms*, 184.

41. See Downs, *Alms*, 184.

42. On redemptive almsgiving in early Christianity, see Downs, *Alms*; Roman Garrison, *Redemptive Almsgiving in Early Christianity*, JSNTSup 77 (Sheffield: JSOT Press, 1993). For rabbinic texts, see Gray, "Redemptive Almsgiving," 155–56. I add that, while Tannaitic writings include meritorious or recompensed giving, they do not do so within the context of a benefactor's sin or atonement.

43. See y. Pe'ah 8:9, 21b (multiple instances), Pesiqta de Rab Kahana 28:3, Lev. Rab. 34:5, 34:7, 34:14, and their discussion in Anderson, *Sin*, 147; Anderson, *Charity*, 25, 31, 67; Gardner, *Origins of Organized Charity*, 184–86; Gray, "Redemptive Almsgiving," 156; Burton L. Visotzky, *Golden Bells and Pomegranates: Studies in Midrash Leviticus Rabbah*, TSAJ 94 (Tübingen: Mohr Siebeck, 2003), 131; Wilfand, *Poverty, Charity*, 54–56, 179–80.

44. E.g., Lev. Rab. 34:5, 8–10 on 25:25; Ruth Rab. 5:4 and 5:9, on 2:19; see Rivka Ulmer and Moshe Ulmer, *Righteous Giving to the Poor: Tzedakah ("Charity") in Classical Rabbinic Judaism, Including a Brief Introduction to Rabbinic Literature*, Gorgias Handbooks (Piscataway, NJ: Gorgias, 2014), 70–71, 74.

depict themselves as recipients of charity and as intercessors whose activities prompt divine recompense.[45]

In contrast to these triadic models, in Tannaitic texts the poor's powers are dampened—they are empowered to initiate the obligation, but the recompense will be meted out to the benefactors by God regardless of the poor's activity.[46] Moreover, while the poor are surely more visible in these texts than others, they function as mere vessels—more so containers into which charity is placed than instruments with agency.

Conclusion

This paper has examined some noteworthy aspects of early rabbinic discussions of charity. First, while predominantly a positive commandment, we also see some texts where charity shades into a negative commandment. Second, in comparison to models of triadic giving, we see that the Tannaim dampen the poor's agency, as they do not fully effect a punishment for the benefactor. That is, these Tannaitic texts cast charity as a negative commandment, but they do so without the full agency or intercession of the poor.

The nature of an obligation can have important implications for care for the poor. Positive obligations rely on the discretion and motivation of individuals and therefore require that someone identify a problem and muster the initiative to act to ensure that a deed is carried out.[47] This can allow for mismatches between what benefactors give and what the poor need, as well as shortfalls due to a lack of individual finances or initiative. Moreover, with positive obligations, a poor person cannot lay claim to a specific asset currently owned by a would-be benefactor—the needy have no inherent claim to be looked after by any particular individual. Claims on a community as a whole can allow for members to shirk individual responsibilities.[48] By contrast, negative obligations provide assets to the poor as they simply require individuals to refrain from interfering. The poor have clear rights over certain goods and claims against another party if they fail to receive those goods. With respect to communal wel-

45. Satlow, "Fruit and the Fruit of Fruit," 245; Yael Wilfand Ben Shalom, "Poverty, Charity, and the Image of the Poor in Rabbinic Texts from the Land of Israel" (PhD diss., Duke University, 2011), 181–82, 190–91.

46. Notably, in t. Pe'ah 4:18 a rich benefactor serves as an intercessor; see the apologetic analysis of this text by Ephraim Urbach, "Treasures Above," in *Hommage à Georges Vajda: Études d'histoire et de pensée juives*, ed. Gérard Nahon and Charles Touati, Collection de la Revue des études juives 1 (Louvain: Peeters, 1980), 117–24.

47. Melinda Jones, "From Welfare to Rights in the Jewish Tradition," in Lieberman and Rozbicki, *Charity in Jewish, Christian, and Islamic Traditions*, 84.

48. Ibid., 84–85.

fare and social solidarity, charity cast as a negative obligation presents certain advantages over depicting it as a positive obligation. In time, the rabbinic tradition would bring together these threads, defining charity in ways that lay bare and harmonize its sense as both a positive and negative obligation.

Interspecies and Cross-species Generation

Limits and Potentialities in Tannaitic Reproductive Science

RACHEL RAFAEL NEIS
University of Michigan

In his article "The Origins of the Matrilineal Principle in Rabbinic Law," and later in his *Beginnings of Judaism*, Shaye Cohen, has suggested that ideas about interspecific reproduction and the classification of resultant offspring, particularly channeled through the biblical prohibition and rabbinic elaborations of *kil'ayim*, were intertwined with considerations about Jewish/non-Jewish offspring.[1] More recently, Charlotte Fonrobert has posited that the "science of blood" in the tractate Niddah underpins rabbinic distinctions between Jewish (specifically, rabbinic, Samaritan), para-Jewish (Samaritan) and non-Jewish communities.[2] Similarly, Gwynn Kessler has argued that rabbinic embryology underpinned a particular ethno-theology about the relationship between Israel and God.[3] All three authors treat types of knowledge that we might describe as rabbinic repro-

1. Shaye J.D. Cohen, "The Origins of the Matrilineal Principle in Rabbinic Law," *AJS Review* 10 (1985):19–53 and Shaye J. D. Cohen, *The Beginnings of Jewishness: Boundaries, Varieties, Uncertainties*, HCS 31 (Berkeley: University of California Press, 1999), 299–302.

2. Charlotte Elisheva Fonrobert, "Blood and Law," *Henoch* 30 (2008): 243–66; Fonrobert, *Menstrual Purity: Rabbinic and Christian Reconstructions of Biblical Gender*, Contraversions (Stanford, CA: Stanford University Press, 2000). In "Blood and Law," Fonrobert gets at the multidirectional and layered ways in which uterine blood science operates beyond gender, to further rabbinic conceptions of Jewish (e.g., rabbinic, Samaritan), para-Jewish (e.g., Samaritan) and non-Jewish identity.

3. Gwynn Kessler, *Conceiving Israel: The Fetus in Rabbinic Narratives*, Divinations (Philadelphia: University of Pennsylvania Press, 2009). For a treatment of the relationship between rabbinic sources on reproduction, ideas of kinship, and the Israeli state, see Susan Martha Kahn, *Reproducing Jews: A Cultural Account of Assisted Conception in Israel*, Body, Commodity, Text (Durham, NC: Duke University Press, 2000). For an incisive analysis of an Amoraic source, see Galit Hasan-Rokem and Israel Jacob Yuval, "Myth, History and Eschatology in a Rabbinic Treatise on Birth," in *Talmudic Transgressions: Engaging the Work of Daniel Boyarin*, ed. Charlotte Elisheva Fonrobert et al., JSJSup 181 (Leiden: Brill, 2017), 243–73.

ductive science (whether animal husbandry, gynecology, or embryology) in terms of their ramified conceptions of Jewishness.[4]

In this article, I also explore some of the same sources as these scholars, reading them as rabbinic biological science and following Tannaitic ideas about the limits and possibilities of reproductive and species nonconformity. I read rabbinic sources in the tractates of Niddah, Kil'ayim, and Bekhorot, as expressions of a science of generation, or a biology, in which nonhuman zoology and human gynecology were entwined both conceptually and even materially in terms of reproductive outcomes. I argue that the rabbis, like other ancient thinkers, understood that creatures of a particular kind (or species), including the human-kind, might deliver a creature that appears to be of a different kind.[5] I show that in the majority of cases the Tannaim believed these species nonconforming offspring *not* to be genuine hybrids, that is, they did not believe that they were the results of cross-species mating. I consider the ways that the rabbis conceptualized such unpredictable generative outcomes and, particularly, the potential gestational entanglements of the human and the nonhuman.

Theories of Reproduction

To begin with, let us note that the rabbis understood that some life forms came into being as a result of "reproduction and multiplication" (*piryah ve-rivyah*, or "sexual reproduction"), whereas others did not but instead emerged from various substances such as water or mud ("spontaneous

---

4. On animals in rabbinic culture, see Beth Berkowitz, "Animal," in *Late Ancient Knowing: Explorations in Intellectual History*, ed. Catherine M. Chin and Moulie Vidas (Oakland: University of California Press, 2015), 36–57; Berkowitz, *Animals and Animality in the Babylonian Talmud* (Oxford: Oxford University Press, 2018). On animality, disability, and rabbinics, see Julia Watts Belser, "Brides and Blemishes: Queering Women's Disability in Rabbinic Marriage Law," *JAAR* 84 (2016): 201–29; on rabbinic intersections of gender, religion, and species, see Mira Wasserman, *Jews, Gentiles, and Other Animals: The Talmud After the Humanities*, Divinations (Philadelphia: University of Pennsylvania Press, 2017), esp. 74-165.

On ancient Jewish sciences, see Annette Yoshiko Reed, "'Ancient Jewish Sciences' and the Historiography of Judaism," in *Ancient Jewish Sciences and the History of Knowledge in Second Temple Literature*, ed. Jonathan Ben-Dov and Seth Sanders (New York: New York University Press, 2014) 195–254.

5. For some of the themes and texts discussed here, albeit with a focus on rabbinic knowledges in the light of critical science studies, feminist science studies, and ancient reproductive thought, see Rachel Neis, "The Reproduction of Species: Humans, Animals and Species Nonconformity in Early Rabbinic Science," *JSQ* 24 (2017): 289–317. In that article, I make the case for reading traditions in Bekhorot and Niddah together given their linguistic and conceptual affinities, their deployment of the classificatory concept of kind (*min*), and their interest in likeness/dissemblance all in contexts of generation. I also consider rabbinic science in the context of imperial, gendered, and species-related dynamics of knowledge.

reproduction").[6] Among those that reproduce via *piryah ve-rivyah*, the rabbis further distinguished between modes of reproduction (e.g., intercourse, spawning, etc.) (see t. Bek. 1:10–11). The question of kind (or species, or *min*) was also a significant one for the rabbis, who sought to elaborate priestly taxonomies, most especially (but not exclusively) in distinguishing among pure and impure species. Whether a creature was sexually or spontaneously produced impinged on determinations of kind. The rabbis, like Aristotle, thought that for the most part kind (or *min*) reproduced like kind. This idea is expressed in their "principle of generation." The Tannaim also understood that material form and appearance was part of what was reproduced in cases of sexual reproduction, and that likeness was a key to sorting origins, parentage, and species designations of newly generated entities. Spontaneous reproduction disrupted this rule, given that one kind of entity (e.g., mud or water) gives rise to another kind (e.g., gnats or the "earth-mouse"; t. Yad. 2:4; m. Ḥul. 9:6).[7]

There were two other phenomena that tested the limits of likeness as a key to assigning species. The first involved the results of cross-species mating (*kil'ayim*), for example, the offspring of a goat and a sheep (a "geep"; t. Bek. 1:13, m. Bek. 2:5) or that of a donkey and a horse (a mule; t. Kil. 5:3, 5:5 and m. Kil. 8:4).[8] The second, perhaps even more confusing, was the case of species-nonconforming offspring that were spontaneously anomalous. In other words, a cow and a bull mated and the cow delivered a creature that is "like a donkey kind" (*ke-min hamor*; m. Bek. 1:2), or a camel (t. Bek. 1:9).[9]

6. See, e.g., Sifra Shemini Parashat 5 (ed. Weiss, 49b), which distinguishes between *sheratsim* that have bones and have sexual intercourse, that do not have bones and do not have sexual intercourse, and the permutations and combinations thereof and b. Shabbat 107b for lice that do not reproduce sexually.

7. The Mishnah is cited according to *Shishah Sidre Mishnah*, ed. H. Albeck (Jerusalem: Mosad Bialik, 1957–1959), with consultation of MS. Kaufmann; the Tosefta according to *Tosefta Kifeshuta*, ed. Saul Lieberman (New York: Jewish Theological Seminary, 1962) or *Tosephta*, ed. M. S. Zuckermandel (Jerusalem: Wahrman, 1970), with consultations of the Primary Textual Witnesses to Tannaitic Literature (https://www.biu.ac.il/JS/tannaim/); the Sifra is cited according to *Sifra*, ed. Isaac H. Weiss (Vienna: Schlossberg, 1862), also with consultation of the Primary Textual Witnesses to Tannaitic Literature. On spontaneously generated insects, see Saul Lieberman, "Light on the Cave Scrolls from Rabbinic Sources," *PAAJR* 20 (1951): 396.

8. For the biblical *kil'ayim* prohibition, see Lev 19:9 and Deut 22:9–11. On the "geep," see C. B. Fehilly, S. M. Willadse, and E. M. Tucker, "Interspecific Chimaerism between Sheep and Goat," *Nature* 307 (1984): 634–36.

9. I do not read m. Bek. 1:2 as referring to results of cross-species unions for two reasons. First, the Mishnah and Tosefta expressly forbid the results of *kil'ayim* as firstborn offerings. Second, they refer explicitly to such cases. Third, in t. Bek. 1:6 (MS Vienna) R. Yosa requires that the one bearing (היולד, masc.) and the one born (הנולד) are the same kind. In the case of species nonconformity, "if it has some of the signs resembling its father" it still qualifies for the firstborn offering (and implicitly in b. B. Qam. 78a).

Tosefta Kil'ayim 5:3 articulates the distinction between species-non-conforming deliveries that are results of cross-breeding and those that are not:

> A horse which delivered a donkey kind (*min*), it is permitted with its mother ['s kind].[10] But if its father was a donkey, it is forbidden with its mother['s kind].
>
> A donkey which delivered a horse kind (*min*), it is permitted with its mother['s kind]. But if its father was a horse, it is forbidden with its mother['s kind].
>
> A ewe which delivered [a goat kind],[11] it is permitted with its mother['s kind]. But if its father was a goat, it is forbidden with its mother['s kind].
>
> A goat which delivered a sheep kind (*min*), it is permitted with its mother['s kind]. But if its father was a sheep (lit., a ewe), it is forbidden with its mother['s kind].
>
> And there is no offering at the altar.[12]

As we see, the Tosefta contemplates two scenarios in which a female horse (a mare) can (seemingly) deliver a donkey kind: through same-species mating and through cross-species mating.[13] According to the Tosefta, the product of cross-breeding (the mule) is not a member of its mother's kind (horse) and therefore may not be mated or yoked with members of the horse species.[14] Here the Tosefta says nothing about the *kil'ayim* delivery's species classification (whether it is distinct from both parents' species, or whether it is its father's kind), however it clarifies that its species classification is *not* matrilineal.

In the case of *same*-species mating, the species-variant delivery is simply classified according to its parentage. A creature born to two horses

10. Lieberman comments in his edition, "a horse that delivered a donkey kind, but its father was also a horse, it is permitted to mate it with a horse" (t. Kil. 5:3, ed. Lieberman, 221).

11. MS Vienna omits (but given in MS Erfurt; Lieberman supplies).

12. MS Vienna (cf. MS Erfurt, which has *pasul*).

13. Lieberman refers to this latter entity as a *nidmeh* (one that appears) (*Tosefta*, 222). This term is attested only in post-Tannaitic sources. See Saul Lieberman, *Tosefta Kifshuta*, Seder Zeraim, vol. 2 (New York: Jewish Theological Seminary of America, 2001), 647, where Lieberman emends סוס שילדה מן החמור to סוס שילדה מין החמור.

14. Cf. t. Kil. 5:5, in which the sages declare that all mules (*haperadot*) are a single kind (*min ehad*) and that therefore mules that are the results of differently gendered unions of horse/donkey parents (i.e. female parent horse and male parent donkey versus female parent donkey and male parent horse) can mate with each other. Rabbi Judah there disagrees, viewing mules of differing parentage as prohibited to one another. However, in t. Kil. 1:8 he prohibits the mating of a female mule with a horse or donkey but allows it with a mule without specifying the parentage of either). Therefore it does not seem that matrilineality is the key decider for Rabbi Judah, at least in the Tosefta's version of his views. In the Mishnah (m. Kil 8:4), Rabbi Judah does seem to espouse a version of the matrilineal principle for species designation (contradicting t. Kil 5:3). See Cohen, *Beginnings of Jewishness*, 299–302.

that looks like a donkey is still a horse, and it is thus not a transgression of the *kil'ayim* prohibition to have it mate or be harnessed with a horse. It cannot, however, be offered (or redeemed) at the temple, as its variation disqualifies it. This is echoed in the tractate Bekhorot, which expands the biblical disqualifying "blemishes" (*mumim*) to include various features of species nonconformity, including animals whose mouths resemble those of pigs, or whose eyes appear to be like those of humans, or whose tails look like those of a pig.[15] It also includes, as mentioned already, cases of more radical species variation like those mentioned in t. Kil 5:3 (e.g., a cow delivering something "like a donkey kind," m. Bek 1:2, or a camel, t. Bek. 1:9). While these creatures may be rejected for cultic purposes, like their human analogs (priests) who are excluded due to species nonconforming features, their species designations are not in question.

These sources make it abundantly clear that various degrees of spontaneously arising species nonconformity can occur, not just in animals but also in humans.[16] We see multiple instances of this phenomenon in rabbinic and other ancient sources, including human women who expel creatures that are "like a kind of domesticated animal, or wild animal, or bird" (m. Nid. 3:2; t. Nid. 4:2) or a woman who was a habitual aborter of a "raven likeness" (*demut orev*; t. Nid. 4:6). In the case of these deliveries by a human, the decision about species designation centers on the degree of nonconformity. This is different from the animal deliveries. While Rabbi Meir includes beings that look completely like animals and birds as human offspring (*valad*), the sages require that such beings bear some minimal human resemblance (*mi-tsurat ha-adam*). The sages thereby effectively admit hybrid-appearing entities delivered by humans, as members of human-kind. Whereas the Mishnah leaves this formal minimal requirement unspecified, the Tosefta confines it to facial features (t. Nid. 4:7).

The Limits and Logics of Species Nonconformity

The Tannaim were not alone in living in a world of unpredictable and variable reproductive outcomes. Nor were they alone in seeking to understand, or at least classify, the species designations of nonconforming deliveries. Those such as Pliny and Soranus, for example, suggested that

15. See, e.g., for the animal whose eye "is round like that of a human," m. Bek. 6:8; t. Bek. 4:11; whose "mouth is like a pig's," m. Bek. 6:8; or for the "tail of a kid goat like that of a pig," m. Bek. 6:9. Bekhorot also talks of interspecies features among human priests, not only extending those pertaining to animals to humans (m. Bek. 7:1), but also adding.

16. Examples of disqualifications of priests include species (or gender) nonconforming features, e.g., those with eyes "as big as a calf, or as small as a goose" (m. Bek. 7:4; t. Bek. 5:3); soles "as wide as a goose" (m. Bek. 7:6), breasts that hang "like a woman's" or an overbite "like a pig's" (m. Bek. 7:5).

variation or "misshapenness," including species nonconformity, was the result of sense impressions during conception.[17] As Ra'anan Boustan has shown, these ideas also had a specifically Near Eastern context, exemplified and inspired by Jacob's exercise in "visual eugenics" (Gen 20:31-42).[18] Sensory data or even affect could interrupt the usual processes of generation as mimesis, introducing different vectors of resemblance instead. In Soranus's example, women viewing monkeys during conception delivered infants of monkey-like appearance (Soranus, *Gyn.* 1.39). Theories such as these would wait to surface in post-Tannaitic materials.

Aristotle, whose theory of generation continued to be influential in late antiquity, understood that resemblance was tied to male seed which acted upon female matter (blood), imparting form to it. Thus, all things being equal, offspring should resemble the male parent. Deviations from this ideal occurred and ranged from female progeny, which Aristotle characterized as the first step toward monstrosity, to the animal (the genus under which the human is subsumed).[19] However, according to Aristotle, even the radically unlike, including species nonconforming, were still properly to be understood as offspring. Aristotle's explanation for deviation was the failure of the (male) seed to master the (female) material.[20] It is clear that Aristotle, like the rabbis, knew of degrees of variation in reproductive outcomes. Rhetorically, and conceptually, part of his explanatory insistence on the failure of male seed to conquer female material was in service of negating other explanations. That is, Aristotle was insistent that, aside from a few known exceptions (e.g., mules), hybrid or radically

17. See Soranus, *Gynecology* 1.39 and 1.47. Owsei Temkin renders both *kakamorphos* and *amorphos* as "misshapen" (Soranus, *Gynecology*, ed. and trans. Oswei Temkin, Publications of the Institute of the History of Medicine, the Johns Hopkins University 2.3 [Baltimore: Johns Hopkins University Press, 1994], 37–38 and 48). Soranus just mentions women; Pliny refers to either parent's sensory impressions (*Nat.* 7.52). For additional versions of this idea in late antiquity, see Rachel Neis, *Sense of Sight in Rabbinic Culture: Jewish Ways of Seeing in Late Antiquity*, Greek Culture in the Roman World (Cambridge: Cambridge University Press, 2013), 36, 39, 131–37, 159–66.

18. Ra'anan Boustan, "Rabbi Ishmael's Miraculous Conception: Jewish Redemption History in Anti-Christian Polemic," in *The Ways That Never Parted: Jews and Christians in Late Antiquity and the Early Middle Ages*, ed. Adam H. Becker and Annette Yoshiko Reed, TSAJ 95 (Tübingen: Mohr Siebeck, 2003), 307–43. See also Neis, *Sense of Sight*, 131–35, 153–56; and Michael L. Satlow, *Tasting the Dish: Rabbinic Rhetorics of Sexuality*, BJS 303 (Atlanta: Scholar Press, 1995).

19. Aristotle, *Gen. an.* 767b8–11 (cf. 767b5–7). See Rosemarie Garland Thomson, *Extraordinary Bodies: Figuring Physical Disability in American Culture and Literature* (New York: Columbia University Press, 2017), 19–20, 27–28, on the Aristotelian link between disability and females.

20. For a reading of Aristotle's account that attends to the potentials of female matter's aleatory character, in which it is dynamic and unpredictable rather than waiting passively and inertly for male seed to act upon it, see Emanuela Bianchi, *The Feminine Symptom: Aleatory Matter in the Aristotelian Cosmos* (New York: Fordham University Press, 2014)

species-nonconforming offspring *could not* come about through interbreeding.

Tannaitic sources do not flesh out a full theory of seed's role in generation aside from a few mentions of the origins of humans in "a (putrid) drop" and a tantalizing source in the Mekhilta.[21] The latter praises the uniquely divine ability to "give a person a son from a drop of water, which resembles (*domeh*) the figure of his father (*le-tsurat aviv*)."[22] We may note echoes of the Aristotelian fixation on the male contribution to form (*tsurah, eidos*), resemblance (*tselamim, eikonin, domeh*), and artistry (*tsayar*). Yet in this Tannaitic source, the agential force of male seed is taken over by the deity, and a female role/material is completely absent.[23] Other than this, the Sifra tantalizingly declares, almost in passing, that God, female parent, and male parent are "three partners in" the offspring.[24] We must await

---

21. These are m. Avot 3:1 (*tipah serukhah,* "a putrid drop"); Midrash Tannaim on Deut 32:2 (*tipah shelzenut,* "a drop of promiscuity"); and Mekhilta de Rabbi Ishmael, Beshallah, 8 (*tipah shel mayim,* "a drop of water"). The more common "emission of seed" (*shikhvat zerah,* Lev 15:16) in Tannaitic sources is not explicitly related to reproduction (e.g., m. Nid. 4:1; t. Nid. 2:8–9; t. Zavim 2:4, 6); some sources describe it as discharged by a woman (e.g., m. Miqv. 8:4). See further Mekhilta de Rabbi Ishmael, *Beshallah,* 8; cf. Mekhilta de Rabbi Shimon bar Yohai 19 and 20.

22. See Mekhilta de Rabbi Ishmael, *Beshallah,* 8: "And it says, 'there is no rock (*tsur*) like our god' (1 Sam 2:2). (Punning:) there is no artist (*tsayar*) like our god. It is characteristic of a human to go to an image maker (*oseh tselamim*) and say to him: make me the figure of (my) father. And wouldn't he (the artist) say to him: bring your father here and let him stand before me, or bring me his *eikonin* (Hebrew for Greek *eikōn*) and I will make his figure? But the holy one blessed be he isn't like this. He gives a person a son from a drop of water (seminal fluid), and it resembles (*domeh*) the figure of his father (*le-tsurat aviv*)."

23. On Greco-Roman gynecology and Palestinian rabbinic sources, see the excellent and nuanced account in Kessler, *Conceiving Israel,* 14–16, 78, 82, 104. On Aristotle's refusal to allow male seed a role other than "form and principle of movement" (*Gen an.* 729a9–11; trans. Peck) versus the female, which provides body and material, through an analogy to how a craftperson gives shape and form without supplying the materials, see *Gen. an.* 729b9–21, 730b4–32. On emissions of male seed and rabbinic masculinity see Marjorie Lehman, "Rabbinic Masculinities: Reading the *Ba'al Keri* in Tractate Yoma," *JSQ* 22 (2015): 109–36. For a gendered reading of rabbinic obstetrics and anatomy of the uterus in the case of a stillbirth, see Christiane H. Tzuberi, "A House inside a House. Mishnah *Ohalot* 7:4," *Nashim: A Journal of Jewish Women's Studies & Gender Issues* 28 (2015): 134–46.

24. Sifra Qedoshim 1:4–7 (ed. Weiss, 86d). The Sifra declares that there is an analogy between the capital sins of cursing God and cursing a person's mother and father, explaining, "the three of them are partners in him (*shutafim bo*)." See Reuven Kiperwasser "'Three Partners in a Person,'" *lectio difficilior* 2 (2009), http://www.lectio.unibe.ch/09_2/kiperwasser.html; Kessler, *Conceiving Israel;* and Judith Reesa Baskin, *Midrashic Women: Formations of the Feminine in Rabbinic Literature,* Brandeis Series on Jewish Women (Hanover, NH: University Press of New England for Brandeis University Press, 2002), 19–22. It is significant that this statement would seem to be unique to human-kind. In later sources, this idea of partnership seems to extend to animal kinds (arguably, real consideration for divine contributions to human formation only occurs in human generation).

post-Tannaitic sources for discussions of generation that resemble the seed-based theories of Aristotle, or for that matter Galen.

As we have seen above, however, even if seed is not their primary conceptual material, the Tannaim do meditate on generation and the limits and possibilities for species nonconformity therein. In the remainder of this paper, I argue that the Tannaim, like Aristotle, understood genuine occurrences of cross-breeding (*kil'ayim*) to be plausible, albeit only in limited instances and that they made similar moves regarding species nonconformity and modes of reproduction. They differed, however, from Aristotlean thought in failing to offer an explanation for spontaneously occurring species nonconformity. I will examine sources in the tractates of Bekhorot and Kil'ayim that consider the limits of generation.

The Limits of Cross-Species Generation

As we have established, the Tannaim contemplated successful cross-species breeding in certain circumstances. These included between donkeys and horses and between sheep and goats, in both combinations of male and female parents. The two tractates in which we find rabbinic discussion of these possibilities, alongside spontaneously anomalous deliveries, are Bekhorot and Kil'ayim. Both tractates have concerns about speciation. In Bekhorot, a blemishless male firstborn animal must be offered to the temple. Thus, a delivery must be established as offspring proper, although, as we will see, it is ultimately dietary laws that establish species designation (given that a member of its parents' kind may be excluded if it has a disqualifying blemish).[25] Kil'ayim, on the other hand, worries about speciation because in order to not transgress the prohibition against mixing kinds, one has to be able to distinguish between them. Kil'ayim thus sorts the conundrum of likeness and difference at the heart of generation whether through cross-species mating or whether spontaneously occurring, while also grappling with the likenesses that occur across different and demarcated kinds (e.g., dogs and wolves; m. Kil. 1:6).

For the purposes of this paper I will treat t. Bek. 1:9–11, one of the most complete passages in which the Tannaim think through the limits and possibilities of cross-species generation (*kil'ayim*) and spontaneously arising variation.

> 9. Rabbi Simon says: what does [Scripture] come to teach you by having *camel* (Lev 11:4) *camel* (Deut 14:7) twice? To include the camel that is born of a cow as if it were born from (*kenolad min*) a camel. And if its head and majority resemble its mother's, it is permitted for eating.

25. See Christine Hayes, "Dietary Laws," *EncJud* 5 (2007) 650–59.

> And the sages say: that which emerges from (*hayotse min*) the impure is impure, and that which emerges from the pure is pure, for an impure animal is not born from[26] the pure, neither is a pure animal born from the impure.[27] And not a large one from a small one, nor a small one from a large one, and not a human (*adam*) from any of them, nor any of them from a human (*adam*).[28]
>
> (10) A pure small domesticated animal gives birth at five months; a large pure domesticated animal at nine months, an impure large domesticated animal at twelve months; a dog at 50 days; a cat at 52 days; a pig at 60 days; a fox and creeping creatures at six months; the wolf, lion, bear, panther, leopard, elephant, baboon and monkey at three years; the snake at seven years.
>
> (11) Dolphins give birth (*molidin*) and grow (*megadlin*) [offspring] like the human (*adam*); impure fish spawn; pure fish lay eggs.

The test for designating the species of the camel born of a cow is not its eligibility for donation to the temple but rather its (im)purity and eligibility for human ingestion. For Rabbi Simon, this camel, even though delivered by a cow, is considered a camel and is thus forbidden for consumption. Whether Rabbi Simon believes the camel offspring to be the result of cross-breeding or spontaneous variation is unclear.[29] However, Rabbi Simon (or a later interpolator) concedes that in a case in which the creature resembles both camel and cow, if its head and the majority of its body bear bovine features, the offspring is edible. We infer that in such a scenario, the hybrid creature is classed as a cow.[30]

The majority refutes Rabbi Simon's view in a thoroughgoing fashion with its principle of generation. The principle is that a creature is always

---

26. Literally "bears from" (יולדת מן). See n. 13 regarding Lieberman's emendation to מין for the phrasing "שילדה מן" in t. Kil 5:3. It is quite possible that such an emendation is warranted here, especially if we compare it to the first citation of the principle in t. Bek. 1:6 and m. Bekh 1:2.

27. See parallels in t. Bek. 1:6, m. Bek. 1:2, t. Kil. 8:5, and b. Bek. 7a.

28. Note that the final line here is to be found only in the version here and in t. Kil. 8:5. Here is the entire parallel at m. Bek. 1:2: "When a cow gives birth to something like a donkey kind or a donkey gives birth to something like a horse kind, it is exempt from the firstborn obligation, as it is written (Ex 34:20) "firstborn donkey" and (Ex 13:13) "firstborn donkey"—twice, [to teach that] the birthing one must be a donkey, and the born one must be a donkey. But what about eating? If a pure kind gives birth to something like an impure kind, it is permissible to eat [the offspring]; if an impure species gives birth to [a creature which] looks like a pure species, it is forbidden to eat [the offspring], *for that which comes from an impure species is impure and that which comes from a pure species is pure.*

29. For Pseudo-Aristotle, *Problems* 878a 20–24, neither variant uterine deliveries "born of corrupted seed" nor worms generated by excrement are to be called offspring; cf. Aristotle, *Gen. an.* 767b–769b, ed. A. L. Peck (LCL, vol. 336). This is regardless of parentage.

30. While this supplement to Simon's exclusion of species-nonconforming offspring may seem surprising, note how it coincides with the majority view about similarly hybridized-appearing offspring in the case of the human parturient in m. and t. Niddah.

classed as the same kind as the one from which it emerges, even if all appearances are to the contrary. This makes the camel born of a cow, a cow. The sages do not contemplate that this delivery is the result of interspecies mating; the rule is not a matrilineal principle of speciation per se.[31] This is apparent in several respects: first, as noted, there is a distinct category for creatures that are considered genuine cross-species offspring: *kil'ayim*.[32] The Tannaim name and discuss these separately, as the offspring of more similar kinds (such donkeys and horses, or sheep and goats).[33] Second, this version of the rule of generation not only reiterates the shorter version in t. Bek. 1:6 (and m. Bek. 1:2), which simply states, "that which emerges from the impure is impure and that which emerges from the pure is pure," but it also adds language of negation. Like the earlier version, it states that kind generates like kind (a version of Aristotle's *anthrōpos anthrōpon gennai*), but it adds that the opposite *cannot* occur.[34] Third, it extends the negation beyond im/pure species to larger and smaller cattle, and even to the human.

Fourth, and finally, immediately after the rule of generation (t. Bek. 1:9), the Tosefta follows with a list of the widely divergent gestational times and modes of a variety of animal kinds, pure, impure, large, small, domesticated, land, and sea (t. Bek. 1:10–11). This conspicuous display of knowledge rhetorically confirms and elaborates the reproductive logics underlying the generation rule. It does so by elucidating the gestational differences and reproductive modes of an assortment of animal kinds that serve as constraints on successful cross-breeding. In other words, taking together this severally joined statement (t. Bek. 1:9–11) clarifies the impossibility of genuine cross-species entities: the Tosefta makes the claim not only that a genuine camel cannot emerge from a cow (i.e., an impure kind

31. Whether there is a matrilineal principle in the case of genuine cross-breeding is a different matter. As we have seen t. Kil 5:3 clarifies that for spontaneously anomalous deliveries, the offspring counts as its parents' kind. This goes to the dispute in t. Kil. 5:5, in which the sages rule that all mules (regardless of which gendered combination of horse/donkey parentage) are one *min*, versus Rabbi Judah, who sees distinct species depending on parentage and considers these forbidden to one another (a kind of sub-*kil'ayim* speciation prohibition). However, this contradicts Rabbi Judah's earlier ruling in 1:8, in which a female mule can be brought to mate with either kinds of male mules. Cohen acknowledges this ambiguity (*Beginnings of Jewishness*, 300–301). It is possible that Rabbi Simon's view may indicate that he does think that this is the result of a cow–camel mating.

32. In any event, as Cohen has argued, the majority view of the sages in the Tosefta does not seem to establish a matrilineal principle of species designation for the offspring of cross-breeding (*Beginnings of Jewishness*, 300–301).

33. T. Kil 5:3; on the use of *kil'ayim* offspring as firstborn donations, see m. Bek. 1:4–5 and t. Bek. 1:13.

34. On Aristotle's repeated maxim, see D. M. Balme, "*Anthropos anthropon gennai*: Human Is Generated by Human," in *The Human Embryo: Aristotle and the Arabic and European Traditions*, ed. G. R. Dunstan (Exeter: University of Exeter Press, 1990), 20–31.

coming out of a pure kind), but also that genuine larger kinds (e.g., cows) cannot be born from smaller kinds (e.g., sheep) and vice versa. The phenomenon of kinds delivering offspring that *look* like different kinds is not in itself negated; the generation principle simply confirms (contra Rabbi Simon?) that such offspring are not genuinely derived from cross-species breeding.

It is noteworthy that the sequence of reasoning in this passage, from cross-species resemblances to reproductive modes and gestational periods echoes Aristotle's musings in *Generation of Animals* (769b23–26). As discussed above, Aristotle explains "the causes of monstrosities" as a failure of the male seed to master the female material. In the human case, he states, this can lead to offspring in which the most "general" remains, in other words, the animal. There, after discussing species nonconformity in human and animal cases (including hybrid entities),[35] Aristotle emphasizes that "in no case are they what they are alleged to be, but resemblances only" (*Gen. an.* 769b18–19). He goes on to declare that interbreeding *cannot* occur, due to "widely different" gestation periods, listing those of humans, sheep, dogs, and oxen. The presence in rabbinic texts not only of ideas but also of sequences of ideas deployed in Aristotle's writing is certainly curious and may tell us something about the bodies of knowledge circulating in early Roman Palestine.[36]

Pressing further on the echoes between Aristotelian and Tannaitic ideas, we have the role of form in the designation of species and more particular kinds of resemblance (*tsurat ha-adam*, m. Nid. 3:2; *tsurat aviv*, Mekhilta deRabbi Ishmael, *Beshallah*, 8), although as noted the role of matter is unstated in Tannaitic sources. The Tannaim distinguish between a creature's species designation and the idealized able, male (animal or human) bodies destined for the temple.[37] The disqualifying *mum* might be viewed as similar to Aristotle's departures from the ideal, or even to his notion of monstrosity (*terata*).[38] In both Aristote-

35. These include phenomena like children with ram or ox heads, or calves with a child's head or a sheep with an ox's head.

36. On possible rabbinic knowledge and inversion of Plato's cave story by Babylonian rabbis, see Charlotte Elisheva Fonrobert, "Rabbi Shimeon bar Yohai's Cave (B. Shabbat 33B–34A): The Talmudic Inversion of Plato's Politics of Philosophy," *AJS Review* 31 (2007): 277–96. For a fascinating gender, race, and queer critical reading of Aristotlean and talmudic sources classifying humans, see Marla Brettscheider, *Jewish Feminism and Intersectionality*, SUNY Series in Feminist Criticism and Theory (Albany: State University of New York Press, 2016), 17–40.

37. Thus, m. Bek. 1:2 and t. Bek. 1:6 and 1:9 distinguish between whether species nonconformity excludes a firstborn from the *bekhor* obligation and whether the creature is a member of its parents' kind (*min*)

38. Aristotle is explicit about how, all things being equal, if the male seed does its job in molding the female matter (blood), the reproductive outcome should be male. For him,

lian and Tannaitic cases, while variation (deviation or *mum*) is marked against an ideal form, it nonetheless fails to impinge on species designation. Finally, the key concept of kind, or *min*, which of course does not precisely map onto a post-Linnean biological taxonomy, seems to be deployed in a sense similar to the Aristotelian *genus/eidos*.[39]

Species Nonconformity and the Human Kind

Putting aside Aristotelian echoes in Tannaitic sources, let us return to the extended principle of generation in t. Bek. 1:9, specifically to its insertion of the human into the general mix of species-nonconforming deliveries. In the context of Bekhorot, the principle declares that species nonconformity can appear across multiple registers of classification: from the distinctly pure/impure kinds, across cattle and larger animal kinds, and even across humans and all of the above ("any of them"). The principle reminds us, however, these are not genuine outcomes of cross-species reproduction.[40]

The only other extended version of the generation principle (with cattle/large animal, and human/animal extensions) is found in t. Kil. 5:8.[41] A reading of this version of the generational principle in its redactional context allows us to see how the principle is deployed to deal with concerns about the place of the human in a world of unstable reproductive outcomes. We observe, first, that the principle in t. Kil. 5:8 parallels m. Kil. 8:5–6, which, after a brief discussion of various types of mules, states:

---

then, any departure from this, including female progeny, is a move toward monstrosity (*Gen. an.* 767b8–10). While the Tannaim make no such claims explicit, one could argue that they are already folded into the requirements for the priest to be a male whose body is heavily regulated into an able-bodied one. On the gendering of disability established by Aristotle, see Rosemarie Garland Thomson, *Extraordinary Bodies: Figuring Disability in American Culture and Literature* (New York: Columbia University Press, 2017), 19–20, 27–28.

39. See Pierre Pellegrin, "Aristotle," trans. Anthony Preuss, in *Aristotle on Nature and Living Things: Philosophical and Historical Studies Presented to David M. Balme on His Seventieth Birthday*, ed. Allan Gotthelf (Bristol: Bristol Classical Press, 1985), 95, in which *genos* and *eidos*, "far from being prefigurations of our notions of genus and species, do not have a *biological* sense: to understand their biological *use*, we must not lose sight of the rules which regulate their *logical* functioning." Modern taxonomists carefully use graduated terms such as *order*, *family*, and *genus*, going all the way down to *species*, which are further inflected with modern notions of evolution and heredity. When I use the term *species* instead of *kind* in discussing rabbinic texts, I mean it in the flexible sense of *min*.

40. This coheres with Rabbi Meir's view in m. Nid. 3:2 (par t. Nid. 4:5), which extends the designation of *valad* to entities that are "like a kind of domesticated animal, wild animal, and bird." As noted, the sages' view there is a bit more qualified.

41. Lieberman observes that the particle "ש" appended to the introductory אין in the Kil'ayim version (which makes no sense) is probably due to scribal transmissional mistake (erroneously copying from a similar text, in this case t. Bek. 1:9).

Adne ha-sadeh are wild animals.
Rabbi Yose says: they convey tent impurity like a human (*ke-adam*).[42]

The Mishnah then continues with discussions about other apparently anomalous kinds, including the hedgehog, the marten, the wild ox, the dog, the pig, the wild donkey, the elephant, and the monkey.[43] These are sorted into wild kinds (*min hayah*) and domesticated kinds (*min behemah*), with debates about all but the last four. The Mishnah closes this short excursus with "and the human is permitted to pull, plow and lead with all of them" (m. Kil. 8:6).

These *mishnayot* that t. Kil. 5:8's generation principle parallels thus raise questions about the place of the human in the world of species distinctions and potential overlaps. The *adne ha-sadeh*, it appears, are human-like wild creatures. Saul Lieberman likens them to the Sifra's *sirenus* (or Siren), a human-like creature of the sea.[44] While the majority of sages view the *adne ha-sadeh* as wild animals, the voice of Rabbi Yose maintains that they possess that most singular and potent of human qualities, the possibility of contaminating with corpse impurity via overhang.[45] The majority distinguish the human from this human-*like* creature. Their position is reminiscent of a logic cited several times in

---

42. M. Kil 8:5. It continues, "The hedgehog and the marten are wild animals. The marten: Rabbi Yose says, Beit Shammai say, an olive's worth conveys impurity when carried, and a lentil's worth if touched." Menahem Mor translates *huldat hasena'im* as "stone marten" (*ha-Hai bi-yeme ha-Mikra, ha-Mishnah veha-Talmud* [Tel Aviv: Grafor-Daftal Books, 1997], 73); cf. Avraham Even-Shoshan, *Milon Even-Shoshan: mehudash u-me'udkan li-shenot ha-alpayim be-shishah kerakhim be-hishtatfut hever anshe mada'* (Tel Aviv: ha-Milon he-Hadash, 2003), 558. The hedgehog and the marten are paired perhaps because they may appear to be reptiles (*sheratsim*) rather than *hayot/behemot* and thus not subject *kil'ayim*. While the majority opinion considers the two animals to be *hayot*, Rabbi Yose attaches a *sheratsim*-type of impurity to the marten. See Sifra, *Shemini*, parashah 4, pereq 6, ed. Isaac Weiss (Vienna, 1862; repr., New York, 1947), 51d, for a discussion of the purity of creatures including the *avne ha-sadeh*, the weasel, the hedgehog, and the monkey. Note MSS Venice and Vatican 31 have *avne hasadeh*, but Vatican 66 and other manuscripts have *adne hasadeh*.

43. M. Kil. 8:6, "The wild ox is a domesticated animal, Rabbi Yose says, a wild animal. The dog is a wild animal, Rabbi Meir says, a domesticated animal. The pig is a domesticated animal, the wild donkey is a wild animal, the elephant and the monkey are wild animals. And the human is permitted to pull, plow and lead with all of them." These animals are all impure kinds except for the "wild ox" (which the sages consider a domesticated animal, against R. Yose, who considers it a wild animal).

44. Lieberman, *Tosefta Kifshuta*, Seder Zera'im, 652–53; Sifra Shemini, 3:7 (ed. Weiss, 49d). For an evocative analysis of the siren as human-like sea creatures in rabbinic and Greco-Roman literature as well as the siren depicted in the Bet Shean mosaic, see Galit Hasan-Rokem, "Leviticus Rabbah 16, 1—'Odysseus and the Sirens' in the Beit Leontis Mosaic from Beit She'an," in *Talmuda de-Eretz Israel: Archaeology and the Rabbis in Late Antique Palestine*, ed. Steven Fine and Aaron Koller, SJ 73 (Berlin: de Gruyter, 2014), 159–89.

45. On this variety of "tent" impurity and on human corpse impurities, see Mira

Kil'ayim, "even though they resemble one another, they are *kil'ayim* with one another," made in order to differentiate between like-appearing kinds (e.g., a dog and a wolf) (see m. Kil. 1:5–6; t. Kil. 1:7–8).[46] If the majority opinion attempts to dispel the specter of human doubles raised by the *adne hasadeh* in m. Kil. 8:5, then the closing statement in m. Kil. 8:6 about the human capacity to pull, plow, and lead with all animals, puts it to rest. The human, it assures us, is not subject to the same vicissitudes of classificatory and reproductive blurriness implied in the whole prohibition of *kil'ayim*. It does not count *as* an animal. Escaping its applications, it in fact sponsors the classificatory project of *kil'ayim*.

Putting Tosefta Kil'ayim's version of the generation principle (t. Kil 5:9) next to these two *mishnayot* both confirms and upsets the position of the human vis-à-vis all other kinds. This is so especially when we juxtapose it with the second halakhah (t. Kil 5:10)—a principle about territorial doubles—that parallels m. Kil. 8:5–6:

> For an impure animal does not give birth to a pure kind, and a pure one to an impure one, neither a large one to a small kind, nor a small one to a large kind, and no human kind from any of them, nor to any of them a human kind. (t. Kil. 5:9)

> Everything that there is in the settlement there is in the wilderness, whereas many entities that are in the wilderness do not exist in the settlement. Everything that is on dry land there is in the sea, whereas many entities that are in the sea are not on dry land. But there is no marten of the sea. (t. Kil. 5:10)

Lieberman reads t. Kil. 5:10 as related to m. Kil. 8:5's discussion of the *adne hasadeh*. This helps us understand the Tosefta as making sense not only of the idea that there is a human-like creature in the wild (the *adne hasadah*) and the sea (the *sirenus*), but also of a quandary motivating many a discussion in Kil'ayim: likeness and difference not only in vertical or genealogical contexts (i.e., a cow giving birth to a donkey-like kind) but also *across* different kinds (e.g., the wolf and the dog; m. Bek. 1:5). It provides an explanation and scheme for why seemingly similar-looking kinds are nonetheless distinctive: these are parallel but genealogically unrelated forms.[47] This is the theory that across three realms: in settled human habi-

---

Balberg, *Purity, Body, and Self in Early Rabbinic Literature* (Berkeley: University of California Press, 2014), 96–121.

46. Note how corpse material's resemblance to human form determines the potency of its impurity (ibid., 109–10).

47. Lieberman observes that t. Kil. 5:10 comments on m. Kil. 8:5. This analysis adds that *both* t. Kil 5:9 and t. Kil 5:10 comment on *both* m. Kil. 8:5 and m. Kil 8:6.

tation, wilderness, and the sea, there are creaturely doubles. And, the rabbinic theory adds, as we draw further from human settlements, there are not only doubles of creatures that we live with, but there is also a surplus of additional creatures. Pliny refers to a more limited version of this theory—one in which every creature has its double in the sea—and explains that the cause is that the fertile sea receives seeds from above and recombines them into a variety of creaturely forms (*Nat.* 9.1.1).

Tosefta Kil'ayim 5:9 is an important complement to 5:10's principle of territorial doubling in that it clarifies the constraints and possibilities of cross-breeding, while also acknowledging that radical variation and species nonconformity in "vertical" reproductive contexts can occur. As significant for this redactional context is that t. Kil. 5:9 is the second instance of an extended principle that includes "no human kind from any of them, nor to any of them a human kind." In other words, it is a version in which the human is folded into the radical variability of reproductive outcomes. Thus, even as this version of the principle of generation excludes the possibility of successful human–animal cross-breeding, it also acknowledges that such outcomes *seem* to occur (e.g., that humans might produce what look like animal forms). So, too, while humans like others have doubles across different realms (per t. Kil. 5:10), the genealogical principle and the principle of doubles, coupled with the special role of the human as a non-animal kind for the purposes of *kil'ayim*, ensures that such doubles are not really human (though this is somewhat disputed per Rabbi Yose). As in m. Kil. 8:5–6, t. Kil 5:9-10 simultaneoulsy unsettles and affirms human distinctiveness.

Tannaitic Prehumanisms

In this article, I present sources from Kil'ayim, Niddah, and Bekhorot as forms of rabbinic knowledge-making about generation. Specifically, I showcase how the rabbis thought the human and the animal to be analogous (conceptually and linguistically) in being subject to unpredictable outcomes even in same-species reproductive scenarios. More than this, I show how the Tannaim went beyond *analogical* human–animal reproductive thinking by enfolding humans and animals within each other's potential reproductive outcomes. Niddah, Bekhorot, and Kil'ayim all, in different contexts, know that even humans are subject to such spontaneous species variation (both radical and partial) in same-species generative processes. At the same time, species integrity is preserved in the knowledge that, across *wide* species variations, mating will not result in cross-species offspring (the principle of generation). Thus, when species nonconformity *does* occur it is classified, despite bodily appearances to the contrary, according to its parentage.

Human distinctiveness is thereby somewhat equivocal. In the case of the human, its unique and even superior role is both implicit and explicit in that it (via the rabbis) is the classifying creature that knows to distinguish animal kinds and to materialize this knowledge by potentially slaughtering, consuming, and breeding them. The human accordingly sponsors the project of classification entailed by the rabbinic program of *kil'ayim*, while itself not being subject to it in quite the same ways as other creatures (at least in contexts of labor; m. Kil. 8:6). At the same time, the very project that maps kinds and their distinctions and similarities also uncovers the specter of the human double, the *adneh hasadeh* (and in the Sifra, of the *sirenus*). The *adne hasadeh,* alongside the phenomenon of species-nonconforming offspring delivered by humans, unsettles the human. Something like this occurs, as I have argued elsewhere, in t. Nid. 4:5 which blurs distinctions between human and animal features.[48] The Tosefta there goes so far as to challenge the vaunted human image (one that just happens to be divine), with its suggestion that aspects of human form, *tsurat ha-adam,* (notably, the eyes) resemble those of animals. We might conclude that Tannaitic biological thought vacillates between ideas of human–animal distinctiveness and commonality.

Shaye Cohen's work on Kil'ayim and the gendered genealogy of Jewishness takes seriously what he describes as the ideological origins of the rabbinic innovation that was the matrilineal principle. [49] Building on the attention to Kil'ayim as ways for thinking not just about animals but also about humans, I have pointed to how cases of species nonconformity that are *not* the results of cross-species mating illuminate the entwined (even if nongenealogical) reproductive biologies of humans and animals. I thus propose a reading of Kil'ayim as biology (and of course as [feminist] science studies and history of science show us, biology is not free of ideology) and as in need of being read with parallels in Bekhorot and Niddah.[50] My focus has been less on the intersections between animal species and ethnoracial biological ideas, and more on the implications and limitations of what it meant to be human in antiquity.

The writings of Charlotte Elisheva Fonrobert on the tractate Niddah and of Gwynn Kessler on Leviticus Rabbah draw out rabbinic theories of gynecology (or the "science of blood") and embryology, respectively.

---

48. Neis, "Reproduction."

49. Cf. Maja Kominko, "Monsters and Barbarians in Late Antiquity," in *The Routledge Handbook of Identity and the Environment in the Classical and Medieval Worlds*, ed. Rebecca Futo Kennedy and Molly Jones-Lewis (London: Routledge, 2016), 373–89; and, in the same volume, Robert Garland, "The Invention and Application of Racial Deformity," 45–61.

50. See Karen Barad, "Getting Real: Technoscientific Practices and the Materialization of Reality," *Differences: A Journal of Feminist Cultural Studies* 10.2 (1988): 87–128; and Donna Jeanne Haraway, *Simians, Cyborgs, and Women: The Reinvention of Nature* (New York: Routledge, 1991).

These authors also attend to how these accounts of human reproduction make for the production of gendered divisions of bio-material labor, upon which markers of Jewishness then hinge.[51] More recently, Max Strassfeld has signaled an approach to the *androginus* in the tractate Bikkurim that sets the *androginus* next to the *koi* as hybrid creatures, deploying transgender theory and critical race theory to show how Tosefta might "shed light on parallel questions of intelligibility and the boundaries of the human."[52] In reading Niddah together with Kil'ayim and Bekhorot, I build upon these scholars' insights to make the case for a broader rabbinic biological science in these tractates, in which humans and animals are not only parallel or analogous but also intersecting and implicated in one another. I sketch a Tannaitic biology that recognized causes beyond parental species identity (e.g., spontaneous species nonconformity and spontaneous reproduction) and that saw resemblances and parallels beyond genealogical relations. There are gendered and political implications to such conceptions.

Scholars have taught us to recognize the ways in which Greek and Roman natural history was indebted to gendered, imperial, and political knowledge-making projects.[53] Tannaitic sources were part of a broader ancient conversation about the generation of living kinds, but these texts claiming to know the reproductive potentials of women and animals were written by male, provincial sub-elite authors under specific socioeconomic and political pressures. Students of imperialism and colonialism, as well as feminist science studies scholars, have sought to get us beyond analytic dualisms such as subordination/resistance or acting/acted upon.[54] Instead,

---

51. On gender and Greek and Roman medicine, see, e. g., Helen King, *Hippocrates' Woman: Reading the Female Body in Ancient Greece* (London: Routledge, 1998); and Rebecca Flemming, *Medicine and the Making of Roman Women:Gender, Nature, and Authority from Celsus to Galen* (Oxford: Oxford University Press, 2001).

52. Max Strassfeld, "Translating the Human: The Androginos in Tosefta Bikurim," *TSQ: Transgender Studies Quarterly* 3 (2016): 587–604.

53. See e.g. Rebecca Fleming, *Medicine and the Making of Roman Women: Gender, Nature, and Authority from Celsus to Galen* (Oxford: Oxford University Press, 2000); and Jason König and Tim Whitmarsh, eds., *Ordering Knowledge in the Roman Empire* (Cambridge: Cambridge University Press, 2007).

54. See, e.g., Mel Y. Chen, *Animacies: Biopolitics, Racial Mattering, and Queer Affect*, Perverse Modernities (Durham, NC: Duke University Press, 2012); Rosi Braidotti, *The Posthuman* (Cambridge: Polity Press, 2013); Cary Wolfe, *"Human, All Too Human," PMLA* 124 (2009): 564–75; Mira J. Hird, "Biologically Queer," in *Ashgate Companion to Queer Theory*, ed. N. Giffney and M. O'Rourke (Aldershot: Ashgate, 2009), 347–62; Diana Coole and Samantha Frost, eds., *New Materialisms: Ontology, Agency, and Politics* (Durham, NC: Duke University Press, 2010); Donna Jeanne Haraway, *When Species Meet*, Posthumanities 3 (Minneapolis: University of Minnesota Press, 2007). On nonhuman entanglement with the human, see, e.g., Myra Hird, "Animal Transex," *Australian Feminist Studies* 21 (2006): 35–50; and Jane Bennett, *Vibrant Matter: A Political Ecology of Things* (Durham, NC: Duke University Press, 2010) 12, 23, 48, 112, 120. Braidotti considers the possibilities in the techno-scientific present, which "writes hybridity into our social and symbolic sphere and as such it challenges all notions of

these scholars encourage us to consider the variety of subjects (whether colonizing people and colonized peoples, or men and women, or scientists and the objects of their study, or even humans and nonhumans) as both constituting *and* constituted.[55]

Such frameworks are useful for the analysis of rabbinic knowledge making, and for getting beyond well-worn analytical grids of influence vs. resistance (rabbis vs. Romans) and authority vs. marginality (Romans vs. rabbis, or rabbis vs. nonrabbinic Jews/women/etc.). Instead, they allow us to track the staggered, relational, mutual, and overlapping dynamics through which Romans, rabbis, women, animals, and other material (or immaterial) entities were constituted and constituting. Without succumbing to either the pole of retrospective scientism (i.e., trying to understand rabbinic zoology in contemporary post-Linnaean taxonomical terms) or that of materialist determinism, such analytic frames can allow us to approach the material lives of ancient humans, animals, and other entities by treating them not solely as passive objects of male/human projects. They enable us to inquire into how the ancient rabbis and others were entangled with and shaped by the "objects" of their knowledge.

The cases I have discussed here of spontaneous species-nonconforming offspring have the potential to disrupt logics of linearity, lineage, and integrity of generative processes. The Tannaim were aware that in some cases an apparently species-nonconforming fetus was not. In t. Bek. 1:7 (par m. Bek. 1:2) they treat finding impure fish inside pure fish and

purity" (*Transpositions: On Nomadic Ethics* (Cambridge: Polity Press, 2006), 99. On racialized, gendered, heteronormative, classed, ableist, speciesist, and imperial or colonial makings of reproductive knowledge, see, e.g., Michelle Murphy, *Seizing the Means of Reproduction: Entanglements of Feminism, Health, and Technoscience,* Experimental Futures (Durham, NC: Duke University Press, 2012); Susan Merrill Squier, *Liminal Lives: Imagining the Human at the Frontiers of Biomedicine* (Durham, NC: Duke University Press, 2004); Kim Tallbear, "Beyond the Life/Not-Life Binary: A Feminst-Indigenous Reading of Cryopreservation, Interspecies Thinking, and the New Materialisms," in *Cryopolitics: Frozen Life in a Melting World,* ed. Joanna Radin and Emma Kowa (Cambridge, MA: MIT Press, 2017), 179–202; Alys Eve Weinbaum, *Wayward Reproductions: Genealogies of Race and Nation in Transatlantic Modern Thought,* Next Wave (Durham, NC: Duke University Press, 2004); Laura Briggs, *Reproducing Empire: Race, Sex, Science, and U.S. Imperialism in Puerto Rico,* American Crossroads 11 (Berkeley: University of California Press, 2003). For an analysis of ethno-racialized politics around Jewish reproduction, see Susan Martha Kahn, *Reproducing Jews: A Cultural Account of Assisted Conception in Israel,* Body, Commodity, Text (Durham, NC: Duke University Press, 2000). On Roman and rabbinic claims to medical knowledge production, see Mira Balberg, "Rabbinic Authority, Medical Rhetoric, and Body Hermeneutics in Mishnah Nega'im," *AJS Review* 35 (2011):323–46.

55. Susan Hekman, "Subjects and Agents: The Question for Feminism," in *Provoking Agents: Gender and Agency in Theory and Practice,* J. Gardiner ed. (University of Illinois Press, 1995), pp. 194-207 and Sirma Bilge, Beyond Subordination vs. Resistance: An Intersectional Approach to the Agency of Veiled Muslim Women," *Journal of Intercultural Studies* 31 (2010): 9-28.

vice versa as instances in which one kind swallowed another. In these instances, explanation is used to disambiguate seemingly unlike entities. In those under treatment in this essay, however, no explanation is given. The cause for non-like generative or bodily material is left open. Perhaps most challenging is how humans were also implicated in these queerings of the expected order of things. While the material impingements of species-nonconforming deliveries or territorial doubles are not necessarily to be romanticized, such events as registered in rabbinic writings also point to the limits of human (male, rabbinic) claims to knowledge about generation, women, and animals. These claims to knowledge are stymied by the material under scrutiny. These potentials of human–animal entanglement or doubling also put a break on the seamless application of self-congratulatory conceptions of the human as *tselem elohim*. The late ancient generative unpredictability and the proliferation of species across territorial realms have the joint effect of upsetting straightforward human-centric accounts of heterosexual, same-species modes of reproduction.[56] While the quest for knowledge of the world by the rabbis was exceedingly capacious, the sources we have examined here register not only how the material (or fetus) "kicks back"[57] but also how "[s]pecies, like the body, are internally oxymoronic, full of their own others, full of messmates, of companions."[58]

56. For studies that historicize and disrupt heterosexualized accounts of reproduction, see, e.g., Emily Martin, "The Egg and the Sperm: How Science Has Constructed a Romance Based on Stereotypical Male–Female Roles," *Signs* 16 (1991): 485–501; Mianna Meskus, "Agential Multiplicity in the Assisted Beginnings of Life," *European Journal of Women's Studies* 22 (2015): 23–39; Marilyn Strathern, *Reproducing the Future: Essays on Anthropology, Kinship, and the New Reproductive Technologies* (New York: Routledge, 1992). On the ways in which chimerism in contemporary technoscience challenges "western heteronormative notions of kinship," see Myra Hird, "Chimerism, Mosaicism and the Cultural Construction or Kinship," *Sexualities* 7 (2004): 217–32.

57. Barad, "Getting Real," 100.

58. Haraway, *When Species Meet*, 165.

Toward a History of Rabbinic Powerlessness

HAYIM LAPIN
University of Maryland

Those who have discussed theory with Shaye Cohen or have heard him talk about it in lectures know that he eschews theory. Readers of a certain age will know that "theory" refers to the rough nexus of Continental philosophy and a healthy dose of Marxian political analysis mobilized for the reading of texts that was transmitted to the American academy beginning in the 1970s and 1980s in particular through departments of comparative literature and became mandatory everywhere throughout the 1990s. This refusal of theory comes from a scholar who has made significant contributions to our understanding of the past as a constructed discourse,[1] and of gender, embodiment, and identity,[2] and of the idea of Jewishness as a historically contingent creation with discrete beginnings.[3] Cohen's primary tool in breaking this new historiographical ground was often quite traditional, even fusty: close philologically informed reading of texts. One could draw out the latent epistemological and theoretical underpinnings of these close readings. Instead, in what follows I take a page out of Cohen's book and pursue a historical question through a reading of a series of passages and work from the texts outward. As it turns out, these passages raise important theoretical implications for how we understand the relationship of rabbis in late antiquity to state authority

Dedicated, of course, to Shaye Cohen, with gratitude. With thanks to Domenico Agostini, Carol Bakhos, Maxine Grossman, Shai Secunda, and Charles Cohen. An early version of this paper was presented in 2012 at the Lubar Institute for Abrahamic Religions, University of Wisconsin, Madison.

1. Shaye J. D. Cohen, "The Significance of Yavneh: Pharisees, Rabbis, and the End of Jewish Sectarianism," *HUCA* 55 (1984): 27–53.

2. Shaye J. D. Cohen, *Why Aren't Jewish Women Circumcised? Gender and Covenant in Judaism* (Berkeley: University of California Press, 2005).

3. Shaye J. D. Cohen, *The Beginnings of Jewishness: Boundaries, Varieties, Uncertainties*, HCS 31 (Berkeley: University of California Press, 1999).

and, in the case of one notable Babylonian tradition, to rabbis' own power or powerlessness.

I take as my starting point the observation that there is an impoverished tradition of internal Jewish power and such a rich one of disempowerment within rabbinic texts.[4] Embedded in the Bible there are texts reflecting a royal ideology of divine selection (especially in Psalms), but the editing of the Bible articulates much more strongly the sense of sin and exile. Redemption, when it comes, is frequently for the righteous few, and human agency is greatly overwhelmed by the divine act.

The creation of the Hasmonean dynasty occasioned some accounts, notably in 1 Maccabees, that celebrated their founders as zealots and remembered for good episodes of forced circumcision and ethnic cleansing.[5] A different history might have given these texts a central place in the self-fashioning of later Jews and their communities, but, in the event, the Judaism that survives today literally has no place for such texts, even within the modern State of Israel that recovered the memory of the Maccabees. The great corpus of rabbinic texts took shape in the absence of power of the kind that late antique Christians, Zoroastrians, or Muslims had to grapple with. Thus, while it is undoubtedly true that we can profitably examine early rabbinic death-penalty discourse as law, and legal discourse as ultimately about power, it remains a near certainty that not a single life was taken in antiquity, or for that matter spared, as a direct result of the application of rabbinic death-penalty law in a formally authorized court.[6]

Let us now turn to the rabbinic texts. In general, it is striking how little rabbinic literature produced in Palestine has to say about contemporaneous rulers.[7] Vespasian (69–79), Titus (79–81), and Trajan (98–117) are mentioned once or more in Tannaitic literature.[8] These traditions are discussed

---

4. For earlier treatments, see, e.g., Jonathan Boyarin and Daniel Boyarin, *Powers of Diaspora: Two Essays on the Relevance of Jewish Culture* (Minneapolis: University of Minnesota Press, 2002); David Biale, *Power and Powerlessness in Jewish History* (New York: Schocken, 1986).

5. 1 Macc 13:46–47 (Gazara); 14:34 (Joppa). See also Josephus, *Ant.* 13.254–256 (destruction of the temple at Mount Gerizim), 257–258 (conversion of the Idumeans), 318–319 (conversion of the Itureans).

6. Beth A. Berkowitz, *Execution and Invention: Death Penalty Discourse in Early Rabbinic and Christian Cultures* (New York: Oxford University Press, 2006).

7. See Shaye J. D. Cohen, "The Destruction: From Scripture to Midrash," *Prooftexts* 2 (1982): 18–19, reprinted in Cohen, *The Significance of Yavneh and Other Essays in Jewish Hellenism*, TSAJ 136 (Tübingen: Mohr Siebeck, 2010), 22–23.

8. E.g., m. Soṭah 9:14; t. Soṭah 15:8 (Vespasian and Titus); Sifra, 'Emor Parasha 8:5 (ed. Weiss 114d) (Trajan, reading ṬRWGYYNWS for MRYYNWS, after Vat. Assemani 66). Hadrian may not be mentioned at all (excepting the problematic Midrash Tannaim, Deut 26:19, ed. David Z. Hoffmann, 262) although there is a reference to Hadrianic (?) pottery, m. 'Abod. Zar. 2:3, t. 'Abod. Zar. 4:7.

in subsequent rabbinic literature, which also includes narratives about the destructions attributed to these emperors and to Hadrian (117–138).[9] After Hadrian, however, almost nothing is said about any ruler but Diocletian (284–305). The reign of Constantine, and the fourth-century emperors, with the possible exception of Julian, are passed over completely.[10]

It is therefore peculiar that Ursicinus, a high-ranking Roman military officer active in the East for much of the 350s, appears in the Palestinian Talmud, and to my knowledge only in the Palestinian Talmud, several times in five distinct traditions.[11] Some scholars connected these stories, and Ursicinus's presence in the region, with a revolt during the reign of the Caesar Gallus (approximately 351–352); while others have questioned the significance, or even the existence, of the revolt. This is a problem we cannot solve here (although I do not believe it is helpful to make the Gallus Revolt a central event in fourth-century Palestinian history), and it seems more useful to consider the range of ways that the memory of Urisicinus, a prominent representative of "the State," is invoked in our passages.

Once, Ursicinus causes damage to the Torah scroll of a community. Twice, Ursicinus demands services from the inhabitants of a settlement. A fourth reference mentions "the days of King Ursicinus" as the occasion of a police action, although it is not clear that Ursicinus is himself the author of that action.[12] Here is our first surprise: Ursicinus was never emperor, although the emperor Constantius reportedly suspected him of having imperial aspirations. If the 350s were still within living memory (some scholars have recently insisted that the Palestinian Talmud was completed within a couple of decades of this date[13]), this is the kind of thing we would expect locals to know, if only because formal deeds and public

---

9. See, conveniently, Mireille Hadas-Lebel, *Jerusalem against Rome*, trans. Robyn Fréchet, Interdisciplinary Studies in Ancient Culture and Religion 7 (Leuven: Peeters, 2005), 127–93. For the traditions about "Antoninus" and Judah the Patriarch, see Martin Jacobs, *Die Institution des jüdischen Patriarchen: Eine quellen- und traditionskritische Studie zur Geschichte der Juden in der Spatantike*, TSAJ 52 (Tubingen: Mohr Siebeck, 1995), 125–54; O. Meir, *Rabbi Yehudah ha-Nasi: Palestinian and Babylonian Portraits of a Leader* [Hebrew] (Tel Aviv: Hakibbutz Hameuchad, 1999), 263–99.

10. Martin Goodman, "Palestinian Rabbis and the Conversion of Constantine to Christianity," in *The Talmud Yerushalmi and Graeco Roman Culture*, vol. 2, ed. Peter Schäfer and Catherine Hezser, TSAJ 79 (Tübingen: Mohr Siebeck, 2000), 1–9. Julian appears in y. Ned. 3:2, 37d, but the parallel passage at y. Shebu. 3:8, 34d has Diocleian. Qohelet Rabbah likely refers to the emperor Julian rather than to Pappus and Lollianus. See Saul Lieberman, "The Martyrs of Caesarea," *AIPHOS* 7 (1939–1944): 413–414.

11. See Hayim Lapin, *Rabbis as Romans: The Rabbinic Movement in Palestine, 100–400 CE* (New York: Oxford University Press, 2012), 144–49, and notes thereto.

12. Torah scroll: y. Meg. 3:1, 74a; services: y. Beṣ. 1:6, 69c; y. Sheb. 4:2, 35c (y. Sanh. 3:6, 21b); police action: y. Yebam. 16:3, 15d (y. Soṭah 9:3, 23c).

13. Ya'aqov Sussmann, "*Ve-shuv 'al yerushalmi neziqin*," *Meḥqere talmud* I (1990): 55–133.

pronouncements were dated to the regnal years of emperors, and coinage included the names and faces of the emperors.

A fifth and final passage provides a second surprise. Two rabbis once came before Ursicinus in Antioch. He rose before them saying, "I see the faces of these in war and I am victorious" (y. Ber. 5:2, 9a). The context of this passage is interesting. It is the third in an escalating series of four anecdotes involving rabbis in interactions with government officials that thematizes the true honor ascribed to men of Torah: *arkhon* (a city official), *antipoṭah* (from the Greek term for *proconsul,* the provincial governor), Ursicinus, and finally *malkhuta,* the seat of the empire.[14] Both the governor and Ursicinus rise before the rabbis, and, in the fourth episode, bolts of lightning from the nape of the rabbi's neck protected him from execution for breach of protocol. Over and above the recurrence of Ursicinus as a royal figure, there is here an echo of the rabbinic version of the Alexander legend, and possibly of Constantine's vision of the Cross. One might legitimately question how far one may push such echoes, but at a minimum the story inserts rabbis and their Torah into the narrative of imperial conquest.

One final surprise comes from further consideration of one of the anecdotes in which Ursicinus demands services: baking bread on the Sabbath. What is interesting about it is that the larger passage in which this appears concerns martyrdom. The passage is in fact deeply ambivalent, juxtaposing the view that requires Jews to submit to death any time they are required to publicly transgress even a minor commandment, with an alternative view that minimizes this requirement. The anecdote about Ursicinus is discussed in the service of the minimizing view. One of the rabbis who permitted baking was challenged about the legality of his position, and he answered, "He [Ursicinus] did not intend to make apostates out of you; he intended only to eat warm bread."

This is as close as the Palestinian Talmud gets to conceding legitimate authority to the state. When the commander of locally quartered soldiers requisitions bread or when, in an earlier case discussed in the same extended passage, taxation demands require that agricultural work for the next season begin before the sabbatical year is through, it is permissible to transgress the Torah. It is only when the state intends apostasy—defined here as making Jews transgress the Torah for its own sake—that martyrdom is required.

The Palestinian Talmud occupies a particular moment, at the turn of the fifth century in northern Palestine. At that moment, the Ursicinus traditions articulate a stance toward governmental authority that is at once

---

14. See Seth Schwartz, *Were the Jews a Mediterranean Society? Reciprocity and Solidarity in Ancient Judaism* (Princeton: Princeton University Press, 2010), 146–49. Schwartz renders *malkhuta* as "the emperor."

compliant, as we have seen, and alienated. There is no question that the representatives of the state come from outside "our" community to make demands of it. "Our" community, in turn, is construed as both local and ethnic: the army comes into the towns of the Galilee or a rabbi travels to Antioch to see Ursicinus, and the world of the Palestinian Talmud is the world of halakhah-observant Israel. Later Palestinian texts, homiletical rather than legal in focus, suggest a sharpening of that alienation as well as hostility, as in the passages that imagine the violent deaths of Roman emperors.[15] This development is no doubt in part a response to the hardening of the imperial position toward the nonorthodox, including Jews, beginning in the latter part of the fourth century and maturing in the sixth and seventh centuries, although it is also in keeping with the general sharpening of communal boundaries among late antique groups.[16]

In contrast to the Palestinian Talmud, the Babylonian Talmud repeatedly cites the tradition that *dina de-malkhuta dina*, "the law of the kingdom is the law." This Talmud was completed significantly later, in late Sasanid Mesopotamia, and the tradition in question is frequently attributed to Samuel, among the earliest representatives of Babylonian rabbinism. The dictum is cited in connection with cases having to do with property law, but these can explicitly intersect with taxation and state rules about ownership. In some cases, the state's role is acknowledged directly and positively: the state may cut down trees to build bridges for common use; documents issued in gentile courts are valid.[17] However, the dialectical character of this Talmud's discourse juxtaposes the principle to traditions

15. See Ra'anan Boustan, "Immolating Emperors: Spectacles of Imperial Suffering and the Making of a Jewish Minority Culture in Late Antiquity," *BibInt* 17 (2009): 207–38.

16. Paula Fredriksen and Oded Irshai, "Chrisitian Anti-Semintism: Polemics and Policies," in *The Cambridge History of Judaism*, vol. 4, *Late Roman-Rabbinic Period*, ed. Steven T. Katz (Cambridge: Cambrdige University Press, 2006), 1005–7; H. A. Drake, *Constantine and the Bishops: The Politics of Intolerance*, Ancient Society and History (Baltimore: Johns Hopkins University Press, 2000), 393–440, for the hardening of views after Julian. Laws are collected in Amnon Linder, ed, *The Jews in Roman Imperial Legislation* (Detroit: Wayne State University Press; Jerusalem: Israel Academy of Sciences and Humanities, 1987). For the sixth and seventh centuries, see Averil Cameron, "The Jews in Seventh-Century Palestine," *Scripta Classica Israelica* 13 (1994): 75–93; Cameron, "Byzantines and Jews: Some Recent Work on Early Byzantium," *Byzantine and Modern Greek Studies* 20 (1996): 249–74.

17. Trees: b. B. Qam. 113b, noting further in that pericope that *sheluḥa de-malka ke-malka*, "the emissary of the king is like the king"; deeds: b. Giṭ. 10b. The other instances are at b. Ned. 28a; b. B. Qam. 113a; b. B. Bat. 55a. A sixteenth-century Yemenite manuscript includes a discussion involving the phrase at b. Sanh. 25b: Yad Harav Herzog 1; Ya'aqov Sussmann et al., *Thesaurus of Talmud Manuscripts*, 3 vols. (Jerusalem: Yad Yitsḥaḳ Ben-Zvi, Friedberg Genizah Project, 2011), no. 7823; Mordechai Sabbato, *A Yemenite Manuscript of Tractate Sanhedrin and Its Place in the Text Tradition* (Jerusalem: Hebrew University, 1998), 81. Geoffrey Herman argues that the phrase enters talmudic discourse in the fourth century, not the early third (*A Prince without a Kingdom: The Exilarch in the Sasanian Era*, TSAJ 150 [Tübingen: Mohr Siebeck, 2012], 204–7).

that do not seem to agree. In one case, according to Samuel himself it is permissible to appropriate property belonging to an idolater: that property is ownerless like the desert. As this is glossed and worked out in the Talmud, the legal issue is narrowed to land sold by an idolater to a Jew who has not yet taken possession. Another Jew may appropriate the land by occupying it, exploiting a gap in legal assumptions about when the transfer of ownership takes place. But, as the Talmud objects, the kingdom has declared that sale requires a deed, and the law of the land is the law, so how can the second Jew simply take possession? The issue is not fully resolved in the passage (b. B. Bat. 54b).

In this last case, the pericope gives expression to a more limited view of the kingdom and its laws. Adherence is not principled and complete—we are the subjects of the Persian king of kings and bound by his law—but rather partial, and tempered by the understanding of local legal workings and the possibilities of personal advantage. In a sense, the Babylonian Talmud is at once less grudging than the Palestinian Talmud in its acceptance of the legitimacy of the state and its administrative and police functions, and at the same time more willing to give voice to a limited, even instrumental, adherence to the state that is in tension with the idea of legitimacy.

Beyond this one, oft-quoted dictum, it is also the case that, in comparison with the Palestinian texts, there are many more narratives about members of the Sasanid dynasty in the Babylonian Talmud, and many of these, if not all, are undoubtedly legendary. A significant group locates rabbis within the orbit of the king or his wife, accepting pious gifts from the queen, giving gifts, or interpreting the king's dreams.[18] These royal stories are not uniformly positive. The fourth-century sage Rava sent ongoing secret gifts to Shapur II, but his property was nonetheless seized (b. Ḥag. 5b).[19] The Talmud has to explain how Shapur I, who promised Samuel that he would not kill any Jews, could have killed twelve thousand in Caesarea Mazaca (b. Mo'ed Qaṭ. 26a).[20] Still, there is rarely the sense, even

---

18. A number of traditions involving Shapur II and his wife are collected in Jacob Neusner, *A History of the Jews in Babylonia*, 5 vols., StPB (Leiden: Brill, 1969), 4:35–56. See also Jason S. Mokhtarian, "Empire and Authority in Sasanian Babylonia: The Rabbis and King Shapur in Dialogue," *JSQ* 19 (2012): 148–80; and now Mokhtarian, *Rabbis, Sorcerers, Kings, and Priests: The Culture of the Talmud in Ancient Iran*, S. Mark Taper Foundation Imprint in Jewish Studies (Berkeley: University of California Press, 2015).

19. The brief anecdote also raises the issue of jealousy or competition among rabbis.

20. The event described may correspond to Shapur's sacking of Caesarea Mazaca in 253 (Zonaras 12.23; see also Sib. Or. 13.90; Inscription of Kirdir from the Ka'abah of Zoroaster (KKZ) 11–13; translated in Michael H. Dodgeon and Samuel N. C. Lieu, *The Roman Eastern Frontier and the Persian Wars (A.D. 226–363): A Documentary History* (London: Routledge, 1991), 55, 44, 56, respectively. For KKZ and parallels in the other inscriptions of Kirdir, see Paul Gignoux, *Les quatre inscriptions du mage Kirdīr: Textes et concordances*, SIr 9 (Paris: Union Académique Internationale, Association pour l'avancement des études iraniennes, 1991), 62;

in these narratives, that the Sasanid regime lacks legitimacy. In the case of Caesarea Mazaca, the inhabitants brought destruction upon themselves by being too noisy.

At the same time, individual rabbis and rabbis as a group are sometimes depicted as working around the laws of the regime. Commenting on an earlier rule that the law of proclaiming the finding of lost objects was relaxed "when confiscators of property ['*anasim*] became numerous,"[21] the Talmud interprets '*anasim* to be the "kingdom," *malkhuta*, which has declared that all lost property belongs to itself. Consequently, rabbis lessened the requirements so as to allow less exposure of lost property to royal eyes.

One last anecdote will help bring me to my final theme. Shila, a rabbi of uncertain identification, once beat a Jewish man for having sex with a gentile woman (b. Ber. 58a).[22] The punished man reported him to the government for judging without authorization. When investigators arrived, they eventually made him an authorized judge, due to Shila's quick thinking and rhetorical skill: Shila quotes a Psalm praising God by way of prayer, and upon being asked its meaning by the authorities, he says, "Blessed be the merciful one who gave a kingdom on earth on the model of heaven, and gave you authority that loves justice." Yet despite this performance of consent to state authority and although the legal practices of the rabbi outside the law are affirmed by the state, the original authority to judge was inherent from the first in the rabbi's community and in the rabbi himself.

This is one of the truly bizarre stories that characterize the Babylonian Talmud, and its interpretation is made difficult by a complicated textual transmission. Four of the witnesses clearly place the story in the Roman empire, even in the city of Rome. Yet the story has been edited, if not com-

---

and D. N. MacKenzie in Georgina Herrmann et al., *The Sasanian Rock Reliefs at Naqsh-i Rustam: Naqsh-i Rustam 6, The Triumph of Shapur I*, Iranische Denkmäler 13 (Berlin: D. Reimer, 1989), 43.

21. Alternatively: '*anasim* is receivers of confiscated property.

22. Using transcriptions in the *The Sol and Evelyn Henkind Talmud Text Databank* (1.3) (n.d.), www.lieberman-institute.com, I have compared the readings in five witnesses, in addition to the standard print edition (which corresponds in most substantive ways to Soncino): Munich (Bayerische Staatsbibliothek 95, Sussmann et al., *Thesaurus*, no. 7204); Paris (BNP 671, Sussmann et al., *Thesaurus*, no. 8208); Oxford (Bodleian, Opp. Add. f. 23, Sussmann et al., *Thesaurus*, no. 627) and the Soncino print edition (1484). Paris and Oxford correspond closely. The other three witnesses vary significantly among themselves. Jonah Frankel, "The Story of Rabbi Sheila," *Tarbiz* 40 (1971): 33–34, republished with changes (and without the stemma) as Jonah Frankel, *The Aggadic Narrative: Harmony in Form and Content*, Helal ben Hayyim (Tel Aviv: Hakibbutz Hameuchad, 1991), 261–63, includes variants from medieval and early modern collections (Yalqut Shim'oni and 'En Ya'aqob) as well. For recent treatments of the story see Mokhtarian, *Rabbis, Sorcerers, Kings, and Priests* 114-115.

posed in the first place, in a Mesopotamian and Sasanian context.[23] One line of transmission, reflected in the Soncino printed edition, omits the connection with Rome and uses Persian terminology.[24] A particular crux in the interpretation of the story is the item called *qolpa*, given to Shila by the authorities when he is made a judge. Possible meanings include strap, rod, axe, and the Persian hat, *kulāf*.[25] The latter three are particularly interesting, because they would locate the rabbi's investiture within Roman or within Sasanian practices. The attendants (*lictors*) of the traditional Roman magistrate carried a bundle of rods and an axe (the *fasces*), while the inscription of Kirdir, the Zoroastrian priest, states that he received the hat and belt from Hormizd, the successor to Shapur I.[26]

Two further features of this story are worth comment. First is the characterization of internal Jewish politics. Shila has plainly lied to the government, claiming that the man had had sex with an ass. In some witnesses, Elijah miraculously appears in the guise of a witness to confirm Shila's claim. In the sequel to this story, Shila defends himself to the Jewish man whom he has beaten, stating that gentiles truly are asses, citing a biblical verse in support. Shila then has to contend with his opponent reporting him for labeling the regime asses, and he murders the man with his new *qolpa* on the principle that this is justifiable self-protection. Here, the instrumental character of the rabbinic view of the state in Babylonia takes center stage: We make use of the government when it suits us and avoid or evade the government at other times; we police our community using our own norms and practices, except when circumstances require us to interact with the state.[27] Elijah's presence suggests that God generally approves, or at least protects his own.

---

23. The expression for slander, *'akal qurṣa*, already attested in Akkadian, is characteristic of the Babylonian Talmud.

24. *Peresteqa*, Middle Persian, *frēstag* [*plystk'*], "messenger"; *harmena*, "command" (F. Rosenthal et al., "Aramaic," *Encyclopedia Iranica* II/3, derive from Parthian **hramān*; see also Moshe Sokoloff, *A Dictionary of Jewish Babylonian Aramaic of the Talmudic and Geonic Periods* [Ramat-GanBar Ilan University Press; Baltimore: Johns Hopkins University Press, 2002], 390 , s.v.)

25. See Sokoloff, *Dictionary of Jewish Babylonian Aramaic*, 993 s.v., and an extensive discussion in E. S. Rosenthal, "For the Talmudic Lexicon: Talmudica Iranica," *Irano-Judaica* 1 (1982): 50–52, arguing in our case in particular for derivation from *kulāf*. Daniel Boyarin prefers a tool like a pickax (citing Akkadian derivation and Syriac parallels) and drawing an analogy with the Roman *fasces* ("Toward the Talmudic Lexicon," *Tarbiz* 50 [1981]: 189–90).. Shaul Shaked leaves open the question of whether *qolpa* represents *kulāf* ("Items of Dress and Other Objects in Common Use: Iranian Loanwords in Jewish Babylonian Aramaic," *Irano-Judaica* 3 (1994): 106.

26. The Ka'aba of Zoroaster (KKZ) 4; Naqš-ī Rustam (KNRm) 9, in the synoptic editions of Gignoux, *Les quatre inscriptions*, 56; and MacKenzie in Herrmann et al., *Sasanian Rock Reliefs*, 39.

27. The important reading of this story by Frankel, "Sheila," 40 n. 17, is at pains to defend a deeper meaning of the story from anti-Semitic readings of its plot alone, citing

The second feature that bears emphasis is Shila's defense of his verdict to the Persian inspectors. Sex with an ass, they tell him, should carry the death penalty. Shila answers, "From the day that we were exiled from our land, we have no authority to kill. You do whatever you want with him." This is strange. The government agent assumes the community has the ability to execute, and the rabbinic judge, who, we will later learn, was not above homicide himself, claims that it does not. The story thus yokes assertive rabbinic judicial power, internal communal policing, and freedom of individual action on the part of Shila to an explicit assertion of powerlessness. Like the tension between the recognition of the legitimacy of state laws with more limited or instrumental views, this yoking of assertiveness and powerlessness seems peculiarly characteristic of Babylonian rabbinism, at least as it is represented by the Babylonian Talmud's latest editors.

This counterintuitive yoking is part of the legacy of late-ancient Babylonian Judaism to the medieval rabbanite world. In many respects, the Babylonian Talmud positions Babylonian rabbis as subordinate to Palestine. Judges in Babylonia were said to be prohibited from assigning penalty payments (*qenasot*) in Babylon, and to the extent that they did so they could be said to be acting as the agents of Palestinian rabbis.[28] This was because, while Babylonian rabbis took the title Rab, they did not have ordination, which resided only in Palestine.[29] The Babylonian Talmud's editors continued to tell and rework stories about how disputes about the precedence among two Babylonian rabbis—understood by the editors as a question of succession to headship of the academy—were settled by referring the matter to Palestine (b. Ber. 64a; b. Hor. 14a). In general, it is difficult to overestimate the significance of Palestinian rabbinic tradition to the formation of the Babylonian Talmud.[30]

Yet all of this relative disempowerment is effectively voluntary and could easily have been overcome by creative argument (as it was, in the ninth and tenth centuries by Babylonian Geonim and their supporters).

Johann Andreas Eisenmenger, *Entdecktes Judenthum*, 2 vols. (Königsberg in Preussen, 1711), 2:212–13 and others.

28. See b. B. Qam. 27b, 84b; b. Ket. 41b.

29. B. San. 14a; cf. y. Bik. 3:3, 65d. However, see Y. Breuer, "'*Rabbi* Is Greater than *Rav*, *Rabban* Is Greater than *Rabbi*, the Simple Name Is Greater than *Rabban*'" [Hebrew], *Tarbiz* 66 (1997–1998): 47–49, which correctly seeks to limit the significance of this tradition.

30. See, most recently, Alyssa M. Gray, *A Talmud in Exile: The Influence of Yerushalmi Avodah Zarah on the Formation of Bavli Avodah Zarah*, BJS 342 (Providence, RI: Program in Judaic Studies, Brown University, 2005); Richard Hidary, "A Rhetorical Reading of the Bavli as a Polemic against the Yerushalmi: Regarding Halakhic Pluralism and the Controversy between the House of Shammai and the House of Hillel," in *Oqimta*, vol. 2 (Ramat Gan: Ruben A. Knoll, 2014), for underlying Palestinian sources for the structure of the Babylonian *sugya*.

Indeed, in connection with the relative merits of Babylonian and Palestinian Torah, Babylonians told stories of the triumphs of Babylonian rabbis over Palestinian.[31] However, rather than assert greater power in principle, the Babylonian Talmud attributes it to its sages in practice. It is my distinct impression that, when the Babylonian Talmud presents rabbis as judging cases, they do so in a wider array of areas and with greater exercise of authority than rabbis in Palestine.[32] They mandate the payment of money on their evaluation of the validity of documents (e.g., b. Yebam. 115b; *b. 'Arak.* 22a); they apply corporal punishment;[33] and they impose the ban (e.g., b. Pesaḥ. 62a; b. Ketub. 111a). Power is played out in other, intrarabbinic ways as well. Interactions between Babylonian rabbis are fraught with tension over rank. To some extent, this represents the squaring off in dialectic warfare between near equals, but by the time the Talmud was completed, the stories are inflected with the imagery of full-blown academies with ranked seating order, headships, and curricula. In fact, the Babylonian Talmud's preoccupation with institutional rank pervades its accounts of Palestine, while little of this exists in surviving Palestinian literature.[34] Even the problem of ordination appears to be almost exclusively a Babylonian preoccupation.[35]

I suggested at the outset that Cohen's sensitive reading of texts often raised important theoretical questions about historical development and long-term implications. In our case, how should we understand the rabbinic legacy of powerlessness? In the first place, as fantasy: the story of Ursicinus rising before rabbis reveals rabbis' "true" importance over and against their apparent insignificance. And the story of Shila is in its own

31. B. B. Qam. 117a, the story of how Kahana, a Babylonian immigrant to Palestine literally unseats the great R. Yohanan with his prowess, if with tragic results. For discussion, and earlier literature on this oft-discussed story, see Geoffrey Herman, "The Story of Rav Kahana (BT Bava Kama 117a-b) in Light of Armeno-Persian Sources," *Irano-Judaica* 6 (2008): 54–86. See also b. Ḥul. 95b.

32. A passage that invokes the rule against exacting fines outside of the land of Israel does so in response to a rabbi doing precisely that (b. B, Qam. 84b). For the absence of enforcement in Palestinian narratives, see Hayim Lapin, "The Rabbinic Class Revisited: Rabbis as Judges in Later Roman Palestine," in *"Follow the Wise": Studies in Jewish History and Culture in Honor of Lee I. Levine*, ed. Zeev Weiss et al. (Winona Lake, IN: Eisenbrauns, 2010), 255–73; Lapin, *Rabbis as Romans*, 98–125.

33. In addition to b. Ber. 58a, which is arguably set in Palestine, see, e.g., b. Ta'an. 24b; b. Giṭ. 19a; and b. Pesaḥ. 113b.

34. The story of Kahana, b. B. Qam. 117a, noted above, reflects this. This characterization is indebted to Jeffrey L. Rubenstein, *The Culture of the Babylonian Talmud* (Baltimore: Johns Hopkins University Press, 2003). The more fully developed Babylonian version of Judah the Patriarch's will in b. Ketub. 103a–b that Shaye Cohen studied in "Patriarchs and Scholarchs," *PAAJR* 48 (1981): 57–85, is a case in point.

35. See Hanokh Albeck, "Semikhah and Minui and Beth Din" [Hebrew], *Zion* 8 (1943): 85–93. I have suggested in *Rabbis as Romans* (83–87) that Palestinian appointments serve a different function and may not be a "Rabbinic" prerogative at all.

uncomfortable way a story about how cleverness and divine providence protect and even empower the disempowered. Perhaps, however, we can also discern here a particular Babylonian rabbinic set of social relations. In its own local context, late-antique Babylonian rabbis may have formed a fairly highly bounded sectarian movement, with a strong internal exercise of power and with a complicated relationship to the outside world expressed in instrumental interaction with external powers and institutions and through an idiom of powerlessness. (At the risk of overgeneralization, modern Haredi Jewish municipalities in the United States, or the complicated relationship of those same communities to the State of Israel, may serve as a model for how this could play out.) To the extent that the Babylonian Talmud became, in the Middle Ages, the touchstone of higher education and scholarly productivity for a broader culture, although differently in Muslim and Christian lands, Babylonian powerlessness became one tool for articulating norms and local power in the context of political and legal subordination. Historical and contemporary debates over Zionism, and the examples of ultraorthodox communities given above suggest that it retains some of its salience.

Hair's the Thing

Women's Hairstyle and Care in Ancient Jewish Society

JOSHUA SCHWARTZ
Bar-Ilan University

Hair grows almost everywhere on the human body. It rarely is left to grow unhindered, though, and is usually styled, cut, trimmed, or shaved. The growing and cutting of hair has been related to control; long hair often stands for freedom or defiance, while short hair is a sign of social regulation, obedience, and disciplined religious or cultural uniformity.[1] In spite of this, there was always some allowance for personal preference, which also made hair a pronounced individuality marker.[2]

The Bible and rabbinic law also contain hair rules and styles. It was forbidden to shave with a (razor) blade against the skin at the five points of the beard (Lev 19:27; b. Mak. 20 a–b), to grow the fringe (m. 'Abod. Zar. 1:3) or cut the hair *komê*, that is trimming the front and leaving the sides to grow (Sipra Aḥare Mot 13:9). The last two either related to Roman ritual or reflected haircuts and hairstyles of the Roman elite.[3]

There has not been a great deal of work on attitudes to hair among ancient Jews. Most of the work up until now relates to the sources dealing with Greco-Roman hairstyles for Jewish men. There has also been some work on the gendered meaning of women's hair in Jewish thought throughout the ages, on hair color in ancient Jewish society, and on haircuts and barbers in ancient Jewish society.[4] The purpose of the present

1. Geraldine Biddle-Perry and Sarah Cheang, "Introduction: Thinking about Hair," in *Hair: Styling, Culture and Fashion*, ed. Geraldine Biddle-Perry and Sarah Cheang (Oxford: Berg, 2008), 3.

2. Edmund Leach, "Magical Hair," *Man, Journal of the Royal Anthropological Institute*" 88 (1957): 147–68; Anthony Synnott, "Shame and Glory: A Sociology of Hair," *British Journal of Sociology* 38 (1987): 381-413 ; Victoria Sherrow, *Encyclopedia of Hair: A Cultural History* (Westport, CN: Greenwood, 2006); Biddle-Perry and Cheang, *Hair*; Howard Eilberg-Schwartz and Wendy Doniger, eds., *Off with Her Head: The Denial of Women's Identity in Myth, Religion, and Culture* (Berkeley: University of California Press, 1995), 85.

3. See Beth A. Berkowitz, "The Limits of 'Their Laws': Ancient Jewish Controversies about Jewishness (and Non-Jewishness)," *JQR* 99 (2009): 145–51 ("Hairstyles").

4. On relevant bibliography and research trends, see in detail the bibliography cited by Joshua Schwartz, "Color and Hair in Rabbinic Literature," in *Between Babylonia and the*

study is to examine hairstyle and hair care of women in ancient Jewish society during the Second Temple period, and mostly during the Mishnah and Talmud periods, as most of the available sources are in rabbinic literature. I begin with covering the hair and hair coverings. Next, I examine what happens when a woman's hair is uncovered. This is followed by hair care and hairstyles. The Jewish material is studied in relation to non-Jewish society. While one might wonder what any of this has to do with the oeuvre of Shaye J. D. Cohen, he has, after all, studied the question of "how do you know a Jew in Antiquity when you see one?" Included in his discussion of this was the question of Jewish clothing. Was a Jew recognized as a Jew by the wearing of particularly Jewish apparel? I ask the same regarding hair. Was a Jewish woman recognized as Jewish by her hairstyle, hair covering, or lack of such?[5] As we shall see, Jewish women could well fit into the world of hair in the Greco-Roman world. When it is possible, I also try to determine the hairstyle customs of a Babylonian Jewish woman, a task less easy than determining the hairstyle habits of the Palestinian Jewish woman.[6]

Covered Hair

Women in Greco-Roman society usually covered their hair in public, and, at the very least, had it bound or braided, although an exception might be made for the ceremonial uncovering of a bride's hair.[7] Unbound hair was acceptable for "nymphs" or for (real) women only in mourning or crisis,[8] or in a state of religious ecstasy, and in the privacy of one's home.[9]

Land of Israel: Studies in Honor of Isaiah M. Gafni [Hebrew], ed. Geoffrey Herman, Meir Ben Shahar, and Aharon Oppenheimer (Jerusalem: Zalman Shazar Center for Jewish History, 2016), 387–99.

5. Shaye J. D. Cohen, *The Beginnings of Jewishness: Boundaries, Varieties, Uncertainties*, HCS 31 (Berkeley: University of California Press, 1999), 25–68 (Chapter 2, "'Those Who Say They Are Jews and Are Not': How Do You Know a Jew in Antiquity When You See One?"). See esp. pp. 31-32 on whether Jewish women in the Roman Empire were veiled. A veil might have covered not only the face but also the hair or parts of it.

6. Do sources in the Bavli reflect Babylonian custom or Babylonian understanding of the Palestinian traditions and reality on which these sources seem to reply?

7. Molly Myerowitz Levine, "The Gendered Grammar of Ancient Mediterranean Hair," in Eilberg-Schwartz and Doniger, *Off with Her Head*, 76–130, here 98–99. The Roman bride wore a yellow veil (*flammeum*) that covered a distinctive hairstyle of six braids. See Jonathan Edmondson, "Public Dress and Social Control in Late Republican and Early Imperial Rome," in *Roman Dress and the Fabrics of Roman Culture*, ed. Jonathan Edmondson and Alison Keith, Phoenix Supplementary Volume 46; Studies in Greek and Roman Social History 1 (Toronto: University of Toronto Press, 2008), 27.

8. See Keith Bradley, "Appearing for the Defence: Apuleius on Display," in Edmondson and Keith, *Roman Dress*, 241. See also Mireille M. Lee, *Body, Dress and Identity in Ancient Greece* (Cambridge: Cambridge University Press, 2015), 155.

9. Levine, "Gendered Grammar," 83–84; Charles H. Cosgrove, "A Woman's Unbound

I first describe covered hair in Greco-Roman society, of girls and then of women, and then Jewish practice.

The Greek girl often made do by braiding or binding her hair, although she might have also cut it, something less likely for a Roman girl, and then worn a hat or a cap.[10] The Roman girl might have had a hairnet or *infulae*, fillets, knotted at intervals with ribbons or with *vittae*, bands wrapped around the hair, which could also hang down in loops. The fillet or *vittae* were sometimes woven into the hair while the nets were not. If the hair was braided, it could be tied with a fillet and *vittae*[11] or braided with a chignon.

Just as their daughters did, adult women in the Greco-Roman world regularly covered their hair and had many options to do so.[12] Thus, there was the *palla*, a mantle of large rectangular cloth that could be brought over the head and was considered a mark of honor, dignity, and social status; or the *pilleus*,[13] a felt brimless hat worn in Greece and Rome; or a *cucullus*, a hood. Hats or caps, though, were only for women with simple hairstyles.[14] Another option was the *mitra*, or turban.[15] As was the case with Greek and Roman girls, the matron might have braided or tied her hair and used an

---

Hair in the Greco-Roman World, with Special Reference to the Story of the 'Sinful Woman' in Luke 7:36–50," *JBL* 124 (2005): 679–84. Hair was unbound, in private, before engaging in sex, licit or otherwise. Prostitutes, however, sometimes displayed unbound hair. See also Guy P. R. Métraux, "Prudery and *Chic* in Late Antique Clothing," in Edmonson and Keith, *Roman Dress*, 288 n. 4.

10. See Lee, *Body, Dress and Identity*, 71–72, 160. On the portrait of a first-century CE Roman girl with hair cut close to the head but with locks extending down the neck, see Susan Walker, "Mummy Portraits and Roman Portraiture," in *Ancient Faces: Mummy Portraits from Roman Egypt*, ed. Susan Walker and Morris Bierbrier, 2nd ed. (London: British Museum, 2000), 97.

11. On knotted fillets and sprang hairnets, see Lee, *Body, Dress and Identity*, 145. On Rome, see Kelly Olson, "The Appearance of the Young Roman Girl," in Edmondson and Keith, *Roman Dress*, 139–57, esp. 145–48.

12. Elaine Fantham, "Covering the Head at Rome: Ritual and Gender," in Edmondson and Keith, *Roman Dress*, 160. See also K. Olson, *Dress and the Roman Woman: Self-Presentation and Society* (New York: Routledge, 2008), 34. The numerous Roman busts of women whose hair was not covered display elaborate hairstyles and represent a minority of upper-class women whose coiffures would have been damaged by a covering. See David W. J. Gill, "The Importance of Roman Portraiture for Head-Coverings in 1 Corinthians 11:2–16," *TynBul* 41 (1990): 252–53. Cf., however, Elizabeth Bartman, "Hair and the Artifice of Roman Female Adornment," *AJA* 105 (2001): 14–16 and pl. 2. A second-century CE bronze of a woman depicts hair encased in a real hairnet. Cf., however, Gill, who claims that the lack of hair covering in marble portraits in Corinth is proof that upper-class women in a Roman colony might have gone bareheaded ("Importance of Roman Portraiture," 251–56).

13. Olson, *Dress and the Roman Woman*, 33–36. Sometimes the *palla* was merged with the Greek *pallium* (cloak). As Roman hairstyles became more elaborate, it became harder to use the *palla*, although it was still effective for partial draping when hairstyles were elaborate only in the front. The *palla* had to be held in place with one hand.

14. Ibid., 53–64.

15. Ibid.

array of headbands and ribbons, the *infulae* or *vittae* mentioned above, or she might have used a fillet.[16] The women's hair, just like their daughters', could also have been covered with hairnets of various types, some with *vittae* or *infulae*. Sometimes the hair being covered, bound, or braided was not real, but a wig, worn out of necessity or design.[17]

The Roman woman had all the necessary equipment for the proper hair covering, and her dressing table would have had snoods, hairbands, shawls, and hairnets.[18] She also would have had combs and hairpins to keep her hair in order or to braid it.[19] The more intricate the hairstyle, the greater the need for hairpins. These would have replaced hairnets, which were not used with elaborate styles.[20] If the woman were well to do, her pins and other accessories might be set with jewels,[21] and some of the accessories might have been gold.[22]

Hair coverings were also common in Jewish society for women of different ages. Jewish girls undoubtedly made use of most or possibly all of the techniques common in the Greco-Roman world. The only real difference between Roman and Jewish girls was that a Jewish girl would likely have covered her bound or braided hair with a hairnet.[23]

Unbound or loose hair was considered sexual and, thus, was frowned upon. There were some exceptions to this, however. When a young woman married and was taken from her father's home to that of her husband-to-be, her hair was ceremoniously left unbound (פרוע)—but not for long (m. Ketub. 2:1). Either during the ceremony or immediately afterwards, her hair was bound again and covered, perhaps with an elaborate head-

16. Ibid., 36–39. There are occasional portrayals in art, such as the red hairband on a Neronian-period Egyptian portrait or the chain across the hair, similarly dated, on another mummy portrait. See Walker, "Mummy Portraits," 38–40.

17. Bartman, "Hair and the Artifice," 74. The wig could either be a half wig, the *galerum* or *galerus*, or the full wig, the *capillamentum*.

18. On the various types of fillets, headbands, and ribbons available to the Greek woman see Lee, *Body, Dress and Identity*, 158. See also Leslie Shumka, "Designing Women: The Representation of Women's Toiletries on Funerary Monuments in Roman Italy," in Edmondson and Keith, *Roman Dress*, 176.

19. Janet Stephens, "Ancient Roman Hairdressing: on (Hair)pins and Needles," *Journal of Roman Archaeology* 21 (2008): 110-132. See also Métraux, "Prudery and *Chic*," in Edmondson and Keith, *Roman Dress*, 272–73. Cf. Lee, *Body, Dress and Identity*, 145.

20. Olson, *Dress and the Roman Woman*, 75–76. Shorter hair needed fewer hairpins. Women who traveled also needed a variety of hairpins.

21. Ibid.

22. Walker, "Mummy Portraits," 51–52, 54–55, 64–65.

23. See below. On the either/or option for Roman women as opposed to Jewish tradition, see Dafna Shlezinger-Katsman, "Clothing," in *The Oxford Handbook of Jewish Daily Life in Roman Palestine*, ed. Catherine Hezser (Oxford: Oxford University Press: 2010), 372. See, however, b. Ned. 30b, which claims that (Jewish) women, married or not, always had their hair covered, while young girls did not. This apparently reflects the practice in Babylonia, not Palestine.

dress such as the "City of Gold" (m. Šabb. 6:1),[24] or with a less elaborate one, reflecting the bride's social circumstances.[25] A woman in mourning also occasionally had her hair unbound, loose and disheveled.[26]

Adult Jewish women had their hair braided, bound, or styled, as well as covered in public.[27] A woman's hair was often held in place by a hairnet (סבכה), often made in the sprang technique, a braiding that stretched threads, producing an elastic fiber suitable for head coverings.[28] There were two types, conical and rectangular, and they were usually made from either linen or wool, but there were more expensive ones even made from gold.[29] The hairnet may have covered all or part of the hair, depending to some extent on whether the hair was braided or not; or the hairnet might have covered buns on the top or back of a women's head.[30] The more elaborate and expensive hairnets had tassels, a base, and even medallions.[31] Sometimes hairpins were used to keep the hair under the net (b. Šabb. 60a).[32]

Mishnah Kelim 24:16 mentions three kinds of hairnets: of a girl, of an old woman, and of a harlot. It does not describe their appearance but

---

24. A "City of Gold" headdress is one of the ornaments with which a woman may not go out on the Sabbath, as it is not considered clothing but a "burden" and she might take it off. The "City of Gold" headdress either had a picture of a particular city on it or was made in the shape of a city or its walls and was probably indeed golden. There are numerous depictions of Tyche, the deity that governed fortune and prosperity, wearing such a headdress. See *Mishnat Eretz Israel, Tractate Shabbat (Moed A-B) Part A with Commentary*, ed. Shmuel Safrai and Ze`ev Safrai (Jerusalem: Liphshitz, 2008), 212–14. B. Šabb. 59a calls it a "Jerusalem of Gold," like that made by Rabbi Aqiva for his wife. See also y. Šabb. 6:1, 7d. M. Soṭah 9:14 relates that during the Trajanic war and persecution, it was forbidden for brides to wear "crowns of brides," and b. Soṭah 49b states that these crowns were the "City of Gold." Instead they wore a "cap (or bonnet) of (fine) wool" (כיפה מילת).

25. See t. Šabb. 4 (5):7, which mentions a generic עטרה, or headdress. The bride might also have worn a festive garland (אצטמא, or *stemma*) (t. Šabb. 4 [5]:7).

26. Pesiqta Rabbati 26 tells of a married woman during the period of the destruction of the First Temple who had lost her seven sons when their house collapsed on them. When meeting the prophet Jeremiah, she wept that she did not know on account of her disastrous situation for whom she should mourn or loosen her hair.

27. See Sipre Num. Naso 11 (ed. Kahana, 1:37–38): "This teaches regarding the daughters of Israel that they used to cover their heads. Cf. b. Ketub. 72b.

28. Petra Linscheid, "Hairnets and Bonnets in Late Roman and Byzantine Egypt," http://www.ucl.ac.uk/museums-static/digitalegypt/textil/hairnets.html.

29. Ibid. See also Antoine De Moor, Cäcilia Fluck, Mark van Strydonck, and Mathieu Boudin, "Radio Carbon Dating of Linen Hairnets in Sprang Technique," *British Museum Studies in Ancient Egypt and Sudan* 21 (2014): 103–20. A gold hairnet from third-century BCE Egypt is on display at the Getty Museum: (http://www.getty.edu/art/collection/objects/19408/unknown-maker-hairnet-greek-220-100-bc/).

30. Linscheid, "Hairnets and Bonnets".

31. Ibid.

32. This refers to an unpierced needle mentioned in m. Šabb. 6:1. The needle, similar to Roman ones, might have had a gold plaque at its head.

rather their purity status. This might explain the somewhat strange choice of nets; that is, there is no net for a "woman" (who is neither old nor a harlot). The net of a young girl was susceptible to *midras* impurity; that is, it might be taken off and one could sit or sleep on it, as it could be the size of a small garment (m. Šabb. 9:5; t. Šabb. 9:7). The old woman did not take off her net to sit on, and thus the net was susceptible only to corpse defilement if it came into contact with impurity; and that of the prostitute never became ritually defiled because it apparently was never worn very long, as she took it off when plying her trade.[33] According to this Mishnah, the young girl might take her net off occasionally; the old woman, hardly or never; and the prostitute rarely had it on. It is hard to reconstruct anything based on this.[34]

Moreover, other hairnet traditions in Tractate Kelim regarding some of these nets do not agree with the details of the traditions just described. Thus, in m. Kelim 28:9, the hairnet of an old woman could become susceptible to *midras* impurity, meaning that she might sit on it after all. This Mishnah does not relate to the net of the young girl, but t. Kelim B. Bat. 2:10 states that the net of the young girl was susceptible (only) to corpse defilement, the opposite of the first Mishnah that we had cited (m. Kelim 24:16), implying that she would not sit on it. Would she sit on her hairnet or not?

Tosefta Kelim B. Bat. 5:16 seems to provide the answer, stating that the young girl placed her net on a chair to sit. It is not clear, though, whether this was done only if the net tore or in general, as the wear and tear on the nets often resulted in their ripping.[35] Mishnah Kelim 28:9 adds that a prostitute would make a garment in the fashion of a hairnet, and, like her hairnet, this garment was not susceptible to impurity because she would not wear it too long. In the final analysis, there are two different traditions regarding the nets of young girls and old women, depending on whether they would sit on them or not. If the net was the only means to hold the hair in place, this might have been a problem, at least for the older woman,

---

33. Roman prostitutes usually did not wear fillets. See Olson, *Dress and the Roman Woman*, 38. In Roman society, a woman with unbound hair or without fillets of any kind might be mistaken for a prostitute. There is no way of knowing if a Jewish prostitute followed the hair custom of Roman prostitutes, although Kelim 24:16 would hint at that possibility. See Luke 7:36–50. A Jewish woman, known as a sinner, unbinds her hair to wipe the feet of Jesus. Sinful she might have been, but normally her hair was bound and probably covered.

34. See our discussion below on m. Šabb. 6:5. There were differences not only between the nets of young women or girls and old women but also between the ribbons, bands, falls, and wigs of young and old. What was appropriate for one was not appropriate for the other, and there were halakhic implications for all of this (y. Šabb. 6:5, 8b; b. Šabb. 64b).

35. T. Kelim B. Bat. 2:10 and 5:16. In the former, the net tears to the extent that it no longer covers most of the hair. In the latter, it is the net of the old women which tears. Obviously, the more expensive nets lasted longer. See t. Šabb. 4 (5): 11; b. Šabb. 57b.

as by taking her net off she uncovered her hair. Yet, as the net was often used in tandem with other hair coverings, it was possible to remove it temporarily. Of course, it is also possible that women would sit on it in the privacy of their own homes and then hair covering was not a problem.

Mishnah Kelim 28:10, also concerned with ritual impurity, mentions braiding the hairnet but provides little helpful detail in terms of the actual braiding.[36] Mentioned are the upper edge and the lower edge of the net and a שביס that fastened it. The words used for the two edges are generic for edges and not net specific. The שביס can be interpreted as a hairband worn around the net, or the net itself, but, as it has a separate status in terms of ritual purity, in this tradition it is a hairband, probably similar to those used by Roman women and discussed above.[37] The Mishnah concludes with one helpful piece of descriptive information, mentioning the strings of the net that are attached or knotted to it.[38] Thus, the סבכה, or hairnet, corresponds to the fillet, and the שביס likely corresponds to the *infulae*, the woolen hairbands knotted with ribbons or strings.

A number of other traditions relate to nets and fillets. Mishnah Šabbat 6:1 mentions objects that a woman cannot wear or with which she may not go outside into the public domain on the Sabbath, as they are not considered clothing or jewelry and she might remove them and carry them from domain to domain, which is forbidden on the Sabbath. Thus, a woman may not go out on the Sabbath with "strings of wool" and "strings of flax" nor with "bands upon her head." The criterion for being "permitted" seems to be whether the strings or bands are sown into the hair or are attached in a manner in which it is unlikely that they will be taken off or loosened. These strings in m. Šabb. 6:1 were likely not attached to the net or sown into the hair and the hairband might have been placed over the net, thus making it removable. It is also forbidden for a woman to go out with סנבוטין or סרבוטין, other types of strings attached to the hair, but not sown into it, and going down from the forehead to the cheeks. Nor could a woman go out with a *kavul* (כבול), a bonnet or cap, which would have been worn on top of the net and, thus, might have been removed.[39]

Mishnah Šabbat 6:5 allows a woman to go out on the Sabbath with a fall made of human hair, her own or someone else's, or animal hair, as this was sown into her own.[40] If the סנבוטין mentioned above were sown

---

36. Linscheid, "Hairnets and Bonnets." Was the sprang technique mentioned above used?

37. Cf. Isa 3:18. See also m. Neg. 11:11 on the שביס as a hairband.

38. Cf. m. Šabb. 15:2. It is permitted to tie or to knot these on the Sabbath.

39. See b. Šabb. 57b: "A rule said in the name of R. Simeon b. Eleazar – It was permissible to go out with anything below the net. It was forbidden to go out with anything above the net."

40. Y. Šabb. 6:5, 8b, and b. Šabb. 64b do not allow young girls to use the hair of old women and vice versa.

into her hair, or the *kavul* was attached in a "permanent" manner or sown into the hair, a woman might go out into the courtyard but not into the public domain, and the same applies to a wig. This would have very much limited her mobility.

Do rabbinic sources reflect reality? There is a natural tendency to be skeptical, but, based on the sources examined so far, the answer would seem to be yes—rabbinic sources do reflect reality. This perception is strengthened by the depiction of many women figures in a number of zodiac floors in ancient synagogue mosaics. These women, albeit not "real" women, have their heads covered with nets.[41] As other female figures in these ancient synagogue floor mosaics had their hair covered also with caps or bonnets, the *kippah,* we turn now to examine this hair covering.

The generic hair covering was the *kippah.* Thus, in the case of two women sitting together, one impure and the other not, the impure one caused the other to be completely defiled, including even "the *kippah* on her head" (m. Zabim 4:1). As we shall see below, the *kippah* is also the generic hair covering mentioned in the *Sotah* ceremony. Tosefta Soṭah 3:3 states that the suspected adulteress had put a scarf (סודרין) on her head to entice her partner and that in the ceremony the priest removed her *kippah* and trampled it. The *kippah* is clearly not the same as the *sudarin,* or scarf, and is to be understood in this instance too as a cap or bonnet. A cap could be worn over a net; the opposite was highly unlikely.[42]

A *kippah* or cap of fine wool could serve as a bridal headdress (b. Soṭah 49b). It was forbidden to wear the *kippah* in the public domain on the Sabbath (b. Šabb. 58a), just like the *kavul* (m. Šabb. 6:1, 5). Both were (woolen?) caps, although we do not know how they differed. Bavli Šabbat 57b also mentions a *bezaina* (בזיינא), which was also apparently a generic hair covering to keep the hair from flying about. It is not clear if this is connected to the *kippah.* In any case, the sages of Babylonia were not always familiar with Palestinian hair matters, and their knowledge probably reflected local custom.[43]

Jewish women also wore full or half wigs or falls, whether for beauty, need, or convenience. Some of these were sown into the hair and some could be removed (m. Šabb. 6:1, 5). The rabbis were not wig experts, as one can see from the tradition in the name of R. Abahu in y. Šabb. 6:5, 8b, that anything that covers the hair and is not the woman's own hair is technically a wig. They did know that a wig could get dirty and that it would

41. Rachel Hachlili, *Ancient Synagogues-Archaeology and Art: New Discoveries and Current Research,* HdO 1.105 (Leiden: Brill, 2013), 574–75.

42. Shmuel Krauss, *Qadmoniyot ha-Tamud, II, 2* (Tel-Aviv: Dvir, 1945), 256.

43. The Babylonian sage Rav Huna, the son of Rabbi Joshua, learned hair-covering practice and halakhah from his sisters.

displease a husband if a woman wore a dirty one (b. Naz. 28b). They also knew that a wig could be a cherished personal item and a mother might pass it down to her daughter (b. 'Arak. 7b).[44] Poor women sometimes had to sell their hair or braids, which were made into wigs or falls (y. Šabb. 6:1, 7d).[45] There is, though, no information regarding whether at this time a wig was considered a proper hair covering for a married woman.[46]

Hair Uncovered: Soṭah

A married Jewish woman covered her hair in public and certainly never went out with it unbound or loose. The exception was during the *Soṭah* ritual for the suspected unfaithful wife.[47] I examine the ritual from the perspective of hair and particularly the rabbinic understanding of Num 5:18 when the priest "loosens her hair" after having first uncovered it: ופרע את ראש האשה.[48]

Mishnah Soṭah 1:5 (= t. Soṭah. 1:7) states that, in the course of the ceremony, the priest "loosens her hair" (וסותר את שערה)[49] and bares her bosom. Rabbi Judah adds that if her bosom (לבה, lit., "heart")[50] was "comely" then neither that nor her hair were exposed. No reason is given for Rabbi Judah's view, but perhaps it is connected to the audience at the ceremony. The ceremony was supposed to elicit shame, but the erotic nature of the loosened hair and the exposed bosom could have had the opposite effect on those viewing the ceremony. As we shall see, the whole purpose of the ceremony was to shame the woman by doing in public what would normally have been done in private. She was accused of enticement and adultery; why take actions that would just heighten her sexual attraction?

---

44. According to b. `Arak. 7b, a woman who says "give my hair to my daughter" means a wig.

45. Rachel, Rabbi Akiva's wife, cut off and sold her braids. The Testament of Job 23:7-10 tells that Job's wife allowed Satan to shear off her hair as payment for bread.

46. The matter is first discussed in the sixteenth century. See, e.g. http://www.kaduri.net/?CategoryID=486&ArticleID=1800.

47. It makes no difference if the ceremony ever took place. For the *Soṭah* ceremony in general, see Ishay Rosen-Zvi, *The Mishnaic Sotah Ritual: Temple, Gender and Misdrash*, JSJSup 160 (Leiden: Brill, 2012). The priest loosens her hair right before she takes the oath as to whether she was faithful or not.

48. On this meaning of פרע, see Ora Cohen, "The Meaning of 'PRIAT ROSH'" [Hebrew], *Beit Mikra* 45 (1990): 177–84; and Amnon Shapira, "'ופרע את ראש האשה' (in Numbers 5:18)," *Beit Mikra* 45 (1990): 274–76.

49. Cf. b. Soṭah 8a. סותר is to be understood as the rabbinic form of the biblical פרע. See the articles of Cohen "Meaning of 'PRIAT ROSH'"; and Shapira, "'ופרע את ראש האשה.'"

50. Sipre Num. Naso 11 (ed. Kahana, 1:37–38) has בית חליצתה, to draw out or expose (the breast). See *Sifre on Numbers: An Annotated Edition. Part II, A Commentary on Piaka'ot 1–58 (The Portion of Naso)*, ed. Menahem I. Kahana (Jerusalem: Magnes Press, Hebrew University, 2011), 132 n. 18.

Who would have seen her hair in this ceremony? According to the Mishnah, the initial stages of the ceremony took place at the Eastern Gate or Nicanor Gate, at the far end of the Women's Court near the Court of the Israelites, a location with the potential of being a rather public area.[51] The Tosefta (t. Soṭah. 1:7) adds to the view of Rabbi Judah that he was afraid at this point that the younger priests, either assisting or just viewing, would be enticed by the loosened hair or bare breasts. The priest actually leading the ceremony stood to the side to avoid looking straight at the woman, but the younger priests might have been able to glance at her.[52] Yerushalmi Soṭah 1:5, 17a adds that the lustful gaze of the young priests would be considered a problem only if she were to be found innocent.

The potential audience seems to change and grow larger during the course of the ceremony. According to m. Soṭah 1:6, after the woman changes clothes and removes jewelry and ornaments so she should be "ugly," "everyone who wishes to see, comes to see, except for her slaves and maid servants," and "all women are permitted to see her" so that they might learn a lesson from her ordeal. Although there seems to be a contradiction in the Mishnah, which mentions both "everyone" and "all women," it is clear that the audience has expanded beyond priests. Sipre Num. Naso 11 has a slightly different version: "All who wish to see should come and see." This actively encourages an audience, as opposed to the more neutral formulation of the Mishnah.[53] The Sipre continues: "both men and women, both near and far are permitted to see her." As for the internal contradiction in the Mishnah mentioned above, b. Soṭah 8b attempts to make the participation of women obligatory, since after all "they," women, are on trial, as every woman is a potential adulteress and should view the ceremony so as to avoid undergoing a similar shaming.[54]

Tosefta Soṭah 3:2–5 continues the description of the ceremony with special attention to hair. Many of the hair actions, by woman or by priest, are symbolic of her supposed inappropriate behavior as an accused temptress, seducer, and adulteress. She put on a beautiful scarf specifically in order to make herself attractive to tempt her potential partner.[55] The woman began her seduction by covering up (her hair) with a beautiful scarf. Therefore, the priest in the ceremony uncovers her and removes her *kippah*, albeit now a plain cap and not a beautiful scarf, and tramples

51. See Joshua Schwartz, "Once More on the Nicanor Gate," *HUCA* 62 (1991): 245–83.

52. In Sipre Num. Naso 11 (ed. Kahana, 1:37–38), this is even clearer: The priest stands behind her. He might have seen her hair but not her bosom. That would make the hair less dangerous than exposing her flesh. Standing to the side relates to both hair and breasts in the same manner.

53. See Kahana, *Sifre on Numbers*, 2:136–37.

54. Ibid.

55. The text should be read as (סודרין) סד[ר]ין, "scarf," not סדין, "sheet." The former implies an act of covering up to make herself attractive while the latter is blatantly sexual.

on it.[56] Thus, in the first stage of the ceremony, it is the hair covering and not the hair that the priest debases by stepping on it. At this stage, the woman's hair is uncovered but is still bound.

The second act of the ceremony as depicted in Tosefta continues to revolve around hair. She had braided or bound it to make herself attractive and to entice her partner, so the priest unbinds her hair, as the woman had certainly done in private.[57] The priest does not dishevel her hair; he does not have to do so. The natural action of most women whose hair has been unbound is to shake it loose. In the seduction, this would have been an act of sexual arousal and of course appropriate only in private. How ironic that she now does so in public and as the ultimate act of her self-shaming. In private, this was part of a plan; in public, it is an involuntary reflex she could not stop.[58]

Not all the sages agreed with all the details of the ceremony as described in the Mishnah and Tosefta. Rabbi Judah, as we saw above, cut back on some aspects of the shaming, such as uncovering her hair, if the woman was beautiful and might still be able to entice at the ceremony. Two additional views are found in Sipre Num. Naso 11. Both Rabbi Ishmael and Rabbi Johanan ben Beroqa were of the opinion that the only action undertaken before the drinking of the bitter waters was the uncovering of the woman's hair or, in the words of Rabbi Johanan, "the daughters of Israel are not to be made more 'ugly' than what is prescribed in the Torah."[59]

Hair and Divorce

Mishnah Ketubbot 7:6 lists those who were considered to have transgressed the law of Moses and Jewish custom.[60] Transgressing the law of Moses included sins such as engaging in intercourse while ritually impure. Transgressing Jewish custom was more a matter of proper behavior. This included actions such as weaving in public in the market or conversing with men. This was immodest behavior but not technically against the halakhah.

How did hair fit into this? The list states that a married woman who goes out in public with her hair loose or disheveled, and obviously uncov-

---

56. Cf., however, Num. Rab., Naso, 9:16, which sees the action of the priest as reflecting the woman's acting like a pagan and going about with her hair uncovered (or unbound).

57. This is according to Codex Vienna of Tosefta (and b. Soṭah 9a).

58. Cosgrove, "Woman's Unbound Hair," 677.

59. Kahana, *Sifre on Numbers*, 2:130–33.

60. See Gen. Rab. 17:8. The requirement for a woman to cover her hair refers back to the sin of Eve and is punishment for her eating from the tree of knowledge, which caused a woman's hair to become sexual.

ered, may be divorced without settlement. Hair in this state might be sexually arousing, and this supposedly had serious repercussions for a continuing normative relationship between husband and wife. For a married woman, the last time she had been allowed in public with her hair unbound was when she was taken on a litter from her father's house to her husband's house and her hair had been unbound during the course of that transfer (m. Ketub. 2:1) when her husband received her like this. Going out again with her hair unbound would signify nonacceptance of her husband's authority. The sympathy was with the husband. The wife lost all claim to her divorce settlement (cf. t. Ketub. 7:6–7).

Mishnah and Tosefta Ketubbot just cited reflect Palestinian tradition. The *sugya* in the Bavli did not understand the Palestinian hair issues. Bavli Ketubbot 72 a–b understands the transgression of the woman as just having her hair uncovered. Placing a basket on her head to transport something might be sufficient as a head covering in place of whatever other head covering the woman had taken off. The *sugya* finds it hard to understand where exactly she had taken off her head covering in a manner that made her liable for divorce. At first, it suggests that this was in the courtyard, but eventually the transgression is located in a passageway between courtyards. In the Bavli, there is little tolerance for any deviation from hair covering norm. In Palestinian tradition, there has to be action with clear sexual connotation.

If uncovered hair was grounds for divorce in Babylonian tradition, this same tradition was absolutely horrified by loose and disheveled hair, which was often associated with demons such as Lilith.[61] An aggadic tradition in b. Sanh. 109b–110a describes the wife of On ben Pelet as being able to keep the supporters of Korah's rebellion against Moses (Num 16:1) away from her husband by simply sitting at the entrance to her tent—that is, "in public"—with her hair untied and disheveled, reflecting a woman mad with grief, as we saw above (see n. 26), or perhaps just a woman who was mad. Even the rebellious supporters of Korah recoiled in horror upon seeing her in such a state and retreated. One can imagine, then, the normative reaction to such an appearance in a public venue like a market.

Mikveh: Washing and Dipping

It was forbidden for a woman immersing herself in a ritual bath, or *mikveh*, to have anything on her body or in her hair that might prevent the water from reaching. Thus, clothing, jewelry, and accessories had to be removed. Before a woman could immerse, however, she had to be clean and that included shampooing her hair and combing it out (y. Ḥag. 4:1; b. B. Qam.

61. B. ʿErub. 100b; b. Nid. 24b; and Num. Rab. 12:3.

82a).[62] How did this washing relate to a woman's regular hair washing? It is unfortunately impossible to determine the frequency of hair washing in ancient Jewish society. It is also hard to know what was used as shampoo in general or by women undergoing ritual immersion. Tosefta B. Meṣi'a 11:32 states that one who engaged in hard, physical, dirty work might have shampooed with natron (or lye) or urine.[63] These are strong substances that would not have been gentle, and it is doubtful that women would have shampooed with them on a regular basis, if at all. The ancient Egyptians used citrus juice to wash hair and wigs, and perhaps Jewish women did so as well. Another common substance for shampooing in the ancient world was a mixture of oil and natron, the oil mitigating the harshness of the natron, but gumming- up the hair and making it difficult to comb out. This may have defeated the purpose of shampooing before ritual immersion but was less critical for a regular shampoo.

One of the most detailed shampooing traditions from the ancient world is found in a poem from fifth-century CE India that describes a courtesan bathing her hair in perfumed oil, ten kinds of astringents, five spices, and thirty-two herbs soaked in water.[64] How common was that type of washing in ancient Jewish or Greco-Roman society? Most women probably used less-complex mixtures of an oil base. There were, however, certain shampoo substances that were forbidden to a woman undergoing ritual bathing such as a lye or natron-based cleanser without oil, which might make the hair brittle, causing it to break off and possibly stick to the woman's body, preventing full immersion. Sand or other "dry shampoos" were forbidden because the hair might stick together, impeding total immersion.[65] There is no mention, though, of oil-based cleansers that might have had the same effect. The temperature of the water for a shampoo was critical. Warm water should be used; cold water was forbidden because it could make the hair brittle and the water might not pass through (b. Nid. 66a–b).

Rabbinic literature does not provide details regarding the types of combs that would be used by women in the ritual bath or in general, but numerous wooden combs have been found in the course of archaeological excavations at sites such as Masada and Wadi Murabba`at. These combs, some simple and some elaborate, for the most part with tiers of teeth on

---

62. As for the substances used, see below. Matted hair though was not an impediment (m. Miqw. 9:3).

63. See also m. Naz. 6:3, which states that the Nazirite is allowed to rub (חופף) and scratch his hair. חופף may mean both rub and shampoo.

64. See Eiluned Edwards, "Air, Devotion and Trade in India," in Biddle-Perry and Cheang, *Hair: Styling, Culture and Fashion,* 160. The reference is to the *Cilappatikaram.*

65. See m. Naz. 6:3. R. Ishmael states that a *nazir* may not rub his head with earth, as it would cause the hair to fall out.

both sides, enabled combing without breaking the teeth, but with teeth close together to remove lice or lice eggs.[66]

As we stated above, nothing could come between water and hair. Even putting hair in one's mouth during immersion might invalidate the immersion (m. Miqw. 8:5). We saw above that there were hairbands and ribbons that had to be removed or loosened before immersion and others that did not, with the criterion being whether they were sown into the hair or not (m. Šabb. 6:1, 5; b. Šabb. 57a–b). A woman was permitted to loosely tie her hair, which would prevent it from floating up but would allow the water to pass through (y. Šabb. 6:1, 7d).

There is also some discussion about how close the shampooing had to be to the immersion. Could a woman shampoo on the eve of the Sabbath but immerse only at night after the conclusion of the Sabbath? (b. Nid. 68a; cf. y. Meg. 4:1, 75a). A priestess, who would immerse daily in order to eat priestly portions in purity, was exempt from shampooing and combing out her hair before and after this immersion, as the rabbis realized that daily shampooing was not good for healthy hair, but a priestess who immersed after completing her period as a menstruant had to shampoo and comb like all other women (y. Pesaḥ. 1:1, 27b).

Hairstyle

Maintaining hair was part of one's individual *kosmos*, and a hairstyle could convey individuality, as well as participation in social structures and even submission to social controls.[67] There are endless ways to deal with hair, and all women do "something" with their hair beyond its natural state. It can be "combed, cut, coloured, curled, straightened, plaited, swept up, tied back, decorated, plucked and shaved."[68] Many of the basic hairstyles in ancient Greco-Roman society were "arrangement-based hair fashions"; that is, the hair need only be cut, parted, restrained, or put up in a particular way to be fashionable.[69] Long hair and short hair meant different things at different times for different cultures. Thus, in ancient Greek society a female slave wore her hair short like a man, as did other women

66. See Yigal Sitri, "Roman Period Wooden Artifacts from the Land of Israel" [Hebrew], *Qadmoniot* 49/152 (2016): 72–73.

67. Bartman, "Hair and the Artifice," 1, 5.

68. See Biddle-Perry and Cheang, "Introduction: Thinking about Hair," 3.

69. See http://www2.cnr.edu/home/sas/araia/RomanHairstyles.html. See this site also on resource-based arrangement; that is, style is based on a specific quality of the hair such as color or length with little concern as to actual arrangement and on combination hair fashions, which tend toward extremes, combining arrangement and resources. This became popular in first-century CE Rome such as with styles that included tall front hair and enormous wreath buns.

in servile status such as hetairai.[70] In Athens, girls wore their hair long, and, as it got longer, it was brought under control with braids, binding, or cutting.[71] Women would wear their long hair in a ponytail or bound in a chignon,[72] but in Sparta adult women kept their hair short, reflecting the regulations of a rigid society.[73]

Roman girls generally had hairstyles simpler than those of grown women. Their hair might be braided, sometimes even loose, or wound into buns, such as the "melon hairstyle," which was twisted back from the crown in sections and wound into a bun at the back of the head.[74] Some girls had more complex styles, perhaps even more elaborate and complex than their mothers', such as a top plait style or rings of curls framing the face, in order to attract suitors.[75]

There were many possibilities for the Roman matron, whether simple or elaborate. Yet it is sometimes difficult to be certain that statuary representations or paintings on caskets portray actual styles, at least normative ones for normative women and not just those of the upper classes or the coiffure whims of the artist.[76]

We have already discussed the unique hair covering of the Roman bride. She also had an elaborate hairstyle called the *seni crines*, perhaps separated into six sections, then twisted and braided on top.[77] The matron could have a special style called the *tutulus*, in which the hair was divided, piled high into a bun, and bound with purple fillets of wool, resulting in a conical shape. It is not clear how long this style persisted, and there are few artistic representations of it.[78]

Upper-class women often had very elaborate styles. One such style in the first–second centuries CE was the *toupet*, which was a towering coiffure of tiers and stories that may have been arranged over padding or greased with animal fat to stay in place.[79] Not everyone, however, was in favor of these styles. The Roman poet Ovid (*Ars.* 3.151–152) advised women to style their hair based on the shape of their face and personality: hanging loose, braided, up in a knot, and even in disarray. There are more

---

70. Lee, *Body, Dress and Identity*, 72, 74. This was not the case, however, in Rome, where prostitutes and their slaves might have had elaborate hairstyles. See Olson, *Dress and the Roman Woman*, 43.

71. Lee, *Body, Dress and Identity*, 71.

72. Ibid.

73. Ibid., 74.

74. Olson, "Appearance of the Young Roman Girl," 145.

75. Ibid., 146. Those who could afford it would adorn their daughter's hair with jewels (148).

76. See Walker, *Ancient Faces*.

77. Olsen, *Dress and the Roman Woman*, 22.

78. Ibid., 39–40. See also Bartman, "Hair and the Artifice," 7.

79. Olsen, *Dress and the Roman Woman* , 70–71.

fashions than acorns on a tree.[80] Just to briefly highlight this, we cite a few styles from mummy portraits of Roman Egypt: central parting, as was the style of the goddess Diana;[81] lightly waved banks of curls at the side; bun at the crown of the head; locks in front; front hair arranged around the brow in two banks of snail shaped curls; ringlets; tiers of curls above the brow and coiled into large plaited bun on crown of head; curly hair cut close to head with locks falling in front of ears; and hair in mass of loose curls piled high on head—and this is just a small part of the rich variety of styles found in these portraits.[82] Palmyrene women wore their hair waved in a simple center-part style.[83] One might get the impression from all this that women changed their style every few years, but the many different artistic representations represent hundreds of years and change was not swift.[84] Elaborate styles required fairly long hair and healthy hair; otherwise the styles were viable only with wigs or falls. Most artistic representations are of younger women, and the styles reflect use of their own hair.

A good description of provincial women's hairstyles that is somewhat contemporaneous with the descriptions from some of the rabbinic writings can be found in the second- to third-century CE North African church father Tertullian. He refers to styles that are simpler than the elaborate Roman styles mentioned above—and thus more representative of normative hairstyles: : "What service, again, does all the labor spent in arranging the hair render to salvation? Why is no rest allowed to your hair, which must now be bound, now loosed, now cultivated, now thinned out? Some are anxious to force their hair into curls, some let it hang loose and flying; not with good simplicity" (*Cult. fem.* 2.8.2).[85] There was also a tendency in the provinces to adopt Roman styles at the expense of local and perhaps even previous "barbarian" styles.[86]

Women's hair required much attention and lengthy grooming sessions, usually at home.[87] Depending on social and economic status, styling might be done by the woman herself, by a professional hairdresser, the *ornatrix*, or by a slave or servant. Sometimes the *ornatrix* and the slave

---

80. Ibid.

81. Bartman, "Hair and the Artifice," 2 n. 7.

82. Walker, "Mummy Portraits," 38–136. See, however, Bartman, "Hair and the Artifice," 22. Sculpture and artistic representation might reproduce real life, but there are exceptions, such as in the case of shoulder locks, an attribute of Venus, although an unlikely style in real life. On the step-by-step recreation of some of the Roman styles, such as a serpentine braid, a strand braid, a tower style, braided bun style and the equipment needed to create these styles, see Janet Stephens, "Ancient Roman Hairdressing: On (hair)pins and needles," *JRA* 21 (2008): 110–32.

83. Bartman, "Hair and Artifice," 17.

84. Ibid., 4, 19.

85. See http://www.tertullian.org/anf/anf04/anf04-07.htm#P431_90321.

86. Bartman, "Hair and Artifice," 6.

87. Ibid., 1, 8.

were identical, and the wealthy woman might have had more than one person working on their hair.[88]

Jewish women adopted many, but not all, of the hairstyles mentioned above, although probably those more popular in the provinces than those in Rome or those in artistic representations depicting the upper classes. Regardless of style, however, a Jewish woman was usually also careful with her hair (b. Šabb. 112a),[89] particularly since most wore their hair long. One tradition even mentions the possibility of a bride under her *huppah* cleaning her dirtied hands with her long hair, and this was actually considered good for her hair (Deut. Rab. 1; cf. Luke 7:36–50). Whatever style was preferred, few, if any, women cut their hair short or off altogether; doing so would result in great discomfort for a woman and was done only under dire circumstances, such as the case of Rachel, Rabbi Akiva's wife, who cut off her braids to sell them to support her husband while he studied, or the wife of Job, who let Satan shear off her hair with scissors as payment for three loaves of bread.[90]

Long hair was often braided and then tied to the back or middle of the head to enable a covering. The rabbis compared the tying of braided hair in the back to a "jewel" (Shir ha-Shirim Rab. 4:1), perhaps also reflecting the apparent popularity of this style (Pesiq. Zutarta [Lekah Tov] 4). A woman might braid her own hair or have it braided by someone else (t. Šabb. 9:13). Rachel, Rabbi Akiva's wife, wore her hair in braids, as we mentioned above, and she probably would have used a simple style that enabled her to cut the braids off and sell them. However, braids might also be elaborate, such as when God himself braided Eve's hair before he brought her to Adam (Gen. Rab. 18:2; b. Šabb. 95a). Because of the often complex nature of braiding, it was forbidden on the Sabbath (m. Šabb. 10:6; y. Šabb. 10:6, 12b);[91] it was considered to be either "building" or "weaving." It was permissible, though, to braid on Festival days (y. Mo'ed Qaṭ. 1:7, 80d).

---

88. Vicki León, *Working IX to V: Orgy Planners, Funeral Clowns and Other Prized Professions of the Ancient World* (New York: Walker, 2007), 17. Bartman, "Hair and Artifice," 8.

89. Thus, a woman was allowed to care for her hair during a period of mourning, as opposed to more stringent regulations for a man (Sem. Avel Rab. 2:1).

90. See y. Šabb. 6:1, 7d; y. Soṭah 9:15, 24c. T. Job 23:7–10. On the social background of these hair-cutting traditions, see Tal Ilan, *Mine and Yours Are Hers: Retrieving Women's History from Rabbinic Literature*, AGJU 41 (Leiden: Brill, 1997), 156–57. During times of war and tribulation, a woman might lose her hair so that it would not be possible to determine whether she was female or male. See Lam. Rab. 4:8. See also Pesiq. Rab. 29 on a similar case in Jerusalem under siege. Starvation causes hair loss.

91. The Mishnah uses גודלת. A form of this word is used for a female hairdresser, who spent a good deal of her time braiding. The Mishnah also forbids an action called פוסקת, which was explained by Maimonides as braiding around the head. Hair coverings could be worn in these cases. *Poseket* might also have been a type of dyeing.

It is not always possible to identify the hairstyle mentioned in rabbinic tradition. Thus, a woman who has very long hair makes it "waves, waves" (y. Mo'ed Qaṭ. 1:7, 80d), perhaps a braid.[92] Women parted their hair (b. Šabb. 60a), straightened it,[93] or put it in ponytails of various sorts (y. Šhab. 6:1, 7d), and often added oil (b. Šhab. 28b).

The Jewish woman might have used a professional hairdresser (m. Kelim 3:3),[94] and the rich might have had servants who performed hairdressing functions.[95] Some sages prohibited Jewish hairdressers from caring for or braiding the hair of a non-Jewish woman so as not to make that woman look more attractive (y. 'Abod. Zar. 1:9, 40b). The stylist, professional or amateur, would have engaged mostly in style and care and rarely in cutting. A late tradition states that Miriam, the mother of Ben Stada (or ben Pandira), identified with Jesus (or Peter) was a hairdresser (b. Šabb. 104b; b. Ḥag. 4b; b. Sanh. 67a). Hairdressing might have also been rather informal, taking place in the courtyard with women braiding one another's hair and using equipment that could double for other purposes (t. Kelim B. Meṣi'a 5:5). Plucking out white or grey hairs was probably done by a woman herself (y. Šabb. 6:1, 7d).

Conclusion

Was there anything particularly Jewish about a Jewish woman in Palestine from the neck up? She might have had her hair covered, but most women in the Greco-Roman world also did so and the same is true regarding a wig or a fall. The Jewish woman's hair might have been braided. This too was not unusual. Would she have had an elaborate hairstyle? That probably depended on her socioeconomic status, and, in any case, her style would have been more in keeping with those popular in the provinces rather than in Rome itself. Hair care was similar throughout the empire and beyond, and same equipment and accoutrements were used.

Was there anything Jewish in the meaning of a woman's hair? The dangers of hair and especially exposed hair seemed to be universal. The dangers were of a potential sexual nature and not of a political or social nature. There does not seem to be a problem with "non-Jewish" styles. Thus, unless there was a particular reason, Jewish women could well fit into the world of hair in the Greco-Roman world.

---

92. See Michael Sokoloff, *A Dictionary of Jewish Palestinian Aramaic of the Byzantine Period* (Ramat-Gan: Bar-Ilan University Press, 1990), s.v. "גלש."

93. See Rashi, Mo'ed Qaṭ. 9b s.v. poseket. Cf., however, Tosafot ad loc., who interpret Rashi as meaning to straighten hair to keep it neat.

94. See Ilan, *Mine and Yours*, 231.

95. M. Qidd. 2:3: שפחה גדלת. This, though, might also mean adolescent daughter. See y. Qidd. 2:2, 62c.

Three Crowns

BURTON L. VISOTZKY
The Jewish Theological Seminary of America

Rabbi Shimeon said, "There are three crowns: The crown of Torah, the crown of priesthood, and the crown of royalty. The crown of a good name is superior to them all."

רבי שמעון אומר שלשה כתרים הם כתר תורה וכתר כהונה וכתר מלכות וכתר שם טוב עולה על גביהן

Pirke Avot chapter 4

When Shaye J. D. Cohen and I studied at the Jewish Theological Seminary almost five decades ago, *Wissenschaft des Judentums* reigned supreme. Philology was a favored tool, particularly of our teacher Rabbi Saul Lieberman. He emphasized *perush hamilim,* the explication of rabbinic terms, as a primary task of the exegete and historian. And so when we were still young men, we learned Greek to supplement our Hebrew and Aramaic, that we might better understand the classical texts of our rabbinic forebears. Shaye himself taught me that accuracy of translation forced a scholar to "take a stand" and be able to defend how one understood a particular passage.[1] It is in this spirit that I assay to translate and explicate three passages from Midrash Bereishit Rabbah, a fifth-century Galilean rabbinic commentary on the book of Genesis. Each passage will refer to Greek literature to help to unpack the text. It seems appropriate as a tribute to a professor of Hebrew literature at so Hellenistic a bastion as Harvard.

This essay honors Prof. Shaye J. D. Cohen. He has continually earned the crown of Torah through his diligent study. He was born to the crown of priesthood. And, as for royalty, well, he is the Littauer Professor of Hebrew Literature and Philosophy in the Department of Near Eastern Languages and Civilizations of Harvard University.

1. Shaye is enough older than me (three years) to have given me this advice about my doctoral dissertation.

כתבו על קרן שור

Early on in Genesis Rabbah, the rabbis comment on the story of creation and the verse "the earth was unformed and void [*tohu vavohu*] and there was darkness upon the depths." In Gen. Rab. 2:4 we read the following pronouncement:

> [והארץ היתה תהו וגו'] ... ר' שמעון בן לקיש פתר קרייה במלכיות ... "וחשך" זו יוון, שהחשיכה עיני ישראל בגזרותיה: שהיתה אומרת לישראל, **כתבו בקרן שור** שאין להם חלק באלהי ישראל[2]

> "And the land was *tohu*" (Gen 1:2) ... Rabbi Shimeon ben Laqish interpreted this verse by referring to the [Four] Kingdoms ... "and darkness" refers to Greece, which darkened the eyes of the Jews with their decrees. She [Greece] said to the Jews, "Write on the horn of an ox, that they have no portion in the God of the Jews."

Here then is our first crown, if you will. Three parts of this midrash require some explication. For the first part, I translated that Rabbi Shimeon "interpreted this verse." The term פתר קרייה is fairly common in the Aramaized text of Genesis Rabbah.[3] Let us stipulate that the קרייה of the passage is the scriptural verse at hand. The verb פתר is related to the Hebrew פשר, which is found regularly among the writings from Qumran, as in the Pesher to Habakkuk.[4] In that corpus, pesher serves as a mode of exegesis in which a verse is interpreted allegorically to refer to the community of Qumran, in what they perceived to be their apocalyptic setting. So, for example, 1QpHab IV, 3–6, ad Hab 1:10b:

> "He [*sic*] laughs at every fortress, piles up earth and captures it" the interpretation of this [*peshro*] concerns the rulers of the Kittim who deride the fortresses of the peoples....

Yet when Genesis Rabbah does its פתר קרייה, while the interpretation of the verse in its gaze is allegorical, it is neither necessarily apocalyp-

---

2. Here following the text of J. Theodor, *Bereschit Rabba*, 2nd printing (Jerusalem: Wahrmann, 1965), 16. Theodor lists parallels in Gen. Rab. 16:4, Lev. Rab. 13:5 and 15:9, y. Ḥag. 2:2, 77d, and Megillat Ta'anit for 27 Iyar (for which see below). Other citations listed by Theodor are later than our Genesis Rabbah text. Cf. Tanhuma Tazria 11, which offers a useful interpretation of our text (see below). All translations are my own.

3. It is used, passim, in the contemporary midrashim Leviticus Rabbah and Song of Songs Rabbah, as well.

4. On *pesher* see, inter alios, Maurya P. Horgan, *Pesharim: Qumran Interpretations of Biblical Books*, CBQMS 8 (Washington, DC: Catholic Biblical Association of America, 1979); Timothy H. Lim, *Pesharim*, Companion to the Qumran Scrolls 3(London: Sheffield Academic Press, 2002); James H. Charlesworth, *The Pesharim and Qumran History: Chaos or Consensus?* (Grand Rapids: Eerdmans, 2006).

tic nor focused on its own time. Rather, while Genesis Rabbah and other contemporary midrashim do פתר קרייה, allegorically (this means that), the interpretation of the allegoresis is most often another verse or concept of Scripture itself. So, the immediately preceding midrash in Genesis Rabbah (2:3) "interprets" the very same verse of Genesis by referring to the biblical "generations" (פתר קרייה בדורות) of Adam, Cain, the generation of Enosh, and the generation of the flood, followed by Abraham, Isaac, and Jacob.

Our text in Gen. Rab. 2:4 "interprets" the verse of Genesis by referring to the biblical concept of the Four Kingdoms (פתר קרייה במלכיות).[5] In truth, rabbinic references to the four kingdoms partake of an apocalypticism similar to that of the Qumran pesher, the difference between Qumran's apocalypticism and Genesis Rabbah's being one of exegetical frequency. In Qumran, the pesher is always apocalyptic in nature. In Genesis Rabbah and other contemporary rabbinic midrashim, the פתר קרייה interprets toward a biblical solution, which most often is not apocalyptic but rather exegetic by reference to another part of Scripture.

Having briefly explicated the use of פתר קרייה, we turn to unpack the part of the Genesis Rabbah text referring to the "[Four] Kingdoms." The term itself originates in the cartoon-like visions of Daniel. He has a nightmare in which he sees a series of bizarre beasts. The explanation of his vision (Dan 7:17) is that "these great beasts, which are four, [refer to the] four king[dom]s that will arise upon the earth." Later in the biblical apocalypse, Daniel is told, "The two-horned ram you saw [refers to] the kings of Media and Persia. The he-goat is the king[dom] of Greece; and the first horn, which is between its eyes, it is the first king" (Dan 8:20–21; and see 2:39–40). Indeed, our midrash follows Daniel's lead and presumes the first three kingdoms to be the Persians, the Medes, and Greece—precisely our textual reading of Greece as "darkness."

What, then, of the dreaded fourth kingdom? Daniel is taught, "The fourth beast [refers to] the fourth king[dom], which will differ from all other kingdoms; it will devour the entire earth, trampling and crushing it" (Dan 7:23). It is easy to surmise that this fourth kingdom was interpreted by the rabbis to refer to Esau/Edom/Rome, the imperial hegemony of their day.[6] In post-Talmudic times, the mysterious fourth kingdom came to be

5. On the four kingdoms, see the dated but still useful H. H. Rowley, *Darius the Mede and the Four World Empires in the Book of Daniel: A Historical Study of Contemporary Theories* (Cardiff: University of Wales Press Board, 1935; repr., Eugene, OR: Wipf & Stock, 2006), passim; John J. Collins, *Apocalypticism in the Dead Sea Scrolls*, Literature of the Dead Sea Scrolls (London: Routledge, 1997) with frequent reference to Daniel and the four kingdoms; and, most recently, Brennan Breed, "Daniel's Four Kingdoms Schema: A History of Re-writing World History," *Int* 71 (2017): 178–89. Most modern readings of the biblical four kingdoms tend toward evangelical interpretations.

6. See Lev. Rab. 13:5, which also depicts Greece decreeing that the Jews "write on the horn of an ox, etc." For the four kingdoms in rabbinic literature, see Rivka Raviv, "The Tal-

seen as Ishmael and the hegemony of Islam.[7] This, like the pesher at Qumran, is an apocalyptic reading of the allegorized text referring to contemporary times. Indeed, if we but refer to the Qumran Pesher to Habakkuk, cited above, we see that it refers to the Kittim, usually understood to mean Rome. Where does Qumran get its term Kittim from? The very same Daniel visions, where we read, concerning the broken kingdom of Greece, that "Ships from Kittim will come against him" (Dan 11:30). Is it a surprise that the Kittim should follow after Greece? We already can read it in Genesis, "The descendants of Yavan/Greece: Elishah and Tarshish, the *Kittim* and the Dodanim" (Gen 10:4).

Now that we have explicated the terms פתר קרייה and four kingdoms, we turn to the odd phrase "write on the horn of an ox." The action depicted here is somewhat opaque. Writing on a horn is referenced elsewhere in rabbinic literature, to be sure. In the matter of Giṭṭin, Jewish divorce documents, a case is raised wherein one has written a *Get* on the horn of a cow or a gazelle.[8] Nevertheless, the vast majority of rabbinic instances of writing on a horn are on an ox horn, similar to our case under discussion. So, let us return to the horn of our dilemma.

There is a seemingly parallel reference to our Genesis Rabah text in Megillat Ta'anit for 27 Iyar, which refers to the "removal of the crown" (איתנטלית כלילא). In the scholion to the passage we read:

> שבימי מלכות יון היו עושין עטרות של ורד ותולין אותן על פתחי בתי עבודה זרה שלהם ועל פתחי החניות ועל פתחי החצרות ושרין בשיר לעבודה זרה **וכותבין על קרניו של שור** ועל מצחי חמורים אין לבעליו חלק בעליון כשם שהיו הפלשתים עושים שנאמר וחרש לא ימצא וגו

> For in the days of the Greek Kingdom they made crowns of roses and hung them upon the entryways of their houses of idol worship, and upon the entryways to the stores and the entryways to the courtyards, and they sang the songs of idol worship. And they wrote upon the horns of an ox and upon the foreheads of donkeys that their owners had no share in the Most High, as the Philistines used to do, as it is said, "No smith was to be found, etc." (1 Sam 13:19).[9]

---

mudic Formulation of the Prophecies of the Four Kingdoms in the Book of Daniel" [Hebrew], *Jewish Studies, an Internet Journal* 5 (2006): 1–20.

7. E.g., Pirqe R. El., ch. 28, apud Carol Bakhos, *The Family of Abraham: Jewish, Christian, and Muslim Interpretations* (Cambridge: Harvard University Press, 2014), 174–76.

8. See m. Giṭ 2:3, which imagines, כותבין ... על הקרן של פרה ונותנין לה את הפרה "Write [the Get] on the horn of a cow, and give her the cow." This is a piquant method of acting out against ones soon-to-be former wife; but apparently it is deemed acceptable for divorcing her according to the majority of the sages of the Mishnah. In the Talmud Yerushalmi's discussion of the Mishnah, ad loc. (ed. Venice 44b), an example of writing a Get on a gazelle's horn is also cited.

9. Following the text of Vered Noam, *Megillat Ta'anit: Versions, Interpretations, History, with a Critical Edition* [Hebrew] (Jerusalem: Hebrew University Press, 2003), 67, with her

The citation of the verse reveals the intention of these two yoked actions. By the Greeks inscribing their animals as having "no share in the Most High," the Jews apparently were forbidden to use them, just as they were forbidden to forge implements of any kind under Philistine rule in the days of Saul and Jonathan. No implements meant no swords or spears, thus the Israelites were impotent. How did this apply to the case cited in the scholion to Megillat Ta'anit? It seems that, once inscribed, the donkeys and oxen could not be used by the Jews, and so the Jews had no animals for plowing. No plowing meant no planting; thus, the Jews were subjected to the Greeks under threat of starvation.[10]

The question for our purposes is whether this text offers any insight into the Genesis Rabbah text we are discussing. Vered Noam dates the two versions of the scholion to "the Talmudic period," and the later hybrid version to the ninth–tenth centuries. That is to say, the text traditions of the scholion are contemporaneous with, or more likely later than, our Genesis Rabbah text. They are equally likely to have been taken from Genesis Rabbah or its parallels in an attempt to explicate the Aramaic text of the Megillah itself.[11] To my mind, the addition of the donkey's forehead to the horns of the oxen makes it a later gloss on the earlier tradition that lacked the donkey.[12] But the tradition of the scholion is on point: somehow the mere inscription onto the horns and foreheads renders the animals unfit for use. We will return to the mode of rendering the animals unfit below.

In one parallel, somewhat later than our text (and perhaps concurrent with what Noam calls "the hybrid scholion"), we find the Tanhuma version of our tradition (Tanhuma Tazria [ed. Warsaw] 11):

'בהרת' זו מלכות יון שהיתה מבהרת על ישראל ואומרת, כל מי שיש לו שור **יחקה על קרן השור**
שאין לו חלק באלהי ישראל, ואם לאו גוזרין עליו הריגה

> "Bright spot" (Lev 13:2) refers to the Greek Kingdom which discolored the Israelites and said to them, "Anyone who has an ox must incise upon the ox's horn that it has no portion in the God of Israel," and if not [the Greeks] decreed upon him/it the death penalty.

---

notes on 191–92. Noam's work is now the standard for Megillat Ta'anit, and her commentary is nonpareil.

10. See the rather baroque, late expansion of this explanation in the *Midrash to Hanukkah* [Hebrew], in A. Jellinek, *Bet ha-Midrasch*, 3rd ed., 6 vols. (Jerusalem: Wahrmann, 1967), 6:1.

11. This makes no reference at all to the "horns of oxen" or the "foreheads of donkeys." For Noam's opinion see her "Megillat Taanit—The Scroll of Fasting," in *The Literature of the Sages*, ed. Shmuel Safrai et al., CRINT 2.3B (Assen: Van Gorcum, 2006), 339–62, esp. 350–56. For more information, see V. Noam," The Scholion to the Megilat Ta'anit: Towards an Understanding of its Stemma" [Hebrew], *Tarbiz* 62 (1992) 55–99.

12. Cf. H. Lichtenstein, "Die Fastenrolle: Eine Untersuchung zur jüdisch-hellenistischen Geschichte," *HUCA* 8–9 (1931–1932): 286.

The Tanhuma is not at all clear about what the effect of the declaration is, but it does get one detail correct. The "writing" of the early text is now taken to be incision into the horn. This is in keeping with the medieval artistic practice of oliphants—incising and carving horns for artistic purposes.[13] The Tanhuma is au courant as to its own practice but doesn't actually tell us much about either the practice of the early Greeks or that of Genesis Rabbah.

For the sake of thoroughness, we note that the prophet Zechariah (14:20-21) includes the following in his messianic vision at the very end of the book:

> On that day, "Holy to the Lord" shall be upon the bells of horses, and the cooking-cauldrons in the House of the Lord will be like the basins before the altar.... Indeed, every cooking-cauldron in Jerusalem and Judea will be holy to the Lord, and all who offer sacrifices shall come and take from them, and boil their [sacrificial meat] in them; nor shall there be Canaanite traders in the House of the Lord of Hosts on that day, any longer.[14]

The text is instructive in that it mentions an inscription "Holy to the Lord" on the bells of horses. This is not the same as an inscription on the horn of an ox, but we are getting warmer. Further, the messianic vision is in keeping with our Genesis Rabbah and Megillat Ta'anit texts that there will be some push-back against the gentiles, represented in Zechariah as Canaanite traders (כנעני). In B. Z. Luria's Megillat Ta'anit commentary adducing this biblical text, he goes so far as to suggest that what actually was inscribed on the ox horns or donkey brows was a dedication to Aphrodite.[15] This is an interesting suggestion; unfortunately, it has no basis in the text.

On the basis of the Giṭṭin materials quoted above, one might conjecture that writing on the horn of an ox and thus denying the God of Israel was a form of divorcing the Almighty. As it were, the Greeks decreed that the Jews write a repudiation of God. In the same tractate Giṭṭin where we read about divorce documents on ox horns, we read, as it were, about God's separation (if not final divorce) from the Jews during the rebellion

---

13. See the fascinating discussion of carved and inscribed ivory tusks from the Islamic period, in Avinoam Shalem, *The Oliphant: Islamic Objects in Historical Context*, Islamic History and Civilization 54 (Leiden: Brill, 2004). I note that these oliphants are all carved on detached tusks. Presumably this is more easily accomplished than it would be were the tusks still attached to the live elephants. My thanks to Nomi Schneck for this reference and for her thorough research assistance on this segment of the essay. This is not the place for the fantastical expansion of the Tanhuma tradition in the Midrash to Hanukkah, as it has no historic basis for its commentary beyond a vivid imagination.

14. See B. Z. Luria, *Megillat Taanit* (Jerusalem: Bialik, 1964), 115–16. Luria's reference to Zechariah (2:12) should be corrected accordingly.

15. Ibid., 115 n. 5.

against Rome and the destruction of the Second Temple (b. Giṭ. 55b–58a). But this, too, is not really suggested by the text of Genesis Rabbah or its parallels.

We do, however, have an explicit reference to the horns of an ox in a sacrificial context in m. Bik. 3:3,[16] which might help us get a bit closer to understanding the allusion in our Genesis Rabbah Text. The Mishnah reads: והשור הולך לפניהם וקרניו מצופות זהב ועטרת של זית בראשו ... עד שמגיעים קרוב לירושלם – "[The pilgrims from afar drove] the ox before them, its horns overlaid with gold and a fillet of olive[-leaves] upon its head … until they neared Jerusalem." The ox is intended to be offered in sacrifice, and its horns have golden decoration on them. Further, the ox is garlanded with a fillet made of olive leaves. A pretty sight, to be sure, but not the same as writing on the horns of the ox or repudiating God with that inscription.

Fortunately, we have a Greek text that speaks of adorning an animal with gold upon its horns and inscribing that gold with a text dedicating it to a god—but not the God of Israel. Philostratus, in his *Life of Apollonius of Tyana*, recounts his hero's journey to the Indus River. There they saw a herd of elephants crossing the river and heard about the exploits of elephants in Alexander the Great's war with King Porus at the battle of the Hydaspes (326 BCE):

> They came upon an elephant near Taxila, the greatest city in India, who was anointed with myrrh by the natives and adorned with fillets. For, they said, this elephant was one of those who fought on the side of Porus against Alexander; and, as it had made a brave fight, Alexander dedicated it to the Sun. And it had, they say, gold rings around its tusks or horns, whichever you call them, and an inscription was on them written in Greek, as follows: "Alexander the son of Zeus dedicates Ajax to the Sun." For he had given this name to the elephant, thinking so great an animal deserved a great name. And the natives reckoned that 350 years had elapsed since the battle, without taking into account how old the elephant was when he went into battle. (*Vit. Apoll.* 2.12; Conybeare, LCL)[17]

Finally, we have someone inscribing on the horns of an animal a dedication to a god! The god is Helios, and the inscription is on the gold ring around the tusk. An elephant is not an ox, nor is a dedication to the god the same as a repudiation of God. But Alexander's dedication sets the animal free to wander and, perhaps, not be worked. One might, therefore, readily imagine other Greeks, of a somewhat later era than Alexander, requiring the negative dedication that this "ox has no portion in the God of Israel." We can now better understand the Genesis Rabbah text.

---

16. See ibid., 116 n. 7, which also must be corrected accordingly.

17. Apollonius flourished ca. 170 CE, so the natives' math is off by a century and a half. With all those wrinkles, it's hard to guess the age of an elephant.

מאין לאין

For our second crown, we read further in the text of Genesis Rabbah 2:4, where we find the report of an encounter between Rabbi Yehoshua and Shimeon ben Zoma. As it appears in Genesis Rabbah, we read:

> כבר היה שמעון בן זומא עומד ותוהא, עבר ר' יהושע שאל בשלומו פעם ופעמיים ולא השיבו, בשלישית השיבו בבהילות, אמר לו מה זו בן זומא **מאיין ולאיין**,[18] אמר לו לא מאיין ר', אמר לו מעיד אני עלי שמים וארץ שאיני זז מיכאן עד שתודיעני מאיין הרגלים, אמר לו מסתכל הייתי במעשה בראשית ואין בין מים העליונים לתחתונים כב' וג' אצבעות ורוח אלהים מנשבת אין כתוב כאן אלא מרחפת כעוף שפורח ומרפרף בכנפיו וכנפיו נוגעות ואין נוגעות, נהפך ר' יהושע ואמר לתלמידים הלך לו בן זומא[19]

> Once, Shimeon ben Zoma was standing confounded. Rabbi Yehoshua passed by and asked after him once, and again, yet he did not reply. At the third attempt, he replied in confusion. He [Yehoshua] said to him, "What's this Ben Zoma? Where from and where to?" He replied, "Nothing from nothing, Rabbi." He said, "I call heaven and earth to witness that I shall not move from here until you tell me where your feet are coming from!"
>
> He said to him, "I was speculating on the Works of Creation, and between the Upper Waters and the Lower Waters there is no more than two to three fingers-breadth. Further, it does not say 'The spirit of God blew,' but rather 'hovered' (Gen 1:2), like a bird that is fluttering, flapping its wings, and its wings touch, yet do not touch." Rabbi Yehoshua turned away and said to his disciples, "Ben Zoma has gone."[20]

Our teacher Rabbi Saul Lieberman wrote about this passage in the appendix to his article "How Much Greek in Jewish Palestine." There Lieberman treated the so-called Gnostic background to our passage rather thoroughly, explaining his detour to such arcana with the memorable line, "Nonsense is nonsense, but the history of nonsense is a very important science."[21] In that spirit, I wish to add two short notes to Lieberman's discussion.

---

18. Here emending the text according to Lieberman, *Tosefta Ki-fshutah*, Hagigah ch. 2, line 28, p. 1292 and n. 14. See, too, Theodor's commentary to this text, referenced below, ad p. 17, line 6, where Theodor attests to the correctness of this reading, as it is found thus in every parallel. The reading in Theodor, מאין הרגלים, is an error due to a dittography from the line below.

19. Genesis Rabbah 2:4, ed. Theodor, p. 17, line 4–p. 18, line 2.

20. My translation, with reference to Saul Lieberman, "How Much Greek in Jewish Palestine?," in *Biblical and Other Studies*, ed. Alexander Altmann, Studies and Texts (Philip W. Lown Institute of Advanced Jewish Studies) 1 (Cambridge: Harvard University Press, 1962), 137–38 and following. The entire article has been reprinted in Lieberman's *Texts and Studies* (New York: Ktav, 1974), 216–34.

21. Lieberman, "How Much Greek?," 135.

The first note is on Rabbi Yehoshua's greeting to Ben Zoma. When Ben Zoma does not reply to him, Rabbi Yehoshua asks, "What's this Ben Zoma? Where from and where to?" Lieberman made a great deal about the rabbinic resonances to this latter phrase, from the most profound existential questions to the most recondite of Gnostic allusions. Surprisingly, the master neglected to provide the Hellenistic background to מאיין ולאיין, as it is found in a number of places in Greek literature.

Possibly contemporary with Rabbi Yehoshua and Ben Zoma, Lucian of Samosata opens his encomium on Demosthenes[22] in dialogue with Thersagorus walking among the Stoa, by asking him, "Where's Thersagorus the poet going? And where's he come from?" ποῖ δὴ καὶ πόθεν; "Where to and where from?"

Of course, the Lucianic text is itself already quoting from Plato's *Phaedrus* §1, which opens with Socrates's greeting to his friend, ὦ φίλε Φαῖδρε, ποῖ δὴ καὶ πόθεν;[23] "O, dear Phaedrus, where to and where from?" In a somewhat later period, Aeneas of Gaza opens his *Theophrastus* with the same greeting.[24] So we must consider the possibility that Rabbi Yehoshua was greeting his friend with a fairly standard conversation starter, which also might have been an allusion to the Greek classics.

The second note is on Ben Zoma's opaque reference to "the spirit of God [hovering] ... like a bird that is fluttering, flapping its wings, and its wings touch, yet do not touch." Lieberman quotes from the Sethian Gnostics,[25]

> The Breath which is between the Darkness which is below the Light which is on high is not a Breath like a gust of wind or a gentle breeze ... but it is like a perfume exhaled from an ointment."

Lieberman is on point with this obscure reference from Gnostic literature likening the Spirit or wind of God to perfume, as we read precisely the

22. Lucian, "In Praise of Demosthenes," trans. M. D. Macleod, *Lucian*, vol. 8, LCL (Cambridge: Harvard University Press, 1967), 239. Here is not the place for a discussion of whether this work is authentically by Lucian (fl. ca. 120–190 CE). If it is pseudo-Lucianic, it likely should be dated to the fourth century (ibid., 237). On Lucian's relevance to rabbinic literature, see Saul Lieberman, *Greek in Jewish Palestine: Studies in the Life and Manners of Jewish Palestine in the II–IV Centuries C.E.* (New York: Jewish Theological Seminary of America, 1942), passim; Burton L. Visotzky, *Golden Bells and Pomegranates: Studies in Midrash Leviticus Rabbah*, TSAJ 94 (Tübingen: Mohr Siebeck, 2003), passim; and on Lieberman's assessment of Lucian, see now Daniel Boyarin, *Socrates and the Fat Rabbis* (Chicago: University of Chicago Press, 2009), esp. 24.

23. Plato, "Phaedrus," trans. H. N. Fowler, *Plato*, vol. 1, LCL (Cambridge: Harvard University Press, 1914), 413. See also the Hebrew translation of Plato (Tel Aviv: Schocken, 1959), 3:351: "פידרוס ידידי, מאין לאן."

24. Aeneas of Gaza, a Christian apologist (fl. sixth century CE), *Theophrastus* §1 (PG 85:871).

25. Lieberman, "How Much Greek?," 139, at n. 27.

same image in Genesis Rabbah on Gen 8:21, "The Lord smelled the pleasing odor,"

רב שילום בשם ר' מנחמא בר רב זעירא למלך שהיה מבקש לבנות פלטין על הים ולא היה יודע איכן לבנותה, מצא צלוחית שלפילייטון והלך לריחה ובנה אותה עליה[26]

> Rav Shilom[27] quoted R. Menahama bar Rav Zeira, [The analogy may be made] to a king who wished to build a palace upon the sea, but did not know where to build it. He found a flask of balsam-perfume[28] and followed its odor. He built the palace upon it.

So we see that, like the Gnostics, the rabbis were familiar with the trope of the perfume scent wafting over the waters. But if we investigate further, we note that Ben Zoma has referenced a bird hovering, the odor of which, I can only suppose, is a far cry from perfumed ointment.

Now Ben Zoma is quite explicit in his imagery of "a bird that is fluttering, flapping its wings, and its wings touch, yet do not touch." Obviously, anyone who has seen a bird about to land upon its nest could invoke such imagery. Yet it is the perfumed ointment that can lead us to Ben Zoma's hovering bird. In an otherwise unnoticed reference in Athenaeus's *Deipnosophistae* 6.257, we can observe precisely the combination of ointments and birds:

> In Paphos there was a practice extraordinarily luxurious to behold and incredible besides.... The king, when he dined, was fanned by pigeons, ay, by nothing else.... He would smear himself with Syrian perfume made of the kind of fruit which, they say, pigeons eat greedily. Attracted by the smell of this they came flying, ready to perch on his head; but slaves who sat by shooed them off. They would rise a little, not much—neither wholly this way nor that, as they say—and so would fan him in such a way that they made a breeze for him that was moderate and not too rough.[29]

Here we find a keen analogue to our statement by Ben Zoma. It is indeed the perfume and the fluttering birds over it to which Athenaeus (fl. ca. 200 CE), a young contemporary of Ben Zoma, draws our attention. Yet, as Rabbi Lieberman has taught us, "Nonsense is nonsense."

26. Gen. Rab. 34:9, ed. Theodor, 319.

27. Or Shalom; see the variants and Theodor's note, ad loc.

28. See Theodor's note on the text, 320.

29. I have followed in large, but not complete, measure the translation of C. B. Gulick, *Athenaeus*, vol. 3, LCL (Cambridge: Harvard University Press, 1929), 159–61.

שהיו שופכין זרען על העצים ועל האבנים

Here, for our third crown, we have a text that is difficult to parse. In commenting on the verse of Gen 6:1, "When men began to increase [לרב] upon the face of the earth, then daughters were born to them;" the midrash teaches: מלמד שהיו שופכין זרען על העצים ועל האבנים.[30] "This teaches that they would pour their seed upon trees and stones."

In essence, Genesis Rabbah has read this verse causally. When men began to increase, then as a result, daughters were born to them. It is almost as though the act of "increase" necessitated the birth of daughters to rectify it. Needless to say, spilling seed upon trees and stones should not result in more births. There is something pernicious about this act of defying God's command to be fruitful and multiply. Indeed, Genesis Rabbah continues: ולפי שהיו שטופים בזנות לפיכך הרבה להן הקב"ה בנקיבות. "Because they were immersed in licentiousness ..." But the word זנות, licentiousness, reads instead in the Paris manuscript and in Midrash Hakhamim[31] as: בזמה, "in lust, unchastity, obscenity, libidinousness, carnality." One might go so far as to suggest sexual perversity of some sort. Because they did what they did, then "the Blessed Holy One increased the number of women."

This makes little sense. What could they have done to result in God's feeling the necessity to increase (miraculously) the number of women? On the face of it, they ejaculated onto the ground. No doubt, our midrash attended here to Gen 6: 12: וַיַּרְא אֱלֹהִים אֶת הָאָרֶץ וְהִנֵּה נִשְׁחָתָה כִּי הִשְׁחִית כָּל בָּשָׂר אֶת דַּרְכּוֹ עַל הָאָרֶץ, "God saw the earth, that it was corrupted; for all flesh had corrupted its way upon the earth." That verse apparently seems to lend force to the rabbis' reading that "they would pour their seed upon trees and stones." We might infer, then, that their heinous sin was masturbation. They spilled semen in vain. They allowed their precious bodily fluids to dribble upon the earth. Theodor suggests that this is the point of the midrash. For him it is focused on the phrase in Genesis "*upon* the face of the earth." Their seed did not even get absorbed into the ground. Rather it was wasted "*upon* trees and stones." Perhaps so, but Theodor does not explain why this should lead God to increase women.

A word about "spilling ... upon trees and rocks." The phrase is found elsewhere in rabbinic literature, again commenting on the earliest Genesis narrative. When Cain killed Abel (Gen 4:8–12), the Mishnah comments on Gen 4:11: "דמי אחיך" שהיה דמו מושלך על העצים ועל האבנים "[Why does the Torah say] 'your brother's blood(s)?' For his blood was poured out upon the trees and upon the stones" (m. Sanh. 4:5).[32] So, blood can also be spilled

---

30. Gen. Rab. 26:4, ad Gen 6:1, ed Theodor, 246.

31. See Theodor's apparatus of variants and notes.

32. So, too, the Yerushalmi and Bavli to this Mishnah. On this verse, see also Gen. Rab. 22:9, ed. Theodor, 216.

upon trees and rocks. The meaning of the problematic phrase is now complicated a bit.

Or take the case of Asaf, who *sang* in Ps 79:1, "O God, the gentiles have entered your domain, they have rendered your sacred tabernacle unfit, and made Jerusalem into ruins." The rabbis point out, "He should have wept [rather than sing a Psalm]!"[33] They reply that Asaf sang, for he was happy God had poured out God's wrath "upon the trees and the stones" and not upon the Jews! [34] Here the pouring of God's wrath upon trees and stones (the sacred tabernacle?) serves to mitigate the punishment of the Jews by displacement of the anger. This further complicates any assumption that there can be one clear understanding of the phrase.

I am troubled to understand how masturbation should lead God either to punish corrupt men or to reward them with more women. Perhaps the problem was not with masturbation, or with Abel's blood, or with God's wrath. Here, too, I suggest that we look to a Greek source to see if we might gain some understanding of the specific phrase in Genesis Rabbah: to pour out seed or semen upon the rocks and trees, שהיו שופכין זרען על העצים ועל האבנים.

Once more I turn to [Pseudo]-Lucian.[35] In his dialogue Erotes (*Amores*) §20, he writes:

> Then luxury, daring all, transgressed the laws of nature herself. And who ever was the first to look at the male as though at a female, after using violence like a tyrant or else shameless persuasion? The same sex entered the same bed. Though they saw themselves embracing each other, they were ashamed neither at what they did nor at what they had done to them, and **sowing their seed, to quote the proverb, on barren rocks**[36] they bought a little pleasure at the cost of great disgrace.

The homophobic sentiments are, of course, no longer our own, but they unfortunately were standard fare among the Greeks and rabbis. What is telling is how [Pseudo]-Lucian describes the same-sex act, with the blithe introduction, *φασίν*, which Macleod idiomatically translates, "to quote the proverb." For Lucian, sex between two men is nothing more than "sowing their seed upon the barren rocks."

---

33. See Midrash Psalms 79 #3 (ed. Buber, 360). See, too, Rashi on b. Qidd. 31b, who alludes to this Midrash; and Lamentations Rabbah ad Lam 4:11 (ed. Buber, 148), where our quotation is from.

34. מזמר אני ששפך הקב"ה חמתו על העצים ועל האבנים ולא שפך חמתו על ישראל. In Midrash on Psalms the verb used is הפיג.

35. [Pseudo]-Lucian, *ΕΡΩΤΕΣ (Affairs of the Heart)* trans. M. D. Macleod, in *Lucian*, vol. 7, LCL (Cambridge: Harvard University Press, 1967), 183; Macleod dates the work to "the early fourth century" (147), the time of Genesis Rabbah.

36. *κατὰ πετρῶν δέ, φασίν, ἀγόνων σπείροντες* (emphasis added to English translation).

I think that our Genesis Rabbah text has a Hebrew equivalent of "the proverb." It accuses the men of that generation of being engaged in immorality (and, as [Pseudo]-Lucian has it "using violence.") They have gay sex, and so God seeks to remedy the situation. It appears that God thought if there were just more women, then homosexuality would disappear. So, more "daughters were born to them." As it turns out, it didn't work. Still doesn't. But understanding this odd phrase in our Midrash through the lens of Greek literature has restored an (unfortunate) idiom from rabbinic vocabulary of the fourth or early fifth century.

Conclusions

I conclude with the hope that these three "crowns" illuminate Genesis Rabbah with light from contemporary Greek sources. And I hope I have honored my colleague Prof. Shaye J. D. Cohen, who wears the crowns of Torah, priesthood, and kingship. Most of all, Shaye wears the crown of a good name.

Ahiqar and Rabbinic Literature

RICHARD KALMIN
The Jewish Theological Seminary of America

There are remarkably close parallels between the book of Ahiqar and a lengthy story in Bavli Bekhorot depicting interaction between R. Joshua ben Hananyah and the Athenian elders. This paper will make two related arguments. The first is that the two compilations drew on a shared storehouse of ancient Near Eastern motifs available in the eastern Roman provinces and east of Byzantium, probably in Mesopotamia. The second is that the very differences between these stories shows the epistemological commitment of Babylonian rabbis to tradition (especially through scriptural exegesis) over empirical observation. The rabbis, that is, knew of and deliberately rejected as foreign the derivation of knowledge from observation of the natural world.

These conclusions support my claim in earlier research that Jewish Babylonia, to a greater degree than earlier scholars imagined, was part of the Mediterranean world, and/or was part of the emerging but never fully realized elite culture forming between Egypt and Mesopotamia, on the one hand, and between Armenia and the Arabian peninsula on the other.[1]

Among the most striking parallels between Ahiqar, the Bavli, and many other ancient compilations from the Middle East is their character as collections of riddling contests. In the most common riddle contest pattern found in the Talmud, with ample parallels throughout the ancient world, a wise protagonist's opponent confronts him with an impossible demand or an unanswerable question. The wise protagonist must respond with alacrity, creating the illusion that he has successfully parried his opponent's thrust. It is less important that he respond cogently to his rival's challenge than that he create the impression that he has matters under control with his speedy and confident response. Alternatively, the wise protagonist creates the impression of infallibility by turning the tables on his opponent and confronting him with an impossible demand or an

To my esteemed teacher, colleague, and friend Shaye J. D. Cohen.

1. Richard Kalmin, *Migrating Tales: The Talmud's Narratives and Their Historical Context* (Oakland: University of California Press, 2014), 1–11 and passim.

unanswerable question of his own. The point of the opponent's question or demand is not to seek knowledge or enlightenment but to humiliate the wise protagonist, and the point of the protagonist's response is not to supply information but to demonstrate that he is not at all unnerved by his opponent's attempt to humiliate him.

Bavli Bekhorot 8b–9a reads as follows:[2]

> The emperor said to R. Joshua ben Hananyah, "How long is the serpent pregnant [before it] gives birth?"
> [R. Joshua ben Hananyah] said to [the emperor], "Seven years."
> [The emperor said to R. Joshua], "Behold, the Elders of the House of Athens mated them and [the female] gave birth in three [years]."
> [R. Joshua said to the emperor], "Those were pregnant beforehand for four [years]."
> [The emperor said to R. Joshua], "But the [snakes in that experiment] had sex [together, and animals don't have sex together when the females are pregnant]."
> [R. Joshua said to the emperor], "[Snakes, when the females are pregnant], have sex [together] like a person."
> [The emperor said to R. Joshua], "But the [Elders of the House of Athens] are wise [therefore they must be correct]."
> [R. Joshua said to the emperor], "We [Jewish sages] are wiser than them."
> [The emperor said to R. Joshua], "If you are so wise, go and defeat them and bring them to me."
> [R. Joshua] said to [the emperor], "How many of them are there?"
> [The emperor said to R. Joshua], "Sixty men."
> [R. Joshua] said to [the emperor], "Make a ship for me that has sixty compartments and every compartment has sixty mattresses."[3]
> [The emperor] made [the ship] for him. When [R. Joshua] arrived [in Athens he entered] a butcher's shop. [R. Joshua] found there a man who who was dressing an animal.
> [R. Joshua] said to [the butcher], "Is your head for sale?"
> [The butcher] said to [R. Joshua], "Yes."
> [R. Joshua] said to [the butcher], "For how much?"
> [The butcher] said to [R. Joshua], "For half a zuz."
> [R. Joshua] gave it to him.
> In the end [the butcher] said to [R. Joshua], "I meant the head of the animal."
> [R. Joshua] said to [the butcher], "[I said to you, 'Your head.'][4] If you want

2. See also Bereshit Rabbah 20:4, ed. Theodor/Albeck, 185.

3. Michael Sokoloff, *A Dictionary of Jewish Babylonian Aramaic of the Talmudic and Geonic Periods* (Ramat-Gan: Bar-Ilan University Press, 2002), 204.

4. The clause in brackets is missing from the printed editions and MS Vatican 119, but it is present in MSS London-BL Add. 15717 (402), Munich 95, and Vatican 120. MS JTS 5529.178–180 (Rab. 1904) reads, "Do you think I was talking about the head of the animal? I was talking about your head."

me to leave you alone, go and show me the entrance to the House of the Athenians."

[The butcher] said to [R. Joshua], "I am afraid, for everyone who shows [the entrance to their House], they kill."

[R. Joshua] said to [the butcher], "Lift a bundle of wood and when you arrive there, set [the bundle] upright like one who is resting."

[R. Joshua] went and found guards outside and guards inside. If they saw the footprint [of someone] entering they killed the [guards] outside, and [if they saw the footprint of someone] leaving they killed the [guards] inside. [R. Joshua] reversed his sandals [and made it seem like he had] exited. They killed the [guards] inside. He reversed his sandals [again] and they killed them all. [R. Joshua] went [inside] and found young people [sitting] above and old people [sitting] below.

[R. Joshua] said [to himself], "If I greet these, the [others] will kill me. They will think, 'We are better [than them] because we are older and they are young.'"[5]

[R. Joshua] said to them [all], "Peace be upon you."

They said to [R. Joshua], "What are you doing [here]?"

R. Joshua said to them, "[I] am a sage of the Jews. I want to learn wisdom from you."

They said to [R. Joshua], "If so, let us ask you [something]."

[R. Joshua] said to them, "Fine. If you defeat [me], do anything you want to me. If I defeat you, eat with me on my ship."

They said [to R. Joshua], "A man who wants a wife [from a particular family] and they do not give [her] to him, should he go [looking for a wife from a family] of higher status?"

[R. Joshua] took a peg[6] [and] stuck it low [into a wall] and it did not enter. [He stuck it] high [into the wall] and it entered. [R. Joshua] said, "This [man] also, he happens [to find] a woman destined for him."[7]

[They said to R. Joshua], "A man who lends [money to another man] and [can only collect] by seizing property [from subsequent buyers], should he lend again?"

[R. Joshua] said to them, "If he goes to a swamp and first cuts a bundle of reeds that he cannot manage, when he cuts more and rests them on top [of the first pile], a man might happen by and help him lift them."

They said [to R. Joshua], "Tell us things that cannot be."[8]

[R. Joshua said to them], "There was a mule that gave birth, and a note

---

5. MS London BL Add. 25717 (402) reads, "[R. Joshua] said to [himself], 'If I greet those sitting below, those sitting above will kill me. They will think, "We are better [than them] because we are older." And if I greet those sitting below, those sitting above will kill me. They will say, "We are superior to them because we are sitting above."'" MSS Munich, Vatican 119, and 120 read like the printed edition. The reading of MSS Munich, Vatican 119 and 120, and the printed edition seems abbreviated, and the reading of MS London BL Add. 25717 (402) is not fully coherent.

6. Sokoloff, *Dictionary of Jewish Babylonian Aramaic*, 803–4.

7. Ibid, 249.

8. Or, "of no value." Ibid, 553.

was hanging from it on which was written, 'The house of my father is owed 100,000 zuz.'"

They said to R. Joshua, "Do mules give birth?"

[R. Joshua] said to them, "These are things that cannot be."

[They said to R. Joshua], "Salt that has spoiled, how does one salt it?"

[R. Joshua] said to them, "With the afterbirth of a mule."

[They said to R. Joshua], "Is there [such a thing as] the afterbirth of a mule?"

[R. Joshua said to them], "And does salt spoil?"

[They said to R. Joshua], "Build us a house in the air."

[R. Joshua] said the [divine] name and he was suspended between heaven and earth.

[R. Joshua] said to them, "Bring up to me bricks and clay [and I will build the house]."

[They said to R. Joshua], "The center of the earth, where [is it]?"

[R. Joshua] pointed with his finger. He said to them, "Here."

They said to him, "Who will prove it?"

[R. Joshua said to them], "Bring ropes and measure."

[They said to R. Joshua], "We have a well in the field; bring it into town."

[R. Joshua] said to them, "Twist ropes for me from bran and I will bring it in."

[They said to R. Joshua], "We have a broken millstone. Sew it up."

[R. Joshua] said [to them], "Spin threads from it and I will sew it."

[They said to R. Joshua], "A garden bed of knives, how does one cut them down?"

[R. Joshua said to them], "With the horn of an ass."

[They said to R. Joshua], "Does an ass have a horn?"

[R. Joshua said to them], "Is there such a thing as a garden bed of knives?"

They brought him two eggs. They asked him, "Which is from a black hen and which is from a white hen?"

He brought them two cheeses. He asked them, "Which is from a black goat and which is from a white goat?"

[They asked him], "A chick that died, from where does its soul exit?"

[He said to them], "From where it entered, it exits."

[They said to him], "Bring to us something that is not worth the damage it causes."

He brought them a reed mat, straightened it out, and it would not fit in the gate.

He said to them, "Bring spades[9] and tear down [the wall]."

They brought spades and tore down the wall. This was something that was not worth the damage it caused.

[R. Joshua] brought all of them [to the ship to sail with him to Jerusalem].

When they saw the sixty mattresses, they said, "All of my colleagues are coming here."

R. Joshua said to the sailor, "Release your ship [so we can set sail]."

---

9. Ibid, 703.

When they were going, [R. Joshua] took dirt from the dirt [of Athens]. [9a]
When [R. Joshua] reached a whirlpool, he filled a vessel with water from the whirlpool. When they arrived [in Jerusalem] he stood them up before the emperor. [The emperor] saw that they were distressed.
[The emperor] said, "These are not they."
[R. Joshua] took some of their dirt and threw it on them. They acted brazenly toward the emperor."[10]
[The emperor] said to [R. Joshua], "Do whatever you want with them."
He brought the water from the whirlpool and threw it into a vessel.[11]
He said to them, "Fill up [the vessel] and bring it [to me]."
They filled [pitchers], poured [the water] into [the vessel] gradually, and it was absorbed.[12] They filled [the vessel] until they dislocated their shoulders, expired, and died.[13]

As noted, there are impressive parallels between the Bavli narrative in Bekhorot 8b–9a and the narrative portions of the book of Ahiqar. The narrative portions of Ahiqar appear to have been composed in Mesopotamia sometime in the seventh century BCE,[14] and the "wisdom sayings" portions of Ahiqar appear to have been composed in northern Syria or Palestine around the same time or even earlier.[15] The earliest extant version of Ahiqar, which combines the narrative portions and wisdom sayings into one more or less coherent book, derives from the fifth-century BCE Upper Egyptian colony of Elephantine.[16]

---

10. Ibid, 1049. Regarding a parallel between R. Joshua's "native soil trick" and Procopius's citation from a "History of the Armenians" (Procopius 1.5.9) (see also Procopius, *De aed.* 3.1.6). See Geoffrey Herman, "The Story of Rav Kahana BT Baba Qamma 117a-b in Light of Armeno-Persian Sources," in *Irano-Judaica*, vol. 6, *Studies Relating to Jewish Contacts with Persian Culture throughout the Ages* (Jerusalem: Ben-Zvi Institute, 2008), 64, 83–84.

11. Ibid, 1203.

12. Ibid.

13. Ibid, 1156.

14. See James Lindenberger, "Ahiqar (Seventh to Sixth Century B. C.): A New Translation and Introduction," *OTP* 2:482–83; I. M. Konstantakos, *The Tale of Ahiqar in Ancient Greece*, vol. 1, *Origins and Narrative Material* (Athens: Stigimi Publications, 2008), 2 of the online summary. Konstantakos observes that the narrative portions of Ahiqar are written in regular imperial Aramaic, with some loanwords from Akkadian, and they reproduce "fairly accurately" conditions at the Neo-Assyrian court. See Erica Reiner, "The Etiological Myth of the 'Seven Sages,'" *Orientalia* NS 30 (1961): 7–8, for support for a Babylonian origin of Ahiqar. On the papyrus of Elephantine, and on the provenance, dating, and textual tradition of Ahiqar, see R. Degen, "Achikar," *Enzyklopädie des Märchens: Handwörterbuch zur historischen und vergleichenden Erzählforschung*, ed. Kurt Ranke et al., 15 vols. (Berlin: de Gruyter,1977), 1:53–59; and J. C. Greenfield, "The Wisdom of Ahiqar," in *Wisdom in Ancient Israel: Essays in Honour of J. A. Emerton*, ed. John Day, Robert P. Gordon, and H. G. M. Williamson (Cambridge: Cambridge University Press, 1995), 43–52.

15. See, e.g., Ioannis Konstantakos, *Akicharos: The Tale of Ahiqar and the Aesop Romance* (Athens: Stigmi Pubications, 2013), vol. 3, online summary, p. 53.

16. Lindenberger, "Ahiqar," 480–84; and Greenfield, "Wisdom of Ahiqar," 47.

The account of Ahiqar's trip to Egypt is the locus of most of the parallels between the Bavli and the translations of Ahiqar. This account is totally missing in the Elephantine papyrus, at least in part because of a lacuna of four papyrus leaves. Due to this lacuna, scholars disagree about how much of Ahiqar's trip to Egypt the original Aramaic story contained.[17] Many of the amplifications found in the later translations of Ahiqar,[18] however, including the account of Ahiqar's visit to Egypt, must have been introduced into the narrative from an early period,[19] since Tobit, the Life of Aesop, and Bavli Bekhorot all presuppose a form of Ahiqar that included many motifs found only in the later translations.[20] The Syriac and Armenian translations of Ahiqar, furthermore, which preserve a more expansive text than the fifth-century BCE Aramaic version, have several parallels to the Eikhah Rabbah compilation (see below) as well as to the book of Tobit and the Life of Aesop. The date and provenance of Tobit and Aesop are unknown, although several scholars suggest a second-century BCE date for Tobit[21] and a first- to third-century CE date for Aesop.[22] We find even more parallels between the Syriac and Armenian translations and the version of the narrative involving R. Joshua and the Athenians in Bavli Bekhorot. According to the consensus of scholars, the Syriac translation of Ahiqar is the oldest and most reliable extant translation of the book. According to this consensus, the Syriac translation derives from late antiquity,[23] and it is likely that the Syriac translation is the source of the Armenian translation, also considered to be very old.[24]

In addition, it is very likely that most of these parallel motifs originated east of Byzantium, where Syriac and Armenian flourished as literary languages, and that the parallels between the Bavli and the translations of Ahiqar derived from the same part of the world. The general

---

17. See Lindenberger, "Ahiqar," 480–81, 498; Greenfield, "Wisdom of Ahiqar," 43, 45, and 48; and Konstantakos, *Tale of Ahiqar in Ancient Greece*, online summary, 9.

18. Lindenberger, "Ahiqar," 480.

19. See ibid., 479; Greenfield, "Wisdom of Ahiqar," 45; and Konstantakos, *Tale of Ahiqar in Ancient Greece*, online summary, 2.

20. On Tobit, see Greenfield, "Wisdom of Ahiqar," 50. On Life of Aesop, see Ioannis Konstantakos, "Characters and Names in the Vita Aesop and in the Tale of Ahiqar, Part 1: Lykoros and Hermippos," *Hyperboreus* 15, no. 1 (2009): 112–13. On the Bavli, see A. Yellin, *Sefer Ahiqar he-Hakham* (Jerusalem, 1937), passim; and Max Küchler, *Frühjüdische Weisheitstraditionen: Zum Fortgang weisheitlichen Denkens im Bereich des frühjüdischen Jahweglaubens*, OBO 26 (Freiburg: Universitätsverlag, 1979), 403–10.

21. See Lawrence M. Wills, *The Jewish Novel in the Ancient World*, Myth and Poetics (Ithaca, NY: Cornell University Press, 1995), 68–92. See, however, Greenfield, "Wisdom of Ahiqar," 46.

22. See Niklas Holzberg, "Eine strukturanalytische Interpretation," in Holberg, *Der* Äsop-*Roman Motivgeschichte und Erzählstruktur* (Tübingen: Narr, 1992), 177–78.

23. See Greenfield, "Wisdom of Ahiqar," 45.

24. See Konstantakos, *Tale of Ahiqar in Ancient Greece*, online summary, 2–3.

pattern of a sage responding to an impossible question or demand with another impossible question or demand, furthermore, is also well attested in ancient Greek and Egyptian literature.

The major similarities between Ahiqar and the Bavli are as follows: the Bavli, in common with the Syriac, Slavonic, and second Armenian translations of Ahiqar, quotes the king saying to the sage, "Do whatever you want with them (him)." In addition, in P.Oxy. 3720 of the Life of Aesop, the Assyrian King Lykoros, agreeing to spare the life of Aesop's adopted son, instructs Aesop to "Do whatever you want with him." Even though the meaning in Ahiqar and in the Bavli is that the king gives the sage permission to kill his antagonist(s), while the king in Aesop is freeing the young man from corporal or capital punishment, the actual words are identical (making allowances, of course, for the rendering into different languages). Another similarity between (1) the later translations of Ahiqar, (2) Aesop, and (3) the Bavli, is the impossible challenge to the wise protagonist to build a castle in the air, the wise hero elevating himself or his agents into the air (in the Bavli, by pronouncing the divine name; in Ahiqar and Aesop, by placing young children on the backs of eagles or on vehicles tied to the birds), and issuing an impossible challenge of his own: to carry building materials either up to him or to the children. Still another similarity between the compilations is that in the Bavli, in Ahiqar, and in Aesop the wise hero is instructed to tell his opponents either something that is impossible or something they have not heard; and in all three texts, central to the wise hero's response is a document of indebtedness for an astronomical sum of money. In the later versions of Ahiqar and in the Bavli, the impossible request to "twist ropes ... from sand" (Ahiqar), or "from bran" (the Bavli) figures prominently.[25] In addition, in both texts the wise hero is instructed to sew up a broken mortar (or millstone), and the protagonist responds by demanding that his antagonist(s) spin threads from the mortar (or millstone) as a precondition for his sewing it up.[26] In the Bavli and in Ahiqar, a king sends a wise protagonist to a foreign land to participate in a riddle contest, and the wise protagonist's life is at risk. In the Bavli the danger is explicit, while in Ahiqar it is implied: Ahiqar had been condemned to death by the Assyrian king, and the king pardons him

---

25. In the Bavli, however, this is R. Joshua's response to an impossible request by the Athenians, while in Ahiqar it is an impossible demand by the pharaoh. Konstantakos notes that the motif of the rope of sand is known to Hellenic tradition as a proverbial expression for something impossible, and that it occurs as such in many peoples' folktales from Europe to India and Tibet (*Akicharos: The Tale of Ahiqar and the Aesop Romance*, 15). On the basis of this motif alone, therefore, we would not have to posit a special relationship between Ahiqar and the Bavli. Given all of the other close parallels between the two works, however, such a relationship between them is not in doubt.

26. See Eli Yassif, "Traces of Folk Traditions of the Second Temple Period in Rabbinic Literature," *JJS* 39 (1988): 228–29.

only because he is needed to represent Assyria in a contest of wits with the Egyptian pharaoh, implying that he will be killed if he loses the contest.

Another crucially important parallel between Ahiqar, Bavli Bekhorot, and Aesop is their character as riddling contests, the specific characteristics of these contests, and what the stories present as sagacious solutions to the riddles. Earlier scholarly work on riddling contests in antiquity provides a key to better understanding the interaction between the protagonists and their opponents, and some of the reasons why ancient audiences viewed such stories as so entertaining and so satisfying.[27]

Jerome Neyrey argues that the rhetorical strategies frequently on display in the Gospel of Mark—and, I would argue, in Ahiqar, Aesop, and Bavli Bekhorot, centuries removed from Mark—were popular in the Greek, Roman, and Mesopotamian world.[28] Neyrey makes a convincing case that in Mark, it was less important that the wise hero's response to a hostile question be logically compelling, and more important that the response be rhetorically effective, that the protagonist reduce his interlocutor to silence by means of a counterargument or, more frequently, a counterquestion that responded to his opponent's impossible question or demand with another impossible question or demand. For the hero to fulfill the impossible demand, it was necessary for his opponent first to fulfill the counterdemand, which meant, in effect, that the hero released himself from the responsibility of fulfilling the demand. In Neyrey's words,

> The sage must say something clever and witty or lose his reputation, because the provocation challenges his role and reputation. While many *chreiai* [stories that conclude with a pronouncement by the wise protagonist—R. K.] report some clever statement by the sage, Mark overwhelmingly presents Jesus responding by answering a question with a counter-question. The question or demand posed to the wise hero was never a disinterested request for information or an invitation to a philosophical debate, but rather a hostile attack designed to embarrass the protagonist, who successfully turned the tables on his opponent, or, occasionally, humiliated him by refusing to deign to respond to such a stupid question from such an unworthy opponent.[29]

Along the same lines, Ioannis Kastantakos describes the impossible questions often found in Greek literature:

> Such questions set a trap for the addressee. They do not admit of a true answer: they aim only at ensnaring the addressee and reducing him to

27. See also the discussion of the parallel in Eikhah Rabbah below.

28. See, e.g., Arrian. *Epict. Diss.* 2.25.

29. Jerome H. Neyrey, "Questions, *Chreiai,* and Challenges to Honor: The Interface of Rhetoric and Culture in Mark's Gospel," *CBQ* 60 (1998): 657–81.

perplexity before an insoluble question. The addressee can escape only if he thinks of some clever reply, which reverses the sophism and turns it against the questioner, entrapping him in his own trap.[30]

We thus find further support for my claim in earlier research that non-Jewish traditions from the eastern Roman provinces, and/or Christian or pagan Mesopotamia, contributed much to the formation of the Babylonian Talmud. Frequently, for reasons not yet entirely clear, non-Jewish traditions contributed more to the Bavli than to the roughly contemporaneous and geographically closer Palestinian rabbinic corpora.

The lengthy story in Bavli Bekhorot, quoted in full above, is not the only long riddling narrative found in rabbinic texts. Eikhah Rabbah 1:1, a Palestinian rabbinic text, shows strong parallels with Bavli Bekhorot.[31]

In Eikhah Rabbah, the Athenians have decided not to guide any stranger to the address he seeks, and the same is true of the sages of Athens in Bavli Bekhorot. The heroes of both compilations follow a man carrying a load of wood, who pretends to stop and rest at the house of the Athenian(s) sought by the Jewish stranger. In addition, in the Bavli the elders bring two eggs to R. Joshua and demand that he tell them whether they come from a white hen or a black hen, and R. Joshua brings two cheeses and asks the Athenians whether they come from a white goat or a black goat. Basically the same thing happens in Eikhah Rabbah in the story of an Athenian and a child in Jerusalem. In Eikhah Rabbah, an Athenian brings a mortar to a tailor in Jerusalem and asks him to sew it up, and the tailor responds by asking the Athenian to spin threads out of a handful of dust so he can sew up the mortar. The same thing happens in the Bavli in an interaction involving R. Joshua and the Athenian sages.[32] It is thus characteristic of both compilations that the wise protagonist responds to absurd questions or demands with equally absurd questions or demands, and on several occasions the initial question and the counterquestion are virtually identical in the two texts. The significance of this phenomenon will be expanded upon below.

It is likely that Eikhah Rabbah and the Bavli independently drew from a common storehouse of traditions, idioms, literary conventions, themes, and motifs deriving from the ancient Near East, from Egypt to Mesopota-

30. In the legend of Alexander the Great and the Gymnosophists in the Alexander Romance, Alexander poses such questions to the Indian sages, and they successfully respond. See Ioannis Konstantakos, "Amasis, Bias and the Seven Sages as Riddlers," *Würzberger Jahrbücher für die Altertumwissenschaft* NS 29 (2005): 15, 23.

31. See the translation and analysis by Galit Hasan-Rokem, *Web of Life: Folklore and Midrash in Rabbinic Literature,* Contraversions (Stanford, CA: Stanford University Press, 2000), 39-66.

32. The only difference is that the story in the Bavli involves a millstone rather than a mortar, but obviously this difference is totally inconsequential.

mia, since some of the details they share are attested in the much earlier book of Ahiqar, the book of Tobit, and the Life of Aesop. It is possible that the storytellers or editors of the Bavli drew material from Eikhah Rabbah,[33] although Eikhah Rabbah cannot have been the exclusive source of the traditions the Bavli shares with earlier compilations, since several of the parallels between Ahiqar and the Bavli are absent from Eikhah Rabbah.[34]

Did the Babylonian Rabbis Receive Ahiqar from the East?

There is no convincing proof that Ahiqar was originally composed in India or Persia and reached rabbinic Babylonia from the East.[35] Significantly, François de Blois observes, "Explicit references to Ahiqar have not been found in Persian literature."[36] In light of the early attestations of the Ahiqar narrative documented above, east of Byzantium and west of Persia, it is difficult to see how Persia or India could be viewed as the place of origin of the story for the Babylonian rabbis.[37]

In addition, while parallels between Persian literature and the Bavli undoubtedly exist, Persian literature was most likely *not* the intermediary through which *Ahiqar* or its many literary motifs reached the Bavli. First, the relevant Persian compilations were edited too late to have served as such an intermediary. Second, linguistically *Ahiqar*, composed in Aramaic

33. It is less likely that storytellers or editors of Eikhah Rabbah drew on the Bavli for some of its source material, since most frequently, rabbinic traditions traveled in the opposite direction, from Roman Palestine to Jewish Babylonia. See Richard Kalmin, *Jewish Babylonia between Persia and Roman Palestine* (New York: Oxford University Press, 2006), passim; Kalmin, *Migrating Tales*, passim. In addition, Eikhah Rabbah was edited approximately a century before the Bavli, decreasing the likelihood that the Bavli served as a source for Eikhah Rabbah.

34. It is also possible that Eikhah Rabbah and the Bavli independently drew from the book of Ahiqar.

35. See A. H. Krappe, "Is the Story of Ahiqar of Indian Origin?" *JAOS* 61 (1941): 280–81; C. J. Brunner, "The Fable of the Babylonian Tree," *JNES* 39 (1980): 191–202, 291–302; and Lindenberger, "Ahiqar," 481 n. 13. For more on riddles in Persian literature, see Miguel Ángel Andrés-Toledo, "Riddles in the Ancient Indian and Iranian Religious Disputes," P. Ruani and M. Timuş, eds. In *"Ils disent que …": La contraverse religieuse Zoroastriens et Manichéens; Actes du colloque organisé du Collège de France, 12–13 juin 2015*, 1–15 of the author's manuscript pages.

36. François de Blois, *Burzoy's Voyage to India and the Origin of the Book of Kalilah wa Dimnah* (London: Rouledge, 1990), 44. See there for a refutation of Cowley's claim (*Aramaic Papyri of the Fifth Century B.C.* [Oxford: Clarendon, 1923], 205–6) that the Old Aramaic Ahiqar was translated from an Old Persian source. See also Lindenberger, "Ahiqar," 491 n. 81.

37. The same is true, for the same reason, of the parallels to Ahiqar in Arabic literature.

and translated into Syriac, would have been far more accessible to Babylonian rabbis than any literature composed in Persian.[38]

The Gestation Period of Snakes: Rabbinic Science or Rabbinic Torah?

Bavli Bekhorot 7b–8b introduces the narrative about the Athenians and R. Joshua ben Hananya, and the narrative begins on b. Bek. 8b and concludes on 9a. Without the introduction provided by 7b–8b, the narrative on 8b–9a pits the wisdom of the Jewish sage R. Joshua against the wisdom of the Athenians, and this wisdom has nothing to do with Torah study. Without b. Bek. 7b–8b, the wisdom of R. Joshua and the Athenians is entirely practical, consisting of the effective observation of nature, the clever use of language, the ability to respond wittily to difficult or impossible questions, and the ability to make effective use of the divine name. In b. Bek. 8b–9a, R. Joshua neither quotes nor analyzes biblical verses, nor does he cite and explicate rabbinic texts; and there is no sign of the usual topics of rabbinic concern: Sabbath observance, tithes, sacrifices, courts, witnesses, purities, and so on. R. Joshua's ability to use the divine name does not establish his identity as a rabbi, since magicians, with whom the rabbis competed for power and authority in Babylonian Jewish society,[39] were also reputed to make effective use of the divine name.[40] And there is no indication that R. Joshua's ability to exploit the power of the divine name results from his wisdom, prayer, piety, or Torah learning.

We also find no trace of the standard give-and-take of Torah study in the dialogue between R. Joshua and the Athenians, which throughout the Talmud takes the form of (1) questions about the biblical source of a postbiblical opinion, followed by attempts to answer the questions, and discussions of these answers; and (2) objections, either in the form of objections from logic or from contradictory traditions, followed by responses to these objections, often continuing on for multiple stages of argument.

The narrative is totally self-sufficient, in no way dependent on the introductory material to be comprehensible. The significant parallels to Eikhah Rabbah and the book of Ahiqar also point to the independent composition of the narrative. In all of these sources, the wisdom of the protagonists is entirely practical, with no hint that God (or the gods) is (are) the

38. See Adam Becker, "The Comparative Study of 'Scholasticism' in Late Antique Mesopotamia: Rabbis and East Syrians," *AJS Review* 34 (2010): 98–99.

39. Kalmin, *Migrating Tales*, 95–129.

40. Joseph Naveh and Shaul Shaked, *Magic Spells and Formulae: Aramaic Incantations of Late Antiquity* (Jerusalem: Magnes, 1993), 18.

source of the power of the sage.[41] In addition, as noted by Susan Niditch and Robert Doran, in traditional wisdom literature the wise hero relies exclusively on his own powers. There is no room for gods (or a God) who intervene(s) on the sage's behalf and enable(s) him to be victorious.[42] R. Joshua in Bavli Bekhorot (divorced from the introductory discussion on 7b–8b), like Ahiqar, relies on his own powers and cleverness.

In Bavli Bekhorot, the discussion begins with the emperor's question to R. Joshua about the gestation period of snakes. R. Joshua answers that the period is seven years, and the emperor responds that the Athenian sages say three years. The Athenians performed an actual experiment, says the emperor, mating a male and a female snake and discovering that the female gave birth three years later. R. Joshua, without the aid of an experiment, responds that the female snake was pregnant for four years prior to the Athenians' experiment, yielding a total of seven years. The emperor answers that animals do not mate when the female is pregnant, so the fact that the snakes mated must mean that the female was not pregnant, hence the gestation period must be only three years. R. Joshua responds that snakes, like humans, do mate when the female is pregnant, so the Athenians misinterpreted the evidence of their senses due to their inadequate knowledge of the natural world. The emperor counters that the Athenians are wise, implying that they know whereof they speak, but R. Joshua responds that in fact the rabbis are wiser. When the emperor challenges R. Joshua to prove his claim, he accepts the challenge, and the stage is set for a competition in Athens between the rabbi and the Athenian sages.

The introductory material in 7b–8b, however, leaves no doubt that, for the later editors who added the introduction to the narrative, R. Joshua's opinion about snakes *is* conventional Torah. First, the tradition in 8a, according to which a snake's gestation period is seven years, is introduced by a technical term indicative of rabbinic provenance: *Tannu Rabbanan,* "Our rabbis taught in a Tannaitic tradition." In addition, in 8a R. Joshua himself[43] responds to the question: "From where [do we derive] these things?" That is, what is the biblical source of the opinion that a snake's gestation period is seven years? R. Joshua responds with a biblical prooftext, which is subjected to exhaustive analysis, in the form of a lengthy series of objections and responses that is the stuff of classic talmudic argu-

41. In the book of Ahiqar, this is true of the narrative depicting the life of the sage, as in Bavli Bekhorot, but in the proverbs section of Ahiqar, there is much mention of the gods. Most modern scholars believe that the narrative and the proverbs of Ahiqar were composed separately.

42. See Susan Niditch and Robert Doran, "The Success Story of the Wise Courtier: A Formal Approach," *JBL* 96 (1977): 186–87, 190–91.

43. According to one of two versions; the other version does not quote the midrash in the name of R. Joshua but rather cites it in the name of Rav, an early third-century CE Babylonian Amora.

mentation. Each objection receives what is, from an ancient rabbinic perspective, an effective response.

Read independently of the introductory material in b. Bek. 7b–8a, the story of the competition between R. Joshua and the Athenians shows that rabbinic empirical knowledge of the gestation period of snakes conflicts with that of the world's acknowledged scientific experts: the Athenians. The introduction reframes the narrative of the Athenian confrontation with R. Joshua, positioning it instead as a demonstration of the superiority of rabbinic derivation of knowledge from Scripture[44] to knowledge derived by non-Jews on the basis of observation alone. Rabbinic derivation of knowledge from Scripture, furthermore, has the advantage of being refined in the crucible of rabbinic argumentation, consisting of a lengthy set of objections and responses, which has the effect of assuring the discussion's audience of rabbis and rabbis-to-be that the rabbinic derivation from Scripture is the only possible conclusion to be drawn from the scriptural verse.

Further insight into the issue of Babylonian rabbinic approval of knowledge obtained via the examination of empirical evidence versus the Palestinian rabbinic tendency to approve of conclusions drawn via the study of traditional sources, is provided by the following dialogue between a philosopher and Rabban Gamliel in Bereshit Rabbah 20:4:[45]

> A certain philosopher wished to know after what period of time a snake gives birth. When he saw them copulating he took and placed them in a barrel and fed them until they bore. When the sages visited Rome he asked them how long it takes a snake to give birth. Rabban Gamliel turned pale [with shame] and could not answer him. R. Joshua, meeting him and seeing his face pale, asked him, "Why is your face pale?" [Rabban Gamliel] said, "I was asked a question and I could not answer it." [R. Joshua] said [to him], "What is the question?" [Rabban Gamliel] said [to him], "After how long does a snake give birth?" [R. Joshua] said to him, "After seven years." [Rabban Gamliel] said [to him], How do you know that?" [R. Joshua said to him], "Because the dog, which is a wild beast, gives birth after 50 days, while it is written, 'You are more cursed than all cattle, and than all beasts of the field,' therefore, just as cattle are 7 times more cursed than the beast, so is the snake 7 times more cursed than the cattle." In the evening, [Rabban Gamliel] went and told [the philosopher], who began to beat his head against the wall, crying out, "All that for which I labored 7 years, this man has come and offered to me on the end of a cane."[46]

44. Perhaps informed by the observation of empirical evidence.

45. Ed. Theodor/Albeck, 185.

46. This is an idiom meaning that Rabban Gamliel discovered the answer with very little effort.

The parallel to the Bavli Bekhorot narrative in Bereshit Rabbah, a Palestinian rabbinic compilation, portrays the issue as one of competition between the power of the unaided evidence of one's senses and rabbinic exegesis of Scripture alone. What the rabbinic protagonist accomplishes in an instant with the aid of Torah study, the gentile sage can only discover after years of labor.

The Rabbis and Empirical Evidence

I noted in an earlier study that until the later layers of the Bavli, and to a much lesser extent the later layers of the Yerushalmi, rabbis do not manifest awareness of the possibility that their opinions might be vulnerable to critique through comparison with conclusions reached via empirical evidence alone.[47] The editing of the Bavli was complete sometime during the sixth or seventh century CE, and the editing of the Yerushalmi was complete in the late fourth or early fifth century CE. It is possible, therefore, that the few indications that later Palestinian rabbis acknowledged the importance of empirical evidence would correspond to the much more frequent acknowledgment that we find in the later layers of the Bavli, were we fortunate enough to possess another century or two of the development of the Yerushalmi. I hope that the present study will constitute a first step toward enabling us to answer this question. Eikhah Rabbah appears to have been edited approximately a century or so later than the Yerushalmi. We might expect, therefore, were the difference between the Bavli and the Yerushalmi partly a function of chronology, to find more relevant material in Eikhah Rabbah than in the Yerushalmi, since Eikhah Rabbah was redacted closer to the time of the final editing of the Bavli.[48]

By the phrase "more relevant material," I mean more material emphasizing the importance of conclusions reached via the observation of empirical evidence, as opposed to or in addition to material emphasizing the importance of conclusions drawn on the basis of the interpretation of Scripture or the reliance on rabbinic authority.

The tendency of the later layers of the Bavli to acknowledge the importance of empirical evidence makes it likely that the opening scene of the Bavli Bekhorot narrative, the dialogue between R. Joshua and the emperor, is a late Babylonian reworking of the parallel in Bereshit Rabbah,

---

47. Richard Kalmin, "Observation in Rabbinic Literature of Late Antiquity," in *The Faces of Torah: Studies in the Texts and Contexts of Ancient Judaism in Honor of Steven Fraade*, ed. Michal Bar-Asher Siegal, Tzvi Novick, and Christine Hayes, JAJSup 22 (Göttingen: Vandenhoeck & Ruprecht, 2017), 359–83.

48. I am grateful to Paul Mandel, who clarified for me the current consensus, to the extent that there is one, about the date of the final editing of Eikhah Rabbah.

despite the fact that it features as its protagonist a Palestinian rabbi of the first half of the second century CE.

It is unlikely that the identity of the protagonist, R. Joshua, should be taken seriously in an effort to determine the story's provenance. First, the story is entirely in Aramaic, and if it were really a tradition deriving from the Tannaitic period we would expect it to be in Hebrew.[49] In addition, R. Joshua was very likely chosen as the protagonist because elsewhere in rabbinic literature he is featured in dialogues with Roman emperors and other Roman dignitaries, as well as with other nonrabbinic figures;[50] and he also solves riddles,[51] including riddles paralleled in the Life of Aesop.[52] The storyteller(s) might also have chosen R. Joshua because, according to one of the two quotation chains on Bekhorot 8a, he authored the statement about the gestation period of snakes.[53]

Summary and Conclusions

This paper attempted to show that several close parallels between Ahiqar and the Bavli indicate that these two compilations drew on a shared storehouse of literary motifs from the eastern Roman provinces and the ancient Near East. This study supported my claim in earlier research that Babylonia, to a greater extent than earlier scholars imagined, was part of the Mediterranean world in late antiquity, and/or part of the cultural unity that was emerging but was never fully realized in the vast territory between Egypt to the west, western Persia to the east, Armenia to the north, and the Arabian peninsula to the south.

The riddle contests in rabbinic literature closely parallel similar narratives preserved in the non-Jewish compilations Ahiqar and the Life of

49. This criterion, however, is not a foolproof indicator of Babylonian Amoraic or post-Amoraic provenance, since some Tannaitic traditions in the Bavli have been translated into Babylonian Jewish Aramaic.

50. See the following notes, and see Bereshit Rabbah 10 (ed. Theodor/Albeck, 75–76) (with Emperor Vespasian); Bereshit Rabbah 28 (ed. Theodor/Albeck, 261–62) (with Emperor Vespasian); Bereshit Rabbah 78 (ed. Theodor/Albeck, 916–18) (with Emperor Vespasian); Qohelet Rabbah 12:5 (with the emperor); b. Ber. 56a (with the emperor); b. Šabb. 119a (with the emperor); b. Šabb. 152a (with the emperor); b. 'Erub. 101a (with a heretic); b. Ḥag. 5b (with the emperor and a heretic); and b. Ḥul. 59b–60a (with the emperor). See also b. Nid. 69b–71a (with the men of Alexandria; there is reason to believe, however, that the men of Alexandria are portrayed as rabbis. See Richard Kalmin, "Observation in Rabbinic Literature of Late Antiquity [part two]," [forthcoming]).

51. See m. Neg. 14:13; and Bereshit Rabbah 17, end; and b. Ber. 56a (with the emperor).

52. See Bereshit Rabbah 64, end, ed Theodor/Albeck, 710–12, esp. 712; b. Ned. 50b (= b. Ta'an. 7a–b [with the daughter of the emperor]); and b. 'Erub. 53b (an unnamed girl and boy).

53. Alternatively, since the story on Bekhorot 8b–9a depicts R. Joshua as the protagonist, his name was added to one of the two versions of the quotation chain on 8a.

Aesop. In the compilations in Eikhah Rabbah and Bavli Bekhorot, as is true of non-Jewish wisdom literature in general, there is no trace of the activity of God, and the wise protagonist's wisdom is entirely practical, having nothing to do with Torah study or the standard preoccupations of rabbinic literature. When the R. Joshua/Athenian Elders story was incorporated into its present context in Bavli Bekhorot, it was naturalized into its rabbinic context by the rabbinization of the issue that gets the discussion off the ground: What is the gestation period of snakes? The story is introduced by a tradition that is identified as rabbinic by virtue of the technical term: *Tannu Rabbanan* ("Our rabbis taught in a Tannaitic source"), and R. Joshua, who dialogues with the emperor in the entirely secular story in 8b–9a, supplies the scriptural source of the Tannaitic opinion, a most rabbinic thing to do ("From where do we derive this?"), and the statement about snakes itself is subjected to a lengthy series of objections and responses, that alternatingly seek to undermine its scriptural foundation but which successfully resolve each one of the objections, leading to the conclusion that the tradition is biblically based.

Guidelines for the Ideal Way of Life

Rabbinic Halakhah and Hellenistic Practical Ethics

CATHERINE HEZSER
SOAS, University of London

Modern Jewish thinkers such as Joseph Soloveitchik and Yeshayahu Leibowitz have emphasized the all-encompassing nature of Judaism, which, in contrast to Christianity with its focus on belief and spirituality, concerns all aspects of daily life. Even aspects of life that one might consider most trivial and mundane such as the questions which household items may or may not be lent to particular neighbors (m. Giṭ. 5:10), how straps can be fastened to cows and donkeys (y. Beṣah 2:8, 61c–d), and what kinds of ingredients are contained in a specific dessert (y. Ber. 6:4, 10c) are halakhically relevant within the wider context of rabbinic religious law for reasons of purity, Sabbath observance, and blessings over meals. As Soloveitchik writes, "Faith is indeed relevant to man not only metaphysically but also practically. It gives his life, even at the secular mundane level, a new existential dimension."[1] Similarly, Leibowitz has stressed that rabbinic halakhah is meant to offer an all-encompassing way of life that concerns all areas of human existence.[2]

In this paper I shall investigate the origins of the rabbinic interest in the intricacies of daily life and the material world, including the body. This interest can be explained only partly by reference to the Hebrew Bible. While the legal portions of the Torah do address issues of (im)purity, agricultural rules, and interpersonal relations, they come nowhere near the all-encompassing scope and detailed scrutiny we find in rabbinic documents and especially in the Talmud. Although the biblical impetus is important, we have to look at Greco-Roman culture to search

1. Joseph B. Soloveitchik, *The Lonely Man of Faith* (New York: Doubleday, 2006; originally published in *Tradition* in 1965), 88.

2. See Yeshayahu Leibowitz, *Judaism, Human Values, and the Jewish State,* ed. Eliezer Goldman (Cambridge: Harvard University Press, 1992), xxiv. Leibowitz points out that political circumstances (e.g., foreign rule; diaspora existence) may prevent certain areas of life from being guided by halakhah, which, in its entirety, must be seen as a utopian system (168).

for possible analogies. Do we find similar attempts to theorize about and provide guidance in all areas of daily life among Greco-Roman philosophers? Can rabbis be viewed as polymaths whose expertise encompassed many areas and who could draw on various sources of knowledge? What was the social, political, and cultural context in which these wide-ranging interests and the presumption to control all areas of their fellow Jews' lives developed? Did rabbis' lack of official authority motivate them to focus on alternative private areas of expertise and control? Can their focus on actual life and practice be considered a reaction to the Christian emphasis on spirituality and the afterlife?

Before I try to answer these questions, I must issue a *caveat*. The wide range of topics and areas of knowledge addressed in rabbinic documents such as the Talmud Yerushalmi must, in the first place, be seen as the product of the talmudic editors' redactional strategy. With the Talmud the editors created a framework for preserving in written format a huge number of rabbinic traditions on diverse themes that had been transmitted for centuries. The variety of issues each individual rabbi dealt with would have been more limited. As far as halakhic expertise is concerned, individual rabbis may have been renowned for their knowledge in particular areas. In areas they were less familiar with they may have consulted colleagues. For example, rabbis who were merchants may have been experts on fraud, rabbis who were farmers would have known about agricultural matters, rabbis who were physicians knew human and animal anatomy.[3] To complement their own knowledge, rabbis are also said to have consulted nonrabbinic experts in particular fields: for example, scribes who were experts in the writing of divorce documents (y. Giṭ. 1:1, 43a), physicians who knew about plants, ointments (b. B. Meṣ. 85b–86a), and the body parts of cows (m. Bek. 4:4).

What I am concerned with here, however, is the more general interest of rabbinic halakhah in the intricate details of human material existence and the claim that rabbinic instructions should govern all areas of their fellow Jews' lives. Rabbinic halakhah as it developed in Roman and early Byzantine times focused on daily life, was wide-ranging in its scope and content, and all-encompassing in its ambition. Why did it emerge in this

---

3. There are references to scholars who were experts in particular areas of law, e.g., m. B. Bat. 10:8 (Shimon b. Nannos as an expert in monetary law). According to Michael Owen Wise, *Language and Literacy in Roman Judaea: A Study of the Bar Kokhba Documents*, AYBRL (New Haven: Yale University Press, 2015), 122: "A number of Rabbi Judah b. Baba's decisions imply expert agricultural knowledge." See also Tzvi Novick, "'Like an Expert Sharecropper': Agricultural Halakhah and Agricultural Science in Rabbinic Palestine," *AJS Review* 38 (2014): 303–20. Hava Tirosh-Samuelson assumes that "[s]everal rabbis (e.g., Yohanan ben Zakkai, Gamaliel II, and Joshua ben Hananya) were expert astronomers, using observed data for the calculation and adjustment of the lunar-solar calendar"("Judaism," in *The Oxford Handbook of Religion and Ecology*, ed. Roger S. Gottlieb [Oxford: Oxford University Press, 2010], 36).

form in the first four centuries CE, and what was the intellectual context of its development?

Biblical Law as the Rudimentary Basis of Rabbinic Halakhah

Biblical law already encompasses many areas of what we would nowadays call "civil law": rules concerning property, the family, inheritance, contracts, damages, labor, as well as "criminal law," that is, offenses that harm other human beings. References to these legal areas are sparse, sporadic, and general, however. Without interpretation and expansion, the practical applicability of these rules would have been limited. For example, there are hardly any regulations concerning divorce apart from taking for granted the husband's right to end the marriage (see Deut 24:1–3).[4] While some biblical rules urge slave owners to manumit their Hebrew slaves in the seventh year of their service (Exod 21:2, Deut 15:12; cf. Lev 25:39–41), the process of manumission and other important aspects of slave law are never addressed.[5] Perhaps most striking is the lack of more detailed instructions concerning Sabbath observance apart from the very general command to rest rather than work (Exod 20:8–11; Deut 5:12–14).[6]

The sporadic references and gaps suggest that biblical instructions for Jewish practice were rudimentary. Israelites are urged to follow certain behavioral rules—the maintenance of the covenantal relationship to God requires action—but they receive little explicit instruction on how to actually live a Jewish life. The focus on the temple with its sacrificial service, with priests acting as communal representatives, may have reduced the need for detailed instructions as far as laypeople's individual piety and practice was concerned.

To some extent, postbiblical Jewish literature, especially wisdom literature, can be considered an intermediate phase in which moral instruc-

---

4. David Instone-Breuer lists the many areas of divorce law that the Torah does not address: legitimate reasons for divorce, return of the dowry, rights of children to their father's estate, maintenance of the woman after divorce, the woman's right to remarry, divorce procedure and witnesses, and so on (*Divorce and Remarriage in the Bible: The Social and Literary Context* [Grand Rapids: Eerdmans, 2002], 23–24).

5. On the development of rabbinic slave law on the basis of the sporadic biblical references, see Catherine Hezser, *Jewish Slavery in Antiquity* (Oxford: Oxford University Press, 2005).

6. For a list of biblical passages referring to the Sabbath, see Lutz Doering, *Schabbat: Sabbathalacha und -praxis im antiken Judentum und Urchristentum*, TSAJ 78 (Tübingen: Mohr Siebeck, 1999), 18–22. Doering summarizes: "Das dekalogische Sabbatgebot untersagt das Tun eines 'jeglichen' Werks. Was unter 'Werk' ... zu verstehen ist, wird nirgends in der Hebräischen Bibel definiert" (22).

tion became more important. This development happened in a Hellenistic cultural milieu, as Ben Sira shows. Ben Sira's moral advice touches on the areas of family, gender, and sexuality, as Ibolya Balla's study explicates.[7] It seems that Ben Sira had some knowledge of Hellenistic philosophy and integrated the Stoic and Cynic ideals of self-control and contentment into his moral teaching.[8]

Before 70 CE, Torah interpretation and instruction also happened among the Pharisees and at Qumran already. The gospels present Pharisees as Torah scholars who advise their Jewish contemporaries in behavioral matters. Steven Fraade has called the Qumran community a "studying community."[9] Nevertheless, the post-70 rabbinic expansion of the Torah to provide practical guidance in all areas of daily life is unprecedented and innovative. Shaye Cohen has already pointed to similarities and differences between pre-70 Pharisees and post-70 rabbis.[10] Pharisees and rabbis shared their interest in Torah interpretation and application to everyday life circumstances. Yet rabbis adopted a pluralistic approach rather than distinguishing their own teachings from those of other contemporary Jewish groups. In fact, no other post-70 Jewish groups that competed with rabbis are known to us.[11] As far as rabbinic innovation is concerned, the biblical basis and the need for religious practice without the temple do not constitute sufficient explanations for the rabbinic attempt to devise rules for all areas of daily life. We should therefore look at contemporary Greco-Roman culture for analogies.

Philosophical Ethics and Rabbinic Halakhah: Instructions for the Ideal Way of Life

Greek philosophy from Aristotle onward aimed to investigate all areas of knowledge, to provide an all-encompassing understanding of nature,

7. Ibolya Balla, *Ben Sira on Family, Gender, and Sexuality,* DCLS 8 (Berlin: de Gruyter, 2011).

8. See, e.g., ibid., 165, with reference to Ben Sira 23:4–6.

9. Steven Fraade, "Interpretive Authority in the Studying Community at Qumran," *JJS* 44 (1993): 46–69.

10. Shaye J. D. Cohen, "The Significance of Yavneh: Pharisees, Rabbis, and the End of Jewish Sectarianism," *HUCA* 55 (1984): 27–53; reprinted in Cohen, *The Significance of Yavneh and Other Essays in Jewish Hellenism,* TSAJ 136 (Tübingen: Mohr Siebeck, 2010), 57–58: "In sum: at no point in antiquity did the rabbis see themselves either as Pharisees or as the descendants of Pharisees"; on the other hand, some rabbis were "latter-day Pharisees [or the descendants of Pharisees] who had no desire to publicize the connection".

11. On this issue, see especially Jodi Magness, "Sectarianism before and after 70 CE," in *Was 70 CE a Watershed in Jewish History? On Jews and Judaism before and after the Destruction of the Temple,* ed. Daniel R. Schwartz and Zeev Weiss in collaboration with Ruth Clements, AJEC 78 (Leiden: Brill, 2012), 69–90.

human life, and the cosmos. Aristotle's *Nicomachean Ethics* was meant to provide instructions on how to lead a good life. *Eudaimonia*—the good as such, not an individually perceived happiness achieved by striving for pleasures—is considered achievable by adhering to virtues such as generosity, temperance, and courage.[12] The ultimate goal of virtuous practice at all levels of society is the good of all citizens in a "well-regulated city."[13] Not so much individual happiness but the functioning of civic society is the aim for which ethical instructions are given. Aristotle considers philosophical contemplation (*theōria*) the supreme practice, just as rabbis considered Torah study more important than anything else. *Theōria* and Torah study are broadly understood as intellectual pursuits that are available to a relatively small literate elite only.[14] The practice of virtue and the observance of the Torah in daily life, to which everyone is called, are subordinated to the higher goals of the common good and worship of God.

A simple secular-religious divide between Aristotelian ethics and rabbinic halakhah is not appropriate. Aristotle associated *theōria* and the striving for virtue with "godlikeness."[15] One could argue that rabbinic halakhic instructions not only were meant as guidelines to proper divine worship but also regulated Jewish civic society at a time when official political and religious authorities were lacking. Thus, both Greek philosophical ethics and rabbinic halakhah aimed at creating encompassing guidelines for communal life in this world and legitimized them by reference to their divine foundation.[16] Despite the many differences as far as the content of these instructions is concerned, their aim—namely, to provide theoretical

---

12. Aristotle was aware of possible misunderstandings of *eudaimonia*; see *Eth. nic.* 1095a–b.

13. Susan Sauvé Meyer, "Living for the Sake of an Ultimate End," in *Aristotle's Nicomachean Ethics: A Critical Guide*, ed. Jon Miller (Cambridge: Cambridge University Press, 2011), 49.

14. On *theōria* as the supreme practice, see A. A. Long, "Aristotle on Eudaimonia, Nous, and Divinity," in Miller, *Aristotle's Nicomachean Ethics*, 92–93, with reference to Aristotle, *Eth. nic.* 1178b. *Theōria* "is the exercise of *sophia*," as Ronald Polansky has pointed out ("Introduction," in *The Cambridge Companion to Aristotle's Nicomachean Ethics* [Cambridge: Cambridge University Press, 2014], 11).

15. See Long, "Aristotle on Eudaimonia," 94–95, with references.

16. On the relationship between rabbinic halakhah and Hellenistic ethics, see also Jonathan Wyn Schofer, "Rabbinical Ethical Formation and the Formation of Rabbinical Ethical Compilations," in *The Cambridge Companion to the Talmud and Rabbinic Literature*, ed. Charlotte Elisheva Fonrobert and Martin S. Jaffee (Cambridge: Cambridge University Press, 2007), 313–19. See also Schofer, *Confronting Vulnerability: The Body and the Divine in Rabbinic Ethics* (Chicago: University of Chicago Press, 2010), 10–11. Schofer defines ethics rather narrowly, however, as ideals and instructions to achieve "well-being" (ibid., 10). He does not compare rabbinic halakhah as such but only what he defines as rabbinic "ethical anthologies," with Hellenistic ethics. He notes,, however, that "certainly not all rabbinic ethics is contained in the ethical anthologies" (ibid.).

tools for the practical functioning of a well-ordered and therefore divinely appreciated or god-like society—is strikingly similar.

Closer to rabbis' own time, Stoic philosophers developed guidelines for a morally good life and society. Christoph Jedan has argued that the ethical instructions of the early Stoic philosopher Chrysippus (third century BCE) are an expression of his "religious world-view."[17] As in Aristotle's *Nicomachean Ethics*, the focus is on virtues here, yet "Stoic virtue ethics is, as an intellectual enterprise, quite different from the virtue ethics formulated by Aristotle."[18] Both Stoic virtue ethics and rabbinic halakhah developed ideals of proper attitudes and behavior that are presented as attainable but would, in reality, have been followed by the respective scholars' disciples and adherents only.[19] Jedan points to the "flexibility and context sensitivity" as well as the "versatility and contentiousness" of the Stoics' practical ethical instructions, an aspect that is reminiscent of rabbinic halakhic diversity.[20]

Both rabbis and Stoic philosophers provided theoretical instructions for the "right" way of living and behaving toward others in this world, instructions that were ultimately based on their religious beliefs. In the first century CE Josephus already noticed similarities between Stoics and Pharisees, when describing the latter as a Jewish *hairesis* or philosophical school (*Vita* 2.3). For his Greek-educated readers this description would have been plausible, given that both Stoics and Pharisees combined theory and practice and instructed their followers on how to best live their lives.

Both Stoics and rabbis concerned themselves with wide-ranging subject matters that required knowledge of a variety of aspects of daily life. The Stoic Posidonius of Apamea (second–first century BCE), for example, is known to have been a polymath whose work dealt with areas such as botany, zoology, geography, and astronomy. "His work was a massive attempt to synthesize philosophy with all other domains of human knowledge."[21] Topics dealt with by philosophers of the Late Stoa included marriage and the family, popular medicine, and food. A few examples must suffice here.

---

17. Christoph Jedan, *Stoic Virtues: Chrysippus and the Religious Character of Stoic Ethics*, Continuum Studies in Ancient Philosophy (London: Continuum, 2009): this is the title of part 1 of his study. On the religious basis of Stoic ethics, see also Keimpe Algra, "Stoic Philosophy," in *The Cambridge Companion to the Stoics*, ed. Brad Inwood (Cambridge: Cambridge University Press, 2003), 153–78.

18. Jedan, *Stoic Virtues*, 1. In appendix 2, Jedan compares Aristotle's and Chrysippus's lists of virtues.

19. Burton L. Visotzky has recently pointed to similarities between Stoic and rabbinic values; see his *Aphrodite and the Rabbis: How the Jews Adapted Roman Culture to Create Judaism as We Know It* (New York: St. Martin's Press, 2016), 139–42. The focus is on tractate Pirqe Avot here.

20. Jedan, *Stoic Virtues*, 7.

21. N. Clayton Croy, "Stoicism and Cynicism," in *The Routledge Encyclopedia of the Historical Jesus*, ed. Craig A. Evans (New York: Routledge, 2008), 606.

At the beginning of his tractate *Advice to Bride and Groom* (*Coniugalia praecepta*) Plutarch (first–second century CE), while claiming not to be a Stoic but nevertheless sharing many concerns with Stoic thinkers, writes: "Of the many admirable themes contained in philosophy, that which deals with marriage deserves no less serious attention than any other" (*Mor.* 2.138 [Babbitt, LCL]).[22] In the following, concrete behavioral instructions are given with reference to earlier traditions: "Solon directed that the bride should nibble a quince before getting into bed" (2.138.1); "In Boeotica, after veiling the bride, they put on her head a chaplet of asparagus (2.138.2)." Metaphors and parables with images from daily life are used to explain matters: "Just as fire catches readily in chaff, fibre, and hares' fur, but goes out rather quickly, unless it holds to some other thing that can retain it and feed it, so the keen love between newly married people that blazes up fiercely as the result of physical attractiveness must not be regarded as enduring or constant, unless, by being centred about character and by gaining a hold upon the rational faculties, it attains a state of vitality" (2.138). Example stories that focus on certain behaviors are mentioned: "Cato expelled from the Senate a man who kissed his own wife in the presence of his daughter" (2.139). He obviously considered such affective behavior between husband and wife in front of their children inappropriate. Plutarch disagrees with Cato and writes, "This perhaps was a little severe" (ibid.). Yet he uses this example to develop an argument a fortiori: "But if it is a disgrace for man and wife to caress and kiss and embrace in the presence of others, is it not more of a disgrace to air their recriminations and disagreements before others?" (ibid.). Further deliberations concern the presence of wives at meals and banquets: their presence at ordinary meals is recommended, whereas they should be excluded from situations in which the husband engages in "licentiousness and debauchery" (2.140).

For some of these recommendations rabbinic analogies could be found. For example, in rabbinic culture women were also excluded from drinking banquets. Women and children's presence at the Passover seder, where the drinking of wine is part of the ritual, constitutes an exception to this rule (m. Pesaḥ. 8:7).[23] What matters more than the specific content, however, and what I am concerned with here, is the phenomenon of Hellenistic philosophers' and rabbis' pretension to govern and control other

22. On Plutarch's relationship to Stoicism, see Jan Opsomer, "Plutarch and the Stoics," in *A Companion to Plutarch*, ed. Mark Beck (Oxford: Blackwell, 2014), 89–102.

23. The Mishnah specifies that women, slaves, and minors should not form separate table fellowships (*havurot*) but should mix with the adult male participants on this occasion. On women's participation in Passover meals, see Judith Hauptman, "Thinking about the Ten Theses in Relation to the Passover Seder and Women's Participation," in: *Meals in Early Judaism: Social Formation at the Table*, ed. Susan Marks and Hal Taussig (New York: Palgrave Macmillan, 2014), 43–57.

people's private sphere and marital life. They used some of the same literary forms to transmit their recommendations: references to earlier views of fellow scholars, metaphors and parables (e.g., the fire metaphor is also repeatedly used in rabbinic writings in a variety of contexts), example stories, and arguments a fortiori.

My second example is from Plutarch's tractate *Advice about Keeping Well* (*De tuenda sanitate praecepta*), which has the literary form of a dialogue between Moschion the physician and Zeuxippus, a Stoic friend of Plutarch. Moschion is said to have criticized philosophers who possess knowledge in subjects such as geometry rather than the machinations of the human body (*Mor.* 2.122). Zeuxippus agrees that matters of health should be part of the philosophical agenda. In the ensuing discussion various insights from ancient popular medicine are mentioned, such as the need to always keep one's hands and feet warm so that heat may not leave the body through the extremities (2.123), or the suggestion that "boiled, baked, or fried foods afford no proper pleasure or gratification to those who are suffering from disease, debauch, or nausea" (2.126). Specific foods and beverages are associated with medical benefits. Symptoms of illnesses are discussed alongside possible remedies. These more specific insights appear alongside more general instructions to exert moderation in food and drink (2.123) and to avoid adultery and licentiousness (2.126).

Rabbis were similarly interested in the body and popular medicine. They also present themselves in conversation with physicians or were physicians themselves.[24] Rabbis would incorporate health professionals' knowledge into their halakhic discussions and advice.[25] They would therefore agree with Zeuxippus that knowledge of the human body, its ailments, and remedies should be part of a public intellectual's repertoire. An additional incentive was the biblical notion that the human body was created by God. Advice concerning bodily matters was therefore not only the domain of physicians but also of religious functionaries. Like Stoic philosophers, rabbis presented themselves as authorities and advisors in all matters concerning human life and did not distinguish between bodily material existence and some kind of higher spiritual sphere. Advice concerning health, food, and eating habits was therefore part of their repertoire. For example, sick people are permitted to decide themselves

---

24. Annette Yoshiko Reed points to "scattered references in the classical Rabbinic literature to Sages said to be experts in … medicinal matters" ("Historiography of Judaism," in *Ancient Jewish Sciences and the History of Knowledge in Second Temple Literature*, ed. Jonathan Ben-Dov and Seth Sanders [New York: New York University Press, 2014], 236). See her n. 132 for source references and secondary literature.

25. See Catherine Hezser, "Representations of the Physician in Jewish Literature from Hellenistic and Roman Times," in *Popular Medicine in Graeco-Roman Antiquity: Explorations*, ed. William V. Harris, Columbia Studies in the Classical Tradition 42 (Leiden: Brill, 2016), 173–97.

whether to fast on a fast day (y. Yoma 8:4, 45a–b). Like Plutarch and Stoic philosophers, they advised their fellow Jews to observe moderation as far as food and drink were concerned. According to a statement attributed to R. Yose b. R. Bun (y. Qidd. 4:12, 66d), "it is forbidden to live in a town that does not have a vegetable garden." This general principle is followed by a warning, attributed to R. Hezeqiah and R. Cohen in the name of Rav: "In the future a person will have to render an account for everything that his eye saw and he did not eat." The warning seems to be directed at a person who refuses to eat certain vegetables. The text advises Jews to make conscious decisions as far as their eating habits are concerned.

The similarity between rabbinic and Stoic concerns is evident also in their distinction between matters that are under human control and others that cannot be controlled. A statement in Epictetus's *Enchiridion*, or *Manual*, is very similar to a rabbinic statement. Epictetus (first–second century CE) writes:

> Of things some are in our power, and others are not. In our power are opinion, movement towards a thing, desire, aversion; and in a word, whatever are our own acts: not in our power are the body, property, reputation, offices (magisterial power), and in a word, whatever are not our own acts. (1.1).[26]

This distinction is the necessary basis of Stoic ethics, for advice for practical living is useful only in areas that are under human control. Diseases of the body, other people's opinions of oneself, inherited wealth, and appointments to offices, on the other hand, are not one's own doing but either inflicted by the gods (body) or dependent on others' actions (reputation, property, offices). Therefore one should concentrate one's efforts on one's own words and practices. Epictetus writes, "If it relates to anything which is not in our power, be ready to say, that it does not concern you" (ibid.).

A similar statement appears in a rabbinic Midrash:

> R. Levi said: Six things [i.e., body parts] serve a human being, three are under his control and three are not under his control. The eye and the ear and the nose are not under his control: he sees what he does not want [to see], he hears and smells what he does not want [to hear and smell]. The mouth and the hand and the foot are under his control: if he wants, he studies Torah; if he wants, he says something wicked; if he wants, he blasphemes and reviles. The hand, if he wants, he distributes charity; if he wants, he steals and kills. The foot, if he wants, he goes to synagogues and study houses; if not, he goes to theatres and circuses." (Gen. Rab. 67:3; my translation)[27]

---

26. Translation with George Long at http://www.perseus.tufts.edu/hopper/text?doc=Perseus%3Atext%3A1999.01.0236%3Atext%3Denc.

27. For a more detailed discussion of this text, see Catherine Hezser, "Self-Control in

Like Epictetus, R. Levi considers some aspects of the body to be out of a person's control. What one can control, however, are the mouth, that is, the opinions and words one utters, and the movements of one's feet and hands. R. Levi does not even mention property, office, and reputation, areas that were as irrelevant to rabbis as to Stoic philosophers. Like Epictetus, R. Levi reckons with humans' ability to make rational choices, to control their behavior and choose actions that are "good" and pleasing to God. Self-control for the purpose of living in accordance with what one perceived to be God's will and for the avoidance of what was seen as transgression was a dominant aspect of rabbinic Judaism.

What rabbis shared with Greek and Hellenistic philosophers, then, was their interest in practical ethics, in providing guidelines on how to live one's life. In both cases these guidelines were based on higher principles and beliefs, but they were quite concrete and encompassed all aspects of life in which decisions about actions had to and could be made. Obviously, some philosophers such as Plutarch and Epictetus were more interested than others in practical ethics. The more theoretical discussion of virtues and vices, good and evil, and primary values by philosophers such as Zeno, as presented by Diogenes Laertius (e.g., 7.83–103), are absent from rabbinic texts.

I do not claim that rabbis of the first four centuries CE were familiar with Plutarch's and Epictetus's writings. Palestinian rabbis lived in a context, however, in which Hellenistic philosophical teachings would have been part of the Greco-Roman cultural *koine* with which local intellectuals would have been familiar, even if they did not possess Greek *paideia*. Palestinian rabbis would have been aware of Hellenistic philosophers who provided partly alternative and partly overlapping moral advice to their popular audiences which, in all likelihood, also included Jews.[28] Based on their biblical heritage, rabbis developed a particularly Jewish type of moral instruction that propagated a lifestyle that was similarly focused on human action in a variety of daily life situations. With Greco-Roman intellectuals they shared the notion that one's inner disposition is revealed in one's actual behavior and practices.[29] This idea converged with the biblical notion that the covenantal relationship required human action.[30] Whereas Hellenistic philosophers instructed their followers to be guided by vir-

---

a World Controlled by Others: Palestinian Rabbinic 'Asceticism' in Late Antiquity," in *Religions in the Roman Empire* 4 (2018): 9–27.

28. On Greek intellectuals in Roman Palestine, see Joseph Geiger, *Hellenism in the East: Studies on Greek Intellectuals in Palestine*, Alte Geschichte 229 (Stuttgart: Franz Steiner, 2014).

29. Anthony Corbeill, *Nature Embodied: Gesture in Ancient Rome* (Princeton: Princeton University Press, 2004), 2.

30. See, e.g., William K. Gilders, "The Concept of Covenant in Jubilees," in *Enoch and the Mosaic Torah: The Evidence of Jubilees*, ed. Gabriele Boccaccini and Giovanni Ibba (Grand Rapids: Eerdmans, 2009), 184–86.

tues in all of their doings, rabbis hoped that their fellow-Jews would realize biblical values in everyday life. Both types of intellectuals developed guidelines for an ideal lifestyle that required control of one's affections.

Early Christianity: From *Physis* to Metaphysics

The early Jesus-movement and the Jerusalem-based branches of early Christianity seem to have been as interested in daily life practices as the Pharisees they allegedly competed with. Not only are teachings that the gospels associate with Jesus concerned with everyday life matters such as adultery and divorce (see Matt 5:27, 31), clothes and food (Matt 6:25, 28), vows (Matt 5:33–34), charity and interpersonal relationships (Matt 5:42–44; Luke 6:27–31), but the parables consistently use images, roles, and situations from daily life and the body to elucidate moral and theological matters: the eye in its relation to the body (Matt 6:22; Luke 11:34), trees and their fruit (Matt 7:17–20; Luke 6:43–44), day laborers, wages, and land owners (Matt 20:1–16). The teachings are concrete and reflect the lives of Palestinian Jews of the first century CE.

Some scholars have already pointed to similarities between the early Jesus tradition and Stoic ethics that can be explained by a "shared intellectual milieu, i.e. a 'philosophical *koine*.'"[31] This is a context that Pharisees and early rabbis would have shared. The Greek-language context in which the editors of the gospels formulated the Jesus-tradition may have given them a greater familiarity with Hellenistic philosophical teachings than most Aramaic-speaking Pharisees and rabbis possessed, although the knowledge of Greek among the latter should not be underestimated. While their actual association with the Pharisaic movement remains doubtful, the Greek-speaking Jews Josephus and Paul suggest that Pharisaism also attracted hellenized Jews.[32]

There is a marked difference between the this-worldliness, concreteness, and practical focus of the Jesus of the gospels, a focus that is evident also in the Didache, and the much more theoretical theological contemplations of Paul and some later patristic writers.[33] The fact that Paul never

31. Evans, ed., "Stoicism and Cynicism," 606.

32. On this connection, see Albert I. Baumgarten, *The Flourishing of Jewish Sects in the Maccabean Era: An Interpretation*, JSJSup 55 (Leiden: Brill, 1997), 46–59. Baumgarten doubts whether Paul can be considered a "typical Pharisee" (49 n. 37). Shaye J. D. Cohen writes of Josephus that "his Pharisaism is of the most dubious quality" (*Josephus in Galilee and Rome: His Vita and Development as a Historian*, Columbia Studies in the Classical Tradition 8 [Leiden: Brill, 1979], 223).

33. On the Didache, see Huub van de Sandt, "Essentials of Ethics in Matthew and the Didache: A Comparison at a Conceptual and Practical Level," in *Early Christian Ethics in Interaction with Jewish and Greco-Roman Contexts*, ed. Jan Willem van Henten and Joseph Ver-

mentions Jesus's teachings as they are transmitted in the gospels has already been emphasized by scholars.[34] New Testament scholars nevertheless maintain that "a continuity in *substance* between Jesus' preaching of the kingdom of God and Paul's gospel of justification" existed.[35] Obviously, Christian theologians have a vested interest in claiming continuity between Jesus and Paul, that is, between the teachings of a first-century Palestinian Jewish street preacher and the Christ of Christian faith. Part of this claim to continuity is the allegedly shared downplaying of Torah observance in favor of belief and the alleged self-identification of Jesus with a divine redeemer figure.

The difference evident here is between a focus on *physis*, that is, nature and humans' lived experience in the world, and what we would call metaphysics, that is, what lies beyond nature or the otherworldly sphere. In Stoic practical ethics, the Jesus tradition, and rabbinic literature metaphysics remains the basis and background for the exploration of humans' daily encounter with others, animals, objects, illnesses, and so on. In other philosophical writings and Paul's letters, on the other hand, metaphysics takes center space. The focus in entirely different, and a greater level of abstraction prevails. Rather than dealing with the more practical aspects of Torah observance that were disputed among Jesus and the Pharisees, Jewish Christians, and rabbis, Paul constructs the abstract categories of faith and righteousness, which he juxtaposes. Salvation through "faith in Jesus Christ" becomes his main slogan. In Gal 2:16 he writes, for example, "A man is not justified by the works of the law but through faith in Jesus Christ." The death and alleged resurrection of Christ becomes the central symbol (see Rom 14:9). This redemption-historical "event" erased human "sins" once for all, so that so-called "works" are no longer necessary or relevant: the "spirit" is received through faith alone (see Gal 3:2, 1 Cor 15:17). In the Letter to the Romans, "righteousness" (*dikaiosynē*) is

---

heyden, Studies in Theology and Religion 17 (Leiden: Brill, 2013), 243–62. Some scholars have also examined Paul's moral teachings in the context of Hellenistic philosophy; see Troels Engberg-Pedersen, *Paul and the Stoics* (Louisville: Westminster John Knox, 2000), 45–49, but the similarities he mentions are rather theoretical, such as *eudaimonia* and striving for a *telos*. Anders Klostergaard Petersen views Paul's alleged emphasis on righteousness on the basis of Stoic virtue ethics ("Finding a Basis for Interpreting New Testament Ethos," in van Henten and Verheyden, *Early Christian Ethics*, 78). Again, the concepts are rather theoretical and general, even in the paraenetic sections of his letters, in contrast to the concrete guidance provided by rabbis. This is not meant, however, to play down the importance of examining Paul's writing on the basis of Stoic philosophy.

34. See Seyoon Kim, *Paul and the New Perspective: Second Thoughts on the Origins of Paul's Gospel*, WUNT 140 (Tübingen: Mohr Siebeck, 2002), 259.

35. See Nikolaus Walter, "Paul and the Early Christian Jesus-Tradition," in *Paul and Jesus: Collected Essays*, ed. Alexander J. M. Wedderburn, JSNTSup 37 (Sheffield: JSOT Press 1989; repr., London: Bloomsbury Academic, 2015), 51.

reinterpreted.[36] It does not refer to practice in daily life. Rather, "the righteousness of God" can be obtained "through faith in Jesus Christ" only (Rom 3:22).

The Pauline letters are full of this kind of abstract terminology and catchphrases that are radically different from the practical ethics, worldliness, and concreteness of the gospels and the rabbinic tradition. What Paul offers his gentile diaspora audience is not an alternative way of life that might compete with the ethics offered by the Stoics and Pharisees. In fact, he dismisses the relevance of any kind of practical ethics as an expression of group identity and beliefs. Behaviors that distinguished Jews from others, such as the refusal to eat non-kosher food—a practice that the Jerusalem-based Jewish Christians continued (see Gal 2:11–13)—are vociferously dismissed. Rather than being replaced by a new Christian set of behaviors, the meaning of "living in Christ" is described in rather general, theoretical terms.[37]

Daniel Boyarin has already pointed to the dualistic nature of Pauline thought: spirit is juxtaposed to body just as faith is juxtaposed to "works-righteousness."[38] This dualism between belief and practice is at odds not only with Judaism but also with practical ethics as an expression of one's values taught by the Stoics and other Hellenistic philosophical schools. As already mentioned above, one's behavior in daily life was seen to be the most important indicator of one's internal disposition. It is not a Greek/Hebrew or philosophical/biblical divide that distinguishes Pauline theology from Pharisaic and rabbinic instructions, then. What could have caused Paul's radical reduction of the Christian message to the abstract concept of "faith in Christ," his dismissal of the relevance of Torah observance, and his caricature of Judaism as "works-righteousness"?[39]

One reason may have been his focus on winning converts in cities and regions outside of Jewish Palestine (see Gal 2:7–8). The Jerusalem-based Jewish Christians around James seem to have continued certain Jewish

---

36. On the meaning of "righteousness" (*dikaiosynē*) in the LXX, Hellenistic Judaism, and Paul, see Ben Witherington III, *Paul's Letter to the Romans: A Socio-Rhetorical Commentary* (Grand Rapids: Eerdmans, 2004), 52–56; J. A. Ziesler, *The Meaning of Righteousness in Paul: A Linguistic and Theological Enquiry*, SNTSMS 20 (Cambridge: Cambridge University Press, 1972), who also traces the use of the term through Hellenistic Judaism, Philo, and Josephus.

37. A. K. Petersen points to Paul's repeated reference to "the virtue of righteousness" as "the pivotal term for describing the new relationship between God and Christ believers" ("Finding a Basis," 78).

38. Daniel Boyarin, *A Radical Jew: Paul and the Politics of Identity*, Contraversions 1 (Berkeley: University of California Press, 1994), 125.

39. Although Paul does mention the necessity to stay away from sin and to live "worthily of God" (1 Thess 2:12), his moral advice remains rather general and is subordinated to his theological instruction. More detailed ethical guidelines are provided only in 1 Thess 4:1–5:22; see James Thompson, *Moral Formation according to Paul: The Context and Coherence of Pauline Ethics* (Grand Rapids: Baker Academic, 2011), 87–110.

practices that distinguished them (Gal 2:12–13).[40] Rather than continuing to argue within Jewish parameters and creating an alternative way of life, Paul threw out the baby with the bathwater. According to him, a new Christian identity was possible only by abandoning all kinds of particularistic lifestyles and concentrating on one unifying belief and symbol only (i.e., salvation through belief in the resurrection of Christ). Lifestyle choices distinguished one set of people from another, Stoics from Epicureans, Pharisees from Jewish Christians. Paul seems to have hoped that this smallest common denominator of a shared belief (and general moral instruction), which he was keen to propagate on his missionary journeys, could unite Jews and gentiles within the newly established Christian communities.[41]

Another reason may have been Paul's greater interest in metaphysics rather than practical ethics, a focus that is shared by some Hellenistic philosophers. Middle Platonism propagated a dualism between body and soul and the superiority of the spirit over the body that stood in striking contrast to Stoic and Epicurean monism with its "materialistic view of human nature."[42] Obviously, Pharisees, rabbis, and Jewish Christians would have felt a much greater affinity with the latter than with the former. As David E. Aune has pointed out correctly, "many monistic and dualistic conceptions of the universe and human nature" circulated in antiquity.[43] Paul would have adapted contemporary philosophical views in an eclectic way and chosen those that fit his own concerns and ideology. He goes so far as to say, "While we are at home in the body, we are absent from the Lord" (2 Cor 5:6); "We … are willing rather to be absent from the body, and to be at home with the Lord" (2 Cor 5:7). By focusing on the spirit and belief rather than on practice and lifestyle, Paul distinguished his newly devised gentile-Christian ideology from both Jewish(-Christian) and Hellenistic philosophical teachings that proclaimed the unity of human nature and the need to practice one's values and beliefs with one's body in all realms of daily life.

In the following centuries, in which Christianity became almost completely gentile, this divide between the focus on daily life practice,

40. On the question whether this James should be considered identical with James the brother of Jesus (cf. Gal 1:19) and the James mentioned by Josephus (*Ant.* 20.200), see James Carleton Paget, *Jews, Christians, and Jewish Christians in Antiquity*, WUNT 251 (Tübingen: Mohr Siebeck, 2010), 193–98.

41. Gerd Theissen and Petra von Gemünden also associate Paul's insistence on righteousness through faith alone with the "universal" appeal of his message (*Der Römerbrief: Rechenschaft eines Reformators* [Göttingen: Vandenhoeck & Ruprecht, 2016], 253).

42. David E. Aune, "Human Nature and Ethics in Hellenistic Philosophical Traditions and Paul: Some Issues and Problems," in *Jesus, Gospel Tradition and Paul in the Context of Jewish and Greco-Roman Antiquity: Collected Essays II*, WUNT 303 (Tübingen: Mohr Siebeck, 2013), 381–97, here 382.

43. Ibid.

on the one hand, and a body-denying spirituality on the other seems to have become stronger and was associated with a divide between Judaism and Christianity. One may argue that post-70 rabbis not only continued the biblical tradition; they also continued a tradition of anthropological monism and practical ethics that was propagated by Plutarch and the Stoics and shared by Jesus and the early Jewish Christians. On the Christian side, the theoretical reasoning of Platonic and Hellenistic metaphysics prevailed. The dogmatic disputes of the fourth century with their definition of "orthodoxy" and exclusion of heretics stood in stark contrast to rabbinic halakhah with its pluralism, flexibility, and concreteness.[44] As Shaye Cohen has already pointed out in his seminal article on Yavneh, rabbis formed a "grand coalition" that agreed to disagree.[45] While they shared certain undisputed monotheistic beliefs, they were free to focus their attention on providing their fellow Jews with guidance in everyday life, a guidance that was both all-encompassing and flexible.

Can the continued rabbinic concern with this-worldly matters and the relevance of daily life practice be considered a reaction to the increasingly abstract and spiritual message of the church fathers with their prioritizing of the soul over the body and the afterlife over life in this world? Rabbinic halakhic discussions and their compilation in the Mishnah and Talmud provide a striking alternative to the writings of Origen, Tertullian, Augustine, and others with their concern about the machinations of the soul, the resurrection of Christ, the identification of heretics, and theological "truth." On the other hand, Christian leaders such as Tertullian were also concerned about certain aspects of worldly practice such as the wearing of the pallium, modest behavior of women, marriage, and celibacy. Rabbis provided an alternative and, from their perspective, more appropriate way of continuing the biblical heritage that remained diverse and flexible within the confines of Judaism, whereas Christian leaders offered a rather restricted and simplified message to an increasingly large and incongruous pool of believers of diverse backgrounds. The development of dogmas and an official hierarchical structure contrasted with disputes and informal collegial interaction as far as late antique Palestinian rabbinic culture was concerned.

---

44. I disagree with Daniel Boyarin, who argues that "Christian writers of Orthodoxy and the rabbis were evolving in important and strikingly parallel ways" (*Border Lines: The Partition of Judaeo-Christianity* [Philadelphia: University of Pennsylvania Press, 2004], 5). Although the editors of rabbinic documents from the Mishnah onward would have made choices between traditions that they included and others that were left out, they provided a variety of viewpoints and presented the rabbinic movement as democratic and pluralistic.

45. Cohen, "Significance of Yavneh," 67.

Some Aspects of Ancient Legal Thought

Functionalism, Conceptualism, and Analogy

YAAKOV ELMAN
Yeshiva University

MAHNAZ MOAZAMI
Columbia University

As this volume was going to press,
Professor Elman passed away.
May his memory be a blessing.

Our honoree has pointed to three signal characteristics of the post-Destruction rabbinic movement: its pluralism, as contrasted to pre-70 sectarianism;[1] its organization as an academy;[2] and the scholastic nature of its discourse, as he described it in his history covering the four centuries abutting the Common Era:

> The Mishnah constructs legal categories, which often appear to be theoretical or abstruse, and then discusses, usually in great detail, the precise definitions and limits of those categories. It creates lists of analogous legal phenomena, and then proceeds to define and analyze every item on the list. It posits legal principles, and devotes much attention to those objects, cases or times which seem to be subject to more than one principle at once, or perhaps to none of the principles at all. These modes of thinking or writing, which can be characterized as *scholastic*, are endemic to the Mishnah, from one end to the other, and are not found in any pre-Mishnaic Jewish document. They will be developed further in the Talmudim.[3]

The foundations of what has become known as Irano-Talmudica were laid at Harvard's Center for Jewish Studies under the directorships of Jay Harris and Shaye Cohen. Our thanks as well to Michael Satlow for his sensitive editing.

1. Shaye J. D. Cohen, "The Significance of Yavneh: Pharisees, Rabbis, and the End of Jewish Sectarianism," *HUCA* 55 (1984): 27-53; quotation from 50.

2. Shaye J. D. Cohen, "Patriarchs and Scholarchs," *Proceedings of the American Academy for Jewish Research* 48 (1981): 57–85

3. Shaye J. D. Cohen, *From the Maccabees to the Mishnah*, 2nd ed. (Louisville: Westminster John Knox, 2006), 207. See also Yaakov Elman, "Order, Sequence, and Selection: The

Elsewhere, in reviewing the complexities of mishnaic Sabbath law, he observes its "passion for cataloguing, classifying, and defining (sometimes) basing its definitions not on real or empirical data, or for that matter on common sense, but on abstract principles and ideas.... It establishes minimal amounts or degrees that must be exceeded if the violator of a prohibition is to incur liability. It assigns great importance to human intention, with the result that the identical acts by different actors can have different legal consequences, depending upon the actors' knowledge and intention," and he concludes:

> The mishnaic sages inherited this law, that practice, or that piece of information from their Second Temple Period predecessors, but they did not inherit the modes of argumentation, the dominant concerns, the logic, or the rhetoric that would come to characterize the Mishnah. These are conspicuously absent from Second Temple sources. The mishnaic sages were not conservators as much as they were innovators; mishnaic Judaism is a new and distinctive kind of Judaism.[4]

Where, then, did this logic come from? And when did it come into use? In assessing the Mishnah's immediate cultural background—that is, Eastern Mediterranean Hellenism, he asserts:

> The Mishnah is, at least to some extent, the repository of legal traditions and procedures that reach back to ancient Mesopotamia. Whether the Mishnah also stands in a relationship with the ancient Mediterranean world, notably Greece, the Hellenistic empires, and Rome, is much debated. Although the Mishnah was composed in a land that was in turn part of the Hellenistic empire of Egypt, the Hellenistic empire of Syria, and the Roman Empire, there is no clear sign that the legal systems of these empires contributed to the form or content of mishnaic law. It is easy to draw parallels and contrasts between mishnaic law and the law of the Hellenistic and Roman Empires, but it is not easy to determine influence or borrowing in either direction.[5]

Specific influences may be difficult to determine, but the thought-world of the Jews during this period may be fairly characterized as hellenized, as Shaye notes in his history.

> All the varieties of Judaism in the Hellenistic period, of both the diaspora *and of the land of Israel,* were Hellenized, that is, were integral parts of the

---

Mishnah's Anthological Choices," in *The Anthology in Jewish Literature,* ed. David Stern (New York: Oxford University Press, 2004), 53–80.

4. Shaye J. D. Cohen, "Judean Legal Tradition and *Halakhah* of the Mishnah," in *The Cambridge Companion to the Talmud and Rabbinic Literature,* ed. Charlotte Elisheva Fonrobert and Martin S. Jaffee (Cambridge: Cambridge University Press, 2007), 121–43; quotations from 138,140.

5. Ibid., 127.

> culture of the ancient world. Some varieties were more Hellenized than others—that is, some were in more intense contact with non-Jews than were others—but none was an island unto itself. It is a mistake to imagine that the land of Judea preserved a "pure" form of Judaism and that the diaspora was the home of adulterated or diluted forms of Judaism. [6]

In this essay, we pursue two different threads of this discussion. First, we argue that the Mishnah itself shows relative development from functional justification of the law to the scholasticism that Shaye noted. That scholasticism was largely a product of its last stages of editing. Second, this emerging rabbinic scholastic approach is seen best not as due to Hellenism per se but instead as a natural process paralleled in Zoroastrian Pahlavi books, where the initial impetus for an analytic/scholastic approach may have been sparked by the prolonged visit of the Athenian Academy. [7] When we compare the Mishnah to the Zoroastrian Pahlavi books, we find this same mixture of functionalism and abstraction, but the Iranian preference for practicality, at least in Sasanian times, kept the latter tendency at bay; among its consequences is the predominance of *rivayāt*-literature (responsa with an emphasis on the "bottom line"), and collections of pithy sayings (moralistic *andarz* literature) over philosophical treatises. The paucity of extended discussions so typical of talmudic discourse can also be explained in this way.

The Mishnah: From Functional to Abstract

In his monograph *Talmudic Reasoning: From Casuistics to Conceptualization*, Leib Moscovitz argues that the development of conceptualization was a gradual if not exactly linear process, even if it did begin before 70 CE.[8] Below we build on this insight, arguing that the Mishnah contains early traditions that begin as "realia based" (to use Moscovitz's terminology) but gradually become framed in a more abstract and scholastic fashion.[9] Here, we will analyze a series of traditions in Mishnah Eduyyot to illus-

---

6. Cohen, *From the Maccabees to the Mishnah*, 29 (italics added).

7. Alan Watson noted a similar dynamic in Roman law (*The Spirit of Roman Law*, The Spirit of the Laws [Athens: University of Georgia Press, 1994], 98).

8. Leib Moscovitz, *Talmudic Reasoning: From Casuistics to Conceptualization*, TSAJ 89 (Tübingen: Mohr Siebeck, 2002).

9. See further ibid., 47; Yaakov Elman and Mahnaz Moazami, "The Quantification of Religious Obligation in Second Temple Judaism—And Beyond," in *Hā-'îsh Mōshē: Studies in Scriptural Interpretation in the Dead Sea Scrolls and Related Literature in Honor of Moshe J. Bernstein*, ed. Binyamin Y. Goldstein, Michael Segal, and George J. Brooke, STDJ 122 (Leiden: Brill, 2017), 96–135; Elman and Maozami, "The Scholasticization of Religion: From Qumran to Ctesiphon," in the Lawrence Schiffman Festschrift (forthcoming); and "PV 5.1–4 in the Context of Late Antique Intellectual History," *BAI* 27 (2017): 13–41.

trate this point. In the next section we show an analogous process in the Zoroastrian Pahlavi books. We now turn to the first Mishnah of a series (m. 'Ed. 1:12–14), which depicts the Houses quite differently than in the rest of rabbinic literature. These cases are grouped together in the first chapter of Mishnah Eduyyot, which itself is redacted on different principles than the rest of the Mishnah, that is, not according to topic but according to tradent. The Hillelites maintain their tradition in all its narrow rigidity, while the Shammaites argue for more flexibility, suggesting that this report relates to a time before the schools attained their usual stances—or images. It is also a case—like m. Pesaḥ. 1:1—where the Houses debate the meaning of an earlier decision, which indicates that these early authorities were indeed heirs of an ongoing tradition. We present only the first part of the Mishnah, which is most relevant to our concerns.

> These are the subjects concerning which the Hillelites reversed [themselves] and taught according to the opinion of the Shammaites: A woman who came from the coastlands [or: from abroad] and said: My husband died—may be married again; [or:] my husband died [without issue]—she must be married by her husband's brother [that is, levirate marriage, as per Deut 25:5]; this is the view of the Shammaites, but the Hillelites say: We have heard so [that the woman's statement be accepted] only in the case of one who came from the harvesting.
>
> The Shammaites said to them: It is the same thing in the case of one who came from the harvest or who came from the olive picking or who came from the sea [or: the coastland]; they mentioned harvest only as an actual occurrence.
>
> Then the Hillelites reversed [themselves] and taught according to the view of the Shammaites.

The Mishnah itself contains a more detailed version, which may represent a later elaboration, but which may nevertheless teach us something of those early days, as it appears in m. Yebam. 15:1–3:

> If a woman and her husband went to the coastland [or: a country beyond the sea] [at a time when there was] peace between him and her [and likewise] peace in the world, and she came back and said: "My husband is dead," she may be married again, but if she said, "My husband is dead [and left no issue]," she may contract a levirate marriage. [If, however, there was peace between him and her, but war in the world, [or if there was] discord between him and her, but peace in the world, and she came back and said, "My husband is dead," she is not believed.
>
> R. Yehudah said: She is never believed unless she comes weeping and her garments are rent. They [the rabbis], however, said to him: She may marry in either case.
>
> The Shammaites said: She [the wife] is permitted to be married and she receives her *ketubah*. The Hillelites said: She is permitted to be married but she does not receive her *ketubah*.

It is clear that the Eduyyot version must be earlier, since it is hard to conceive of an editor deleting details essential to understanding the text. The Yevamot version seems to be an elaboration of the earlier text in order to make it more understandable to a later generation. This later version, however, still bears the earmarks of an earlier period, not only because of the framework of debate and reconciliation, and of the fact that the Houses have not assumed their usual stances, but also because these considerations ("peace in the world," and "peace between the spouses") are not the subject of later discussion. This is not to suggest that these aspects were rejected; m. Yebam. 15:4 addresses the issue of whether the testimony of family members who are likely to be at odds is accepted in the case of the report regarding a dead husband. Whether the Houses included subjective factors in their discussions requires separate treatment.[10]

Moscovitz describes the Hillelite position as "strict constructionist." [11] Labeled or not, though, the concept/principle is necessary to complete the argument in this case. Moreover, we assume, with Adiel Schremer and Aharon Shemesh, that one major transition in this period was that from mimetic to analytic presentations, of whatever sort.[12] If this is so, we are viewing these cases in terms of the levels of analysis applied to them. We should also note that the use of analogy is also implicit here: do we regard the wife's testimony as equivalent to a man's. Moreover, as Moscovitz notes, the issue is the scope of the law as transmitted. The Hillelites are cautious; they do not wish to extend the precedent unduly by analogizing too much.[13]

Nevertheless, we must not press this point too strongly, since there are other issues on which one or another of the Houses departs from its usual stance; some are already listed in m. 'Ed. 4:1–12. Indeed, the Hillelites tend to strictness on marital issues even as they are lenient on others, as m. 'Ed. 1:3 illustrates.

There may also be a terminological clue to dating the tradition. Some sixty years ago, Yitzhak Baer suggested that *medinat ha-yam* referred

---

10. See Howard Eilberg-Schwartz, *The Human Will in Judaism: The Mishnah's Philosophy of Intention*, BJS 103 (Atlanta: Scholars Press, 1986), but he studies the Mishnah as a unit.

11. Moscovitz, *Talmudic Reasoning*, 69.

12. See Adiel Schremer, "'[T]He[Y] Did Not Read in the Sealed Book': Qumran Halakhic Revolution and the Emergence of Torah Study in Second Temple Judaism," in *Historical Perspectives: From the Hasmoneans to Bar Kokhba in Light of the Dead Sea Scrolls: Proceedings of the Fourth International Symposium of the Orion Center for the Study of the Dead Sea Scrolls and Associated Literature, 27–31 January 1999*, ed. David M. Goodblatt, Avital Pinnick, and Daniel R. Schwartz, STDJ 37 (Leiden: Brill, 2001), 105–26, esp. 117. While Schremer stresses the movement from mimetic religion to "book religion," we wish to stress the use of analogy. See Aharon Shemesh, *Halakhah in the Making: The Development of Jewish Law from Qumran to the Mishnah*, Taubman Lectures in Jewish Studies 6 (Berkeley: University of California Press, 2009), 95–96.

13. We will discuss the issue of analogy in legal reasoning below.

specifically to the coast of Eretz Israel and dated before the Hasmonean kingdom, when the seacoast was foreign territory, a suggestion that was revived by David Goodblatt some two decades ago.[14] Of course, this does not mean that this was the meaning it had in Roman times or that the Houses understood it that way. Given the entire context of this case, however, it seems more likely that its venue is "overseas" rather than the coast of Roman Palestine.

The upshot is that we may have here a precious remnant of an early rabbinic debate that dates from a time when the Judean world opened to travel "overseas," where untoward happenings may be expected to occur—and, in this case, women's testimony may have to be accepted. It also considers the effects of war and peace, perhaps pointing to a time around Ptolemy's sacking of Jerusalem in 63 BCE.

It would seem that this uncertainty stems from a lack of agreed-upon guidelines of "statutory construction" and that the Hillelites were feeling their way, so to speak. What then were the circumstances surrounding this uncertainty? We must assume that we are standing at the beginning of an analytic/scholastic approach to halakhah, presumably triggered by new circumstances—couples going abroad or beyond the reach of reliable reports and by the need to decide on the status of the wife's testimony, since we have nothing else to go on. Dare we analogize from the case handed down by tradition to the one in the Mishnah? And if we do not, what are we left with on which to base a decision? Must the wife remain "chained" to her (possibly) dead husband? As we shall see, the very next mishnah stresses the principle that the world was created to be inhabited; if a childless widow cannot remarry, that principle is violated. If considerations such as these were in play, we again have a case of functionalist analysis.

Note that there is no "book" text available for either side to resort to in this case. While the institution of levirate marriage is of biblical origin (Deut 25:5–10), there is nothing in the biblical text regarding determination of death. Moreover, while women's testimony in general seems to have been held invalid in Hellenistic times, there is a marked difference between the approaches of m. 'Ed. 1:12 and m. Yebam. 15:1–3 to the question. In the former, the issue for the Hillelites seems to have been the question of how likely it is that the husband would have died during the various scenarios mentioned, while in the latter the question is more subjective: how likely is it that the wife is telling the truth, or how likely is her inference regarding her husband's death to be accurate?

Pahlavi literature provides an illustrative parallel to this issue, but first we should briefly survey that literature. There are seven Pahlavi sources worth considering in this respect. Four are more or less completely pre-

---

14. David Goodblatt, "'Medinat ha-Yam'—Mishor he-Hof," *Tarbiz* 64 (5755/1995): 13–37.

served: a seventh-century law book, "The Book of a Thousand Decisions" (Mādayān ī Hāzar Dādestān, hereafter MHD); a late fifth-century translation and commentary on an Avestan (a Zoroastrian "biblical book"), which is devoted to pollution (corpse and menstrual) and purification (the Pahlavi Vidēvdād, otherwise known as the Vendidad, hereafter PV); and a sixth-century super-commentary on the legal parts of the latter, "Commentary on Chapters of the Vidēvdād" (Zand ī Fragard ī Jud-Dēw-Dād, hereafter ZFJ). There are also fragmentary Avestan commentaries whose lemmata and comments are preserved, one on priestly training (Hērbedestān) and one on the liturgy (Nērangestān). Finally, there is a ninth-century "halakhic" handbook, Šāyast-nē-Šāyast ("Proper/Improper," hereafter: ŠnŠ), similar to other such gaonic works composed within the matrix of Islamic book culture. In these books are preserved hundreds of comments by over two dozen late Sasanian authorities, in some cases dozens of comments attributed to one *dastwar*, whose approach to the Avesta and to Zoroastrian ritual law can thus be discerned.[15]

The issue of accepting a woman's testimony in court became a hotly debated one among Iranian jurists in the sixth and seventh centuries, when the Black Plague and wars seem to have decimated the class of male landowners, whose place was taken by their women.[16] That debate is to be found in the early seventh-century Sasanian lawbook MHD and concerns the right of a Sasanian landowner's widow to represent her dead husband's estate in court. But in PV 16.2 the issue is uncertainty about determining the onset of menses.

> (I) When she knows today that "I was in menses yesterday," then from the moment of knowing (she should avoid) direct contact (with) other things. There is one who says thus: *Tahīg* is from the beginning, while the other stages (begin) from the moment when she knows it.[17]

As Mahnaz explains, *tahīg* "seems to be a source of impurity or time for waiting for a menstruating woman to become clean." There seems to be a dispute as to how far we take her testimony, perhaps similar to the issue

---

15. See Philippe Gignoux, "La controverse dans le Mazdéisme tardif," in *La controverse religieuse et ses formes*, ed. Alain Le Boulluec, Patrinoines: Religions du livre (Paris: Cerf, 1995), 127–49; and Yaakov Elman, "Toward an Intellectual History of Sasanian Law: An Intergenerational Dispute in Hērbedestān 9 and Its Rabbinic Parallels," in *The Talmud in Its Iranian Context*, ed. Carol Bakhos and M. Rahim Shayegan, TSAJ 135 (Tübingen: Mohr Siebeck, 2010), 21–57.

16. Yaakov Elman, "Marriage and Marital Property in Rabbinic and Sasanian Law," in *Rabbinic Law in Its Roman and Near Eastern Context*, ed. Catherine Hezser, TSAJ 97 (Tübingen: Mohr Siebeck, 2003), 227–76.

17. PV, ed. Moazami, 376–77. References to PV will be to Mahnaz Moazami's edition, *Wrestling with the Demons of the Pahlavi Widēwdād: Transcription, Translation, and Commentary*, Iran Studies 9 (Leiden: Brill, 2014).

in m. 'Ed. 1:1 and m. Nid. 1:1, which involves Hillel and Shammai. The dispute seems to relate to the difference between "the moment of knowing" (*az dānistan*) and "from the beginning" (*az bunīh*)—that is, awareness and sure knowledge. In the immediately preceding paragraph we have:

> (H) If there is a door or a window in front, then it should be opened with the *finger, (in case) of doubt it is allowed, if she does not examine her genitals. Gōgušnasp said: Also in certainty it is allowed (not to examine her genitals).[18]

The point seems to be that, since she is allowed to rely on her internal feeling/awareness even in cases of doubt and thus forgo a physical examination, this is all the more so when she is certain that the feeling is accurate.[19] PV then proceeds to a case in which there is an interval between awareness and knowledge. This is similar to a debate in the Mishnah where the two early authorities, Hillel and Shammai, debate the same issue as Gōgušnasp and the anonymous redactor in PV, an analysis of which we must defer to another occasion. Menstrual impurity is an area of ritual law in which even the most conservative cleric would tend to trust women's testimony, if only to avoid having to deal with the physical effects of menstruation. In any case, PV 6.2H represents an important instance of the turn to conceptualization."[20]

The next mishnah in our series ('Ed. 1:13) deals with another case in which the Hillelites come to accept the Shammaites' view; the parallel (m. Giṭ. 4:5) is essentially the same except for the substitution of *i efshar* ("it is impossible") for *eino yakhol* ("he cannot").

Here the Hillelites initially compare a jointly owned slave to property,[21] but the Shammaites point out that, in the case of a slave, there is a human dimension that must be considered, and so that what began as a case of "competing analogies" came to have functionalist considerations as well. Which then is the more relevant analogy of a half-slave/half-free individual, to chattel or to a free human being? A biblical verse is then

18. PV, ed. Moazami, 376–77.

19. Ibid: (I) When she knows today that "I was in menses yesterday," then from the moment of knowing (she should avoid) direct contact (with) other things. There is one who says thus: *tahīg* is from the beginning, while the other stages (begin) from the moment when she knows it.

20. See Yaakov Elman, "The Other in the Mirror: Iranians and Jews View One Another: Questions of Identity, Conversion and Exogamy in the Fifth-Century Iranian Empire," *BAI* 19 (2009): 15–26; 20 (2009): 25–46; in particular, see 29–30 in the latter part.

21. Slaves are considered equivalent to real estate for certain monetary transactions, since the word *naḥalah* is applied to them in Lev 25:46 in a halakhic midrash cited in b. B. Qam. 62b, 117b, b. B. Meṣ. 57b, and elsewhere, though the original midrash seems not to have survived in our texts of the *midreshei halakhah*; see Rashi *ad* B. Qam. 117b, s.v. שהוקשו לקרקעות.

cited to determine the Torah's policy, and, as noted above, this "policy decision" may have a bearing on the case of the widow.

This case differs from the usual and expected pattern not only in that the Hillelites are more stringent but also in that they initially ignore individual human needs while the Shammaites do not! Once again, it seems that the list reflects an early period in Houses' debates. We have absolutely no information on the internal dynamics or structure of the "Houses," or the internal politics that may have gone into the decision-making process for the early period of their history. Judging from the famous incident in which the Shammaites prevailed by force (y. Šabb. 1:4), this was presumably an anomalous situation, simply because the rabbis as a group could not have functioned in that manner—or, perhaps a holdover from an earlier period of sectarian tension within the proto-rabbinic group (Pharisees?).[22] In our case we have no idea who among the Hillelites proposed the first solution, and who accepted the Shammaite proposal, and who or what they represented.

This also suggests that this debate dates from a time before functionalist or nominalist considerations were admitted into the debate without further ado.[23] This is not to say that the Shammaites were the first to suggest such considerations, since we find "motive clauses" in the Pentateuch, especially in the book of Deuteronomy,[24] but for human jurists to take upon themselves such responsibility requires another step and considerable self-confidence on the part of the jurist legislator.

Here a Zoroastrian parallel that, like the motive clauses of Deuteronomy, occurs in the *Avesta* itself and in the name of Ohrmazd, a text that deals with the problem of how to regard one who commits an inadvertent sin—the heinous sin of feeding a fire with wood polluted with dead matter deposited by even a fly. In the ancient Videvdad 5.3–4 Ohrmazd shows himself to be a thoroughgoing nominalist in Mahnaz's rendering of the Middle Persian translation of and commentary on that declaration:

---

22. See Cohen, "Significance of Yavneh."

23. The debate over nominalism and realism in Qumran and rabbinic literature has been intense and fruitful. It began with some observations by Yohanan Silman, "Halakhic Determinations of a Nominalistic and Realistic Nature: Legal and Philosophical Considerations" [Hebrew], *Diné Yisrael* 12 (1984–1985): 249–66. More recently, see Christine Hayes, "Legal Realism and the Fashioning of Sectarians in Jewish Antiquity," in *Sects and Sectarianism in Jewish History*, ed. Sacha Stern, IJS Studies in Judaica 12 (Leiden: Brill, 2011), 119–48; Jeffrey L. Rubenstein, "Nominalism and Realism Again," *Diné Yisrael* 30 (2015): 79–120; Vered Noam, *Mi-Qumran ad la-Mahapehah ha-Tannait: Hebetim bi-Tefisat ha-Tum'ah*, (Jerusalem: Yad Ben Zvi, 2010), 221–264; and Christine Hayes, *What's Divine about Divine Law? Early Perspectives* (Princeton: Princeton University Press, 2015), 195–235.

24. See Rifat Sonsino, *Motive Clauses in Hebrew Law: Biblical Forms and Near Eastern Parallels*, SBLDS 45 (Chico, CA: Scholars Press, 1980).

> 5.3 (A) Ohrmazd answered: Neither carried by the dog, nor carried by the bird, nor carried by the wolf, nor carried by the wind, nor carried by the fly, dead matter causes a man to sin [it does not make one sinful, though it makes one impure].
>
> 5.4 (A) For if these corpses, which are carried by the dog, carried by the bird, carried by the wolf, carried by the wind, and carried by the fly, were to cause a man to sin [they would become sinners] (B) right away [this would have happened soon (after death)], my entire material world would have been searching the destruction of righteousness [the path to duty and good deeds would have been blocked to them]. Howling would be given to (descend upon) that soul [their souls would have been howled and chased from paradise]; everybody would be a *tanāpuhl* sinner [would have been a sinner deserving of death], (C) because of the great amount [due to the excessiveness] of these corpses who die on this earth.[25]

To be precise, Ohrmazd asserts that the man is not a sinner; that is to say, offering polluted firewood to the fire in circumstances such as this does not constitute a "sin" (the glossator attempts to limit Ohrmazd's leniency by defining sin here as a *tanāpuhl* sin, one of the more heinous sins), though the wood is polluted. We suggest that even according to Christine Hayes's definition of nominalism ("a legal approach that tends to assume the mind-dependent reality of" legal categories, determinations, and judgments), Ohrmazd is a nominalist because, although the creator of reality, he modifies his law in functionalist terms.[26] As noted above, there is also the problem of competing analogies, as in PV 3.14, where the question concerns the prohibition of carrying a dead body "alone": Are two humans required, or can a large quadruped substitute for one of the humans?

> 3.14 (T) When (the dead body) is tied down over large cattle and (one) pulls it, it is not clear to me (U) (if it) so happens as (if it were removed) by the strength of a man or two men. (V) Rōšn said: (If) it so happens (i.e., if it were removed) by the strength of two men.[27]

Rōšn was most likely a disciple of Abarg—thus two generations beyond our earliest corpus of Pahlavi debates and to be dated to the mid-fifth century, but still relatively early in Pahlavi literature. Moscovitz makes an important observation on the use of analogy, based on one of Zechariah Frankel:

> Tannaitic legal analogies occur more frequently in the Tosefta than in the Mishnah and predominate in the teachings of earlier tannaim, especially

---

25. PV, ed. Moazami, 122–23.
26. See Hayes, *What's Divine about Divine Law?*, 197.
27. PV, ed. Moazami, 76-77.

> in disputes between Beit Shammai and Beit Hillel and between R. Joshua and R. Eliezer, although such reasoning sometimes occurs in the teachings of later tannaim. Why analogies are used more often by (or attributed more frequently to) earlier tannaim is unclear, although it seems unlikely that this reflects the happenstance preservation of earlier analogies and/or the loss of later ones. The chronologically uneven preservation of such analogies suggests that what we have accurately reflects what there was, even if particular tannaitic analogies were lost with the passage of time. Perhaps the more extensive use of legal analogy is due to the fact that such reasoning reflects a comparatively early stage of legal development, which preceded the formation of (explicit) legal principles.[28]

He further observes:

> Why this is so is not clear, although it might be due to either literary or historical factors (and these explanations are not mutually exclusive). Thus, the practical "bottom line" of the Mishnah might have led to the exclusion of discursive material, including analogical argumentation. Alternatively, analogical argumentation might have appeared in earlier, more pristine versions of tannaitic teachings of the sort sometimes preserved in the Tosefta (see chapter 1, at n. 67). However, such material might generally have been excluded from the Mishnah, parts of which might be later and more carefully (and aggressively) edited than the Tosefta.[29]

In other words, analogical arguments could have been excluded for the same reason as halakhic midrash, at whose root, it should be noted, stand various types of analogical reasoning: *qal va-homer*, *gezerah shavah*, *heqesh*, *binyan av*, and so on. Nevertheless, a fair amount of discursive material does exist in the Mishnah. Moreover, analogies stand at the heart and root of legal reasoning, as Frederick Schauer notes in his *Thinking like a Lawyer*:

> Analogical reasoning is widespread throughout the legal system, and it comes as no surprise that many commentators have sought to explain the mechanism by which lawyers use analogies in making arguments and judges use analogies in justifying their decisions....
>
> What distinguishes the good arguments from the bad ones ... is not that the good arguments are based on similarity whilst the bad ones are not, because both are based on similarity. Rather, the good arguments appear to draw on a relevant similarity, while the bad arguments draw on similarities that are not legally relevant at all, even though those similarities might be relevant for other purposes.[30]

---

28. Moscovitz, *Talmudic Reasoning*, 235–36.

29. Ibid., n. 30.

30. Frederick Schauer, *Thinking like a Lawyer: A New Introduction to Legal Reasoning* (Cambridge: Harvard University Press, 2006), 92–94.

This is of course the case when a legal system is up and running, but when it is just getting started, jurists-to-be are searching for ways of *judging* relevance, as in those cases in which the Hillelites, not yet assuming the role that posterity has assigned them, seem somewhat at sea and finally agree with the Shammaites.

We have examined two mishnahs that in our estimation preserve some flavor of early tannaitic discourse and have compared them to some Pahlavi parallels. While we intend to examine this topic elsewhere in greater depth and breadth, we feel that enough has been presented here to indicate the fruitfulness of such comparative work, and that even our earliest remnants of such material indicate that issues of the nominalist–realist debate and that of the question of competing analogies, the use of scriptural texts, and the beginning of conceptualization can be traced to the earliest layer of both literatures.

Pahlavi Scholasticism

A century and a half ago, Friedrich Spiegel, a pioneer in the study of Pahlavi texts, wrote:

> I fear no contradiction when I suggest that in these glosses the same Semitic influence is active that we can recognize in the translations (i.e., the *zand*). Namely, we may compare the very similar work of the Babylonian Jews here. The Parsee glosses may be reasonably categorized under the two rubrics of the Aggada and Halakha; while the glosses to the Vendidad are more halakhic, the ones to the Yasna belong more to the Aggada.[31]

Spiegel opens up another unstated but fruitful comparison with the Mishnah. Like the Mishnah, the Pahlavi law books were redacted, and we can see a development within them from more functional approaches to, on the redactional level, a more scholastic one.

While the Zoroastrian texts are less explicit in their analysis and hardly ever present direct debates between disputants, it is clear, as Spiegel saw, that the Pahlavi texts are of the same genre as the rabbinic ones and reflect a scholastic mind-set of making subtle distinctions. For example, PV 6.5C rules that, "when a single hair remains on the earth, the entire earth up to the water is unclean up to the length and breadth of the body just as (it) lies." This raises the question of why the pollution does not continue beyond the water table. In 6.5G-J the text continues:

31. Friedrich Spiegel, *Einleitung in die traditionellen Schriften der Parsen* (Vienna: K. K. Hof, 1856), 92.

> (G) Whatever is made one with the earth, when one dies on it, one makes the earth polluted; that which is made separate does not (make the earth polluted), but bricks, dust, and sand, too, are of this kind. (H) These, such as small particles of ash, gravel, plaster, dust, flour, (when) one with the other are made separately in their own substance they are made one; (when) with the earth, they are separate. (I) Of stone and of plaster, Abarg said: It is made one. Gōgušnasp said: Only that much space (which is actually adjoining). (J) Stone, when they let it (lie) with (that is, on) the earth, will be clean in due time. If they dig and wash it, it will be clean on the spot. If they dig it, but do not wash it, it will never be clean.[32]

Before analyzing this passage, a word on relative chronology would be helpful. According to ŠnŠ, there were two lines of Zoroastrian tradition, one begun by Ādur Ohrmazd, and one by Ādur Farnbay Narsēh, both of whom are mentioned only once in the Pahlavi books. The former had a disciple, Gōgušnasp, who is mentioned twenty-five times in those books, and the latter had a disciple named Sōšāns, who is mentioned seventy-four times. They in turn had disciples named Mēdōmāh and Abarg, who are mentioned some twenty-five and seventy times, respectively. Though Sōšāns and Gōgušnasp seem to have been contemporaries whose disputes are recorded, Sōšans's major disputant is Kay Ādur Bozēd (forty-three times).[33] Thus, the passage above is atypical in that Abarg disputes his master's colleague, Gōgušnasp, rather than Mēdōmāh, Gōgušnasp's disciple. In ZFJ, the super-commentary on PV mentioned above, schools or groups of *dastwa*rs, seem to have coalesced in the course of the sixth century, the Abargites and the Mēdōmāhites, named after those well-known authorities, and a third, the Pēšagsīrites. These schools continue to dispute among themselves, though the creative voices are those of two redactors. It is important to note, however, that the anonymous redactors do not attribute their innovations to their named predecessors, and this despite the fact that Iranian cultural and religious texts were transmitted orally. Indeed, the Bavli's insistence on oral transmission is simply a reflex of a general Sasanian trope.

Now to return to our passage (6.5G), which lays down a rule to account for why pollution does not extend past the water table: the water line represents a boundary beyond which the pollution cannot pass, because the polluted earth is no longer "made one" with the earth below the water line.

In 6.5G the redactor states the rule in general terms and then immediately applies it to substances such as "bricks, dust, and sand," that is,

---

32. PV, ed. Moazami, 166–67.

33. The standard edition is that of Jehangir C. Tavadia, *Šāyast-nē-Šāyast: A Pahlavi Text on Religious Customs* (Hamburg: Friedrichsen, De Gruyter, 1930), 28–29. The figures are taken from Gignoux, "La controverse dans le Mazdéisme tardif" and the table on p. 147. However, his article does not mention ZFJ.

particulate matter that is "made one" in itself and thus transmits pollution within its own conglomeration of material, and possibly altogether (that is, a heap of bricks, dust, and sand altogether), but not to the earth upon which the heap lies.

Stone and plaster, however, are clearly a different matter (pun intended), and thus Abarg and Gōgušnasp disagree on whether it is or it is not "made one." Stone is clearly part of the landscape, and thus the earth, but it is not particulate, and so we have a disagreement over which principle holds greater weight, as Shaye points out in regard to the Mishnah. However, in the spirit of *ham-dādestān*, "agreement," the rabbinic *lo nehlequ ela*, "they disagreed only in regard to," the redactor finds (or delimits) an area in which the two *dastwar*s might agree (6.5J), thus obviating the necessity of deciding between them. We can hardly determine whether this is so; we have only the redactor(s)' word for it. When we examine ZFJ 11.4–11.5, however, parallel to PV 6.5E (not presented here due to lack of space), the final opinion of three is the most complex; its placement may signal the redactor(s)' determination that it is the regnant one.

As noted above, none of this discussion appears in the ancient Avestan text; the more relevant question for us, however, is, how much, if any, of G-H is implied by the dispute in I? Could Gōgušnasp and Abarg have disputed the status of stone and plaster without the more general questions having been addressed? We suggest that their discussion involved the usual case of someone dying within a house, and how far the pollution runs. G-H and J are scholastic elaborations due to the redactor(s).

Nevertheless, "made one" and "made separate" are abstractions of the basic principle of pollution—contagion, that pollution is spread by contact, the rabbinic *tum'at magga'*, which is an abstract noun derived from the biblical verb *naga'* ("to touch"), a concept that underlies much of the ancient Vidēvdād and is expressed by the Middle Persian *pahikōftan* ("to strike"), or, to denote a more intimate form of contact, *gumēxtan* ("to mix"). Likewise, we should point to a more distant form of "contagion," the rabbinic *ohel* ("tent" or "overshadowing"), where corpse matter pollutes by overshadowing or when a person overshadows corpse matter, or something like a tree overshadows both. In Zoroastrian law, however, the demonness of dead matter is smitten by certain species of dogs and birds, and, in the case of the latter, "when it casts its shadow over (the dead body) [*sāyag*]).[34] In ZFJ, however, the super-commentary on PV, "shadowing" may also *transmit* pollution:

> [440:2.4] If a bird [flying] above casts [its shadow], unless it is by way of direct contact [with the corpse], he does not become polluted.

---

34. PV 7.2D, ed. Moazami, 184–85. It should be noted that this teaching is transmitted by Sōšāns, one of the earliest teachers for whom we have a large corpus of materials.

> If the bird is not among those birds that smite the she-demon of dead matter, even then it is such [that one only is impure if he comes into direct contact with the *nasāy*].[35]

Along with abstract conceptualization comes a more functionalist perspective that leads to leniencies, especially in the laws governing pollution, as in PV 5.4S:

> (S) When the dead matter has reached the gates of the village and the stream of running water, the faithful and the teachers of the Mazdayasnian religion allow (the use of the gate) for the same work; (this also applies to) the furthermost gate.

The tendency toward leniency on the part of Abarg, consonant with Ohrmazd's nominalist position, is also similar to the rabbinic determination that doubtful impurity in public spaces is decided leniently,[36] and may be seen in another decision of Abarg's, this one reported in ŠnŠ 2.73–74,[37] in a recent, as-yet-unpublished edition by Oktor Skjærvø:

> 2.73 (As for) a herd in which there is a sheep that has eaten a dead thing, and a wood in which there is a tree containing a dead thing,
> and a firewood-container in which there is a piece of firewood containing fat, (about these) Abarg said: The implication is that it is not appropriate to make the herd and wood (a case of) "being in doubt" (and so needing testing), but (all) the firewood is useless.
> 2.74 (As for) a door/gate that a dead thing touches: about the gate of a village or town they agreed that it should be left to be used as before, about the outermost gate they disagreed:
> Gōgušasp said: The implication is that it should be left (as such) because it is (considered) appropriate.
> Sōšyans said: The implication is that it is not (considered) appropriate.
> About the other doors, they were agreed that it is not appropriate.

Here we have a case in which dead matter certainly touches a gate, but both Gōguš(n)asp and Sōš(y)ans, Abarg's teacher, agreed that, despite the certainty, the town gate must remain in use. This is certainly public domain. In contrast, "the other doors," that is, those within the town, are not to be continued in use until proper purification is accomplished; these doors serve private domains. The intermediate case is in dispute, with Sōš(y)ans (Abarg's teacher) ruling that it is not to remain in use, and Gōguš(n)asp (Mēdōmāh's teacher) disagreeing. Sōš(y)ans is the earliest

---

35. ZFJ 2.5, from Mahnaz's edition in preparation.
36. Sifre Numbers, Naso 7, ed. Horovitz, 13.
37. See also ibid., 57, for a rendering of the text.

authority of whom we have a substantial number of statements; he tends to be literal-minded and strict. In one notable case, Abarg disagrees with him.[38] Nevertheless, it is important to note that both agreed to the use of the village gate, despite the certainty of the presence of dead matter. (Presumably, the dead matter was removed before the gate's use resumed.)

Conclusion

Shaye's observation that the Mishnah is scholastic and abstract rather than functionalist in its final form requires us to differentiate between that final form and its earlier traditions. Moreover, the resemblance of this redactional layer to the conceptual reasoning of Roman law, where practical considerations are seldom in evidence, suggests that this mishnaic characteristic may have been influenced by Roman legal culture, which in turn was the result of the study of Greek philosophy by Roman jurisconsults who were more interested in displaying their erudition than providing practical solutions to legal problems, as Alan Watson has suggested.[39]

Hellenism certainly came to Iran by 519 CE, when members of the Athenian Academy were expelled and took shelter in the Sasanian court of Xusrō I, and thus PV shows some of the same characteristics, and some early authorities show evidence of conceptualist thinking in PV, especially Gōgušnasp.[40]

---

38. See further Elman, "Toward an Intellectual History of Sasanian Law."
39. Watson, *Spirit of Roman Law*, 72–73.
40. Yaakov has already shown one example of this in PV 5.4; see Elman, "Other in the Mirror," *BAI* 20:29.

The Role of Disgust in Rabbinic Ethics

JEFFREY L. RUBENSTEIN
New York University

The emotion of disgust has received increasing attention in social, political, biological, psychological, legal, and moral discourse in recent years.[1] In a much-discussed essay published in *The New Republic*,[2] the philosopher and ethicist Leon Kass emphasized the "wisdom of repugnance" and appealed to disgust as an innate moral compass. Our inherent disgust at bestiality, necrophilia, and (so Kass claims) human cloning, proves that these practices are inherently immoral. Martha Nussbaum, on the other hand, has explored—and exposed—the role of disgust in opposition to same-sex marriage, gay rights, and related issues and has argued that disgust should have no (or almost no) impact on law and public policy.[3] In her opinion, multicultural, liberal, and rights-based societies such as our contemporary Western civilizations should not recognize a "disgust based morality" but rather should base law and morality on the criterion of harm. Because what disgusts one individual (e.g., eating meat, watching

---

Among the courses I took in my first year of study at the Jewish Theological Seminary in 1985 were two with Dr. Shaye J. D. Cohen. Dr. Cohen's expert pedagogy, sharp humor, and brilliant scholarship made a deep impression on me, and I count him among my scholarly role models. It is a privilege to contribute to this volume in his honor.

1. On disgust in general, see William Ian Miller, *The Anatomy of Disgust* (Cambridge: Harvard University Press, 1997); Susan B. Miller, *Disgust: The Gatekeeper Emotion* (Hillsdale, NJ: Analytic Press), 2004; P. Rozin, J. Haidt, and C. McCauley, "Disgust," in *Handbook of Emotions*, 3rd ed., ed. Michael Lewis and Jeanette M. Haviland-Jones (New York: Guilford, 2008), 757–76; Rachel Herz, *That's Disgusting: Unraveling the Mysteries of Repulsion* (New York: Norton, 2008); Daniel Kelly, *Yuck: The Nature and Moral Significance of Disgust*, Life and Mind (Cambridge, MA: MIT Press, 2011); Winfried Menninghaus, *Disgust: Theory and History of a Strong Sensation*, trans. J. Golb, Intersections (Binghamton: State University of New York Press, 2012).

2. Leon R. Kass, "The Wisdom of Repugnance," *The New Republic* 216.22 (1997): 18–26. A similar version appeared as "The Wisdom of Repugnance: Why We Should Ban the Cloning of Humans," *Valparaiso University Law Review* 32 (1998): 679–705.

3. Martha Nussbaum, *From Disgust to Humanity: Sexual Orientation and Constitutional Law*, Inalienable Rights (New York: Oxford University Press, 2010); see too her *Hiding from Humanity: Disgust, Shame, and the Law* (Princeton: Princeton University Press, 2004).

boxing, homosexual sex, a certain politician) may not disgust another and may even be enjoyable to others, Nussbaum finds disgust a poor arbiter of morality. Yet Nussbaum recognizes the important function of disgust within a given tribe, culture, or religion, even as she emphasizes the often deleterious use of disgust to characterize and demean the "Other" over against the majority, or dominant, group.

Disgust, together with other emotions, has been relatively neglected in scholarship on rabbinic Judaism.[4] In this paper, I would like to examine a few sources that illustrate the role of disgust in rabbinic ethics. I will argue that disgust functions in two different, and almost opposing, ways. On the one hand, rabbinic sources encourage us to suppress and overcome instinctive feelings of disgust at particular others to enable us to act with compassion toward them. On the other hand, rabbinic passages encourage the mobilization of feelings of disgust as a means to avoid sin. Disgust can be triggered either through the imagination, by calling to mind and pondering disgusting things, or through the direct experience of disgusting substances. Rabbinic moral life thus entails a tricky balance of resisting the undeserved, illegitimate disgust we spontaneously feel toward particular others, which may cause us to sin toward them, and yet welcoming and even seeking the deserved, legitimate disgust we should experience at those who tempt us to transgress.

Rabbi Plimo Meets Satan

The following story, which appears in b. Qidd. 81a–b, provides a good entry point to our topic:[5]

---

4. See, however, Sasha Stern, *Jewish Identity in Early Rabbinic Writings*, AJEC 23 (Leiden: Brill, 1997), 57–71; and Ari Mermelstein, "Beauty or Beast? The Pedagogical Function of Metaphor and Emotion in Midrashim on the Law of the Lovely Captive" (forthcoming). Charlotte Elisheva Fonrobert, for example, plays down the importance of disgust as a component of the rabbinic laws of menstrual impurity: "Like few other cultures, rabbinic Judaism in this tractate transforms blood and bodies into language, analyzes the nature of blood and pads, of births and abortions or miscarriages. One detects no sense of embarrassment, shame, or disgust in those pages of the Talmud, feelings familiar to those of us who have grown up in the cultural context of the West" (*Menstrual Purity: Rabbinic and Christian Reconstructions of Biblical Gender*, Contraversions [Stanford, CA: Stanford University Press, 2003], 1; see also 17–18). Rabbinic sources, following the Bible, employ a number of roots for disgust, including מאס, שקץ, געל, זהם, טמא. I know of no comprehensive philological study of these lexemes, which is clearly a desideratum for future research.

5. Text according to the Vilna printing. Manuscript variants are minor and not significant for my purposes here. For additional scholarship on this story, see the excellent study by Admiel Kosman, "Pelimo and Satan: A Divine Lesson in the Public Latrine," *CCAR Journal* 57 (2010): 3–13; Avraham Walfish, "Creative Redaction and the Power of Desire: A Study of the Redaction of Tractate Qiddushin: Mishnah, Tosefta, and Babylonian Talmud" [Hebrew], *Jew-*

[A] Plimo was in the habit of saying each day, "An arrow in Satan's eye!"	פלימו הוה רגיל למימר כל יומא גירא בעיניה דשטן
[B] One day, on the eve of the Day of Atonement, he [Satan] appeared to him [disguised] as a poor person.	יומא חד מעלי יומא דכיפורי הוה אידמי ליה כעניא
[B1] He came and knocked on the door. They brought him a loaf of bread.	אתא קרא אבבא אפיקו ליה ריפתא
[B2] He said to them, "On such a day as this—everyone should be inside and I remain outside?!" They brought him inside, and they brought him a loaf of bread.	אמר ליה יומא כי האידנא כולי עלמא גואי ואנא אבראי עייליה וקריבו ליה ריפתא
[B3] He said to them, "On such a day as this—everyone [has a seat] at the table and I remain alone?!" They brought him and sat him at the table.	אמר ליה יומא כי האידנא כולי עלמא אתכא ואנא לחודאי אתיוהו אותבוהו אתכא
[C] He [Satan] was sitting, and his body became filled with boils and sores, and he was doing disgusting things with them (e.g. picking at the sores). He [Plimo] said to him, "Sit nicely!" He [Satan] said to him, "Give me a cup." They gave him a cup. He coughed and threw up phlegm into it (the cup.) They rebuked him.	הוה יתיב מלא נפשיה שיחנא וכיבי עליה והוה קעביד ביה מילי דמאיס א"ל תיב שפיר אמר ליה הבו לי כסא יהבו ליה כסא אכמר שדא ביה כיחו נחרו ביה
[D] He [Satan] fell down dead. They heard it being said, "Plimo killed a man! Plimo killed a man!"	שקא ומית שמעו דהוו קאמרי פלימו קטל גברא פלימו קטל גברא
[E] He [Plimo] ran away and hid himself in a latrine. He [Satan] went after him. He [Plimo] fell down before him.[6]	ערק וטשא נפשיה בבית הכסא אזיל בתריה נפל קמיה

ish Studies, an Internet Journal 7 (2008): 64–66. Walfish provides manuscript variants (59–60) and lists some additional bibliography (65 n. 84).

6. It is possible to take the text to mean that Satan fell down before Plimo, but I do not think this interpretation reads smoothly. See the commentary of the Maharsh"a ad loc.

[F] When he [Satan] saw how much he [Plimo] was suffering, he revealed himself to him.	כי דחזייה דהוה מצטער גלי ליה נפשיה
He [Satan] said to him, "Why do you speak thus?"	אמר ליה מאי טעמא אמרת הכי
He [Plimo] said to him, "How then should I speak?"	ואלא היכי אימא
He [Satan] said to him, "The master [=you] should say, 'May the Merciful One rebuke Satan'" (cf. Zech 3:2).	אמר ליה לימא מר רחמנא נגער ביה בשטן

Plimo,[7] a sage who prides himself on his piety, routinely taunts Satan by saying each day "An arrow in Satan's eye." That is, Plimo expresses the confidence that he can defeat Satan were Satan to do "battle" with the sage and attempt to make him sin. (In this passage "Satan" is functionally equivalent to the "evil inclination" that tempts one to sin.[8]) This phrase is used elsewhere in the Talmud by Rav Hisda, who states, "The fact that I am superior to my colleagues is because I married at the age of sixteen, and had I married at fourteen, I would have said to Satan, 'An arrow in your eye'" (b. Qidd. 29b–30a). Rav Hisda's comparatively early marriage spared him from sexual temptation and sin, and, had he married at an even younger age, he would have been so impervious to depravity that he could have provoked Satan to battle, secure that his "arrows" and (figurative) armaments would defeat the weapons of the Adversary. The phallic imagery of the arrow and the penetration of an orifice in Rav Hisda's statement fit the context of sexual temptation, but in Plimo's case the sense is broader: he considers himself completely righteous and therefore not susceptible to any type of transgression.[9]

Satan, having been provoked, resolves to test Plimo (B1–B3). He comes to his house in the guise of a beggar on the eve of the Day of Atonement while Plimo and his family enjoy the meal before the fast. Plimo or members of Plimo's family first bring the beggar some bread outside, as perhaps is their routine when vagrants come to the door. When Satan persists and asks to come in to the warmth of the house, Plimo and his family acquiesce but seat him alone in a separate room, not at the table with the family. Only when he remonstrates again do they admit him to

7. "Plimo" or "Pelimo," though an unusual name for a rabbi, appears in about a dozen rabbinic passages. However, he may have been chosen as protagonist of this story because his name evokes the Greek word *polemos*, meaning "battle" or "strife," a fitting name for this battle cry.

8. See b. B. Bat. 16a, where Resh Laqish states that "Satan, the evil inclination and the angel of death are all one."

9. We should note, however, the grotesque aspect of the bodily orifice being penetrated, as the grotesque recurs later in the story.

full fellowship with them and offer him a seat at the table. We understand that Plimo reluctantly and begrudgingly extends hospitality to the needy; he is hardly the paragon of piety he believes himself to be. Satan, the beggar, wants not only food and drink but the warmth of human fellowship, companionship, and inclusion—but this is denied him.

With his deep bag of tricks, Satan has not finished bringing Plimo's failings to light. Not only does he afflict himself with suppurating sores all over his body, but he acts in a disgusting manner too, perhaps picking at his scabs and flicking them in the air, or squeezing his boils such that pus exudes from them [C]. Plimo and his family cannot stomach such behavior, and they instruct the visitor to knock it off and sit appropriately for the important meal. Now Satan ratchets up his antics by requesting a cup to drink—apparently he had only been given bread to this point—and coughing up phlegm and spittle into the cup. This proves too much for Plimo and Plimo's respectable family. Rather than show compassion or act to ameliorate the suffering, they rebuke Satan for such revolting conduct.[10]

Satan now pretends to die [D]. The news apparently spreads quickly throughout the neighborhood. Exactly who said "Plimo killed a man" is not completely clear. It could be the neighbors, and they need not mean that Plimo committed murder, but that he was somehow responsible for a man's death. It is also possible that Plimo imagined that he heard such words, taking his anxieties as reality. Or it may have been Satan speaking, projecting his voice like a ventriloquist. Whether the words are real or imagined, Plimo becomes distraught and flees to an outhouse, a public latrine [E].

Not yet through with Plimo, Satan pursues him here. We do not know what went through Plimo's mind when he beheld the beggar, now looking very much alive. He may have thought that this was the beggar's spirit or ghost, harassing him for causing the death. Or he may have thought it was a demonic vision inflicted upon him as punishment. Plimo falls down before the poor man, a sign of contrition and atonement, and certainly of capitulation.

At this point Satan takes mercy on Plimo, reveals himself to the sage, and brings home the lesson: Plimo should not have "spoken thus," should not have boasted "An arrow in the eye of Satan" [F]. Plimo is hardly a consummately righteous figure, as Satan easily defeated the sage by inducing him to sin. Now Plimo takes his lumps and accepts Satan's admonition, humbly asking about the appropriate language. Satan teaches the sage to

10. Clearly this scene is a kind of reversal of the book of Job, where Satan afflicts Job with boils all over his body. The suppurating sores exuding pus and the spitting are other grotesque elements.

ask God for help in resisting temptation, "Let the Merciful One rebuke Satan" (based on Zech 3:2). Even the sages are susceptible to moral failings and in need of divine assistance to maintain their piety.

Disgust features prominently in the story and is explicitly emphasized when Satan "does disgusting things" with his boils, the details of which the storyteller mercifully leaves to our imaginations. Skin diseases, sores, and imperfections are considered disgusting in almost every culture, as are bodily secretions such as phlegm, which Satan expectorates in front of the dinner guests.[11] Plimo fails the test of righteousness by his insensitive and callous reactions to the disgusting body and secretions of his guest.[12] Minimally he ought to have expressed compassion at the illness and suffering of a fellow human being, and perhaps even have gone beyond the call of duty and offered to summon a doctor or to procure a salve. Instead Plimo adds insult to injury by humiliating the stranger, instructing him to "sit nicely" in front of all the diners, and then rebuking him in their presence.[13] Plimo has failed Satan's test, failed to suppress his natural feelings of revulsion so as to act with sympathy and kindness.

The denouement therefore appropriately takes place in the latrine, a disgusting place, where human waste is eliminated, also an almost universal source of revulsion.[14] Plimo is brought down from his haughtiness, his sense of self-righteousness and superiority, to the place that collapses all distinctions between rich and poor, high and low, powerful and weak. All humans must excrete waste each day, a reminder of our common humanity and fundamental equality. In a stark contrast to the rarified atmosphere of the holy meal, where food is ingested, Plimo winds up in the structural opposite, the foul-smelling locale where food is eliminated. Plimo's overconfidance has been replaced with abject submission, as he learns that he is no better than others in resisting sin.

Sensitized to the theme of disgust in the story, we might interpret two other narrative elements accordingly. First, Plimo's fleeing from the dead

---

11. On skin, see W. Miller, *Anatomy of Disgust*, 51–60; Kelly, *Yuck!*, 49; S. Miller, *Disgust*, 17–19; Menninghaus, *Disgust*, 52–58. On bodily secretions, see Rozin, Haidt, and McCauley, "Disgust," 757–61; W. Miller, *Anatomy of Disgust*, 89–108; Herz, *That's Disgusting*, 48–52; S. Miller, *Disgust*, 37–38; Kelly, *Yuck!*, 28–29.

12. See the interesting story in b. Qidd. 39b, where a Roman noblewomen (*matronita*) tries to seduce R. Hanina bar Pappi. The rabbi recites a magic formula that covers his body with scabs and boils. Alas, the noblewoman performs a magical act and heals him!

13. I assume that the plural "they rebuked him" refers to Plimo and his servants, or Plimo and his family, who have learned his ways. Even if the pronoun refers to all the guests, it includes Plimo, who, as host, should have taken the lead and shown compassion.

14. See b. Šabb. 10b, "A bathroom is different as it is disgusting"; b. Šabb. 46a, "a chamber pot with excrement is disgusting"; and see the sources collected in Baruch M. Bokser, "Approaching Sacred Space," *HTR* 78 (1985): 279–99. On human waste as a near universal source of disgust, see Rozin, Haidt, and McCauley, "Disgust," 757; Miller, *Anatomy of Disgust*, 135–36.

body may also be motivated by disgust. Corpses are considered among the leading sources of disgust in many cultures. Bodies rot quickly and often become infested with maggots and worms; humans may even have evolved the disgust reflex instinctively to avoid the danger of ingestion or contact with such rotting matter.[15] According to the psychologist Paul Rozin, death is the "chief elicitor" of disgust that ranks highest on the scale of disgust he developed.[16] Moreover, the diseased flesh of the beggar-Satan would give the appearance of a decaying and diseased corpse. Here too Plimo fails to act virtuously, shirking his responsibility to care for the dead. The storyteller may even intend to evoke the *meit mitzvah*, a body with no one to care for its burial. To tend to a *meit mitzvah* is among the most important commandments, yet here Plimo cannot overcome his feeling of disgust to fulfill this obligation.

Second, Plimo's initial reluctance to invite the beggar to the table may also have been motivated by disgust, and not simply by the unwillingness to have an undesirable and potentially annoying guest. Beggars and indigents often reek badly, having less access to bathing and hygiene, especially in antiquity, and often must wear the same clothes for days or weeks on end. Moreover, aristocrats in many cultures believe that the poor give off a stench, whatever the reality.[17] We could understand that Plimo, having whiffed the vile odors of the filthy and disheveled vagrant, at first declines to welcome him into the home, then attempts to keep him in the foyer or a separate room, and only when importuned acquiesces to seat him at dinner.

A fascinating intertext may help us understand the storyteller's message regarding the moral challenge of disgust. Catherine of Siena, a famous medieval Christian "holy woman," Benedictine, and mystic (1347–1380), drank the pus exuding from the sores of those she attended, rubbed her nose in the secretions, and ate scabs and lice in order to overcome her nausea at such ailments. Once, when she was dressing the cancerous sore on the breast of an old woman that exuded a foul stench, Catherine vomited.

15. Kelly, *Yuck!*, 28. Menninghaus, *Disgust*, 1: "The decaying corpse is therefore not only one among many foul smelling and disfigured objects of disgust. Rather, it is *the* emblem of the menace that, in the case of disgust, meets with such a decisive defense, as measured by its extremely potent register on the scale of unpleasurable affects. Every book about disgust is not least a book about the rotting corpse."

16. See "Food for Thought: Paul Rozin's Research and Teaching at Penn," http://www.sas.upenn.edu/sasalum/newsltr/fall97/rozin.html: "This finding led Rozin and his research associates to conclude that 'the most threatening aspect of humans' animalness is their mortality, and that disgust serves as a defense against pondering mortality.' Human consciousness, as it were, accesses the pre-existing distaste system, and all its involuntary mechanisms of revulsion physically force us to avoid contemplating our undeniable predicament: we are animals that must die."

17. W. Miller, *Anatomy of Disgust*, 235–54.

She judged this to be the work of the devil causing her own flesh to revolt, and addressed her body as follows:

> I shall make thee not only to endure the savor of it, but also to receive it within thee. With that she took all the washing of the sore, together with the corrupt matter and filth; and going aside put it all into a cup, and drank it up lustily. And in so doing, she overcame at one time, both the squeamishness of her own stomach and the malice of the devil.[18]

As Catherine faced the old, sick woman, she understood that she was being tested by the devil, as was Plimo in the talmudic story. In contrast to Plimo, she resolved to approach, not reject, the source of repugnance, so as to transcend it. The talmudic storytellers do not expect this exaggerated level of piety (admittedly bordering on madness; Catherine died in her early thirties, and this diet could hardly have helped) from Plimo, but they do require a little more kindness. Indeed, throughout history pious caregivers who ministered to lepers, cared for social outcasts, and prepared dead bodies for burial, have had to transcend feelings of revulsion. Plimo, our talmudic storytellers would have us understand, must do no less.

"Who Varies the Forms of the Creatures"

The rabbis believed that all human beings are created in the image of God. Yet they also understood that it is sometimes difficult to appreciate that theological truth when confronted with the sight of people who strike us as ugly and disgusting. The Talmud contains two blessings to be recited upon beholding people with abnormalities and deformities.

> One who sees an Ethiopian, a person with red skin, one with [unusually] white skin, a hunchback, a dwarf, or a person with a malformed mouth, recites, "Blessed is He who varies the forms of the creatures."
>
> [One who sees] a person with missing limbs, or a blind person, or one with a flattened head, or a lame person, or one who suffers from boils, or one who is pock-marked, recites "Blessed is the true Judge." (b. Ber. 58b) [19]

---

18. W. Miller, *Anatomy of Disgust*, 158–59. See too Caroline Walker Bynum, *Holy Feast and Holy Fast: The Religious Significance of Food to Medieval Women*, New Historicism (Berkeley: University of California Press, 1987), 144, 182. For interesting parallels to the encounter of Satan in the latrine, see Martha Bayless, *Sin and Filth in Medieval Culture: The Devil in the Latrine*, Routledge Studies in Medieval Literature and Culture 2 (New York: Routledge, 2012).

19. There is uncertainty as to the identification of some of these conditions and some variation in the explanations of the talmudic commentators.

The first blessing, the Talmud explains, applies to (what we would call) natural deformities, conditions that originated "in his mother's womb," while the second pertains to those whose condition resulted "after he was born," presumably from diseases and accidents (b. Ber 58b).

All of these conditions are considered disgusting in many cultures. Imperfections of skin, whether in color, texture, or other aspects of appearance, are prime sources of revulsion. Beauty is associated with pure, smooth, and unblemished skin of the right color (depending on the culture), and ugliness and disgust with flawed, scarred, wrinkled, pocked, spotted, furrowed, hairy, rough, folded, discolored, blotchy, mottled, or bulging skin of the wrong color.[20] Skin is the primary and ultimate boundary between one individual and another, between "me" and what is "not me," and constitutes a crucial barrier to potentially dangerous fluids, substances, gases, and diseases that emanate from another individual.[21] It is therefore possible that a disgust reflex evolved to skin abnormalities, although there will inevitably be a culturally specific component as well. We can therefore readily understand why the black-skinned Ethiopian, red- and white-skinned individuals (perhaps albinos are intended) mentioned in the first blessing, and those suffering from boils and pockmarks, referenced in the second blessing, would have elicited disgust.[22]

Physical deformities such as dwarfism and gigantism, and other malformations of the human body, including missing limbs and misshapen appendages, are also common cross-cultural sources of horror and disgust:[23]

> Another aspect of disgust that relates to the body is when the external form is unusually distorted or mutilated. This includes physical deformities, gore, amputees, the very ugly and those who are morbidly obese or skeletally thin.... Mutilation-deformity disgust is also elicited when

---

20. See n. 10.

21. W. Miller, *Anatomy of Disgust*, 51–53; Kelly, *Yuck!*, 49.

22. Black skin, in particular, has been a source of revulsion both in Western culture and in some Jewish sources, so it is not surprising that it begins the first list. See Abraham Melamed, *The Image of the Black in Jewish Culture: A History of the Other*, trans. Betty Sigler Rozen, RoutledgeCurzon Jewish Studies (New York: Routledge, 2003). (But see Goldenberg's savage review of Melamed's book in *JQR* 93 [2003]: 557–79.) Cf. David M. Goldenberg, *The Curse of Ham: Race and Slavery in Early Judaism, Christianity, and Islam*, Jews, Christians, and Muslims from the Ancient to the Modern World (Princeton: Princeton University Press, 2003), 250. And see George Yancy, *Black Bodies, White Gazes: The Continuing Significance of Race* (Lanham, MD: Rowman & Littlefield, 2008), 7: "[T]he governing norms of white philosophical anthropology marked Black bodies as disgusting and occluded from the realm of the conceptually white *anthropos*." See too pp. 243–62.

23. W. Miller, *Anatomy of Disgust*, 105; Menninghaus, *Disgust*, 78–84: "As a counter-image to the ideally beautiful state of *eternal youth* and the *springtime of life*, death thus represents the repellent vanishing point or last station of the disgust-series comprised by folds, wrinkles, openings, excrescences, and dismembered limbs" (80).

> normal bodies have been maimed in some way that we aren't attracted to, even when no blood or serious harm seems involved.[24]

Almost every deviation from the norm of an intact, symmetrical body tends to be associated with ugliness and revulsion, and the greater the deviation, the greater the potential to disgust.[25] In fact, in the late nineteenth century many American cities passed so called "ugly laws" that forbade mutilated and deformed people from appearing in public. The legislation passed in 1881 by the Chicago City Council, for example, prohibited "any person who is diseased, maimed, mutilated or deformed in any way, so as to be an unsightly or disgusting object, to expose himself to public view."[26] The hunchback, dwarf, amputee, malformed mouth, and flattened head mentioned in the blessings are therefore likely to provoke a reaction of disgust. Likewise those who are lame and blind—presumably the blindness marked in some way, either by missing or misshapen eyes, or signaled by a cane or other implement, as we do today—would also be viewed with revulsion.[27]

The talmudic blessings are calculated to reframe the instinctive and/or culturally mediated reaction of disgust that the viewer experiences upon seeing other human beings in these states. The first blessing reminds the viewer that these people too are created by God, and that the varied forms of humans are part of the grandeur of God's creation which enriches the world. Elsewhere the Mishnah teaches that "humanity was created as a singleton," that is, Adam was created alone, "to tell of the greatness of God. For a human being stamps many coins with one seal, and they are all identical to each other. But the supreme King of Kings, the Holy Blessed one, stamps every human being with the seal of the first man, and not one is identical to his fellow" (m. Sanh. 4:5; b. Ber. 37a). Thus, the diversity of human appearances, shapes, and sizes in and of itself testifies to God's greatness in creating a mechanism that resulted in an infinite variety of forms that all descended from the same human being. The blessing "who varies the forms of his creatures" extends that theological principle to atypical or abnormal appearances, directing the beholder to keep his or her emotions in check and concentrate rather on the divine element in all creation.

The second blessing, "Blessed is the true judge," is the same blessing that is recited upon hearing bad news or news of a death in the family (m. Sanh. 9:2; b. Ber. 59b). It acknowledges divine providence and the hand of God in all happenings, good and bad alike. The blessing helps the viewer

---

24. Herz, *That's Disgusting*, 39.

25. Ibid., 168.

26. Susan Schweik, "Ugly Laws," in *Encyclopedia of Disability*, ed. Gary L. Albrecht, 5 vols. (Thousand Oaks, CA: Sage, 2006), 4:1575.

27. See W. Miller, *Anatomy of Disgust*, 90–91, 203.

understand that such unfortunate ailments are in some way part of God's plan, or at least a function of God's decree, and therefore must be accepted along with other negative experiences. Ideally, this awareness tempers the initial disgust reflex, which, if allowed to express itself fully, might cause the afflicted individual embarrassment and humiliation. There is also an unfair tendency to blame those we hold in revulsion for their own condition, for inflicting their disgustingness upon us.[28] The blessing neutralizes this inclination by asserting divine responsibility. It therefore assists and encourages adherents to rise to the moral challenge of suppressing disgust and reacting with compassion and sympathy.

Disgust and Humility

When disgust precludes compassion toward others or causes humiliation, it must be overcome. But when disgust functions to prevent, rather than to induce, sin, it should be cultivated. Consider the following teaching from m. 'Abot 3:1:

Akavia ben Mahalalel says: Keep your eye on three things, and you will not come to sin: Know from where you came, and to where you are going, and before Whom you are destined to give an account and a reckoning.	עקביה בן מהללאל אומר, הסתכל בשלושה דברים, ואין אתה בא לידי עבירה--דע מאיין באת, ולאיין אתה הולך, ולפני מי אתה עתיד ליתן דין וחשבון
From where did you come? From **a putrid drop**.	מאיין באת, **מטיפה סרוחה.**
And to where are you going? To a place of **dust, worms, and maggots**.	ולאיין אתה הולך, **למקום רימה ותולעה.**
And before Whom are you destined to give an account and a reckoning? Before the King of Kings, the Holy One, blessed be He.	ולפני מי אתה עתיד ליתן דין וחשבון, לפני מלך מלכי המלכים הקדוש ברוך הוא

This tradition emphasizes the disgusting origins and ends of human life, repulsive bookends that suggest everything in between, namely, our entire lives, is not free of disgust. Every human being originated in a "putrid drop" of semen and will ultimately decay in the grave, the body doomed to rot and fill with worms and maggots. This miserable, inescap-

28. W. Miller, *Anatomy of Disgust*, 203. "Probably the greatest homage we pay to our anxiety about condemning those who disgust us is our constructions of stories making the stigmatized blamable in the restricted sense demanded by guilt.... If we cannot quite blame the blind for their blindness we get around it by blaming them for not remaining invisible."

able fate of humans contrasts sharply with the eternal and majestic King of Kings, before whom all souls justify themselves in the next world.

As noted above, dead bodies themselves are prime sources of disgust, as are maggots, worms, other insects and creeping things. Bodily secretions, especially those that emerge from genitals, are considered repulsive in many cultures. Semen is a source of impurity in biblical and rabbinic law and also is associated with disgust in other rabbinic sources.[29] Meditating on the lowly and disgraceful nature of oneself should instill a sense of humility and inhibit feelings of arrogance and haughtiness, which are undesirable or even sinful traits.[30] Thus, the Mishnaic commentator Ovadia of Bertinuro explains, "One who contemplates that he came from a 'putrid drop' will be saved from pride. And one who contemplates that he is destined to go 'to a place of dust, worms, and maggots,' will be saved from illicit desire, and from lust for money."[31] Contemplation of our ignominious origins will obviate the sin of pride, while the focus on the repulsive fate of the body will preclude illicit sexual desire, as one will see the object of lust not as a beautiful and alluring man or woman but as a sack of filth and corruption. Likewise, for Bertinuro, greed for riches will be tempered by picturing one's rancid corpse—why strive to amass a fortune when all material possessions can do nothing to forestall such a fate?

Disgust and Sexual Sin

Bertinuro's interpretation of disgust's potential to thwart "illicit desire" (*ta'avah*) features in several rabbinic narratives, including the following story from 'Abot R. Nat. A 16:2.[32]

When he (Rabbi Akiba) travelled to Rome, he was slandered to the governor. The governor sent him two beautiful women. He had them bathe and anoint themselves, and he adorned them like brides for their grooms. They fell upon the Rabbi the entire night: This one said, "Come be with me." That one said, "Come be with me."	כשהלך (ר' עקיבא) לרומי אוכילו קורצא אצל שלטון אחד, ושיגר לו שתי נשים יפות. רחצום וסכום וקשטום ככלות חתנים, והיו מתנפלות עליו כל הלילה. זאת אומרת חזור אצלי, וזאת אומרת חזור אצלי.

29. See b. 'Abod. Zar. 68b; and Rashi, s.v. *uleta'ameikh*.

30. Catherine of Siena too was motivated by humility; see W. Miller, *Anatomy of Disgust*, 157–62.

31. Ovadia of Bertinuro, commentary to m. 'Abot 3:1.

32. *Avot d'Rabbi Natan*, ed. S. Schechter (London, 1887), 32a; Hans-Jürgen Becker, *Avot de-Rabbi Natan: Synoptische Edition beider Versionen*, TSAJ 116 (Tübingen: Mohr Siebek, 2006), 166–67.

But he sat between them and spat,[33] and did not look at them.	והיה יושב ביניהם ומרקק, ולא פנה אליהן.
The next morning they went and complained to the governor. They said, "Death is preferable to us than to be given to a man like that."	הלכו להן והקבילו פני השלטון, ואמרו לו: שווה לנו המות משתתננו לאיש הזה.
The governor summoned Rabbi Akiba and said to him: "Why do you not do with these women as is customary for men to do with women? Are they not beautiful? Are they not human beings like you? Did He who created you not also create them?"	שלח וקרא לו, אמר לו: מפני מה לא עשית עם הנשים הללו כדרך שבני אדם עושים לנשים? לא יפות המה, לא בנות אדם כמותך הן, מי שברא אותך לא ברא אותם?
Rabbi Akiba said to him: "What can I do, for their stench came upon me from carrion, un-kosher meat, and reptiles?" [Some texts read: "Their stench came upon me **like** that of carrion and swine?"[34]]	אמר לו: מה אעשה, ריחן בא עלי מבשר נבלות וטרפות ומבשר שרצים (נוסח אחר: כבשר נבלות וכבשר חזיר)

In this story, R. Akiba is the target of some unspecified slanderous accusation, and the Roman governor, apparently seeking more concrete evidence of wrongdoing, attempts to entrap the rabbi in a sex scandal, a ménage à trois with two gentile women. R. Akiba resists the seductresses, who are so insulted by his rejection of their sexual advances that they return to the governor complaining in hyperbolic terms about this mistreatment. When the governor asks R. Akiba to explain his refusal to sleep with these beautiful and desirable women, the rabbi responds that their foul stench made it impossible to engage in sexual congress.

Leaving aside the obscure and convoluted logic of this narrative (Why does the governor need to entrap R. Akiba rather than just arrest him? Why choose this tactic? And what crime is involved in sleeping with two slaves or prostitutes?), we should note the role of disgust as a counter to sin. When the courtesans "fall upon" R. Akiba in an attempt to seduce him, he spits and refuses to look at them, presumably focusing on his spittle instead. Spit is frequently identified as a disgusting substance in talmudic sources, as it is in many cultures (b. Ber. 62b; b. Ḥag. 15b).[35] Even

33. Some text witnesses omit "spit."

34. This reading is found in the parallel version of the story published in Pesiqta de Rab Kahana, "Liqutei midrash," ed. Bernard Mandelbaum (New York: Jewish Theological Seminary, 1987), 461.

35. W. Miller, *Anatomy of Disgust*, 97-98; Kelly, *Yuck!*, 28; Herz, *That's Disgusting*, 35–37, 179.

the thought of swallowing one's own saliva once expectorated into a cup will occasion disgust. In this way R. Akiba stimulated his own disgust reflex as a bulwark against the machinations of the temptresses. The focus on the spittle and the emotion of revulsion helped inhibit feelings of sexual arousal.

In his response to the Roman governor R. Akiba explains that, despite their physical beauty, he could not have sex because he was overwhelmed by a disgusting odor. Some manuscripts refer to carrion (*neveilot*), that is, meat from animals that died naturally and were not ritually slaughtered, and to non-kosher meat, that is, meat from animals that had internal defects in their main organs,[36] and reptiles, while others mention pig explicitly. All of these are proscribed by the Jewish dietary laws and would therefore be considered repulsive to a rabbi (carrion and various reptiles are considered repulsive to eat in many cultures). There are also textual variants as to whether the odor came *from* such types of meat or the odor of the women "came upon" the Rabbi *like* the odor of these animals. The former reading suggests that the women had consumed such meat in their previous meals and the odor remained on their bodies, or came from their mouths when they breathed, having been incorporated somatically. The latter probably implies that the women did not emit any such odor, but R. Akiba, through a mental process, imagined the women eating such a diet, apparently a typical gentile diet (or the rabbinic conception of a typical gentile diet), and experienced revulsion at such thoughts. Because the Roman governor bathed and anointed the women in an effort to beautify them, I prefer the latter reading. The different readings entail slightly different didactic points. According to the first reading, a physical odor exudes from the women themselves and assaults R. Akiba's senses involuntarily. Overcome by disgust, he cannot become aroused. According to the second reading, R. Akiba must proactively stimulate his disgust reflex, as he did by spitting, so as to refrain from sin. Realizing the danger of being seduced by two determined women, he deliberately conjured up a source of disgust associated with these women and thereby succeeds in preserving his virtue. As opposed to the case of Plimo, in situations like this disgust should be cultivated and encouraged, rather than suppressed and overcome.

A more graphic (and misogynistic) variation of this theme, that is, the mobilization of disgust to obviate sexual sin, appears in a late midrashic tale about a student of R. Akiba:

> It happened of a student of R. Akiba who sat before 24,000 disciples that he once went out to the marketplace of the harlots. He saw there a harlot woman and fell in love with her, and a messenger brought mes-

36. Roughly; the technical definition of a *tereifah* is more complicated.

sages between them throughout the day until evening. That evening she ascended on the rooftop and saw him sitting at the head of his disciples like a general, and the Angel Gabriel was standing at his right hand. She said to herself, "Alas for this woman [= me], for all the sufferings of Gehennom [hell] are designated for her. A great man like that, who resembles a king—this woman [= me] afflicts him, such that when she dies and passes from this world she will inherit Gehennom. But if he accepts her [words], she can save both him and her from the punishments of Gehennom."[37]

When he came to her, she said to him: "My son! Why are you losing your life in the World to Come for one hour (of pleasure) in this world?" But his passion did not cool down until she said to him, "The place you love is the dirtiest and filthiest of all the limbs, a sack full of excrement and refuse, and no living creature can stand its smell."[38] Yet his passion did not cool down until she grabbed his nose and put it on her genitals.[39] When he smelled its odor he was disgusted, and never married a woman. A divine voice went forth and said, "The woman So-and-so and the man So-and-so are destined for life in the World to Come."

This bizarre narrative (bizarre even by rabbinic standards[40]) in some ways is the mirror image of the previous source. Instead of the women attempting to seduce the rabbi and the rabbi heroically resisting, the rabbi pursues the woman, who heroically resists. Indeed, the prostitute is the true heroine, a kind of inverse femme fatale who saves the holy rabbi from temptation and sin. Instead of the rabbi activating his own disgust reflex by spitting and smelling (or imagining the smell of) the noxious odors of his seductresses, the prostitute first attempts to stimulate the rabbi's

37. *Eliyahu Zuta*, ed. Meir Ish-Shalom (Vienna, 1904; repr. Jerusalem: Wahrmann, 1949), chapter 22, pp. 39–40: מעשה בתלמיד אחד מתלמידי ר' עקיבא שהיה יושב בראש עשרים וארבעה אלפים תלמידים, פעם אחת יצא לשוק של זונות וראה שם אשה זונה ואהב אותה, והיה שליח משתלח בינו לבינה עד עת הערב, לעת הערב עלתה על הגג וראתה אותו כשהוא יושב בראש התלמידים כשר צבא והיה גבריאל עומד על ימינו, אמרה [בלבה] אוי לה לאותה אשה שכל מיני פורענות של גיהנם צואת לה, אדם גדול כמו זה שהוא דומה למלך תענינו אשה זאת וכשמתה ובטלה מן העולם יורשת גיהנם, אלא אם יקבלנה הרי היא מצלת אותו (ולעצמי) [ולעצמה] מדינה של גיהנם, וכיון שבא אצלה אמרה לו, בני מפני מה אתה מאבד חיי העוה"ב בשביל שעה אחת בעוה"ז, לא נתקררה דעתו עד שאמרה לו, בני מקום שאתה אוהב מלוכלך ומטונף מכל אברים [חמת מלא צואה וזבל] ואין כל בריה יכולה להריח ריחו, ולא נתקררה דעתו עד (שתפשו) [שתפשתו] בחוטמו (והניחו) [והניחתו] על אותו (קבר) [הקבר], כיון שהריח ריחו נמאס בפניו ולא נשא אשה (מעולם) [לעולם], יצתה בת קול ואמרה אשה פלונית ואיש פלוני (מזומן) [מזומנין] לחיי העוה"ב.

38. Cf. b. Šabb. 152a.

39. *Qever*. On *qever* referring to the uterus, see Marcus Jastrow, *A Dictionary of the Targumim, the Talmud Babli and Yerushalmi and the Midrashic Literature* (New York, 1893; repr. New York: Judaica Press, 1989), 1313, s.v. קֶבֶר.

40. See Ish-Shalom's note, *Eliyahu Zuta*, ad loc. "I know of no similar story." However, the story of R. Eleazar b. Dordia, who travels to a famous prostitute in a distant land but is saved from sinning when she farts just before intercourse, has something in common (b. ʿAbod. Zar. 17a).

disgust reflex by telling him of the repugnant stench of female genitalia, and, when that fails, forcing him to smell her genitals. Here too the strategy succeeds: the disgust tactic is so effective the rabbi could never bring himself to marry for the rest of his life (an interesting breach of rabbinic norms, incidentally, but not our concern here).[41] In place of R. Akiba saved from this-worldly arrest and punishment by the Roman official, both the student and the prostitute are saved from otherworldly punishment in Gehennom and are guaranteed entry into the World to Come. Again disgust is construed in a positive manner, having an appropriate and even necessary role in the constant struggle to avoid sin.

In sum, disgust operates in two different and even opposing ways in the rabbinic moral economy. On the one hand, disgust poses a moral challenge: involuntary feelings of disgust, whether instinctual, culturally determined, or a combination of both, toward the poor, the socially marginal, the dismembered, the handicapped, and the diseased, must be suppressed. Failure to overcome one's disgust, and certainly outward expressions of disgust that humiliate such others, is sinful, whereas suppression of disgust so as to show kindness and compassion contributes to virtuous character and ethical good. On the other hand, disgust should be cultivated, even actively stimulated, as a means to avoid sin. This can be done daily, through contemplation of the disgusting origin, fate, and even fundamental nature of the self and of all human beings, so as to instill humility and guard against pride. Likewise, disgust should be mobilized when one is tempted by sexual and other sins as a means of resisting the allures of the flesh or other illicit acts. What the Talmud states of the sexual inclination (*yetser*), "Always let the left hand drive away and the right hand draw near" (b. Sanh. 107b), might aptly be said of disgust too.

---

41. See Daniel Boyarin, *Carnal Israel: Reading Sex in Talmudic Culture*, New Historicism 25 (Berkeley: University of California Press, 1993), 134–36.

The Place of Shabbat

On the Architecture of the Opening Sugya of Tractate Eruvin (2a–3a)

CHARLOTTE ELISHEVA FONROBERT
Stanford University

As is well known, the "opening" *sugya* of a tractate or sometimes of a chapter in the Babylonian Talmud is a textual phenomenon that has exercised the minds of scholars from the beginnings of talmudic scholarship. From Geonic days, to the "Wissenschaft" scholars in Europe in the nineteenth and early twentieth century, and their successors in Israel, it was such talmudic *sugyot* in particular that lent themselves to the question of the making of the Talmud.[1] Thus, the "mother" of all opening *sugyot* in this long line of argument has been the opening *sugya* of Tractate Qiddushin, exhorted by Rav Sherira Gaon in his *Iggeret* as a product of the so-called Saboraim, successors of the Amoraim.[2] The Wissenschaft scholars continued that line of argument and mainly sought to expand the list of *sugyot* for which Saboraic provenance could be argued. Following Nehemiah Brüll, Avraham Weiss identified other *sugyot* that exhibited characteristics similar to the opening *sugya* of Tractate Qiddushin.[3]

This contribution to the Festschrift honors Shaye J. D. Cohen's work on Sabbath law, e.g., "Sabbath Law and Mishnah Shabbat in Origen *De Principiis*," *JSQ* 17 (2010): 160–89; as well as his editorial and translation work for the Oxford Study Mishnah, for which he translated and annotated Mishnah Shabbat, while I did Mishnah Eruvin. This piece therefore serves as a reflection of my work on the sister tractate of Shabbat. I would like to thank especially Michael Satlow, Marjorie Lehman, and Gil Klein for their helpful suggestions.

1. One of the most recent discussion of and revisions to the theories of the making of the Talmud has been presented by Moulie Vidas in his *Tradition and the Formation of the Talmud* (Princeton: Princeton University Press, 2014). His careful and thoughtful analysis of the first *sugya* of Bava Qamma (2a–3b) constitutes a major piece for his rethinking of the work of the *stam*, the anonymous voice of the *sugya*. However, the position of the *sugya* as opening *sugya* as such does not matter to his analysis.

2. B. M. Lewin, ed., *Iggeret Rav Sherira Gaon* (1921; repr., Jerusalem: Makor, 1962), 71. See also Avinoam Cohen, "Regarding the Nature of Saboraic Halakhah: The Bavli's *Sugya* at the Beginning of Kiddushin and the Geonic Reception," *Dinei Israel* 24 (2007): 161–214.

3. N. Brüll, "Die Entstehungsgeschichte des Babylonischen Talmuds als Schriftwerk," in *Jahrbücher für jüdische Geschichte und Literatur II*, ed. N. Brüll (Frankfurt, 1876) 43ff.). A.

As far as the "opening *sugya*"—or the *petihah*, as Weiss refers to it—as a textual phenomenon is concerned, the discussion has mostly been dominated by efforts to identify formal criteria, in the service of dating the material in the textual genesis of the Bavli, such as first and foremost the anonymity of the material.[4]

In this discussion, however, another question has mostly fallen by the wayside. That is, the chronological or textual-historical relationship of opening *sugyot* to the rest of the tractate or to the Talmud as a whole is only one question that can be raised about the particular textual phenomenon. But what were to happen if we ask about the literary or conceptual relationship that these particular *sugyot* have with the rest of the tractate?[5] If we agree that opening *sugyot* are well edited and among the latest editorial work of the Talmud, then can we ask how far opening *sugyot* serve to *introduce* and not just "open" a tractate?[6] Much as introductions to books

---

Weiss attributes the introductory sections to what he identifies as the younger Saboraim (*Saboräer*) (*Ha-yetzirah shel ha-Sabora'im* [The Literary Activities of the Saboraim], Hebrew University lecture of 31 December 1952, pbl. by Magnes Press). He identifies especially and primarily the opening segments as examples of the Saboraic teachings (explanations and assumptions) that became part of the talmudic text itself. He lists seven examples of opening *sugyot* that he considers to be totally "Saboraic": Eruv. 2a; Yebam. 2b; Qidd. 2a–3b, Ned. 2b–3a, Naz. 2a–b, Soṭah 2a, Šeb. 2b–3a, p.44 n.62. Weiss (*Ha-yetzirah shel ha-Sabora'im*, 9) cites Brüll's note and provides additional examples (13–14). I should say that his formulation does not include the term *sugya*, as in a clearly defined unit of talmudic discourse. He writes of "die zu Anfang mehrerer Tractate sich befindenden *Erörterungen*," the generic German term for discourses. His list in fact includes segments of text of a variety of length that may or may not fall in the category of what one would refer to as *sugya*. Hence, Weiss refers to the beginning segment of Eruvin as a "note."

4. Other criteria hover somewhere on the border of form and substance, such as the presumed interest of the shapers of such *sugyot* in the precise language of the first mishnaic paragraph of the tractate, or in the place of the relevant mishnaic tractate in the *seder*; see Weiss, *Ha-yetzirah shel ha-Sabora'im*, 9, following Brüll. Yaakov Elman specifies the substantive criteria even more, such as the focus on grammatical issues in the opening *sugya* of Qiddushin ("The World of the 'Sabboraim': Cultural Aspects of Post-Redactional Additions to the Bavli," in *Creation and Composition: The Contribution of the Bavli Redactors (Stammaim) to the Aggada*, ed. Jeffrey L. Rubenstein, TSAJ 114 (Tübingen: Mohr Siebeck 2005), 383–85. Jeffrey Rubenstein also made the case for the long sequence of aggadic material at the beginning of Tractate Avodah Zarah to be read as an "opening *sugya*" (*Talmudic Stories: Narrative Art, Composition, and Culture* (Baltimore: Johns Hopkins University Press, 1999), 212–42.

5. This has been argued to great effect by Mira Wasserman for the opening of Tractate Avodah Zarah. Building on Rubenstein's identification of that opening as belonging in the genre of opening *sugya*, she discusses how that opening *sugya* does the work of "literary" introduction to the first chapter and the tractate as a whole (*Jews, Gentiles, and Other Animals: The Talmud after the Humanities*, Divinations (Philadelphia: University of Pennsylvania Press, 2017), 36–73.

6. Brüll writes that "wahrscheinlich wurden damit [CEF: opening *sugyot*] die Lehrvorträge, die dann den talmudischen Text zu Grundlage hatten, *eingeleitet*" ("Die Entstehungs-

are often written or edited only after the main body of the book is finished, can one think of "introductory" *sugyot* as *hakdamot*, "forewords," intended to introduce the study of a tractate and its conceptual or intellectual underpinnings? Are they therefore shaped with aesthetic and conceptual or theoretical concerns in mind, and not just by purely formal criteria as identified by scholars like Brüll and Weiss?[7] Arguably, it is this aspect that might allow us to ask different questions about the shaping of rabbinic "thought."

In this contribution I will focus on one particular opening *sugya*, that of Eruvin.[8] My goal is to show not only that this *sugya* is purposefully and artfully composed,[9] and that it is a post-Amoraic composition that in its main section draws on earlier Amoraic material,[10] as well as supplementing later distinct segments, but also that the final architects[11] of the *sugya* in the form in which we have it in front of us had meta-halakhic, conceptual criteria in mind when they added the various seemingly disparate parts together. Those criteria provide a conceptual framework for the study of Tractate Eruvin as a whole, lending the tractate, beyond its task of following the course of study paved by the mishnaic tractate, the veneer of an overarching intellectual project.

From the *sugya* emerges a map of building structures that bear what I want to describe as *inherent* Jewish meaning in various ways: Sukkah, Temple and its sub-structures, as well as biblical structures. All of these structures are called upon to "think with" for the discussion of the one that is the least obviously "Jewish" or "halakhic," and that is the subject of the

---

geschichte," 47). It is not entirely clear to me how he imagines this, but he does not elaborate, so there is little to go on.

7. See Louis Jacobs, "The Talmudic *Sugya* as a Literary Unit," *JJS* 24 (1974): 119–26.

8. The boundaries of this or any *sugya* as a literary unit are not always self-evident. Uri Zur determines the first *sugya* (*sugyat ha-petihah*) to continue to b. Eruv. 10a, the next lemma of the mishnaic paragraph (*Or Israel: Editorial Considerations in the Redaction of Sugyot in Tractate Eruvin of the Babylonian Talmud, Chapter 1–3* [Hebrew] [Lod: Haberman Institute for Literary Research, 1999], 17 n. 2). Within that long *sugya*, which, for Zur "serves as ornamentation" (vii), he determines further subdivisions. By his definition a *sugya* is all of the textual material related to one mishnaic paragaph (13 n. 1). I focus here on 2a–3a as a textual unit, based on the substantive criteria suggested in this essay.

9. Jacobs presents a number of models ("Talmudic *Sugya*"). Moulie Vidas essentially follows and builds on Jacobs "in looking at the *sugya* as a carefully planned literary construct" (*Tradition and the Formation*, 28). So in a sense my reading of the opening *sugya* of Eruvin presented here adds to the ever-growing library of *sugyot* as our primary talmudic texts.

10. As pointed to by Weiss, *Ha-yetzirah shel ha-Sabora'im*, 13.

11. There is no perfect way to refer to the hand that provided the final shape of the *sugya*. Some scholars use "authors of the *sugya*" (Vidas, *Tradition and the Formation*, e.g., 41). I find "architects" an apt term for the purpose of this essay about the talmudic map of Jewish building structures.

tractate and is ritually replicated to this day, namely, the ordinary, generic alleyway,[12] the urban street of mishnaic (and talmudic) days.[13] The Mishnah moves the urban alleyway into the foreground of Sabbath law, in fact opens its Tractate Eruvin with it, prompting the architects of the Bavli's introductory *sugya* to provide this seemingly nondescript urban structure with Jewish resonance of various rhetorical registers. The Sabbath in a manner of speaking is *located*, not only pragmatically in residential spaces where Jews are assumed to dwell—the home, the urban street, the town—but also with respect to a much larger conceptual map of Jewish memory, architecture, and cultural or even theological geography. Before we can proceed with investigating the stakes of this project, we need to outline this map.

Between Urban Street and Temple: The Tannaitic Texts

Like its sister tractate Shabbat,[14] the mishnaic tractate of Eruvin opens with a focus on residential space, the former on the domestic dwelling,

12. The presumption for the opening paragraph of the mishnaic tractate, discussed below, is not only that structurally the alleyway is walled, but that it is a cul-de-sac, although the language does not specify this. M. Shabbat 16:1 mentions an open or a through street (*mavoi mefulash*) versus one that is "not a through street" as backdrop for the halakhic dispute there, but in Eruvin the Mishnah uses only the generic term (*mavoi*), which engenders extensive discussions in the Bavli as to what type of alleyway is implied.

13. I use alley, alleyway, and street interchangeably throughout this essay, mostly for convenience and stylistic reasons. Talmudic literature has a variety of terms to refer to urban and extra-urban foot and vehicular traffic-ways, which have been discussed in a variety of contexts. See, e.g., Gil Klein, "Spatial Struggle: Intercity Relations and the Topography of Intra-Rabbinic Competition," in *Religious Competition in the Third Century CE: Jews, Christians, and the Greco-Roman World*, ed. Jordan D. Rosenblum, Lily C. Vuong, and Nathaniel P. DesRosiers, JAJSup 15 (Göttingen: Vandenhoeck & Ruprecht, 2014), 153–67. Klein focuses on the Palestinian rabbinic texts, and especially the Galilean towns of Sepphoris and Tiberias. On the urban built environment as the setting for mishnaic discourse, with a focus on the *bayit*, the *shuq*, and the *ḥatzer* (the shared courtyard), see Cynthia Baker, *Rebuilding the House of Israel:Architectures of Gender in Jewish Antiquity*, Divinations (Stanford, CA: Stanford University Press, 2001). For socio-archaeological work on the street in contemporaneous Roman urban environment, see Mary Beard, "Street Life," the second chapter of her magisterial *Pompeii: The Life of a Roman Town* (London: Profile Books, 2008). On the importance of the street to thinking about the city, see Jane Jacobs's classic *The Death and Life of Great American Cities* (New York: Random House, 2011 [orig. 1961]). I focus here on the alley (*mavo'*), a smaller urban passageway that connects walled, shared courtyards (*chazerot*). In Tractate Eruvin such alleyways function as the urban connective tissue between residences beyond the shared courtyards.

14. On the suggestion that Mishnah Shabbat and Eruvin were originally one tractate, see A. Goldberg, following J. N. Epstein, in his critically annotated edition of MS Kaufmann, *Perush la-Mishnah: Masekhet Eruvin* (Jerusalem: Magnes, 1986). There is no manuscript evidence for this. Nonetheless, Eruvin is obviously dependent on Shabbat.

the home (*bayit*),[15] the latter on the urban alleyway. The opening teachings of both mishnaic tractates, Shabbat and Eruvin, focus on the boundary of their respective residential spaces, Shabbat on the entry (or window) into the house, Eruvin on the entry to the urban alleyway. However, whereas in m. Shab. 1:1 the house serves as a backdrop only for staging a halakhic case scenario, in m. Eruv. 1:1 the entry turns into the subject of halakhic reflection itself:

> If an [entry to an][16] alleyway is higher than twenty cubits
> one should reduce it.
> Rabbi Judah says: This is not necessary.
> And one wider than ten cubits
> one should reduce it.
> But if it has the shape of a doorway,
> then even if it is wider than ten cubits,
> one does not need to reduce it. [m. Eruv. 1:1][17]

This teaching in Tractate Eruvin is in fact somewhat surprising with its injunction to adjust the height of the entrance to the urban alleyway, surprising because it is not obvious why such an alleyway, or the urban street, should need a doorway or a shape of a doorway, or even less obvious, why its height should be adjusted. This is not merely a case of the normal assumption of mishnaic didactics that every teaching assumes that one already knows all other teachings. Rather, it is simply not clear why the mundane alleyway or its entrance should be a subject of interest to rabbinic halakhah. Minimally, therefore, the effect of this ruling is to turn the urban alleyway into a halakhically relevant space, one that becomes subject to halakhic reflection, if only for the purposes of the Sabbath. The alley is thus lifted out of the fabric of the built environment of Jewish urban life with which the authors of the Mishnah would be familiar to become endowed with halakhic purposefulness. In and of itself the

---

15. M. Shabbat 1:1 stages the halakhic concern about the boundary between the abstract "inside" and "outside," across which one is prohibited to transport anything on the Sabbath, at the entrance (or window?) of a residential house, with a "poor person" (*'oni*) outside (*ba-hutz*), and the householder (*ba'al ha-bayit*) inside (*bif'nim*).

16. The mishnaic term *mavoi* (biblical *mavo*) generally refers to the entire structure of the alleyway, but in this opening statement it seems to refer to the entryway that marks the border between the public realm and the alleyway. See also A. Goldberg, *The Mishna Treatise Eruvin Critically Edited* (Jerusalem: Magnes, 1986), 1. The medieval commentators, beginning with Rashi, mostly assume that in fact the term here refers specifically to the crossbeam mentioned in 1:2 only.

17. Translations of the rabbinic texts are my own. For translation of mishnaic texts in this paper I follow the procedure of the *Oxford Study Mishnah* (forthcoming), edited by the honoree of this Festschrift, Shaye Cohen, together with Hayim Lapin and Robert Goldenberg. The translation is based on the printed Vilna edition, with important differences in the best manuscripts (Kaufmann and Parma) mentioned in the footnotes where relevant.

alley is not necessarily a *Jewishly* significant space, and certainly not one familiar in any way from biblical or postbiblical law, but the rabbis of the Mishnah turn this preexisting subunit of the urban landscape, prosaic as it may seem in its residential functionality, into a *halakhic* project.[18] Later in the tractate (m. Eruv. 7:6–10), that halakhic project emerges as what is termed the *shittuf mevo'ot*,[19] the "partnering of alleys," a ritual performance involving symbolic food sharing, a public declaration thereof by the ritual actor(s), and fictive property transfer, all staged in the alleyway.[20] The ritual performance is designed essentially to transform a collectivity of residents in an alley into a residential community, in order to allow the residents to "share the road" and to make use of it on the Sabbath the way one would on any other day of the week, by carrying into it, depositing objects or moving items around within it.

The prominence of the street in Sabbath law in the Mishnah indeed seems puzzling, and so the various para- and post-mishnaic reflections on this mishnaic text, from the Tosefta to our opening *sugya* in the Babylonian Talmud, connect the street that frames and situates rabbinic Sabbath law to a structural space that above all bears inherent Jewish significance and meaning, namely, the Temple.

The Tosefta glosses our mishnaic teaching in the following way:

> If an alley-entry is higher than twenty cubits,
> *more than the doorway (pitḥo) of the sanctuary (hekhal),*
> it needs to be reduced.
> ...[21]
> A width beyond ten cubits,
> *more than the doorway of the* hekhal,
> It needs to be reduced.
>
> (T. Eruv. 1:1; my emphases)[22]

18. I am uncertain whether halakhic is an appropriate or sufficient term here for this project, since the *shittuf mevo'ot* and its smaller-scale cousin the *eruv ḥatzerot* are in fact rabbinic ritual innovations and therefore might more effectively be described as ritual projects in the veneer of halakhic rhetoric.

19. The Mishnah (m. Eruv. 6:8 and esp. 7:6-10) uses only the verbal form, as in "how do they make a partnering [*mishtatefin*] in the alley?" (7:6). Cf. also m. Eruv. 8:1, for the partnering of *tehumim*. The Tosefta has the nominal form (t. Eruv. 6:1, *shittuf mavoi*).

20. On the surprising role of women in this ritual, see Judith Hauptman, "Women in Tractate Eruvin: From Social Dependence to Legal Independence" [Hebrew], *Mada'ei ha-Yahadut* 40 (2000): 145–58, as well as my own "Gender Politics in the Rabbinic Neighborhood: Tractate Eruvin," in *A Feminist Commentary on the Babylonian Talmud*, Introduction and Studies, ed. Tal Ilan et al.;Tübingen: Mohr Siebeck, 2007), 43–61.

21. The omitted phrase, an instruction on how to reduce the height, is not central to the line of thought pursued here.

22. My translation of the Toseftan texts is based on S. Lieberman's critical edition, *The Tosefta* (New York and Jerusalem: Jewish Theological Seminary, 1962; repr., 2002).

The Toseftan gloss here repeatedly, and therefore seemingly emphatically invokes the doorway of the Temple's sanctuary building as a reference point for the entry to the urban alley, thereby in pronounced fashion transforming the prosaic tone of the Mishnah. Still, as a gloss only, it is no more than suggestive so its purpose is not entirely clear: it may be of a hermeneutic nature, in that the *baraita* focuses on the detail of the measurement in the mishnaic paragraph and implicitly connects the teaching in Eruvin with the architectural data of the Temple's structures as the Mishnah teaches them elsewhere.[23] Alternately, it is possible that the Tosefta seeks to add a theological component, a remark on the centrality of the Temple to all things architectural, however ephemeral.[24] The gloss might suggest a literary analogy or have in mind an actual guideline for the design of urban streetways, as an injunction not to build higher than "the church" in town.

Either way, the Temple and its sanctuary are hereby invoked as a reference point, and the urban street is thus connected with the sanctuary's doorway. According to the Tosefta's teaching, the alley's entryway is to gesture toward the Temple's sanctuary—in a manner of speaking, to bow to it—as the Temple seems to radiate into the generic, halakhically manipulated city that forms the backdrop of mishnaic Sabbath law. It is this gesture that occupies the architects of the opening *sugya* in the Bavli's tractate, only to dismiss it after a convoluted discussion.

Between Sacred and Profane Architecture: The Bavli's Eruvin *Sugya*

In the following I discuss the discursive arc of the opening *sugya* in the Bavli, without focusing on all the textual and argumentative details for which there is no space here. As an overview, the *sugya* consists of three sections that will be discussed here: first, the brief introductory segment that compares the beginnings of the mishnaic tractates Sukkah and Eruvin (2a); then the main section (2a–3a) based on a teaching attributed to the early Amora Rav[25] that compares and develops the analogy with the

23. Namely, in Tractate Middot, and here specifically 4:1, according to which "the height of the doorway of the sanctuary [*hekhal*] is twenty cubits and the width ten cubits." The Bavli's *sugya* makes this connection explicitly; see below.

24. See Naftali Cohen, *The Memory of the Temple and the Making of the Rabbis*, Divinations (Philadelphia: University of Pennsylvania Press 2013), esp. chapter 4, "Constructing Sacred Space" (73–91).

25. The Yerushalmi's opening *sugya*, which is shared by Tractates Sukkah (1:1, 51c) and Eruvin (1:1, 18b) as a textual parallel, starts with a similar teaching, including an attribution to Rav, but records a dispute over that attribution: "Rabbi Yosi taught it without attribution [*stam*], Rabbi Aha in the name of Rav" (Saul Lieberman, *Talmud Yerushalmi: According to Ms.*

Temple buildings, which in its conclusion the *sugya* will dismiss as mistaken;[26] inserted into this section we find a longer, complicated exegetical discussion (2a–b), clearly set apart in style (biblical exegesis), rhetoric (anonymous), and contents from the discussion about Rav's teaching. The goal of tracing the *sugya*'s discursive arc is, first, to demonstrate that the *sugya* is carefully and purposefully composed, which is less surprising. But second, and perhaps more importantly, my purpose is to show that the *sugya*'s architects were guided not only by formal criteria but by substantive considerations as well. The latter in particular will allow us to raise more seriously the question why some of these discursive choices were made in the opening *sugya* to Tractate Eruvin. Like the opening *sugya* of Qiddushin, Pesaḥim, and other tractates, the architects of this *sugya* engage in a meta-halakhic reflection process.[27] In fact, the red thread that holds the parts of the composite *sugya* in Eruvin together, I suggest, is the motif of building structures with various Jewish valences, beginning with the *sukkah*, followed by the Temple and its building structures (sanctuary/ *hekhal* and entry hall/ *'ulam*), supported by the foremost biblical building structures, the tent of meeting (*ohel mo'ed*), the tabernacle (*mishkan*), and its courtyard enclosure (*ḥatzer*). And these are not all, as we shall see. The architects of the *sugya* arrange these building structures so as to form a wide conceptual frame within which to endow the mishnaic focus on the urban street with Jewish significance. Allow me to elaborate.

As we have seen in the introduction above, the *sugya* opens with a brief segment, discussed in the literature, comparing the opening mishnaic teachings of Eruvin and Sukkah,[28] both of which are linked by virtue of the measurement of height (twenty cubits) that they share: Neither a *sukkah* nor the alley's entry is to be higher than twenty cubits. Given the parallel measurement, the editors raise the question about the different

---

Or. 4720 (Scal.3) of the Leiden University Library with Restorations and Corrections [Jerusalem: Academy of the Hebrew Language, 2001]), 451, 635.

26. Actually, the *sugya* does not simply end with this dismissal of Rav's teaching, attributed to Rav Nachman bar Yitzchaq (3a). Once the *sugya* reaches a conclusion with regard to Rav's derivation of the alley's entry from the Temple's buildings, the harmonizing anonymous editorial voice proceeds to ask about the relationship between Rav Nachman's conclusion here in Eruvin, and the seemingly similar teaching attributed to Rabbah with regard to the *sukkah* (b. Sukkah 2a). Possibly, the same hand that added the first segment comparing the beginning of Sukkah and Eruvin, added this final discussion to frame the main segment on the comparison of Temple and alleyway, centered on Rav's teaching.

27. Elman suggests that this is in fact a characteristic element of the genre of opening *sugyot* altogether, which prompts him to assume a different audience from the rest of the Bavli. He writes, "the fact that these sugyot are irrelevant to both the halakhic and the aggadic processes that characterize the rest of the Bavli may indicate that the audience for which they were intended was different from that of the rest of the Bavli" ("World of the 'Sabboraim,'" 384 [and similarly elsewhere]). I will discuss this further in my conclusion.

28. Via a *tenan ha-tam* formula, paralleled in b. Sukkah 2a.

halakhic language employed in both, the simple prohibition in the case of the *sukkah* (*pasul*) as opposed to the instruction to adjust in the case of the alley (reduce). This short segment, shaped entirely by the Bavli's anonymous editorial voice, with an almost verbatim parallel at the beginning of Sukkah, may have been placed here precisely for these purely formal reasons.[29] But beyond the formal interests that may have prompted this late insertion, it also introduces the *sukkah* as the very first analogous structure to consider for the subsequent discussion of the restructuring of the street entry for the purpose of the *shittuf* (Sabbath partnership).

The second and main segment starts with the citation of an Amoraic teaching attributed to Rav transmitted by his student Rav Yehudah.[30] This main section of the *sugya* formally is devoted to an analysis of the dispute in the mishnaic paragraph between its anonymous teaching, the majority sages,[31] and Rabbi Yehudah, based on Rav's analysis thereof.

> Rav Yehudah said in the name of Rav:
> The sages [in the mishnah] learned it from the doorway of the sanctuary [*hekhal*], while Rabbi Yehudah learned it from the entry-hall [*'ulam*].[32]

Rav suggests that the mishnaic sages derived their limitation of the alleyway's entry at maximally twenty cubits from the Temple's sanctuary building (*hekhal*) in the Temple, while the mishnaic Rabbi Yehudah from its entry-hall (*'ulam*), or rather their respective doorways. This teaching, which forms the basis of the talmudic analysis that follows, is presented as Rav's, independently of the Tosefta's *baraita* discussed above. As we will see, the *sugya*'s architects know the *baraita*, as it is cited later on, curiously with the claim that Rav also knew and actually misunderstood it. Here at the *sugya*'s beginning, Rav ostensibly bases his argument on the formal connection of Eruvin's teaching to the Temple structures as they are taught in Mishnah Middot. At least that is the connection that the

29. In addition, the segment has no precise parallel in the Yerushalmi's opening *sugya*, although we ought to consider also that the Yerushalmi starts both Tractate Eruvin and Tractate Sukkah with a parallel *sugya*. Brüll ("Die Entstehungsgeschichte," 43) and, following him, Epstein (*Amoraim*, 51), Weiss (*Ha-yetzirah shel ha-Sabora'im*), as well as Zur (*Or Israel*, 19) consider this segment to be added late, perhaps by the latest Saboraim, based on these formal criteria. The talmudic discussions repeatedly create linkages throughout these two tractates, but that cannot be pursued here in detail. For a list, see Epstein, *Amoraim*, 51.

30. Cf. the Yerushalmi's opening *sugya*—with a parallel at the beginning of Sukkah (y. Sukkah 1:1, 51c).

31. In the Yerushalmi referred to as *rabbanan*, in the Bavli as both *hakhamim* by Rav, and *rabbanan* in the anonymous layer.

32. Translations from the Bavli follows the Vilna text, which I compare with MS Munich (online) and the first printed edition, produced by Bomberg in Venice (Jerusalem, 1948, facsimile). For the first *sugya*, the major manuscripts are MS Munich (1342) and MS Vatican 127, and significant differences will, as always, be noted.

sugya's architects make explicit with a reference to that mishnaic teaching, stitched together from two different contexts in the Mishnah:

> ... since we learn [elsewhere] in the Mishnah:
> "The height of the doorway of the sanctuary [*hekhal*] is twenty cubits and the width ten cubits," (m. Mid. 4:1)
> "and of the entry-hall [*'ulam*] the height is forty cubits and the width twenty." (m. Mid. 3:7)[33]

If, so the citation implies, the *'ulam* was that high and served as Rabbi Yehudah's model for the alley's entry, he would of course not require a reduction. Both Tannaitic opinions in Eruvin, therefore, like Rav's teaching, would take the Temple as their model, just from different structures within it.

In many ways, Rav's teaching seems entirely unremarkable, since the Temple as supreme paradigm makes eminent talmudic sense, and the related Tannaitic tradition preserved in the Tosefta makes that same connection, as we have seen above. In addition, the Yerushalmi's *sugya* starts with a tradition invoking a similar version of Rav's teaching, albeit without elaborating much on it. Nonetheless, the architects of the Bavli's *sugya* set out to undo the linkage of the alley with the Temple. When the *sugya* picks up the discussion again (2b), after the exegetical interlude to which I'll return momentarily, its anonymous voice undoes first the entry hall's doorway as the ostensible model for Rabbi Yehudah in the Mishnah, and subsequently the sanctuary's doorway as model for the majority sages.

It first asks whether the Mishnah's Rabbi Yehuda really thought of the entry hall (*'ulam*),[34] since in light of a selection of Tannaitic sources this would seem rather difficult to maintain.[35] In conclusion, Rav Ḥisda, an Amora two generations after Rav, argues that Rav, in his effort to make the connection between street and Temple, must clearly have been misled by the very *baraita* that we also know from the Tosefta, discussed above:

---

33. These citations from m. Middot may or may not be part of "Rav's" voice. Syntactically it certainly works as part of his statement, making this part of the early Amoraic statement. Text-historically it is also possible that these citations have been added by the *sugya*'s architects. For my purpose this does not make a difference at this point.

34. B. Eruvin 2b, "But did Rabbi Judah really derive [his concept of the alley's entry] from the *'ulam*?"

35. There are two objections, the first from the continuation of the mishnaic paragraph itself, and the second from a teaching that is introduced as a *baraita* (*ve-hatanya*): "An entryway that is higher than twenty cubits—it needs to be reduced, but Rabbi Yehudah validates it till forty or fifty cubits." Such a teaching is not recorded in any Tannaitic collection at our disposal, but the Yerushalmi's opening *sugya* states that "Rabbi Ḥiyya taught [*tenai*] even forty or fifty cubits; Bar Qappara taught even a hundred cubits for the height." In the Bavli, then, Rabbi Ḥiyya is transformed into Rabbi Yehudah, in order to design the argument against Rav there.

> Rav Ḥisda said: The following *baraita* misled Rav,
> as it is taught:
> "If an alley-entry is higher than twenty cubits,
> *more than the doorway* [pitḥo] *of the* hekhal,
> it needs to be reduced."
> He reasoned: Since the rabbis [*rabbanan*] derived [the alley] from the sanctuary's doorway, Rabbi Yehudah learned [the alley's entry] from the entry-hall's doorway.
> But not so! Rabbi Yehudah [rather] learned from the doorway of kings. (2b)

Rav, so argues Rav Ḥisda, put two and two together wrongly when he learned the *baraita*, that we also know from the Tosefta. Rav thought that if the sages used the *hekhal* to think with, Rabbi Yehudah by the same token must also have used the Temple to think with, just a different structure, namely, the doorway of the *'ulam*. But, so Rav Ḥisda, Rav was wrong. In fact, Rabbi Judah would have had something else entirely in mind. Namely, he was thinking of the "doorway of kings" (*pitḥa di-melakhim*), palatial structures, a suggestion—I might add—that remains strangely undeveloped in this talmudic *sugya*.[36] Rav Ḥisda's proposition radically changes the understanding of the dispute in the Mishnah. It is now no longer one between two different Temple building structures as models for the alley's entry, both sacred, but between Temple and royal palace, between sacred and political architecture. Each of these models would lend the street's meaning a very different resonance. This is where the *sugya* leaves Rabbi Yehudah's opinion,[37] without adding any more to develop this analogy or model, but again, we note that another building structure is added to the map.

Turning to the majority sages in the Mishnah (*rabbanan*) and the *hekhal* as their supposed model for the street in the *sugya*'s concluding section, the architects of the *sugya* take the metaphorical wrecking ball to it as well: "As to the Rabbis, did they really derive [*gemirei*] [the alley's entry's] from the doorway of the *hekhal*?" (2b). As before, the logic of various Tannaitic texts puts Rav's suggested analogy in question,[38] and, as before, the final resolution is attributed to an Amoraic teacher, to the fourth generation Rav Naḥman bar Yitzḥaq:

---

36. That is, this is all there is to this. The *sugya* does not pursue this analogy or its source any further, no biblical or rabbinic reference. Rashi (ad loc.) suggests simply that, in general, palatial doorways are just very high. As far as I can tell, the phrase is a *hapax legomenon* in rabbinic literature. Does this even evoke biblical memory, as in the palace of the Davidic monarchs, or is this a generic reference to royal architecture?

37. Meiri, rephrasing as "the gates of the palaces of kings," understands the *sugya* to consider this to be Rabbi Yehudah's reason (Beit ha-Behirah, *Eruvin* 1:1, 2a).

38. Again, I am skipping the various Tannaitic sources against Rav's analogy for brevity's sake, as their analysis is not essential to the line of thought I pursue here.

> Rav Naḥman bar Yitzḥaq said:
> Without Rav['s teaching at the beginning of the *sugya*] the two Tannaitic teachings would not contradict each other.
> As far as the sages and their teaching about the [height of the] crossbeam [for the alley's entry] is concerned—that is because of "perceptibility" [*mishum hekeira*].
> And regarding what the *baraita*[39] taught—"more than the doorway of the *hekhal*"—that was merely a mnemonic sign [*simana de'alma*]. (3a)

Rav Naḥman resolves a hypothetical contradiction between the Tannaitic teachings, as to whether indeed the *hekhal* did or did not serve as a model to think with, by suggesting first of all to remove Rav altogether from the discussion. This allows him to reinterpret the rationale behind the mishnaic sages' opinion as having an entirely pragmatic purpose. When they limited the height of the alley's entry they did not think of the Temple at all but were concerned about people's ability to recognize the crossbeam above the alley as a structural element, one that demarcates the residential alley within from what lies outside, the space of the *shittuf mevo'ot* from that which lies beyond.

That leaves the Tosefta's *baraita* and its self-same suggestion, but Rav Naḥman reduces that even more authoritative teaching to a mere mnemonic sign, without substantive reference, a signpost. The height of the alley's entry, therefore, according to this conclusion, has little to do with the actual Temple and is designed above all for its functional purpose as a signpost to the residents within, signaling a boundary between the space within and without.

Thus, the opening *sugya* is built on Rav's initial analogy of street and Temple buildings, which moves the Temple building symbolically into the urban landscape. The alley's entry, whether by design or by analogy, is now understood to be patterned after the Temple's doorways. But over the course of its analysis, the *sugya* questions that teaching and explains why Rav was surely mistaken with making the Temple the model for the street, and ends up, if anything, with removing the Temple from the Mishnah's civic urban landscape. The end result of the *sugya*'s analysis would seem to be that the sages in the Mishnah are understood as considering the crossbeam a mere boundary marker that must be recognizable to the residents within. Rabbi Yehuda, on the other hand, is assumed to have a structural model in mind, namely, royal palaces. At the same time, of course, after so much discussion, the Temple has become part of the mental landscape that is superimposed onto the urban landscape.

39. The *baraita* that we also know from the Tosefta, containing the gloss regarding the Temple's sanctuary. The *sugya* cites this *baraita* in its argument against Rav.

Biblical Models for the Urban Alleyway

Let me turn to the exegetical segment that the *sugya*'s architects insert right after the opening citation of Rav's teaching, to show how they expand their map of Jewish structures to think with even further. In brief, this segment can be subdivided further into three parts. The first part proposes that the mishnaic dispute about the height of the alley's entry is based on a difference in interpretation of a biblical verse mentioning the "entrance of the tent of meeting" (Lev 3:2, *petaḥ ohel mo'ed*): "[The sacrifice of well-being] shall be slaughtered at the entrance of the Tent of Meeting."[40] The second part discusses the relationship between *mishkan* and *mikdash* based on that verse. Finally, the third part of the segment explores the question whether the mishnaic teaching about the alley's entrance is not in fact derived from the entrance of the tabernacle's enclosure or courtyard (*ḥatzer*).[41] From this overview it already appears that the biblical building structures form the red thread through this segment of biblical exegetical discourse, stitched together by an anonymous hand. Given that it switches rhetorical register from the surrounding main segment of the *sugya*, it clearly stands textually apart from it.

Now let me develop this outline a little further, to tease out the valences in play for the architects of Eruvin's *sugya*. The exegetical segment, as is to be expected, is carefully stitched into the *sugya*'s discussion of Rav's teaching by its architects, in that they propose that both parties of the mishnaic dispute on the alley's entrance, the majority sages and Rabbi Yehuda, "interpreted [*darshu*] the same verse" (2a, with reference to Leviticus 3:2), only differently with respect to how the Temple structures, entry hall, and sanctuary can be mapped onto the biblical tent of meeting. The *sugya*'s architects propose that what underlies the mishnaic dispute is in fact different theories of the status of sanctity inherent to each structure:

---

40. The "entrance of the tent of meeting" (*petaḥ ohel mo'ed*) is of course mentioned numerous times in the Torah. I am not sure why the architects of the *sugya* would have chosen this particular verse here. According to J. Milgrom the Priestly tradition has the tent of meeting located in the center of the desert camp (e.g., Num 2:17, 3:38), while the epic tradition has it located outside the camp (e.g., Num 11:24–27, 12:4–5, etc.); see his extensive note in *Leviticus 1–16: A New Translation with Introduction and Commentary*, AB 3 (New York: Doubleday, 1991), 139–43. See also Benjamin D. Sommer, "Conflicting Constructions of Divine Presence in the Priestly Tabernacle," *BibInt* 9 (2001): 41–63. Sommer demonstrates the contrast between the P and the E sources' depiction of the biblical tabernacle. The Priestly writers variously call the structure *mishkan, ohel mo'ed* and *ohel ha-'edut* (tent of the pact) while the Elohistic writers only use *ohel mo'ed*.

41. The construction of the tabernacle's *ḥatzer* is described in Exod 27:9–19. The introduction of the biblical *ḥatzer* here reads like a literary foreshadowing of the discussions of the *eruv ḥatzerot*, the *eruv* of courtyards, later in the courtyard, the centerpiece of the tractate, after which it is named.

And both [mishnaic opinions] interpreted the same verse: "[The sacrifice of well-being] shall be slaughtered at the entrance of the Tent of Meeting."
For the sages held:
the sanctity [*kedushah*] of the sanctuary [*hekhal*] and the sanctity of the entry-hall [*'ulam*] are each distinct, and when it is written:
"... the doorway of the tent of meeting" — it is written with reference to the *hekhal* (only).
But Rabbi Yehudah held:
the sanctity of the *hekhal* and of the *'ulam* are one and the same, and when it is written:
"... the doorway of the tent of meeting" — it is written with reference to both (*hekhal* and *'ulam*). (2a)[42]

The *sugya* now moves away from discussing Rav's teaching and the question of the analogy between the alley's entrance and the entrance of the Temple structures to the question of the analogy between the Temple structures and the biblical tent of meeting. At the same time it evokes the concept of sanctity of space into the discussion of the design of the alley's entry. The trajectory of introducing the sanctity of the Temple's structures here, at the beginning of Eruvin, almost forces us to consider the question of how much, if any, *kedushah*, or sanctity, is in fact introduced into the Mishnah's urban map by the sugya's architects.

This exegetical move, where both parties in the mishnaic dispute would apply the same biblical structure (*ohel mo'ed*) to different structures in the Temple, seems forced even to the *sugya*'s architects.[43] It prompts them to raise the question that shapes the second part of this exegetical

42. There are a number of talmudic intertexts for this argument. First, of course the famous list of the ten degrees of sanctity of m. Kelim 1:6–9, which lists the space between the entry hall and the altar, and the sanctuary itself on different levels of sanctity (1:9). That mishnaic list is discussed b. Yoma 43a–b. In Yoma (44a), the Talmud attributes to the fourth generation Amora Rava the teaching that the sanctity of the entry hall and sanctuary are on the same level, while the anonymous editors reject that teaching and insist at that *sugya*'s conclusion that both have a different level of sanctity. Cf. b. Zev. 14a (also Rava who considers the equal level of sanctity for both) and b. Zev. 58b and 59a (where the anonymous voice considers if the mishnaic Rabbi Yehudah held that both entry hall and sanctuary had the same level of sanctity).

43. I am skipping the brief suggestion of an alternative suggestion (*'i-ba'eit 'eima*) piece, fascinating as it is, again for brevity's sake. This suggestion has Rabbi Judah hypothetically relying on a different verse, one that, much to the annoyance of the medieval commentaries, does not exist anywhere in the Masoretic Text: "since it is written 'to the entrance of the entryhall of the House.'" The Tosafist R. Isaac (2a, *lemma dikhtiv*) suggests that phrase is stitched together from two verses in Ezekiel, 40:48 and 47:1. If we were to accept this suggestion, one could read this strange argument as an indirect reference to Ezekiel's map of the Temple precinct in Ezek 40–43. On Ezek 40–48 as offering what he describes as "the most coherent ideology of place ... of all the texts preserved in the biblical canon," see famously Jonathan Z. Smith's chapter "To Put in Place" in his *To Take Place: Toward Theory in Ritual*, CSHJ (Chicago:

segment, namely whether in fact the verse does apply to the Temple at all, or rather to the biblical tabernacle itself: "[Anonymous:] But is not this text written with respect to the tabernacle [*mishkan*]?"(2a). If, so the reasoning goes, the "entrance of the tent of meeting" (Lev 3:2) is in fact part of the biblical tabernacle, it could obviously not be used as a model for the Temple, and therefore not by the disputants in Mishnah Eruvin as an indirect reference for the street entrance.

In what follows, however, the *sugya*'s architects muster biblical verses as well as talmudic cross-references to show that in fact the biblical tabernacle (*mishkan*) and the Temple (*mikdash*) are at times used interchangeably.[44] This line of reasoning ends with the famous verse, in which the divine voice enjoins Moses to convey to the Israelites: "And let them make Me a sanctuary [*mikdash*], that I may dwell [*ve-shakanti*] among them" (Exod 25:8).[45] *Miskhkan* is called *mikdash*, just as *mikdash* is called *mishkan*, and the "entrance of the tent of meeting" theoretically still holds as a reference to the entrance to the Temple sanctuary. As we are contemplating the alley's entry, we have now been led backwards in Jewish memory from the Temple, its stationary sanctity of place in the *hekhal* and *'ulam*, to the *ohel moed* and the *mishkan*, God's dwelling place in the Torah's story. God's mobile biblical dwelling "among us" now is placed right at the alley's entry.[46]

This would seem like a nice climax for this exegetical segment in the *sugya*. However, the *sugya's* architects take us one step further and explore the entrance to the enclosure or courtyard of the tabernacle (*petaḥ sha'ar*

University of Chicago Press, 1987), 47–73. On the relationship between Ezekiel's map and the one construed in m. Middot, see N. Cohen, *Memory of the Temple*, esp. 84–89.

44. The use of Lev 3:2 with reference to the Temple by an Amora, here Rav Yehudah in the name of Shmuel, in the context of the talmudic discussion of the order of the well-being offering, is cited several times elsewhere in the Talmud, b. Yoma 62b, b. Naz. 45a. The cross-referencing of *mishkan* and *mikdash*—"*mishkan* is called *mikdash*, and *mikdash* is called *mishkan*"—and the biblical support texts, including their interpretation, presents an almost verbatim parallel with a segment found in a larger discussion in b. Shev. 16b, all the way up to the citation of Exod 25:8. Since b. Shev. 16b constitutes a longer discussion on the relationship between *mishkan* and *mikdash*, it seems most likely that the architects of our *sugya* cite this exegetical segment from there.

45. The parallel text in b. Shev. 16b adds Exod 25:9 to make the cross-referencing clearer since that verse explicitly uses the term *mishkan*, rather than just its verbal form: "Exactly as I show you, the pattern of the Tabernacle (*tavnit ha-mishkan*) ... so shall you make it."

46. Sommer ("Conflicting Constructions of Divine Presence") discusses the tension between models of stationary sacred center and peripatetic or ambulatory sacred centers within biblical literature and even within the P source, or—drawing on J. Z. Smith—between locative and utopian models. Sommer adds his own category of a locomotive ideology of religion to capture P's theology (48). In light of his article, the talmudic reading of the relationship between *mishkan* and *mikdash* would require more discussion than I can pursue here. But it suggests that the *mishkan* as model for the shaping of the street entrance in *Eruvin* evokes the dynamic of mobility for this particular boundary.

hae-ḥatzer) as a potential model for the alley's entry, now with regard to the width of the entrance:

> [Anonymous:] Whether majority rabbis or Rabbi Yehudah, perhaps they both could learn from the doorway of the gate of the [tabernacle's courtyard] (2b).

This is not the place to reconstruct the mathematical equation based on the measurements in the list of various verses tied together to make their case (Exod 27:14, 18; 38:15). Let me just underline that of the two arguments offered by the anonymous talmudic voice finally rejecting the biblical courtyard's entrance as a model for the street entrance, one insists outright on the distinction between a "regular doorway" (*petaḥ stama*) and the "doorway of the courtyard's gate" (*petaḥ sha'ar ḥatzer*).[47] The anonymous voice simply differentiates between what might apply to the biblical tabernacle and a regular street entryway and refuses the mapping of one onto the other.

This exegetical excursion, then, maps biblical structures onto the mishnaic dispute. It starts with the *ohel mo'ed* (Lev 3:2), endowing the *hekhal* and *'ulam* with sanctity. The *ohel mo'ed* morphs into the *mishkhan*, which in turn is equated with the *mikdash*, both of which move God into the midst of the Israelites and therewith into the urban streets of Eruvin. It leaves us at the gates of the courtyard of the *mishkan*, now linked to the alley's entry. The actual gain in terms of the question that the *sugya* started out, namely, as to the origins of Eruvin's requirement of shaping the entrance to the residential alley as a doorway may remains utterly uncertain, considering that some associative links are dismissed outright. At the same time, the red thread has become more obvious. It seems as if the structuring of this segment is driven by a desire to introduce and arrange as many biblical building structures as possible around the alley's entry, to create a veritable map of structures with various degrees of inherent Jewish meaning and valence—namely, biblical memory, the link back to the time of the Israelites wanderings, their own mobility, and the mobility of the structures that they moved around with them, that moved the divine indwelling with them. The exegetical segment, therefore, contributes to making the opening *sugya* of Eruvin the only *sugya* in all of the Bavli to arrange all these structures into one discursive context. Adapting J. Z. Smith's reading of Ezekiel[48] to talmudic literature: of all the *sugyot* preserved in the talmudic canon, this one—as it discusses the significance of the urban

47. Again, the discussion of the *ḥatzer* provides biblical resonance for the *eruv ḥatzerot*, the *eruv* of shared courtyards that receives sustained halakhic discussion in the tractate later on (especially in the sixth chapter).

48. Smith, *To Take Place*, 47–73.

street—is perhaps the most comprehensive in terms of offering a coherent ideology of place I tried to fix it] in talmudic thought.

Conclusion

By all the standard formal criteria established in talmudic scholarship it is beyond any doubt that this opening *sugya* is post-Amoraic. In the shape that it has come to be preserved, it can be considered a fairly late textual artifact in the chronology of the making of the Talmud. As we have seen, previous talmudic scholarship has established the late addition of the first segment comparing Eruvin and Sukkah. For the other segments, we have seen that the architects of the *sugya* were familiar with a number of other talmudic *sugyot*, as in the exegetical segment that shares discussions about the relationship of *mishkan* and *mikdash* with other contexts in the Bavli and draws on those contexts.

We have been able to make visible the design that holds the various composite parts together. The *sugya*'s architects invested a significant amount of effort in expanding the repertoire of building structures with which to make sense of the Mishnah's focus on the urban street in Sabbath law. In the main segment, it is the Temple, its *hekhal* and its *'ulam*, that are tested as models or reference points, a proposal attributed to earlier voices, both Rav, one of the earliest Amoraim, and to a *baraita*. In the conclusion of the *sugya*, its architects refer to a pragmatic explanation—attributed to a later Amoraic teacher—for the particular social and urban context: the residents have to be able to notice the entrance to the street as an entrance, to notice a structure that frames the street, that sets it aside from that which is beyond, and this and only this is the reason for the dispute in the Mishnah. According to the analysis of the *sugya's* architects, then, the street remains profane. At the same time, in terms of the intellectual and discursive energies invested in the *sugya*, its architects have mapped out a theory of Jewish space within which Sabbath law is located, in which a variety of structures are linked to each other. In the end the street is not just a street. It resonates with a virtual map of structures alive in Jewish liturgy and memory. In this sense, the opening *sugya* works well as an introduction to the tractate, since it not only analyzes the stakes of the dispute of the opening mishnaic paragraph, but in doing so it creates an expansive map of a Jewish mental landscape.

In order to make the case for reading the opening *sugya* as an introduction to the tractate and its halakhic project, which Talmud and Mishnah refer to as the *shittuf mevo'ot*, the equivalent of the *eruv ḥatzerot* or *eruv* of courtyards and in contemporary shorthand simply the *eruv*, let me return once more to Yaakov Elman's—in his own words—"unduly speculative" suggestion that the opening *sugyot* of tractates are geared to an audience different from the rabbinic academic audience for the rest of the tractate. If the subjects dealt with in such *sugyot*, so his reasoning goes, "are sometimes peripheral not only to the tractate but even to the mishnah to which they are attached,"[49] their audience must be peripheral as well, a "radically different audience," perhaps "the political and financial supporters of the yeshiva" in attendance of the lecture. Our opening *sugya* would seem to fall into the category of what Elman thinks of as "peripheral" subject matter, since it deals with meta-halakhic issues. Perhaps Elman's *ba'alei batishe* donors to the geonic *yeshiva* needed to be treated to a discourse that made sense of what might otherwise seem as a far stretch of rabbinic halakhic discussions. I don't know whether this is the case, or whether such a *Sitz im Leben* for the opening *sugyot* could ever be demonstrated. It does seem, however, that, even if so, the Bavli's makers decided to make such *sugyot* anything but peripheral by including them in the tractate—in decidedly nonperipheral places no less—thereby at the very least joining peripheral and yeshiva "audiences," making them textually one.

My equally speculative suggestion, therefore, would be to consider these *sugyot* as introductions to the tractate at hand, not so much to its halakhic subject matter(s) per se but as a framing device. If, as Mishnah Eruvin suggests, the Sabbath is located at the home, in the shared courtyards, and in the street, as Mishnah Eruvin would have us believe, that location becomes meaningful and significant in light of the map of Jewish space as Eruvin's opening *sugya* maps it for us.

49. Elman, "World of the 'Sabboraim,'" 391.

An Analysis of Sugyot Containing the Phrase *Lo Savar Lah Mar* in the Babylonian Talmud

JUDITH HAUPTMAN
Jewish Theological Seminary of America

Halakhic anecdotes are short narratives that describe how an Amora carried out a stated rule. They abound in the Babylonian Talmud.[1] A typical *sugya* presents a halakhah and then analyzes it in detail. Some *sugyot* end with an anecdote that reports how an Amora implemented the rule under discussion. Upon reading several hundred of these short episodes, I arrived at the conclusion that they were incorporated into the *sugya* not to praise the piety of the Amora but to suggest that he may modify the halakhah when carrying it out. If we compare the statement of the halakhah to the report of the Amora's performance, it is easy to see that they differ from each other in small but significant ways. By including these anecdotes in their magnum opus, the editors of the Talmud are suggesting that halakhah changes over time.[2]

This article focuses on a subset of halakhic anecdotes, those that contain the phrase *lo savar lah mar* ("Doesn't the master hold the following

My heartfelt thanks to Shaye J. D. Cohen for his help, advice, and encouragement over many years of friendship. A better colleague would be hard to find.

1. They also abound in the Jerusalem Talmud. This study, however, is only about the Babylonian Talmud.

2. Although other scholars have already noted that the implementation of a halakhah often differs from the statement of the halakhah, they have not suggested that this is consistently true or that the talmudic editors themselves endorse the possibility of halakhic modification. Barry Wimpfheimer argues that some talmudic stories seriously engage the law, that the narrative is antinomian only in the sense that it resists the statutory presentation of the law, and that legal narrative presents a far richer palette [than the law itself] (*Narrating the Law: A Poetics of Talmudic Legal Stories*, Divinations [Philadelphia: University of Pennsylvania Press, 2011], 11, 18, 27). The stories he analyzes are, for the most part, considerably longer than the very short legal episodes I address herein. My focus in this article is on halakhic changes instituted by senior scholars and the techniques they used to bring these changes about.

opinion?").[3] In all thirty-five sugyot in which this phrase appears,[4] the Amora who asks this question is the student or junior colleague of the Amora to whom it is addressed. The *lo savar lah mar* narratives follow a pattern: they begin with a statement of a halakhah followed by the report of a student who sees his mentor carry out the halakhah differently from the way it was prescribed. The student then asks his mentor, Aren't you familiar with the halakhah that suggests a somewhat different mode of behavior? The narrative ends with the mentor, in response, defending his action, usually by arguing that the cited rule does not address his particular set of circumstances. The senior scholar has thus modified the rule, shrinking the number of cases to which it applies. I suggest that the inclusion in the BabylonianTalmud of this kind of halakhic anecdote shows that, according to its editors, a halakhah can change even after it becomes an accepted rule of Jewish practice.

A close reading of seven of the thirty-five *sugyot* will present evidence for this hypothesis.[5] An eighth *sugya* (presented first) will provide a basis for comparison. It contains a halakhic anecdote but not the phrase *lo savar lah mar*.

1. Bavli Baba Qamma 119a, Collecting Charity from Women

ת"ר: לוקחין מן הנשים כלי צמר ביהודה וכלי פשתן בגליל, אבל לא יינות ושמנים וסלתות. . . ..
אבא שאול אומר: מוכרת אשה בארבעה וחמשה דינר, כדי לעשות כפה לראשה; . . . גבאי צדקה לוקחין מהן דבר מועט, אבל לא דבר מרובה. . .
רבינא איקלע לבי מחוזא, אתו נשי דבי מחוזא רמו קמיה כבלי ושירי. קביל מינייהו.
א"ל רבה תוספאה לרבינא: והתניא גבאי צדקה מקבלין מהן דבר מועט, אבל לא דבר מרובה!
א"ל: הני לבני מחוזא דבר מועט נינהו.

3. I have already presented papers on halakhic *sugyot* containing the term *iqla* ("he visited") and *hava qa'imna* ("I was standing"), at the AJS conferences in 2016 and 2017. I also presented a paper on halakhic anecdotes at the World Congress of Jewish Studies in 2013 (plenary session). My article in *Nashim*, "The Talmud's Women in Law and Narrative," 28 (spring 2015) 30–50, addresses the issue of halakhic anecdotes, in particular those that feature women. See also my article "The Talmudic Rabbi as Holy Man," in *Rabbi–Pastor–Priest: Their Roles and Profiles through the Ages*, ed. Walter Homolka and Heinz-Günther Schöttler, SJ 64 (Berlin: de Gruyter, 2013), 1–23.

4. See Ber. 24b, 28b (2x), 41b, 42a (2x), 42b, 43b, 46a (2x), 50b; Shab. 11a, 50b, 55a, 95a, 109a, 136a; Eruv. 15a, 24a, 68a, 102b; Pesaḥ. 86b, 103b; Yoma 78a; Sukkah 7a, 19a; Yevam. 106a, 106b; Giṭ. 7a; Qidd. 81b; B. Qam. 113a; Menaḥ. 35b, 37b, 42a; Nid. 66a. These *sugyot* were located via a Bar Ilan database search.

5. Translations of the *sugyot* are my own, based on the Soncino translations.

A *baraita*: One may purchase woolen garments from women in Judea and linen garments [from women] in the Galilee but not wine or oil or fine flour.... Abba Shaul says: a woman may sell [products from the door of her cottage] for four or five denarii, to make herself a kippah for her head.... Charity collectors may take small donations from women but not large ones....

Ravina visited Bei Mehoza [to collect charity]. The women of Bei Mehoza came and threw chains and bracelets at him [as donations]. He accepted [these items] from them.

Said to him Rabbah Tosfa'ah: Have we not learned that charity collectors may accept [only] small donations from women but not large ones?!

He responded: for the people [i.e., women] of Mehoza these are small donations.

According to the opening *baraita*, a charity collector is permitted to accept only a small donation from a woman. She is likely to be giving him money of her own that she earned by the sale of homemade products, as the *baraita* permits. Were she to make a large donation, she is assumed to be taking money from her husband without his consent. An anecdote reports that Ravina, a charity collector, arrived at Bei Mehoza. The women there, to whom he apparently pitched his charity, tossed their precious jewelry at him. He accepted their donations. Rabbah Tosfa'ah, Ravina's student, challenges him by noting that the *baraita* permits accepting only small donations from women and these are clearly large. Ravina responds that, for the rich women of Mehoza, a donation of precious jewelry is "small." He thus views the *baraita*'s terms "small" and "large" as relative, not absolute.

I suggest that Ravina interpreted the *baraita* anew in order to justify his accepting large donations from the women of Mehoza. His interpretation, as reasonable as it is, does not appear to have been considered by him in advance. His student, Rabbah Tosfa'ah, clearly did not know it. This halakhic modification, that "large" and "small" are relative terms, was created by him on the spot in response to criticism by a student, and not via give-and-take on the *baraita* with colleagues in the study hall. Ravina's comment ends the *sugya*. No Amoraic analysis follows. Note that the halakhah of this *sugya* is thus made up of two parts: the *baraita* itself and Ravina's new interpretation of one clause. This halakhic anecdote is typical in that an Amora deviates from a stated rule, his student questions his behavior, and he responds by modifying the rule to accommodate his situation.[6]

---

6. A feminist sidebar: In other *sugyot*, the women of Mehoza are characterized as pampered, as persons who eat without working for their upkeep (b. Shab. 33a). In this *sugya*, they are characterized as generous with their funds. It seems to me that this detail paints a somewhat different picture of them. Yes, say the male authors of these various statements,

The next seven *sugyot* all contain the phrase *lo savar lah mar*.

2. Bavli Shabbat 11a, Refusing Hospitality

ואמר רבא בר מחסיא אמר רב חמא בר גוריא אמר רב: יפה תענית לחלום כאש לנעורת.
אמר רב חסדא: ובו ביום. ואמר רב יוסף: אפילו בשבת.
רב יהושע בריה דרב אידי איקלע לבי רב אשי, עבדי ליה עיגלא תילתא.
אמרו ליה: לטעום מר מידי.
אמר להו: בתענית יתיבנא.
אמרו ליה: ולא סבר ליה מר להא דרב יהודה, דאמר רב יהודה: לוה אדם תעניתו ופורע?
אמר להו: תענית חלום הוא, ואמר רבא בר מחסיא אמר רב חמא בר גוריא אמר רב: יפה תענית לחלום כאש לנעורת, ואמר רב חסדא: ובו ביום, ואמר רב יוסף: אפילו בשבת.

Said Rava bar Mehasia said R. Hama bar Guria said Rav: Fasting cancels a [bad] dream as fire consumes straw.

Said R. Hisda: provided it is on the same day. And R. Yosef added: even on the Sabbath.

R. Joshua breih d'R. Idi visited the home of R. Ashi. They prepared a young calf for him, and said to him: let the master taste [this delicacy].

He said to them: I am in the midst of a fast.

They said to him: Does not the master hold the view of R. Judah that a person may borrow against a fast and then repay?

He said to them: It is a fast for a [bad] dream. Rava bar Mehasia said in the name of R. Hama bar Guria who said in the name of Rav: Fasting cancels a [bad] dream as fire consumes straw. And R. Hisda commented: provided it is on the same day [as the dream]. And R. Yosef added: even on the Sabbath.

This passage is the last one in a series of statements by Rava bar Mehasia in the name of R. Hama bar Guria in the name of Rav. A person who has had a bad dream can neutralize the dream's dire predictions by means of a fast. R. Hisda adds that he needs to fast on the same day as he dreamt the bad dream, and R. Yosef further notes, even if that day is the Sabbath, when fasting is generally forbidden. An anecdote reports that R. Joshua breih d'R. Idi visited the home of R. Ashi. The household staff, that is, his wife and servants, prepared delicacies for the guest but he refused to eat them, claiming he was fasting. Not giving up, they then asked him, doesn't he accept the ruling of the Amora R. Judah that a person who needs to fast can borrow against the fast and pay it back later, that is, postpone the fast?[7] They clearly want him to eat the food they prepared

---

we husbands pamper our wives, which may reflect well on our ability to support them. But these women are willing to give up the jewelry that we lavish on them to those in need.

7. To "postpone a fast" means to eat a meal today, for instance, in response to a host's offer of hospitality, but to "pay back" the fast later on, that is, to fast on another day.

for him. He, however, remained steadfast in his refusal, citing the view that he has to fast that very day. He apparently understands R. Judah's statement about postponing a fast as referring to other fasts and not to a fast for a bad dream. His answer ends the anecdote. There is no Amoraic or *stama* comment on the anecdote. If so, the minor halakhic correction was accepted: most fasts may be postponed but not a fast for a bad dream.

Note that the household staff—women and servants—engage in a halakhic exchange with the visitor.[8] It is they who bring R. Judah's comment about postponing a fast to R. Joshua breih d'R. Idi's attention. It is also possible that R. Ashi's students are among the staff that engages in conversation with the guest. If that is the case, then it is these same students who, the anecdote claims, prepared delicacies for the guest.[9]

3. Bavli Berakhot 43b, Order of Blessings

תנו רבנן: הביאו לפניו שמן והדס, בית שמאי אומרים: מברך על השמן ואחר כך מברך על ההדס; ובית הלל אומרים: מברך על ההדס ואחר כך מברך על השמן. אמר רבן גמליאל: אני אכריע. שמן זכינו לריחו וזכינו לסיכתו, הדס לריחו זכינו לסיכתו לא זכינו.

אמר רבי יוחנן: הלכה כדברי המכריע.

רב פפא איקלע לבי רב הונא בריה דרב איקא, אייתו לקמייהו שמן והדס, שקל רב פפא בריך אהדס ברישא והדר בריך אשמן.

אמר ליה: לא סבר לה מר הלכה כדברי המכריע?

אמר ליה, הכי אמר רבא: הלכה כבית הלל.

ולא היא, לאשתמוטי נפשיה הוא דעבד.

A *baraita*: they brought before him oil and myrtle: the School of Shammai says that he first recites a blessing on the oil and then on the myrtle; but the School of Hillel says that he first recites a blessing on the myrtle and then on the oil. Said Rabban Gamliel: I will decide. As for oil, we benefit from its pleasing odor and its ability to anoint; as for myrtle, we benefit from its pleasing odor but it cannot be used to anoint.

Said R. Yohanan: the halakhah is according to the "decider."

R. Pappa visited the home of R. Huna breih d'R. Iqqa. They brought before him oil and myrtle. He took the myrtle and recited a blessing on it and afterwards recited a blessing on the oil.

---

8. This interpretation supports my claim that women were more knowledgeable halakhically than they are usually given credit for. See the next note; and see my article "A New View of Women and Torah Study in the Talmudic Period," *Jewish Studies, an Internet Journal* 9 (2010): 249–92, http://www.biu.ac.il/JS/JSIJ/9-2010/Hauptman.pdf.

9. The Soncino translation sidesteps the issue of who it is that cites the view of R. Judah to the guest. The Rishonim do not comment on this matter. On students fulfilling the role of servants, see Catherine Hezser, *The Social Structure of the Rabbinic Movement in Roman Palestine*, TSAJ 66 (Tübingen: Mohr Siebeck, 1997), 332-334.

> Said to him R. Huna breih d'R. Iqqa: doesn't the master hold the view of the "decider"?
>
> He [R. Pappa] responded: thus said Rava, the halakhah is like the School of Hillel.
>
> This is not so. He did this to avoid criticism.

The Schools of Hillel and Shammai disagree about the order of blessings at the end of a meal. According to the School of Shammai, if both oil and myrtle are brought out at the same time—oil for cleaning one's hands and myrtle for its pleasing odor (Rashi, s.v., *shemen v'hadas*)—one first recites a blessing on the oil and only afterwards on the myrtle. But according to the School of Hillel, one first recites a blessing on the myrtle and only afterwards on the oil. Rabban Gamliel decides the matter based on the differing uses of oil and myrtle. He says that one first recites a blessing on oil, for one benefits both from its odor and from its ability to anoint, and then recites a blessing on the myrtle, for one benefits only from its pleasing odor. R. Yohanan determines the halakhah to be according to Rabban Gamliel, which means oil first and then myrtle. An anecdote reports that R. Pappa visited the home of R. Huna breih d'R. Iqqa and recited a blessing first on myrtle and only then on oil. The host asked him if he doesn't hold that the halakhah is according to the decider, Rabban Gamliel, who ruled like the School of Shammai, that is, first recite a blessing on oil and only then on myrtle. He responds that Rava decided the halakhah like the School of Hillel and therefore one should favor the myrtle over the oil.

The problem is that nowhere in the Talmud is there a statement that Rava decided the halakhah in this circumstance like the School of Hillel. Moreover, it is hard to imagine that Rava would fix the halakhah against the determination of both Rabban Gamliel and R. Yohanan. Instead of admitting that he made a mistake, R. Pappa, it seems, attributed a statement to Rava that he never made. To my surprise, the *stama d'gemara* goes on to say that Rava did not issue such a statement, and, further, that R. Pappa claimed that Rava said it in order to exonerate his own behavior.[10] I suggest that this is one case of many in which an Amora, when put on the spot by the question *lo savar lah mar*, either fabricates a statement or else interprets an earlier halakhah in a way it was never intended to be understood in order to defend his own lapse of halakhic behavior. Whether this conversation took place as reported, or whether it was edited or even fabricated by

10. ולא היא - לא אמר רבא הלכתא כבית הלל אלא רב פפא אכסיף לפי שטעה והשמיט עצמו בכך, "This is not so—Rava did not say that the halakhah is like the School of Hillel. Rather, R. Pappa was embarrassed that he erred and so he avoided criticism in this manner" (רש"י מסכת ברכות דף מג עמוד ב). The root שמט means to slip away. This is the only case I know of in which the *stama* says one should disregard the view of the defending Amora.

the *stama*, the point remains the same: a senior scholar, when challenged by a junior scholar, may modify a rule, on occasion for his own benefit.

4. Bavli Yevamot 106b, How to Recite Verses at a *halizah* Ceremony

אמר אביי: האי מאן דמקרי גט חליצה, לא ליקרי לדידה "לא" לחודיה ו"אבה יבמי" לחודיה, דמשמע אבה יבמי, אלא "לא אבה יבמי"; ולא ליקרי לדידיה "לא" לחודיה "חפצתי" לחודיה, דמשמע חפצתי לקחתה, אלא "לא חפצתי לקחתה".

רבא אמר: אפסוקי מילתא היא, ואפסוקי מילתא לית לן בה.

רב אשי אשכחיה לרב כהנא דקמצטער ומקרי לה לא אבה יבמי, אמר ליה: לא סבר ליה מר להא דרבא?

אמר ליה: מודה רבא בלא אבה יבמי.

Said Abaye: One who is reading aloud [the words of] a *halizah* document for the childless widow, let him not separate the word "does not" [*lo*] from "agrees to enter into levirate marriage with me" [*avah yabmi*], because that would mean that he [the levir] agrees to enter into levirate marriage [with her], but rather read [without a break] the words "does not" and "agrees to enter into levirate marriage with me." And when reading aloud for the levir, he should not separate the words "does not" [*lo*] and "wish" [*khafazti*] because that would mean that he, the levir, does wish to enter into levirate marriage with her. Rather he should read [without a break] "I do not wish to marry her."

Rava said: It is just a brief pause and does not matter.

R. Ashi found R. Kahana making a painful effort to recite the phrase "he does not wish to enter into levirate marriage with me" [without a break]. He said to him, doesn't the master hold, according to Rava, that a brief pause does not matter?

He answered him: Rava concedes [to Abaye] that the words "he does not wish to enter into levirate marriage with me" [must be read without any pause at all].

This passage deals with the ritual of *halizah* and its accompanying document.[11] Abaye warns judges not to pause between reciting the words "does not" and "wish to enter into levirate marriage with me" so that the widow will not think that the levir does, in fact, want to enter into levirate marriage with her. Similarly, a judge should not pause between "I do not" and "wish" so that the levir will not think the judge is saying that he wishes to marry her. Rava disagrees and says that a pause is too brief

---

11. A discussion in b. Yevam. 106a refers to a *halizah* document (גט חליצה). Rashi comments (s.v., *ein kotevin get halizah*) that she can present such a document prior to remarriage to prove her marital availability. It functions like a divorce document, which also is designed to serve as proof of marital availability.

to be misleading, either from her perspective or his. An anecdote relates that R. Ashi encountered R. Kahana, his mentor, as he was having trouble reading the phrase "he does not wish etc." without a break.[12] He asked his teacher, don't you accept the rule of Rava that one need not concern himself about a brief pause? R. Kahana responds that, although Rava, in general, overlooks a brief pause, regarding the words "he does not wish to enter into levirate marriage with me" he concedes to Abaye that there should be no pause at all. That is, in response to the criticism of R. Ashi, R. Kahana cites a teaching of Rava that affirms his efforts to read the words "he does not wish to enter into levirate marriage with me" without the slightest pause. The anecdote ends the *sugya*.

Again, the problem is that Rava's statement, as cited by R. Kahana, does not appear anywhere else in the Talmud. In this instance, as in others, it seems that R. Kahana, when criticized by his student, fabricated Rava's concession on the spot. Had Rava agreed with Abaye concerning the words "he does not wish to enter into levirate marriage with me," but disagreed regarding "I do not wish to marry her," it stands to reason that he would have said so, most likely in this context. But he did not. It is possible that R. Kahana is embarrassed that he did not remember Rava's teaching that one may overlook a small pause, or that he agrees with Abaye and disagrees with Rava on this matter, but instead of saying so, he attributes to Rava a statement he never made. R. Kahana has thus modified the halakhah of *halizah* recitation, making it stricter in order to defend his own behavior.

5. Bavli Berakhot 24b, Spitting during Prayer

. . . דאמר רב יהודה: היה עומד בתפלה ונזדמן לו רוק מבליעו בטליתו, ואם טלית נאה הוא מבליעו באפרקסותו.

רבינא הוה קאי אחורי דרב אשי, נזדמן לו רוק, פתקיה לאחוריה.

אמר ליה: <u>לא סבר לה מר להא דרב יהודה</u> מבליעו באפרקסותו?

אמר ליה: אנא אנינא דעתאי.

. . . For R. Judah said: if someone was standing in prayer and saliva accumulated [in his mouth], he may spit it out into his tallit. If it is a fine tallit, he may spit it out into his undergarment.

Ravina[13] was standing behind R. Ashi when saliva accumulated [in his mouth]. He spat it out behind him.

---

12. There is no explanation as to why a person would have trouble reading these few words without a pause. Perhaps the Amora was old and was experiencing physical challenges.

13. The text in the Vilna Shas is not clear as to who is standing before whom. In all cases of *lo savar lah mar*, however, it is the junior scholar who asks this question to the senior

He said to him: does not the master hold the rule of R. Judah that one spits into his undergarment?

He said to him: I am delicate.

According to the Amora R. Judah, it is disrespectful to spit on the ground during prayer. If saliva does accumulate in a person's mouth, he may spit it out into his tallit, that is, his overgarment. If he does not wish to soil his tallit, he may spit it out into his undergarment. In all cases, the one who spits needs to make sure that the spittle is not visible to others. An anecdote relates that Ravina was once standing behind R. Ashi during prayer and saw that R. Ashi spat behind himself. Ravina asked his senior colleague, don't you hold like R. Judah that during prayer one should spit only into one's garment? R. Ashi responded that he spat on the ground because he is delicate, that is, he cannot tolerate spittle on his overgarment or undergarment. This is the end of the discussion.

There is no reason to think that R. Judah intended to exclude delicate people from his rule. It is more likely that R. Ashi adjusted the halakhah in response to the criticism of his student. When caught spitting on the ground behind him, in violation of R. Judah's dictum, R. Ashi, on the spot, introduced his delicacy as an extenuating circumstance. It is likely, however, that Ravina would have known that his teacher is delicate. A similar argument is made by R. Gamliel (m. Ber. 2:6). He bathed far too soon when mourning his wife, citing grounds of delicacy. R. Ashi is thus expanding the number of rules a delicate or fastidious person may break. It again appears that an Amora, when caught in the act of violating a halakhah, devised a defense on the spot. In this case, as in a number of others, the defense appears to be self-serving.

6. Bavli Shabbat 95a, Sprinkling a Floor on the Sabbath

אמימר שרא זילחא במחוזא, אמר: טעמא מאי אמור רבנן, דילמא אתי לאשויי גומות, הכא ליכא גומות.

---

scholar. It follows that R. Ashi, the senior scholar, is the one who spit, and it is Ravina, the junior scholar, who asks him *lo savar lah mar*. The Soncino translation says that Ravina spit and R. Ashi asked *lo savar lah mar*. That is wrong. This is an instance in which a review of all thirty-five instances of *lo savar lah mar* enables me to determine how to translate several ambiguous phrases in this passage. Munich 95 has a slightly different, more clear text: אמר רבינא הוה קאימנא אחוריה דרב אשי ונזדמן לו רוק ופתקיה לאחורי אמרי ליה, "Said Ravina: I was standing behind R. Ashi and saliva chanced upon him and he spat it out behind me."

The differences between Munich 95 and the Vilna Shas are that there is a *vav* before *nizdamen*, which suggests it is Ravina speaking of R. Ashi who spat, and the word אמרי, which means "I said," suggests that Ravina, the narrator of the anecdote, is the one who said *lo savar lah mar* to R. Ashi, and not vice versa.

רבא תוספאה אשכחיה לרבינא דקא מצטער מהבלא,
ואמרי לה מר קשישא בריה דרבא אשכחיה לרב אשי דקא מצטער מהבלא,
אמר ליה: לא סבר לה מר להא דתניא: הרוצה לרבץ את ביתו בשבת מביא עריבה מלאה
מים ורוחץ פניו בזוית זו, ידיו בזוית זו, רגליו בזוית זו, ונמצא הבית מתרבץ מאליו?
אמר ליה: לאו אדעתאי.
תנא: אשה חכמה מרבצת ביתה בשבת.

> Amemar permitted sprinkling [the floor with water on the Sabbath] in Mehoza. He [further] said: why did the rabbis [forbid sprinkling on the Sabbath], lest one come to even out depressions [in the floor]. Here there are no depressions [in the floor].
>
> Rabbah Tosfa'ah encountered Ravina [on a Sabbath] suffering from the heat.
>
> And some say it was Mar Qashisha son of Rava who encountered R. Ashi suffering from the heat.[14]
>
> He said to him: doesn't the master hold that which was taught in a Tannaitic text: one who wishes to sprinkle his home on the Sabbath, brings a basin full of water and washes his face in this corner, his hands in that corner, his feet in another corner, and the house is sprinkled on its own!?
>
> He responded: it did not occur to me.
>
> A Tannaitic text: a wise woman sprinkles her home on the Sabbath.

Amemar permitted the people of Mehoza to sprinkle their floor with water on the Sabbath in order to cool the room off. He goes on to explain that in earlier times sprinkling water on the Sabbath was forbidden because of the possibility of evening out depressions (לאשוויי גומות) (see b. Shab. 141a). However, there is no such concern in Mehoza, where floors are made of stone, not earth. An anecdote reports that Rabbah Tosfa'ah encountered Ravina suffering from the heat on the Sabbath, probably in Mata Mehasia, where he lived and where the floors are not made of stone.[15] He asks his mentor if he is willing to act on the following *baraita*'s advice of sprinkling the floor by washing hands here, face there, and so on. Ravina responds that utilizing such a strategy never occurred to him. The meaning of his answer is not clear. He is probably saying that he does not oppose sprinkling the home in that manner on the Sabbath but did not think of it himself. In this instance, the mentor accepts the advice of the student and does not defend his (lack of) action. As for halakhic change, it is the student who applies the floor-washing technique on the Sabbath to cooling a home on the Sabbath.[16] The mentor seems willing to go along with this strategy.

---

14. This alternate attribution is omitted in Munich 95. And following the question, *lo savar lah mar*, the words *ha detanya* appear twice in succession. See n. 18 below.

15. If the Amora suffering from the heat is R. Ashi, he lived in Sura. One has to assume that there, too, the floors are not made of stone.

16. The context in the Yerushalmi, how to get around the law (*ha'aramah*), suggests that

The *sugya* continues with a short *baraita* which states that a wise woman knows how to sprinkle her floor on the Sabbath. There is no explanation of how she does that. The Yerushalmi contains a similar assertion, not as a *baraita* but as a *memra*.

Talmud Yerushalmi (Venezia) Shabbat 2:7, 5c

רבי ירמיה ור' זעירה בשם ר' חייא בר אשי אשה פיקחת מדיחה כוס כאן קערה כאן תמחוי כאן ונמצאת מרבצת את ביתה בשבת

R. Yirmiyah, R. Zeira in the name of R. Hiyya bar Ashi: A wise woman washes a cup here, a bowl there, a basin somewhere else, and it turns out that she washes her floor on the Sabbath.

This passage explains in detail how a woman can function on the Sabbath: she can wash a cup here, a bowl there, and so on, and in this way her floor gets sprinkled on its own. It appears that the Bavli reformulated the Yerushalmi text, and, in the process, turned a *memra* into a *baraita* and replaced a woman washing dishes with a man washing himself. I point this out because, in nearly all cases, when a student says to his teacher, "doesn't the master hold the opinion of R. X," he cites a *memra*, not a *baraita*. This *sugya*, as it reads today in the Vilna Shas, presents just a vestige of the Yerushalmi *memra* about a woman, following the so-called *baraita* about a man.[17] The *sugya* thus implies that the woman copied the action of the man who invented the strategy, even though the opposite is true.

The inclusion in the *sugya* of this opaque "*baraita*" leads one to suspect that the Bavli editor consciously and tendentiously rewrote the Yerushalmi *memra*. He may have done so to put a better argument in Rabbah Tosfa'ah's mouth, so that he can offer Ravina a *baraita* that speaks of a man and thereby persuade him to adopt the heat-reducing strategy. It is also possible that the term *detanya*, which follows the words *lo savar lah mar*, is a later addition to the text by an early editor who (mistakenly) considered any Hebrew teaching to be Tannaitic.[18]

7. Bavli Giṭṭin 7a, Crowns for Brides

א"ל ריש גלותא לרב הונא: כלילא מנא לן דאסור?
א"ל: מדרבנן, דתנן: בפולמוס של אספסיינוס גזרו על עטרות חתנים . . . .
אדהכי קם רב הונא לאפנויי, א"ל רב חסדא, קרא כתיב: (יחזקאל כא:לא) כה אמר ה' אלהים הסר המצנפת והרם העטרה זאת לא זאת השפלה הגבה והגבוה השפיל, וכי מה

---

the point of her actions is to wash the floor without intending to, perhaps to keep down the dust. It does not seem likely that her goal is to cool the room off.

17. This is a second time that the same Yerushalmi *memra* is called a *baraita* in the Bavli.

18. See previous note.

ענין מצנפת אצל עטרה? אלא לומר לך: בזמן שמצנפת בראש כ"ג עטרה בראש כל אדם, נסתלקה מצנפת מראש כ"ג נסתלקה עטרה מראש כל אדם.
אדהכי אתא רב הונא, אשכחינהו דהוי יתבי, א"ל: האלהים! מדרבנן, אלא חסדא שמך וחסדאין מילך.
רבינא אשכחיה למר בר רב אשי דהוה גדיל כלילא לברתיה, א"ל: לא סבר לה מר הסר המצנפת והרם העטרה?
א"ל: דומיא דכ"ג בגברי אבל בנשי לא.

The exilarch said to R. Huna: from where do we learn that garlands are forbidden?

He answered: it is a rule of the rabbis, as we learn in a Mishnah (m. Soṭah 9:14), "during the invasion of Vespasian, they decreed against [the wearing of] garlands [*atarot*] for bridegrooms ..."

R. Huna then arose to relieve himself.

Said to him R. Hisda [to the exilarch]: There is a Scriptural source for it. [We read in Ezek 21:31,] "Thus said the Lord God, remove the mitre and lift up the crown" ... What is the connection between a mitre and a crown? This juxtaposition comes to teach that when the mitre is on the head of the High Priest, a crown may be placed on the head of ordinary persons; when the mitre is removed from the head of the high priest, the crown must be removed from the head of ordinary persons.

At this time R. Huna returned and found the two of them sitting [and conversing]. He said to them: it is from the rabbis [and not from Scripture, as you suggest], but your name is Hisda, [meaning favor], and your words match your name.

Ravina encountered Mar Bar R. Ashi weaving a garland for [the wedding of] his daughter. He said to him: doesn't the master hold the teaching "remove the mitre and lift up the crown"?

He answered: This applies to men, who are like the high priest, but not to women.

The *sugya* opens with two Amoraim visiting the exilarch.[19] He asks one of them, R. Huna, from where in Scripture can one deduce that neither a bride nor a groom may go out with a garland on their head? The Amora answers that this rule is rabbinical. He then leaves the room for a period of time. In his absence, the other visitor, R. Hisda, says to the exilarch that the ban on garlands is derived from a verse, which means it is not rabbinical but scriptural. Since the prophet Ezekiel says that one should remove the mitre and the crown, one may deduce from the juxtaposition of these words that, if the high priest no longer dons a mitre, it is forbidden for ordinary people to go out in a crown. That is, after the destruction of the Second Temple, brides and grooms could no longer wear fancy

19. See Geoffrey Herman, *"A Prince without a Kingdom": The Exilarch in the Sasanian Era, TSAJ 150* (Tübingen: Mohr Siebeck 2012), for a discussion of Babylonian Amoraim and their relationship with the exilarch.

headgear to their wedding celebrations. R. Huna returns and insists that the rule is from the rabbis, not from Scripture, but still offers high praise to R. Hisda for his midrashic derivation. Is R. Huna speaking sarcastically when he praises R. Hisda? Very likely yes. Since seemingly straightforward answers in other anecdotes turn out to have been sarcastic, it is possible that in this case, as well, the praise is really criticism.[20]

An anecdote then reports that Ravina encountered Mar bar R. Ashi weaving a garland, or crown, for his daughter's wedding. He asked him, "don't you hold the view of R. Hisda that when the high priest no longer wears a mitre, ordinary people are also forbidden to wear crowns," implying that Mar bar R. Ashi should not be preparing a crown for his daughter's wedding. Mar bar R. Ashi answers that R. Hisda's ban applies only to men and not women, because the verse speaks of the high priest, a man. That ends the anecdote. Mar bar R. Ashi has thus supported reintroducing fancy headgear for brides.

In this case, too, I claim that the criticized Amora produces an answer on the spot in order to justify his behavior. Mar bar R. Ashi, chided by Ravina for weaving a garland for his daughter's wedding, justifies his action by claiming that R. Hisda banned garlands for men only, permitting them for women. The wording of R. Hisda's midrash does not sit well with this interpretation, since the Amora speaks of *kol adam*, that is, ordinary persons, men and also women. But to justify his action, Mar bar R. Ashi reinterprets R. Hisda's midrash, restricting the ban to men. Mar bar R. Ashi thus cancels the Mishnah's decree against garlands for brides. This Amora lived in the last Amoraic generation, about five hundred years following the destruction of the Second Temple. Perhaps, in his opinion, the decree no longer had any relevance. By limiting the scope of a midrash, Mar bar R. Ashi, benefited women, brides in particular.

8. Bavli Baba Qama 113a, Missing a Court Date

אמר רבא: האי מאן דכתיב עליה פתיחא על דלא אתי לדינא, עד דאתי לדינא לא מקרעינן ליה . . .

אמר רב חסדא: קובעים זמן שני וחמישי ושני, זמנא וזמנא בתר זמנא, ולמחר כתבינן.

רב אסי [צ"ל רב אשי] איקלע בי רב כהנא, חזא ההיא איתתא דאזמנה לדינא בפניא, ובצפרא כתיב עלה פתיחא.

א"ל, <u>לא סבר לה מר להא דאמר רב חסדא</u>: קובעין זמן שני וחמישי ושני?

א"ל: ה"מ גברא דאניס וליתיה במתא אבל איתתא כיון דאיתה במתא ולא אתיא מורדת היא.

20. See, e.g., b. Ḥul. 111b, Rav's comment about Shmuel; and b. Ber. 41b, R. Himnuna's comment to R. Hisda.

> Said Rava: A person against whom a Petiha has been written for not showing up in court, it is not torn up until the person [actually] comes to court....
>
> Said R. Hisda: [In a legal summons], we cite the person to appear on a Monday, [then on] a Thursday, and [then on the following] Monday, one after the other. [If the person still does not show up], on the morrow we write [a Petiha].
>
> R. Ashi was visiting the home of R. Kahana. He saw [there] a woman who was asked to appear in court in the evening [and did not show up], and in the morning a Petiha was written against her.
>
> He said to him: doesn't the master hold what R. Hisda said, that one sets three court dates in succession, a Monday, [and then a] Thursday, and [then the following] Monday?
>
> He answered: that applies to men only, for they are sometimes unable to appear on the appointed date because of circumstances that keep them out of town. But a woman, since she is always in town, if she does not appear, she is a *moredet* [a rebellious woman].

A *petiha* is the declaration of a ban for disobeying the judges. In a discussion of court procedures, Rava says that if a *petiha* was written for someone who does not show up in court on the appointed date, it is not torn up until he shows up. R. Hisda comments that a person is given three successive court dates—a Monday, a Thursday, and a Monday. If he does not show up on any of those days, the judges issue a *petiha* against him. An anecdote reports that R. Ashi visited the home of R. Kahana and saw there a woman who had been summoned to appear before R. Kahana the previous evening but did not show up. The next morning he wrote a *petiha* against her. R. Ashi asked his mentor why he wrote the *petiha* so soon since, according to R. Hisda, one gives a person three chances and she was given just one. He answers that R. Hisda gives men three chances to show up because they are often on the road; women are always in town and so they get only one court date.

As we saw above regarding garlands for brides, we see here an Amora who justified his behavior with a claim that the rule of an earlier Amora does not apply to an entire category of people, in both cases women. Here, too, it seems that the Amora issued this limitation on the spot in response to criticism. There is no indication whatsoever in the statement of R. Hisda that he intended it to apply to men only. Unlike Mar bar R. Ashi, who made a change that benefited women, R. Kahana modified the law in a way that harmed women. The moral voice is that of R. Ashi, who feels a woman was wronged in that she was treated more harshly than the law allowed. But he is silenced by his mentor who says that the law has good reason to treat men more leniently than women.

Conclusions

Through analysis in this article of seven *sugyot* that contain the phrase *lo savar lah mar,* and another twenty-five that also contain the phrase, I conclude that an Amora who implements a halakhah on occasion gives himself permission to change it. In response to the pointed critique of a student, a senior Amora will justify his "errant" behavior in a number of different ways: by claiming that his circumstances are not addressed by the rule, by interpreting a verse anew, by identifying a class of people to whom the rule does not apply, by making a claim that he is delicate and so the law does not apply to him, by fabricating a new rule but attributing it to an earlier Amora, and even, on occasion, by admitting he never heard of the rule under discussion.[21] I argue that nearly all anecdotes containing the phrase *lo savar lah mar* present a modification of halakhah. Their inclusion in the Talmud loudly broadcasts the editors' view that Amoraim may change a halakhah in the course of carrying it out. Even after a halakhah leaves the "study hall," [22] it may be altered.

In most cases of *lo savar lah mar,* a student critiques his mentor or a senior scholar. It may not seem reasonable, at first glance, that a student would attack a teacher, but upon reflection it becomes clear that there is logic to this phenomenon. Had the criticism been by the teacher of the student, halakhah could not develop because a student may not innovate halakhically. But when a student or junior colleague criticizes a senior colleague, the senior colleague has the opportunity to introduce halakhic change. In most cases of *lo savar lah mar,* the Amora modifies the halakhah in the direction of leniency. In a few cases, he modifies it in the direction of stringency.

We also saw that in the *sugyot* containing the phrase *lo savar lah mar,* the halakhah that is cited by the student is that of an Amora.[23] The underlying assumption of a student is that an Amora is not allowed to disagree with the halakhah of another, earlier Amora. In the thirty-five *lo savar lah mar* sugyot, the criticized Amora does not disagree outright with the rule of the earlier Amora. In response to the question "does not the master hold

---

21. It is of interest that these techniques are the same ones used throughout the Talmud to resolve contradictions between two prescriptive halakhot.

22. The study hall need not be a bricks-and-mortar building. I use this phrase to indicate acceptance of the halakhah by a group of rabbis at a particular point in time. Later rabbis, I argue, may modify that accepted halakhah.

23. If it were the halakhah of a Tanna, the question would have been formulated as "have we not learned in a mishnah" (*vehatenan*) or "have we not learned in a *baraita*" (*vehatanya*).

like R. X?" the criticized Amora affirms the halakhah of the earlier Amora but modifies it somewhat.

All of the anecdotes containing the phrase *lo savar lah mar,* and most other halakhic anecdotes,[24] appear at the end of a unit of discussion. There is no Amoraic commentary on them. I posit that its absence supports my theory that halakhot are often composed of two parts: the version that emerges from the "study hall" as cited earlier in the *sugya,* and the adjustment of the halakhah that results from real-life implementation, as presented by the anecdote. One might say, therefore, that the anecdote gets the "last word."[25]

24. As I have argued in various presentations on this topic. See n. 2.

25. The notion of *ma'aseh rav,* meaning that the actual implementation of a rule decides the halakhah, is already present in the Talmud and even more so in the early commentators. But *ma'aseh rav* is not what I have been discussing here. This term does not suggest that the implementation of the halakhah differed from its formulation. It just means that if Tannaim or Amoraim dispute a rule, then an actual occurrence, a *ma'aseh,* will determine which view to accept. That has not been my concern here. For example: regarding the dispute among Rishonim regarding whether women may recite a blessing when donning tefillin (or any other mitzvah from which they are exempt), Tosafot (b. Eruv. 96a) say that the fact that Beruriah did recite a blessing when donning tefillin is a case of "*ma'aseh rav,*" meaning that her action indicates that the halakhah is like Rabenu Tam, who says that women may recite a blessing when performing a mitzvah from which they are exempt.

Living on the Edge

Jews, Graffiti, and Communal Prayer in Extremis

KAREN B. STERN
Brooklyn College

Nearly fifteen hundred years ago, generations of seafarers carved reverential messages into the rocky slopes surrounding Grammata Bay along the northwestern coast of the Cycladic island of Syros in Greece, where they sought temporary refuge during nautical expeditions. Sometimes they inscribed their writings on isolated rocks. At other times, they carved their messages beside, or directly over, those of their predecessors. Yet most of their compositions followed common formulas. Writers invoked the "Lord," or "Christ," described themselves as god's servants, recorded their own names, mentioned their family members, associates, or crewmates, and requested divine assistance during their collective and forthcoming journeys at sea.[1] Some concluded their sentiments with the expression "Amen." And while centuries have passed since writers carved these entreaties into the shoreline, scores of examples remain legible today.

A cursory review of these seaside graffiti reveals two significant patterns. First, many examples contain written expressions that replicate those frequently documented in early Christian prayers from other contexts.[2] Liturgies and monumental inscriptions, recited and recorded in late ancient basilicas and churches, addressed the divine in similar ways: they proclaimed the humbleness of their writers (as servants or slaves of god), requested divine favors, and often concluded with expressions of "Amen."[3] The scratched messages from Grammata Bay, however, retain a

1. See the collection of materials in Georges Kiourtzian, *Recueil des inscriptions grecques chrétiennes des Cyclades: De la fin du IIIe au IIe siècle après J.-C.*, Travaux et mémoires du Centre de recherche d'histoire et civilisation de Byzance, Collège de France, Monographies 12 (Paris: De Boccard, 2000), 134–200 (henceforth *RIGCC*), including nos. 113, 114, 117.

2. For broader discussions of Christian prayer in antiquity, see Anne Marie Yasin, *Saints and Church Spaces in the Late Antique Mediterranean: Architecture, Cult, and Community*, Greek Culture in the Roman World (Cambridge: Cambridge University Press, 2009).

3. Distinct modes of prayer are considered in P. W. van der Horst, "Silent Prayer in Antiquity," *Numen* 41 (1994): 1–25.

second consistent element, otherwise absent from their literary and monumental counterparts inside churches and basilicas: details about diversities in the religious identifications and geographic origins of their late ancient authors. Christians, as it seems, were not the only ones responsible for carving these prayer graffiti around Grammata Bay. Closer inspection of the seventy published examples of late ancient graffiti from this part of Syros, rather, reveals that some of their inscribers included seafaring Jews as well as Christians.[4] This heterogeneity of authorship flouts traditional expectations, informed by textual traditions, about the exclusivity of ancient Jewish or Christian prayer communities and activities around the Mediterranean. It also demonstrates, more broadly, how critical is the consideration of isolated inscriptions such as these toward improved insights into ranges of Jewish devotional behaviors in late antiquity.

Graffiti from Syros are not well known to students of early Jewish history: their contents are terse and opaque and their locations and numbers appear marginal to scholars more interested in the developments of Jewish life in centers of literary production in Palestine and Babylonia. But a review of inscriptions from coastal Syros, alongside those from inland entrepôts around the Mediterranean and Arabia demonstrate something most significant: how deeply interconnected, in many places, were certain activities of prayer and writing among Jews, Christians, and their neighbors. Samples of graffiti from disparate and isolated locations in the Cyclades (Syros), the arid eastern deserts of Egypt (El-Kanaïs), and isolated rocks and structures in the outer reaches of Arabia exemplify how pervasively did sailors, traders, wanderers, and travelers who traversed the seas and deserts engage in devotional practices together, inclusive of their diverse origins and god-beliefs.[5] This essay thus suggests that graffiti preserve rare but significant evidence for how ancient Jews used acts of writing and prayer to modify and engage with the linguistic, social, professional, cultic, religious, and cultural customs of their non-Jewish neighbors. Attention to examples of this phenomenon in a diversity of times and locations, moreover, shows how pervasive were such types of practices in remote trading centers and routes throughout the ancient world.

Specific terminologies and understandings inform associated considerations of graffiti writing and cognate practices in Greece, Egypt, and

4. The precise total is unclear. *RIGCC* includes sixty-six entries from Syros, but multiple examples include texts or fragments that were written by multiple authors (see 198–200). The original numbers surely exceed the amount of the published examples.

5. My use of the word *pagan* below serves as a problematic and justifiably contested shorthand to describe persons who did not identify themselves as Jews or Christians. See more extensive discussion of the use of this term in Karen B. Stern, *Writing on the Wall: Graffiti and the Forgotten Jews of Antiquity* (Princeton: Princeton University Press, 2018), 177 n. 1.

Arabia. The category of graffiti, for instance, as I deploy it below, serves as a type of shorthand to describe a subset of inscriptions more generally. Throughout the ancient world, many people—Jews and non-Jews alike—drew graffiti (technically, carved writing) in places that they visited and worshiped.[6] These writings often integrate pictures and differ from monumental inscriptions in several ways: they constitute sui generis acts of writing and commemoration on the part of their authors; their applications are chronologically secondary to the construction of surrounding spaces; and their appearances are not necessarily predicated upon preliminary acts of donation or dedication.[7]

The authorship of many of these texts, however, remains somewhat uncertain, even when the inscriptions include personal names. In some cases, individuals carved these graffiti themselves, while, at other times, they probably asked individuals with more refined writing or rock-carving skills to incise them on their behalf. The contingencies informing such decisions (of whether to write one's own message or to ask another to do it in one's stead) remain difficult to reconstruct and respond as much to rates and ranges of literacy among their authors (agents) as to the technical challenges posed by carving letters and words into hard stone.[8] When I use the terms *authors* or *writers* below, therefore, I do so as shorthand to describe the inscriptions' agents—those whose desires impelled the creation of associated messages (even if it was only under their direction, rather than by their very hands, that their messages were incised).

Also central to this evaluation is an expanded definition of prayer, which encompassed acts of writing such as those considered here.[9] As I suggest above and argue more extensively elsewhere, such a classification is reasonable and useful, because so many graffiti employ the same terms and reflect the same purposes as prayers otherwise embedded in liturgies and monumental inscriptions. Their messages address the divine directly, describe supplicants in a relational way (often by redefining their agents as slaves or servants of god) and detail their appeals to the divine for assistance in general or particular circumstances.[10] Even in retrospective inscriptions—including those that offer thanks for writers' safety during

6. For more extensive discussion of the definition of *graffiti,* see Stern, *Writing on the Wall,* 13–20.

7. For additional consideration of related points, see Jennifer Baird and Claire Taylor, eds., *Ancient Graffiti in Context,* Routledge Studies in Ancient History 2 (New York: Routledge, 2011), 4–8.

8. Questions of authorship remain significant and are considered in other contexts. See Stern, *Writing on the Wall,* 22–23.

9. Ibid., 78–80.

10. See Reuven Kimelman, "Rabbinic Prayer in Late Antiquity," in *The Cambridge History of Judaism,* vol. 4, *The Late Roman-Rabbinic Period,* ed. Steven Katz (Cambridge: Cambridge University Press, 2006), 573–611.

journeys already completed—several examples replicate the syntax of thanksgiving prayers by attributing their authors' survivals or salvation to divine favor. While selected numbers of graffiti from Greece, Egypt, and Arabia, which I consider briefly below, necessarily and simultaneously fulfill broad ranges of additional functions (whether economic, political, professional, personal, or interpersonal), their social, cultural, and devotional aspects remain the focus of the following discussion. Rather than address the theological beliefs of supplicants, therefore, the ensuing analysis considers acts of writing as behaviors of worship, which necessarily responded to and transformed surrounding landscapes and communities.

Syros

The shores of Syros retain some of the clearest examples of links between public writing and prayer during the Roman period. By late antiquity and after the reorganization of the Roman Empire, the island of Syros in the Greek Cyclades had fallen under the distinct administration of *Provincia Insularum*, of which Rhodes was the capital.[11] While Hermoupolis was the capital of the island, Grammata Bay served as its principal port. Roughly a half-hour boat ride from Kini, itself across the island, the Bay was a place where sailors, shipowners, and traders of various origins temporarily congregated in the middle of their journeys.[12] It was along its coasts that sailors and traders carved their messages, which anticipated and commemorated their journeys by sea.

Chronologies of inscriptions found on Grammata Bay correspond with significant political and theological shifts throughout the region: earlier studies classified as "pagan" fifty-five messages from its rocky coastline and written in earlier periods,[13] but greater numbers of published examples (at least seventy-five in number) include texts that nominate individuals with distinctly Christian names, record sentiments that are diagnostically Christian, and incorporate images of Christograms or Latin crosses.[14] The latter group of messages likely dates to the fourth through seventh centuries CE, although only one graffito from this group includes

11. *RIGCC*, 136.

12. Ibid., 135.

13. Klonas Stéphanos, "'Επιγραφαὶ τῆς Νήσου Σύρου," in Ἀθήναιον 3 (1874): 517–25, 648–56; reprinted in K. Στεφανος, Ἐπιγραφαὶ τῆς Νήσου Σύρου τὸ πλεῖστον ἀνέκδοτοι μετὰ τοπογραφικῶν καὶ ἱστορικῶν παρατηρήσεων περὶ τῆς ἀρχαίας Σύρου καὶ δύο λιθογραφικῶν πινάκων (Athens, 1875), nos. 13–24.

14. See *RIGCC*, pl. XX–XXII. My tabulation of the number of Christian texts includes the enumeration in Kiourtzian but counts the unedited fragments in no. 136 as individual inscriptions in addition to the total.

a clear date.[15] The majority of inscribed texts from this area of Syros thus derive from periods of later Roman and Christian hegemony, even if examples abound from earlier eras.

The population in Grammata Bay was seasonally inundated with merchants, sailors, shipowners, or those otherwise engaged in maritime enterprises.[16] Authors of local graffiti along the shore recorded in their writings the ranges of positions they occupied that related to shipping industries and trade.[17] Some graffiti name specific ships on which inscribers worked; others explicitly document the writings and concerns of shipowners, captains, or sailors.[18] Several of the graffiti, moreover, record designations that reflect their writers' diverse ethnic and geographic origins. Texts record some authors' connections to farther-flung places, including Naxos, Rhodes, Miletos, Smyrna, Bithynia, Hydra, and Tyre.[19] In carving similar messages, in similar scripts, languages, and manners around Grammata Bay, however, these travelers also exhibited their embrace of a local and regional practice of writing graffiti as an aspect of preparing for (or reflecting on) their maritime voyages.[20]

As indicated above, most graffiti from late ancient Syros follow common syntactical, linguistic, and orthographic features for the region. They betray clear Christian associations through explicit invocations of "Lord" or "Christ" and inclusions of scratched crosses beside and beneath several inscriptions. Their graffiti thus include syntactical patterns that resemble those of their pagan predecessors but integrate specifically Christian imagery, vocabulary, or concepts.[21]

Two messages among them, however, include distinct elements that differently index the identifications of their authors. One such message reads:[22] Κ(ύρι)ε βοήθη τῷ̣ δού-| λο̣ σου Εὐνομίο̣| κὲ πάσῃ̣ τῇ̣ συνπλοί|ᾳ̣ αὐτοῦ

15. Also see *RIGCC* no. 129. Similar groupings of texts are in *RIGCC* nos. 20, 136, 138. Only a few of these may derive from a much later period (early eleventh century; nos. 87, 88, 89b).

16. On the seasonality of ancient travel, see Michail D. Bukharin, "Greeks on Socotra: Commercial Contacts and Early Christian Missions," in *Foreign Sailors on Socotra: The Inscriptions and Drawings from the Cave Hoq*, ed. Ingo Strauch, Vergleichende Studien zu Antike und Orient 3 (Bremen: Hempen, 2012), 519–20.

17. On the culture, juridical, and political power of maritime traders in the Greek world, see C. M. Reed, *Maritime Traders in the Ancient Greek World* (Cambridge: Cambridge University Press, 2003), 27–33.

18. Inscriptions that name ships include *RIGCC* nos. 71, 92, 103, and 107; those that name personnel and their concerns are abundant and include *RIGCC* nos. 130, 131, and 133.

19. These toponyms and ethnics are recorded in *RIGCC* nos. 6, 14, 47, 25–26, 101, 108, 122, and 131.

20. Kiourtzian records examples from throughout the Cyclades, including those in Amorgos, Ios, Delos, Kythnos, Melos, Paros, Naxos, and elsewhere in *RIGCC*.

21. Compare examples in Stéphanos, "Ἐπιγραφαὶ τῆς Νήσου Σύρου," 517–25.

22. Transcription from *RIGCC* no. 108; pl XXXIV.

Ναξίοις ("Lord! help your servant Eunomios and all of his crew, Naxians"; *RIGCC* nos. 108, 174= IJO I Ach72); while a second one invokes: ἐπὶ ὠνώματος Θ(εο)ῦ ζõν[τος] | Είωρτύλις [?Ἰουδα]ῖος | σωθὶς ὑπὲρ [εὐπλ]ύα[ς?] ("In the name of the living God, Heortylis the Jew (?), having returned safely, for a good voyage (?)"; *RIGCC* no. 118 = IJO I Ach73).[23] Most features of the syntax, script, and expressions in these texts are locally conventional among Christian authors, but other of their elements stand out differently and thereby highlight their writers' devotional, political, and cultural particularities.

The first example largely replicates local writing conventions and only indexes Jewish association through its pictorial elements. Following local custom, for instance, its Greek text appears within a tabula ansata frame. The style, syntax, and orthography of the message, moreover, are mostly indistinguishable from those of other prayers written around the Bay: the text directly addresses "the Lord" using the conventional abbreviation for Κύριε (KE overscored by a horizontal bar), solicits help for the writer (self-described as the Lord's "servant" or "slave"), and uses the term *συνπλοία* to describe the crew, the ship, and its effects (*RIGCC* no. 108).[24] The writer and crew described in this text, like many other local examples, are allogenic (in this case, from Naxos) and likely passed through Syros during the courses of their longer journeys. The personal name of the writer of the text (Εὐνομιος) is also regionally common in periods of earlier and later antiquity.[25] Only one element of this text, then, distinguishes this message somewhat from others and explicitly indicates its association with a Jew rather than a Christian—the deep engraving of a menorah and two other symbols—perhaps a lulav and an amphora of some kind—into the upper right corner of the tabula.[26] This menorah is visually prominent and responds to the contours of the text; it occupies a greater proportion

---

23. Translations from David Noy, Alexander Panayotov, and Hanswulf Bloedhorn, *Inscriptiones Judaicae Orientis*, vol. I (Tübingen: Mohr Seibeck, 2004) [henceforth IJO I], Ach72 and Ach73. Compare also the imprecation in Michail D. Bukharin, "Greeks on Socotra: Commercial Contacts and Early Christian Missions," in Strauch, *Foreign Sailors on Socotra*, 501–39, here 532, 535.

24. The text even uses the irregular orthography for the dative here, also quite common in surrounding inscriptions; see discussion in commentary in IJO I, Ach72.

25. Friedrich Preisigke, *Namenbuch enthaltend alle griechischen, lateinischen, ägyptischen, hebräischen, arabischen und sonstigen semitischen und nichtsemitischen Menschennamen, soweit sie in griechischen Urkunden (Papyri, Ostraka, Inschriften, Mumienschildren usw.) Ägyptens sich vorfinden* (1922; repr., Amsterdam: A. M. Hakkert, 1967); discussion in IJO I, Ach72.

26. Menorahs are not necessarily incontrovertible symbols Jewish presence, as discussed in Steven Fine, "When Is a Menorah 'Jewish'? On the Complexities of a Symbol under Byzantium and Islam," in *Age of Transition: Byzantine Culture in the Islamic World*, ed. Helen Evans (New York: Metropolitan Museum of Art, 2015), 38–53. Bereft of any explicit Christian association, however, the menorah carvings on Syros seem to be more certainly associated with Jewish use.

of the tabula ansata than do most of the crosses in comparable inscriptions. The relative prominence and clarity of the menorah and associated symbols therefore remain significant and suggest that the writer carved them to be seen clearly and beside the adjacent (and otherwise locally conventional) message.

A second text that once incorporated similar iconography is found nearby (*RIGCC* no. 118; IJO I, Ach 73). The syntax of this text is more unusual for local inscriptions from Grammata Bay. Rather than naming the "Lord" ("Κύριε" or "Christ"), the incipit of the text calls out "In the name of the living God," ἐπὶ ὠνώματος Θ(εο)ῦ ζον[τος]. The context for this divine epithet is unclear. Even if scholars have variously connected this formula to others in the Septuagint and New Testament (e.g., LXX Deut 4:33; and Rev 15:7), the phrase remains otherwise unattested on Syros and in inscriptions associated with Jews from elsewhere.[27] Moreover, while the text incorporates some locally conventional abbreviations (including the bar over the theta to indicate "Θεος"), both the personal name (Εἰωρτύλις) and its prayer formulation remain locally unusual. For instance, most of the inscriptions from Grammata Bay, including the previous example, request divine assistance for a safe forthcoming voyage, but this inscription is (as David Noy calls it) "retrospective"—it offers thanks for a journey already successfully completed.[28]

Still other features differentiate the latter graffito from other local examples. The first of these is the word [?Ἰουδα]ῖος in line 2, even if this reading remains decidedly uncertain. Second, and more definitive, is the presence of a clearly drawn menorah, with a bisecting bar, on the left side of the inscription, as attested in the original squeeze impression.[29] This documented element has since disappeared but associates the text (and thereby the author) with a Jewish context. Other sentiments in the inscription, which remain both locally unattested and regionally unconventional, may reflect its agent's particularly Jewish perspectives, beliefs, or modes of worship, but associated hypotheses necessarily remain speculative without additional information about its inscriber.

Given these uncertainties, how might we understand this and the previous inscription from Grammata Bay and their locations beside other imprecations of explicitly polytheistic or Christian association? At minimum, the position and contents of the texts demonstrate their authors' direct engagement with specific features of local maritime culture: namely, the practice of carving messages into rocks around Grammata

27. For discussion of this point, see the commentary of IJO I, Ach73; and *RIGCC* no. 118.

28. Noy, Panayotov, and Bloedhorn emphasize this aspect of the inscription in comparing it to examples from El-Kanaïs, in the commentary of IJO I, Ach73.

29. As represented in Stéphanos's and Hillier's squeeze published in *IG* xii 5.1 1903, no. 712, 99; Stéphanos, "Επιγραφαὶ τῆς Νήσου Σύρου," 88 no. 99; discussed in IJO I, Ach73 (244).

Bay to beseech the divine for safety and sustenance before (or following) trips at sea.

That Jews would be among writers on Syros, similarly occupied with maritime trade and professions, of course, is not surprising. Multiple ancient sources attest to Jews' roles as shipowners, captains, sailors, and seafarers throughout the Mediterranean as well as in the Aegean and elsewhere.[30] Common features of a life at sea, among Jews and non-Jews alike, predicted that seafaring and shipowning Jews would share the same needs, challenges, and concerns as their non-Jewish peers, whether regarding the safety or well-being of their cargo or crew, or their wishes to evade mortal dangers at sea (such as inclement weather or piracy). Surrounded by the writings of their peers and anticipating (or reflecting on) comparable uncertainties during nautical expeditions, Jewish seafarers on Syros carved messages along the coastline (over pagan antecedents and beside their Christian neighbors) in several locally conventional ways—as one means to assure (or give thanks for) their success. Self-identified Jews thus expressed these imperatives in the same basic ways as their neighbors, individual variability notwithstanding.

Any observer's particular vantage, of course, informs her interpretation of these texts and their broader significance (or lack thereof) in local and cross-regional contexts. From a theological perspective, for instance, one could regard graffiti associated with Jews as dramatically distinct from other written messages around Grammata Bay. The explicit invocations of "Christ" in many texts, and the clear incisions of a menorah in others, could betray their inscribers' vastly discrepant beliefs and practices, theologies, orientations, and cultural contexts. From a sociological perspective, by contrast, one could take a different view. One could argue that, while slight differences are apparent in the syntax (whether one or another message invokes "Lord" as opposed to "Christ") and iconography (inclusions of crosses versus drawings of menorahs) in some of these graffiti, the vast preponderance of their features point to common behaviors of writing and praying: messages are carved into the rocks in similar places, in the same languages, with the same vocabulary, and for the same purposes, beside other local examples. Regardless of one's precise perspective, however, certain patterns remain definitive: pagan seafarers, along with the Jews and Christians, who visited Syros's rocks after them, prepared for their voyages in identical ways by performing similar activi-

---

30. On Jews, ships, rabbinic texts, and their portrayals of maritime life and seafaring, see Daniel Sperber, *Nautica Talmudica*, Bar-Ilan Studies in Near Eastern Languages and Culture (Ramat-Gan: Bar-Ilan University Press, 1986); and Catherine Heszer, *Jewish Travel in Antiquity*, TSAJ 144 (Tübingen: Mohr Siebeck, 2013), 186–89. For the regional resonance and use of ship images in mortuary contexts, see Karen B. Stern, "Ships, Jews, and Death: A Consideration of Nautical Imagery in Levantine Mortuary Contexts," *Images* 19 (forthcoming).

ties of carving devotional graffiti, even if they appealed to different deities when doing so.

When focusing on the big picture, of course, one could remain quite skeptical and argue that the number of graffiti associated with Jews from Syros remains rather negligible: they represent only 3 percent of contemporaneous published examples. Yet given the percentages of inscriptions associated with Jews throughout the Mediterranean, one could argue equally that this number remains statistically significant. The mere presence of these texts and their incorporation of limited indices of Jewishness (despite broader local conventionalities) indeed document otherwise-overlooked dynamics of local maritime and devotional culture, embraced by some Jews as well as Christians.

This diversity in the authorship of devotional graffiti, moreover, seems to have been mutually acceptable to contemporaneous Jewish and Christian inscribers. Ancient Jewish writers carved their messages close to those authored by Christians. At the same time, Christians did not efface the menorah symbols and associated texts from Syros, written alongside their own; the menorahs remained unscathed until more recent periods of modernity.[31] This reality contrasts to the fate of several paleo-Christian ("pagan") inscriptions, which ancient Christian writers carved over with their own messages during the same periods.[32] These patterns of epigraphic and precatory coexistence, then, suggest something more palpable: that ancient Jews and Christians found their activities of graffiti writing sufficiently acceptable that they did not efface differently identified examples.[33]

Some might wish to explain further the fundamental similarities of Jews' and Christians' messages by hypothesizing that their authors might have employed the same sets of local inscribers to do the work for them. This reasonable possibility would account for the comparable syntax, uses of abbreviations, and geographic locations of many of the inscriptions, which Jews and Christians carved into adjacent portions of rock. But the paleography of these writings remains diverse (suggesting multiple hands of application, through time) so other hypotheses are equally likely to account for their similarities. One could easily imagine, for instance,

---

31. The menorah in *RIGCC*, no. 118, was effaced only in the more recent past, as evidenced by the discrepancy between recent autopsy and the original squeezes of the inscription. See the discussion of this point in IJO I, 244.

32. As there was ample space to carve into Syros's rocky shore, such instances of overwriting appear to be deliberate. Examples of this include *RIGCC* no. 83; photo in *RIGCC*, pl. XXVII.

33. See cognate discussions in Annabel Wharton, "Erasure: Eliminating the Space of Late Ancient Judaism," in *From Dura to Sepphoris: Studies in Jewish Art and Society in Late Antiquity*, ed. Lee I. Levine and Zeev Weiss, JRASup 40 (Portsmouth, RI: Journal of Roman Archaeology, 2000), 195–214.

that Jewish, as well as Christian seafarers and their predecessors, might have adopted common formulas for prayers at sea, which they exacted in writing on land, because they had similar needs: they lived together, traveled together, and occupied the same ships and ports together. They faced similar fates and fears together. They might have prayed to different gods, but they also might have understood or appealed to those gods in similar ways. Indeed, they might have carved the same types of messages into the local rocks as an appropriate and locally conventional ritual to perform before a voyage. Regardless of disparities in the theological views and terminologies, or the personal preferences of inscribers, therefore, Jews, Christians, and their pagan predecessors inscribed messages into the desolate rocks surrounding Grammata Bay over centuries, for similarly stated purposes—for directly soliciting divine attention, intervention, and protection at sea. Jews, in writing such messages, thus simultaneously wrote and prayed beside their Christian peers and colleagues.

El-Kanaïs

Heterogeneous communal writing and devotional practices are evident also in places farther inland, where Jews similarly wrote graffiti, as did their neighbors, to document their prayers and offerings of thanksgiving to the divine. Indeed, in a place and time that seems worlds apart from the rocky coastlines of the Cyclades, Jews and their peers wrote messages of gratitude in graffiti, which they deposited around shrines and sanctuaries to Pan in the Eastern desert of Egypt. Pan was worshiped throughout Egypt in periods of earlier antiquity, but the regnant Ptolemaic dynasty particularly promoted the god's veneration from the third century BCE.[34] Pan (and his local manifestation as Min) was particularly popular as a patron and protector of Egypt's desert wanderers. Worshipers at regional shrines, therefore, frequently merged attributes of Pan with those of Min to synthesize local as well as hegemonic features of the cult.

Epithets in inscriptions at several shrines to Pan throughout the eastern desert reflect and reinforce the importance of the god to traders, among the most directed of desert travelers. Monumental inscriptions and graffiti, for example, herald the god as "Pan-who-walks-in-the-moun-

34. The sudden proliferation of shrines to Pan throughout the eastern desert in Egypt materializes these energies, as described in C. E. P. Adams, "Travel and the Perception of Space in the Eastern Desert of Egypt," in *Wahrnehmung und Erfassung geographischer Räume in der Antike,* ed. Michael Rathmann (Mainz am Rhein: Philipp von Zabern, 2007), 211–20, here 212. This pattern is broadly documented by André Bernand, who also considers shifts in shrine construction and use during the Roman period (*Pan du d*ésert [Leiden: Brill, 1977], 1–5). Roman rerouting of trade routes assured the decline of sanctuaries and way stations, such as those in El Kanaïs; this fact assists the dating of the Greek inscriptions from the site.

tains," "Pan-companion-on-campaigns," and, most clearly "Pan-giver-of-good-roads."[35] Such epithets recur also around the Paneion in El-Kanaïs in the Eastern desert, where a sanctuary and open cliffs surround a built shrine for the god, which simultaneously served as locus of refuge and worship for those who traversed the surrounding landscape.

An inscription discovered near the Paneion in El-Kanaïs reveals that Seti I credited himself with the foundation of the site, which subsequently served as a critical way station for travelers in the eastern desert between the Red Sea and the Nile Valley, fewer than sixty kilometers away from Edfu on the route to Berenice.[36] Ptolemaic kings, however, edified and renovated the cult building in the third century BCE; the presence of multiple dedicatory inscriptions around the shrine dates its reconstruction to the rule of Ptolemy II Philadelphos (ca. 254 BCE). Despite the longevity of El-Kanaïs as a cult center and caravansary, therefore, most of the Greek graffiti date to the Ptolemaic period. [37] The Paneion of this era, however, served as more than just a desert shrine. Itinerants could stop there to find water and refuge for themselves and for their animals amid the punishing expanse of the desert. Their dedicatory inscriptions and graffiti, which pervaded the surfaces of the shrine and surrounding cliffs, explicitly invoked the god's protection for these purposes. Travelers who self-identified as Ἰουδαῖοι also contributed their own writings.

While Arabic and Latin graffiti appear throughout the landscape, André Bernand published only the Greek inscriptions from the Pan shrine and along the cliffs that surrounded it. Contents of these ninety-two messages range from "signature" graffiti, which list personal names, to proud assertions about the number of times that writers had successfully reached the shrine during their regional journeys (often one, two, or three times). Still other texts serve as miniature biographies of the traders who passed through the place. In the process of thanking Pan for sustenance, several writers recounted their dangerous journeys by land and sea, which they survived to arrive in the sanctuary, including their survival in the face of battle, the hunt, distant voyages, or the

35. On these points, see Adams, "Travel and the Perception of Space," 212.

36. Rachel Mairs, "Egyptian 'Inscriptions' and Greek 'Graffiti' at El Kanais," in Baird and Taylor, *Ancient Graffiti in Context*, 151–61; Adams, "Travel and the Perception of Space," 212.

37. Bernand reprints Henri Gauthier's earlier plans of the built shrine in Bernand, *Le Paneion d'El-Kanaïs: Les inscriptions grecques* (Leiden: Brill, 1972), pl. II (figs. 1–2). Most of the writings from the Paneion (particularly those in Hieratic or Arabic) have evaded careful publication. Only a handful of Bernand's inscriptions (nos. 55–59b) seem to be from the imperial period. Related points considered in Bernand, *Le Paneion*. Most of the graffiti in Bernand are Hellenistic and predate Roman changes to regional trade routes. See the discussion of this point in Adams, "Travel and the Perception of Space," 212–13.

inevitable perils of sea travel.[38] Still others simply record their names and offer more general words of thanks to Pan for their survival in the face of unspecified challenges during protracted journeys.

Among the published Greek writings from the site, at least two identify their authors as Jews or Judeans (Ἰουδαῖοι). One of these reads, "Bless God. Theodotos son of Dorion the Ἰουδαῖος, returned safely from overseas,"[39] while another acclaims, "Praise the God. Ptolemaios, son of Dionysios, Ἰουδαῖος."[40] Both texts explicitly invoke *τὸν θεόν*, or "the God," but only the first explicitly names a reason for the author's gratitude ["(he) returned safely from the sea"]. Little about these inscriptions differentiates them particularly from neighboring examples: the names and patronymics of their writers, the use of the Greek language, scripts, and syntax collectively adhere to regional convention in offering divine blessing or praise.

Of course, the primary feature to suggest that Ἰουδαῖοι wrote these inscriptions (as opposed to any other types of travelers) is that they explicitly say so. Appearance of the word (Ἰουδαῖος) thus remains significant in these texts and triggers considerations of ongoing debates concerning the appropriate sense of the term.[41] A second significant feature of these inscriptions is their mutual inclusions of the word for God (τὸν θεόν), rather than a direct invocation of the god Pan. No other inscriptions found around El-Kanaïs include this more generalizing term for divinity, but this feature also appears significant when assessing the theological proclivities of their agents.[42]

While the inclusion of the term Ἰουδαῖος and the absence of a specific reference to Pan initially appear to index differently than other examples, other aspects of these inscriptions remain locally typical. Each message

---

38. One such example describes a carpenter's survival following his dangerous escapades hunting elephants. The textual message is flanked by a graphic depiction of an elephant. See the image and text in Bernand, *Le Paneion*, no. 9b; pl. 54.1–2; see also nos. 6, 15, 55, 71, 86, 26, 47, 64, 8, 42, 90; also Adams, "Travel and the Perception of Space," 218, fig. 4.

39. *CIJ* ii 1537= William Horbury and David Noy, *Jewish Inscriptions of Greco-Roman Egypt* (Cambridge: Cambridge University Press, 1992) (henceforth *JIGRE*), no. 121. Textual transcriptions and translations from El-Kanaïs modify those of *JIGRE*.

40. *JIGRE* no. 122 = *CIJ* ii 1538 = Bernand, *Le Paneion*, no. 34; letter heights of 12–15 mm; reading in Bernand, *Le Paneion*, no. 34: εὐλόγει τὸν θεόν. | Πτολεμαῖος | Διονυσίου | Ἰουδαῖος.

41. Discussions of related points are unabated. As Shaye Cohen famously suggested in *The Beginnings of Jewishness*, for instance, "before the end of the second century B.C.E." the translation of the word *Ioudaios* (Ἰουδαῖος) as "Jew" is "wrong, because before that point these words always and everywhere mean 'Judean,' not 'Jew'" (*The Beginnings of Jewishness: Boundaries, Varieties, Uncertainties*, HCS 31 [Berkeley: University of California Press, 1999], 104, 105). See also recent discussions in Cynthia Baker, *Jew*, Key Words in Jewish Studies 7 (New Brunswick, NJ: Rutgers University Press, 2017), 1–11.

42. The precise ending of this inscription additionally challenges meaningful assessment, because it could be in the accusative case for either a masculine or neuter noun—either way, the noun could be rendered in English diversely as "the God" or "the god"—each translation with significantly different theological implications.

is carved in Greek, follows orthography conventional for the site, and includes sentiments that correspond with those in other examples, carved merely centimeters away. Even their inclusions of ethnic information (Ἰουδαῖος) strictly reflect local custom. Writers and travelers at El-Kanaïs enjoyed flaunting the distances they traveled and their far-flung origins in their inscriptions. Nearly 40 percent of graffiti from El-Kanaïs include comparable ethnic or toponymic designations, as graffiti throughout the complex identify the origins of their writers in Cyrene, Macedonia, and Crete.[43] When regarded differently, therefore, the texts that describe their writers (or their fathers) as Ἰουδαῖοι exhibit a locally normative pattern. Writers who advertised their lineage or divine thanks in this way might or might not have directly originated in Judea, just as their "Macedonian" neighbors might or might not have traveled directly from Macedonia. But these writers chose to present themselves in similar ways and likely for comparable purposes, in identifying foreign origins, flaunting the distance of their travels, and thereby exhibiting their triumphs of survival during grueling journeys through desolate landscapes, such as those surrounding El-Kanaïs.

Past evaluations of these texts have assessed their omissions of direct invocations to Pan as significant.[44] This may be true: unlike messages on Syros, in which the generic term (θεόν) is common in inscriptions of appeal or thanksgiving, this is not the case at El-Kanaïs, where slightly more than half of the messages directly nominate Pan. Yet the omission of Pan's name is not entirely particular to these inscriptions either.[45] The messages written by Ἰουδαῖοι might thereby fall into that broader (if a slight minority) category of inscribers who expressed gratitude about their arrival at the site, without their specific nomination of the resident god.[46]

Perhaps most important to evaluations of the El-Kanaïs graffiti (of Ἰουδαῖοι and non-Ἰουδαῖοι alike), therefore, is the degree to which the texts that include the term conform to the spatial, linguistic, and stylistic features of local writing practices. Inscribers applied their words of praise and thanksgiving to the cliffs surrounding the Pan sanctuary, just as did most of their Macedonian and Egyptian peers. Most graffiti from El Kanaïs, including those of Ἰουδαῖοι, indeed, reflect their authors' awareness

---

43. Mairs "Egyptian 'Inscriptions,'" 155; Bernand, *Le Paneion*, 33.

44. See also Allen Kerkeslager, "Jewish Pilgrimage and Jewish Identity in Hellenistic and Early Roman Egypt," in *Pilgrimage and Holy Space in Late Antique Egypt*, ed. David Frankfurter, RGRW 134 (Leiden: Brill), 99–225.

45. Slightly more than 40 percent of all recorded inscribers at El-Kanaïs do not mention Pan in their inscriptions at all.

46. Without the inclusion of Ἰουδαῖος in the same inscriptions, of course, editors would not have regarded the abstract reference to deity as worthy of note. Only when paired with the inclusion of the word Ἰουδαῖος, does the reference to a more abstract divinity assume greater significance.

of common "rules" of participation. Graffiti are syntactically repetitive, and their authors scratched them close to, but not directly on top of, other texts (as was customary elsewhere in the Hellenistic and Roman world (such as in Pompeii, or in late ancient Syros, for that matter).[47] Ἰουδαῖος graffiti, in each of these respects, conform to the implicit rules of local graffiti discourse; they obey standards of content, placement, and respect for other inscriptions and thereby demonstrate their authors' awareness of local writing conventions.

The Ἰουδαῖοι who wrote their messages at El-Kanaïs, as well as others who deposited their writings on site, endured similar difficulties while conducting trade, hunting, or campaigning over desert lands and through the nearby Red Sea. They participated in local practices of writing and prayer by carving their thanksgiving messages to the divine into the rocks of the Pan sanctuary. Thus, whether graffiti artists identified themselves as traders, soldiers, miners, or hunters, and whether they announced that their birthplaces were in Punt, Crete, Macedonia, or Judea, they all participated in a common feature of regional culture: they applied comparable graffiti in proximate spaces to praise god and to celebrate the improbability of surviving harsh climates and protracted voyages. If one emphasizes the social dimensions of graffiti writing, one might not care so much about to which precise god, or to which precise aspect of a god, individual writers directed their praise. Rock faces of El-Kanaïs, in all cases, constituted appropriate and effective places to offer thanks to deity, for both Ἰουδαῖοι and their neighbors. In writing their prayers in and around a sanctuary to Pan, Ἰουδαῖοι (Judeans/Jews) thus performed the same activities as did their peers and, presumably, for the same stated reasons, as they took temporary refuge and used a chisel on stone to commemorate the improbability and the precariousness of their safety. The adjective or toponym of Ἰουδαῖος in this part of Egypt in the Hellenistic period, indeed, may demonstrate yet another feature of the term's capaciousness: perhaps it classified the geographic origins and/or diverse ranges of political identification of individual inscribers, alongside information about their theological beliefs and devotional practices, which encompassed activities of thanksgiving performed in a Pan shrine.[48]

---

47. Some Theban examples exhibit such overwriting; see, e.g., Jules Baillet, *Inscriptions grecs et latines des tombeaux des rois ou syringes à Thèbes*, MIFAO 42 (Cairo: Institut français d'archéologie orientale du Caire, 1920), pl. 13b, 17c, 18; also ibid., "Les graffiti," 107–16. Dialogical features of graffiti placement are reflected in graffiti position and context, e.g., Bernand, *Le Paneion*, nos. 71, 4; Mairs "Egyptian 'Inscriptions,'" 162.

48. On the consideration of related points and on the appropriate translation of the word Ἰουδαῖος, see discussion in n. 41 above.

Arabia and Beyond

There are additional places in the ancient world, well outside of Grammata Bay and El-Kanaïs, where other self-identified Jews also engaged in merged practices of prayer and writing beside their neighbors of various origins and theological proclivities. Abundant evidence exists for carvings of graffiti, of comparable sorts, on stone outcroppings throughout the deserts of Arabia, where Jews, Nabateans, and Arabs commemorated their historical presence by writing their own prayers beside each other.[49] These patterns are well chronicled in publications of Robert Hoyland and Christian Robin.[50] The rock cliffs of Arabia thus preserve additional evidence of places where Jews carved their prayers with their peers, beyond the confines of the Cyclades and the eastern Egyptian desert.

Multiple examples of devotional graffiti of these kinds appear in northwest Arabia, but other examples also appear farther to the south in Arabia Felix.[51] One such text, which probably dates to the fifth century CE, was discovered in Zafār; it follows common formats for regional messages by including the name of the author and his request for remembrance before a human or divine audience.[52] Carved into stone and open cliffs and upon built structures, it declared in Hebrew: "Yahūdah wrote (it): may he be remembered for good: amen, *shalom*, amen!" [53] This message exhibits features that align with those that Joseph Naveh has classified as forms of prayers throughout the region, which request remembrance of a named writer and often before a specific deity. Its specific deployment of Hebrew and inclusion of a diagnostically Jewish name (*Yahūdah*) distinguish the author and his devotional or cultural identification, even if other features of the content and location of the message remain more conventional.[54] Throughout the deserts of Arabia, wanderers and trad-

49. Joseph Naveh, "Graffiti and Dedications," *BASOR* 235 (1979): 27–30.

50. Robert Hoyland, "Jews of the Hijaz," in *New Perspectives on the Qur'an: The Qur'an in Its Historical Context 2*, ed. Gabriel Said Reynolds (London: Routledge, 2011), 91–116; Christian Robin, "Le Judaïsme de Himyar," *Arabia* 1 (2003): 107.

51. These inscriptions from northwest Arabia are considered in Hoyland, "Jews of the Hijaz," and in Stern, *Writing on the Wall*, 71–76.

52. I use the masculine pronoun here, because, to this point, I have not located examples of Arabian graffiti associated with women writers. The search for women writers of Arabian inscriptions remains ongoing.

53. Robin, "Le Judaïsme de Himyar," 107. This graffito appears beside a more extensive Aramaic dedicatory inscription that names "*Yhwd' Ykf* ... with the prayer of his people Israel," which suggests that its inscriber and the monumental inscription were associated with Jews (107).

54. The word *šlm*, for instance, is ubiquitous in Nabataean inscriptions of a similar sort, even if it was vocalized differently in the Hebrew. Words, such as *amen* were also included in regional and cross-regional Christian inscriptions, as seen above. See further Stern, *Writing on the Wall*, 56.

ers carved thousands of similar writings, which, much like this example, recorded their names, requested the attention of passersby, and begged for their (good) remembrance by a deity. But only a small percentage of such writings, whether in northwest or southern Arabia, such as this one, retain features of Jewish association. This message, like so many written throughout Arabia, appears beside others of similar type—in this case in Hebrew script. The text therefore modifies a common message, and a common regional practice of writing graffiti, as a means to draw attention to the Jewish writer (*Yahūdah*) and request his remembrance by human and divine audiences.

Carvings of these types of devotional graffiti are not unique to Arabia and its travel routes. Rather, such graffiti are particularly clustered in places where traders, travelers, sailors, and merchants most converged and convened in antiquity. More concentrated collections of these types of graffiti often appear in more geographically defined spaces, such as shrines or isolated land masses and particularly in extreme or remote locations. For instance, inside the cave of Hoq on Socotra off the coast of Yemen in the Indian Ocean, over many centuries, travelers of diverse origins, who spoke and wrote in different languages (including Greek and Indic dialects) and who demonstrated diverse religious proclivities, used different forms of drawing and writing to pray next to and with each other. Their writings, in multiple languages, followed the syntax and conventions demonstrated above—they include messages of thanksgiving after travel, prospective prayers for safety, and explicit requests for remembrance before human and divine audiences.[55] In Hoq, writers also celebrated the improbability of their survival, having traversed arid deserts and navigated dangerous straits and seas. Synthetic and collective activities of prayer and writing are therefore not exclusive to Syros, El-Kanaïs, and Zafār but are conventional in all sorts of centers and routes where traders and sailors came together in desolate landscapes—pagans, Jews, and Christians alike.

Assessment

Acts of carving graffiti to pray around shorelines, cliffs, and deserts might appear somewhat strange to modern sensibilities. Today, graffiti are rarely associated with acts of prayer, but rather, are more conventionally classified as behaviors of vandalism or disrespect. Moreover, places of prayer, in the modern world, are most frequently segregated among and between

55. Useful assessments of these are chronicled in Ingo Strauch, "The Indian Participants of Trade: The Historical Perspective," and Strauch, "Concluding Remarks: The Discoveries in the Cave Hoq: A Short Evaluation of their Historical Meaning," in *Foreign Sailors on Socotra*, 346–60, 540–44.

religious groups. Jews might pray alongside other Jews inside synagogues, Christians with other Christians in churches, and Muslims inside mosques, but more rarely do these prayer communities, environments, and associated activities overlap and intersect.[56] But whether along the rugged coastlines of Grammata Bay in the Cyclades or throughout the expanses of the eastern Egyptian or Arabian deserts, some ancient people extolled their connections with their natural environments, the divine, and with each other in ways different from how many modern people might anticipate—by carving requests for ongoing aid and support, and thanksgiving, as collectives. In these places, Jews engaged in acts of devotional writing alongside and with their Christian neighbors and their variously polytheistic predecessors and peers. These patterns are consistent despite contrasting and conflicting evidence presented in ancient literary sources.

Literary works of the rabbis, for instance, prescribed for Jews to conduct their devotional activities exclusively (syntactically, theologically, and spatially) and apart from their non-Jewish neighbors.[57] Hellenistic, Roman, and subsequent Christian writers from earlier and later antiquity, in tandem, similarly emphasized how vast were chasms between their own modes and activities of worship and those practiced by contemporaneous Jews (and inappropriately behaving Christians); such differences, indeed, appear to be prescriptive and constitutional (even if Jews and Christians, occasionally "transgressed").[58] Later medieval writers additionally elaborated on received literary and religious traditions concerning fissures between ancient Jewish and Christian devotional behaviors and prayer environments.[59] But examples from graffiti remain instructive in illuminating how overly generalizing, and how misleading, are many of these diachronic literary accounts and their associated representations. Locations of the preceding inscriptions indeed offer rare but significant

56. Exceptions to this pattern appear in modernity in specific settings, such as office buildings or hospitals, which may include "multipurpose" rooms for prayer.

57. For efforts to differentiate Jewish prayer, see m. Meg. 4:8–9; b. Meg. 24b; cf. b. Ber. 34b. See also William Horbury, "The Benediction of the *Minim* and Early Jewish–Christian Controversy," *JTS* 33 (1982): 19–61. For general comments on the *minim* and their identification and polemical use in the Mishnah, see Shaye Cohen, *From the Maccabees to the Mishnah*, 3rd ed., LEC 7 (Louisville: Westminster John Knox, 2014), 241–48.

58. Examples of these points abound and include the works of Manetho and Tacitus from earlier periods (including, for Manetho, *Aegyptiaca*, trans. W. G. Waddell, LCL [Cambridge: Harvard University Press, 1964], 126; Tacitus, *Hist.* 5.2–5). Ancient Christian writers developed the perspectives of their pagan predecessors. Examples include writings of Tertullian (*To the Nations* [*Ad nationes*] 1.12.3–4) and Cyril of Alexandria (*On Worship in Spirit and in Truth* [*De adoratione*] 3.92.3). Chrysostom's famous diatribes against Christian presence in synagogues (*Against the Jews* [*Adversus Judaeos*], 1), moreover, have suggested that the presence of Christians in synagogues was not unusual in Syrian Antioch.

59. Medieval commentators on Jewish texts often underscore these points, as is evident in Ovadiah Bartenura's commentary on m. Meg. 4:8–9.

evidence for overlapping regional and local prayer traditions among polytheists, Christians, and Jews, who worked and traveled along the habitable margins of the ancient world.

After all, the contingencies of life often counter the ideals prescribed by Jewish or Christian editors and authors. Certain professional occupations disproportionately drew individuals (regardless of whether or not they were Jews) into extreme desert and maritime environments. Travel and trade in these places required individuals' ongoing presence in punishing landscapes that challenged their efforts to obtain the bare necessities of life—whether fresh drinking water and food for themselves and for their animals; spaces for shade or shelter from sun, wind, or rain; or safety from theft or brigandage. The prayers that individuals verbalized and wrote in these locations and under associated conditions, therefore, simultaneously responded to such realities as necessary features of their professional, social, economic, and daily existence.

What, then, initially impelled hundreds of people to respond to such dangers by carving writings, such as those found in the rocks around Grammata Bay or on cliffs around El-Kanaïs? One explanation relates to local customs. Whether in antiquity or modernity, graffiti and cognate writings often proliferate in clusters; people tend to write in the same places (and in the same ways) that their peers have already written.[60] This explanation may account, at least partly, for the popularity of devotional graffiti in certain times and places on designated surfaces in Greece, Egypt, Arabia, and elsewhere. Jews, in these places, might have simply followed local custom: by writing graffiti prayers, they did what their peers had done before them. Environmental contexts of the same graffiti, however, suggest even more developed rationales. Conditions of maritime travel were precarious in antiquity, and seafarers wished to solicit divine assistance, in multiple ways, to assure factors that predicted successful voyages, including favorable winds and weather at sea, the health and safety of ships' personnel and cargos, and good fortune in evading pirates.[61] Desert travel required commensurate sequences of luck and success, as overland traders contended with drought, dwindling supplies,

60. Baird and Taylor, *Ancient Graffiti in Context*, 7.

61. Conditions of maritime trade are considered in multiple volumes, including Christoph Schäfer, ed., *Connecting the Ancient World: Mediterranean Shipping, Maritime Networks and Their Impact* (Rahden: Marie Leidorf, 2016). Piracy, of course, consistently scourged maritime traders: for this reason, its confrontation is notably mentioned as one of the achievements of Augustus in his Res gestae 3.1; 25.1. On the latter point, see Robert L. Hohlfelder, "An Archaeological Addendum to the *Res Gestae*: Unifying the Maritime World of Imperial Rome," in Schäfer, *Connecting the Ancient World*, 91–104, here 95. See also Lionel Casson, *Travel in the Ancient World* (London: Allen & Unwin, 1974), 149–62; Reed, *Maritime Traders*, 8, 21, 48; and Lionel Casson, *Ships and Seamanship in the Ancient World* (Baltimore: Johns Hopkins University Press, 1995), 300–314.

and marauders. Messages within coastal graffiti around Grammata Bay, as well as some found farther southeast in El Kanaïs and Arabia, indeed, reflect these diverse realities and conditions. But, unlike countless numbers of verbal prayers that once transmitted comparable messages and requests, which Jews and other travelers once vocalized to supplicate their gods for protection in the same places, the durable media of their writings in stone assured their exceptional documentation.[62] Their writings, in many cases, still call out from their original surfaces.

One might wonder, however, whether Jews and their neighbors might have written prayers together only in more remote locations, or whether they might have done so also in more densely populated areas? Limited features of the archaeological record suggest that such practices were regionally determined and were equally apparent in more urban environments.[63] One might ask, therefore, why examples from more extreme locations (with respect to ancient patterns of settlement or climate) should merit independent consideration here? The answers are clear. First, graffiti from remote areas document the lives of individuals whose modes of social, professional, and devotional engagement are otherwise often omitted from the literary record. Second, and in complement, these types of graffiti augment the data available for investigating how and where ancient Jews prayed and with whom throughout multiple corners of the ancient world. These types of evidence thus contribute to improved understandings of the breadth of ancient Jewish prayer practices in antiquity in diverse geographic locations and social and economic circumstances.[64]

Religious traditions and literary texts incline scholars to regard ancient Jews as peoples who necessarily prayed separately from their neighbors. Yet examinations of different types of data, including certain graffiti, inspire new ways to interpret archaeological and epigraphic vestiges of ancient behaviors. Fundamental similarities in written prayer expressions in graffiti, let alone in the professional pursuits of Jewish and non-Jewish inscribers, suggest that in certain natural landscapes—including Syros, El-Kanaïs, Zafār, and Hoq—all types of people, whether they originated in Naxos, Macedonia, Crete, Judea, Yemen, or the Indian subcontinent, wrote their prayers alongside each other and for similar reasons. In so

62. Similar inscriptions are found elsewhere in Greece, and many are listed in *RIGCC*, 137 n. 13 and include those found in Messenia (*IG* V.1:1538–55); on Thasos (*IG* XII.8:581–86). Others are identified in Mirabello on Crete and in Grama on the Albanian coast. For the latter groupings, see, respectively, F. Chapouthier, "Inscriptions antiques gravées sur le roc dans le gulf de Mirabello," *BCH* 59 (1935): 376–81; and N. Ceka and M. Zeqo, *Monumentet* 28 (1984): 131–33.

63. Greater proportions of graffiti associated with Jews derive from contexts elsewhere, such as burial caves, synagogues, and even civic spaces. For broader discussions of these points, see Stern, *Writing on the Wall*, 12–20.

64. Concerning this argument, see Stern, *Writing on the Wall*, 35-79.

doing these writers (whether Jews, Christians, Pan worshipers, or early Muslims) ultimately formed collective prayer communities together—even if those communities looked different from we might anticipate.[65]

In *The Beginnings of Jewishness*, Shaye Cohen asked, "[h]ow did you know a Jew in antiquity when you saw one"?[66] Cohen systematically considered answers according to multiple categories, including "looks," "clothing," "speech," "names," and "occupations," and ultimately concluded that one could not truly tell by outward appearances alone. Instead, he pointed out, that "one could make reasonably plausible inferences [concerning who was a Jew in antiquity] from what you saw."[67] The examples considered above engage with Cohen's methods and conclusions by evaluating selected groupings of graffiti from the Cyclades, eastern Egyptian desert, and southwestern Arabia. If one applied the question "how do you know a Jew in antiquity when you see one?" to these inscribed data, for instance, one arrives at conclusions that correspond with the answers Cohen once offered. One might not be able to tell who was a Jew on Syros or in El-Kanaïs, based on watching him carve prayers into rocks, but one could make inferences by scrutinizing the details of his messages. Many ancient Jews offered prayers periodically in ways and spaces apart from their non-Jewish peers, but examples from graffiti thus demonstrate another complementary reality: sometimes, *in extremis*, Jews and their non-Jewish neighbors, wrote and repeated prayers in the same ways and alongside each other.

---

65. A related point concerns the possibility that Jews could have written their graffiti beside and just like their neighbors but could have *understood* their practices somewhat differently. For example, in the modern day, situations such as those described above (participation in or completions of successful travel by sea or survival in the desert, alongside release from prison or survival from sickness) would merit the recitation of the so-called Gomel prayer. The Gomel appears to manifest traditions described in rabbinic texts (e.g., m. Ber. 4.4 and 4.6). One might wonder whether the graffiti prayers described above, which Jews offered in Syros, El-Kanaïs, and Zafār, might exhibit devotional traditions that led to the development of the Gomel prayer, or whether they demonstrate independent and similar phenomena of celebrating the improbable survival of difficult circumstances.

66. Cohen, *Beginnings of Jewishness*, 25–68, here 67.

67. Ibid., 67.

"Epigraphical Rabbis" in Their Epigraphical Contexts

JONATHAN J. PRICE
Tel Aviv University

In 1981, Shaye Cohen published a pioneering article called "Epigraphical Rabbis," in which he assembled fifty-nine cases of persons identified as rabbis in inscriptions and determined that few if any could be identified securely as a rabbi from rabbinic literature.[1] He concluded that "rabbi" was not a formalized title and could be used by community leaders who were not part of the rabbinic establishment as represented in talmudic literature. "Even in antiquity, not all rabbis were Rabbis"; thus the sphere of influence of rabbinic Judaism was limited even in Eretz Israel. Rabbis were, furthermore, not leaders in synagogues.

The reactions to this article have focused mainly on, who was a rabbi (either mentioned in the Talmud, or a sage of written and oral Torah with similar method and status); when talmudic rabbis became prominent; and where.[2] There has also been an interesting methodological debate about

1. Cohen's roster included one "rabbi" from a papyrus letter from the Judean Desert and a late addition from Qazrin ("Epigraphical Rabbis," *JQR* 72 [1981]: 1–17; reprinted with additional instances not affecting his conclusions in his *The Significance of Yavneh and Other Essays in Jewish Hellenism*, TSAJ 136 [Tübingen: Mohr Siebeck, 2010], 227–43).

2. The main responses include the following: Stuart S. Miller has addressed the issue repeatedly, his two most important publications on the matter are "'This Is the Beit Midrash of Rabbi Eliezer ha-Qappar' (Dabbura Inscription)—Were Epigraphical Rabbis Real Sages, or Nothing More Than Donors and Honored Deceased?," in *Talmuda de-Eretz Israel: Archaeology and the Rabbis in Late Antique Palestine*, ed. Steven Fine and Aaron Koller, SJ 73 (Berlin: de Gruyter, 2014), 239–73, citing his treatments of the issue in previous publications, and Miller, *Sages and Commoners in Late Antique 'Ereẓ Israel: A Philological Inquiry into Local Traditions in Talmud Yerushalmi*, TSAJ 111 (Tübingen: Mohr Siebeck, 2006), 427–45. See also Hayim Lapin, "Epigraphical Rabbis: A Reconsideration," *JQR* 101 (2011): 311–46; Fergus Millar, "Inscriptions, Synagogues and Rabbis in Late Antique Palestine," *JSJ* 42 (2011): 253–77; Ben Zion Rosenfeld, "The Title 'Rabbi' in Third- to Seventh-Century Inscriptions in Palestine Revisited," *JJS* 61 (2010): 234–56; Catherine Hezser, *The Social Structure of the Rabbinic Movement in Roman Palestine*, TSAJ 66 (Tübingen: Mohr Siebeck, 1997), 119–23; Lee I. Levine, "Bet Še'arim in Its Patriarchal Context," in *"The Words of a Wise Man's Mouth are Gracious" (Qoh 10,12): Festschrift for Günter Stemberger on the Occasion of His 65th Birthday*, ed. Mauro Perani, SJ 32 (Berlin: de Gruyter, 2005), 197–225; Tessa Rajak, "The Rabbinic Dead and the Diaspora Dead

whether the rabbinic corpus and inscriptions should be treated separately or as mutually informative.[3] My purpose in this article, offered in respect to Shaye Cohen, who was one of my dissertation advisers, is not to enter the fray regarding who was what kind of rabbi or Rabbi when and where, since I cannot add anything to that debate. Rather, I shall turn the focus on epigraphical features of the inscriptions: their place, setting, date, and other circumstances of the production and display that could affect their content, even the decision to use the term *rabbi*. My treatment will not turn the topic on its head but rather offer refinements of how to read and interpret the epigraphic evidence.

"Epigraphical context" refers to all the factors that can influence the content and quality of an inscription. The physical setting is crucial. A donor's inscription set in the mosaic floor of a synagogue near the entrance to the building will have a different purpose, audience, and kind of inscriber (level of professionalism, relation to the subject of the text); will use different formulae and epigraphic conventions; and will transmit different biographical and other information, from those of a wall inscription painted by a relative to identify the deceased interred in a loculus within a sealed catacomb. A synagogue in a coastal city has a different audience from one in the remote interior, as do, mutatis mutandis, synagogues in Iudaea/Palaestina and a Greek-speaking province like Asia Minor. By the same token, a Greek inscription at the entrance to a synagogue in a coastal city had a different audience and frequency of visits than did the halakhic text at Rehov or the long text in the mosaic floor in Ein Gedi, addressed specifically to the insular Aramaic-speaking community in each place.[4] Physical setting and purpose could affect even whether a person's titles are mentioned, or how. A rabbi mentioned on a synagogue floor or wall, and who has paid for it, is presenting himself to the community and the visitors—sometimes many visitors, if the synagogue is big, important, and located in a well-trafficked area—as he wants to be recognized in public, and as he wishes to be remembered as benefactor. In a private context such as a closed family burial cave, a person—who did not necessarily choose the wording of his own epitaph, or even its language—was identified as he was known to his family; the choice of men-

at Beth She'arim," in *The Jewish Dialogue with Greece and Rome: Studies in Cultural and Social Interaction*, AJEC 48 (Leiden: Brill, 2002), 479–99; Jodi Magness, "The En-Gedi Synagogue Inscription Reconsidered," *EI* 31 (2015): 123–31.

3. See primarily Miller ("This Is the Beit Midrash") and Rosenfeld ("Title 'Rabbi'"), arguing that the same word in different contemporary media should be considered to mean the same thing unless there is a good reason to think otherwise. Since only two inscriptions show rabbis performing a rabbinical function (see below), inscriptions alone afford no idea, apart from etymological, of what "rabbi" could have meant or what a rabbi might do.

4. Joseph Naveh, *On Mosaic and Stone: The Aramaic and Hebrew Inscriptions from Ancient Synagogues* [Hebrew] (Jerusalem: Israel Exploration Society, 1978), nos. 49 and 70.

tioning any title including rabbi reflects how they wished to remember him, how they thought he would want to be remembered, or even how family members could distinguish him from someone else of the same name. As we will see, "rabbi" was not fused to a man's name.

Moreover, "setting" includes the epigraphic usages in the immediate environment: epitaphs in different places—individual necropoleis, or cities, or regions—provided different information, but in a locally uniform manner. Compare, e.g., the virtual template epitaphs at Zoar with the different formulae used at Jaffa or in Rome or on the Jerusalem ossuaries[5]—all different sets of formulae. Another example of localization is the occurrence of the "curses of Deuteronomy" on Jewish epitaphs from Phrygia, which are unique in Jewish epigraphy; they are an imitation of the curses in non-Jewish epitaphs from the same region and occur only there, as a Jewish version of the local idiom.[6] And so forth: epigraphy was sensitive to local formulae and idioms, the local "dialect," as it were. Moreover, it can be demonstrated that people brought their epigraphical idioms with them when they traveled; we will see a good example of this below, in examining the Palmyrene catacombs at Beth She'arim.

Epigraphical setting also includes, naturally, chronology. Almost all of the epigraphical rabbis appear in texts dating from the third to the seventh centuries CE, covering the formative phase of rabbinic literature. It should be assumed that the title "rabbi" was fluid in this long period and that its prevalent meaning in the third century was not the same as its prevalent meaning just before the Arab conquest[7]—and, again, it could have been used differently in public and private contexts. Even strong critics of Cohen's thesis agree that רבי or בן רבי on first-century ossuaries from Jerusalem are names or respectful nicknames rather than titles of religious or legal authority. But the informal use of a term out of respect and even affection in the first century should be expected to continue even as the term was adopted by a specialized group as a title of authority two hundred to three hundred years later, and afterwards when that usage became less specialized and more general. Semantic uniformity satisfies scholars, but messiness is human reality: former meanings coexist with the new ones, especially in different settings. Moreover, it should be asked—although I cannot attempt an answer in this article—whether a "rabbi" in a remote and insular community like Ein Gedi had the same significance,

---

5. For Zoar, see Yiannis E. Meimaris and Kalliope I. Kritikakou-Nikolaropoulou, *Inscriptions from Palaestina Tertia* [Greek], Meletemata 41 (Athens: National Hellenic Research Foundation, 2005); for Aramaic, see, e.g., articles in Hebrew by Joseph Naveh in *Tarbiz* 64 (1995): 477–98, and 69 (2000): 619–36, and by Sacha Stern and Haggai Misgav in *Tarbiz* 74 (2005): 137–52. For Jaffa, see *CIIP* III, 2174–2255. For Jerusalem ossuaries, see *CIIP* I, 18–608.

6. *IJO* II, nos. 173, 174, 213 with commentary by Walter Ameling ad loc.

7. See esp. Lapin ("Epigraphical Rabbis: A Reconsideration") and Miller ("This Is the Beit Midrash") for strong discussion on this point.

functions, even process of acquisition, as in a more cosmopolitan synagogue like that in Sepphoris.[8]

It has been observed by others that of all the ancient inscriptions mentioning rabbis, only two texts actually portray rabbis in what can be considered a rabbinical function, and neither of those cases (obviously) is an epitaph or donor inscription. This does not mean that other epigraphical rabbis were not part of the so-called rabbinical movement or class, only that just two appear in an actual rabbinic function. The first is the much-discussed basalt lintel from the Golan:[9]

זה בית | מדרשו | שהלרבי |אליעזר הקפר

This is the *Beth Midrash* (House of Study) of Rabbi Eliezer Ha-Qappar

Putting aside the question whether Rabbi Eliezer Ha-Qappar is the same as the talmudic rabbi of the same name and title, a House of Study, the premier institution of rabbinic literature, is identified at the entrance to the building as somehow closely identified with—founded by and/or using the system of—a learned rabbi. He was not necessarily still alive when the inscription was incised; nor would his presence have been required at the founding of a study house based on his teaching far from where he actually lived (if that was the case). While the epigraphical R. Eliezer and the talmudic one may or may not have been the same person, that question is not crucial to including the rabbi on the Golan in the rabbinic "movement."[10] This only highlights the utter absence of any synagogue[11]—where rabbis are commemorated as donors—or any other kind of place identified with a rabbi in a specifically rabbinic role.

The second text in which rabbis function as Rabbis was not discussed by Cohen and some of his critics: the halakhic text in the floor pavement

---

8. One can only speculate wistfully about the information lost in the inscriptions from synagogues in places like Caesarea and Gaza.

9. Dan Urman, "Jewish Inscriptions from Dabura in the Golan" [Hebrew], *Tarbiz* 40 (1971): 406–8; Naveh, *On Mosaic and Stone*, no. 6 [Hebrew]. See important discussions by Lapin and Miller, and by Shamma Friedman, *Studies in the Language and Terminology of Talmudic Literature* [Hebrew] (Jerusalem: Academy of the Hebrew Language, 2014), 410–26.

10. Miller has the most detailed discussion of this inscription, citing previous treatments ("This Is the Beit Midrash"). On the matter of the rabbinical "movement," he is most sensible (272): "practically all rabbis by the amoraic period, epigraphical or literary, were teachers of 'Torah' who belonged to a still inchoate network of teachers of Torah. Some, including many an epigraphical rabbi even when unknown to us from rabbinic writings, may have belonged to the self-selecting group responsible for these texts; others were less closely associated with the literary rabbis, but still belonged to the evolving 'movement' if only because they shared the same devotion to conveying the meaning of 'Torah.'"

11. Note Rabbi Samuel, archisynagogos from Phrygia (*CIIP* I.2, 1001). On the Rabbis' ambivalence toward synagogues, see Lee I. Levine, *The Ancient Synagogue: The First Thousand Years* (New Haven: Yale University Press 2000), 446–63.

at the Reḥov synagogue.[12] Since the inscription quotes talmudic texts, the mention of Rabbis is not surprising. In line 10 it is written, at the end of a list of towns in which seventh-year produce was forbidden: "Rabbi permitted Kefar Tsemah," referring to Rabbi Yehudah Ha-Nasi, and quoting the text in t. Shevi'it 4:6; as Miller remarked, the laconic statement creates "the impression that people in Late Antiquity would have been familiar with who 'Rabbi,' i.e. Judah ha-Nasi was (and why not?)." The second mention of rabbis is in line 26, where it is stated that חוששין לו רבותינו "our rabbis are apprehensive" of adding new places to Eretz Israel lest its produce require tithing; these words are not in any extant parallel talmudic text, so that whether it is a lost talmudic text or "our rabbis" refers to local figures remains uncertain.[13] In both instances, the rabbis are religious and legal authorities recognized at least by the synagogal community at Reḥov in the fourth to seventh centuries CE; the first rabbinical reference and possibly the second refer to figures who could have had little directly or personally to do with this agricultural community.[14]

In what follows I shall deal directly only with the epigraphical rabbis from Iudaea/Palaestina. This is partly the result of space limitations in this volume. Iudaea/ Palaestina is also where most of the inscriptions with rabbis were found, and it is the main area of activity of the Rabbis of the Mishnah and Jerusalem Talmud. There are no inscriptions from the rabbinic academies in Sura, Pumbedita, or Nehardea in Babylonia. The closest we come is the Jewish inscriptions from Edessa, Dura Europos, and Palmyra, which, however, mention no rabbis.[15] We shall see below that rabbis do appear in the burials of Palmyrenes at Beth She'arim, and on Aramaic incantation bowls from Babylonia. But "epigraphical context" requires place, architectural or physical setting, reasonable idea of date, and comparative epigraphy from the vicinity.

Jaffa

The Jewish necropolis in Jaffa was in use from the third to the sixth centuries; this chronological parameter must be stressed since some post-Cohen

---

12. The bibliography is huge; for a reliable text, see Naveh, *On Mosaic and Stone*, no. 49; and the fundamental discussion in Hebrew by Jacob Sussmann in *Tarbiz* 43 (1974): 88–158; 45 (1976): 213–57; Miller (see n. 2 above); Steven D. Fraade, "The Rehov Inscriptions and Rabbinic Literature: Matters of Language," in Fine and Koller, *Talmuda de-Eretz Israel*, 225–38.

13. Miller suggests a third alternative: "sages of Torah who carried on for those who preceded them in the actual texts—that is, the inscription is asserting that "Rabbis of today" (i.e., *rabboteinu*) have their doubts on the matter at hand *just as their predecessors did*" ("This Is the Beit Midrash," 258; italics original).

14. It should also be mentioned that a certain rabbi who is the son of Lazar is mentioned in one of the unpublished inscriptions from the painted plaster walls.

15. Cf. *IJO* III, s.v., the places mentioned.

arguments have been based on presumed earlier or later dates.[16] Unlike the necropolis at Beth She'arim, which was in use during the same time and administered as a commercial enterprise for a large "catchment area,"[17] the necropolis at Jaffa apparently served mostly the population of the city. This enabled in Jaffa, unlike Beth She'arim, a local epigraphic idiom and pattern.[18] The Jaffa necropolis was huge, extending over perhaps one hundred dunams in present-day Abu Kabir, and containing hundreds of burial caves; the modern city has destroyed or covered up most of them, and only about thirty to forty[19] caves in one corner of the burial ground were excavated in any way that can be called a controlled manner. Eighty-one inscriptions have been recovered from what must have been hundreds or thousands. Even these relatively few texts provide strong evidence that caves were purchased and organized by family groupings, which is to be expected, since it is the confirmed practice in almost every Jewish burial cave from antiquity.

The excavated caves in Jaffa all have a similar, relatively modest design, consisting of a sunken vestibule with adjoining stairs, a door or sealable opening to one or more rooms with loculi; arcosolia are rare. The openings to the burial chambers were usually less than one meter high, as were the passageways between chambers; interiors were cramped, ceilings relatively low (compared to Beth She'arim). The outer entrances were fitted with a stone door or blocked with stone slabs; in a few, the door had been removed and replaced by slabs while the tomb was still in use. Often an inscription was attached to the outside rock face near the cave entrance (marked by a recessed area the shape and size of the stone) identifying the ownership of the tomb and even offering details about the purchase. All the other inscriptions, identifying the deceased, were *inside* the chambers, placed near or even inside the loculi, which themselves were often sealed.

Thus, the epitaphs at Jaffa were mostly not public texts and were not normally seen by anyone but family members, who had to open the stone door or remove covering slabs and crouch down into the cave, sometimes not even being able to stand up inside. The only possibly public inscrip-

---

16. Jonathan J. Price, "The Necropolis at Jaffa and Its Relation to Beth She'arim," in *Judaea-Palaestina, Babylon and Rome: Jews in Antiquity*, ed. Benjamin Isaac and Yuval Shahar, TSAJ 147 (Tübingen: Mohr Siebeck, 2012), 211–22; the more accurate dating of the necropolis is based on a remarkable MA thesis by Avner Ecker, "The Abu Kabir Necropolis of Jaffa" (Jerusalem: Hebrew University, 2010).

17. The phrase is used by Rajak in her influential article "Rabbinic Dead and the Diaspora Dead," 479–99.

18. See the commentaries pointing out significant formulaic patterns in *CIIP* III, 2174–2255.

19. Exact number are unknown, since the excavations in the 1950s, 1960s, 1970s and 1990s were never properly published, and even the location of some them is unknown today; Ecker assembled the available evidence.

tions in the Jaffa necropolis were the ownership inscriptions attached to outside wall near the entrances of some caves, but these also, because of the sunken vestibules, were not readily visible from the surface and could be seen only by someone who walked down the stone stairs and stood in front of the entrance.

One fragmentary epitaph preserves בן רבי "son of Rabbi ..."; two inscriptions contain the name of someone whose name is preceded by "rabbi"; and two more have been considered rabbinical because of the designation *berabbi*.[20] Four of the five are in Hebrew or Aramaic, which is rare in the Greek-dominated necropolis. The first is too fragmentary to say much useful, except that someone in this inscription, named in the missing portion of the text, was the son of a rabbi who was also named in the missing portion. Unless, of course, *ben Rabbi* was a kind of respectful title like that found in the first century, but this does not seem likely.

More is known or can be surmised about the two inscriptions that were obviously displayed on the outside façade of caves and clearly identifying the owners as rabbis. The first, that of Yudan son of Rabbi Tarfon (*CIIP* III, 2205), is a rectangular marble slab, made to be fitted into a wall (it was not found in a controlled excavation but was brought by workers to a collector in the early twentieth century). The text is inside a tabula ansata and reads:

הדא קבורתא דיודן ברה | דרבי טרפון בירבי נוח נפש זיכרונו | לברכה שלום

This is the grave of Yudan son of Rabbi Tarfon *berabbi*. His soul is at rest. May his memory be a blessing. Peace.

The announcement "This is the grave" and the design and shape of the slab, with a smoothed back, indicate that it was fitted near the entrance of the burial complex and pertained to the entire complex. The owner was a distinguished son of a rabbi, or the son of a distinguished rabbi, depending on who is described by *berabbi*.

The second "external" inscription (*CIIP* III, 2200) was also incised on a smoothed white marble slab; it is broken but was once a regular square or rectangle and would have been, like the previous one, fitted into the wall by the cave entrance. This one is unusual not only because it is bilingual but also in the relation of the two scripts to each other.

הקבר הזה שלרב | יודן הכהן ברב. | נוח נפש. שכן לוד

Ῥαβι Ἰόδα | υἱὸς Ἰωνά|θα

This grave is of Rav Yudan the priest, *berabb(i)*. His soul is at rest. Resident of Lod.
Rabi Ioda son of Ionatha.

---

20. *CIIP* III, 2197, 2205 and 2200, and 2239, 2233.

This inscription originally consisted solely of the three lines of Hebrew text, which were inscribed in neat, professional square letters identifying the owner, a distinguished rabbi priest—here it is indisputable that ברב or ברב(י) applies to Rav (or Rabbi) Yudan, and means "the honorable" (or "son of a rabbi," which is less likely given the Greek text). It is possible that the first two Hebrew lines were inscribed in Rabbi Yudan's lifetime according to his instructions, and the third line was added after his death by his family. What is certain is that the Greek text is a later addition by a less professional hand, the irregular letters are added above and below the Hebrew chaotically, the initial *iota* of Ἰόδα was at first forgotten and then squeezed in (the final iota of Ῥαβι confused the inscriber). The reason for the Greek addition can only be guessed, but since the inscription was on the outer rock face, it was addressed to whoever could see it by descending to stand in front of the tomb, and perhaps it was felt that the distinguished rabbi should be identified in Greek as well. The information offered in Greek is different: Yudan/Iouda's father is identified by name Ionatha (Jonathan—note that he does not bear the title rabbi), Yudan's title Rabi is retained at the expense (space was cramped) of both his priestly status and the honorific ברב(י). Thus, the author of the Greek addition felt that "rabbi" was the most important thing to advertise about Yudan, more important than his priestly status and his honorific *berabbi,* for which there was not enough space. The precise calculation is not of course known: it may have been felt that "priest" and *berabbi* had less functional significance or were a lesser or more private matter—or some other thought beyond recovery.

Before considering the last two texts from Jaffa, which are identified as "rabbinical" solely on the basis of the term *berabbi,* I would like to suggest with considerable caution—since it is somewhat in defiance of great rabbinical scholars—that a reassessment is in order of those individuals identified as rabbinical solely on the basis of this term in its various forms, *berabbi/berebbi/birebi,* and so on. The topic is complex and voluminous. Shamma Friedman required two hundred pages to show that the original meaning of the term as בן/בר רבי ("son of a rabbi") informs almost every instance in rabbinic literature *as well as* the contemporary documents such as inscriptions.[21] This opinion contradicts the view expressed by other scholars that the term developed from "son of rabbi" into a general term of respect, following Rashi, who translates the term as בן גדולים or "son of a respectable or important person."[22]

This term is perhaps one instance in which the medium does make a difference. The only epigraphic instance in which it unquestionably

21. Friedman, *Studies in the Language,* 227–429.

22. Saul Lieberman, *Greek in Jewish Palestine: Studies in the Life and Manners of Jewish Palestine in the II–IV Centuries C.E.,* 2nd ed. (New York: P. Feldheim, 1965), 157. Miller, *Sages and Commoners.*

means "son of Rabbi ..." is in Beth She'arim: רבי יהשוע בירבי הלל אטיון, "Rabbi Yehoshua *berabbi* Hillel Ation."[23] The other instances are postpositive and problematic as nameless patronyms,[24] nor are they even, without the aid of rabbinic parallels, a clear sign of rabbinic status. The pivotal question, as with the matter of "epigraphical rabbis" from the start, is the connection between talmudic terminology and realities, on the one hand, and the realia of the inscriptions that were written by many people from many different places and different sectors of the population, on the other.

More decisive are two other factors. In three or four of the six cases in which *berabbi* appears without the designation of its holder as rabbi, the inscription is in a private setting, a closed context; that is, while the title of respect was genuine, it was not perforce a title with public recognition or standing in every documented case. The Jaffa examples will illustrate.[25] The first is a well-rendered text that reads Σαμου|ήλ Γάλ|λου βηρ|εβι. שלום (*CIIP* III, 2233). Now it is true that this slab has come down to us without context—and its present location is not known—but it has the form of the epitaphs used inside the caves to mark individual tombs or loculi. Not only is there no indication of ownership, but the names are broken across lines (a practice shunned in the "external" inscriptions from Jaffa) and the final *shalom* was commonly used as a greeting to or from the deceased. This inscription is the only surviving instance of *berabbi* in Greek; it was an honorific that may have been used on certain occasions during Samuel's life or as a regular attribution; it was certainly how his family wished his name to be preserved in death.

The last epitaph from Jaffa reads simply תנחום | בירבי | שלום "Tanḥum *Berebbi*, Peace" (*CIIP* III, 2239). The same consideration applies here as to the Greek Samuel βηρεβι: this was an epitaph identifying a specific burial within a cave not visited by the public. It was how his family remembered him; this of course does not exclude the use of Tanḥum's honorific in public, but it does anchor it in a private context. He may have been a rabbi, too.

Although it originally meant only "son of rabbi," the term *berabbi* does not seem to mean that invariably *in the epigraphic evidence*, and its equivalence even as a rabbinic title is debatable. Given that it took on different connotations in spoken language—which even Friedman acknowledges—it cannot be expected to have maintained an identical meaning in every location throughout this period.

23. Nahman Avigad, *Beth She'arim*, vol. 3 (Jerusalem: Massada, 1976), 243 no. 16 (Catacomb 20).

24. It is not always clear whether in X son of Y *berabbi* the term refers to father or son; see Cohen, "Epigraphical Rabbis," 234 n. 7; Friedman, *Studies on the Language*, 261.

25. See also Cohen, "Epigraphical Rabbis," nos. 16 (Beth She'arim), 42 (Beth Alfa), possibly 56 (Susiya, depending on what the epithet goes with), the ossuary from H. Rimmon, and the epitaph from Zoar. In another possible instance, Ada Yardeni reads כהן ברבי in line 2 of the inscription at Dalton, Naveh no. 107.

Thus, in Jaffa, "rabbi" was a public title advertised in inscriptions placed in the public view, at least in the surviving evidence. It is possible that other rabbis are contained in the epitaphs set up *inside* the caves but not mentioned as such in that closed context. It is unorthodox to say, but still it should not automatically be assumed that all of a person's titles, including rabbi, would be mentioned in every inscription in every context, especially one in which no one but the family would read it.

Rabbi or Not?

The possibility that, depending on the setting and context, a person's titles, even rabbi, would not necessarily always be mentioned in an inscription (especially an epitaph), becomes quite clear when we notice the instances in which the same person is mentioned with and without the title. In the third register of the first and original part of the Aramaic text in the synagogue floor at Ein Gedi:[26]

דכירין לטב יוסה ועזרון וחזיקיו בנוה דחלפי

> May they be remembered for good: Yose and Ezron and Ḥezkiayhu the sons of Ḥalfi.

In the fourth and last register, in less ordered writing obviously added later by a different hand, Yose is a rabbi:

רבי יוסה בר חלפי חזקיו בר חלפי דכירין לטב | דסגי סגי הנון עבדו לשמה דרחמנה. שלום.

> Remembered for the good be Rabbi Yose son of Ḥalfi (and) Ḥezkiayhu son of Ḥalfi who did a great amount on behalf of the Merciful One. Peace.

Cohen's explanation that Yose "became a rabbi" between the two phases sounds reasonable. But Ein Gedi is full of secrets, including what is meant by "whoever reveals the secret of the town to the gentiles" in the third register. The meaning and process of Yose's rabbinic title in Ein Gedi (not necessarily the same process as in Tiberias, for example) are obscure to us, and we really cannot exclude other remote but epigraphically possible explanations, such as that the first mosaicist was afraid it would not fit in the line, or the second mosaicist was a greater stickler for titles, and so forth. In his first mention, what Yose and the others did is not specified—most likely monetary benefaction. In the last register, the commemorated "did a great amount on behalf of the Merciful One"—not very specific, but this could be something more than contributions, such as resolving conflicts (the inscription promises divine punishment for "everyone who causes conflict between two people"), making his rabbinic status more important.

---

26. Naveh, *On Mosaic and Stone*, no. 70.

Yet, if the anomaly at Ein Gedi can be explained simply as a promotion, without resorting to far-fetched explanations, the same thing in Beth She'arim catacombs cannot be. In cave 1, hall 7, we find on the archway between rooms 3 and 4, painted in red:[27]

[רב]י יוסף
בן יצחק

Ῥιββι Ἰωσῆ
ὅσιος υἱὸς
Εἰσακίου
θάρσει Μ----

Rabbi Yosef son of Yitzḥak.
Ribbi Iose *hosios* ("the holy") son of Eisakios

The restoration of רבי in line 1 is secure based on the remaining letter traces and the Greek parallel. R. Yosef's grave was in this hall, but the placement of this inscription has it refer to the entire chamber and not a single burial: R. Yosef is the patriarch, perhaps also the legal owner of the plots. In the same room, the occupant of one of the caves is specifically identified in a text painted beside a tomb:[28]

υἱὸς Ἰωσῆ
רבי ὅσ[ι]ος ὧδε κῖτε
θά[ρσει]

The son Iose *hosios* lies here. Courage!
[in Hebrew] Rabbi.

There is no doubt that Iose = Yosef is the same person in each inscription, not only because of the close family groupings in each chamber but also because of the distinctive ὅσιος in each text. In his son's epitaph, Yosef's rabbinic title was left off. A different inscriber added it in Hebrew (immediately or some time afterwards), without Yosef's name.[29]

Finally, in the same room, painted in red over an arcosolium:[30] Ἰωσήφ ὅσιος "Joseph *hosios* ('the holy')."

---

27. Moshe Schwabe and Baruch Lifshitz, *Beth She'arim*, vol. 2 (Jerusalem: Hebrew University of Jerusalem, 1974), no. 41.

28. Schwabe, *Beth She'arim*, , vol. 2, no. 43.

29. That רבי wasn't part of the original text is clear; see Moshe Schwabe, *BIES* 5 (1937): 86 [Hebrew]. In the same way, Hebrew words were added on the side of a Greek inscription in Cave 3 (Benjamin Mazar, *Beth She'arim*: *Report on the Excavations During 1936–1940*, vol. 1 (Jerusalem: Massada Press, 1957), 126, Schwabe no. 88), another burial complex for Palmyrenes; adding text on the side was a Palmyrene epigraphic practice; see below.

30. Schwabe, *Beth She'arim*, vol. 2, no. 44.

This is in fact R. Yosef's actual burial (see Schwabe, *Beth She'arim*, vol. 2, no. 44), a place of honor in an arcosolium, and he strikingly is named in Greek with his distinctive ὅσιος but without his title Ῥιββι; the same scrupulous Hebrew inscriber in no. 43 left this brief text alone. Thus, it is only in the first inscription, which is an identification of the entire family tomb, that R. Yosef is identified fully, in Hebrew and Greek, with his rabbinic title and his patronym and his honorific ὅσιος, which is perhaps like בירבי. The ceremonial or official function of that inscription may account for the full display of titles, but it shows that "Rabbi" was detachable from Yosef. The second inscription marks the grave of Rabbi Yosef's son; the father is named with the same honorific ὅσιος, but the rabbinic title is left off; apparently the Greek inscriber did not think the title necessary in the patronym, but this bothered the Hebrew inscriber, who added it. This wasn't a correction of an inadvertent admission: the three Greek inscriptions were written as intended, apparently.

The same phenomenon can be found elsewhere in hall G of cave 1, where Ῥ Εισάκιος Μοκίμου, "Rabbi Eisakios (son) of Mokimos," appears in four Greek inscriptions, in two of which—a general ownership label on a lintel and the epitaph marking his burial place—his title of rabbi is mentioned, whereas in the other two (one of which seems a general label!), his title is not mentioned.[31] If the family tree constructed by Schwabe is correct, this Isaac was the great uncle of Rabbi Yosef mentioned in the room on the other side of the corridor. (The title of rabbi skipped a generation, if the information is correct.)

It *may* be significant that the missing rabbinic titles are all in Greek inscriptions. One may speculate—but it remains rank speculation—that in the Hebrew epigraphic idiom, a rabbinic title was felt to be less separable from the personal name than in Greek the idiom. It follows that there are probably more "epigraphical rabbis," that is, individuals who could be called rabbi in some context, than are visible in the epigraphical evidence. There are no practical consequences from this second point, since we cannot count or assess what we cannot see, but it is worthwhile keeping it in mind when viewing the visible evidence overall: generalizing conclusions about numbers and status of "rabbis" should be avoided when some epigraphic names without the title could have had the title "rabbi" in other inscriptions or other contexts. It was not an inseparable part of one's name, at least in Greek.

It is relevant that catacombs 1–4 at Beth She'arim belonged to Jews from Palmyra. This was noticed and emphasized by the first modern excavators of the site, and is evident not only from the presence of Palmyrene script and names and the use of the ethnic Παλμυρηνός, but also—

31. Schwabe, *Beth She'arim*, vol. 2, nos. 18 and 20 vs. 19 and 23.

more important for the present study—the use of Palmyrene epigraphic customs. For example, the use of vertical writing,[32] the insertion of text around or beside other text,[33] the use of the word חבל,[34] calling the grave נפש or נפשא[35]—all these are typical features of Palmyrene epigraphy,[36] but unique in Beth She'arim. Jews from abroad brought epigraphic idioms with them, as can be shown for other caves of "foreigners" in the necropolis; whether the deceased and the inscribers actually lived in Eretz Israel, and what generation they were, is idle speculation that does not affect the variety of epigraphical idioms and the lack of a local template in Beth She'arim. For the Palmyrenes, a certain epigraphical relation to the title rabbi may also have been imported. It should be noted that in Palmyrene non-Jewish Aramaic epigraphy, the roots רב and רבי are (naturally) used to mean "leader" or "head," such as leaders of the priesthood.[37] This may or may not have affected the Palmyrene Jews' understanding of "rabbi," but it could help explain when they decided to use it in their inscriptions; that is, the title is mentioned when the official function is relevant to context, but not invariably.

The Other Rabbis at Beth She'arim[38]

Aside from the "rabbis" in the Palmyrene catacombs, all but two of the remaining Beth She'arim rabbis[39] were found in two caves, and these are the rabbis for whom some scholars have suggested a talmudic or patriar-

---

32. Mazar, *Beth She'arim*, vol. 1, nos. 12, 83, 101, 132.

33. Ibid., no. 126, Schwabe, *Beth She'arim*, vol. 2, no. 88.

34. Mazar, *Beth She'arim*, vol. 1, nos. 67, 130.

35. Ibid., nos. 12, 91, 126, 132.

36. Delbert R. Hillers and Eleonora Cussini, *Palmyrene Aramaic Texts*, Publications of the Comprehensive Aramaic Lexicon Project (Baltimore: Johns Hopkins University Press, 1996); Jean Cantineau et al., *Inventaire des inscriptions de Palmyre*, Publications du Musée national syrien de Damas 1 (Beirut: Impr. catholique, 1930–1975).

37. Hillers and Cussini, *Palmyrene Aramaic Texts*, 408–9. The forms ῥιββι and ῥιβ are also exclusive in the Beth She'arim inscriptions, except for two plaques found near synagogue that were, however, epitaphs taken from the Palmyrene caves; see discussion in *CIIP* V, forthcoming.

38. The date of the Beth She'arim necropolis has been convincingly determined to range from the second to the sixth centuries CE: see Fanny Vitto, "Byzantine Mosaics at Beth She'arim: New Evidence for the History of the Site," *'Atiqot* 28 (1996): 115–46; Gabriela Bijovsky, "Numismatic Evidence for the Gallus Revolt: The Hoard from Lod," *IEJ* 57 (2007): 187–203; Zeev Weiss, "Burial Practices in Beth She'arim and the Question of Dating the Patriarchal Necropolis," in *"Follow the Wise" (B Sanhedrin 32b): Studies in Jewish History and Culture in Honor of Lee I. Levine*, ed. Zeev Weiss et al. (Winona Lake, IN: Eisenbrauns, 2010), 205–29; Weiss, "Burial Practices in Beth She'arim and the Date of the Patriarchal Necropolis" [Hebrew], *Zion* 70 (2010): 265–90.

39. ῥ]αβὶ Ἱερών[υμος] in cave 16 and ῥ|αβὶ Ε|ἰούδα] in cave 25.

chal connection: three rabbis in five texts (three Hebrew and two Greek) in cave 14, and twelve rabbis in eleven Hebrew inscriptions from cave 20. These rabbis have been much discussed; I shall make one general observation that will serve the limited purpose of this article.

The typical catacomb at Beth She'arim was approached by walking down uneven carved steps into an excavated courtyard several meters below the ground surface (which could not necessarily be seen by a pedestrian walking casually above). The catacomb was entered through one or more entrances off the courtyard, usually through a carved door that could be locked and was usually less than a meter high, often not much higher than half a meter. The size, internal spaciousness, ornament, level of finish, and overall investment in the catacombs varied considerably—much more than in the excavated caves in Jaffa—but these shared features ensured their function as closed private spaces: they were not open like synagogues and churches, porticoes, basilicas, or other public spaces whose architectural structures invited visitors to come in and see what was on offer. The entrances were closed by small if elegant locked doors; cave ceilings were usually high enough to allow standing but space inside rooms was efficiently used for multiple burials in the form of troughs in arcosolia or loculi covered by slabs; maneuvering space, light, and air were sufficient for small numbers, that is, families visiting and tending to the graves, but not for public display; inscriptions were usually painted or (less often) inscribed by an amateur hand; individuals were identified by inscriptions next to their burials; and family identity or ownership was indicated by a text in a general space like an entrance archway. Ornament varied as did epigraphic idioms, according to the origin of the families; figurative art was found in eight of the thirty-three caves.[40] While some investment was indeed made in the façades and interior ornament of tombs, and while some elaborate poetic inscriptions were found inside the caves, I do not think that the catacombs were usually thrown open to visitors like tourist sites in antiquity. The inscriptions could be detailed, unique and original, charming, but generally—with some prominent exceptions like the poetic texts that were set up in public places[41]—they look like homemade affairs, directed toward relatives and (perhaps) close friends who visited the tomb on certain significant occasions during the year, or to add a burial.

---

40. Zeev Weiss, "Hellenistic Influences on Jewish Burial Customs in the Galilee during the Mishnaic and Talmudic Period" [Hebrew], *EI* 25 (1996): 356–64.

41. The two long Greek poetic inscriptions on marble plaques, that of Ioustos (Justus) son of Leontios (Schwabe, *Beth She'arim*, vol. 2, no. 127) and that of Karteria (ibid., no. 183), were both installed in public places: Justus in the only mausoleum at Beth She'arim, and Karteria in the courtyard of catacomb 18, that is, *outside* the cave for all to see. Karteria's epitaph says that a certain Zenobia brought her bones to the site, suggesting a possible connection with Palmyra; the Greek of the inscription does not necessarily represent local knowledge.

This is true for all excavated caves except 14 and 20. As Avigad wrote, cave 14 "differs completely from the thirteen preceding catacombs—in its large dimensions, in the layout of its spacious rooms, in the forms of its tombs, and in its external architecture. In general features only catacomb 20 is similar to catacomb 14."[42] In cave 14, a broad staircase led the visitor into an expansive courtyard. Hall A[43] has a monumentally high façade, with arches and pillars, constructed of ashlar masonry; the main entrance is an unusual double door under a high arch, the entrance itself is 1.7 meters high, even if a smaller door to the left, just over one meter high, was probably used more frequently, and the inside lock of the double door means that the double door was used for ceremonial occasions—the point being that there *were* such occasions designed for relatively large audiences.[44] The interior of Hall A was also uncharacteristic of the Beth She'arim pattern: unlike efficient use of walls and floors, the rooms were relatively spacious (3 m high) and had few burial spaces. Above the catacomb, in the open air, was constructed a large place of assembly with benches. The buried rabbis here have the names Rabbi Shimon, Rabbi Gamaliel, and Rabbi Aniana.

Catacomb 20, the largest cave discovered in Beth She'arim, is even grander than 14, with a spacious courtyard and a high constructed façade that had three double-doored entrances under pillared archways—again, the kind of monumental welcoming entryway used in Roman public architecture, as Avigad pointed out. The interior of catacomb 20 is branching and massive and contains different kinds of burials and inscriptions, but, significantly, the cave contains a large and unique (for Beth She'arim) concentration of sarcophagi. More than 130 were found. Sarcophagi are not only expensive and space-consuming modes of burial, but they stand on the floor in the open room instead of being hidden in troughs or in loculi behind slabs; if they are carved on four sides, they were meant to be viewed from all sides. The rabbis buried in cave 20 were all (in the surviving evidence) interred in sarcophagi: Rabbi Gamaliel ben Nehemiah, Rabbi Yehudah ben Rabbi Gamaliel, Rabbi Anianah, Rabbi Yudan ben Rabbi Miyashah, Rabbi Yehoshua ben Levi, Rabbi Gamaliel ben Rabbi Eliezer, and Rabbi Hillel ben Rabbi Levi. These rabbis in sarcophagi, whoever they were, were part of the public display for which the tomb was designed. Above catacomb 20 is a large meeting area with benches and an

42. Avigad, *Beth She'arim*, vol. 3, 42. The universal assumption is that all the rabbis in caves 14 and 20 were from Eretz Israel; there is little reason to think otherwise, but nothing is certain.

43. The other two halls in cave 14, called B and C, were more modest, somewhat later than A, and contained no rabbinical inscriptions.

44. Avigad thought that the multi-arched façade "derived from the multi-arched arcade so characteristic of Roman architecture" (*Beth She'arim*, vol. 3, 51).

apsidal niche, like the one above 14: only these two burial complexes had such constructed open meeting areas.

Catacombs 14 and 20, which contain most of the rabbis at Beth She'arim—especially those with the suggestive names—were built to welcome and impress visitors. The architecture, starting with large ornate entrances, invited them in as if to a gallery. Although burial caves, they were designed and, I assume, used as public spaces. In this they are different from all the other excavated caves at the site. It is easy and natural to suppose that the rabbinical titles account for the splendor and even public nature of the tombs: the rabbis had been important public figures. But it is to be remembered that both burial complexes were large and contained many more individuals—and perhaps family groupings—than the rabbis and their families. From an epigraphic point of view it is possible that, instead of the rabbinic titles being the reason for the setting, the setting was the reason for the titles. Clearly the rabbinic titles were important to the families in the tombs, but why, and what exactly that importance was, cannot be judged from the documents themselves, or from projection back from later experience.[45] The wealthy families who commissioned catacombs 14 and 20 did so as a display of wealth and status, certainly; display of status included the rabbinical titles held by some members of the families. The evidence from the Palmyrene caves at Beth She'arim shows that the rabbinical title was detachable from the name: the setting and perhaps language determined when it would be used.

Conclusions

The title rabbi, at least in Greek, was detachable from the name and was not mentioned every time the name was inscribed. The tendency was for "rabbi" to appear in inscriptions in outstanding public contexts, such as donor inscriptions in synagogues and display tombs. The occasion influenced the use of the title, instead of the other way around. This was of course not an iron-clad rule, but it is the trend and tendency. There was less a felt need to use the title in private, closed contexts.[46] An extreme example that makes this point is the donor advertising his benefaction in the synagogue at Susiya: מרי רבי איסי הכהן המכובד בירבי, "Mari ('my master'),

45. Lapin suggests another intriguing possibility, namely, a family preference to use "rabbi" as a social marker; he notes that one of the rabbis in cave 20 was only seventeen years old (Avigad, *Beth She'arim*, vol. 3, no. 26).

46. Rosenfeld says something similar, concluding that use of the title in a public context implies general acceptance and understanding of the title ("Title 'Rabbi,'" 255-56). Miller suggests that the use of "rabbi" in a formal setting such as a synagogue mosaic or in epitaphs had to have been more than a common way of expressing respect (*Sages and Commoners*, 442).

Rabbi Isi/Isai, the priest, the honorable, *berabbi*"[47]—he vowed his contribution to the synagogue at the wedding feast of his son, Rabbi Yoḥanan the priest (and) scribe *Berabbi* (רבי יוחנן הכהן הסופר בירבי), so the donation is as public as it can be. R. Isi is identified by five different terms indicating public status, and his son has four titles; one wonders whether their epitaphs, if in closed, private burial caves, were as elaborate.

Since there is an obvious development in the meaning of the term *rabbi* from first-century ossuaries to public texts from late antiquity, there is no reason to think that at any stage it acquired an *exclusive* meaning in all epigraphic contexts. Moreover, the lesser frequency of the title in Greek may, as usually assumed, indicate an aversion of rabbis to Greek, but it may also reflect a less-solid tendency to mention it in a Greek inscription: each epigraphical language had its customs and idioms. Thus, the absence of rabbis in the fairly large set of Jewish inscriptions from Rome does not perforce indicate an absence of rabbis there (whatever that title meant locally). The title may simply not have been used in the only epigraphical context we have for Roman Jews, where Hebrew is sparse. Iudaea/Palaestina is unusual as the only place in the ancient world in which Hebrew and Aramaic *Jewish* inscriptions outnumber Greek; this was not true at Beth She'arim, but that necropolis had a rather international composition, unlike any other place so far discovered from that period in the region.

Appendix: Exclusions and Additions

Lapin did the most radical surgery to Cohen's roster (but could not consider the seven additions in Cohen's revised list). Cohen's nos. 12–13 and 41 are excluded by Lapin because they are unverifiable; nos. 2–3, because of their probable late date; and nos. 49 (Jerusalem ossuary), 58 (papyrus letter from the Judean Desert) and Cohen add. = *JIWE* 1:186 (Spain) because of modified readings. I agree with these exclusions. It is unnecessary, however, to exclude Cohen no. 50[48] on the grounds that בן רבי is a name and not a title, which is conjecture and, even if true, is a phenomenon that could continue in later periods.

Lapin's additions should now be permanent in the roster:[49]

- Lapin no. 6, a magic bowl from Iraq mentioning רב יוסף בר אימא דאימא.
- Lapin no. 7, a papyrus from Egypt with לרב יעקב בר יצחק.

47. *CIIP* IV, 3868; Miller, *Sages and Commoners*, 253–54.

48. Cohen himself admits that his no. 51 is a modern forgery ("Epigraphical Rabbis," in *Significance of Yavneh*, 232).

49. Lapin, "Epigraphical Rabbis," 333–43.

- Lapin nos. 14–15: רבי תנחום and אבה רבי from Qazrin.
- Lapin no. 19: רבי עלא ואחוי, near Tiberias.
- Lapin no. 21, רבי יודן, Sepphoris, making *CIJ* 989 and 990 two inscriptions.[50]
- Lapin no. 22: רבי יהושע | בר לוי קפרה, Sepphoris.
- Lapin no. 23 שלנחום ושליעקב בניו של רבי הוסוכי Ναουμ κὲ Ιακωβ υἱοὶ τοῦ ῥαββὶ Ἡσυχίου, Sepphoris.
- Lapin no. 24 רבי [י]סא היורורה, Sepphoris.
- Lapin no. 66 דרבי סימון ביריבי, Zoar.
- Lapin nos. 67–68 רבי ת[נחום] and ורבי שמעון הכהן, "unverified" Sepphoris.

In addition, as seen above, Miller, Rosenfeld, and Millar et al. correctly include the two mentions of rabbis in the Reḥov inscription. However, the addition of a certain R. Bisna from Jaffa (Rosenfeld, Miller) is based on a mistaken reading and cannot be accepted (see *CIIP* III, 2247).

Fergus Millar includes a certain [ר]ב מתיה from Thella/Yesud Ha-Maala,[51] which is S. Klein's correction of an obviously mistaken reading of a lost text—too speculative for inclusion in the catalogue.

Rosenfeld seeks further to add a doubtful inscription from around Sepphoris, purportedly with the title "rabbi,"[52] but this was rightly excluded by both Cohen and Lapin as unsupportable. Rosenfeld also includes רב יעקב בר יצחק mentioned in a letter from around Lod, which is too doubtful to be included, and an inscription from Caesarea, Ἰακκώβου Δασσᾶ ἰοῦ | Γάδη, which he misreads (following Schwabe) as Δασσαίου, thus rendering the name of the Amora Jacob son of Dosi, but even his misreading does not have a rabbinic title.[53]

Finally, there are additional inscriptions to be included in any future discussion of epigraphical rabbis.

1. Caesarea, fragmentary marble plaque: [--]דרבי[--] (*CIIP* II, 1610).
2. Caesarea, marble plaque: θήκη | Ραβη, in which Ραβη could be either a name or a title (*CIIP* II, 1541).
3. Sepphoris, on lintel of burial cave: שמואל ויעקב ומנחם בניו של רב יוסה ספרה ואניאנה בר רב פתחיה.[54]

---

50. For the Sepphoris additions, see Mordechai Aviam and Aharoni Amitai, "The Cemeteries of Sepphoris," *Cathedra* 141 (2012): 6-26 (Hebrew).

51. Millar, "Inscriptions, Synagogues and Rabbis," 271; S. Klein, "Zwei Synagogeninschriften aus Galiläea," *Palestina-Studien* I.4 (1928): 59–60.

52. Rosenfeld, "Title 'Rabbi,'" 242.

53. See the discussion in *CIIP* II, 1481.

54. Aviam-Amitai 19 no. 8 = Joseph Naveh, "Inscriptions in Hebrew and Aramaic from Sepphoris" [Hebrew], *Atiqot* 49 (2005): 113–15.

4. Sepphoris, unpublished: הדין משכבה דרבי תנח[ום] | ורבי שמעון כהנה הונה ש[לום].[55]
5. Jericho, limestone slab: דבנה זייג | ריש צבורה | דר/די..בריה | דמרי ושלתי ורבי ואתתיה |.[56]
6. Hijaz (third century CE), ברכה/עטיר בר/למנחם ורב ירמיה.[57]
7. Magical texts. This is a source that has not been fully explored (nor will it be here); the use of such texts is even less straightforward than other kinds of inscriptions. Cohen and Lapin list one, a Rabbi Eliezer son of Esther on an amulet. Shaul Shaked offers a partial list from incantation bowls:[58] Rav Dimi, Rav Seḥora son of Immi, Rav Ashi son of Maḥlafta, Rav Yosef bar Imma d-Immeh, Ḥanina bar Rav Yatma, Rav Mari bar Mama, Rav Malḥlafa son of Khwardukh, Rav Alḥma son of Alḥat. Bowls also mention Mar Zutra bar Gilai and Mar Zutra bar Ukkamay. Shaked points out the uncertainty about whether "rabbi" "is a title of office or merely an honorific address." The mentioned rabbis are hard to identify as talmudic sages since they are usually identified by their matronymic. The incantation bowls come from Babylonia, dating mostly after the completion of the Babylonian Talmud. It may be disconcerting to some to see rabbis as the clients of magic.

55. Aviam-Amitai 19 no. 10.

56. Ada Yardeni and Jonathan J. Price, "A New Aramaic Dedicatory Inscription from Israel," *Scripta Classica Israelica* 24 (2005): 125–33.

57. Hayim Z. Hirschberg, "New Jewish Inscriptions in the Natabaean Sphere" [Hebrew], *Eretz Israel* 12 (1975): 142–48, here 146; the inscription had in fact been published already by J. T. Milik (see Hirschberg).

58. Shaul Shaked, "Rabbis in Incantation Bowls," in *The Archaeology and Material Culture of the Babylonian Talmud*, ed. Markham J. Geller, IJS Studies in Judaica 16 (Leiden: Brill, 2015), 97–120.

Palaestina Secunda

The Geohistorical Setting for Jewish Resilience and Creativity in Late Antiquity

LEE I. LEVINE
The Hebrew University of Jerusalem

From the reign of Diocletian (284–305 CE) and throughout the fourth century CE, the provincial system of the Roman Empire underwent some one hundred changes, including the subdivision of existing provinces and the addition of new ones. From about fifty provinces beforehand, this number jumped to some 104.[1] The reasons behind most of these changes seem to relate to the societal upheavals caused by barbarian incursions along Rome's northern and eastern borders that aroused a deep angst among the population in the third century and, in turn, led to unrest in Rome and elsewhere for over half a century (ca. 235–284).[2] Together with this turmoil, the triumph of Christianity under Constantine in the fourth century was once regarded as a difficult period for the Jews, setting the stage for the travails of the Middle Ages that lasted well over a millennium. The assumption that the fourth century was the harbinger of

---

It is a pleasure to contribute this study in honor of a friend and colleague who is renowned for his knowledge, diligence, and creativity in the field of ancient Jewish history.

1. For a comprehensive overview of this phenomenon, see Joonas Sipilä, *The Reorganisation of Provincial Territories in Light of the Imperial Decision-Making Process: Later Roman Arabia and Tres Palaestinae as Case Studies*, Commentationes Humanarum Litterarum 126 (Helsinki: Societas Scientiarum Fennica, 2009), 103–30; see also Stephen Williams, *Diocletian and the Roman Recovery* (New York: Methuen, 1985; repr., New York: Routledge, 1997), 104–5, 221–23. On the crisis in the third century generally and in Palestine in particular, see Michael Avi-Yonah, *The Jews of Palestine: A Political History from the Bar Kokhba War to the Arab Conquest* (New York: Schocken, 1976), 89–136; Timothy D. Barnes, *The New Empire of Diocletian and Constantine* (Cambridge: Harvard University Press, 1982); Williams, *Diocletian*, 15–231; Adam Ziolkowski, "The Background to the Third-Century Crisis of the Roman Empire," in *The Roman Empire in Context: Historical and Comparative Perspectives*, ed. Jóhann P. Árnason and Kurt A. Raaflaub, Ancient World—Comparative Histories (Chichester: Wiley-Blackwell, 2011), 111–33.

2. Alan K. Bowman, Peter Garnsey, and Averil Cameron, eds., *The Cambridge Ancient History*, vol. 12, *The Crisis of Empire, A.D. 193–337*, 2nd ed. (Cambridge: Cambridge University Press, 2005).

an era of Jewish suffering, discrimination, and even persecution has held sway in Jewish historiography until the last few generations. This paper will suggest that such a perception requires serious reconsideration, that is, that Rome was, in fact, largely supportive of the Jewish population's social, communal, religious, and cultural agendas.

The reorganization of the empire under Diocletian and his successors was driven by Rome's desire to fortify its frontiers in the face of the many successful external attacks by its neighbors and the turmoil wreaked in their wake. Additional factors, such as economic, social, geographic, demographic, ethnic, and religious considerations, also may have played a role in determining provincial borders.[3]

No fewer than seven or eight changes were implemented in both Palestine and Arabia[4] that affected their southern and eastern regions, that is, the Negev, Sinai, and southern Transjordan. The title *Prima* was added to the province of *Palaestina* around the turn of the fifth century, following the creation of *Palaestina Secunda* and *Palaestina Salutaris* (or *Tertia*) (fig. 1). A precise date is difficult to ascertain for these last additions since the two sources documenting these changes do so post facto, and only generally. For example, the Theodosian Code states:

> In consideration of the interests of the border militia and of the landholders throughout First, Second and Third Palestine, a regulation has been issued to the effect that, when a fixed rate of commutation prices has been paid, the exaction of payments in kind shall be suspended.... Given on the tenth day before the kalends of April at Constantinople in the year of the eighth consulship of Honorius Augustus and the third consulship of Theodosius Augustus.—March 23, 409. (Codex Theodosianus 7.4.30)[5]

Clearly, then, by the end of the first decade of the fifth century Palestine had already been divided into three provinces.

A second source, Notitia Dignitatum Orientis, a document listing the deployment of the Roman army throughout the eastern empire and dated between 395 and 413 CE, also attests to the existence of these two new provinces, *Secunda* in the north and *Salutaris* in the south.[6] Thus, both

---

3. Sipilä, *Reorganisation of Provincial Territories*, 57–102.

4. Israel Shatzman, "From *Iudaea* to the Three Provinces of *Palaestina*: The Framework of the Roman Administration in the Land of Israel from the First to the Early Fifth Century CE," in *Arise, Walk through the Land: Studies in the Archaeology and History of the Land of Israel in Memory of Yizhar Hirschfeld on the Tenth Anniversary of His Demise* [Hebrew], ed. Joseph Patrich, Orit Peleg-Barkat, and Erez Ben-Yosef (Jerusalem: Israel Exploration Society, 2016), 6; Sipilä, *Reorganisation of Provincial Territories*, 149–90.

5. Clyde Pharr, trans., *The Theodosian Code and Novels, and the Sirmondian Constitutions*, Corpus of Roman Law 1 (Princeton: Princeton University Press, 1952), 162.

6. Otto Seeck, ed., *Notitia Dignitatum* (Berlin: Weidmann, 1876; repr., Frankfurt am Main: Minerva, 1962), 48–49. On the Notitia generally, see Arnold H. M. Jones (*The Later*

FIGURE 1. The division of Palestine into three provinces in the Byzantine period. Prepared by Ḥani Davis. Used by permission.

of these sources indicate that *Palaestina Secunda* was created sometime around the end of the fourth or the beginning of the fifth century.[7]

Regarding a more precise date, Israel Shatzman has argued that in four laws cited in the Theodosian Code (12.1.55 from 363 CE, 11.36.28 from 383 CE, 11.30.42 from 384 CE, and 10.16.40 from 385 CE) only the name *Palaestina* is noted (without any accompanying numerical designation of *Prima, Secunda,* or *Tertia*), from which he deduces that there was as yet no subdivision of the province and therefore a division would have occurred only soon thereafter, in 388–392.[8] Shatzman also cites Jerome, in his *Commentary on Genesis*, written between 389 and 392, wherein he notes that the biblical Gerar (Gen 20:1–2; 26:6, 20, 26) was located in the recently created province of *Palaestina Salutaris* ("not long ago," *ante non grande tempus*).[9]

Palaestina Secunda included the central and eastern Galilee, the central and southern Golan Heights, the Jezreel and Bet Shean Valleys, the northern Gilead, and the River Valley east of the Jordan. To its south the province was bordered by the Gilboa and Samaria mountain ranges, to the west by the Carmel mountain range and the Zebulun Valley, to its north by Phoenicia, to the northeast by Panaeas in the northern Golan, and to the east by *Provincia Arabia*. Eleven cities were located in this province—Scythopolis (Bet Shean), Pella, Gadara, Abila, Capitolias, Hippos (Susita), Tiberias, Helenopolis, Diocaesarea (Sepphoris), Maximianopolis, and Gaba; [10] its capital was Scythopolis, a well-established Roman city located on a major trade route running from Syria to Egypt (fig. 2). Archaeological finds indicate that Scythopolis underwent extensive renovations in the latter part of the fourth century and thereafter,[11] due in part to the destruction a generation earlier resulting from the earthquake of 363 or

---

Roman Empire, 284–602: A Social, Economic, and Administrative Survey, 3 vols. [Baltimore: Johns Hopkins University Press, 1964], 2:1417–50, esp. 1421), who dates the composition of this work sometime between 395 and 413.

7. A later attestation for the existence of this division can be found Justinian's Novella 103, dating to 536, which discusses the turmoil caused by the Samaritan rebellion of 529; see Philipp Mayerson, "Justinian's Novel 103 and the Reorganization of Palestine," *BASOR* 269 (1968): 65–71. The Greek chronicler Malalas (fl. 491–578 CE), for his part, claims (mistakenly) that the emperor Constantine created *Palaestina Secunda* and *Palaestina Tertia*; see Philipp Mayerson, "Libanius and the Administration of Palestine," *ZPE* 69 (1987): 258 n. 11; see also Leah Di Segni, "The Administration of Palestine from Diocletian to the Muslim Conquest" (in press).

8. Shatzman, "From *Iudaea*," 6.

9. *Qu. hebr. Gen.* 21.30–31 [CCSL 72:26]. See Philipp Mayerson, "'Palaestina' vs. 'Arabia' in the Byzantine Sources," *ZPE* 56 (1984): 228–30; Walter D. Ward, "'In the Province Recently Called Palestine Salutaris': Provincial Changes in Palestine and Arabia in the Late Third and Fourth Centuries C.E.," *ZPE* 181 (2012): 289–302.

10. Shatzman, "From *Iudaea*," 5.

11. Yoram Tsafrir and Gideon Foerster, "Urbanism at Scythopolis-Bet Shean in the Fourth to Seventh Centuries," *Dumbarton Oaks Papers* 51 (1997): 99–126; Leah Di Segni, "New Epigraphic Discoveries at Scythopolis and Other Sites of Late-Antique Palestine," in *Atti del*

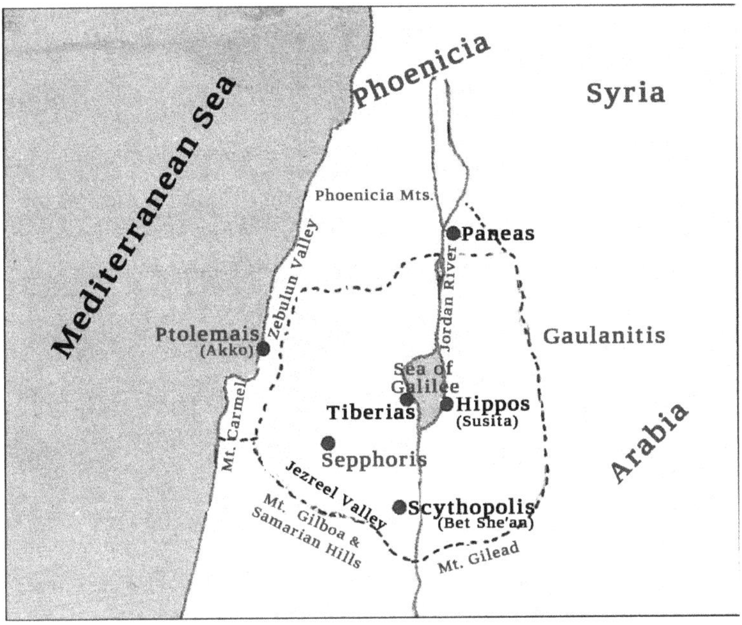

FIGURE 2. The borders of *Palaestina Secunda* in the Byzantine period. Prepared by Ḥani Davis. Used by permission.

perhaps owing to the city's now-enhanced status as the capital of this new province, or both.[12]

Scythopolis was one of the ten cities of the Decapolis in ancient Palestine that formed an alliance and were listed as such for the first time by Josephus.[13] The city enjoyed two periods of unusual growth and development, one in the second century CE (from the reigns of Trajan and Hadrian to those of Antoninus Pius and Marcus Aurelius) and another in the fourth century CE, when it became the capital of *Palaestina Secunda*. In the latter era, Scythopolis contained a rather heterogeneous population of pagans, Samaritans, Jews, and Christians. While the pagans had originally dominated the city for centuries, this population began to decline in the fourth century CE, as attested by remains of its many temples and idols found

XI. Congresso internazionale di epigrafia greca e latina, Roma, 18–24 settembre 1997, 2 vols. (Rome: Quasar, 1999), 2:625–42.

12. Yoram Tsafrir, "Scythopolis," in *Late Antiquity: A Guide to the Postclassical World,* ed. Glen W. Bowersock, Peter R. L. Brown, and Oleg Grabar (Cambridge: Belknap Press of Harvard University Press, 1999), 687–88; Gabi Mazor, "Bet Shean: The Hellenistic–Early Islamic Periods: The Israel Antiquities Authority Excavations," *NEAEHL* 5:1628–34.

13. Emil Schürer, *The History of the Jewish People in the Age of Jesus Christ (175 B.C.–A.D. 135),* rev. and exp. ed. by Geza Vermes, Fergus Millar, and Martin Goodman, 3 vols. (New York: T&T Clark, 1973–87), 2:125–27, 142–45.

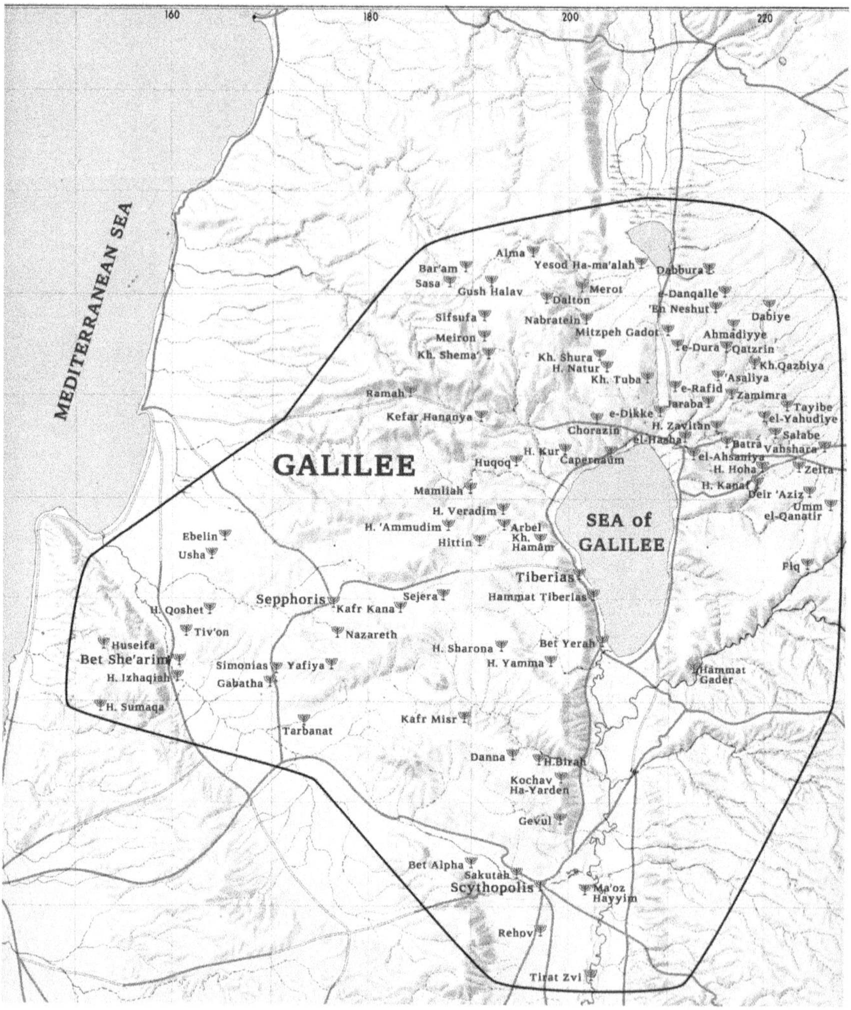

FIGURE 3. Jewish settlements and synagogues in *Palaestina Secunda*. Prepared by Ḥani Davis. Used by permission.

in archaeological excavations.[14] The Jewish population remained in the city and its environs throughout antiquity and boasted some five synagogues, all dating to the sixth century.[15] When the Samaritans settled in Scythopolis

14. Tsafrir and Foerster, "Urbanism at Scythopolis-Bet Shean," 125–46.

15. The two synagogues associated directly with the city were the Leontis building in its southwestern part, and another just outside the city wall to the north (identified as either Jewish or Samaritan). Beyond the city boundaries were three others, Bet Alpha to the west,

in the Roman-Byzantine period, the city played an important role in their rebellions against the imperial government in the fifth and sixth centuries. Finally, with the transition of the empire from the fourth century onwards, Christians and their institutions gradually gained control of the city.

Throughout late antiquity, Scythopolis was endowed with lavish buildings and monuments typical of any important Roman city.[16] Given its pivotal geographical location between the sea and inland highways (the Via Maris and the Via [Traiana] Nova) as well as between the large cities to the south and northeast (Alexandria and Damascus, respectively), many roads converged in Scythopolis, which was graced with multiple gates, *propylaea*, colonnaded streets, an impressive civic center, and marketplace (*agora*). Baths were also built there, especially several large ones to the east and west, as well as a *bouleutērion*, *nymphaea*, pagan temples, churches, a theater, and a hippodrome (converted into an amphitheater in the later fourth century). A plethora of inscriptions attesting to a wide range of officials, patrons, and buildings was also discovered there.[17] Only toward the end of the sixth century did the city cease to flourish, and in 635 CE it was conquered by the Arabs.[18]

Beyond the above-noted references to the Theodosian Code and the Notitia, we have no idea who was responsible for creating this province, when exactly it was done, and why at this time. The usual reasons for such provincial adjustments, especially the addition of other provinces, are discussed extensively by Joonas Sipilä.[19] However, given the paucity of available data, there seems to be no way of ascertaining which of these options, if any, are applicable, and Sipilä himself posits no specific suggestion in this case.[20]

Given this quandary, I would like to address a heretofore neglected dimension that focuses on the social and demographic nature of the territory designated as *Palaestina Secunda* (fig. 3). Three aspects demand attention in this regard:

Ma'oz Ḥayyim to the east, and Reḥov to the south; see Lee I. Levine, *The Ancient Synagogue: The First Thousand Years*, 2nd ed. (New Haven: Yale University Press, 2005), 215–20.

16. Benny Arubas, Gideon Foerster, and Yoram Tsafrir, "The Hellenistic–Early Islamic Periods at the Foot of the Mount: The Hebrew University Excavations," *NEAEHL* 5:1636–41.

17. For a general statement regarding late antique Palestine and Arabia in this respect, see Leah Di Segni, "Late Antique Inscriptions in the Provinces of Palaestina and Arabia: Realities and Change," in *The Epigraphic Cultures of Late Antiquity*, ed. Katharina Bolle, Carlos Machado, and Christian Witschel, Heidelberger althistorische Beiträge und epigraphische Studien 60 (Stuttgart: Franz Steiner, 2017), 287–322.

18. Tsafrir and Foerster, "Urbanism at Scythopolis-Bet Shean," 135–46.

19. See Sipilä, *Reorganisation of Provincial Territories*, 57–130, 149–90.

20. Ibid., 57–102.

1. First and foremost, this region was the dominant area of Jewish settlement in the country whose creation as a separate region had a profound effect on the cultural and religious life of its Jewish inhabitants. It was home to the largely Jewish cities of Tiberias (seat of the patriarichate in its prime at this time; see below) and Sepphoris, both major urban centers of rabbinic activity. The centrality and importance of these two Galilean cities are widely recognized by Jewish and Christian literary sources and are corroborated by rich archaeological finds.
2. Given the ethnic-religious demography of *Palaestina Secunda*, it stands to reason that the most important and most ubiquitous archaeological data represented in this region are its ancient synagogues. Since the synagogue had become the central Jewish communal institution by this era, and given the fact that *Palaestina Secunda* contained the largest concentration of Jewish communities in the world, its ninety-or-so synagogues constituted almost 85 percent of the total number known to date in late antique Palestine.
3. The legal standing of the Jews vis-à-vis the Byzantine authorities is best documented for the fourth and early fifth centuries by the Theodosian Code, which is generally considered the most authoritative and accurate indication of how Jews were regarded and treated throughout this period. Thus, notwithstanding the tensions and pressures that had already surfaced in the fourth century under Byzantine-Christian rule, recent research on the Jews, Jewish institutions, and Jewish society suggests that such challenges should be viewed today as relatively marginal and that, in fact, Jewish society at large enjoyed a significant measure of prosperity, political stability, and cultural vitality at this time.[21]

---

21. See Lee I. Levine, "Jews and Judaism in Palestine (70–640 CE): A New Historical Paradigm," in *The Faces of Torah: Studies in the Texts and Contexts of Ancient Judaism in Honor of Steven Fraade*, ed. Michal Bar-Asher Siegal, Tzvi Novick, and Christine Hayes, JAJSup 22 (Göttingen: Vandenhoeck & Ruprecht, 2017), 403–12; Levine, "The Emergence of the Patriarchate in the Third Century," in *Envisioning Judaism: Studies in Honor of Peter Schäfer on the Occasion of His Seventieth Birthday*, ed. Ra'anan Boustan et al., 2 vols. (Tübingen: Mohr Siebeck, 2013), 2:256–58. This suggested reconstruction differs radically from that suggested by Zeev Safrai and Uzi Leibner in recent years regarding the decline of Jewish life in the Galilee from the third to fifth centuries.

For a summary of these proposals and subsequent critiques, see Zeev Safrai, *The Missing Century: Palestine in the Fifth Century: Criticism, Growth and Decline*, Palästina Antiqua 9 (Leuven: Peeters, 1998); Gabriela Bijovsky, "The Currency of the Fifth Century C.E. in Palestine: Some Reflections in Light of Numismatic Evidence," *Israel Numismatic Journal* 14 (*Studies in Memory of Leo Mildenberg*) (2000–2002): 196–210; Uzi Leibner, "Settlement Patterns in the Eastern Galilee: Implications Regarding the Transformation of Rabbinic Culture in Late Antiquity," in *Jewish Identities in Antiquity: Studies in Memory of Menahem Stern*, ed. Lee I. Levine and Daniel R. Schwartz, TSAJ 130 (Tübingen: Mohr Siebeck, 2009), 269–95; Leibner, *Settlement and History in Hellenistic, Roman, and Byzantine Galilee: An Archaeological Survey of the Eastern Galilee*, TSAJ 127 (Tübingen: Mohr Siebeck, 2009); and comments of Jodi Magness, "Did Galilee Experience a Settlement Crisis in the Mid-Fourth Century?," in Levine

We will begin our discussion of this previously "neglected dimension" noted above—which has been overlooked in the traditional historiography of the period—with a brief overview of the status of the Jews prior to the creation of *Palaestina Secunda*. For several centuries beforehand, already in the time of Rabbi Judah I (ca. 200) and to a great extent throughout much of the following century as well, Jewish life seems to have suffered only minimally, thriving with the support of the Roman government.

Using the Theodosian Code as a basis for assessing Jewish legal standing,[22] one finds that the subjects of legislation for the early fourth century were relatively few and primarily concerned specific areas within the religious sphere that separated Jew from Christian, for example, the prohibition against circumcising Christians, persecuting Jewish converts to Christianity, and proselytizing to Judaism. The legislation protected Christians who abandoned Judaism in order to return to their original faith, punished Jews who purchased or proselytized non-Jewish slaves or confiscated the properties of Christian proselytes, and limited the number of Jews seeking asylum in churches.[23]

Following this legislation at the outset of Christian rule and continuing for several decades thereafter (ca. 360–380), there was virtually no anti-Jewish legislation that attacked the Jews per se or their institutions and beliefs. Even during the final twenty years of the fourth century, negative laws remained relatively limited in number and marginal in impact.[24] In contrast, a large number of laws were issued to protect and even enhance Jewish rights and privileges, including the protection of synagogues from

---

and Schwartz, *Jewish Identities*, 296–313; Magness, "Did Galilee Decline in the Fifth Century? The Synagogue of Chorazin Reconsidered," in *Religion, Ethnicity, and Identity in Ancient Galilee: A Region in Transition*, ed. Jürgen Zangenberg, Harold W. Attridge, and Dale B. Martin, WUNT 210 (Tübingen: Mohr Siebeck, 2007), 259–74. See also the more recent reservations of Hayim Lapin, "Population Contraction in Late Roman Galilee: Reconsidering the Evidence," *BASOR* 378 (2017): 127–43.

22. Amnon Linder, *The Jews in Roman Imperial Legislation* (Detroit, MI: Wayne State University Press), 67–82; Jill Harries, *Law and Empire in Late Antiquity* (Cambridge: Cambridge University Press, 1999).

23. Linder, *Jews in Roman Imperial Legislation*, nos. 6, 8, 10, 11, 12, 26. Added to this is the repeal of Jewish exemptions from curial duties in certain areas of the empire; whether this was beneficial or harmful to the Jews is unclear (no. 29, 398 CE).

24. Consider, for example, the following rulings (in Linder, *Jews in Roman Imperial Legislation*): Jewish religious officials were no longer exempted from curial duties (no. 15, 383 CE; no. 29, 398 CE); Christians were forbidden to participate in Jewish (as well as pagan and Manichaean) cults (no. 16, 383 CE); Christian slaves could no longer be owned or proselytized (no. 17, 384 CE); Jews could not intermarry with Christians (no. 18, 388 CE; no. 22, 393 CE); Jewish converts were not to be accepted in churches (no. 26, 397 CE); taxes could no longer be collected for the Patriarch (no. 30, 399 CE); Jews were obligated to serve on curiae (no. 31, 399 CE).

destruction and spoliation owing to their status as recognized religious institutions.[25]

In addition, this latter legislation also featured laws enhancing Jewish autonomy and rights regarding, for instance, maritime practices for Jewish and Samaritan communities in Egypt; the authority of Jewish leaders to excommunicate and revoke excommunications; Jewish autonomy in fixing prices in their markets; the confirmation of the power of Jewish courts; the resumption after a hiatus of five years of the permission granted to Patriarchs to collect taxes from Jewish communities in the West; the reinforcement of the Patriarch's position vis-à-vis opposition within the Jewish community and outside it as well;[26] and, finally, the dramatic declaration regarding the overall protection and enhancement of the Patriarchate comparable to what was enjoyed by the Christian clergy:

> The Jews shall be bound to their rites; while we shall imitate the ancients in conserving their privileges, for it was established in their laws and confirmed by our divinity, that those who are subject to the rule of the Illustrious Patriarchs, that is the Archisynagogues, the patriarchs, the presbyters and the others who are occupied in the rite of that religion, shall persevere in keeping the same privileges that are reverently bestowed on the first clerics of the venerable Christian Law. For this was decreed in divine order also by the divine Emperors Constantine and Constantius, Valentinian and Valens. Let them therefore be exempt even from the curial liturgies, and obey their laws.[27]

To gain an even greater appreciation of the relative status and security of the Jewish community throughout the fourth century, the above laws should be compared to those relating to Christian heretics, pagans, and other contemporary minority groups. Indeed, an examination of Roman laws from late antiquity reveals the extent of Roman tolerance among the ruling political and imperial elites in contrast to the more aggressive and hostile policies fostered within ecclesiastical circles.

Even an event once considered disastrous for the Jews in the mid-fourth century, such as the supposed Gallus revolt of 351–352,[28] has of late been severely minimized in its extent and scope. Once presumed to have been of major proportions, the revolt is now regarded by most scholars

---

25. Ibid., no. 14 (370 CE), no. 21 (393 CE), and no. 25 (397 CE): "Your Excellent Authority shall order the governors to assemble, in order that they shall learn and know, that it is necessary to repel the assaults of those who attack Jews, and that their synagogues should remain in their accustomed peace."

26. Ibid., no. 19 (390 CE), no. 20 (392 CE), no. 24 (396 CE), no. 28 (398 CE), no. 34 (404 CE), no. 23 (396 CE), respectively.

27. Ibid., no. 27 (397 CE).

28. Avi-Yonah, *Jews of Palestine*, 176–81.

as, at most, a localized skirmish. Both historical sources and archaeological remains once considered authoritative are viewed today as, at best, highly problematic; it is claimed that the literary sources, owing to the tendentiousness of their Christian ecclesiastical authors who magnified this Jewish failure, excessively influenced the interpretation of archaeological material. The excavations conducted over recent years exposed only a limited number of destruction layers and, subsequently, a highly controversial dating (owing to the far better documented earthquake of 363 that caused extensive damage), rendering the evidence for a destruction around 352 far from conclusive.[29]

Finally, late fourth- and early fifth-century Galilee witnessed the construction of four remarkably impressive synagogue buildings, attesting to flourishing and well-endowed Jewish communities. One synagogue (Capernaum) was monumental in size; another (Ḥammat Tiberias) contained a richly decorated mosaic floor featuring, for the first time, pagan and Jewish motifs amid a plethora of Greek inscriptions; and two others (Sepphoris and Ḥuqoq) had elaborate mosaic floors containing a diverse and heretofore unattested range of biblical motifs. The art in these four structures is distinctly hellenized, and the architecture in the synagogue at Capernaum is most unusual. The first two buildings are dated to the late fourth century and the latter two to the early fifth century, that is, just prior to and following the formation of *Palaestina Secunda*.

Capernaum

Unique in a variety of ways, this richly decorated synagogue building was first and foremost a structure of monumental proportions erected at a Christian pilgrimage site in the late fourth and fifth centuries; it dwarfed the remains of an octagonal church built soon thereafter (fig. 4). The synagogue was built of white limestone, in contrast to the surrounding buildings, including the church, that were constructed of local black basalt. The synagogue stands on an artificial platform and consists of three parts; the

29. See Saul Lieberman, "Palestine in the Third and Fourth Centuries," *JQR* 36 (1946): 329–44; Joseph Geiger, "The Last Jewish Revolt against Rome: A Reconsideration," *Scripta Classica Israelica* 5 (1979): 250–57; Peter Schäfer, "Der Aufstand gegen Gallus Caesar," in *Tradition and Re-Interpretation in Jewish and Early Christian Literature: Essays in Honour of Jürgen C. H. Lebram*, ed. Jan W. van Henten et al., StPB 36 (Leiden: Brill, 1986), 184–201; Menahem Mor, "The Events of 351–352 in Palestine: The Last Revolt against Rome?," in *The Eastern Frontier of the Roman Empire: Proceedings of a Colloquium Held at Ankara in September 1988*, ed. David H. French and Christopher S. Lightfoot, 2 vols., BAR International Series 553 (Oxford: B.A.R., 1989), 335–53; Günter Stemberger, *Jews and Christians in the Holy Land: Palestine in the Fourth Century* (Edinburgh: T&T Clark, 2000), 161–84; Gabriela Bijovsky, "Numismatic Evidence for the Gallus Revolt: The Hoard from Lod," *IEJ* 57 (2007): 187–203.

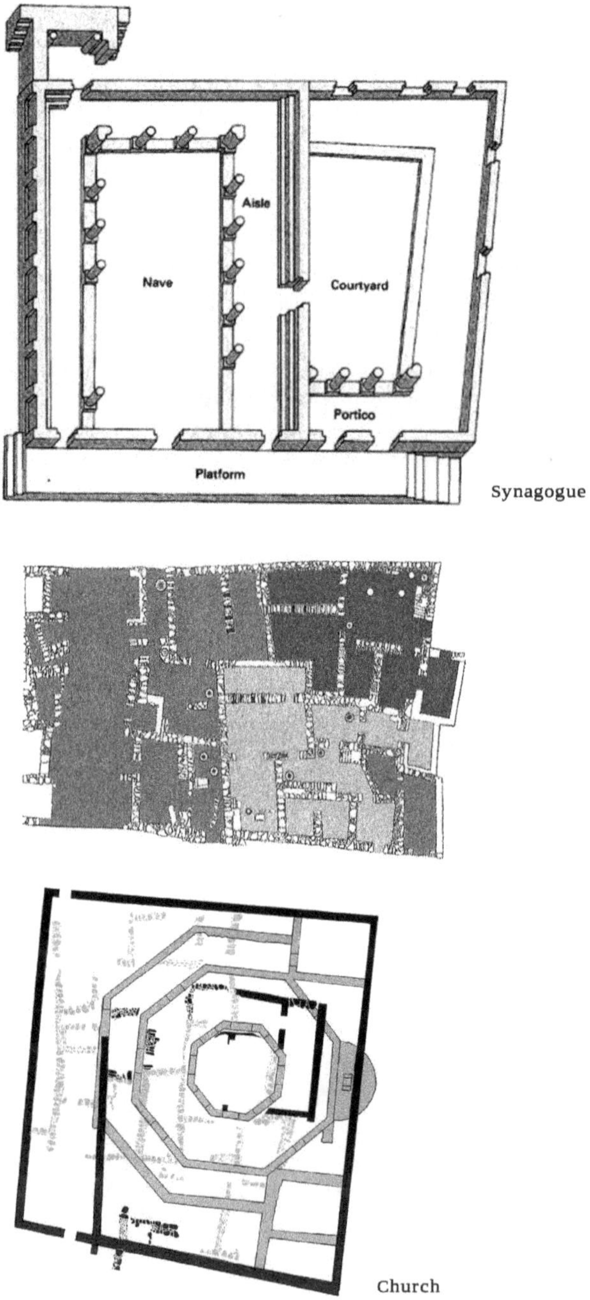

FIGURE 4. The synagogue and nearby church in Capernaum. Adapted from drawing by Mattila in "Capernaum, Village of Naḥum," 224. Used by permission.

sanctuary itself, paved with large flagstones, contained sixteen columns and is divided into a nave and three aisles, with stone benches on three sides of the hall. A courtyard lies east of the building, and a porch stands in front of the building. The main entrances to the synagogue faced south and were flanked by two *bimas*, or *aediculae*.

Capernaum and its remains are of special interest to Christians owing to the important role the town played in Jesus's activities as described in the New Testament, where it is mentioned sixteen times (e.g., Mark 1:21; 2:1; Matt 4:13; 8:5; 11:20–24; Luke 4:23–24, 31–37; John 2:12; 4:46–53), second only to Jerusalem. The synagogue and its immediate environs were acquired in the late nineteenth century by the Franciscans, who conducted a series of limited excavations at the site.

It was only from 1968 to 1986, however, that two Franciscan fathers, Virgilio Corbo and Stanislao Loffreda, undertook extensive excavations that produced a massive amount of archaeological evidence (over twenty-five thousand coins and large amounts of pottery), clearly demonstrating that the synagogue was built several hundred years later than heretofore assumed, that is, in the late fourth and fifth centuries (instead of the late second and third centuries).[30] Despite some reservations, particularly by Israeli scholars,[31] this late dating has now become the *communis opinio* and has been corroborated by many excavations of other Galilean and all Golan synagogues conducted since the 1970s, all attesting to a fourth- to sixth-century date of construction.[32]

The building is distinguished by its rich interior and exterior stone ornamentation; cornices, capitals, friezes, and lintels were decorated with eagles, sea horses, lions, as well as floral and geometric reliefs. One Corinthian capital features a carved menorah flanked by a shofar and incense shovel, and a frieze depicts a wheeled structure (a building or a chariot?)

---

30. Stanislao Loffreda, "The Late Chronology of the Synagogue of Capernaum," *IEJ* 23 (1973): 37–42; Loffreda, "Capernaum," *NEAEHL* 1:292–95; see also James F. Strange, "The Capernaum and Herodium Publications (review)," *BASOR* 226 (1977): 65–73. The excavators have made a distinction between the synagogue building with its main hall and porch to the south, and the atrium built on its eastern side later on, in the fifth century. An even later date of construction is argued by Jodi Magness, who suggests a sixth-century date ("The Question of the Synagogue: The Problem of Typology," in *Judaism in Late Antiquity*, part 3, *Where We Stand: Issues and Debates in Ancient Judaism*, vol. 4, *The Special Problem of the Synagogue*, ed. Alan J. Avery-Peck and Jacob Neusner, HdO 1 (Leiden: Brill, 2001), 1–48, esp. 18–26.

31. Michael Avi-Yonah, "Some Comments on the Capernaum Excavations," in *Ancient Synagogues Revealed*, ed. Lee I. Levine (Jerusalem: Israel Exploration Society, 1981), 60–62; and, in the same volume, Gideon Foerster, "Notes on Recent Excavations at Capernaum," 57–59.

32. For a summary of this change in scholarly opinion, see Levine, *Ancient Synagogue*, 319–26; see also Sharon L. Mattila, "Capernaum, Village of Naḥum, from Hellenistic to Byzantine Times," in *Galilee in the Late Second Temple and Mishnaic Periods*, vol. 2, *The Archaeological Record from Cities, Towns, and Villages*, ed. David A. Fiensy and James R. A. Strange (Minneapolis: Fortress, 2015), 217–26.

FIGURE 5. The zodiac on the mosaic floor of the synagogue in Ḥammat Tiberias (see the figure of the sun god Helios in the center of the zodiac). In Dothan, *Hammath Tiberias*, fig. 27.1. Used by permission of the Israel Exploration Society.

in relief that has been interpreted as representing the wilderness tabernacle or some other portable Torah shrine.

The redating of the Capernaum synagogue in light of the Franciscan excavations has not only led to a comprehensive reevaluation of the entire corpus of Galilean and Golan synagogues, as noted above, but has also had far-reaching ramifications regarding the status of the Jews in Byzantine-Christian society generally. If the Jews indeed erected synagogues throughout the Byzantine era, some of considerable size and prominence (such as the one in Capernaum) and others of an unusually high artistic level (as in Ḥammat Tiberias; see below), such a phenomenon would seriously impact our understanding of the Jewish political, economic, social, and religious status at this time.

This is particularly true in Capernaum. Not only was this a recognized Christian holy site, but the subsequent building of a large magnificent synagogue that dwarfed the nearby church signals a new reality wherein the Jews constituted a political, economic, social, and perhaps even religious prominence vis-à-vis other local communities, Christians included. It is impossible to imagine that such a situation could have existed without the consent of the Byzantine authorities, be they local, provincial, or imperial.

Ḥammat Tiberias

Excavated by Moshe Dothan in 1961,[33] this synagogue was clearly associated with Patriarchal circles and even with the Patriarch himself. The main donor to this building, one Severus, is identified on two occasions as "disciple (or protégé, θρεπτός) of the Illustrious Patriarchs," once in an inscription in the eastern aisle of the sanctuary and again in the longest of the eight dedicatory inscriptions located in the northern panel of the nave. In the latter setting Severus is accorded unusual prominence: each of the other seven inscriptions occupies one square while that of Severus fills two.[34] Thus, mention of the Patriarch was arguably the most significant feature among the epigraphic remains of this building.

The dominant role of Greek in this synagogue floor, together with its striking mosaic, clearly indicates the cosmopolitan cultural orientation of its donors and probably of many, if not most, of this congregation. The acculturation within Patriarchal circles is documented for some three hundred years, from the very first (proto-) stage under Rabban Gamaliel II (around the turn of the second century) until that of Rabban Gamaliel VI (the last of this dynasty's line in the early fifth century). Such acculturation was clearly expressed by the liberal and tolerant attitude toward figural and even pagan art, a phenomenon that undoubtedly would have upset many contemporary sages (and others).[35]

This nexus between Patriarchal and urban aristocratic circles, the latter represented by the wealthy synagogue benefactors noted above, goes a long way toward explaining the significant degree of acculturation and the strikingly high quality of the Tiberian synagogue mosaics, which can be rightfully considered the most elegant and "hellenized" of their kind in all ancient Jewish art (fig. 5). Besides its overall high quality, the art of this synagogue is of the highest standard in antiquity and compares favorably with that of contemporary Antioch, which was considered the main venue of eastern Roman art at this time. Here we find the earliest depiction of

---

33. Moshe Dothan, *Hammath Tiberias: Early Synagogues and the Hellenistic and Roman Remains* (Jerusalem: Israel Exploration Society, 1961).

34. Ibid., 54–60.

35. See Lee I. Levine, *Visual Judaism in Late Antiquity: Historical Contexts of Jewish Art* (New Haven: Yale University Press, 2012), 443–55.

a cluster of finely executed Jewish symbols, which were emulated many times in subsequent years; of no less significance is the first portrayal of the zodiac signs and Helios in synagogue art, a pattern that was imitated at a half dozen other Jewish sites, but rarely, if ever, at Christian ones.

By the turn of the fifth century Jews were accorded repeated assurances that their central institutions were being protected and granted a large measure of autonomy in how they were built and decorated: the Patriarch was approaching the zenith of his power and authority near the turn of the fifth century; Jewish practices and observances were reconfirmed in imperial law; and synagogues flourished presumably with strong imperial backing.

Thus, the creation of *Palaestina Secunda*, a region dominated by Jews, may be regarded as constituting yet another step in imperial Rome's support of the Palestinian Jewry's communal needs.

The benefits of this political and geographic arrangement seem to be abundantly evident throughout the ensuing centuries, which witnessed the flourishing of Jewish cultural and religious creativity together with the ongoing construction of synagogues boasting impressive artistic, architectural, and epigraphic remains (see below). It is not surprising, then, that, even after the establishment of this new province at the outset of the fifth century, two other impressive synagogues were erected, one in Sepphoris and one in Ḥuqoq, each reflecting stable and flourishing Jewish communities in the eastern Galilee.

Sepphoris

The Sepphoris synagogue was discovered in 1993. Its impressive mosaic floor, boasting seven panels (many of which are subdivided) instead of the usual three found in most ancient synagogues, includes a panel with a dedicatory inscription flanked by two lions; a panel with the cluster of Jewish symbols as in Ḥammat Tiberias; two panels depicting the wilderness tabernacle, including a portrayal of the high priest Aaron (almost entirely destroyed); the zodiac theme with the sun replacing the usual figure of Helios; and, finally, two partially preserved scenes from the book of Genesis—the Aqedah (Binding of Isaac) and Sarah standing at the entrance to her tent.

The various themes portrayed here have generated a number of theories regarding their purpose—an anti-Christian polemic, ideas of promise and redemption, motifs illustrating early synagogue *piyyutim*, and an emphasis on local priestly prominence in the city.[36]

---

36. Zeev Weiss, *The Sepphoris Synagogue: Deciphering an Ancient Message through Its*

Figure 6. Mosaic from the synagogue at Ḥuqoq depicting Samson carrying the gates of Gaza on his shoulders. Photo by Jim Haberman. Reproduction by permission of Jodi Magness.

Ḥuqoq[37]

A second early fifth-century synagogue appears in Ḥuqoq, located north of Tiberias, near the northwestern coast of the Sea of Galilee. Ongoing excavations have produced in a few short years a remarkably wide range of biblical mosaic depictions—several scenes of Samson (see, e.g., fig. 6), the tower of Babel, Noah and the ark, the splitting of the Red Sea, and Jonah and the whale. In addition, a scene of the zodiac and Helios was found there, as well as the most unusual postbiblical scene of a Greek general or king accompanied by Greek soldiers meeting (in what appears to be a friendly encounter) a Jewish leader, probably a high priest, with Jewish soldiers.[38]

Archaeological and Socio-Historical Contexts (Jerusalem: Israel Exploration Society and Institute of Archaeology, Hebrew University, 2005), 225–62; Levine, *Visual Judaism*, 267–77.

37. Given the fact that a final report of this most unusual find has yet to be published, our comments must remain limited.

38. Jodi Magness et al., "Huqoq (Lower Galilee) and Its Synagogue Mosaics: Preliminary Report on the Excavations of 2011–13," *JRA* 27 (2014): 339–47.

The Byzantine-Christian Period: Diachronic and Synchronic Factors

In Jewish and non-Jewish culture, diachronic and synchronic dimensions are regularly intertwined. Both must be considered even though they differ in importance from subject to subject, from one period to the next, not to speak of from one scholar's assessment to another. Was a given society forged by its past history (diachronic) or by its contemporary milieu (synchronic)? In what follows, I will focus on the latter dimension, not only because it was usually ignored or dismissed in earlier Jewish historiography of the period, but even more so because the appearance of considerable amounts of new archaeological and Genizah material over the last decades has highlighted more than ever this synchronic phenomenon.

We shall, nevertheless, begin our discussion by briefly noting those areas in which the diachronic factor in late antiquity remained significant. For example, the economic prosperity of Palestine at this time was not the foremost result of Christianization, but is indeed reflected in the many building projects in the cities and among a number of local ethnic and religious groups, Jews included, as early as the third and fourth centuries.[39] Continuity is likewise evident in Jewish settlement patterns, which remained fairly stable from the late second–third centuries onward. The creation of *Palaestina Secunda* merely formalized this pattern, which focused on Jewish life in the Galilee, Golan, Bet Shean and its environs, and the Jezreel Valley. The major languages used by Jews—Aramaic, Greek, and Hebrew—also remained constant, as did the model of local communal leadership and the centrality of the synagogue, which likewise carried over from the Roman period.[40]

Yet, alongside these elements of continuity, major changes took place in Jewish society of the Byzantine era, particularly in *Palaestina Secunda*. Jews found themselves in a new psychological, social, and religious milieu even as Byzantine-Christian rule attempted to move toward greater homogeneity and strived to diminish the earlier multifaceted social and religious matrices of the Roman Empire.

An examination of the changes and innovations in Jewish society at this time significantly reinforces the claim that the Byzantine period should be viewed as a unique historical era. The many new components in Jewish life of late antiquity can be best (and in many cases, only) explained in terms of models and stimuli stemming from the wider Byzantine-Christian

---

39. Doron Bar, "Geographical Implications of Population and Settlement Growth in Late Antique Palestine," *Journal of Historical Geography* 30 (2004): 1–10.

40. Levine, *Visual Judaism*, 387–402.

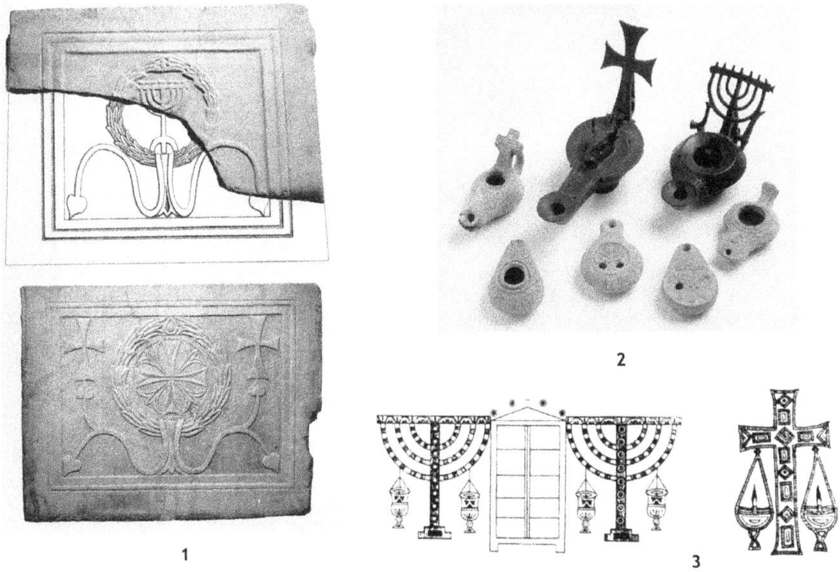

Figure 7. The use of the menorah and cross in Jewish and Christian contexts in the Byzantine period: (1) Chancel screens from Ḥammat Gader and Masu'ot Yitzḥaq; (2) oil lamps with the menorah and cross from Jerusalem; (3) lamps suspended from *menorot* and a cross. Photos/drawings in Yael Israeli, *In the Light of the Menorah: Story of a Symbol* (Jerusalem: Israel Museum, 1999), 155, 159. Used by permission of the Israel Museum and the Israel Antiquities Authority.

culture taking shape at this time (fig. 7).[41] Through this synchronic prism of late antiquity we will examine a range of phenomena emanating from the growing corpus of Jewish material and literary remains.

Burgeoning synagogue construction. As noted, Byzantine synagogues dating from the fourth through seventh centuries constitute the bulk of synagogue remains from antiquity. These would include synagogue structures throughout Palestine, the Galilee, the Golan, the Bet Shean area, and the southern parts of the country. Not coincidentally, the construction of public buildings in the Galilee by both Christians and Jews took place almost simultaneously, rendering the chronological and geographical propinquity too coincidental to ignore. Thus, it seems logical and compelling to

41. See in greater detail Levine, *Visual Judaism*, 206–21; as well as Seth Schwartz, *Imperialism and Jewish Society, 200 B.C.E. to 640 C.E.*, Jews, Christians, and Muslims from the Ancient to the Modern World (Princeton: Princeton University Press, 2001), 179–202.

link the building of synagogues in the Byzantine period with what was taking place in the nearby Christian sector.[42] What remains unclear, however, is whether the construction of these synagogues was a direct result of Christian activity or of a flourishing economic situation that encouraged such building by both populations (and for the Samaritans as well in the fourth century), or a combination thereof.

Synagogue architecture. Throughout Jewish history, synagogue buildings invariably have reflected the regnant styles and models of contemporary architecture. Most synagogues from the Byzantine period (the most striking example being Bet Alpha) followed the basilical model of churches in that era that featured a nave, side aisles, apse, narthex, and courtyard; other synagogues appropriated variants of that model.

Synagogue sanctity. The religious component of the synagogue had become especially ubiquitous and prominent in late antiquity. While rabbinic sources and material remains from the earlier Roman period have preserved some evidence of this development, owing to the dearth of physical remains it is impossible to determine how widespread this phenomenon was before the fourth century. From the fourth–fifth centuries on, however, synagogues everywhere acquired a significant measure of sanctity, as is evident in their orientation, art, and inscriptions.

Moreover, the fact that the sanctity of people, objects, and places became paramount and universal in late antiquity generally cannot be ignored. It is difficult to imagine that Christian concern with holy places in the fourth century, the redefinition of Palestine as "the Holy Land," and the sanctity attributed to churches, saints, and relics could not have but impacted the Jews and their synagogues.[43]

Piyyut. Religious poetry flourished in the Byzantine synagogue during the sixth and seventh centuries. Although the language and content of this liturgical genre drew heavily on earlier Jewish sources such as the Bible and midrash, its actual appearance in late antiquity is significant because a similar liturgical genre also flourished in contemporary Christian and

42. Mordechai Aviam, "Christian Galilee in the Byzantine Period," in *Galilee through the Centuries: Confluence of Cultures, Second International Conference on Galilee in Antiquity*, ed. Eric M. Meyers, Duke Judaic Studies 1 (Winona Lake, IN: Eisenbrauns, 1999), 281–300.

43. See Peter R. L. Brown, *The Cult of the Saints: Its Rise and Function in Latin Christianity*, Haskell Lectures on History of Religions NS 2 (Chicago: University of Chicago Press, 1981); Brown, *Society and the Holy in Late Antiquity* (London: Faber & Faber, 1982); Robert L. Wilken, *The Land Called Holy: Palestine in Christian History and Thought* (New Haven: Yale University Press, 1992); Levine, *Ancient Synagogue*, 236–49; Levine, *Visual Judaism*, 337–59.

Samaritan contexts. This has been most persuasively argued by Ophir Münz-Manor and Wout van Bekkum,[44] who claim that the fourth and fifth centuries witnessed the simultaneous emergence of Jewish, Samaritan, and Christian religious poetry (the latter in both Syriac and Greek) and that they all share many poetic, thematic, and conceptual characteristics. These similarities clearly indicate that such parallels were part of a common religious creativity in late antiquity that abandoned all antecedents, be they ancient Mesopotamian, biblical, rabbinic, or Greek. For instance, when comparing the poems, and especially the *kontakia*, of Romanos, the leading Christian poet of the sixth century, with the *Qedushta* of the contemporary Jewish *paytan* Yannai, it becomes clear that both compositions were produced at virtually the same time and that there was some sort of indirect, if not more substantive, contact between them.[45] One wonders whether synagogue *piyyut* would have emerged expressly at this time were it not for the existence of a similar Christian or Samaritan genre. While a definitive answer to this question is beyond the purview of our sources, I suspect not.

Magic. The publication of documents on magic from the Cairo Genizah, together with similar talmudic evidence and the discovery of related archaeological material, indicates that many Jews in late antiquity believed in the efficacy of magical practices in solving daily matters.[46] What is striking is that the use of amulets, incantation bowls, and literary forms, as well as soliciting heavenly forces (usually angels) with similar ritual ceremonies (often accompanied by prayer or some other sort of incantation), were popular among pagans and Christians as well at this time. Indeed, engaging in practical magic appears to have been universal in late antiquity (and earlier as well), appealing to both intellectual elites (rabbis, Christian clergy, and Neoplatonists) and the common people.

---

44. Ophir Münz-Manor, "Liturgical Poetry in the Late Antique Near East: A Comparative Approach," *JAJ* 1 (2010): 336–61; Wout J. van Bekkum, "The Hebrew Liturgical Poetry of Byzantine Palestine: Recent Research and New Perspectives," *Prooftexts* 28 (2008): 232–46.

45. Joseph Yahalom, "*Piyyûṭ* as Poetry," in *The Synagogue in Late Antiquity*, ed. Lee I. Levine (Philadelphia: American Schools of Oriental Research and the Jewish Theological Seminary, 1987), 122.

46. See, inter alios, Philip S. Alexander, "Incantations and Books of Magic," in Schürer, *History of the Jewish People*, 3/1:342–79 ; Peter Schäfer, "Jewish Magic Literature in Late Antiquity and Early Middle Ages," *JJS* 41 (1990): 75–91; Joseph Naveh and Shaul Shaked, *Amulets and Magical Bowls: Aramaic Incantations of Late Antiquity* (Jerusalem: Magnes, 1985); Naveh and Shaked, eds., *Magic Spells and Formulae: Aramaic Incantations of Late Antiquity* (Jerusalem: Magnes, 1993); Michael D. Swartz, "Jewish Magic in Late Antiquity," in *The Cambridge History of Judaism*, vol. 4, *Late Roman–Rabbinic Period*, ed. Steven Katz (Cambridge: Cambridge University Press, 2006), 699–720; Gideon Bohak, *Ancient Jewish Magic: A History* (Cambridge: Cambridge University Press, 2008).

Astrology. Jewish interest in astrology from the Second Temple period through late antiquity has likewise merited scholarly attention over the last several generations.[47] Both literary sources and archaeological material have contributed to this growing corpus of evidence, beginning with Qumran and including fragments of late antique astrological texts from the Cairo Genizah. Jews were indeed part of the astrological discourse of the age, making use of the Greco-Roman material then in circulation while adding elements having a distinct Jewish character, such as Hebrew words for labeling the zodiac signs in synagogue mosaics.

Apocalyptic literature. Several Jewish apocalyptic compositions (for example, Sefer Zerubbabel, were written in the late sixth and early seventh centuries, very likely in response to the unsettling conditions of the time and especially the military confrontations between Persia and Byzantium.[48] Following the biblical book of Daniel, these wars were perceived as a struggle between two empires that would precede the end of days and usher in the messianic era (Daniel's fifth kingdom). Similar eschatological responses to the Persian conquest of Jerusalem appear among Christian sources as well.[49] Thus, both Jewish and Christian writers reacted to similar contemporary political upheavals from their own religious perspectives.

Hekhalot literature. Although there has been a general consensus of late that the mystical traditions found in this literature had already crystallized by late antiquity, significant differences of opinion remain regarding the role of the Byzantine-Christian realm in this development. While many scholars have posited continuity from the Second Temple era, others have suggested a late antique context for this literary genre.[50]

---

47. James H. Charlesworth, "Jewish Interest in Astrology during the Hellenistic and Roman Period," *ANRW* 2.20.2 (1987): 926–50.

48. See John C. Reeves, *Trajectories in Near Eastern Apocalyptic: A Postrabbinic Jewish Apocalypse Reader*, RBS 45 (Atlanta: Society of Biblical Literature, 2005).

49. Günter Stemberger, "Jerusalem in the Early Seventh Century: Hopes and Aspirations of Christians and Jews," in *Jerusalem: Its Sanctity and Centrality to Judaism, Christianity, and Islam*, ed. Lee I. Levine (New York: Continuum, 1999), 260–72.

50. On continuity from the Second Temple period, see Gershom Scholem, *Major Trends in Jewish Mysticism* (New York: Schocken, 1941), 40–79; Itamar Gruenwald, *From Apocalypticism to Gnosticism: Studies in Apocalypticism, Merkabah Mysticism and Gnosticism*, BEATAJ 14 (Frankfurt am Main: P. Lang, 1988); Rachel Elior, *The Three Temples: On the Emergence of Jewish Mysticism* (Oxford: Littman Library of Jewish Civilization, 2004), 232–63. On the late antique context, see Peter Schäfer, *The Origins of Jewish Mysticism* (Tübingen: Mohr Siebeck, 2009), 243–330, 339–48; Martha Himmelfarb, "Heavenly Ascent in the Relationship of the Apocalypses and the Hekhalot Literature," *HUCA* 59 (1988): 73–100; Guy G. Stroumsa, "Religious Dynamics between Christians and Jews in Late Antiquity (312–640)," in *The Cam-*

Whatever the case, it seems rather certain that the balance of continuity and innovation in the mystical traditions of late antiquity witnessed a surge of activity regarding the theory and practice of mysticism among both Jews and Christians. In fact, some interesting parallels have been drawn between the Byzantine-Christian context, the development of contemporary Jewish mysticism, and the role of Byzantine-Christian chronographers in the transmission of earlier Second Temple pseudepigraphic sources to the authors/redactors of later mystical and midrashic works.[51]

Aggadic midrashim. The Byzantine period witnessed the appearance of a new rabbinic genre—the aggadic midrash—the earliest of which dates to late antiquity: Genesis Rabbah; Leviticus Rabbah; Pesiqta d'Rav Kahana; Lamentations Rabbah; Qohelet Rabbah; and perhaps others.[52] Virtually all we know about Palestinian rabbinic culture from this era comes from such midrashim, which are a far cry in content and quantity from the mainly (though not exclusively) halakhic works of the third and fourth centuries.

How might the emergence of this important genre at this time be explained? Indeed, these collections of commentaries and sermons focusing on the biblical narrative may be viewed as parallel to the commentaries and sermons (*catena*) of contemporary church fathers, leading us to conclude that this type of Jewish creativity may have been influenced by Christian practice.[53] Alternatively, these similar Jewish and Christian literary works may be the product of a common Zeitgeist that yielded similar responses in both religions.

Jewish art. The phenomenon of a unique and creative Jewish art is a significant innovation of late antiquity. Although appearing on a limited scale in the third century, a far broader range of Jewish art forms gained popularity under Byzantine-Christian rule, when many of the most Jewish

---

bridge History of Christianity, vol. 2, *Constantine to c. 600*, ed. Augustine Casiday and Frederick W. Norris (Cambridge: Cambridge University Press, 2007), 691–725; Stroumsa, "To See or Not to See: On the Early History of the Visio Beatifica," in *Wege mystischer Gotteserfahrung: Judentum, Christentum und Islam / Mystical Approaches to God: Judaism, Christianity, and Islam*, ed. Peter Schäfer, Schriften des Historischen Kollegs. Kolloquien 65 (Munich: Oldenbourg, 2006), 67–80.

51. Annette Y. Reed, "From Asael and Šemihazah to Uzzah, Azzah, and Azael," *JSQ* 8 (2001): 132–36; Reed, *Fallen Angels and the History of Judaism and Christianity: The Reception of Enochic Literature* (New York: Cambridge University Press, 2005), 13–16, 233–77.

52. Hermann L. Strack and Günter Stemberger, *Introduction to the Talmud and Midrash* (Minneapolis: Fortress, 1992), 300–322; Avigdor Shinan, "The Late Midrashic, Paytanic, and Targumic Literature," in Katz, *Cambridge History of Judaism*, 4: 678–91.

53. Nicholas de Lange, "Jews in the Age of Justinian," in *The Cambridge Companion to the Age of Justinian*, ed. Michael Maas (Cambridge: Cambridge University Press, 2005), 403–5.

motifs (symbols and biblical scenes and figures) found parallels among Jews throughout the Byzantine-Christian world (fig. 8).[54]

Given the religious revolution transpiring under the Byzantine Empire, when the center of Rome's territorial empire was moved to Constantinople, religious identity emerged as a primary factor in contemporary art. It was in this context that Jews began using symbols and creating artistic forms in sync with their neighbors, which served, inter alia, to bolster their self-identity.

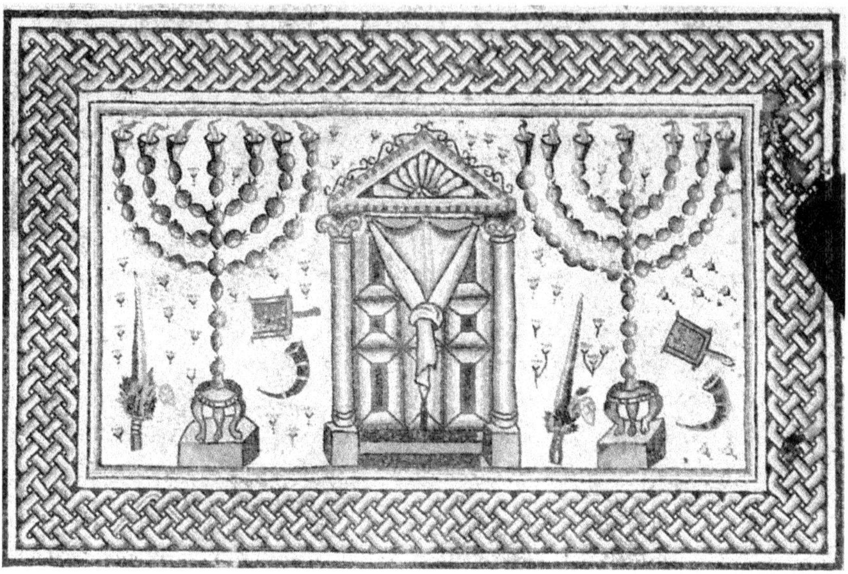

FIGURE 8. Depiction of Jewish symbols on the mosaic floor of the synagogue in Ḥammat Tiberias. In Dothan, *Hammath Tiberias*, fig. 29.1. Used by permission of the Israel Exploration Society.

Conclusion

The rise of Christianity in the fourth century inaugurated a new era for Jews that would continue for some three hundred years, until the Arab conquest in the seventh century. Throughout this era Jews were actively engaged in a broad range of cultural endeavors stimulated in no small measure by Christianity and its penetration into all aspects of the empire. Despite the church's aspirations for compliance and unity, the Byzantine Empire remained heterogeneous among Orthodox Christians and those

54. On this topic, see Levine, *Visual Judaism*, 225–467 (chs. 11–22).

outside the fold. J. Hillis Miller has aptly noted the complexity of each period in this light: "Periods differ from one another because there are different forms of heterogeneity, not because each period held a single coherent view of the world."[55] The unique diversity of this era accorded it a special character; it had inherited Roman traditions yet was under Christian rule, and it had a significant ideological component yet was less rigid than what was to crystallize in the Middle Ages.

If the term "late antiquity" is indicative of processes of renewal, vitality, and creativity in society generally, then one can easily identify parallel developments within the Jewish sphere as well. Instances of Jewish creativity in the material and literary realms of *Palaestina Secunda* can be most fully appreciated if viewed in the wider historical context in which they coalesced, namely, the Byzantine-Christian realm. This multifaceted creativity and resilience, together with a growing sense of vulnerability, characterized this particular era in ancient Jewish history.

---

55. Joseph Hillis Miller, "Deconstructing the Deconstructors," *Diacritics* 5 (1975): 31.

Did Constantine Really Prohibit (All) "Conversion to Judaism" in 329?

A Rereading of Codex Theodosianus 16.8.1

ROSS S. KRAEMER
Brown University

The final sentence of a law of Constantine issued in 329 CE is regularly read to contain a blanket prohibition of conversion to Judaism. In its first, longer sentence, Codex Theodosianus (16.8.1.1) sternly warns that Jews who attack their former coreligionists who have become Christians will be burned to death.[1] A second, briefer final sentence warns: "si quis vero ex populo ad eorum nefarium sectam accesserit et conciliabulis eorum se adplicaverit, cum ipsis poenas meritas sustinebit." What precisely this prohibits is the focus of this piece, but at a minimum, it declares that any one "of the people" who joins with (the Jews) will be liable, with them, for the punishments deserved.[2] The first part of the law, Cod. theod. 16.8.1.1, was reiterated in somewhat different form in 335. That law repeated a prohibition against Jews circumcising non-Jewish purchased slaves (*mancipia*), but did not reiterate the provision of Cod. theod. 16.8.1.2.[3]

This essay draws extensively on my new book on Jews in the late antique Mediterranean diaspora in the wake of Christianization, forthcoming from Oxford University Press.

1. In the interests of space, I have minimized here discussions of other aspects of this law. I treat these extensively in my forthcoming book (Kraemer, *Jews*).

2. Cod. theod. 16.8.1. Latin and English translation in Amnon Linder, *The Jews in Imperial Roman Legislation* (Detroit, MI: Wayne State University Press, 1987) (hereafter *JRIL*), no. 8. Latin and French translation in Jean Rougé and Roland Delmaire, *Les lois religieuses des empereurs romains de Constantin à Théodose II (312–438)*, vol. 1, *Code Théodosien Livre XVI*, SC 497 (Paris: Cerf, 2005). For an additional English translation, see Clyde Pharr, *The Theodosian Code and Novels, and the Sirmondian Constitutions: A Translation with Commentary, Glossary and Bibliography*, in collaboration with Theresa Sherrer Davidson and Mary Brown Pharr, Corpus of Roman Law 1 (Princeton: Princeton University Press, 1952; repr., Union, NJ: Lawbook Exchange, 2001).

3. Sirmondian Constitutions 4, in *JRIL*, no. 7; Latin and French translation in Jean Rougé and Roland Delmaire, *Les lois religieuses des empereurs romains de Constantin à Théodose*

In this brief tribute to my long-time friend and short-time colleague at Brown, Shaye Cohen, I argue against this reading.[4] I propose instead that the entire law pertains to those persons who took part in physical attacks on Jews who had become Christians, and that the final sentence of the law extends the penalties applicable to Jews for these crimes to others who joined in these attacks.

Although I cannot pursue these issues in depth here, I am well aware of the practical and theoretical impediments to reconstructing the intentions of those who wrote and authorized the law, as well as how it may initially have been construed. The law was then, and remains now, ambiguous and susceptible to multiple readings. We owe its preservation to the collators of the Theodosian Code, who did not always transmit the original laws in their entirety.[5] We seem to lack the full contextual and prefatory information this law would initially have had. We know very little about the drafters of the law, including Christian lobbyists, imperial advisers or professional lawyers. Nevertheless, I believe it is possible to argue the case for this reading.

The interpretation of Cod. theod. 16.8.1.2 as a prohibition of non-Jews becoming Jews is exemplified in the commentary of Amnon Linder, in his major edition of Roman laws pertaining to Jews and Jewish religion.[6]

II (312–438), vol. 2, *Code Théodosien Livre I–XV, Code Justinien, Constitutions Sirmondiennes,* SC 531 (Paris: Cerf, 2009), 484–87. The earlier law concerning the circumcision of slaves is Cod. theod. 16.9.1 (Linder, *JRIL,* no. 11; Rougé and Delmaire, *Les lois religieuses* 1:484–87), Constantine II in 339.

4. I have known Shaye Cohen more than thirty years, during which I have benefited immensely from his scholarship and friendship. But I owe him a special debt for the role he played in bringing me to Brown in 2000, particularly in his capacity as chair of the search committee.

5. For some helpful overviews on the collection and transmission of the Code, see Tony Honoré, *Law in the Crisis of Empire, 379–455 A.D: The Theodosian Dynasty and Its Quaestors with a Palingenesia of Laws of the Dynasty* (Oxford: Oxford University Press, 1998), 123–53; Jill D. Harries, *Law and Empire in Late Antiquity* (Cambridge: Cambridge University Press, 1999); and John F. Matthews, *Laying Down the Law: A Study of the Theodosian Code* (New Haven: Yale University Press, 2000).

6. I take the scholarship of Linder and Capucine Nemo-Pekelman here as representative of modern scholarly positions on these laws: Linder, *JRIL;* Capucine Nemo-Pekelman, *Rome et ses citoyens juifs (IVe–Ve siècles),* Bibliothèque d'études juives: Histoire 35 (Paris: Honoré Champion, 2015). Selected bibliography on Jews in imperial Roman law includes Jean Juster, *Les juifs dans l'Empire Romain: Leur condition juridique,* économique *et sociale,* 2 vols. (Paris: Paul Geuthner, 1914); A. M. Rabello, "The Legal Condition of Jews in the Roman Empire," in *ANRW* 2.13 (1980): 662–762; Rabello, "The Attitude of Rome Towards Conversions to Judaism (Atheism, Circumcision, Proselytism)," in *Towards a New European Ius Commune: Essays on European, Italian and Israeli Law in occasion of 50 years of the EU and of the State of Israel,* ed. A. Gambaro and A. M. Rabello, Jerusalem: Harry and Michael Sacher Institute for Legislative Research and Comparative Law, 1999), 37–68; reprinted in Rabello, *The Jews in the Roman Empire: Legal Problems, from Herod to Justinian,* Collected Studies, CS 645 (Aldershot: Ashgate, 2000), number XIV (with original pagination).

Linder titles the entry "Persecution of Converts and Proselytism."[7] The former is shorthand for Jews who "persecuted" other Jews who had become Christians, while the latter is shorthand for the persecution of those who became Jews (that is, proselytes), and perhaps those who abetted them (who engaged in proselytism).

This interpretation is similarly exemplified in a recent study of Jews in the laws of the fourth and fifth centuries CE by Capucine Nemo-Pekelman, who sees the law further as the first wholesale prohibition against conversion to Judaism.[8] She, too, redescribes the law as pertaining to conversion, titling her discussion of it: "La conversion au judaïsme comme *crimen publicum*."[9] Nemo-Pekelman is mildly uneasy that a blanket prohibition of non-Jews becoming Jews would seem to be a violation of the "spirit" of the Edict of Milan in 313, which she takes to have granted citizens the right to their chosen religious practices. Rather than reconsider what this law penalizes, she proposes that it was "conceived and formulated" not by Constantine, nor by his professional legal advisers, but "by the church hierarchy,"[10] for whom, presumably, such an inconsistency was not troubling.

It is important to note that if Cod. theod. 16.8.1.2 is a ban on conversion, the two sentences of the law are concerned with substantially different matters. The first makes it a capital offense for Jews to attack other Jews who had become Christians, in response to actual instances, or at least accusations, of such behavior. The second pivots to a different offense, that of the "quis ... ex populo" whose conversion to Judaism is taken to be described in the verbal clauses "ad eorum nefarium sectam accesserit et concilabulis eorum se adplicaverit." Scholars who take Cod. theod. 16.8.1.2 to prohibit conversion do not see any dissonance here and appear to presume that the unifying interest of the law is in conversion—protecting Jewish converts to Christianity from angry Jews in the first sentence, and forbidding non-Jews from becoming Jews in the second. Although a law combining these two concerns is not impossible, it is by no means self-evident that this accurately explains how these two prohibitions are actually related. A hint that, on the contrary, both sentences pertain to the same transgression may be found at the outset of Cod. theod. 16.8.1.1,

---

7. Linder, *JRIL*, p. 124.

8. Nemo-Pekelman, *Rome et ses citoyens juifs*, 124 (with fuller discussion, 120–24).

9. Ibid.: "conversion to Judaism as a criminal offense." She disputes older views that the Romans had long prohibited non-Jews taking up Jewish practice (119–24). If this law does not prohibit conversion, this argument becomes moot.

10. Nemo-Pekelman relies on Edoardo Volterra's analysis of laws written by expert jurists and those probably composed by Christian lobbyists: for references, see Nemo-Pekelman, *Rome et ses citoyens juifs*, 126 n. 49. Volterra did not identify this law as the work of Christian lobbyists, but Nemo-Pekelman proposes it was (*Rome et ses citoyens juifs*, 127). See also the notes in Rougé and Delmaire, *Les lois religieuses*, 1:487.

when the legislator says that the provisions of the law are in force *post hanc legem*, that is, "after this law [has been given]." Such language is not repeated in the second sentence, which is at least consistent with the interpretation that it is all one law, and that both sentences pertain to the same activity, attacks on Jews who had become Christians.

Cod. theod. 16.8.1.2 and 16.8.7

The interpretation of Cod. theod. 16.8.1.2 as a blanket prohibition of conversion is regularly enhanced by reading it in tandem with 16.8.7, given in 353 in the name of Constantine II.[11] It reads in full, "Si quis, lege venerabile constituta, ex Christiano Iudeus effectus sacrilegis coetibus adgregetur, cum accusatio fuerit conprobata, facultates eius dominio fisci iussimus vindicari," with the crucial portions underlined. Scholars routinely presume that this law, too, criminalizes conversion to Judaism. Linder characterizes it as "a partial return to the legal rule established at the end of the third century," according to which a (male) Roman citizen who became a Jew would be subject to the twofold penalty of exile and confiscation of property.[12] Cod. theod. 16.8.7, by comparison, pertains only to Christians and imposes only confiscation and not exile.[13]

Because Nemo-Pekelman thinks both laws pertain to conversion, she proposes that Cod. theod. 16.8.7 may have been a rescript—a response to a judge who sought clarification of the (otherwise unspecified) "merited punishment(s)" prescribed for a Christian who became a Jew in Cod. theod. 16.8.1.2. This law provides an answer: total confiscation of assets.[14] Were this to be correct, it might suggest that "quis ... ex Christiano Iudeus" similarly clarifies who, exactly, was intended by the earlier phrase "quis ... ex populo." She also thinks that the underlined language provided a basis for establishing the guilt of the person accused. It had to be shown both that the person had become "Iudeus," and had been joined to the sacrilegious "assemblies."[15]

The interpretation of the law of 353 as a prohibition of conversion is facilitated by supplying a conjunctive that the Latin text lacks, at least as we now have it, so that "ex Christiano Iudeus effectus" becomes one act

11. Cod. theod. 16.8.7; *JRIL*, no. 12. For discussion of the date and other matters, see Linder, *JRIL*, pp. 151–52; also Rougé and Delmaire *Les lois religieuses*, 1:380.

12. The *Sentences* of Paul 5.22.3-4, Linder, *JRIL*, no. 6.

13. Linder, *JRIL*, p.152.

14. Nemo-Pekelman thinks the forfeiture must be all assets, because the law does not specify a proportion (*Rome et ses citoyens juifs*, 129).

15. Nemo-Pekelman offers a fascinating if speculative consideration of how a judge or arbitrator might have established this (*Rome et ses citoyens juifs*, 130).

and "sacrilegis coetibus adgregetur" becomes another.[16] In my view, the insertion of a conjunction between these two phrases comes at least in part from the perception that Cod. theod. 16.8.7 is analogous to 16.8.1.2. If the latter alludes to two processes of some sort, the former should as well. Syntactically, however, the insertion of any conjunction seems unnecessary. The law reads perfectly well by taking "quis ex Christiano Iudeus effectus" as the transgressor of the law, and "sacrilegis coetibus adgregetur" as the transgression: "If one (who has) become Jew from Christian is joined to their sacrilegious gatherings...." The phrase "ex Christiano Iudeus effectus" ("one become Jew from Christian") is comparable to the phrase "ex Iudaeo Christianum factum" as the term for a Jew who has become a Christian in the restatement of the law of 329 in the Sirmondian Constitutions in 335 and in numerous other examples.[17] This suggests that the construction "x become y" functions in these laws as a nominative, rather than as the description of a second action. If such phrasing does function as a complex nominative, it might suggest that, in fact, becoming "Iudeus ex Christiano" is not what the law here prohibits. It may intend to distinguish such a person from other non-Jews who subsequently became *Iudeus*. In this law, the "ex Christiano Iudeus effectus" was liable for a specific act: "sacrilegis coetibus adgregetur."

I have long had reservations about the general arguments exemplified by Linder and Nemo-Pekelman, especially the classification of non-Jews interested in Jewish religious practices as either "proselytes" or "godfearers/sympathizers."[18] Their readings of Cod. theod. 16.8.1 strike me as governed more by the assumptions that scholars bring to questions of how non-Jews might have affiliated themselves with Jews than about what

---

16. Pharr, *Theodosian Code*, 467: "If anyone should be converted from Christianity to Judaism <u>and</u> should join their sacrilegious gatherings"; Linder, *JRIL*, p.153 n. 4: "if someone shall become Jew from Christian <u>and</u> shall be joined to sacrilegious assemblies." Rougé: "si un chrétien se convertit au judaïsme <u>et</u> participe à leurs réunions sacrilèges," (Rougé and Delmaire, *Les lois religieuses*, 1:381). Only Nemo-Pekelman supplies "or": "si un chrétien s'est fait juif <u>ou</u> a rejoint leurs assemblées sacrilèges" (*Rome et ses citoyens juifs*, 129). Whether "effectus" (as opposed to "factus est") implies that others have played a determinative role in this change is immaterial to my point here.

17. Sirmondian Constitutions 4; *JRIL* (above). Cod. theod. 16.8.5 contains a brief extract from that law: it is unlawful for Jews to disturb or injure "eum, qui ex Iudaeo Christianus factus est" ("one who has become Christian, having been a Jew"). See also Cod. theod. 16.7.1, Theodosius I in 381, depriving "qui ex christianis pagani facti sunt" ("those who have become 'pagan' from Christian") of their right to make wills; Cod. theod. 16.8.19, a law of Honorius at Ravenna in 409, targeting persons called "quis ex christiana fide" for taking up "the name of Jews."

18. See esp. Ross S. Kraemer, "Giving Up the Godfearers," *JAJ* 5 (2014): 61–87; reprinted in *Crossing Boundaries in Ancient Judaism and Early Christianity: Ambiguities, Complexities, and Half-Forgotten Adversaries; Essays in Honor of Alan F. Segal*, ed. Andrea Lieber and Kimberly Stratton, JSJSup 177 (Leiden: Brill 2016), 169–99.

the laws intend to prohibit. But I only recently realized there might be a more serious difficulty with the interpretation of Cod. theod. 16.8.1.2 as a wholesale ban on whatever is meant by the language of "conversion to Judaism." Like many such recognitions, this one was somewhat serendipitous. Intending to write on the gendered dynamics of these laws, I reread Rougé's French translation of Cod. theod. 16.8.1.2. Although I had read it many times before, I was startled to realize that Rougé's translation casts the entire second sentence in a different light. "Si quelqu'un du peuple se joint à leur secte impie et participe à leurs groupements séditieux, il supportera, avec eux, les châtiments mérités," "If any one of the people joins up with their impious sect and participates in their seditious bands, he will suffer, with them, the merited punishments."[19] Rougé died in 1991 and left no explanations of his translation decisions.[20] The notes subsequently prepared by Delmaire provide no further discussion.[21] Consistent with the implication of Rougé's translation, the Sources chrétiennes volume titles the entire law "contre les juifs qui lapide ceux d'entre eux qui sont devenus chrétiens" ("against the Jews who stoned those among them who had become Christians") with no other reference to conversion. Although I am not certain that "seditious bands" ("groupements séditieux") is the most felicitous translation of "sacrilegis coetibus," it facilitates an entirely different interpretation that may be a more accurate reading of the initial law. I subsequently realized that A. M. Rabello raised the possibility of a related, but not identical, reading of the law in a 1999 article, discussed further below.[22]

To argue my position here, it helps to highlight the aspects of the law that do not sit easily with the reading exemplified by Linder and Nemo-Pekelman. First and perhaps foremost, if Cod. theod. 16.8.1.2 is a prohibition of conversion, why is it so oblique and circumlocutious? Why does it not simply say, "it is forbidden for anyone to become a Jew"? Why does the law not refer to the assemblies of the Jews as "synagogues"? If it is a broad prohibition of conversion, why is it necessary to specify that the "quis" is "ex populo"? Who, precisely, does this designate? Why does it say that the offenders will receive, *with them*, those merited punishments? Who is the referent of "them"? Why do "they" merit punishment(s)? And why does Cod. theod. 16.8.1.2 not specify the "punishments deserved" ("poenas meritas") for whatever transgression it envisions? I will consider all these features of the law shortly, but it is worth a brief consideration of

19. Rougé and Delmaire, *Les lois religieuses*, 1:369: my English translation of the French.

20. Ibid., "Avant Propos" (no pagination).

21. It is not clear that Delmaire even recognized this as an issue.

22. Rabello, "Attitude of Rome towards Conversions." The bibliography for this law in Rougé and Delmaire, *Les lois religieuses*, 1:368, does not cite Rabello's article.

one feature it lacks—any reference to circumcision. If Cod. theod. 16.8.1.2 is about "conversion," is this absence at all curious?

Prior Roman laws criminalizing circumcision do not necessarily equate the procedure with non-Jews becoming Jews, but the two are closely linked in the late third-century law preserved in the *Sentences* of Paul.[23] Subsequent laws, particularly those pertaining to the circumcision of enslaved non-Jewish males in Jewish households, clearly link the two. A notable instance is the law of 335, which repeats the provisions of Cod. theod. 16.8.1.1 against attacking Jews who had become Christian and forbids the circumcision of enslaved non-Jewish males, but not the provisions of Cod. theod. 16.8.1.2.[24] With many scholars, Linder appears to assume that any prohibition of conversion necessarily entailed a prohibition of circumcision (presumably at least for males, although he does not say this explicitly).[25] I had at one point wondered whether the absence of any reference to circumcision could be due to an imperial recognition that both females and males sometimes became Jews, and thus laws that banned circumcision were not comprehensive. But were that to be the case, it is notable that the laws against circumcising slaves show no comparable concern for the "conversion" of enslaved females.

A more detailed comparison with Cod. theod. 16.8.7, concerning the transgressions of the Christian become Jew ("quis ex Christiano Judeus effectus") is illluminating. In Cod. theod. 16.8.1.2, the penalty for whatever transgression is presumed is to be the same as the penalty merited for some unspecified "them." In Cod. theod. 16.8.7, the penalty is vindication of property to the imperial treasury. If Nemo-Pekelman is correct that Cod. theod. 16.8.7 was a rescript clarifying the joint punishments in Cod. theod. 16.8.1.2, we need not explain the differential punishments. But alternatively, the punishments are different because the crimes are different: Cod. theod. 16.8.7 targets the (free, male) Christian-become-Jew, whose crime merits vindication of property, while 16.8.1.2 penalizes a different crime, that of assaulting Jews become Christians.

Codex Theodosianus 16.8.1.2 contains no explicit statement that the charges must be proven; 16.8.7 is explicit, by contrast, that the apostate Christian's property may be vindicated to the state only after the accusation of such actions has been proven. Moreover, this law applies only to Christians who have become Jews and cannot be read as a generic blanket prohibition on non-Jews becoming Jews.

---

23. Above, n. 13.

24. Above, n. 4.

25. This is apparent in his parenthetical identification of the two: "A reference to the punishments on proselytism (circumcision) evolved during the second and third centuries" (Linder, *JRIL*, p. 131 n. 18).

Further, although Cod. theod. 16.8.7 is universally presumed to reflect a prohibition on Christians becoming Jews,[26] why, here too, does it not just say this? Why not have a law that simply read "quis ex Christiano Judeus effectus ... facultates eius dominio fisci iussimus vindicari," with or without provisions for proving the accusation? What is the value added by the phrase "sacrilegis coetibus adgregetur"? Further, if the behavior criminalized is the same as that of Cod. theod. 16.8.1.2, namely, "conversion to Judaism," why is the language different? In a literary composition we might just argue that the use of different language may be attributed to a desire for rhetorical flourishes and posturing. But if Cod. theod. 16.8.7 criminalizes the same behavior as 16.8.1.2, why not repeat the earlier legislation more closely? To argue that this rephrasing *is* that repetition begs the question.

Rereading Cod. theod. 16.8.1

In my view, these and other questions can be answered, and the features of Cod. theod. 16.8.1 be better explained if the law was not two separate (if thematically connected) prohibitions but a single cohesive law. Its first sentence pertains to Jews who engaged in violent acts against Jews who had become Christians, and were liable to be burned to death, while the second sentence pertained to others who joined them in this violence. I will endeavor to demonstrate this through a clause by clause analysis of Cod. theod. 16.8.1.2.

> Si quis vero ex populo ad eorum nefarium sectam accesserit et conciliabulis eorum se adplicaverit, cum ipsis poenas meritas sustinebit

The phrase "ex populo" does considerable heavy lifting in the arguments that this law bans conversion, mostly focusing on the referent of *populus*. In a long note, Linder acknowledges that *populus* could sometimes just designate "Christians," a shorthand for *populus dei,* the people of God. Nevertheless, he concludes that here it is more likely to designate "the population of either the universal Empire or of particular cities and regions."[27] But his entire discussion here is predicated on his perception that Cod. theod. 16.8.1.2 prohibits conversion to Judaism, and his primary concern is the extent of the prohibition.

Little consideration is devoted by Linder and others to the preposition *ex,* on the apparent assumption that it simply designates membership in a class. This is unquestionably sometimes the case. Cod. theod. 16.5.8, a

26. See, e.g., Rabello's list, "Attitude of Rome towards Conversions," 56.
27. Linder, *JRIL*, p. 131 n. 15.

law of Theodosius I in 381, confiscates the churches of several dissident Christian groups, including those who are "ex dogmate Aeti," "who hold to the positions of Ethius."[28] In other cases, however, including several contemporaneous instances, the use of "ex" signals former membership in a class. The clearest instance is perhaps Cod. theod. 16.2.20—Gratian, at Rome in 380, referring to "ecclesiastici aut ex ecclesiasticis," "ecclesiastics or former ecclesiastics." Cod. theod. 16.5.7.2, another law by Theodosius I at Constantinople within two months of 16.5.8, designates the children of Manicheans who have become Nicenes as "qui licet ex manichaeis."[29] Still other instances are ambiguous or perhaps bear multiple meanings. The law of Theodosius I, also in 381, depriving Christians who became "pagani" of their testamentary rights, targets "qui ex christianis pagani facti sunt" (Cod. theod. 16.7.1), language comparable, as noted earlier, to that of 16.8.7 ("quis ex Christiano Iudeus factus"). Does it mean to convey that these persons used to be Christians but are now "pagani," or does it mean to specify that it targets Christians who have taken up "pagan" practices but not others who have done so, for instance Jews or Samaritans?[30] Or does it, perhaps, mean both? For most scholars who take this law to prohibit conversion, the subtle implications of the preposition are immaterial. The exception, as we shall see, is Rabello.

The interpretation of "quis ... ex populo" in Cod. theod. 16.8.1.2 depends to some degree on how one reads the two verbal clauses that immediately follow: "ad eorum nefarium sectam accesserit et conciliabulis eorum se adplicaverit." If these clauses describe conversion in some sense, the phrase "quis ... ex populo" designates non-Jews who "convert to Judaism," and *populus* most likely has the broader connotation Linder ascribes to it: anyone other than a Jew, since, at least hypothetically, anyone who was not born a Jew might choose to become one.[31] But if the legislator meant to specify persons who had "become" Jews in some sense (that is, those "formerly of the people"), why would the law not state this unequivocally, for example, "Si quis ex populo Iudeus

---

28. The other persons targeted here are, however, described with the simple construction "nullus Eunomianorum atque Arrianorum," "no one of the Eunomians and the Arians," and it seems difficult to see a meaningful distinction in these two phrasings. Cod. theod. 16.5.69, a law of Theodosius II against the Nestorians in 435, uses "nullus ex" and "nulli ex" to designate membership in a particular group of persons.

29. Cod. theod. 16.5.7 and 16.7.1 were issued days apart (8 May 381 and 2 May 381): Cod. theod. 16.5.8 was issued that July. Honoré attributes all the laws between 10 January 381 and 30 December 382 to the same *quaestor*: he cannot provide an identification for this person but thinks he may have been a lawyer and was definitely a Christian (Honoré, *Law in the Crisis*, 40). As he shows, many *quaestors* can be identified by distinct linguistic practices.

30. It seems possible that the use of *Christiani* here might actually designate "orthodox" Christians but not Arians, etc.

31. Linder, *JRIL*, p. 131 n. 15

effectus [or factus est]," in line with Cod. theod. 16.8.7,[32] as does Cod. theod. 16.8.7 in 353?

In my view, "Si quis ... ex populo" is the complement to the earlier "si quis" in Cod. theod. 16.8.1.1, which must, by virtue of the opening address of the law as well as its content, implicate Jews. The first sentence of the law, then, pertains to any Jew who dares to attack other Jews who have taken up Christian worship of God, while the second sentence penalizes "quis ... ex populo" who participate in such attacks, as Rougé appears to have read the law. The use of the preposition *ex* here simply designates membership in a class. *Populus* itself would then almost certainly mean persons who were neither Christians nor Jews, since it seems virtually inconceivable that the legislator would imagine Christians to have joined in attacks on Jews who had now joined their own ranks. But it may not simply be a synonym here for *pagani,* since it might also have included Samaritans.

> si quis vero ex populo ad eorum nefarium sectam accesserit et conciliabulis eorum se adplicaverit cum ipsis poenas meritas sustinebit

These two clauses bear by far the most weight in perceptions that Cod. theod. 16.8.1.2 bans conversion to Judaism. Yet this is not nearly as obvious as it seems to some scholars. As we saw in the discussion of "quis ... ex populo," those who drafted legislation in these years were clearly capable of unambiguously denoting a person who had become a Jew (or a Christian). If these clauses are intended to criminalize persons for becoming Jews, its writers have chosen to use extremely roundabout language to do so. To imagine that these clauses are circumlocutious for reasons we cannot determine is, of course, not impossible, but it is somewhat of a circular argument. Importantly, to see Cod. theod. 16.8.1.2 as a ban on non-Jews becoming Jews forces scholars not only to read both clauses as indirect accounts of such behavior and to explain the choice of such circumlocutious language but also to explain why there are two such clauses and not merely one.

Linder offers no explanation for this indirect language. Instead, he presumes that such derogatory language was natural for laws written by or for Christian legislators.[33] His discussion focuses on the denigration of

---

32. I am uncertain whether "effectus" and "factus [est]" are here synonyms, or whether they carry slightly different resonances. Pharr avoids the issue by translating "quis ex Christiano Iudeus" in Cod. theod. 16.8.7 as "should be converted from Christianity to Judaism" (Pharr, *Theodosian Code,* 468). Linder takes it as more or less a synonym for "factus est": "shall become Jew from Christian" (*JRIL* p. 153).

33. For a compelling analysis of the strategic use of this language, see, however, M. V. Escribano Pano, "The Social Exclusion of Heretics in *Codex Theodosianus* XVI," in *Droit, religion et société dans le Code Théodosien: Troisièmes journées d'étude sur le Code Théodosien, Neu-*

Jews with terms such as "nefaria secta," or even "conciliabula," which he sees as a deliberate derogatory alternative for "concilia," although he acknowledges that "'[c]onciliabulum' was not an uncommon synonym to 'ecclesia,'" in the early fourth century.[34] The failure of this particular law to designate assemblies of Jews as "synagogues" goes unremarked,[35] apparently on the assumption that the drafters of these laws chose vituperative language whenever possible, even if such imprecise language might undercut the efficacy of these laws as the basis for legal prosecution.[36]

Linder seems to solve the problem of the double clauses by projecting a two-stage model of "conversion" (which he sees made explicit in the language of Cod. theod. 16.8.7), in which the putative convert first somehow "becomes" a Jew and then is accepted in the Jewish assembly (described not, however, as a synagogue but in more derogatory terms). Nemo-Pekelman solves the problem by reading into this language a subtle allusion to two different social processes for adopting Jewish practices and ideas. "[A]d eorum nefarium sectam accesserit" denotes "full proselytism," while "conciliabulis eorum se adplicaverit" denotes a looser association of non-Jews with Jewish practices, "partial proselytism."[37]

This is not, of course, how she translates the passage, which she renders fairly literally: "entre dans leurs secte nefaste et se mêle à leurs conciliabules" ("enter into their nefarious sect and join oneself to their 'conciliabula'").[38] But she thinks this *really* means "anyone of the people [who] formally enters into the Jewish sect, or hangs out informally in their gatherings," will be liable as described. She does not appear to see that this creates a significant problem that her translation masks. In her view, this law actually describes two separate and mutually exclusive acts, since one cannot be both a semi-proselyte and a full proselyte at the same time. Yet the syntax of the text says something different: it says that the trans-

châtel, 15–17 février 2007, ed. Jean-Jacques Aubert and Philippe Blanchard, Recueil de travaux publiés par la Faculté des lettres et sciences humaines 55 (Geneva: Université de Neuchâtel, 2009), 39–66.

34. Linder, *JRIL*, p. 131 n. 17. But all other uses of *conciliabula* in the Theodosian Code are to assemblies of dissident Christians, not Jews, in laws dating between 379 and 389: 16.5.5; 16.1.2; and 16.5.19.

35. Leonard V. Rutgers has argued that Christians eventually imputed sufficiently negative connotations to the term *synagogue* that Jews began to designate their gathering places by other terms (*Making Myths: Jews in Early Christian Identity Formation* (Leuven: Peeters, 2009), 79–115, esp. 110.

36. Nemo-Pekelman's discussion of Cod. theod. 16.8.7 as a clarification of "*poenas meritas*" in 16.8.1.2 nods to this general problem, but she does not seem to see that it applies to use of circumlocutious language elsewhere.

37. My use of this language, as well as the language of "conversion" to reproduce the ideas of others should not be mistaken for assent to the accuracy of these categories; see Kraemer, "Giving Up the Godfearers."

38. Nemo-Pekelman, *Rome et ses citoyens juifs*, 125.

gressor engages in two distinct illicit actions: "ad eorum nefarium sectam accesserit" and "conciliabulis eorum se adplicaverit." A third alternative, of course, would be take these clauses as two different ways of describing the same transgression, although this does not solve the problem of the circumlocutious language.[39]

There is, of course, a simpler explanation: these clauses do not describe non-Jews taking up Jewish religious practices. Rougé's translation, and its implicit interpretation of these clauses, has none of these drawbacks. It does not require us to impose a very different set of meanings onto language for which a more straightforward interpretation is available. It does not require us to explain why this law means one thing (no one may become a Jew, or, in Nemo-Pekelman's reading, no one may become either a full proselyte or a partial proselyte) but chooses deeply indirect language in which to say something that could have been said quite directly.

Instead, it takes these clauses more seriously at face value to penalize any "one of the people [who] joins up with [*accesserit*] their impious sect and participates in their seditious bands [*conciliabulis*]." It takes seriously both the syntax and structure of the sentence to denote two different but related offenses: joining up (or perhaps associating) with the (vilified) Jews and participating with them in the acts previously depicted in the law. Although I continue to have some reservations about Rougé's translation of "conciliabula" as "seditious bands," I take it to intend a derogatory term for a group (or groups) of Jews engaged in the kinds of antisocial, anti-imperial behavior for which Jews are punished by "crematio" in the first portion of the law.

> si quis vero ex populo ad eorum nefarium sectam accesserit et conciliabulis eorum se adplicaverit cum ipsis poenas meritas sustinebit

The linch-pin of my reading comes in two words of the final phrase: "cum ipsis poenas meritas sustinebit." Interestingly, neither Linder nor Nemo-Pekelman comments on this language, whose translation, at least—"with them"—is relatively straightforward. Presumably these are "the Jews," but if Cod. theod. 16.8.1.2 prohibits conversion, why is this the case? "[C]um ipsis" cannot intend to subject converts to the punishments for which Jews are liable simply by virtue of being Jews, since it was not a crime to be born a Jew, nor to remain one. Hypothetically, "they" might be those (Jews) who instigate or facilitate these conversions, but such a suggestion presumes that the law pertains to conversion and then seeks an interpretation of "cum ipsis" that fits into the paradigm. Here, too,

39. If Nemo-Pekelman is correct that the language of this law was drafted by Christian lobbyists, and one thinks it is about conversion, one might speculate that the use of parallel clauses emulates the parallelism of some Biblical Hebrew poetry.

in other laws, such actors are more explicitly described, so the question remains why this law does not do so.[40]

For Rabello, however, "cum ipsis" triggers his tentative suggestion, considered further below, that the law here "does not concern the crime of apostasy as such, but only levels the threatened punishment against those who, although they are not Jews by birth ... join the Jews in attacking the converts."[41] For Rabello, however, if the law is then not a prohibition of conversion, it is nevertheless still about converts. The words I have excluded in the ellipsis read "but only proselytes or sympathizers to Judaism," signaled by his reading of the phrase "ex populo" as "formerly of the people."

In my view, "cum ipsis" provides perhaps the best clue to the true intent of the law. Those "of the *populus*" who join with Jews in attacks on other Jews who have become Christians will suffer punishment "with them." Here, too, all the problems with forcing "cum ipsis" into a paradigm of conversion dissipate. This interpretation is strengthened by the last phrase in Cod. theod. 16.8.1.1, which mandates that any Jew found to have attacked former coreligionists will be burned "cum omnibus suis participibus"—with all those who participated with them (in these acts). It is thus the immediate lead-in to Cod. theod. 16.8.1.2, a juncture ignored by scholars who see 16.8.1.2 as essentially a separate prohibition whose only connection to 16.8.1.1 is a common concern with conversions. But if 16.8.1 is a complete unit, all of which pertains to attacks on Jews who have become Christians, 16.8.1.2 now makes explicit just who those "omnes" are. The law penalizes not Jews who have participated but any others who might do so, Jews or non-Jews.

> si quis vero ex populo ad eorum nefarium sectam accesserit et conciliabulis eorum se adplicaverit cum ipsis poenas meritas sustinebit

Nemo-Pekelman and Linder only indirectly consider the failure of Cod. theod. 16.8.1.2 to specify the punishment for the presumptive conversion, with divergent implicit explanations. Equating "proselytism" with circumcision, Linder observes that there was already a body of law concerning the punishments for these activities that apparently accounts

40. Cod. theod. 16.8.22 (Theodosius II in 415), the edict demoting the Jewish Patriarch Gamaliel, contains a provision making it illegal for the Patriarch "or one of the Jews" to do something that might be construed as circumcising not just enslaved males but free ones as well, but the phrase "one of the Jews" may be a later addition, extending the chastisement of Gamaliel to Jews more generally. A law of Honorius in 409 apparently penalizes those who compel others to abandon Christianity and become Jews, as well as those Christians who become Jews, but there are complex issues with the interpretation of this law beyond the scope of this contribution: Cod. theod. 16.8.19, *JRIL*, no. 39, discussed in Kraemer, *Jews*.

41. Rabello, "Attitude of Rome towards Conversions," 61.

for why they are not spelled out. That is, he appears to assume that the violators of Cod. theod. 16.8.1.2 have been circumcised, and thus "the merited penalties" are those articulated in the *Sentences* of Paul, noted earlier.[42] There, (male) Roman citizens who allowed themselves or their (male) slaves to be circumcised were to be permanently exiled to an island, and their property confiscated. Significantly, circumcised slaves were not penalized, presumably on the assumption that they lacked legal capacity to consent and therefore could not be held liable. (In the law of 335, circumcised slaves were given their liberty.) Neither the *Sentences* of Paul nor Cod. theod. 16.8.1.2 addresses the culpability and penalties for Jews who might have encouraged or facilitated these circumcisions, although the former prescribes the execution of doctors (*medici*), who presumably performed the circumcision.[43]

Nemo-Pekelman similarly does not consider this question directly. But whereas Linder thinks that the law invokes "merited punishments" that are already sufficiently known, she seems to think that this was not the case, and that the law of 353 was a response to a request for guidance on the proper penalties, as previously noted. Rabello explicitly cites Cod. theod. 16.8.1.2 to support his claim that "Roman-Christian legislation did not immediately fix a punishment for the proselyte; it left this entirely to the discretion of the judge,"[44] seeming to side with Nemo-Pekelman's view that the law gave judges latitude. This is, however, antithetical to his alternative hypothesis that the law makes converts to Judaism who assaulted converts to Christianity liable to the punishments "cum ipsis," that is, with the Jewish perpetrators in Cod. theod. 16.8.1.1, namely, death by burning.

A very close reader of the text will notice that Cod. theod. 16.8.1.2 speaks of plural punishments (*poenas*), while 16.8.1.1 specifies only a single penalty: death by burning. If these are in fact the same, we might have expected to see the use of the singular. But the same very close reader will also notice that the punishment in the first sentence does actually have two parts: the perpetrator will be consigned to the flames ("flammis dedendus est") and burned ("et ... concremandus"). Whether this sufficiently accounts for the use of "poenas" is beyond our ability to ascertain, for the many reasons noted at the outset of this contribution. But overall, here again, the simpler reading resolves the seeming incongruities and oddities produced when the law is taken to prohibit conversion. Because these other persons have committed the same crime as the Jews who

42. Above, n. 13.

43. Linder notes that this was already the punishment for physicians who performed castrations (*JRIL*, p. 119 n. 6, citing Hadrian's rescript in the *Digest* 48.8.4.2).

44. Rabello, "Attitude of Rome towards Conversions," 59. The failure to specify the penalty would be unusual for laws that criminalized circumcision, as well as many other acts prohibited to Jews.

have attacked new Christians, they, too, will "suffer the deserved punishment(s)" already specified in the law, namely, death by burning.

Rabello's Proposition

As I have already indicated at several points, my thesis that Cod. theod. 16.8.1 is a unified law concerned entirely with penalizing violence against Jews who had become Christians, both by their former coreligionists and others, is similar in some respects to the hypothesis that Rabello briefly floats, but it differs in others. Rabello, too, recognized that "cum ipsis" could well signal that Cod. theod. 16.8.1.2 extends to others the prohibition against attacks on Jews who had become Christians. In Rougé's translation, and in my reading, these others are anyone else who might participate, for whatever reasons, and the two verbal clauses describe that participation in association with Jews. Rabello, however, envisions that these other persons were not Jews by birth—to whom the first part of the law speaks—but persons who had taken up Jewish practices and religious beliefs by choice. This is how he construes the two verbal clauses, envisioning, as does Nemo-Pekelman, that this could entail either "full" or "partial" proselytes. Unlike her, however, Rabello does not argue that this distinction is discernible in the differing language of the two verbal clauses. Rather, for him, it is signaled in the description of these persons as "ex populo," construed to mean "formerly but no longer 'of the people.'" Interestingly, were he to be correct that Cod. theod. 16.8.1.2 extends the penalties of 16.8.1.1 to converts, it implies that such persons would not have been considered Jews under Roman law. If they were, they would already have been liable under the language of Cod. theod. 16.8.1.1, and 16.8.1.2 would either be superfluous, or applicable only to those "partial proselytes."[45] In the end, this interpretation remains, for Rabello, at best an intriguing suggestion, which he may not have fully pursued because it is, as I have already noted, difficult to reconcile with his other reading of the law.

In my view, "non-Jews become Jews" might have been among the persons who participated with the Jews in these attacks, but they need not have been. These persons might equally have been sympathizers of a

45. Questions about the legal status of persons who "became Jews" are beyond the scope of this contribution. Nevertheless, it is interesting to consider whether becoming a Jew was merely illegal (to whatever extent it seems to have been so). Scholars who take this law to prohibit conversion often frame the issue as one of religious choice (e.g., Nemo-Pekelman, who worries that this law contradicted Constantine's so-called "edict of toleration"). But one might wonder whether a non-Jew becoming a Jew entailed a category error. Did Roman (Roman/Christian) law recognize as Jews persons who were not born to Jewish parents? Could such persons claim the various *privilegia* ("exemptions") and protections that Roman laws, including late antique Roman laws by Christian emperors, granted to Jews?

different sort, who saw Christians as a threat for any number of reasons: hostile practitioners of traditional Roman religion; dissident Christians who opposed Jews joining themselves to the "wrong" sorts of Christians and were happy to make common cause; Samaritans, who had their own quarrels with both Jews and Christians, and even perhaps just certain young men willing to engage in violence for any reason or no reason at all.

The Possible Implications of Cod. theod. 16.8.6

My hypothesis that neither Cod. theod. 16.8.1.2 nor 16.8.7 points to a wholesale prohibition of non-Jews becoming Jews may be further bolstered by Cod. theod. 16.8.6, a rather enigmatic ruling issued in 339 by Constantine II.[46] Women who had previously worked in an imperial weaving workshop in some unidentified location had left that establishment under circumstances that are unspecified and had apparently been associating in some fashion with Jews. (These workshops produced textiles and uniforms for the imperial administration and the military, and the women and men who worked in them were effectively slaves, bound to the workshop for life.)[47] The edict ordered the women returned to the establishment. The law is explicit that in the future, Jews who "join" (*iungo*) Christian women to their "shameful acts" (*flagitium*) will be subject to capital punishment.

Scholars have generally read this law to prohibit either inducing Christian women to become Jews (or facilitating such change in some way), or else marriage between Jewish men and Christian women. These divergent readings are fueled by the law's somewhat opaque language, especially the opening clause: "As pertains to the women whom the Jews led to 'consortium' in their 'turpitudinis'"(or perhaps, "the women whom the Jews, in their 'turpitudinis,' led to 'consortium'").[48] Similarly unclear is the use of *flagitium,* to which the Jews must not "join" Christian women, and perhaps the verb *iungo* ("join") itself.

If this law responds to a specific incident in which Jewish men induced some imperial women weavers, perhaps Christians, to become Jews (and leave the workshop),[49] and if the law of 329 was really a wholesale prohibition of non-Jews becoming Jews, we might expect Cod. theod. 16.8.6 to punish the weavers for adopting Jewish practices. Yet nothing in the law

46. Cod. theod. 16.8.6 (*JRIL,* no. 11). It was issued on the same day as Cod. theod. 16.9.2, which forbade Jews to purchase non-Jewish slaves or to circumcise such slaves.

47. Nemo-Pekelman, *Rome et ses citoyens juifs,* 148; Rougé and Delmaire, *Les lois religieuses,* 1:377 n. 3; Linder, *JRIL,* p. 149 n. 8.

48. So Nemo-Pekelman *Rome et ses citoyens juifs,* 148: other translators generally follow the first translation.

49. For more detailed consideration of this episode, see Kraemer, *Jews,* forthcoming.

suggests that this occurred. The weavers are returned to their forced labor in the workshop, with no other punishment decreed.[50]

The lack of any punishment for the men involved in this incident is also quite curious, given that the law prescribes capital punishment for whatever it is that Jewish men might do in the future with Christian women. Perhaps the disposition of the case against the men was handled elsewhere, in a rescript or edict we do not have. But in the absence of such evidence, it seems that either the law aims to criminalize something that was previously not explicitly unlawful, or the men had not done what the law prohibits going forward.[51] If the men were instrumental in the weavers becoming Jews, this would suggest that not only was it not yet illegal for the women to do so, but it was not yet illegal for the men to induce them to do so. Henceforth, of course, things will apparently be different, but even then, this law does not constitute a blanket prohibition of non-Jews becoming Jews: it is, at most, a prohibition on Jewish men inducing Christian women to become Jews, punishable by death.[52]

Conclusion

Codex Theodosianus 16.8.1.2 is thus unlikely to be a blanket prohibition of non-Jews becoming Jews, tacked on somewhat awkwardly to 16.8.1.1, which sentenced to death by burning those Jews who attacked their former coreligionists who had become Christians. Instead, it is best understood as the second part of the same law, extending that penalty to others, probably only non-Christians, who joined with the Jews in such egregious and offensive behavior. Even subsequent laws in the fourth century seem at most to be narrower prohibitions against Christians, especially free males, becoming Jews.

---

50. Consistent with Nemo-Pekelman's observation (*Rome et ses citoyens juifs*, 149–50) that (later) laws pertaining to fugitives from such establishments penalize those who harbored them, and not the weavers, this might imply that their only offense was ceasing to labor at the workshop, and that they were not, in fact, found guilty of having "become Jews."

51. Subsequent laws pertaining to wayward weavers suggest a very different scenario, in which the men had been ordered to return the weavers by a specified date and had done so, thus avoiding legal liability for their past actions: see Kraemer, *Jews*, forthcoming.

52. Alternatively, if this law pertains to conversion, the treatment of the weavers does not accord with the punishments prescribed in both Cod. theod. 16.8.7 (vindication of property) and 16.8.1.2 ("crematio")—assuming for the moment that the latter law proscribed becoming Jewish—because laws pertaining to those who became Jews applied only to free men, and not to free women or to enslaved persons, male or female. But I cannot pursue this here.

Taming the Jewish Genie

John Chrysostom and the Jews of Antioch in the Shadow of Emperor Julian

ARI FINKELSTEIN
University of Cincinnati

In recent years Shaye Cohen has taken to challenging other scholars who read social reality out of John Chrysostom's homilies, *Against the Judaizers* (*Adversus Judaeos*). I can hear his voice rising in consternation as he challenges the reality behind Chrysostom's portrayal of porous borders between Christians and Jews. He is certainly correct to point out that there is no evidence of Jews keeping Christian practices. Even Chrysostom claims Jews do not celebrate Christian holy days (*Adv. Jud.* 4.3.9 [PG 48:876]). On the other hand, there are far too many sources claiming that some Christians practiced Jewish ancestral laws and gathered in the synagogue. In Antioch alone, we have John Chrysostom, the Apostolic Constitutions, Emperor Julian's *Against the Galileans*, and canon law from the Synod of Antioch in 341 CE.[1] In this contribution to my mentor's Festschrift, I examine how John Chrysostom is particularly troubled by the vitality of Jewish law and Jewish institutions among some Christian communities in late fourth-century Antioch, the very same issues that Emperor Julian had sought to strengthen over twenty years earlier when he wrote *Against the Galileans* and attempted to rebuild the Jerusalem temple. Not only does Chrysostom employ the Jerusalem temple's destruction to invalidate Jewish festivals, as Christine Shepardson explains,[2] but he also responds to Jewish and Judaizing claims that the temple, sacrifice, and priests will

1. Not to mention third- and early fourth-century Christian works like the Didascalia Apostolorum and the Pseudo-Clementine literature, all written elsewhere in Syria but circulating in Antioch in the late fourth century.

2. Christine Shepardson, "Paschal Politics: Deploying the Temple's Destruction against Fourth-Century Judaizers," *VC* 62 (2008): 233–60. Ephrem also uses the temple's destruction to attack Christianity and predates Chrysostom's *Judaizers*. However, Ephrem wrote in Syriac, which Chrysostom could not read. For Chrysostom's descriptions of Jews, see Christine Shepardson, "Between Polemic and Propaganda: Evoking the Jews of Fourth Century Antioch," *JJMJS* 2 (2015): 147–82.

soon return. At issue for both men was the power of the image of the Jew among Christians (and Hellenes) in Antioch and its role in the making of orthodoxy.[3] While Julian sought to bring Christians back to the observance of their Jewish ancestral laws by playing up their efficaciousness, Chrysostom attacked Jews by declaring Jewish law invalid in the absence of the temple. He did so because he believed Jews posed a significant challenge to his attempt to define Christian orthodoxy. In effect, Chrysostom sought to tame the Jewish genie that Julian had unleashed years earlier.[4]

There is a direct link between Julian and John Chrysostom. The future church leader grew up in Antioch, reaching adolescence during Julian's stay there in the fall of 362 into the winter of 363. He would have witnessed the impact of that emperor's mischievous rhetorical use of Jews on the dynamics of Jews, Christians, and Hellenes in Antioch. This seems to have affected Chrysostom. He mentions Julian's attempt to rebuild the temple no fewer than eight times in his works.[5] Both he and Julian were alive to the fluid nature of Christian identities in the city. When Julian arrived in the summer of 362 Christians were split among three factions.[6] The situation in Chrysostom's Antioch of the mid to late 380s was again in flux. Under Theodosius I, imperial support for *homoousian* Christianity enabled Chrysostom to reshape the city of Antioch along orthodox *homoousian* lines.[7] Just as Julian sought to hellenize Antioch using Jews,

---

3. On Hellenes, see my forthcoming book *The Specter of the Jews: Emperor Julian and the Rhetoric of Ethnicity in Syrian Antioch* (Berkeley: University of California Press, 2018). The term Hellenes functions for Julian as a super-*ethnos*, with land, gods, language, culture (*paideia*) and cult. They are an "imagined community" which he constructs.

4. Christine Shepardson claims that Julian's attempt to rebuild the temple inflamed anti-Jewish rhetoric. See her "Controlling Contested Places: John Chrysostom's Adversus Iudaeos Homilies and the Spatial Politics of Religious Controversy," *JECS* 15 (2007): 483–516, here 492.

5. Chrysostom, *De Babyla contra Julianum et gentiles* 119. See John Chrysostom, *Discours sur Babylas*, ed. and trans. Margaret A. Schatkin, SC 362 (Paris: Cerf, 1990), 258–61; John Chrysostom, *Apologist*, trans. Margaret A. Schatkin and Paul W. Harkins, FC 73 (Washington, DC: Catholic University of America Press, 1985), 146–47; John Chrysostom, *Against the Judaizers* 5.11 (PG 48:900–901, 905); John Chrysostom, *Discourses against Judaizing Christians*, trans. Paul W. Harkins, FC 68 (Washington, DC: Catholic University of America Press, 1979), 136–40, 6.2 (PG 48:905); *Against Jews and Gentiles* 16 (PG 48.835); *Homilies on Matthew* 4.1 on Matt 1:17 (PG 57:39); *Commentary on the Psalms* 110.4 (PG 55:285); *In Praise of St. Paul* 4.6 (PG 50:489); *Homilies on the Acts of the Apostles* 41.3 (PG 60:291). See Robert L. Wilken, *John Chrysostom and the Jews, Rhetoric and Reality in the Late 4th Century*, Transformation of the Classical Heritage 4 (Berkeley: University of California Press, 1983), 130.

6. Robin Ward, "The Schism at Antioch in the Fourth Century" (PhD diss., King's College, London, 2003).

7. Fourth-century Christians were split in a number of ways. One major disagreement was whether Jesus, the son of God the Father, was separate from the Father in substance or whether they shared the same substance. The former group was called *homoians* and the latter were *homoousians*. Various fourth-century emperors supported one group or the other. Ultimately, *homoousians* won the day under Theodosius I in the 380s.

Chrysostom was confronted with the embeddedness of Jews in local Antiochene culture. Chrysostom attempted to disarm Jewish idioms in the city's landscape, diabolizing Jews with vicious rhetoric and instilling what Shepardson calls *topophobia*, in an effort to alter how Christians perceived Jews.[8]

Julian

Emperor Julian's stay in Antioch from the late summer of 362 through 5 March 363 was an unhappy one. He had high hopes that the city would welcome his hellenizing program particularly because of its rich Hellenic history and the presence of the temple of Apollo in the nearby neighborhood of Daphne, an important place for Neoplatonist philosophers because of its ancient oracle.[9] Very quickly Julian discovered that Christians, their practices and growing spatial claims in the city and its territory, threatened Hellenic ritual. Meanwhile, Hellenes did not take to the emperor's attempt to encourage them to attend temples and sacrifice (Julian, *Misop.* 362AB). With the onset of winter, Julian rededicated himself to his hellenizing campaign, writing several works that established the correct mixture of ethnic gods who had always secured Rome's well-being, and correct worship that would guarantee the gods' beneficence.[10] As he gathered himself to write *Against the Galileans*, Julian obtained copies of the work of Celsus, which he accessed via Origen's *Against Celsus*,[11] many of the works of the third-century philosopher Porphyry of Tyre, including *Philosophy from Oracles*, *On Abstinence*, and likely *Against the Christians*,[12] and also Eusebius of Caesarea's *Preparation of the Gospels* and

8. Christine Shepardson, *Controlling Contested Places: Late Antique Antioch and the Spatial Politics of Religious Controversy* (Berkeley: University of California Press, 2014), chapter 4; Dayna S. Kalleres, *City of Demons: Violence, Ritual, and Christian Power in Late Antiquity* (Berkeley: University of California Press, 2015).

9. Julian, *Misop.* 367C. See Julian, *Œuvres complètes*, vol. 1, part 2, *Lettres et fragments*, ed. and trans. Josef Bidez (Paris: "Les Belles Lettres," 1932; repr., 1972).

10. Susanna Elm, *Sons of Hellenism, Fathers of the Church: Emperor Julian, Gregory of Nazianzus, and the Vision of Rome*, Transformation of the Classical Heritage (Berkeley: University of California Press, 2012), 2.

11. Marie-Odile L. Boulnois, "Le *Contre les Galiléens* de L'empereur Julien: Répond-il a *Contre Celse* d'Origène?," in *EN KALOIS KOINOPRAGIA: Hommage à la mémoire de Pierre-Louis Malosse et Jean Bouffartigue*, ed. Eugenio Amato, Revue des études tardo-antiques, Supplément 3 (Nantes: Association Textes pour l'histoire de l'Antiquité tardive, 2014), 103–28.

12. In recent years scholars have raised questions about the content of this work. See articles in Irmgard Männlein-Robert, ed., *Die Christen als Bedrohung? Text, Kontext und Wirkung von Porphyrios' Contra Christianos*, Roma aeterna 5 (Stuttgart: Franz Steiner, 2017); Sébastien Morlet, ed., *Le traité de Porphyre contre les chrétiens: Un siècle de recherches, nouvelles questions; Actes du colloque international organisé les 8 et 9 septembre 2009 à l'Université de Paris IV-Sorbonne* (Paris: Institut d'Études Augustiniennes, 2011); Porphyry, *Contra Christianos:*

Demonstration of the Gospels book 1.[13] From these writings Julian learned how to think ethnographically to order and hierarchize his empire.[14] Jews could be positioned to attack Christians but also, using Porphyry's tactic of reading particularistic barbarian wisdom from certain wise nations like the Hebrews, could be ethnic exempla employed to shape Hellenic identity and sometimes even sources for Hellenic wisdom lost since Plato's death.[15] This argument depended on how Jews were placed relative to Hebrews. Hebrews were highly valued in these works. Neoplatonist philosophers and Christians alike believed that Hebrews were an ancient wise people. To Porphyry, the third-century Neoplatonist philosopher, Hebrew and Babylonian wisdom were the most reliable sources of Hellenic wisdom. Porphyry's student and Julian's guru, Iamblichus of Chalcis, also appears to have held Hebrew wisdom highly, although he favored the wisdom of the Chaldeans (Babylonians) above all others. Christians put Hebrews to a different use. Writing in the early fourth century, Eusebius of Caesarea claimed that Hebrews were the wisest of nations (*Praep. ev.; Dem. ev.* 1). Using ethnic reasoning, he argued that Jews ceased being the successors of the Hebrews once their temple was destroyed, as they could no longer practice their ancestral laws. For all intents and purposes, the Jewish *ethnos* became a defunct entity. Meanwhile, Christians, he argued, became their successors—the "true Israel." As Andrew Jacobs argues, Eusebius's argument served to historicize the Jews, rendering them inert tools with which he could develop Christian orthodoxy.[16] *Against the Galileans* was the first of a number of works Julian wrote in a span of three months to mention Jews. While in the first part of the work he attacks Hebrews as inferior to Hellenes, in the final part he attacks Christians for failing to follow Jewish ancestral laws. Julian uses ethnographic rhetoric to describe Jews.

Attempting to weaken Christian ethnic identity Julian set out to prove that Jews were indeed the Hebrews. He demonstrates that their practices more closely follow Hebraic law than do the Christians and thereby proves

---

Neue Sammlung der Fragmente, Testimonien und Dubia, ed. and trans. Matthias Becker, Texte und Kommentar 52 (Berlin: de Gruyter, 2016); Ariane Magny, *Porphyry in Fragments: Reception of an Anti-Christian Text in Late Antiquity*, Ashgate Studies in Philosophy and Theology in Late Antiquity (Burlington, VT: Ashgate, 2014).

13. Jean Bouffartigue, *L'empereur Julien et la culture de son temps*, Collection des *études* augustiniennes, Série Antiquité 133 (Paris: Institut d'Études Augustiniennes, 1992).

14. Todd S. Berzon, *Classifying Christians: Ethnography, Heresiology, and the Limits of Knowledge in Late Antiquity* (Berkeley: University of California Press, 2016), 36.

15. Jeremy M. Schott, *Christianity, Empire, and Religion in Late* Antiquity, Divinations (Philadelphia: University of Pennsylvania Press, 2008), 57–59. On ethnic exempla see Aaron P. Johnson, *Religion and Identity in Porphyry of Tyre: The Limits of Hellenism in Late Antiquity* (Cambridge: Cambridge University Press, 2013), 202.

16. Andrew S. Jacobs, *The Remains of the Jews: The Holy Land and Christian Empire in Late Antiquity*, Divinations (Stanford, CA: Stanford University Press, 2004), 27–34.

Eusebius false. Now he positioned Jews to attack Christians. In Julian's hands, Jews are Judeans, an *ethnos* that possesses a land, a god, a temple, and ancestral laws. By placing Judeans on his ethnic map, Julian normalizes Jews within his Platonic empire in which each nation has an ethnarchic god assigned by the Demiurge. Christians are Galileans, a non-*ethnos*. The Galilee never had a single *ethnos* associated with it nor a central city or ancestral laws, and, therefore, Christians have no place on his map.[17] In the final part of *Galileans*, Julian highlights Jewish ancestral laws, which some Christians in the city still kept and which were problematic to maintaining orthodox Christianity. He shows that Jewish law, far from being defunct, remains efficacious. This is particularly the case for Jewish sacrifice, Jewish priesthood, dietary laws, Passover and other festivals, and circumcision. Many of these are issues Chrysostom also addressed. Julian's argument was planted on fertile soil. Eusebius's image of the Jews did not mesh well with the lived experiences of Christians in places like Antioch. The city was home to a large Jewish community whose members were perceived to be authentic purveyors of a hoary Christian past.

Julian on the Temple

Julian's plan to rebuild the Jerusalem temple stirred a Christian backlash. A renewed temple would underscore Jewish vitality. Not only could Jews worship their god there through sacrifice, but Jesus had prophesied its destruction and promised that it would never again be rebuilt (Matt 24:2). This is not to say that Julian's attempt to rebuild the temple was a wholly anti- Christian act. The logic of *Galileans* suggests that it was mainly the realization of the emperor's ethnological arguments. Jews would return to their city and temple as Judeans and worship their god in accordance with their ancestral laws. These laws contained mysterious divine wisdom such that worship of the Jewish god supported Julian's hellenizing program and its theurgic Neoplatonist salvific goals.[18] Meanwhile, Jews served as an example to Hellenes of proper ethnic behavior and thereby shaped Hellenic identity. They sacrificed in temples at a time when not all Hellenes revered temples as holy spaces (*Misop.* 344C). Even Hellenes who still sacrificed did not necessarily do so in temples.[19]

To the extent that the rebuilding program was anti-Christian, Julian

17. Julian goes out of his way to show that Christians have no need and no connection to Jerusalem.

18. Julian presents Jews as a mystery cult. These groups understood the true meaning of sacrifice and performed acts of theurgy. Elsewhere I argue that Jewish sacrifice contains theurgic markers (*Specter of the Jews*, chapter 1).

19. Julian, *Ep.* 98 (a letter to Libanius). Julian, Œuvres *completes*, ed. Bidez, vol. 1, part 2. In *Galil.* 306A, Julian characterizes the Jerusalem temple as *tou naou*, and "as the Jews call

saw it as an opportunity to right the Flavian dynasty's mischaracterization of the cosmic order.[20] When Constantine built the Church of the Holy Sepulcher, Eusebius wrote that the god of that place was Jesus, who was Plato's Divine Intellect (*On Christ's Sepulcher* 12.16). To link his dynasty with the Christian god, Constantine placed his palace on its grounds. Julian dissociated the Flavian dynasty from its connection to Jesus by returning Jerusalem to the Jews and by fixing its ethnic god to Jerusalem after ensconcing that god in the emperor's cosmic order.[21] The rebuilding of the temple and Julian's promise to pray with the Jews there symbolized the normalization of Jews qua Judeans as an *ethnos* within the empire.[22] In his *Life of Constantine* 3.33, Eusebius of Caesarea claimed that the Church of the Holy Sepulcher stood facing the ruins of the Temple Mount, a symbol of Christianity's replacement of the Jews as inheritors of the covenant with God. Had Julian been successful, there would have been no need to remove the Church of the Holy Sepulcher. The new structural reality would have caused a Christian exiting the compound of the church to fall under the shadow of a renewed temple with its sacrificial cult. This would have disrupted any narrative of truth to Jesus's claim that the temple would fall and never again be rebuilt and certainly would have upended Christian attempts to replace a "defunct" Jewish *ethnos*.

Chrysostom on the Temple

The absence of the temple is a claim repeated many times in *Against the Judaizers*.[23] Chrysostom uses its absence to attack the validity of Jewish rituals, especially their festivals and fasts. First, however, he must deal with Jewish (and Christian) counterclaims that Jerusalem will be returned to the Jews and the temple will be rebuilt.[24] It seems that in late fourth cen-

---

it the most holy place" (*tou hagiasmatos*), to stress that the temple in Jerusalem was the true center of the sacrificial cult. Jews model here proper sacrificial behavior.

20. Julian, *Or.* 7.234C *Against Heracleius*. Julian, *Œuvres complètes*, ed. Bidez, vol. 2, part 1, *Discours de Julien*.

21. See Finkelstein, *Specter of the Jews*, chapter 6.

22. Julian, *Letter to the Community of the Jews* (*The Works of the Emperor Julian*, ed. and trans. Wilmer Cave Wright, 3 vols., LCL 13, 29, 157 (Cambridge: Harvard University Press, 1923), vol. 3.

23. This list is in no way comprehensive: Chrysostom, *Adv. Jud.* 3.3.6 (PG 48.868), 4.4.3–4, 7 (PG 48.876), 4.5.2 (PG 48.878), 4.6.7–9 (PG 48.880), 4.7.6 (PG 48.881), 5.1.3 (PG 48.883), 5.1.7 (PG 48.884), 5.4.2 (PG 48.889), 5.11.4–5 (PG 48.900), 5.11.10 (PG 48.901), 6.4.3 (PG 48.908), 6.5.5 (PG 48.911).

24. Before late fourth century, Christian authors argued that the temple's destruction proved that God had rejected the Jews and the ritual of sacrifice. After Julian, the destruction of the temple fulfilled Jesus's prophecy of the temple's destruction. See Shepardson, "Paschal Politics", 239-258.

tury Antioch, the Jerusalem temple still had the power to excite Christian minds. Julian's failure to rebuild the temple seems to have encouraged Christian and Jewish beliefs that it would soon be rebuilt. Chrysostom takes his audience through the prophecies of Daniel and Jesus on the temple's destruction (*Adv. Jud.* 5.8.7–8 [PG 48.897–98]). This argument reaches its fever pitch when he recounts Julian's failed attempt to rebuild the temple. Julian's failure, he argues, is a miracle demonstrating the truth of Jesus's prophecy and the truth of Christianity and its triumph over Jews. Proof is not only in the temple's destruction in the past but can be witnessed by Christians today, says Chrysostom, if they go to Jerusalem and see the "bare foundation" left from Julian's attempt to rebuild it. In *Adv. Jud.* 5.11.10 (PG 48.901) Chrysostom writes:

> Even today, if you go into Jerusalem, you will see the bare foundation, if you ask why this is so, you will hear no explanation other than the one I gave. We are all witnesses to this, for it happened not long ago but in our own time. Consider how conspicuous our victory is. This did not happen in the times of the good emperors; no one can say that the Christians came and prevented the work from being finished. It happened at a time when our religion was subject to persecution, when all our lives were in danger, when every man was afraid to speak, when Hellenism flourished. (trans. Harkins, 140)

The import of Julian's failure to rebuild the Jerusalem temple might not be grasped by Chrysostom's flock, who were used to Christian supremacy in the age of Theodosius I. This is why he emphasizes the anti-Christian persecution of Julian so as to highlight the miracle.

Nevertheless, Jews whisper that Jerusalem will soon be theirs again (*Adv. Jud.*. 7.1.4 [PG 48.916]). Chrysostom is certain this will never happen. Or is he? At least one of his arguments indicates otherwise. In Chrysostom's recounting of Julian's temple rebuilding effort, he imagines that Julian successfully rebuilt the temple and the altar but that his effort failed owing to the lack of heavenly fire to light the altars (*Adv. Jud* 5.11.7 [PG 48.900]).[25] This claim is remarkably similar to an anti-temple argument implied in the letter sent to Egypt which is appended to the beginning of 2 Maccabees (1:19). There the author, arguing for the legitimacy of the Second Temple, asserts that the fire of the temple was found. Chrysostom's claim is oddly placed given that he will soon argue that Julian's failure to rebuild the temple proves Jesus and Christianity correct. Why, then, this sidebar attempt to discredit the temple? Most likely he intends to discredit any future temple that might be rebuilt. Led by Apollinaris of Laodicea, who lived and taught in Antioch and

---

25. On the other hand, *Adv. Jud.* 5.12.11 and 8.5.4 show a more confident Chrysostom.

preached an imminent millennialism during which the temple would be rebuilt, the topic of the rebuilding of the temple was very much a live issue for Christians in Antioch—and one might imagine for Jews as well.[26] Chrysostom's argument that a future temple lacked basic items like the *parokhet* (veil), the high priest, and the heavenly fire, a claim repeated elsewhere in *Judaizers*, is an attempt to inoculate Christianity from any such successful rebuilding effort.[27] One cannot help but think that the recent memory of Julian's attempt to rebuild the temple moves Chrysostom to protect Christianity should anything go wrong. The pathos in Chrysostom's retelling of Julian's rebuilding attempt may reflect his own past emotional ordeal, which would suggest that he feared another rebuilding attempt.

Julian on Jewish Sacrifice

Closely related to the topic of the temple is sacrifice. In *Galileans* frag. 72 = 305D–306A, Julian makes the astounding claim found nowhere else that Jews still sacrifice.

> [305D] Now I should remind you of the things I said earlier and for what purpose I said those things. For why, after you have abandoned us, will you not accept the Law of the Judeans nor remain faithful to the teachings by that man [Moses]? Surely some sharp-witted person will say, "But the Judeans also do not sacrifice." But I, for my part, will expose him, being terribly blind, for, first, you do not keep the customs of the Judeans. Second, they do sacrifice [*thyousin*] in private places [*en adraktois*].
>
> [306A] Even now all things the Judeans eat are consecrated [*hiera*]; they pray before sacrificing, and they give the right shoulder [*ton dexion ōmon*] to the priests as first fruits [*aparchas*]. Having been deprived of the temple, or as they customarily call it, their holy place [*tou hagiasmatos*], they abstain from offering to God the first fruits of the offerings. But you, why, having invented a new sacrifice [*kainēn thysian*], do you not sacrifice, since you do not need Jerusalem?[28] (my translation)

---

26. Pieter W. van der Horst, "Jews and Christians at Antioch at the End of the Fourth Century," in *Christian–Jewish Relations through the Centuries*, ed. Stanley E. Porter and Brook W. R. Pearson, JSNTSup 192 (London: T&T Clark, 2000), 228–38; Oded Irshai, "Dating the Eschaton: Jewish and Christian Apocalyptic Calculations in Late Antiquity," in *Apocalyptic Time*, ed. Albert I. Baumgarten, SHR 86 (Leiden: Brill, 2000), 113–53.

27. Chrysostom, *Adv. Jud.* 4.7.6 (PG 48.881) to discredit the Festival of Trumpets; 6.5.6 (PG 48.911)

28. For a discussion of these passages, see Finkelstein, *Specter of the Jews*, chapters 4 and 5.

Here Julian responds to Eusebius's claim that Christians are the "true Israel."[29] In the preceding passages Julian outlines Hebrew sacrifice on the Day of Atonement; according to frag. 72 = 305D–306A, Jews continue the tradition of Hebrew sacrifice. Importantly, Jewish private sacrifice remains efficacious, since it consecrates the meat they eat. Thus, contrary to Eusebius's claim in book 1 of *Demonstration of the Gospel*, sacrifice could take place in the absence of the temple. In fact, the efficaciousness of Jewish private sacrifice is bound up in its consumption. This is meant to be read in conjunction with 305B, where Julian quotes Lev 16:15 to prove that Moses did not consider the meat of the sacrifice to be impure. Julian thus removes one of the Christian grounds of objection to sacrifice. On the other hand, the Christian Eucharist is a "new" sacrifice because it bears no relation to Hebrew sacrifice. Christians had maintained that the Eucharist was an atonement sacrifice, using sacrificial language and images of the temple to depict it, while the officiating bishop acted as high priest.[30] Giorgio Scrofani demonstrates that mid-fourth-century church leaders often associated temple imagery with the Eucharist using terms like *naos archiereus thysiastērion* and *hagia tōn hagiōn* to support their arguments that the Eucharist was a true atonement sacrifice.[31] He points out that this argument countered the practices of Judaizers who celebrated the Day of Atonement with the Jews. Real atonement, Julian argues, comes from proper animal sacrifice and not from Christian prayer and the Eucharist. To counter Eusebius's depiction of Christians as the "true Israel," Julian highlights the incongruence between the Eucharist and sacrifice in the Bible in the face of what he characterizes as continuing Jewish sacrifice, which resembled its ancient forerunner.[32]

Meanwhile, Julian adopts Syrian eucharistic trappings to depict Jewish private sacrifice. By doing so, he demonstrates that it achieves everything that the local Syrian Eucharist does including expiation.[33] Fourth-century

---

29. Julian, *Galileans*, frag. 62 = 253A. All references to *Against the Galileans* follow the edition of Emanuela Masaracchia: *Giuliano imperatore: Contra Galilaeos* (Rome: Edizioni dell'Ateneo, 1990); Bouffartigue, *L'empereur Julien et la culture*, 387.

30. Daniel C. Ullucci, *The Christian Rejection of Animal Sacrifice* (Oxford: Oxford University Press, 2012), 91.

31. Giorgio Scrofani, "'Like the Green Herb': Julian's Understanding of Purity and His Attitude Towards Judaism in Contra Galilelos," *Journal for Late Antique Religion and Culture* 2 (2008): 1–16, here 5.

32. Julian highlighted the incoherence of Christianity's positions on sacrifice by laying out their contradictory claims. Christians claimed that (1) Jews no longer sacrifice (frag. 72 = 305D); (2) sacrifices can no longer be consumed by heavenly fire (frag. 83 = 343C); (3) sacrifice is sanctioned only in Jerusalem (frag. 85 = 351D); (4) the Eucharist is ritual sacrifice (frag. 72 = 306B) and therefore Christians had no need for Jerusalem; and (5) sacrifice was impossible since Jesus was the most perfect sacrifice.

33. See Eusebius,*Vit. Const.* 3.28; Gregory Nazianzen, *Or.* 10.4; Tertullian *Bapt.* 17.1; Scrofani "'Like the Green Herb,'" 5.

eucharistic liturgies from Syria identified the Eucharist with the Hebrew *kippur* (expiation) and considered it a sacred mystery.[34] In this case, the fact that Jewish private sacrifice occurs in private/hidden places (*en adraktois*) might be explained as a parallel to the mystery of the Eucharist.[35] Cyprian of Carthage and later John Chrysostom argued that the Eucharist and its ministers were equivalent to sacrifices and priests of the temple, respectively.[36] Meanwhile the Eucharist was accompanied by prayers and firstfruit offerings.[37] In the Eastern Church, the *anaphora*, or the prayer piece of the Eucharist, contained the word "offering" (*qorbana*).[38] Julian's addition of firstfruit offerings to the priests in 306A also parallels the firstfruit offerings of the Eucharist. In total, Julian showed that Jewish private sacrifice performs all of the functions of Moses's and Aaron's expiatory sacrifices and more closely resembles them than does the Eucharist because they are animal sacrifices. As a result, Jewish private sacrifice was the true successor to Hebrew sacrifice.[39] Meanwhile, Julian called the Eucharist "new"

34. Louis Ligier "Autour du sacrifice eucharistique (anaphores Orientales et anamnese juive de Kippur)," *NRT* 82 (1960): 40–55, here 52–53. Like Moses's sacrifices, the Eucharist took on expiatory meaning.

35. It also has parallels to the idea present in Aphrahat's work that prayer is an offering that should be made in secret. See Sebastian P. Brock, "Fire from Heaven: From Abel's sacrifice to the Eucharist: A Theme in Syriac Christianity," in *Papers Presented at the Eleventh International Conference on Patristic Studies Held in Oxford, 1991*, ed. Elizabeth A. Livingstone, 5 vols., StPatr 24–28 (Leuven: Peeters, 1993), 2:229–43, here 239.

36. Andrew B. McGowan, *Ancient Christian Worship: Early Church Practices in Social, Historical, and Theological Perspective* (Grand Rapids: Baker Academic, 2014), 54.

37. Justin Martyr also describes a Roman community of Syrian origin praying before they eat their meal (*1 Apol.* 67). See McGowan, *Ancient Christian Worship*, 36.

38. A. Gelston, "Sacrifice in the Early East Syrian Eucharistic Tradition," in *Sacrifice and Redemption: Durham Essays in Theology*, ed. S. W. Sykes (New York: Cambridge University Press, 1991), 118–25, here 119–20.

39. Julian may have had bona fide information that Jews sacrificed either from seeing the slaughter of the paschal lamb, about which we have information about this time from patristic sources, or he witnessed Jewish slaughter of animals for the purpose of consumption. Christian leaders claim that Jews continued to slaughter the Passover lamb. See Augustine, *Gen. Man.* 1.23:40 (PL 34.192), and his *Retract.* 1.10.2; Zenon, *On Exodus* (PL 11.521). See also Jean Juster, *Les juifs dans l'Empire Romain: Leur condition juridique, économique et sociale*, 2 vols. (Paris: Paul Geuthner, 1914), 1:357. Alternatively, Julian heard about this practice from Libanius, who employed Jews, or from someone else. Another possible source is Deut 18:3, which requires that a person slaughtering meat away from the temple give the priests the shoulder, jaw, and maw. Later interpretation of this verse interpreted the shoulder as the *right* shoulder, likely as a result of conflation with Lev 7:32–34. We see evidence of this in the Temple Scroll from Qumran (11QT XX, 14–16; XXI, 1–4). The following sources identify the shoulder as the *right* shoulder: Josephus, *Ant.* 4.74; m. Ḥul. 10:4; a *baraita* in the Babylonian Talmud (b. Hul. 134b); a variant version of a fourth-century Bohairic text of the Septuagint (For the Bohairic text on Deuteronomy 18:3 see Melvin K. H. Peters ed., *LXX, A Critical Edition of the Coptic (Bohairic) Pentateuch, Volume 5, Deuteronomy* (Chico, CA: Scholars Press, 1983), 61); and Targum Pseudo-Jonathan (seventh century) (Targum Pseudo-Jonathan Deuteronomy 18:3. For further reference see Ernest G. Clarke, *Targum Pseudo-Jonathan: Deuteron-*

and so denigrated it as something unconnected to the ancestral traditions of the Hebrew past.

Elsewhere, Julian seems familiar with Jewish sacrifice of the paschal lamb. He is aware of Christians who claim that they cannot keep the Sabbath, "*nor sacrifice/slaughter the lamb in the Jewish manner*, nor do they eat the unleavened bread" because these cannot be done outside of Jerusalem (*Galileans* frag. 85; my translation).[40] Julian may be borrowing a Jewish claim and/or a Judaizing claim that Jews continued to sacrifice the paschal lamb, or perhaps they are responding to Julian's claim that Jews continued to sacrifice. We do know that the Tannaim—the rabbis of the first through early third centuries—thought that some Jews believed they were sacrificing when they slaughtered the Passover lamb.[41] These rabbis seek to control the range of meanings Jews attribute to the slaughter of the Passover lamb, fearing that Jewish ritual around such slaughter bears the markers of sacrifice. Some scholars believe that Jews continued to sacrifice after the temple's destruction in 70 CE and not necessarily on Passover.[42] While one of these narratives is picked up by the Amoraim—the rabbis of the third through fifth centuries—it is hard to discern contemporary Jew-

---

omy (Collegeville, Minn.: The Liturgical Press, 1984), 52) . On the other hand, many of these earlier sources do not specify which shoulder ought to be given: See Philo, *Spec.* 1.147, and Targum Onkelos. (Targum Onkelos on Deut 18:3. For further reference see *Targum Onkelos to Deuteronomy: An English Translation of the Text with Analysis and Commentary* [trans. I. Drazin; Jersey City, N.J.: Ktav, 1982]). However, Julian does not quote Deut 18:3 as is his custom and patristic sources never interpret this passage. For this reason, along with the fact that he fails to cite the jaw and the maw among the items Jews give to priests, I doubt Julian knew of this passage.

40. See Cyril of Alexandria, *Against Julian* 10, 31.

41. See the stories in m. Pesaḥ. 4:4; m. Beṣah 2:7; cf. m. Ed. 3:11. See Baruch M. Bokser, *The Origins of the Seder: The Passover Rite and Early Rabbinic Judaism* (Berkeley: University of California Press, 1984), 101–5; t. Aḥilot 3:9 (Beit Dagan), 18:18 (Ashkelon). There are two conflicting instructions in the Torah for the roasting and eating of the Passover lamb. See Exod 12; cf. Philo, *Spec.* 2.148; and Deut 16:5–6. There is a recurring rabbinic story about "Theudas, the Roman," a Jew, who the rabbis claim taught the Jews of Rome to eat their Passover lambs *mequlas,* in a manner similar to the paschal lamb sacrifice in the temple. Their concern that Theudas misled Roman Jews into believing they were engaged in sacrifice seems to reflect real anxiety that other Jews do not adhere to rabbinic orthodoxy. See t. Beṣah 2:15; Baruch M. Bokser, "Todos and Rabbinic Authority in Rome," in *Religion, Literature, and Society in Ancient Israel: Formative Christianity and Judaism,* ed. Jacob Neusner et al., New Perspectives on Ancient Judaism 1 (Lanham, MD: University Press of America, 1987), 117–30. The story's location in Rome provides the best testimony of a rabbinic understanding of far-flung diaspora Jews who purchased lambs to roast on the nights of Passover.

42. See Friedenthal, *Litteraturblatt des Orients X* (Leipzig, 1849). J. Derenbourg argued the opposite (*Essai sur l'histoire et la géographie de la Palestine d'après les Thalmuds et les autres sources rabbiniques* (Paris: Imprimerie Imperiale, 1867), 480–82. In more recent years, Kenneth W. Clark has argued that sacrifice continued on the Temple Mount until 135 CE ("Worship in the Jerusalem Temple after AD 70," *NTS* 6 [1959–1960]: 269–80); see also Alexander Guttmann, "The End of Jewish Sacrifice," *HUCA* 38 (1967): 137–48.

ish practice of sacrifice in this period.[43] The only evidence that Jews continued to sacrifice in these centuries comes from the leaders of the church, who state that Jews continued to sacrifice the Passover lamb. In general, we should be suspicious of their reliability. Nevertheless, Augustine's testimony seems to be the most reliable. In *On Genesis against the Manichaeans* 1.23:40 (*PL* 34.192), he writes that Jews sacrifice their lambs on Passover. When Christians complain, he offers a retraction claiming that Jews slaughter their lambs rather than sacrifice (*Retract.* 1.10.2). If there was an intra-Jewish dispute on the permissibility of sacrifice in the fourth century, evidence of it has been lost. We do know, however, that Christian leaders depended on an end to legal Jewish sacrifice to support their own claims that Jewish ritual had ended with the destruction of the temple.

Chrysostom on Sacrifice

Julian's arguments about the persistence of Jewish sacrifice would have presented Christian leaders with a serious challenge. Christian discourse on sacrifice was built on its estimation that Jewish sacrifice ceased after the destruction of the temple in 70 CE, a position that was crucial to Christian sacrificial substitution (e.g., the Eucharist) and to Christians' self-understanding as successors to the ancient Hebrews. Thus, any lingering Jewish sacrifice was a source of anxiety for the church leaders, whose power was at stake.[44] Julian played on this anxiety by characterizing as sacrifice Jewish acts of ritual nonsacral slaughter that were common in Antioch. Eusebius's argument that Jewish ritual was defunct could not be effective against witnessed Jewish slaughter, carefully and realistically interpreted as sacrifice. There is also the possibility that some fourth-century Antiochene Jews thought of their nonsacral ritual slaughter as sacrifice, although there is no evidence to support this.

If there were Jews who sacrificed, Chrysostom seems unaware of it. In general, he assumes that Jewish sacrifice ended with the destruction of the temple, and he uses this fact to invalidate Jewish festivals such as Passover and Trumpets (the Jewish New Year).[45] These he declares invalid, as they required sacrifice in the Jerusalem temple. All celebrations outside

43. Y. Pesaḥ. 7:1, 34a. Similar versions are found in y. Beṣah 2:7, 61c and y. Mo'ed Qaṭ. 3:1, 81d.

44. This also explains the Christian overreaction to Augustine's perceived claim that Jews continued to sacrifice (*Gen. Man.* 1.23.40 [PL 34:192]). In *Retract.* 1.10.2, Augustine withdrew and explained his claim of continued Jewish sacrifice. See Paula Fredriksen, *Augustine and the Jews: A Christian Defense of Jews and Judaism* (New York: Doubleday, 2008), 309.

45. For Passover, see Chrysostom, *Adv. Jud* 4.4.3–7 (PG 48.876–77); for Trumpets, see 4.7.5–6 (PG 48:881–82).

of the temple were therefore an abomination.[46] This use of sacrifice as a counterargument to invalidate current Jewish ritual practices is found in a contemporary Christian Antiochene source, the Apostolic Constitutions, which claims that Jewish sacrifice was impossible in the absence of the temple.[47] It is possible that the Christian need to refute Jewish sacrifice was so powerful that Christians never admitted its existence. Any attempt to renew sacrifice would have garnered a strong Christian response. This might explain the Christian reaction to Augustine.

Julian on Priests

Jewish priests are important constituent elements of the Judean *ethnos*, and Julian views Jewish priests primarily as a model for Hellenic priests. Jews have an important place for priests in their society, and Jews live the life of the *hieratikoi bioi* (*Galileans* 238C), literally, "holy men" or priests, who share characteristics with Julian's local priests. What is striking in *Galileans* frag. 72 = 305D–306A is that priests remain an active part of Jewish ritual life, a rather surprising observation given that there was no functioning temple. Yet Julian claims that priests continue to collect their priestly gifts. In contrast to Christian bishops, who claim to be successors of the Jewish priests and high priests, Julian demonstrates that Jewish priests retain their privilege of collecting the right shoulder as firstfruits. Most likely Julian is referring to a Jewish ritual either he or members of his coterie witnessed.[48] According to Deut 18:3, Jews are required to offer priests the shoulder, cheeks, and maw of any sacrifice/slaughter of meat.[49] Since Julian is in the habit of quoting or paraphrasing biblical passages, the nonalignment of his statement with the biblical passage suggests that he witnessed this practice or had knowledge of it from his ally, Libanius, who employed Jews in his fields outside the city of Antioch.[50]

Julian also seems to refer to Jewish priests in his *Letter to the Community of the Jews*, even though he never mentions them directly. We can

46. Chrysostom, *Adv. Jud.* 1.7. Jews of the Bible neither sacrificed nor sang hymns in another land (4.4.2 [PG 48.876]), nor did they observe such fasts outside of Jerusalem (Chrysostom, *Adv. Jud* 4.5.2 [PG 48.878]).

47. Apostolic Constitutions 6.25. For a similar earlier claim see the Didascalia 26.

48. Libanius employed Jewish tenant farmers (*Ep.* 1098).

49. The verb *thyo* in Greek, like *zābaḥ* in Hebrew, can be translated as either "sacrifice" or "slaughter." In later Jewish tradition, from Josephus in the first century CE and the rabbis, the shoulder became the right shoulder. Julian is the only non-Jew to observe the custom. Aside from Julian, only b. Ḥul. 132a and 133a remark that Jews fulfilled this commandment. Geoffrey Herman, "The Priests of Babylon in the Talmudic Period" (MA thesis, Hebrew University of Jerusalem, 1998), 54 n. 215.

50. This is not surprising, since Christians never commented on it.

detect a priestly presence in his portrayal of Judean worship, which is similar to biblical images of the priest praying with arms outstretched toward heaven and focused in concentrated prayer on the worship of God in the temple.[51] This is how Julian describes all prayer in *Galileans* frag. 11 = 69B, and it corresponds with the emperor's depiction of Judeans as priests. Jewish concentrated prayer in this letter is a model for Hellenes and, once sacrifice was added at the temple, would animate the sacrifice. Now that he was rebuilding the temple and returning Jews to Jerusalem, he required a priestly caste to run the temple. Julian's removal of taxes on Jews should be seen in light of his policy of an abatement of taxes on cities in order to revive their civic cults but also more generally as his attempt to free up Jews, presented as priests, to engage in worship full-time, as Julian himself says. Removing these taxes would allow Jews to forgo working. This is not dissimilar to Julian's exemption of Hellenic priests from the financially burdensome *curiae*.

Recent arguments that the letter demonstrates a later hand are convincing.[52] However, there are good reasons to believe that the letter does contain an authentic Julianic core.[53] The letter asks that Jews pray to their god for Julian as he is about to fight the Persians and refers to the resettlement of Jews in Jerusalem to worship their god. This represents Julian's realization of his ethnographic rhetoric in *Galileans*, and the renormalization of Jews as Judeans in the Roman empire. In his effort to absolve Jews of financial responsibilities, which he believes deter people from prayer, Julian claims to have written the Jewish Patriarch to remove his *apostolē* tax. The voluntary removal of the *apostolē* would enable the Jews to restart their temple half-shekel tax. As Lee Levine argues, this did not likely come at the Patriarch's expense.[54] Julian refers to him as *aidesimotatos*, which is equivalent to *illustris* and *clarissibus* and therefore seems to raise the Patriarch's status. It is possible that Julian was creating a dyarchy along messianic lines. Jews would be led by the lineage of the House of David as the Patriarch claimed, and by the high priests, and they would, thereby,

---

51. See 1 Kgs 8:22, Neh 8:6, Ps 28:2, Ezra 9:5, Dan 12:7, Lam 3:41, Sir 50:20.

52. Peter Van Nuffelen, "Deux fausses lettres de Julien l'Apostat (La Lettre aux Juifs, *Ep.* 51 [Wright], et la lettre à Arsacius, *Ep.* 84 [Bidez]," *VC* 55 (2001): 131–50.

53. See Finkelstein, *Specter of the Jews*, appendix. Julian's use of *hiketeia* for prayer suggests Neoplatonic theurgic prayer and is the same word used by Julian's mentor, the theurgic Neoplatonist Iamblichus of Chalcis. No Christian would have used this term.

54. Lee I. Levine, "Contextualizing Jewish Art: The Synagogues at Hammat Tiberias and Sepphoris," in *Jewish Culture and Society under the Christian Roman Empire*, ed. Richard Kalmin and Seth Schwartz, Interdisciplinary Studies in Ancient culture and Religion 3 (Leuven: Peeters, 2003), 92–131, here 108–10. Julian does not mention Jewish high priests. However, since he clearly is restoring the Judean *ethnos* and was aware of biblical models, it seems reasonable to argue that he intended to reinstitute the role of the Jewish high priest. See Zech 4:14. The text imagines a dyarchy between the high priest Yehoshua ben Yehozadak and Zerubabel, the descendant of David.

model the leadership Julian sought for Hellenes (Julian, *Ep.* 89b.296bc). All in all, Jewish priests are full of vitality in Julian's works of early 363, and he seems to restore them to their former leadership position within the Judean *ethnos*.

Chrysostom on Priests

In his effort to demonstrate that Jewish ancestral laws are no longer efficacious, Chrysostom also emphasizes the absence of Jewish priests, pointing on two separate occasions to the lack of Jewish priests in *Judaizers*. Without a high priest, there is no one to oversee the sacrifices in a future temple, so that even if one believed that the temple would be rebuilt, Judaism lacks the personnel to make this happen. But Chrysostom also addresses possible Jewish counterclaims to the absence of priests. In *Adv. Jud.* 6.5.5-6 Chrysostom writes:

> (6) Where are the things you held as solemn, where is your high priest, where are his robe, his breastpiece, and stone of declaration? Do not talk to me about those patriarchs of yours who are hucksters and merchants and filled with iniquity. Tell me, what kind of priest is he if the ancient oil for anointing priests no longer exists nor any other ritual of consecration? What kind of a priest is he if there is neither sacrifice, nor altar, nor worship? [Harnack, Fathers of the Church]

Chrysostom picks up on a Jewish claim likely proclaimed by the Patriarch that he was the high priest. This in addition to his claim of being a descendant of King David. It was on this basis that he likely laid claim to the priestly gifts, gifts Julian claimed were still being offered to actual Jewish priests.[55] Chrysostom's broadside attacks the Patriarch's claim to fill the role of the high priest as a sham, which is only part of his larger argument that Jews are defunct. He will not allow Jews to have any vestiges of leadership. Like the case of the heavenly fire in the temple, this argument seems to be designed to inoculate Christianity from a possible future restoration of the temple. If there was no high priest, sacrificial ritual would be illegitimate.

There was much at stake for Christian leadership in the viability of Jewish priests. Christian bishops claimed the authority of the high priest. We find it first in 1 Corinthians, where Old Testament priesthood is analogous to Christian leadership (1 Cor 9:13–14). Paul's analogy continues to

---

55. Most scholars argue that there is no clear evidence that the Jewish Patriarch claimed to be the high priest and collected priestly tithes. However, Genesis Rabbah 80 and Epiphanius's *Panarion* 30 can be read to corroborate Chrysostom's claim that the Patriarch claimed to be the high priest and therefore would have collected priestly gifts.

shape the thought and practice of the later Syrian church.[56] In the eighth chapter of the Apostolic Tradition, thought to have been written in Syria and to be later than the rest of the work, not only does the theme of priests determine the tasks of the bishop, but prayer beseeches God to grant the bishop the spirit of the high priesthood.[57] In the third century, the Didascalia Apostolorum says that every bishop is a high priest,[58] a claim repeated in the Apostolic Constitutions 2.26.4, likely written in Antioch in Chrysostom's time.[59] We also find that temple priests serve as a model for Christian bishops in Eusebius's works.[60] Chrysostom's anti-Jewish priestly argument seeks to preserve Christian appropriation of historicized temple priests. As a priest and later bishop of Constantinople, Chrysostom's own authority was at stake.

The Maccabean Martyrs between Julian and Chrysostom

Controlling Jewish sites in the Antiochene landscape was important to both Julian's and Chrysostom's projects. One such site was the Maccabean reliquary possibly located in Daphne.[61] Gregory Nazianzen's *Homily* 15, dated to 362/363 offers us the earliest evidence of a Christian cult of the

56. The Didache designates the prophet as a "high priest." See Hippolytus, *La tradition apostolique, d'après les anciennes versions*, trans. Bernard Botte, 2nd ed., SC 11 (Paris: Cerf, 1968), 42–46.

57. Bryan Alan Stewart, "'Priests of My People': Levitical Paradigms for Christian Ministers in the Third and Fourth Century Church" (PhD diss., University of Virginia, 2006), 65.

58. Didascalia 9; and Apos. Con. 2.26, in Marcel Metzger, *Les Constitutions Apostoliques*, 3 vols., SC 320, 329, 336 (Paris: Cerf, 1985–1986), 1:236.

59. Apostolic Constitutions 1.6 (Metzger, 1:116–18). For a discussion of this perspective in the Didascalia, see R. Hugh Connolly, *Didascalia Apostolorum* (Oxford: Clarendon, 1929), lxii–lxiv. See Didascalia 8; Apos. Con. 2.25 (Metzger, 1:228–30). Stewart, "'Priests of My People,'" 118. Stewart identifies a bishop-as-priest typology in Apos. Con. 1.6.

60. Eusebius's use of Christian priests appears to be bound up in his supersessionist argument. He uses Old Testament priestly models of leadership to undergird the authority of the Christian bishops. See Eusebius, *Hist. eccl.* 10.3.3.

61. My reading of the evidence suggests that there was a reliquary based in a cave called Matrona's as Chrysostom describes it. Plaguing this issue have been inconclusive and contradictory sources. It is not at all clear where the church of the Maccabean martyrs was located, how many Maccabean churches there were, or whether the relics of the martyrs were in Daphne or in the Kerateion. For an overview, see Martha Vinson, "Gregory Nazianzen's Homily 15 and the Genesis of the Christian Cult of the Maccabean Martyrs," *Byzantion* 64 (1994): 166–92; Lothar Triebel, "La polémique anti-juive der makkabäischen Märtyrer in Antiochia am Orontes," *ZAC* 9 (2005): 464–95; Wendy Mayer and Pauline Allen, *The Churches of Syrian Antioch (300–638 CE)*, Late Antique History and Religion 5 (Leuven: Peeters, 2012); Shepardson, *Controlling Contested Places*, 114-15.

Maccabean martyrs.[62] Its beginnings likely coincide with Julian's stay in Antioch. Jewish worship at the site is inconclusive, although not impossible given the Jewish practice of praying at the tombs of prophets in the Second Temple period.[63] On the other hand, a full-blown Jewish cult of the Maccabean martyrs is unlikely. In Julian's *Letter to Theodorus*, his high priest of Asia, a fellow Neoplatonist and, like Julian, a student of the Neoplatonist theurgist Maximus of Ephesus, the emperor writes admiringly of the Jews' willingness to die for their laws rather than taste pig. The reference is likely taken from Porphyry's *On Abstinence* 2.61, another Neoplatonist philosopher whom both Julian and Theodorus likely read. Porphyry writes:

> For it would be a terrible thing, that while the Syrians do not taste fish and the Hebrews pigs ... and even when many kings strove to change them they preferred to suffer death rather than to transgress the law, we choose to transgress the laws of nature and the divine orders because of fear of men or some evil-speaking coming from them.[64]

As Peter Schäfer points out, of the *ethnē* Porphyry lists above, only the Jews in the time of Antiochus IV died in order to keep their dietary laws.[65] In Antioch, where the Maccabean martyrs were believed to be buried, any person hearing this argument would have associated Julian's reference with these martyrs. Julian here is drawing on Porphyry's mining of Jewish wisdom in his cross-cultural endeavor to reconstitute Hellenic wisdom lost after Plato.[66] However, he alters Porphyry's wording of Jewish wisdom, by adding language taken from the Apostolic Decree. Here is Julian in the *Letter to Theodorus*:

> Therefore, when I saw that there is among us great indifference about the gods and that all reverence for the heavenly powers has been driven out by impure and vulgar luxury, I always secretly lamented this state of things. For I observed that adherents to the doctrines ... [MS Spanheim: of the Judeans] are so ardent in their belief that they would choose to die for it, and to starve and die rather than taste pork [MS Spanheim: or any animal that had been strangled] or had the life squeezed out of

62. See Vinson, "Gregory Nazianzen's Homily 15."

63. Pieter W. van der Horst, "The Tombs of the Prophets in Early Judaism," in *Japheth in the Tents of Shem: Studies on Jewish Hellenism in Antiquity*, ed. Pieter W. van der Horst, CBET 32 (Leuven: Peeters, 2002), 119–37.

64. See Menahem Stern, *Greek and Latin Authors on Jews and Judaism*, 3 vols., Fontes ad res Judaicas spectantes (Jerusalem: Israel Academy of Sciences and Humanities, 1974–1984), vol. 1, n. 454, 434-35.

65. Peter Schäfer, *Judeophobia: Attitudes Towards the Jews in the Ancient World* (Cambridge: Harvard University Press, 1997), 75–76.

66. Schott, *Christianity, Empire, and Religion in Late Antiquity*, 58.

> it; whereas we are so apathetic about religious matters that we have forgotten the customs of our forefathers, and therefore we actually do not know whether any such rule has ever been written down. But these Judeans are for their part godfearing, seeing that they worship a god who is truly most powerful and most good and governs this world of sense, and as I well know, is worshiped by us also under other names. They act correctly, in my opinion, if they do not transgress the laws; but they err in one matter in that, while reserving their deepest devotion for their own God, they do not conciliate the other gods also; but the other gods they think have been allotted to us Gentiles only. This error they have taken to such foolish extremes in their barbaric conceit. But those who belong to the impious sect of the Galileans that spreads its disease ... (my translation)

Despite the passage's appearance in a letter to a Hellenic priest, for a number of reasons it is likely that it also appeared in *Galileans* in a fragment that is no longer extant. It shares several important ideas with *Galileans*. First, the triangulation of Hellenes with Jews and Christians is not only present but is used in the exact same manner as it is in *Galileans*. Just as Judeans share with Hellenes matters pertaining to sacrifice, temples, altars, and purifications in *Galileans* (frag. 72 = 306B), as well as matters pertaining to the priestly life (frag. 58 = 238), so too in the *Letter to Theodorus* Julian suggests that Jewish dietary laws may be practices that Hellenes ought to keep.[67] In both works, Julian compares Jews favorably with Hellenes but finds the former deficient in their refusal to worship more than one God. Further, the flow of the argument in the *Letter to Theodorus* matches that of *Galileans* but works in reverse. Julian extols Jews for keeping their ancestral laws in the letter but then goes on to attack them for refusing to worship more than the one god. Jewish worship of one god is still preferable to Christian worship of a corpse, an argument that gets cut off here in the *Letter to Theodorus* likely by a Christian offended by the claim.[68] In *Galileans* these arguments work in the exact reverse. Julian denies that Jesus is a divine being, (frag. 79–80 = 327A–333D), calling him a corpse, which leads him to attack the Christian worship of other dead people, the martyrs (frag. 81 = 335BC). Either Julian is writing both works at the exact same time, or, more likely, he took a passage from *Galileans* and inserted it in his *Letter to Theodorus*. If this passage also appeared in *Galileans*, it would have been heard by Christians in synagogues and churches and in the *bouletērion*.

---

67. Julian, *Letter to Theodorus*, 453D. Giorgio Scrofani explains Julian's use of Jewish dietary laws to model Julian's understanding of purity and his attitude toward Judaism in *Against the Galileans* ("'Like the Green Herb,'" 6–7, 11-12).

68. See Wright, *Works of the Emperor Julian*, 3:61 n. 2.

The message to Christians is that they ought to be keeping the dietary laws just as the Apostolic Decree requires. This is an argument that would have reverberated among Christians in Antioch, where some kept Jewish law, likely including dietary laws, and where the Apostolic Decree was contested.[69] Julian also subtly suggests that real martyrs die for their ancestral laws, not for a corpse. The observance of ancestral law was a principal goal of Julian's hellenizing program. Each *ethnos* was to worship its own god in accordance with its ancestral laws. Christians stood out for not having ancestral laws. The law that they ought to have kept—Jewish law—they rejected.

One can well imagine that Julian's arguments could have had an impact on Christians as they witnessed other Christians worshiping at the reliquary of the Maccabean martyrs. Rather than Christian saints capable of interceding with God, the Maccabean martyrs could now be understood as Jewish martyrs who died for their faithful observance and their refusal to contravene their dietary laws. Julian sought to encourage Christian attraction to Jewish law and thereby weaken the boundaries separating Christians and Jews. It was precisely the authenticity of Jewish law, practices, and holy sites that caused some Christians to cleave to Jewish practices and synagogues. Now Julian hoped to affect how Christians understood their martyred past, with the ultimate goal of weakening Christian orthodoxies and bringing more Christians to Jewish life.

Chrysostom and the Maccabean Martyrs

The Maccabean martyrs and their connection to Jewish law are also the subject of one of Chrysostom's homilies. In contrast to Julian's view, the Maccabean martyrs did not die for their laws, argues Chrysostom in *On Eleazar and the Seven Sons* (PG 63:525).[70] Instead they were murdered for Christ. In *On Eleazar* 6 Chrysostom writes:

> So then, that they displayed considerable courage by competing in those times is absolutely clear. That they received their wounds for Christ's sake, this I will now attempt to demonstrate. Tell me for what reason did they suffer? "Because of the law," you say, "and the edicts that lie within the law." If then, it is apparent that it was Christ who gave that law, is it not clear that, by suffering for the law, they displayed all of that boldness

---

69. There is no direct evidence in Julian's time that Christians kept dietary laws. However, there is evidence in the Didascalia Apostolorum, written in Syria mostly in the third century and circulating in Antioch, that some Christians kept dietary laws. The Apostolic Decree forms the framework for the Apostolic Constitutions.

70. See Daniel Joslyn-Siemiatkoski, *Christian Memories of the Maccabean Martyrs* (New York: Palgrave Macmillan, 2009), 44.

> for the lawgiver? Come, then, let us demonstrate this today: that it is Christ who gave the law.[71]

Chrysostom offers proof from Jeremiah (38:31-33), who argued that God would give a new covenant. He quite matter-of-factly claims that Jesus gave the new covenant. Since Jeremiah says the one who will give the new covenant also gave the old covenant it is clear to Chrysostom that Jesus gave both covenants. Therefore, when the Maccabean martyrs died for the laws of the covenant they were in fact worshipping the lawgiver, Jesus.

It is not entirely clear where Chrysostom delivered this homily. Wendy Mayer favors Constantinople slightly,[72] where another church to the Maccabean martyrs stood. However, it is equally possible that this sermon was delivered in Antioch. If so, Chrysostom's association of the sacrifice of the Maccabean martyrs takes place against a backdrop of intra-Christian competition over the correct meaning and site of the Maccabean martyr reliquary. Sometime in the 380s, Theodosius I sponsored a basilica church in the Kerateion, which claimed to be the home of the Maccabean martyr relics. This site belonged to the *homoousians*.[73] Meanwhile, the original reliquary of the Maccabean martyrs was perhaps associated with *homoians* but almost certainly with Christians who stressed the Jewish background of the Maccabean martyrs who died for their observance of the law.

If the Antiochene provenance of *On Eleazar* and *Against the Judaizers* is correct, this homily demonstrates that Jewish law continued to be a major attraction to Christians in the city of Antioch two decades after Julian.[74] Chrysostom feels the need to reorient the understanding of the Maccabean martyrs as people who died rather than violate their dietary laws to the understanding of them as proto-Christians who died on behalf of Christ. Attraction to Jewish law made the Apostolic Decree a lightning rod for interpretation as Christians fought over exactly which laws of the Old Testament they ought to keep. This is likely why Julian used it.

Julian had attempted to use Jewish willingness to die for their ancestral laws as a model for ideal martyrdom. Willingness to die for Christ was not real martyrdom. At the same time, he reminded Christians that the apostles required that they keep the dietary laws. By not living up to their Maccabean heroes they were in breach of their own ancestral laws. Years later Chrysostom sought to redefine the Maccabean martyrs as people who died for Jesus, their lawgiver. To do so he disentangles and reframes

71. John Chrysostom, *The Cult of the Saints*, trans. Wendy Mayer (Crestwood, NY: St. Validimir's Seminary Press, 2006), 125.

72. Ibid., 119.

73. See n. 7 above.

74. We do not have any information to confirm or deny Greco-Roman attraction to Jews, their god, and practices in this period.

the laws from the Maccabean martyr stories in order to strengthen Christian *homoousian* claims to the Maccabean martyrs and to weaken their connection to the specifics of Jewish law.

Against the Jews or the Judaizers?

In recent times John Chrysostom's *Adversus Judaioi* has been translated as *Against the Judaizers*. The logic is that it is Christians who keep Jewish practices who are Chrysostom's real target. Therefore, his argument is not really with Jews as much as it is with Judaizing Christians. If Jews are targeted it is only as a rhetorical device designed to convince Christian Judaizers that Jewish law, institutions, and heroes are invalid and dangerous.[75] If true, under current scholarly heresiological paradigms, the Judaizers would be heretics, falling between orthodox Christians and Jews, who should be presented as an inferior but legitimate "other."[76] Chrysostom's arguments, however, do not follow heresiological principles. There is no question that Chrysostom targets Judaizers, but he most certainly attacks Jews directly and declares Jewishness dead. He does so because Jews pose a real threat to Christians in late fourth-century Antioch. Building Christian orthodoxy depended on taming Jewish ritual efficacy. The nature of this fourth-century anti-Jewish rhetoric is by no means limited to Chrysostom, but his words are meant to play out over the Antiochene landscape, one that had heard a very different argument about Jews only two decades earlier.

Conclusion

When Rome became Christian, a process begun in earnest in the mid-380s with the support of Emperor Theodosius I, Christianity came to define *Romanitas*. This process differed from locale to locale.[77] In Antioch,

75. For the debate on whether Chrysostom's homilies are directed against Jews or Judaizers, see Marcel Simon, "La polémique anti-juive de S. Jean Chrysostome et mouvement judaisant d'Antioche," in *Annuaire de l'Institut de Philologie et d'Histoire Orientales et Slaves* 4 (1936): 403–21; Harkins, "Introduction," in *Discourses against Judaizing Christians*; Klaas Smelik, "John Chrysostom's Homilies against the Jews: Some Comments," *Nederlands theologisch tijdschrift* 39 (1985): 194–200; A. M. Ritter, "John Chrysostom and the Jews: A Reconsideration," in *Ancient Christianity in the Caucasus*, ed. Tamila Mgaloblishvili, Caucasus World (Richmond: Curzon, 1998), 141–54; van der Horst, "Jews and Christian at Antioch," 229-232; Shepardson, *Controlling Contested Places*, 100 n. 25; Kalleres, *City of Demons*, 281 n. 3.

76. Daniel Boyarin, *Border Lines: The Partition* of *Judaeo-Christianity*, Divinations (Philadelphia: University of Pennsylvania Press, 2004).

77. Like recent articulations of Romanization, this process was inherently local, negotiated rather than imposed, and ongoing in nature. See Greg Woolf, "Beyond Romans and

Christian leaders had to reckon with the embeddedness of Jews in local culture just as Julian had done two decades earlier. For Chrysostom, the road to orthodoxy forced him to confront the powerful Jewish symbols deemed authentic and legitimate by a group of Christians in Antioch. These symbols had to be shown to be powerless. As Chrysostom tried to occupy and control greater amounts of life and space in the city of Antioch, he was forced to deal with Jewish spaces and practices there. This meant affecting how people understood themselves and their culture. Asking Christians to reevaluate how they looked at and valued Jews, their laws, practices, institutions, and heroes, was difficult particularly because of society's unconscious acceptance of Jewish idioms within the local culture. Weaning Christians from Jewish law required tough language, and Chrysostom rose to the occasion. Chrysostom seeks to put the Jewish genie, weaponized and released by Julian, back in the bottle, by proving Jews are a defunct *ethnos*, as Eusebius had done earlier in the century. Chrysostom's scalding rhetoric reflects the fact that Jews were viewed by many Christians not as defunct but as vital, authentic, and therefore legitimate. Julian had raised the stakes of Christians' attraction to Jews. Now Jews were a real threat to Christianity both in his day and in the future should a temple be rebuilt. Unfortunately, Chrysostom's report on Julian's attempt to rebuild the temple and his hostile attitude toward the Jews supported Christian anti-Jewish attitudes for generations.[78]

Natives," *World Archaeology* 28 (1997): 339–50; Woolf, *Tales of the Barbarians: Ethnography and empire in the Roman West*, Blackwell Bristol Lectures on Greece, Rome, and the Classical Tradition (Chichester: Wiley-Blackwell, 2011).

78. David Levenson argues that Chrysostom may have known of an anonymous *homoian* tradition that reported on Julian's attempt to rebuild the temple. He demonstrates that this tradition was passed on to many future Christian leaders who wrote about the same events. See Levenson, "The Ancient and Medieval Sources for the Emperor Julian's Attempt to Rebuild the Jerusalem Temple," *JSJ* 35(2004): 409–60, here 418 n. 33.

Reinventing Yavneh in Sherira's Epistle

From Pluralism to Monism in the Light of Islamicate Legal Culture

YISHAI KIEL

The Hebrew University of Jerusalem, Faculty of Law

Shaye Cohen has irrevocably changed the way we think about the emergence of rabbinic Judaism in the aftermath of the temple's destruction in 70 CE against the foil of the sectarian movements that pervaded the Second Temple period. Prior to the publication of "The Significance of Yavneh,"[1] scholars tended to depict the rabbinic gathering at Yavneh—whether portrayed as a founding moment or a historical era—which ultimately yielded the Mishnah and other Tannaitic works, as suffused with an air of crisis and urgency, a fact that resulted in the formation of a grand coalition centered on the proto-rabbinic Pharisees. The new rabbinic coalition was said to have been characterized by internal consensus and monism and motivated by an exclusivist and antipluralistic agenda aimed at demarcating a new Jewish "orthodoxy" while excluding sectarian forms of faith and practice. The rabbinic gathering at Yavneh was further credited, according to this paradigm, with the expulsion of Jewish Christians and other "heretics" from the synagogue, the composition of *birkat ha-minim* centered on the denunciation of sectarians, and the undertaking of a canonization project aimed at establishing a scriptural canon purged of all and any traces of heresy.[2]

In contrast to this influential paradigm, which depicted the rabbinic gathering at Yavneh as some sort of Jewish equivalent to the Council of

1. Shaye J. D. Cohen, "The Significance of Yavneh: Pharisees, Rabbis, and the End of Jewish Sectarianism," *HUCA* 55 (1984): 27–53; reprinted in *The Significance of Yavneh and Other Essays in Jewish Hellenism*, TSAJ 136 (Tübingen: Mohr Siebeck 2010), 44–70. References to pages in this article refer to the reprinted edition.

2. For this long-standing paradigm, see, e.g., W. D. Davies, *The Setting of the Sermon on the Mount* (Cambridge: Cambridge University Press, 1966), 271–77; Martin Goodman, "The Function of 'Minim' in Early Rabbinic Judaism," in Goodman, *Judaism in the Roman World: Collected Essays*, AJEC 66 (Leiden: Brill, 2007), 163–74. The contours of this paradigm were summarized in Cohen, "Significance of Yavneh," 45–46 (further literature cited on 46 n. 2).

Nicaea and its orthodox heritage, Shaye Cohen has persuasively argued that the ethos and legacy of Yavneh were neither exclusive nor monistic but rather inclusive and pluralistic.[3] The emerging rabbinic movement was indeed committed to the elimination of Jewish sectarianism, but this was accomplished not by a discourse of orthodoxy and heresy but rather by one of inclusion, pluralism, and tolerance, in which all parties "agreed to disagree." The clearest articulation of this ethos is found in the Mishnah, the ultimate expression of rabbinic aspirations and views, which incorporates the insights of the Yavnean rabbis and their successors. As clearly put by Cohen, "no previous Jewish work looks like the Mishnah because no previous Jewish work, neither biblical nor post-biblical, neither Hebrew nor Greek, neither from the land of Israel nor from the diaspora, attributes conflicting legal and exegetical opinions to named individuals who, in spite of their differences, belong to the same fraternity."[4]

In connection with Cohen's deconstruction of the monistic image of the rabbinic gathering at Yavneh, several scholars have further sought to demythologize different aspects of Yavneh's image as a site of orthodoxy and exclusion, as a gathering permeated by an air of crisis and urgency, as a locus of scriptural canonization, and as the bedrock of *birkat ha-minim* and the expulsion of Jewish Christians from the synagogue.[5] In the present article, in honor of Shaye Cohen's inestimable contribution to the study of ancient Judaism, I seek to problematize, stratify, and complicate the pluralistic/monistic legacy of Yavneh by sketching the unfolding of the Yavnean myth from its inception in Tannaitic literature, through its maturation in the Babylonian Talmud, and finally to its reinvention in the Geonic era. Following a survey of the status quaestionis on the pluralistic image of Yavneh in the classical talmudic corpus, I will focus on a closer textual examination of the deconstruction of the pluralistic Yavneh and the reconstruction of a monistic and centralist ethos of Yavneh in the

---

3. Cohen lists four major flaws in the prevailing paradigm: (1) it is overly simplistic; (2) it assumes that Yavneh was suffused with an air of crisis, while, in fact, "the air of crisis which pervaded the apocalypses of Baruch and Ezra is conspicuously absent from tannaitic literature"; (3) it is based on disjointed reports in rabbinic literature; and, most importantly, (4) it misses the tolerant and inclusive ethos of the emerging rabbinic movement ("Significance of Yavneh," 46).

4. Ibid.

5. For Yavneh and scriptural canonization, see, e.g., Jack P. Lewis, "Jamnia Revisited," in *The Canon Debate*, ed. Lee Martin McDonald and James A. Sanders (Peabody, MA: Hendrickson, 2002), 146–62. For Yavneh and post-destruction trauma, see David Goodblatt, "The Jews of Eretz-Israel in the Years 70–132," in *Judea and Rome: The Jewish Revolts* [Hebrew], ed. Uriel Rappaport (Jerusalem: Am Oved, 1983), 155–84. For Yavneh, *birkat ha-minim*, and the expulsion of Jewish Christians from the synagogue, see, most recently, Ruth Langer, *Cursing the Christians? A History of the Birkat Ha-Minim* (Oxford: Oxford University Press, 2012), 16–39.

Epistle of Rav Sherira Gaon b. Hanina,[6] in the light of contemporaneous Islamicate[7] rhetoric concerning consensus and unanimity (Arabic *ijmā'*; Middle Persian *ham-dādestānīh*) of the jurists and the nation at large. In this context, we will see that Sherira, not unlike some of his contemporaries, sought to project his innovative monistic jurisprudence back onto a glorious mythical past.

Considering its historiographic orientation, Sherira's epistle was utilized mainly by historians as a source for reconstructing the intellectual history of rabbinic Judaism from the third to the tenth centuries. At the same time, scholars have attempted to expose the ideological agenda underlying the epistle, which include Sherira's assertion of the preeminence of the Babylonian rabbinic tradition vis-à-vis that of Palestine, the relative preeminence of the academy of Pumbeditha vis-à-vis that of Sura, the authenticity of the Davidic genealogy of the Exilarchate, and anti-Qaraite polemic.[8] Certain institutional, historiographic, and literary features of the epistle were further situated in the broader context of Syriac and Arabic literature.[9]

In the present article, I provide a jurisprudential reading of Sherira's epistle. By this, I do not mean to suggest that the epistle contains a full-

---

6. On Sherira's epistle, see in general Robert Brody, "Epistle of Sherira Gaon," in *Rabbinic Texts and the History of Late-Roman Palestine*, ed. Martin Goodman and Philip Alexander, Proceedings of the British Academy 165 (Oxford: Oxford University Press, 2010), 253–64; Brody, *The Geonim of Babylonia and the Shaping of Medieval Jewish Culture* (New Haven: Yale University Press, 1998), 20–25. For a critical edition of Sherira's epistle, see Benjamin M. Lewin, ed., *Igeret rav sherira gaon: Mesuderet bi-shnei nusḥa'ot: nusaḥ sefarad ve-nusaḥ tzarfat 'im hilufei girsa'ot mi-kol qitvei-ha-yad ve-qitvei ha-genizah she-ba-'olam* (Haifa: Itzkowsky, 1921).

7. For the term *Islamicate*, see Marshall G. S. Hodgson, *The Venture of Islam: Conscience and History in a World Civilization*, 3 vols. (Chicago: University of Chicago Press, 1974), 1:59; Lena Salaymeh, *The Beginnings of Islamic Law: Late Antique Islamicate Legal Traditions* (Cambridge: Cambridge University Press, 2016), 9.

8. See, e.g., Isaiah Gafni, "On the Talmudic Chronology in Iggeret Rav Sherira Gaon," *Zion* 52 (1987): 1–24; Gafni, "On the Talmudic Historiography in the Epistle of Rav Sherira Gaon: Between Tradition and Creativity," *Zion* 73 (2009): 271–96; Robert Brody, "On the Sources for the Chronology of the Talmudic Period," *Tarbiz* 70 (2000): 75–107; Gerald Blidstein, "Oral Torah: Ideology and History in the Epistle of Sherira Gaon," in *Religious Knowledge, Authority, and Charisma: Islamic and Jewish Perspectives*, ed. Daphna Ephrat and Meir Hatina, Utah Series in Turkish and Islamic Studies (Salt Lake City: University of Utah Press, 2014), 73–87. See, however, the careful assessment in Brody, *Geonim of Babylonia*, 20 n. 5.

9. See Joseph David, "As Explained in the Book of Adam: The History of Halakha and the Mythical Perception of History in the Late Geonic Period," *Tarbiz* 74 (2005): 577–601; Adam Becker, *Fear of God and the Beginning of Wisdom: The School of Nisibis and Christian Scholastic Culture in Late Antique Mesopotamia*, Divinations (Philadelphia: University of Pennsylvania Press, 2006), 107–10; Talya Fishman, "Claims about the Mishnah in the Epistle of Sherira Gaon: Islamic Theology and Jewish History," in *Beyond Religious Borders: Interaction and Intellectual Exchange in the Medieval Islamic World*, ed. David Freidenreich and Miriam Goldstein, Jewish Culture and Contexts (Philadelphia: University of Pennsylvania Press, 2012), 65–77; Simcha Gross, "When the Jews Greeted Ali: Sherira Gaon's Epistle in Light of Arabic and Syriac Historiography," *JSQ* 24 (2017): 122–44.

fledged theory of the law, certainly not one that approximates contemporary legal theory. I simply maintain that, alongside its historiographic value, the epistle should be appreciated from a legal-theoretical perspective as an attempt to provide the theoretical underpinnings of (actual or idealized) legal activity in the late Geonic era. Specifically, I argue that Sherira's jurisprudential adherence to legal monism and centralism, a position diametrically opposed to the pluralistic ethos espoused in the classical talmudic tradition, was couched in an innovative retelling of the founding mythical events that allegedly constituted rabbinic Judaism: the gathering at Yavneh guided by Rabban Yohanan ben Zakkai and the composition of the Mishnah guided by Rabbi Yehudah the Patriarch some 130 years later.[10] The distinctive narrative/mythical framework in which Sherira's monistic jurisprudence is cast lends itself to the type of analysis advanced by Robert Cover, both in terms of the reciprocity of *nomos* and narrative in general[11] and in terms of the interplay of jurisprudence and constitutional myths of origin.[12]

Legal Pluralism versus Legal Monism

Legal theorists have long debated the question of whether a legal system, as such, is necessarily defined as a monistic, unitary, and hierarchal system of legislation and adjudication, connected with a centralized political power and backed up by its sanction.[13] In contrast to the perception of law as inherently monistic and centralized, which dominated legal scholarship for most of the twentieth century, the emerging idea of legal pluralism was predicated on the assumption that the state is not the sole guardian of law, envisioning instead a model of overlapping, intersecting, and coinciding legal systems and normative orders that include both state

---

10. I will thus use the terms *Yavneh* and *Yavnean* in this context to refer broadly to the postdestruction consolidation/formation of rabbinic Judaism.

11. For the reciprocity of *nomos* and narrative, see Robert Cover, "The Supreme Court, 1982 Term—Forward: Nomos and Narrative," *Harvard Law Review* 97 (1983): 4–68. For the application of Cover's theory of *nomos* and narrative in the field of rabbinics, see, e.g., Steven Fraade, "Nomos and Narrative before Nomos and Narrative," *Yale Journal of Law and the Humanities* 17 (2005): 81–96; Barry S. Wimpfheimer, *Narrating the Law: A Poetics of Talmudic Legal Stories*, Divinations (Philadelphia: University of Pennsylvania Press, 2011), 9–24.

12. For the interplay of constitutional myth and jurisprudential theory, see Robert Cover, "Obligation: A Jewish Jurisprudence of the Social Order," *Journal of Law and Religion* 5 (1987): 65–66 (juxtaposing the foundational myths of Sinai and the Social Contract underlying Jewish and Western legal cultures).

13. For legal centralism and monism, see, e.g., Hans Kelsen, *Pure Theory of Law*, trans. Max Knight (Berkeley: University of California Press, 1967), 205–8; John Austin, *The Province of Jurisprudence Determined* [1832], ed. Wilfrid E. Rumble, Cambridge Texts in the History of Political Thought (Cambridge: Cambridge University Press, 1995), 9–19.

and nonstate forms of law.[14] Indeed, more recent currents in legal theory, international law, critical legal studies, political science, and law and religion reflect a growing appreciation of nonstate forms of law and the importance of negotiating multiple and simultaneous normative systems.[15]

The debate surrounding legal monism vs. legal pluralism pertains not only to the question of negotiating the coexistence of multiple normative systems of state and nonstate law within a given society or the coexistence of alternative institutions within a single legal order,[16] but also the challenge involved in the containment of multiple, often conflicting, positions within a single legal institution, be it legislative or judicial.

Since the rise of legal pluralism in recent decades, rabbinic law was often invoked in the literature as a counterexample or alternative to the traditional perception of law in Western legal theory as centralized and monistic, echoing instead a pluralistic, antihierarchal, and decentralized legal model.[17] Beyond the stateless nature of Jewish law, which can be seen perhaps as a contingent dimension of the system, the pluralistic model offered by rabbinic law was often construed as an inherent feature of the system, which emphatically celebrates multivocality and polysemy.[18] Some of the programmatic talmudic assertions to that effect include, "these and these are the words of the living God" (אלו ואלו דברי אלהים חיים) (y. Yebam. 1:6, 3b; b. Eruv. 13b; b. Giṭ. 6b) and "they [the disputing positions] were all given at the hand of a single shepherd"[19] (כולם מרועה אחד ניתנו). In fact, legal pluralism was perceived as so fundamental to the rabbinic legal system that it was regularly associated with, and projected back onto, the founding constitutional moments of rabbinic Judaism, especially the rabbinic gathering at Yavneh after the temple's destruction and the sub-

---

14. For legal pluralism see, in general, John Griffiths, "What Is Legal Pluralism?" *Journal of Legal Pluralism and Unofficial Law* 24 (1986): 1–55; Brian Tamanaha, "Understanding Legal Pluralism: Past to Present, Local to Global," *Sydney Law Review* 30 (2008): 375–411. Robert Cover's realization that the law is not limited to statutes, rules, and institutions but encompasses foundational narratives that provide meaning to normative communities has also contributed to a pervasively "pluralistic" view of the law, one in which multiple interpretive communities simultaneously identify their paradigms for normative behavior. See Cover, "Nomos and Narrative."

15. To name just a few recent contributions: Emmanuel Melissaris, *Ubiquitous Law: Legal Theory and the Space for Legal Pluralism*, Law, Justice, and Power (London: Routledge, 2009); Paul Schiff Berman, *Global Legal Pluralism: A Jurisprudence of Law Beyond Borders* (Cambridge: Cambridge University Press, 2012).

16. Griffiths, "What Is Legal Pluralism?," 5.

17. See especially the discussion of Cover's views in Suzanne L. Stone, "In Pursuit of the Counter-Text: The Turn to the Jewish Legal Model in Contemporary American Legal Theory," *Harvard Law Review* 106 (1993): 828–29, 834–36.

18. The vast literature confirming this assertion will be surveyed below.

19. B. Ḥag. 3b; t. Soṭah 7:11-12, in Saul Lieberman, ed., *The Tosefta*, 4 vols. (New York: Jewish Theological Seminary of America, 2002), 194–95.

sequent composition of the Mishnah more than a century later. Whether the full-fledged pluralistic legacy of Yavneh emerged already in Tannaitic literature or only in the editorial stratum of the Babylonian Talmud, it is clear that by the sixth-century the myth of the founding council at Yavneh was understood as a touchstone of rabbinic pluralism, multivocality, and polysemy. Indeed, it is precisely this pluralistic image of Yavneh that was bequeathed by the classical rabbis to posterity. Sherira's epistle, by contrast, contains a very different account of the founding moments of rabbinic Judaism, which are emphatically characterized by legal monism and permeated by a rhetoric of consensus, unanimity, and centralism.[20]

The role of monism and consensus in Sherira's account is significantly illuminated by recourse to positivist legal theory,[21] since legal positivism was often connected with a monistic perception of the law. I refer here not only to the centralist-monistic tendencies characteristic of earlier theorists

---

20. For an overview of rabbinic attitudes to pluralism/monism, see Hanina Ben-Menahem, Neil S. Hecht, and Shai Wosner, *Controversy and Dialogue in the Jewish Tradition: A Reader,* Publication of Boston University Institute of Jewish Law 31 (London: Routledge, 2005), 17–63; Richard Hidary, *Dispute for the Sake of Heaven: Legal Pluralism in the Talmud,* BJS 353 (Providence, RI: Brown Judaic Studies, 2010), 1–36. For the different meanings associated with pluralism/monism consider the following distinctions: (1) Interpretive/hermeneutic polysemy should be distinguished from legal pluralism in the sense of diversity of legal opinions. (2) Interpretive polysemy should be distinguished from literary notions of the inherent indeterminacy of texts as such. (3) Interpretive polysemy should also be distinguished from predilection to dialectics and argumentation. (4) The textual praxis of legal pluralism should be distinguished from its thematization through self-conscious ideological statements. (5) Practical or "particular" pluralism should be distinguished from theoretical, philosophical, or "universal" pluralism. The former type of pluralism tolerates the existence of legal diversity but can maintain (with Ronald Dworkin) that there is, theoretically, a single correct answer to every legal question. The latter type adheres to theoretical diversity and the possibility of several correct answers to any given legal question. (6) Historical and other contingent explanations of pluralism—for example, the idea that diversity is the result of a mess-up in transmission or interpretation—should be distinguished from an ahistorical account of pluralism as an essential facet of the legal tradition. (7) Descriptive accounts of legal pluralism should be distinguished from evaluations/assessments of legal pluralism in terms of a positive or negative phenomenon. (8) Literary depictions of legal pluralism should be distinguished from a reality of legal pluralism attesting to the system's mode of operation. (9) The notion of theoretical/philosophical pluralism should be distinguished from the theological question of whether or not "God's truth" coincides with a logical or theoretical truth. (10) Pluralism internal to a legal system or institution should be distinguished from the type of pluralism governing competing legal orders or institutions. (11) Finally, judicial pluralism, in the sense of enabling dissents in court decisions, should be distinguished from legislative pluralism.

21. For the major concerns and debates of legal positivism, see Andrei Marmor, "Exclusive Legal Positivism," in *The Oxford Handbook of Jurisprudence and Philosophy of Law,* ed. Jules L. Coleman, Kenneth Einar Himma, and Scott J. Shapiro (Oxford: Oxford University Press, 2004), 104–24; and, in the same volume, Kenneth E. Himma, "Inclusive Legal Positivism," 125–65.

such as John Austin and Hans Kelsen,[22] who viewed the law as connected with a centralized and unitary political power, but also to contemporary positivist theorists heirs to H. L. A. Hart, who highlight social convention as the basis of law. Although Hart himself was committed to theoretical pluralism insofar as the adjudication of hard cases,[23] his theory rests on the assumption that the law is essentially a social artifact while its criteria of validity depend on convention. According to the conventionality thesis, a set of agreed-upon criteria of legal validity, which constitute a society's rule of recognition, determine the authoritative sources of the law from which valid rules are deduced.[24] A valid rule of recognition must meet two basic conditions: (1) the criteria of validity are accepted and agreed upon by the legal officials as standards of their own conduct; and (2) citizens generally comply with the rules validated through the conventionally accepted legal sources.[25] In this context, the function of the accepted criteria of validity that form a society's rule of recognition is not merely epistemic, providing certainty to the law,[26] but also, and more importantly, constitutive. In other words, it is social convention, reflected in the agreement of legal officials and the general compliance of citizens, that establishes the authoritativeness vested in the identified legal sources.[27]

Viewed in this light, I will argue that Sherira's account reflects not only centralist convictions but also insistence on the constitutive role of consensus, both of the jurists and the nation at large, in establishing the canonicity of the Mishnah as a legal source. The revelatory origin of the substantive rules notwithstanding, Sherira employs the idea of legal consensus, not simply on an epistemic level to solve the problem of uncertainty, but also on a constitutive level, so as to validate and ratify the canonical status of the Mishnah as a binding legal source. While the substantive rules stem

---

22. See Kelsen, *Pure Theory of Law*, 202–8; Austin, *Province of Jurisprudence*, 9–19. For a recent analysis of these and other early positivist theories, see Gerald J. Postema, "Legal Positivism: Early Foundations," in *The Routledge Companion to Philosophy of Law* (London: Routledge, 2015), 31–47.

23. For Hart's debate with Dworkin on this matter, see, e.g., Brian H. Bix, "Natural Law Theory," in *A Companion to Philosophy of Law and Legal Theory*, ed. Dennis M. Patterson (Malden, MA: Wiley-Blackwell, 2008), 221–24.

24. H. L. A Hart, *The Concept of Law*, 2nd ed. (Oxford: Oxford University Press, 1994), 79–99.

25. Ibid., 92. For theoretical justifications of the conventionality thesis, see, e.g., Andrei Marmor, "Legal Conventionalism," *Legal Theory* 4 (1998): 509–31; Marmor, "Exclusive Legal Positivism," 105–9; Himma, "Inclusive Legal Positivism," 129–35; Jules Coleman, "Incorporationism, Conventionality, and the Practical Difference Thesis," *Legal Theory* 4 (1998): 381–425; Leslie Green, "Positivism and Conventionalism," *Canadian Journal of Law and Jurisprudence* 12 (1999): 35–52.

26. For the idea that social convention provides certainty, see Hart, *Concept of Law*, 94–96.

27. Marmor, "Exclusive Legal Positivism," 107.

from divine revelation, Sherira argues that it is ultimately social convention, reflected in the consensus of the jurists and the nation at large, that confirms and ratifies the exclusive status of the Mishnah as normatively binding.[28]

Legal Pluralism in Classical Rabbinic Literature

In an attempt to refine the discussion surrounding the pluralistic/monistic legacy of Yavneh in classical rabbinic literature, Daniel Boyarin suggested two important interventions in Cohen's new paradigm:[29] First, he argues that the inclusive portrayal of Yavneh is the product, neither of the "real" first-century Yavneh nor of Tannaitic reconstructions of it, but rather of the redactors of the Babylonian Talmud, who "were so successful in hiding themselves that they were able to retroject those patterns and make it seem as if they were a product of a 'real' Yavneh of the first century."[30] The inclusive and pluralistic portrayal of Yavneh is best described, according to Boyarin, in terms of "talmudic mytho-poesis" rather than as "talmudic historiography or memory of the early (tannaitic) period."[31] It is only in the fifth or sixth century, with the literary and cultural activity of the talmudic redactors that "the significant 'Yavneh' of which Shaye Cohen speaks came into being."[32]

While Cohen seems to refer to a more general sense of pluralism, multivocality, and polysemy—be it theoretical or practical—which is arguably typical of rabbinic literature at large, Boyarin focuses on a specific ethos characteristic of the Babylonian Talmud, which refuses a "bottom line" and cherishes endless debate and dialectical argumentation for its own sake.[33] Situating rabbinic pluralism in a broader context of the "end of dialogue" in antiquity,[34] Boyarin traces a diachronic development from an earlier ethos of controlled dialogue in pursuit of epistemic "truth" to one of "sensibility

---

28. For the relation between legal theory and revelatory theology, see Yishai Kiel, "Normative Canonization and Revelatory Theology in the Geonic, Islamic, and Zoroastrian Traditions" (forthcoming).

29. Daniel Boyarin, *Border Lines: The Partition of Judaeo-Christianity*, Divinations (Philadelphia: University of Pennsylvania Press, 2004), 151–201. See also Boyarin, "Anecdotal Evidence: The Yavneh Conundrum, 'Birkat Hamminim', and the Problem of Talmudic Historiography," in *The Mishnah in Contemporary Perspective*, ed. Alan J. Avery-Peck and Jacob Neusner, 2 vols., HdO 65 (Leiden: Brill, 2006), 2:1–35; Boyarin, "Dialectic and Divination in the Talmud," in *The End of Dialogue in Antiquity*, ed. Simon Goldhill (Cambridge: Cambridge University Press, 2009), 217–41.

30. Boyarin, *Border Lines*, 152.

31. Ibid.,154.

32. Ibid., 155. See also Boyarin, "Anecdotal Evidence," 11.

33. On this point, see also Jeffrey L. Rubenstein, *The Culture of the Babylonian Talmud* (Baltimore: Johns Hopkins University Press, 2003), 39–53.

34. Boyarin, "Dialectic and Divination."

of the ultimate contingency of all truth claims, one that goes even beyond the skepticism of the Platonic academy."[35] This, however, does not mean that the earlier Tannaitic Yavneh was not pluralistic and inclusive. Although the latter does not reflect interpretive indeterminacy, an ethos of endless argumentation for its own sake, and epistemic doubt about truth claims, the Tannaitic Yavneh represents an important break from Second Temple Judaism, as, for the first time in Jewish history, an authoritative legal work consciously records dissenting positions on an equal footing.

Second, Boyarin notes that Tannaitic pluralism should be qualified in yet another way, since "this pluralism is pluralism only when looked at from a very particular, rabbinic insider's perspective. When viewed in terms of the dual canonization of the textual forms of Christianity and Judaism, it—like the patristic corpus from which it is otherwise so different—is a highly efficient means for the securing of a 'consensual' orthodoxy."[36] In other words, one must pay attention not only to the overt pluralistic and inclusive rhetoric but also to the mechanisms of exclusion of those who are not part of the "legitimate" rabbinic coalition.[37] Viewed in this light, the pluralistic ethos of the rabbis also partakes at the same time in a discourse of orthodoxy and heresy quite similar to that of contemporaneous patristic literature. This point, however, hinges on the relative significance one attaches to the category of *minim* and *minut* in Tannaitic culture.[38]

In a critique of Boyarin's construction of Yavneh's pluralistic ethos as a product of late Babylonian rabbinic culture, Steven Fraade argued that interpretive polysemy and legal multivocality are, in fact, amply attested in Tannaitic literature, in terms of both textual praxis and ideological/theological thematization.[39] In this context, he deems the expressly pluralistic statements of the Babylonian Talmud (e.g., "These and these are the words of the living God") to be a fuller and more dramatically narrativized and theologized expression of interpretive polysemy and legal multivocality, but an expression that, nonetheless, is already thematized (perhaps more subtly) in Tannaitic literature. "In reality, however, our earliest rabbinic texts exhibit both tendencies, muddying the waters of Boyarin's paradigm, which cannot tolerate the coexistence of the two tendencies in the same texts (or historicized textual layers) and which, there-

35. Boyarin, *Border Lines*, 153.

36. Ibid., 153.

37. See also Hidary, *Dispute for the Sake of Heaven*, 35–36.

38. On this question, see also Adiel Schremer, *Brothers Estranged: Heresy, Christianity, and Jewish Identity in Late Antiquity* (Oxford: Oxford University Press, 2010), 3–24; David M. Grossberg, *Heresy and the Formation of the Rabbinic Community*, TSAJ 168 (Tübingen: Mohr Siebeck, 2017), 50–91.

39. Steven Fraade, "Rabbinic Polysemy and Pluralism Revisited: Between Praxis and Thematization," *AJS Review* 31 (2007): 37.

fore, requires their arrangement in linear historical sequence."[40] Thus, in line with Cohen's observation quoted above regarding the unprecedented attempt of the rabbis to attribute "conflicting legal and exegetical opinions to named individuals who, in spite of their differences, belong to the same fraternity,"[41] Fraade notes that, in none of the Second Temple antecedents of classification and rearrangement of the scattered and sporadic instructions of the Torah, "does the legal material in need of sorting encompass contradictory rulings."[42]

Be the nature of Tannaitic pluralism as it may, several scholars have argued for systematic differences between Palestinian and Babylonian rabbinic attitudes to legal pluralism. Hanina ben-Menahem argued that the Palestinian and Babylonian Talmuds fundamentally differ with regard to judiciary power and the ability of judges to deviate from the letter of the law. He finds that the Palestinian rabbinic insistence on strict judicial conformity to the law and its application is connected with a broader appreciation of uniformity of practice and opinion, whereas the Babylonian rabbinic flexibility on this matter and their willingness to accept the power of judges to exceed the limits of the law are connected with a broader tendency to tolerate and even advocate legal pluralism.[43]

Shlomo Naeh traced important diachronic developments concerning two of the most famous programmatic rabbinic statements connected with legal pluralism.[44] Thus, he argues that the expression "these and these are the words of the living God" (y. Yebam. 1:6, 3b; b. Eruv. 13b; b. Giṭ. 6b). did not initially refer to legal disagreement between the sages but rather to political sectarianism and divisiveness. It is only later on, in the Babylonian Talmud, that this statement came to be associated with legal pluralism.[45] Similarly, the rabbinic homily asserting that "they were all given at the hand of a single shepherd" (b. Ḥag. 3b; t. Soṭth 7:11–12 [ed. Lieberman, 194–95]) initially (in the Tosefta) refers to the problem of recitation and organization of memory in the context of oral transmission, and only later, in the Babylonian Talmud, is associated with legal pluralism.[46]

---

40. Ibid., 7; see also 39.

41. Cohen, "Significance of Yavneh," 46.

42. Fraade, "Rabbinic Polysemy," 15.

43. Hanina Ben-Menahem, *Judicial Deviation in Talmudic Law: Governed by Men, Not by Rules*, Jewish Law in Context 1 (New York: Harwood Academic, 1991), 86–98.

44. Shlomo Naeh, "'Make Your Heart Many Rooms': Another Look at the Utterances of the Sages about Controversy," in *Renewing Jewish Commitment: The Work and Thought of David Hartman* [Hebrew], ed. Avi Sagi and Zvi Zohar (Jerusalem and Tel Aviv: Shalom Hartman Institute and Ha-kibbutz Ha-Meuhad, 2001), 851.

45. Ibid., 862. Compare also Boyarin, *Border Lines*, 157–60; Hanina Ben-Menahem, "Is There Always One Uniquely Correct Answer to a Legal Question in the Talmud?," *Jewish Law Annual* 6 (1987): 168; Christine Hayes, *What's Divine about Divine Law: Early Perspectives* (Princeton: Princeton University Press, 2015), 175 n. 10.

46. Naeh, "Make Your Heart Many Rooms." Compare Steven Fraade, "'A Heart of

Finally, Richard Hidary argued that the Palestinian and Babylonian Talmuds reflect diverging approaches to practical or "particular" legal pluralism. Examining a range of talmudic topics—the status of rules of adjudication (*kelale pesiqa*); the status of local custom (*minhag*); the nature of the rabbinic prohibition against forming factions (*agudot*); the nature of the split between the Houses of Shammai and Hillel; traditions concerning dissenting sages; the law of the rebellious elder (*zaqen mamre*); and the question of nonconformity in the case of an erroneous decision of the court—he finds that the Babylonian Talmud is systematically more tolerant than the Palestinian Talmud to differences in practice and interpretation.[47]

Legal Monism in Sherira's Epistle

No matter where exactly one stands on the question of the unfolding of rabbinic pluralism and the evolvement of the Yavnean myth in the classical talmudic corpus, by the time of the redaction of the Babylonian Talmud, the founding rabbinic gathering at Yavneh was broadly imagined as a touchstone of legal pluralism, multivocality, and polysemy. In what follows, we will see that Sherira's account of the founding moments in the emergence of rabbinic Judaism differs fundamentally from the talmudic antecedents. Sherira's retelling of the origin story of rabbinic Judaism amounts, in fact, to a deconstruction of the pluralistic ethos of classical rabbinic literature along with its mythical foundation.

According to Sherira's epistle, prior to the temple's destruction the content of the Oral Torah revealed at Sinai was unanimously agreed upon and legal disputes were few and far between. In the absence of a textually demarcated version, each master was free to teach the Oral Torah to his students in any style or manner he fancied, but this situation did not generate content-related diversity.[48] However, with the crisis surrounding the temple's destruction and the ensuing Roman persecution, doubts and disputes surrounding the content of the Oral Torah proliferated among the rabbis:

> As long as the temple was in existence … and wisdom proliferated … and there was disagreement among them only with regard to ordination (b. Ḥag. 16a). And even when Shammai and Hillel came forth, they disagreed on only three matters, as we have learned, "Rav Huna said:

Many Chambers': The Theological Hermeneutics of Legal Multivocality," *HTR* 108 (2015): 113–28.

47. Hidary, *Dispute for the Sake of Heaven*, 40–41 (summary of the evidence).

48. On Sherira's idea of fluid articulation and set content, see Blidstein, "Oral Torah," 73–87; Brody, *Geonim of Babylonia*, 278–79.

> Shammai and Hillel disagreed on three matters" (b. Shabb. 15a). And after the temple was destroyed they went to Betar and it too was laid waste and the rabbis were dispersed in every direction.[49] And due to confusion, persecution, oppression and calamity, they did not administer (to their masters) properly[50] and disputes proliferated from the time of Rabban Yohanan ben Zakkai's death, when Rabban Gamliel II (took his place) and R. Dosa ben Harkinas and others of the generation of old were still alive. And although the (opinions of the) House of Shammai were rejected and the law was established according to the House of Hillel (b. Eruv. 13b), they were still disputing other matters in the generation of Rabban Gamliel II, as (evinced by the disputes between) R. Eliezer, who belonged to the House of Shammai (b. Shabb. 130b), and R. Yehoshua, both of whom were disciples of Rabban Yohanan ben Zakkai.[51]

Interestingly, Sherira stresses that disputes multiplied among the rabbis, not immediately following the temple's destruction but mainly "from the time of Rabban Yohanan ben Zakkai's death." Later in the epistle, he explains that Rabban Yohanan ben Zakkai's tenure at Yavneh was a peaceful interim, characterized by centralized rabbinic authority and legal monism, amid a traumatic period. It was only after the death of Rabban Yohanan ben Zakkai, therefore, that disputes proliferated. The latter's tenure at Yavneh is described by Sherira in the following passages:

> And after (the tenure of) Rabban Shimon b. Gamliel, who was killed, Rabban Yohanan ben Zakkai came forth, and he lived at the time of the temple's destruction. And when Vespasian let him out (of besieged Jerusalem), his students R. Eliezer and R. Yehoshua went out with him. And he demanded of Vespasian (to spare) the dynasty of the house of Rabban Gamliel (and Yavneh and its sages).[52] And when Rabban Yohanan ben Zakkai and the sages reached a state of tranquility at Yavneh, he enacted ten enactments, of which it is said in the Mishnah: "once the temple was destroyed, Rabban Yohanan ben Zakkai enacted" (m. Rosh Hash. 4:1–4;

49. Sherira is summarizing here the failure of the two major Jewish revolts in Palestine, in 66–70 and 132–136 CE, and the destruction of the two cities connected with these revolts, Jerusalem and Betar.

50. That is, the students did not take proper care to register and record their masters' teachings. For the various meanings of *shimush ḥakhamim*, see Yishai Kiel, "The Authority of the Sages in the Babylonian Talmud: A Zoroastrian Perspective," *Shenaton Ha-mishpat Ha-ivri* 27 (2012–2013): 145–47.

51. Based on the edition of Lewin, 10–11 (French recension). The translation is my own.

52. The clause "Yavneh and its sages" is added in the Spanish recension of the epistle following Rabban Yohanan ben Zakkai's request of Vespasian according to b. Giṭ. 56a. For the different version of Vespasian's "gift," see the recent summary and discussion in Meir Ben Shahar, "The Prophecy to Vespasian," in *Josephus and the Rabbis* [Hebrew], ed. Tal Ilan and Vered Noam, 2 vols. (Jerusalem: Ben Zvi, 2017), 2:604–64.

> m. Sukkah 3:12). First, he was in Bror Hayyil (b. Sanh. 32b) and then he came to Yavneh.[53]
>
> And it was an important time when they reached a state of tranquility after the temple's destruction. At that time, they sat down in order to retrieve their laws, which were as if lost (to them) due to the calamity of destruction and persecution and the disputes of the Houses of Shammai and Hillel.[54]

According to Sherira, Rabban Yohanan ben Zakkai's peaceful tenure at Yavneh was a time of restoration, backed up by Vespasian's imperial authorization, in which the sages were able to overcome internal strife and the recent dispersion and loss of rabbinic tradition. This period of unity, which was followed again by an age of diversity and persecution, prefigured another peaceful era: the tenure of Rabbi Yehudah the Patriarch ("Rabbi") more than a century later. Aided by imperial authorization and the unanimous submission/agreement of his colleagues, Rabbi was able to (partly) restore the original state of legal monism and unanimity that prevailed prior to the temple's destruction:

> Heaven bestowed authority upon Rabbi together with his Torah, for his entire generation was subservient to him all his years. As we have learned (b. Giṭ. 59a): "Rava the son of R. Abba said, and some say (it was) R. Hillel the son of Rabbi: from the days of Moses until Rabbi, we have not found Torah and authority combined in one person." … In his days, the rabbis were spared all persecution due to the love Antoninus had for him (b. Abod. Zar. 10b). He [Rabbi] then decided to arrange/systematize the laws, so that the rabbis would recite them uniformly rather than each his own version. Since, those early rabbis before the destruction of the temple … were aided from heaven and the underlying rationales of the Torah were as clear to them as the law given to Moses at Sinai and there was no difference (of opinion) and no dispute (among them), as we have learned (t. Ḥag. 2:9; t. Sanh. 7:1; b. Sanh. 88b): "(It says in a) *baraita*: R. Yose said: initially, there was no dispute in Israel … once the students of Shammai and Hillel increased, who did not properly administer (to their masters), disputes proliferated in Israel and the Torah became as two. And the sages who came afterwards in the days of Rabban Gamliel and his son R. Shimon were still debating and arguing and there were disputes among the Tannaim and it was not possible for them all to recite uniformly. And in the days of Rabbi, their matters were aided, so that the words of the Mishnah seemed as if pronounced by the Almighty himself and they were like a sign and wonder.[55]

---

53. Ed. Lewin, 74–75 (French recension).
54. Ed. Lewin, 12 (French recension).
55. Ed. Lewin, 21–23 (French recension).

While the state of textual and stylistic uniformity (*peh ehad*) achieved with the composition of the Mishnah differs from the state of unanimity that prevailed before the temple's destruction, which was characterized by agreement of content and stylistic fluidity, Sherira seems to suggest that Rabbi had, in some sense, restored the initial state of legal monism, in which "the underlying rationales of the Torah were as clear to them as the law given to Moses at Sinai and there was no difference (of opinion) and no dispute" (ולית חלוף ולית פלוגתא). Sherira acknowledges, of course, that at least some of the disputes that emerged in the Tannaitic period were not resolved by Rabbi and his generation but rather were recorded in the Mishnah for posterity. He insists, nonetheless, that Rabbi strove to resolve, or at least minimize, the disputes to the best of his ability, in an attempt to restore the original state of unanimity. In this context, stylistic uniformity constitutes only one aspect of a broader project of substantive unification and systematization of rabbinic law.

In the course of his celebration of legal monism and the value of unanimity, Sherira quotes from the talmudic corpus rather selectively, while conveniently neglecting the classical ethos of pluralism, multivocality, and polysemy. He quotes neither the idea that "these and these are the words of the living God" nor that "they were all given at the hand of a single shepherd," stressing instead that "initially, there was no dispute in Israel ... once the students of Shammai and Hillel who did not properly administer (to their masters) multiplied, disputes proliferated in Israel and the Torah became as two."[56] In so doing, Sherira does not only reject the notion of theoretical pluralism (i.e., the existence of multiple correct answers to a given legal question), but voices intolerance toward practical pluralism, attributing the emergence of disputes to the unfortunate historical contingencies of persecution and inattentiveness.[57]

Sherira's selective quoting from the classical talmudic corpus is evident in another important context, namely, his discussion of the reasons for, and legal ramifications of, Rabbi's decision to record minority opinions:[58]

---

56. For Sherira's selective quoting in this regard, see Blidstein, "Oral Torah," 75.

57. Compare David Sklare, *Samuel ben Ḥofni Gaon and His Cultural World: Texts and Studies, Études* sur le judaïsme médiévale 18 (Leiden: Brill, 1996), 255–57; Marc Herman, "Systematizing God's Law: Rabbanite Jurisprudence in the Islamic World from the Tenth to the Thirteenth Centuries" (PhD diss., University of Pennsylvania, 2016), 82–86.

58. For the possible impact of Roman law, see, e.g., Yaakov Elman, "Order, Sequence, and Selection: The Mishnah's Anthological Choices," in *The Anthology in Jewish Literature*, ed. David Stern (New York: Oxford University Press, 2004), 65–70 (mentioning also comparable Syriac and Persian parallels from a later period). Cf. Jacob Neusner, "The Mishnah in Roman and Christian Contexts," in *The Mishnah in Contemporary Perspective*, ed. Alan J. Avery-Peck and Jacob Neusner, 2 vols., HdO 65, 87 (Leiden: Brill, 2002–2006), 1:121–34.

> And he [Rabbi] also mentioned in it [the Mishnah] the essence and root of all rabbinic disputes. Since there were rabbis who heard (the teachings of) those dissenting authorities and dissenting minorities and (then) recited those teachings anonymously. If someone were to hear them, the one who heard them might come to err. But since it is explained (in the Mishnah) that such and such has occurred, doubt is lifted as it says in the Mishnah: "R. Yehudah said: why were the words of the individual mentioned amongst those of the majority—to annul (their legal validity)' (m. ʿEd. 1:6). For, if a person says 'I have thus heard,' we say to him 'you heard the words of rabbi so and so, but the halakhah was not decided in accordance with his opinion.'"[59]

Sherira's quotation from Mishnah ʿEduyot 1:6 to the effect that minority opinions were mentioned in the Mishnah only in order to deny their legal validity ironically relies on a minority position (R. Yehudah) that seems to contradict the anonymous voice of the Mishnah (m. ʿEd. 1:5), according to which it is taught: "why do they record the opinion of the individual against that of the majority, as the law is decided in accordance with the opinion of the majority? So that if a subsequent court approves of the opinion of the individual, it may rely on him."[60] In stark contrast to the monistic position of R. Yehudah adopted by Sherira, the underlying logic of the anonymous Mishnah is rather similar to the argument voiced in contemporary debate in support of the norm of publishing court dissents and concurrences. As put by Cass Sunstein, "a dissent might turn out to have desirable effects on the future development of the law. Perhaps Justices will eventually view it persuasive."[61] It would seem that Sherira consciously subverts the Mishnah's pluralistic ethos expressed in the idea that dissents were recorded for the sake of future development of the law. Instead, he prefers the monistic position attributed to R. Yehudah, according to which dissents were recorded in the Mishnah only in order to annul their legal validity and make sure they are not followed.

As part of the narrative framework for his monistic theory of the law, Sherira reconstructs a series of constitutional moments in the early history of rabbinic Judaism—beginning with the gathering at Yavneh and ending with the composition of the Mishnah—in which a state of monism and unanimity prevailed among the sages. Indeed, he portrays these founding moments in terms of the restoration of a glorious past. His reconstruction of these moments as a cornerstone of legal monism, however, seems to under-

---

59. Ed. Lewin, 29–30 (French recension).

60. Compare also t. ʿEd. 1:4, and see the discussion in Hanina Ben-Menahem, "Controversy," in *Windows onto Jewish Legal Culture: Fourteen Exploratory Essays*, ed. Hanina Ben-Menahem, Arye Edrei, and Neil S. Hecht, 2 vols. (London: Routledge, 2011), 1:20–21.

61. Cass Sunstein, "Unanimity and Disagreement on the Supreme Court," *Cornell Law Review* 100 (2015): 802–3.

mine and subvert the pluralistic retrojection of Yavneh and its ethos of multivocality and polysemy that dominates the classical talmudic corpus.

Beyond the submission/consensus of the sages surrounding Rabbi's codification project, Sherira stresses that the Mishnah was, at the same time, unanimously accepted by the entirety of Israel:[62]

> But the reliance of Israel is on those laws (contained in the Mishnah) and all of Israel have accepted them, as we have witnessed, in faith, and there is not a single person who disputes this matter.[63]

> And when everyone saw the beauty of the Mishnah's arrangement and the truth of its reasoning and the precision of (its) words, they all abandoned those (other) tannaitic teachings they had been reciting. And these halakhot (contained in the Mishnah) spread throughout Israel and became our halakhot.[64]

While the Mishnah purportedly encompasses the revelatory content of the Oral Torah and is endowed with textual, stylistic, and organizational "perfection" similar to the inimitable characteristics attributed to the Qur'an,[65] its authority and canonicity as a normative source rest not on these qualities but on the social fact that the Mishnah was unanimously accepted as authoritative by the sages and the nation at large. Notably, consensus does not function in this equation as an independent legal source, but rather as a social mechanism of validation and ratification of the Mishnah's canonical status.[66] Sherira sought, therefore, to ground the authority and validity of the system's sources—that is, the Mishnah and Talmud—in social convention, reflected in the unanimous acceptance of these sources by the sages (the system's "officials") and the entirety of Israel ("general compliance"), thus satisfying the fundamental positivist conditions for a valid rule of recognition.

Sherira's monistic reconstruction of the constitutional moments in the

---

62. Compare David Weiss Halivni, "The Reception Accorded to Rabbi Judah's Mishnah," in *Jewish and Christian Self-Definition*, vol. 2, *Aspects of Judaism in the Graeco-Roman Period*, ed. E. P. Sanders, A. I. Baumgarten, and A. Mendelson (Philadelphia: Fortress, 1981), 204–12.

63. Ed. Lewin, 30 (French recension).

64. Ed. Lewin, 30 (French recension).

65. See Fishman, "Claims about the Mishnah," 67; Talya Fishman, *Becoming the People of the Talmud: Oral Torah as Written Tradition in Medieval Jewish Cultures*, Jewish Culture and Contexts (Philadelphia: University of Pennsylvania Press, 2011), 41–42. For the inimitable characteristics of the Qur'an, see Richard C. Martin, "Inimitability," in *Encyclopaedia of the Qur'ān*, ed. J. D. McAuliffe (Leiden: Brill, 2001), 526–36.

66. A similar mechanism of social validation seems to govern the Babylonian Talmud's authority as well (ed. Lewin, 90–91). Cf. Maimonides's Introduction to Mishneh Torah 14; Gideon Libson, "Maimonides' Halakhic Writing against the Background of Muslim Law and Jurisprudence of the Period," in *Maimonides: Conservatism, Originality, Revolution* [Hebrew], ed. Aviezer Ravitzky, 2 vols. (Jerusalem: Shazar, 2008), 1:280 n. 102.

emergence of rabbinic Judaism—the gathering at Yavneh and the composition of the Mishnah—should be examined, however, not only from an abstracted jurisprudential perspective but also in a concrete historical context. The "historicity" of Sherira's account, to be sure, lies not in the events he depicts but rather in the cultural context of the Abbasid period in which he himself operated and to which he responded. In that sense, the unity and consensus surrounding Rabban Yohanan b. Zakkai's legal activity at Yavneh and Rabbi's codification project seem to reflect Sherira's discomfort with the schisms and disputes that pervaded his own time, both within the Rabbinite community (as described in the second part of the epistle) and between Rabbinite and Qaraite authorities, and his longing for the restoration of unanimity and consensus.

Legal Consensus in Early Islamic Legal Thought

Sherira's monistic jurisprudence, grounded in a founding myth of unanimity, should be appreciated not only in the historical context of intra-Jewish polemics and schisms but also in the light of contemporaneous Islamicate discourse on legal consensus, connected with the Islamic concept of *ijmāʿ*.[67]

While the nature and scope of *ijmāʿ* were subject to much debate in early Islamic jurisprudence, many jurists seem to hold that consensus provides epistemic certainty to matters not firmly rooted in the revealed sources. Others go even farther in asserting that the Qur'an and Hadith derive their very authority and validity as legal sources from the social fact of consensus. While the authority of the Qur'an and Hadith is vested in revelation, it is argued, it is only through consensus that this authority is validated. Thus, adherence to the content of the revealed sources is predicated on the assumption of social convention confirming their legal validity.[68] One of the major points of contestation surrounding the Islamic doctrine of consensus concerns the question of whether *ijmāʿ* refers to

67. For Sherira and the Islamic doctrine of *ijmāʿ*, see, e.g., Blidstein, "Oral Torah," 13; Uziel Fuchs, *The Geonic Talmud: The Attitude of Babylonian Geonim to the Text of the Babylonian Talmud* [Hebrew] (Jerusalem: Magnes, 2017), 108 n. 52. The present discussion will delve deeper into this suggestion, while extending the comparison to Zoroastrian views on consensus. The literature on *ijmāʿ* is vast, but see esp. Wael B. Hallaq, "On the Authoritativeness of Sunni Consensus," *International Journal of Middle East Studies* 18 (1986): 427–54; Aron Zyzow, *The Economy of Certainty: An Introduction to the Typology of Islamic Legal Theory*, Resources in Arabic and Islamic Studies 2 (Atlanta: Lockwood, 2013), 113–56; Joseph Lowry, *Early Islamic Legal Theory: The Risāla of Muḥammad Ibn Idrīs Al-Shāfiʿī*, Studies in Islamic Law and Society 30 (Leiden: Brill, 2007), 319–58.

68. See, e.g., Hamilton A. R. Gibb, *Mohammedanism*, 2nd ed. (Oxford: Oxford University Press, 1962), 96; N. D Anderson and N. J. Coulson, "Islamic Law in Contemporary Cultural Change," *Saeculum* 18 (1967): 26. Cf. Zyzow, *Economy of Certainty*, 114 ("An examination of the classical texts, however, does not support these great claims made for *ijmāʿ*").

the agreement of the Islamic nation at large (*'umma*) or only that of the jurists.[69] In the present context, I note that both types of consensus contemplated by Islamic jurists—namely, that of the jurists and that of the nation at large—are similarly reflected in Sherira's epistle. The authority of the legal sources is based on their unanimous acceptance by officials, on the one hand, and general compliance, on the other hand.

Scholars have noted that *ijmāʿ* is alluded to by other rabbinic authorities as well (using either the Arabic term or a Hebrew equivalent), a fact that seems to suggest the participation of rabbinic authorities in a broader Islamicate discourse focused on legal consensus.[70] Some of the rabbinic authorities who mention *ijmāʿ*—whether by accepting, rejecting, or limiting its authority—include Saʿadya Gaon,[71] Samuel ben Ḥofni Gaon,[72] Hayya Gaon,[73] Yehudah Ha-Levi,[74] and Maimonides,[75] to name just a few. In fact, the varying rabbinic accounts of legal consensus largely reflect the range of Islamic usage, spanning from consensus of the nation at large, through the unanimous agreement of the jurists, to various permutations of the agreement of the many.

In the present context, I note that Sherira's subversion of the classical rabbinic ethos of legal pluralism, his innovative reconstruction of rabbinic legal theory (and its mythical underpinnings) through the lens of legal monism, and the central role he assigns to consensus and unanimity in this framework, are significantly illuminated by contemporaneous Islamic discourse. For both Sherira and his Muslim contemporaries, consensus of the jurists or the nation at large functioned, both in terms of epistemic certainty and corroboration of the content of revelation and in terms of social validation/ratification of the legal sources.

---

69. For the different positions, see Joseph Schacht, *The Origins of Muhammadan Jurisprudence* (Oxford: Clarendon, 1950), 88–94; Zyzow, *Economy of Certainty*, 121–25; Lowry, *Early Islamic Legal Theory*, 321–22, 350–54; Wael Hallaq, *A History of Islamic Legal Theories: An Introduction to Sunnī Uṣūl al-Fiqh* (Cambridge: Cambridge University Press, 1997), 27–28.

70. For recent summaries and discussions, see, e.g., Gideon Libson, *Jewish and Islamic Law: A Comparative Study of Custom during the Geonic Period*, Harvard Series in Islamic Law 1 (Cambridge: Islamic Legal Studies Program, Harvard Law School, 2003), 68–76; Herman, *Systematizing God's Law*, 66–69. For an attempt to trace the origins of *ijmāʿ* in the earlier talmudic tradition, see Judith Romney Wegner, "Islamic and Talmudic Jurisprudence: The Four Roots of Islamic Law and Their Talmudic Counterparts," *American Journal of Legal History* 26 (1982): 25–71, here 39–44, 55–58.

71. Moshe Zucker, "Qeṭaʿim mi-kitāb taḥṣīl al-sharāʾiʿ al-samāʿīya le-rasag," *Tarbiz* 41 (1973): 373–410, here 404–5.

72. Sklare, *Samuel ben Ḥofni Gaon*, 163.

73. Fishman, *Becoming the People of the Talmud*, 50–51; Fuchs, *Geonic Talmud*, 107–8.

74. Ehud Krinis, "The Arabic Background of the Kuzari," *Journal of Jewish Thought and Philosophy* 21 (2013): 1–56, here 50.

75. Libson, "Maimonides' Halakhic Writing," 278–85.

Consensus and Constitutional Myth in Islamicate Zoroastrianism

Not unlike the classical rabbinic endorsement of legal pluralism, the Pahlavi Zand (the oral redaction of which can be dated with some probability to the Sasanian period) reflects ubiquitous interpretive polysemy and diversity of opinions, with very few attempts to reconcile, harmonize or otherwise systemize the conflicting positions.[76] A conscious statement to that effect, likely reflecting theoretical (and not merely practical) pluralism, is attributed to the sixth-century[77] scholar-priest Kay-Ādur-bōzēd:

> Kay-Ādur-bōzēd said: that is, the teachers of old (*pōryōtkēšān*) did not teach the Avesta without dissent, (but, regarding) this decision they were unanimous (*ham-dādestān*).[78]

In line with the pluralistic ethos advocated in classical rabbinic sources, Kay-Ādur-bōzēd seems to hold that diversity and multivocality are essential features of the legal tradition, going back to the revered teachers of old. While he does not go as far as asserting theological pluralism in a manner similar to statements found in the classical rabbinic tradition (e.g., "these and these are the words of the living God"), he certainly understands legal pluralism to be an essential facet of the legal system, rather than a mere historical contingency. Legal diversity is the result of neither persecution nor inattentive students, but an essential feature of the legal system.

The ethos of legal pluralism that governed the Zoroastrian legal tradition in the Sasanian period underwent a major shift toward legal monism

---

76. For diversity and disputes in the Zand, see Philippe Gignoux, "La controverse dans le mazdéisme tardif," in *La controverse religieuse et ses formes*, ed. Alain Le Boulluec (Paris: Cerf, 1995), 127–49; Alberto Cantera, *Studien zur Pahlavi-Übersetzung des Avesta* (Wiesbaden: Harrassowitz, 2004), 164–239; Shai Secunda, "On the Age of the Zoroastrian Sages of the Zand," *Iranica Antiqua* 47 (2012): 317–49; Kiel, "Authority of the Sages," 157–60. For institutional-judicial diversity in the Sasanian period, see, e.g., Shaul Shaked, "Administrative Functions of Priests," in *Proceedings of the First European Conference of Iranian Studies Held in Turin, September 7th–11th, 1987 by the Societas Iranologica Europaea*, ed. Gherardo Gnoli and Antonio Panaino, 2 vols., Serie orientale Roma 67 (Rome: Istituto Italiano per il Medio ed Estremo Oriente, 1990), 1:261–73; Touraj Daryaee, *Sasanian Persia: The Rise and Fall of an Empire* (New York: I. B. Tauris, 2009), 126–33; Janos Jany, *Judging in the Islamic, Jewish and Zoroastrian Legal Traditions: A Comparison of Theory and Practice* (Farnham, Surrey: Ashgate, 2012), 54–68; Uriel I. Simonsohn, *A Common Justice: The Legal Allegiances of Christians and Jews under Early Islam* (Philadelphia: University of Pennsylvania Press, 2011), 25–62.

77. For the dating of this jurist, see Secunda, "On the Age," 343.

78. Nirangestān 2.28.43 (cf. Firoze M. Kotwal and Philip G. Kreyenbroek, eds., *The Hērbedestān and Nērangestān*, 4 vols. (Paris: Association pour l'avancement des études iraniennes, 1992–2009), 3:102–3.

in the early Abbasid period. It is in this context that the concept of legal consensus (*ham-dādestānīh*) comes to the fore of the jurisprudential discourse. Indeed, the range of opinions on the nature and scope of legal consensus found in Geonic and Islamic sources is similarly reflected in contemporaneous Pahlavi writings.[79] Certain Pahlavi accounts from the Abbasid period present consensus as an independent source of law on a par with the textual authority vested in the Avesta and Zand. Thus, for example, the eighth book of the Dēnkard asserts, "And regarding that the judge should make a decision from the Avesta and Zand or from the consensus [*ham-dādestānīh*] of the good."[80] It is not entirely clear whether the consensus of the "good" (generally, a reference to Zoroastrians in good standing) refers in this passage to the entire community of the faithful or only to scholar-priests. But, in any event, this account of consensus as a source of law differs considerably from earlier references to consensus, especially those found in the Sasanian collection of (real and hypothetical) case law, the Mādayān ī Hazar Dādestān ("Book of a Thousand Judgments"), in which *ham-dādestānīh* is employed in a much narrower and anecdotal sense to denote the agreement of particular jurists on a particular legal matter.[81]

In other Pahlavi traditions from the Abbasid period, *ham-dādestānīh* functions, not as a source of law but rather as a mechanism of social validation and epistemic and theological corroboration. Mānuščihr, a ninth-century Zoroastrian jurist and high priest[82] who understood the doctrine of consensus in this manner, reconstructed a founding myth in which the consensus of jurists serves to ratify and validate the normative and canonical authority of the textual sources of the law, the Avesta and Zand. In fact, Mānuščihr's account is remarkably similar to Sherira's monistic

---

79. For the relationship between the Islamic doctrine of *ijmā'* and the Zoroastrian doctrine of *ham-dādestānīh*, see, e.g., Jany, *Judging*, 171–78; Jany, "The Four Sources of Law in Zoroastrian and Islamic Jurisprudence," *Islamic Law and Society* 12 (2005): 291–332, here 301–2. Cf. Kiel, "Authority of the Sages," 156–57.

80. Dēnkard 8.20.69, in Dhanjishah Meherjibhai Madan, ed., *The Complete Text of the Pahlavi Dinkard* (Bombay: Society for the Promotion of Researches into the Zoroastrian Religion, 1911), 712; Mark J. Dresden, ed., *Dēnkart: A Pahlavi Text, Facsimile Edition of the Manuscript B of the K.R. Cama Oriental Institute Bombay* (Bombay: K. R. Cama Oriental Institute; Wiesbaden: Harrassowitz, 1966), 541.

81. See, e.g., Mādayān ī Hazar Dādestān 41.5, 46.14, 4.4–9, 42.5–9; Mādayān ī Hazar Dādestān (Part 2) 11.12–17; Nirangestān 2.28.43 (quoted above). And see Jany, "Four Sources," 301–2.

82. On Mānuščihr, see Mahmoud Jaafari-Dehaghi, *Dādestān ī Dēnīg*, part 1, *Transcription, Translation and Commentary*, Studia Iranica 20 (Paris: Association pour l'avancement des études iraniennes, 1998), 23–26. A critical edition and translation of the first two of Mānuščihr's epistles was published piecemeal by Maneck Kanga. For the parts quoted below, compare Maneck F. Kanga, "Epistle 1, Ch. 4, of Mānuščihr ī Juwān-jamān: A Critical Study," *Indian Linguistics* 27 (1966): 46–57.

reconstruction of the constitutional moments of the emergence of rabbinic Judaism. According to Mānuščihr, the sixth-century Sasanian King Xusrō, known from other Pahlavi sources to engage in the fighting-off of heresies and false doctrines,[83] summoned a council of jurists who were charged with the canonization of the sacred Zoroastrian Tradition:[84]

> It was like when Weh-šābuhr showed in the assembly of Xusrō of immortal soul, king of kings, son of Kawād, the twenty-one divisions (of the Avesta and Zand)[85] so that the sages abided by it. And they sealed a document [*nibišt āwišt*] so that it was the way the sages (agreed) with it and as it had been decided. And, afterwards, the sages agreed with all the decisions he showed them and they were unanimous [*ham-dādestān*]: to regard (them) as something special, as being on the level of certainty, and in firm usage.[86]

Not unlike Sherira's depiction of the canonization of the Mishnah by Rabbi, Mānuščihr envisions the canonization of the Avesta and Zand by Weh-šābuhr, a Zoroastrian jurist and high priest (*mowbedān mowbed*) who lived during the reign of Xusrō.[87] Like the favorable attitude exhibited by Antoninus toward Rabbi and the imperial authorization of his codification project (and the permission granted by Vespasian to Rabban Yohanan ben Zakkai to conduct his legal restoration project in Yavneh), Mānuščihr stresses that the canonization of the Avesta and Zand took place at a council summoned and authorized by the Sasanian king Xusrō. As with the elevated status of the Mishnah according to Sherira, Mānuščihr emphasizes the unique normative, epistemological, and revelatory status of the Avesta and Zand ("to regard them as something special, as being on the level of certainty, and in firm usage"), which were believed to contain the complete articulation of Ahura Mazda's law revealed to Zarathustra.[88] Furthermore, as with the undivided submission of Rabbi's colleagues,

83. See Dēnkard 4.15–21 (ed. Madan, 412–13; ed. Dresden, 321–22); Shai Secunda, *The Iranian Talmud: Reading the Bavli in Its Sasanian Context*, Divinations (Philadelphia: University of Pennsylvania Press, 2013), 59.

84. Another report of Xusrō's council focuses on the "fighting off of heresy" and grapples with disbelief in the authoritativeness of the Zand. See Zand ī Wahman Yasn 2.1–4. See Carlo G. Cereti, ed., *The Zand ī Wahman Yasn: A Zoroastrian Apocalypse*, Serie Orientale 75 (Rome: Istituto Italiano per il Medio ed Estremo Oriente, 1995), 134 (transcription), 150 (translation); Secunda, "On the Age," 321–24.

85. For the twenty-one *nasks* of the Avesta and Zand, see Yuhan Vevaina, "Enumerating the *Dēn*: Textual Taxonomies, Cosmological Deixis, and Numerological Speculations in Zoroastrianism," *HR* 50 (2010): 111–43.

86. Epistles of Mānuščihr 1.4.17–18 ([T420–421]); trans. Prods Oktor Skjaervo (private communication).

87. For the historical identification of this figure, see Secunda, "On the Age," 323–25.

88. See Yishai Kiel, "Reinventing Mosaic Torah in Ezra-Nehemiah in the Light of the Law (*dāta-*) of Ahura Mazda and Zarathustra," *JBL* 136 (2017): 325.

Mānuščihr stresses the unanimous agreement of Weh-šābuhr's colleagues at the council and their submission to his decisions.

According to Mānuščihr, consensus (*ham-dādestānīh*) functions not merely as a mechanism of epistemic corroboration ("being on the level of certainty") but also as a form of social validation of the canonical and authoritative status of the Avesta and Zand as legal sources. In this context, consensus does not function as an independent source of law (although, as we have seen, other Pahlavi accounts indeed construe consensus in such a manner), but rather as a form of social convention that serves to ratify and validate the authoritative status of the Avesta and Zand as normative sources. Despite the revelatory origin of the contents of the Avesta and Zand, it is, in the end, the agreement of the jurists that bestows normative authority upon the Avesta and Zand as binding legal sources. In line with Sherira's reconstruction of the founding mythical gathering at Yavneh, which prefigured and ultimately led to the Mishnah's canonization by virtue of the unanimous agreement of the jurists, Mānuščihr similarly reconstructs the founding mythical moment in which the Avesta and Zand were canonized and Ahura Mazdā's revelation to Zarathustra was textually demarcated by Weh-šābuhr and the unanimous agreement of his colleagues in the assembly of Xusrō. For Mānuščihr, not unlike Sherira, the consensus of the jurists functions not as an independent source of law but more in line with a positivist convention validating the legal sources.

In sum, we saw that Sherira's monistic and centralistic attempt to revolutionize rabbinic jurisprudence, couched in the retelling of the founding moments of rabbinic Judaism—the gathering at Yavneh and the Mishnah's codification—is significantly informed by contemporaneous Islamicate legal culture and its fixation with legal consensus. While various Jewish, Muslim, and Zoroastrian authors participated in this broader discourse, we saw that Sherira's account is particularly illuminated by contemporaneous attempts to situate the jurisprudential shift from legal pluralism to monism that took place in the early Abbasid period in the context of a myth of origins narrating the founding moments of the tradition's canonization.

Sherira was not "influenced" by the surrounding Islamicate legal culture so much as he was an integral part of it. The present findings join those of other studies in portraying a complex and dynamic picture of cultural exchange in the Abbasid period, in the context of which Jewish, Islamic, and Zoroastrian jurists—who were members of distinct, and yet intersecting, normative communities—engaged in a mutual effort to constitute and create legal meaning within the confines of their respective communities, but, at the same time, negotiated these particularities within the broader framework of Islamicate legal culture.

On Medieval Jewish Prophecy

From "Deus Vult" to "The Will of the Creator"

IVAN G. MARCUS
Yale University

Jewish tradition claims that biblical prophecy ended with the early Second Temple figures Haggai, Zechariah, and finally Malachi (My Messenger). And although a rabbinic tradition maintains that "a sage is preferable to a prophet" (*hakham 'adif mi-navi*), an oracular voice (*bat qol*) continued to be relied on for some matters.[1] Beyond late antiquity, different types of Jewish prophecy persisted into medieval times. To date, scholars have provided various examples, and there is a diverse bibliography on the subject, but we do not yet have a comprehensive study.[2] In honor of a

1. For rabbinic reference to the end of prophecy, see b. B. Bat. 14b, and for the saying, see b. B. Bat. 12a. In addition, see Ephraim E. Urbach, "Matai Paseqah ha-Nevu'ah?" *Tarbiz* 17 (1945): 1–11; Abraham Joshua Heschel, "'Al Ruah ha-Qodesh bimei ha-Beinayim," in *Alexander Marx Jubilee Volume*, ed. Saul Lieberman, 2 vols. (New York: Jewish Theological Seminary, 1950), Hebrew volume, 175–208; Heschel, *Prophetic Inspiration after the Prophets: Maimonides and other Medieval Authorities*, edited by Morris M. Faierstein (Hoboken, NJ: Ktav, 1996); Alon Goshen-Gottstein, "'The Sage Is Superior to the Prophet': The Conception of Torah through the Prism of the History of Jewish Exegesis" [Hebrew], in *Limmud ve-Da'at be-Mahshavah Yehudit* [*Study and Knowledge in Jewish Thought*], ed. Howard Kreisel, 2 vols. (Beer Sheva: Ben-Gurion University of the Negev, 2006), 2:37–77; Elliot R. Wolfson, "'Sage is Preferable to Prophet': Revisioning Midrashic Imagination," in *Scriptural Exegesis: The Shapes of Culture and the Religious Imagination; Essays in Honour of Michael Fishbane*, ed. Deborah A. Green and Laura S. Lieber (Oxford: Oxford University Press, 2009), 186–210; and Aaron Rothkoff, "Bat Kol," in *EncJud* (2007) 3:213.

2. See Philip S. Alexander, "A Sixtieth Part of Prophecy: The Problem of Continuing Revelation in Judaism," in *Words Remembered, Texts Renewed: Essays in Honour of John F. A. Sawyer*, ed. Jon Davies, Graham Harvey, and Wilfred G. E. Watson, JSOTSup 105 (Sheffield: Sheffield Academic, 1995), 414–33; L. Stephen Cook, *On the Question of the "Cessation of Prophecy" in Ancient Judaism*, TSAJ 145 (Tübingen: Mohr Siebeck, 2011); Joseph Dan, "The End of Prophecy and Its Significance to Jewish Thought" [Hebrew], *Alpayyim* 30 (2007): 257–88; Fazlur Rahman, *Prophecy in Islam: Philosophy and Orthodoxy*, Ethical and Religious Classics of East and West 21 (London: Allen & Unwin, 1958); Matt Goldish, *The Sabbatean Prophets* (Cambridge: Harvard University Press, 2004); Boaz Huss, "'A Sage Is Preferable than a Prophet': Rabbi Shimon Bar Yohai and Moses in the Zohar" [Hebrew], *Kabbalah* 4 (1999): 103–39; Niels Christian Hvidt, *Christian Prophecy, The Post-biblical Tradition* (Oxford: Oxford University Press, 2007); Moshe Idel, "Lawyers and Mystics in Judaism: A Prolegomenon for a State of

much-admired colleague and longtime friend, I offer these musings as a small contribution to that story, developed out of an earlier Hebrew essay now significantly revised. [3]

Collective Christian Prophecy in 1095

In the late eleventh and twelfth centuries, groups of Christians and Jews living in medieval Europe willingly and suddenly engaged in unprecedented religious practices. Although a charismatic pope's words triggered the first acts, the Christians who obeyed him believed that God was speaking to them directly in a form of prophetic revelation. Jews, too, were swept away to act in totally unprecedented ways, confident that God was commanding them to do things that others condemned as murder. The religious enthusiasm provoked by this medieval prophetic moment then ended as suddenly as it had begun, but it left an indelible impression on Western Christian and Jewish imaginations.

The first case is the outbreak of religious enthusiasm that occurred in connection with the beginnings of what became the First Crusade and Jewish innovative martyrdom practices that accompanied a horrific set of anti-Jewish attacks in medieval Germany. Both the Crusader attacks and the Jewish acts of martyrdom were triggered by a belief that God was revealing his will in imminent acts of "collective prophecy."

The beginning of what became the First Crusade, an armed pilgrimage to liberate Christian holy places in Jerusalem, was a speech that Pope Urban II made on the 27th of November, 1095, at the Council of Clermont.

Prophecy in Jewish Mysticism," [NYU] Straus Institute Working Paper No.10/10, 2010; Alex P. Jassen, *Mediating the Divine: Prophecy and Revelation in the Dead Sea Scrolls and Second Temple Judaism*, STDJ 68 (Leiden: Brill, 2007); Marjorie Reeves, *Influence of Prophecy in the Later Middle Ages: A Study in Joachimism* (Oxford: Clarendon, 1969; repr., Notre Dame, IN: University of Notre Dame Press, 1993); Gershom G. Scholem, "Abraham Abulafia and the Doctrine of Prophetic Kabbalah," in his *Major Trends in Jewish Mysticism* (New York: Schocken Books, 1961), 119–55; Scholem, *Ursprung und Anfänge der Kabbala*, SJ 3 (Berlin: de Gruyter, 1962), 110–18; Hillel Schwartz, *The French Prophets: The History of a Millenarian Group in Eighteenth-Century England* (Berkeley: University of California Press, 1980); Benjamin D. Sommer, "Did Prophecy Cease? Evaluating a Re-evaluation," *JBL* 115 (1996): 31–47; and Bertrand Taithe and Tim Thornton, eds., *Prophecy: The Power of Inspired Language in History 1300–2000*, Themes in History (Thrupp, Stroud, Gloucestershire: Sutton, 1997). See esp. Moshe Idel, "Prophets and Their Impact in the High Middle Ages: A Sub-Culture of Franco-German Jewry," in *Regional Identities and Cultures of Medieval Jews*, ed. Javier Castaño, Talya Fishman, and Ephraim Kanarfogel (London: Littman Library of Jewish Civilization in Association with Liverpool University Press, 2018), 285–337.

3. Ivan G. Marcus, "Mi-'Deus Vult' ve'ad 'Rezon ha-Borei': Idiologiyot Datiyot Qizoniyot u-Mezi'ut Historit bi-Shenat Tatnu ve-Ezel Hasidei Ashkenaz," in *Yehudim mul ha-Zelav: Gezeirot Tatnu be-Historiah u-ve-Historiografiah*, ed. Yom Tov Assis et al. (Jerusalem: Magnes, 2000), 92–100.

Although the speech itself has not been preserved, different witnesses reported what he said.[4] From the Latin reports, it is clear that the pope did not mention the Jews, but a religious fervor emerged in that audience, and it led to a chain of events that affected some Jews in the Rhineland and in central Europe.

Among the arguments that Urban used to motivate the French knights to leave home and make an armed pilgrimage to Jerusalem was an appeal to their military prowess in the past. Instead of killing one another, he told them, they should go and liberate the Church of the Holy Sepulcher and save their Christian brothers in the East, whom the infidel Turks were polluting and killing. If they would go and avenge these acts of barbarism and cruelty, the fighters for God would receive papal forgiveness for the punishments due for their sins. The pope's promise that if French knights and barons went East to kill the enemies of the faithful they would be able to atone for their past sins was a powerful message that crusaders could interpret in unexpected ways and produce different and unanticipated consequences.[5]

What was the underlying religious authority behind this call to armed pilgrimage to Jerusalem? In light of the fact that the pope made the speech, we might first think that papal authority alone was the source behind the call to take up arms and become pilgrims to oust the Turks. But how did the audience understand the religious authority behind the message they heard? We find a clue about this in the Latin narrative of Robert the Monk. Toward the end of his account he reports the following: "When Pope Urban had said these and very many similar things in his urbane discourse, he so influenced to one purpose the desires of all who were present, that they cried out, 'It is the will of God! It is the will of God!'" (*Deus vult! Deus vult!*). The pope then proceeded to interpret what he had just heard:

> My beloved brethren, today is manifest in you what the Lord says in the Gospel, "Where two or three are gathered together in my name there

---

4. On the speech, see D. C. Munro, "The Speech of Pope Urban II at Clermont, 1096," *American Historical Review* 11 (1905): 231–42.

5. On the development of the idea of a holy or just war in Christian history, see Carl Erdmann, *The Origin of the Idea of Crusade*, trans. Marshall W. Baldwin and Walter Goffart (Princeton: Princeton University Press, 1977). Erdmann's influential book played down Urban II's direct and unexpected significance in shaping the idea of the Crusade and attributed it instead to earlier canonists. For convincing arguments that the Urban speech was the main factor that suddenly created the new idea of the Crusade, see John Gilchrist, "The Erdmann Thesis and the Canon Law, 1083–1141," in *Crusade and Settlement: Papers Read at the First Conference of the Society for the Study of the Crusades and the Latin East and Presented to R. C. Smail*, ed. Peter W. Edbury (Cardiff: University College Cardiff Press, 1985), 37–45. That Urban's goal was not, as Erdmann would have it, mainly to aid Byzantine Christians but also to liberate Jerusalem from the beginning, see Jonathan Riley-Smith, *The Crusades: A Short History* (New Haven: Yale University Press, 1987), 6–8.

> am I in the midst of them" [Matt 18:20]. Unless the Lord God had been present in your spirits, all of you would not have uttered the same cry. For although the cry issued from numerous mouths, yet the origin of the cry was one. Therefore I say to you that God, who implanted this in your breasts, has drawn it forth from you.[6]

Whose authority, then, underlay the pope's call? The will of God as the pope transmitted it through his apostolic authority within the church? Or was it rather the more potent and uncontrollable direct inspiration of God that was, as even the pope himself said, somehow known directly to the future crusaders themselves?

We may think of the latter as a case of collective prophecy, a group's claim that they can directly intuit God's will independent of any institutional sources of religious authority. If, indeed, as the pope's interpretation of the passage from Matthew indicated, the spirit of God was in the knights listening to his speech, why should we be surprised if these same knights, or others who heard about the events at Clermont, should decide to go out to fight other enemies of the faithful, such as the Jews, even though they were theoretically protected against Christian violence by centuries of papal and more recent imperial policies?

The same Urban II who preached what became the First Crusade also called attention to the need to fight infidel enemies closer to home, not the Jews but the Muslims in Iberia. Urban wrote a letter to the Catalonian counts of Besalú, Empurias, Rousillon, and Cerdaña and urged Christian knights not only to go and fight the enemies in the East but also to liberate "a church so near you," the church of Tarragona.[7] In that letter, Urban differed from his predecessor, Pope Alexander II, who wrote a letter in 1063 to Spanish bishops in which he indicated that war was to be waged only against the Muslims in Spain, but that the Jews were to be protected.[8]

In view of the religious enthusiasm the pope aroused in 1095 and his failure to indicate that the Jews should be protected, it was easy for lay knights and barons to jump to the conclusion that on their way to Jerusalem there might be other "enemies among us," namely, the Jews of Germany. As Jonathan Riley-Smith has noted, the Christian knights who led

---

6. Roberti Monachi, *Historia Iherosolimita* 1.1–2, in *Recueil des historiens des croisades: Historiens occidentaux* [RHC, occ.] (Paris: Imprimerie royale, 1844–95), 3:727–30; English translation in Louise Riley-Smith and Jonathan Riley-Smith, eds., *The Crusades: Idea and Reality, 1095–1274* (London: Edward Arnold, 1981), 44.

7. Paul Kehr, *Papsturkunden in Spanien: Vorbereiten zur Hispania Pontificia: I. Katalonien* (Berlin: Weidmann, 1926), 287–88. Riley-Smith and Riley-Smith, *Crusades*, 40.

8. See H. Liebeschütz, "The Crusading Movement in Its Bearing on the Christian Attitude towards Jewry," *JJS* 10 (1959): 107. The letter of Pope Alexander II to the Spanish bishops is available in PL 146:1386D, and in Shlomo Simonsohn, *The Apostolic See and the Jews*, vol. 1, *Documents, 492–1404* (Toronto: Pontifical Institute of Mediaeval Studies, 1988), #37, 35–36.

the armies and mobs that invaded the Rhineland Jewish communities in 1096, could well confuse avenging the Jews' killing of Christ, in the past, with attacking the hostile Muslim Turks in the East, in the present. For them, vengeance against both was part of the familiar institution of a vendetta, a blood feud to seek revenge on those who were their enemies.[9] This attitude was encouraged, even though it was contrary to all charters of protection and canon laws, because the knights thought the spirit of God within them told them to do it: "Deus vult! Deus vult!"

There is abundant evidence that the crusaders who attacked the Jews in Germany in the spring and summer of 1096 were thinking of them as nearby enemies who deserved revenge. We see this clearly in several Hebrew and Latin sources some of which put attributed speeches into the mouths of the crusaders just before the attacks. We find them in the three Hebrew chronicles on the riots and acts of martyrdom in 1096.[10] Near the beginning of the so-called Solomon bar Samson account, we read:

> Now it came to pass that as they passed through the towns where Jews dwelled, they said to one another: "Look now, we are going a long way to seek out the profane shrine and to avenge ourselves on the Ishmaelites, when here, in our very midst, are the Jews—they whose forefathers murdered and crucified him for no reason. Let us first avenge ourselves on them and exterminate them from among the nations so that the name of Israel will no longer be remembered, or let them adopt our faith and acknowledge the offspring of promiscuity." [11]

---

9. Jonathan Riley-Smith, "The First Crusade and the Persecution of the Jews," in *Persecution and Toleration: Papers Read at the Twenty-Second Summer Meeting and the Twenty-Third Winter Meeting of the Ecclesiastical History Society* (ed. W. J. Sheils, Studies in Church History 21 (Oxford: Ecclesiastical History Society, 1984), 51–72, esp. 66–72.

10. Eva Haverkamp, ed., *Hebräische Berichte* über *die Judenverfolgungen während des Ersten Kreuzzugs*, Monumenta Germaniae Historica, Hebräische Texte aus dem Mittelalterlichen Deutschland 1 (Hannover: Hahn, 2005) (EH). The three Hebrew chronicles were published in Abraham Habermann, *Sefer Gezeirot Ashkenaz ve-Zarefat* (Jerusalem, 1946) (H). The translation is Shlomo Eidelberg, trans. and ed., *The Jews and the Crusaders: The Hebrew Chronicles of the First and Second Crusades* (1977; repr., Hoboken, NJ: Ktav, 1996) (E).

For the textual relationship of the three chronicles, see EH, 85–129. As to the factual or literary character of the three texts, see Ivan G. Marcus, review of *European Jewry and the First Crusade*, by Robert Chazan (Berkeley: University of California Press, 1987), *Speculum* 64 (1989): 685–88; Jeremy Cohen, review of *European Jewry*, by Robert Chazan, *American Historical Review* 93 (1988): 1031–32; Robert Chazan, "The Facticity of Medieval Narrative: A Case Study of the Hebrew First Crusade Narratives," *AJS Review* 16 (1991): 31–56, which repeats earlier arguments. Cf. Robert Chazan, *God, Humanity, and History: The Hebrew First Crusade Narratives* (Berkeley: University of California Press, 2000), 138–39 (the correct citation that I mistakenly cited from his *Medieval Stereotypes and Modern Antisemitism* [Berkeley: University `of California Press, 1997] in Ivan G. Marcus, "A Jewish-Christian Symbiosis: The Culture of Early Ashkenaz," in *Cultures of the Jews: A New History*, ed. David Biale [New York: Schocken, 2002], 506 n. 45).

11. EH, (615); H, 24; E, 22.

A few lines after these words, in connection with the pope's speech found in the same Hebrew narrative:

> Why should we concern ourselves with going to war against the Ishmaelites dwelling about Jerusalem, when in our midst is a people who disrespect our god—indeed, their ancestors are those who crucified him. Why should we let them live and tolerate their dwelling among us? Let us commence by using our swords against them and then proceed upon our stray path.[12]

Similar speeches are attributed to the crusaders in the chronicles of Rabbi Eliezer bar Nathan and in the so-called Mainz Anonymous.[13]

In addition to versions of an attributed speech found in the three Hebrew chronicles, there is another Hebrew version in the composition of Ovadiah the Proselyte, a former Christian whose composition has been preserved in the Cairo Geniza. It sheds additional light on the crusaders' mentality from a Christian convert:

> [And when they were determined] to go to Jerusalem, [one said to the other], "Why are we [going to a distant land, to] our enemies, when here in our own land [and towns dwe]ll our enemies and those who hate [our religion. Why should we leave] them with our wives?" [And an outcry was heard in the Franks' camp.][14]

Two Christian texts in Latin provide additional evidence that crusaders were making the a fortiori argument that, if they were going all the way to Jerusalem to kill the enemies of God, they should first deal with the Jews who are the enemies of Christ at home. In his *Autobiography*, Abbot Guibert of Nogent says the following about an incident in Rouen in Normandy: "After traversing great distances, we desire to attack the enemies of God in the East, although the Jews, of all races the worst foes of God, are before our eyes. That's doing our work backward."[15] This comparison is found also in a letter that Peter the Venerable, abbot of Cluny, sent to Louis VII, king of France, in 1146:

> What good is it to pursue and persecute the enemies of the Christian faith in far and distant lands if the Jews, vile blasphemers and far worse than

12. EH, (609); H, 27; E, 26.

13. On the former, see EH, (561); H, 72; E, 80; for the latter, EH, (539); H, 93; E, 99.

14. Alexander Scheiber, "Ein aus arabischer Gefangenschaft befreiter christlicher Proselyt in Jerusalem," *HUCA* 39 (1968): 170.

15. Guibert de Nogent, *De vita sua* 2.5 in *Recueil des historiens des Gaules et de la France*, ed. M. Bouquet et al., 24 vols. (Paris, 1738–1904), 12: 240: "Cum ante oculos nostros sint Judei, quibus inimicitior existat gens nulla Dei." For the translation, see *Self and Society in Medieval France: The Memoirs of Abbot Guibert of Nogent*, ed. John F. Benton, Medieval Academy Reprints for Teaching 15 (Toronto: University of Toronto Press, 1984), 134–35.

> the Saracens not far away from us but right in our midst, blaspheme, abuse, and trample on Christ and the Christian sacraments so freely and insolently and with impunity?[16]

In addition to making the a fortiori argument that the crusaders who are going off to the East to kill the enemies of Christ should surely do so closer to home where the Jews are, a parallel argument is made about the pope's offer to the crusaders to remit their sins. In Clermont, Urban II had told the crowd that he would remit the earthly punishment due for the crusaders' sins. Applying the same a fortiori logic as before to the pope's offer: "A proclamation was issued: 'Whosoever kills a Jew will receive pardon for all his sins.'"[17]

Pope Urban II did not even hint at any connection between this reward and killing Jews, the enemy living nearby. Still, if the crusaders could equate the enemy Jews with the enemy Turks as deserving of death, they could also imagine that their reward would be the same for killing a Jew at home as well as a "pagan" enemy abroad. Here, too, we see the consequences of a belief that each side could know the will of God in a direct, unmediated way.

Collective Jewish Prophecy in 1096

The Jewish narrators of the events of 1096 understood that the Jews of the Rhineland, not only the crusaders, were able to intuit the will of God directly in a form of collective prophecy. It was the Jews' awareness of God's will that made them turn away from typical political and even military acts of defense and assume that God now wanted them to carry out unprecedented acts of ritual sacrifice of their children and self-sacrificial martyrdom. [18]

We see this in a story about a young man named Barukh ben Isaac,

---

16. Peter the Venerable, *The Letters of Peter the Venerable*, ed. Giles Constable, 2 vols., Harvard Historical Studies 78 (Cambridge: Harvard University Press, 1967), no. 130, 1:328; and see the English translation in Jeremy Cohen, *Living Letters of the Law: Ideas of the Jew in Medieval Christendom* (Berkeley: University of California Press, 1999), 247.

17. EH, (539); H, 94; E, 100.

18. See Ivan G. Marcus, "From Politics to Martyrdom: Shifting Paradigms in the Hebrew Narratives of the 1096 Crusade Riots," *Prooftexts* 2:1 (January 1982): 40-52. Although the narrative structure of a political phase, followed by a martyrological one, is most pronounced in the narrative attributed to Solomon bar Samson, it is found also in the Mainz Anonymous. See the political phase in EH, (535); H, 96; E, 103 [Worms]; EH (531–527); H, 98–100; E, 105–106 [Mainz]. The martyrological phase follows in EH, (535–531); H, 96–97; E, 103–105 [Worms] and in EH, (525–519); H, 101–104; E, 106–114 [Mainz]. In each case, the turning point between the two stages is the Jews' awareness that it is the will of God that they die as martyrs. Cf. Chazan, *European Jewry and the First Crusade*, 308–9 n. 21.

who claimed that he had heard someone crying in the synagogue. [19] It turned out, however, that no one was there: "Upon hearing this, we cried out: 'Ah, Lord God! Wilt Thou make a full end of the remnant of Israel?'" Then they went and reported the occurrence to their brethren who were concealed in the court of the count and in the bishop's chambers, and all knew that this decree was of God.[20]

As in the episode of Barukh ben Isaac, reported in the longest of the three chronicles, the other two Hebrew chronicles also claim that the Jews can know the will of God directly. For example, in R. Eliezer bar Nathan's narrative: "They hastened to fulfill the will of their Creator, not wishing to flee just to be saved for temporal life, for lovingly they accepted Heaven's judgment."[21] Similarly, in the Mainz Anonymous, the narrator assumes that the Jews know the will of God when he says, "When the people of the Sacred Covenant saw that the Heavenly decree had been issued and that the enemy had defeated them, they all cried out."[22]

In all of these First Crusade texts, then, we see evidence of religious enthusiasm that prevailed according to which it was possible for Christians and Jews to know immediately the will of God. According to this knowledge, some crusaders killed Jews or forcibly converted them, against the norms of both church and state, and some Jews ritually slaughtered their families and themselves as sacrifices, in unprecedented acts.

It was important for the Jewish martyrs to know that it was the will of God that they take the lives of their families and their own. Some Jews looked back critically at what the Jewish martyrs' confidence had acted out then. Among these is the remark of a Tosafist in a commentary on Gen 9:5:

> It once happened that a certain rabbi slaughtered many children during a persecution because he was afraid they would be forced to become Christians. Another rabbi there got furious with him and called him a murderer, but the first one ignored him. The (second) rabbi said, "If I am right, let the other rabbi die a horrible death." And so it happened that Christians caught [the first rabbi], skinned him alive and put sand in his wounds. Soon the persecution ended and had he not slaughtered the children, they would have been saved.[23] (my translation)

19. EH (607); H, 28; E, 27–28. Compare the episode in the Latin and Hebrew chronicles of how Christians interpreted the behavior of a goose as an omen portending it was the will of God that they go on a Crusade. See Albertus Aquensis, *Historia Hierosolymitana/Liber Primus Christianae Expeditionis* 1.30 in RHC, occ., 4:295; Guibert de Nogent, *Gesta per Francos* 1.32 in RHC, occ. 4:251; EH, (607, 531); H, 28, 98; E, 27, 106.

20. EH, (607); H, 28-29; E, 27-28 (quotation from 28).

21. EH, (553); H, 75; E, 83.

22. EH, (527); H, 100; E, 109.

23. See *Da'at Zeqeinim* (Livorno, 1783), f. 4b to Gen 9:5.

Although scholars have noted the absence of legal precedent for the behavior of ritual homicide and suicide described in the sources about the martyrdom of 1096, some have proposed literary models such as the behavior of temple priests or that the defenders of Masada who took lives of other Jews and then their own after the fall of Jerusalem. According to those literary traditions, it was permissible, indeed required, that certain Jews take their own lives and even kill one another, when it was God's will that the temple be destroyed. The decision that their sacrifice was God's will followed from a sense that they could decipher it then and there.[24]

Sage Prophecy in Sefer Hasidim

The idea of an intuitive ability to decipher the will of God is also an important feature of individuals in the pietistic circle surrounding Judah *he-hasid* (d. 1217), the Jewish pietists of medieval Germany or *hasidei ashkenaz*.[25] The source of religious authority in German Jewish *hasidut* is predicated on the ability of the advanced *hasid* or *hakham* to understand the hidden will of God, sometimes called "the will of the Creator" (*rezon ha-borei*), terms that refer to the source but not the content of the revelations.[26]

How do the Hasidim know they are fulfilling the God's hidden will? Rabbi Judah b. Samuel *he-hasid* wrote down thousands of moralistic stories, biblical comments, and commands in anonymous compilations of a book called "Sefer Hasidim," and in his compilation of some seventy commands (*Zava'ah*). He makes it clear that the authority underlying these teachings was a form of divine inspiration or prophecy. Although his father, R. Samuel b. Qalonimos ha-Zaqen, was known as "the prophet"

---

24. See Yitzhak Baer, "Mavo" to Habermann, *Sefer Gezeirot*, 4; Avraham Grossman, "Shorashav shel Qiddush ha-Shem be-Ashkenaz ha-Qedumah," in *Qedushat ha-Hayyim ve-Heiruf ha-Nefesh*, ed. Isaiah Gafni and Aviezer Ravitzky (Jerusalem: Merkaz Shazar, 1993), 102–5; David Goodblatt, "Suicide in the Sanctuary: Traditions on Priestly Martyrdom," *JJS* 46 (1995): 10–29.

25. See Ivan G. Marcus, *"Sefer Hasidim" and the Ashkenazic Book in Medieval Europe*, Jewish Culture and Contexts (Philadelphia: University of Pennsylvania Press, 2018), 45–74.

26. Although Haym Soloveichik refers to the idea of a hidden divine will as a "theme" in *Sefer Hasidim* ("Three Themes in Sefer Hasidim," *AJS Review* 1 [1976]: 311–57, passim), it has little substantive meaning since *hasidut* (pietism), by definition, exceeds the ordinary demands of Jewish law, custom, and pious practices as embodied in the product of biblical revelation and rabbinic norms. The demands of pietism must by definition be based on an additional dimension of the divine will that God may reveal to a few or that some may seek out on their own. Whether acquired passively or actively, the idea of a hidden divine will does not indicate the *contents* in any form of pietism, including German *hasidut*. See Ivan G. Marcus, *Piety and Society: The Jewish Pietists of Medieval Germany*, Etudes sur le judaisme médiéval 10 (Leiden: Brill, 1981), 1–17 and Marcus, *"Sefer Hasidim" and the Ashkenazic Book*, 136 n. 38.

(*ha-navi*), Judah, too, had a reputation for prophetic ability.[27] Some passages in *Sefer Hasidim* suggest an idea of immanent and spontaneous religious inspiration that may benefit the sage.[28]

For example, a sage whom people ask questions that he cannot answer is to pray for direct divine guidance in such occasions:

> When people bring a question about what is forbidden or permitted or (seek) any advice to a sage, before he answers, he should say: "May it be Your will, my Creator, *that you teach me* the correct approach so that the one who asks does not fail and true Torah be in my mouth and no evil be found on my lips."[29](my translation)

Judah *he-hasid* refers to God helping a sage when he is about to give specific advice to someone:

> In the verse, "The Lord was pleased for His righteousness' sake to make the teaching great and glorious" (Isa. 42:21), the first letters of these words encode (the word which means) and (the spirit of God) descended (on someone: *va-tizlah*).... So, if a sage who is asked about something that he does not know, as soon as he is asked, the spirit of wisdom descends upon the sage and he knows (the answer to) the question, it means that the Holy One, blessed be He, wants (the sage) to answer (the questioner). Since (the sage) knows the answer because of (God's) help, (the sage should) tell (the questioner the answer). But if (the questioner) asks him

27. On Samuel, see Avraham Epstein, "R. Shmuel he-Hasid b. R. Qalonimos ha-Zaqen." *Ha-Goren* 4 (1903): 81–101, reprinted in *Dat ve-Hevrah be-Mishnatam shel Hasidei Ashkenaz*, ed. Ivan G. Marcus (Jerusalem: Merkaz Shazar, 1986), 25–46; on Judah as a prophet, see Jerusalem, National Library of Israel, Hebrew MS Oct. 3182, published in Eli Yassif, ed., *Me'ah Sippurim Haser Ehad: Aggadot Ketav Yad Yerushalayim ba-Folklore ha-Yehudi shel Yemei ha-Beinayim* (Tel Aviv: Haim Rubin Tel Aviv University Press, 2013), 177 (no. 7) and note on 268. Among scholars who have referred to Judah *he-hasid* as a prophet, see Yitzhaq Baer, "Ha-Megamah ha-Datit-ha-Hevratit shel 'Sefer Hasidim,'" *Zion* 3 (1938): 12; but cf. Soloveitchik, "Three Themes," 312 n. 1.

28. See, too, Judah D. Galinsky, "The Significance of the Form; R. Moses of Coucy's Reading Audience and his Sefer ha-Mizvot," *AJS Review* 35 (2011): 293–321, esp. 299 and 309; and of related interest, Israel Ta-Shma, "'Shei'lot u-Teshuvot min ha-Shamayim,'" *Tarbiz* 57 (1988): 51–66; reprinted in Ta-Shma, *Keneset Mehqarim: 'Iyyunim ba-Sifrut ha-Rabbanit bimei ha-Beinayim* (Jerusalem: Mosad Bialik, 2010), 4:112–29, esp. 126–29; and Ephraim Kanarfogel, "Dreams as a Determinant of Jewish Law and Practice in Northern Europe during the High Middle Ages," in *Studies in Medieval Jewish Intellectual and Social History: Festschrift in Honor of Robert Chazan*, ed. David Engel, Lawrence Schiffman, and Elliot Wolfson, Supplements to the Journal of Jewish Thought and Philosophy 15 (Leiden: Brill, 2012), 111–43, esp. 124–25.

29. *Sefer Hasidim*, Parma, Biblioteca Palatina MS H 3280 [De Rossi 1133; hereafter SHP], 1569; *Sefer Hasidim*, former Jewish Theological Seminary Boesky 45 (FJTSB45), 662; *Sefer Hasidim*, Cambridge, Cambridge University Library, Add. 379 (Cambridge Add. 379), 474. On the two-dozen manuscripts of *Sefer Hasidim*, see Marcus, *"Sefer Hasidim" and the Ashkenazic Book*, 87–112.

> something and the sage (is not helped by) the spirit of God descending, so that he (does not) learn the answer, it means that God does not want (the sage) to answer (the questioner).[30] (my translation)

Moreover, one who receives such divine guidance is obligated to write it down so that the substance of the will of God not be lost:

> "Who has plumbed the mind of the Lord" (Isa 40:13). For the Holy One, blessed be He, decrees who becomes wise and in what his wisdom consists how many years and how much he will have. He decrees that he will produce one book or two or three. This is also true with regard to learning or to solving biblical verses or other secrets. And to whomever the Holy One blessed be He has revealed things but does not write it down, though he can do so, steals from the One who revealed (it) to him. For they were revealed to him only to be written down, as it is written, "The secret of the Lord is to those who fear Him; to them He makes known His covenant" (Ps. 25:14) and it is written, "Your springs will gush forth" (Prov 5:16).[31](my translation)

There are connections between the Jewish martyrs of 1096 and Hasidei Ashkenaz that have not yet been explored. Between the persecutions of 1096 and the Hasidei Ashkenaz there were about two generations, and both phenomena occurred in the Rhineland towns and in Regensburg. In *Sefer Hasidim*, the author remembers 1096 but assumes that he and the other *hasidim* are living not in a time of persecution: "Consider, if it were a time of persecution, you would undergo suffering or death for the Holy One, blessed be He, ... and all the more should you do something that is less difficult, that you overcome your impulse."[32]

According to this view, a *hasid* is a Jew who is always ready to martyr himself by committing suicide but lacks the opportunity to do so. Meanwhile, he must learn a fortiori from the martyrs how to be a *hasid*. *Hasidut* demands of him that he conquer his passions (*ytizro*) by means of doing *hasidut*, and this way of living is a kind of *qiddush ha-shem* at a time of relative peace and security. *Sefer Hasidim* also refers to specific incidents that occurred during the riots, as Joseph Hacker proved.[33] From these stories we see evidence of the awareness among the *hasidei ashkenaz* that they were living two generations after the martyrs of 1096.

In addition, Hasidei Ashkenaz internalized an ideology of private inspiration about the hidden will of God that we find earlier as collective

30. SHP 794; FJTSB45, 310; *Sefer Hasidim*, Bologna, 1538 (SHB), 290.

31. SHP, 1950; FJTSB45, 3; Cambridge, Add. 379, 557; SHB, 538.

32. SHP, 2; FJTSB45, 5; SHB, 155: a passage from R. Samuel b. Qalonimos' *Sefer ha-Yir'ah*.

33. SHP, 198; FJTSB45, 101; SHB, 197 and SHP, 1922; Cambridge, Add. 379, 541 and Joseph Hacker, "Gezeirot Tatnu (1096)," *Zion* 31 (1966): 229–30.

prophecy among the Jewish martyrs of 1096, because both drew on the same ancient Palestinian and southern Italian traditions that shaped the Jewish martyrs of 1096 and Hasidei Ashkenaz.[34]

We should also remember that because these examples from the First Crusade and Hasidei Ashkenaz illustrate a spontaneous belief about an ability to know the will of God, each lasted only a short time and soon disappeared as a historical factor. The anti-Jewish crusader ideology, the Jewish model of martyrdom, with a few exceptions,[35] and the vision of a social program of Hasidei Ashkenaz did not persist for long.[36] Nevertheless, Jews remembered these cases of immanent prophecy in Europe for some time to come.

A comprehensive study of postbiblical prophecy still remains to be undertaken. It might consider not only moments of crisis, as illustrated here, when religious hysteria spilled over from one culture to another. It would also look at forms of Jewish and Christian revival that sometimes developed within established religious structures or at other times challenged them. For example, the German Pietists were active rabbinic leaders of their time even though a sense of prophetic inspiration underlay some of their teachings. In Christian society, various heretical voices based themselves on prophetic claims to challenge the Christian order. An awareness of divine prophecy, then, could generate religious enthusiasm from within or provoke newly grounded forms of group tension and even violence. The dynamics of these and other expressions of medieval prophecy need to be studied more carefully.

---

34. See Robert Chazan, "The Early Development of Hasidut Ashkenaz," *JQR* 75 (1985): 199–211, who links 1096 and Hasidut Ashkenaz on the theme of the will of God. For earlier roots into southern Italy or Palestine, see Robert Bonfil, "Bein Erez Yisrael le-Bavel," *Shalem* 5 (1977): 1–30; Peter Schäfer, "The Ideal of Piety of the Ashkenazi Hasidim and Its Roots in Jewish Tradition," *Jewish History* 4 (1990): 9–23; and Moshe Idel, "Lawyers and Mystics in Judaism: A Prolegomenon for a State of Prophecy in Jewish Mysticism," [NYU] Straus Institute Working Paper No.10/10, 2010, 27: "My second assumption is that the prophetic drive, and its continuation—to be sure with many changes, since the apocalyptic literatures—but especially the Hekhalot literature, reached Europe via Italy, and had an impact on the Hasidei Ashkenaz and other circles in Germany and France, which resorted explicitly to the term prophet in many cases, statistically speaking more than it has been done in any other Jewish center beforehand."

35. Two exceptions are the episode at York in 1190 and the Shepherds' Crusade riots in southern France. See Ephraim of Bonn, *Sefer Zekhirah*, ed. Avraham Habermann (Jerusalem: Mosad Bialik, 1970), 70; R. B. Dobson, *The Jews of Medieval York and the Massacre or March 1190*, Borthwick Papers No. 45 (York: St. Anthony's Press, 1974); Malcolm Barber, "The Pastoureaux of 1320," *JEH* 32 (1981): 143–66; and David Nirenberg, *Communities of Violence: Persecution of Minorities in the Middle Ages* (Princeton: Princeton University Press, 1996), esp. 43–68.

36. Marcus, *Piety and Society*, 130–132; idem, *"Sefer Hasidim" and the Ashkenazic Book,"* 45–74.

Hitler and Antiochus, Hellenists and *Rabbinerdoktoren*

On Isaak Heinemann's Response to Elias Bickermann, 1938

DANIEL R. SCHWARTZ
The Hebrew University of Jerusalem

According to Shaye J. D. Cohen's *From the Maccabees to the Mishnah,* "the most striking feature of the Hellenistic period is its spectacular finish": the chain of events that began with Antiochus IV Epiphanes's profanation of the temple and persecution of Judaism and quickly turned into the Maccabean revolt and, two decades later, the end of Seleucid rule in Judea.[1] The present study, contributed in gratitude and friendship by one who has been reading Cohen's works and learning from them for nearly four decades, is offered in the hope that he too will find it interesting to think about what and how our predecessors of not too long ago thought about the origins of that chain of events in the second century BCE.

The basic facts of Antiochus Epiphanes's decrees against Judaism are fairly well documented. According to several ancient sources (especially 1 Macc 1 and 2 Macc 6 but also other interesting passages including Dan 7 and 11, As. Mos. 8–9, and Diodorus Siculus, *Bib. hist.* 34/35.1.3–4[2]), Antiochus established a pagan cult in the temple of Jerusalem, coerced the Jews to participate in it, forbade circumcision, forced Jews to eat forbidden foods, burned Torah scrolls, and, in general, forbade the practice of Judaism. As 2 Macc 6:6 put it, it was even forbidden to admit to being Jewish. These decrees played a serious role in touching off the Maccabean revolt that led, eventually, to the establishment of the Hasmonean state.

In contrast, the question *why* Antiochus Epiphanes imposed these decrees, which seem to have been unprecedented in antiquity and also

1. Shaye J. D. Cohen, *From the Maccabees to the Mishnah,* LEC 7 (Philadelphia: Westminster, 1989), 14–15.

2. Menahem Stern, *Greek and Latin Authors on Jews and Judaism,* 3 vols., Fontes ad res Judaicas spectantes (Jerusalem: Israel Academy of Sciences and Humanities, 1974–1984), 1:182–85.

to contradict all we would expect from a polytheistic monarch, is hardly addressed in the ancient sources. Nevertheless, it has occupied scholars for centuries. Numerous suggestions have been made, based on this or that interpretation of this or that source or combination of sources but also influenced by this or that contemporary trend or issue. Indeed, there is no dearth of historiographical studies that survey the various suggestions and contextualize them, explaining how each functioned in its respective time and place. This is often done, of course, as part of a scholar's opening move, clearing the deck before proposing a new explanation.

Thus, for the two main examples of the mid-twentieth century, both Elias Bickermann in 1937[3] and Victor Tcherikover in the 1950s[4] opened their studies by surveying various theories and showing their weaknesses, after which each proposed his own explanation. Bickermann, after surveying several earlier theories and contextualizing them, argued that Antiochus issued his decrees because Jewish Hellenists, such as Jason and Menelaus (known especially from 2 Macc 4–5), convinced him to do so in support of their effort to modernize the Jews and make them part of the broader Hellenistic world. Tcherikover, in contrast, for whom Bickermann's suggestion was the most recent of the five he surveyed and found wanting, argued instead, mostly on the basis of a close reading of 2 Macc 5, that nationalist Jews of Judea had rebelled against Antiochus's rule in a bid for independence. For Tcherikover, accordingly, the king's decrees against Judaism—as later Hadrian's at the time of the Bar Kokhba revolt—are to be understood as retaliatory measures meant to hit the Jewish rebels where it hurt.

It is not too difficult to contextualize those two suggestions. Bickermann explicitly compared the hellenizers of the second century BCE to German Reform Jews of the nineteenth century, the founders of a type of Judaism quite current in the Germany in which Bickermann lived in the 1920s and 1930s.[5] Moreover, as Albert Baumgarten has shown, it seems

3. Elias Bickermann, *Der Gott der Makkabäer: Untersuchungen über Sinn und Ursprung der makkabäischen Erhebung* (Berlin: Schocken, 1937). An English translation (but without the footnotes) was published as Elias Bickerman, *The God of the Maccabees*, SJLA 32 (Leiden: Brill, 1979) and was included in Bickerman, *Studies in Jewish and Christian History: A New Edition in English Including* The God of the Maccabees, ed. Amram Tropper, 2 vols., AJEC 68 (Leiden: Brill, 2007), 2:1025–1149. (At different times of his life B. spelled his name differently. In this article, which focuses on his *Gott der Makkabäer*, I use "Bickermann" throughout, except when citing publications that give his name as "Bickerman.")

4. Tcherikover's article on Antiochus's decrees was first published in Hebrew, in *Eshkolot* 1 (1953–1954): 86–109. It was reprinted in several collections but is most easily available in English as chapter 5 of his *Hellenistic Civilization and the Jews* (Philadelphia: Jewish Publication Society of America, 1959), 175–203. That volume is a translation of the second edition of Tcherikover's Hebrew work (which appeared in 1962/63).

5. See Bickermann, *Gott der Makkabäer*, 132. For the view that it was this nineteenth-century analogy that explains Bickermann's view (away), see K. Bringmann, "Die Verfolgung

likely that Bickermann was also thinking of Russian Jewish communists and maybe Russian Jewish reformers as well—of the types he will have known in his earlier days in Russia.[6] As for Tcherikover, he is not explicit about his models and inspiration, but they should be obvious when we note that Tcherikover's reconstruction of a Jewish national revolt in the 160s BCE jelled in Jerusalem a few years after the Israeli War of Independence (1948). Indeed, note that the very next chapter in Tcherikover's work (but only in the second edition, of 1959–63 [see n. 4], not in the first, of 1930) was entitled "The War of Liberation" (in the Hebrew original: *milḥemet hashiḥrur*, the common name for the 1948 war) and that it complained about theologians "who have arrogated to themselves a monopoly of the study of Jewish history,"[7] who dismissed the political side of the rebellion's etiology. That Jews were interested in having their own state was a notion very well at home in Tcherikover's historical context.

Perhaps it is superfluous, but I will nevertheless underline, before going on, that the fact that a scholar's theory is inspired by the context in which he or she lives does not, in and of itself, show the theory is not valid. While Benedetto Croce is right that all history is current history, some ancient history is also ancient history. Whether Bickermann's theory is true, that is, whether it corresponds to what really happened in the 170s and 160s BCE, or whether Tcherikover's theory is, or whether perhaps some other theory should be preferred, is not an issue I am addressing. Nor do I wish to focus on contextualizing Bickermann's theory or Tcherikover's, although that would be interesting and there is more to say about them; for both, I note, it would be very interesting to pursue the relation of their ideas to those of their teachers at the University of Berlin in the Weimar years, especially Eduard Meyer.[8]

Rather, the present study focuses on a single influential study that appeared between Bickermann's and Tcherikover's: Isaak Heinemann's 1938 response to Bickermann, entitled "Wer veranlaßte den Glaubenszwang der Makkabäerzeit?" ("Who Brought on the Religious Persecution in the Maccabean Period?").[9] By focusing precisely on who "brought on"[10]

---

der jüdischen Religion durch Antiochos IV: Ein Konflikt zwischen Judentum und Hellenismus?," *AuA* 26 (1980): 176–90, here 179; also Bringmann, "Elias Bickermann und der 'Gott der Makkabäer,'" *Trumah* 17 (2007): 9–10.

6. A. I. Baumgarten, *Elias Bickerman as a Historian of the Jews: A Twentieth Century Tale*, TSAJ 131 (Tübingen: Mohr Siebeck, 2010), 240–69.

7. Tcherikover, *Hellenistic Civilization*, 206. This was a common theme; see Baumgarten, *Elias Bickerman*, 181 (on Eduard Meyer and Hans Lewy).

8. On Meyer on ancient Judaism, see Christhard Hoffmann, *Juden und Judentum im Werk deutscher Althistoriker des 19. und 20. Jahrhunderts*, SJMT 9 (Leiden: Brill, 1988), 133–89.

9. Isaak Heinemann, "Wer veranlaßte den Glaubenszwang der Makkabäerzeit?," *MGWJ* 82 (1938): 145–72.

10. It appears that Heinemann formulated the title of his article with care, for "veran-

Antiochus's decrees, Heinemann took aim at Bickermann's central thesis, and Baumgarten correctly characterized it as the "most trenchant" of the critical reviews of *Gott der Makkabäer*.[11] Indeed, it has often been recognized as a central refutation of Bickermann's thesis;[12] writing in 1978, Bickermann himself, who did not give up his thesis, recognized Heinemann's article as "the most incisive (and still worth reading) review" of his book and responded to it at some length.[13] Somewhat surprisingly, however, Heinemann's article seems not to have been the object of attention directed at contextualizing it historically. In what follows, I will address that desideratum, focusing on three main points raised, one way or another, by Heinemann's article.

1. "Gleichschaltung"

The first point builds on an obvious datum: both Bickermann's monograph and Heinemann's response were published in Nazi Germany, when Hitler was at the height of his power. That context must be taken very seriously. True, Bickermann had written about the issue well before the Nazis' rise to power: as early as 1928, in a detailed study of the books of Maccabees, he specifically addressed the question of what engendered

---

laßen" is more nebulous than "cause" or "be responsible for" and so can mean something less direct. The entry in a contemporary dictionary, for example, offered a whole list of verbs beginning with "cause" but continuing with "occasion" and "bring about" (K. Breul, *Heath's New German and English Dictionary*, ed. J. H. Lepper and R. Kottenhahn [Boston: Heath, 1939]), and that in *Duden Bedeutungswörterbuch: 24000 Wörter mit ihrem Grundbedeutungen*, ed. Paul Grebe et al., Der große Duden 10 (Mannheim: Bibliographisches Institut, 1970) makes the breadth of possibilities very clear: "auf irgendeine Weise dahinwirken, daß etwas Bestimmtes geschieht oder dass jmd. etwas Bestimmtes tut" ("to bring about, one way or another, that something in particular happens or that someone does something particular"). The title of Heinemann's study thus encompassed not only the argument that he offered at length—that the Jewish hellenizers did not in fact *cause* the persecution—but also the "bottom line" of his article, discussed in the third part of the present essay, about the tragic role they nevertheless played in "bringing it on."

11. See Baumgarten's "bibliographical note" at the end of Bickerman, *The Jews in the Greek Age* (Cambridge: Harvard University Press, 1988), 310.

12. Tcherikover, *Hellenistic Civilization*, 473 n. 18; Bringmann, "Die Verfolgung der jüdischen Religion," 181; Bringmann, "Elias Bickermann," 10; Stern, *Greek and Latin Authors*, 1:185. Note, in this connection, that Heinemann's article is the only study cited by Tcherikover (183–85) in his discussion and rejection of Bickermann's thesis, and that, in turn, a reference to those pages by Tcherikover is the only source citation supplied by Jonathan A. Goldstein, some twenty years later, in his footnote rejecting Bickermann's thesis: *1 Maccabees: A New Translation with Introduction and Commentary*, AB 41 (Garden City, NY: Doubleday, 1976), 159 n. 336.

13. See Bickerman, "Preface to English Translation," in his *God of the Maccabees*, xii–xiii (reprinted in his *Studies in Jewish and Christian History*, 2:1030–31); also Baumgarten, *Elias Bickerman*, 243–44. See also n. 33 below.

Antiochus's decrees, and already then he raised the possibility that the Jewish Hellenists had been the main movers.[14] Nevertheless, his *Gott der Makkabäer*, a decade later, developed the thesis in much more detail and also presented it with a pathos that undoubtedly reflects the times of persecution in which it appeared.[15] What about Heinemann's response?

Heinemann, we should first note, was very active in Jewish community life. He was the rector and, by 1938, the main remaining scholar at the Jewish theological seminary of Breslau and editor of the *Monatsschrift für Geschichte und Wissenschaft des Judentums* (in which his response to Bickermann was the lead article in its May–June 1938 issue); he also served in numerous other Jewish communal functions.[16] I take it to be axiomatic that no such person writing in Germany of 1938 about the persecution of Jews in antiquity could do so without thinking of what was going on around him. Indeed, Heinemann is quite explicit about the way he looked around his contemporary world (as we all do) in order to understand the past: at numerous points in his response to Bickermann he refers to modern events in order to make his points about antiquity. Thus, for example, when Heinemann points out that pious Jews of the second century BCE may have taken umbrage at departures from tradition although the departures were innocuous from the point of view of Jewish law, he adduces, as an example, the opposition of ultra-Orthodox Jews of Palestine, in his day, to the widespread use of Hebrew as a vernacular language.[17] Similarly, a few pages later Heinemann clarifies the importance of Antiochus III's charter of the Judeans' rights at the outset of Seleucid rule of Judea (Josephus, *Ant.* 12.138ff.) by comparing it to the Balfour Declaration.[18]

---

14. E. Bickermann, "Makkabäerbücher (I. und II.)," PW 14/1 (1928), cols. 779–97, here 794–96.

15. See esp. Martha Himmelfarb, "Elias Bickerman on Judaism and Hellenism," in *The Jewish Past Revisited: Reflections on Modern Jewish Historians*, ed. David N. Myers and David B. Ruderman, Studies in Jewish Culture and Society (New Haven: Yale University Press, 1998), 199–211, here 206–8; Baumgarten, *Elias Bickerman*, 248–49.

16. On Heinemann and his oeuvre, see A. Altmann, "In Memoriam—Isaak Heinemann," *JJS* 8 (1957): 1–3; Ephraim E. Urbach, "Prof. Isaak Heinemann" [Hebrew], in *Ḥokhmat Yisrael be-Maarav Eiropa*, vol. 1, ed. Simon Federbusch (Jerusalem: Neumann, 1958), 219–22; Hoffmann, *Juden und Judentum*, 219–32; Renate Heuer, ed., *Lexikon deutsch-jüdischer Autoren*, 20 vols. (Munich: Saur [vols. 1–16]; Berlin: de Gruyter [vol. 17–20], 1992–2012), 11:30–37. For Heinemann's writings see Heuer, *Lexikon*; also Hanna Emmrich, "Isaak Heinemanns Schriften," *MGWJ* 80 (1936): 294–97; and the continuation in *Das Breslauer Seminar: Jüdisch-Theologisches Seminar (Fraenckelscher Stiftung) in Breslau, 1854–1938*, ed. Guido Kisch (Tübingen: Mohr Siebeck 1963), 396–97.

17. Heinemann, "Wer veranlaßte den Glaubenszwang," 147 n. 7.

18. Ibid., 154. Note also 147 n. 6 (on modern Jewish sports associations), 158 (modern complaints about the superficial westernization of primitive cultures), and 168 (even today it is difficult, in Palestine, for the government to put its hands on tax evaders). For another case of this (Heinemann's reference, in a 1919 article on ancient anti-Semitism, to World War I and contemporary discussions concerning war guilt), see Hoffmann, *Juden und Judentum*, 228.

Against that background, and also given the fact that at least as late as 1931 the question of who was responsible for Antiochus's decrees did not exist for Heinemann,[19] I think we should be especially interested in a particular word in the formulation of Heinemann's main thesis. That thesis is that not the Jewish hellenizers (as Bickermann argued) but, rather, Antiochus himself initiated the decrees. This thesis has two main parts: a positive argument—that Antiochus had his own reasons for imposing the decrees—and a negative argument—that the Jewish hellenizers would not have encouraged Antiochus to impose decrees against Judaism. In the first, positive part of Heinemann's thesis, 1 Macc 1:41 is the key to the whole issue. It states that Antiochus imposed the decrees because he wanted to unify his kingdom. However, if 1 Maccabees put that in quasi-biblical terms, saying that Antiochus's goal was that all should "become one people,"[20] Heinemann phrases the matter in other terms:

> Daß er seine Verfügung durch den Gedanken an die Reichseinheit begründet hat, ist außerordentlich wahrscheinlich, da die Seleukiden, im Gegensatz zu den Ptolemäern, zwar nicht gerade auf eine "Gleichschaltung," aber doch auf eine Anpassung der verschiedenen Reichskulturen hingearbeitet haben.[21]
>
> [That he based his edict upon the notion of imperial unity is extremely likely, for the Seleucids, as opposed to the Ptolemies, strove, if not precisely for a *Gleichschaltung*, nevertheless for the assimilation of the different cultures of the empire.]

In a footnote (his n. 41) appended to *Gleichschaltung*, Heinemann refers his readers to Aage Bentzen's 1937 commentary on Daniel, where Bentzen

---

19. See Heinemann, "Antisemitismus," PWSup 5 (1931), cols. 5–6—a discussion of Antiochus's motives without any reference to the possibility of Jewish influence on him. Similarly, note that, although already in 1919 Heinemann had argued that a certain Strabonic text depends on Posidonius ("Poseidonius über die Entwicklung der jüdischen Religion," *MGWJ* 63 [1919]: 113–21), he saw no reason to inquire whether Posidonius had derived the relevant notion from previous thinkers. Note, in addition, that in his 1931 "Antisemitismus" (cols. 34–35) he even took it for granted that Posidonius *did* build on such predecessors and popular ideas: "Im Gegensatz zu den Rhetoren greift Poseidonius, sicherlich bewußt, auf die Gesichtspunkte der philosophischen Darsteller des Judentums zurück.... So gewiß sich in der Durchführung dieser über alle Parteischablone erhaltenen Betrachtung die Eigenart des Philosophen und Historikers [= Poseidonius] auswirkt, so beruhen doch ihre Grundzüge auf weit verbreiteter Betrachtungsweise." It was only in his 1938 response to Bickermann that Heinemann saw the need to assert the opposite, namely, that the notion to which he refers was so typical of Posidonius that it could not have been current earlier; see at n. 32 below.

20. It seems likely that the original Hebrew text will have been taken, by those who knew their Bible, as an implicit comparison of Antiochus to the Shechemites of Gen 34:16, 22, whom Jews of course took to be the villains of the story.

21. Heinemann, "Wer veranlaßte den Glaubenszwang," 163–64.

uses the term in his discussion of Antiochus's policy, making specific reference to 1 Macc 1:41–42.[22] Readers of Heinemann's article, however, will have readily understood Heinemann's use of that term as an allusion (conscious or not) to their own times. Indeed, it seems that, even without the cues supplied by *Reichseinheit* and *Reichskulturen*, *Gleichschaltung* must have pointed them directly to their own context, for the term—in the sense of "bringing into line," "unifying," "making all march to the beat of the same drummer"—was one of the Nazis' favorites. As Victor Klemperer put it, the word was "ungeheuerlich repräsentativ für die Grundgesinnung des Nazismus" ("monstrously representative of the basic attitude of Nazism").[23] As has been noted by lexicographers, apart from electrical engineering (where it refers to the ability to close or break numerous circuits simultaneously) the term was not at all in use before the Nazi period; there was no entry for it in the 1929 tenth edition of Duden's *Rechtschreibung*, but there was by the eleventh, which appeared in 1934.[24] That is, the term came in, in a big way, with Hitler and the Nazis. Whether we look at their 1933 laws "zur Gleichschaltung der Länder mit dem Reich" or at the widespread usage of the term that same year in the context of abolishing professional unions and taking control of the press, the word and the theme were omnipresent in the parlance of Nazi policy.[25] And, as has been observed,[26] the word and the theme were again very popular in 1938, in connection with the annexation (*Anschluß*) of Austria to the Reich in March 1938—when Heinemann must have been busy preparing his response to Bickermann, which appeared later that spring. All in all, it seems clear that in Germany of 1938 one simply could not use *Gleichschaltung* without alluding to Nazi laws and policies. In the present case, moreover, Heinemann's adjacent references to *Reichseinheit* and *Reichskulturen* will have underscored the point all the more.[27]

---

22. Aage Bentzen, *Daniel*, HAT 1/19 (Tübingen: Mohr Siebeck, 1937), 50–51 (2nd ed. [1952], 81–82). Bentzen, in his brief discussion, writes that Antiochus wanted to effect a Hellenistic *Gleichschaltung* of his kingdom that would "also" (*zugleich*) help it resist Parthian expansion, but he does not suggest what Antiochus's main reason was for desiring the *Gleichschaltung*.

23. Victor Klemperer, *LTI: Notizbuch eines Philologen*, 22nd ed. (Stuttgart: Reclam, 2007), 207–8 (Eng. *The Language of the Third Reich* [London: Athlone, 2006], 144). (LTI [Lingua Tertii Imperii] was Klemperer's term for the language of the Third Reich.) Klemperer was cited by Cornelia Schmitz-Berning, *Vokabular des Nationalsozialismus* (Berlin: de Gruyter, 1998), 278 n. 167.

24. See Thorsten Eitz and Georg Stötzel, *Wörterbuch der 'Vergangenheitsbewältigung': Die NS-Vergangenheit im öffentlichen Sprachgebrauch* (Hildesheim: Olms, 2007), 271 n. 601.

25. As Klemperer (above, n. 23) notes, the term's popularity resulted in its being the subject of satire as early as late 1933.

26. Schmitz-Berning, *Vokabular des Nationalsozialismus*, 278.

27. See Eugen Seidel and Ingeborg Seidel-Slotty, *Sprachwandel im Dritten Reich: Eine kritische Untersuchung faschistischer Einflüsse* (Halle: Verlag Sprache und Literatur, 1961),

True, Heinemann qualifies his ascription of this policy to Antiochus; he writes that the Seleucids strove not precisely for a *Gleichschaltung* but only for something similar. But in context that is merely a scholarly pose meant to avoid the appearance of coming to the topic with an attitude that is too crassly dictated by contemporary circumstances. Despite this, Heinemann goes on to say that the Seleucids, and especially Antiochus Epiphanes, did strive for cultural unity within the kingdom, and he even opines that 1 Macc 1:41's reference to the demand that all become one people echoes the king's actual words. That all fits *Gleichschaltung* well.

Thus, my first point is that, if Bickermann found it difficult to imagine that a Hellenistic king would attempt to impose cultural or religious unity upon his subjects and therefore found himself forced to look for others who could have influenced the king to do so, Heinemann, in his context, had no such difficulties. Heinemann's context, and his active involvement in it and in the German Jewish community's struggle to maintain itself within it, made it quite easy for him to imagine a government trying to impose such unity upon its subjects. In that respect, Heinemann's *Sitz im Leben* was very different from that of Bickermann, who had left Germany for France in 1933, after little more than a decade in Germany—and even when there had not considered himself a German Jew.[28]

2. Hellenism instead of *Volkssitte* = Apostasy?

My second point has to do with the negative part of Heinemann's response to Bickermann: his vigorous denial of the likelihood that Jewish Hellenists would have attempted to move Antiochus to impose the decrees. Heinemann bases this on several claims. One is the general agreement of the sources that Antiochus was responsible—a point that is basically true but overstated by Heinemann.[29] Another, more important argument is Heine-

70–71; K. Pätzold, "Gleichschaltung," in *Enzyklopädie des Nationalsozialismus*, ed. Wolfgang Benz, Hermann Graml, and Hermann Weiß (Stuttgart: Klett-Cotta, 1997), 490–91; Schmitz-Berning, *Vokabular des Nationalsozialismus*, 277–80; Eitz and Stötzel, *Wörterbuch der 'Vergangenheitsbewältigung,'* 270–76.

28. See Baumgarten, *Elias Bickerman*, 108–11.

29. Heinemann overstates it in two ways. First, in his discussion of the ancient sources that ascribe the decrees to Antiochus himself ("Wer veranlaßte den Glaubenszwang," 150–53), he does not recognize the fact that, even if others influenced the king, ancient authors may not have known that or may have preferred to ignore such details. Second, after belatedly admitting (153) that 2 Macc 13:4 and its parallel at *Ant.* 12.384 do have Lysias claiming, retrospectively, that a Jewish hellenizer, Menelaus, was to blame for all the troubles—texts that were Bickermann's very point of departure (*Gott der Makkabäer*, 153)—Heinemann belittles the importance of those texts. He insists that "kein Historiker weiß etwas von der Schuld des Menelaus" ("no historian has anything to say about Menelaus's guilt"), so Lysias's claim must be only ex post facto scape-goating. This sounds like special pleading, for why should

mann's rejection of Bickermann's suggestion that the Jewish hellenizers in Jerusalem held, like various nineteenth-century scholars and reformers (to whom Bickermann alludes[30]), historicizing beliefs that today we associate with biblical criticism and the history of religions: beliefs that undermine the authority of Jewish law by arguing that it was of human and even post-Mosaic origin. Such a belief concerning Jewish law may be found in Diodorus Siculus, apparently going back to Posidonius[31]—but even Posidonius was born only some three decades after the death of Antiochus Epiphanes. Heinemann, who was a specialist in Posidonius's thought (see below, n. 42), argued, in his response to Bickermann, *silently retracting a view he had once posited before the need arose to deal with Bickermann's thesis,* both that such beliefs were not yet current among Greek thinkers prior to Posidonius and that, even if they were, Hellenism in Jerusalem of the second century BCE was probably too superficial to pick up such scientific theories.[32]

For some reason, this particular argument of Heinemann has aroused the most subsequent discussion.[33] It is undoubtedly an important argument. Much more basic for Heinemann, however, seems to have been his insistence that, just as the ancient sources distinguish between the hellenizers' innovations and Antiochus's persecutions, so too must the modern historian recognize that there is a chasm between hellenizing and apostatizing. For Heinemann, it was of fundamental importance to make that point and to argue that, all the more so, there is a chasm between hellenizing, on the one hand, and attempting to force other Jews to give up Judaism, on the other.

For Heinemann, insistence on these points is based on the principle that the Jewish religion requires the observance of Jewish religious law but not adherence to a more general and folksy Jewish way of life—what he terms *Volkssitte*. As long as hellenization applied only to the latter, hellenizers did not abandon Judaism, for only the abandonment or violation of religious law constitutes apostasy.[34]

---

we should accord this passage of 2 Maccabees less weight than the silence of the same work in its earlier chapters?

30. See n. 5 above.

31. See Stern, *Greek and Latin Authors*, 1:184.

32. See Heinemann, "Wer veranlaßte den Glaubenszwang," 156–59 and n. 19 above.

33. Note, for example, that it is at only at this point of his argument with Bickermann that Tcherikover cites Heinemann with approval (*Hellenistic Civilization*, 473 n. 18); so too Bringmann, "Die Verfolgung der jüdischen Religion," 181; and it is also the focus of Hoffmann's discussion in *Juden und Judentum*, 242–43. As Baumgarten notes in his "bibliographical note" in Bickerman's *The Jews in the Greek Age* (310–11; as also in *Elias Bickerman*, 245), that volume is basically Bickermann's "fully nuanced response" to this part of Heinemann's criticism.

34. Note here that L. Levin's characterization of Heinemann's position as if "the line that he drew was between those who did and did not accept the binding character of the

Thus, although Heinemann readily admits that the Jewish reformers of Antiochus's day were very enthusiastic about Hellenism but only lukewarm about the Jewish religion,[35] right at the outset of his discussion he nonetheless insists that although Jason, the first of the prominent hellenizers, strongly opposed Jewish popular practices, he hardly violated Jewish religious law ("scharf gegen die jüdische Volkssitte, aber nur in begrenzten Umfang gegen das jüdische Religionsgesetz verstoßen" [146]). Thus, Jason was a very far cry from Antiochus, whose edicts deliberately strove to abolish the Jewish religion ("bewußt die Beseitigung der jüdischen Religion anstreben" [146]). In this passage, we clearly see that, for Heinemann, *Religion* amounts to the observance of religious law, while everything else about being Jewish is merely *Volkssitte* and nonessential.

Specifically, in the same vein, Heinemann goes on to insist that the adoption of the Greek hat (2 Macc 4:12) was totally innocuous from a religious point of view ("eine religiös so unverfängliche Neuerung" [146]) and that "auch die Einführung des Gymnasion ist nicht, wie Bi[ckermann, S.] 63 meint, 'nach dem jüdischen Gesetz verpönt'" ("even the introduction of a gymnasium is not, as Bickermann [p. 63] thought, prohibited by Jewish law"), for however unhappy Jews might be about what went on in gymnasia, "ein Verbot des Gymnasion ist im jüdischen Schrifttum nirgends zu lessen" (146–147 ["a prohibition of the gymnasium is nowhere to be found in Jewish writings"]). True, Heinemann does go on (ibid.) to point to three of the hellenizers' innovations that were "religiös anfechtbar" (could be criticized from a religious point of view), but he minimizes the import of all three, for:

1. sexual contact with non-Jewish women,[36] although admittedly a violation of "religious ethic," does not constitute "planmässige religiöse Reform" (programmatic religious reform);
2. it is an overstatement to characterize the concealment of circum-

body of traditional halakha as a whole" (preface to his English translation of Heinemann, *The Reasons for the Commandments in Jewish Thought: From the Bible to the Renaissance* [Boston: Academic Studies Press, 2008], xv) is somewhat less than precise, insofar as it does not distinguish between halakha and tradition.

35. Heinemann, "Die Verfolgung der jüdischen Religion," 148: "Daß die jüdischen Hellenisten der Weltkultur helle Begeisterung entgegenbrachten, für ihre Religion dagegen nur sehr laue Gefühle hegten, ist gar nicht zu bezweifeln" ["It is not at all to be doubted that the Jewish Hellenists responded to the world culture with hearty enthusiasm, while for their own religion, in contrast, they retained only lukewarm feelings"]).

36. For this Heinemann cites ἐζευγίσθησαν in 1 Macc 1:15, which (as is especially suggested by 2:24–26) seems to be echoing *ṣmd* in Num 25:3, 5. Other relevant sources include a talmudic reference to a "Hasmonean court" that prohibited sexual relations with a non-Jewish woman (b. Sanh. 82a) and the polemics of Jubilees 30. For a review of the evidence and doubts about the extent of the phenomenon see Martha Himmelfarb, "Levi, Phinehas, and the Problem of Intermarriage at the Time of the Maccabean Revolt," *JSQ* 6 (1999): 1–24.

cision as "Abfall vom heiligen Bunde" (rebellion against the holy covenant—1 Macc 1:15) since it applies to only one law; and

3. sending funds to subsidize pagan sacrifices at games in Tyre (2 Macc 4:18-20) would not have been much of a violation of Jewish law, and anyway probably even Jason did not intend the funds to be used that way.[37]

This distinction between *Volkssitte* and what is entailed by the real Jewish *Religion*, namely, religious *law*, with the consequent insistence that one can abandon the *Volkssitte* without violating the *Religion*, is a cardinal argument for Heinemann. It seems to me that, in order to understand this distinction and to understand why Bickermann was not impressed by it, we must realize that Heinemann was brought up in, and remained devoted to, the version of modern German Orthodoxy associated with the name of Rabbi Samson Raphael Hirsch (1808–1888), who insisted that Jews could and should live in both worlds.[38] This type of Orthodoxy, usually termed neo-Orthodoxy, had to entail, in real life, a limiting of the sphere addressed and claimed by Judaism, so as to leave space for life in contemporary German culture—and the way that was done was by reducing Judaism to Jewish law as opposed to a more total way of life. As Mordechai Breuer has shown, such a reduction of "being Jewish" to observance of Jewish religious law was often criticized by self-critical Orthodox (who complained that "apart from their religious life, Jews had ceased to be Jews"), but in practice one could summarize the stance of most German Orthodox Jews as "We want to do nothing in contradiction to the provisions of the *Shulchan Aruch* [i.e., the authoritative code of Jewish law], but we do not want everything we do to derive from it."[39]

---

37. Here Heinemann specifically contradicts Bickermann (*Gott der Makkabäer*, 64), who had assumed, following the plain meaning of 2 Macc 4:19–20, that Jason had wanted the money to go for sacrifices.

38. For Heinemann's Hirschian upbringing, see Urbach, "Prof. Isaak Heinemann," 219. Several of Heinemann's publications are devoted to Hirsch; see n. 16 above. On Hirsch's approach, see Noah H. Rosenbloom, *Tradition in an Age of Reform: The Religious Philosophy of Samson Raphael Hirsch* (Philadelphia: Jewish Publication Society of America, 1976), and Robert Liberles, *Religious Conflict in Social Context: The Resurgence of Orthodox Judaism in Frankfurt am Main, 1838–1877*, Contributions to the Study of Religion 13 (Westport, CT: Greenwood, 1985).

39. Mordechai Breuer, *Modernity within Tradition: The Social History of Orthodox Jewry in Imperial Germany* (New York: Columbia University Press, 1992), 24, 26 (quoting publications of 1870 and 1876). True, it seems that Breuer took the latter passage (*Die Angriffe des Herrn Rabbiner Süskind zu Wiesbaden gegen die Statuten der Israel. Religionsgesellschaft zu Frankfurt a. M.* [Frankfurt a. M.: Kauffmann, 1876], 10) out of context: the assertion was made by an Orthodox spokesman defending the fact that his community's rules *were even more stringent*, in defense of the religious community, than those of the *Shulchan Aruch*. A candid assertion by an Orthodox Jew that he does not want everything he does to be governed by Jewish law

Indeed, Heinemann was a salient example of that type of attitude. Heinemann, whose major works were devoted to Philo of Alexandria, including a large monograph about Philo's relationship to both Jewish and Greek culture,[40] expressed intense admiration for Philo's success at living in both worlds. That is natural, for Heinemann too lived in both worlds: his Berlin doctoral dissertation, written in Latin, concerned a prominent Athenian of the seventh–sixth century BCE, Solon,[41] and his major work of the 1920s was a two-volume monograph on the metaphysics of the Hellenistic philosopher Posidonius.[42] He wrote these works while teaching both at the University of Breslau and at the Jewish theological seminary of Breslau. There was no way such a scholar could easily accept the notion that his forerunners of the second century BCE were, simply due to their penchant for Hellenism, to be blamed for an attempt to destroy Judaism.

Perhaps even more basically, we should note that Heinemann not only had been brought up in a Hirschian circle but also had studied at a Jewish theological seminary—the Orthodox Hildesheimer Rabbinerseminar in Berlin—whose graduates were required to earn a doctorate from a university if they wanted to be ordained by the seminary. The latter demand exposed them to the scorn of traditionalist circles, for whom German *Rabbinerdoktoren* symbolized everything that was incompatible with true religion.[43] In response, someone like Heinemann simply had to insist that admiration for Hellenistic culture was, in and of itself, a chasm away from anti-Judaism. Indeed, in support of his claim that education in a gymnasium was not contrary to Judaism, Heinemann—who taught in his family's Jewish *Privatlyzeum* in Frankfurt for many years, a school that emphasized "scientific" education (*horribile dictu*—even for girls)[44]—-spe-

---

would be—as Breuer himself notes (23)—out of character. Nevertheless, Breuer's point that this was, by and large, their true stance seems to be well founded. For an idea of the world of the Frankfurt Jewish *Gesetzestreue* among whom Heinemann grew up, see his account of his father's role in the schism in the Frankfurt Jewish community: "Zur Umbildung der Frankfurter Gemeinde in den Jahren 1876/77," *Frankfurter Israelitisches Gemeindeblatt*, September 1932, 6–7 (this newspaper is accessible online via the "Compact Memory" website, under the title *Gemeindeblatt der Israelitischen Gemeinde Frankfurt am Main*).

40. Isaak Heinemann, *Philons griechische und jüdische Bildung: Kulturvergleichende Untersuchungen zu Philons Darstellung der jüdischen Gesetze* (Breslau: Marcus, 1932). For surveys of Heinemann's oeuvre, see n. 16 above.

41. Isaak Heinemann, *Studia Solonea* (diss., Berlin; Berlin: Vogt, 1897).

42. Isaak Heinemann, *Poseidonios' metaphysische Schriften*, 2 vols. (Breslau: Marcus, 1921–1928).

43. For such criticism, see, e.g., Daniel R. Schwartz and Christhard Hoffmann, "Early but Opposed, Supported but Late: Two Berlin Seminaries Which Attempted to Move Abroad," *Year Book of the Leo Baeck Institute* 36 (1991): 270, 283.

44. On the Heinemann'sches Institute (Israelitische höhere Mädchenschule und Pensionat), which was directed by Heinemann's father and stepmother, and his own teaching there for around two decades, see Paul Arnsberg, *Die Geschichte der Franfurter Juden seit der Französischen Revolution*, 3 vols. (Darmstadt: Roether, 1983), 2:79–80, 3:182–84. An advertise-

cifically points to Jewish participation in games in the gymnasia of ancient Alexandria as evidence that such participation was not a violation of Jewish law.[45] Similarly, he points to Philo for support of the assertion that circumcision is just one law among many, and therefore concealing it does not constitute abrogation of the covenant.[46] As Maren Niehoff has shown, German scholars of *Wissenschaft des Judentums* frequently pointed to the Alexandrian model as "a paradigm for acculturation, modernization and pluralism within Judaism."[47] But that entails a definition of Judaism limited to the more or less narrow bounds of religious law alone, to the exclusion of the more inclusive *Volkssitte* that amounts to a way of life—a way of life in which being Jewish fills up so much space and time that little is left for going to gymnasia or for symbiosis with any other culture. German Jewish Orthodoxy had to leave such a *Volkssitte* behind in order to participate in the world of *Bildung* and scholarship at large, and Heinemann speaks here for the many who did just that.

Bickermann came from another world. In the Eastern European world in which Bickermann was raised, religious Judaism was still very traditional; that is, it was usually assumed to be, for those who adhered to it, an entire way of life and not just the relatively narrow domains addressed by religious law *sensu stricto*.[48] In the absence of a distinction between the

---

ment for the school in *Frankfurter Israelitisches Familienblatt*, 2 September 1904, p. 7, first says it offers girls "gründliche wissenschaftliche" education, only thereafter adding also "häusliche und gesellschaftliche"; so too ibid. 31 August 1917, p. 7.

45. Heinemann, "Wer veranlaßte den Glaubenszwang," 147, n. 8. He refers to H. Idris Bell, *Juden und Griechen im römischen Alexandreia*, Behefte zum "Alten Orient" 9 (Leipzig: Hinrich'sche, 1926), 26, who cites in this context the fifth column of Claudius's letter to the Alexandrians (P. London 1912).

46. Heinemann, "Wer veranlaßte den Glaubenszwang," 148. He gives no specific reference to Philo for this point. Indeed, his position is surprising and seems to have been influenced by the needs of his critique of Bickermann. A few years earlier, without such a context, Heinemann had emphasized that Philo treats circumcision separately ("völlig ausserhalb der Hauptgliederung") at the outset of *De specialibus legibus* 1, before turning to the specific laws (*Philons griechische und jüdische Bildung*, 176–77). See also Heinemann's own outline of the structure of *De specialibus legibus*, which precedes his translation of the work (*Die Werke Philos von Alexandria in deutscher Übersetzimg*, ed. Leopold Cohn [Breslau: Marcus, 1910], 2:8): Philo's opening discussion of circumcision precedes his discussion of the first and second commandments.

47. Maren R. Niehoff, "Alexandrian Judaism in 19th Century *Wissenschaft des Judentums*: Between Christianity and Modernization," in *Jüdische Geschichte in hellenistisch-römischer Zeit: Wege der Forschung; Vom alten zum neuen Schürer*, ed. Aharon Oppenheimer (Munich: Oldenbourg, 1999), 9–28 (quotation from 27). See esp. 22–25 on work at the Breslau Seminary, and 25 on the rise of Philonic studies—which was at the heart of much of Heinemann's work. For a similar turn to the Alexandrian example by younger contemporaries of Heinemann, see Moses Hadas, "Judaism and the Hellenistic Experience: A Classical Model for Living in Two Cultures," *Commentary* 222 (August 1956): 119–24, along with readers' responses, 375–76.

48. For this contrast, see, e.g., Eli Lederhendler, "Modernity without Emancipation or Assimilation? The Case of Russian Jewry," in *Assimilation and Community: The Jews in*

latter and mere *Volkssite*, that was a stance that tended to make any deviation from Jewish tradition, even from those practices that Heinemann's Orthodox world would deem to be mere *Volkssitte*, a departure from Judaism. That was a Jewish world in which, as the Yiddish phrase would have it, a Greek had no place at all in a Sukkah; as mentioned above, a *Rabbinerdoktor* was something of a joke. Reverting to our Hellenists of the second century BCE, it seems that, if Heinemann reflected German circumstances, Bickermann's theory reflects those of Eastern Europe.[49]

In sum, my second point is that Heinemann's context made him used to the idea that Jews could be Orthodox by observing Jewish law (but not necessarily all the folksy traditions that had accreted to it) and nonetheless be Hellenists. Bickermann, in contrast, was led by his eastern European upbringing to see the abandonment of a Jewish way of life, even if that applied only to what Heinemann would marginalize as mere *Volksitte* as opposed to religious law, as tantamount to leaving the fold entirely.

3. Jewish Representatives with Only Loose and Lukewarm Attachment to Judaism

My third and final point about Heinemann's article pertains especially to its concluding remarks. They too, I believe, deserve much more attention than they have received. After an entire article dedicated to exonerating the Jerusalem Hellenists of Antiochus's day of responsibility for the king's persecution of Judaism, Heinemann turns about-face in the last four sentences of the article and asserts that Antiochus would not have begun his

Nineteenth-Century Europe, ed. Jonathan Frankel and Steven J. Zipperstein (Cambridge: Cambridge University Press, 1992), 324–43. For a somewhat paradoxical corollary, see Adam S. Ferziger, *Exclusion and Hierarchy: Orthodoxy, Nonobservance, and the Emergence of Modern Jewish Identity*, Jewish Culture and Contexts (Philadelphia: University of Pennsylvania Press, 2005), 166–68, 186–87: in Eastern Europe, the fact that great masses of Jews continued to adhere to tradition allowed Orthodox authorities to feel less threatened and, therefore, more inclusive toward nonobservant Jews. That is, however, a legal implication. Sociologically, the gap between Eastern European traditionalists and nonobservant Jews could be much greater than the one between German Orthodox (such as Heinemann) and nonobservant Jews, whose lifestyles might be quite similar, apart from some circumscribed aspects of life defined by religious law.

49. Note, for example, the 1886 case discussed by Ferziger (*Exclusion and Hierarchy*, 166–68), in which a prominent Orthodox rabbi in Germany, Esriel Hildesheimer, wanted to deny a noncircumcised boy the right to celebrate his bar mitzvah, in order to make a point about the importance of religious practice. In rejecting that suggestion, the just-as-prominent Lithuanian rabbi with whom Hildesheimer consulted, Isaac Elhanan Spektor, emphasized that legally the child was a Jew and also expressed the fear—which apparently did not worry Hildesheimer—that Hildesheimer's policy might drive such people into apostasy and even into anti-Semitism. That is the kind of suspicion that Bickermann bespoke.

persecution of Judaism had he thought it would encounter serious resistance. This leads him to conclude that the Jewish hellenizers of Jerusalem did share some of the guilt (*eine gewisse Mitschuld*):

> Sie haben die völlige Ausmerzung des Judentums, die Antiochos nach Möglichkeit durchführen versuchte, nicht veranlaßt, und in ihrer großen Mehrheit schwerlich gewollt; aber ernstlichen Widerstand brauchte der König von ihrer Seite allerdings nicht zu befürchten. Und es war das Unglück des Judentums, daß Antiochos seine [= des Judentums – DRS] innere Kraft nach Männern bemaß, die ihm vertraut waren, mit den Überlieferungen ihrer jüdischen Gemeinschaft aber nur noch in sehr loser Verbindung standen.[50]

> [They did not initiate the complete eradication of Judaism, which Antiochus attempted to carry out if at all possible, and the great majority of them hardly desired it—but the king did not need to fear any serious resistance on their part. And it was the misfortune of Judaism, that Antiochus measured its inner strength according to those men with whom he was familiar—people whose attachment to the traditions of their Jewish community was, by then, only very loose.]

That is the very end of the article, Heinemann's parting shot. My impression is that any sentence written by a German Jew in 1938, placed so prominently at the conclusion of an article and beginning the final sentence with a lapidary reference to "das Unglück des Judentums," must be read in light of the contemporaneous situation—especially since the sentence includes nothing (such as *damaligen*) that limits its relevance to the ancient case under discussion. Heinemann, that is, seems to be bespeaking the view that, had those the Nazis took to be representing Judaism had more of an attachment to it, the Nazis would not have undertaken their program aimed at suppressing Judaism. This amounts to a complaint that those who were representing the Jews to the Nazis had only a loose attachment to Judaism and its traditions, and to blaming them for thus making the Nazis think that an attempt to eradicate Judaism could easily succeed.

Whom did Heinemann have in mind? Did he, in fact, have anyone specific in mind? His wording, about Jews whose attachment to Judaism was only very loose (or "lukewarm" [n. 35]) is a general and stereotypical way of referring to nontraditional Jews and so need not point to anyone in particular.[51] Indeed, so far I have not found anything explicit enough to

---

50. Heinemann, "Wer veranlaßte den Glaubenszwang," 172.

51. Compare, for example, Toni Cassirer's general reference to German Jewish refugees in the 1930s "die nur noch eine ganz lose Verbindung zum Judentum hatten" (*Mein Leben mit Ernst Cassirer* [Hildesheim: Gerstenberg, 1981], 234). Cf. also Todd M. Engelman's account of liberal German Jews in England of the mid-nineteenth century: "their attachment

allow for anything more than a guess. Nevertheless, as a work in progress in which one seeks help and input from friends and colleagues, I will not abstain from that guess, however painful it might be.

German Jews were represented collectively, to the Nazi government, by the Reichsvertretung der deutschen Juden (National Representative Body of German Jews). So it was named when founded in 1933, and even when it was demonstratively downgraded in 1935 to Reichsvertretung der Juden in Deutschland ("... of the Jews in Germany"), it retained its designation as the body representing (*vertreten*) the Jews to the German government.[52] Its director from the outset was Otto Hirsch (1885–1941); its first and only president was Leo Baeck (1873–1956). Hirsch was an important lay leader of liberal Judaism;[53] Baeck, the foremost liberal rabbi in Germany of his day.[54]

Now it just so happens that there was considerable competition between Heinemann and Baeck, who were of almost the same age. This had, first of all, an institutional basis. There were three rabbinical seminaries in Germany, and, while Heinemann had studied at the Orthodox Hildesheimer rabbinical seminary in Berlin and had spent much of his career at the traditionally oriented seminary in Breslau, Baeck, although he began his higher Jewish studies in Breslau (1891–1894), deliberately left it for a more liberal institution.[55] He completed his studies in Berlin—not at Hildesheimer's, but, rather, at the third German rabbinical seminary—the liberal Lehranstalt für die Wissenschaft des Judentums, founded by Abraham Geiger, the real founder of German Reform Judaism. Baeck was ordained by the Lehranstalt in 1897 and, eventually, would teach there for decades, beginning in 1913.[56] Anyone familiar with competition among

---

to Judaism was lukewarm ... maintained a loose attachment to Judaism" ("German Jews in Victorian England: A Study in Drift and Defection," in Frankel and Zipperstein, *Assimilation and Community*, 74).

52. See Esriel Hildesheimer, *Jüdische Selbstverwaltung unter dem NS-Regime: Der Existenzkampf der Reichsvertretung und Reichsvereinigung der Juden in Deutschland*, Schriftenreihe wissenschaftlicher Abhandlungen des Leo Baeck Instituts [SWALBI] 50 (Tübingen: Mohr Siebeck, 1994); Otto Dov Kulka, ed., *Dokumente zur Geschichte der Reichsvertretung der deutschen Juden 1933–1939*, vol. 1 of *Deutsches Judentum unter dem Nationalsozialismus*, SWALBI 54 (Tübingen: Mohr Siebeck, 1997).

53. See P. Sauer, "Otto Hirsch: Director of the Reichsvertretung," *Year Book of the Leo Baeck Institute* 32 (1987): 341–68.

54. There is a huge literature about Baeck. See, inter alia, Leonard Baker, *Days of Sorrow and Pain: Leo Baeck and the Berlin Jews* (New York: Macmillan, 1978); and Heuer, *Lexikon deutsch-jüdischer Autoren*, 1:289–98.

55. See the anecdotes in Baker, *Days of Sorrow*, 21.

56. See *Zweiunddreissigster Bericht der Lehranstalt für die Wissenschaft des Judentums in Berlin* (Berlin: Itzkowski, 1914), 8, 58–75 (Baeck's inaugural lecture, "Griechische und jüdische Predigt"). For Baeck's ordination there, see Baker, *Days of Sorrow*, 26. At times in its history the Lehranstalt was termed "Hochschule"; I use "Lehranstalt" throughout.

scholars, and among academic institutions, can imagine what it was like to have two Jewish institutions of higher learning, representing two diametrically opposed versions of Judaism, in the same city—at times, indeed, on the very same street (Artilleriestrasse). If, for example, in 1897, while Heinemann was studying at the Hildesheimer seminary, a prominent professor at the Lehranstalt allowed himself to complain publicly that the Judaism of Hildesheimer's was hidebound and deathlike,[57] we can easily imagine what clichés were common at Hildesheimer's about the lack of serious devotion to Judaism at the Lehranstalt. Certainly Esriel Hildesheimer himself was full of burning anger and unbounded scorn for the Lehranstalt, which he characterized as devoted to the destruction of Judaism.[58] Those were the kinds of clichés Heinemann will have imbibed, as a youthful scholar, with regard to the institution with which Baeck was to stay affiliated throughout his life, and Heinemann's move to Breslau will not have engendered any need to back far away from such clichés.

Moreover, note that only about a year before Heinemann responded to Bickermann, the Reichsvertretung had tried, in a move presided over by Baeck in a committee in which the deck was stacked and so Heinemann's protest was quite outnumbered, to amalgamate the Berlin Lehranstalt and the Breslau seminary into one institution. That came to naught, but must have engendered a lot of hot air and resentment.[59]

Baeck's work competed with Heinemann's in a more personal way as well. Note, first of all, that early in his career Baeck turned to apologetics: his *Das Wesen des Judentums* (1905), which responded to Adolf von Harnack's *Das Wesen des Christentums* (1900) and the way it portrayed Judaism, put him on the map quite prominently.[60] But what he did in that

---

57. See Heymann Steinthal, *Über Juden und Judentum: Vorträge und Aufsätze*, ed. Gustav Karpeles, Schriften herausgegeben von der Gesellschaft zur Förderung der Wissenschaft des Judentums (Berlin: Poppelauer, 1906), 246–47. In this lecture (originally published in the *Allgemeine Zeitung des Judenthums*, 4 June 1897, 270) celebrating the first quarter-century of the Lehranstalt, Steinthal contrasts its living Judaism to the historical Judaism of the Breslau seminary and the dead Judaism of Hildesheimer's.

58. For Hildesheimer's intense hostility both to the Lehranstalt and to the Breslau seminary, see David Ellenson, *Rabbi Esriel Hildesheimer and the Creation of a Modern Jewish Orthodoxy* (Tuscaloosa: University of Alabama Press, 1990), 75–84.

59. On this episode, see Kulka, *Dokumente zur Geschichte der Reichsvertretung*, 302–7. True, the Reichsvertretung's committee on rabbinical training (see ibid., 304) had one representative from each of the three seminaries. But it was chaired by Baeck himself; two of its members were from the Allgemeiner Rabbinerverband Deutschlands, which also happened to be chaired by Baeck (see Kulka, *Dokumente*, 455 [and see Ellenson, *Rabbi Esriel Hildesheimer*, 85, on avoidance of it by the Orthodox]); and the Lehranstalt was allowed a representative for its general studies program, apart from one for its rabbinical program. Thus, of the seven members of the committee, five were in Baeck's camp. According to Kulka (303 n. 5), no more is known of this plan.

60. For an English version, see Leo Baeck, *The Essence of Judaism* (1936; repr., New York: Schocken, 1961; German original 1905). On its context and reception, see Baker, *Days of Sor-*

volume, in searching for the *Wesen* (essence) of Judaism as opposed to all its secondary and tertiary accretions, was just what Heinemann was doing: looking for the Jewish religion in its most circumscribed form, without its *Volkssitte*, so as to allow for a major involvement in Western culture beside it. The fact that Baeck sought to achieve that same end by seeking Judaism in its most universalist form, identifying its essence as faith and morality and ascribing law only a secondary function (preservation of the community that observes true religion), whereas Heinemann basically equated Judaism with Jewish law, made the difference between them quite polar.[61] Moreover, Baeck devoted much of his research and writing to ancient rabbinic literature and to its Hellenistic context, thus plowing a field that very frequently was the same as the one worked by Heinemann[62]—and it is not at all surprising that Baeck is one of the few scholars with whom Heinemann troubles to argue in his volume on Philo, once even underscoring his point with an exclamation point.[63]

In sum: Baeck and Heinemann represented academic institutions that competed with each other and varieties of Judaism that frequently evinced contempt for each other; and they competed with each other personally as well, working with similar materials and on similar themes. But Heinemann, in Breslau, played virtually no role in national Jewish leadership and representation to the Nazis. Baeck, in Berlin, was at its helm—and anyone could see, in 1938, that things were not going well.

Thus, although I would prefer to find something that explicitly backs up this hunch, it appears quite likely that academic competition plus inner-Jewish tensions could, in the pressure cooker in which German Jewry found itself in 1938, with everyone looking for someone to blame,

---

row, 42–47. For an eastern Jewish response to Baeck's work that denounces it as the work of "ein moderner Rabbiner" and totally scorns it, see [Elias] Jakob Fromer, *Das Wesen des Judentums* (Berlin: Hüpeden & Merzyn, 1905), esp. 181–82 n. 60.

61. For Heinemann, see above, after n. 33. As for Baeck, see esp. *Das Wesen des Judentums* (Berlin: Nathansen & Lamm, 1905), 151 (Eng., *Essence of Judaism*, 263). Here, daringly appropriating the mishnaic distinction (m. Avot 1:1) between basic laws ("Torah") and other, secondary laws that were merely "fences" to ensure that the Torah would not be violated, Baeck (who goes on to protest definitions of "Torah" that limit it to law), defines all of Jewish ritual law, including such basics as the Sabbath and dietary laws, as mere "ceremonial laws" that were only fences around true "Religion."

62. Note already his inaugural lecture at the Lehranstalt (n. 56 above), and see his collection *Aus drei Jahrtausenden: Wissenschaftliche Untersuchungen und Abhandlungen zur Geschichte des jüdischen Glaubens* (Berlin: Schocken, 1938). For English versions of some of his studies of ancient Judaism, see Leo Baeck, *Judaism and Christianity* (with a biographical introduction by Walter Kaufmann; New York: Leo Baeck Institute, 1958); also Baeck, *The Pharisees and Other Essays*, with an introduction by Krister Stendahl (New York: Schocken, 1966).

63. See Heinemann, *Philons griechische und jüdische Bildung*, 47 n. 4 (Baeck interprets a text very one-sidedly ["in sehr einseitiger Beleuchtung"]) and 61–62 n. 5 (Heinemann scolds Baeck for holding that those who thought less of priesthood than of the Torah are therefore to be understood as opposing the priesthood.).

lead people like Heinemann to imagine that if only the Nazis had to deal with more traditional Jews than the Leo Baeck type—namely, with Jews whose attachment to Judaism was not (so Heinemann thought) so lukewarm and loose[64]—they would not think they could get away with things so easily. That is the direction in which Heinemann's closing complaint about the hellenizers seems to point.[65]

In sum, I suggest that (a) Heinemann's willingness to characterize Antiochus's policy as *Gleichschaltung*, (b) his insistence that hellenizing Jews were not apostates and were far from imposing apostasy, and (c) his complaint that they were too lukewarm about their Judaism and therefore—since they represented Judaism in the eyes of the government—let the government think it could easily suppress Judaism, are all to be understood as reflecting his own particular location in the world of German Jewry in the intense years in which he wrote, half a decade after the Nazis' rise to power. This is only as should be expected.

64. See the quotations in n. 35 and at n. 50.

65. It is interesting to imagine how the end of Heinemann's article would have been received, and the look on his face, had he given it in 1938 as a lecture in the Lehranstalt.

Abel J. Herzberg's *The Memoirs of King Herod*

The Interaction between a Tragic Tyrant and His Subjects

JAN WILLEM VAN HENTEN
University of Amsterdam/Stellenbosch

This contribution is a modest expression of my immense gratitude for Shaye Cohen's long-standing guidance in scholarship and his friendship. It interacts with his work on Josephus as well his keen interest in European culture and society. In his *Beginning of Jewishness*, which I use as a standard work in one of my MA classes, Herod the Great figures as the first case study with the leading question "Was Herod Jewish?"[1] The answer is complex. Shaye concludes that the historical Herod was certainly Jewish, but he also points out that the rabbis thought differently and the answer ultimately depends on whom you ask: "Herod was either a *Ioudaios* (that is, a Judean and Jew), a blue-blooded Judean, an Idumean, and therefore not a Judean, an Idumean and therefore also a Judean, an Idumean and therefore a half-Judean, an Ascalonite, a gentile slave, an Arab, or–the Messiah!"[2] The Dutch lawyer Abel J. Herzberg (1893–1989) was fascinated by the figure of Herod, and, interestingly, he answers the question whether Herod was a Jew in a different and ultimately negative way.

Herzberg was a leading figure in Dutch Jewry before the Second World War, primarily due to his strong commitment to the Zionist cause. During the war he was first interned, with other members of the Jewish elite, in Barneveld, a village in the Netherlands. In January 1944 he and his wife were transferred to Bergen Belsen. Herzberg and his family survived, but the experience affected them deeply.[3] Herzberg wrote several works

1. Shaye J. D. Cohen, *The Beginnings of Jewishness: Boundaries, Varieties, Uncertainties*, HCS 31 (Berkeley: University of California Press, 1999), 13–24.

2. Ibid., 23.

3. This is apparent from his books about the persecution of the Jews but also from his word of thanks during the presentation of the P. C. Hooft prize; see the next section and the

about the persecution of the Jews during the war, varying from very factual to highly personal and emotional reports. After the war he was a controversial and less prominent figure among the Jews in the Netherlands, but he became a popular author and public figure in Dutch society at large, especially after the publication of his *Letters to my Grandson* (1964), which explains Herzberg's Jewish heritage—his family originated from the Baltic region—to his grandson, who was living in Israel.[4] Herzberg composed several retellings of biblical and historical writings, focusing on Miriam, King Saul, King Herod, and other figures. The most interesting work of this type concerns the pseudo-autobiographical *Memoirs of King Herod* (*De memoires van koning Herodes*) from 1974.[5] What is the relevance of the Herod figure for Herzberg, and what caused his fascination for this king, who ruled ca. two thousand years ago?

Although Herod's image in recent historical studies has become more positive, the king has mostly been remembered as a wicked and cruel tyrant, mainly on the basis of the New Testament. This is Herzberg's point of departure.[6] A crucial factor in Herod's remembrance is the dramatic brief passage about the murder of the innocents in the story of the birth of Jesus (Matt 2:16–18),[7] which is represented many times, for instance, in Italian Renaissance art.[8] Herzberg repeatedly argues that this murder is a myth, but he still considers Herod to have been a tyrant,[9] in line with our main source about the king, Flavius Josephus. Josephus characterizes Herod in an exceptional passage in *The Jewish War* as the most savage tyrant ever (*War* 2.84), an image he maliciously elaborates in *The Jewish*

---

written version of his word of thanks, Literatuurmuseum 2 QUE Correspondentie Herzberg, A.J. (1–2). The murder of Wilhelm Spiegel, Herzberg's brother-in-law, in his own house in Kiel affected Herzberg deeply (Arie Kuiper, *Een wijze ging voorbij: Het leven van Abel J. Herzberg* [A wise person went by: The life of Abel J. Herzberg][Amsterdam: Querido, 1997], 115).

4. Abel J. Herzberg, *Brieven aan mijn kleinzoon: De geschiedenis van een joodse emigrantenfamilie* (The Hague: Bakker/Daamen, 1964).

5. Abel J. Herzberg, *De memoires van koning Herodes* (Amsterdam: Querido, 1974; reprinted in 1986 and in 1993 as part of Herzberg's collected writings, *Verzameld werk* 1 [Amsterdam: Querido, 1993], 7–218); Willem M. Visser, *Abel J. Herzberg*, Grote ontmoetingen 34 (Nijmegen: Gottmer; Brugge: Orion, 1979), 74–75.

6. See, among the host of recent studies, esp. Peter Richardson, *Herod: King of the Jews and Friend of the Romans*, Studies on Personalities of the New Testament (Columbia: University of South Carolina Press, 1996); Geza Vermes, *The True Herod* (London: Bloomsbury, 2014); and Adam Marshak, *The Many Faces of Herod the Great* (Grand Rapids: Eerdmans, 2015).

7. As stated also by Herzberg, "Het laatste woord over Herodes, de geschiedenis van een tyran," *Maatstaf* 4 (1956–1957): 178–84, here 178.

8. Giotto included it in the fresco cycle in the Scrovegni Chapel in Padua (1303–1305), and Giovanni Pisano depicted it on two sculpted pulpits made in Pistoia (1301–1311); for details, see Jules Lubbock, *Storytelling in Christian Art from Giotto to Donatello* (New Haven: Yale University Press, 2006), 39–147.

9. Herzberg, "Het laatste woord," 179. Kuiper, *Een wijze*, 414; 424–25.

Antiquities.[10] The Byzantine scholar Photius (*Bib.* 238) gives the deathblow to Herod's positive image by combining Matthew's story with passages from Josephus.[11] The result is obvious from a wide range of references to Herod as a wicked tyrant, including Shakespeare's phrase "out-Heroding Herod" (*Hamlet* 3.2) and more recently Mark Rich's script for *The Nativity Story*, which depicts Herod as vicious tyrant and a pawn of the Roman Empire.[12]

Herzberg's work is a fascinating case of the reception history of King Herod. Like Josephus, he returns to the figure of Herod in a second book. The city authorities of Amsterdam commissioned a play from Herzberg in 1953, and he decided to devote it to Herod. Because his key character was so complex and difficult to understand without a historical context, he made an unusual decision to publish the play together with a detailed historical introduction and epilogue: *Herod: The History of a Tyrant* (1955).[13] The play was staged about ten times in 1955, but not afterwards apart from an abridged version for TV in 1973. Its reception was mixed; some critics thought it was long-winded.[14] The New Israelite Weekly (*Nieuw Israëlitisch Weekblad*) commented that some of the scenes missed "a Jewish atmosphere," which could easily have been added, such as the prayer of the dying and the lighting of the *hanukkiah* on the last evening of Hanukkah.[15] Herzberg himself was not satisfied with the final result. He returned to Herod and wrote an elaborate history of the king in the 1970s in the form of detailed fictional memoirs in the tradition of the famous *Mémoires d'Hadrien* by Marguerite Yourcenar.[16] As one would expect, the *Memoirs* deal with Herod's plans, emotions, and personal reflections, but they also highlight the interaction between Herod and the Jewish people, the

---

10. Jan Willem van Henten, "Constructing Herod as a Tyrant: Assessing Josephus' Parallel Passages," in *Flavius Josephus: Interpretation and History* (eds. J. Pastor, P. Stern and M. Mor; JSJSup 146; Leiden: Brill, 2011), 193-216.

11. Photius, *Bibliothèque*, ed. and trans. René Henry, 9 vols., Collection des universités de France (Paris: Les Belles Lettres, 2003), 5:142–43.

12. *The Nativity Story*, directed by Catherine Hardwicke (New Line Cinema, 2006).

13. Abel J. Herzberg, *Herodes: De geschiedenis van een tyran* [Herod: The history of a tyrant] (Amsterdam: De Arbeiderspers, 1955).

14. For the reception of the play as well as the book, see Kuiper, *Een wijze*, 421–28.

15. Siegfried E. van Praag, *Nieuw Israëlitisch Weekblad*, 20 June 1955. The author nevertheless concludes that Herzberg is very much himself in the play and deeply Jewish (Kuiper, *Een wijze*, 427).

16. Marguerite Yourcenar, *Mémoires d'Hadrien* (Paris: Plon, 1951). Hadrian's memoirs have been lost like Herod's. Herzberg may have followed up the advice of a publisher, Jan van Loghum Slaterus, who refused to publish *Herodes: De geschiedenis van een tyran* because Herod was a minor tyrant and not an interesting figure and the work contained far too many details. Van Loghum Slaterus suggested that a novel would be a more suitable genre; see the letter by Jan van Loghum Slaterus dated 21 April 1954, Literatuurmuseum 2 QUE Correspondentie Herzberg, A.J. (1-2); Kuiper, *Een wijze*, 422.

king's main subjects, as well as his foreign policy and relationship with Augustus and other prominent political figures such as Marc Antony and Cleopatra.[17] In this brief contribution I will offer brief introductions to Herzberg's biography and his *Memoirs* and then aim to discuss three issues: (1) Herzberg's presentation of Herod in his second work about the king; (2) his interpretation of Judaism in the time of Herod, which is closely related to the Herod figure; and (3) a brief attempt to explain Herzberg's fascination with Herod in a synthesis that also contextualizes his presentation of Herod by connecting it to relevant statements in public or his personal correspondence.

Brief Biography

Abel Herzberg was born in Amsterdam on 17 September 1893, and he died in Amsterdam at the advanced age of ninety-five on 19 May 1989.[18] His parents came from Latvia and Lithuania and both settled in the Netherlands in 1882. Herzberg was a lawyer by profession, who specialized in the legislation for beverages, including alcoholic drinks.[19] He was already a Zionist activist in his early years, being, among other things, involved in the foundation of the Jewish Youth Organization (Joodse Jeugdfederatie). He was also the editor of the magazine *Hatikwah* of the Dutch Zionist Student Organization (NSZO). Later on he became a member of the Dutch Zionist League (Nederlandse Zionistenbond), of which he was president from 1934 to 1939.[20] During the war Herzberg first was director of a labor camp for young Jews at Wieringen. He was interned in camp De Biezen at Barneveld in March 1943, where he joined the so-called Barneveld group, a group of "meritorious" Jews who were not "set to work" due to

17. In a letter to the director Reinhold Kuipers of the publishing house Querido, dated 22 September 1973, Herzberg states that it concerns a completely new work ("volledig nieuw werk"); Literatuurmuseum 2 QUE Correspondentie Herzberg, A.J. (1-2). Cf. an undated memo by Herzberg about his *Memoires*, Literatuurmuseum 20A HERZ H Herodes, pp. 1–2.

18. See details in the extensive biography by Kuiper, *Een wijze*. See also Connie Kristel, *Geschiedenis als opdracht: Abel Herzberg, Jacques Presser en Lou de Jong over de jodenvervolging* [History as dedication: Abel Herzberg, Jacques Presser, and Lou de Jong about the persecution of the Jews] (Amsterdam: Meulenhoff, 1998), 27–47; *De digitale bibliotheek voor de Nederlandse letteren*: http://www.dbnl.org/auteurs/auteur.php?id=herz001; *De Bibliografie van de Nederlandse taal- en literatuurwetenschap*: http://www.bntl.nl/bntl/?wicket:interface=:21.

19. In 1932, Herzberg published a lengthy monograph on the new license act of 1931: *De nieuwe drankwet met toelichting* (Rotterdam: Nijgh en Van Ditmar, 1932). He finished his law practice when he was eighty years old; see the invitation to farewell drinks by the law firm Stibbe and Blaisse, dated 11 April 1973, Literatuurmuseum 2 QUE Correspondentie Herzberg, A.J. (1-2).

20. Kristel, *Geschiedenis als opdracht*, 29.

their continuing usefulness to Dutch society.[21] Herzberg apparently merited this due to his expertise in the new Dutch licensing act. Almost all members of this group survived the Second World War. At Barneveld, Herzberg and his wife opted for a Palestine certificate, which implied that they had to be transferred to Bergen-Belsen, from where they would be enabled to move to Palestine on the basis of an exchange program, which in fact never happened (January 1944–April 1945). After the war Herzberg started practicing law again, but he also turned to writing, focusing deliberately on the general audience, which was not appreciated by some of the representatives of the Jewish community.[22]

Herzberg is the author of about twenty books, mostly fiction, including several works that are retellings of biblical episodes.[23] Three of his books, *Amor fati* (1946), *Kroniek der Jodenvervolging* [Chronicle of the persecution of the Jews] (1950), and *Tweestromenland: Dagboek uit Bergen Belsen* [Land between rivers: Diary from Bergen-Belsen] (1950) concern the Second World War. They describe Herzberg's personal experiences and reflections in camp Bergen-Belsen, where he stayed from January 1944 to April 1945.[24] Herzberg had been a Zionist during his entire life and a strong supporter of the State of Israel. He seriously considered moving to Israel but never could bring himself to cut the knot, as two of his children did. Herzberg's collected writings appeared in 1993–1996.[25] He won the P. C. Hooft prize in 1972, which is a prestigious literary prize in the Netherlands named after a famous Dutch poet from the golden age.[26] Since 1990, an annual lecture by a prominent Dutch speaker is organized

---

21. Herzberg, *Kroniek der jodenvervolging* [Chronicle of the Persecution of the Jews] (Arnhem: Van Loghum Slaterus, 1950; Amsterdam: Meulenhof, 1951); Jacques Presser, *Ondergang: De vervolging en verdelging van het Nederlandse jodendom, 1940–1945* [Ruin: The persecution and extermination of Dutch Jewry, 1940–1945] (The Hague: Nijhoff, 1965); Kuiper, *Een wijze*, 196; Kristel, *Geschiedenis als opdracht*.

22. Kristel, *Geschiedenis als opdracht*, 35, 37–38, 42.

23. *Saul's dood: Drama in zeven tonelen* [Saul's death: Tragedy in seven scenes] (1958); *Twee Verhalen: De oude man en de engel Azriël. Mordechai* [Two stories: The old man and the angel Azriel. Mordecai] (Amsterdam: Querido, 1982); *Mirjam* [a children's book] (1985); *Aartsvaders: Het verhaal van Jakob en Jozef* [Patriarchs, the story of Jacob and Joseph] (Amsterdam: Querido, 1986) (Kuiper, *Een wijze*, 377).

24. *Amor fati: Zeven opstellen over Bergen-Belsen* (Amsterdam: Moussault, 1946), seven essays about Bergen-Belsen originally published in *De Groene Amsterdammer; Kroniek der jodenvervolging*, a distanced factual report about Bergen-Belsen; *Tweestromenland: Dagboek uit Bergen-Belsen* [Land between rivers: Diary from Bergen-Belsen] (Arnhem: Van Loghum Slaterus, 1950), a highly personal and emotional diary secretly written in the camp (the two streams—Judaism and Nazism—are two incompatible principles of life that came together in the camps). Kuiper, *Een wijze*, 11; Kristel, *Geschiedenis als opdracht*.

25. Abel J. Herzberg, *Verzameld werk*, 3 vols (Amsterdam: Querido, 1993–1996).

26. The report of the committee refers to the extraordinary quality of Herzberg's work on Herod from 1955, Literatuurmuseum 2 QUE Correspondentie Herzberg, A.J. (1-2).

in memory of Herzberg by the debating center De Rode Hoed and *Trouw*, one of the main newspapers in the Netherlands.

Herzberg's *Memoirs of King Herod*

Paratextual information gives us already a hint of what the aim of the *Memoirs* may have been. The jacket blurb and preface introduce Herod the Great and his very bad reputation. They also mention the king's lost memoirs, which he composed as an apology for Augustus, Herod's most important patron and friend. Herzberg attempts to revive these memoirs, not as an apology for the emperor but as an autobiography for the future generations of the kingdom.[27] He indicates that Herod dictated these memoirs to his loyal secretary Nicolas of Damascus when he was old and ill. Nicolas is indeed addressed many times as secretary in the book. Herzberg makes the fictional status of the work explicit by stating that his book is deliberately selective and also includes details that are not found in any of the historical sources. He adds that the work "may in general follow the historical line transmitted to us, but novelistic excursions appeared to be unavoidable."[28]

A brief epilogue offers a retrospect of the Herod figure. It refers to his being an astute businessman, his wealth, and his final will. It continues with his reputation starting with Augustus's alleged famous saying "I'd rather be Herod's pig than Herod's son."[29] Herzberg concludes that Herod's reputation is mixed: some admired him because of his strategic vision as well as his political and diplomatic skills, but the Jews "say of him that he sneaked to the throne like a fox, ruled like a tiger and died like a dog."[30] This conclusion is telling because of its ambiguity and open-endedness. Herod was a successful but merciless ruler, and Jews and non-Jews held very different opinions of him. The differentiation between Jews and non-Jews may build on statements by Josephus in his *Antiquities*. Herzberg does not formulate a verdict for Herod; the readers have to find out for themselves, but paradoxically he also refers to the Jewish blessing "Blessed be the True Judge" (*barukh dayan emet*), said when some-

27. This is also pointed out by Herzberg in the undated memo about *De memoires*, Literatuurmuseum 20A HERZ H Herodes, p. 1. Cf. the much shorter fictitious memoirs in Richardson, *Herod*, 315–18, which are modeled on Augustus's *Res gestae*.

28. Herzberg, *De memoires*, 6: "In het algemeen is in dit boek de ons overgeleverde historische lijn gevolgd, maar romantische uitstapjes bleken onvermijdelijk."

29. Macrobius, *Sat.* 2.4.11 (Menahem Stern, *Greek and Latin authors on Jews and Judaism*, Fontes ad res Judaicas spectantes, 3 vols. (Jerusalem: Israel Academy of Sciences and Humanities, 1980), 2:665–66.

30. Herzberg, *De memoires*, 280: "De joden zeggen van hem, dat hij naar de troon geslopen is als een vos, geregeerd heeft als een tijger, en gestorven is als een hond."

body dies and during the funeral service. Herzberg assumes that Herod's Jewish subjects would have said this when the king died, including Menahem the Essene, who predicted that Herod would become king.[31] This ending of the epilogue is all the more intriguing because Herzberg stated that he did not believe in a transcendent God.[32] A snippet of paratextual information points in a different direction. There is a page between the table of contents and the actual memoirs, which contains a quotation from the book of Daniel (8:23–25). There is no comment whatsoever, but it is obvious that "the king of bold countenance who will stand up against the prince of princes" in these verses is here associated with Herod. The end of the quotation is telling: "But he shall be broken, but not by human hands" (Dan 8:25 NRSV). It matches the end of the epilogue; the verdict and punishment of the king are left to God.[33]

Herzberg introduces his book as a novel and a fictional autobiography, but an informed reader may conclude that the work has a hybrid character. As a matter of fact, Herzberg relies heavily on Josephus, and in certain ways the book looks like a historical work. A detailed map of Herod's kingdom and genealogical tables of the Hasmonean and Herodian families support this impression. Many of the details in the *Memoirs* seem to derive from Josephus's version of Herod's story in the *Antiquities*, which sets Herod in a less favorable light than the depiction of him in the *War*.[34] Nevertheless, as the preface of Herzberg's book indicates, other details have been added. The order of the events differs sometimes considerably from Josephus's narrative.

The beginning and end of the *Memoirs* situate Herod at the end of his life: the king is ill and knows he will die soon. This situation brings him to the decision to tell the truth and dictate the story of his life to his secretary, Nicolas of Damascus. The work is consistently written in the first person. It has a loose structure in six chapters and describes Herod's life more or less in chronological order, starting with the king's father and grandfather and his youth (ch. 1). It ends with the final events of Herod's rule, including the death of his oldest son, Antipater, and the episode of the golden eagle. But as indicated already, Herzberg sometimes went against the chronological order so as to emphasize certain things. This happens

31. "Geloofd zij Hij, die oordeelt naar waarheid," *De memoires*, 281.

32. Herzberg acknowledged that he had a religious consciousness that led to specific moral standpoints; see the interview with his friend Huub Oosterhuis in the newspaper *De Tijd*, 12 September 1986.

33. Herzberg deviates from Josephus's report here; Josephus makes it obvious, especially in *Antiquities*, that Herod's severe suffering during his final illness was God's punishment.

34. Jan Willem van Henten, "Herod the Great in Josephus," in *A Companion to Josephus*, ed. H. H. Chapman and Z. Rodgers, Blackwell Companions to the Ancient World 110 (Chichester: Wiley-Blackwell, 2016), 235–46.

already at the very beginning of the book, where Herod reflects on the most dramatic event in his life, the death of his wife Mariamme:

> I, Herod, king of Judea, seated on the throne in the city of Jerusalem, have murdered my wife. I don't hide it, I rather shout it out. There is no use in denying it any longer. Nicolas, whom I ordered to write my history, tried to whitewash me. I read what he has written. He didn't succeed. Nobody will believe him. His words ring false.[35]

A few lines further on Herod indicates that he wants to tell the truth about himself. And he starts with Mariamme, because her death dominates all his memories.[36] He realizes that he murdered Mariamme's sons as well and piled one crime on another, and, contrary to Josephus's reports, he accepts punishment for that.[37] He even acknowledges that Mariamme was innocent.[38]

This is a powerful dramatic beginning of the novel, which leads to the pertinent question why Mariamme nevertheless was executed? Herzberg provides two answers: (1) Herod made a miscalculation concerning his judges, and (2) Mariamme refused to ask for mercy. As stated by Salome, Herod acknowledges that he had appointed the judges himself and had indeed accused and convicted Mariamme, but he adds that he aimed for a license to save his own honor as well as Mariamme's life. The judges should have acquitted Mariamme because they knew she was innocent, but they didn't do that because they didn't want to be responsible for the consequences. Herod follows this up with an ironic lamentation about the corruption of justice:

> Judges! What are judges? They sentence only in order to proclaim what the king prefers to hear. The king or who else who may be in power over the country. What is justice? A beautiful dress for an ugly woman.[39]

35. *De memoires*, 13: "Ik, Herodes, koning van Judea, zetelend in de stad Jeruzalem, heb mijn vrouw vermoord. Ik verberg het niet. Ik schreeuw het liever uit. Het heeft geen zin het nog langer te ontkennen. Nicolaüs, die ik heb opgedragen mijn geschiedenis te schrijven, heeft geprobeerd mij schoon te wassen. Ik heb gelezen wat hij geschreven heft. Het is hem niet gelukt. Geen mens die hem geloven zal. Zijn woorden klinken vals."

36. See also *De memoires*, 222.

37. Herod considers God an accomplice for this (*De memoires*, 18).

38. *De memoires*, 14. See also 235–43, 258. Herzberg reads Josephus selectively here (cf. *War* 1.441–444; *Ant.* 15.82–87, 223–231). In the brief and straightforward report of *War*, Herod decides to execute Mariamme, but he regrets it terribly afterwards. The *Antiquities* report is much more complex and entails two episodes: during the first one Herod believes Mariamme is innocent, but in the second one he has her convicted and sentenced to death but aims to transfer her to one of his fortresses (15.230). Salome persuades him finally to have Mariamme executed. In *De memoires*, 14, Herod acknowledges that Salome lied about Mariamme, because she was carried away by jealousy and hatred.

39. *De memoires*, 15: "Rechters! Wat zijn rechters? Zij vonnissen alleen maar om te ver-

The second point concerns mercy as the final option to save Mariamme. Herod wanted to grant his wife mercy, and he even visited her in prison. She was too proud and stubborn, however, to ask for mercy, which is in line with Josephus's characterization of Mariamme in *Antiquities*.[40] Herod even blames the victim here: "Mariamme, Mariamme, why did you do this to me?"[41]

The next section (2) explains the treason of Soemus, which led to Mariamme's downfall. It also recounts who Nicolas of Damascus was.[42] The chronological survey of Herod's life starts in section 3, beginning with Herod's father and grandfather.[43] The dramatic beginning of the book focusing on the execution of Mariamme sets the tone for the rest. Herod is very open and communicative about his own opinions and feelings in his report. His emotional involvement in many events jumps from the paper, so to speak. Herzberg builds here on dramatic sections in Josephus's report and even embellishes them. One example is the flight of Herod's family from Jerusalem to Masada, after the Parthians and Herod's opponent Antigonus got control over Jerusalem. Josephus tells this in passing in *War* (1.264), but he offers a more detailed and dramatic report in *Antiquities* (14.352–358), which highlights the suffering of the women involved and also depicts Herod more negatively than does the *War* passage. It includes the telling detail that Herod lost control over himself (14.356). Herzberg elaborates the report in *Antiquities*, by adding further details and offering a very lively description of this journey. He further dramatizes the scene of the accident of Herod's mother:

> Until suddenly the wagon on which my mother sat overturned and she fell upon the rocks. I lost my mind then for a moment, and as a fool I blamed everyone, because my mother was lying there, pale and with glazed eyes, so that I thought she was dead. I had no desire to continue the trip with this gang, a gang which had become a funeral procession. They all stood around me, a packed crowd, speechless. I shouted: "Do something, help her," but nobody moved.[44]

---

kondigen wat de koning het liefst hoort. De koning of wie anders de macht mag hebben in het land? Wat is recht? Een mooi gewaad voor een lelijke vrouw."

40. Jan Willem van Henten, "Blaming the Women: Women at Herod's Court in Josephus's *Jewish Antiquities* 15.23–231," in *Women and Gender in Ancient Religions: Interdisciplinary Approaches*, ed. Stephen P. Ahearne-Kroll, Paul A. Holloway, and James A. Kelhoffer, WUNT 263 (Tübingen: Mohr Siebeck 2010), 153–75.

41. *De memoires*, 16: "Mariamme, Mariamme, waarom heb je mij dit aangedaan?" Cf. 153, 219.

42. *De memoires*, 16–20.

43. *De memoires*, 20–34.

44. *De memoires*, 120: "Totdat opeens de wagen waarop mijn moeder zat, kantelde en zij tegen de rotsen sloeg. Ik heb toen een ogenblik mijn bezinning verloren, ik heb als een redeloze iedereen de schuld gegeven, want mijn moeder lag daar, bleek en met glazen ogen,

This passage highlights Herod's deep love for his mother but also illustrates what seems to be a structural flaw in his character: he is able to communicate neither with the people around him nor with his subjects (below), a kind of disconnection that predicts failure at this stage of the work. However, Herzberg leaves out the detail that Herod almost took his own life in his panic when the wagon of his mother overturned. Ironically, he came to his senses when Mariamme grabbed him and shook him, a detail that is missing in Josephus. As a result, Herod successfully took the lead in fights against Parthian and Jewish enemies, so that the convoy arrived safely at Masada.[45]

The final section of the *Memoirs* (8) concerns the king's last days, with the destruction of the golden eagle in the Jerusalem temple and the death of his son Antipater as important events. Herzberg builds once again on Josephus's *Antiquities* (17.185–187) when he describes Antipater's end. Antipater tried to bribe the jailer when everyone in the palace thought Herod had died, so that he could take over the throne. When Herod heard this, he immediately ordered the execution of his son, whom he characterizes as a parricide and murderer of his brothers. In addition to recounting the material from Josephus, Herzberg briefly and dramatically describes how Herod responded to Antipater's death after the officer brought him the message. Herod had a flashback: he sees how Antipater as a beautiful young boy left the palace with his mother Doris, who was sent away, as we know, because Herod was going to marry Mariamme. More specifically Herod sees Antipater looking at him with a reproaching look in his big black eyes, which caused Herod, king of Judea, to begin to weep.[46] This tragic note basically concludes the memoirs. Herzberg does not explain why Herod started to cry, but this can be filled in when we know more about his interpretation of the Herod figure below.

The very last lines of the book link up with its beginning and refer once more to Nicolas of Damascus. Herod asks him, "Did you write everything down, Nicolas? I have nothing else to tell. But don't put away your writing materials. I still have to change my will."[47] This ending is tragic as well

---

zodat ik dacht dat ze dood was. Ik had geen lust meer om met deze bende verder te gaan, een bende die een begrafenisstoet was geworden. Zij allen stonden daar om mij heen, een opeengepakte massa, sprakeloos. Ik schreeuwde: 'Doe dan toch wat, help haar,' maar niemand verroerde zich."

45. Another embellishment concerns Herod's reception by Cleopatra in Alexandria, which is expanded into a juicy story (*De memoires*, 128–35, 183–89; cf. Josephus, *War* 1.279; *Ant.* 15.96–103). Interestingly, Cleopatra's mockery of Herod triggers his plan to become the king of Judea (*De memoires*, 133).

46. *De memoires*, 278.

47. *De memoires*, 278.

as ironic, because we know from Josephus that Herod changed his will several times; Antipater was the beneficiary in the penultimate version.[48]

Herzberg's Interpretation of Herod

In line with Josephus's portraits, in *De memoires* Herod is an avid builder, a military genius, and a clever and successful friendly king of the Romans.[49] More importantly, Herzberg points out that Herod had a mission for the Jewish people. When the king describes his entrance to Jerusalem after capturing the city, he notes that he was hoping for a fruitful cooperation with his subjects. He is filled with concern for his people and honestly thinks that he will act in the best interest of the people and the city of Jerusalem.[50] The continuation of the *Memoirs*, however, shows that the king's intended fruitful interaction with his Jewish subjects turned out badly. Herod's intentions become clear immediately after the capture of Jerusalem, because he characterizes himself right away as a reformer of Judaism and an emancipator of the Jews. He wants to "throw open the windows and let some fresh air enter" in the provincial town of Jerusalem. He aims at leveling out the religious and spiritual barriers between the Jews and other nations by introducing "modern" Greek and Roman customs at the court with the help of Nicolas of Damascus, as he indicates already when he introduces Nicolas.[51] Herod wants to demolish the spiritual walls around Jerusalem ("de geestelijke muren rond die stad te slechten") and turn it into a cosmopolitan city, which will be admired by everyone.[52] Herod's ambitious building program, and especially the renovation and expansion of the temple, would be a good illustration of this policy, and Herzberg does devote a section of his *Memoirs* to this subject, but he highlights one episode in order to elaborate Herod's policy and also make the point that the king utterly failed in this respect.[53]

This episode concerns Herod's quadrennial games in Jerusalem in honor of Augustus (Josephus, *Ant.* 15.268–291), who defeated Marc Antony and Cleopatra VII during the Battle of Actium (31 BCE). Herod considers Augustus to be the redeemer of humankind who would bring humans all over the world together and allow each nation to live in accordance with

48. Richardson, *Herod*, 33–38.

49. Another correspondence with Josephus is that Herod has the support of God (*De memoires*, 157–58, 166).

50. *De memoires*, 162, 227.

51. *De memoires*, 19–20: "'Nicolaüs, smijt de ramen open, laat de lucht van de moderne vrije wereld naar binnen stromen.'" Cf. *Herodes*, 110, 230.

52. *De memoires*, 20, 225.

53. *De memoires*, 221–32.

its own customs. He is proud to be the emperor's deputy in Judea.[54] The most famous performers of their time were contracted for these prestigious games in honor of Augustus, and the most successful plays at other locations were on stage in Jerusalem for an entire week. Terrific horse races were organized as well. Jerusalem was full of strangers during this week—musicians, acrobats, wrestlers, and other athletes. Herod remarks sarcastically that the Jerusalemites made a lot of money out of the games. But the salient point is that the Jews did not come to watch the games because they were horrified by them. That only Greeks, Romans, Syrians, Samaritans, Arabs, soldiers, and non-Jewish servants came to the theater and the arena was a shock to Herod.[55] He recalls that the games were a disaster and even an occasion for people to conspire against him—for no reason, in his opinion. The conspirators wrongly thought that the trophies put next to the theater (Josephus, *Ant.* 15.272, 276–278, 287) were images of humans. Herod knew very well that such images were forbidden by the Ten Commandments and he would never violate these. He realized in hindsight that the Jews used every occasion to stand up against him.[56] For similar reasons, the impressive renovation and expansion of the temple complex were also a failure from the perspective of the Jews, because of the eagle set on top of the main entrance gate to the sanctuary—a telling symbol of Rome.[57]

When Herod describes the future for the Jews, he uses the modern rhetoric of a reformer. The Jews had a simple choice: under Herod's guidance they could go along with the course of nations and become citizens of the free world, free cosmopolitans so to say, or they would always remain a subjugated and backward nation.[58] Jerusalem was its own enemy; it didn't realize that Herod was the guarantor of its freedom. There was no longer room for the traditional narrow-minded views of the Jews, which were backward and hidebound. The Jews should enjoy the fruits of civilization, which came from Hellas and Rome.[59] One can easily interpret statements such as these as a policy to assimilate completely to the gentile world, but that is not Herod's intention, as becomes apparent from other passages. Although Herod's own faithfulness to Jewish practices is ambiguous in the *Memoirs*, Herod's view of himself as a ruler clearly implies that he

---

54. *De memoires*, 229, 264.

55. *De memoires*, 221–22.

56. *De memoires*, 224. This conclusion may be supported by several passages in *Antiquities*, which suggest that Herod had a security problem, but there is little evidence for it in *War* (Jan Willem van Henten, "Rebellion under Herod the Great and Archelaus," in *The Jewish Revolt against Rome: Interdisciplinary Perspectives*, ed. Mladen Popović, JSJSup 154 (Leiden: Brill, 2011), 241–70.

57. *De memoires*, 230–32.

58. *De memoires*, 22.

59. *De memoires*, 67–68.

tried to respect Jewish religion and enable his Jewish citizens to live in accordance with Jewish practices. He sees no difference between his role in Judea and that abroad, where he acts as an important advocate for the Jews in the diaspora, by helping them when injustice was done to them or when they were unable to live in line with Jewish practices.[60] Thus, Herod advocates a kind of reform Judaism that was open to Greco-Roman culture, and he presents himself as a benevolent political patron of the Jews in Israel as well as the diaspora.

Herod sees himself, in fact, as the ideal *trait d'union* between Rome and a unique nation, which unfortunately was inclined to rebel against every foreign authority because of its convictions.[61] Both the king's respect for the Jewish practices and his assessment that the Jews were a rebellious nation are obvious in a section where Herod informs Augustus, his new patron, about the Jews, the various groups, the temple, their religion, and their messianic expectations. He explains that the Jews were a nation that was very difficult to govern, but he also defends them:

> I have not accused the Jews; I defended them, as their king. I pointed at the importance of their beliefs, at their moral strength and determined character, but also at the consequences of this for their attitude toward Rome. How there always was a possibility that they would rebel and how you had to contain this.[62]

Herod assumes that the Jews have a problem with authority, because the God of Israel determines the life of the Jews to such an extent that they do not tolerate earthly powers put over them.

Herzberg is ambiguous about Herod's personal involvement in Jewish religion, which may reflect his own ambivalence about it. At certain times Herod seems to be a secular Jew, but sometimes he is faithful to Jewish practices. Herzberg writes that Herod could not bring himself to say the daily prayers as king[63] and that he grew up with the Jewish practices but took a dislike to them as a boy. He does not keep *kashrut* at Rome during the festivities after being appointed king, as well as on several occasions when he was traveling.[64] Elsewhere, however, he acknowledges the God of Israel and reminds his readers that he renovated the temple in a glo-

---

60. *De memoires*, 228–29.

61. *De memoires*, 68.

62. *De memoires*, 216: "Ik heb de joden niet aangeklaagd, ik heb hen, als hun koning, verdedigd. Ik heb op de grote waarde gewezen, van wat zij geloofden, op hun zedelijke kracht en op hun onveranderlijke karakter, maar ook op de gevolgen die dit had en wel hebben moest voor hun houding tegenover Rome; hoe daardoor altijd opstandigheid kon worden gewekt en hoe je dat zou moeten beheersen."

63. *De memoires*, 34.

64. *De memoires*, 145.

rious way.[65] Herod claims he never attempted to violate the sacredness of the temple. He considers himself to be Jewish and ordered Nicolas to prove without any doubt that he descended from the forty-two thousand Jews who returned from Babylon to Judea. He knows the Torah very well.[66] At the same time, Herod is also a pragmatist who seriously believes that the traditional religious views of the Jews are not beneficial. One example concerns a reference to Hillel's golden rule ("What is hateful to you, do not do to your fellow: this is the whole Torah; the rest is the explanation; go and learn" [b. Shab. 31a]). Herod comments, "I would like to know how you can rule Judea with such slogans."[67] The picture becomes even more complex during a trip to Rome, which points to a pragmatic attitude of double participation: Herod recollects that he sacrificed to Poseidon at Rhodes on his way to Rome but also that he went to pray in a small synagogue there.[68]

Obviously Herod defined a very ambitious mission for himself, but he knows at the end of his life that he has failed terribly. He appears to be a tragic figure in the *Memoirs*, a hunted man and a puppet of God and the gods:

> Sometimes I think that this whole tragedy, which happened in Judea, was invented by one of them [the gods] in order to entertain them all. So, in my own way I too may be a believing person. I played my role and wait for their applause.[69]

Herod also realizes that his family history was deeply tragic, in line with Josephus's presentation of Herod's failure to control the struggles of the factions at his court and the execution of Mariamme and three of his sons. Herod confesses that he never had a happy family life. As long as he was present at his court he was able to hush up the struggles, but when he was away hostilities broke out between the factions in his family.[70] His marriage with Mariamme was tragic as well. He loved her deeply, but she spoiled it by her attitude and by lobbying for her brother, who had to become the new high priest.[71] Herod considered the return of a Has-

---

65. *De memoires*, 66, 230–32.

66. *De memoires*, 24–25.

67. *De memoires*, 39. Herod thinks that the Jews are narrow-minded. He concludes that they only believed in what could be read in the old books (26).

68. *De memoires*, 141. Elsewhere Herod comes close to being an agnostic: he doesn't know which gods he should call upon, but he also accepts that the gods of Olympus or the invisible God of Sinai will punish him (13).

69. *De memoires*, 59.

70. *De memoires*, 205, 219, 242.

71. *De memoires*, 152–53; also 172–73, 207–8, 219.

monean leader a great step backwards, which reminded him of the succession of Saul and the preference of David over Saul ("Saul made havoc among thousands but David among tens of thousands" [1 Sam 18:6–7]).[72] It was highly unfortunate that nobody believed that the drowning of the young Aristobulus during a party in his honor was an accident and that none of Herod's friends defended his innocence.[73] Since then Mariamme's attitude to Herod cooled considerably.

Herod's interaction with his Jewish subjects was another tragedy. He claims that his heart was always with his subjects, but he knows that their heart was never with him.[74] Menahem the Essene (Manaemus in Josephus) already predicted Herod's failure when he announced to the young Herod that he would become king.[75] Herod disagrees with Menahem's assessment of him as king and claims that he always has been just and that he loved his people. Later on, Herod laments that Menahem runs him ragged and sneaks into his room when he is afraid of the murderer who comes to have his revenge. Menahem's prediction became a curse for Herod—which, in his opinion, he did not deserve.[76] The curse points to another tragic aspect of Herod as king, which goes beyond Josephus: Herod failed completely as a ruler; despite all his endeavors, he did not fulfill his mission to emancipate the Jews and make them assimilate to the outside world protected by the Romans. He was hated by his ungrateful subjects, who frustrated him in his plans whenever they could, as we will see in the final section.

Herzberg's Presentation of the Jews in the *Memoirs*

The picture of the Jews in the *Memoirs* is complex, although the actual information about Jewish persons and groups is limited. A few times Herod mentions the various groups of Jews, as we know them from contemporary sources. One passage concerns Menahem the Essene's prediction that Herod would become king. It includes a description by Menahem in the first person that briefly characterizes the Pharisees, Sadducees, and Essenes. Menahem dislikes the Pharisees and the Sadducees. The Pharisees did not live up to what they were preaching, and the Sadducees were only craving for money.[77] The Pharisees did not recognize the Hasmonean

72. *De memoires*, 172–73.
73. *De memoires*, 196.
74. *De memoires*, 25.
75. *De memoires*, 62–66; cf. Josephus, *Ant.* 15.373–379.
76. *De memoires*, 66.
77. *De memoires*, 63–64; cf. *Herodes*, 32–33, about the Pharisees.

rulers, nor did they welcome Herod's marriage with Mariamme.[78] One passage clearly presents the Pharisees in a negative light. When Herod starts to describe the party thrown by Alexandra after the king's decision to appoint Aristobulus III (Alexandra's son and Mariamme's brother) as high priest, he says about the Pharisees, "All had come, only the Pharisees were absent. They always broke away from the others when they were drinking, laughing and singing. They preferred to do that in their own way, among each other."[79] The Pharisees reflect here Herod's overall criticism of the Jewish people: the observance of the Jewish practices went hand in hand with a particularistic attitude and the refusal to assimilate and incorporate Greek and Roman customs, and enjoy the benefits of the common world as a result.

By way of a flashback, Herod says that Judea was the most bitter experience of his life. His Jewish subjects didn't love him; they were waiting for his death. He states that he tried out several strategies and that he meant well, but the Jews forced him to use violence many times.[80] He was a stranger and an outcast to them, an Edomite, who would better be killed. In his paranoia he says, "Who possessed a dagger was lying in wait for me. Any poison that was prepared was meant for me."[81] Herod considers Jerusalem to be a cruel city, which devours its inhabitants, but blames their king for that. The city would have been lost if Herod had not domesticated it. The Jerusalemites blamed him for throwing their money around and demanding extreme taxes, but they didn't realize that Herod's projects were to their own benefit.[82]

Looking back at a successful trip to Marc Antony during which he had to account for Aristobulus's death, Herod notes that after his return he was not received in a friendly fashion by the Jerusalemites and that he deliberately had provoked the pious by riding a horse on the Sabbath. He wanted to signal that he, as king, created his own rules and that he would follow those.[83] There is a similar statement after Herod's successful return from his journey to Octavian, after the Battle of Actium (31 BCE): "I was entitled to have a triumphal procession and I would have received one everywhere, but not in Jerusalem. There they only have triumphal processions with palm branches and Torah scrolls, and, when I actually appeared, with invisible flags of hatred."[84]

78. *De memoires*, 103.

79. *De memoires*, 194.

80. *De memoires*, 17.

81. *De memoires*, 45: "Wie een dolk bezat, loerde op mijn leven. Geen gif werd bereid, of het was voor mij bestemd." See also 23, 65, 68.

82. *De memoires*, 230–32.

83. *De memoires*, 206–7.

84. *De memoires*, 212: "Ik had recht op een triomftocht en had hem ook overal ter wereld

At the end of his *Memoirs*, Herod states that the destruction of the golden eagle, which was standing on a main gate of the sanctuary, was his greatest humiliation by his subjects.[85] The eagle was his most costly votive offering to God, and taking it down at midday was a sacrilege.[86] Herod recalls, after the arrest of the perpetrators, a dialogue with Judah, one of the sages who took the initiative to demolish the eagle, which shows once again that the views of Herod and those of his people were incompatible:

> The Jews were silent and bowed their head. Only Judah spoke: "We have been faithful to the law of God, and God doesn't want an image in the temple."
>
> Then I shouted out: "Judea, Judea, the will of God is that Rome rules. Could I have done differently? Could I have accounted towards Rome that I had taken away the eagle? This eagle is the symbol of Rome, and if Caesar Augustus had asked me where the eagle would have been, should I have said that God is superior to Rome and that the law of Moses is superior to his law?... Is this eagle not in your own interest? You think you have destroyed it, but you have destroyed yourself, and if you continue this way, you will yourself destroy the holy temple."[87]

Before the perpetrators were burned on the stake, they protested against Herod, they pointed out that his rule was illegal and they ridiculed him with quotations from Scripture.

In short, the relationship between Herod and his Jewish subjects was hopeless. The king had an ambitious mission to reform and emancipate the Jews by assimilating them to a great extent to the non-Jewish milieu, but he failed to persuade them to accept this mission with open arms and turned to force and brutal measures, which had a contrary effect. The interaction between the tyrannical king and his Jewish subjects was an ongoing miscommunication that could result only in the repression of the Jews.

---

gekregen, behalve in Jeruzalem. Daar houden ze alleen maar triomftochten met wetsrollen en palmtakken en, als ik verscheen, met onzichtbare vlaggen van haat."

85. *De memoires*, 273.

86. *De memoires*, 274. In Herzberg, *Herodes*, 292, Herod himself implies that the eagle was a symbol of his own power and, at the same time, was dedicated to God.

87. *De memoires*, 274: "De joden zwegen en bogen het hoofd. Alleen Juda sprak: 'Wij hebben de wet van God gehoorzaamd, en God wil geen beeld in de tempel.' Toen heb ik het uitgeschreeuwd: 'Judea, Judea, de wil van God is dat Rome regeert. Kon ik dan anders? Had ik tegenover Rome kunnen verantwoorden die adelaar weg te laten? Die adelaar is het symbol van Rome, en als Keizer Augustus mij had gevraagd waar dit gebleven was, had ik hem dan moeten antwoorden dat God boven Rome stond en de wet van Mozes boven de zijne?... Is die adelaar dan niet in jullie belang? Jullie denken dat je hem hebt verwoest, jullie hebt je zelf verwoest, en als je zo doorgaat, verwoesten jullie je heilige tempel zelf.'"

Conclusion

Why did Herod the Great as a historical figure fascinate Abel Herzberg so much that he devoted two literary works to him? Arie Kuiper, Herzberg's biographer, assumes that Herzberg associated the cruel king with the Nazi persecution of the Jews.[88] Herzberg was very much interested in the explanation of the incomprehensible behavior of the Nazis,[89] but he points out important differences between Herod and the Nazis in an interview after the publication of his play in 1955.[90] He acknowledges that the law of the jungle ruled in both cases, but he emphasizes that Herod did not set up a totalitarian system and placed no controls on religious views. Nor did he eliminate people's moral consciousness, as Hitler did.[91] Herzberg's view of the historical Herod is complex and nuanced, and he admires the king's ambitious project of the rebuilding of the temple and even concludes that Herod was no less talented than Augustus and Marcus Agrippa.[92] Herod was a very successful general and politician, but he was unable to win his wife Mariamme's affection. Mariamme represents the entire Jewish people here: Herod is unable to win the hearts of his Jewish subjects and turns to force and murder to persuade them. In the end, he is a very self-centered, lonely, and tragic figure.[93]

Two other interrelated reasons may explain Herzberg's interest in Herod better. Herod is not an isolated figure for Herzberg; the interaction between Herod and his Jewish subjects is the salient point. Herod's attempt to reform and assimilate the Jews to the surrounding world in order to save them resulted in their rejection of him as a foreign tyrant, and this response paradoxically led to the survival of the Jews. This dialectic process is a lesson for eternity for Herzberg, and he saw it as his task as a novelist to elaborate such lessons in his books.[94] Additionally, Herod's

---

88. So Kuiper, *Een wijze*, 425: "Herod was of all ages and one is almost inclined to say that Herzberg had met him in Bergen-Belsen" ("Herodes was van alle tijden en men is bijna geneigd te zeggen: Herzberg had hem in Bergen-Belsen ontmoet").

89. Literatuurmuseum 2 QUE Correspondentie Herzberg, A.J. (1-2), p. 6.

90. "Gesprek met Abel. J. Herzberg," *De Boekenkorf* 2 (1955): 9-10, Gemeente Amsterdam Stadsarchief 929, https://archief.amsterdam/inventarissen/inventaris/929.nl.html.

91. Ibid., 10: "Ik voor mij geloof niet, dat men zonder geestelijke grondslag tot politieke machtsvorming kan komen. Hitler heeft het geestelijk inzicht uitgeschakeld." The phrase "geestelijk inzicht" is ambiguous; it can mean "spiritual view" or "moral consciousness." The latter seems more plausible.

92. Ibid.: "Hij was een enorm knappe kerel, hij deed niet voor Augustus of Agrippa onder."

93. Herzberg, "Het laatste woord," 183.

94. Literatuurmuseum 2 QUE Correspondentie Herzberg, A.J. (1-2), p. 3. How the Jews were able to survive without a fatherland was a leading question for Herzberg (Kuiper, *Een wijze*, 118–20).

rule was part of the crucial period before 70 CE, which is, for Herzberg, a major formative period for the Jewish people, which not only formed the basis for the people's survival as a nation but also coined its main significance for humankind.[95] In an undated document about the *Memoirs*, Herzberg discusses these points by suggesting an analogy between the political situation in Herod's period and the relationship between the State of Israel and the countries around it in his own time. He highlights that Judea succeeded in preserving its own unique culture and outlook upon life ("uitzonderlijke levensopvatting en cultuur") after 70 CE, as Israel did in the twentieth century.[96] The precise nature of this unique outlook upon life seems to vary for Herzberg. Sometimes it is the struggle against heathendom and the evil passions of humans and the faithfulness to God and the Ten Commandments.[97] Sometimes it boils down to humaneness. In his noticeable words of thanks for the P. C. Hooft prize, Herzberg observed, "sometimes the victims of inhumanity become the bearers of humaneness."[98] He illustrates this with a very moving memory from his period in Bergen-Belsen. In the concentration camp he coincidentally came upon a dying woman with a heavily mutilated face, who must have suffered terribly. She held a book in her hands, which had already grown stiff. It was not the Bible but a copy of Spinoza's *Ethics*, which triggered a quotation from this book for Herzberg: "[the intellectual love of the mind towards God] is part of the infinite love wherewith God loves himself" ("God heeft zichzelf lief met oneindige geestelijke liefde" [*Ethics* 5.36]). Herzberg partially explains the meaning of these words from the context of Spinoza's passage and interprets it as a guideline for a humane life inspired by love, magnanimity, and peace. It is obvious from this perspective that Herod the Great, in Herzberg's view, not only plays the role of a heathen catalyst of Jewish history who triggers a process that enables Jews to express and disseminate the ideal of humaneness that forms the heart of the Jewish immaterial heritage; but, despite all his positive qualities, Herod is also a prime example of an inhumane person—self-centered, corrupted by power, incapable of empathizing with others, and merciless.

---

95. In "Gesprek met Abel. J. Herzberg," 10, Herzberg points out that he had wanted to write about this period for a long time because of its enormous problems—spirit versus power and culture versus politics, and the moral victory of the Jews because they remained a nation after their political downfall. See also Kuiper, *Een wijze*, 425.

96. Literatuurmuseum 20A HERZ H Herodes, 2. See also p. 2: "It is remarkable that despite all differences in political relationships in the Middle East in antiquity forces have been opposing each other which make one think of those of our own time" ("Het is merkwaardig dat—bij alle verschil in politieke verhoudingen—in het Midden-Oosten in de Oudheid krachten tegenover elkaar hebben gestaan, die doen denken aan die van onze tijd"). Cf. Kuiper, *Een wijze*, 425–26.

97. Kuiper, *Een wijze*, 129, 381.

98. Literatuurmuseum 2 QUE Correspondentie Herzberg, A.J. (1-2), p. 6.

It is time to return to the question that forms the starting point of this essay: Was Herod Jewish? In spite of some ambiguities for Herzberg, the answer is no. Herod aimed at a radical modernization of Judaism by introducing Greek and Roman customs and taking away most barriers between Jews and gentiles, so that the Jews would leave their old fashioned and narrow-minded views behind and go along with the course of the nations. That he failed to persuade his Jewish subjects to embark on this path was ultimately a blessing, because it helped them to maintain their Jewish identity and survive as a nation with a unique significance for humankind.

Study Is Greater, for Study Leads to Action

LEONARD GORDON
Temple Beth Sholom, Framingham, Massachusetts

> Does [the reconstruction proposed here] have implications for contemporary practice?... I am speaking to those who accept, as I do, a modern, historical approach to Jewish tradition. Does my analysis have Halakic implications?
>
> The answer is no. Jewish law, like other legal systems, is based on precedent, and what the historian can contribute to Halaka is the collection of precedents and the analysis of legal history. But history and Halaka are autonomous disciplines, each with its own methods, assumptions, and goals, and the historian cannot tell the jurist which precedent to follow or which decision to adopt.[1]

Shaye Cohen reminds us that while historians often deal with issues that may have contemporary ramifications, drawing the connections between classical texts and contemporary concerns is a complex enterprise. For the fruits of historical research to be relevant to religious practice, religious leaders make determinations outside of the purview of the historian's work of data gathering and reconstructions of the past. Cohen's assertion is an expression of respect for a process that parallels scholarship; it is also a cautionary statement, one designed to liberate historians of religion to proceed with their research and analyses free from the worry about either possible implications for contemporary choices or misuse of their scholarship.

But those of us who are in the business of contemporary practice do, of course, make connections between classical sources and contemporary issues, often dependent on the work of historians to contextualize and interpret those sources and make sense of the evolution of ideas and practices in changing contexts and historical circumstances. Whether we are making halakhic determinations for new situations or, less con-

1. Shaye J. D. Cohen, "The Matrilineal Principle in Historical Perspective," *Judaism* 34 (1985): 5–13, here 13.

sequentially, using Jewish wisdom as a resource for debates about contemporary ethical dilemmas or thorny questions of public policy or social justice, practitioners using Jewish sources face resistance and skepticism from Judaic scholars and secularists alike. Scholars whose work is steeped in ancient texts often discourage drawing connections between past and present because they are aware of the pitfalls of selective application of history's lessons. Because interpretations are often equivocal, the danger of eisegesis significantly increases when the interpreter is leaning toward a particular outcome. Secularists are equally wary of looking to the religious past to find warrants for particular positions on issues of pressing current concern. They find that those who cite religious texts often do so to preclude rather than advance dialogue and compromise, and they are aware of a tendency among religious practitioners to cherry-pick texts from within a multifarious tradition, and as non-experts in the tradition, they are disadvantaged by their inability to identify counterexamples, competing interpretations, or other strategies for engaging with long, complex histories of interpretation. Jewish public policy professionals may intuit that Judaism has a relevant contribution to make to contemporary debates and may feel a principled commitment to including Judaism in the conversation, but the path for doing so is not well cleared.

In this small tribute to my teacher, Shaye Cohen, I want to speak to the challenge for rabbis engaged with social-justice work and committed to using Jewish sources in our work and conversations. Many of us who find inspiration in classical sources for engaging in social-justice work want to move beyond trendy appeals to the vague Jewish mystical ideal of *tikkun olam* (repairing the world) and the democratizing claim based in Genesis that "all human beings are made in the divine image" as the sum and substance of the guidance Judaism offers in our own arguments about present issues. Judaism, Jewish texts, and the Jewish historical experience are rich in wisdom and information about the issues that concern us today and often help us stand outside of our own moment and locate contemporary issues in a broader context. By reducing Judaism's contribution to social-justice work to such phrases as *tikkun olam*, we risk trivializing the complexity of Jewish wisdom, and we turn over a critical area of life, the common good, to those who approach policy questions from sometimes narrow secular perspectives.

Time and again when I sit at the table in Jewish organizations alongside lawyers and public policy professionals, lip service is paid to Judaism, and then the conversation shifts into one that would be indistinguishable from what could be heard in any secular gathering discussing similar issues. Conscious of a long rabbinic tradition that gives precedence to Jewish learning over doing good deeds on the grounds that right action results from study (see b. Qidd. 40b), I am convinced that social-justice work in a Jewish context is best anchored in Jewish learning and the Jewish system of *mitzvoth*. In a version of a rabbinic formulation, we can endlessly debate whether *torah* (learning) or good deeds take precedence, but they are mutually dependent, and without grounding in *torah*, work to accomplish good deeds rests on a weaker foundation. The challenge is to address the reasonable objection, shared by Jewish historians and secularists, and turn to Jewish sources in ways that have integrity.

After first citing one exemplary instance of a Jewish policy statement made with no reference to Judaism and suggesting some Jewish sources that might have strengthened that position, I sample the discussion among practitioners about the place of Jewish sources in contemporary Jewish debates. While there are persuasive, principled reasons to avoid concluding that "Judaism says" this or that about a current concern, there are Jewish social justice activists and ethicists who insist that, however much the sources may be equivocal or equivocate, it behooves us to consider Jewish tradition with a wide lens and extrapolate what we may call Jewish principles to inform our own deliberations.[2] In so doing, we make visible the Jewish sensibility that rationalizes Jewish organizational pronouncements on public affairs. Finally, I conclude with my own analysis of the legal debate about whether convicted felons who have served their time should be legally permitted to vote. Ranging around Jewish sources that do indeed contradict one another, I am convinced—and would hope to persuade others—that reading into the preponderance of sources, and the general sensibility they convey about Jewish values and priorities, offers good reasons to favor reinstating to the voting rolls people who have served sentences.

Hydrofracking: What Makes a Viewpoint Jewish?

Once a year, the Jewish Council for Public Affairs (JCPA) meets to review resolutions on the major issues of the day. The introduction to the resolution on Hydrofracking in 2012 from a recent JCPA Plenum is a good example of an appeal to balancing competing principles without reference to this strategy as having particularly Jewish resonances:

> This resolution addresses natural gas and oil extraction by the combination of horizontal drilling and hydraulic fracturing, otherwise known as

---

2. In *Creating Judaism: History, Tradition, Practice* (New York: Columbia University Press, 2006), Michael L. Satlow argues persuasively that "Judaism" itself is not easily defined. Essentialist and normative definitions obscure the "diversity of Jewish practice and belief" (5), and the corrective conceptualization of "Judaisms" neglects Judaism's unifying features. Adapting Wittgenstein's model of "family resemblance," Satlow proposes, instead, that we think about Judaism as a "family of traditions" that may be plotted onto maps of identity, textual canons, and religious practices.

> hydrofracking. The JCPA does not have policy specific to hydrofracking, but has existing policies including support for "expansion of America's energy infrastructure with sensitivity to our natural environment" and "ensuring that all people are protected from environmental pollutants and benefit from access to clean water." The resolution calls for support of regulations, policies, and research to limit the environmental and health impacts of hydrofracking.[3]

Although there is no reference to Jewish texts or tradition, Jewish history is full of debates about how to deal with balancing competing goods in times of financial limitations as well as traditions that stress environmental stewardship, providing compelling models for how we might deal with such issues today.[4] Meir Tamari, for example, examines the values that informed Jewish tax policy and the production of public budgets in rabbinic and medieval times. Recognizing the desire of majorities within communities to reduce tax burdens, he identifies those areas, such as education, feeding and clothing the poor, caring for widows and orphans, and redeeming captives, which needed to be funded as a basic communal obligation. Similarly, contributions to basic communal infrastructure, such as synagogues, cemeteries, and rituals baths (*mikvehs*) were "not options open to communal decisions."[5] Extending this logic of our basic obligations to the well-being of the community, today we might well include preventing environmental degradation as such a basic function of government. In raising protection of the environment to the level of a core Jewish communal priority, we can also turn to the tradition of stewardship, rooted in the exegesis of the verse, "The earth is the Lord's and all that is in it" (Ps 24:1 NRSV). Politically, this verse puts a check on human claims to political sovereignty; environmentally, it reminds us that our job is to preserve that which does not belong to us but is in our trust. Dan Fink writes that "our challenge is to be loving caretakers of the earth. This position is grounded in God's commandment to Adam to work the soil and watch over the world (Gen 2:15)."[6] The simple recognition that rabbinic Judaism saw urgency in identifying categories of social responsibility for which taxation is mandated, no matter the popular resistance to taxation, clarifies that Judaism, as a religious system, must continue to evaluate those categories under changing conditions.

---

3. Jewish Council for Public Affairs, resolution on Hydrofracking. Adopted by the JCPA Plenum in 2012. Posted on May 17, 2012, http://engage.jewishpublicaffairs.org/blog/comments.jsp?blog_entry_KEY=6341&.

4. See, e.g., Meir Tamari, *"With All Your Possessions": Jewish Ethics and Economic Life* (New York: Free Press, 1987); and Ellen Bernstein, *Ecology and the Jewish Spirit: Where Nature and the Sacred Meet* (Woodstock, VT: Jewish Lights, 1998).

5. Tamari, *"With All Your Possessions,"* 213.

6. Bernstein, *Ecology and the Jewish Spirit*, 237.

The Debate: Why Jewish Public Policy Prefers Secular Terms of Debate

The suspicion of those who address contemporary questions using classical sources is reasonable. There is a perception that rabbis cherry-pick those texts that fit their preexisting political beliefs and then call that Judaism. Shakespeare characterized our problem in the words of Antonio in *Merchant of Venice*: "*even the devil* can cite scripture for his purpose" (I.iii.98). Jacob Petuchowski reminds us that the breadth of Jewish writing on legal subjects necessarily means that a wide range of perspectives can be found, further complicating the task of the contemporary Jewish ethicist: "If, as Shakespeare has rightly seen, even the devil can cite Scripture for his own purposes, then the post-biblical literature of the Jews provides an infinitely wider field replete with citations for the devil—or anyone else—to cull."[7]

Indeed, a single chapter in Deuteronomy captures the dilemma of those seeking guidance from the biblical tradition on such a core issue as the conduct of warfare. Contrast Deut 20:10, "When you draw near to a town to fight against it, offer it terms of peace" with Deut 20:16, "But as for the towns of these peoples, that the LORD your God is giving you as an inheritance, you must not let anything that breathes remain alive." Is Deuteronomy stressing the importance of peacemaking or advancing a model of obliterating one's enemy?

A similarly powerful set of contrasts can be found in the New Testament. For a simple example, in the gospel accounts of the Beatitudes one can contrast Matt 5:3 "Blessed are the poor in spirit" with Luke 6:20 "Blessed are you who are poor." Is Jesus speaking to those struggling with faith in a radically new situation, or is Jesus addressing the poor and offering them hope in the face of their material lacks. Paul presents contrasting attitudes toward women's relative position. In 1 Cor 11:3 we read that "Christ is the head of every man, and the husband is the head of his wife," a text that builds a "great chain of being," locating husbands as intermediaries between God and women. Galatians 3:28 offers the stark contrast that, "There is no longer Jew or Greek, there is no longer slave or free, there is no longer male and female, for all of you are one in Christ Jesus."

If in the core texts of Judaism and Christianity we can find such strikingly divergent statements on such fundamental issues as war and peace and social hierarchies, we clearly have some work to do in constructing a faith-based approach to public policy. Even if many rabbis and church leaders continue to speak about contemporary issues as if the problem of

7. Jakob J. Petuchowski, *Freedom of Expression in the Jewish Tradition*, Jewish Perspectives (New York: American Jewish Committee, 1984), 1.

connecting classical sources to contemporary issues does not exist, scholars have long recognized that the path from sacred text and tradition to contemporary policy is more treacherous. Jewish scholars have reflected on the problematics of selecting texts and building links between classical sources and contemporary concerns. Jacob Neusner writes:

> For Judaism, as for any historic religious tradition, you cannot make things up as you go along, or say what sounds right or feels good, calling it "Judaism." True, you are right for yourself in whatever you say. But to speak to someone else in the framework of Judaism, you must speak a common language, the conversation is three-sided: you, the other person, and the great body of law and theology called Torah.[8]

Norman Lamm struggles to define the relationship between divine law and our obligation to promote social good. "Yet it is no simple matter to determine how Judaism evaluates the man–man duties vis-à-vis the man–God obligations. Man's social responsibilities derive their ultimate validity from the divine law, yet there is a certain independence about them."[9] By referencing "a certain independence," Lamm hedges on articulating the nature of the autonomy of rules governing human relationships, but he feels compelled to recognize that there is no neat way to go from divine law to social policy. Echoing Cohen, Norman Solomon makes the point more dramatically: "Is there logically a way to derive firm practical conclusions from traditional texts? The answer is negative; one can by all means *relate* practical conclusions to traditional texts, but one cannot *derive* them logically, *more geometrico*."[10] Like Cohen, both secular and religious scholars are wary of the direct application of Jewish sources to particular positions on specific issues. The JCPA's generalized statement of goodwill in regard to considerations relevant to hydrofracking honors that modest approach. And yet, those of us whose practice and values derive from a living Jewish tradition are often resistant to sidelining Jewish wisdom when we deliberate on matters of urgent concern today.

In the effort to use the Jewish textual and legal traditions to address practical moral and ethical questions, the approach of traditional halakhic decision making will fail us. Judaism, in its complexity, multivocality, and historic diversity, provides resources for positons that different readers will identify as both moral and immoral. Prooftexts famously can be found in Scripture and tradition that support wars of annihilation, slavery, oppression of outsiders, and the subjugation of women. Nevertheless,

8. Jacob Neusner, *Tzedakah: Can Jewish Philanthropy Buy Jewish Survival* (Chappaqua, NY: Rossel Books, 1982), 4.

9. Norman Lamm, *The Good Society: Jewish Ethics in Action* (New York: Viking, 1974), 7.

10. Norman Solomon, *The Analytic Movement: Hayyim Soloveitchik and His Circle*, SFSHJ 58 (Atlanta: Scholars Press, 1993), xii.

we are not without resources for developing grounded Jewish responses to contemporary issues, even issues never contemplated before our time (in realms such as technology and gender fluidity).[11] In what follows I propose a strategy that acknowledges complexity and contradiction and suggests the advantage of an oblique approach to ethical dilemmas. The strategy advocates for culling texts from an array of mutually reinforcing sources that can be connected to one another and can guide our thinking without enforcing certainty.

Not So Fast: Identifying Jewish Principles and a Jewish Sensibility in Contemporary Debates

Although some may find greater coherence in the prophetic tradition of ethical monotheism, other genres of biblical texts and the diverse traditions—legal, philosophic, and mystical—of postbiblical, rabbinic Judaism create a rich and complex body of texts from which to draw what we may identify as core Jewish values. Jill Jacobs recognizes the problem of connecting classical texts to current issues but begins the process of doing so by identifying meta-principles that may provide a firmer platform on which to build claims for "Jewish" policy positions. She is willing to posit that classic texts may not offer any specific directives on the most pressing issues we face today but that Judaism nevertheless provides us with critical guidance about how to do our work. "Judaism does not dictate a clear cut answer to every—or even any—social or economic issue.... [A]ncient texts ... can inform our own approaches to current issues, challenge our assumptions, and force us to consider alternative approaches."[12] Louis Newman shares that view. There are unprecedented questions arising in our day, but we can nevertheless apply principles that guided earlier decision making by a process of careful analogy. Newman writes, "Jewish ethics must grow out of an encounter with traditional texts. But that encounter must begin by acknowledging the ambiguity of the texts and the complexity of applying them to unprecedented situations."[13]

In his foreword to Jacobs's book, Elliot Dorff responds implicitly to Neusner's critique of those who make up a Judaism in the image of their own politics. Dorff finds in Judaism a core set of values that can guide us in developing public policies:

---

11. See, for example, the introductory discussion by Elliot N. Dorff and Louis E. Newman in *Contemporary Jewish Ethics and Morality: A Reader*, ed. Dorff and Newman (New York: Oxford University Press, 1995).

12. Jill Jacobs, *There Shall Be No Needy: Pursuing Social Justice through Jewish Law and Tradition* (Woodstock, VT: Jewish Lights, 2009), 2–3.

13. Louis E. Newman, "The Ambiguity of Jewish Ethics," *Sh'ma* 34 (2004): 6, 8.

> [W]e are not importing a foreign set of moral ideas to the Jewish tradition. Much less are we simply adopting the current politically correct fad. We are instead applying the central vision of the Jewish tradition of who we are and ought to be—the same vision that shaped Jewish law from its inception—to the moral demands that we must strive to fulfill beyond the minimal requirements of the law.[14]

For Dorff, the core value statement is *lifnim m'shurat ha-din* (judging beyond the literal/narrow requirements of the law). Law alone is not enough. It must be supplemented by narrative, by the human story and human needs, which sometimes means going beyond and sometimes even going against the law as literally understood. Dorff derives his convictions in this way:

> *Kofin al middat s'dom* (we coerce a person not to act according to the trait of the people of Sodom, who cared only for themselves and not for others); *mi-shepara* (cursing people publicly in court who renege on their agreements, even if those agreements have not reached the stage where they can be legally enforced); and *ru'ach chakhamim einah nochah heimenu* ("the spirit of the Sages is not pleased with him").[15]

The last principle relates to times where an individual acts within the letter of the law but still the rabbis are displeased with their actions. Dorff then adds a category introduced by Nachmanides (1194–1270): "*(N)aval b'rshut ha-Torah* (a scoundrel within the bounds—or 'with the permission'—of the Torah)."[16]

Turning to the narrative tradition, Dorff emphasizes the many ways in which the experience of being enslaved and being strangers needs to inform one's behavior as a host, ensuring that there is one law for all peoples. In b. Soṭah. 14a, God provides a model for human action in the opening and closing scenes of the five books of Torah, first by clothing Adam and Eve when they lament their nakedness and then by burying Moses. Neither of these is a major deed, but both are exemplary of the kinds of acts that build a caring community, one in which people assume responsibility for the well-being of others.

In seeking to identify additional general principles found in multiple sources in the history of Judaism to inform the work of Jewish public policy, we might include the values of compromise, pluralism, and the setting of human limits (humility). For example, explaining how justice is achieved, we read in b. Sanh. 6b that mediation is favored over the discovery of the elusive goal of achieving strict justice:

---

14. Elliot Dorff, "Foreword," in Jacobs, *There Shall Be No Needy*, xii–xiii.
15. Ibid., xiv.
16. Ibid. For the reference to Naval, see 1 Sam 25.

> Rabbi Yehoshua ben Korcha says: It is a mitzvah to mediate a dispute, as it is written, "render in your gates judgments that are true and make for peace" (Zech 8:16). Is it not the case that where there is strict judgment there is no true peace, and in a place where there is true peace, there is no strict judgment? But what kind of justice includes genuine peace? You must say: mediation.[17]

Similarly, David Kraemer spells out a theory of truth that underpins the value of compromise in the Babylonian Talmud: "the form of the Bavli embodies a recognition that truth, divine in origin, is on the human level indeterminable. For this reason, at least in part, the Bavli considers alternative approaches to the truth but methodically seeks to avoid privileging one over another."[18] The preference for compromise over a single truth is further reinforced in a comment on Deuteronomy's call for justice: "'Justice, justice, pursue' (Deut 16:20). (The word justice is used) once for strict judgment (*din*) and once for compromise" (b. Sanh. 32b).

Mishnah Eduyyot ("On Testimonies") provides extensive reflection on the value of compromise and the rationale for including multiple perspectives to attain wholeness in the new rabbinic community. Eduyyot 4:8 contains the dramatic proposition that the two great schools around which the disagreements of the early rabbinic generations are organized, the Schools of Shammai and Hillel, transcended disagreements about purities (food) and family law (marriage) in order to eat and marry across sectarian boundaries.

> And although (the School of Shammai) declare ineligible (women) whom the (the School of Hillel) pronounce eligible, nevertheless the House of Shammai did not refrain from marrying women from (the families of) the House of Hillel, and the House of Hillel (did not refrain) from marrying women from the House of Shammai. And (despite) all (of the disputes concerning the rules of) cleanness and uncleanness, concerning which these declared clean what those declared unclean, they did not refrain from using one another's belongings in matters affected by (the rules of) cleanness.[19]

Finally, the value of humility, of holding our political views lightly is advanced often in rabbinic texts, classical and medieval. Even with the best of intentions, we have all experienced that sometimes we are wrong and that things do not turn out as we anticipated. In the medieval Jewish

---

17. Unless otherwise noted, translations are my own.

18. David Kraemer, *The Mind of the Talmud: An Intellectual History of the Bavli* (New York: Oxford University Press, 1990), 7.

19. For further discussion of Mishnah Eduyyot as an extended essay on compromise, see Leonard Gordon, "Where the Circle Begins: Tractate Eduyyot as an Introduction to the Mishnah," *Conservative Judaism* 59.3 (2007): 49–65.

community, the moral hazard risked in the redemption of captives was an ongoing concern, and one that continues to have resonance today. If you pay ransom, more captives might be taken. If you do not redeem a captive, they might languish in the hands of their captors. The Mishnah and later Maimonides's *Code of Jewish Law* reflect on the dilemma and its solution:

> We do not ransom captives for more than they are worth because of *tikkun ha'olam* (the better ordering of the world; often translated: repairing the world). We do not help captives escape because of *tikkun ha'olam.* (m. Giṭ. ["On Bills of Divorce"] 4:6)

> We do not redeem captives for more than they are worth because of *tikkun ha'olam,* so that enemies should not pursue them to kidnap them. And we do not help captives escape because of *tikkun ha'olam* so that captors should not make their chains heavier or add more guards. (Maimonides, *Code of Jewish Law, Laws of Gifts to the Poor* 8:12)

Howard Lesnick of the University of Pennsylvania Law School expresses the overarching principle that I am advocating here. He argues that, in Judaism, a decision needs to conform not to a specific source such as the Bible, nor accord with one authoritative rabbi, but rather, the basis of a decision's authoritativeness in Judaism is "its coherence with the web of prior rulings."[20] Jacobs, Dorff, and Lesnick all affirm the possibility—indeed the importance—of turning to Jewish resources for analyzing contemporary concerns. Nevertheless, each recommends assuming a wide perspective from which one can ascertain general principles based on an aggregate of relevant examples.

The Case of Voting Rights to Convicted Felons

With this principle in mind, I offer one specific case, which I chose specifically for the lack of direct precedent in biblical or rabbinic culture: the issue of restoring voting rights to convicted felons, something now decided in the United States state by state, creating a patchwork of conflicting rulings. A prisoner from a state that allows prisoners to vote, for example, might be serving his time in a prison in a state that does not.

First, a classic biblical passage dealing with crime and restitution: "When someone steals an ox or a sheep, and slaughters it or sells it, the thief shall pay five oxen for an ox and four sheep for a sheep" (Exod 22:1). A mishnaic ruling spells out what is implicit in Exodus: restitution completes the punishment and returns the offender to the usual web of social relationships.

---

20. Howard Lesnick, *Religion in Legal Thought and Practice* (New York: Cambridge University Press, 2010), 187.

> Anyone who is liable to punishment by premature death [*karet*], who has been flogged is exempt from liability to premature death, as it is said, And your neighbor will be degraded in your sight (Deut 25:3)—Once a person has been flogged, they are considered your neighbor. (m. Mak. 3:15)

In the Mishnah's cognate document, Tosefta, this point is deepened through a reflection on Yom Kippur, the Day of Atonement. Confession for past sin on this day completes the process of atonement and need not be repeated the following year.

> Concerning sins about which one has made confession on the previous Day of Atonement, one does not have to include them in the confessions of the upcoming Day of Atonement, unless the person did those same transgressions (during the intervening year). (t. Kip. 4:15)

One principle underlying the emphasis on moving forward is the high value placed on human dignity, which, according to b. Ber. 19b "takes precedence over a negative precept of the Torah." In b. B. Meṣ. 58b we find a list of three crimes for which a person is never forgiven (does not re-ascend from Gehenna), one of which is assaulting human dignity by giving another person an evil epithet, even in a case where the person has grown accustomed to the nickname. The Talmud recognizes that the power of labels and "nicknames" can adhere to a person and then limit their future. Such a principle might well apply to permanently labeling someone a "felon," even after his or her time is served. By restricting voting rights on the basis of a label, the label effectively becomes a permanent identity.

The Talmud's desire to facilitate reentry and remove the stigma of past misdeeds extends to a case in which it may limit restitution:

> If a person stole a beam and builds it into a grand building, the House of Shammai say that the person must demolish the entire building and return the beam to its owner. And the House of Hillel say that the victim can claim only the value of the beam, as a rule instituted for the sake of not placing obstacles in the path of those who would repent. (b. Giṭ. 55a)

Israel, which bases its legal system on both British and classical Jewish law, has recently weighed in on this question in an especially dramatic case, upholding the voting rights of the individual who denied such rights to the entire citizenry of the State by assassinating the Prime Minister. The High Court of Justice ruled that, in the absence of specific statutory authorization, the State could not revoke the voting rights of the person convicted of assassinating Prime Minister Yitzhak Rabin.[21]

---

21. Melissa Weintraub, "Kvod Ha-Briot: Human Dignity in Jewish Sources, Human Degradation in American Military Custody," http://www.truah.org/resources/human-dignity-in-jewish-sources-human-degradation-in-american-military-custody/.

In constructing this tradition that places a high value on reintegration, I acknowledge that Judaism is not univocal, and along with traditions that point toward reintegration, Deut 23:3 condemns certain peoples as incapable of change and unfit to enter the community: "No Ammonite or Moabite shall be admitted to the assembly of the LORD even to the tenth generation, none of their descendants shall be admitted to the assembly of the LORD." Notably, however, the book of Ruth, which tells the story of a Moabite who becomes a direct foremother of the Davidic (messianic) line, may have identified this heroine as a Moabite precisely as a critical reflection on the law that permanently stigmatizes Moabites.

What I have tried to illustrate here is an approach to applying Judaism to current policy issues that recognizes the complexity of the tradition and the lack of direct precedent but that does not shy away from saying that there is both a Jewish approach to questions of social policy and a multiplicity of Jewish texts that must be aggregated to inform contemporary discussions. Rather than choose prooftexts, policy makers do well to discern not a single "Jewish answer" but rather a response informed by Jewish texts and history relevant to the debate. However subjective this Jewish response may seem to be, the effort to discover precedents in the Jewish experience or textual tradition gives living Judaism a voice in contemporary conversations. I hope that both in presenting the problem and suggesting paths to a solution I have opened up the question in ways that have implications for all of us who think about faith and the common good.

Shaye Cohen may be right that the historian has no conclusive results to offer the practitioner that will determine, based on fixed precedent, how to make decisions. Our best historians of Judaism, like Cohen, identify values and processes that are implicit and recoverable and that shed light on how contemporary ethicists and those who make decisions about Jewish public policy might conduct inquiries rooted in Jewish history and Jewish texts. Since contemporary Jewish organizations do weigh in on secular policy issues *as* Jewish organizations, it seems irresponsible to do so without honoring the longstanding commitment of Jewish legalists to base opinions and rulings on Jewish learning, both textual and historical. Referencing rabbinic Judaism's capacity to yield conflicting results as a rationale for marginalizing the tradition weakens our work by rejecting the obligation to study as a basis for right action. Indeed, discerning Jewish sensibilities requires a studious disavowal of that devil who quotes Scripture for his own purposes. Instead, maximizing Jewish learning means gathering as many varied sources for study as we can, so that we bring to our policy debates a nuanced reading of how Jewish values can be applied to the thorny questions before us today.

Dicing and Divination

New Approaches to Gambling in Jewish History

JONATHAN D. COHEN
University of Virginia

When scholars write about the history of gambling, their studies invariably begin with the platitudinous claim that gambling is an inescapable enterprise. Traces of gambling have been found in nearly every society regardless of era, location, religion, or culture. Consequently, scholars often open their analysis by claiming that games of chance represent an activity intrinsic to human civilization. Arguments about the inevitability of gambling, however, implicitly push scholars to focus on specific games, particularly those recognizable to modern gamblers. What better way to show the timelessness of gambling than by drawing parallels between the games of the twenty-first century and those of 21 BCE? Both societies played games with dice, for instance. Therefore, gambling reveals not only historical details about each era but also that risk and uncertainty represent fundamental aspects of human nature.

In this essay, I take a slightly different view to examine gambling in Jewish antiquity. The narrative of ubiquitous gambling leads to a focus on certain types of games but not others. Even risky endeavors that look like gambling but lack certain elements presumed to be crucial to gambling, such as the exchange of money, are often not considered gambling. Through an investigation of gambling in ancient Jewish society, I contend that the use of lotteries and astragals for divinatory purposes should be considered a form a gambling and, therefore, that gambling was an important and commonplace component of ancient Jewish life. Numerous sources cite lotteries as tools of divination, and this chapter provides a theoretical and textual case for scholars to consider these drawings as gambling.

Furthermore, I assess the possibility that ancient Jews incorporated religious practice into their betting. Given the widespread belief in divine influence over lottery drawings and the thin line between gambling and divination, it proves likely that Jewish gamblers viewed their betting as determined by divine forces. Previous scholars—particularly Joshua

Schwartz—have provided illuminating studies of the rabbinic approach to gambling as well as the dynamics of gambling in Jewish antiquity. Borrowing from new scholarship in the fields of gambling studies and the history of gambling, I broaden the category of what constitutes gambling and illustrate gambling as a serious activity with important theological, historical, and social implications.

Any study of gambling in Jewish antiquity must begin by acknowledging the paucity of available textual and archeological evidence. Compared with scholars of twentieth-century gambling or betting in the Middle Ages, scholars of ancient times must rely on fragments, small game pieces of uncertain ownership, and doctrinal decrees littered with esoteric terminology. This lack of sources creates a void between studies of ancient times and the latest research on the topic, which focuses almost exclusively on living subjects. For example, over the past few decades, *The Journal of Gambling Studies* and *International Gambling Studies* have been devoted primarily to analysis of compulsive gambling—habits, addiction development, and treatment solutions. Meanwhile, historical studies of gambling have relied on either social, political, or business history, focusing on the machinations of gaming operators, legislation to restrict or facilitate the expansion of gambling, and the lives and betting practices of casual and professional gamblers.[1] Studies of compulsive gambling are often built on statistical data, whereas historical studies rely on archival documents beyond those available to scholars of antiquity.

Nonetheless, scholars have made do with the available source material and have illustrated that gambling represented a common phenomenon in Jewish antiquity. Joshua Schwartz has written a number of studies of Jewish gambling in the Greco-Roman period, and he has collected and analyzed the rabbinic passages that illuminate how Jewish authorities approached gambling. I offer a brief summary of these texts: Mishnah Rosh Hashanah 1:8 bans gamblers from providing testimony regarding the new moon or providing any testimony except for the forms of testimony that women were permitted to bring. Mishnah Sanhedrin 3:3 bans gamblers from providing testimony regarding monetary matters, though Rabbi Judah specifies that this prohibition holds only if gambling is their sole occupation, indicating that gambling was sufficiently prevalent to necessitate a rabbinic distinction between professional and casual gamblers. Like these other sources, Mishnah Shevu'ot 7:4 groups gamblers with seedy characters—such as usurers or traffickers in produce from the

1. See the works cited throughout this study and, for example: Charles T. Clotfelter and Phillip J. Cook, *Selling Hope: State Lotteries in America* (Cambridge: Harvard University Press, 1989); Ann Fabian, *Card Sharps and Bucket Shops: Gambling in Nineteenth-Century America* (New York: Routledge, 1999); and David G. Schwartz, *Suburban Xanadu: The Casino Resort on the Las Vegas Strip and Beyond* (New York: Routledge, 2003).

shmita year—in order to explain the reliability of their oaths regarding monetary claims. Finally, like the first two mishnaic sources, Tosefta Sanhedrin 5:2 deals with gamblers as witnesses and explains the steps these individuals need to take to reclaim their legalistic legitimacy.[2] Schwartz goes into detail on each of these texts and, in a revision of his previous work, argues that, because of the popularity of gambling in Hellenistic-Roman society, Jewish authorities in Palestine came down strongly against both casual and professional gamblers. Babylonian Jewish authorities, on the other hand, had no such exposure to Roman life and took a far more lenient approach to betting.[3] Significantly, all of these texts use the term *hamesacheq be-kubya'*, literally, "the dice player," as synecdoche for "gambler." The repeated use of this phrase indicates either that the rabbis assumed that all gamblers were dicers and vice versa, or that dicing was so common that it stood in for all forms of gambling.

Games of chance also appeared in other aspects of ancient Jewish life. For instance, Joshua uses a lottery to determine the distribution of the land of Israel (Josh 18–19), one of seventy-eight references to lotteries (*gorallot)* in the Hebrew Bible.[4] Later texts make further use of lotteries in nonmonetary contexts. Mishnah Shabbat 23:2 permits a household to cast lots to determine the order in which food portions are distributed, provided that the drawing does not determine the *size* of each person's portion. The Mishnah notes that using a lottery to determine portion size is prohibited because it would constitute a form of dice playing (*mishum kubiya'*), implying either a general rabbinic ban against gambling or a more specific decree against distributing basic resources—such as food—through games of chance.[5] Tosefta Shabbat 17:4 permits similar lotteries within households and even permits wedding parties to cast lots on the Sabbath to determine the size of each guest's portion. Amram Tropper postulates that these texts use lotteries as an impartial method either to promote social equality (at a wedding) or to ensure the fair treatment of young children (in the household).[6]

---

2. This summary is drawn from Joshua Schwartz, "Jews at the Dice Table: Gambling in Ancient Jewish Society Revisited," in *Envisioning Judaism: Studies in Honor of Peter Schäfer on the Occasion of His Seventieth Birthday*, ed. Ra'anan S. Boustan et al., 2 vols. (Tübingen: Mohr Siebeck, 2013), 131–32. For a survey of talmudic approaches to gambling, see William Galston, "The Memory of Sin: Gambling in Jewish Law and Ethics," in *Gambling: Mapping the American Moral Landscape*, ed. Alan Wolfe and Eric C. Owens (Waco, TX: Baylor University Press, 2009), 213–26.

3. J. Schwartz, "Jews at the Dice Table," 130.

4. Frederick H. Cryer, *Divination in Ancient Israel and Its Near Eastern Environment: A Socio-Historical Investigation*, JSOTSup 142 (Sheffield: JSOT Press, 1994), 276.

5. J. Schwartz argues that Babylonian Amoraim inserted the reference to dicing to specify that gambling was permitted generally but forbidden on the Sabbath ("Jews at the Dice Table," 135).

6. Amram Tropper, "The Economics of Jewish Childhood in Late Antiquity," *HUCA* 76 (2005): 215–16.

Previous examinations of ancient Jewish gambling are largely centered on these mishnaic-era texts. Scholars such as Schwartz and Leo Landman have adjudicated the meanings of the Mishnah's and Tosefta's prescriptions on gambling, what activities constituted gambling in ancient Israel, and how religious authorities treated gamblers.[7] Yet such legalistic discussions of permissible and impermissible forms of betting mostly leave out the gamblers themselves. Borrowing from innovations in the field of social history, recent historical scholarship on gambling has focused on how individuals incorporate gambling into their daily lives and how gambling relates to their political, cultural, and religious beliefs. Meanwhile, scholarship on Judaism and gambling, whether focused on ancient times or the twentieth century, often focuses on Jewish doctrine without including actual gamblers. The laws fall under scrutiny, but the people subjected to them do not.

The work of Dan Judson provides a notable and useful exception. In his study of synagogue-hosted bingo in the United States, Judson analyzes the rulings on gambling from the Mishnah through the Shulchan Aruch and Rambam; the responsa of Orthodox, Conservative, and Reform rabbis in addressing whether synagogues could raise money from gambling; and the experience of Jewish communities as they handled these doctrinal decisions while trying to balance their religious values with their monetary needs.[8] Judson's primary focus on the mid-twentieth century allows a larger source base than is available for the study of antiquity, but his work provides a model of how scholars should balance analysis of legalistic religious doctrine with an investigation of individual experience.

This type of grassroots-level analysis is important because actual gambling practices may differ sharply from doctrinal decree. As Chloe Taft and Michelle Robinson illustrate, the lives of gamblers are often far different from the intention of authorities. Taft and Robinson show how, despite exertions of managerial control, casino card dealers can carve out spaces for autonomy in the gambling process.[9] So, too, it is possible that

---

7. Leo Landman, "Jewish Attitudes toward Gambling: The Professional and Compulsive Gambler," *JQR* 57 (1967): 298–318; Landman, "Jewish Attitudes toward Gambling II: Individual and Communal Efforts to Curb Gambling," *JQR* 58 (1967): 34–62; Joshua Schwartz, "On the Prohibition against Eating Nuts on the Eve of Rosh ha-Shanah," *Talilei Orot*, 7 (1997): 112–15; J. Schwartz, "Pigeon Flyers in Ancient Jewish Society," *JJS* 48 (1997): 105-119; J. Schwartz, "Play and Games," in *The Oxford Handbook of Jewish Daily Life in Roman Palestine*, ed. Catherine Hezser (Oxford: Oxford University Press, 2010), 641–53.

8. Dan Judson, "Sanctity, Pragmatism, and Paying the Bills: The Controversial Use of Bingo in Synagogues," in *All In: The Spread of Gambling in the Twentieth Century United States*, ed. Jonathan D. Cohen and David G. Schwartz (Reno: University of Nevada Press, 2018), 202–19.

9. Chloe E. Taft, *From Steel to Slots: Casino Capitalism in the Postindustrial City* (Cambridge: Harvard University Press, 2016), 113–16; Michelle Robinson, "In the Lion's Den:

ancient Jews ignored—or were unaware of—rabbinic edicts surrounding the propriety of gambling. Unfortunately, the personal, improvisational, and hidden nature of these gambling practices contributes to the scarcity of records from gamblers in both modern and ancient times. It may prove impossible to construct social histories of any aspect of life in ancient Palestine, but scholars should consider the strong possibility that lived reality differed from rabbinical decree.

In particular, when looking closely at the dynamics of ancient gambling, future studies should consider the possibility that Jews incorporated religious practice into their gambling. The rabbinic stance on gambling is clear, and Schwartz has outlined the popular games of the period and the types of people who might have played them—particularly soldiers.[10] Yet, beyond these historical details, scholars have not investigated the distinctly religious nature of gambling. Romans, Jews, Assyrians, and Greeks all gambled. But to what extent was Jewish gambling actually *Jewish*?

This question proves particularly poignant because of the connection between Christianity and gambling. Theologian Kathryn Tanner suggests that conservative Protestants oppose gambling not only because they believe it represents an immoral leisure activity but also because of its threatening theological implications: "Ironically, Christianity has a critical view of gambling because of what it shares with it." In her reading of Blaise Pascal, Tanner contends that Christianity, like gambling, is built around an invisible, unknowable system of grace, the possibility that a select, lucky few may be rewarded. "Religious life and games of chance are both ways of dealing ... with life's precarious prospects."[11] Christianity offers a logical structure to the universe: everything that happens is part of a divine plan. Gambling, on the other hand, privileges randomness and luck, thereby flying in the face of a divinely ordered system. Despite—or perhaps *because* of—these theological parallels, Christian gamblers frequently invoked their faith to aid their betting, as evidenced by twentieth-century American lottery winners who thanked God for their jackpots as well as by the ancient Roman owner of a game board with an inscription calling for Jesus to help him win dice games.[12]

Upon initial examination, ancient Judaism does not appear to feature

---

Evangelicals on the Las Vegas Strip and the Meaning of Billy Graham's 1978 Crusade," in J. Cohen and D. Schwartz, *All In*, 185–87.

10. Joshua Schwartz, "Gambling in Ancient Jewish Society and in the Greco-Roman World," in *Jews in a Greco-Roman World*, ed. Martin Goodman (Oxford: Clarendon, 1998), 161.

11. Kathryn Tanner, "Grace and Gambling," in Wolfe and Owens, *Gambling*, 227–56, here 228.

12. Nicholas Purcell, "Literate Games: Roman Urban Society and the Games of *Alea*," *Past and Present* 147 (1995): 19 n. 70; on religion and modern lottery winners, see Jonathan D. Cohen, "For a Dollar and a Dream: State Lotteries and American Inequality" (PhD diss., University of Virginia, 2019).

any such overlap of gambling and theology. Schwartz argues that "gambling did not function within a religious framework," as Jewish authorities in Palestine opposed gambling because of its association with Roman culture, not because it offered a competing form of religion. In fact, Schwartz contends that there was no connection whatsoever between religious practice and gambling and that players did not offer prayers to aid their bets. His conclusion rests in part on "where-there's-smoke-there's-fire" logic: "If there had been religious issues involved the sages would have come down on gambling with a much heavier hand."[13] Because the rabbis did not caution against the integration of theology and gambling, this must not have been a common issue in ancient society. If gamblers had been prone to connecting religion and gambling, the rabbis would have spoken against it, especially given the overall disdain religious authorities in Palestine showed to nearly all forms of Jewish betting.

Scholarship in the field of gambling studies, however, may reshape possible approaches to religion and gambling in Jewish antiquity. Recent works take capacious approaches to gambling, studying various forms of wagering and various games of chance that might have previously been excluded from the category of gambling.[14] According to the *Oxford English Dictionary*, "gambling" refers to the "action, practice, or pastime of playing games for stakes, as cards, dice, etc." Significantly, these stakes do not have to be monetary, nor does gambling refer only to bets conducted for leisure. Any use of a game of chance to guide a decision-making process or distribute resources can be considered a form of betting.[15]

Thus, given the lack of sources regarding the experience of gamblers in Jewish antiquity, divination should be considered alongside traditional—monetary—gambling in studies of betting in Jewish antiquity. Frederick Cryer notes that ancient Israel was a "magic society" in which divinatory rituals were ubiquitous, as they were elsewhere in the biblical, Hellenistic, and Roman periods. These magical practices, Cryer notes, were not merely the preserve of a priestly elite but were prevalent "at the popular level … there was a broad base of magical usage in Israelite society."[16] Through the drawing of lots or the casting of bones, divination often resembled what in historical retrospect looks like gambling. The impulse behind gambling is a similar impulse behind divination: decisions by lottery were meant to bring order to the universe by ceding human control.

---

13. J. Schwartz, "Jews at the Dice Table," 130, 145.

14. See, e.g., Gerda Reith, *The Age of Chance: Gambling in Western Culture* (London: Routledge, 2002); Jackson Lears, *Something for Nothing: Luck in America* (New York: Penguin, 2004); David G. Schwartz, *Roll the Bones: The History of Gambling* (New York: Gotham, 2006).

15. "Gambling, n.", *Oxford English Dictionary* online (Oxford: Oxford University Press, 2018), www.oed.com/view/Entry/76450.

16. Cryer, *Divination in Ancient Israel*, 324–25.

As gambling historian David G. Schwartz notes, in ancient society, "the line between divination and gambling [was] blurred."[17]

Therefore, divination offers insight into how gambling worked for ancient Jews as well as into their possible incorporation of religious faith into games of chance. A few examples illustrate the gambling elements inherent in these divination practices and the importance of lotteries as decision-making tools. In Ezek 21, God instructs the prophet to mark out two roads for the king of Babylon, one road leading the king to war against the Ammonite city of Rabbah and the other to Jerusalem. The prophet explains that the king will stop at the fork in the road

> to seek an omen: He will cast lots with arrows, he will consult his idols, he will examine the liver. Into his right hand will come the lot for Jerusalem, where he is to set up battering rams, to give the command to slaughter. (Ezek 21:21–22 NIV)

Ezekiel declares that Nebuchadnezzar will consult animal innards—a common divination practice—and will use lots to determine the target of his invasion. The result will not be random, nor will it be determined by an idolatrous power, as Nebuchadnezzar presumably intended. Rather, God will shape the outcome, as the destruction of Jerusalem represents God's punishment of the Israelites. The possibility that Nebuchadnezzar might march to war against Rabbah instead of Jerusalem is crucial to this story: the king could have received an omen to attack the Ammonite city, but God ensured that he drew the lot for Jerusalem. The Israelites, then, represent the losers in this game of chance.

The most famous biblical appearance of lotteries occurs in the book of Esther. Though the narrator does not mention God at any point, midrashic interpretations locate a secret role of divine intervention throughout the story, particularly in the recurrence of lotteries (*purim*), which represent an avenue for heavenly interference. Abraham D. Cohen contends that *"the 'pur' is nothing less than the intentional symbol of chance-fate,* which at once conceal, and appear to govern these very same events." On the surface, Esther's story is guided by coincidence, for instance, Mordechai's fortunate position, which allows him to overhear the plot against the king, as well as Haman's presence in the outer court just as Achashverosh's is pondering a reward for Mordechai. But Cohen argues that, through the lottery, "God acts behind the veil of causality and chance, on behalf of the people of Israel ... By delivering [the Jews] one month to the day before Passover, God showed them anew his providential care for them."[18] The

17. D. Schwartz, *Roll the Bones*, 3.

18. Abraham D. Cohen, "'Hu Ha-goral': The Religious Significance of Esther," *Judaism* 23 (1974): 87–94, here 89 (emphasis original).

result of Haman's genocidal drawing was shaped by a protective God who ensured that the Jewish victory would occur one month before the Passover holiday, thereby illustrating God's care for the Jews, even in exile. If Haman had drawn a different day—perhaps one closer to the date of the drawing—Esther may not have had time to intervene with Achashverosh. The fate of the Jews was indeed at risk in Haman's lottery, but the result of the drawing was a divine symbol meant to illustrate the power of God's protection.

A potential caveat about these sources is the fact that, in Ezekiel and Esther, the lots are not conducted by Jews. The use of lotteries for divination—and the divine intervention in the results of the drawings—may have been conducted exclusively among non-Jews. As Brent A. Strawn notes, however, almost every reference to lots in the Old Testament entails either Israelites conducting the lottery, God playing a role in the results, or lots related to tribal issues or the land of Israel. In fact, of the five lots conducted by non-Israelites, four "reflect an intra-Israelite perspective" according to Strawn, including, for example, Haman's lottery in the book of Esther.[19]

Sources about Israelites conducting drawings are similar to those from Ezekiel and Esther. For example, in 1 Sam 10, Samuel chooses the Israelite king through a lottery that first selects the tribe of Benjamin, then Matri's clan, and then Saul. In the previous chapter, God had told Samuel that God would send a Benjaminite to Samuel the following day, and, by the time of the lottery, readers know that Saul has already been anointed. Barring the possibility that Samuel rigged the drawing—by placing only Benjamin's name in the drawing of the tribe, then only Matri's name in the drawing of the clan, and then only Saul's name in the drawing of clan members—it appears that Samuel conducted a fair lottery and that the prophet knew God would intervene to select Saul (regardless of the logistical difficulties of a lottery that accounted for every clan in every tribe). Samuel knew the results prior to the drawing, but, for the Israelite audience that appears to have been in attendance, Samuel's selection would have felt like a modern lottery drawing, with the winner crowned king. Even if they believed that God would shape the results, given Saul's shock at his selection, we can assume that many of those present may have believed that anyone could have been the individual selected.

Two additional sources examine regular individuals in ancient Jewish society using a lottery to ascertain divine will. At the end of Acts 1, the apostles return to Jerusalem following Jesus's ascension. Peter cites from the book of Psalms (69:25 and 109:8), arguing that the group needs to

---

19. Brent A. Strawn, "Jonah's Sailors and Their Lot Casting: A Rhetorical-Critical Observation," *Bib* 91 (2010): 66–76, here 70.

select a new apostle to replace Judas. The two nominees are Joseph (also known as Barsabbas/Justus) and Matthias:

> Then they prayed, "Lord, you know everyone's heart. Show us which of these two you have chosen to take over this apostolic ministry, which Judas left to go where he belongs." Then they cast lots, and the lot fell to Matthias; so he was added to the eleven apostles. (Acts 1:24–26 NIV)

Whether they would have viewed it this way or not, the apostles gambled to determine their final member. As with the appointment of the king generations earlier as well as the distribution of Jesus's garments at the foot of the cross following the crucifixion (Matt 27:35), for Joseph and Matthias the selection of lots probably felt like a lottery drawing: God would determine the outcome, and one would be the winner accepted as an apostle and the other the loser.

Finally, lotteries make two significant appearances in Josephus's *Jewish War*. In improbably parallel stories, Jewish soldiers besieged by Romans at Jotapata (3.361–391) and then at Masada (7.390) use lotteries to structure acts of collective suicide. As Shaye J. D. Cohen notes, however, the Masada narrative is replete with implausible or simply impossible details. After the Romans broke through the Sicarii defenses, it is unbelievable that they promptly decamped, thereby allowing time for dramatic oration and even more dramatic mass suicide. As a result, Cohen concludes, it is likely that there was no lottery at Masada or, at the very least, that any lottery drawing occurred on a far smaller scale than the selection of several hundred names, as Josephus claims.[20] Josephus inserted the story of the lottery in Masada for dramatic effect and to draw a parallel between his experience in the siege at Jotapata and that of the Sicarii at Masada.

The lottery at Jotapata in book 3 of *Jewish War* offers a clear indication of the relationship of chance, fate, and gambling in ancient Jewish society. When his mutinous forces resolve to commit suicide, Josephus proposes a lottery: the first person whose name is drawn will be killed by the second person, the second person by the third, and so on. With no plans to die in the cave, Josephus "staked his life on one last throw," as he likens his desperate attempt to convince the soldiers to accept his scheme to a dice roll. Fortunately for Josephus, the men approve his plan, content that Josephus will be killed along the way. Yet Josephus survives, because he wins the lottery: "Shall we put it down to divine providence or just to luck," he writes, but Josephus draws one of the final two lots and convinces the final man to surrender with him. Josephus makes explicit what many of the texts cited above only imply: that a lottery drawing is directly con-

---

20. Shaye J. D. Cohen, "Masada: Literary Tradition, Archaeological Remains, and the Credibility of Josephus," *JJS* 33 (1982): 385–405, here 396.

trolled by divine intervention. Despite the relatively small probability that his would be among the final two names, the fact that Josephus's lot falls among the last two indicates that some greater force was responsible for shaping the outcome of the lottery.

Thus, if Israelites lived in a society that not only used games of chance for important decisions but also openly acknowledged that God actively shaped the results of lottery drawings, then it seems certain that some Jews must have integrated religion into their wagering. Importantly, notwithstanding the reference to luck in Josephus's lottery at Jotapata, ancient society had no concept of mathematical probability. "Randomness," Nigel Pennick contends, ironically serves as "a form of well-defined structure inherent in the universe."[21] As a result, what in the twenty-first century might be attributed to chance or luck would instead be ascribed to the divine. This explains the prevalence of lotteries as tools of decision making in an era before introduction of lotteries for money.[22] Yet many gambling games involved dice, which were also used as tools of divination. But if ancient society did not view lotteries as random, then how could they view dice as random?[23]

It seems likely that some ancient dice players viewed the results of their wagers as shaped in some way by supernatural forces. My own research indicates that twentieth-century lottery winners view their gambling wins as gifts from God, confirmation of their divine favor, similar to the way proponents of divination would have interpreted the results of their own lottery drawings. Though Joshua Schwartz finds no evidence for religious gambling, the lack of a rabbinic decree against religious gambling cannot suffice as evidence given the context and the likelihood of a gap between rabbinic decree and lived experience.

Furthermore, the field of anthropology has long been concerned with the study of magic, the belief in the connection between two objects without physical association. Psychologists have illustrated that magical thinking is an intrinsic part of the gambling experience, often in the form of "superstition."[24] In a seminal study, Ellen Langer deems such practices

---

21. Nigel Pennick, *Games of the Gods: The Origin of Board Games in Magic and Divination* (London: Rider, 1988), ix.

22. There appear to have been lotteries in China around this period, and Roman elites held lotteries to distribute prizes at dinner parties. But the first lottery that would be recognizable to modern gamblers—which included the sale of tickets—dates to approximately fifteenth-century Italy (D. Schwartz, *Roll the Bones*, 16–17, 27, 83–84).

23. On lotteries as divination tools and the use of dice in Assyria, see Pennick, *Games of the Gods*, 31–32; and Eric D. Huntsman, "And They Cast Lots: Divination, Democracy, and Josephus," *Brigham Young University Studies* 36 (1996–1997): 365–77.

24. E.g., James M. Henslin, "Craps and Magic," *American Journal of Sociology* 73 (1967): 316–30; Rosa Bersabé and Rosario Martínez Arias, "Superstition in Gambling," *Psychology in Spain* 4 (2000): 28–34; Allen J. Windross, "The Luck of the Draw: Superstition in Gam-

"the illusion of control," as gamblers counteract randomness by taking steps that they believe—incorrectly—will increase their odds, such as selecting meaningful lottery numbers.[25] Even if Jews in Babylon and Palestine did not connect their gambling with recognizable religious practices, it proves likely that some form of supernatural belief was tied up in their betting. Significantly, the lone archeological evidence of Jewish gambling was a loaded die found in Jason's Tomb in Jerusalem.[26] Likewise, the Slavonic version of *Jewish War* claims that "divine providence or ... luck" had nothing to do with Josephus winning the lottery at Jotapata; instead, "he counted the numbers cunningly and so managed to deceive all the others," fixing the results by not placing his name in the drawing to begin with.[27] The rigging of a die and the manipulating of a lottery indicate not only the possibility of cheating but also the desire to exert control over the randomness of gambling. Josephus and the Jewish gambler may have known that the results of their games would be interpreted as divine will regardless of the outcome, so they shifted the odds in their favor, an impulse as ubiquitous as gambling itself.

Gambling may be inevitable, but it looks different in different times and places, sometimes radically so. Scholars of all eras—in this case Jewish antiquity—should reflect not only on the legalistic prohibitions concerning gambling but also, to the degree possible, on the gamblers and the games themselves. In this way, it becomes clear that divination at the very least parallels gambling or in fact represents a form of gambling that was practiced throughout Jewish antiquity. Future analysis of the relationship of divination and gambling will reveal the precise role of betting in ancient society and what exactly these practices illustrate about social and religious life.

---

bling," *Gambling Research* 15 (2003): 63–77; Jackie Joukhador, Alex Blaszczynski, and Fiona Maccallum, "Superstitious Beliefs in Gambling among Problem and Non-Problem Gamblers: Preliminary Data," *Journal of Gambling Studies* 20 (2004): 171–80; Ohtsuka Keis and Chi Chuen Chan, "Donning Red Underwear to Play Mahjong: Superstitious Beliefs and Problem Gambling among Chinese Mahjong Players in Macau," *Gambling Research* 22 (2010): 18–33; Marina D'Agati, "'I Feel Like I'm Going to Win': Superstition in Gambling," *Qualitative Sociological Review* 10 (2014): 80–101.

25. Ellen Langer, "The Illusion of Control," *Journal of Personality and Social Psychology* 32 (1975): 311–28. See also Stuart A. Vyse, *Believing in Magic: The Psychology of Superstition* (Oxford: Oxford University Press, 2000).

26. J. Schwartz, "Gambling in Ancient Jewish Society," 160.

27. Josephus, *The Jewish War*, trans. G. A. Williamson (London: Penguin Books, 1959; repr., 1981), 470.

Bibliography of the Writings of Shaye J. D. Cohen

Prepared by
MENACHEM BUTLER
Harvard Law School

1979

1. *Josephus in Galilee and Rome: His Vita and Development as a Historian.* Columbia Studies in the Classical Tradition 8. Leiden: Brill, 1979.

1980

2. "A Virgin Defiled: Some Rabbinic and Christian Views on the Origins of Heresy." *USQR* 36 (1980): 1–11.
3. Review of *A Hidden Revolution*, by Ellis Rivkin. *JBL* 99 (1980): 627–29.
4. "Women in the Synagogues of Antiquity." *Conservative Judaism* 34.2 (November–December 1980): 23–29.

1981

5. "The Beauty of Flora and the Beauty of Sarai." *Helios: A Journal of Classics and Comparative Studies* 8.2 (Autumn 1981): 41–53.
6. Review of *Greek and Latin Authors on Jews and Judaism*, vol. 2, by Menahem Stern. *Conservative Judaism* 35.1 (Fall 1981): 88–89.
7. "Epigraphical Rabbis." *JQR* 72.1 (July 1981): 1–17.
8. "Patriarchs and Scholarchs." *PAAJR* 48 (1981): 57–85.
9. "Sosates the Jewish Homer." *HTR* 74 (1981): 391–96.

1982

10. "The Destruction: From Scripture to Midrash." *Proof* 2 (1982): 18–39.
11. Review of *The Jews in Hellenistic and Roman Egypt*, by Aryeh Kasher. *JQR* 72 (1982): 330–31.
12. "Yavneh Revisited: Pharisees, Rabbis, and the End of Jewish Sectarianism." Pages 45–61 in *Society of Biblical Literature 1982 Seminar Papers*. Edited by Kent Harold Richards. Chico, CA: Scholars Press, 1982.

13. "Masada: Literary Tradition, Archaeological Remains, and the Credibility of Josephus." Special issue, Yigael Yadin Festschrift, *JJS* 33.1–2 (1982): 385–405.
14. "Josephus, Jeremiah, and Polybius." *History and Theory* 21 (1982): 366–81.
15. "Alexander the Great and Jaddus the High Priest according to Josephus." *AJS Review* 7–8 (1982–1983): 41–68.

1983

16. "Conversion to Judaism in Historical Perspective: From Biblical Israel to Post-Biblical Judaism." *Conservative Judaism* 36.4 (Summer 1983): 31–45.
17. "Jacob Neusner, Mishnah, and Counter-Rabbinics: A Review Essay of *Judaism: The Evidence of the Mishnah.*" *Conservative Judaism* 37.1 (Fall 1983): 48–63.
18. "The Prohibition of Intermarriage: From the Bible to the Talmud." Special issue, "Essays in Honor of Robert Gordis," *Hebrew Annual Review* 7 (1983): 23–39.

1984

19. "The Significance of Yavneh: Pharisees, Rabbis, and the End of Jewish Sectarianism." *HUCA* 55 (1984): 27–53.
20. Review of *Women Leaders in the Ancient Synagogue,* by Bernadette Brooten. *USQR* 39 (1984): 240–43.
21. Review of *State and Society in Roman Galilee,* by Martin Goodman. *American Historical Review* 89 (1984): 1315–16.
22. "The Temple and the Synagogue." Pages 151–74 in *The Temple in Antiquity.* Edited by Truman Madsen. Provo, UT: Brigham Young University Press, 1984.

1985

23. "The Origins of the Matrilineal Principle in Rabbinic Law." *AJS Review* 10.1 (Spring 1985): 19–53.
24. "The Matrilineal Principle in Historical Perspective." *Judaism* 34.1 (Winter 1985): 5–13.
25. Review of *Two Powers in Heaven,* by Alan Segal. *AJS Review* 10.1 (Spring 1985): 114–17.
26. Review of *II Maccabees: A New Translation and Commentary,* by Jonathan Goldstein. *JAOS* 105 (1985): 799–800.

1986

27. Review of *Josephus: The Historian and His Society,* by Tessa Rajak. *JBL* 105 (1986): 350–52.

28. "Was Timothy Jewish (Acts 16:1–3)? Patristic Exegesis, Rabbinic Law, and Matrilineal Descent." *JBL* 105 (1986): 251–68.
29. "Parallel Historical Tradition in Josephus and Rabbinic Literature." Pages 7–14 in *Proceedings of the Ninth World Congress of Jewish Studies 1985, Division B, Volume 1.* Jerusalem: World Union of Jewish Studies, 1986.
30. "The Political and Social History of the Jews in Greco-Roman Antiquity: The State of the Question." Pages 33–56 in *Early Judaism and Its Modern Interpreters.* Edited by Robert Kraft and George W. E. Nickelsburg. BMI 2. Atlanta: Scholars Press, 1986.
31. "Anti-Semitism in 'Antiquity': The Problem of Definition." Pages 43–47 in *History and Hate: The Dimensions of Anti-Semitism.* Edited by David Berger. Philadelphia: Jewish Publication Society, 1986.

1987

32. *From the Maccabees to the Mishnah.* LEC 7. Philadelphia: Westminster, 1987.
33. Ed., with Edward L. Greenstein, David Marcus. *Ancient Studies in Memory of Elias Bickerman.* Special issue, *JANES* 16–17 (1984–1985). New York: Jewish Theological Seminary of America, 1987.
34. "Elias J. Bickerman: An Appreciation." Pages 1–3 in *Ancient Studies in Memory of Elias Bickerman.* Special issue, *JANES* 16–17 (1984–1985). Published in 1987.
35. "Solomon and the Daughter of Pharaoh: Intermarriage, Conversion, and the Impurity of Women." Pages 23–37 in *Ancient Studies in Memory of Elias Bickerman.* Special issue, *JANES* 16–17 (1984–1985). Published in 1987.
36. "Pagan and Christian Evidence on the Ancient Synagogue." Pages 159–81 in *The Synagogue in Late Antiquity.* Edited by Lee Levine. New York: Jewish Theological Seminary of America, 1987.
37. "Respect for Judaism by Gentiles in the Writings of Josephus." *HTR* 80 (1987): 409–30.

1988

38. Review of *Jewish Settlement in Judaea after the Bar Kochba War,* by Joshua Schwartz. *JAOS* 108 (1988): 311–12.
39. "What Really Happened at Masada?" *Moment* 13.5 (July–August 1988): 28–35.
40. "Roman Domination." Pages 205–35 in *Ancient Israel: A Short History from Abraham to the Roman Destruction of the Temple.* Edited by Hershel Shanks. Washington, DC: Biblical Archaeology Society, 1988.
41. "History and Historiography in the *Against Apion* of Josephus. Special issue, "Essays in Jewish Historiography." *History and Theory* 27 (1988): 1–11.

1989

42. "Crossing the Boundary and Becoming a Jew." *HTR* 82 (1989): 13–33.
43. Review of *On Pagans, Jews, and Christians,* by Arnaldo Momigliano. *Classical World* 83 (1989): 134–35.

1990

44. Ed., with Edward L. Greenstein, *The State of Jewish Studies.* Detroit: Wayne State University Press, 1990.
45. "The Modern Study of Ancient Judaism." Pages 55–73 in *The State of Jewish Studies.* Edited by Shaye J. D. Cohen and Edward L. Greenstein. Detroit: Wayne State University Press, 1990.
46. Review of *Jewish Symbols in the Greco-Roman Period,* by Erwin R. Goodenough. *HR* 70 (1990): 488.
47. "The Rabbinic Conversion Ceremony." *JJS* 41 (1990): 177–203.
48. Review of *The Ruling Class of Judaea,* by Martin Goodman. *Classical Philology* 85 (1990): 164–166.
49. "Religion, Ethnicity, and 'Hellenism' in the Emergence of Jewish Identity in Maccabean Palestine." Pages 204–23 in *Religion and Religious Practice in the Seleucid Kingdom.* Edited by Per Bilde et al. Åarhus: Åarhus University Press, 1990.

1991

50. Review of *Appeasement or Resistance and Other Essays on New Testament Judaism,* by David Daube. *Religious Studies Review* 17 (April 1991): 176.
51. Review of *Judas Maccabaeus,* by Bezalel Bar-Kochva. *American Historical Review* 96 (1991): 850–51.
52. "Can a Convert to Judaism say 'God of our Fathers'?" *Judaism* 40 (1991): 419–28.
53. "Menstruants and the Sacred in Judaism and Christianity." Pages 273–98 in *Women's History and Ancient History.* Edited by Sarah Pomeroy. Chapel Hill: University of North Carolina Press, 1991.
54. "Adolf Harnack's 'The Mission and Expansion of Judaism': Christianity Succeeds Where Judaism Fails." Pages 163–69 in *The Future of Early Christianity: Essays in Honor of Helmut Koester.* Edited by Birger A. Pearson. Minneapolis: Fortress, 1991.

1992

55. "Purity and Piety: The Separation of Menstruants from the Sancta." Pages 103–15 in *Daughters of the King: Women and the Synagogue; A Survey of History, Halakhah, and Contemporary Realities.* Edited by

Susan Grossman and Rivka Haut. Philadelphia: Jewish Publication Society, 1992.

56. "Morton Smith (1915–1991)." *PAAJR* 58 (1992): 37–40.
57. "The Place of the Rabbi in the Jewish Society of the Second Century." Pages 157–73 in *Galilee in Late Antiquity*. Edited by Lee I. Levine. New York: Jewish Theological Seminary of America, 1992.
58. "Was Judaism in Antiquity a Missionary Religion?" Pages 14–23 in *Jewish Assimilation, Acculturation, and Accommodation: Past Traditions, Current Issues, and Future Prospects; Proceedings of the Second Annual Symposium of the Philip M. and Ethel Klutznick Chair in Jewish Civilization Held on Sunday–Monday, September 24–25, 1989*. Edited by Menahem Mor. Lanham, MD: University Press of America, 1992.
59. "Can a Convert to Judaism have a Jewish Mother?" Pages 19–31 in *Torah and Wisdom: Studies in Jewish Philosophy, Kabbalah, and Halacha in honor of Arthur Hyman*. Edited by Ruth Link-Salinger. New York: Shengold, 1992.
60. "Judaism to the Mishnah: 135–220 CE." Pages 195–223 in *Christianity and Rabbinic Judaism: A Parallel History*. Edited by Hershel Shanks. Washington, DC: Biblical Archaeological Society, 1992.

1993

61. Ed. *The Jewish Family in Antiquity*. BJS 289. Atlanta: Scholars Press, 1993.
62. Ed., with Ernest S. Frerichs. *The Diasporas in Antiquity*. BJS 288. Atlanta: Scholars Press, 1993.
63. "'Those Who Say They Are Jews and Are Not': How Do You Know a Jew In Antiquity When You See One?" Pages 1–45 in *The Diasporas in Antiquity*. Edited by Shaye J. D. Cohen and Ernest S. Frerichs. BJS 288. Atlanta: Scholars Press, 1993.

1994

64. "Is 'Proselyte Baptism' Mentioned in the Mishnah? The Interpretation of M. Pesahim 8:8 (= M. Eduyot 5:2)." Pages 278–92 in *Pursuing the Text: Studies in Honor of Ben Zion Wacholder on the Occasion of His Seventieth Birthday*. Edited by John C. Reeves and John Kampen. JSOTSup 184. Sheffield: Sheffield Academic, 1994.
65. "Morton Smith and His Scholarly Achievement." Pages 1–8 in *Josephus and the History of the Greco-Roman Period: Essays in Memory of Morton Smith*. Edited by Fausto Parente and Joseph Sievers. StPB 41. Leiden: Brill, 1994.
66. "*Ioudaios to genos* and Related Expressions in Josephus." Pages 23–38 in *Josephus and the History of the Greco-Roman Period: Essays in Memory of Morton Smith*. Edited by Fausto Parente and Joseph Sievers. StPB 41. Leiden: Brill, 1994.

67. "Judaism at the Time of Jesus." Pages 3–12 in *Jews and Christians Speak of Jesus.* Edited by Arthur Zannoni. Minneapolis: Fortress, 1994.

1995

68. Review of *The Death of Herod: An Essay in the Sociology of Religion,* by Richard Fenn. *AJS Review* 20 (1995): 176–78.
69. Review of *Mission and Conversion,* by Martin Goodman. *JJS* 46 (1995): 297–300.
70. "Foreword." Pages xi–xv in *The Jews of Egypt: From Rameses II to Emperor Hadrian,* by Joseph Mélèze-Modrzejewski. Philadelphia: Jewish Publication Society, 1995.
71. "Le fondement historique de la matrilinéarité juive." Pages 109–24 in *La loi juive à l'aube du xxi*[e] *siècle.* Edited by Rivon Krygier. Paris: Messer, 1995.

1996

72. Ed., *Studies in the Cult of Yahweh,* by Morton Smith. 2 vols. RGRW 130. Leiden: Brill, 1996.
73. "Preface." Pages vii–viii in vol. 1 of Morton Smith, *Studies in the Cult of Yahweh.* Edited by Shaye J. D. Cohen. RGRW 130. Leiden: Brill, 1996.
74. "In Memoriam Morton Smith." Pages 279–85 in vol. 2 of Morton Smith, *Studies in the Cult of Yahweh.* Edited by Shaye J. D. Cohen. RGRW 130. Leiden: Brill, 1996.
75. "Ioudaios: 'Judaean' and 'Jew' in Susanna, First Maccabees, and Second Maccabees." Pages 211–20 in vol. 1 of *Geschichte – Tradition – Reflexion: Festschrift für Martin Hengel zum 70. Geburtstag.* Edited by Peter Schäfer. Tübingen: Mohr Siebeck, 1996.
76. Review of *Sabbath and Synagogue,* by Heather McKay. *JBL* 115 (1996): 736–37.
77. "Gentiles and Jewish Studies." *JSQ* 3 (1996): 185–92.
78. "Are There Tannaitic Parallels to the Gospels?" *JAOS* 116 (1996): 85–89.
79. "Did Martial Own a Circumcised Jewish Slave?" Pages 59*–66* in *The Jews in the Hellenistic-Roman World: Studies in Memory of Menahem Stern.* Edited by Isaiah M. Gafni et al. Jerusalem: Shazar, 1996.

1997

80. "Why Aren't Jewish Women Circumcised?" *Gender and History* 9.3 (November 1997): 560–78.
80. Review of *The Stranger within Your Gates,* by Gary G. Porton. *CBQ* 59 (1997): 393–95.
82. "Bring Back the 'God-Fearers'?" *Sh'ma* 27/534 (16 May 1997): 3–5.

83. "The Unfinished Agenda of Jewish–Christian Dialogue." *Journal of Ecumenical Studies* 34.3 (Summer 1997): 326–29.

84. "Were Pharisees and Rabbis the Leaders of Communal Prayer and Torah Study in Antiquity? The Evidence of the New Testament, Josephus, and the Church Fathers." Pages 99–114 in *The Echoes of Many Texts: Reflections on Jewish and Christian Traditions; Essays in Honor of Lou Silberman.* Edited by William G. Dever and J. Edward Wright. BJS 313. Atlanta: Scholars Press, 1997.

1998

85. "The Conversion of Antoninus." Pages 141–71 in vol. 1 of *The Talmud Yerushalmi and Graeco-Roman Culture.* Edited by Peter Schäfer. TSAJ 71. Tübingen: Mohr Siebeck, 1998.

86. Review of *Greek Jewish Texts from the Cairo Genizah,* by Nicholas de Lange. *JQR* 89.1–2 (July–October 1998): 182–84.

87. "On Murdering or Injuring a Proselyte." Pages 95–108 in *Hesed Ve-Emet: Studies in Honor of Ernest S. Frerichs.* Edited by Jodi Magness and Seymour Gittin. BJS 320. Atlanta: Scholars Press, 1998.

88. With John Meier and Peter Steinfels, "The Jewishness of Jesus." Pages 24–55 in *No Religion Is an Island: The Nostra Aetate Dialogues.* Edited by Edward Bristow. New York: Fordham University Press, 1998.

1999

89. *The Beginnings of Jewishness: Boundaries, Varieties, Uncertainties.* HCS 31. Berkeley: University of California Press, 1999.

90. "Were Pharisees and Rabbis the Leaders of Communal Prayer and Torah Study in Antiquity? The Evidence of the New Testament, Josephus, and the Early Church Fathers." Pages 89–105 in *The Evolution of the Synagogue: Problems and Progress.* Edited by Howard Clark Kee. Harrisburg, PA: Trinity Press International, 1999.

91. "The Temple and the Synagogue." Pages 298–325 in *The Early Roman Period.* Vol. 3 of *The Cambridge History of Judaism.* Edited by William Horbury, W. D. Davies, and J. Sturdy. Cambridge: Cambridge University Press, 1999. Written in 1985.

92. "The Rabbi in Second-Century Jewish Society." Pages 922–90 in *The Early Roman Period.* Vol. 3 of *The Cambridge History of Judaism.* Edited by in William Horbury, W. D. Davies, and J. Sturdy. Cambridge: Cambridge University Press, 1999. Written in 1983.

93. "Purity, Piety, and Polemic: Medieval Rabbinic Denunciations of 'Incorrect' Purification Practices." Pages 82–100 in *Women and Water: Menstruation in Jewish Life and Law.* Edited by Rahel R. Wasserfall. Brandeis Series on Jewish Women. Hanover, NH: University Press of New England for Brandeis University Press, 1999.

94. "Judaism under Roman Domination: From the Hasmoneans through the Destruction of the Second Temple." Pages 57–69 in *From Mesopotamia to Modernity: Ten Introductions to Jewish History and Literature.* Edited by Burton Visotzky and David Fishman. Boulder: Westview, 1999.

95. "Judaism." Pages 528–29 in *Late Antiquity: A Guide to the Postclassical World.* Edited by G. W. Bowersock, Peter Brown, and Oleg Grabar. Harvard University Press Reference Library. Cambridge: Belknap Press of Harvard University Press, 1999.

96. "Mishnah." Page 582 in *Late Antiquity: A Guide to the Postclassical World.* Edited by G. W. Bowersock, Peter Brown, and Oleg Grabar. Harvard University Press Reference Library. Cambridge: Belknap Press of Harvard University Press, 1999.

97. "Talmud." Pages 715–16 in *Late Antiquity: A Guide to the Postclassical World.* Edited by G. W. Bowersock, Peter Brown, and Oleg Grabar. Harvard University Press Reference Library. Cambridge: Belknap Press of Harvard University Press, 1999.

98. "Tosefta." Page 730 in *Late Antiquity: A Guide to the Postclassical World.* Edited by G. W. Bowersock, Peter Brown, and Oleg Grabar. Harvard University Press Reference Library. Cambridge: Belknap Press of Harvard University Press, 1999.

2000

99. Ed., *The Synoptic Problem in Rabbinic Literature.* BJS 326. Providence, RI: Brown Judaic Studies, 2000.

100. "Introduction." Pages vii–xiii in *The Synoptic Problem in Rabbinic Literature.* Edited by Shaye J. D. Cohen. BJS 326. Providence, RI: Brown Judaic Studies, 2000.

101. "Some Thoughts on 'The Attitude toward *mamzerim* in Jewish Society in Late Antiquity.'" *Jewish History* 14 (2000): 171–74.

102. "False Prophets (4Q339), Netinim (4Q340), and Hellenism at Qumran." *Journal of Greco-Roman Christianity and Judaism* 1 (2000): 55–66.

2001

103. "Between Judaism and Christianity: The Semi-Circumcision of Christians according to Bernard Gui, His Sources, and R. Eliezer of Metz." *HTR* 94 (2001): 285–321.

104. "Hellenism in Unexpected Places." Pages 216–43 in *Hellenism in the Land of Israel.* Edited by John Collins and Greg Sterling. CJAn 13. Notre Dame, IN: University of Notre Dame Press, 2001.

2002

105. "Judaism without Circumcision and 'Judaism' without 'Circumcision' in Ignatius." *HTR* 95 (2002): 395–415.

106. "Preface." Pages xvii–xxi in Jeffrey Rubenstein, *Rabbinic Stories*. Classics of Western Spirituality. New York: Paulist Press, 2002.

2003

107. "A Brief History of Jewish Circumcision Blood." Pages 30–42 in *The Covenant of Circumcision: New Perspectives on an Ancient Jewish Rite*. Edited by Elizabeth Wyner Mark. Brandeis Series on Jewish Women. Hanover, NH: University Press of New England for Brandeis University Press, 2003.

2004

108. "Does Rashi's Torah Commentary Respond to Christianity? A Comparison of Rashi with Rashbam and Bekhor Shor." Pages 449–72 in *The Idea of Biblical Interpretation: Essays in Honor of James L. Kugel*. Edited by Hindy Najman and Judith H. Newman. JSJSup 83. Leiden: Brill, 2004.

2005

109. *Why Aren't Jewish Women Circumcised? Gender and Covenant in Judaism*. Berkeley: University of California Press, 2005.
110. Review of *Playing a Jewish Game*, by Michele Murray. *American Historical Review* 110 (2005): 1233.

2006

111. "Preface to the Second Edition." Pages xiii–xiv in *From the Maccabees to the Mishnah*. 2nd ed. Louisville: Westminster John Knox, 2006.
112. Review of *The Talmud Yerushalmi and Greco-Roman Culture, vol. 3*, edited by Peter Schäfer. *JSJ* 37 (2006): 489–90.

2007

113. Ed., with Joshua J. Schwartz, *Studies in Josephus and the Varieties of Ancient Judaism: Louis H. Feldman Jubilee Volume*. AJEC 67. Leiden: Brill, 2007.
114. With Joshua J. Schwartz, "In Appreciation of Louis H. Feldman." Pages viii–viii in *Studies in Josephus and the Varieties of Ancient Judaism: Louis H. Feldman Jubilee Volume*. Edited by Shaye J. D. Cohen and Joshua J. Schwartz. AJEC 67. Leiden: Brill, 2007.
115. "'Your Covenant That You Have Sealed in Our Flesh': Women, Covenant, and Circumcision." Pages 29–42 in *Studies in Josephus and the Varieties of Ancient Judaism: Louis H. Feldman Jubilee Volume*. Edited by Shaye J. D. Cohen and Joshua J. Schwartz. AJEC 67. Leiden: Brill, 2007.
116. "The Judaean Legal Tradition and the Halakhah of the Mishnah." Pages 121–43 in *The Cambridge Companion to Rabbinic Literature*.

Edited by Charlotte Elisheva Fonrobert and Martin Jaffee. Cambridge: Cambridge University Press, 2007.

117. "Are Women in the Covenant?" Pages 25–42 in *A Feminist Commentary on the Babylonian Talmud.* Edited by Tal Ilan. Tübingen: Mohr Siebeck, 2007.
118. Review of *Marked in Your Flesh: Circumcision from Ancient Judaism to Modern America,* by Leonard Glick. *AJS Review* 31 (2007): 167–68.

2008

119. "'Common Judaism' in Greek and Latin Authors." Pages 69–87 in *Redefining First-Century Jewish and Christian Identities: Essays in Honor of Ed Parish Sanders.* Edited by Fabian Udoh et al. CJAn 16. Notre Dame, IN: University of Notre Dame Press, 2008.

2009

120. "Why Study Talmud." Pages 119–28 in *Why Study Talmud in the 21st Century.* Edited by Paul Soken. Lanham, MD: Lexington Books, 2009.

2010

121. *The Significance of Yavneh and Other Essays in Jewish Hellenism.* TSAJ 136. Tübingen: Mohr Siebeck, 2010.
122. "The Name of the Ruse: The Toss of a Ring to Save Life and Honor." Pages 25–26 in *'Follow the Wise': Studies in Jewish History and Culture in Honor of Lee I. Levine.* Edited by Zeev Weiss et al. Winona Lake, IN: Eisenbrauns, 2010.
123. "Sabbath Law and Mishnah Shabbat in Origen De Principiis." *JSQ* 17 (2010): 160–89.

2011

124. "From Permission to Prohibition: Paul and the Early Church on Intermarriage." Pages 259–91 in *Paul's Jewish Matrix.* Edited by Thomas G. Casey and Justin Taylor. Bible in Dialogue 2. Rome: Gregorian & Biblical Press; Mahwah, NJ: Paulist, 2011.
125. "Judaism to the Mishnah: 135–220 CE." Pages 211–38 in *Christianity and Rabbinic Judaism: A Parallel History.* Edited by Hershel Shanks. Revised 2nd ed. Washington, DC: Biblical Archaeological Society, 2011.
126. "The Letter of Paul to the Galatians." P. 332 in *The Jewish Annotated New Testament.* Edited by Amy-Jill Levine and Marc Zvi Brettler. New York: Oxford University Press, 2011.
127. "Judaism and Jewishness." Pages 513–15 in *The Jewish Annotated New Testament.* Edited by Amy-Jill Levine and Marc Zvi Brettler. New York: Oxford University Press, 2011.

128. "Josephus." Pages 575–77 in *The Jewish Annotated New Testament.* Edited by Amy-Jill Levine and Marc Zvi Brettler. New York: Oxford University Press, 2011.

2012

129. "Dancing, Clapping, Meditating: Jewish and Christian Observance of the Sabbath in Pseudo-Ignatius." Pages 29–51 in *Judaea-Palaestina, Babylon and Rome: Jews in Antiquity.* Edited by Benjamin Isaac and Yuval Shahar. TSAJ 147. Tübingen: Mohr Siebeck, 2012.
130. Review of *The Image of the Jews in Greek Literature,* by Bezalael bar-Kochva. *American Historical Review* 117 (2012): 908–9.

2013

131. "Antipodal Texts: B. Eruvin 21b–22a and Mark 7:1–23 on the Tradition of the Elders and the Commandment of God." Pages 965–83 in *Envisioning Judaism Studies in Honor of Peter Schäfer on the Occasion of his Seventieth Birthday.* Edited by Ra'anan S. Boustan, et al., eds., (Tübingen: Mohr Siebeck, 2013), 965-983
132. "In Between: Jewish-Christians and the Curse of the Heretics," in Hershel Shanks, ed., *Partings: How Judaism and Christianity Became Two* (Biblical Archaeology Society, 2013), 207-236
133. Review of Matthias Thiessen *Contesting Conversion, Catholic Biblical Quarterly* 75 (2013): 379-381

2014

134. "Preface to the Third Edition." Pages xi–xii in *From the Maccabees to the Mishnah.* 3rd ed. Louisville: Westminster John Knox, 2014.
135. "The Presbyterians and I." *Marginalia,* 22 July 2014.
136. Review of *Outside the Bible,* edited by Louis H. Feldman, James L. Kugel, and Lawrence H. Schiffman. *The Seforim Blog,* 25 July 2014, http://seforim.blogspot.com/2014/07/.

2016

137. "Sabbath Labor Prohibitions in 'The Book of the Laws of Countries' by Bardaisan the Syrian." [Hebrew]. Pages 169–82 in *Between Babylonia and the Land of Israel: Studies in Honor of Isaiah M. Gafni.* Edited by Geoffrey Herman et al. Jerusalem: Shazar, 2016.

2017

138. "Judaism and Jewishness." Pages 592–96 in *The Jewish Annotated New Testament.* Edited by Amy-Jill Levine and Marc Z. Brettler. 2nd ed. Oxford: Oxford University Press, 2017.

2018

139. "The Ways That Parted: Jews, Christians, and Jewish-Christians, ca. 100–150 CE." Pages 307–39 in *Jews and Christians in the First and Second Centuries: The Interbellum 70–132 CE.* Edited by Joshua Schwartz and Peter J. Tomson. CRINT 15. Leiden: Brill, 2018.

Index

CPSIA information can be obtained
at www.ICGtesting.com
Printed in the USA
BVHW070918301018
530644BV00008B/2/P

9 781946 527127